Learn AppleScript

The Comprehensive Guide to Scripting and Automation on Mac OS X, Third Edition

**Hamish Sanderson and
Hanaan Rosenthal**

Apress®

Learn AppleScript: The Comprehensive Guide to Scripting and Automation on Mac OS X, Third Edition

ISBN-13 (pbk): 978-1-4302-2361-0

ISBN-13 (electronic): 978-1-4302-2362-7

Publisher and President: Paul Manning
Lead Editor: Douglas Pundick
Technical Reviewer: David A. Coyle
Editorial Board: Clay Andres, Steve Anglin, Mark Beckner, Ewan Buckingham, Gary Cornell, Jonathan Gennick, Jonathan Hassell, Michelle Lowman, Matthew Moodie, Duncan Parkes, Jeffrey Pepper, Frank Pohlmann, Douglas Pundick, Ben Renow-Clarke, Dominic Shakeshaft, Matt Wade, Tom Welsh
Coordinating Editor: Debra Kelly
Copy Editor: Bill McManus
Compositor: MacPS, LLC.
Indexer: BIM Indexing & Proofreading Services
Artist: April Milne
Cover Designer: Anna Ishchenko

Distributed to the book trade worldwide by Springer-Verlag New York, Inc., 233 Spring Street, 6th Floor, New York, NY 10013. Phone 1-800-SPRINGER, fax 201-348-4505, e-mail orders-ny@springer-sbm.com, or visit www.springeronline.com.

For information on translations, please e-mail rights@apress.com, or visit www.apress.com.

Apress and friends of ED books may be purchased in bulk for academic, corporate, or promotional use. eBook versions and licenses are also available for most titles. For more information, reference our Special Bulk Sales–eBook Licensing web page at www.apress.com/info/bulksales.

The source code for this book is available to readers at www.apress.com.

Contents at a Glance

Contents

Foreword

One of the inherent tensions in product design is the balance between generality and specificity. Products are designed to appeal to a wide range of users, yet each individual has specific needs and problems that cannot be anticipated.

Custom products are usually much more expensive than generic ones. This is true for clothing, automobiles, medicine, and of course software. Custom products are also more difficult to create. Even worse, a person's needs may change over time, so something that worked when it was purchased may not be as useful in another time or situation.

Unlike physical products, software is infinitely malleable. In theory, at least, it can do (almost) anything you want and be specialized to your needs. In practice, software designers have to anticipate what users are most likely to want. Building in every possible option would make the software very powerful but completely unusable. With this in mind, Mac software developers tend to focus on simplicity and elegance. This is a cultural value that has grown up with the Mac OS and now permeates every aspect of the Mac experience. The idea is to carefully design just the right product while avoiding unnecessary features.

But what if the end result is not quite right for you? When it comes to software, the human usually learns to adapt to fit the software, rather than the other way around. It's as if the tailor adjusts your body to fit the suit, rather than the suit to fit you. But there is another solution, which is to make the software itself more customizable. Again, it's not possible to anticipate everything that anyone would want. This is a difficult problem, then, to build software applications that are simple and elegant, yet infinitely customizable to suit unknown needs.

This is the vision behind AppleScript: to enable users to extend, combine, and customize software to suit their own specific needs. AppleScript is not just a scripting language. It is an approach to customizable and extensible software development, which has been adopted by hundreds of applications on the Mac. AppleScript is designed to create a network effect in software, where the more applications that use AppleScript the better it is for everyone. This is a grand vision, but the reality is not so simple. Scripting and customizing applications is not something that everyone does every day. It requires some technical knowledge and practical examples to follow.

This book is an essential guide to AppleScript and related technologies. The key value of the book is that it integrates a clear presentation of the vision and purpose of AppleScript with the mundane technical details of writing scripts and getting useful work done. When talking about scripting, it's easy to get lost in the details. When writing a foreword, like this, it's easy for me to present a grand vision that seems appealing. The benefit of this book is that it combines and connects the vision with the practical reality.

Dr. William Cook
Associate Professor
Department of Computer Science
University of Texas at Austin
AppleScript Architect and Engineering Manager
Apple Computer, 1991–1993

About the Authors

Hamish Sanderson is a 10-year veteran of AppleScript and a professional automation developer living and working in the UK. Over the years he has contributed a range of useful libraries and utilities to the AppleScript community and pops up with some regularity on the various AppleScript mailing lists. He is also the author of the highly regarded appscript library, which brings AppleScript-style application scripting support to the Python, Ruby, and Objective-C languages on Mac OS X. He can be reached at hhas@users.sourceforge.net.

Hannan Rosenthal is the founder of Custom Flow Solutions LLC. He started his media automation consulting firm in 1990, whose clients are now The New York Times, Thomson Reuters, Associated Press, and Fidelity Investments. Since then he helped reshape the workflow of numerous publishing companies creating systems that save their owners millions of dollars and thousands of hours annually.

Hanaan is a speaker in MacWorld Expo and Seybold Seminars. Hanaan and his wife, Johanne, home-school their two children and restoring their solar-powered Victorian home in Providence, RI. In his spare time, Hanaan likes to pour concrete kitchens, sculpt, photograph, write and generally get into trouble in any way possible. He can be reached at applescript@hanaan.com.

About the Technical Reviewer

David A. Coyle earned his Ph.D. in thermochronology in 1992. Research in thermal modeling and crustal evolution at the Max-Planck Institute for Nuclear Physics (Heidelberg, Germany) lead to a career in software development. David has been concentrating on Apple technologies since 1997 and is a certified Apple System Administrator.

Acknowledgments

We would like to thank the many people who have worked long and hard to make this book possible.

Many thanks to our guest authors—Emmanuel Levy, Harald Monihart, Ian Piper, Shane Stanley, Barry Wainwright, and Craig Williams—for sharing their knowledge and experience with us.

Many thanks to David Coyle for helping to get the technical details right and to Bill McManus for ensuring all of the other words made sense too.

Many thanks too to Rob and Mark for their feedback on draft chapters and to Debra, Douglas, Kylie, Clay, and the rest of Apress for supporting this project through a long and sometimes arduous development process.

Lastly, many thanks to Dr William Cook for gracing us with his insights into the philosophy and goals of AppleScript and to all of the AppleScript engineers, application developers, and community members for a network effect where the copious sharing of knowledge and enthusiasm is every bit as important as the myriad interactions of bits and bytes.

Introduction

Welcome to the third edition of *Learn AppleScript: The Comprehensive Guide to Scripting and Automation on Mac OS X*. This book will teach you the principles and practices of controlling the many "AppleScriptable" Mac OS X applications using the AppleScript scripting language included in Mac OS X.

The title of this book represents a challenge: just how do you create a comprehensive guide to a subject as broad and deep as automating your Mac with AppleScript?

While we do cover every aspect of the AppleScript language in extensive detail, obviously we cannot hope to cover every last scriptable application on the market today. Instead, we will explain the core principles by which all scriptable applications operate, before exposing you to a broad range of very different applications—from simple and familiar tools such as TextEdit and Finder, through popular lifestyle applications such as Mail and iTunes, and on to professional productivity programs such as Microsoft Office and Adobe InDesign.

Although you may not use all of these applications in your daily routine, we hope that you will take the time to explore them here. Exploring the wide range of applications covered here will help to familiarize you with the many similarities (and differences) found among scriptable applications today—knowledge that will provide essential guidance and inspiration as you go on to learn and use other scriptable applications for yourself.

While this book is designed for Mac users who have never scripted before, we have ensured that there is plenty of material here to engage more experienced AppleScripters, as well as professional programmers coming to AppleScript from other languages. So without further ado, let's look at how you can get the most out of this book whatever your background is.

If You Have Never Scripted Before...

If you have never scripted before, don't worry! This book was designed with you foremost in mind.

Part 1 of the book will start you off with a very gentle introduction to AppleScript and application scripting concepts and techniques. Learning to script is not a five-minute task; there is a lot of information to absorb, and it takes time and practice to master. To help you get to grips with these subjects, Chapter 2 divides them into eight "Key Concepts"—four for the AppleScript language, four for application scripting—to provide you with a roadmap of what you will learn over the course of the book and help you to fit the pieces together as you go. Chapter 3 then leads you through the process of creating your first practical AppleScript.

Part 2 begins with an introduction to Mac OS X's AppleScript Editor, where you will write and test the majority of your scripts throughout this book. Next, Chapter 5 takes you on a grand tour of the four key concepts behind application scripting, helping you develop a robust understanding of this incredibly powerful technology in preparation for Part 3 of the book. Chapters 6 to 17 then guide you through the first three key concepts that underpin the AppleScript language itself, equipping you with all the knowledge you need to start writing scripts of your own. Chapters 18 and 19 cover the fourth key concept behind AppleScript, although as this material is more advanced you might wish to skip it for now and come back to it later when you are ready to learn more.

Part 3 of the book provides you with lots of opportunity to put your newfound knowledge to practical use, as you explore a wide range of popular scriptable Mac OS X applications in Chapters 20 to 23 and learn how to extend the functionality of the AppleScript language through the use of scripting additions.

As your confidence grows, you might like to tackle some of the larger, more advanced applications covered in Chapters 24 to 28. Or you might wish to return to Chapters 18 and 19 to complete your knowledge of AppleScript's most advanced language features before Chapter 30 launches you into the exciting world of GUI application development with Snow Leopard's new AppleScriptObjC bridge.

If You Are Already an AppleScript User...

If you are an existing AppleScript user keen to expand your knowledge and hone your skills, you will find lots of valuable information throughout this book, particularly in Parts 2 and 3. I recommend you start with a quick read through Part 1, just to familiarize yourself with the planned structure of the book, before diving into the areas of Parts 2 and 3 that interest you the most.

As with previous editions, Part 2 provides an extensive reference to every facet of the AppleScript language itself, while Part 3 gets down and dirty with the practical business of automating your desktop. However, this new edition expands both the breadth and depth of our coverage of AppleScript and application scripting with several hundred pages of completely new material!

In addition to ensuring a robust understanding of basic AppleScript features—objects, commands, operators, variables, and flow control statements—we dig deeply into the more advanced and obscure corners of AppleScript. Chapters 7 and 17 include detailed discussion of Unicode text and text file encodings—essential background knowledge for reading and writing text files in AppleScript. Chapter 17 clarifies the sometimes confusing world of AppleScript's alias, file, and POSIX file classes, explaining just how they work and how to use them effectively.

Chapters 18 and 19 provide detailed coverage of handlers and script objects—powerful features for organizing large, sophisticated scripts. Along the way, we show you how to package your handlers as reusable libraries for easy sharing between many scripts and provide an AppleScript-friendly introduction to object-oriented programming as you learn how to design and use your own "classes" of objects. With the introduction of Snow Leopard's exciting new AppleScriptObjC bridge, these features and techniques are more important to AppleScript developers than ever before.

Chapter 22 will help you navigate the practical issues involved in installing and using scripting additions across a range of Mac OS X architectures: PowerPC and Intel, 32- and 64-bit. Guest author Ian Piper also contributes an introduction to advanced text processing with the popular Satimage scripting addition.

As before, we cover a good range of popular Mac OS X applications—including the Finder, Mail, iCal, and the ever-present iTunes—giving you plenty of opportunity to hone your automation skills. In addition, two new guest chapters provide in-depth coverage of a number of important productivity applications. Chapter 24, contributed by Harald Monihart and Barry Wainwright, explores the iWork and Microsoft Office application suites, while Chapter 26 provides an extensive introduction to one of the great heavyweights of Mac OS X automation, Adobe InDesign, under the guidance of InDesign scripting expert, Shane Stanley.

Chapter 27 explains the ins and outs of integrating the AppleScript language with the powerful, if cryptic, Unix command line that lies just beneath the surface of the Mac OS X operating system, while Chapter 28 explores the highly versatile Satimage Smile platform in the company of guest author Emmanuel Levy.

In Chapter 29, we step back from the day-to-day practicalities of AppleScripting to examine the bigger picture behind scripting and programming in general. While this chapter is by no means required reading, we hope that it will provide valuable inspiration and practical knowledge that will aid you as you look to design, debug, and optimize your scripts more effectively.

Finally, in Chapter 30, guest author Craig Williams introduces you to one of the most exciting AppleScript developments of recent years: Snow Leopard's new AppleScriptObjC bridge. AppleScripters can now directly harness the enormous power of Mac OS X's Cocoa programming frameworks to develop highly polished and capable GUI applications of their own.

If You Are an Experienced Programmer...

If you are an experienced programmer looking to develop some AppleScript skills, you will find this book to be a valuable reference guide.

While the AppleScript language itself is surprisingly small and simple, the English-like syntax can take some getting used to if you are more familiar with dot-style languages such as Python and Ruby or curly-brace languages such as Objective-C and Java. Remember, AppleScript syntax is designed to be easily read by nonprogrammers, so the trade-offs it makes are different from those made by these other languages, but with a little time and practice I'm sure you'll get the hang of it too.

The real challenge will be in forming a full and accurate understanding of how application scripting works. AppleScript's command and reference syntax may resemble that of object-oriented programming—but don't be fooled by appearances! AppleScript's conceptual roots lie as much in procedural and relational database programming as in the more familiar world of OOP. (To use a rough analogy, think of sending Apple events as a bit like sending XPath queries over XML-RPC.) While we may not employ such technical terms throughout this book, the information you need to make sense of this powerful, if unusual, technology is all in there.

You may find the pacing a little slow for your taste and the detailed discussion of basic programming language concepts such as variables, values, and flow control to be somewhat redundant at your level. However, all the essential information you require is in here: the features and capabilities of the AppleScript language, and the principles and practices of application scripting. Nor do we shy away from "advanced" AppleScript topics such as module management and object-oriented programming with script objects, or essential optimization techniques for getting the best performance out of your application automation code.

We recommend you quickly skim the introductory material in Part 1 before moving on to the real meat in Parts 2 and 3. You'll find Chapters 6 and 12 especially valuable in understanding how application scripting works, while Part 3 provides lots of hands-on experience in working with a wide range of scriptable applications and explains how to integrate AppleScript with the Unix command line and Objective-C/Cocoa environments.

Resources

Here are some links to useful online AppleScript-related resources:

- The Apple web site provides several AppleScript-related mailing lists (`http://www.lists.apple.com/mailman/listinfo`), including the AppleScript-Users mailing list, which is a great place to meet other AppleScript users and get your questions answered. An AppleScript bulletin board is also available at `http://discussions.apple.com` (you'll find it in the Mac OS X Technologies section).

- The Apple web site's developer section (`http://developer.apple.com`) includes a range of AppleScript-related material aimed at intermediate and advanced AppleScript users and scriptable application developers, such as the AppleScript Language Guide reference documentation.

- MacScripter (`http://www.macscripter.net`) is a terrific community-driven web site where you can find scripting additions, AppleScript code shared by other scripters, a BBS, and many other AppleScript-related resources.

- The Mac OS X Automation web site (`http://www.macosxautomation.com`) provides useful information on AppleScript and other automation technologies found in Mac OS X. The AppleScript section includes links to a range of other AppleScript-related web sites.

- More-advanced readers might also wish to check out Dr. William Cook's HOPL III conference paper on the early history of AppleScript. Dr. Cook's paper provides many fascinating insights into the philosophy and workings of the AppleScript language and application scripting technologies and is available from his web site (`http://userweb.cs.utexas.edu/users/wcook`) as a downloadable PDF.

Many other AppleScript-related web sites exist that I haven't included here. Some are given in later chapters, others can be found via the previous links provided or by searching online.

Formatting Conventions Used in This Book

To aid readability, we have used a few simple formatting conventions in this book:

- The ¬ symbol is used in example scripts to indicate where a long line of code has been wrapped to fit the printed page. AppleScript also uses this symbol to indicate line continuations, so you can type it as-is if you wish, but its position may change when the script is compiled. Alternatively, you can omit both this symbol and the line break that follows it and allow the entire line to wrap naturally within the AppleScript Editor window.

- The `-->` character sequence at the start of a line is used to indicate a typical value returned by a script when it is run and is not . The double-hyphen sequence (`--`) is also used by AppleScript to indicate a single-line comment, so it doesn't matter if you type this line when entering a script into AppleScript Editor (though see the next point).

- Where a return value indicated by the `-->` character sequence is too long to fit on a single line, it may be spread across subsequent lines like this:

```
--> {application file "Address Book.app" of folder "Applications" of
      startup disk of application "Finder", application file "Automator.app"
      of folder "Applications" of startup disk of application "Finder", ...}
```

  If you choose to type this text into AppleScript Editor, make sure you remove all of the line breaks so that it appears as a single line, otherwise the script will not compile correctly.

▓ We regularly use the phrase "application object" to mean any object that is defined by a scriptable application—a folder object, a playlist object, and so on. Most scriptable applications also define a top-level object whose class is application, so when we discuss these objects in particular, the word "application" is shown in monospace text to make the distinction clear; for example, "the Finder's application object."

Errata

We have made every effort to ensure that there are no errors in the text or code. However, mistakes happen, and we recognize the need to keep you informed of any mistakes as they're discovered and corrected. An errata sheet will be made available on the book's main page at http://www.apress.com. If you find an error that hasn't already been reported, please let us know.

The scriptable applications used in this book were the latest versions available at the time of writing, though newer releases may appear over time. While scripts written for one version of an application will usually work with newer versions, this is not always the case. If you discover a script no longer works due to non-backwards-compatible changes in the software used, please let us know and we will try to address such issues where possible.

Part I

Welcome to AppleScript

Chapter 1

Introducing AppleScript

AppleScript is a scripting language for automating your Mac. With AppleScript's help, many tasks that you would normally perform with the mouse and keyboard can be turned over to your Mac to deal with, freeing you up to get on with more interesting or important things.

What is AppleScript good for? AppleScript's greatest strength is its ability to communicate with hundreds, if not thousands, of Mac OS X applications. This makes it ideal for all kinds of application scripting tasks—anything from simple, one-off scripts that you run once to perform a particular task, up to large, complex workflows that will perform vital functions for months or even years to come. In fact, most of the power of AppleScript comes not from the language itself, but from the applications it talks to.

What makes AppleScripting worthwhile? Although many of the tasks you carry out on your Macintosh are interesting and unique, many other, day-to-day tasks are boring and repetitive, requiring you to perform the same sequence of actions over and over again. If you write some scripts to take care of the latter, the time you save can be spent on more of the former.

Automating with AppleScript: From Small Tasks to Large

AppleScript is great for creating small, simple scripts, each of which performs a single task many times over—providing significant, immediate benefits to even the most casual of users. In the hands of an experienced developer, AppleScript can also scale to large and complex tasks, to assemble a whole series of professional Mac applications into powerful and sophisticated workflows.

Let's consider an example of each.

Automating Small Tasks

Creating small, simple scripts is the ideal way for you to start to become familiar with AppleScript. AppleScript lets you easily create a script, test it, save it as a file or application, and start using it. This quick turnaround for truly useful utilities is part of the winning recipe that makes AppleScript so great.

A few years ago I was teaching an Adobe Photoshop class, and during my five-minute break, a colleague told me about a problem a client of his, a prepress house, was having. The client couldn't print lines in QuarkXPress documents that were thinner than 0.25 point and was spending hours correcting every document. By the end of my break I had written the following script, saved it as an application, and handed it to him:

```
tell application "QuarkXPress 4.01"
    tell every page of document 1
        set width of (every line box whose width < 0.25) to 0.25
    end tell
end tell
```

The prepress shop was thrilled with the "utility" we had scrambled to program for them. Because the client got this one for free, its return on investment (ROI) can't be measured in terms of money. But just for kicks, we *can* figure out the ROI in terms of time. Again, I created the script in five minutes. Without the script, it took an employee of the prepress facility ten minutes to fix an average file manually, and this prepress facility printed ten files a day. Using these numbers, the time investment paid for itself *5000 times over* during the first year (5 minutes invested saved approximately 100 minutes a day, which corresponds to 500 minutes in a five-day work week, or 25,000 minutes in a 50-week work year). This sounds a bit over the top, but it's not. Little AppleScript efforts can make a big difference.

Automating Large Tasks

While AppleScript doesn't sweat the small stuff it can also be the base for large-scale custom integrated systems. Large-scale automated solutions can provide impressive savings in time and money over the long term, but they can also require significant time and work to develop in the first place. Before you convert a long and complex manual workflow into an AppleScript-based one, the first thing you need to do is determine whether or not the process will be worth automating.

For example, here is a process that is not so suitable for automation:

> You read the client's instructions file to figure out what corrections the client wants. If the client wants an image to be color-corrected, you open the image in Photoshop and apply curves until it looks better. Otherwise, just correct the typos in the InDesign document.

This process is much too arbitrary and relies on the operator's human qualities such as the ability to perform color correction and to correct typos. Although you might manage to identify one or two small tasks that could be streamlined by the addition of small utility scripts, the overall process will work best if left as a manual workflow.

Here is a better candidate for automation:

> When you get a job from a client, you search for the client in your FileMaker Pro database to locate the job information. If the job is marked "urgent," you notify the imaging room via e-mail to expect the job within ten minutes. You open the Adobe InDesign document and verify that all the fonts were provided. You make sure the document contains the number of pages indicated in the electronic job ticket; if it doesn't, you make a note in the database and e-mail the client from Mail. After you finish all these tasks, you use the Finder to make a copy of the "job" folder in the "archive" folder on the server, and you send another copy to the "in" folder on the production server. You repeat these steps for all jobs that arrived last night.

This is a process for which AppleScript is perfect because

- It deals with lots of information, all of it in electronic form.

- It follows clear, logical rules in deciding what to do with that data.

- It must be repeated, step for step, for each one of the many client jobs that arrive.

- Accuracy is important, as any mistakes will mean time and money are lost.

Note that all the steps in the process happen in software applications. The operator has to know how to use FileMaker Pro to search for and enter data; how to use InDesign to check fonts, pages, and so on; how to use Mail to send e-mail messages; and how to use the Finder to move folders. The great news is that all of these applications include extensive AppleScript support.

Controlling these and many other applications is one of AppleScript's main strengths. AppleScript can give commands to applications and get information from applications, such as retrieving the data in a FileMaker Pro record or the number of pages in an InDesign document.

When to Automate (or Not)?

Regardless of whether you write small- or large-scale scripts, one key question to ask yourself is always the same: is the task worth automating? In other words, is the time and/or cost of creating an automated solution less than the time and/or cost of doing the job manually?

For example, a task that probably won't benefit from automation is the retouching of photographs. Although there may be many photographs to process (repetition), each photograph is sufficiently unique that a human operator will be required to decide exactly what changes—adjustments to highlights and shadows, removal of blemishes, and so on—are necessary on a case-by-base basis.

However, even with tasks that require extensive manual intervention, you may find that certain aspects of the job can be performed by a well-aimed script, making the human operator's job a bit easier. For example, if a client requires a low-resolution JPEG thumbnail to be created for each of the original, high-resolution images, you could ask the retoucher to save a second copy of each file once they have finished correcting it. Alternatively, the retoucher could save all of their finished files to a folder and then run a script that opens each file in turn and resaves it as a JPEG file to another folder, enabling the retoucher to get on with the next client's work while the script runs.

The Golden Triangle: Scriptable Applications, the AppleScript Language, and the Scripts You Write

Have you ever traveled to a foreign country where you don't speak the local language and are unfamiliar with local customs? Until you find your way around the place, it's easy to feel a bit overwhelmed by it all, perhaps even intimidated. If this is your first trip into the world of AppleScript, or scripting in general, you will probably start getting this feeling very shortly.

What you need is a map; one that provides a general overview of the entire territory, shows you where the important landmarks lie, and points you toward some of the safer, simpler, and/or more interesting paths that you can go on to explore for yourself. This chapter is...not that map. In fact, this chapter is more of a map to the real map, which you'll meet in the next chapter. For now, I want to introduce you to three basic concepts in the AppleScript world: scriptable applications, the AppleScript language, and the scripts you write.

What Is a Scriptable Application?

As a Macintosh user, you likely already use many Mac OS X desktop applications, are familiar with the graphical user interfaces (GUIs) that these applications present—menus, buttons, text boxes, and so on—and know how to manipulate these GUIs using a keyboard and mouse.

However, did you know that many of these applications also have a *second interface*, one that's invisible to ordinary human users but can be freely accessed by other Mac OS X applications running on the same or even other machines? This invisible interface allows one Mac application to take control of another—for example, to open a file, manipulate its content, and save it again. In some cases, applications may interact in this way purely for their own benefit; for example, the operating system occasionally tells all the currently running applications to quit themselves so that it can safely shut itself down. More often than not, however, these invisible application interfaces are actually being used by *scripts* written by human users, to perform actions for *our* benefit. In honor of this type of usage, we commonly refer to the application being controlled as a "scriptable application."

The driving force behind these hidden application interfaces is a special sort of instruction, known as an *Apple event*, that can be passed from one running application to another. The AppleScript language not only knows how to speak Apple events, it was created with exactly that purpose in mind.

TIP: Applications that understand Apple events are often also referred to as "AppleScriptable applications," although technically AppleScript is not the only language that can speak Apple events.

I will talk a little more about Apple events later in the book, although in day-to-day scripting you rarely should need to think about them yourself because AppleScript looks after these low-level details for you.

Application scripting is such a large and important subject that it will take a couple of full chapters just to build up a basic understanding of all the concepts and features behind it, plus several more to really see what it can do when used to interact with real-world applications such as Finder, iTunes, Mail, FileMaker Pro, Adobe InDesign, Microsoft Word…the list of possibilities goes on and on!

For now, there are a couple of really basic application scripting concepts I'd like to introduce you to, partly to give you an idea of what to expect and partly to whet your appetite for what's to come. These two concepts are *objects* and *commands*.

Introducing Objects

Objects are things. A kettle is a thing. A dog is a thing. In scriptable applications, the things you deal with are pieces of information: a piece of music, a QuickTime movie, an e-mail message from a friend or colleague, and so on. Some pieces of information may even bemade up of smaller, simpler pieces of information: a movie consists of both an audio track and a video track; an e-mail message has a subject, a sender, one or more recipients, and a message body.

A Mac application has its own ways of representing these pieces of information in its GUI, in a form that human users can understand. For example, an e-mail message in Mail is represented by a window, and each section of the message is represented by a different text box in that window. Similarly, the application's scripting interface needs to represent these pieces of information in a form that other applications can understand. These representations are called *objects*.

However, although making all this information visible to you and your scripts is great, information on its own isn't enough to do anything useful—you also need some way to usefully manipulate that information. Which brings us to our second concept: commands.

Introducing Commands

Commands are instructions. "Boil" is an instruction. "Sit" is an instruction. All desktop applications should respond to a few standard commands such as run, open (to open one or more files), and quit. Individual applications may also define additional commands for themselves—for example, iTunes provides commands for starting and stopping the playback of music and movies; Mail provides commands for creating a new outgoing e-mail message and sending it.

These commands allow a scriptable application to be manipulated by other programs, just as the menus and buttons in its GUI allow it to be manipulated by human users. If the open and quit commands sound familiar, that's probably because most applications have Open and Quit menu options with the same names that fulfill the same functions, if not necessarily in exactly the same way (the open command does not use a file chooser dialog box, for example).

What's more, many commands can be combined with objects to perform all sorts of specific and sophisticated operations. For example:

- Boil the kettle.
- Tell the dog to sit.

Okay, so I don't actually know of any Mac OS X applications that support these two particular operations. However, before we look at some real application commands, I need to introduce the other two concepts in the golden triangle…

What Is the AppleScript Language?

The first thing you should know about today's computers (if you haven't already noticed) is that they are dumb; really, really dumb. To do anything useful at all, they require extremely simple, absolutely precise instructions. I'm not just talking about "play the first music track in iTunes" or "send the frontmost e-mail message in Mail" either; I mean "read 4 bytes of data from memory location X, sum it with 4 bytes of data from memory location Y, and store the result in memory location Z" simple.

Obviously, creating complex modern desktop applications like iTunes or Mail directly using such low-level instructions would take an extremely long time. To speed up software development (and no doubt preserve their sanity too), computer programmers have created their own higher-level instruction sets that sit on top of the very low-level instructions used by your computer's hardware. This allows them to write much simpler statements such as "z = x + y" and leave the computer to take care of all the nitpicky details involved in fiddling with bits and bytes. These high-level instruction sets are called *programming languages*. They provide a sort of halfway house between the extremely primitive instructions used by computer hardware and the incredibly complex and sophisticated languages normally used by humans; a place where humans and computers can meet and (hopefully!) understand each other.

Over the years, many of these languages have been created to cater to a huge range of different tasks: advanced mathematics, heavy-duty business data management, general system administration, desktop- and web-based application development, and so on. While many of these languages have been designed for programmers by programmers, every so often a language comes along that is designed to appeal to nonprogrammers—ordinary users like you and me—as well. AppleScript is one such language.

Originally developed by Apple in the early '90s, and included in every version of Mac OS since System 7.1, AppleScript is, at its heart, a pretty simple tool. It provides objects to represent various basic types of information that scripters regularly work with (numbers, text, etc.), along with commands and other kinds of instructions that can be used to manipulate that information. In addition, it provides several extremely useful structures that can be used to control if and when these instructions should be performed, and a couple of particularly powerful features that more advanced scripters can use to organize their code.

None of these features is unique to AppleScript, however; many other scripting languages also have them. So what makes AppleScript so special? Two features stand out in particular.

The first is AppleScript's ability to speak Apple events, allowing it to communicate with scriptable Mac OS X applications. Other languages can use Apple events as well, but only AppleScript builds this ability into the very heart of the language itself. That's how important application scripting is to AppleScript, and it is very, *very* good at it.

The second is the exceptionally readable, "English-like" appearance of AppleScript code. This makes it especially attractive to Mac users who have important tasks that they'd like to automate, but who don't have a lot of time to spend learning a more traditional scripting language. Even if you have never written a single line of program code, often you can get a good overall idea of what an existing AppleScript will do when you run it just from looking at it. Take another look at the prepress script I showed you earlier:

```
tell application "QuarkXPress 4.01"
   tell every page of document 1
      set width of (every line box whose width < 0.25) to 0.25
   end tell
end tell
```

Even if you don't know any AppleScript—or any QuarkXPress, for that matter—you can probably tell just from reading the preceding script that it's going to go through a QuarkXPress document and thicken up any lines that are too thin to print.

Of course, before you can begin writing your own code, you need to learn a bit about exactly *how* the AppleScript language works. Still, I think you'll agree; being able to see *what* a piece of AppleScript code does just by looking at it is pretty impressive.

Which brings us to our final concept...

What Is a Script?

A *script* is a set of instructions for a computer to perform, written in a text-based language that both humans and computers can understand. Mac OS X includes a number of popular scripting languages as standard, allowing you to start scripting straight out of the box. The aim of this book is to teach you how to read and write scripts using the AppleScript language in particular.

Every script starts with an idea; for example, "I want to clean up my desktop by moving everything on it into a folder named after today's date." Mind you, having ideas is the easy bit. The key to writing a successful script is explaining these ideas to AppleScript using only grammar and vocabulary that it is familiar with, and in sufficient detail that it knows exactly what you want done. One of the first steps to becoming a skilled AppleScript user is realizing just how much you must "dumb down" everything you say to it. If your script does not follow AppleScript's grammatical rules, AppleScript will not be able to read it. If your instructions contain words that AppleScript is unfamiliar with, it won't know how to carry them out. And if you aren't precise enough in explaining what you want done, don't be surprised if AppleScript gets confused and does something different from what you intended.

Obviously, if you are completely new to AppleScript, it will take a little while to learn enough of the language and how to use it to create really interesting and powerful scripts of your own. Even automating a seemingly simple task such as cleaning up your desktop will require some bits of knowledge that won't be fully explained for several chapters to come. However, it would be a pity to leave this chapter without some sort of hands-on introduction to the language itself, so let's start with something really simple: writing a script to display the traditional programmers' greeting, "Hello World!"

Your First AppleScript: Hello World!

The first thing you need to start creating your "Hello World!" script is something to write it in. Open the folder named Utilities in your Mac's main Applications folder. You will see several applications within this folder—the one you're interested in is AppleScript Editor, which is Apple's standard tool for creating, viewing, and running AppleScript code.

> **NOTE:** On Mac OS X 10.5 and earlier, the AppleScript Editor application is named Script Editor and can be found in /Applications/AppleScript.

Double-click the AppleScript Editor icon to start it up. Upon launching, AppleScript Editor automatically creates an empty document similar to the one shown in Figure 1–1.

Figure 1–1. *An empty AppleScript Editor document*

Into this window, type the following line:

```
display dialog "Hello World!"
```

At this point, your script is just an ordinary piece of text that could mean anything to anyone. The first bit of AppleScript magic occurs when you click the Compile button in the window's toolbar, so do that now.

Notice anything different? Assuming you typed your text exactly as shown, it should have changed from purple text displayed in the Courier font to a mixture of blue and black text set in Verdana. Figure 1–2 shows how the window should look before and after the Compile button is clicked.

Figure 1–2. *Compiling the "Hello World!" script*

What just happened? When you clicked the Compile button, AppleScript Editor asked AppleScript to read the text you typed and see if it could make sense of it. As you probably guessed, I didn't choose the phrase display dialog at random, or wrap the "Hello World!" message in quote marks without good reason. display dialog is the name of a command that instructs AppleScript to display a dialog box onscreen. The quote marks around the phrase "Hello World!" indicate that it is a piece of textual information. Put these two things together, and you have a script that tells your Mac to display the text "Hello World!" in a dialog box. Click the Compile button, and AppleScript checks that your script's grammar, or *syntax*, is correct. If it is, AppleScript translates your text into the precise operations that will be carried out when the script is run: create an object representing the phrase "Hello World!" and then perform a command named display dialog using that object. As a final courtesy, AppleScript gives AppleScript Editor a nicely colored version of your original text that makes it easy for you to see which bit is which while confirming that it has understood the text that you've typed.

Now that your script is ready to go, all that remains is to run it. To do this, just click the window's Run button. Figure 1–3 shows what happens when you do this.

Figure 1-3. *Running the "Hello World!" script*

Congratulations! You've now written and run your first successful AppleScript!

Summary

In this chapter, you were introduced to AppleScript and application scripting—what they're good for, and a little bit about how they work. In particular, you were introduced to two key concepts: objects, which are pieces of information, and commands, which are instructions to manipulate that information.

You also created your first successful script: a traditional "Hello World!" greeting that combines an object with a command to display the text "Hello World!" in a dialog box onscreen.

The next chapter maps out these and other key concepts in a bit more detail, providing you with a bird's-eye view of AppleScript's world that will help to prepare you for the in-depth coverage of these concepts in Part 2.

Chapter 2

AppleScript in Principle

Learning how to script for the first time can be a daunting prospect. Although you do not need to learn every last feature and technique of scripting to create your own successful scripts, you do have to know a certain amount of information before you can really start scripting.

Part 2 of this book will explore each major feature of AppleScript in its own chapter. Although this approach allows you to study each feature in lots of detail, it has one obvious disadvantage: until you have read and digested all of those chapters, it is very difficult to see exactly how all the different pieces of the AppleScript jigsaw puzzle fit together. Don't worry, though, because you won't be going in empty-handed.

The purpose of this chapter is to provide you with a broad map of AppleScript's world. Think of it as a tourist guide that briefly describes all the major landmarks you will visit on your impending trip. Although reading about what each place is like is no substitute for actually going there, having a rough idea of what to expect means you won't spend the entire journey feeling like you have no idea of where you're off to next or why.

The first two sections of this chapter will help you to make sense of application scripting and the AppleScript language. The first section breaks down application scripting into four easy-to-remember "key concepts." Each key concept is introduced in turn, with a brief explanation of what it is, what part it plays in the grand scheme of things, and how it relates to the other key concepts. The second section does the same for the AppleScript language itself, breaking it down into its four key concepts and introducing each one in turn. After you've been introduced to all eight key concepts, the final section describes just what it is that makes AppleScript special.

In Chapter 3, you will put this initial knowledge to practical use as you develop your first serious script. Part 2 of the book will gradually fill in all the gaps.

Enough introduction—let's get started.

The Four Key Concepts of Application Scripting

In application scripting, there are four key concepts to understand:

- How applications represent information as objects
- How applications manipulate objects using commands
- How applications organize their objects into object models
- How applications describe their objects and commands in dictionaries

Chapter 1 briefly introduced the first two of these concepts, *objects* and *commands*, but they are such an essential part of application scripting that we'll go over them again, along with the latter two concepts that have yet to be introduced.

Chapter 5 will fill in all the details that you need to know to script applications for yourself, and in Part 3 of the book you will put all of this knowledge to work automating many popular OS X applications.

How Applications Represent Information As Objects

The purpose of most desktop applications is to enable users to work with information. For example, TextEdit is used to create or view textual data; iTunes is used to manage and listen to audio data; Adobe Illustrator is used to manipulate graphics data; and so on.

Each of these applications provides a graphical user interface (GUI) to allow human users to interact with that information. For example, Figure 2–1 shows the main playlist window from iTunes' GUI.

As you can see, the playlist window has three main parts: a left-hand sidebar that displays its playlist data, the main list area where track data can be viewed, and a toolbar across the top containing buttons for controlling playback.

iTunes also provides a second, invisible interface that allows nonhuman users—specifically other applications—to view the same data, though in a different way. This *scripting interface* represents each piece of data (every playlist, every track, and so forth) as an *object*. Although human users cannot view these objects directly, we can observe them indirectly through scripting languages such as AppleScript (hence the term "scripting interface"). To demonstrate, open a new window in AppleScript Editor (/Applications/Utilities/AppleScript Editor.app) and type the following line:

```
tell application "iTunes" to get the first playlist
```

Figure 2–1. *iTunes' main playlist window displaying its data (playlists and tracks)*

Now click the Run button to compile and run this script. The script will ask iTunes for its first playlist object, and iTunes will return a result that looks something like this:

```
--> library playlist id 414 of source id 41 of application "iTunes"
```

What you're seeing here isn't the actual playlist object—objects that belong to a particular application only ever exist within that application—but rather a set of directions, called a *reference*, that describes how to find that object within iTunes. We'll talk about references a bit more in the discussion of the next two key concepts: how applications manipulate objects and how applications organize their objects.

iTunes' track and playlist objects also contain lots of useful information about themselves. For example, if we want to know the name of each playlist, we can ask for it like this,

```
tell application "iTunes" to get the name of every playlist
```

and iTunes will return a list of names like this:

```
--> {"Library", "Music", "Movies", "Podcasts", "Purchased", "Party Shuffle",
     "Genius", "Music Videos", "My Top Rated", "Recently Played", ...}
```

We can ask for lots of other information as well, such as the total playing time (in seconds) of the "Recently Played" playlist:

```
tell application "iTunes" to get the duration of playlist "Recently Played"
--> 39066
```

We can already get this sort of information from iTunes' GUI, of course, but that interface has been created specifically for human users and would be very clumsy and difficult for other applications to use. By providing a second interface that is designed especially for programs to use, iTunes allows nonhuman users such as AppleScript to access the same data, but in a format that they find convenient to work with.

Of course, being able to see data isn't much use if we can't do anything with it, which brings us to our second key concept...

How Applications Manipulate Objects Using Commands

Representing data as objects is only one piece of the puzzle. A scriptable application must also provide nonhuman users such as AppleScript with a way to manipulate that data. Remember, objects only live within the application that defines them, so we need some way of telling an application what we want it to do with those objects.

In a GUI, we would use controls such as menus and buttons to perform actions such as opening a text file in TextEdit, playing a track or playlist in iTunes, or deleting a line in Illustrator. In application scripting, the feature used to perform an action is called a *command*.

Once again, both menus and commands have the same overall goal—to manipulate an application's data—but the way each works is specially tailored to suit the type of user who is using it. For example, to start iTunes playing, a human user would click the "play" button at the top of iTunes' playlist window or select the Controls ➤ Play item in iTunes' menu bar. To start playing iTunes from AppleScript, we send a command named play to the iTunes application:

```
tell application "iTunes" to play
```

Create a new AppleScript Editor document, type this line into it, click the Run button, and iTunes will begin playing.

So far, so good, but what if we want to tell iTunes to play a particular playlist? A human user must perform two separate tasks to accomplish this: click the desired playlist to select it, and then click the Play button to start playing the selection. However, this two-step approach is unnecessary when a script is in control. Instead, many application commands allow you to specify the object or objects you want them to work with. For example, iTunes' play command will let you refer to a track or playlist object immediately after the command's name.

Let's try this now by telling iTunes to play the playlist named "Top 25 Most Played". First, here's how we'll identify the playlist we're interested in:

```
playlist "Top 25 Most Played"
```

This is a reference, albeit a simple one, that identifies the playlist object we're interested in by its name (the part within the double quotes).

Next, write this reference after the play command in your earlier script:

```
tell application "iTunes" to play playlist "Top 25 Most Played"
```

Finally, click the Run button to compile the script and run it. iTunes will immediately begin playing the tracks in your Top 25 playlist.

> **NOTE**: The "Top 25 Most Played" playlist is one of the standard playlists in iTunes, although the name may vary on non-English systems. If your Top 25 playlist is named differently, just change the playlist name used in the preceding script to match the playlist name shown in iTunes' GUI.

How Applications Organize Their Objects into Object Models

So far we have looked at how an application's scripting interface represents individual pieces of data to its nonhuman users as objects, and how it allows those users to manipulate that data by sending commands to the application. For our third key concept, let's take a look at how scriptable applications organize their objects.

Many users have to deal with large quantities of different kinds of data, so to make all that data manageable, applications need to organize it somehow. For example, a typical iTunes user may own thousands, or even tens of thousands, of music tracks in their library. An easy way to organize this library is to collect related tracks together—for example, all the tracks by a particular artist, all the tracks that fit a romantic mood, and so on—and put each set of tracks in a playlist of their own. Figure 2–2 shows a collection of tracks gathered together in a single user-defined playlist, as seen in iTunes' GUI.\Remember that a lot of the information we see in iTunes' GUI can also be seen in its scripting interface. How the GUI represents information to its human users may or may not resemble the way that the scripting interface represents the same information to its software-based users, of course. In this case, though, the similarities are actually very strong.

Just as the GUI shows tracks as being contained by a playlist, so does the scripting interface represent track objects as being contained by a playlist object. The diagram in Figure 2–3 illustrates how this *containment structure* appears from AppleScript's point of view.

Figure 2–2. *iTunes' main playlist window displaying a number of tracks collected together in a user-defined playlist*

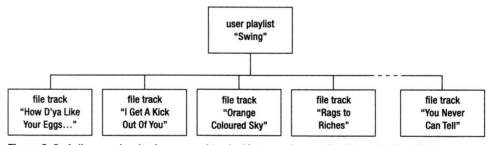

Figure 2–3. *A diagram showing how several track objects can be contained by a playlist object*

This ability of a playlist object to contain track objects is just part of a larger containment structure: in turn, playlist objects are contained by other objects called *sources*, and all these source objects are contained by a single `application` object. This entire structure is what's known as an *object model*. Almost every scriptable application has an object model, and the way that an application's object model is laid out is unique to that application.

Organizing objects into object models makes them easier to manage, particularly in applications such as iTunes that can easily contain many tens of thousands of objects.

Figure 2–4 shows a simplified example of a typical iTunes object model (I've omitted some less important parts of the object model and cut down the number of tracks shown for sake of space). This should give you some idea of what AppleScript can see when it talks to iTunes' scripting interface.

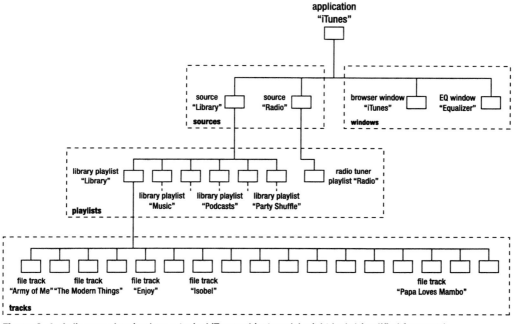

Figure 2–4. *A diagram showing how a typical iTunes object model might look (simplified for space)*

Of course, now that iTunes has nested all of its track objects within playlist objects, and all of its playlist objects within source objects, and all of its source objects within its main `application` object, scripting interface users such as AppleScript will need some way of locating objects within this structure.

This is where references come in, providing directions through the object model to the objects you want to use. For example, the following reference identifies the first track object of the first playlist object of the first source object:

```
tell application "iTunes"
    track 1 of playlist 1 of source 1
end tell
```

How Applications Describe Their Objects and Commands in Dictionaries

Having learned about objects, commands, and object models, you probably are wondering how on earth you are supposed to determine what kinds of objects and commands a scriptable application provides, and how those objects are organized into an object model. The answer to this question is simple: every scriptable application contains its own built-in documentation, called a *dictionary*, that lists all the commands that are available to use and describes each different kind, or *class*, of object you will find within the application's object model.

We have a lot more information to get through in this chapter, including the four key concepts of the AppleScript language, so we'll resume the examination of dictionaries in Chapter 5, which discusses all the concepts behind application scripting in a lot more detail. In the meantime, Figure 2–5 shows part of iTunes' dictionary to give you a rough idea of what a typical application dictionary looks like when viewed in AppleScript Editor.

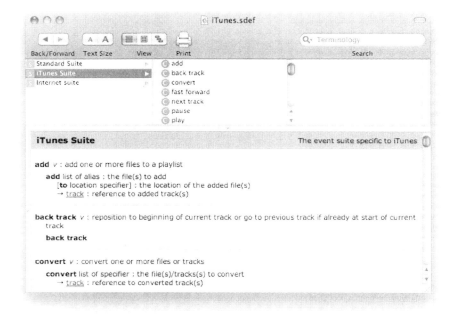

Figure 2–5. *Part of iTunes' built-in dictionary, displayed in AppleScript Editor's dictionary viewer*

The Four Key Concepts of the AppleScript Language

Now that you are familiar with the four key concepts behind application scripting in general, let's proceed to the four key concepts behind the AppleScript language itself:

- How AppleScript represents information as objects
- How AppleScript manipulates objects using commands, operators, and variables
- How AppleScript makes decisions on what to do and when to do it
- How AppleScript organizes code using handlers and script objects

Although this section is not very long, it is important—in Part 2 of the book we will spend a great deal of time exploring the many pieces that make up the AppleScript language, so it's a good idea to know beforehand how and where each of those pieces is supposed to fit in the overall picture.

Let's get started.

How AppleScript Represents Information As Objects

Like scriptable applications, a big part of AppleScript's job is to manipulate information, so it probably won't surprise you to hear that AppleScript can create and work with objects of its own. Although AppleScript objects, like application objects, are used to represent information, there are a few differences in how they behave.

The first difference is that AppleScript objects are much simpler than application objects. Application objects normally represent quite specialized pieces of information: windows and documents in TextEdit, playlists and tracks in iTunes, paths and layers in Illustrator, and so forth. AppleScript objects represent the most basic building blocks you can use in your scripts: simple things like numbers, pieces of plain text (called *strings*), and dates. Here are some examples as you would write them in your scripts:

```
42
3.14
"Hello World!"
date "Sunday, May 17, 2009 12:41:13 PM"
```

Some types of AppleScript objects are a little fancier in that they can contain other objects. For example, here's a list object containing my weekly lottery numbers:

```
{2, 3, 17, 18, 43, 45}
```

The second difference is that AppleScript objects, unlike application objects, don't live in an organized object model. Instead, AppleScript objects can exist independently within a running script, appearing anywhere they like. Don't worry though if this sounds a bit unruly: AppleScript provides its own set of features for keeping objects well organized—more on this in the next section.

The third difference between AppleScript objects and application objects is that because AppleScript objects are not tied to any single application, they can be used anywhere. For example, in the earlier "How Applications Represent Information As Objects" section, you saw how to ask iTunes for the names of its playlists:

```
tell application "iTunes" to get the name of every playlist
--> {"Library", "Music", "Movies", "Podcasts", "Purchased", "Party Shuffle",
    "Genius", "Music Videos", "My Top Rated", "Recently Played", ...}
```

As you can see, iTunes returns an AppleScript object—specifically a list object containing several string objects. We can now manipulate these objects directly in AppleScript or use them in other application commands.

Chapters 6 to 10 will present the various types of objects available in AppleScript, and you will find them used throughout the book.

How AppleScript Manipulates Objects Using Commands, Operators, and Variables

Not only can AppleScript represent information as objects, it allows you to manage and manipulate those objects too. AppleScript provides three important features for working with objects: commands, operators, and variables.

Using Commands

You already met commands in the earlier discussion of how to manipulate application objects. Well, AppleScript provides various commands of its own too, and even allows users to define their own commands. For example, AppleScript's built-in count command allows you to count the number of characters in a string object,

```
count "Hello World!"
--> 12
```

or the number of items in a list object:

```
count {2, 3, 17, 18, 43, 45}
--> 6
```

Using Operators

Operators are similar to commands in that they are also used to manipulate objects. Unlike commands, however, operators have their own syntax and you cannot define new operators of your own—you can only use the operators that are already built into AppleScript itself.

AppleScript has 25 operators in total. These include math operators that allow you to perform simple math calculations on numerical objects, comparison operators that let you compare two objects to see if they are the same or different, and a very handy "concatenation" operator that you can use to join two strings or two lists together. Here are several examples to give you an idea of how operators are used:

```
1 + 2
--> 3

16 / 2.5
--> 4.0

"HELLO" is equal to "hello"
--> true

99 < 3.5
--> false

"Hello " & "World!"
--> "Hello World!"

{2, 3, 17, 18, 43, 45} & {6}
--> {2, 3, 17, 18, 43, 45, 6}
```

Using Variables

Unlike commands and operators, which are used to manipulate objects, variables are what we use to store objects when we *aren't* working with them.

Think of a variable as a box. Whenever a script has an object that it will need to use again later, it can put it in this box for safe storage while it goes off and does other things. Later on, when it needs to use that object again, it can retrieve it just by finding the box it put it in earlier. To make these storage boxes easy to identify, each one has its own name, or *identifier*.

For example, the following line of code defines a list object containing my lottery numbers and assigns (puts) it in a variable (box) named "lucky_numbers":

```
set lucky_numbers to {2, 3, 17, 18, 43, 45}
```

Later on, if I want to use this list object again, I can retrieve it by referring to my lucky_numbers variable:

```
lucky_numbers
--> {2, 3, 17, 18, 43, 45}
```

Best of all, we can combine all of these features together. For example, if I want to check that I have exactly six numbers in my lucky number list, I can do so as follows:

```
(count lucky_numbers) is equal to 6
--> true
```

I will discuss all of these features—commands, operators, and variables—in a lot more detail in Part 2 of the book.

How AppleScript Makes Decisions on What to Do and When to Do It

The third key concept in AppleScript is that running scripts have the ability to decide what they should do and when they should do it. Roughly speaking, a script may face three kinds of questions when manipulating data:

- Should I do this?
- How often should I do that?
- What should I do if things go wrong?

Happily, AppleScript provides several valuable features for dealing with each one of these questions.

Conditional statements allow a script to decide if an action should be taken. A conditional statement always starts with the word if at the beginning of a line and normally ends with the words end if on a later line. Here is an example:

```
if 2 + 2 is equal to 4 then
   display dialog "Two plus two is four."
end if
```

Repeat statements allow a script to control the number of times the action is performed. A repeat statement always starts with the word repeat at the beginning of a line and ends with the words end repeat on a later line. Here is an example:

```
repeat 15 times
    display dialog "Hello again!"
end repeat
```

Finally, *try* statements allow a script to catch and clean up the mess caused when an action unexpectedly (or expectedly) backfires. A try statement always starts with the word try at the beginning of a line and ends with the words end try on a later line. Here is an example:

```
try
    3 / 0
on error
    display alert "Oops! Can't divide by zero."
end try
```

We're not going to explore how these features work now—we'll do that in Chapters 14 and 15. However, it is useful to know the purpose of each and be able to recognize them when you see them, as they are used in example scripts throughout this book.

How AppleScript Organizes Code Using Handlers and Script Objects

The first three key concepts in AppleScript—representing data, manipulating data, and making decisions—all share a common purpose: to make your scripts do things. The final key concept is different: instead, it is concerned with how you organize the code that goes into your scripts.

Why should your code be organized?

Well, the first bit of news is that if you write only small utility scripts, your code usually doesn't need much, if any, organization to solve your problems successfully. Also, when you're beginning to learn how to script, you'll have more than enough to do just learning the basic features needed to do anything at all. For these sorts of simple scripts, you just start typing at the beginning of the script and keep on going until you reach the end. As long as the completed script compiles and runs and is easy to test and debug, this is the easiest way to get the result you want.

The second bit of news is that once you have mastered the basics, you will probably want to create more powerful and ambitious scripts. This is where good organizational skills become increasingly important, because the real trick to developing medium- to large-scale scripts successfully isn't writing the code, but rather preventing that code from growing so knotty and complicated that it becomes impossible to understand. Chaotic code is extremely difficult to test and debug effectively, or to modify later if you need to add new features. Any time you change one part of the code, it's all too easy to break other parts without even realizing it—too many pieces are entangled with too many other pieces for you to keep track of them all.

Obviously, what larger scripts need is a bit of discipline. The trick here is to break down large, complicated tasks into several smaller, simpler pieces that are easier to understand and manage. This approach requires two things: good design skills—which you can learn with time and practice—and language features.

We will discuss good design techniques in later chapters, after you have had a chance to familiarize yourself with the basic tools of the trade—that is, the features provided by the AppleScript language. When it comes to organizing your code, AppleScript provides two features that you can use: handlers and script objects.

Script objects are a particularly powerful feature that are not needed for most tasks in AppleScript, so I won't say anything further about them here. More advanced scripters can learn about them in Chapter 19.

Handlers are a simpler feature that many scripters find increasingly useful once their scripts grow beyond one or two dozen lines of code. Using script handlers allows you to define your own commands using only AppleScript code. That's right—not only can you use the thousands of existing commands provided by scriptable applications, you can create your own commands too, custom-tailored to your exact needs!

Even if you only write short and simple scripts that don't require a highly structured design, you may find that using handlers is a useful way to package some commonly used pieces of code. For example, you can package the code to find and replace a piece of text within a string as a handler named `find_and_replace`. Then, any time you write a script that needs to perform a find and replace operation, just paste your `find_and_replace` handler into your script somewhere and send a `find_and_replace` command each time you want to use it.

Many of the longer examples in this book use handlers to define these sorts of simple convenience commands. Several go one step further and use handlers to organize their overall structure, breaking a long, complex task down into several smaller, simpler sections that are easier to test, modify, and understand. You can easily identify these handlers because the first line of the handler always begins with the word on or to, followed by the handler's name. The last line of the handler consists of the word end followed by the handler's name again. Between these two lines is the code that will run when the handler is called.

Here is a very simple example of a handler called `square_root` that takes a number, calculates its square root, and returns it:

```
on square_root(the_number)
    return the_number ^ 0.5
end square_root
```

And here is an example of a `square_root` command that uses this handler to calculate the square root of 25:

```
square_root(25)
--> 5.0
```

Looking at the preceding handler, you may be wondering exactly how the calculation part works—after all, doing math in AppleScript won't be covered until Chapter 8.

However, this brings us back to one of the great benefits of using handlers: as long as you know that the handler named square_root calculates the square root of a number, you don't actually need to know *how* it does it. Just call it, and it does all the work for you. It's that simple!

Tying It All Together: What Makes AppleScript Special

Now that you've had a general tour of AppleScript, let's finish off with a brief look at its most distinctive characteristics—or what makes AppleScript "AppleScript."

The English-like Syntax

Some people love it. Some people hate it. Almost everyone will agree: it's certainly different! Yes, I'm talking about AppleScript's famously "English-like" appearance.

What's so special about it? Well, AppleScript's word-based syntax makes it amazingly easy for an ordinary Mac user to look at a piece of AppleScript code and get a pretty clear idea of what that code will do when it is run...*even if she doesn't know any AppleScript herself*. This makes AppleScript unusually quick to get started in, as the first step of learning any new language is figuring out how to read it.

The downside of AppleScript grammar is that it gives you very few clues as to how precisely the script will carry out a particular task. For example, if you see the word count in a script, is that the name of a command, a variable, or some other feature? What about count lines—is that a single name, "count lines," or two separate names, "count" and "lines"? Figuring out these sorts of fine technical details for yourself can take some time and effort, particularly if you have to search through application and scripting addition dictionaries to find the information you need to interpret the code correctly.

More traditional scripting languages typically use various symbols—dots, curly braces, parentheses, and so on—to indicate exactly what type of structure you are looking at; for example, count(lines) would be a command, count, that takes an object stored in a variable named lines. Traditional languages also avoid using spaces within keywords; for example, count_lines would clearly be a single name. The downside of this sort of traditional scripting language syntax is that until you've learned exactly what all these squiggles and signs actually mean, the entire script will appear completely cryptic and you won't be able to tell what it does at all.

In other words, all scripting languages make trade-offs in their choice of syntax. AppleScript's trade-off is that in order to write scripts for yourself, you need to have a good grasp of the various vocabularies used by scriptable applications and AppleScript itself. On the other hand, a well-written AppleScript can be wonderfully elegant and easy to read when you want to find out what the script does—and it is this readability that makes AppleScript so attractive and approachable to many Mac users who might otherwise dismiss scripting as something that's intended for "professional" programmers only.

Built-in Application Scripting Support

Scripting applications is such a huge part of what AppleScript does that it can be easy to forget that the AppleScript language and a scriptable application are actually two very different things. The ease with which we can forget about those differences and just get on and do things is largely due to the almost seamless integration of the AppleScript language with the Apple event technology that applications can use to communicate with one another.

While other languages can also use Apple events through external add-ons, AppleScript is almost unique in having this ability built directly into the language itself. This makes it very convenient to use, as application scripting in AppleScript "just works" straight out of the box. It also allows the language to integrate application-defined keywords directly into the user's code, giving scripts their distinctive English-like appearance.

If the merging of these two technologies has a downside, it's that sometimes it can be a little tricky to tell if the objects and commands you're working with belong to AppleScript itself or to one of the applications that the script is controlling. Often this difference isn't really important: AppleScript-defined objects have many similarities with application-defined objects, and both behave in much the same way in a lot of situations. Sometimes, though, the differences are big enough that they can catch you unawares when you expect an object to behave one way only for it to do something else instead, like cause an error.

One of the tricks to mastering AppleScript is knowing what the similarities and differences are between application objects and AppleScript objects, and being able to tell which kind of object you're dealing with at any point in your script. With the help of this book and plenty of practice, this is something you will get good at in time, and your scripts will become more elegant and reliable as a result.

Attaching Scripts to Applications

Attachability is the ability to hook, or "attach," a script to a desktop application so that the script can be triggered by the application itself. This can be tremendously useful when you need a script to run automatically: just attach it to an application, and when the application does whatever it is you're interested in, it will let your script know about it.

Unfortunately, while external scripting interfaces are common among Mac applications, support for attachability is much less widespread. Even applications that do allow you to attach scripts often only provide notifications of one or two types of events, which may or may not be the ones that you're actually interested in.

Still, attachability is supported in quite a few areas and can be used for a variety of tasks. Here are a few examples:

- System Events (a hidden utility application included in Mac OS X that provides many useful AppleScript-related features) can attach scripts to folders in the file system. A Folder Action script will be triggered when files are added to, or removed from, the folder it is attached to. For example, you might create a drop folder named Upload to Website on your desktop that automatically zips and uploads any files that are dragged and dropped onto it.

- Apple's Mail application can attach scripts as e-mail rules so that they are triggered when an e-mail message arrives, allowing the script to process that message automatically. For example, the script might scan the message content for the time and location of a weekly meeting and then create an entry in iCal for that meeting.

- AppleScript Editor can attach scripts to its context menu, allowing you to run them with a right-click. AppleScript Editor already includes a number of handy context menu scripts for inserting commonly used chunks of code into your script document, and you can easily add more.

While most of the example scripts provided in this book are designed to run directly from AppleScript Editor, later chapters include several attachability-based examples. You can also try modifying some of the stand-alone examples to make them work as folder actions.

> **NOTE:** You may sometimes hear the term Open Scripting Architecture, or OSA, used in discussions of AppleScript. This is the plug-in system that attachable applications use to load the AppleScript language plug-in so that they can run scripts written in AppleScript. In theory, other scripting languages can also be packaged up as OSA components, but to date AppleScript is the only language that provides full OSA support.

The AppleScript Community

Throughout this chapter I've described the key features and concepts that make up scriptable applications and AppleScript. To finish, I'd like to mention one last "feature" of AppleScript: the many people who support and use it. AppleScript has been on the go for more than a decade and a half now, and in that time an enthusiastic and supportive community of developers and users has built up around it.

Within the AppleScript community you will find all sorts of people from many different walks of life: from teenage hobbyists with a pressing need to tidy their vast iTunes music collections, to full-time workflow developers creating powerful automation systems for the publishing industry; from the Mac users who had never written a line of code before, to the professional software developers who produce the scriptable applications that make AppleScript the success it is today.

Many members of the AppleScript community have worked with the language for years, building up considerable knowledge of both the AppleScript language and the many different applications it can be used to control—information and experience that they are only too happy to share with others.

So whether it's a trip to Apple's AppleScript Users mailing list to pop a quick question, or a shopping trip around MacScripter.net's huge collection of third-party scripts for a ready-made solution or something to pull apart and learn from, the AppleScript community is there to help you. And perhaps one day soon, as a skilled AppleScripter yourself, you might do the same for others.

> **TIP:** The introduction to this book includes links to many useful AppleScript resources, including community web sites, mailing lists, and discussion boards.

Summary

This chapter has provided a quick tour of all the major landmarks in the world of AppleScript and application scripting, telling you what they are and showing where they fit in the overall picture.

The first section introduced the four key concepts behind application scripting: how applications represent information as objects, how these objects can be manipulated by commands, how objects are assembled into object models to make them easier to manage, and how all these structures are described in dictionaries.

The second section introduced the four key concepts behind the AppleScript language itself: how AppleScript also represents information as objects; how these objects can be manipulated and managed using commands, operators, and variables; how scripts can make decisions on what to do and when; and the advanced features that AppleScript provides for organizing code in larger, more complex projects.

Part 2 of this book will cover all these features in exhaustive detail. Before you get to that, however, you'll have some fun in the next chapter as you write your first "real" AppleScript.

Chapter 3

AppleScript in Practice

Now that you have a general idea of what makes AppleScript and application scripting tick, it's time to roll up your sleeves and create your first serious AppleScript.

As a heavy-duty Mac user, I frequently drop interesting-looking web links, text clippings, zip files, and so forth onto my desktop "to put away later." Of course, what actually happens is that I never do get around to filing them away myself; instead, my desktop turns into such a mess that in the end I make myself a new "desktop archive" folder and throw everything into that. Although I might never get around to organizing these files properly, my desktop is nice and clean again—at least until I start accumulating a fresh pile of random files.

Given how bad I am at doing my own housekeeping, wouldn't it be much more convenient if my Mac could take care of this tedious task for me? Well, with AppleScript's help, it can!

The Project: Tidy Desktop

In this project, we'll create a simple yet useful housekeeping script that cleans up your desktop by moving any files that are on it into a newly created "desktop archive" folder. Along the way, we'll also explore some of the basics of AppleScript grammar, and try out some of the concepts discussed in Chapter 2.

Before we begin, however, I'm going to show you the finished script itself:

```
set date_string to date string of (current date)
set folder_name to "Desktop Archive for " & date_string

tell application "Finder"
    set archive_folder to make new folder at home ¬
        with properties {name:folder_name}
    move every file of desktop to archive_folder
end tell
```

Presenting the completed code up front may seem a little like cheating—however, this book isn't a homework exercise, and the aim of this project isn't simply to create a finished script. Instead, the real goal is to help you understand how you, as a scripter, can get from an initial idea to a successful working product.

So now that you know what the finished script looks like, you can focus on the entire journey without having to wonder what the destination might be. Enjoy the ride!

> **TIP:** Don't get stressed if you find the rest of this section too much to take in at first. Just go with the flow, read the text, and do the exercises. All the points covered here will be repeated in great detail throughout the book.

Planning the Script

The goal of this script is to move all the files from the desktop into a newly created "archive" folder. The folder's name should include the date on which the folder is created, so that users know when the items the folder contains were moved there.

Now that we know what the script should do, we can break down the process into individual steps. This is a pretty simple project, with three steps in total:

1. Create the folder name, which will look something like "Desktop Archive for Friday, January 8, 2010".

2. Create a new folder with this name. To keep things simple, we'll create the folder in the current user's home folder.

3. Move all the files that are currently on the desktop into this new folder.

Having identified each of the steps involved, we can figure out what sort of features we need to perform each task:

- For the first step, we need some way to get today's date as a piece of text (for example, "Friday, January 8, 2010"). AppleScript provides all the features we need to obtain this information, as you'll see later in the chapter.

- For the second and third steps, we need to manipulate the file system. The Finder provides excellent AppleScript support, making it the ideal tool to use here.

- We need some way to assemble the full file name by joining the "Desktop Archive for " text with the date text. For this job, we use AppleScript's concatenation operator (&).

- We need some way to store the various pieces of information that our script creates and uses. AppleScript variables fit the bill perfectly.

Okay, that's our plan of action. Let's start turning it into actual code.

Writing the Script

Whereas our plan identifies three steps in total, I will cover the development of the script in two main sections: one covering the AppleScript-only part of the script (step one), the other covering the Finder automation part (steps two and three).

As we work through this project, I will also go over some of AppleScript's basic syntax (grammar) rules—these appear as sidebars within the main project description. Although reading about AppleScript grammar isn't nearly as interesting as developing the project itself, it's a good idea for you to get familiar with the basic constructs and jargon now so that you can more easily follow the discussion of the example scripts that are presented later in the book.

Creating the Folder Name

The aim of this step is to create a name for our new archive folder. Obviously, you need somewhere to write this script, so start up AppleScript Editor if it isn't already running (/Applications/Utilities/AppleScript Editor.app) and choose File ➤ New to create a new script document.

The process of creating the folder name is actually made up of two smaller steps. The first part is to get the current date as a piece of text. The second part is to join the date text with the other half of the folder name, "Desktop Archive for ".

Getting Today's Date As Text

To get today's date, type the following code into AppleScript Editor:

```
current date
```

As you might guess, current date is the command that returns the current date and time when it is run. In fact, run it now. Just click the Run button at the top of the script window, and AppleScript Editor will compile and run this command, and display the result at the bottom of the window. Figure 3–1 shows a typical result.

Did you notice that the text you typed was initially formatted as purple Courier? This formatting indicates code that has not yet been compiled. When you clicked the Run button, AppleScript Editor asked AppleScript to compile your code and then run it. Compiling the script is an essential step before running it: among other things, AppleScript checks whether or not your script's syntax (grammar) is correct.

> **TIP:** You can check your script's syntax at any time by clicking the Compile button. This compiles the script but doesn't run it. It's a good idea to compile your script frequently as you write it so that you can quickly identify and correct any syntax problems that occur.

Figure 3–1. *The result of running the* `current date` *command in AppleScript Editor*

After you successfully compile the script, the font and the color of the text both change. Suddenly, AppleScript understands what you're saying…although whether or not it knows how to do what your script is telling it to do is a different question—one that's answered only when you actually run the script.

Now that we have a date object representing the current date and time, the next task is to obtain the date part as a string object.

> **NOTE:** This book talks a lot about "strings." "String" is the traditional computing jargon for a text-based object, as in "a string of characters." In Mac OS X 10.4 and earlier, `string` was also the name of one several different types of text objects used by older versions of AppleScript. When AppleScript 2.0 was introduced in Mac OS X 10.5, it greatly simplified things by introducing a single, one-size-fits-all text type. It also created a bit of confusion by naming this new type `text` instead of the more familiar `string`. Chapter 7 discusses this topic in much more detail; for now, just regard the terms "text" and "string" as interchangeable.

As discussed in Chapter 2, many objects contain extra pieces of information about themselves, and AppleScript objects are no exception. Date objects, for example, allow you to extract individual pieces of information: the year, the name of the month, the day of the month, the number of seconds that have passed since midnight, and so on.

For this exercise, the data we want is stored as a *property* of the date object. This property is called `date string`, and to get its value we use a reference:

```
date string of (current date)
```

Type this into your script window and run it, and you will get a result similar to the following:

`"Friday, January 8, 2010"`

This is our string object. You can tell it's a string object because AppleScript displays it as a piece of text enclosed in a pair of straight double quotes. More on strings in a moment.

You may notice a couple of other things about our growing script. The first point of interest is the use of the word of—well, we're asking for a property *of* an object, so it's only natural that AppleScript should have an of keyword especially for constructing this reference. I will discuss references in great detail in Part 2 of this book, so I'll skip the rest of the details for now.

The second thing you'll notice is that we put parentheses around our original current date command. Although AppleScript is pretty good at making sense of the code you write, there are times when it needs a little extra help in deciding which bits are which. By adding parentheses, we make it clear to AppleScript that it should treat current date in a particular way when compiling the script.

ABOUT APPLESCRIPT GRAMMAR: EXPRESSIONS

Let's try an experiment. Delete the opening and closing parentheses for a moment, and try compiling the script without them:

`date string of current date`

Alas, when you click Compile this time, an syntax error occurs: "Expected expression but found command name." What on earth does that error message mean? Well, you already have some idea of what a command is: it's a type of instruction you can send to scriptable applications and AppleScript—in this case, the current date command.

What's an expression? Well, in AppleScript grammar, an expression is any piece of code that returns an object when evaluated. For example, `"Hello World!"` is an expression. So is 2. More complex expressions can be constructed using operators; for example, `2 + 2 is equal to 4`.

I'll talk more about expressions in later chapters; for now, the point I want to make is that commands, weirdly enough, *aren't* considered to be expressions. The reason for this is simple: although most commands do return an object, they *aren't required* to do so, and some don't. As a result, when we try to use a command in a place where AppleScript expects an expression—in a reference, for example—we get a syntax error instead.

Fortunately, you can clarify your intentions ("yes, I really do mean to use a command there") by wrapping your command in parentheses. Not only does this tell AppleScript that it should treat that particular piece of code as a single unit within the larger script, a pair of parentheses is also considered to be an expression itself, so AppleScript is happy once again.

Inconsistencies such as this make AppleScript grammar a bit more tricky to learn than it ought to be, but, hey, no language is perfect. With time and practice, however, you will get used to it—quirks and all.

Now that we have our string object, we should probably store it somewhere for safe keeping. For this, we use a variable. Let's call this variable date_string—not very imaginative, I know, but we only need it for a short time, so there's no need to get fancy. (In later chapters I'll discuss good naming practices for your own variables.)

To assign an object to a variable, we use AppleScript's built-in set command. Here's how our code should now look:

```
set date_string to date string of (current date)
```

Our date string of (current date) expression goes on the right side, after the keyword to (which is a part of the set command). Our variable name, date_string, appears after the keyword set. Now when AppleScript evaluates the expression, the object it returns is stored safely in the date_string variable. Later on, our script can retrieve this object again when it needs to use it for something.

Okay, so the first line of our script is done. Compile it, run it, and make sure that it works. If all goes well, you should see the string object appear in the bottom half of the script window. If not, check your code carefully, fix any mistakes, and try again until it does work.

Putting the Name Together

Let's pick up the pace a little now. We have the second half of our file name, but we still need the first half. Begin the second line of the script by typing the following:

```
"Desktop Archive for "
```

Take care to use straight double quotes, not single or curly ones, and be sure to put a space after the word for exactly as shown.

ABOUT APPLESCRIPT GRAMMAR: LITERALS

Let's take a closer look at what we've just written:

```
"Desktop Archive for "
```

In grammatical terms, this is called a *literal*; in this case, a literal string object. Why "literal"? Because it's how we [literally] write an AppleScript object as AppleScript code. A string literal, for example, consists of the actual text wrapped in a pair of double quotes. Other types of objects have different literal representations: a literal number object is written as, well, a number; a literal list object is indicated by a pair of curly braces; and so on.

Literals are also considered to be expressions, which means that when AppleScript evaluates our literal string, it will create a string object that contains the text that we wrote inside the quotes.

We can now join this string object with the other string we stored earlier in the date_string variable. To do this, we use my own personal favorite AppleScript operator: the concatenation operator. This is written as an ampersand (&) symbol with one object on the left and the other on the right. Here's how our second line looks when we put these pieces together:

```
"Desktop Archive for " & date_string
```

Finally, because we're being especially tidy in this project, we can assign the result of this new expression to another variable, this time called `folder_name`. Here's how our script now looks:

```
set date_string to date string of (current date)
set folder_name to "Desktop Archive for " & date_string
```

Compile it, run it, and check that it gives the proper result, which should look something like the output shown in Figure 3–2.

Figure 3–2. *The result of running the first two completed lines of the script*

In particular, did you remember to insert a space between `for` and the day of the week? Remember, AppleScript does exactly what you tell it do, so if you don't put a space between the two parts of our file name, the two words will run together as "…forWednesday…" when AppleScript joins them together.

Once you're satisfied that everything is working correctly, it's time to move on to the next step: creating the archive folder.

Interacting with the File System

Now that we have the name for our new desktop archive folder, we are ready to create the folder and move the contents of our desktop into it.

The AppleScript language itself does not include any features for working with the file system, so we need to look for another way to do this. As I've already discussed, AppleScript's greatest feature is its ability to control "scriptable" Mac applications, so the answer is to look for an application that knows how to work with the file system and provides some sort of scripting interface.

In fact, Mac OS X provides us with several options we could use, such as the hidden System Event application that provides a wide range of useful features for AppleScript to use, or perhaps the Unix command-line tools that live further down in the operating system. There are even some third-party file managers available that include AppleScript support, such as Cocoatech's Path Finder.

For this project, however, we will go with the most obvious solution, Mac OS X's Finder application. Finder has a well-designed scripting interface that is elegant and (once you know a bit of AppleScript) straightforward to use.

We will explore the Finder's scripting interface in much more detail in later chapters, so for now I will only cover the essential points that you need to know to get this project up and running. Let's start by looking at how we tell AppleScript that we'd like to talk to the Finder.

> **CAUTION:** Application scripting interfaces, unlike GUIs, do not come with an Undo feature! When manipulating the file system (or doing anything else with AppleScript that might affect important files or work), make sure you have sufficient backups prepared in case anything goes wrong. If you run a script and it destroys your files, either by design or by accident (for example, due to a bug), the last thing you want is to lose that information forever!

Addressing the Finder

In Chapter 2, you learned that the way to make scriptable applications do things is to send them commands. Before writing our commands, however, we need to tell AppleScript where to send them. In this case we want to send them to the Finder, so the first step is to identify the Finder application in our script. Here is the code for doing this:

```
application "Finder"
```

This structure is what's known as an *object specifier*, because it is used to identify, or specify, an object of some sort. Object specifiers are mostly used when identifying objects that live within other objects; however, AppleScript also uses them to create several types of AppleScript objects from scratch, such as date, file, and—as seen here—application objects.

ABOUT APPLESCRIPT GRAMMAR: OBJECT SPECIFIERS

Object specifiers can be a rather tricky concept to wrap your head around at first, so before we go any further, let's spend a little time getting acquainted.

Here is our object specifier from a moment ago:

```
application "Finder"
```

You saw another example of an object specifier earlier in the chapter when we ran the `current date` command; in that case, AppleScript Editor displayed the resulting date object as an object specifier that looked similar to this:

```
date "Friday, January 8, 2010 1:41:32 PM"
```

What is the point of an object specifier? Well, as you've already seen, AppleScript provides special literal syntax for creating several basic types of objects: a numerical object is written as one or more digits, a string object is written as the text itself surrounded by double quotes, and so on.

However, many other types of objects do not have a custom syntax in AppleScript, so we need a more general way of creating or identifying those objects. The solution here is to use an object specifier, which is written as the type, or *class*, of the object we want, followed by an object of some sort.

If the object being specified is an AppleScript object, AppleScript creates that object from scratch. If it is an object in a scriptable application, AppleScript creates a reference to that object. In either case, the second part of the object specifier—the object part—provides AppleScript with all the information it needs to create or identify the object we want. For example, a `date` specifier takes a string object describing the date and time we want the newly created date object to have. For our `application` specifier, we use a string object containing the name of the application we're interested in, which in this case is the Finder.

One last thing: if you type in the following line and run it,

```
application "Finder"
```

the result will also appear as:

```
application "Finder"
```

When displaying an object back to the user, AppleScript generally uses the same syntax that you would use yourself when typing in that object as a literal in your script. This makes it really easy for you to see exactly what sort of object was returned. (There are one or two exceptions to this rule—for example, `POSIX file` specifiers are written one way but displayed another—but we'll deal with those quirks when we get to them.)

Now that we have an `application` object that identifies the application we want to control, we need some way to direct our commands at it. Once again, AppleScript provides us with a language feature for exactly this task: the `tell` statement. Here is the syntax for AppleScript's `tell` statement:

```
tell target_object

end tell
```

A `tell` statement (or "tell block") controls where commands are sent. Normally when AppleScript executes a command in a script, it sends the command to the script itself. If the script knows how to handle that particular command, then great—AppleScript lets the script handle it. On the other hand, if the script doesn't recognize the command, AppleScript then sends the command to the application running the script. If the application doesn't understand the command either, AppleScript gives up and reports an error.

Although this process is great if you want to send a command to your script, or to the application running the script (in this case, AppleScript Editor), it isn't useful if you want to send the command to some other application, such as the Finder. To send our commands to the Finder, we have to redirect them away from our script and at the application object created by our `application "Finder"` specifier.

To do this, take the preceding `tell` statement and replace the *target_object* bit with `application "Finder"`. Here is how the resulting code should look:

```
tell application "Finder"

end tell
```

Now when AppleScript executes this piece of code, any commands that appear within these two lines will be directed at the Finder application by default. With this arrangement, you will be able to direct commands to any scriptable application on your Mac—all you need to do is change the application name to the one you want. Powerful stuff!

ABOUT APPLESCRIPT GRAMMAR: STATEMENTS

Let's look at this new piece of code:

```
tell application "Finder"

end tell
```

In AppleScript, this structure is known as a *statement*—a *compound statement* to be exact. A compound statement consists of an opening line and a closing line. The opening line starts with a keyword that tells you what sort of statement it is—for example, the keyword `if` indicates a conditional statement while the `tell` keyword indicates a `tell` statement.

The other kind of statement is a *simple statement*, which consists of a single line. The first two lines in our script, with which we create our folder name, are both simple statements. For example, this is a simple statement:

```
set date_string to date string of (current date)
```

The advantage of a compound statement is that it can contain any number of other statements. This allows the compound statement to control how the statements within the block are executed when the script runs. For example, a conditional statement can decide if the code it contains should be run or ignored, whereas a `tell` statement specifies the default object that commands within the block should be sent to.

Okay, now that we have the Finder's attention, let's give it something to do.

Creating the Archive Folder

The first thing we want the Finder to do is to create a new folder. This folder should appear within the user's home folder, and it should use as its name the string object that we created earlier and stored in the `folder_name` variable. Let's start with the "making the folder" bit, and then build up from there.

To create new objects in the Finder, we use the `make` command. The documentation for this command appears in the Finder's built-in dictionary, but we'll have plenty of time to explore application dictionaries in later chapters. For now, just follow along as I construct the command a piece at a time.

First, type the make command's name inside the tell block, like this:

```
tell application "Finder"
make
end tell
```

Now click the Compile button. As you can see, the script compiled successfully...always a good first sign.

> **TIP:** AppleScript cleans up any extra spaces and tabs when you compile the script, so don't bother tidying them yourself. AppleScript also automatically indents any lines that appear within compound statements to make the overall structure of the code easier to see. For readability's sake, you may find it useful to insert blank lines between some statements—AppleScript leaves those alone.

However, if you try to run the script now, you will get an error, because telling the Finder just to "make" isn't enough. You also need to tell it *what* to make—in this case, a folder object. Here is the code to do this:

```
tell application "Finder"
    make new folder
end tell
```

This indicates the class of object we want created: folder. When the script runs, this object will be passed to the Finder as part of the make command. The make command can take several values at once, however, so we need to label these values so that the make command knows which is which. Having scripted the Finder before, I already know that the label for this particular parameter is new, so that's what I've used here. Just copy what I've written for now, and in Chapter 5 I'll show you how to look up this information for yourself.

Now compile and run this script. If all goes well, Finder should create a new untitled folder on the desktop. Congratulations! You've just created your first object in another application. Figure 3–3 shows this script in action.

As you can see, the Finder has created a new folder on the desktop, which is the default location it uses if you don't specify a location yourself. You may notice something else of interest here: when the make command finished executing, it returned a reference to the newly created folder object. This is something we will make use of later.

So far we've prompted the Finder to create a new folder for us, but we'd really like to refine this process a bit. The first task is to tell the Finder exactly *where* to make the folder—specifically, in the user's home folder.

Figure 3-3. *The result of telling the Finder to make a new folder*

Normally, when we want to identify an object somewhere in the Finder's object model, we have to create a reference to that location ourselves. On this occasion, however, the Finder conveniently provides a built-in shortcut that will provide this reference for us. This shortcut is named home, and it's a property of the Finder's application object. (Don't worry what that means for now; all will become clear in Chapter 5 when we explore application scripting in depth.) To use this shortcut in the make command, just add the label at followed by the word home:

```
tell application "Finder"
    make new folder at home
end tell
```

If you run the script now, Finder will create a new untitled folder in your home folder.

The last bit of refinement is to tell Finder what the newly created folder should be called. To do this, we need to retrieve our custom folder name string (which we stored earlier in the folder_name variable for safekeeping), and then have the make command use this value as the folder's name when it creates it. This bit will take longer to explain, so for now I will just show you the code for it:

```
tell application "Finder"
    make new folder at home with properties {name:folder_name}
end tell
```

Run this script now, and you should see a new folder with a name like "Desktop Archive for Friday, January 8, 2010" appear in your home folder.

CAUTION: One limitation of the current script design is that if you run the script more than once on the same day, the Finder will report an error like this: "The operation could not be completed because there is already an item with that name." Obviously this script isn't quite as intelligent as it could be—I'll discuss how it might be improved in the final section of this chapter. For now, I recommend that each time you test the script, you first check that it creates the archive folder and moves all the existing desktop files into it. Once you're satisfied that it has worked correctly, move those files manually back to the desktop and drop the empty archive folder into the Finder's Trash before running the script again.

We will need to refer to this folder again when we move our desktop files into it, so to finish this statement, insert an AppleScript set command to capture the folder reference returned by the make command in a variable named archive_folder:

```
tell application "Finder"
    set archive_folder to make new folder at home ¬
        with properties {name:folder_name}
end tell
```

You might notice I've rearranged the make command a bit in the previous bit of code. The whole line was getting a bit long, so I took advantage of another little AppleScript feature, the line-continuation symbol (¬), to spread the code over two lines for neatness. It is still a single simple statement, but the continuation symbol allows me to insert a line break safely into the middle of it. When AppleScript sees the continuation symbol, it simply continues reading on the next line as if the line break didn't exist at all. To insert a continuation symbol, just press Alt+L (users with non-US keyboard layouts may need to use a different key combination).

TIP: AppleScript Editor also allows you to press Alt+Return to insert a continuation symbol followed by a return.

Moving the Files

Our final task is to move all the files from the desktop into our new archive folder. For this we use another Finder command, conveniently called move. The move command can move a single object to another location, or, if we refer to several objects at once, it can move them all together—a very elegant and powerful feature!

Here is how we refer to all the files on the desktop:

```
every file of desktop
```

This deceptively simple-looking reference is the key to the simplicity of our script. I won't explain exactly how it works here—that's another job for Chapter 5—but rest assured it does exactly what it claims to do: specify every single file on the Finder's desktop.

Let's put the final command together. Insert a new line before the end tell line and type the following:

```
move every file of desktop to archive_folder
```

When this line runs, the reference to every file of the desktop is created from scratch, while the reference to our archive folder is retrieved again from the archive_folder variable. Both references are then passed to the Finder as part of our move command. When the Finder receives this command, it finds all the files identified by the first reference, and moves them into the location identified by the second one. It's that simple!

Final Thoughts

Congratulations on creating your first practical AppleScript! Obviously, I've kept this particular exercise as simple as possible for the sake of readers who are completely new to scripting, but hopefully it has given you some idea of the potential power available in AppleScript.

Over time, you will pick up additional knowledge and skills that will enable you to design and write much more powerful scripts entirely on your own. As you work through this book, you might consider revisiting earlier projects such as this one and trying to improve and enhance them yourself, either for practice or for your own personal use. With that in mind, here are some ideas on how you might develop this project further...

Improving Reliability

When developing and testing a new script, you will often discover additional problems that you hadn't considered when you originally came up with the idea. In this case, you may have noticed that while the Tidy Desktop script is pretty good at moving files into a newly created archive folder, it does run into problems when an archive folder for the same day already exists.

You will also find that often more than one way exists to solve a particular problem. For example:

- You could do nothing. If the script fails, it fails, and the user will just have to accept that. In fact, there are plenty of situations where this is the proper thing to do: for example, if a FileMaker Pro script requires a particular database but the database file cannot be found, there's no point in the script trying to proceed any further. That said, it is often useful to provide the user with a more helpful description of the problem than just a raw application error. We'll look at ways of dealing with unexpected errors in Chapter 15. We'll also look at ways of presenting error messages and other basic information to users in Chapter 16.

- You could ask the user for help. For example, if the script needs to create a new folder but another folder with the same name already exists, the script could display a dialog box asking the user to enter a different folder name or to choose a different location in which to create the new folder instead. Chapter 16 also explains how to present file Open and Save dialog boxes to users.

- You could take care of the problem yourself. In the case of the Tidy Desktop script, the best solution might be to start by checking if an archive folder for today already exists. If it does, just skip the "make new folder" step and move the desktop items directly into the existing folder. We'll look at how to make these sorts of decisions in later chapters, particularly in Chapter 14.

In fact, once you've gained a bit more knowledge and experience, I recommend you revisit this and other early example scripts and see if you can improve them yourself. It's good practice, and will help to improve your design and testing skills. And perhaps you'll even find some of these scripts to be useful.

Adding Features

In addition to improving reliability, there are many ways in which you could modify or extend the Tidy Desktop script in future to better fit your own needs. Here are a few ideas:

- You could make the script easier to use by saving it as a standalone mini-application that the user can run just by double-clicking it in the Finder. Or you could install it in the system-wide Script menu, allowing the user to launch it from their own menu bar. We'll look at these options in Chapter 4.

- You could create the archive folders in the user's Documents folder, or allow the user to set the location they want as a preference option. You'll learn how to construct your own references to application objects in Chapter 5, and Chapter 11 includes a section on storing values such as user settings between runs. And don't forget Chapter 16 for help on displaying file and folder chooser dialog boxes.

- You could extend the script to tidy away folders as well as files. Just add an extra line, move every folder of desktop to archive_folder, to the end of the tell application "Finder" ... end tell block. Or you could restrict the script so that only document files or text clippings are filed away. Chapter 5 looks at how to broaden or narrow your references to identify different types of objects. (Just take care not to refer to every item of desktop, however, as that would include all visible disks as well!)

▪ You could modify the script so that different types of items are filed away in separate locations. For example, you might move all text files to your Documents folder, image files to your Images folder, video files to Movies, and so on. Chapter 5 discusses how to construct references that perform these kinds of filtering operations based on individual attributes of your objects, such as file name extensions.

Once again, I encourage you to come back to this project later on and try your hand at adding these and other enhancements yourself.

Documenting Your Code

Creating good documentation isn't only for AppleScript engineers and scriptable application developers. As a script writer, you will also find it useful to record useful bits of information about the code you write. To help you in this task, AppleScript provides a commenting feature that allows you to insert ordinary text within your script.

For small, quick scripts that you write once, run once, and then throw away, you likely don't need detailed documentation—you can probably keep any important information you need in your head as you go, or make a quick note on the side. However, when developing large, complex scripts or scripts that may be in use for many months or years to come, good, detailed explanations can make a great deal of difference should you or another scripter ever need to maintain or modify that script.

To add a single line of text that you want the script to ignore, precede it with a double hyphen (--) or hash symbol (#). Any text starting after the double hyphen or hash symbol, all the way to the end of the line, will compile as an inline comment; for example:

```
display dialog "Hello World!" -- This is a comment
display dialog "Hello World!" # This is another comment
```

You can comment out whole blocks of text as well. You do that by starting the block with (* and ending it with *). Here's an example:

```
(*
Tidy Desktop

ABOUT
This script cleans up the user's desktop by moving all of its contents
into a dated 'Desktop Archive' folder.

HISTORY
- 2009-07-01 - v1.0; first release

KNOWN ISSUES
- If the desktop archive already exists, the make command will raise
  an error.

TO DO
- Modify the script so that it only creates a new archive folder if
  one doesn't already exist.
*)
```

This type of comment is great for longer explanations you want to add to your scripts. Adding a sort of executive summary at the start of the script is a great way to explain what the code does and how it does it.

Adding comments is essential if you or someone else needs to add functionality or fix a bug in a piece of code that was written several months (or even years) ago. It is amazing how difficult it can be to decipher even your own scripts after a while, after you no longer remember what the different parts of the script are supposed to do.

For example, even in a simple script like Tidy Desktop, you might want to include a note explaining why it doesn't include the current time in the file name:

```
(*
Note: I originally tried using 'current date as text' to include the time as well,
but found that Finder gives an error as colons (e.g. "12:00:00 PM") are illegal in
file names. One solution would be to find and replace all the colons with a hyphen
(-) or period (.), but for now I'll just use the date only.
*)
set date_string to date string of (current date)
```

Summary

In this chapter, you worked through the process of creating your first "real-world" AppleScript, putting into practice many of the concepts that were introduced in Chapter 2: AppleScript objects, commands, operators, and variables; and application objects and commands.

These first three chapters provide only a taste of things to come, of course. In Part 2 of the book, you will learn about all of these features in much more detail, along with other features that you have yet to use, such as application dictionaries, conditionals and repeat loops, and so on—knowledge you can use to build your own scripts entirely from scratch.

Understanding AppleScript

Chapter 4

Writing Scripts in AppleScript Editor

Before we start exploring application scripting and AppleScript in detail, in this chapter we are going to take a closer look at the main tool we will use in this book to create, save, and run scripts: AppleScript Editor.

AppleScript Editor is a simple application for writing and running AppleScripts. You can find it in your Mac's `/Applications/Utilities/` folder. The following sections describe AppleScript Editor's main features, starting with script windows, and then moving on to other important features such as dictionary viewer windows, the Library window, and preference options.

> **NOTE:** On Mac OS X 10.5 and earlier, the AppleScript Editor application is named Script Editor and can be found in `/Applications/AppleScript/`. There are a few other differences as well, which I'll point out as we go.

Working with Script Windows

AppleScript Editor's script windows are where you edit and test your scripts. Figure 4–1 shows a typical script window. To create a new script window for yourself, just select File ➤ New in AppleScript Editor's menu bar.

As you can see, the script window is divided into two parts: the top pane is the area where you can write your script, and the bottom pane is used by AppleScript Editor to display various kinds of useful information.

The toolbar at the top of the window contains four buttons for performing basic AppleScript actions: Record, Stop, Run, and Compile. A fifth button, Bundle Contents, is only available when the script is saved in certain formats.

Figure 4–1. *A script window in AppleScript Editor*

At the bottom of the window are two buttons for changing the contents of the bottom pane: Description and Event Log. When the Event Log option is selected, the three buttons that appear immediately beneath the divider—Events, Replies, and Result (the default)—allow you to control what is shown.

> **NOTE:** In Mac OS X 10.5 and earlier, Script Editor has three buttons at the bottom of the script window: Description, Result, and Event Log. These provide access to the same information, just in a slightly different way.

Compiling a Script

Once you've typed some AppleScript code into the main window, the first thing to do is to ask AppleScript to compile it. To do this, click the Compile button in the window's toolbar or select Script ➤ Compile in AppleScript Editor's menu bar. AppleScript checks your code to see if its syntax (grammar) is correct. If all is well, a tidied up version of your source code appears in the top pane of the window. If a problem exists, AppleScript Editor highlights the part of your code that's causing the problem and presents an error dialog box explaining why AppleScript couldn't compile it.

TIP: When typing AppleScript code, it's a good idea to click the Compile button regularly. This allows you to check for any obvious typos as you work, and neatly indents any nested blocks of code for you. You can also see how AppleScript has understood the various words in your script: an AppleScript keyword, for example, is displayed as bold black text; an application-defined keyword as blue or purple text; a user-defined variable or handler name as green text; and so on.

Running and Stopping a Script

The Run button, as its name suggests, is used to run the script that's shown in the window's top pane. If the script isn't already compiled, AppleScript Editor automatically compiles it for you before running it.

If you need to force a running script to stop—for example, if you've just realized it's doing something wrong—just click the Stop button. You can also start and stop scripts by using the Script menu in AppleScript Editor's menu bar, or by pressing Cmd+R.

Recording a Script

Here's recording in a nutshell: you click the Record button in AppleScript Editor, perform some action in another application, and AppleScript Editor records that action in the AppleScript language.

Okay, if recording a script is so easy, why do you need to write a script ever again? Good question. Here's the answer:

- Although recording is nice, most applications aren't recordable. The recordability feature is rare, because application developers have to put in a lot of extra work to add it.

- When you record a script, you get computer-generated AppleScript code consisting of a series of application commands, and nothing else. If your script needs any conditional statements, repeat loops, variables, or handlers, you will have to add these yourself.

Recording scripts is great if you can't figure out how to script a specific aspect of an application, and you're lucky enough to be using an application that supports recording. For instance, the Mac OS X Finder has some limited support for recording, which can make your life a little easier when performing simple operations such as arranging Finder windows on your desktop.

To test it, start a new script window in AppleScript Editor and click the Record button in the toolbar. Then, create some new windows in the Finder, move them, rename some files or folders, and move them around. When you are done, click the window's Stop button, and then look at its top pane of AppleScript Editor to see the recorded actions. As you will see, some simple operations, including opening windows and creating and renaming folders, are recorded in AppleScript Editor as AppleScript commands, whereas others, such as moving and duplicating files, are ignored.

> **TIP:** Another option for recording and replaying GUI interactions is Automator's Watch Me Do feature, first introduced in Mac OS X 10.5. Although recorded Automator actions cannot be edited or modified to the same extent as recorded AppleScripts, Automator recording does not require any special support from individual applications, so it can be used much more widely than AppleScript recording.

Viewing the Result of Running a Script

Many scripts return a final result when you run them. You can view this value in the bottom part of the script window—just select the Event Log tab and click the Result button if they aren't already selected. (Figure 4–1 at the start of the chapter showed a typical script result.) This is the view you will use most often, whether to observe the normal result of running a script or to check values returned while testing and debugging parts of a larger script.

> **TIP:** Starting in Mac OS X 10.6, if a script stops running due to an unexpected error, the Result pane displays all the error information provided by AppleScript to help you debug your code. You will learn all about errors and how to deal with them in Chapter 15.

Viewing the Events Sent by a Running Script

As I mentioned in Chapter 1, Mac OS X uses a special data structure, known as an Apple event, to exchange commands between running applications. Whenever a script directs a command at an application (or scripting addition), AppleScript converts the command into an Apple event, allowing it to travel outside of the script and on to its intended destination.

When the Events button of the Event Log tab is selected, AppleScript Editor allows you to "spy" on all the Apple events that the script is sending, along with any replies it receives (if the Replies button is also selected). This can be very useful when debugging scripts that interact with other applications. Figure 4–2 shows a simple script and the log it created while running.

Figure 4–2. *Viewing the Event Log*

> **NOTE:** In Mac OS X 10.5 and earlier, Script Editor's script windows use a slightly different approach. There, you need to switch between the Event Log and Result panels by clicking the buttons at the bottom of the window. Also, the Event Log panel records events only while it is visible.

Adding a Description to a Script

Clicking the Description tab at the bottom of the script window in AppleScript Editor reveals a large text field. You can write a description for your script and use the Format menu to change the text's type size, font, and color as you like, or copy and paste in styled text from another application such as TextEdit. You can also have that formatted text appear in a dialog box every time your script application launches. We'll look at how to do this in the "Customizing the Startup Screen" section later in the chapter.

Viewing Application Dictionaries

You can view the built-in documentation, or *dictionary*, of any scriptable application or scripting addition using AppleScript Editor's dictionary viewer. You can open a dictionary viewer in several different ways:

- Select File ➤ Open Dictionary in the menu bar and choose one or more entries from the list of installed applications.

■ Drag-and-drop an application or scripting addition file onto AppleScript Editor's application icon in the Finder.

■ Double-click an application or scripting addition name in AppleScript Editor's Library window.

Figure 4–3 shows a typical dictionary window showing part of TextEdit's dictionary.

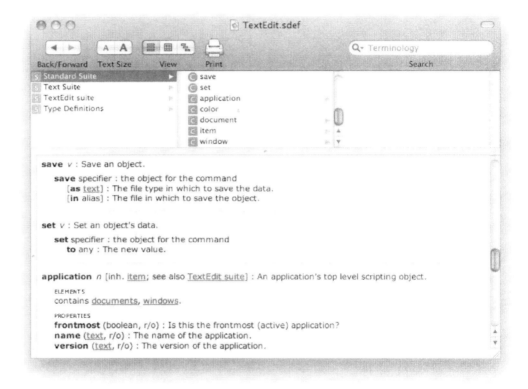

Figure 4–3. *A dictionary viewer window displaying part of TextEdit's dictionary*

You will learn how to use the dictionary viewer in Chapter 5. For now, let's move on to examining AppleScript Editor's other features.

Other Useful AppleScript Editor Features

Script and dictionary windows are the two main features of AppleScript Editor, but it has plenty of other useful tools built into it as well, such as the Library window, the Result and Event Log History windows, and customizable script formatting preferences. The following sections look at these and other features.

Using the Library Window

AppleScript Editor's Library window is an extremely handy feature if you write AppleScripts on a regular basis. It provides a shortcut for opening the dictionaries of your favorite applications and scripting additions. To open the Library window, just select Window ➤ Library from AppleScript Editor's menu bar.

Figure 4–4 shows a typical library.

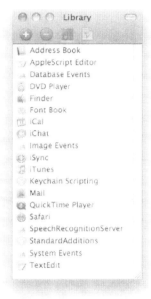

Figure 4–4. *The Library window*

As you can see, the Library window comes with a selection of Apple-installed applications and scripting additions already present. You can easily add new entries or remove existing ones by clicking the "+" and "–" buttons in the window's toolbar.

To open an application or scripting addition dictionary, just double-click the item you're interested in, or select one or more items from the list and click the "bookshelf" icon in the window's toolbar.

The Library window has one further trick up its sleeve: if you select an application name and click the toolbar icon that looks like a script file, AppleScript Editor creates a new script document containing a `tell application ... end tell` block that's ready be to filled in.

Navigating to a Handler in a Script

In addition to the features discussed earlier, script editing windows have a couple of less obvious features that will be of interest to more advanced users. One of these features is the handler navigation menu that appears directly beneath the window's toolbar, as shown in Figure 4–5.

TIP: You can show and hide the navigation bar at any time by choosing View ➤ Show/Hide Navigation Bar.

Figure 4–5. *The script navigation menu—in this example, the* open *handler has been chosen.*

If you are working on a long script that contains a number of user-defined handlers, you can use this menu to jump instantly to the point in the script where a particular handler is defined. Just click the handler menu and pick the name of the handler you want.

TIP: The menu to the left of the handler navigation menu contains the name of the language (AppleScript) that the script is written in. In theory, the language selection menu allows you to select other OSA languages to write your scripts in, but because AppleScript is the only OSA language included in Mac OS X, you normally can ignore this menu.

Viewing the Event Log History

The Event Log History window (Window ➤ Event Log History) keeps track of all script results in chronological order. Figure 4–6 shows a typical Event Log History window. Notice that the right pane has Events, Replies, and Result buttons, which work exactly the same here as they do in a script window.

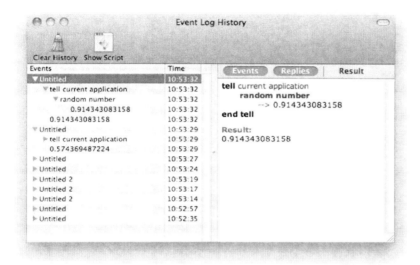

Figure 4–6. *I ran the "random number" script multiple times, and the Event Log History feature captured them all.*

In addition, the Event Log History window allows you to view historical "snapshots" of any script that is run as long as the history window is already open. This can be particularly useful when testing and debugging scripts. For example, if you run a script, make some changes, and then run the script again, the Event Log History window will remember what the script looked like each time it was run. To view the older version of the code, just select the earlier entry in the history window and click the Show Script button in its toolbar.

> **TIP:** If you would like AppleScript Editor to record events even when the Event Log History window is not open, uncheck the "Log only when visible" check box in the History panel of AppleScript Editor's Preferences window.

Scripting the AppleScript Editor

AppleScript Editor itself is scriptable. AppleScript can tell AppleScript Editor to make new script documents, manipulate their source code, compile and execute them, and save them to files. For example, run the following script; it will create a new script document named "My Script" and then compile and execute it:

```
tell application "AppleScript Editor"
    set script_doc to make new document with properties {name:"My Script"}
    set text of script_doc to "say date string of (current date)"
    compile script_doc
    execute script_doc
end tell
```

Using Context Menu Scripts

Try Ctrl-clicking the script window to see the context menu that pops up. The bottom half of the context menu contains a range of useful scripts, organized by kind, that will do everything from inserting tell statements, repeat loops, and conditional statements to adding error handlers. All of these scripts can be found in the /Library/Scripts/Script Editor Scripts/ folder, which you can open by choosing Open Scripts Folder from the context menu. Users who have administrator access can add their own context menu scripts by placing them in this folder.

Viewing the Bundle Contents Drawer

The Bundle Contents drawer is another "hidden" feature of script windows. When you are editing a compiled script or script-based application that has been saved as a *bundle*, clicking the Bundle Contents icon in the window's toolbar opens a drawer that allows you to view and modify any resource files that are contained in the bundle.

> **NOTE:** A bundle is a special "file" format that looks and behaves like an ordinary file in the Finder but is really a folder in disguise. For instance, Mac OS X applications (.app files) are almost always bundle based—the bundle contains all the resource files (icons, images, sounds, etc.) that the application needs to do its job.

Figure 4–7 shows the extra resource files that are included in a typical bundle-based script application created by AppleScript Editor.

Figure 4–7. *Viewing the contents of a bundle-based applet*

You will find the Bundle Contents drawer to be most useful when you are preparing script applications that require extra support files to do their job. Although you could distribute the applet and its supporting files grouped together in a single folder, if the user doesn't need to know about the support files, then a much better solution is to hide all the support files inside the application bundle. As well as being tidier, this stops the user from breaking your applet by fiddling with the support files or moving them to a different location where they can't be found.

To copy a file into the bundle, just drag it into the Bundle Contents drawer. You can edit the bundle contents in other ways by clicking the drop-down menu at the top of the drawer.

Later chapters will discuss how your applet's main script can use commands from the Standard Additions scripting addition to locate and read these files when it needs them.

Setting the Script Formatting Preferences

AppleScript Editor has a number of user-configurable preferences that you can access via its application menu. One item of particular interest is the Preferences window's Formatting panel, shown in Figure 4–8, where you can change the fonts, sizes, colors, and other formatting that AppleScript applies to your source code when compiling a script.

To change the formatting styles used, first select a category (Language keywords, Comments, Variables and subroutine names, etc.) and then use AppleScript Editor's Font menu to alter its settings. (If you don't yet know what all the different category names mean, don't worry: all these terms will be explained in the following chapters.)

Figure 4–8. *The Formatting panel in AppleScript Editor's Preferences window*

TIP: An especially useful tip provided by AppleScript engineer Christopher Nebel is to change the style for application keywords so that they are underlined. This will also underline any spaces within keywords, making it easy to see where each keyword begins and ends; for example, `path to startup disk` will appear as <u>`path to`</u> <u>`startup disk`</u>. To do this, go to the Formatting panel and use Shift-click to select all the application-related keyword styles (Application keywords, Command names, Parameter names, etc). Next, select Font ➤ Show Fonts to bring up the Fonts palette. Click the pop-up menu in the top-left corner of the Fonts palette and select the Single underline style.

Now that we've completed our tour of AppleScript Editor's graphical interface, let's move on to examining the various file formats that we can save our scripts in, and the features and benefits of each.

Saving Scripts

After you've written a script in AppleScript Editor, you'll probably want to save it so that you can use it again later, distribute it to other users, and so forth. There are four basic file formats you can use: text, script, script bundle, and application. Table 4–1 provides a brief summary of each.

Table 4–1. *Basic AppleScript File Formats*

Format	Description	Extension	Icon
Text	The script's source code, saved as a plain text file	`.applescript`	
Script	A compiled script file	`.scpt`	
Script bundle	A bundle-based compiled script file	`.scptd`	
Application	A simple stand-alone application, often called an *applet*	`.app`	

To save a script in AppleScript Editor, just select File ➤ Save As. Figure 4–9 shows a typical Save dialog box. Notice the various menu and check box options near the bottom of the dialog box—these will be discussed in the following sections.

> **NOTE:** In Mac OS X 10.5 and earlier, Script Editor could save applets in two different formats: single file ("Application") and bundle based ("Bundle Application"). The old single-file format, which only runs natively on PowerPC-based Macs, has been made obsolete by the newer bundle-based format, which can run natively on 32- and 64–bit Intel Macs as well as PowerPC. As of 10.6, AppleScript Editor *always* saves applets in the new bundle-based format.

Figure 4–9. *A typical Save dialog box in AppleScript Editor*

Text-Based Scripts

The most basic format for saving script files is plain text. A plain text script file has the file name extension .applescript and contains only the uncompiled source code for the script. To save a script as plain text, select the Text option from the File Format menu in AppleScript Editor's Save dialog box.

The main advantage of the plain text file format is that it can be opened and viewed in any plain text editor—TextEdit, BBEdit, TextWrangler, and so on. Another benefit is that you do not need to have installed the applications and scripting additions used by the script to be able to open and read the code. However, most of the applications that actually run AppleScripts expect a complied script file, so you probably won't use the plain text format very often.

Compiled Scripts

A compiled script file is AppleScript's default file format, and its file name ends in either .scpt or .scptd. (The extra "d" indicates the script file uses Mac OS X's special bundle format, which we'll discuss later.) To save a script as plain text, select the Script (or Script bundle) option from the File Format menu in AppleScript Editor's Save dialog box.

What is the difference between a compiled script and plain text? The big difference is that AppleScript converts the original source code from AppleScript's hallmark English-like syntax into a cryptic-looking binary format that can only be understood by the AppleScript interpreter. A compiled script file containing the simple script `display alert "Hello!"` looks like the following when viewed raw in Bare Bones Software's BBEdit:

```
FasdUAS 1.101.10ˇˇˇˇ
lˇ ˇˇ
Iˇˇˇˆˇ .sysodisAaleRTEXT
m±Hello!ˇˆˇ ˇˇˇˑ ˇˑˇˇˇˇ
.aevtoappnullÄê****   ˇˇˇˇˆˇ1ˇˇ.aevtoappnullÄê****
k
ˇÛˇÛˇˇˆˇÛˇÛ.sysodisAaleRTEXTˇ1‡jascr
ˆfifi≠
```

To convert, or *decompile*, a compiled script file back into human-readable AppleScript code, just open it again in AppleScript Editor or another AppleScript editor such as Smile or Script Debugger.

The compiled script file format has several advantages:

▨ You can be certain that a compiled script file does not contain any syntax errors because it has to be successfully compiled in order to save it. (AppleScript code that cannot be successfully compiled can still be saved in plain text format, however.)

▨ Compiled scripts can contain data as well as code, allowing compiled scripts to retain important values from one run to the next. Not all applications support this feature, but when they do it can be very useful. We'll cover this ability in more detail when looking at script properties in Chapter 11.

▨ Compiled scripts can be loaded into other scripts. Chapter 19 will discuss how more-advanced scripters can use this feature to share frequently used pieces of code across many other scripts in a very neat and efficient way.

Saving Scripts As Run Only

When saving a script in compiled format, you can choose the Run Only option to lock the contents of your script so that it can no longer be read or edited by you or anyone else.

> **CAUTION:** Before you save a script as Run Only, always save an editable copy of your script under a different name first. Once a compiled script is saved as Read Only, it cannot be decompiled. If you forget to keep an editable version of your script, or accidentally save over it with your read-only version, you will have to rewrite the entire script from scratch if you ever need to change it later on!

I personally never lock any of my scripts. As a consultant, I want my clients to open my scripts and look at them. All they can say is, "Wow, we better not touch that stuff!" For me, locking a script would be like Apple locking the containers of its computers so you couldn't open them.

Sometimes, however, saving scripts as Run Only is a good idea. The obvious reason is to protect your scripting secrets, especially if your scripts are distributed to a mass audience. Another reason is to prevent the users of the scripts from messing them up, intentionally or unintentionally.

Saving Scripts As Bundles

Most of the time you will probably save your compiled scripts as ordinary .scpt files. If you want to save a compiled script using Mac OS X's special bundle format, select the Script bundle option from the File Format menu in AppleScript Editor's Save dialog box.

When you do this, two things happen. The first is that AppleScript Editor changes the file name extension from .scpt to .scptd to indicate it is a bundle-based script. The second is that the Bundle Contents button in the script window's toolbar becomes active (normally it is grayed out), allowing you to open the Bundle Contents drawer and examine the contents of the bundle file.

Figure 4–10 shows the internal layout of the files and folders in a script bundle.

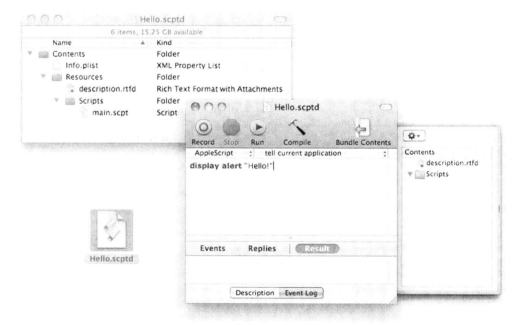

Figure 4–10. *The structure of a basic script bundle, viewed in the Finder (top left) and AppleScript Editor (bottom right)*

You can add additional files and folders to the script bundle by dragging them into the Bundle Contents drawer, or by clicking the drop-down menu at the top of the drawer. Later chapters will look at some of the useful things you can do with bundles.

Script-Based Applications (Applets)

Although the compiled script format is fine for scripts that will be used by other applications, wouldn't it be great if users could also run your scripts directly just by double-clicking them in the Finder? Guess what—they can! Just select the Application option from the File Format menu in AppleScript Editor's Save dialog box, and AppleScript Editor will save your script as a stand-alone mini-application, or *applet*, that you can run just like any other Mac application.

In fact, why not try this right now? First, create a new document in AppleScript Editor (File ➤ New) and type the following line of code:

```
display alert "Hello!"
```

Next, select File ➤ Save As to bring up the Save dialog box, select the Application option in the File Format menu, name the file Hello.app, and click Save. Finally, find your Hello applet in the Finder and double-click it. The applet will launch and display the dialog box shown in Figure 4–11.

Figure 4–11. *The dialog box displayed when the applet is run*

Click the OK button to dismiss the dialog box and allow the script to proceed. Once the script finishes running, the applet will quit automatically.

Applets are an ideal format to use when writing scripts for other people. They simply download the applet, unzip it, and double-click the applet icon to run it—no extra installation is needed!

Droplets

Droplets are script applets with a twist: they can process files that are dropped on them.

To turn an applet into a droplet, simply include an open handler somewhere in it. Don't worry if you don't understand exactly what an open handler is yet; we'll explore handlers in much more detail in later chapters.

Figure 4–12 shows the code for a very simple droplet that tells you how many files and folders were dropped on it.

Figure 4–12. *The basic droplet script*

Figure 4–13 shows the result of dropping three items onto the droplet in the Finder.

Figure 4–13. *The result of dragging and dropping some files onto the droplet*

Notice how the applet icon now includes a diagonal arrow to indicate that it's a droplet.

Stay-Open Applets

If you want an applet to behave more like a regular desktop application and stay open until the user quits it manually, just enable the Stay Open check box in the Save dialog box. Stay-open applets have the advantage that they can respond to more than one event. For example, if you resave the script in Figure 4–12 as a stay-open applet, once it's launched, you can drag files and folders onto it as often as you like. Figure 4–14 gives another example—perhaps you can guess what it does when saved as a stay-open applet and then launched in the Finder? (If not, don't worry: you'll learn all about using the idle handler in Chapter 18.)

Figure 4–14. *A simple example of a stay-open applet*

Saving Applets As Run Only

Checking the Save dialog's Run Only check box causes an AppleScript applet to be saved in run-only form to prevent anyone from viewing or modifying its source code. Remember to save an editable copy under a different file name first in case you need to modify its code in the future!

Customizing the Startup Screen

When saving a script applet, you can check the Startup Screen check box, found in the Save dialog box. The next time the applet runs, the text you typed in the Description panel of your AppleScript Editor script window will display in a rather crude welcome window.

Figure 4–15 shows the script's Description panel, which will be displayed when the script applet is launched if the Startup Screen check box is checked when the applet is saved.

Figure 4–15. *You can add formatted text to the Description panel in the AppleScript Editor script window. This text can be displayed when the script applet starts.*

At this point we've covered all of the essential applications you will need to begin developing and using your own scripts. Before we finish, however, let's take a quick look at several advanced tools that are worth exploring once you've gained a bit more AppleScript experience.

Other Tools for Writing and Running AppleScripts

Although this chapter has focused on using Apple's AppleScript Editor application to create and run AppleScripts, plenty of other useful tools are available to AppleScript developers and users. Before we move on to the next chapter, let's take a moment to look at some of the main options, several of which we'll explore further in later chapters.

The System-wide Script Menu

The system-wide Script menu is an extremely useful Mac OS X extra that lets you run compiled AppleScripts directly from your menu bar. The Script menu comes with dozens of useful scripts already installed, and you can easily add your own scripts to it as well.

The system-wide Script menu is disabled by default. To enable it, simply go to the General panel of AppleScript Editor's Preferences dialog box and check the "Show

Script menu in menu bar" option. Once enabled, the Script menu sits neatly on the top-right corner of the menu bar, alongside the usual Mac OS X "menulets" for controlling volume levels, AirPort settings, and so on. Figure 4–16 shows the open Script menu.

> **NOTE:** In Mac OS X 10.5 and earlier, you can use the AppleScript Utility application in /Applications/AppleScript/ to enable the Script menu and set its preferences.

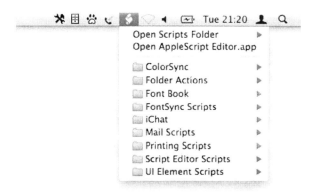

Figure 4–16. *The open Script menu*

To run a script from the Script menu, simply select it from the menu. To open a script using the default AppleScript editor, select a script from the menu while holding down the Option key.

The Script menu contains two additional items on top of the scripts and script folders. The first item, Open Scripts Folder, opens the folders where the Script menu's scripts are stored, making it easy to add and remove your own. The second item, Open AppleScript Editor.app, provides a handy shortcut for launching the AppleScript Editor application.

Where Are the Menu Scripts Stored?

As you can tell from looking at the menu shown in Figure 4–16 (or by gazing at your own Script menu), it already has quite a few scripts. These scripts are provided by Apple and come already installed in the /Library/Scripts/ folder of your startup disk.

The Script menu can contain up to three sets of scripts separated by divider lines.

The first set of scripts are those installed in /Library/Scripts/ and can be run by any user. If you want to hide these scripts so that they don't appear in the Script menu, just uncheck the "Show Computer scripts" option in the General panel of AppleScript Editor's Preferences window.

The second set of scripts are those installed in your own personal ~/Library/Scripts/ folder and are only available to you. Because your own Scripts folder is empty by default, you won't see anything here initially. We'll look at how to add your own scripts to this location in just a moment.

The third set of scripts are those that you want to "belong" to one particular application. For example, you may have written a script for tidying up your Finder desktop. If you want this script to be visible in the Script menu *only* when the Finder is frontmost, just put it in ~/Library/Scripts/Applications/Finder and the Script menu will hide or show it depending on what application is active at the time.

Adding Your Own Scripts

Adding your own scripts to the Script menu is easy. Just select the Scripts folder that you want from the Script menu's Open Scripts Folder submenu, and the folder will open in the Finder.

To open the system's /Library/Scripts/ folder, choose the Open Scripts Folder ➤ Open Computer Scripts Folder option. Anyone can open and view these scripts in AppleScript Editor, but you will need an administrator password if you want to add, remove, or modify scripts in this folder.

Unless you want to share your menu scripts with other users on your Mac, the usual place to put them is in ~/Library/Scripts/. To open this folder, choose Open Scripts Folder ➤ Open User Scripts.

To add exclusive scripts for an application, activate that application (the Finder, for example), and then from the Script menu, choose Open Scripts Folder ➤ Open Finder Scripts Folder. Any scripts you place in that folder will appear only when the Finder is active. If a folder for that application doesn't exist, it will be created as you make your selection.

> **TIP:** While the system-wide Script menu is usually used to run AppleScripts, it can also run scripts written in other scripting languages such as Perl, Python, Ruby, and bash. Just copy these scripts into one of the Script menu's Scripts folders and they're ready to go!

Third-Party AppleScript Editors

In the world of third-party AppleScript editors, two names stand out in particular: Satimage's Smile and Late Night Software's Script Debugger.

Smile

Satimage Software, the developers of Smile, describe it as "a programming and working environment based on AppleScript." To put it another way, Smile is both an AppleScript editor *and* a highly customizable platform that more advanced users can build on to suit their own particular needs.

Like AppleScript Editor, Smile can be used to write and run AppleScripts. A built-in dictionary viewer provides easy access to application dictionaries, while an extensive scripting interface allows many aspects of Smile to be controlled from AppleScript. On top of this, Smile adds many interesting features of its own, including "terminal" windows where you can type in or select any piece of AppleScript code and instantly compile and run it; scriptable graphics windows that you can use to create graphs, illustrations, and other images; and a simple toolkit for creating and adding your own GUI dialog boxes to Smile.

Smile is available from the Satimage web site at http://www.satimage-software.com. Several versions are provided: the standard Smile, which is free to download and use, and two commercial options—SmileLab, which can be used for advanced data processing tasks, and SmileServer, which can be used to build web applications in AppleScript.

We will explore several of Smile's more powerful and interesting features later on in this book.

Script Debugger

Late Night Software proudly describe their Script Debugger as "The Ultimate AppleScript Tool," and I don't think many AppleScripters would disagree with them.

Like AppleScript Editor, Script Debugger focuses on one task in particular: developing AppleScripts. However, whereas AppleScript Editor provides only the basic tools required to create and run scripts, Script Debugger is crammed full of powerful and sophisticated features aimed at making intermediate and advanced AppleScripters' lives as easy as possible.

An advanced dictionary viewer ensures that every ounce of useful information is squeezed out of application dictionaries and displayed to users, while an interactive object browser allows users to explore the object models of running applications and examine their contents in detail. Advanced testing features make it easy to run individual handlers within a larger script to check that they work correctly, while clever packaging tools can examine scripts and tell you what applications and scripting additions they rely on.

Script Debugger's best-known feature, of course, is its powerful interactive AppleScript debugger. The debugger allows you to pause and resume running scripts so that you can examine their data at any time, and if anything goes wrong in your script, Script Debugger can immediately provide extensive details on where the problem occurred and what the script was doing at the time. We'll take a look at debugging scripts with Script Debugger in Chapter 29.

Script Debugger is available as a free demo or commercial purchase from the Late Night Software web site at http://www.latenightsw.com.

Developing GUI Applications

Although AppleScript's main goal is to control other Mac OS X desktop applications, it can be used to create them, too! A couple of options exist: Satimage's Smile and the new AppleScriptObjC framework introduced in Mac OS X 10.6. We'll look at these later in the book.

> **NOTE:** In Mac OS X 10.5 and earlier, the standard Apple tool for developing GUI applications with AppleScript was AppleScript Studio. However, although it is still possible to maintain existing Studio-based projects in 10.6, AppleScriptObjC is now the standard platform for all new development.

Command-Line Tools

Whereas AppleScript's natural home is the Mac OS X desktop, many other scripting languages happily live and work within Mac OS X's Unix command-line environment. Not to be outdone by the competition, AppleScript has responded with its own set of command-line tools, including osacompile and osadecompile, which allow you to compile and decompile AppleScripts from the command line, and osascript, which allows AppleScripts to be run directly from the Mac OS X command line.

We will look at the various ways in which AppleScript and the Unix command line can work together in Chapter 27.

Summary

In this chapter we looked at the basic tools for creating and running AppleScripts that every AppleScript user should be familiar with: AppleScript Editor and the system-wide Script menu. We also studied the various file formats that scripts can be saved in, comparing the features and benefits of each.

One feature of AppleScript Editor that we haven't really looked at yet is its powerful dictionary viewer, used to examine the built-in documentation of scriptable applications and scripting extensions. We will cover this in the next chapter, as you discover exactly how application scripting works.

Chapter 5

Understanding How Application Scripting Works

While the AppleScript language can be used for many general scripting tasks, by far the most common and important use for it is automating desktop applications—which isn't surprising, as this is the main reason it was created in the first place. In fact, often when people talk about "AppleScripting," they don't just mean scripting with the AppleScript language, but application scripting as a whole! One point I make throughout the book is that the AppleScript language is pretty small on its own. It has merely five commands and a handful of objects. What makes AppleScript so powerful is the ease with which it can interact with hundreds of scriptable applications and scripting additions, getting them to do all the hard work so you don't have to!

As you become an experienced scripter, you will learn the individual commands and objects of specific applications that you need to script. First, though, you need to learn the common features and behaviors that all scriptable applications share.

In Chapter 2, I introduced you to the four key concepts of scriptable applications:

- How the application represents your data as *objects*

- How the application lets you manipulate these objects using *commands*

- How the application organizes its objects into an *object model*

- How the application documents its objects and commands in a *dictionary*

In this chapter I will fill in all the details: how application objects are structured, how commands are used, how the object model operates and how you navigate it, and how to understand the information provided by the application dictionary.

> **TIP:** While reading through this chapter and the chapters that follow it, remember to refer back to Chapter 2 any time you need to remind yourself how the pieces fit together. Also, don't worry if you don't understand everything the first time you read it—after all, it is a very large quantity of information to digest all at once!

A Quick Application Scripting Example

An application's scriptability consists of two realms: objects and commands. Objects represent the important pieces of information in your application, such as documents, pages, and paragraphs. Commands are actions that you tell the application to perform: save (a document), make (a new page), delete (a paragraph), and so on.

For instance, Apple's TextEdit application includes a command named open that is used to open text files. When TextEdit receives an open command, it reads each text file you told it to open and creates a new document object containing the file's contents.

Figure 5–1 shows how to open a file named TODO.txt that is located in the home folder of the user named hanaan on the hard disk named Macintosh HD.

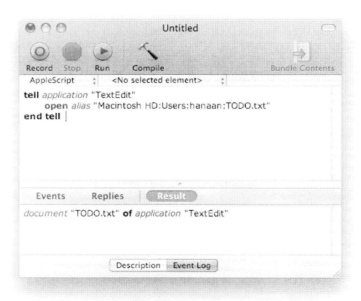

Figure 5–1. *Sending an* open *command to the TextEdit application to open a text file*

TIP: Notice the `alias "..."` expression in Figure 5–1. When the script runs, this creates an AppleScript object that identifies a particular file, folder, or disk—in this case, the `TODO.txt` file. AppleScript's alias objects will be fully explained in Chapter 17. For now, all you need to know is that TextEdit's open command requires one or more alias objects that identify the text file(s) you want it to open.

When the script runs, as you'd expect, a new window containing the file's text appears in TextEdit's graphical user interface (GUI).

However, that's not all that happens. Beneath the surface, TextEdit creates a new document object that contains the text from the file and is responsible for managing any changes that you may make to it. And since TextEdit is scriptable, you can see this object directly from AppleScript, and manipulate it too.

In fact, the last thing that the open command does, once it has read the file into a new document object, is to return a *reference* to the new document object, as shown in the Result pane in Figure 5–1.

As you will see later in the chapter, references are a vital part of working with objects in a scriptable application, with each reference acting as a series of directions that allows you to locate a specific object (or objects) within the application's object model. In this case, the reference `document "TODO.txt" of application "TextEdit"` identifies a document object named "TODO.txt" within the application named "TextEdit".

NOTE: If you want to try the script in Figure 5–1 yourself, just create a text file named `TODO.txt` in your home folder and replace the hard disk and user folder names in the script to match your own. A number of the scripts in this book that work with files use hard-coded paths like this for simplicity, but as every user's file system is different, you may need to tweak these paths for the scripts to work correctly on your Mac.

Understanding Objects

Objects have three important characteristics: class, properties, and elements. Let's consider each of these in turn.

How Objects Are Categorized by Class

Humans love to categorize things; it's part of our nature. With applications representing lots of different kinds of data—disks, folders, and files in Finder; tracks and playlists in iTunes; and so forth—it's not surprising that the different kinds of objects that appear in scriptable applications should be categorized too.

We describe all objects of a particular type as belonging to the same *class*. For example, in the Finder, all of the objects describing mounted disks belong to the disk class; in TextEdit, all of the objects representing your open documents are members of the document class.

Knowing the class of an object is essential for figuring out what you can and can't do with it. For example, if you are dealing with an object of class disk, you can be pretty certain that it has a name (for example, "Macintosh HD") and a format (HFS+, NTFS, UFS, etc.), can contain any number of files and folders, and can be ejected from the system (assuming it isn't the startup disk). If you are dealing with an object of class folder, you can safely assume that it also has a name and can contain files and folders, but doesn't have a format and can't be ejected. If you are dealing with an object whose class is document file, then you can assume that it too has a name, that it doesn't contain any files or folders, and that you can tell the Finder to open it in the application that created it.

> **NOTE:** The Finder may have thousands of document file objects—each one unique—yet all of these document file objects have exactly the same structure. This structure is defined by the Finder's document file class and can be viewed in AppleScript Editor's application dictionary viewer. You will learn how to do this in the "Understanding Application Dictionaries" section later in the chapter.

To identify the exact class that a particular object falls into, scriptable applications normally provide each object with a property named, not surprisingly, class. The value of the class property is the name of the class that the object belongs to.

For instance, in Figure 5–1, you saw that TextEdit's open command returned a reference to an application object. Script 5–1 sends a second command, get, asking TextEdit for the class of the object being referred to. As you might guess, the class of the object in this case is document.

Script 5–1.

```
tell application "TextEdit"
    open alias "Macintosh HD:Users:hanaan:TODO.txt"
    get class of result
end tell
--> document
```

Notice how the class name appears as a keyword. Don't confuse class names with AppleScript strings, which appear as text surrounded by double quotes. Class names are application-defined symbols; strings are user-defined text.

Incidentally, AppleScript values also have a class property:

```
class of "Hello, World!"
--> text
```

Even class name objects have a `class` property:

```
class of document
--> class
```

There is a bit more to the class-based categorization scheme than I've described so far, but we'll get to that later.

Introducing Object Properties

Properties are the object's traits. If your car was an object in the application of your life, its properties would include the car's color, manufacturing year, make, model, plate number, and so on. Each property appears only once in an object. Your car can't have more than one plate number, for example.

A Finder object of class `document file` may have properties such as the size, creation date, and icon position of the file, while an InDesign object of class `image` may include properties describing the image's rotation angle, resolutions, and bounds.

Here are some of the properties you can find in an iTunes object of the class `user playlist`:

```
name (text) : The name of the playlist

duration (integer, r/o) : The total length of all songs (in seconds)

special kind (none/Audiobooks/folder/Movies/Music/Party Shuffle/
           Podcasts/Purchased Music/TV Shows/Videos, r/o) : Special playlist ¬
  kind

parent (playlist, r/o) : Folder which contains this playlist (if any)
```

Each description consists of the property name in bold, followed by the class of object it contains in parentheses, and finally a brief description of its purpose.

For example, the `name` property contains an AppleScript string (an object of class `text`), which is the name of that playlist—"Library", "Music", "Movies", "Top 25 Most Played", or whatever.

Notice that most of the properties shown here are marked `r/o`, which is short for "read-only." You can get the current value of a read-only property using AppleScript, but you cannot modify it. Only the `name` property allows you to get *and* set its value however you like.

In most cases, the properties of an application-defined object describe the ordinary, day-to-day details of that application object. Most of these properties contain plain old AppleScript values such as numbers and text. For example:

```
tell application "iTunes" to get name of playlist 1
--> "Library"

tell application "iTunes" to get duration of playlist 1
--> 43145
```

A few of these properties contain symbol-style values, known as *constants*, which are defined by the application itself.

> **NOTE:** You may also occasionally see constant objects referred to as "enumerations," "enumerated types," or "symbols," which are terms commonly used in other programming languages.

Constants are typically used when the value of a property needs to be one of a number of predefined options; think of it as a "multiple-choice" setting. For example, the special kind property of an iTunes playlist must contain one of the following constant objects only: none, Audiobooks, folder, Movies, Music, Party Shuffle, Podcasts, Purchased Music, TV Shows, or Videos. For instance:

```
tell application "iTunes" to get special kind of playlist "Library"
--> none
```

```
tell application "iTunes" to get special kind of playlist "Movies"
--> Movies
```

Notice how each constant is made up of a word (or phrase). You can tell that it is a constant rather than a text object because text objects are displayed as a pair of double quote marks with the text in between. Instead, each constant is defined as a keyword in the application dictionary, allowing you to write it directly in your script.

> **TIP:** Another way you can tell that the result is a constant is that AppleScript Editor will show application-defined constant keywords as plain purple text, whereas AppleScript objects appear in black. (This is assuming you are running Mac OS X 10.6 and haven't changed the default settings in AppleScript Editor's Formatting preferences, of course.)

In special cases, an object property will contain not an AppleScript object but another application object, or—to be exact—a *reference* to another application object. For example, if a playlist object is stored inside a playlist folder, as shown in Figure 5–2, then its parent property will contain a reference to the playlist folder that contains it.

Figure 5–2. *A playlist folder containing several playlists, as seen in iTunes' GUI*

If you are dealing with one of these nested playlist objects and need to know what playlist folder it is in, you can find out just by asking the playlist object, like this:

```
tell application "iTunes" to get parent of playlist "80's Music"
--> folder playlist id 147 of source id 43 of application "iTunes"
```

The resulting reference object is a bit cryptic to look at, but it is pointing to the object that represents the playlist folder named "Music by Decade" in the preceding example. To check this, ask the folder playlist object for its name:

```
tell application "iTunes" to get name of parent of playlist "80's Music"
--> "Music by Decade"
```

Another good example is the home property of the Finder's main application object. This contains a reference to the current user's home folder. This isn't the only way to locate the user's home folder, but it provides a very convenient shortcut for identifying it quickly and reliably:

```
tell application "Finder" to get home
--> folder "hanaan" of folder "Users" of startup disk of application "Finder"
```

A particularly interesting feature provided by most scriptable applications is the properties property. When you get the properties property of an application object, the result is an AppleScript object, called a *record*, that contains the current values of many or all of the object's properties:

```
tell application "Finder" to get properties of home
--> {class:folder,
    name:"hanaan",
    index:3,
    displayed name:"hanaan",
    name extension:"",
    extension hidden:false,
    container:folder "Users" of startup disk of application "Finder",
    disk:startup disk of application "Finder",
    position:{-1, -1},
    desktop position:missing value,
    bounds:{-33, -33, 31, 31},
    kind:"Folder",
    label index:0,
    locked:false,
    description:missing value,
    comment:"",
    size:missing value,
    physical size:missing value,
    creation date:date "Sunday, October 4, 2009 10:11:37 AM",
    modification date:date "Wednesday, March 3, 2010 10:53:05 PM",
    icon:missing value,
    URL:"file://localhost/Users/hanaan/",
    owner:"hanaan", group:"staff",
    owner privileges:read write,
    group privileges:read only,
    everyones privileges:read only,
    container window:container window of folder "hanaan"
            of folder "Users" of startup disk of application "Finder"}
```

This can be a great way to find out lots of information about an object, particularly when exploring an application's object model in AppleScript Editor to see what it contains.

Introducing Object Elements

The elements of an application object play a very different role from its properties. Whereas properties provide basic information about the object itself, and occasionally provide a useful shortcut to another object of interest, the *only* purpose of an application object's elements is to tell you about the other application-defined objects it *contains*. In particular, while an object can only have one of each property, it can have any number of elements you like, including none at all. You can also perform a much wider range of actions on elements, compared to properties. In addition to getting an object's existing elements, you can add new ones, delete them, move or duplicate them, and so on.

All application objects contain properties, although not all have elements. For example, in the Finder, a folder can contain other folders, application files, document files, and so forth. These nested files and folders are represented as elements of the folder object that contains them. By comparison, files in the file system don't contain other items, so while file objects have properties, they don't have any elements.

Here are the different types of objects that a Finder folder object can contain:

- Folders
- Alias files
- Application files
- Document files
- Internet location files
- Clippings
- Packages

Most of these should sound familiar, since you deal with these file system objects all the time in the Finder's GUI. Folder objects represent folders in the file system, document files (.txt, .jpg, .doc, etc.) contain information, clippings are desktop clipping files (.textClipping, .pictClipping), and so on. The only one that might not be obvious is "package," a special format that appears as a file but is really a folder in disguise, but you'll find out more about packages later on in the book.

For example, the script shown in Figure 5–3 asks the Finder for all of the folder elements of the current user's home folder.

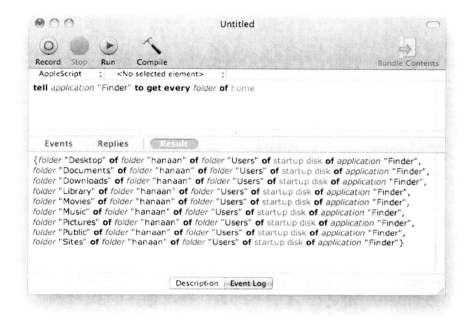

Figure 5–3. *Asking the Finder for all the* `folder` *elements of a folder object returns a list of references, one to each element.*

When you run the script, the result is a whole list of references, each one identifying a particular `folder` element contained by the folder object that represents the user's home folder.

You can refer to the elements of an object in various ways, including by position (index), by name (if they have one), all at once, or even by testing them to see if they match your exact requirements by using the powerful whose clause. We'll study these and other *reference forms* later on in the "More on Constructing References" section.

In Figure 5–3, I used a reference to all of the `folder` elements of the home folder, while each of the references returned identified each `folder` element according to its name.

In the following iCal example, I refer to the first event element of the `calendar` element named "Home":

```
tell application "iCal"
    event 1 of calendar "Home"
end tell
```

If I run this script, the result is a fresh reference to the object that was found:

```
--> event id "E0BE7912-6D89-4831-9B48-05621C1D9F2A"
        of calendar id "EE4AE213-DB53-460A-82A9-0BB856FC3890"
        of application "iCal"
```

This reference identifies elements in yet another way, by using unique identifiers. Although it may not be so pretty to look at, because iCal gives each of its objects a unique ID that never changes, this kind of reference is highly reliable if you need to find that particular object again later on in a script.

Understanding elements is key to understanding how objects are organized into an object model. There is a lot more still to learn, but let's not get ahead of ourselves. We'll come back to elements soon enough in the "Understanding the Application Object Model" section, but for now let's spend a bit of time discussing the second key concept in application scripting: commands.

Understanding Commands

Compared to objects, commands are a breeze to understand. Yet commands are every bit as crucial to application scripting as objects. Commands *make things happen*, and without them, all of those valuable objects would be utterly useless.

Most of the commands you use in AppleScript are defined by scriptable applications. One application command may create a new document in TextEdit; another may play a song in Apple iTunes. Other commands could create new files and folders, send e-mails, or resize images...the list of possibilities is almost endless!

> **NOTE:** Scriptable applications are not the only sources of commands for scripts to use. Commands can also be defined by *scripting additions*, special plug-ins that add useful commands for working with AppleScript's own built-in objects. For example, the Standard Additions scripting addition provides commands for displaying dialog boxes, reading and writing files, and so on. In addition, AppleScript provides five *built-in* commands (get, set, copy, count, and run), and you can define your own commands by adding *script handlers* to your AppleScripts.

So, what makes up a command?

For starters, every command must have a *name*. For example, earlier in the chapter you encountered the command called open that is provided by TextEdit for opening text files.

In addition, many commands can also have *parameters*. These are objects, provided by your code, that will be passed to the application to use when processing the command.

In order for the command to have an effect, it must be *sent to an object*. This object is known as the command's *target*. When working with scriptable applications, the target is an object that represents the application.

Many commands return objects as their *result*. If a command fails for some reason, an *error* will be generated instead.

The following sections will explore each of these concepts in turn.

Introducing Command Names

Every command has a name. When an `application` object receives a command, it checks whether it contains a *handler* with the same name. If it does, it responds to the command by executing the code in the handler.

Here are some common application-defined command names: `make`, `move`, `duplicate`, `delete`, and `close`. You will see these names frequently, as most scriptable applications provide these commands for manipulating objects in their object models. Some applications also provide commands for performing more specialized tasks, such as `play`, `check syntax`, and `shut down` (found in iTunes, AppleScript Editor, and System Events, respectively). There are even a few commands that all applications will understand, whether they are scriptable or not: `run`, `activate`, `open`, and `quit`.

Here are some examples of simple commands:

```
tell application "TextEdit"
    activate
end tell

tell application "iTunes"
    play
end tell

tell application "System Events"
    shut down
end tell
```

Introducing Command Parameters

Most command handlers require extra information to do their jobs. The command itself must supply the values to use—we call these values *parameters*. For example, the following `open` command requires a single parameter, an AppleScript alias object identifying the file you want to open in TextEdit:

```
tell application "TextEdit"
    open alias "Macintosh HD:Users:hanaan:Notes.txt"
end tell
```

Some commands, such as `open`, take a *direct parameter*, where the value appears immediately after the command name.

Many commands also take *labeled parameters*, where each value is identified by a keyword. For example, the following `make` command requires a labeled parameter that tells it the class of object to create:

```
tell application "TextEdit"
    make new document
end tell
```

The parameter's label is `new` and its value is an object representing the class name: `document`.

At most, a command can have one direct parameter, but it can have any number of labeled ones. For example, the Finder's duplicate command, which is used to duplicate files and folders, has the following definition:

```
duplicate v : Duplicate one or more object(s)
    duplicate specifier : the object(s) to duplicate
        [to location specifier] : the new location for the object(s)
        [replacing boolean] : Specifies whether or not to replace items in the
            destination that have the same name as items being duplicated
        [routing suppressed boolean] : Specifies whether or not to autoroute items
            (default is false). Only applies when copying to the system folder.
    --> specifier : to the duplicated object(s)
```

This command takes a direct parameter along with three labeled parameters, named to, replacing, and routing suppressed:

- The direct parameter is a reference to the Finder object, or objects, to be copied; in this case, one or more files and/or folders.

- The to parameter is a reference to the object (in this case, a folder or disk), where the items are to be copied to.

- The replacing parameter is a value that tells the handler for the duplicate command whether it should overwrite any existing items that have the same names as the items being copied.

- The parameter named routing suppressed is a holdover from the days of Mac OS 9, when copying control panel, font, and extension files to the system folder would automatically put them in the appropriate subfolders.

The following script demonstrates how to copy every document file on the current user's desktop into their Documents folder:

```
tell application "Finder"
    duplicate every document file of desktop ¬
        to folder "Documents" of home ¬
        replacing false
end tell
```

As you can see, we are using the Finder's duplicate command, giving it three parameters to work with:

- The direct parameter is a Finder reference to all of the document files on the user's desktop: every document file of desktop.

- The to parameter is a reference to the user's Documents folder: folder "Documents" of home.

- The replacing parameter is an AppleScript object, false.

You'll notice I haven't included a routing suppressed parameter. While some application commands require all parameters to be supplied by your script, other commands may allow some or all parameters to be omitted. When you do not supply an optional parameter, the application will use a sensible default value instead. In this case, if you omit the `routing suppressed` parameter, the Finder will use the default value of `false`.

If you want, you can also omit the `to` and/or `replacing` parameters. Omitting the `to` parameter causes the Finder to make copies in the same folder, just as if you select the files in the GUI and choose **File ➤ Duplicate**. If you omit the `replacing` parameter, the `duplicate` command will use the default value, which is `false`. This will cause the `duplicate` command to generate an error if you try to replace any existing files in the `Documents` folder. (If the `replacing` parameter is `true`, any existing files will be replaced without warning, so be careful.)

There is one more thing you will notice about this command. When you compile it, AppleScript magically transforms the `replacing false` part into `without replacing` to make it easier to read. We'll discuss this further in Chapter 12.

Commands Must Be Targeted at Objects

To have an effect, a command must be sent to an object that knows how to handle it. When scripting other applications, this is an object of class `application` that represents the program you want to script. Here is the basic syntax for creating an `application` object:

```
application application_name_or_path
```

To make targeting commands easy, AppleScript provides the `tell` block statement, which you already met in Chapter 3. You can use a `tell` block to specify the default target for all the commands inside the block, which can be especially convenient when you want to direct several commands to the same location.

Here is the syntax for AppleScript's `tell` statement:

```
tell target_object
    -- One or more statements here...
end tell
```

If the `tell` block contains only a single statement, then you can, if you wish, shorten it to this:

```
tell target_object to some_statement
```

In Script 5–2, the target for the `sleep` command is the System Events application.

Script 5–2.

```
tell application "System Events"
    sleep
end tell
```

Here's how the script works:

1. When the `application "System Events"` expression is executed, it creates an object of class `application` identifying System Events.

2. The `tell` block makes this object the default target for all of the commands inside the block.

3. When the `sleep` command inside the `tell` block is run, it is sent to the object identified by the `tell` block, `application "System Events"`.

4. The `application` object transforms this command into an *Apple event*, a special data structure that Mac OS X uses to pass commands between GUI applications, and sends it to System Events.

5. System Events recognizes this command as one of its own, and performs the appropriate action—putting your Mac to sleep, in this case. The part of the application that responds to the command is called a *handler*.

> **NOTE:** If the target application is not already running, AppleScript will automatically launch it before sending it the command. This is normally the behavior you want. However, if you wish to find out if an application is running before sending it commands, you can check the `application` object's `running` property first. We'll discuss this and other features of `application` objects in the "More on `application` Objects" section later in the chapter.

Commands Can Return Results or Report Errors

Many commands return an object as a result. With some commands, usually those that process data, returning a value is their only purpose. For instance, you can use the Finder's `exists` command to check for the presence of a particular file, folder, or disk. The result is an AppleScript object (either `true` or `false`) that tells you whether or not the desired item could be found:

```
tell application "Finder"
   exists folder "Applications" of startup disk
end tell
--> true
```

Other commands may perform an action and then return a useful value related to the outcome of that action. For example, the purpose of the Finder's `make` command is to create a new file or folder on one of your disks, which it does. In addition, it returns a reference to the object it just created:

```
tell application "Finder"
   make new folder at home
end tell
--> folder "untitled folder" of folder "hanaan"
      of folder "Users" of startup disk of application "Finder"
```

This can be useful if you need to refer to that object later in the script: just assign the returned reference to a variable, and the next time you need it you can get it from the same variable. In the following script, the second line stores the reference to a newly created folder in a variable named the_folder. The third line then retrieves the reference from that variable and uses it as the parameter to the Finder's open command to open the folder onscreen:

```
tell application "Finder"
    set the_folder to make new folder at home
    open the_folder
end tell
```

Commands that run into unexpected problems while performing a task usually generate an error to let the script know that something has gone wrong. For example, unless you happen to have a thousand folders in your home folder, the open command in the following script will raise an error when you try to run it:

```
tell application "Finder"
    open folder 1000 of home
end tell
```

The message describing this error is "Finder got an error: Can't get folder 1000 of home." In addition to a human-readable description, other information such as error number codes and the value that caused the problem may be provided, allowing scripts to work out what the problem is and try to sort it out themselves, if they want.

NOTE: Chapter 15 will explain errors and error handling in detail.

At this point, we have still not covered the finer details of working with application commands, but don't worry; what you have learned here is more than enough to get you started. We will come back to the subject in Chapter 12 when we discuss commands in general.

Now that you've filled out your knowledge about how individual objects and commands work, it's time to proceed to the third key concept in application scripting: how scriptable applications organize their objects into an object model.

Understanding the Application Object Model

Perhaps the most compelling part of scripting an application is working with its object model. The object model is used to organize large amounts of program data so that you can navigate it effectively to find the information that you want. Most scriptable applications have an object model—only those with particularly simple or limited scripting support can do without one.

Earlier in the chapter you learned how individual application objects are structured. Each object in a scriptable application usually has one or more properties containing simple AppleScript values such as numbers and text that tell you something about that object. In addition, some application objects can also contain other application objects, either stored in properties or represented as elements. In turn, some of those objects may contain other objects, and so on, until the position of every last scriptable object in the application has been identified.

This type of structure is called an *object model*, and the way it fits together is described as a *containment hierarchy*.

Let's now look at exactly how the object model of a scriptable application is put together.

How Objects Can Contain Other Objects

Although different applications have different types of objects (the Finder has files and folders, Adobe InDesign has pages and text frames, and so on), most applications' object models follow the same overall structure: a single, top-level object of class `application` that contains a number of objects, some of which contain other objects, and so on.

To understand this structure, imagine a large office building. (This building is equivalent to a scriptable application.) The building is divided into floors, each floor is divided into offices, and an office may have desks and people in it. Every office has a specific address that anyone in the building can use to find it.

Figure 5–4 shows a cutaway view of the building to help you visualize its internal structure.

Once you know how the building is laid out, you can easily find your way around it. For instance, the receptionist's desk is the third office on the second floor. The office also has a name, "Reception", so another way you could identify it would be by saying "the office named 'Reception' on the second floor." Notice that you can identify the desired office by two different approaches: by its position and by its name.

In AppleScript, locating objects in order to script them is the first order of the day. Scriptable applications use a similar method of organizing their objects as our fictional office building. For example:

- The Finder application has disk objects that can contain file and folder objects. Folders can have files or more folders.

- In InDesign, you have document objects, each of which contains page objects. The pages may contain, among other things, text frames that can contain words and characters.

- In FileMaker Pro, you have database objects that can have tables with fields and records.

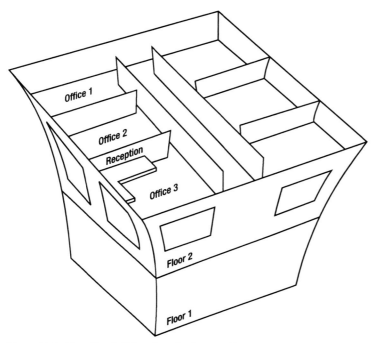

Figure 5–4. *The office building described as an object model*

How AppleScript Refers to Application Objects

Just as you can follow a set of directions to arrive at a specific office in a building, so can AppleScript provide a set of directions to locate a particular object (or, in some cases, several objects at once) in an application's object model. We call this set of directions a *reference*.

> **NOTE:** When talking about application references, the *AppleScript Language Guide* for Mac OS X 10.5+ uses the term *object specifier*, while AppleScript Editor uses just *specifier*. However, every AppleScript user I know says *reference*—the traditional term since AppleScript was invented—so we will continue to call them references throughout this book.

Identifying objects in scriptable applications is also similar to the building example. For instance:

- In the Finder, you can refer to the document file named "report.txt" in the third folder of the disk named "Server".

- In InDesign, you can refer to the fifth text frame of page 2 in the document named "Annual Report.indd".

- In FileMaker Pro, you can refer to the cell named "Last Name" in record 5 of the table named "Contact" of the front database.

Each application has completely different types of objects, but the way each object model works is pretty much the same.

Here is how we can write these directions in AppleScript itself:

```
tell application "Finder"
    document file "report.txt" of folder 3 of disk "Server"
end tell

tell application "Adobe InDesign CS3"
    text frame 5 of page 2 of document "Annual Report.indd"
end tell

tell application "FileMaker Pro"
    cell "Last Name" of record 5 of table "Contact" of database 1
end tell
```

HOW ENGLISH-LIKE CAN APPLESCRIPT CODE BE?

One of AppleScript's most striking features is that, if you wish, you can make your scripts look remarkably close to written English. For example, the document file named "report.txt" in the third folder of the disk named "Server" is not just natural English—it also makes a perfectly good AppleScript reference when written inside a tell application "Finder" ... end tell block.

For starters, notice how the appears several times in the reference. You can insert the keywords almost anywhere in your code—they don't do anything except make your code look more English-like. The reference also uses third folder instead of folder 3 and disk named "Server" rather than disk "Server".

You do have to be careful, though. Just because AppleScript allows you to make your code *look like* English, it doesn't mean that AppleScript can actually *understand* English. Although AppleScript's grammar and vocabulary may be more flexible than that of most programming languages, they still follow their own particular set of rules—and these rules are strictly enforced. For example, when talking to InDesign, AppleScript allows you to say the fifth text frame of page 2 but *not* the fifth text frame on page 2, even though either phrase would be acceptable in English. The AppleScript compiler will recognize either of or in when used as prepositions in a reference, but not on, which has a totally different purpose as far as AppleScript is concerned.

In practice, although AppleScript does allow for some clever phrasing, most scripters ultimately prefer to keep their code simple and consistent and avoid the fancy but nonessential stuff. For example, document file "report.txt" of folder 3 of disk "Server" may not look as attractive as the more "natural" phrasing shown previously, but it is clear and to the point. (Plus, it takes less work to type!) As you use AppleScript more, you will come to find the coding style that best suits you.

You can assemble references in several different ways. For instance, the reference

```
tell application "Finder"
    application file "TextEdit.app" of folder "Applications" of startup disk
end tell
```

can also be written using AppleScript's possessive 's form, like this:

```
tell application "Finder"
    startup disk's folder "Applications"'s application file "TextEdit.app"
end tell
```

Both approaches work in exactly the same way, so just use whichever one you find most readable.

A third option is to build up the reference one bit at a time using nested `tell` blocks:

```
tell application "Finder"
    tell startup disk
        tell folder "Applications"
            application file "TextEdit.app"
        end tell
    end tell
end tell
```

This produces exactly the same reference as before—you can check this by running all three scripts in AppleScript Editor and comparing the results. In each case, Finder will return a new reference that looks like this:

```
--> application file "TextEdit.app" of folder "Applications"
            of startup disk of application "Finder"
```

Nested `tell` blocks make it easy to use the same reference across several commands without having to type it out each time. Script 5–3 gathers some information on the currently playing track in iTunes and displays it to the user.

Script 5–3.

```
tell application "iTunes"
    play
    set the_track_name to name of current track
    set the_album to album of current track
    set the_artist to artist of current track
end tell
display dialog "Now listening to " & the_track_name ¬
        & " of " & the_album & " by " & the_artist & "."
```

The code works, but is somewhat repetitive when identifying the current track property. With a longer reference, this would become even more awkward to read and maintain. Script 5–4 eliminates the repetition by using a `tell` block to identify the application object's `current track` property as the starting point for assembling references within the block.

Script 5–4.

```
tell application "iTunes"
    play
    tell current track
        set the_track_name to name
        set the_album to album
        set the_artist to artist
    end tell
end tell
display dialog "Now listening to " & the_track_name ¬
        & " of " & the_album & " by " & the_artist & "."
```

How do these `tell` blocks work? Well, there are two ways you can compose a literal reference in your code: as an *absolute* reference, or as a *relative* reference. An absolute reference describes the object where the entire search begins. In application scripting, this is always an `application` object. For example, the following literal references are all absolute because they start by identifying the `application` object representing TextEdit:

```
application "TextEdit"
document 1 of application "TextEdit"
name of document 1 of application "TextEdit"
```

AppleScript can evaluate these references to obtain the objects you want without any further information.

A relative reference, on the other hand, doesn't specify the root object. For example, these expressions will all be treated as relative references:

```
name of document 1
document 1
name
```

Because AppleScript can't resolve a reference unless it knows where to begin its search, it assumes that any relative reference must be part of a larger reference. To find the missing piece of the reference, it looks at the current default target of the script. Initially, the default target is the script itself, but as we discussed in the earlier "Understanding Commands" section, you can use `tell` blocks to define a new default target for statements within the block. For example:

```
-- The default target is initially the current script

tell application "TextEdit"

    -- The default target is now application "TextEdit"

    tell document 1

        -- The default target is now document 1 of application "TextEdit"

        name

    end tell

    -- The default target here is application "TextEdit"

end tell

-- The default target here is the current script
```

When AppleScript evaluates the `name` expression, it knows that this is the name of a property in an application object, so it uses the enclosing `tell` blocks to expand this into a full reference: `name of document 1 of application "TextEdit"`. Once AppleScript has assembled the full reference, it can decide what to do with it (in this case, get the value of the property from TextEdit).

A word of warning when using nested `tell` blocks: sometimes applications use the same names for both properties and classes—for example, TextEdit has both a text property and a text class. If AppleScript encounters the text keyword by itself, it will assume you are using text as the name of a class, not a property, and return the class name, text:

```
tell application "TextEdit"
  tell document 1
    text
  end tell
end tell
--> text -- This is not what you wanted!
```

In this situation, you need to modify your code to make it clear to AppleScript that you are using text as a property name within a larger reference, like this:

```
tell application "TextEdit"
  text of document 1
end tell
```

Or, like this:

```
tell application "TextEdit"
  tell document 1
    text of it
  end tell
end tell
--> "Hello, World!" -- Much better!
```

> **NOTE:** it is a special AppleScript variable that always contains a reference to the target of the current tell block. You will learn more about this and other special variables in Chapter 11.

Script 5–5 shows a more complex example that opens the current user's home folder window, repositions it, sets it to list view sorted by date, and displays the folder sizes. (Once you know a bit more about Finder scripting, why not try rewriting this script without any nested tell blocks, just to see what a difference they make?)

Script 5–5.

```
tell application "Finder"
  tell home
    open
    tell container window
      set bounds to {40, 40, 800, 800}
      set current view to list view
      tell its list view options -- Equivalent to: tell list view options of it
        set calculates folder sizes to true
        set sort column to column id modification date column
      end tell
    end tell
  end tell
end tell
```

Now that you know the principles by which an application object model operates, let's put that knowledge to the test by exploring a real, live example: the Mac OS X Finder.

Exploring a Typical Object Model

A good way to get your head around object models is to dive straight in and explore one. One of the best applications to start with is the Finder. In addition to being well designed and not too complicated, the Finder's GUI presents the structure of the file system in much the same way as its scripting interface.

> **NOTE:** Some of the following examples use file, folder, and disk names that are specific to my computer. Before running these scripts yourself, modify them as necessary to use file, folder, and disk names that appear on your own file system.

To begin your exploration, choose the Go ➤ Computer option from the Finder's menu bar. This will show a window somewhat similar to the one in Figure 5–5, displaying all of your mounted volumes.

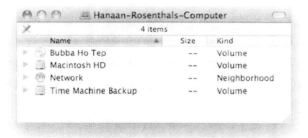

Figure 5–5. *A Finder window that displays the currently mounted volumes*

The Finder represents mounted volumes as objects of class disk, so let's try getting all of the disk elements of the Finder's main application object. Figure 5–6 shows the script and a typical result.

As you can see, the result of the script in Figure 5–6 is a list of references. The first thing you will notice is that all but one of the references are of the following form:

```
disk "volume name" of application "Finder"
```

Each of these disk objects is identified by its name: "Bubba Ho Tep" and "Time Machine Backup". As long as you do not have two or more disk objects with the same name, you can be confident that each of these references identifies a different volume in the file system.

The one exception is the following reference:

```
startup disk of application "Finder"
```

Figure 5–6. *An AppleScript that returns a list of references to the currently mounted volumes*

The Finder is clever enough to know that one of the mounted volumes must be the one you booted the operating system from, so it provides a special shortcut that allows you to locate that volume even if you don't know its name in advance. This shortcut takes the form of a property named `startup disk` that appears in the Finder's main `application` object.

Many scriptable applications use properties like this to provide useful shortcuts to particularly important or useful objects in their object models.

You can refer to the `startup disk` property in your own code like this:

```
tell application "Finder"
    startup disk
end tell
```

When you run this script, the Finder returns another reference:

```
--> startup disk of application "Finder"
```

If you know the startup disk's name, you can refer to it using that as well. For example, my startup disk is named "Macintosh HD", so I can refer to it by name:

```
tell application "Finder"
    disk "Macintosh HD"
end tell
```

Once again, when you run the script, the result is

```
--> startup disk of application "Finder"
```

Notice that the reference returned by the application is not necessarily the same as the one you gave it. A well-designed scriptable application will return whatever reference it thinks will be most useful to you the next time you need to refer to a particular object.

Now let's explore the file system more deeply. In Figure 5–7, I have dug down to the Sites folder of my home folder, where I can see a document file, index.html, as well as another folder, images.

Figure 5–7. *Viewing a portion of the file system hierarchy in the Finder's GUI*

The Finder's scripting interface also represents the file system structure as objects nested within other objects, allowing us to dig down into it in much the same way.

From Figure 5–7, you can see that the Macintosh HD volume contains a number of folders: Applications, Developer, Library, System, and Users. The Finder's GUI displays each folder as a folder icon followed by the folder's name. Similarly, the Finder's scripting interface represents each folder as an object of the folder class. If you are interested in these folders, you can use AppleScript to ask for references to all of them, as shown in Script 5–6.

Script 5–6.

```
tell application "Finder"
    every folder of disk "Macintosh HD"
end tell
--> {folder "Applications" of startup disk, folder "Developer" of startup disk,
    folder "Library" of startup disk, folder "System" of startup disk,
    folder "Users" of startup disk}
```

Or you can ask for just one folder in particular; for example:

```
tell application "Finder"
    folder "Users" of disk "Macintosh HD"
end tell
```

Here, I am asking the Finder to look in its application object for an element of class disk whose name is "Macintosh HD". Once it finds that object, it should look in it for an element of class folder whose name is "Users".

Next, I'll locate my home folder, named hanaan, which is in the Users folder:

```
tell application "Finder"
    folder "hanaan" of folder "Users" of disk "Macintosh HD"
end tell
```

As this is where I keep all of my personal files, it is a very useful place to get to. Once again, the Finder's designers anticipated this and added another shortcut property, home, to the Finder's main application object. This allows me to get to my home folder with much less effort:

```
tell application "Finder"
    home
end tell
```

If I run the previous two scripts, both return the exact result—a complete step-by-step reference to the object that represents my home folder:

```
--> folder "hanaan" of folder "Users" of startup disk of application "Finder"
```

> **NOTE:** You may notice that the preceding scripts do not specify a particular command for the application to perform using the given reference. In these cases, AppleScript will automatically send a get command to the target application, asking it to resolve the reference for you. We will discuss how these "implicit gets" work in Chapter 12.

Let's build a reference to the index.html document file in the Sites folder now, taking advantage of the home property of the Finder's application object while we're at it. Script 5–7 shows the easiest way to construct this reference.

Script 5–7.

```
tell application "Finder"
    document file "index.html" of folder "Sites" of home
end tell
```

Although you can refer to the same file like this,

```
tell application "Finder"
    document file "index.html" of folder "Sites" of ¬
        folder "hanaan" of folder "Users" of disk "Macintosh HD"
end tell
```

using the home property makes the code shorter. It also avoids any need to hard-code the home folder and startup disk names for one particular user, making the code much more portable.

> **TIP:** A good way to see different Finder references is to select a file, folder, or disk anywhere in the Finder's GUI and then run the following code: `tell application "Finder" to get selection`.

Let's try a few more examples for practice. First, let's ask for the `name` property of every folder in the current user's home folder:

```
tell application "Finder"
    name of every folder of home
end tell
--> {"Desktop", "Documents", "Downloads", "Library", "Movies", "Music", ...}
```

Or, what if we want a reference to the disk or folder that is displayed in the frontmost Finder window? Here's how we do it (assuming the window exists):

```
tell application "Finder"
    target of Finder window 1
end tell
--> folder "Applications" of startup disk of application "Finder"
```

Notice how we refer to the Finder window by numerical index. Previous examples have identified elements by name or, by using the `every` keyword, all at once. However, elements normally appear in a particular order—window elements, for example, are ordered so that the frontmost window is window 1, the window behind it is 2, and so on—so another option is to refer to elements by position. The `target` property contains a reference to the folder that is displayed in that window.

The next example digs down into the Finder's desktop window object to get the coordinates of the desktop window, which is handy if you are writing a script to reposition other Finder windows on the desktop:

```
tell application "Finder"
    bounds of container window of desktop
end tell
--> {0, 0, 1680, 1050}
```

Lastly, here's another corner of the Finder's object model for you to consider:

```
tell application "Finder"
    Finder preferences
end tell
--> Finder preferences of application "Finder"
```

Once again, we are referring to an application object property, `Finder preferences`, that contains another application property. The result in this example is unremarkable—just a fresh reference to the property itself—but dig deeper and things get more interesting. The `Finder preferences` property contains a one-off object of class `preferences` that can be used to get and set various Finder preferences.

For instance, the preferences object contains a property, `new window target`, that contains a reference to the disk or folder that is initially displayed when you choose **File ➤ New Finder Window** (⌘+N) in the GUI:

```
tell application "Finder"
   new window target of Finder preferences
end tell
--> startup disk of application "Finder"
```

This property is editable, so you can easily use a `set` command to change its value to a different reference:

```
tell application "Finder"
   set new window target of Finder preferences ¬
         to folder "hanaan" of folder "Users" of startup disk
end tell
```

Now when I create a new Finder window in the GUI, it will initially show the contents of my home folder instead of my startup disk.

While the Finder's designers could have added these preferences properties directly to the main `application` object, tucking them away in their own dedicated object is a bit tidier. Incidentally, another application that likes to organize properties into "preferences" objects is Adobe InDesign, which we'll cover in Chapter 26. There, though, you'll be dealing with many dozens of properties at a time—so neatness really is a virtue!

> **TIP:** A great way to explore live objects in an application object model is by using Late Night Software's Script Debugger (http://www.latenightsw.com). Like AppleScript Editor, Script Debugger's Dictionary view can display class and command definitions from the dictionary. However, it also provides a powerful expandable Explorer view, allowing you to examine the actual objects that currently exist in the application, along with their properties and elements.

All application object models fit together according to the same basic rules, so once you know how to navigate the object model of, say, the Finder, the same techniques will serve you well when you go on to script other applications, from very simple applications such as TextEdit all the way up to powerful and sophisticated applications like InDesign.

Understanding the general rules by which application object models are put together is essential to finding your way around those object models, but it is not the only knowledge you require: you must also understand exactly how the objects (and commands) in a particular application are structured. This brings us to our fourth key concept of application scripting: how scriptable applications document these structures in their application dictionaries.

Understanding Application Dictionaries

Every scriptable application has a scripting dictionary that defines all the application's commands and classes available for use with AppleScript. The dictionary supplies two things: the keywords that AppleScript will need to compile your scripts, and some basic human-readable documentation, consisting of a short description of each command and class, what it does, and the features it provides.

Some applications include additional information such as sample code and notes in their dictionaries, making it easier to understand how to use them. Others may prefer to supply this sort of information as separate documentation. Unfortunately, all too many applications do not provide anything beyond the essential details required by the dictionary format.

One of the challenges in learning an application's scripting interface is learning your way around its dictionary. Large, complicated applications such as Microsoft Word and Adobe InDesign can have massive dictionaries to pour through, and even the dictionaries of smaller, simpler applications such as Finder and iTunes can take a while to understand.

To make dictionaries easier to digest, they are normally broken up into several sections, or *suites*, each defining a number of classes and/or commands that share a common purpose or are otherwise related to each other.

> **TIP:** Remember, *classes* describe the structure of the objects you work with, and *commands* are what you use to manipulate those objects.

For example, the Standard Suite that appears in most application dictionaries defines a number of basic classes such as application, document, and window and sets out the basic functionality for these features. It also defines a number of commands for performing common operations on application objects, including creating new objects (make), moving existing objects around the object model or making fresh copies of them (move and duplicate), or even deleting objects completely (delete).

There are a few quirks as to how class and command information can be laid out in a dictionary, but we'll discuss these quirks as we go. For now, let's dive in and start exploring a few application dictionaries in order to understand them better. Of course, to do this we'll need some way to view them, so it's time to bring up AppleScript Editor and investigate the one big feature we skipped over in Chapter 4: the dictionary viewer.

Introducing AppleScript Editor's Dictionary Viewer

To view an application's dictionary in AppleScript Editor, choose File ➤ Open Dictionary, pick the application you're interested in, and click Open. Or, if you are in the Finder, you can drag and drop the application you're interested in onto AppleScript Editor's icon and AppleScript Editor will open its dictionary automatically.

> **TIP:** You can add frequently used applications to AppleScript Editor's Library palette (**Window ➤ Library**), allowing you to open their dictionaries quickly with a simple double-click. See Chapter 4 for more information on this feature.

If the application does not have a dictionary, AppleScript Editor will display the following message: "Unable to read the dictionary of the application or extension because it is not scriptable."

Even if an application does not have a dictionary, all is not lost: you can still use the standard run, open, activate, and quit commands on it, and if you really must automate it, then you may be able to control its GUI directly from AppleScript using GUI Scripting, which we'll look at later in the book. Fortunately, many applications do provide at least some level of AppleScript support, so once you've established that an application is scriptable, the next step is to read its dictionary to figure out exactly what scripting features it provides.

For this exercise, choose File ➤ Open Dictionary, select the Finder application from the list, and click Open to bring up its dictionary in a new viewer window. Figure 5–8 shows how the viewer window will initially look.

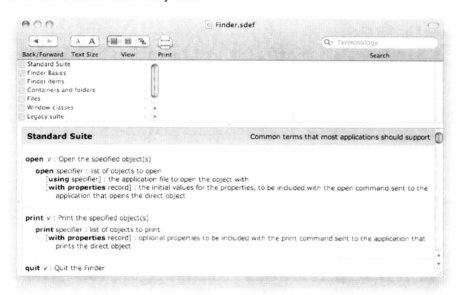

Figure 5–8. *Viewing the Finder's dictionary in AppleScript Editor*

The AppleScript Editor dictionary viewer window is divided into three parts: the toolbar at the top, the navigation browser beneath it, and the main terminology view at the bottom.

The toolbar contains a number of useful controls, most of which are self-explanatory. The most important ones are the View buttons and the Search field. The Search field is great when you want to find a particular word: just type it in, and a list of all matching entries will immediately appear. The View buttons let you control how the application dictionary is displayed in the navigation browser.

The main terminology view at the bottom of the window is where the definitions of the application's classes and commands are displayed. We'll discuss how to interpret the information in the next section. By default, the terminology view shows the entire contents of the application's dictionary, although you can use the navigation control to narrow down what is displayed.

The navigation control beneath the toolbar provides a convenient summary of the dictionary's contents and also allows you to jump quickly to one particular part of the dictionary just by selecting one or more items in each column. How the dictionary is displayed here depends on the View mode you have selected in the toolbar. From left to right, the three View buttons allow you to browse the dictionary by suite (the default view), by containment, or by inheritance.

When the dictionary viewer window is first opened, you will see two things: a list of all of the dictionary's suites in the left column of the navigation control, and all of the dictionary's command and class definitions in the main terminology view. While you can scroll the dictionary view up and down to find the entries you want, a quicker way to navigate is by clicking the name of a suite in the navigation section. When you do this, the terminology view shows only the classes and commands in that suite. The navigation control also updates to show the names of the commands and classes in that suite. Figure 5–9 shows how the dictionary viewer looks after selecting the Finder Basics suite

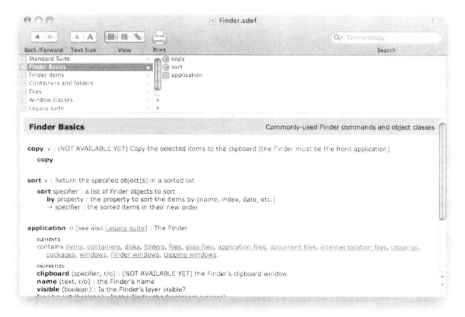

Figure 5–9. *Viewing the Finder Basics suite*

Notice how each name is preceded by a colored icon: a square orange icon containing the letter *S* indicates a suite name, command names are marked by the letter *C* in a blue circle, while the letter *C* in a purple square tells you that you're looking at a class name.

NOTE: While most class definitions describe objects that are part of the application's object model, some class definitions are used to describe the structure of AppleScript record objects instead. For instance, the print settings class in TextEdit's dictionary actually describes a record structure used by TextEdit's print command. You will learn more about records in Chapter 10.

How Classes Are Documented

In an application dictionary, a class is simply a description of all the features you can find in a particular type of object. Early in the chapter, I explained how an application object can have properties and, in many cases, elements as well. Let's now look at how to find out exactly what properties and elements are available for a particular class of objects.

The Finder Basics suite contains only three entries: two commands, copy and sort, and the main application class. This is probably the most important class in any scriptable application, and the one you will look at first. The reason for that is obvious: as you learned in the previous section, every application's object model has a single root object whose class is application. Now that you have access to the Finder's dictionary, you can find out exactly what properties and elements its main application object provides.

To display only the application class definition, click the application entry in the navigation browser, as shown in Figure 5–10.

TIP: To view more than one command or class at a time, just hold down the Shift key when clicking in the middle column of the navigation view to make a multiple selection. (You can also Shift-click in the other columns as well, although you can only make multiple selections in one column at a time.)

At the top of the terminology pane is the name of the class, application, followed by the letter *n*. AppleScript Editor's dictionary viewer likes to distinguish classes (which describe objects) and commands (which describe actions) using the letters *n* and *v*, short for *noun* and *verb*, just like in a traditional English language dictionary.

Following the letter *n* is a pair of square brackets. This tells you how this class definition relates to other class definitions in the same dictionary. We'll discuss this further in later sections. The line then ends with a short comment describing the class.

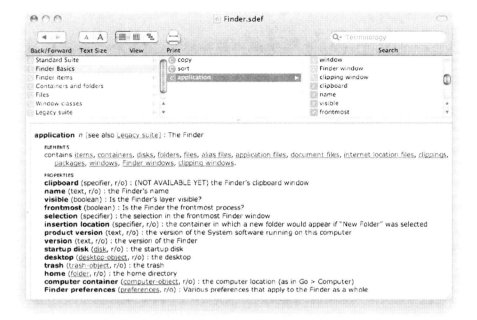

Figure 5–10. *Viewing the* `application` *class*

You'll also notice that the right column in the navigation pane now lists the names of all the properties and classes defined by the class. Properties are indicated by purple squares containing the letter *P*, and elements are indicated by orange squares containing the letter *E*. Clicking the name highlights the corresponding line in the main terminology pane.

> **NOTE:** Calling object classes "nouns" and commands "verbs" in the dictionary viewer makes some sense; after all, in human languages, nouns are the names of objects, while verbs are the names of actions you can perform on those objects. However, the technical terms *class*, *object*, and *command* are more precise in their meaning, so we will stick with them for the rest of the book.

Viewing the Properties and Elements Defined by a Class

Under the section labeled PROPERTIES, you will see a list of property names, each one highlighted in bold. Each property name is followed by a pair of parentheses. This tells you the class of object the property contains, and may also contain r/o to indicate that the property is read-only. Finally, there is short description of the property's purpose.

For example, you can see from Figure 5–10 that the Finder's `application` class has a name property containing an object of class text; that is, an AppleScript string. Further down, you can see that it has a property named home containing an object of class folder. (Technically, the home folder contains a reference to an object of class folder, but that's a minor distinction we won't worry about here.) This time, the class name is displayed as a blue underlined link. Clicking this link takes you directly to the definition of the Finder's folder class, where you can learn about the structure of folder objects, including any properties and elements that they have.

The ELEMENTS section lists the names of the application object's elements. Each element name corresponds to the name of an application-defined class; the only difference is that the dictionary viewer normally uses the plural version of the class name. Each element name is displayed as a blue underlined link, allowing you to jump directly to the class in question just by clicking it.

For example, disks are listed as one of the elements of the application class definition, which tells you that the Finder's main application object can contain any number of objects of class disk. Clicking the disks element name takes you directly to the description of the disk class.

> **TIP:** See the "Introducing Object Properties" and "Introducing Object Elements" sections earlier in the chapter for more discussion of properties and elements.

How Inheritance Describes Features Shared Between Classes

So far, we've looked at how the application class is documented in the Finder's dictionary. This is quite an easy class to read, as all of its properties and elements are listed in the one place (except for the old desktop picture property, which is tucked away in the Legacy suite). Many classes take a bit more work to understand, however. For example, let's consider how the Finder's folder class is documented.

First, click the Finder's Containers and Folders suite in the navigation section of the dictionary viewer to bring up a list of all classes in the suite. Next, click the folder class to view its definition, as shown in Figure 5–11.

How strange—you can see the description of the folder class, but there doesn't seem to be anything in it! Surely a folder object must have some properties and elements?

The answer to this riddle lies in the first line of the class definition, inside the square brackets, where it says inh. container > item. The "inh." part is short for *inheritance*, and what this means is that some (or all) of the folder class's properties and elements actually come from another class in the Finder dictionary. In this case, the folder class inherits a number of its attributes from the container class (which in turn inherits some of its attributes from the item class).

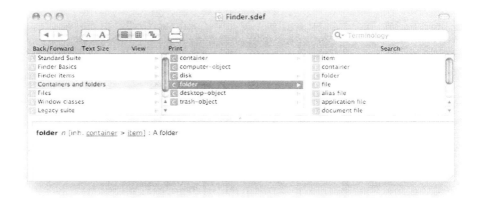

Figure 5-11. *Viewing the* `folder` *class definition in the Finder's dictionary*

Okay, then, let's look up the `container` class to see what we're missing. Click the `container` link to bring up the class definition, shown in Figure 5–12.

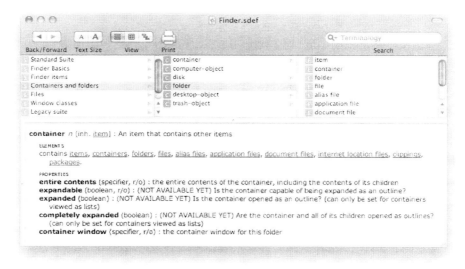

Figure 5-12. *Viewing the* `container` *class definition in the Finder's dictionary*

That's more like it—now we can see what types of elements a folder object can have. We can also see some of the properties you'd expect to find in a folder object, though it still looks like we're missing a few.

No problem: according to the first line of the class definition, the `container` class inherits in turn from the class named `item`, so click that link to bring up the `item` class definition, as shown in Figure 5–13.

Figure 5–13. *Viewing the item class definition in the Finder's dictionary*

The item class doesn't inherit from any other classes, which means at last we've found the rest of the properties available in folder objects.

The container and item classes are interesting cases. Unlike the folder class, which describes the folder objects you work with in your scripts, the container and item classes do not describe actual objects in the Finder's object model. Instead, they are defined solely as a foundation for other classes, such as folder, to build on.

You may be wondering why the Finder's designers would go to all of this trouble, instead of sticking everything into the folder class. Well, the reason is simple: many of the basic properties of a folder object can also be found in other types of Finder objects, such as disks and document files. Every disk, folder, and document file in the file system has a modification date, for example, so rather than write the modification date property three times—once in the disk class, once in the folder class, and again in the document file class—and then doing the same for all of the other properties they have in common, it makes much more sense to document all of these properties in a separate class, item, and then indicate that the disk, folder, and document file classes all possess the properties listed in the item class (plus any additional properties that they define for themselves).

Similarly, some (though not all) file system objects, such as disks and folders, can contain other objects as elements. To better organize the dictionary, the Finder's designers have created another class, container, that defines all the attributes from which any file system object that contains other file system objects can inherit.

Now that you know how to find out all the properties and elements for one particular class, let's step back and take a look at the Finder's inheritance hierarchy in full. Figure 5–14 provides an overview of all the classes defined in the Finder dictionary, showing which classes inherit from which.

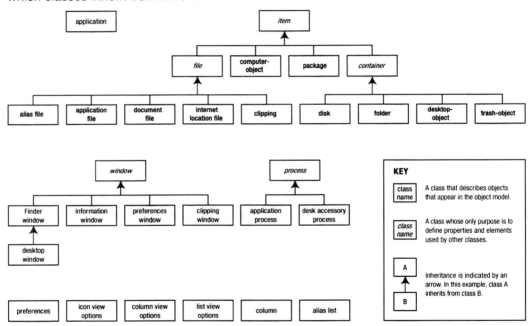

Figure 5–14. *The Finder's complete class inheritance hierarchy*

> **TIP:** When viewing a class definition in the dictionary viewer, you can include all of its inherited properties and elements by checking the "Show inherited items in dictionary viewer" option in the General panel of AppleScript Editor's Preferences window.

In addition to making the dictionary more compact by avoiding unnecessary repetition, a careful study of class inheritance also tells you which behaviors different classes of objects will have in common. For instance, if you know the item class defines name, comment, and label properties, then you know that all disk, folder, and file objects will contain these properties.

Understanding inheritance is also valuable when referring to the elements of an object. For example, if you ask for every file element of a folder object, you will get a list of references identifying all of the alias files, application files, document files, internet location files, and clippings contained by that folder:

```
tell application "Finder"
   get every file of folder "Pictures" of home
end tell
--> {document file "9781430223610.gif" of folder "Pictures" ...,
     alias file "iChat Icons" of folder "Pictures" ...,
     document file "iPhoto Library" of folder "Pictures" ...}
```

You can narrow this request by picking an element class that is further down the inheritance hierarchy; for instance, asking for the folder object's document file elements will return references to objects of class document file only:

```
tell application "Finder"
   get every file of folder "Pictures" of home
end tell
--> {document file "9781430223610.gif" of folder "Pictures" ...,
     document file "iPhoto Library" of folder "Pictures" ...}
```

Or you can broaden this request by asking for the container's item elements. This will give you references to all of its disks and folders as well as all of its files:

```
tell application "Finder"
   get every file of folder "Pictures" of home
end tell
--> {folder "New Artwork" of folder "Pictures" ...,
     folder "Unsorted Images" of folder "Pictures" ...,
     document file "9781430223610.gif" of folder "Pictures" ...,
     alias file "iChat Icons" of folder "Pictures" ...,
     document file "iPhoto Library" of folder "Pictures" ...}
```

A useful, if not always reliable, feature of AppleScript Editor's dictionary viewer is the ability to browse classes according to their inheritance hierarchy. To do this, click the right View button in the toolbar, as shown in Figure 5–15.

Unfortunately, the dictionary viewer is a bit limited in that it only shows classes that ultimately inherit from the item class, and only then if the item class is actually visible in the dictionary. Hopefully, this shortcoming will be fixed in a future release, but it may work well for some applications and can help you to develop a feel for the way that inheritance works.

Figure 5–15. *Viewing the inheritance hierarchy for Finder's* `alias file` *class*

> **CAUTION:** Don't confuse the inheritance hierarchy with the containment hierarchy. Inheritance tells you what features objects have in common; containment tells you which classes of objects can be nested inside which other classes of objects.

Class Definitions Can Be Spread Across More than One Suite!

Returning to the top line in the `application` class description (refer to Figure 5–10), you will see a note telling you to look in the Legacy suite, so click the `Legacy suite` link to jump directly there.

As you can see from Figure 5–16, it's not just the Finder Basics suite that defines a class named `application`; the Legacy suite lists an `application` class as well!

You might be wondering how a scriptable application can have two different classes with the same name. In fact, there is still only a single `application` class in the Finder; however, its definition has been split into two parts—one appearing in the Finder Basics suite and the other in the Legacy suite.

Many applications take this slightly odd approach to documenting classes. For example, Cocoa-based applications such as TextEdit and Mail often list the features of `application` and `document` classes that exist in all Cocoa applications in their Standard Suites. Features that are only found in that particular application are then listed in a separate suite—for example, most of the definition for Mail's `application` class appears in its Mail suite, along with other Mail-only features.

Figure 5–16. *The Legacy suite contains a second* `application` *class definition!*

This habit of splitting some class definitions across several suites is usually more accidental than deliberate. It is most common in Cocoa applications, an odd side effect of the way that Mac OS X's Cocoa Scripting system is designed.

In the Finder, though, splitting the `application` class's definition was a deliberate decision. The Legacy suite lists features that were originally added to the Finder in the pre–OS X days but have since moved to OS X's own dedicated System Events application. These features still work in the Finder, though Apple does recommend that you use System Events (which you'll learn about in Part 3) instead.

> **NOTE:** Cocoa Scripting is the name of the framework that provides all Cocoa-based applications with much of their AppleScript support (and a few quirks too).

Now that you know how to discover the properties and features provided by objects, let's look at how you can explore an application's containment hierarchy using the dictionary viewer.

Browsing the Containment Hierarchy

Let's play a little more with the dictionary viewer's navigation options. You've already seen how to browse classes by suite and by inheritance. Now let's try exploring classes according to containment structure.

To switch the navigation pane to the containment view, click the middle View button in the toolbar. When you do this, the navigation section changes from displaying classes and commands by suite to displaying the `application` class in the leftmost column. (Actually, you will see two "application" entries—this is due to one of the quirks I hinted at earlier, but don't worry about it for now.)

Now you can browse the application dictionary according to the elements of each class. Each time you click a class name that has an arrow to its right, a new column appears listing the classes of its elements. Take a look at Figure 5–17 to see what I mean.

Figure 5–17. *Browsing the Finder's dictionary by its containment hierarchy*

In Figure 5–17, I started by clicking the application entry with the arrow next to it, which gives me a list of all the classes of elements the Finder's application object can have. Let's say I want to build a reference to a document file, starting with the disk it is on, so I click the disk entry in the second column. That shows me all the classes of elements a disk object can have; I figure the file is probably in a folder, so I click folder next...and so on, until I click the document file entry, which doesn't have any elements of its own.

One disadvantage of the dictionary viewer's containment view is that it only lists the elements defined by each class; it does not include any properties that contain references to other application objects, such as the Finder's startup disk and home properties. It also gets a bit confused when the same class name appears in different suites (this is why there are two application entries shown in Figure 5–17, for example). Still, even with these shortcomings, it can be a useful tool when you're trying to understand how an application's object model is laid out.

Another option is to draw your own containment diagram as you read through the dictionary. This is a bit more work, but it's a good way to learn. The diagram in Figure 5–18 describes the main part of the Finder's containment hierarchy.

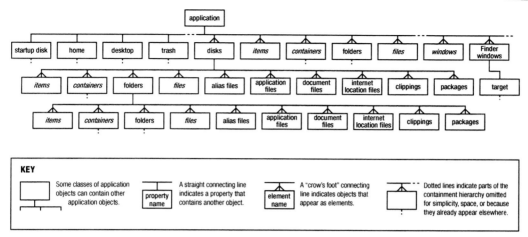

Figure 5–18. *A diagram of the Finder's containment hierarchy*

At the top is the main `application` object. The next row shows the contents of the `application` object. On the left are properties that contain other application objects; on the right are its elements. (Some of the less important properties and elements are omitted for space.)

The most important elements of the main `application` object are the `disk` elements, so I have expanded on that part of the diagram to show most of the elements that an object of class `disk` can have, and so on.

You'll notice that I've used dotted lines to indicate where parts of the diagram have been omitted. For instance, folder objects can contain other folder objects, which can contain other folder objects, and so on indefinitely, so I've truncated that bit for obvious reasons. The `home` property of the main `application` object contains a folder object, but as the containment structure for folders is already shown elsewhere in the diagram I've not repeated it. Less interesting classes of objects, such as clippings and packages, have been left out as well. The art of drawing a good containment diagram is to include enough information to give you a feel for its structure, but not so much that it becomes impossibly complicated to follow.

You'll also notice that the connecting lines to properties and elements are different. Since each property only appears once in an object, I have indicated this one-to-one relationship with a straight line. On the other hand, a single object can have any number of elements—one, many, or even none at all—so the connecting lines end in crow's feet to indicate this one-to-many relationship. (Incidentally, I borrowed this notation from the world of database programming, which is also where the inventors of AppleScript took some of their ideas from.)

Finally, I have written the names of some elements in italics. That is to remind me that asking for these elements will return references to several different classes of objects. For instance, asking for, say, `file` elements will return objects of class `alias file`, `application file`, `document file`, and so on, whereas asking for `document file` elements will return objects of class document file only. Refer to the earlier section on inheritance for more details on this aspect of scriptable application behavior.

> **CAUTION:** Don't confuse the containment hierarchy with the live object model. The containment hierarchy only tells you how to reach different classes of objects. To find out exactly what objects your application currently contains, you need to send lots of get commands to the running application and see what comes back, or use Script Debugger's Explorer view, which does this for you.

How Commands Are Documented

An application's dictionary will describe all of the commands that the application recognizes. Some applications define relatively few commands that are widely used on many different classes of objects. Others provide lots of specialized commands to perform different tasks. Well-designed applications tend to follow the first approach, although it does depend to some extent on the type of application.

Most scriptable applications include a Standard Suite, which is one of the recommended suites provided by Apple. The Standard Suite contains commands for creating and deleting objects, and moving them around the object model. These commands are usually similar from application to application. Other suites may contain commands that are unique to that particular application. For example, the Finder Items suite in the Finder's dictionary includes an empty command for emptying the Finder's Trash.

As we discussed earlier, a command is made up of a name followed by any number of parameters. Figure 5–19 shows the definition for the Finder's move command.

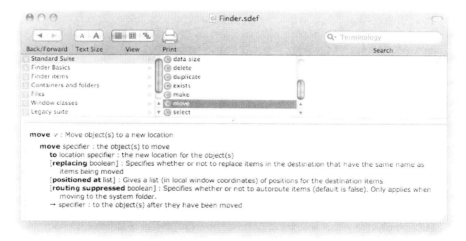

Figure 5–19. *Viewing the move command definition in the Finder's dictionary*

The first line starts with the command's name, move, followed by the letter *v*, which is short for "verb." That tells you that you are looking at the definition of a command. (Remember, AppleScript Editor's dictionary viewer likes to refer to objects as nouns and commands as verbs.) This is followed by a short description of what the command does. In this case, the move command is used to move one or more objects from their original position in the object model to a new location.

The rest of the definition tells you how to write the command in your script. Naturally, you begin with the command's name, move. The move command requires a direct parameter, which is a reference to the object, or objects, that you wish to move. In the dictionary, the class of the direct parameter is shown immediately after the command name—in this case, it is specifier. (AppleScript Editor's dictionary viewer uses the term "specifier" to mean "reference.") Following this is a colon (:), which indicates that the rest of the line is a brief description of the parameter's meaning.

For example, if you wish to move every document file on the current user's desktop, you would use the reference every document file of desktop as the move command's direct parameter.

Many application commands take a direct parameter, This is often a reference to the object (or objects) you wish to manipulate.

The next parameter that the Finder's move command requires is the location where the object(s) should be moved to. This parameter is given as a labeled parameter, named to. A dictionary-defined command can have at most a single direct parameter, but it can have any number of labeled parameters. In the dictionary, the parameter name is followed by the class of the object you need to use. The to parameter requires a reference to the point where the objects should be moved to, which the dictionary describes as a location specifier (a reference to the point where the object/s will be inserted).

For example, if you want to move your document files from the desktop to the Documents folder, the value of the to parameter would be folder "Documents" of home.

The move command has one direct parameter and four labeled parameters in total, although only the direct and to parameters are required. The dictionary indicates which parameters are optional by surrounding them in square brackets. You can supply values for these parameters if you want, or you can leave them out of your command, in which case the application will use their default values instead.

Here is how the assembled command looks:

```
move every document file of desktop to folder "Documents" of home
```

Of the three optional parameters that the move command accepts, the most useful one is the replacing parameter. Although the dictionary isn't helpful enough to tell you itself, once you start using the Finder's move command, you will soon find out that its default value is false. In other words, if you try to copy a file or folder to a location where another file or folder of the same name already exists, the move command will generate an error telling you that it is not allowed to replace that item. If you want the Finder to overwrite any existing files or folders of the same name, you will have to specify your own `true` value for the `replacing` parameter.

> **NOTE:** When compiling a script, AppleScript may reformat Boolean parameters for readability. For instance, `move some_item to new_location replacing true` will compile as `move some_item to new_location with replacing`. More on this in Chapter 12.

If the command returns a result, the last line of the command's definition indicates the class of the value returned—in this case, a new reference (`specifier`), followed by a brief description.

Now that you've learned how to read application dictionaries, let's discuss the things that they *don't* tell you.

Application Dictionaries Don't Tell You Everything!

Although dictionaries are an essential part of application scripting, they are often not as good as they could or should be. Some dictionaries may simply be buggy or broken. Others may be poorly thought out, inventing nonstandard commands for tasks that could be performed using the standard set of application commands, or duplicating lots of properties across multiple classes instead of establishing a good, clean inheritance structure between these classes.

However, even well-designed dictionaries rarely provide all of the information you need to script applications effectively. This is partly the fault of the dictionary format itself: the original AETE ("Apple Event Terminology Extension") format was very limited in the kinds of information it could contain, and even the newer SDEF ("Scripting Definition") format does not force application developers to document every detail.

The best application developers supply additional documentation and examples, either included in the optional sections of an SDEF-based dictionary, or as separate files on their websites. Microsoft and Adobe are particularly good at this, for example.

Other applications provide only the basic dictionary, leaving you to figure out the missing details for yourself. (Surprisingly, this includes quite a few Apple applications.)

> **NOTE:** A lack of good documentation can make learning to script applications something of a challenge. If you find an application's scripting documentation to be inadequate, don't be afraid to contact the application developer with a polite request for improvements.

One of the biggest challenges for application scripters is working out which classes of objects can be used in which commands. For instance, although the Apple iTunes dictionary will reveal the `make` command and the `track` class, iTunes doesn't allow you to combine the two to create a new `track` object. Thus, a command such as the following, although it looks as though it ought to work correctly, will just generate an error when you run it:

```
tell application "iTunes"
    make new file track at playlist 1 with properties ¬
        {location:alias "Macintosh HD:Users:hanaan:Music:some.mp3"}
end tell
-- iTunes got an error: Can't make class file track
```

Fortunately, there are ways to create and copy tracks in iTunes, although you'll have to wait until Chapter 21 to find out how.

Similarly, the Finder dictionary contains the class window and the command duplicate, but that doesn't mean you can duplicate a window. (You can, however, use the make command to create a new window that displays the contents of the desired folder or disk.)

Some class definitions may include a RESPONDS TO section that tell you which commands accept objects of this class as their direct parameter, but many dictionaries do not provide this information. Even in those that do, this section may not list every command that can be used.

Labeled parameter descriptions can be even more vague. For instance, the to parameter in the Finder's move command requires an insertion location reference, but doesn't say exactly how this reference should be constructed. As you gain experience in application scripting, you will develop a good idea of what tends to work and what doesn't. We'll discuss some of the approaches you can try later, in Chapter 12.

While figuring out the correct parameters to commands is usually the greatest challenge, even simple features like properties may require some investigation.

Consider the container property defined by the Finder's item class, or the entire contents property defined by the container class. Although I didn't include them in the earlier containment diagram (refer to Figure 5–18), these properties do contain references to other Finder objects and can be extremely useful for certain tasks. The container property gives you a reference to the folder or disk that contains a file or folder object. The entire contents property allows you to refer to all of the files and folders within a disk or folder, no matter how deeply nested they are (though in practice, it's best used on small segments of the file system, as it becomes impossibly slow with large numbers of items).

The challenge of the container and entire contents properties is that the Finder dictionary does not tell you very much about the values they contain. Each property claims to contain a value of class specifier—that is, a reference—but doesn't say what sort of object (or objects) it refers to. With the container property, it is reasonable to guess that if your object is a file or folder, the container property will contain a reference to an object of class folder or disk. The entire contents property is less obvious, however.

One way to find out is to perform some tests. For instance, the following scripts confirm the nature of the container property:

```
tell application "Finder"
   container of home
end tell
--> folder "Users" of startup disk of application "Finder"

tell application "Finder"
   container of folder "Users" of startup disk
end tell
--> startup disk of application "Finder"
```

When you ask for the contents of the entire contents property, the result is a list of references, like this:

```
tell application "Finder"
   get entire contents of folder "Pictures" of home
end tell
--> {folder "Holidays June 2009" of folder "Pictures" of folder "hanaan"
         of folder "Users" of startup disk of application "Finder",
      document file "9781430223610.gif" of folder "Pictures" of folder "hanaan"
         of folder "Users" of startup disk of application "Finder",
      alias file "iChat Icons" of folder "Pictures" of folder "hanaan"
         of folder "Users" of startup disk of application "Finder",
      document file "iPhoto Library" of folder "Pictures" of folder "hanaan"
         of folder "Users" of startup disk of application "Finder",
      document file "005.jpg" of folder "Holidays June 2009"
         of folder "Pictures" of folder "hanaan" of folder "Users"
         of startup disk of application "Finder",
      document file "007.jpg" of folder "Holidays June 2009"
         of folder "Pictures" of folder "hanaan" of folder "Users"
         of startup disk of application "Finder", ...}
```

Does this mean the entire contents property contains a list of single file references? The answer is: no. Once again, this is a case of the Finder returning the value that it thinks you want, which is not necessarily the value that is actually there. In fact, the entire contents property contains a multi-item reference. If you get the property directly, the Finder guesses that you want a list of references to the individual items and returns that. Because the property contains an application object reference, though, you can go further into the object model if you want. For example, Script 5–8 shows how to narrow your request if you are only interested in document files, while Script 5–9 goes even further, by retrieving only the file names.

Script 5–8.

```
tell application "Finder"
   get every document file of entire contents of folder "Pictures" of home
end tell
--> {document file "9781430223610.gif" of folder "Pictures" of folder "hanaan"
         of folder "Users" of startup disk of application "Finder",
      document file "iPhoto Library" of folder "Pictures" of folder "hanaan"
         of folder "Users" of startup disk of application "Finder",
      document file "005.jpg" of folder "Holidays June 2009"
         of folder "Pictures" of folder "hanaan" of folder "Users"
         of startup disk of application "Finder",
      document file "007.jpg" of folder "Holidays June 2009"
         of folder "Pictures" of folder "hanaan" of folder "Users"
         of startup disk of application "Finder", ...}
```

Script 5–9.

```
tell application "Finder"
    get name of every document file of entire contents of folder "Pictures" of home
end tell
--> {"9781430223610.gif", "iPhoto Library", "005.jpg", "007.jpg", ...}
```

You can even manipulate all of these object directly using other commands such as set and move. For example, to set their label colors:

```
tell application "Finder"
    set label index of every document file of ¬
        entire contents of folder "Pictures" of home to 7
end tell
```

The amount of control that is available through such a humble-looking property is impressive, although you would hardly guess this from its dictionary definition, and even experimenting for yourself may not give you the full story.

Given the limitations of application dictionaries and frequent lack of supplementary documentation, you should also make a point of studying scripts written by other AppleScript users, lots of which are available online, and reading the AppleScript mailing lists and bulletin boards for valuable insights and tips. You'll also find that as you grow more experienced, you will become better at guessing the sort of things that are most likely to work for a particular application, based on what you've found to work (or not work) on others.

Now that we've discussed the four key concepts of application scripting, let's proceed to fill in some of the finer details, beginning with AppleScript's application objects.

More on *application* Objects

As you now know, an application object model consists of objects that contain other objects, which in turn contain yet more objects, and so on. The result is a tree-shaped structure that starts from a single point and then branches out repeatedly until every scriptable object within the application appears somewhere within that structure.

The base of this object tree is always represented by an object of class application. Let's now look in detail at how these application objects work.

Creating *application* Objects

Obviously, the first thing you need to know is the name of the application you want to talk to—for example, Finder, iTunes, or TextEdit. However, having the name of an application alone is not sufficient; if it was, you could just write code like this:

```
tell Finder to get name of startup disk
```

If you do that, though, you will get an error, as AppleScript won't understand what you mean by Finder. (As you will find out in later chapters, what you have there is a variable named "Finder", which is not what you need here.)

You must be a lot more specific, and tell AppleScript in absolutely precise terms that what you want is an object that represents the Finder application. To do this, you must tell AppleScript to construct an `application` object for you.

Identifying Applications by Name

In AppleScript, an `application` object is represented by the keyword `application`, followed by (in most cases) the name of the application written in double quotes, like this:

```
application "Finder"
application "iTunes"
application "TextEdit"
```

The `application` keyword indicates the kind of object we want to create, which is (you guessed it) an object of class `application`.

The double quotes are used in AppleScript source code to indicate the beginning and end of an AppleScript text object, or string. The strings shown here represent the names of applications we're interested in talking to: Finder, iTunes, and TextEdit.

Put these two simple structures together—the `application` keyword followed by a string—and we have a new structure called an *object specifier*, so called because it identifies, or *specifies*, the exact object we want.

> **CAUTION:** Be aware that AppleScript always uses the application's default English name, even on non-English systems.

Identifying Applications by Path

Identifying applications by name is the most commonly used approach, but it is not the only way. You can also specify applications by their full path, like this:

```
application "Macintosh HD:Applications:FileMaker Pro 10:FileMaker Pro.app"
```

The path is a string consisting of the name of the volume, followed by the names of any folders, and finally the full name of the application itself.

The main disadvantage of that approach is that, because the exact location of the application is hard-coded in the script, the code is not as portable: other Macs may use different names for their startup disks. All the same, it can come in very useful if you have several applications with the same name and need to specify one of them in particular.

Identifying Applications by Bundle ID

In Mac OS X 10.5 and later, you can also identify applications using their bundle identifier, which is basically an Internet domain–style name written backward. For instance, Apple own the apple.com domain, so its applications use bundle IDs beginning with com.apple followed by the application name (written without spaces or other funky characters, of course). Examples include com.apple.Finder, com.apple.iTunes, and com.apple.TextEdit.

To create an application object using a bundle ID, you need to use a slightly fancier version of the application specifier, consisting of the application keyword followed by an id keyword, followed by a case-insensitive string containing the bundle ID, like this:

```
application id "com.apple.Finder"
application id "com.apple.iTunes"
application id "com.apple.TextEdit"
```

The main advantage of using bundle IDs is that, unlike an application file name, which anyone can change at any time, the bundle ID is stored safely within the application itself—and once an application has been assigned a bundle ID, it normally keeps that ID for life. This makes it a very reliable way to identify a particular application.

For example, some applications such as Adobe Photoshop like to alter their file names to reflect each new version that comes out. So a script that refers to application "Adobe Photoshop CS3" won't automatically recognize Adobe Photoshop CS4 if you have that installed. However, if you refer to it using application id "com.adobe.photoshop" then it will work regardless of what version you have installed, as all versions of Photoshop have the same bundle ID.

> **NOTE:** Occasionally, different versions of an application will use different bundle IDs. For example, the new QuickTime Player X in Snow Leopard has the ID com.apple.QuickTimePlayerX, while the older QuickTime Player 7 (which has a different scripting interface) uses com.apple.quicktimeplayer. This can be handy if you have both versions installed on your Mac, as you can use an application id ... specifier to target the one you want.

Identifying Applications by Remote URL

There is one other way you can identify scriptable applications from AppleScript: by eppc:// URL. When Mac OS X's Remote Apple Events feature is enabled, eppc:// URLs can be used to control applications that are running on a completely different machine! This is a very cool feature but it's not something you are likely to need straightaway, so we'll skip it for now and come back to it later, in Chapter 12.

> **TIP:** If you write app instead of application in your code, AppleScript will expand it for you when the script is compiled.

The Standard Properties of *application* Objects

In addition to any properties and elements defined by the application dictionary, application objects come with several useful properties already built in: class, name, id, version, running, and frontmost.

The class property contains the name of the object's class. Its value is always application (which, like all class names, is an object of class class):

```
class of application "Finder"
--> application
```

The name property contains the name of the application; for example:

```
name of application id "com.adobe.photoshop"
--> "Adobe Photoshop CS4"
```

The id property contains the bundle ID of the application; for example:

```
id of application "iTunes"
--> "com.apple.iTunes"
```

The version property contains a piece of text representing the application's version number; for example:

```
version of application "Chess"
--> "2.4.1"
```

The running property contains one of two values, true or false, that tells you whether or not the application is currently running; for example:

```
running of application "Finder"
--> true
```

Lastly, the frontmost property tells you whether or not the application is the active application in your Mac's GUI. Its value is also one of true or false.

All of the properties are read-only; that is, you can get their existing values, but you cannot set them to different values yourself. Only AppleScript can change their values; for example, the value of the running property will change when an application launches or quits.

One advantage of using these properties is that AppleScript does not have to launch the application in order to obtain their values. For example, if you would like to tell iTunes to start playing *only* if it is already running, you can use the following script:

```
tell application "iTunes"
    if running then
        play
    end if
end tell
```

Here, the tell ... end tell block identifies the application object for iTunes as the current target for any commands. The second line gets the value of the application object's running property. If the value is true, it executes the code inside the if ... end if block—in this case, a simple play command. On the other hand, if the value of the `running` property is `false`, then the `if ... end if` block (which is also known as a *conditional* statement) does nothing.

Another benefit of these built-in properties is that even if the application itself is not scriptable (such as the built-in Chess application, shown previously), you can still use these properties to get some basic information about it.

> **NOTE:** Except for the standard `class` property, these built-in properties are only available in Mac OS X 10.5 and later. Older versions of AppleScript do not provide these `application` object properties as standard; however, many scriptable applications define their own name and `version` properties in their dictionaries, and you can always use Mac OS X's invisible System Events application to find out if they are running or frontmost. The new built-in properties are definitely more convenient, however.

How AppleScript Compiles *tell application ...* Blocks

AppleScript has one more trick up its sleeve when it comes to `application` objects and `tell` blocks. As you know, each scriptable application you deal with defines its own set of keywords for scripts to use. For AppleScript to compile a script successfully, it needs to know what each of the keywords used in your code means.

So how does it know which dictionary to look in each time it encounters an application-defined keyword? The solution is clever, yet simple: whenever AppleScript encounters a `tell` block whose target is an `application` object, it uses the `application ...` specifier to determine the application dictionary it should use when compiling keywords within the `tell` block.

Normally, when we write application object references, we start with a `tell application ...` block, like this:

```
tell application "TextEdit"
    every paragraph of text of document 1
end tell
```

In theory, you can write the same reference as follows, without any `tell` blocks:

```
every paragraph of text of document 1 of application "TextEdit"
```

The catch here is that this code will only compile if AppleScript recognizes all of the keywords used without any help from the application dictionary. Fortunately for the preceding reference, AppleScript defines a number of application-related keywords by default—`paragraph`, `text`, and `document`. Other keywords will not be understood without help from an enclosing `tell application ... end tell` block. For instance, try to compile the following line in AppleScript Editor:

```
every document file of desktop of application "Finder"
```

The problem here is that the keyword `document file` means nothing to AppleScript, so a compilation error occurs: "Expected 'from', etc. but found class name." The exact wording is often unhelpful, but the general meaning is clear. Rearrange the Finder-related keywords so that they appear within a tell application "Finder" ... end tell block, and the code compiles as intended:

```
tell application "Finder"
    every document file of desktop -- This line compiles correctly
end tell
```

> **TIP:** There is another way to persuade AppleScript to compile keywords outside of a tell application ... end tell block: the using terms from statement. This statement comes in handy when you need to compile application-defined keywords outside of a tell block, or where the application name can only be determined when the script is run; for instance, application ("Adobe InDesign CS" & version_number). We'll discuss this further in later chapters.

Now that you know the ins and outs of identifying applications, let's move on to examine in depth the many different ways in which you can construct references to objects within those applications.

More on Constructing References

As you know, a key part of application scripting is constructing references to the object (or objects) within the object model that you want a command to manipulate. If you can't point to the right object, your script will not function as expected, if at all.

The different ways of pointing to an object are called *reference forms*. The simplest reference form identifies a property of an object.

There are a number of reference forms for identifying an object's elements. A single element may be specified in any of the following ways:

- By index (either a numerical value or one of several keyword options)
- By name, if it has one
- By unique ID, if it has one
- By its position relative to (that is, before or after) another element

Multiple elements may be specified as follows:

- By range
- By test condition (also known as a whose clause)
- All of them (using the every keyword)

In addition, when creating, copying, and moving objects, you can also refer to a point before, after, or in between existing elements when you want to specify a location where the object should be inserted.

TIP: Multi-item references can be extremely powerful when used in application commands that know how to process them, allowing you to manipulate many objects using a single command.

The following sections will help you understand the different reference forms and how to use them.

Referring to Properties

Properties are easy to refer to: just write the name of the property you want, and when the script is run, the application will locate the object stored in that property.

Here are some examples for you to try:

```
tell application "Finder"
    selection
end tell

tell application "iTunes"
    name of current track
end tell

tell application "Adobe InDesign"
    properties of document preferences of active document
end tell
```

Referring to Elements

Whereas referring to a property is as simple as adding the property name to your reference, referring to an element or elements of an object is a more complex, two-part process. Not only do you have to specify the class of elements you want, you also have to tell the application how to identify the element or elements of that class that you are interested in.

NOTE: Remember, you can use your knowledge of the application's inheritance hierarchy to identify objects that belong to several related classes or that belong to a single class only. For instance, in the Finder, referring to item elements of a specific folder encompasses all items including folders, files, applications, and so on. Referring to the folder's file elements narrows the request to file objects only, and you can go further still by referring to a specific class of file, such as document file.

The following sections look at the different ways in which you can identify the element or elements that you want, based on characteristics such as the order in which they appear within an object, their names, unique IDs, whether their properties and elements meet certain conditions, and so on.

Identifying All Elements

In many situations, you will want a reference to all the elements of a particular object, such as all paragraphs of a TextEdit document, all files of a folder in the Finder, or all pages of an InDesign document.

To indicate a reference to all elements, you use the keyword every, followed by the name of the class of elements you want:

```
every element_name of some_object
```

Here are some examples:

```
tell application "Address Book"
    every person
end tell

tell application "Finder"
    name of every folder of home
end tell

tell application "TextEdit"
    every word of text of every document
end tell
```

Alternatively, you can omit the every keyword and use the plural class name instead:

```
tell application "TextEdit"
    words of text of documents
end tell
```

Both approaches work exactly the same, so just use whichever one you find easier to read.

Identifying an Element by Its Index, or Position

The by-index reference form uses a whole number, or integer, to identify an element by its position. To use the index reference form, you type the element's class name followed by the position of the specific element you want:

```
element_class index_number
```

For instance, to get the third file of the second folder of the first disk in Finder:

```
tell application "Finder"
    file 3 of folder 2 of disk 1
end tell
```

Notice that the first element of an object is referred to as item 1. This is known as *one-based indexing*.

CAUTION: Traditional programmer-oriented languages use *zero-based indexing*, where the first item's index is 0, not 1. Languages such as AppleScript that are designed for ordinary users generally prefer one-based indexing, however, because that is how humans usually count.

The index reference form uses the order of the elements in the way the application defines that order. In the Finder, for the most part, the files are arranged alphabetically. In page-layout applications, the order of page elements is determined based on their stacking order; the topmost item is always item 1. The order of some objects, such as pages and paragraphs, is easy to determine.

The index reference form is particularly convenient for referring to the frontmost document, since document elements are always ordered from front to back. Thus, to address commands to the front document, just direct them to document 1. The following script counts the number of words in the front TextEdit document:

```
tell application "TextEdit"
   tell document 1
      count every word
   end tell
end tell
```

TIP: If you don't find this sort of phrasing "English enough" for your tastes, you can even use keywords—first, second, third, etc.—instead of index numbers 1 to 10, or you can write any index number like this: 1st, 2nd, 3rd, and so on; for example: first character of 19th word of tenth paragraph of 1st document.

The index reference form works from the back as well by specifying negative numbers. The last item is also item –1, one before the last item is –2, and so on. For example, to bring the backmost window in the Finder to the front:

```
tell application "Finder"
   select window -1
end tell
```

There are four more keywords you can use when identifying a single element by position: front (which is the same as first), last, middle, and some. As it sounds, these keywords identify a single element based on its position in the collection of elements. The meanings of the front/first, last, and middle keywords should be obvious enough, identifying the first, last, or middle element of an object. The some keyword is especially neat, because it allows you to pick an element completely at random. Here are some examples:

```
tell application "Finder"
   close front window
end tell

tell application "TextEdit"
   get middle word of last document
```

```
end tell

tell application "iTunes"
    play some track
end tell
```

Identifying an Element by Its Name

Many application-defined objects contain a name property, allowing you to identify that object *by name*. As a general rule, if the class definition includes or inherits a name property, then you can refer to objects of that class by name.

Sometimes it is up to you to name an object in the first place; for example, you can assign unique names to page items in an Adobe Illustrator document, making them easy to identify in the future. In most cases, the objects are already named and all you have to do is refer to the object by name in your script.

You can identify an element by name using the following syntax:

```
element_class named name_text
```

However, the named keyword is optional, so in practice it is normally written like this:

```
element_class name_text
```

For example, to open a folder named "Applications" on a disk named "Macintosh HD":

```
tell application "Finder"
    open folder "Applications" of disk "Macintosh HD"
end tell
```

> **TIP:** If you find it easier to read, you can insert the keyword named between the element's class name and name. For example, `folder "Applications"` can also be written as `folder named "Applications"`.

The following script creates a new AppleScript Editor document named "My Script" and then refers to that document by name:

```
tell application "AppleScript Editor"
    make new document with properties {name:"My Script", ¬
        contents:"tell application \"Finder\" to activate"}
    execute document "My Script"
end tell
```

By-name references tend to be a bit more reliable than by-index references. Let's say your script identifies a TextEdit document according to its position, like this:

```
tell application "TextEdit"
    tell document 1
        -- Some commands to manipulate the document...
    end tell
end tell
```

This is fine if the document you want to work in is always the frontmost document in TextEdit's GUI. However, if the order of TextEdit's document elements changes halfway through—for example, because you minimized the document window or opened another text file—then the rest of your commands will end up manipulating a different document from the one you started on.

However, if you can identify an element by its name, it is much easier to keep track of the element you want (assuming the value of the object's name property doesn't change, of course). The only catch is if an object has two or more elements with identical names. In this situation, the application will use the first of these elements and ignore the rest. This isn't an issue with some applications such as the Finder, where each element of an object has to have a unique name, but it is something you need to be aware of when dealing with, say, document elements in TextEdit or AppleScript Editor.

Fortunately, there is a third reference form that can reliably locate the same object every time, even if the object does move around or find itself among identically named neighbors…

Identifying an Element by Its Unique ID

Although names are useful, some applications provide an additional identifier for some or all of their objects: a *unique ID*. When the application creates an object, it assigns a unique ID to an object's id property. As a general rule, if the class definition includes or inherits an id property, then you can refer to objects of that class by ID. The id property is read-only, which means that it cannot be changed once the object is created. Also, no two objects within the application can share the same ID.

A by-ID specifier consists of the element class, followed by the keyword id, followed by the ID value itself.

```
element_class id id_value
```

For example, when you ask Safari for its window objects, the result is a list of by-ID references:

```
tell application "Safari" to get every window
--> {window id 293 of application "Safari", window id 294 of application "Safari"}
```

The unique and unchanging nature of object IDs makes them especially useful to your scripts. Although the index or name of an object might change over time—for example, when the object is renamed or moved to a different position—its ID is permanent. If your script needs to store a by-index or by-name reference to an object, and the object's position or name changes, the next time you try to use that reference to locate the object, you could easily end up with a completely different object instead. However, if you can get a by-ID reference instead, then you can be certain that the next time you use that reference, it will still be pointing to the same object as before (assuming that object still exists, of course).

Different applications may use different ID formats. For example, iTunes uses whole numbers (integers) as object IDs:

```
tell application "iTunes"
  get playlist 1
end tell
--> library playlist id 44 of source id 43 of application "iTunes"
```

In Address Book, each person object's ID is a long and cryptic-looking piece of text:

```
tell application "Address Book"
  get id of person 1
end tell
--> "DE1F7D95-2FC6-4F0A-89ED-5ED52C0CE1D9:ABPerson"
```

Only the application itself knows what a particular ID value means, so when constructing by-ID references from scratch, you should only use ID values that have come from the application. Also, some applications may use different ID values the next time they are launched, so you should be cautious of reusing by-ID references or ID values provided by the application on a previous run.

Applications that assign unique IDs to most or all of their objects include Address Book, iCal, iTunes, and Adobe InDesign. Other applications such as Finder, TextEdit, and Adobe Illustrator don't use IDs nearly as much (or not at all), so you will have to make do with whatever by-index and/or by-name references they do provide.

Identifying an Element Before or After Another Element

A *relative* reference identifies an element that is positioned before or after another element. The syntax is as follows:

```
class_name before element_reference
```

```
class_name after element_reference
```

For instance,

```
tell application "TextEdit"
  paragraph before paragraph 3 of document 1
end tell
```

requires that paragraph 3 of document 1 of application "TextEdit" will be a valid reference in order for it to be valid itself. If there's no paragraph 3, then you can't use the reference paragraph before paragraph 3 or paragraph after paragraph 3.

The following example selects the photo that follows the currently selected photo:

```
tell application "iPhoto"
  set current_selection to item 1 of (get selection)
  select photo after current_selection
end tell
```

When using relative references, bear in mind that the application will decide what the previous or next element actually is. For example, if you have selected a photo in one iPhoto album, when you run the preceding script, the next photo selected might be in a completely different album.

Identifying a Range of Elements

The *range* reference form allows you to reference an entire range of elements, instead of one element at a time. You do this by identifying the first and last elements in the range you want, using the following syntax:

```
plural_class_name first_element thru last_element
```

You can use through instead of thru if you prefer. The following syntaxes also work:

```
plural_class_name from first_element thru last_element
```

```
every class_name from first_element thru last_element
```

You can specify the first and last elements in several ways. The simplest option is to use index numbers. The following script will reference a range of records in a FileMaker Pro database:

```
tell application "FileMaker Pro"
  records 12 thru 16 of database 1
end tell
```

The next example minimizes all TextEdit windows except the frontmost one:

```
tell application "TextEdit"
   set miniaturized of windows 2 thru -1 to true
end tell
```

Although this is the most common approach, you can also use strings where that makes sense. For example, you could refer to a range of people in your Address Book by name:

```
tell application "Address Book"
   people "Rachel Andrews" thru "Sarah Jones"
end tell
```

A third option is to use short references to the start and end elements themselves. For example,

```
tell application "TextEdit"
   words 2 thru 4 of text of document 1
end
```

is really just shorthand for this:

```
tell application "TextEdit"
   words (word 2) thru (word 4) of text of document 1
end
```

The start and end points are relative references, word 3 and word 6, that will be expanded using the reference to the container object, text of document 1 of application "TextEdit", as the base reference. In most applications, this isn't a particularly useful way to write references, but some applications allow you to use different classes of elements for the start and end points. For instance, the following script obtains several words from a text frame in Adobe Illustrator:

```
tell application id "com.adobe.illustrator"
   contents of words 2 thru 4 of text frame 1 of document 1
end tell
```

```
--> {"funny", "thing", "happened"}
```

That's fine if all you want are the words themselves, but what if you want all of the text between the first and last words? In Illustrator, to identify a section of text, you refer to the text frame's text elements, like this:

```
tell application id "com.adobe.illustrator"
    contents of text 3 thru 22 of text frame 1 of document 1
end tell
--> "funny thing happened"
```

However, that assumes you know the exact character positions of the first and last words. Fortunately, Illustrator allows you to use relative references to the start and end points in the text range, like this:

```
tell application id "com.adobe.illustrator"
    contents of text (words 2) thru (word 4) of text frame 1 of document 1
end tell
--> "funny thing happened"
```

Identifying Elements Using the whose Clause

The whose clause, also known as the *by-test* reference form, is one of the most powerful features provided by scriptable applications. It gives you the ability to identify elements whose property and/or element values meet certain criteria. For instance, you might ask the Finder to identify all files that are larger than 10MB, or perhaps you want iTunes to locate every track from a particular album that has a 100 percent rating.

Here is the basic syntax:

```
plural_element_class whose test_expression
```

You can write where instead of whose if you prefer—both words mean exactly the same thing to AppleScript. You can also use every *class_name* instead of the plural class name if you find it easier to read.

Script 5–10 asks the Finder to identify all files larger than 10MB anywhere in the user's Documents folder, while Script 5–11 gets all the names of all the tracks belonging to the album "Kings of Swing" with a 100 percent rating.

Script 5–10.

```
tell application "Finder"
    every file of entire contents of folder "Documents" of home ¬
        whose size > (10 * 1000 * 1000)
end tell
```

Script 5–11.

```
tell application "iTunes"
    name of every track of library playlist 1 ¬
        whose album = "Kings of Swing" and rating = 100
end tell
```

What makes whose clauses so powerful is that the application itself is responsible for testing each object. Not only does this save you from having to write the test code yourself, the code runs far more quickly. The whole operation is performed in a single command, with the application doing all of the hard work for you.

Let's look in more detail at how the test expression in a whose clause is constructed. Here is the test from Script 5–10:

```
size > (10 * 1000 * 1000)
```

As you can see, the first reference contains a property name, `size`. When the application evaluates the whose clause, it loops over each of the elements being tested. It then evaluates any relative references within the test clause—in this case, `size`—against the element. So the script asks for the size of file 1, then file 2, and so on. Once the value to be tested has been retrieved, the test is performed—in this case, checking whether the size value is greater than 10,000,000 bytes (10MB).

Notice how the original script expressed this number as a multiplication calculation, `10 * 1000 * 1000`. This part is actually evaluated by AppleScript before it sends the reference to the target application. The only operations that scriptable applications know how to perform are comparison tests, containment tests, and Boolean tests—any other operations and commands must be performed by AppleScript first. (You'll learn more about these operations in later chapters.)

Here is the test clause from Script 5–11:

```
album = "Kings of Swing" and rating = 100
```

Here we have two comparison tests being performed—one to check the value of a track object's `album` property, and one to check the value of the track's `rating` property. The results of the two tests are combined by a Boolean operator, and, that returns `true` only if both tests pass. If the entire test passes, then the track object is included in the result; if one or both tests fail, then the object is skipped.

Let's look at a couple more examples. First, Script 5–12 uses a whose clause to identify all of the Illustrator text frames that contain no text and delete them.

Script 5–12.

```
tell application id "com.adobe.illustrator"
    delete every text frame of document 1 whose contents = ""
end tell
```

Script 5–13 shows another example, this time using Address Book.

Script 5–13.

```
tell application "Address Book"
    get name of first person whose (email_address is in (value of every email))
end tell
```

This example searches for a person with a particular e-mail address. Notice that e-mails are stored as elements of the person object, so you can't simply write `every person whose email is` *email_address*. Fortunately, Address Book is pretty clever at interpreting even fairly complex whose clause tests, so you can ask it to look through each email element's value property to see whether the desired address is in any of them. Had this powerful whose clause not been available, you would have had to use a pair of nested AppleScript loops to search through each `email` element of each person object one at a time—a rather more laborious and far slower solution than getting Address Book to do all the hard work for you.

Referring to Insertion Locations

All of the previous reference forms have been concerned with identifying objects stored in properties or as elements of other objects. The insertion reference form is different: it identifies a point before or after an existing element. Insertion references are normally used in commands that create, duplicate, or move objects to indicate the place where the object being created or moved should be inserted.

There are two ways you can specify the insertion location. First, you can pick a position before the first element or after the last element of an object:

```
beginning of plural_element_class
```

```
end of plural_element_class
```

This approach works even if no previous elements exist.

Alternatively, if you have a reference to an existing element, you can specify an insertion point before or after that:

```
before element_reference
```

```
after element_reference
```

Because insertion references do not identify an application object, you can only use them in certain commands—typically make, move, and duplicate. For example, TextEdit's make command requires an insertion location when adding new paragraphs to a document, as demonstrated by Script 5–14.

Script 5–14.

```
tell application "TextEdit"
    make new paragraph ¬
        at end of paragraphs of text of document 1 ¬
        with data "A new paragraph\n"
end tell
```

> **NOTE:** Some applications require a reference directly to the object into which the new object will be inserted, rather than an insertion point reference. This is often the case with older applications such as the Finder and iTunes. Modern Cocoa-based applications normally use insertion location references, although some parts of the reference may be omitted for convenience; for example, `end of paragraphs of text of document 1` may also be written as `end of text of document 1`.

Summary

In this chapter, you learned about the four key concepts behind application scripting: how applications represent your data as objects, how applications allow you to manipulate these objects using commands, how these objects are organized into an object model, and how application dictionaries document all of this information. This is a lot of material to digest, so let's spend a bit of time reviewing it.

To begin with, you discovered exactly what makes an object an object. First, you learned how objects are categorized by class. Two objects of the same class may contain very different data, but their overall structures are exactly the same. For instance, the Finder contains many thousands of folder objects, all with different names and containing different files and subfolders. Because you know that all of these objects belong to the folder class, you can be certain that they will always have a name property and file and folder elements, and can be manipulated in the same ways.

You learned how objects can have properties that describe their various characteristics: name, class, position, color, and so on. Properties can also contain references to other objects within the application. These are often provided as convenient shortcuts to objects that are of particular importance to scripters—for instance, the home property of the Finder or the current track property in iTunes.

You learned how some objects can contain other objects as elements. Although an object can only ever have one of each property, it can have any number of elements: one, many, or even none at all. For example, a user playlist in iTunes may contain any number of file-based tracks, each of which appears as a file track element of the playlist object.

After exploring the structure of application objects, you next looked at how application commands are constructed. You learned that every command must have a name, and many have parameters too. Each parameter is a reference or AppleScript object that will be passed to the scriptable application as part of the command. Some application commands have a single direct parameter that appears directly after the command name, some have one or more labeled parameters where each value is identified by a keyword-based label, and some commands have both.

Once you learned how to write commands, you learned how commands must be sent to a target object in order to do their jobs. In the case of application commands, the target is an object of class application that represents the scriptable application you wish to manipulate. You also saw how to use AppleScript's tell statement to specify an application object as the default target for all commands within the tell block.

Lastly, you learned how application commands may return values as results—these values may be new application object references or AppleScript values (or a mixture of both). Or, if the application is unable to perform the desired command, it will report an error instead.

With the basic building blocks of application scripting now under your belt, you discovered how applications organize their scriptable objects into object models, allowing these objects to be explored and manipulated from other applications. You saw how application objects can be contained within other application objects, usually as elements, though sometimes in properties too. You also spent some time looking at how to refer to objects using references. Each reference acts as a set of directions, telling the application how to navigate through the object model to the object (or, in some cases, multiple objects) that you wish to work with. You then got some practice exploring a typical object model (the Finder's) and constructing references to its objects.

Having explored the mechanics of application scripting, you then learned how to read the core documentation that comes with every scriptable application: the dictionary. You learned how to translate the information provided by the dictionary—class and command definitions—into a practical understanding of the types of objects a scriptable application provides, how these objects may fit together to form the object model (the containment hierarchy), and how to write commands to manipulate these objects.

You also learned about inheritance, which is the system by which several classes may share common features defined by another class. For instance, the item class in the Finder is inherited by the container and file classes, which in turn are inherited by the disk and folder classes, and the alias file, application file, document file, and other file-related classes.

Although you will never meet an object of class item, container, or file in the Finder's object model, you will meet plenty of objects of class disk, folder, alias file, application file, and so on. Knowing how these classes are related to one another tells you what features objects of these classes have in common—for instance, they all contain name properties, since this is defined by the item class, while disks and folders all have folder and file elements of various sorts, as these are defined by the container class. You also discovered that a good understanding of the application's class inheritance hierarchy gives you greater control over the class or classes of objects you can identify when referring to an object's elements. For instance, asking for all of the item elements of a folder gives you its subfolders and all of its files; asking for the file elements gives you all of its files but not its folder; and asking for its document files gives you its document file objects only.

Having now covered the four key concepts of application scripting, you spent a bit of time exploring the application class, learning about the various ways in which you can identify target applications: by name, by file path, by bundle ID, and by eppc:// URL (although we will leave the details of the last one until Chapter 12). You also found out about the useful properties that all application objects provide by default, allowing you to get information such as the application's name, version, and running status without even having to send any commands.

Finally, you spent some time filling in the remaining knowledge needed to construct references to application objects. Referring to properties is very simple; just give the property's name. Referring to elements requires a bit more work: in addition to indicating the class of element you want, you also have to specify exactly which element (or elements) you are interested in, based on their position, name, unique ID, or whether they fall within a given range or meet a particular set of requirements—or you even can just specify all of them.

Because AppleScript's application scripting features are so deeply integrated into the language itself, it can sometimes be a little difficult to see where the language features end and the features provided by scriptable applications begin. Still, this chapter should provide you with some appreciation of how scriptable applications work, while the rest of the chapters in Part 2 of the book educate you on every aspect of the AppleScript language itself.

Although the real hands-on application scripting material does not begin until Part 3 of the book (Chapters 20 to 30), you will get some practical experience of application automation along the way, as sample scripts and projects demonstrate how AppleScript features can be combined with scriptable applications to perform all sorts of powerful, interesting, and fun tasks. Just remember: any time you encounter a piece of code that involves application scripting, you can come back to this chapter to check up on any details you are unsure of.

In the next chapter, we begin our exploration of the first of our AppleScript key concepts: how the AppleScript language represents information as objects of its own.

Chapter 6

Learning to Work with AppleScript Objects

Now that we've discussed the principles of application scripting in detail, let's turn our attention to the AppleScript language itself.

Chapter 2 introduced you to the four key concepts that underlie AppleScript (and other scripting languages):

- How AppleScript represents information as objects

- How AppleScript manipulates objects using commands, operators, and variables

- How AppleScript makes decisions on what to do and when to do it

- How AppleScript organizes code using handlers and script objects

I will cover the last two concepts—making decisions and organizing your code—later in the book, in Chapters 14, 15, 18, and 19. For now, I want to spend some time exploring the first two concepts.

Although AppleScript is a fairly small language, it will still take us some time to cover all the important aspects of representing and manipulating data. To simplify the process, I have broken down this coverage into a number of chapters.

The first two sections in this chapter map out the two key concepts in a bit more detail, describing how data is represented by AppleScript objects and introducing the features that you can use to manipulate these objects. The final section in this chapter introduces you to the first of several AppleScript classes: the boolean class.

Chapters 7 to 10 will describe some of the more powerful objects you will meet in AppleScript: numbers, strings, dates, lists, and records. Chapters 11 and 12 will fill in the remaining details on working with variables and commands, and Chapter 13 will complete your understanding of operators and coercions.

Let's get started.

How AppleScript Represents Information As Objects

As previous chapters have mentioned, both AppleScript and scriptable applications represent individual pieces of information as *objects*. Application objects are fairly complicated structures that represent application-specific data—documents, playlist tracks, calendar events, and so on—and are found only in scriptable applications. AppleScript objects are much simpler structures that represent the most basic pieces of information that your scripts can work with: numbers, plain text, dates, and so forth. Unlike application-defined objects, AppleScript objects can live within the AppleScript language itself and can easily be passed from one application to another.

Now let's take a look at how AppleScript objects are structured and how they behave.

Although objects in AppleScript are not the same as the objects you find in application object models, they are not that different, either. You can create new objects, you can get information about objects, you can manipulate objects using commands and other features, and some objects can even be used to hold other objects.

What Kinds of Objects Does AppleScript Provide?

In Chapter 5 you saw how application dictionaries categorize different kinds of application objects according to their class: document, window, disk, track, and so forth. The AppleScript language categorizes its own objects in exactly the same way, describing each object as belonging to a particular class.

Here are the main classes of objects you will find in AppleScript:

- class
- constant
- boolean
- integer
- real
- text
- date
- alias
- file
- POSIX file
- list
- record
- data
- script object
- application
- reference

Some of these class names should be self-explanatory: for example, an object of class `integer` represents a whole number (integer); an object of class `text` represents a piece of plain text; an object of class `list` is an ordered collection of other objects. Other classes such as `boolean`, `alias`, and `script object` aren't as obvious, but don't worry: they will all be explained in this and later chapters.

Creating New Objects

Creating new objects is especially easy in AppleScript. Creating a new application object requires the use of an application command such as `make`, but you can create a new object just by typing its literal representation in your script and running it.

For example, type `89` in your script, and when AppleScript executes that code it will create a new integer object representing the number 89. Run the code `"Hello World!"`, and AppleScript will create a new text object containing the phrase "Hello World!"

AppleScript provides special syntax to represent several basic classes of object in your code; for example, a pair of double quote marks indicates where a text object, or string, begins and ends:

```
"Hello World!"
```

Other types of object, such as dates, do not have their own special syntax but instead use AppleScript's standard object-specifier syntax, consisting of the class name followed by a string containing the raw data to be used in creating that object:

```
date "Wednesday, July 1, 2009 3:45:20 PM"
```

> **TIP:** A newly created AppleScript object remains in existence only for as long as it is in use. If you want to keep hold of an object so that you can use it again later in your script, you can do this by storing it in a *variable*. More details on variables are provided later in the chapter.

Getting Information from Objects

In Chapter 5, you learned that an application-defined object normally possesses one or more properties containing information about that object. For example, every object has a `class` property that tells you what kind of object it is:

```
class of 89
--> integer
```

```
class of "Hello World!"
--> text
```

Some objects may have additional, built-in properties; for example, text, list, and record objects also have `length` properties that tell you how long they are:

```
length of "Hello World!"
--> 12
```

```
length of {"Hello", " ", "World", "!"}
--> 4
```

Some classes of AppleScript objects even allow you to define your own properties. For example, here is a record object containing two properties, name and age:

```
{name:"John Smith", age:900}
```

Some objects also have elements. For example, to extract a word from a larger string, just refer to the word element you want:

```
word 2 of "Hello World!"
--> "World"
```

In addition to working with their properties and elements, you can also manipulate objects using various AppleScript features. We'll look at these features next.

How AppleScript Works with Objects

When working with objects in scriptable applications, there is one way to manipulate them: by sending commands to the application. AppleScript objects can also be manipulated with commands, but this is not the only way: AppleScript provides two other important features for manipulating objects: operators and coercions. In addition, it provides a fourth feature, variables, that allows you to store objects within your script so that you can use them again later.

Let's look at each of these in turn.

Manipulating Objects with Commands

For a language that spends so much time sending commands to other applications, AppleScript has surprisingly few commands built into it: just five, in fact.

Fortunately, there are a couple of ways to provide AppleScript with access to additional commands: by installing special application plug-ins, called *scripting additions*, and by defining your own commands in your scripts.

Introducing the Five Built-in Commands

The AppleScript language defines just five commands itself: get, set, copy, count, and run.

The first two commands, get and set, are used to retrieve and assign objects that are stored within variables, or as properties or elements of other objects. For example:

```
set the_variable to "Hello World!"
get the_variable
--> "Hello World!"
```

If the get and set commands sound familiar, that's because AppleScript also uses these two commands to get and set properties and elements within application objects. As with application scripting, you hardly ever need to write explicit get commands in your script, because AppleScript will automatically retrieve a value for you when you refer to the property, element, or variable where it is stored. So, for example, although you can retrieve a value like this,

```
get length of "Hello World!"
--> 12
```

it is normal to omit the get part and just write this:

```
length of "Hello World!"
--> 12
```

The copy command works a lot like the set command in that it assigns values to properties, elements, and variables. There is one big difference, however: whereas the set command assigns the value you give it, the copy command makes an *exact copy* of the original value and assigns that instead.

> **NOTE:** The difference between set and copy becomes very important when working with objects such as lists and records whose contents can be modified by AppleScript. We'll discuss this issue in detail in Chapter 12.

The fourth built-in command, count, can be used to count the number of characters in a string, the number of elements in a list, or the number of properties in a record.

The final command, run, can be used to do what its name suggests: run a script.

Later chapters will explore all five built-in commands in greater detail, so for now let's move on and look at the ways in which extra commands can be added to supplement AppleScript's own.

Introducing Scripting Addition Commands

Scripting additions are plug-ins that provide additional commands for AppleScript to use. Mac OS X ships with one important scripting addition, Standard Additions, already included, and there are plenty of third-party scripting additions available that you can install yourself.

The Standard Additions scripting addition, for example, provides AppleScript with a range of commands for displaying simple dialog boxes and reading and writing files, among other things. In fact, the very first script you wrote in this book used one of the Standard Additions commands, display dialog, to show a "Hello World!" message onscreen:

```
display dialog "Hello World!"
```

Third-party scripting additions may add commands for other tasks, such as changing a string to all-uppercase or all-lowercase text, performing trigonometric math calculations, working with XML data, and so on.

The next few chapters will describe several Standard Additions commands that are of particular use when working with numbers, strings, and dates. Later chapters will explore other areas in which scripting addition commands are used, and Chapter 22 will cover all the technical aspects of using scripting additions, including where and how to install your own. For now, however, you don't need to worry about the technical details, so just use the Standard Additions commands as if they were a part of the language itself.

Introducing User-Defined Commands

One of the more advanced, but very cool, features of AppleScript is that it allows you to define your own commands using the language itself. This feature becomes increasingly useful as your scripts grow larger and more complex, as it allows you to organize chunks of AppleScript code into neat little packages, called *handlers*, that your script can then run by sending itself some commands.

For example, you might define one handler to find and replace a particular piece of text within a larger string, and another handler to take a list and sort its items into ascending order. In Chapter 2, I showed a very simple example of a command handler called square_root that takes a number, calculates its square root, and returns it:

```
square_root(25)
--> 5.0

on square_root(the_number)
    return the_number ^ 0.5
end square_root
```

Writing your own handlers from scratch is a topic best left for later on in the book—Chapter 18, to be exact—but this shouldn't stop you from copying and using some of the prewritten handlers provided in the following chapters. Although user-defined commands normally use a syntax that is slightly different from AppleScript- and scripting addition-defined commands, their goal is the same: to manipulate data.

So far in this chapter, I've talked about objects and commands in AppleScript. Although some technical differences may exist between these objects and commands and the objects and commands you find in scriptable applications, the basic concepts are not too different. Now, however, it's time to introduce a brand new feature to you, one that you won't find in scriptable applications: the *operator*.

Manipulating Objects with Operators

What are operators? Well, you might be a little disappointed to hear this, but they are not really all that different from commands, as the goal of both operators and commands is to manipulate data. (Some languages don't even bother with operators at all, and just use regular commands to provide all their functionality.)

All AppleScript operators take either a single object (unary operators) or a pair of objects (binary operators), perform some sort of calculation, comparison, or other transformation, and return a new object as a result. In grammar terms, we refer to the objects that are passed to an operator as *operands*, and to the combination of operator and operand(s) as an *operation*. For example, in the following math operation, the addition operator, +, has two operands, 2 and 5, that appear on either side:

```
2 + 5
```

When this operation is executed, the addition operator calculates the sum of the two numbers and returns a new value, 7, as the result.

What Makes Operators Special?

Although it is tempting to think of an operator as just a special kind of command, it is important to know what the differences are.

The first unique feature of operators is that they can be provided only by the AppleScript language itself. In addition, the number of operators that AppleScript provides is completely fixed: there are 26 in total.

The second characteristic of operators is that they are *expressions*. This means that they will *always* return an object. Most commands also return an object, but some do not— unlike operators, it's up to the command's designer to decide whether or not the command should return a result.

The third feature is that each operator has its own special syntax provided by the language itself. For example, the concatenation operator, which previous chapters have already mentioned, is written as an ampersand, &, symbol, with the two objects that are being joined appearing on either side:

```
"Hello " & "World!"
```

The final distinguishing feature of operators is that AppleScript has its own special set of rules that it follows when evaluating two or more nested operator expressions. You will need to learn these rules in order to combine operators effectively; fortunately, most of the rules that govern evaluation order are pretty intuitive, as they are designed to be consistent with the rules of math you learned in school. For example, the rules for evaluating an expression containing several math operators are the same as the rules used in regular math: multiplication and division operations are performed before addition and subtraction, while calculations within parentheses are carried out before the calculations outside of them. Here are a couple of examples to illustrate:

```
2 + 3 / 5
--> 2.6
```

```
(2 + 3) / 5
--> 1
```

In the first example, the division operation takes precedence over the addition operation, so it is calculated first: 3 divided by 5 returns 0.6, and this is added to 2 to produce the final result, 2.6. In the second example, the parentheses have even higher priority than division, so 2 and 3 are added first to give 5, which is then divided by 5 to produce 1.

Don't worry too much about operator precedence for now: the next few chapters will fill in any details as they're needed, and Chapter 13 will provide a full summary of AppleScript's precedence rules, for your future reference.

Let's now take a quick look at the different kinds of operators that AppleScript provides.

What Kinds of Operators Does AppleScript Provide?

AppleScript's 26 operators can be broken down into several different groups according to what they do. The following sections provide a brief summary of each of these groups to get you started; subsequent chapters will explain in detail the operators that are relevant to the objects being discussed.

The Concatenation Operator

Probably the most used operator in AppleScript is the concatenation operator, &.

To *concatenate* means to join together. For example, AppleScript's concatenation operator can concatenate two strings to create a new string, two lists to produce a third list, and two records to create a third record:

```
"Hello " & "World!"
--> "Hello World!"

{1, 2, 3} & {3, 2, 1}
--> {1, 2, 3, 3, 2, 1}

{name:"John Smith"} & {age:900}
--> {name:"John Smith", age:900}
```

Chapters 7 and 10 will look at this very useful operator in more detail.

Math Operators

Next are the math operators, which are used to work with numbers (integer and real values). Table 6–1 lists the available math operators and their names, and provides a brief summary of what they do.

Table 6–1. *Math Operators*

Operator	Name	Description
+	Addition	Adds the left and right numbers.
-	Negation (with one operand)	Converts the single number to its right from positive to negative or from negative to positive.
-	Subtraction (with two operands)	Subtracts the right number from the left number.
*	Multiplication	Multiplies the left and right numbers.

Operator	Name	Description
/	Division	Divides the left number by the right number.
div	Integral division	Returns the number of times the right number fits whole in the left number.
mod	Remainder (modulo)	Subtracts the right number from the left number repeatedly until the remainder is less than the right number and returns the final remainder.
^	Exponent	Raises the left number to the power of the right number.

Chapter 8 will explain in a lot more detail how you can use these math operators.

Comparison Operators

Comparison operators basically ask a simple question: is the left operand less than, greater than, or the same as the right one? The result of a comparison can be either true or false. Table 6–2 summarizes the six comparison operators available.

Table 6–2. *Comparison Operators*

Operator	Name	Description
=	Is equal to	Returns true if both operands are the same.
≠	Is not equal to	Returns true if the operands are different.
<	Is less than	Returns true if the left operand is less than the right operand.
≤	Is less than or equal to	Returns true if the left operand is less than or equal to the right operand.
>	Is greater than	Returns true if the left operand is greater than the right operand.
≥	Is greater than or equal to	Returns true if the left operand is greater than or equal to the right operand.

I will discuss throughout the next four chapters where and how you can use these operators.

Containment Operators

Containment operators check whether one object can be found inside another, returning true or false as a result. AppleScript provides six containment operators—these are listed and described in Table 6–3.

Table 6–3. *Containment Operators*

Operator	Description
starts with	Returns true if the second operand appears at the start of the first.
ends with	Returns true if the second operand appears at the end of the first.
contains	Returns true if the second operand appears anywhere within the first.
does not contain	Returns true if the second operand does not appear in the first.
is in	Returns true if the first operand appears anywhere within the second.
is not in	Returns true if the first operand does not appear in the second.

All of these operators can be used on strings and lists, and some can be used on records as well. We'll look at using containment operators in Chapters 7 and 10.

Boolean Operators

AppleScript has three Boolean operators—and, or, and not—that are used when working with Boolean values. I'll discuss these operators in the "Working with Boolean Objects" section later in the chapter.

The Coercion Operator

Coercion is the process of converting an object of one class to a comparable object of another class. For instance, the value 5 is an integer, and the value "5" is a string. You can't do math with "5", and you can't concatenate 5 to another string as long as it is an integer. So, to do math with the string value "5", you must convert it, or *coerce* it, into a number. Similarly, to use the number value 5 in a string, you must coerce it into a string.

To perform coercion operations, you use the coercion operator, as. This takes two operands: the left operand is the object to be coerced, and the right operand is the name of the class you want to convert it to. For example:

```
5 as text
--> "5"
```

> **NOTE:** AppleScript also has the ability to coerce objects automatically in certain situations. We refer to this process as *implicit coercion*, to distinguish it from explicit coercions performed using the as operator.

The *a reference to* Operator

The last operator in AppleScript is a `reference to`. This is a more advanced feature that you won't need to use very often, so I won't say anything more about it here. Chapter 13 will explain what this operator does, after you've finished learning about the different types of objects it can be used with.

Coercing Objects

As I mentioned when discussing AppleScript's coercion operator (`as`), coercion is the process of converting an object of one class into an equivalent object of another class. In fact, there are two ways in which coercions can happen.

The first way in which a coercion occurs, as previously described, is when your script uses the `as` operator to instruct AppleScript to perform the conversion—what we call an *explicit* coercion. In the following example, the `current date` command returns an object of class `date` that represents the current date and time:

```
current date
--> date "Wednesday, July 1, 2009 3:45:20 PM"
```

If we want to get the date and time as a string object instead, we can easily convert the original date object by coercing it to an object of class `text`:

```
(current date) as text
--> "Wednesday, July 1, 2009 3:45:20 PM"
```

The second way in which a coercion occurs is when you pass an object to a command or operator that requires a different class of object from the one you gave it. In this situation, the command or operator will often try to coerce the supplied object to the required class by itself—what's known as an *implicit* coercion.

For example, AppleScript's math operators all require either whole numbers (integers) or decimal numbers (reals) as operands:

```
3 + 5
--> 8
```

However, you can also use other classes of objects as operands, just as long as those objects are capable of being coerced to numbers. For example, if you pass two strings, AppleScript will automatically attempt to coerce them to numbers before performing the addition:

```
"3" + "5"
--> 8
```

Of course, this will only work as long as each string contains only numerical characters; if you try to pass strings that don't make sense as numbers, you will get a coercion error instead:

```
"Hello" + "World"
-- AppleScript error: Can't make "Hello" into type number.
```

You will discover which coercions can be applied to each class of AppleScript objects in this and subsequent chapters. Chapter 13 provides a convenient cross-reference to all the operators and coercions found in AppleScript

Storing Objects in Variables

Variables are the "memory" of AppleScript. Unlike commands and operators, variables are not used to manipulate objects. Instead, their job is to store objects while you aren't using them. Any time you have an object that you will need again later in your script, you can assign that object to a variable. Whenever you need to use that object again, you can retrieve it simply by referring to the variable you stored it in.

Every variable has a user-defined name, or *identifier*, that you give it when you first assign an object to it. It is this name that you use when you want to refer to the variable again later on.

To assign a value to a variable, you use AppleScript's set command. Let's try an example. Open a new AppleScript Editor window, and type the following:

```
set the_city to "Providence"
```

This statement assigns a string, "Providence", to a variable named the_city. AppleScript recognizes the_city as a user-defined identifier because it is a single piece of unquoted text that is not a known keyword. Because the word "Providence" is in quotes, AppleScript knows it's literal text, not an identifier.

When you run this code, the variable the_city will have the string "Providence" assigned to it. To retrieve the string object, just refer to the_city again:

```
the_city
--> "Providence"
```

Let's take this example a little further. First, type another statement to assign a second object to a variable named the_state:

```
set the_state to "Rhode Island"
```

Now you can do something with these variables. Type the following line:

```
set my_greeting to "Hello, I live in " & the_city & ", " & the_state
```

Here we retrieve the strings stored earlier in our two variables, the_city and the_state, and use three concatenation operators (&) to join these and other strings together to form a new string. Lastly, we assign this new string to a third variable, my_greeting.

To finish this example, we can use a command, display dialog, to display the completed greeting in a dialog box:

```
display dialog my_greeting
```

Figure 6–1 shows the completed script, and the dialog box that is displayed when the script is run.

Figure 6–1. *The completed script, using variables, concatenation operators, and a* `display dialog` *command to display a text message*

How Are Identifiers Written?

When naming a variable, you must follow several rules in order for your code to compile correctly. The rules for writing a valid identifier will be covered fully in Chapter 11, but for now here are the main ones you need to know:

- It must start with an alphabetic character (a–z, A–Z) or underscore (_).

- It can contain any number of additional alphabetic characters, digits (0–9), and underscores.

- It cannot be the same as a keyword defined by a scriptable application (this only applies within an application `tell` block), an installed scripting addition, or AppleScript itself.

NOTE: Identifiers are case insensitive; however, once you use a variable in a script, AppleScript will remember how you typed it, and anywhere else that you use it, AppleScript will change the case of the characters in the variable to match the same pattern you used the first time.

Where Can Variables Be Used?

When you define a variable in one part of your script, other parts of your script may or may not be able to see that variable. For example, a variable that is defined inside a handler normally can be accessed only by the code within that handler—the rest of your script cannot see it. This area of visibility is referred to as the variable's *scope*.

WHAT'S THE POINT OF VARIABLE SCOPES?

As a new scripter, you may find variable scopes frustrating to deal with: you create a variable in one section of your script and later try to use it in another…only to have AppleScript insist that the variable doesn't exist! You might think AppleScript is just being obstructive…and it is, but for a very good reason. As you will learn in later chapters, restricting the visibility of a variable within your script can be an incredibly powerful technique for keeping your code manageable.

For example, suppose you have a 1000-line script, and every one of those lines appears in the same scope. This means that each variable in your script could be manipulated by up to a 1000 different lines of code! Whereas, if the same code is divided across 50 different handlers, you only have to look at 20 lines of code when figuring out what happens to a variable whose scope is limited to one of those handlers.

For now, I just want you to get a rough idea of how and where variables can be defined and used. For example, if you define a variable in one scope, you can refer to that variable from anywhere in the same scope. On the other hand, if you write its name in a second, unrelated scope, what you actually have is two completely separate variables which happen to use the same name.

Imagine you work in the accounts department under a boss named George. As long as you work in that department, whenever you mention "the boss," everyone knows you are referring to George. If you move temporarily to the marketing department, which has a different boss, Sue, now when you talk about "the boss," everyone knows you are referring to Sue. When you return to your original department, "the boss" will once again refer to George. And if you leave employment altogether, referring to "the boss" will no longer have any meaning at all.

Let's express this glittering career path in AppleScript:

```
work_in_accounts()
display dialog "Now I've retired, my boss is " & the_boss

on work_in_accounts()
    set the_boss to "George"
    display dialog "Working in accounts for " & the_boss
    work_in_marketing()
    display dialog "Back working in accounts for " & the_boss
end work_in_accounts

on work_in_marketing()
    set the_boss to "Sue"
    display dialog "Now working in marketing for " & the_boss
end work_in_marketing
```

So, what happens when this script runs?

Well, AppleScript starts by running any statements at the top level of the script—in this case, the two lines at the top of the script. The first line sends a `work_in_accounts` command to the script, causing it to execute the statements in the `work_in_accounts` handler. Here we create a variable named the_boss and assign it an object, `"George"`. We can then refer to the_boss to retrieve that object and use it, in this case to display the message "Working in accounts for George".

Next we send a `work_in_marketing` command, causing AppleScript to run the statements in the `work_in_marketing` handler. Here we create a new variable. This variable is also named the_boss, but because it is in a separate handler, it is not related to the the_boss variable in the `work_in_accounts` handler.

How can we tell that these variables are unrelated, even though they have the same name?

Well, once the `work_in_marketing` handler displays its own dialog message, "Now working in marketing for Sue", it runs out of statements to execute, so AppleScript returns to the `work_in_accounts` handler at the same point it left it. And the next message displayed is... "Back working in accounts for George". As you can see, the value of the_boss in the `work_in_accounts` handler was not affected by the set the_boss to `"Sue"` statement in the `work_in_marketing` handler, because the variables that are visible in one handler are not visible inside the other, and vice versa. We call these variables *local*, because their scope is limited to a single handler.

Finally, the script finishes running the `work_in_accounts` handler, and returns to executing the top-level statements. However, when it tries to run the final top-level statement, rather than displaying a "Now I've retired, my boss is..." message, an error occurs instead: "The variable the_boss is not defined."

Of course, handlers wouldn't be very useful if there wasn't some way to pass values from one to another, so AppleScript provides ways to do that. You can even make variables visible throughout the entire script, by defining them as *properties* or *globals*.

For now, you're not moving about departments, so you have nothing to worry about. As long as a script doesn't contain any user-defined handlers, you can be sure that using a certain variable name always refers to the same variable. Later chapters will discuss in great detail the implications of using variables in handlers, global and local variables, and properties.

Now that you know a bit more about AppleScript objects in general, it's time to examine some of the more important AppleScript classes in detail, beginning with the `boolean` class.

Working with Boolean Objects

The `boolean` class (named after the inventor of Boolean logic, George Boole) is one of the simplest classes you will meet in AppleScript. There are only two objects of this class: `true` and `false`. Despite its simplicity, however, it is still a very important class, and Boolean objects are used throughout AppleScript, particularly in the area of decision-making, where many questions ultimately resolve to simple "yes" or "no"—true or false—answers.

AppleScript provides three Boolean logic operators specially for working with Boolean objects: and, or, and not. In Boolean operations, both operands and the result are Booleans. Several other AppleScript operators—in particular, the comparison and containment operators—also return Boolean values as their results. Boolean operators are often used in complex expressions to combine the results of two or more containment and/or comparison operations.

AppleScript does not provide any commands specifically for working with Boolean values. However, many commands also use Boolean values as parameters or as return values—for example, the Finder's exists command returns true or false depending on whether or not the object you're referring to can be found.

Boolean Operators

The meaning of the operators and, or, and not is pretty self-explanatory, much like the use of these words in the English language. For example, in a Boolean and operation, if the left operand is true *and* the right operand is true, the resulting value will be true too.

Using and, or, and not correctly in AppleScript does require a little care, however. Although it's okay to say something like "If the score is 9 or 10, then say 'Excellent!'" in English, if you try that in AppleScript, you'll get an error when you run it because 10 is not a Boolean value. You have to phrase the test expression in strictly logical terms: the_score is 9 or the_score is 10.

Let's look at each of these operators in turn, beginning with the simplest one, not.

The *not* Operator

The not operator takes a Boolean value as its sole, right-side operand and returns the opposite Boolean value. If the operand is true, the result is false. If the operand is false, the result is true.

The following script snippets show the not operator in action:

```
not true
--> false

not false
--> true

not (1 + 2 = 3)
--> false
```

Because the expression (1 + 2 = 3) results in the Boolean value of true, putting the not operator before it reverses the result to false.

The not operator is useful in various situations. One is reversing a Boolean value when testing its value in a conditional statement. Here's a practical example that creates a folder named "TO DO" on your desktop if it doesn't already exist:

```
tell application "Finder"
    if not (folder "TO DO" of desktop exists) then
        make new folder at desktop with properties {name:"TO DO"}
    end if
end tell
```

The *and* Operator

The and operator takes two Boolean operands and returns true only if both operands are true. If either operand is false, it returns false. Here are some examples of the and operator in action:

```
true and true
--> true

true and false
--> false

false and true
--> false

false and false
--> false
```

And here are some practical examples of using and:

```
if (email_address contains "@") and (email_address contains ".") then
    -- Create and send an email here...
else
    -- Display an "invalid email address" error dialog here...
end if
```

Or, if you just want a variable whose value is true or false, use something like this:

```
set is_valid_address to (email_address contains "@") and (email_address contains ".")
```

Notice the use of the parentheses. They are not required in this case, but they visually distinguish the different operations, making the code easier to read.

To check if a variable, x, is within a range of numbers, say between 10 and 20 inclusive, you can use the following statement:

```
if (x ≥ 10) and (x ≤ 20) then
    -- Do something here...
end if
```

The *or* Operator

The or operator takes two Boolean operands and returns true if either operand is true. If both operands are false, it returns false. Here are a few examples:

```
true or true
--> true

true or false --> true

false or true --> true

false or false --> false

if (email_address ends with ".net") or ¬
    (email_address ends with ".com") or
    (email_address ends with ".org") then
  -- Do something here...
end if
```

How Boolean Operators Are Evaluated

One important feature when using the and operator is that if the value of the left operand, which is evaluated first, is false, the right operand will never get evaluated. This is useful in situations where you have two test expressions joined by an and operator, and attempting to evaluate the second test when the first one had already returned false would cause an error.

To demonstrate, consider the following example:

```
tell application "TextEdit"
  if (document 1 exists) and (text of document 1 is not "") then
    -- Process the document's text here...
  end if
end tell
```

Look at the and operator in the second line. The command on its left side checks whether document 1 exists, while the expression on its right checks whether document 1 has any text. If AppleScript saw that the document didn't exist but went on to ask for its text anyway, this would cause TextEdit to raise a "Can't get document 1" error.

Fortunately, AppleScript is smarter than this and knows that if the first operand is false, the and operation's eventual result must always be false as well. This means AppleScript knows there's no point in getting the second operand, and therefore no need to evaluate the second expression, so it doesn't get it. If the document does not exist, the entire and operation immediately returns false, and AppleScript moves straight to the next statement without any trouble.

The or operator is "short-circuited" in a similar fashion; however, in its case, the right operand is ignored when the left one is already true.

Boolean-Related Coercions

AppleScript allows you to coerce Boolean values to several other classes of objects: integer, text, and list.

When coercing true and false objects to integers, the result is always 1 or 0:

```
true as integer
--> 1
```

```
false as integer
--> 0
```

If you coerce true and false to strings, the result is either "true" or "false":

```
true as text
--> "true"
```

```
false as text
--> "true"
```

You can also coerce Boolean values to lists, where each list contains the original object, true or false:

```
true as list
--> {true}
```

```
false as list
--> {false}
```

The reverse coercions also work: 1, "true", and {true} can all be coerced to true, and 0, "false", and {false} will all coerce to false.

There is one more coercion that you can perform with Boolean values: you can coerce them to boolean too:

```
true as boolean
--> true
```

```
false as boolean
--> false
```

In fact, all objects in AppleScript can be coerced to their own class. This might not sound very useful in itself, but it can come in handy in some situations where you are not quite sure what class of object a command or other piece of code may give you. To be sure that you get the class of object that you need (or an obvious error message if the value is completely unsuitable), just add an explicit coercion. We'll look at this technique in later chapters, once we've covered the other AppleScript features you will need.

Summary

In this chapter, you learned more about AppleScript objects in general: what they are, what kinds (classes) of objects are available, how they can be manipulated using commands, operators, and coercions, and how they can be stored in variables.

This chapter also introduced you to the first of several important and commonly used objects in AppleScript: the two Boolean values, true and false. You learned what these objects are used for, and what operators and coercions could be used to manipulate them.

In the next chapter, we will look at what is perhaps the single most important class in AppleScript: text.

Chapter 7

Working with Text

One of the tasks you will find yourself doing a lot in AppleScript is working with text in one way or another. This chapter covers the many aspects of text manipulation in AppleScript.

We will begin with a bit of background on how computers make sense of human-readable text. Next, we will study the various properties and elements of AppleScript's text objects, along with the standard operators and commands you can use to manipulate those objects. We will also spend some time exploring AppleScript's text item delimiters—a key feature when breaking text apart or joining it together.

Once you understand the principles behind working with text in AppleScript, we will round off the chapter with a couple of projects that put this knowledge to practical use.

Introducing Text

Text is found everywhere in Mac OS X: the content of TextEdit and Word documents, as file and folder names in the Finder, track titles in iTunes, e-mail addresses in Mail…the list is endless. Given the huge importance of text in Mac applications, it will come as no surprise that AppleScript provides its own built-in support for representing and manipulating text within the language itself.

When talking about text objects in the AppleScript language, we normally refer to them as *strings*, which is the traditional programmer term for them (as in, "a string of characters"). I find that talking about "strings" sounds less silly than talking about "texts" and also helps to distinguish AppleScript's built-in text objects from the similarly named but unrelated text objects that belong to scriptable applications such as TextEdit, Safari, and Mail.

In source code, you indicate a string literal as any number of characters between two straight double quotes—for example, "Hello World!". Simply having Hello World in the script without quotes would cause the script to not compile.

As with any other object, you can assign a string to a variable using AppleScript's set command:

```
set my_greeting to "Hello World!"
```

This line assigns "Hello World!" to the variable my_greeting.

You can do many other things with AppleScript strings, of course, but before we get into that topic, I'll take you on a quick trip through time to give you a better understanding of how representing text on computers works today.

A Brief History of Text

In 1440, Johannes Gutenberg invented the first mechanical printing press. Five hundred years later, the first digital electronic computers were built. This was a big step backward for text representation, but fortunately they've caught up a lot since then.

When Is Text Not Text?

When it comes to text, computers have a big problem: they only understand numbers! Every bit of information that goes through your modern Mac's fancy multicore CPU has to be represented as a number of one sort or another. Those numbers, in turn, are represented by bytes of memory. Each byte consists of 8 bits, and the value of each bit can be either 0 or 1.

You calculate the actual number as follows. Starting with the number 0, if the least-significant bit is 1, you add 2^0 (two raised to the power of zero), or 1. If the next bit is 1, you add 2^1, or 2. If the third bit is 1, you add 2^2, or 4, and so on. When you get to the eighth bit, if it is 1, you add 2^7, or 128. Once you've done this, the total sum is the decimal number represented by that byte. Figure 7–1 shows some examples.

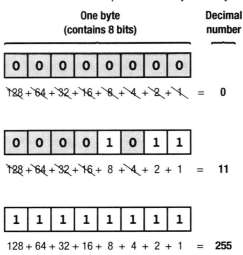

Figure 7–1. *How bits and bytes are used to represent numbers*

In total, then, a single byte can represent a total of 256 unique numbers (or 2 to the power of 8). To represent larger numbers, just use more bytes: 2 bytes can represent 65,536 different numbers (or 2 to the power of 16), 4 bytes allows 4,294,967,296 different numbers (or 2 to the power of 32), and so on.

Now, this might sound a bit basic, but don't forget that bits and bytes are the fundamental building blocks used to construct every single program on your Mac—the operating system, all your applications, and AppleScript itself—so even though they're hidden away under all those higher layers, their influence is still felt.

Getting back to text… Whereas computer hardware deals only with numbers, the more biological among us expect some decent home comforts. Although the very earliest programmers had no choice but to toggle in raw digits on primitive mechanical switches, as computer hardware became more powerful, they soon began to look for better solutions. Programmers soon figured out that they could represent each character in the alphabet as a different number, allowing computers to "understand" human-readable text. (Well, sort of understand, anyway.) And so was born the *character set*.

Understanding Character Sets

A character set maps human-readable character symbols, or "glyphs," to CPU-friendly numbers. One early character set that is still with us today is ASCII (American Standard Code for Information Interchange). ASCII is a small character set consisting of a mere 128 characters: uppercase and lowercase A to Z, numbers 0 to 9, a handful of arithmetic and punctuation characters, space, tab, and special "control" characters for things like creating line breaks, moving the text cursor, and even ringing the mechanical bell on old-style computer consoles!

Figure 7–2 shows the full ASCII character set. As you can see, the first 32 entries are used as special control characters—the ones you normally need to know about are ASCII 9, the horizontal tab, and the two line break characters, ASCII 10 (line feed) and ASCII 13 (carriage return).

	0	1	2	3	4	5	6	7	8	9	10	11	12	13	14	15
0	NUL	SOH	STX	ETX	EOT	ENQ	ACK	BEL	BS	HT	LF	VT	FF	CR	SO	SI
16	DLE	DC1	DC2	DC3	DC4	NAK	SYN	ETB	CAN	EM	SUB	ESC	FS	GS	RS	US
32		!	"	#	$	%	&	'	(	)	*	+	,	-	.	/
48	0	1	2	3	4	5	6	7	8	9	:	;	<	=	>	?
64	@	A	B	C	D	E	F	G	H	I	J	K	L	M	N	O
80	P	Q	R	S	T	U	V	W	X	Y	Z	[	\	]	^	_
96	`	a	b	c	d	e	f	g	h	i	j	k	l	m	n	o
112	p	q	r	s	t	u	v	w	x	y	z	{			}	~	DEL

Figure 7–2. *The ASCII character set*

Despite its limitations, ASCII proved to be very popular. As the name implies, it was designed mostly for an American, or English-speaking, audience consisting mostly of programmers, and it contained all the characters needed by that audience. Mind you, ASCII was not the only character set around: different companies and countries would often develop rival character sets containing whatever characters they thought most appropriate...although, like ASCII, they were limited to a fairly small number of characters.

Early computers were extremely expensive and limited in power, so it was essential to make every byte (that word again!) count. As a result, character set designers would often use a single byte to represent each character. After all, a single byte can represent 256 different numbers—more than enough to hold all the characters in the English alphabet, plus digits, punctuation, and a few other useful or cool symbols as well.

With the advent of low-cost microchips and the invention of the IBM PC and Apple Macintosh, computers rapidly spread into homes and offices around the world. That gave rise to an urgent need for operating systems such as Mac OS and Windows to represent the characters found in the many different human languages, so new character sets were invented to meet these local needs.

The Problem with Character Sets

Alas, all this enthusiasm for inventing more and more little character sets was creating a real problem. With all these character sets using the same numbers, often a number that represented a particular symbol in one set would represent a completely different symbol in another!

Perhaps you can see the problem emerging here: if computers represent everything as numbers, including the characters in saved text files, what happens if you create that file using one character set and then open and display it with another?

Take a look at Figure 7–3 and Figure 7–4, which show two of the character sets that were used on Mac OS 9 and earlier, MacRoman and MacCyrillic.

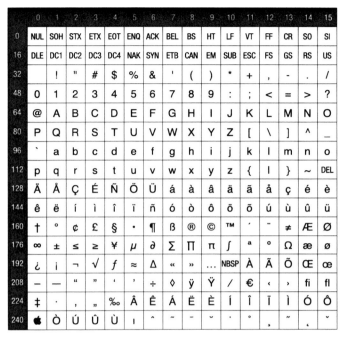

Figure 7–3. *The MacRoman character set*

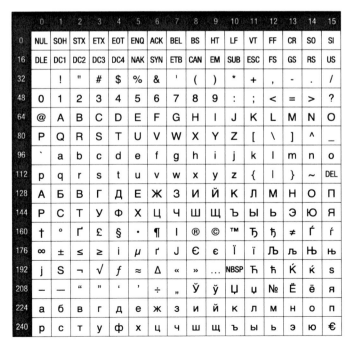

Figure 7–4. *The MacCyrillic character set*

MacRoman was used to represent text in English and other Western languages, and MacCyrillic was used for Russian and other Slavic texts.

The first thing you'll notice about these character sets is that they actually have quite a few characters in common: in fact, the first 128 characters of both character sets are identical to the ASCII character set (I told you ASCII was popular), providing a degree of compatibility between them. The remaining 128 symbols are mostly very different, however, being tailored to the specific requirements of Western or Slavic languages.

For example, the phrase "привет мир" can be successfully represented in MacCyrillic, but not in MacRoman, which doesn't contain the needed glyphs. However, let's think about what "привет мир" in MacCyrillic really means in terms of bits and bytes—that is, how each symbol is represented as a number.

Here are the characters from our text, with the corresponding MacCyrillic byte values beneath them:

```
п    р    и    в    е    т         м    и    р
239  240  232  226  229  242  32   236  232  240
```

Okay, so that seems straightforward enough. But wait a moment: what if we open a plain text file containing this text in, say, TextEdit? Well, if we know it contains MacCyrillic-encoded text, we can tell TextEdit to interpret the bytes in the file using that character set. However, what if we don't know it's Russian text, and open it as if it's a MacRoman-encoded file (the default on US and Western European Macs)? Here are the previous byte values, with the corresponding MacRoman characters beneath them:

```
239  240  232  226  229  242  32   236  232  240
 Ô        Ë    ,    Â    Ú          Ï    Ë
```

Clearly, "Ô Ë,ÂÚ ÏË " is not the same thing as "привет мир", yet both are represented by exactly the same sequence of bytes. So, interpreting the raw bytes using the wrong character set renders a piece of text completely incomprehensible. This makes text worryingly fragile, especially when it is stored in something like a plain text file that doesn't allow you to indicate the correct character set to use as part of the file itself. If you don't know where the file came from, you have to guess which character set to use, and if you guess wrong, there's a good chance the file will display onscreen as a lot of nonsense.

Requiring users to pick different character sets in this manner obviously wasn't a good start, but there was worse to come: what if a single character set didn't contain all the glyphs you needed to use in a particular document? As a workaround, font developers created special symbol fonts—Mac OS 9's Symbol and Zapf Dingbats fonts are two classic cases—that replaced the usual alphanumeric glyphs with custom ones. But because these fonts were using the same numerical values, 0–255, to represent wildly different symbols from conventional fonts such as Times and Courier, all you had to do to make a text document impossible to read was change its font settings from one font to another!

Unicode to the Rescue!

Faced with the growing chaos of varying character sets and ad hoc workarounds for the many limitations of those character sets, software companies *finally* did the sensible thing and got together to design a permanent solution. The result was the appropriately named *Unicode* character set—a single giant character set, large enough to hold all the glyphs from all languages in common use today, with loads of room left over for future growth as well.

> **NOTE:** To accommodate all these different glyphs—up to a million, in fact—Unicode generally uses multiple bytes to represent each character. You won't need to worry about this until you start reading and writing Unicode text files directly, so we'll leave that discussion until Chapter 17.

Admittedly, Unicode isn't without a few flaws of its own...it was designed by a committee, after all. For example, many accented characters can be represented as either a single glyph (such as é) or a combination of two glyphs, (e and ´), which can cause unwary programs all sorts of embarrassment when trying to compare the two (since a single digit is not, from the processor's point of view, the same as two digits). Smarter software will be aware of these little quirks, however, and deal with them appropriately. And even with its imperfections, virtually everyone agrees that Unicode is a huge step forward over the old chaos.

With every single glyph assigned to its own unique number (or *code point*), as long as you know that the character set to use is Unicode, you will never have to worry about a particular number translating to any other symbol than the one it is meant to be.

Even the font developers have gotten on board with Unicode compatibility. Although Symbol, Zapf Dingbats, and other "special" fonts are still around today, instead of mapping their glyphs to numbers 0–255, they now map them to the correct Unicode code points, so that there is no risk that changing a font setting on a piece of text will cause completely different symbols to appear.

> **TIP:** Many Mac applications provide a palette where you can view and select characters from anywhere in the Unicode character set. Just look under the Edit menu for a Special Characters option. You can also obtain Unicode character charts from `www.unicode.org/charts`.

Introducing Text in AppleScript 2.0

With the advent of Mac OS X, Unicode took its place firmly at the center of Apple's operating system, and since then has spread through the vast majority of modern desktop applications (indeed, nowadays it is pretty rare to encounter an application that doesn't support it unless that application is particularly old or ill-maintained).

Although AppleScript took a little while to catch up, with the release of AppleScript 2.0 in Mac OS X 10.5, Unicode finally became *the* text format used throughout the entire

AppleScript language. Unicode text was supported in earlier AppleScript versions (via the `Unicode text` class), but it lived rather awkwardly alongside AppleScript's older, non-Unicode text classes (`string` and `international text`) and could be painful to work with at times; you could not use Unicode characters within your scripts' source code, for example. With AppleScript 2.0, Apple replaced all the extra complexity and mess with a single Unicode-based `text` class and Unicode-aware source code.

It is worth noting that some older, non-Unicode-aware Carbon applications may still use the old `string` and `international text` classes themselves. However, as soon as non-Unicode text objects from those applications are passed to AppleScript, they are automatically converted to AppleScript's own Unicode-based strings. Similarly, when passing AppleScript strings to those applications, as long the application is properly designed, it should automatically translate back without any problem (assuming the strings don't contain any characters outside of the character set used by the application).

> **NOTE:** The main purpose of this chapter is to explain how text works in AppleScript 2.0 and later. However, you will still often encounter older scripts written for Tiger and earlier, particularly when looking for scripts online, so I will cover the main differences later in the chapter, in the section "How AppleScript Text Works in Tiger."

Now that you've digested a bit of background on how computers represent text data, let's get started on the good stuff: using text in AppleScript.

How to Write Literal Strings in AppleScript

Although you can include any characters in a string, some of them need a slightly different treatment if you want to use them in a literal string in your script. For instance, consider double quotes. Since a double quote is the character that specifies the start and end of a string, how can you include quotes in a literal string? If you write the following,

```
set my_text to "Choose the file named "Read Me" and open it"
```

AppleScript will get confused and think the literal string ends at the second double quote (`"Click on the file named "`), and what comes after that won't compile.

The error you get, shown in Figure 7–5, is almost philosophical. I'm glad that AppleScript at least found itself...

Figure 7–5. *AppleScript expected end of line but found "me".*

The error message does not say exactly what is wrong with the code, but at least it points you in the general direction of the problem. The first step to take when an compilation error makes no sense is to check whether you left some quote open somewhere.

To properly include a straight double quote character (") in a string, you have to *escape* it by adding a backslash character (\) in front of it. Here is the previous example again, this time with the quote marks around the phrase "Read Me" correctly escaped:

```
set my_text to "Choose the file named \" Read Me\" and open it"
```

Here's another problem: with the backslash acting as the special escape character in a string literal, what do you do if you want to include the backslash character itself in a string? For instance, if you want to display a dialog box asking users not to use the backslash character, you will need to use it yourself. To do that, you can simply escape it with another backslash character, like this: \\. For example, here is how you would write C:\user\docs\readme.txt as a literal string in AppleScript:

```
set windows_file_path to "C:\\user\\docs\\readme.txt"
```

The script in Figure 7–6 displays a backslash character inside double quotes. Fancy stuff!

Figure 7–6. *The script and the resulting dialog box*

Another way you can include the double quote character is by simply using AppleScript's built-in quote variable, which contains a predefined string object with a single double quote character in it. This might look a little odd at first because the quote variable doesn't go inside the quotes, of course. Using this variable, the previous script line would look like this:

```
set my_text to "Choose the file named " & quote & "Read Me" & quote & " and open it"
```

Other characters you should know about are the tab, return, and line feed characters. These two characters won't give you a hard time—just the opposite; you can include them in a string in a few ways.

The first option is to type them directly, which is simple enough.

The second way to include these characters within a literal string is by typing \r for return and \t for tab. Both \r and \t will normally be replaced with returns (ASCII 13) and tabs (ASCII 9) as soon as you compile the script; the similar combination of \n will be replaced with a line feed (ASCII 10) character. See Figure 7–7 and Figure 7–8 for an example.

Figure 7–7. *The script before it has been compiled*

Figure 7–8. *The script after it has been compiled*

White-space characters can often be difficult to tell apart, and because white space within strings can affect how your scripts work, you often need to know exactly what tab, return, and/or linefeed characters your string literals contain. AppleScript Editor allows you to disable the default behavior by selecting the "Escape tabs and line breaks" option in the Editing panel of the Preferences window. This makes all tab and line break characters inside literal strings appear as \t, \r, or \n. Now if you type your script as shown in Figure 7–8 and compile it, the compiled script will appear as shown in Figure 7–7!

The third way you can obtain tab, return, and line feed characters is by referring to the corresponding built-in variables. AppleScript has five constants: quote (which you looked at already), space, tab, return, and (new in 10.5) linefeed. You can then use the concatenation operator (&) to join everything together:

```
set my_own_menu to "coffee" & tab & "$1.15" & linefeed & "donut" & tab & "$0.65"
```

The Properties of Text

AppleScript's text class defines several properties—class, length, quoted form, and id—that allow you to obtain various bits of information from strings.

The class Property

The value of the class property is always text:

```
class of "Hello World!"
--> text
```

So, for example, if you have an object in a variable and need to find out if it is text or not, you can use a test like this:

```
if class of some_object = text then
    -- Do something with the text here...
else
    -- It's not text, so do something else...
end if
```

The length Property

Because a string is made of characters, the length of the string is the number of characters it has in it. To get the length of a string, just ask it for the value of its length property. Here is how you do that:

```
length of "rope"
--> 4
```

The result is a number, in this case the number 4 since the string "rope" has four characters.

The quoted form Property

The quoted form property can be used to escape a string so that it can be used safely in a Unix shell script. I'll discuss this property when we cover the do shell script command in Chapter 27.

The id Property

As I discussed earlier in the chapter, each character that can appear in a string corresponds to a unique number, or code point. In Mac OS X 10.5 and later, you can obtain these code points by asking the string for the value of its `id` property. For example:

```
id of "A"
--> 65
```

id of "नमस्कार दुनिया"
```
--> {2344, 2350, 2360, 2381, 2325, 2366, 2352,
     32, 2342, 2369, 2344, 2367, 2351, 2366}
```

As you can see, asking for the ID of a single-character string returns a single number, whereas a multicharacter string returns a list of numbers. The syntax is a bit odd, but it gets the job done.

To go in the other direction, you need to use a `character id ...` specifier with the following syntax:

```
character id integer_or_list_of_integers
```

For example:

```
character id 65
--> "A"
```

```
character id {2344, 2350, 2360, 2381, 2325, 2366, 2352, ¬
     32, 2342, 2369, 2344, 2367, 2351, 2366}
```
--> "नमस्कार दुनिया"

CAUTION: When using the `character id` specifier, make sure it appears outside of any `tell application...` blocks. Otherwise AppleScript will think you are referring to `character` elements in the target application, and because scriptable applications aren't familiar with this particular reference form, the result would be an application error.

The Elements of Text

A large part of working with text is being able to break apart a string and manipulate different pieces of it. AppleScript's text class defines several types of elements for doing this: `character`, `word`, `paragraph`, `text`, and `text item`. The next few sections explain the first four; `text item` elements are a bit more complex, though, so I'll cover them later in the chapter, in the "Working with Text Item Delimiters" section.

Characters

To break a string into characters, you have to use the keyword `characters` to refer to all of the string's `character` elements, along with the `get` command:

```
get characters of "tic-tac-toe"
```

You can also drop the word get and write the following:

```
characters of "tic-tac-toe"
```

Or you can write every character of ..., which has the same meaning as characters of ...:

```
every character of "tic-tac-toe"
```

Whichever style you use, the result will be the same: a list object containing all the characters of the string, with each character taking up one item in the list:

```
--> {"t", "i", "c", "-", "t", "a", "c", "-", "t", "o", "e"}
```

So now you know that AppleScript can split a string into characters. What you also need to know is how to extract chunks of strings for use in your script. To put it in context, slicing up strings and turning chunks of them into new strings is one task as a scripter you will do all the time: figuring out what date a job is due based on the date embedded in the file name, parsing out text files and using the information there, cleaning out unwanted characters taken from different sources, formatting phone numbers, and so on. The list is endless.

The first and most commonly used tool you have is the ability to extract a character from a string by specifying its index. This method is called the *index reference form*, since you refer to a character (in this case) by its position among the other characters.

An easy example is as follows:

```
character 5 of "AppleScript"
```

As you likely determined already, the result of the preceding expression is a one-character string, "e".

Here are a couple more examples:

```
character 1 of "AppleScript"
--> "A"
```

```
character 11 of "AppleScript"
--> "t"
```

And since I'm talking AppleScript here, and not some other, no-fun programming language, you can also write the following:

```
fifth character of "AppleScript"
--> "e"
```

```
first character of "AppleScript"
--> "A"
```

```
last character of "AppleScript"
--> "t"
```

Let's go back a step and look at the term last character. Of course, using this kind of syntax is useful for that last character, or even the one before it, but what about the one before that? You're in luck, because AppleScript has the perfect solution! The last character is also known to AppleScript as character -1 (that is, minus one). The reason why this is so cool and so useful is that you can use a number to look for a specific character by counting from the end of the string, not the beginning. Using that negative-index reference style, you can write the following,

```
character -3 of "AppleScript"
```

which will return the character i.

For your reference, Figure 7–9 shows you different ways you can refer to different characters in a string.

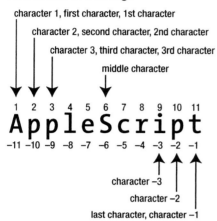

Figure 7–9. *Referring to characters in a string*

Looking at Figure 7–9 you can also see that the word middle is a valid reference form, although I've never used that one.

Another way to refer to a character is to use the arbitrary reference form some. The reference some character of the_string returns a random character from a string:

```
set the_string to "AppleScript"
set a_random_character to some character of the_string
```

So far, you've seen how to refer to individual characters by index, or all characters at once. But what if you want to get several adjoining characters out of a larger string? Fortunately, there is one more reference form supported by AppleScript strings: the *range reference form*.

To specify a range of characters, you write the keyword characters followed by the position of the first character, then the keyword thru, and finally the position of the last character. For example:

```
characters 1 thru 4 of "tic-tac-toe"
--> {"t", "i", "c", "-"}
```

```
characters 3 thru -3 of "tic-tac-toe"
--> {"c", "-", "t", "a", "c", "-", "t"}
```

```
characters -3 thru -1 of "tic-tac-toe"
--> {"t", "o", "e"}
```

You'll notice that the keyword thru isn't fully spelled out as through. Say "thank you" to the AppleScript team for locking the grammar police in the closet that day. As one who uses the word thru in quite a few AppleScript statements, I'm grateful. Using the full spelling through is completely legal, however.

Working with individual character elements is sometimes useful in scripts, though it is more common to work with larger chunks, such as words, paragraphs, or ranges of text. So let's move on to the next kind of text-related elements: words.

Words

As you would expect, you can also break down text into individual words. Doing this also returns a list, but, unlike breaking text into characters, which retains the integrity of the text, breaking text into words cleans out any characters that are considered word delimiters.

Let's start with a little example. Type the following into a new AppleScript Editor document and run it:

```
get every word of "oh my word"
```

The result is a list of strings, where each string contains a single word from the original string:

```
--> {"oh", "my", "word"}
```

What you might not notice right away, you're sure to realize with the next example:

```
words of "3-day forecast, starting 5/12/2009"
--> {"3", "day", "forecast", "starting", "5", "12", "2009"}
```

When you ask for the words of a string, you get a list of the words, but the dashes, commas, slashes, and so on are nowhere to be seen. Punctuation marks and white space are not considered to be words and thus are not included. Other symbols may or may not be considered words; for example:

```
words of "Pay me $10"
--> {"Pay", "me", "$", "10"}
```

```
words of "Give me 100%"
--> {"Give", "me", "100"}
```

As you might guess, you can also ask for an individual word or a range of words:

```
word 3 of "You keep using that word."
--> "using"
```

```
words 5 thru -3 of "I do not think it means what you think it means."
--> {"it", "means", "what", "you", "think"}
```

The precise rules that AppleScript relies on when deciding what is or isn't a word are complicated and may vary according to system settings or Mac OS version—and the language being used. For example, the following expression successfully breaks up the Japanese phrase "user name" into words, even though there are no spaces in Japanese text:

```
words of "ユーザ名"
--> {"ユーザ", "名"}
```

In general, although word elements can be very useful for extracting human-readable words out of regular text, you should probably use a more precise method, such as text ranges or text item delimiters, when you need absolute control over how a string is broken up.

Paragraphs

Much like breaking strings into words, you can break strings into paragraphs. The logic behind a paragraph is much simpler. The first paragraph in the string starts at the beginning of the string and ends at the first instance of one of the following:

- A carriage return character (ASCII character 13), which is the standard line break indicator on Mac OS 9 and earlier and which is still used in places on OS X

- A line feed character (ASCII character 10), which is the standard line break on Unix and is often used on OS X

- A carriage return character followed by a line feed character, which is the standard line break on Windows

If you have only one paragraph (and there's always at least one paragraph, even if the string is empty!), then that one paragraph ends at the end of the string. If you have more than one paragraph, then the second paragraph starts right after the first line break and ends right before the next one, and so on. The last paragraph ends at the end of the string.

Take, for example, Script 7–1. It starts with a simple string that contains five paragraphs (one of which is empty) and asks AppleScript to return every paragraph. The result is a list in which every list item is a string that contains one paragraph from the original text.

Script 7–1.

```
set my_string to "This is a line
The next line is here
I'm third

Last paragraph"

every paragraph of my_string
--> {"This is a line", "The next line is here", "I'm third", "", "Last paragraph"}
```

Text Ranges

Earlier you saw how to extract a sequence of characters as a list of single-character strings, but what if you want to extract them as a single string instead?

A common novice approach is to extract a list of characters and then use AppleScript's as operator to convert, or *coerce*, it into a single piece of text, like this:

```
(characters 5 thru 7 of "tic-tac-toe") as text -- Not a good way to get text ranges
--> "tac"
```

Although this approach may appear to do what you want, it isn't very efficient and can easily lead to unexpected errors, as you will discover later in the chapter when I discuss how list-to-string coercions actually work.

Fortunately, AppleScript provides a far better way to extract one string from another, by referring to a string's text elements. This type of reference always has the following form:

```
text start_position thru end_position of the_string
```

For example:

```
set the_string to "Necessity is the mother of taking chances."
set sub_string to text 9 thru 18 of the_string
--> "y is the m"
```

This is a particularly useful way to reference text, so let's look at a quick practical example.

Let's say that you have a file name, "JB445091_UTFg12.zip", and you need to extract the client's account number, which is the six-digit number starting from the third character.

Let's start by assigning the string to a variable so that it is easier to work with:

```
set job_file_name to "JB445091_UTFg12.zip"
```

For this exercise, the file name is given as a literal string. In a larger working script, you would probably retrieve it from the Finder using a get command.

The first step in obtaining the client's account number is to refer to the text range that starts at character 3 and ends on character 8 (that's six characters in all, since the start and end indexes are inclusive):

```
set account_number_string to text 3 thru 8 of job_file_name
```

Once you've extracted a string containing only the account number information, the second and final step is to coerce this string into an integer by using the as operator:

```
set account_number to account_number_string as integer
```

If you prefer, you can combine the last two lines into one:

```
set account_number to (text 3 thru 8 of job_file_name) as integer
```

The expression in the first set of parentheses produces a string, and as integer at the end coerces that string into an integer.

Now run the script in AppleScript Editor. The result should be the client's account number, 445091.

Another point I will discuss later is that the error-free execution of the script depends on the extracted characters being all digits. You'll learn more about that when I talk about coercing text later in the chapter.

As you can see, text ranges are already pretty useful to work with, but they have one more trick up their sleeves. You already know how to extract a range of text from one character to another, but what if you want to start and finish on a whole word or paragraph?

As you found out in Chapter 5, scriptable applications often allow you to identify the start and end positions using "mini" references to the exact elements you want to begin and end on. The good news is that AppleScript strings also allow you to do this: you can begin and/or end on a character (the default), a word, or a paragraph.

For example, let's say you want to extract all the text that lies between two words (inclusive). Here is how you do it:

```
set the_string to "Necessity is the mother of taking chances."
set sub_string to text (word 3) thru (word -2) of the_string
--> "the mother of taking"
```

Pretty slick, huh? You can use the same technique when referring to character, word, and paragraph ranges too, although I find it is most often useful when working with text ranges.

At this point, we have covered almost all the elements of AppleScript strings. We have one more type of element, text item, still to cover, but before we get to that, let's look at the more general features that AppleScript provides for working with strings.

Operators and Commands

Extracting information from strings via their properties and elements is obviously useful, but if that was all we could do with strings, we'd probably get rather bored with them before very long. Happily, AppleScript provides a number of commands and operators for manipulating strings in other ways, so we'll look at these next.

Joining Strings

You already saw the concatenation operator at work in Chapter 3, but now you'll look at how it operates on strings in a bit more detail.

Concatenating two strings always returns a string result. For example:

```
"Hello, " & "World!"
--> "Hello, World!"
```

That makes sense. What else would it return? Well, try the following in a new script window:

```
set the_price to "$" & 6
```

The result is "$6".

The difference here is that you concatenated a string to a number. AppleScript took the liberty to coerce the number into text for you, so the result is the same as if you had treated the 6 as text in this way:

```
set the_price to "$" & "6"
```

You get the same result.

However, let's see what happens when you switch places:

```
set the_price to 6 & " Dollar"
```

The result this time is different. Because the first operand (the item you operate on) is a number and not a string, AppleScript figures that returning a list is safer than returning a string. The result, then, is a list of two items, a number and a string:

```
--> {6, " Dollar"}
```

To prevent that from happening, you have to use the coercion operator, as, to convert the number to a string yourself.

The as operator converts an object of one class into an object of another class. In this case, you should first coerce the number (which is an object of class integer) to a string (an object of class text), like this:

```
set the_price to (6 as text) & " Dollar"
```

Now the result is a single string—"6 Dollar"—just as you wanted.

CONCATENATE WITH CARE

Take care! A common mistake here is to join the two values using the following:

```
6 & " Dollar" as string
```

This may seem to work okay sometimes, but it hides a nasty bug because it works by first creating a two-item list, {6, "Dollar"}, and then coercing that list to a string. If AppleScript's text item delimiters property (which you'll meet shortly) is set to any value except an empty string, you'll find extra characters mysteriously inserted into the result! To avoid such unpleasant surprises, always write it as (6 as string) & " Dollar" instead.

Comparing Strings

What about the other operators? Well, many operators compare one string to another. These operators are =, ≠, <, ≤, >, and ≥—otherwise known as is equal to, is not equal to, is less than, is less than or equal to, is greater than, and is greater than or equal to.

Let's start with the simple ones: comparing two strings for equality. It's easy to understand how you can see whether strings are equal; consider the following operations. This one,

```
"Ice cream" = "carrot"
```

returns false. And this one,

```
"Me" ≠ "You"
```

returns true.

Incidentally, AppleScript allows each of these operators to be written in any of several ways: as symbols, words, or phrases. This makes no difference to how your script runs, but it does allow you to write your code in whichever style you think reads best. Here are the various alternatives, or *synonyms*, AppleScript provides for the = and ≠ operators:

```
"Ice cream" is "carrot"
"Ice cream" equals "carrot"
"Ice cream" is equal to "carrot"
"Me" is not "You"
"Me" is not equal to "You"
```

> **TIP:** Operator synonyms are a neat feature that can help to make your code easier to read. You can find a summary of all available operator synonyms in Chapter 13.

Let's look at some more string comparisons. How about the following statement?

```
"555-1212" = "5551212"
--> false
```

Or the following one?

```
"ASCII" = "ascii"
--> true
```

The result of the first operation is false because the first operand has an extra hyphen in it, whereas the result of the second one is true because AppleScript normally ignores case when comparing two strings. AppleScript makes a number of assumptions by default about what characteristics of the text you want to consider or ignore while comparing text. You can overrule these assumptions with special considering and ignoring clauses that allow you to ignore or consider certain conditions. More details on considering and ignoring clauses are coming up shortly.

Much like the is equal to and is not equal to operators, the is less than and is greater than operators always return a result as a Boolean.

To determine in a script whether one string comes before another string, use the is less than operator, which can be written in any of several ways:

```
"a" comes before "b"
"a" < "b"
"a" is less than "b"
--> true
```

Similarly, the is greater than operator checks whether the first parameter is greater than the second or appears later in the sorting chain:

```
"a" comes after "b"
"a" > "b"
"a" is greater than "b"
--> false
```

Use the is greater than or equal to operator to see whether one value is either the same as or greater than another:

```
"a" ≥ "b"
"a" is greater than or equal to "b"
--> false
```

And you can use the is less than or equal to operator to see whether one value is the same as or less than the other:

```
"a" ≤ "b"
"a" is less than or equal to "b"
--> true
```

You may be wondering exactly how AppleScript decides if one string comes before or after another string. The answer is…it's a bit complicated.

With old-fashioned character sets such as MacRoman, one character is considered less than or greater than another character depending on whether the first character appears before or after the second one in the MacRoman character table. Unicode is much more sophisticated, however, and decides the ordering based on meaning as well as physical position in the Unicode character set.

For example, consider three characters, 0, ?, and A. In the ASCII character set, ? is at code point 63, so it comes after 0, which is at code point 48, but comes before A, which is at code point 65. In Unicode, the first 128 characters are also based on ASCII, so these characters occupy exactly the same code points:

```
id of "0" --> 48
```

```
id of "?" --> 63
```

```
id of "A" --> 65
```

However, when you try to compare them as Unicode strings, you will find that ?—along with other punctuation marks—actually comes before both 0 and A, although 0 still comes before A as before:

```
"?" < "A" --> true
```

```
"?" < "0" --> true
```

```
"0" < "A" --> true
```

A full discussion of how Unicode determines which characters come before or after other characters is beyond the scope of this book. You might want to research Unicode sorting rules on your own if you are going to perform tasks such as sorting a list of strings into order, as they will affect the final result. In general, though, the Unicode rules are based on what human users would consider a common-sense sorting order, so it seems quite natural for AppleScript to follow them.

Checking for Strings Within Strings

Several operators can be used to check for strings within other strings. These operators are starts with, ends with, contains, and is in.

As their names suggest, the starts with and ends with operators check whether a string appears at the start or end of another string, respectively, and return true or false as the result. For example:

```
"Don't let schooling interfere with your education." starts with "Don't let school"
--> true
```

```
"Action speaks louder than words but not nearly as often." ends with "words"
--> false
```

The contains operator checks whether the string given as the second operand appears anywhere in the string that is the first operand:

```
"Name the greatest of all inventors. Accident." contains "vent"
--> true
```

The is in operator does about the same thing, only it checks whether the first string appears within the second:

```
"necessary evil" is in "Work is a necessary evil to be avoided."
--> true
```

As with the comparison operators, the result of containment operations can be influenced by considering and ignoring clauses, so let's look at those next.

Considering and Ignoring Attributes

AppleScript allows you to consider or ignore various attributes of text when doing string comparisons. These attributes are (in alphabetical order) case, diacriticals, hyphens, numeric strings, punctuation, and white space. By default, when comparing strings, AppleScript ignores case and numeric strings but considers the rest.

To change how strings are compared, you have to wrap your comparison tests in a considering or ignoring statement, depending on your intention. These statements have the following syntax:

```
considering attribute [, attribute ... and attribute ] ¬
    [ but ignoring attribute [, attribute ... and attribute ] ]
    -- One or more statements...
end considering

ignoring attribute [, attribute ... and attribute ] ¬
    [ but considering attribute [, attribute ... and attribute ] ]
    -- One or more statements...
end ignoring
```

As you can see, you can specify the attributes to be considered and those to be ignored either in separate statements, or combined into one statement if you want to specify both at the same time. You can specify as few or as many attributes as you want; any attributes that are omitted remain at their current settings.

Let's start with a simple example: comparing two strings for equality. The default AppleScript behavior is to ignore the case of characters, so asking AppleScript to consider the case of characters will yield a different result. Simply stating the following,

```
"A" = "a"
```

returns true, and since AppleScript ignores the case of characters by default, the following statement returns true as well:

```
ignoring case
    "A" = "a"
end ignoring
```

If you want to take the case of the strings into consideration, then you need to wrap the comparison test in a considering case ... end considering block, like this:

```
considering case
    "A" = "a"
end considering
```

The result of the preceding script snippet is false.

In a recent project, I had to add to a system a feature that would determine whether the content of a Microsoft Excel sheet had changed. The solution was to save every worksheet as a text file and then compare the most recent text file with the older version of that file. Initially, I used the following line:

```
set files_match to (read file_a) = (read file_b)
```

The statement simply compares two strings that are returned from the read command (which you will explore in depth later in this book). The problem with this solution is that if someone simply fixed a capitalization problem in a worksheet, AppleScript would still think the text of the files is identical. The script was retrofitted with the considering case clause, like this:

```
considering case
    set files_match to (read file_a) = (read file_b)
end considering
```

This time, even a simple change of capitalization would show.

The diacritical, hyphen, and punctuation consideration attributes work slightly differently. Each of these refers to a set of special characters that can be ignored when comparing strings. All are considered by default, so using them in a considering clause won't normally change the result, but using them in an ignoring clause will.

The ignoring diacriticals clause allows you to ignore any accent marks so that the following statement returns a true result:

```
ignoring diacriticals
    "Résumé" = "Resume"
end ignoring
--> true
```

The ignoring hyphens clause allows you to ignore hyphens in the text:

```
ignoring hyphens
    "1-800-555-1212" = "18005551212"
end ignoring
--> true
```

CAUTION: In Mac OS X 10.5 and earlier, the `ignoring` hyphens clause ignores only hyphen (minus) characters. In 10.6 and later, typographical dashes such as an en dash or em dash are also ignored.

The `ignoring punctuation` clause allows you to ignore punctuation marks. Here's an example:

```
ignoring punctuation
    "That's all, right? Now!" = "Thats all right now."
end ignoring
--> true
```

NOTE: The Unicode character set defines which characters are punctuation and which aren't. You can find out about these and other Unicode rules at `www.unicode.org/standard`.

The `ignoring white space` clause allows you to ignore spaces, tabs, line feeds, and return characters when comparing strings:

```
ignoring white space
    "Space craft" = "Spacecraft"
end ignoring
--> true
```

The `considering numeric strings` clause is useful when comparing strings that contain a mixture of text and numbers; for example:

```
"Chapter 5.pdf" comes before "Chapter 10.pdf"
--> false -- Not the answer you wanted!

considering numeric strings
    "Chapter 5.pdf" comes before "Chapter 10.pdf"
end considering
--> true
```

Considering numeric strings is also very useful when comparing version numbers. Because application version numbers are conveyed as strings and commonly contain multiple decimal points (for example, 1.4.2) or more than one digit per part (for example, 2.13.9), converting them into a number often isn't possible, or safe. For that reason, version numbers are best compared as strings.

Take, for instance, these two version numbers (expressed as strings): "1.5.8" and "1.5.10". If looked at simply as sequences of characters, the "8" in the first string is greater than the "1" at the same position in the second string. Therefore, the following script returns true:

```
"1.5.8" > "1.5.10"
--> true
```

However, in the world of numbers, we know that 10 comes after 8, so the result we actually want is `false`. Considering numeric strings will correct that, as you can see here:

```
considering numeric strings
   "1.5.8" > "1.5.10"
end considering
--> false
```

Using a single considering or ignoring statement might be sufficient for your needs, but what if you need to specify more than one attribute? For that you can use multiple parameters and even nest clauses.

Say you're writing a quick-fire question-and-answer game. Although you need the words to be correct, you want to be lenient when it comes to case, diacriticals, dashes, and spaces.

Here is how you can evaluate the accuracy of the answer:

```
ignoring case, diacriticals, hyphens and white space
   set is_answer_correct to user_answer = actual_answer
end ignoring
```

This will ensure that if the expected answer is "El Niño", the responses "elnino", "El nino", "Elñino", and "El-Nino" will also register as correct.

What if you do want to consider the case of the answer but also want to give some slack over the rest? Your statement would look like this:

```
considering case but ignoring diacriticals, hyphens and white space
   set is_answer_correct to user_answer = actual_answer
end considering
```

You can also nest considering and ignoring statements inside one another; for example:

```
considering case
   ignoring diacriticals
      ignoring hyphens and white space
         set is_answer_correct to user_answer = actual_answer
      end ignoring
   end ignoring
end considering
```

One final thing to remember when using considering and ignoring blocks: if you send a command from inside a considering or ignoring statement, the attributes you specify might also affect the code that handles the command. For example:

```
offset of "s" in "AppleScript"
--> 6

considering case
   offset of "s" in "AppleScript"
end considering
--> 0 -- A lower-case "s" wasn't found!
```

Whether or not this happens depends on the particular handler you called. Most scriptable applications and scripting additions always ignore case and consider everything else, and simply ignore any attributes specified by your script (the Standard Additions offset command is one of the exceptions). On the other hand, user-defined handlers that appear in scripts are *always* affected:

```
on is_pdf_file(file_name)
    return file_name ends with ".pdf"
end is_pdf_file

set file_name to "DN301002.PDF"
considering case
    is_pdf_file(file_name)
end considering
--> false -- Oops!
```

This can cause hard-to-trace bugs in larger scripts where user-defined handlers that perform text-related operations are called from within considering/ignoring statements. If you need to, you can protect sensitive code against this problem by wrapping comparison and containment operations in their own considering/ignoring blocks that specify exactly the attributes you need at the time; for example:

```
on is_pdf_file(file_name)
  ignoring case but considering diacriticals, hyphens, punctuation and white space
        return file_name ends with ".pdf"
  end ignoring
end is_pdf_file

set file_name to "DN301002.PDF"
considering case
    is_pdf_file(file_name)
end considering
--> true
```

The count Command

In addition to the length property, you can also use the count command to get the number of characters of a string. For example:

```
count "Hello World!"
--> 12
```

You can even use the optional each parameter to indicate exactly which class of element you want to count (without it, the default value is item, which in this case means each character):

```
count "Hello World!" each word
--> 2
```

Personally, though, I prefer to use a reference to the desired elements instead—it gives the same answer but makes the code easier to read:

```
count words of "Hello World!"
--> 2
```

The offset Command

The offset command, which is defined in the String Commands suite of the Standard Additions dictionary, is useful for figuring out where a certain substring starts in another string.

The result of the offset command is an integer that indicates the position of the first instance of the substring in the main string, or 0 if the substring is not found.

Here's a simple example of the offset command:

```
offset of "@" in "steve@apple.com"
--> 5
```

Script 7–2 uses the offset command to extract the domain name from a valid e-mail address.

Script 7–2.

```
set the_email_address to "info@store.apple.com"
set the_offset to offset of "@" in the_email_address
set the_domain to text (the_offset + 1) thru -1 of the_email_address
--> "store.apple.com"
```

Coercing to and from Text

To convert an object of one class into an object of another class, you use a coercion. Some coercions occur automatically when needed—for example, when using the concatenation operator, &, to join a number onto the end of a string, AppleScript first coerces the number into a string for you:

```
"Joe" & 90 -- The second operand is automatically coerced to text
--> "Joe90"
```

Other times, you can use the as operator to coerce objects yourself; for example:

```
42 as text
--> "42"
```

AppleScript supports a number of coercions for text objects.

You can, of course, coerce any text object to text:

```
"Hello World!" as text
--> "Hello World!"
```

In other words, the result of coercing text to text is the text object you already had. That might not seem useful, but it's good to know that AppleScript won't mess with your text when you do this. For example, if your script has a variable that ought to contain text but might be a number or something else, just coerce its value to class text and then you can be 100 percent sure.

AppleScript also allows you to coerce text to boolean, integer, real, alias, and POSIX path, as long as the content of the string is appropriate for that class:

```
"true" as boolean
--> true

"false" as boolean -- Or any string other than "True"
--> false

"16" as integer
--> 16
```

```
"-3.3333" as real
--> -3.3333

"Macintosh HD:Applications:TextEdit.app" as alias
--> alias "Macintosh HD:Applications:TextEdit.app:"

"/Applications/TextEdit.app" as POSIX file
--> file "d1:Applications:TextEdit.app"
```

If AppleScript is unable to coerce the string to the desired class, a coercion error (number –1700) will occur:

```
--"forty-two" as integer
-- Error: Can't make "forty-two" into type integer.
```

You can also coerce a string to a single-item list:

```
"Hello World!" as list
--> {"Hello World!"}
```

Any objects of class boolean, integer, real, alias, or POSIX path can be coerced to class text:

```
true as text
--> "true"

"false" as text
--> "false"

16 as text
--> "16"

-3.3333 as text
--> "-3.3333"

(alias "Macintosh HD:Applications:TextEdit.app") as text
--> alias "Macintosh HD:Applications:TextEdit.app:"

(POSIX file "/Applications/TextEdit.app") as text
--> "d1:Applications:TextEdit.app"
```

> **NOTE:** Coercing an alias or POSIX file object to text always gives a colon-delimited HFS file path. If you want a slash-delimited POSIX file path instead, you should ask the object for the value of its POSIX path property instead. We'll cover these objects in detail in Chapter 17.

In addition, there are a few other classes you can coerce to text: date, class, and constant (although you cannot coerce them in the other direction). For example, here's how you coerce a date to text:

```
set the_date to date "Tuesday, September 15, 2009 19:03:55"
the_date as text
--> "Tuesday, September 15, 2009 19:03:55"
```

> **TIP:** Chapter 9 will explain how to convert between dates and text in much more detail.

And here are some examples of coercing class names (document, Wednesday) and a constant (no):

```
document as text
--> "document"

Wednesday as text
--> "Wednesday"

no as text
--> "no"
```

Finally, you can coerce a list to text as long as the list contains text objects, or objects that can be coerced to text. If the list contains only a single item, the result is straightforward:

```
{"That's no ordinary rabbit!"} as text
--> "That's no ordinary rabbit!"
```

If the list contains multiple items, however, things become a little more complex because *text item delimiters* become involved. I will discuss how list-to-text coercions work in more detail later in the next section.

Working with Text Item Delimiters

Yet another AppleScript pearl, text item delimiters, is a property built into AppleScript, and it's useful for a whole range of text manipulations.

The text item delimiters property is used in two situations: when splitting a string into a list of smaller strings and when coercing a list of strings into one big string.

Splitting Strings with Text Item Delimiters

AppleScript allows you to split a string by searching for a substring (or several substrings) and breaking the string wherever the substring is found. To do this, you use the text item element defined by AppleScript's text class and the text item delimiters property, which is defined by AppleScript itself and can be accessed from anywhere in the script.

By default, AppleScript's text item delimiters property is set to {""}, which means asking for every text item element of a string is the same as asking for every character of a string. Where things start to get exciting is when you set AppleScript's text item delimiters property to a different value.

Let's take a phone number, 800-555-1212, and see what happens when you change AppleScript's text item delimiters property to "-".

Start a new script window, and enter the following script text:

```
set text item delimiters to "-"
get every text item of "800-555-1212"
```

Run the script, and the result will be the following list of strings:

```
--> {"800", "555", "1212"}
```

Figure 7–10 shows how this works.

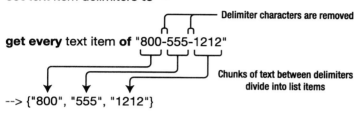

set text item delimiters **to** "-"

Delimiter characters are removed

get every text item **of** "800-555-1212"

Chunks of text between delimiters
divide into list items

```
--> {"800", "555", "1212"}
```

Figure 7–10. *Breaking up a string after setting the* `text item delimiters` *property to a hyphen*

As you can see, the delimiter substrings themselves are discarded, and anything in between them ends up as items in the resulting list.

Splitting strings into lists is one way you can use text item delimiters, but you can also use them within larger references. For example, Script 7–3 shows another way to extract the domain name from an e-mail address, this time by using text item delimiters to split the string on the "@" symbol.

Script 7–3.

```
set the_email_address to "info@store.apple.com"
set text item delimiters to "@"
set the_domain to text item -1 of the_email_address
--> "store.apple.com"
```

When referring to a string's `text` elements, a really neat trick is to use a reference to a text item as the start or end point. Script 7–4 shows how to extract the parent folder from a POSIX path string by extracting a substring that goes from the start of the original string up to (but not including) the final slash character.

Script 7–4.

```
set the_path to "/Users/hanaan/Work/todo.txt"
set text item delimiters to "/"
set the_parent_path to text 1 thru (text item -2) of the_path
--> "/Users/hanaan/Work"
```

As you can see, the starting point for the text range is given as 1—that is, character 1. The end point for the range is specified by a relative reference, `text item -2`, that identifies the second-to-last text item in the path string (in this case, "Work"). The result is a string that contains all the text that was found at the start and end points plus everything in between.

By default, text item delimiters are case insensitive but match everything else exactly. For example:

```
set text item delimiters to "e"
text items of "PLEASE read my résumé!"
--> {"PL", "AS", " r", "ad my résumé!"}
```

However, you can use considering and ignoring statements to make them consider case or ignore diacriticals as well:

```
set text item delimiters to "e"
considering case and diacriticals
    text items of "PLEASE read my résumé!"
end considering
--> {"PLEASE r", "ad my résumé!"}

set text item delimiters to "e"
ignoring case and diacriticals
    text items of "PLEASE read my résumé!"
end ignoring
--> {"PL", "AS", " r", "ad my r", "sum", "!"}
```

One thing you may have noticed about the text item delimiters property is that the default value is a list object containing a single string. Usually you only want to split a string on a single delimiter string. In that case, you can assign the delimiter string directly to the property (for example, "/"), although you can wrap it up as a single-item list if you prefer ({"/"}). In Mac OS X 10.6 and later, however, you can also split a string using multiple delimiters.

Script 7–5 uses this new feature to clean up phone numbers by removing any parentheses, spaces, and hyphens.

Script 7–5.

```
set the_phone_number to "(800) 555-1212"
set text item delimiters to {"(", ")", "-", " "}
set the_list to text items of the_phone_number
```

Create a new document in AppleScript Editor, and type in the code as shown. When you run it, the result will be the following list of substrings:

```
--> {"800", "", "555", "1212"}
```

In case you're wondering, the second item in the list comes from between the closing parenthesis and the space character that immediately follows it. Because there are no non-delimiter characters between these two delimiters, the result is an empty string.

The script isn't complete yet—we still need some way of joining the remaining pieces back together, but it's a good start. The next section will look at how we can combine this list back into a single string.

Combining List Items into a Single String

The other function of the text item delimiters property is to provide padding between items when coercing a list into a string.

Let's finish the code started in Script 7–5. Script 7–6 adds the final two lines: the first to set the current text item delimiter to an empty string; the second to coerce the list back into a single string.

Script 7–6.

```
set the_phone_number to "(800) 555-1212"
set text item delimiters to {"(", ")", "-", " "}
set the_list to text items of the_phone_number
set text item delimiters to ""
set the_cleaned_phone_number to the_list as text
```

Now when you run the script, the result will be as follows:

```
--> "8005551212"
```

As you can see, when the `text item delimiters` property is set to an empty string, the list items just squish together.

Let's try another example. Script 7–7 shows how to turn a list of strings into a single string with each item separated by a comma and a space.

Script 7–7.

```
set shopping_list to {"bread", "milk", "butter", "cream", "Wensleydale cheese"}
set text item delimiters to ", "
set shopping_text to shopping_list as text
display dialog "Remember to buy " & shopping_text & "."
```

Figure 7–11 shows the assembled text that appears in the dialog box when the script is run.

Figure 7–11. *The assembled string displayed in a dialog box*

As you may have noticed, although most of our delimiters have been single-character strings, multicharacter strings also work. In Script 7–8, the `text item delimiters` property is set to the string `"mississippi"`:

Script 7–8.

```
set text item delimiters to "mississippi"
set the_secret_message to ¬
    "memississippiet mississippime mississippiamississippit fimississippive"
set the_items to text items of the_secret_message
set text item delimiters to ""
set the_message to the_items as string
-->"meet me at five"
```

One more thing before we move on: generally, getting and setting the `text item delimiters` property is pretty straightforward, but there is one gotcha you need to watch out for. Any time you need to address the `text item delimiters` property from inside an application's tell block, you must make it clear to AppleScript *exactly* whose `text item delimiters` property you are referring to.

To demonstrate, try running the following script:

```
tell application "Finder"
    set text item delimiters to ":"
end tell
```

The result of this will be an error: "Finder got an error: Can't set text item delimiters to ":"." That's because, unless you tell it otherwise, AppleScript assumes you are referring to a property named `text item delimiters` in the target application. Since most applications, including the Finder, don't have a property by this name, they will throw an error to let you know this.

Fortunately, the solution is a simple one: just make it clear that you are referring to a property of AppleScript itself. To do this, you need to identify the `AppleScript` object, which is where the `text item delimiters` property is found; for example:

```
tell application "Finder"
    set AppleScript's text item delimiters to ":"
end tell
```

Now the script will successfully set AppleScript's `text item delimiters` property to the desired value, exactly as you intended.

Finding and Replacing Text

One use of the `text item delimiters` property is to perform a simple search and replace on strings inside AppleScript. You do this by setting the value of the `text item delimiters` property to the text you want to replace and splitting the text you want to search in into a list. This will remove the search text. Next you set the `text item delimiters` property to the replacement text and combine the list back into a string.

For this example, we will look at a simple way to take template text containing placeholders and personalize it. Imagine that you have a string that is part of some legal text you need to insert at the end of a document. The text was prepared in advance with the placeholders and looks like this: "Let it be known that [company] is responsible for any damage any employee causes during [company]'s activity while in the conference."

Let's imagine that this text is stored as a string in the variable form_text. You also have another variable, called company_name, which will be set to the string "Disney Inc." for these purposes.

Script 7–9 shows the code that will replace the text "[company]" with the specified company name.

Script 7-9.

```
1. set form_text to "Let it be known that [company] is responsible for any damage" ¬
     & " any employee causes during [company]'s activity while in the conference."

2. set text item delimiters to "[company]"
3. set temporary_list to text items of form_text
4. set text item delimiters to "Disney Inc."
5. set finished_form to temporary_list as text
6. set text item delimiters to ""
7. return finished_form
```

You can study the intermediate workings of this script by temporarily inserting a return temporary_list statement after line 5. The value of the temporary_list variable is as follows:

```
--> {"Let it be known that ",
    " is responsible for any damage any employee causes during ",
    "'s activity while in the conference."}
```

Note how the "[company]" placeholder is omitted from the temporary list shown previously.

Now, remove the temporary return statement so that the rest of the script can run as well. The value of the finished_form variable is this text: "Let it be known that Disney Inc. is responsible for any damage any employee causes during Disney Inc.'s activity while in the conference."

How AppleScript Text Works in Tiger

The transition to 100 percent Unicode support in Leopard was undoubtedly the biggest change to occur in the AppleScript language since it was first released in 1993. Sure, the implementation of AppleScript may have changed a lot since then, moving from 68K processors to PPC and then Intel, jumping from Mac OS 9 to Mac OS X, and growing 64-bit support along the way.

None of these behind-the-scenes changes really affected how scripters interacted with AppleScript, though: scripts written even on early versions of AppleScript continued to work, with perhaps just an occasional quick recompile needed.

With the switch to full Unicode, however, AppleScript finally decided to shake things up. Some scripts that worked for years on AppleScript 1.x suddenly required alterations to run smoothly on AppleScript 2.0; although the transition was remarkably smooth considering the amount of change involved, some non-backward-compatible alterations were pretty much inevitable.

As older operating systems such as Tiger fade away, this will become less of a concern for users; however, there are still many older AppleScripts available online that may not have been updated for Leopard. To help you to understand and update old scripts, the next few sections briefly discuss the main "highlights" of working with AppleScript text in Tiger and earlier.

The Many Different Classes of Text

Before Leopard, AppleScript provided multiple classes to describe text objects: string, styled text, international text, and Unicode text. As you might imagine, this could be a bit of a mess to work with at times.

AppleScript's original string class could only represent a limited range of characters. When dealing with older applications that don't support Unicode, Mac OS X picks an old-style character set to be your "primary encoding." Your system's language settings determine the exact character set used—for example, for English and most other European languages, the MacRoman character set, which contains 256 characters, is used. If your system language is Japanese, then the primary encoding will be the MacJapanese character set, which contains several thousand characters. In Tiger and earlier, this primary encoding was used by AppleScript objects of the string class, and also for your source code.

The styled text class was a bit different. Although it was based on your primary encoding, it also held font information. This meant that if your primary encoding didn't contain a particular glyph, a styled text object might still be able to represent it if it could find it in one of the non-Unicode "special symbols" fonts (Symbol, Zapf Dingbats, etc.). This allowed it to represent a larger range of characters than the string class, although still far fewer than could be found in Unicode. One of the quirks of styled text objects was that when you ask them for their class, the result would be string, which meant you could never be entirely sure if you were dealing with a regular unstyled string or a styled one.

The international text class was Apple's own attempt to come up with a Unicode-like standard for representing text, back before Unicode itself was created. Once Unicode came along, this format quickly became redundant, although it lingered for a while in some older applications that had adopted it before Unicode was available.

Finally, the Unicode text class was AppleScript's response to the growing availability of Unicode support in the classic Mac OS, allowing scripts to work directly with Unicode-based text. (The new text class that appears in Mac OS X 10.5 and later is equivalent to the old Unicode text class.) This was a later addition to AppleScript, which probably goes some way toward explaining the multitude of other classes that had already appeared by the time it was introduced.

Working with the Various Text Classes

As AppleScript source code in Tiger and earlier was based on the system's primary encoding, any literal strings in your script would be of the string class; for example:

```
set the_text to "it's all text"
class of the_text
--> string
```

Text coming from other sources such as scriptable applications could be in any format, depending on whether or not the application supported Unicode, needed to work with characters outside the user's primary encoding, and so on. You could also coerce text from one text class to another; for example:

```
set the_text to "it's all text" as Unicode text
class of the_text
--> Unicode text
```

Coercing text of class Unicode text to the string class would also work (the result was actually a styled text object), although any characters that couldn't be represented would be replaced with "?" characters.

Comparing strings of different classes but with the same content returns a true result; for instance:

```
set string_text to "it's all text"
set unicode_text to "it's all text" as unicode text
string_text = unicode_text
--> true
```

However, if you want to check that a given object is some kind of text, but aren't sure if its class is string or Unicode text, then you have to check for both possibilities. For example:

```
if class of the_text is in {string, Unicode text} then
    -- Do something with the text here...
end if
```

If you need the script to run on Mac OS X 10.5 and later as well as on 10.4 and earlier, you also have to check for a third option, text, as that is the class of all text objects in 10.5 onward:

```
if class of the_text is in {text, string, Unicode text} then
    -- Do something with the text here...
end if
```

Another significant difference between string and Unicode text objects is in how the less-than and greater-than comparisons work. As discussed earlier, Unicode defines its own logical rules that determine whether one character comes before or after another, regardless of their physical position in the Unicode character set. With older character sets such as MacRoman, character order is decided purely by position. For example,

```
("?" as Unicode text) < ("0" as Unicode text) -- Comparing Unicode characters
--> true
```

but,

```
"?" < "0" -- Comparing MacRoman characters
--> false
```

The final difference I'll mention here is in how splitting text with text item delimiters works. Strings of class Unicode text respect the script's current considering/ignoring case and diacriticals attributes when getting text item elements. For example:

```
set text item delimiters to "e"
ignoring case and diacriticals
    text items of ("PLEASE read my résumé!" as Unicode text)
end ignoring
```

```
--> {"PL", "AS", " r", "ad my r", "sum", "!"}
```

This matches the behavior of text in AppleScript 2.0.

When dealing with objects of class `string`, however, all `considering`/`ignoring` attributes are ignored and an exact, case-sensitive match is performed instead:

```
set text item delimiters to "e"
ignoring case and diacriticals -- This won't work on text of class string
    text items of "PLEASE read my résumé!"
end considering
--> {"PLEASE r", "ad my résumé!"}
```

If you need text item delimiters to perform case-insensitive matching in Tiger or earlier, you need to make sure your text is coerced to class `Unicode text` before you begin. Similarly, if you want to perform a case-sensitive match but aren't quite sure what class the text is, you'll want to enclose the code in a `considering case ... end considering` block just to be sure.

There are several other differences between the `string` and `Unicode text` classes as well—for example, how `word` elements are determined and which coercions are supported—but because these differences are less important, we won't bother going into them here.

> **TIP:** If you do need to support Tiger and earlier, refer to the original *AppleScript Language Guide* included in Apple's Developer Tools for more information. This mainly covers AppleScript 1.3.7, but much of the content still applies to Tiger's AppleScript, and a list of more recent changes can be found in the AppleScript Release Notes on Apple's developer site (`http://developer.apple.com`).

The ASCII number and ASCII character Commands

Prior to Mac OS X 10.5, AppleScript provided two Standard Additions commands, `ASCII number` and `ASCII character`, for converting single-character strings to and from their corresponding code points. However, as their names suggest, these commands did not support Unicode text, and were only good for working with ASCII and other single-byte-based character sets.

The `ASCII number` command takes a one-character string as its parameter and returns a number from 0 to 255 that indicates its position in the MacRoman character table (or whatever the user's primary encoding is). For instance, the statement `ASCII number space` will return 32, which is the code point of the space character.

The opposite command is `ASCII character`, which accepts a number from 0 to 255 as its parameter and returns the character for that code point. For instance, the statement `ASCII character 36` will return the one-character string $.

Try the following script:

```
display dialog "I love the big " & ASCII character 240
```

While executing the script, AppleScript evaluates the ASCII character 240 command. Assuming your primary encoding is MacRoman, this returns a string containing the Apple logo character, as shown in Figure 7–12.

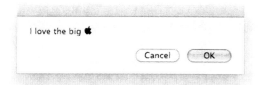

Figure 7–12. *The dialog box displaying MacRoman text with ASCII character 240*

If your primary encoding is a different single-byte character set, then you may get a different symbol instead. As for multibyte character sets such as MacJapanese, they don't work at all well with ASCII number and ASCII character, which are only designed to handle single bytes—another reason why the changes to text handling in AppleScript 2.0 are so welcome.

NOTE: The ASCII number and ASCII character commands still exist in the Standard Additions scripting addition in Leopard and later, but their use should be avoided unless your scripts need to run on Tiger or earlier. Instead, use the text class's id property and the character id specifier to convert AppleScript strings to their corresponding code points and back. This will ensure you get the correct results, no matter what your text might be.

Example Projects

Let's put your new knowledge of AppleScript text to good use in a couple of projects.

The first project is a fairly simple but useful one: defining a new command that will find and replace text in AppleScript. This is a common task, so you will no doubt find this code useful in your own scripts as well.

The second project involves extracting meeting information from an e-mail message in Mail and creating a new iCal entry for it. This task is a bit more specialized, but it demonstrates nicely how AppleScript code can work together with scriptable applications to carry out sophisticated tasks.

Defining a Find-and-Replace Command

Performing find and replace operations with text item delimiters is such a common task that it's worth defining our own find_and_replace command just for this purpose. To do this, we will create a user-defined handler named find_and_replace that we can add to any script that needs it. Although we won't cover handlers properly until later in the book, it won't do any harm to dabble in them a little now.

Let's start by planning the find_and_replace command itself. We've already picked a name for it, so the next step is to decide what parameters it needs.

Just like application commands, user-defined commands can accept any number of objects as parameters. Those objects are then passed into the handler, which can use them however it likes. The principle is the same in both cases, although the syntax for user-defined commands is a bit different.

Anyway, to find and replace a substring within a larger string, the find_and_replace command needs to supply three string objects to the handler: the string to be modified, the substring to search for, and the string that will be inserted in its place. Once the handler is done, it will return a new, modified string as its result.

Once we know what parameters the handler can take, we can begin writing it. A user-defined handler statement consists of an opening line, a closing line, and any number of statements in between. The first line must begin with the keyword on, followed by the handler name, in this case find_and_replace. After the handler name comes a pair of parentheses containing the names of the variable to which each of our three parameter strings will be assigned. Let's call these the_text, search_text, and replacement_text. The last line of the handler consists simply of the keyword end, followed by the name of the handler again.

Here is how the handler looks so far:

```
on find_and_replace(the_text, search_text, replacement_text)
    -- Find-and-replace code goes here...
end find_and_replace
```

Next, we'll fill in the lines of code that will perform the actual find-and-replace work. Take another look at lines 2 to 7 of Script 7–9 to remind yourself how it did this part:

```
2. set text item delimiters to "[company]"
3. set temporary_list to text items of form_text
4. set text item delimiters to "Disney Inc."
5. set finished_form to temporary_list as text
6. set text item delimiters to ""
7. return finished_form
```

Line 2 sets AppleScript's text item delimiters to the string to be found, and then line 3 breaks up the original string according to this delimiter and stores the resulting list in a temporary variable. Line 4 sets the text item delimiters to the text to insert into the gaps, and line 5 coerces the temporary list back into a string. Line 6 resets the text item delimiters to their default value; although you don't have to do this, some AppleScripters consider it good manners to do so. Line 7 returns the finished result.

The only changes we have to make to this code are to replace the hard-coded delimiter strings with the `search_text` and `replacement_text` variables and rename the other variables to something a bit more generic (`the_text` and `finished_text`).

Because this handler may be used in a variety of situations, we'll also improve the way that it manages the `text item delimiters` property. Instead of simply setting the property to an empty string, we will preserve its current value at the start of the handler and restore it at the end. That way, a script can set the `text item delimiters` property to a particular value, send some `find_and_replace` commands, and then safely perform some other tasks using the delimiters it set earlier.

Let's put it all together. Here is the assembled handler after these tweaks have been made:

```
on find_and_replace(the_text, search_text, replacement_text)
    set old_delims to text item delimiters
    set text item delimiters to search_text
    set temporary_list to text items of the_text
    set text item delimiters to replacement_text
    set finished_text to temporary_list as text
    set text item delimiters to old_delims
    return finished_text
end find_and_replace
```

Now, whenever you want to perform a find-and-replace job on an AppleScript string, all you need to do is add this handler to your script. For example, Script 7–10 shows the result of rewriting Script 7–9 to use the new `find_and_replace` handler.

Script 7–10.

```
set form_text to "Let it be known that [company] is responsible for any damage" ¬
        & " any employee causes during [company]'s activity while in the conference."
set finished_form to find_and_replace(form_text, "[company]", "Disney Inc.")

on find_and_replace(the_text, search_text, replacement_text)
    set old_delims to text item delimiters
    set text item delimiters to search_text
    set temporary_list to text items of the_text
    set text item delimiters to replacement_text
    set finished_text to temporary_list as text
    set text item delimiters to old_delims
    return finished_text
end find_and_replace
```

Run it, and the result should be exactly the same as before.

Now, you might be wondering what the point was of reworking this particular script to use a handler—after all, it hasn't made it any shorter or simpler. True; but now that you've written the handler once, you can quickly add it to *any* script that needs it, instead of rewriting the find-and-replace code from scratch.

There are also times when you need to find and replace text in several different areas of a script. Without a handler, you would need to copy and paste the find-and-replace code multiple times, making your code larger and more complicated than necessary.

You can avoid this situation by adding a single `find_and_replace` handler and using multiple `find_and_replace` commands instead.

> **TIP:** If you want to consider case or ignore diacritical marks when finding and replacing text, just wrap your individual `find_and_replace` commands in the appropriate `considering`/`ignoring` blocks and AppleScript will automatically apply those attributes to the code in your `find_and_replace` handler.

Transferring Meeting Arrangements from Mail to iCal

From my experience, looking at the words and paragraphs components of strings can be extremely useful. Either breaking down a text file into paragraphs and looping through them or referencing the paragraphs of a string one by one is essential, and asking for every word of some text is great for finding the information you need.

As an exercise, let's create a script that will parse some text and use the information. The script is one I actually use myself for scheduling purposes. One of my large clients has scheduling software that sends e-mails to me whenever I'm scheduled to be part of a meeting. The e-mails are well formatted, and their content is completely predictable and reliable, because a computer generates them. The e-mail contains, in plain text, information about the location and time of the meeting and some other general information. The goal of the script you are going to create is to convert these e-mails into events in your iCal calendar.

We will start by creating the script as a single flow, from top to bottom. The first part will gather the text from the message in Apple's Mail application. Then, we will extract the actual meeting information from that text, and we will end by adding a new event to iCal with the information we've collected.

> **NOTE:** When designing a script for other people to use, you should make the script as reliable and safe to use as you can; for example, by checking that the user selected a suitable message in Mail before processing it, and halting the script with a helpful explanation: "Please make sure an e-mail message containing meeting arrangements is selected in Mail's message viewer window, and run this script again." This sort of user-friendly error handling takes time to design and develop, and makes scripts larger and more complex, but it ensures that different errors are reported to the user in a way they can understand and deal with. For now, we'll leave out any special error checking or reporting code in order to keep the project as simple as possible, but once you've learned how to deal with errors in Chapter 15, you can always add your own improvements.

Getting the Message from Mail

The script will start by extracting the raw information from Mail. We will assume that there's a message selected and that it contains text formatted to our expectations.

Like many applications, Mail provides a `selection` property that identifies the current graphical user interface (GUI) selection. The `selection` property belongs to the `application` object and therefore can be accessed from within the initial application `tell` block.

In Mail, like some other applications, the `selection` property contains a list that can include any number of items or no items at all; in this case, it holds only a single item, and we need to retrieve it to get its text.

Before you start writing here, make sure the Mail application is running. Type the content of the message from the following text into a new outgoing e-mail and send it to your own e-mail address:

Meeting Reminder

Subject: Preapproval of the meeting proposed in the initial proposal draft

When: Friday, October 2, 2009, 8:30 AM to 9:30 AM (GMT–05:00) Eastern Time

Where: Break Room in the Marketing Wing

Next, pick up your new mail, and make sure this message is selected in the inbox of Mail's message viewer window. This message will serve as your test data as you write and test this script.

I realize you might not be using Mail, or that you might prefer to ignore this task while developing and testing the rest of the script. If so, you can insert the following code instead:

```
set message_text to "Meeting Reminder
Subject: Preapproval of the meeting proposed in the initial proposal draft
When: Friday, October 2, 2009, 8:30 AM to 9:30 AM (GMT-05:00) Eastern Time
Where: Break Room in the Marketing Wing"
```

This will create the dummy text within AppleScript itself and assign it to the variable named message_text. This way you can bypass Mail and get right to cleaning the text in the next section.

All this, by the way, isn't just logistics that relate strictly to learning AppleScript from this book; these are different tasks you should perform while writing actual scripts, including creating dummy data, creating objects in an application to use in testing, and so on.

Assuming you are a fan of Mail, let's begin by looking at how we can extract the message content. For this exercise, we'll assume the user will select the e-mail message they want and then run the script manually. There are other approaches we could use—for example, using a Mail rule to run the script automatically whenever a new e-mail arrives—but this way is simplest to understand and also an ideal first step because it's quick and easy to test out.

To get a list of the currently selected e-mail messages, we use the `selection` property of Mail's application object. Figure 7–13 shows that the `selection` property is defined as part of the `application` class's definition in the Mail suite.

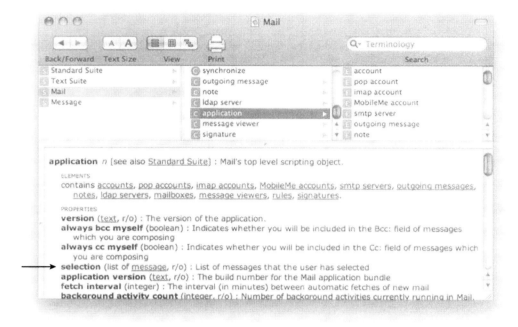

Figure 7–13. *Part of the Mail application's dictionary, showing the* `selection` *property of the main* `application` *class*

Write the following lines, and run the script:

```
tell application "Mail"
   get selection
end tell
```

Assuming you have selected only the test e-mail that you just sent to yourself, the result is a list containing a single reference to the selected message object. Here is a typical example of this:

```
--> {message id 70854 of mailbox "INBOX" of account "your.name@example.org"
   of application "Mail"}
```

Since we want only the first reference and not the entire list, let's change the script to get the first item of the list:

```
tell application "Mail"
   get item 1 of (get selection)
end tell
```

NOTE: Notice that we're using `item 1 of (get selection)` here instead of `item 1 of selection`. That's because we have to get the entire list out of Mail first and then use AppleScript to extract the item we want.

Now that we have a reference to the message we're interested in, let's go all the way and extract the text. In Mail, every message object has a `content` property that includes the body text of the message. You can see this in Mail's dictionary if you look at the `message` class definition in the Message suite, as shown in Figure 7–14.

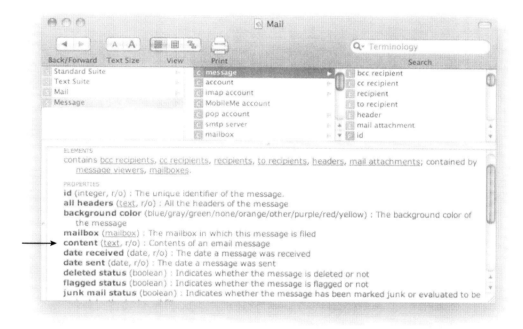

Figure 7–14. *Part of the Mail application's dictionary, showing the* content *property defined by the* message *class*

What we need is to get the value of the selected message's `content` property into a variable. Here is how:

```
tell application "Mail"
    set the_message to item 1 of (get selection)
    set message_text to content of the_message
end tell
```

Run this script, and the result should be a string that looks like this:

```
--> "Meeting Reminder
Subject: Preapproval of the meeting proposed in the initial proposal draft
When: Friday, October 2, 2009, 8:30 AM to 9:30 AM (GMT-05:00) Eastern Time
Where: Break Room in the Marketing Wing"
```

Notice that the message text has four paragraphs and that the information we want is concentrated in paragraphs 2, 3, and 4.

Parsing the Message Text

Now that we've retrieved the raw message text, the next step is to break it down and extract the bits we want.

Let's add the lines of code that assign the contents of these paragraphs to different variables. We will make the identifiers of these variables as descriptive as you can:

```
set message_subject_line to paragraph 2 of message_text
set message_dates_line to paragraph 3 of message_text
set message_location_line to paragraph 4 of message_text
```

Now we can start to turn the text into the information we need. If you examine iCal's dictionary, you can see that it includes an event class. That is the class of the object we need to create. Figure 7–15 shows the definition for iCal's event class in AppleScript Editor's dictionary viewer.

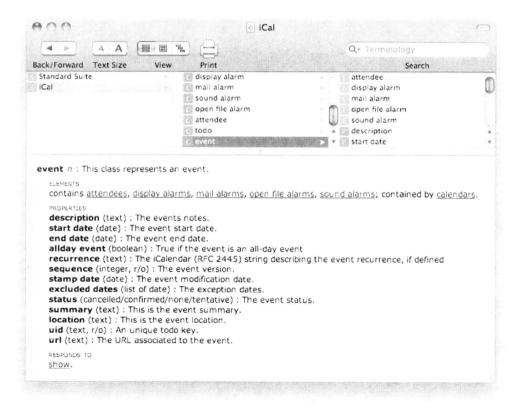

Figure 7–15. *Viewing the definition of iCal's event class in AppleScript Editor*

As you can see, an event object has over a dozen properties (including the ones defined by the parent item class), out of which five are of interest to us: start date, end date, summary, location, and status.

Of these four properties, start date and end date need an object of class date, summary takes a string, and the status property takes one of the following iCal-defined constants: none, cancelled, tentative, or confirmed.

Anyway, the next job is to create four variables that hold objects ready to go into the first four of these properties. We'll call these variables start_date, end_date, the_summary, and the_location. For the status property, we will just insert the confirmed value directly.

The next portion of the script will mold the plain text we got from the message into data that will fit into these variables. Let's start with a couple of easy ones: summary and location. These are both just text descriptions, and the text in the message_subject_line and message_location_line variables is almost perfect as it is. The only thing we'll do to improve them is remove the label at the start of each line.

Since we know that each label always consists of a single word, we will ask AppleScript for the text range beginning at the second word and ending at the end of the string. Add the following line:

```
set the_summary to text (word 2) thru -1 of message_subject_line
```

Run the script to make sure it works. The result is as follows:

```
--> "Preapproval of the meeting proposed in the initial proposal draft"
```

Now do the same for the message location line and test that as well:

```
set the_location to text (word 2) thru -1 of message_location_line
--> "Break Room in the Marketing Wing"
```

Next, we need to attend to the dates. Let's start by breaking down the message_dates_line variable into words. Because this task is a bit more complex, you might find it helps to work in a separate, temporary document in AppleScript Editor until you have a solution, so create a new document and then type the following code to assign a dummy value to a message_dates_line variable there:

```
set message_dates_line to ¬
    "When: Friday, October 2, 2009, 8:30 AM to 9:30 AM (GMT-05:00) Eastern Time"
```

The first task is to figure out exactly how to break this text down to get the words we need, so type the following:

```
words of message_dates_line
```

Run the script, copy the result, and paste it in any text editor or into a blank script window. We will use that text as a reference, allowing us to see what the different words are and their order.

The result should be a list with 17 items:

```
--> {"When", "Friday", "October", "2", "2009", "8", "30", "AM", "to",
    "9", "30", "AM", "GMT", "05", "00", "Eastern", "Time"}
```

A quick analysis reveals that items 3, 4, and 5 contain the date; items 6, 7, and 8 make up the start time; and items 10, 11, and 12 make up the end time.

In AppleScript, a date object contains both a date and a time. In fact, if we don't specify a time, AppleScript assigns midnight of that date as the time.

In this case, we will create two strings: one will have the date and the start time, and the other will have the same date and the end time. We will then convert these strings into date objects so that they can be used by iCal.

First, though, we need to assemble the strings. Here is one way we can do it:

```
set the_meeting_date to ¬
    word 3 of message_dates_line & space & ¬
    word 4 of message_dates_line & ", " & ¬
    word 5 of message_dates_line
set the_start_time to ¬
    word 6 of message_dates_line & ":" & ¬
    word 7 of message_dates_line & space & ¬
    word 8 of message_dates_line
set the_end_time to ¬
    word 10 of message_dates_line & ":" & ¬
    word 11 of message_dates_line & space & ¬
    word 12 of message_dates_line
```

Let's examine these variables. Add the following line:

```
return the_meeting_date
```

What you will get is a string containing the date only, "March 2, 2001". You can do the same with the other variables to examine their values for accuracy.

Although this approach will do the job, another, more elegant solution is to use some more fancy text range references to get the substrings we want directly:

```
set the_meeting_date to text (word 3) thru (word 5) of message_dates_line
set the_start_time to text (word 6) thru (word 8) of message_dates_line
set the_end_time to text (word 10) thru (word 12) of message_dates_line
```

You can probably guess which technique I like most—if only because it saves me a bunch of typing!

The next two lines concatenate the date string and each of the strings containing the start time and end time and convert them into date objects:

```
set start_date to date (the_meeting_date & space & the_start_time)
set end_date to date (the_meeting_date & space & the_end_time)
```

Run the script to see how AppleScript has converted each date-time string into a date object. As long as you give AppleScript some sort of a date containing at least the month, day, and year, it'll take it from there and make it into a date it can understand.

> **NOTE:** The way in which AppleScript converts date strings to date objects depends on your system settings. This example assumes you're using US-style dates or similar. If your settings are different and the script reports an error when creating date objects, go to the Formats tab of the Language & Text panel in System Preferences and temporarily change the region to United States while testing this script. I'll discuss these issues in further detail in Chapter 9, and also look at an alternative way to create date objects that will always work, regardless of a user's date and time preferences.

Once you are happy with your date parsing code, copy those lines into the main script. Now that the text parsing code is complete, it's time to begin the final stage.

Creating the Event in iCal

At this point, we have all the information that our script needs neatly formatted into dates, text, and so on. Now let's create the event in iCal.

iCal's object model starts with the application object, which contains calendar elements, each of which can contain event elements. To create a new event object, we must first identify an existing calendar object that will contain this event. Since a working iCal application must have at least one calendar element, we can safely talk to calendar 1. Here is the tell block we will use to talk to iCal:

```
tell application "iCal"
    -- Commands go here...
end tell
```

I always complete the tell blocks first before inserting the command. This is a way to eliminate nagging little typos that will steal more debugging time than they deserve.

Now, type the following line in the tell block:

```
make new event at end of calendar 1 with properties ¬
    {start date:start_date, end date:end_date, ¬
    summary:the_summary, location:the_location, status:confirmed}
```

This statement starts with the make command. The new parameter is event, which is the class of the object we're creating. The at parameter indicates where the new event object should appear, in this case at the end of calendar 1's existing event elements. iCal is smart enough to work out that end of calendar 1 really means end of elements of calendar 1, which saves some extra typing. Also, as part of the make command, we can specify initial values for some or all of the new object's properties. This is a fast and efficient way to set the start date, end date, and so on.

Script 7–11 shows the finished script.

Script 7–11.

```
-- Get the message text from Mail
tell application "Mail"
```

```
      set the_message to item 1 of (get selection)
      set message_text to content of the_message
   end tell

   -- Parse the message text
   set message_subject_line to paragraph 2 of message_text
   set message_dates_line to paragraph 3 of message_text
   set message_location_line to paragraph 4 of message_text

   set the_summary to text (word 2) thru -1 of message_subject_line
   set the_location to text (word 2) thru -1 of message_location_line

   set the_meeting_date to text (word 3) thru (word 5) of message_dates_line
   set the_start_time to text (word 6) thru (word 8) of message_dates_line
   set the_end_time to text (word 10) thru (word 12) of message_dates_line

   set start_date to date (the_meeting_date & space & the_start_time)
   set end_date to date (the_meeting_date & space & the_end_time)

   -- Create the iCal event
   tell application "iCal"
      make new event at end of calendar 1 with properties ¬
         {start date:start_date, end date:end_date, ¬
         summary:the_summary, location:the_location, status:confirmed}
   end tell
```

Make sure that you've deleted or commented out any temporary test code, check that your test mail message is still selected in Mail, and run the script to find out if it works! If all goes well, a new event should appear in iCal, as shown in Figure 7–16.

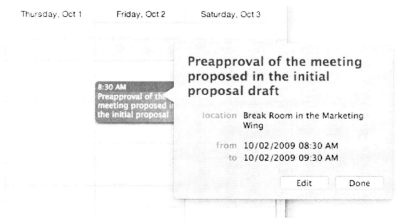

Figure 7–16. *The iCal event created using the information from the Mail message*

Summary

Whew! As you can see, text in AppleScript is a pretty big subject, so let's take a moment to review what you've learned before we move on to the next topic.

We started with a quick crash course on how computers deal with text in general. You learned that computer hardware doesn't understand human-readable text, only numbers, so the operating system and applications rely on character sets to map different characters (glyphs) to numbers (code points) that computers can understand. You were introduced to some of the character sets that have been used over the years, including ASCII, MacRoman, and Unicode. You learned about the shortcomings of the older character sets and why the modern replacement to them, Unicode, is a good thing in general.

Fortunately, you won't have to worry about character set issues too much when working in AppleScript because from Mac OS X 10.5 onward the entire language is based on Unicode and nothing else. You will have to deal with them when you start reading and writing text files directly in AppleScript, but we'll cover those issues later on in Chapter 17.

Having gotten all the boring background and jargon out of the way, we next looked at the various properties and elements that AppleScript's text class defines for extracting information from AppleScript text objects (or *strings*, as most scripters like to call them). You learned how to extract individual characters, words, and paragraphs from strings, and how to retrieve a substring by referring to the original string's text elements.

Next we covered the various operators you can use to concatenate, compare, and coerce strings, followed by the standard commands, count and offset, that you can use to measure strings and search them.

In the "Working with Text Item Delimiters" section, we looked at the coolest string-related feature of all: text item delimiters. You discovered how to pull a piece of text apart using the text item delimiters property and the string's text item elements, and how to put it together again using a list-to-text coercion. We looked briefly at how to use these techniques to find a particular phrase in a piece of text and replace it with another.

Finally, following a quick reference section to help you understand how text works differently in pre-Leopard versions of AppleScript (useful if you need to write, maintain, or update Panther- or Tiger-based scripts), we developed a couple of practical projects that involve text manipulation.

The first project created a custom find_and_replace handler that your own scripts can use to find and replace text in any string, simply by sending a find_and_replace command to themselves.

The second project produced a complete script that can extract information from a pre-formatted e-mail message in Mail and then parse out the important details and put them into iCal as a new event. Integrating desktop applications in this way is the biggest reason for learning and using AppleScript in the first place. As you can see, it is possible to achieve some impressive results with just a little bit of AppleScript "glue" code and some powerful scriptable applications at your disposal.

Now that you've got your head around AppleScript strings, it's time to move on to the next class (or classes) of objects you'll use in AppleScript: numbers.

Chapter 8

Working with Numbers

No matter what you do in AppleScript, numbers and math are everywhere—page layout automation, database interaction, and system administration; all require some kind of number manipulation. Some of my graphic-intensive scripts even forced me to pick up a trigonometry book and figure out triangles, sines, and cosines! Throughout the book, you will be attacking number problems and using the concepts covered in this chapter.

Introducing Integers and Reals

AppleScript supports two classes of numbers: `integer` and `real`. An integer is a whole number without a decimal fraction and with no potential of ever getting one. Integers can, however, be negative numbers. Real numbers, on the other hand, have decimal points, even if the decimal point is ceremonial, like in the case of the real 1.0. It's equal in value to the integer 1, but it is a real nonetheless.

When you do math, some operations return reals and some return integers. This generally isn't an issue because reals and integers can be used pretty much interchangeably in AppleScript. You can always use an integer in any situation where a real number is expected, and you can usually use a real number in place of an integer (though if it has a fractional part, AppleScript may round it to the nearest whole number for you).

Here are some examples of integers,

```
0
3
-712
536870911
```

and some examples of reals:

```
3.0
-0.017
8591.2
4.51E+19
1.577E-10
```

You can find out the exact class of a number by getting the value of its `class` property:

```
class of 2003
--> integer
```

```
class of 1.5
--> real
```

Real numbers have the tendency to be written using exponential notation, which is the scientific form of a number used to shrink the length of a number while (for the most part) not changing its value. You can write large numbers in AppleScript in their long form (say, 120,000,000), but as soon as the script is compiled, these long numbers get converted to their exponential forms, which can prove irritating.

For example, try to write the following in a new AppleScript Editor window:

```
10000.0
```

When you compile the script, the number will change to this:

```
1.0E+4
```

In mathematical terms, the number breaks down into the coefficient, which is always a number from 1.0 up to, but not including, 10.0, and the exponent, which is the number appearing after the E, in this case +4.

> **NOTE:** Using traditional scientific notation, 10,000 would be written as 1.0×10^4. However, you can't use true multiplication signs or superscript text in AppleScript code, so an equivalent "E notation" is used instead.

In other words, AppleScript tells you, "I moved the decimal point four spots to the left." Move the decimal point back, and you have your 10,000 back.

It's simple, really! If you take the number 12345678.7654321 and compile it in a script window, it will be displayed as 1.23456787654321E+7. All you have to do is shift the decimal point seven spaces to the right to get the number 12345678.7654321.

The same decimal-shifting idea works with negative exponential numbers. That doesn't mean the number itself is negative, just that the direction of the decimal point is. For example, 1.0E-4 is actually 0.0001. Notice the decimal point moved four spots to the right. Move the decimal, and you get the number.

> **TIP:** AppleScript automatically displays any real number that is less than 0.0001 or greater than 10,000 using E notation; otherwise, the number is displayed as is.

Operators and Commands

AppleScript provides a number of math operators for performing simple arithmetic operations, while its comparison operators, which you used in the previous chapter to compare text, are equally adept at performing numerical comparisons. The Standard Additions scripting addition defines two math-related commands, round and random number. The following sections will look at how each of these operators and commands can be put to good use when working with numbers.

Math Operations

Although you can use numbers in many ways that require no more than some counting skills, when you think numbers, you probably think math. I personally love math and look forward to solving any challenging operations a script may require.

The operators you can use with numbers are the familiar ones such as addition, subtraction, division, and so on, and some less often used ones such as div and mod.

Table 8–1 lists and describes the operators you can use with numbers.

Table 8–1. *Math Operators*

Operator	Name	Description
+	Addition	Adds the left and right numbers.
-	Negation (with one operand)	Converts the single number to its right from positive to negative or from negative to positive.
-	Subtraction(with two operands)	Subtracts the right number from the left number.
*	Multiplication	Multiplies the left and right numbers.
/	Division	Divides the left number by the right number.
div	Integral division	Returns the number of times the right number fits whole in the left number.
mod	Remainder (modulo)	Subtracts the right number from the left number repeatedly until the remainder is less than the right number and returns the final remainder.
^	Exponent	Raises the left number to the power of the right number.

Adding, Subtracting, Multiplying, and Dividing Numbers

AppleScript's four basic math operators—addition, subtraction, multiplication, and division—work just as you would expect them to. Here are some examples:

```
5 + 3
--> 8

12 - 8.5
```

```
--> 3.5

3 * 10
--> 30

10 / 4
--> 2.5

7.5 / 2
--> 3.75
```

Notice that integers and reals can be freely mixed together in calculations.

In the following script, I will show how to create a handler that takes a list of numbers and returns a record with a few mathematical facts regarding the list. The resulting record will include the list average, the highest number in the list, and the lowest number in the list. If you fed the following list to the handler,

```
{10, 3, 5, 4, 13}
```

you'd get the following record as the result:

```
{average:7.0, high:13, low:3}
```

Here is the complete script:

```
1. math_facts({10, 3, 5, 4, 13})

2. on math_facts(numbers_list)
3.     set high_number to item 1 of numbers_list
4.     set low_number to item 1 of numbers_list
5.     set numbers_total to 0
6.     repeat with i from 1 to count numbers_list
7.         set the_number to item i of numbers_list
8.         if the_number > high_number then set high_number to the_number
9.         if the_number < low_number then set low_number to the_number
10.        set  numbers_total to numbers_total + the_number
11.    end repeat
12.    set the_average to (numbers_total / (count numbers_list))
13.    return {average:the_average, high:high_number, low:low_number}
14. end math_facts
```

I started by creating three variables, on lines 2, 3, and 4. These variables, for the most part, will hold the values that will return the handler's result. The variables are high_number, low_number, and numbers_total, which will be used to get the list average at the end.

The repeat loop between lines 6 and 11 is the main loop that goes through the numbers in the list and analyzes each number to see whether it fits in the high number or low number spots and to add it to the numbers total.

Line 8 determines whether the currently processed number is larger than the value stored in the high_number variable. If it is, that number will become the new value of the high_number variable. This way, when the repeat loop concludes, the high_number variable will contain the highest number from the number_list variable. Line 9 is responsible for determining the lowest number in a similar fashion.

Line 12 calculates the average of all the numbers by dividing their total, stored in the variable numbers_total, by the number of items in the list.

Line 13 puts all this information into a neatly labeled record and returns it.

Negating Numbers

To convert a number from positive to negative, or vice versa, simply add the minus sign before it, even if the number is in a variable:

```
set n to 500
set reverse_n to -n
--> -500
```

In this situation, the minus operator is the unary *negation* operator, not the binary *subtraction* operator that allows you to subtract one number from the other. (*Unary* means an operator has only one operand; *binary* means an operator has two of them.)

The following user-defined handler uses the negation operator to calculate the absolute value of a given number:

```
on abs_num(n)
    if n < 0 then set n to -n
    return n
end abs_num
```

Let's say you need to calculate the difference between two distances. The subtraction operation may return a positive or negative number depending on which operand is larger; however, the final result should always be a positive number. How can we ensure this? The solution is simple: just add the abs_num handler to the script and, once the subtraction is performed, use an abs_num command to get the absolute value of the result:

```
set d1 to 23
set d2 to 45.5
abs_num(d1 - d2)
--> 22.5
```

Calculating the Integral and Remainder

Now let's look at the mod and div operators. Although mod and div are used less often than other math operators, when you need them, they really shine.

mod and div deal with how many instances of a number can fit inside a different number without breaking. For instance, div can tell you that 2 can fit three times in 7.5, while mod will tell you that after you fit 2 in 7.5 three times, the remainder is 1.5:

```
7.5 div 2
--> 3
```

```
7.5 mod 2
--> 1.5
```

Why is this so great? Well, I'll discuss a couple of uses of div and mod. First, what if you want to take a large number of seconds and show it as minutes and seconds? You can do something like this:

```
set total_seconds to 735
set the_minutes to total_seconds div 60
set extra_seconds to total_seconds mod 60
set the_time to (the_minutes as text) & ":" & extra_seconds
--> "12:15"
```

Second—say you are printing postcards—what if you need to fit four postcards per page, and the number of postcards changes from job to job? If a job has 27 postcards, how many whole pages will you need? You need the following calculation:

```
set total_postcards to 27
set postcards_per_page to 4
set whole_pages to total_postcards div postcards_per_page
if whole_pages mod postcards_per_page ≠ 0 then
    set whole_pages to whole_pages + 1
end if
return whole_pages
--> 7
```

27 div 4 returns 6, because 4 fits 6 times into 27, so we know we will completely fill six pages. We then use the mod operator to check whether we need a partially filled page at the end. If the remainder is 0, it means that the division is perfect—for example, 24 postcards would fit exactly onto 6 pages. But if the remainder is not 0, then you need to add a page for the remaining postcards.

You can also use the mod operator to check whether a number is whole or not:

```
on is_whole_number(n)
    return n mod 1 = 0
end is_whole_number
```

n mod 1 calculates the fractional part of the number; for example, 2.0 mod 1 returns 0.0, while 3.3 mod 1 returns 0.3. We then check whether this value is 0—if it is, we know the original number was whole, and if it isn't, we know it must have had a fractional part:

```
is_whole_number(2.0)
--> true

is_whole_number(3.3)
--> false
```

Using the Exponent Operator

The final math operator we'll look at is the exponent (^) operator, which raises the left operand to the power of the right operand. For example, to calculate the cube of 2, use the following:

```
2 ^ 3
--> 8.0
```

To calculate the square root of 9, use the following:

```
9 ^ 0.5
--> 3
```

The following example combines the exponent operator to calculate the distance between two points—with a little help from Greek mathematician Pythagoras:

```
on distance_between_two_points(x1, y1, x2, y2)
    set dx to x1 - x2
    set dy to y1 - y2
    return ((dx ^ 2) + (dy ^ 2)) ^ 0.5
end distance_between_two_points
```

The `distance_between_two_points` handler takes four parameters representing the X and Y coordinates of each point. The next two lines work out the horizontal and vertical distances, which represent the lengths of the two short sides of a right-angled triangle. The last line employs the Pythagorean theorem ($a^2 + b^2 = c^2$, or *The square of the hypotenuse of a right triangle is equal to the sum of the squares on the other two sides*) to calculate the length of the longest edge of the triangle, or the distance between the two points.

For example, given the points (1, –2) and (4, 2), we can calculate the distance between these two points as follows:

```
distance_between_two_points(1, -2, 4, 2)
--> 5.0
```

Comparison Operations

You also have the comparison operators, which return a Boolean object (that is, `true` or `false`). Table 8–2 describes the comparison operations you can use with numbers.

Table 8–2. Comparison Operators

Operator	Name	Description
=	Is equal to	Returns `true` if both operands are the same.
≠	Is not equal to	Returns `true` if the operands are different.
<	Is less than	Returns `true` if the left operand is less than the right operand.
≤	Is less than or equal to	Returns `true` if the left operand is less than or equal to the right operand.
>	Is greater than	Returns `true` if the left operand is greater than the right operand.
≥	Is greater than or equal to	Returns `true` if the left operand is greater than or equal to the right operand.

> **TIP:** On a US-style keyboard, type Option-equal (=) to insert the ≠ symbol, Option-comma (,) to insert ≤, and Option-period (.) to insert ≥. Or you can use plain English equivalents if you prefer: `is not equal to`, `is less than or equal to`, and `is greater than or equal to`—see Chapter 13 for more information on operator synonyms.

Here are some examples:

```
3 = 6
--> false

7.0 = 7
--> true

3.7 ≠ -5
--> true

0.5 > -39
--> true

14 ≥ 14
--> true

-2 < -5
--> false

0.7 ≤ 0.5
--> false
```

> **CAUTION:** If you are used to working in other scripting languages, take care. Most languages use = to assign values to variables, == to compare for equality, and != to compare for inequality. In AppleScript, using == and != will prevent the script from compiling, while the = symbol performs a comparison, not an assignment.

Comparing Reals Can Be Trickier Than You Think

So far, working with numbers seems straightforward—and it is…usually. Unfortunately, there is one caveat, which has to do with the way that computer hardware represents real numbers.

Consider the following code:

```
0.7 * 0.7
```

Run it, and AppleScript Editor displays exactly the result you'd expect: `0.49`. Now run the following:

```
0.7 * 0.7 = 0.49
```

The result should be `true`, right? Well, try it and see:

```
0.7 * 0.7 = 0.49
--> false
```

Yikes, that makes no sense at all! Aren't computers meant to be precise and predictable? Well, they are predictable (when you know what to expect), but being 100 percent precise can be surprisingly difficult for some tasks. The problem is that the computer hardware uses a limited number of bits to represent real ("floating-point") numbers: 64 bits to be exact. Some real numbers can be perfectly represented in 64 bits or less, but others are only an approximation—close enough for most purposes, but not absolutely accurate.

Because the limited precision of real numbers is due to the limitations of the underlying hardware, it is something that all programmers have to live with, regardless of the language they're using.

> **CAUTION:** Just to add to the confusion, the tiny rounding errors that exist in some real numbers aren't always visible within AppleScript. For example, 0.49 is really 0.4899999999999, but appears as 0.49 in source code and script results. So everything looks okay on the surface, but it could give you an unwanted surprise if you aren't aware of what's going on underneath.

For most tasks involving real numbers, the slight loss of precision isn't a practical problem—the results are "good enough." In situations where absolute precision is really needed—most often when comparing one real number against another—you just have to allow a certain amount of leeway. For example, rather than using a simple equality test, a safer solution is to check that the number you're testing is within a certain range, like this:

```
set error_margin to 1.0E-10
set the_number to 0.7 * 0.7
the_number > (0.49 - error_margin) and the_number < (0.49 + error_margin)
--> true
```

As long the lower limit of the range is fractionally less than the number you want and the upper limit is marginally above the number you want, this will compensate for any imprecision that might exist in the numbers used.

Performing Multiple Comparisons

Comparison operators can be quite boring when used one at a time. However, when you gang them up, you can create some mighty powerful, and also rather confusing, expressions.

A simple expression may look like this:

```
the_age ≥ 18
```

This evaluates whether the value of the variable the_age is equal to or greater than 18. This expression will return true or false. You can combine this simple expression with other simple expressions to carry out a complex task. Suppose you need to write a statement that will approve or reject a credit card application. You'd need to check for a number of true-or-false conditions such as age, household income, bankruptcies, credit ratings, current debts, and so on.

You can use AppleScript's three Boolean logic operators—and, or, not—to combine two or more simple comparison expressions into a powerful compound expression.

For example, Script 8–1 includes a compound expression that uses multiple comparison operations and no less than nine logical operators to connect everything.

Script 8–1.

```
set is_applicant_approved to ¬
    age ≥ 18 and ¬
    ((bankruptcies = 0 and credit_rating > 700 and debt < 20000) ¬
        or (bankruptcies = 0 and credit_rating > 500 and debt < 10000)) ¬
        or (bankruptcies = 0 and debt > 1000 and will_give_up_first_born)
```

Introducing Operator Precedence

When several operations are combined to create a more complex expression, AppleScript follows a strict set of rules, known as *operator precedence* rules, to decide the exact order in which operations should be performed.

Chapter 13 will explain AppleScript's precedence rules in full, but while we're on the subject of math-related operations, let's take a quick look at how the precedence rules for math operators work. Fortunately, the precedence rules for AppleScript's math operators are much the same as the rules you learned in high school math class, so you should find them fairly easy to remember.

First up, we have the negation (unary minus) operator, -. This has the highest precedence of all math operators, so a negation operator in front of a positive number always gives you a negative number.

Next, we have the exponent operator, ^. Since the negation operator has higher precedence, if you write an expression like this,

```
-2 ^ -2
```

AppleScript will evaluate each of the negation operators first, giving us –2 and –2. It then uses these two values as operands to the exponent operator, to produce the final result (0.25).

Following the exponent operator, we have several operators all with equal precedence: multiplication (*), division (/), integral division (div), and remainder (mod). And beneath these we have the addition (+) and subtraction (binary minus, -) operators, which also have the same level of precedence as each other. This means that if you write an expression like this,

```
3 + 2 * 6 - 4 / 8
```

the multiplication and division operations will be evaluated first, since they have the highest precedence in this case. This gives us the following intermediate result:

```
3 + 12 - 0.5
```

The addition and subtraction operations have equal precedence, so they are simply evaluated from left to right to give us the final result:

```
14.5
```

Other operators, such as comparison and Boolean logic operators, have lower precedence still, so in a large, complex expression that contains a mixture of math, comparison, and logic operations, the math operations will normally be performed first, then the comparison operations, and finally the logic operations.

Sometimes the default evaluation order is the one you want, in which case you don't need to do anything more to your code. However, often you'll want AppleScript to follow a different order. By grouping parts of a larger expression within parentheses, (and), you can force AppleScript to resolve the smaller expression within the parentheses before evaluating the larger expression around it. For example, given the following complex expression,

```
(3 + 2) * (6 - 4) / 8
```

the smaller expressions within parentheses are resolved first. At this point, the calculation looks like this:

```
5 * 2 / 8
```

The remaining operations are then evaluated to produce the final result:

```
1.25
```

> **CAUTION:** Take care to position your parentheses correctly, especially if they are deeply nested. Poorly placed parentheses may prevent your script from compiling or cause it to error or produce the wrong result when run.

The *round* Command

Rounding numbers is an important aspect of scripting and programming. Although the round command rounds the number you provide as its direct parameter, you can perform many tasks with the command if you make some modifications to it.

Let's look at the round command in detail. To begin with, the round command takes a direct parameter, which is a real number. The result returned by the round command is an integer.

To test the basic function of the round command, start a new script window, type each of the following lines, and run each line separately to get the result. I included the result on separate lines here:

```
round 1.5
--> 2

round 2.2
```

```
--> 2

round -6.4
--> -6
```

You can fine-tune the behavior of the round command by using its optional rounding parameter. The rounding parameter has five possible values, all of which are constants: up, down, toward zero, to nearest (the default option), and as taught in school. The following sections explain how each option affects the round command's behavior.

Rounding Up

As it sounds, rounding up always rounds to the next higher integer. Here are some examples:

```
round 1.1 rounding up
--> 2

round 5.5 rounding up
--> 6

round -2.9 rounding up
--> -2
```

Rounding Down

The opposite of rounding up, rounding down always rounds to the next lower integer. Here are some examples:

```
round 1.7 rounding down
--> 1

round 5.5 rounding down
--> 5

round -2.1 rounding down
--> -3
```

Rounding Toward Zero

rounding toward zero acts the same as rounding down with positive numbers, and with negative numbers it acts like rounding up would. In other words, it simply "chops off" the decimal portion of the number. Here are a few examples:

```
round 17.5 rounding toward zero
--> 17

round -2.5 rounding toward zero
--> -2
```

Rounding to Nearest

rounding to nearest is the default behavior that will be used if none other is specified. It works as follows:

- If the fractional part is less than .5, AppleScript rounds toward zero.

- If the fractional part is greater than .5, AppleScript rounds away from zero.

- If the fractional part is .5 and the whole part is an odd number, AppleScript rounds away from zero.

- If the fractional part is .5 and the whole part is an even number, AppleScript rounds toward zero.

These rules may sound a bit fussy, but they ensure that exactly half of all numbers round upward and exactly half round downward. This bias-free technique of rounding numbers prevents your results from becoming skewed over time due to cumulative errors. Here are some examples:

```
round 5.5 rounding to nearest
--> 6
```

```
round 4.5 rounding to nearest
--> 4
```

Rounding As Taught in School

rounding as taught in school works almost the same as rounding to nearest, except that numbers whose decimal part is .5 are *always* rounded away from zero. Here are some examples:

```
round 5.5 rounding as taught in school
--> 6
```

```
round 4.5 rounding as taught in school
--> 5
```

```
round -2.5 rounding as taught in school
--> -3
```

> **TIP:** As you can see, the round command only knows how to round to the nearest whole number. Later in the chapter, we will define a new command, `round_to_decimal_places`, for rounding to a specific number of decimal places.

The *random number* Command

What's a programming language without the ability to generate random numbers? "Incomplete" is the answer. Like other languages, AppleScript has a command for generating random numbers named, unsurprisingly, `random number`. You can provide the `random number` command with a number of optional parameters to make it work for you in many ways.

Random Number Result

The `random number` command returns a result that can be either an integer or a real, depending on whether the parameters you provided are reals or integers.

Parameters

You can use the `random number` command as is, without any parameters. The result in that case is a real number from 0 to 1, as shown in Figure 8–1.

Figure 8–1. *The* `random number` *command used without parameters*

The direct parameter you can use is a number, either a real or an integer, following the command. Try this:

```
random number 5
```

The result is an integer from 0 to 5. Next, try this:

```
random number 5.0
```

Now the result is a real number with up to 12 decimal places, also from 0.0 to 5.0. You can also use the range parameters `from` and `to`, like so,

```
random number from 20 to 30
```

or like so:

```
random number from 20.0 to 30.0
```

Note that if you provide a direct parameter as well as `to`/`from` parameters, only the direct parameter is used. For instance, the following command generates an integer from 0 to 3, not a real from 20.0 to 30.0:

```
random number 3 from 20.0 to 30.0
```

The final parameter, with seed, is a bit obscure. It allows you to get the same sequence of "random" numbers each time your script runs.

Okay, so isn't asking for a nonrandom sequence of numbers contrary to the concept of random numbers? Aren't random numbers supposed to always be random? Well, yes, but random number actually uses a *pseudo-random* number generator to produce its results.

Truly random numbers are surprisingly hard to obtain on modern computers, which are designed to be predictable and precise, for obvious reasons. A pseudo-random number generator works around this limitation by obtaining an initial "seed" number calculated from reasonably unpredictable operating system information such as the current date and the times between user input. It then uses some clever math calculations to generate a random-looking sequence of numbers from that seed.

Normally when you run a script that uses the random number command, you want the random numbers to be different each time. Sometimes, however, it is useful to get the same sequence of numbers each time—for example, when repeatedly testing a script. In this case, you can reset the pseudo-random number generator by calling random number once beforehand, giving it a with seed parameter of your choice.

For example, type the following script into AppleScript Editor and run it several times:

```
-- Seed the pseudo-random number generator
random number with seed 1

-- Now generate a non-random sequence of random numbers
set the_numbers to {}
repeat 10 times
    set end of the_numbers to random number from 1 to 100
end repeat
the_numbers
--> {65, 48, 6, 15, 79, 27, 89, 78, 65, 50}
```

As you can see, it returns the same sequence of numbers each time. Try changing the seed number to a different amount, and you will get a different, but still repeatable, sequence.

Any time you want to get an unpredictable sequence of numbers, just disable or delete the random number with seed... command, and random number will go back to using the seed provided by the system.

Coercing to and from Numbers

AppleScript allows you to coerce integer values to several other classes of values: boolean, real, text, and list. Real values can be coerced to integer, text, and list.

The following integer-to-Boolean coercions are supported:

```
0 as boolean
--> false
```

```
1 as boolean
--> true
```

true and `false` can also be coerced back to 1 and 0 again. Trying to coerce other integers to Booleans will give an error, however:

```
3 as boolean
--> Error: Can't make 3 into type boolean.
```

Integers can be coerced directly to reals, for example:

```
678 as real
--> 678.0
```

Reals can also be coerced to integers, but the process is a little more complex.

If the decimal portion is .0, the resulting integer is equal to the original real number:

```
-17.0 as integer
--> -17
```

When the real number has a fractional part, AppleScript follows the same rules as it follows for the round command's rounding to nearest option. That is, it rounds to the nearest whole number *except* when the fractional part is exactly .5, in which case it rounds to the nearest *even* number.

Here are some examples:

```
3.3 as integer
--> 3
```

```
3.7 as integer
--> 4
```

```
3.5 as integer
--> 4
```

```
4.5 as integer
--> 4
```

Integers and reals can be freely coerced to text; for example:

```
1000 as text
--> "1000"
```

```
4.3E+17 as text
--> "4.3E+17"
```

You can also coerce in the other direction, but only if the string contains a correctly formatted number—any other characters will result in a coercion error:

```
"1000" as integer
--> 1000
```

```
"1000" as real
--> 1000.0
```

```
"$1,000,000" as integer
--> Error: Can't make "$1,000,000" into type integer.
```

If you don't want to specify the exact class of number, AppleScript also allows you to coerce to the special number pseudo-class. AppleScript then chooses the most appropriate class for you, depending on whether or not the number has a fractional part:

```
"43" as number
--> 43

"-3.14" as number
--> -3.14
```

Example Projects

Let's finish off with three practical projects that put integers and reals to good use. For the first exercise, you'll develop an enhanced rounding command, `round_to_decimal_places`, which can round a real to a given number of decimal places. The second exercise will produce a simple Blackjack game using basic arithmetic and comparison operators. The final exercise will create a handy kitchen timer application, using the `div` and `mod` operators to perform time-related calculations.

Defining a Round-to-Decimal-Places Command

When you simply round a real number, you get an integer as a result. That's good for some things, but what if you want to round to a certain number of decimal places instead? Take, for example, currency formatting. If you need to calculate a price, you need two decimal points.

In this project, you are going to use AppleScript to calculate the 7 percent Rhode Island state sales tax. For a product that costs $4.99, the total cost with tax will be $5.3393. Using the round command on its own would give you $5, but what you want is $5.34. The solution involves dividing and multiplying the number before and after rounding it.

Here is the script, which is followed by a line-by-line breakdown:

```
1. set the_price to 4.99
2. set sales_tax to 0.07
3. set price_with_tax to the_price + (the_price * sales_tax)
4. price_with_tax * 100
5. round result rounding as taught in school
6. set price_with_tax to result / 100
```

In lines 1 and 2, you assign values to some variables you will use in the script. This is still a good idea even if the values never change. The sales tax is 7 percent, or 0.07. This value is assigned to a well-named variable, `sales_tax`, making its purpose obvious at a glance, especially if it is used in multiple places in your script.

Line 3 multiplies the price and the sales tax values, and then adds the result to the price before tax to obtain the exact price with tax included, which is 5.3393.

Lines 4 to 6 perform the rounding operation. In line 4, you multiply the result by 100. You do this because any real number with two decimal points multiplied by 100 should be whole. To figure out the number to use, you can raise 10 to the power of the number of decimal places you want. Get it? You want to end up with two decimal places, so you do 10^2 to get 100.

To make that result whole, you round it in line 5, using the rounding parameter with the value as taught in school to ensure that a price ending with half a penny or more rounds up to the next penny.

To give the resulting number its two decimal places back, you divide it by 100 in line 6.

> **NOTE:** Lines 4 and 5 in the preceding example don't assign any variables. You could use a temporary variable if you wanted to, but this example used AppleScript's special result variable instead. This is a built-in variable that automatically holds the result of the previous expression. You can do that here because the result of each expression is only used in the following line. The result of line 4 is used in line 5, and the result of line 5 is used in line 6. Chapter 11 will explain this variable in more detail.

Generally, as you math whizzes already know, if you take a number (N) and first multiply it by another number (M) and then divide it by that same number (M), you get your original number. You're counting on that fact, but you've added a little twist: you rounded the number in the middle.

Now that you've worked out the basic process for rounding to a fixed number of decimal places, you need to develop a general-purpose handler that can round to a custom number of decimal places. The handler, called round_to_decimal_places, will accept two parameters:

- The number to round in the real value class.

- The number of decimal places. This will be a small integer that tells the handler what precision you want. For instance, a value of 2 turns 1.66667 to 1.67.

Script 8–2 shows the complete handler, which is followed by a brief explanation of the steps.

Script 8–2.

```
1. on round_to_decimal_places(the_number_to_round, the_decimal_precision)
2.    set multiplier to 10 ^ the_decimal_precision
3.    the_number_to_round * multiplier
4.    round result
5.    return result / multiplier
6. end round_to_decimal_places
```

I already discussed steps 3 through 5 earlier. You multiply the number you want to round and then you round it and divide it by the same number to return it to its original range.

The neat feature here is how you got to the number you need to multiply and divide by. Line 2 takes the number of decimal places that you want, and raises the number 10 by that number. For example, if you want to end up with three decimal places, you do this calculation: 10 ^ 3. The result is 1000, which then is used in the rounding operation.

For example, suppose you want to round 5.1234 to 2 decimal places. Just add the round_to_decimal_places handler to your script, along with the following command:

```
round_to_decimal_places(5.1234, 2)
```

Run the script, and the command returns 5.12.

You can even use a negative integer for the precision, in which case digits to the left of the decimal point will be rounded to 0 as well as any on the right:

```
round_to_decimal_places(1234.567, -2) as integer
--> 1200
```

One last thing: notice that line 2 expects the decimal precision value to be a whole number. What happens if the user then passes a non-whole number by accident? Well, the multiplier value will not be an exact multiple of 10. For example, round_to_decimal_places(1.2345, 2.1) would give a multiplier of 125.892541179417. This would change the number 1.2345 to 155.41434208599 instead of just shifting the decimal point to the right, giving a final result of 1.231208763823—not what you want at all!

While you can use this handler as it is, it would be good to protect against this possibility. The solution is to check beforehand whether the number provided has a fractional part, and throw an error if it does. The following conditional statement uses the is_whole_number handler from earlier in the chapter to check the decimal precision value, and throws an error if it is unsuitable:

```
if not is_whole_number(the_decimal_precision) then
    error "The decimal precision parameter was not a whole number."
end if
```

Add this code to Script 8–2 immediately before line 2, and the improved round_to_decimal_places handler is good to go. (When pasting this handler into your scripts, remember to add the is_whole_number handler as well.)

Blackjack!

To cap off the short random-number topic, I thought it would be appropriate to invite you to play a little game of Blackjack.

To keep the script short and simple for the sake of the example, I have simplified a few rules. In the AppleScript Blackjack game, an ace is always 1, cards 2 to 10 keep their face values, a jack is 11, a queen is 12, and a king is 13.

If this is too much for your purist self, I suggest you add the necessary lines of code to make the game complete, such as to allow an ace to be 1 or 11.

As for my script, here's how I went about it: the two players are the dealer and you. Each of you has a hand of cards. The information regarding that hand is kept in a record. Each player has their own record that includes two properties labeled total and hand. The total property contains your total score that shows whether either of you reached or passed 21, and the hand property contains a string that's used to show you the cards you have and to show the dealer's hand at the end of the game. In that string, cards may appear like so: [5][K], meaning you have a five and a king.

> **NOTE:** Notice that I'm storing each player's information in a compound value called a *record*, which is a collection of properties. Each property consists of a unique label (or name), which is an identifier, and a value. To get or set a property's value, you refer to it by its label. Records are often used to package up closely related pieces of information. You can find more details about records in Chapter 10.

This is how the player's record typically looks:

```
{total:18, hand:"[10][8]"}
```

Later in the script, you'll use the hand property to display the dealer's hand to the player, like this:

```
display dialog (dealer's hand)
```

> **TIP:** You can write the above reference using the more common <property> of <object> style if you like, though on this occasion I find the <object>'s <property> style to be easier to read.

You start the script by setting up some basic variables. The first is a list of cards, presented in the way they should be displayed. So if the drawn card is 12, for instance, you can ask for item 12 of card_marks and get the string "[Q]". You can use that to build the visual display of the hands:

```
set card_marks to {"[A]", "[2]", "[3]", "[4]", "[5]", "[6]", ¬
    "[7]", "[8]", "[9]", "[10]", "[J]", "[Q]", "[K]"}
```

You also initialize the dealer's hand and the player's hand:

```
set dealer to {total:0, hand:""}
set player to {total:0, hand:""}
```

Then you continue by picking cards for the dealer. You simply repeat in a loop until the dealer's card total reaches 17 points or more. If the dealer gets more than 21, the dealer instantly loses:

```
-- Set up dealer hand
repeat
    set drawn_card to random number from 1 to 13
    set dealer's total to dealer's total + drawn_card
    set dealer's hand to dealer's hand & item drawn_card of card_marks
```

Get that last statement? drawn_card is an integer from 1 to 13 (random, of course). You associate the card number with the card symbol by using the integer value in drawn_card to get the corresponding string item from the list stored in the variable card_marks; for instance, if the number drawn is 1, then asking for item 1 of the card_marks list will give you "[A]".

The following conditional statement first checks whether the card total exceeded 21. If it did, the dealer has lost, so a victory message is displayed and then the script stops running. If the card total reached 17 but didn't go beyond 21, then the dealer rests and the script is instructed to leave the repeat loop.

```
if dealer's total > 21 then
    display dialog "Dealer busted. You won! " & return & return & ¬
        "Dealer's hand:  " & dealer's hand buttons {"OK"}
    return
else if dealer's total ≥ 17 then
    exit repeat
end if
end repeat
```

The next segment of the script sets up the player's initial hand by drawing the first two cards and adding them to the player's total:

```
-- Draw first two player cards
repeat 2 times
    set drawn_card to random number from 1 to 13
    set player's total to player's total + drawn_card
    set player's hand to player's hand & item drawn_card of card_marks
end repeat
```

Next, you create a similar loop to the one that built the dealer's hand, but here you interrupt the loop with a dialog box asking the player to either hit or stay.

First, you start the loop:

```
-- Draw any additional player cards
repeat
```

Next, you check whether the player has just busted, in which case the loop should not proceed any further:

```
-- Draw any additional player cards
repeat
    if player's total > 21 then
        set the_outcome to "You busted!"
        exit repeat
    end if
```

On the other hand, if the player is still in the game, then the following line displays the player's hand and requests an action:

```
    display dialog "Your hand:" & return & player's hand buttons {"Hit", "Stay"}
```

Figure 8–2 shows the kind of dialog box that is displayed here.

Figure 8–2. *The player is prompted for the next move.*

Next, the script acts on the decision made by the user:

```
if button returned of result is "Stay" then
    if player's total > dealer's total then
        set the_outcome to "You won!"
    else
        set the_outcome to "You lost!"
    end if
    exit repeat
end if
set drawn_card to random number from 1 to 13
set player's total to player's total + drawn_card
set player's hand to player's hand & item drawn_card of card_marks
end repeat
```

If the player stays, the loop exits. Otherwise, it proceeds to draw a fresh card and then starts over again.

The final task, which is performed once the last loop has exited, is to display the outcome of the game:

```
-- Display the outcome
display dialog the_outcome & return & "* * *" & return & ¬
    "Your hand:  " & player's hand & return & return & ¬
    "Dealer's hand:  " & dealer's hand buttons {"OK"}
```

Figure 8–3 shows a typical result.

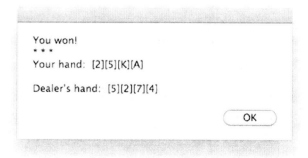

Figure 8–3. *You won!*

That's it for the example, but I'll give you some exercises to prove your super AppleScript ability. Feel free to e-mail your solutions to me.

1. Make the 11, 12, and 13 cards (jack, queen, and king) have a value of 10, not their actual card value as I've programmed them.

2. Make the ace, or 1, have a value of either 1 or 11. This can be quite a challenge since you will need to run an unknown number of scenarios to determine what the dealer's best number is under 21 and when the player exceeds their limit.

3. Put the whole game in a repeat loop, and assign a starting cash allowance of, say, $1,000. Give the player the ability to bet money on each game and add or subtract the bet amount at each round.

Kitchen Timer

To finish off the chapter, I will show you how to create a simple kitchen timer. To keep things simple, you will use a TextEdit document to display the countdown. The document's text will change every second to reflect the remaining time. When the countdown reaches zero, the script will beep several times to alert you that your food is ready.

Here is the script in its entirety:

```
1. set dialog_reply to display dialog "How many minutes?" default answer "120"
2. set total_time_in_minutes to text returned of dialog_reply as integer

3. tell application "TextEdit"
4.     activate
5.     set timer_doc to make new document with properties {text:"00:00:00"}
6.     set size of text of timer_doc to 60
7.     set bounds of window 1 to {100, 100, 400, 250}

8.     repeat with total_minutes_left from (total_time_in_minutes - 1) to 0 by -1
9.         set hours_left to total_minutes_left div 60
10.         set minutes_left to total_minutes_left mod 60
11.         repeat with seconds_left from 59 to 0 by -1
12.             set formatted_time to ¬
                    my pad_with_zero(hours_left) & ":" & ¬
                    my pad_with_zero(minutes_left) & ":" & ¬
                    my pad_with_zero(seconds_left)
13.             set paragraph 1 of text of timer_doc to formatted_time
14.             delay 1
15.         end repeat
16.     end repeat
17. end tell

18. repeat 10 times
19.     beep
20.     delay 0.5
21. end repeat
```

```
22. on pad_with_zero(the_number)
23.    if the_number < 10 then
24.       return "0" & the_number
25.    else
26.       return the_number as text
27.    end if
28. end pad_with_zero
```

As you can see, there are several parts to this script. Let's look at each part in turn.

The script starts by displaying the dialog box shown in Figure 8–4. This asks the user to enter the number of minutes to count from; the default value is 120 minutes.

How many minutes?

120

Cancel   OK

Figure 8–4. *Asking the user to input the number of minutes to count down*

Line 2 takes the text the user typed in the dialog box, converts it to an integer, and stores this integer in a variable, `total_time_in_minutes`, so that it can be used later in the script.

Line 3 identifies the TextEdit application that your script will use to display the countdown, and the `activate` command on line 4 brings it to the front.

Lines 5 to 7 set up the window in which the countdown will be displayed. Line 5 creates a new TextEdit document containing some initial text: "00:00:00". Line 6 increases the size of the text to make it easy to see, and line 7 adjusts the window to a more sensible size.

Lines 8 to 17 make up the main part of the script, which consists of two repeat loops, one inside the other. The outer loop (lines 8 to 17) counts down the number of whole minutes left, while the inner loop (lines 11 to 16) counts down the number of seconds left in each minute. Actually, just like a real timer, the script starts counting from one second earlier than the requested time. To achieve this, the outer loop calculates its starting value by subtracting 1 from the value of the `total_time_in_minutes` variable and then counting to 0 by increments of –1. Each time the outer loop repeats, the inner loop starts at 59 seconds and counts down to 0.

Lines 9 and 10 are where you take the total number of minutes left and separate that number into hours and minutes. The first expression returns the whole number of hours left:

```
total_minutes_left div 60
```

The second expression returns the number of minutes left over:

```
total_minutes_left mod 60
```

For example, if the value of `total_time_in_minutes` is 135, the first expression will return 2, as 60 divides evenly two times in 135. The second expression will return 15, because after you fit 60 into 135 twice, you have a remainder of 15.

The inner repeat loop counts the seconds for each minute. It starts from 59, the number of remaining seconds in that minute, and ends at 0.

Line 12 is responsible for formatting the hour, minute, and second numbers as two-digit strings and then joining them together. For example, if the hours, minutes, and seconds are 2, 15, and 0, respectively, you want the finished text to be "02:15:00". Although AppleScript knows how to convert integers to strings, it doesn't provide a built-in command for adding leading zeros, so you'll use your own command, `pad_with_zero`, to perform this formatting for you. I'll discuss the handler for this command in a moment; for now, all you need to know is that it takes an integer and returns it as a two-digit string. Notice how each `pad_with_zero` command has a my keyword in front of it: because you're using these commands inside of a `tell` block, you must explicitly instruct AppleScript to send them to the current script, not to the target of the `tell` block (TextEdit). Once you have your two-digit strings, you use the concatenation operator, &, to join them all together.

Looking next at the `pad_with_zero` handler defined on lines 22 to 28, it takes a single parameter, which is the integer to format, and returns a string. If the number is less than 10 (assume only non-negative integers are used), you use the concatenation operator (&) to join it to the string "0" to create a two-digit string. Otherwise, you use the coercion operator (as) to convert it to a string as is. For example, if the handler is fed the integer 5, it'll return "05".

Line 13 updates the TextEdit document with the resulting string. Line 14 adds a one-second delay between each update of the countdown window.

When both repeat loops reach zero, the script proceeds to lines 18 to 22, where it beeps repeatedly to inform the user that their time is up. Figure 8–5 shows the countdown window as it appears in TextEdit.

Figure 8–5. *The countdown window displayed in TextEdit*

Summary

In this chapter, you explored the two classes of objects that AppleScript uses to represent numbers: integer (used for whole numbers only) and real. You learned how to perform math and comparison operations on numbers, how to round real numbers to whole values, and how to generate numbers at random. You then put this knowledge to use by developing a custom command for rounding numbers to a given number of decimal places, a fun card game, and a simple timer program.

In the next chapter, you will learn how AppleScript represents another frequently used piece of everyday information: the humble date.

Chapter 9

Working with Dates

Dates play an essential part in everyday life—imagine a world without dates! You'd never know if you were on time, and you'd miss out on all kinds of important events, even your birthday! As you might expect, dates are also important in programming. Think of how dates come into play in the applications you use every day—your operating system, your e-mail client, a lot of the web sites you regularly visit, and so on.

In this chapter, you'll learn how to use dates in AppleScript. As you're about to find out, the date class in AppleScript is versatile and has many hidden aspects that are worth exploring. I'll cover working with dates, using date objects' properties, and performing simple and complex date operations.

Introducing Dates

In AppleScript, objects of class date hold information about a specific second in time. That second includes information about the date, including the time, day, month, and year on which that second falls.

To create a date value, you use a *date specifier*, which is written as the word date followed by a string that describes the date in human-readable form, such as:

```
date "Monday, January 12, 2009 12:00:00 AM"
```

AppleScript provides some flexibility when interpreting that string; for example, you can also write the previous date as date "Jan 12 2009, 12 am" or date "1/12/2009", and AppleScript will figure it out for you. You should note, though, that the way it interprets that string can vary from user to user, depending on their system preferences; I'll discuss this shortly.

> **CAUTION:** For simplicity, this book assumes your Mac is set to use the default US-style date and time formats in the Formats tab of System Preferences' Language & Text panel. If your date and time settings are different, you may need to modify the date-processing code in a few of the scripts.

To create a simple date, start a new window in AppleScript Editor, and type the following:

date "2/3/09"

Now compile the script. As you can see in Figure 9–1, AppleScript takes the liberty of reformatting your date and adding to it the missing time, which is midnight of the date you specified by default. (If your date formatting preferences are set differently, then you may get a different result—more on this in the next section.)

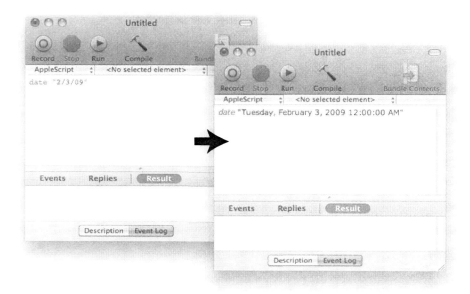

Figure 9–1. date "2/3/09" *before and after it's compiled on a US-style Mac system*

You can, of course, also specify your own time, and this is the time AppleScript will use—try this:

date "2/3/09 1:54 PM"

On Macs that use US date and time formats, AppleScript compiles this specifier as follows:

date "Tuesday, February 3, 2009 1:54:00 PM"

Understanding Date and Time Formats

When AppleScript reads or displays a date string, it interprets it according to the settings in the Language & Text panel of System Preferences. (In Mac OS X 10.5 and earlier, the Language & Text panel is named International.)

Figure 9–2 shows the Formats tab in the Language & Text panel of System Preferences, which you use to modify the format of the date and time for the current user. Although you can change these settings, it may not be a good idea because other applications may rely on them.

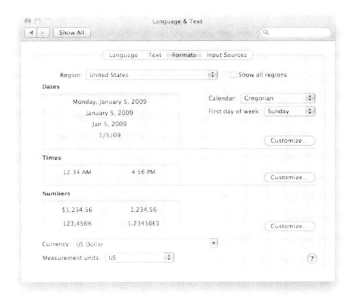

Figure 9–2. *The Formats tab in the Language & Text panel of the Mac OS X System Preferences*

Figure 9–1 shows what appears on my own Mac, which uses the US-style "month/day/year" date format when it creates a date object from the string "2/3/09". Other AppleScript users may get different results, however. A UK-based Mac will normally use a "day/month/year" format, in which case the same date string is interpreted as "2 March 2009" instead, and a Swedish user who uses "year/month/day" will end up with "9 March 2002". Other times they'll get an error; for example, if the string is "2/15/09", then a US-style Mac will read it as "15 February 2009", but Swedish and UK users are told it's an "invalid date and time" because they don't have a 15th month of the year! Weekday and month names are similarly affected. For example, a French-speaking Mac will understand "12 janvier 2009". An English-speaking Mac won't but will understand "12 January 2009" instead.

These sorts of inconsistencies are a result of AppleScript's desire to be user-friendly, of course, and are often convenient when writing and running your own scripts. When sharing your scripts with other users, however, you may sometimes need to tweak any date-related code a little to ensure the scripts work smoothly.

Because the user of the computer on which the script runs is able to change the date format, the script is unreliable for many purposes. For instance, if you want to extract the month from the date, you should avoid using string manipulation like this:

```
word 2 of (the_date as text)
```

That may give the desired result if the host Mac uses default US-style date and time formatting, where a date object looks like this:

```
date " Tuesday, March 2, 201012:00:00 AM"
```

When converted to a string, the second word is "March". The same code could break, however, if the preferences are changed later or the script is run on a different Mac. For example, if the Mac uses UK-style dates, the same date object would look like this:

```
date "Tuesday, 2 March 2010 00:00:00"
```

Coercing this date to text and asking for the second word of the resulting date string would give you "2", not "March", as intended.

This issue, however, becomes moot when you become familiar with the properties of date objects, which provide a much better way to do things. I'll discuss those properties in a bit.

Forming Dates On-the-Fly

AppleScript does have a few default behavior patterns it uses to convert your date strings into a date object. These are important when your script needs to take different values and make up date objects from them. For instance, your script may need to create a date object containing the first day of the month or let the user input a date and make sure AppleScript understands it.

The following date specifiers will all compile properly into date objects (on a US-style Mac; some users may need to tweak them to make them work on their Macs):

```
date "03/03/03"
--> date "Monday, March 3, 2003 12:00:00 AM"

date "5/1/2012"
--> date "Tuesday, May 1, 2012 12:00:00 AM"

date "Feb 28 5:50 AM"
--> date "Saturday, February 28, 0005 12:00:00 AM"

date "3:30 AM"
--> date "Sunday, February 14, 2010 3:30:00 AM"
```

I originally ran these examples on February 14, 2010. Some will return slightly different results if you run them yourself on a different day.

Here are the main rules that AppleScript follows when converting strings into dates:

- The date string must contain a date, a time, or a date followed by a time. If you specify only a date without the time, the default time will be midnight on the date you specified. If you specify only a time without the date, AppleScript will use the date on which the date specifier was evaluated. An invalid date or time will produce an error.

- The format of the date part must match one of the formats shown in the Dates section of the Formats tab in System Preferences' Languages & Text panel. (You can click the Customize button there to view and/or edit the formats used.) You can omit the weekday name if you wish, but the day, month, and year must all appear in the order shown, otherwise an error will occur.

- The format of the time part must match one of the formats shown in the Times section of the Formats tab. You can omit the number of seconds if you wish, but you must give the hours and minutes, and if 12-hour time is used, then you must also include either AM or PM as shown. (You cannot specify a time zone, however, as AppleScript dates do not support this.)

Let's look more closely at the previous date specifiers, before and after AppleScript compiles them.

`date "03/03/03"` compiles as this:

```
date "Monday, March 3, 2003 12:00:00 AM"
```

AppleScript had to tack on the time, which is, by default, midnight.

`date "5/1/2012"` compiles as this:

```
date "Tuesday, May 1, 2012 12:00:00 AM"
```

`date "Feb 28 5:50 AM"` compiles as this:

```
date "Monday, February 28, 2005 12:00:00 AM"
```

Oops! What happened here is that the year hasn't been specified, so AppleScript took the first digit you intended to use for the time and used it for the year. AppleScript ignored the minutes specified because it was looking for an "hours" number by then, and 50 didn't make sense.

`date "3:30"` compiles as this:

```
date "Sunday, February 14, 2010 3:30:00 AM"
```

Here, the time was understood as 3:30 AM, and the date is the date on which the script was compiled.

The following example prompts the user to enter a date as text, and then uses this string to create a date object.

```
display dialog "Enter date (e.g. 3/15/2010):" default answer ""
set user_date to text returned of result
set the_date to date user_date
```

Line 1 of the script asks the user to enter a date and gives a format to follow. Figure 9–3 shows the dialog box.

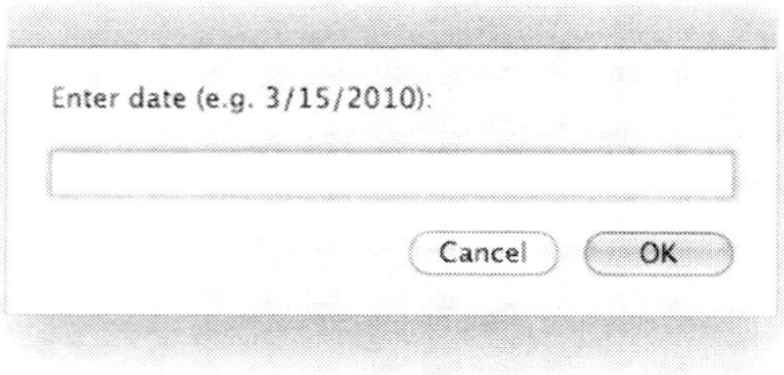

Enter date (e.g. 3/15/2010):

Cancel   OK

Figure 9–3. *The input dialog box asks the user to enter a date.*

Line 2 assigns the user's typed text to the user_date variable. The value of user_date is a string that was returned from the display dialog command.

Line 3 retrieves this string from the user_date variable and uses it in a date specifier. If the user entered a valid date, then the result is a date object; otherwise, AppleScript will report an "Invalid date and time" error.

> **CAUTION:** Prior to Mac OS X 10.6, AppleScript dates lacked support for some languages and non-Gregorian calendars. These limitations were finally addressed in 10.6; however, the one downside of these improvements is that AppleScript is now much more strict when parsing date strings. In particular, older versions of AppleScript would accept a partial date string and fill in the missing information for you, but this is no longer the case. For example, date "1" is a valid date specifier in 10.5, but not in 10.6. As a result, older scripts that rely on this behavior will need to be updated to run correctly on 10.6.

Specifying a Time Relative to a Date

A nice feature of AppleScript's date values is that they allow you to obtain a particular time relative to a given date. You do this using a simple reference of the following form:

```
date time_string of date_value
```

For example, the following script creates a date that points to 5 PM today:

```
date "5:00 PM" of (current date)
```

> **TIP:** The current date command returns a date object describing the current date and time. More on this later in the chapter.

AppleScript allows you to write the of keyword as relative to if you'd like; they both mean the same thing. This may make the code more readable, like so:

```
date "6:30 AM" relative to date "September 1, 2009"
```

If you enter this expression and compile it, AppleScript will just change it to a single date literal:

```
date "Tuesday, September 1, 2009 6:30:00 AM"
```

However, if you use variables, this may be useful, as in the following example:

```
set the_date to (current date)
set the_time to "4:00 PM"
date the_time relative to the_date
--> date "Sunday, February 14, 2010 4:00:00 PM"
```

The result shown here, and in many other places in the book, depends on the date you run it.

> **CAUTION:** When specifying a time relative to a date, remember that the format of the time string must match one of the time formats set in the Language & Text panel of System Preferences; otherwise, an error will occur.

The Properties of Dates

So, parsing the date as a string to extract the individual pieces, such as the month, weekday, hour, and so on, isn't such a good idea. For these items, you can turn to the properties built into date objects.

The class Property

The first property is class. The value of class is always date. The class property is useful to check whether the value stored in a variable is of class date.

The year Property

The year property contains an integer representing the year of the given date:

```
year of date "Sunday, February 14, 2010 4:00:00 PM"
--> 2010
```

The month Property

The month property contains a value representing the month of the given date. The value of the month property is one of the following 12 AppleScript constants: January, February, March, April, May, June, July, August, September, October, November, or December. For example:

```
month of date "Sunday, February 14, 2010 12:00:00 AM"
--> February
```

NOTE: Because month values are constants, not strings, they are not affected by the Mac's language settings. For instance, running `month of date "domingo 14 de febrero de 2010 4:00:00 p.m."` on a Spanish-speaking Mac will also return the constant `February`.

You can coerce these month constants into strings (which works well for English-speaking users); for example:

```
June as text
--> "June"
```

You can also coerce them into numbers, like this:

```
December as integer
--> 12
```

For example, to get the current month as a number, you'd do this:

```
month of (current date) as integer
--> 5
```

The day **Property**

The day property contains an integer representing the day of the month:

```
day of date "Sunday, February 14, 2010 4:00:00 PM"
--> 14
```

The weekday **Property**

The weekday property can contain one of these constants: Sunday, Monday, Tuesday, Wednesday, Thursday, Friday, or Saturday:

```
weekday of date "Sunday, February 14, 2010 4:00:00 PM"
--> Sunday
```

You can also coerce the weekday constants into integers, like this:

```
Sunday as integer
--> 1
```

Because AppleScript represents weekdays using constants, not localized strings, you can safely perform comparisons without having to worry about the language settings of the Mac that is running the script.

Script 9–1 puts both of these features to use in a script that every busy office worker should have.

Script 9–1.

```
1. set today to current date
2. if today's weekday is in {Saturday, Sunday} then
3.    display dialog "No work today!"
4. else if today's weekday is Friday then
5.    display dialog "Thank goodness it's Friday!"
```

```
6. else
7.    set days_left to 6 - (today's weekday as integer)
8.    display dialog "Only " & days_left & " more days till the weekend!"
9. end if
```

Line 1 uses the `current date` command to get a date object containing today's date and time. Lines 2 to 9 then perform a number of tests on this date and display different messages depending on what day of the week it is. First, line 3 checks whether the date falls on a weekend. If the value of the date's weekday property is either Saturday or Sunday, then it is safe to go back to bed. If not, then line 4 checks whether the date's weekday property is Friday, in which case freedom is only a few hours away. Otherwise, line 7 coerces the weekday to an integer and uses this number to calculate the number of days left before the weekend arrives.

The hours **Property**

The `hours` property contains the hours of the time of the current date. For example:

```
hours of date "Sunday, May 31, 2009 4:54:04 PM"
--> 16
```

The result here is 16, not 4, because the value of the `hours` property is based on the 24-hour clock. You can use `hours` in a simple `if ... then` loop as follows to give you an alert when it's lunchtime:

```
if (hours of (current date) is 12) then display alert "Lunch!"
```

The minutes **Property**

This property is similar to `hours`, but contains the minutes in the time contained in the date object:

```
minutes of date "Sunday, May 31, 2009 4:54:04 PM"
--> 54
```

The seconds **Property**

This property is similar to `minutes` and `hours`, but contains the seconds in the time contained in the date object:

```
seconds of date "Sunday, May 31, 2009 4:54:04 PM"
--> 4
```

The time **Property**

The `time` property of a date object contains the number of seconds that have passed since midnight of the given date. For example:

```
time of (date "Sunday, May 31, 2009 4:00:00 PM")
--> 57600
```

The date string **Property**

The date string property contains a string that represents the date portion of the date object. For example:

```
date string of (current date)
--> "Sunday, February 14, 2010"
```

The Dates portion of the Formats tab of the Language & Text panel of System Preferences, shown earlier in Figure 9–2, determines the exact format of the date string property.

The short date string **Property**

The short date string property contains a string that represents a short version of the date portion of the date object. For example:

```
short date string of (current date)
--> "2/14/10"
```

The Dates portion of the Formats tab of the Language & Text panel of System Preferences determines the exact format of the short date string property.

The time string **Property**

The time string property is a string that contains the time portion of the date object. For example:

```
time string of (current date)
--> "5:44:23 PM"
```

The Times portion Dates of the Formats tab of the Language & Text panel of System Preferences determines the exact format of the time string property.

Setting Date Properties

AppleScript date objects are surprisingly flexible. Not only can you get their years, months, days, hours, minutes, and seconds, you can also *set* them to new values! For example:

```
set the_date to date "Sunday, May 31, 2009 4:00:00 PM"
set day of the_date to 1
the_date
--> date "Friday, May 1, 2009 4:00:00 PM"
```

In fact, you can set the year, month, day, hours, minutes, or seconds property of a date object to any positive integer; any excess will simply roll over:

```
set the_date to date "Sunday, May 31, 2009 4:00:00 PM"
set day of the_date to 33
the_date
--> date "Tuesday, June 2, 2009 4:00:00 PM"
```

In the preceding example, the day property is set to 33, but because there are only 31 days in May, the date automatically rolls over to June 2.

You can set the month property to either a month constant or the equivalent integer. For example,

```
set month of the_date to 8
```

has the same effect as

```
set month of the_date to August
```

Take care when modifying the properties of an existing date object. If another part of your script is also using the same object, it will also be affected by that change. This can easily result in confusing behavior or unexpected errors if you aren't careful.

If you want to copy an existing date object before making changes, just use AppleScript's built-in copy command. For example:

```
set date_one to date "Thursday, January 7, 2010 8:30:00 PM"
copy date_one to date_two
set day of date_two to 1
set time of date_two to 0
{date_one, date_two}
--> {date "Thursday, January 7, 2010 8:30:00 PM",
    date "Friday, January 1, 2010 12:00:00 AM"}
```

Chapter 11 will cover the built-in copy command in more detail.

The following example shows how to create a new date object from integers instead of the usual date string:

```
on make_date(the_year, the_month, the_day, the_hours, the_minutes, the_seconds)
    set the_date to current date
    set year of the_date to the_year
    set day of the_date to 1
    set month of the_date to the_month
    set day of the_date to the_day
    set hours of the_date to the_hours
    set minutes of the_date to the_minutes
    set seconds of the_date to the_seconds
    return the_date
end make_date
```

The user-defined make_date handler takes six parameters representing the year, month, day, hour, minute, and second values for the date, and returns a newly created date object. This approach can be especially useful in situations where you need to create new date objects from user input but cannot rely on date strings to be one particular format (for example, if your script is to be run by users in multiple countries).

To use this handler, just add it to your script, and then send a make_date command to your script, like this:

```
make_date(2012, 6, 3, 5, 40, 0)
--> date "Sunday, June 3, 2012 5:40:00 AM"
```

The make_date handler contains a couple of interesting design details.

First, the handler uses the current date command to create an initial date object. You could use a regular date specifier here if you prefer, but if you do, remember that the script will only compile if the format of the date string matches the format chosen in the Language & Text preferences of the Mac it is being compiled on. Using the current date command avoids this issue, making the handler just as portable in source form as it is in compiled form.

Once a date object has been created, the rest of the handler simply sets its properties to the desired values. The second thing that might puzzle you about the handler's design is that it sets the date's day property twice—first to 1, then to the final value. Why is this necessary? Well, remember that AppleScript will automatically roll over any excess when you set the day property's value, so if the current date is June 30 and you try to create a date for February 28, changing the date's month to February would give February 30...which immediately rolls over to March 2! Setting the day to 1 before setting the month avoids any risk of accidental rollover, ensuring that the date returned by the handler is the one the user asked for.

Operators and Commands

You can use various operators and commands when working with dates, including the full range of comparison operators, two math operators, and the current date and time to GMT commands.

Comparison Operators

As with numbers, dates can be compared. Table 9–1 lists the comparison operators that can be used with dates.

Table 9–1. *Comparison Operators*

Operator	Name	Description
=	Is equal to	Returns true if both operands are the same.
≠	Is not equal to	Returns true if the operands are different.
<	Is less than	Returns true if the left operand is less than the right operand.
≤	Is less than or equal to	Returns true if the left operand is equal to or less than the right operand.
>	Is greater than	Returns true if the left operand is greater than the right operand.
≥	Is greater than or equal to	Returns true if the left operand is equal to or greater than the right operand.

Here are some examples of date comparisons:

```
date "Friday, July 3, 2009 12:00:00 AM" = date "Sunday, July 5, 2009 12:00:00 AM"
--> false

date "Wednesday, July 1, 2009 12:00:00 AM" > date "Sunday, May 31, 2009 4:00:00 PM"
--> true
```

Take particular care when comparing two dates to see if they are equal. Consider the following example:

```
set birth_date to date "7/27/2010"
if (current date) = birth_date then
    display dialog "Happy Birthday!"
end if
```

You may expect the script, if run on July 27, 2010, to display a dialog box, right? Wrong—when you run line 2 of the preceding script, the resulting date is Monday, July 27, 2010 *12:00:00 AM*. This means the script displays the dialog box only if it runs at exactly midnight!

You have a few ways to remedy this problem. One is to compare the day, month, and year separately. Another approach is to set the time properties of both dates to 0 before performing the comparison. A third option is to use the is less than (<) and is greater than or equal to (≥) operators to see if the current date is within a certain range:

```
set start_of_birthday to date "7/27/2009"
set end_of_birthday to date "8/28/2009"
if (current date) ≥ start_of_birthday and (current date) < end_of_birthday then
    display dialog "Happy Birthday!"
end if
```

Script 9–2 is a simple file synchronization script that looks at a version of a file both in the server and on the local hard drive. If the hard drive version of the file is newer, the file is copied over to the server version.

Script 9–2.

```
1. tell application "Finder"
2.    set documents_folder to folder "Documents" of home
3.    set backup_folder to folder "Backup Files" of disk "Backup Server"
4.    set file_name to "Accounts Database.fp7"
5.    -- Get modification date of the original file
6.    set original_file to file file_name of documents_folder
7.    set original_modification_date to modification date of original_file
8.    -- Get modification date of the backup file
9.    set backup_file to file file_name of backup_folder
10.    set backup_modification_date to modification date of backup_file
11.    if original_modification_date > backup_modification_date then
12.        duplicate original_file to backup_folder with replacing
13.    end if
14. end tell
```

Line 1 targets the Finder, which is the application you'll use to get the modification dates for the files and perform a fresh backup if it is needed.

Lines 2 and 3 identify the folders where your original and backup files are located, and line 4 supplies the name of the file you're interested in.

Lines 6 to 10 obtain the modification dates for the two files. Line 11 compares these dates, and if the original file is newer than the backup file, then line 12 copies the original file to the backup folder, automatically replacing the previous backup file.

Math Operators

When performing math operations on dates, generally you will be performing one of two tasks: subtracting seconds from or adding seconds to a date to get a different date, or subtracting one date from another to get the number of seconds in between.

Table 9–2 shows the math operators that can be used with dates.

Table 9–2. *Math Operators*

Operator	Name	Description
+	Addition	Adds a whole number of seconds to a date.
-	Subtraction (with two operands)	Subtracts one date from another, or a whole number of seconds from a date.

Here are some examples:

```
(date "Sunday, May 31, 2009 9:00:00 AM") + 3600
--> date "Sunday, May 31, 2009 10:00:00 AM"

(date "Sunday, May 31, 2009 9:00:00 AM") - 3600
--> date "Sunday, May 31, 2009 8:00:00 AM"

(date "Sunday, May 31, 2009 10:00:00 AM") - (date "Sunday, May 31, 2009 8:00:00 AM")
--> 7200
```

The following sections look at how these operators can be used.

Some Useful Constants

To assist you in performing date arithmetic, AppleScript was fitted with several date-related constants describing the number of seconds in various periods of time. You can use these constants in your scripts without having to remember their numerical values. Here are the constants and their values:

- minutes = 60
- hours = 3600
- days = 86,400
- weeks = 604,800

Don't confuse these global variables with the date object properties explained previously. These predefined variables belong to AppleScript itself and can be used anywhere in the script. To get the idea, type the following script, and run it:

```
display dialog weeks
```

This displays the value of the weeks constant, which is 604,800.

So, what exactly do these numbers mean, and what are they good for? They help you perform date-related calculations using specific time spans such as days or weeks.

Let's look at the last two scenarios. If you want to check what the date is going to be three weeks from today, you can use the following script:

```
(current date) + 1814400
```

The number 1814400 is the number of seconds in three weeks. Now, I don't expect you'll want to remember that, let alone figure out the number of seconds in, say, five weeks, three days, and two hours! Because the constant weeks is equal to the number of seconds in one week, you can get the same result like this:

```
(current date) + (3 * weeks)
```

Here are some more examples:

```
(date "Sunday, May 31, 2009 9:00:00 AM") + (6 * days)
--> date "Saturday, June 6, 2009 9:00:00 AM"

(date "Sunday, May 31, 2009 9:00:00 AM") + (12 * hours)
--> date "Sunday, May 31, 2009 9:00:00 PM"

(date "Sunday, May 31, 2009 9:00:00 AM") - (1 * weeks)
--> date "Sunday, May 24, 2009 9:00:00 AM"
```

So, where are the years and months constants? Well, the number of seconds in a month or in a year isn't fixed; therefore, they can't be defined as constants.

Expect much more fun with these constants in the next section.

Calculating Time Differences

When you want to see the time difference between two dates, AppleScript gives you an *integer* result; you can obtain this by using the subtraction operator (binary -) to subtract one date from the other. The resulting integer is the number of seconds between the two dates. At first it looks a bit funny, especially when trying to figure out things such as how long Frank Sinatra lived for:

```
set date_born to date "Sunday, December 12, 1915 12:00:00 AM"
set date_died to date "Thursday, May 14, 1998 12:00:00 AM"
set seconds_lived to date_died - date_born
--> 2.6009856E+9
```

The result of that script tells you Frank lived for a little more than 2.6 billion seconds, but what if you want to make a little more sense out of that number? If you want to know how many minutes, hours, days, or weeks were in that period, you can divide it by the values of AppleScript's built-in minutes, hours, days, and weeks constants. Script 9–3 will ask users for their birthday and tell them how long they have lived.

Script 9–3.

```
1. set dialog_reply to display dialog "Enter your date of birth" ¬
        default answer "" buttons {"weeks", "days"}
2. set birthday_string to text returned of dialog_reply
3. set increment_chosen to button returned of dialog_reply
4. try
5.    set birthday to date birthday_string
6. on error
7.    display dialog "Bad date format!"
8.    return
9. end try
10. set age_in_seconds to (current date) - birthday
11. if increment_chosen = "weeks" then
12.    set age_in_weeks to age_in_seconds div weeks
13.    display dialog "You have been alive " & age_in_weeks & " weeks"
14. else
15.    set age_in_days to age_in_seconds div days
16.    display dialog "You have been alive " & age_in_days & " days"
17. end if
```

This method works well with predictable increments such as weeks or days. However, if you just want to know the age in years, then you are better off comparing the date components: year, month, and day. You have to compare all three, because just comparing years may leave you with the wrong answer. Look at this example:

```
set birthday to date "Wednesday, October 31, 1979 12:00:00 AM"
set today to date "Thursday, July 10, 2003 12:00:00 AM"
set age to (year of today) - (year of birthday)
```

The script returns a result of 24, which is the difference between 1979 and 2003. However, this person won't turn 24 for three more months! You could use the following trick:

```
set birthday to date "Wednesday, October 31, 1979 12:00:00 AM"
set today to date "Friday, July 10, 2009 12:00:00 AM"
set age_in_days to (today - birthday) / days
set age_in_years to age_in_days div 365.2425
set extra_days to round (age_in_days mod 365.2425) rounding down
"You are " & age_in_years & " years and " & extra_days & " days old."
--> "You are 29 years and 252 days old."
```

Although not perfectly accurate, I used the number 365.2425, which is about the number of days (on average) per year, taking into account leap years.

Another method would be to compare the two dates' year, month, and day values separately. If the month in your birthday comes after the month in today's date, then you have to reduce the year difference by one year. However, if the months are the same, then the day has to be compared, and the same rule applies: if the day in your birthday comes after the day in today's date, then you have to reduce the year difference by one year. If the days are the same, then guess what: it's your birthday! Script 9–4 shows how you can go about doing that.

Script 9–4.

```
set birthday to date "Wednesday, October 31, 1979 12:00:00 AM"
set today to date "Friday, July 10, 2009 12:00:00 AM"
set age_in_years to (year of today) - (year of birthday)
if (month of birthday) > (month of today) then
    set age_in_years to age_in_years - 1
else if (month of birthday) = (month of today) then
    if (day of birthday) > (day of today) then
        set age_in_years to age_in_years - 1
    end if
end if
age_in_years
--> 29
```

The current date Command

The current date command is part of Standard Additions. The command takes no parameters and returns a date object containing the current date and time, such as date "Sunday, February 14, 2010 10:15:09 PM".

When used as part of a larger operation, the current date command likes to be enclosed in parentheses. Actually, AppleScript is quite aware of that and will many times enclose it, as well as other commands, with parentheses when the script is compiled.

The usefulness of the current date command never ceases to amaze me. Just imagine how many times a day you turn to someone to ask what time or what date it is...okay, so its usefulness goes beyond knowing the current date and time. For one, it's a way to get a unique timestamp on which you can perform several operations. You can use the result of the current date command to figure out the time it takes to run a script, as shown in the following example:

```
set start_time to current date
-- Your script here...
-- More script...
-- A few more statements...
set end_time to current date
set time_in_seconds to end_time - start_time
display dialog "The script took " & time_in_seconds & " seconds to run!"
```

> **NOTE:** Although you can time medium to long scripts with the current date command as shown previously, because of its low precision, for short scripts or script portions it's better to use a third-party scripting addition such as AppleModsTools, which includes an AMTime command that is precise to the millisecond. You'll find the AppleModsTools scripting addition at http://applemods.sourceforge.net.

The `time to GMT` Command

Another date-related command, `time to GMT`, returns the time difference between the time zone of the computer that runs the script and Greenwich mean time (GMT). The result is returned in seconds, which means that if you want to extract any useful information from it, such as the number of hours, you have to divide it by the number of seconds in an hour.

Script 9–5 will return the time difference between your time zone and GMT (provided of course that the time zone is properly set on your computer).

Script 9–5.

```
1. set time_difference to (time to GMT) / hours
2. if time_difference mod 1 = 0 then
3.    set time_difference to time_difference as integer
4. end if
5. if time_difference < 0 then
6.    set time_difference to -time_difference
7.    set the_message to "You are " & time_difference & " hours behind GMT"
8. else if time_difference > 0 then
9.    set the_message to "You are " & time_difference & " hours ahead of GMT"
10. else
11.    set the_message to "Your time zone is GMT"
12. end if
13. display dialog the_message
```

You start the script by getting the time difference and dividing it by the value of AppleScript's built-in hours constant, 3600, which is the number of seconds in an hour.

Line 1 returns a real number, but most time zones lie on the hour (0.0, 2.0, –8.0, and so on), and you'd like those numbers to display without the .0 at the end, so you use lines 2–4 to prettify them. Line 2 checks whether the number is a whole number by using the `mod` operator to divide by 1 and get the remainder. If the remainder is 0, then it's a whole number, and line 3 can safely coerce it to an integer; time zones with an extra 0.25 or 0.5 hour in them remain untouched. The conditional statement that starts on line 5 and ends on line 12 forms a different message depending on whether the time zone of the user is before GMT, after it, or the same.

If the time zone is before GMT, then the value stored in the `time_difference` value has to be made positive for the dialog box message. That happens on line 6, which uses the negation operator (unary -) to convert the negative number into a positive number.

Example Projects

Let's finish off this chapter with a couple of date-based projects. For the first project, you'll create a useful maintenance script that will delete any files in a specified folder that are older than a certain number of weeks. In the second project, you will develop an AppleScript-based alarm clock that plays a user-selected audio file when it is time to wake up.

Deleting Old Files

For this exercise, you will create a script that looks at a folder's contents and deletes every file that's older than a specified number of weeks. For example, you could use this script to keep your Downloads folder tidy by throwing away any files that haven't been moved to a permanent location after a set length of time.

This script will have two main stages. First, you need to prompt the user to enter the number of weeks and then, after the user responds, calculate what the date was that number of weeks ago. This will be the expiration date. Then, you check the modification date of each file. If it is less than the expiration date, it means the file is more than that number of weeks old and you can delete it. For testing purposes, instead of deleting the file, you can just set its label to red.

Creating the Script

In this script, you will use a property that holds the path to the folder you want to clean out. The script will start by checking whether that path is valid—in other words, whether the folder specified actually exists. If it does not exist, the user will be prompted to choose a new one.

Although this is the way the script will start, you will write that portion last. I know that in the previous example you started with the file-choosing portion, commented it out for development purposes, and reinstated it at the end, but don't worry—both ways work. For testing purposes, you should create a folder and put some assorted files in it.

You will use the Finder application to identify and delete any out-of-date files in the folder. The Finder's powerful whose clause allows you to perform this entire operation using a single command!

Before you start programming the Finder, you need to have a folder path to work with for testing purposes and an integer indicating the number of weeks old the file has to be in order to be marked. Although specifying the integer isn't a big issue, providing a path may be a bit irritating. I really like to make life easy for myself, so I have saved myself some time by creating a little lazy workaround. For the workaround, start a new script, type the command choose folder, and run the script. The choose folder command will force you to choose a folder and return a path to that folder, as shown in Figure 9–4.

Figure 9–4. *The result of the* `choose folder` *command*

The script in Figure 9–4 is a throwaway script. You can copy the resulting string (without the `alias` keyword) to your real script and then close this one without saving.

The script starts with two variables: `folder_path`, which holds the path pointing to the folder you want to clean, and `weeks_old`, which will be the integer specifying how many weeks old the file has to be to be deleted (or have its label changed, in this case). Here is the initial stage of the script:

```
set folder_path to "Macintosh HD:Users:hanaan:Desktop:Desktop Stuff:"
set weeks_old to 12
```

The next step is to script the part that calculates what the date was *N* weeks ago. I used 12 weeks in my script, which ensures that some of the files in my test folder will be affected and some will not.

The date calculation statement is rather simple, and like many other statements in AppleScript, you can write it on a single line or spread it out over several lines. The single-line version is as follows:

```
set expiration_date to (current date) - (weeks_old * weeks)
```

The following part of the script will tell the Finder how to treat the old files:

```
tell application "Finder"
   tell (every file of folder folder_path whose creation date < expiration_date)
      set label index to 2
   end tell
end tell
```

Notice how you can use a single command to address only the files you want. In the final version of the script, the statement that now says set label index to 2 will simply say delete.

Adding the User Interaction Portion

The final stage of the script will get the user involved. You need to make sure the user understands what the script will do. You will also allow the user to change the settings stored in script properties—that is, the folder that will be cleaned and the number of weeks.

You start by changing the first two variables into properties with an initial value. Then, you add the code to check the current value of the properties. Remember that even though you assign a value to the properties when you write the script, this value will be changed by user activity, and the new values will stick.

After the properties are declared, the first real part of the script checks whether the folder path is valid and makes sure the number of weeks specified isn't zero or less. If all is well, you show a dialog box reminding the user that the files in a specific folder that are older than a specific date will be deleted. When the OK button is clicked, you will go ahead with the process. Script 9–6 shows the script with the added properties and conditional statement.

Script 9–6.

```
property folder_path : ""
property weeks_old : 0

-- Verify folder
tell application "Finder"
   set folder_exists to folder folder_path exists
end tell
if not folder_exists then
   set folder_path to choose folder with prompt "Pick a folder to clean:"
   set folder_path to folder_path as text
end if

-- Verify weeks
if weeks_old < 1 then
   set dialog_reply to display dialog ¬
         "Delete files that are how many weeks old?" default answer "5"
   set weeks_old to (text returned of dialog_reply) as integer
end if

set expiration_date to (current date) - (weeks_old * weeks)
tell application "Finder" to set folder_name to name of folder folder_path
set short_date to short date string of expiration_date

display dialog "Files in folder \"" & folder_name & ¬
      "\" that were created before " & short_date & " will be deleted."

tell application "Finder"
   tell (every file of folder folder_path whose creation date < expiration_date)
      set label index to 2
   end tell
```

```
end tell
```

Let's see what was added to the script in this round and what is still missing.

The "verify folder" section uses the Finder to check that folder_path contains a valid path to a folder or a disk:

```
-- Verify folder
tell application "Finder"
    set folder_exists to folder folder_path exists
end tell
if not folder_exists then
    set folder_path to choose folder with prompt "Pick a folder to clean:"
    set folder_path to folder_path as text
end if
```

You start by creating a Finder reference, folder folder_path, that identifies the folder you're interested in. You then pass this reference to the Finder's exists command, which returns true if a folder or disk exists at that location. If the path is not valid or the Finder finds a file there instead, the command returns false, and the user will be asked to choose a different folder.

The "verify weeks" section checks whether the weeks_old property is less than 1:

```
-- Verify weeks
if weeks_old < 1 then
    set dialog_reply to display dialog ¬
        "Delete files that are how many weeks old?" default answer "5"
    set weeks_old to (text returned of dialog_reply) as integer
end if
```

What it doesn't do nicely is verify that the user entered a value that can be coerced into an integer. If the user tried to be funny and enter "Five", for instance, the script would choke when trying to coerce the result into an integer.

The next thing to do is create the message to allow the user to bow out of the deal and cancel. This message will contain the folder's name, which is obtained using the Finder and assigned to a variable named folder_name:

```
tell application "Finder" to set folder_name to name of folder folder_path
```

It will also contain the short version of the expiration date, which you get by asking the date object for the value of its short date string property:

```
set short_date to short date string of expiration_date
```

You then assemble the message string using the concatenation (&) operator and use a display dialog command to display it onscreen:

```
display dialog "Files in folder \"" & folder_name & ¬
    "\" that were created before " & short_date & "will be deleted."
```

Figure 9–5 shows a typical dialog box displayed by this command.

Figure 9–5. *The dialog box informing the user of the action that follows*

> **NOTE:** Notice the use of quotes in the dialog box text. If you look at the script, you will see that in order to include a double quote inside a literal string, you need to escape it; in other words, you need to put a backslash before it, like this: \".

Now that the script is fully assembled, it's time to test it. Create a test folder in your home folder, and copy into it some older and newer files that you can safely use for testing purposes.

Next, run the script. As this is the first time the script has been run, the "verify folder" and "verify weeks" code will ask you to enter new values. Choose the test folder and enter the number of weeks at which files should be deleted (choose a number that is less than the age of your older test files).

If the values you have entered are valid, the script will display a dialog box similar to the one shown in Figure 9–5, allowing you to confirm your selection. Click OK, and then check that all the files that are older than the expiration date have had their label colors correctly set to label 2.

Once you are completely satisfied that the script is working correctly, just replace the set label index to 2 line with a delete command and your script is ready to use.

> **NOTE:** The next time you run the script, you will be asked to re-enter the folder and weeks values because recompiling the script causes it to forget the values that were previously stored in the folder_path and weeks_old properties. You'll learn more about script properties in Chapter 11.

Alarm Clock

The script presented in this section woke me up every morning when I had to be in Boston for a few months. For this script to be useful, it requires two pieces of information: what time you want to wake up and which song you want playing when you wake up. You will retrieve both of these values using dialog boxes that prompt the user to pick a time and then a song. You'll also store these choices in properties so that the user has to pick them only if they need to be changed. Like other scripts you looked at earlier, this one contains several repeat loops. Two endless repeat loops ensure that the script does not proceed until the user has entered valid information and is happy with it. (We will look at this user interaction technique in more detail in Chapter 16.) Once that's done, the script will wait in a third repeat loop until it's time for the alarm to go off.

Script 9–7 shows the script in its entirety.

Script 9–7.

```
1. property wakeup_tune_file : missing value
2. property requested_time : "7:00"

3. if wakeup_tune_file is missing value then
4.    set wakeup_tune_file to choose file ¬
             with prompt "Pick a wakeup tune:" of type {"public.audio"} ¬
             without invisibles
5. end if
6. tell application "Finder" to set song_name to name of wakeup_tune_file

7. set tomorrow_date to (current date) + (1 * days)
8. repeat
9.    set wake_dialog to display dialog "Enter time you want to wake up:" ¬
             default answer requested_time buttons {"Stop", "OK"} default button "OK"
10.    if button returned of wake_dialog is "Stop" then return
11.    set requested_time to text returned of wake_dialog
13.    try -- See if time entered is OK
14.       set wakeup_date to date requested_time of tomorrow_date
15.       exit repeat
16.    on error -- Invalid time string
17.       try
18.          display dialog "Not a valid time. Please try again."
19.       on error number -128 -- User canceled
20.          return
21.       end try
22.    end try
23. end repeat

24. repeat
25.    display dialog "The song \"" & song_name & "\"" & return & ¬
             "should wake you up on: " & return & wakeup_date ¬
             buttons {"Change Song", "OK"} default button "OK" giving up after 15
26.    if button returned of result is "Change song" then
27.       set wakeup_tune_file to choose file ¬
                with prompt "Pick a wakeup tune:" of type {"public.audio"} ¬
                without invisibles
28.       tell application "Finder" to set song_name to name of wakeup_tune_file
29.    else
30.       exit repeat
31.    end if
32. end repeat

33. repeat until (current date) ≥ wakeup_date
34.    delay 10
35. end repeat

36. tell application "QuickTime Player"
```

```
37.    activate
38.    open wakeup_tune_file
39.    tell document 1
40.        set audio volume to 1.0
41.        play
42.    end tell
43. end tell
```

Let's go over the script's major parts.

In lines 3 to 6, you choose the song file and extract the file's name into a variable. Note that you have the user choose a file only if the property wakeup_tune_file is set to the default setting of missing value. That means these lines will be executed only the first time the script runs. Later in the script, in lines 26, 27, and 28, you give the user a chance to change the song file.

The following part, which starts on line 7 and ends on line 23, allows you to figure out and verify the wakeup time and date. You start this block with line 7, where you simply figure out tomorrow's date:

```
set tomorrow_date to (current date) + (1 * days)
```

You will later apply a new time to the date object stored in the tomorrow_date variable. This takes place on line 14:

```
set wakeup_date to date requested_time of tomorrow_date
```

Line 8 starts a repeat loop that ends on line 23. The purpose of that loop is to qualify the text the user typed as a valid date. The time the user was asked to provide has to be a time string, such as "7:00 am", that can be converted into a date.

The script first stores the string the user entered in the requested_time variable. It then tries to convert this value into a date. This happens in lines 13 through 22. If the conversion is successful, line 15 will exit the repeat loop. If the conversion fails, the try statement will capture the error, and the on error portion of the statement will be executed.

Within this on error section, you start a new try statement, which is intended to allow the user to cancel. You ask the user to enter a new date, but you give them a way out this time. If the user clicks the Cancel button, the display dialog command raises a "User canceled" error. This is caught by the inner try block, which executes the return statement in its on error section, causing the script to stop. This happens on lines 19 and 20.

Line 25 will then collect all the information and will use a self-dismissing dialog box to let the user know when the clock is going to play which song and allow the user to change the tune that'll play, as shown in Figure 9–6.

The song "Burning down the house.mp3"
should wake you up on:
Tuesday, March 16, 2010 7:00:00 AM

            (Change Song)   (OK   )

Figure 9–6. *The script displays a dialog box that allows the user to change the song. The dialog box will give up (close by itself) after 15 seconds.*

Lines 24 through 32 allow the user to change the song file.

Lines 33 through 35 create a loop that makes the script wait until the wakeup time is reached. The repeat until ... loop statement checks whether the current date is the same as or later than the wakeup date. If it is, the loop exits automatically; otherwise, it executes the delay command to wait ten seconds before trying again.

> **NOTE:** If you need to cancel this loop, press Cmd-period. Later in the book, Chapter 18 will introduce you to idle handlers, which can be used to perform this kind of periodically repeating task in a more efficient and user-friendly way.

The final part of the script starts on line 36 and ends on line 43. (Mac OS X 10.5 users: change line 40 to set sound volume to 256.) This tells the QuickTime Player application to open the chosen music file and play it loudly.

Summary

This chapter introduced you to date objects, used by AppleScript to represent dates and times. You learned how to convert strings into dates and vice versa, how to get and set individual properties of date objects, and how to perform date-based math calculations.

In the next chapter, you will learn about AppleScript's list and record classes, used to create collections of other objects.

Chapter 10

Working with Lists and Records

Two of AppleScript's most powerful and interesting classes are `list` and `record`. Unlike simpler objects such as numbers and strings, which represent "flat" data, a list or record object is actually a *collection* of other AppleScript objects. In this chapter, you will learn how list and record objects are structured and the different types of tasks they can be used for.

Introducing Lists and Records

Before we go into the details, let's begin with a quick introduction to lists and records and compare them to one another.

What Is a List?

In technical terms, a list is an ordered collection of objects. In less technical terms, though, what does that mean? A simple example will help to clarify.

Imagine you are preparing to go to the supermarket. If, unlike me, you are organized, the first thing you will do is write down a list of all the things you need to buy; for example: milk, bread, eggs, sugar, cabbage, and ham. In AppleScript, you could represent each of these items as a string and put the items into a list, like this:

```
{"milk", "bread", "eggs", "sugar", "cabbage", "ham"}
```

These items appear in a specific order and are grouped together in a single list object that can be passed around the script just like any other object. A list may be empty, or it may contain any number of items. Each item can be anything you like. Because the items appear in a specific order, you can identify them by position. For example, if I ask you what the fourth item is, you will look for item 4 of the list and tell me that it is "sugar".

You can insert new items at the beginning or end of a list. For example, if you remember that you need to buy boot polish, you can put that after "ham", making the list one item longer. You can replace an existing item, too—for example, you might replace "bread" with "bagels". Or you can concatenate two lists to create a new list containing all the items from both lists.

All in all, a list is a flexible and expandable storage solution when you have a collection of similar values that you want to group together, often in a particular order.

As you've seen in the scripts in previous chapters, a *list literal* is written as a pair of curly brackets, with each item separated by a comma. Here are some more examples:

```
{1, 2, 3, 4, 5} -- A list of integers
{"make", "love", "not", "war"} -- A list of strings
{"B", true, 2, "me"} -- A mixed list
```

What Is a Record?

Like a list, a record is a collection of values, but in a record every item is labeled. When working with records, you use the label to identify an item. Unlike lists, it's not possible to refer to a record's items by position, because their order is not fixed.

Imagine a page in an address book, divided into a number of sections, each of which contains a different piece of information. Each section has a different label that describes the information it contains: one for the person's name, one for their birthday, another for their home address, another for their home phone number, yet another for their mobile phone number, and so on. For example:

```
Name:           James Ho
Birthday:       1/24/84
Home Address:   39 Main Street, Anytown
Home Phone:     305 555 6189
Mobile Phone:   212 555 1754
```

If you need to look up a particular piece of information, you can refer to it by its label. For example, if you want to phone your friend at home, you would look at the entry labeled "Home Phone."

AppleScript records take the same approach. In your script, you define a record to hold a number of values that belong together. This allows you to pass these values around your script in a single group. Each entry, or *property*, in the record consists of a label and a value. The structure of the record is defined in your source code—you cannot add and remove properties while your script is running, but you can get and set their values as you like.

A record literal in AppleScript is written as a pair of curly brackets, with each property separated by a comma. Each property's label must be an AppleScript keyword or a user-defined identifier; its value can be anything. You separate the label and the value with a colon. Here are some examples:

```
{frontmost:false, class:application, version:"3.2.1", name:"Safari"}
{job_id:131, job_file:alias "Macintosh HD:Users:Hanaan:A61432.indd", is_urgent:true}
```

And here is our earlier address book entry rewritten as an AppleScript record:

```
{name:"James Ho", birthday:date "Tuesday, January 24, 1984 00:00:00", ¬
    home_address:"39 Main Street, Anytown", home_phone:"305 555 6189", ¬
    mobile_phone:"212 555 1754"}
```

How Are Lists and Records Used in Scripts?

To understand the difference between what role a list plays in your script versus what role a record plays, consider again your address book. The address book contains information about people: names, telephone numbers, e-mail addresses, and so on.

A list is perfect for storing lots of similar values that you're going to process all in the same way; for example, you might want to create a list of e-mail addresses so you can send a newsletter to each one. Here's an example:

```
{"james12345@example.net", "jml@example.com, "etc@example.org"}
```

Other times you might need to treat all the information for one particular person as a single group, such as when handing it to a script that will generate a selection of letterheads and business cards for that person. Each value has a different meaning, so using a record rather than a list to group them makes more sense because it allows each value to have a clear, descriptive label:

```
{name:"James Ho", mobile_phone:"212 555 1754", email:"james12345@example.net"}
```

Working with Lists

As discussed earlier in the chapter, a list is an ordered collection of objects. The following sections will discuss in detail how you can work with the items of a list, but first let's look at some of the places where lists may appear.

One common way to obtain a list is to get multiple elements from an AppleScript or application object. For example, the following line asks an AppleScript string for all its word elements:

```
get every word of "It was a dark and stormy night."
--> {"It", "was", "a", "dark", "and", "stormy", "night"}
```

The result is a list of strings, each one containing a single word from the original string.

The next example asks the Finder for the names of only those `file` elements that represent files larger than 100MB in size. The result is a list of strings, each one the name of a file:

```
tell application "Finder"
    get name of every file of folder "Movies" of home whose size > 100000000
end tell
--> {"HouseOnHauntedHill.mp4", "LastManOnEarth.mp4", "LittleShopOfHorrors.avi"}
```

Another way you might obtain a list is to create an empty list and then add items to it over time. For example, let's say you have a workflow script that needs to keep a log of its activities. One approach would be to create a new, empty list when the script starts running, add each new message to the end of the list as the script does its thing, and finally coerce the entire list into a single string, which can then be written to a text file.

The following statement creates a new, empty list and assigns it to a variable named log_list:

```
set log_list to {}
```

You can then insert new items at the end of the list one at a time, like this:

```
set end of log_list to "Beginning job at " & (short date time of current date)
```

Eventually you will have a list that looks something like this:

```
{"Beginning job at 3:41:29 PM", "Reading database Products.fm7",
    "Opening Template 1.indd", ..., "Finished job at 3:47:01 PM"}
```

All you need to do then is set AppleScript's text item delimiters to a return or linefeed character, coerce the list to class text, and write the result to a date-stamped text file.

Now that you've seen some of the ways that lists are used, let's take a closer look at how they actually work.

The Properties of a List

Being a bit more complex than other AppleScript classes, the list class defines several read-only properties that allow you to obtain different kinds of information from lists. The properties are class, length, rest, and reverse.

The *class* Property

The class property always contains the same value, which is list:

```
class of {1, 2, 3}
--> list
```

The *length* Property

The length property of a list holds an integer describing the number of items it contains. For example:

```
length of {"John", "Paul", "George", "Ringo"}
--> 4
```

The *rest* Property

Getting the rest property of a list returns a new list containing all the items of the original list except for the first one. For example:

```
rest of {"don't", "talk", "while", "you", "eat"}
--> {"talk", "while", "you", "eat"}
```

If the list contains only a single item, the value of its rest property is an empty list:

```
rest of {"time"}
--> {}
```

The *reverse* Property

As you might guess, asking for the reverse property of a list returns a new list that contains the same items but in reverse order. For example:

```
reverse of {"start", "middle", "nearly there", "finish"}
--> {"finish", "nearly there", "middle", "start"}
```

The Elements of a List

Because the purpose of an AppleScript list is to contain other objects in an ordered sequence, it is not surprising that these items appear as elements of the list. Although list objects are in many ways less powerful than application objects that have elements—for example, AppleScript lists don't support the powerful *whose* clause reference form recognized by most application objects—you can still manipulate list objects in plenty of ways. And because lists are general-purpose objects, there is no restriction on the class or number of items they can contain.

The following sections look at how you can get, set, add, and "remove" list items.

Getting Items

Once you have a list, you often need to be able to retrieve items from it. To do this, you normally refer the list object's item elements. For example, to get a single item from a list, you would use the following syntax (the get keyword is optional, as usual):

```
get item index of the_list
```

List items are always identified by position, so if you're counting from the beginning of the list, the first item is at index 1, the second is at index 2, and so on. For example:

```
item 1 of {"a", "b", "c", "d", "e", "f"}
--> "a"

item 5 of {"a", "b", "c", "d", "e", "f"}
--> "e"
```

Alternatively, you can count back from the end of the list by using negative indexes instead, in which case the last item is at index –1, the second-to-last item is at index –2, and so on:

```
item -2 of {"a", "b", "c", "d", "e", "f"}
--> "e"

item -5 of {"a", "b", "c", "d", "e", "f"}
--> "b"
```

You can also refer to the first, last, and middle elements like this:

```
first item of {"a", "b", "c", "d", "e", "f"} -- Equivalent to asking for item 1
```

```
--> "a"

last item of {"a", "b", "c", "d", "e", "f"} -- Equivalent to asking for item -1
--> "f"

middle item of {"a", "b", "c", "d", "e", "f"}
--> "c"
```

Or you can get an item completely at random:

```
some item of {"a", "b", "c", "d", "e", "f"}
```

In addition to getting single items, you can also get a range of items using the following syntax (you can write through instead of thru if you prefer):

```
get items start_index thru end_index of the_list
```

Here are some examples:

```
items 2 thru 5 of {"a", "b", "c", "d", "e", "f"}
--> {"b", "c", "d", "e"}

items -2 thru -1 of {"a", "b", "c", "d", "e", "f"}
--> {"e", "f"}
```

And, of course, you can ask for all of the list's items:

```
every item of {"a", "b", "c", "d", "e", "f"}
--> {"a", "b", "c", "d", "e", "f"}
```

The result here is a new list containing all the original objects from the old list. This is useful if you want to make a copy of the original list without also duplicating the objects it contains. You can also copy lists using AppleScript's built-in copy command, but this duplicates each of the original list items as well. This doesn't make a difference if the items are all simple objects like numbers and strings, but it will affect the result if they are lists or records, as you may not want them to be duplicated too.

> **NOTE:** We'll look at the effects of the copy command on lists and records in Chapter 12.

If the script tries to get an item in a list that is out of range, the script will throw a "Can't get reference" error (error –1728), which is a common runtime error:

```
item 4 of {"a", "b", "c"}
-- Error: Can't get item 4 of {"a", "b", "c"}
```

As you've already seen, a list can contain objects of any class. But what if you want to extract only the items of a specific class, such as just the strings or integers? AppleScript has an easy way to do this, too. All you have to do is ask for the class of items you want, like so:

```
every string of {"I", "Love", "You", 2, true}
--> {"I" ,"Love" ,"You"}
```

Setting Items

You can use the set command to replace any existing item in a list with a new value, like this:

```
set item index of the_list to new_value
```

For example:

```
set my_list to {"A", "B", "C"}
set item 2 of my_list to "Z"
my_list
--> {"A", "Z", "C"}
```

Adding Items

You can add new items to either the beginning or end of an existing list.

To insert an item at the end of a list, use the set command as follows:

```
set end of the_list to new_value
```

For example:

```
set my_list to {1, 2, 3}
set end of my_list to 4
my_list
--> {1, 2, 3, 4}
```

Similarly, to insert an item at the beginning of a list, use the set command as follows:

```
set beginning of the_list to new_value
```

For example:

```
set my_list to {1, 2, 3}
set beginning of my_list to 4
my_list
--> {4, 1, 2, 3}
```

"Removing" Items

Although it is not possible to delete list items directly, you can work around this limitation by using existing list features, in particular, the ability to get a range of elements. The trick here is to construct a new list containing all the items except the one you don't want. For example, to "remove" the third item of a five-item list, you get a sublist containing all the items to the left of item 3 and another sublist containing all the items to the right of it, and then join these two lists to produce the final four-item list:

```
set the_list to {"a", "b", "c", "d", "e"}
set new_list to (items 1 thru 2 of the_list) & (items 4 thru 5 of the_list)
new_list
--> {"a", "b", "d", "e"}
```

Here's an example of how you'd use this principle in a script:

```
set the_list to {"a", "b", "c", "d", "e"}
set item_to_remove to 3
set new_list to (items 1 thru (item_to_remove - 1) of the_list) ¬
    & (items (item_to_remove + 1) thru -1 of the_list)
new_list
--> {"a", "b", "d", "e"}
```

This code isn't quite ready for general use, however. Although it works for any item in the middle of the list (2, 3, or 4), it will raise a "Can't get reference" error for the first or last item of the list as it tries to get an item that's out of range:

```
set the_list to {"a", "b", "c", "d", "e"}
set item_to_remove to 1
set new_list to (items 1 thru (item_to_remove - 1) of the_list) ¬
    & (items (item_to_remove + 1) thru -1 of the_list)
-- Error: Can't get items 1 thru 0 of {"a", "b", "c", "d", "e"}
```

To deal with those two "corner cases," you have to add a conditional statement that checks where the item is in the list and does things differently if it's at the start or end. As a finishing touch, we'll also turn this script into a useful little handler that you can use in your own scripts. Script 10–1 shows the completed result.

Script 10–1.

```
on remove_item_from_list(the_list, index_to_remove)
    if index_to_remove = 1 then
        set new_list to rest of the_list
    else if index_to_remove = length of the_list then
        set new_list to (items 1 thru -2 of the_list)
    else
        set new_list to (items 1 thru (index_to_remove - 1) of the_list) ¬
            & (items (index_to_remove + 1) thru -1 of the_list)
    end if
    return new_list
end remove_item_from_list
```

And here is an example of how to use it:

```
set the_list to {"a", "b", "c", "d", "e"}
set new_list to remove_item_from_list(the_list, 1)
--> {"b", "c", "d", "e"}
```

Operators and Commands

You already used the concatenation operator, &, to join two lists together. List objects also support a variety of comparison and containment operators, which all return a Boolean value. The built-in count command can also be used on lists. For other tasks, such as removing or sorting items, you can always define your own commands.

Concatenating Lists

You join lists together with the concatenation operator, &. Whenever you use the concatenation operator to combine two lists, you get a single list as a result, comprising the items from the list to the left of the operator followed by the items from the list to the right. Here are a few examples:

```
{1, 2, 3} & {4 ,5 ,6 }
--> {1, 2, 3, 4 ,5 ,6}

{"a", "b"} & {"c"} & {"d", "e", "f"}
--> {"a", "b", "c", "d", "e", "f"}

{{name:"Jon", age:35}} & {{name:"Susan", age:39}, {name:"Kate", age:24}}
--> {{name:"Jon", age:35}, {name:"Susan", age:39}, {name:"Kate", age:24}}

1 & 2
--> {1, 2}
```

The first three examples are easy enough to understand, but what's going on with the last one? Well, any time you use the concatenation operator, the first thing it does is check if the class of the left operand is text, list, or record, as those are the only types of objects it knows how to join. If the operand is of any other class—in this case, integer—it is automatically coerced to a single-item list, allowing the concatenation operator to work with it. The right operand is then coerced to the same class as the left operand (another single-item list, in this example), and these two single-item lists are joined together to produce a new list.

Comparing Lists

As with any other class of objects, you can compare two lists to check whether they're equal or not. For example:

```
{1,2,3} = {1,2,3}
--> true

{"background.tif", "icon.tif"} = {"icon.tif", "background.tif"}
--> false

{true, true, false, true} ≠ {true, true, true}
--> true
```

You can't, however, use the <, >, ≤, and ≥ operators to check whether one list is greater or smaller than another.

Checking for Sublists

You can check whether parts of a list match parts of another list. The operators you use to do that are starts with, ends with, contains, and is in. You can also use does not start with, does not end with, does not contain, and is not in to check whether there isn't a match.

The *starts with* Operator

The starts with operator checks whether one list (the right operand) matches the start of another list (the left operand). The following statements all return true:

```
{1, 2, 3, 4} starts with {1}
{1, 2, 3, 4} starts with {1, 2}
{1, 2, 3, 4} starts with {1, 2, 3, 4}
```

Now, what if the right operand isn't a list? For example:

```
{1, 2, 3, 4} starts with 1
```

AppleScript's containment operators require that both operands are of the same class, so AppleScript starts by coercing the right operand into a list to match the class of the left operand and then performs the actual containment test as follows:

```
{1, 2, 3, 4} starts with {1}
--> true
```

The *ends with* Operator

The ends with operator works mostly the same way as the starts with operator but instead checks whether the right-hand list matches the end of the left-hand list. For example:

```
{1, 2, 3, 4} ends with {3, 4}
--> true
```

The *contains* Operator

You can use the contains operator to check whether one list contains another list:

```
{1, 2, 3, 4, 5} contains {3}
--> true
```

```
{1, 2, 3, 4, 5} contains {3, 4}
--> true
```

```
{1, 2, 3, 4, 5} contains {4, 3}
--> false
```

Script 10–2 shows how you can use the contains operator to check whether the startup disk contains the essential folders. (Of course, you can check that in other ways, but you're currently looking at lists.) The script first creates a list using the list folder command and then checks whether the default folders are part of that list.

Script 10–2.

```
tell application "Finder"
    set names_list to name of every folder of startup disk
end tell
if names_list contains "Applications" and ¬
        names_list contains "Library" and ¬
        names_list contains "System" and ¬
        names_list contains "Users" then
    display dialog "Startup disk has all key folders"
else
    display dialog "Startup disk is missing some key folders"
end if
```

The result of the second line is a list containing the names of every folder of the startup disk. The fourth line then checks whether the list contains the four strings "Applications", "Library", "System", and "Users". Because each `contains` operation is separated with the Boolean operator and, the comparisons operate independently, and the startup disk is approved only if all four values are found.

The *is in* Operator

Lastly, the `is in` operator checks whether the left operand is contained by the list in the right operand. Here are some examples:

```
{1, 2} is in {1, 2, 3}
--> true
```

```
{"a", "c"} is in {"a", "b", "c"}
--> false
```

```
{1, 2} is in {1, 2, 3}
--> true
```

```
"treasure" is in (words of "treasure chest")
--> true -- The actual test is: {"treasure"} is in {"treasure", "chest"}
```

Here are a few more examples—see whether you can spot which one has the counterintuitive result:

```
{2, 4} is in {1, 5, 2, 4, 3, 0}
--> true
```

```
{2, 4} is in {{1, 5}, {2, 4}, {3, 0}}
--> false
```

```
{{2, 4}} is in {{1, 5}, {2, 4}, {3, 0}}
--> true
```

The second example is a good reminder that AppleScript's containment operators actually check for a matching range, not a single item. This doesn't matter most of the time, but it can catch you when working with lists of lists unless you're careful.

More Uses for Containment Operators

Although you will study conditional, or `if`, statements in much more detail in Chapter 14, I wanted to explain here how using lists can make certain `if` statements simpler. Sometimes you will want to perform an operation only if a variable has a specific value. This is an easy comparison:

```
if the_variable = "this value" then
    -- Do something...
end if
```

What if, however, you want to check the variable's value against options? For instance, what if you want to perform an operation only on weekends?

One option is to write a separate equality test for each option and use the or operator to link them together:

```
if the_weekday = Saturday or the_weekday = Sunday then
    -- Do something...
end if
```

Although this particular example is still manageable, imagine how unwieldy it would be when checking against 10 or 20 possibilities. The solution is to replace all the is-equal operations and their connecting or tests with a single is in test, like this:

```
if {the_weekday} is in {Saturday, Sunday} then
    -- Do something...
end if
```

Not only is this code simpler to read, but it's also easier to modify later if you need to add and remove items from the list in order to change the conditions.

Counting Lists

Using the count command on the list returns the number of items in the list:

```
count {"John", "Paul", "George", "Ringo"}
--> 4
```

This is equivalent to asking for the value of the list's length property.

Coercing to and from Lists

AppleScript allows lists to be coerced to and from several different classes of object.

Most AppleScript objects can be coerced to a single-item list; for example:

```
1 as list
--> {1}

"Hello, World!" as list
--> {"Hello, World!"}

alias "Macintosh HD:Applications:" as list
--> {alias "Macintosh HD:Applications:"}
```

The one exception to this rule are AppleScript records: coercing a record to a list results in a list containing the record's values. We'll look at this later in the chapter, in the "Coercing from Records" section.

Perhaps the most frequently used coercion is from a list of strings (or other objects that can be coerced into strings) to a single string. Chapter 7 has already shown you how to break up a string into a list of substrings and join them back together again, but let's go over it again quickly here.

Let's start with a list of words:

```
set the_list to {"It", "was", "a", "dark", "and", "stormy", "night"}
```

To join these words back into a single string, we coerce the list to class text, like this:

```
the_list as text
```

Of course, when coercing a list into text, there's one catch: the strings will be joined together in different ways, depending on the current value of AppleScript's `text item delimiters` property. With the default setting, which is an empty string, the strings are joined directly together:

```
--> "Itwasadarkandstormynight"
```

If you want to use a different separator, you need to set the text item delimiters first; for example:

```
set AppleScript's text item delimiters to {" "} -- A single space
the_list as text
--> "It was a dark and stormy night"
```

> **CAUTION:** I recommend that you *always* set AppleScript's text item delimiters immediately before coercing a list to text, just in case another part of your script changed them previously. If you don't do this, your list-to-text coercion could end up using the wrong delimiter, resulting in a different string from the one you expected.

If the list contains a single item, you can coerce the list to any class that you can coerce the item itself to; for example:

```
{date "Saturday, August 1, 2009 00:00:00"} as text
--> "Saturday, August 1, 2009 00:00:00"
```

Processing List Items with a Repeat Loop

Often, the purpose of collecting items in a single list is so that you can easily go through that list later and do something with each item. Take cooking mashed potatoes, for instance: you start by standing in front of the potato bin in the store, picking up each potato, and putting only nice ones in your bag. When you get home, you take out each potato in your bag and peel it.

Notice that both of these tasks—filtering out the potatoes you want from a larger collection and preparing your potatoes for the pot—involve repetition, where each item is processed one at a time. In AppleScript, you can repeat an action or series of actions by using a `repeat` statement. We'll cover `repeat` statements fully in Chapter 14; however, I would be remiss not to mention them briefly here, given how often repeat loops are used when working with list objects.

You can get at every item of a list in succession in a couple of ways, and both ways involve a repeat loop of some sort. The idea is to have the loop take a list item and assign it to a variable within the loop. The rest of the code in the loop can then refer to that variable in order to process the object. Once it's done, the loop starts over with the next list item, and so on until all the items have been processed.

Let's start by going through the potato bin and picking the ones we want. Script 10–3 shows our potato-filtering script. Because AppleScript lists, unlike application objects, don't support the powerful whose filtering clause, we need to do our own filtering using a repeat loop and a conditional block.

Script 10–3.

```
1. set potato_list to {"small potato", "big potato", "banged potato", "round potato"}
2. set nice_potato_list to {}
3. repeat with i from 1 to (length of potato_list)
4.     set the_potato to item i of potato_list
5.     if {the_potato} is not in {"banged potato", "moldy potato"} then
6.         set end of nice_potato_list to the_potato
7.     end if
8. end repeat
9. nice_potato_list
--> {"small potato", "big potato", "round potato"}
```

Lines 1 and 2 start by defining two lists and assigning them to variables: potato_list, which contains a list of all the potatoes in the bin, and nice_potato_list, which contains the list we'll add all the undamaged potatoes to.

Next, lines 3 to 8 create the repeat loop that is responsible for processing each potato in potato_list. For this example, we'll use a repeat with...from...to... loop, which counts from one number to another, assigning the current count to a variable on each repetition. In this case, we're counting from 1 to the number of potatoes in potato_list and assigning the current count to variable i.

Line 4 uses the value of variable i to get the corresponding item from the main potato list and assigns it to variable the_potato.

Lines 5 to 7 then check if the potato is banged or moldy, and if it isn't, add it to the nice potato list. Once that's done, the loop begins over again, increasing the value of i by 1, until all the potatoes have been dealt with.

Once we get home, we use another loop to process the items in our nice potato list:

```
set nice_potato_list to {"small potato", "big potato", "round potato"}
repeat with the_potato_ref in nice_potato_list
    tell application "Kitchen"
        peel the_potato_ref
        add the_potato_ref to cooking pot
    end tell
end repeat
```

This example uses a different type of repeat statement, just to let you compare them. A repeat with...in... loop takes a list and assigns each list item—or, more precisely, a reference to each item—to a variable. This can be a particularly elegant loop to use when working directly with lists, although because it provides references to the items rather than the items themselves, it can easily catch you out if you aren't careful. But don't worry about this for now—all will become clear in Chapter 14.

In the preceding example, you start with a list of potatoes. As you loop through the list, with each repetition the loop variable, the_potato_ref, is assigned a reference to an item of the list, beginning with the first item and ending with the last. Within the loop, we tell a fictitious application, Kitchen, to peel the potato and then add it to the cooking pot.

Sorting Items in a List

AppleScript provides few built-in commands for working with lists, so you will often need to add your own code for performing common tasks such as searching and sorting. In this section, we'll look at how to sort list items using a simple, if inefficient, algorithm called *bubble sort*.

Because sorting lists is a general task, we will define our own general-purpose bubblesort command. To do this, we add a user-defined handler named bubblesort to our script. This handler takes a single parameter, which is the list you want sorted. (I should also note that I did not invent bubble sort. It's a standard sorting algorithm that has been around for decades and is often taught to beginners due to its simplicity.) Script 10–4 shows the handler in its entirety.

Script 10–4.

```
1. on bubblesort(the_list)
2.     set is_sorted to false
3.     repeat until is_sorted
4.         set is_sorted to true
5.         repeat with i from 1 to (length of the_list) - 1
6.             if item i of the_list > item (i + 1) of the_list then
7.                 set {item i of the_list, item (i + 1) of the_list} to ¬
                       {item (i + 1) of the_list, item i of the_list}
8.                 set is_sorted to false
9.             end if
10.        end repeat
11.    end repeat
12. end bubblesort
```

Once you've added the bubblesort handler to your script, you use it by sending a bubblesort command to your script, with the list you want sorted as the command's parameter. The handler will then arrange the items of the original list into ascending order. For example:

```
set the_list to {"Dell", "Apple", "HP"}
bubblesort(the_list)
the_list
--> {"Apple", "Dell", "HP"}
```

Notice how the contents of the original list have been rearranged by the bubble sort routine. If you do not want the original list to be affected, you should make a copy of it first—for example, by asking for every item of the_list—and sorting the new list instead:

```
set the_list to {"Dell", "Apple", "HP"}
set new_list to every item of the_list
bubblesort(new_list)
new_list
--> {"Apple", "Dell", "HP"}
```

Let's now look briefly at how the bubble sort algorithm shown in Script 10–4 works. As you can see, it uses two nested repeat loops.

The outer loop (lines 3 to 11) will keep repeating while the list's items are not all in ascending order.

The inner loop (lines 5 to 10) is responsible for putting the items into the correct order. It does this by comparing every value with the next value in the list. It loops through the values from the first to the next-to-last one. Each value is paired with the following value in turn, and the two are compared. The script starts by comparing the first item to the second item, then the second item to the third, the third to the fourth, and so on. If the first value in the pair is greater than the second value, then the two values switch places and are placed back into the list at the original spots. For example, if the list is {100, 400, 200, 50}, then it'll start by comparing 100 to 400; because 100 is less than 400, nothing will happen. However, when items 2 and 3 (values 400 and 200) are compared, they will be flipped, because 400 is less than 200. The result will be changing {400, 200} with {200, 400}, resulting in {100, 200, 400, 50}. What actually happens is that the two values in every pair of numbers are sorted in relation to each other.

Once each value has been moved to the appropriate position relative to the others, the outer loop detects that the list is now in order and stops repeating, allowing the handler to exit.

> **NOTE:** Because of the amount of repetition involved, bubble sort is only suitable for sorting small lists. As lists get larger, bubble sorting becomes too slow to be practical. In Chapter 29 we will look at how you can improve performance by using a more efficient sorting algorithm.

Working with Records

Although lists are wild things with items that only you and your scripts know the meaning of, the objects contained in records are meticulously labeled. Records make complex information easier to understand and manage by presenting it as a neatly labeled, self-describing structure.

The following examples illustrate the differences between a list and a record:

```
--This is a list:
{"Bob", 24, true, 55000}
```

```
--This is a record:
{name:"Bob", age:24, married:true, income:55000}
```

The list contains four items: the values "Bob", 24, true, and 55000. Each value is stored and retrieved according to its index (position) in the list.

The record contains the same four values, only now each one is stored in a property. Each property consists of a label, which is either a keyword (normally a property name) or a user-defined identifier, and a value.

Being a portable, self-describing set of information, records are often used as the result of commands that need to return several pieces of related data. A good example is the display dialog command provided by the Standard Additions scripting addition. What's particularly interesting about this command is that, depending on the parameters you give it, the record you get as a result may have different items in it. Figure 10–1 and Figure 10–2 show two different uses of the display dialog command along with their results once the dialog boxes are dismissed.

Figure 10–1. *The* display dialog *command with the* default answer *parameter used*

Figure 10–2. *The* display dialog *command with the* giving up after *parameter used*

The display dialog command returned a different result in each case. Both records contain a button returned property, but the first record has an additional text returned property while the second has an extra gave up property. It is up to you to know what result to expect and how to deal with it when it comes, because you're the one deciding which parameters to include with the command.

Another area where you will find records used is in the `properties` property provided by many application objects. This property holds a record containing all (or most) of the object's properties. This is convenient when you want to get the values of multiple properties: instead of getting each value one at a time, you just ask the object for the value of its `properties` property, and it returns them all at once. The following example shows the range of information you get when you ask for the properties of a movie document in QuickTime Player:

```
tell application "QuickTime Player"
   properties of document 1
end tell
--> {data size:219194941, audio volume:0.0, modified:false,
      current audio compression:missing value, name:"Nosferatu.mp4",
      current microphone:missing value, output muted:false,
      duration:5059.68796666667, current movie compression:missing value,
      current screen compression:missing value, data rate:40034,
      current camera:missing value, presenting:false, playing:true,
      class:document, file:file "Macintosh HD:Users:hanaan:Movies:Nosferatu.mp4",
      natural dimensions:{320, 240}, looping:false, time:602.823945871, rate:1.0}
```

Getting the properties of an object as a record is also a useful learning aid when familiarizing yourself with the application's object model.

Getting and Setting the Properties of a Record

By default, records have two properties, `class` and `length`. The `class` property contains the class of the object, which is normally `record`, and the `length` property normally contains the number of properties in the record:

```
class of {name:"Bob", age:24, married:true, income:55000}
--> record

length of {name:"Bob", age:24, married:true, income:55000}
--> 4
```

The neat thing about records, however, is that they are not limited to the standard properties defined by AppleScript. On top of these, you can define any additional properties of your own. Each property must be specified in your source code—you cannot add or remove properties while the script is running. However, you can get or set each property's value any time you like.

Let's take our previous record and assign it to a variable, the_dude, so that it's easier to work with:

```
set the_dude to {name:"Bob", age:24, married:true, income:55000}
```

This record contains four properties defined by us: name (a commonly used keyword provided by AppleScript), age, `married`, and `income` (which are identifiers we've made up).

To obtain a value from this record, you need to create a reference to the property that holds the value you want. Because the record's structure—that is, how many properties it has and what their names are—is defined in the script's source code, the references you use to access these properties must be defined in the source code too. For example, the_dude's record contains a property with the identifier age, so to obtain the age value from the record, you write a reference to the record's age property:

```
age of the_dude
--> 24
```

Or, if you want to make the get command explicit, you write the following:

```
get age of the_dude
```

You can use the set command to assign new values to a record's properties. Here's an example:

```
set the_dude to {name: "Bob", age: 24, married: true, income: 55000}
set income of the_dude to 75000
the_dude
--> {name: "Bob", age: 24, married: true, income: 75000}
```

By now, you might be wondering: since records allow you to define any properties you like, what happens if you define a property named class or length? Let's try it:

```
set the_dude to {class:"person", name: "Bob", age: 24, married: true, income: 55000}
class of the_dude
--> "person"
```

As you can see, our custom class property overrides the built-in one, allowing us to indicate what this particular record structure represents—that is, a person. Adding a custom length property to a record has the same effect—asking for the record's length returns whatever value the custom length property currently holds, rather than the number of properties in the record.

Some scriptable applications also use this feature when they want to represent relatively simple pieces of structured data that don't need to be full-blown application objects. For example, Adobe Illustrator uses records to represent different types of color values—RGB, CMYK, and so on. Each record contains a custom class property that indicates exactly what type of color it is. For example:

```
tell application "Adobe Illustrator"
    fill color of path item 1 of document 1
end tell
--> {class:CMYK color info, cyan:0.0, magenta:0.0, yellow:0.0, black:100.0}
```

> **NOTE:** Remember, a record is a collection of properties whose structure is defined at *compile time*. If you want to store values under keys that are only known at runtime—for example, if your keys are strings—then you need to use a different structure. One option would be to use Mac OS X's faceless Database Events application, which we'll cover in Chapter 25. Another possibility is to invent your own data structure using a combination of lists and records, and then define a number of commands for adding and removing values. We will look at how to do this in Chapter 18.

Operators and Commands

AppleScript records support a few operations—concatenation, and some comparison and containment tests—and a single command, count. Let's look at each of these in turn.

Concatenating Records

You concatenate records the same way you concatenate lists: by using the concatenation operator, &. The following is a simple record concatenation operation:

```
{model:"Focus", year:2008} & {maker:"Ford"}
--> {model:"Focus", year:2008, maker:"Ford"}
```

If the two records contain the same property, the property from the left operand is used and the property from the right operand is discarded:

```
{model:"MBP17", RAM:4096} & {RAM:2048, speed:2800}
--> {model:"MBP17", RAM:4096, speed:2800}
```

Notice that both of the original records contained the property RAM, but the result only contains the RAM value from the left one.

Comparing Records

You can test whether or not two records are equal. For instance, the following comparison returns true, even though the properties appear in different order:

```
{model:"Focus", year:2008, maker:"Ford"} = {year:2008, maker:"Ford", model:"Focus"}
--> true
```

Checking for Subrecords

You can use the contains, is in, does not contain, and is not in containment operators to check whether or not a record contains another record. For example:

```
{year:2008, model:"Focus", maker:"Ford"} contains {model:"Focus"}
--> true

{year:2004} is in {year:2008, maker:"Ford", model:"Focus"}
--> false
```

Once again, the order of the properties is not important, only their names and values.

Coercing from Records

AppleScript allows records to be coerced into lists. Coercing a record into a list creates a list containing the value of each property from the original record. For example:

```
{year:2008, maker:"Ford", model:"Focus"} as list
--> {2008, "Ford", "Focus"}
```

Counting Records

You can count the number of properties in a record by using the count command:

```
count {name: "Bob", age: 24, married: true, income: 55000}
--> 4
```

Notice that whereas the count command and length property can be used interchangeably when working with strings and lists, things are different with records. Remember, a script or application may define any record properties it requires. If a record defines a property named length, asking the record for its length property will return that value instead. Using the count command always returns the actual number of items in the record:

```
length of {x:32, y:79, length:55, height:60}
--> 55

count {x:32, y:79, length:55, height:60}
--> 4
```

Mind you, I'm not sure why you'd ever want to find out the number of properties in a record, but the feature is there if you need it.

Example Project: Measuring Word Frequency in TextEdit

We'll finish this chapter with an example project that combines the use of lists and records to measure how often words appear in a TextEdit document.

Counting the frequency of words is an interesting project; although the solution is not too complicated, it may not be obvious if you haven't solved this sort of problem before. So, before I show you the source code, let's consider what's involved.

Planning the Script

Consider the following famous piece of text from Charles Dickens' *A Tale of Two Cities*:

> *It was the best of times, it was the worst of times, it was the age of wisdom, it was the age of foolishness, it was the epoch of belief, it was the epoch of incredulity, it was the season of Light, it was the season of Darkness, it was the spring of hope, it was the winter of despair, we had everything before us, we had nothing before us, we were all going direct to Heaven, we were all going direct the other way—in short, the period was so far like the present period, that some of its noisiest authorities insisted on its being received, for good or for evil, in the superlative degree of comparison only.*

The goal is to find out how often words appear in this text—for example, "the" appears 14 times, "best" appears once, and so on. If you were doing this manually, you would keep a tally of words on a piece of lined paper as you read through the text. Each time you encountered a new word, you would write it on a new line and put a tally mark next to it. Each time you encountered a word that already appeared on the paper, you would add another mark to that line, as shown in Figure 10–3.

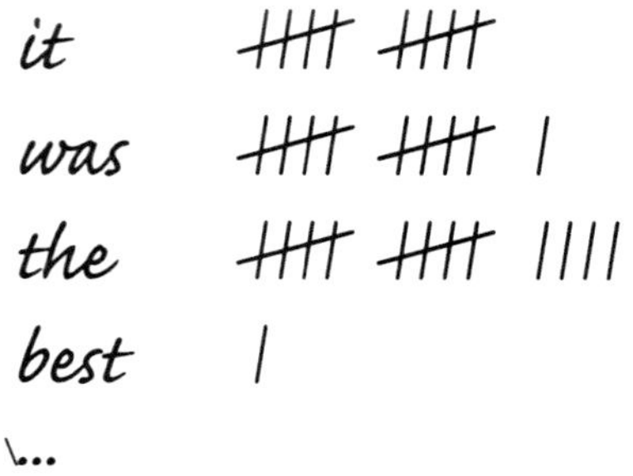

Figure 10–3. *Tallying the word frequency by hand*

Using AppleScript, the process is not too different. Instead of a piece of lined paper, we will use a list to hold all the unique words we find. We also need to track how many times each word appears, so we will store the word and its associated count as a record with two properties: the_word and the_count. For example:

```
{the_word:"the", the_count:14}
```

Each time we encounter a new word, we add a new record for that word to the word frequency list and set its the_count property to 1. Whenever we encounter a word that's already in the list, we retrieve the record for that word and increase the value of its the_count property by one. In a nutshell, this is the core of our solution.

Once we've completed the main word counting logic, we will enhance the basic script by assembling our word counts into a neatly formatted string and inserting it into a new TextEdit document for the user to see.

Developing the Script

Now that we've discussed how the script will work, let's start putting it together. We'll begin by asking TextEdit for a list of all the words in the front document:

```
-- Get a list of words from the front TextEdit document
tell application "TextEdit"
   set word_list to every word of document 1
end tell
```

You should test this code by creating a new TextEdit document with some words in it and then running the script. The result should be a list of word strings, like this:

```
--> {"It", "was", "the", "best", "of", "times", "it", "was", "the", "worst",
    "of", "times", "it", "was", "the", "age", "of", "wisdom", "it", "was",
    "the", "age", "of", "foolishness", ...}
```

Next we define the main list that will track the frequency of each word:

```
-- Define a list to store the number of times each word appears.
-- Each item in the list will be a record with the following structure:
-- {the_word:<text>, the_count:<integer>}
set word_frequency_list to {}
```

Notice that I'm adding descriptive comments to this script. If this were a throwaway script that you would use only once, you probably wouldn't bother adding any comments unless they would help you in planning the design. On the other hand, if you intend to keep the script around for a while, adding comments that remind you what each stage of the script does will help you if you need to modify the script in the future.

Next we begin the main loop that will process each word in the original list:

```
-- Loop through the words in the master list
repeat with the_word_ref in word_list
```

The repeat with...in... loop assigns a reference to the list item to variable the_word_ref, but we want the string itself, so we will extract it from the reference and assign it to a new variable, the_current_word, for use in the rest of the loop:

```
    -- Extract the word string from the reference and assign it to a variable
    set the_current_word to contents of the_word_ref
```

> **TIP:** Don't worry if all this stuff about repeat with...in... loops and references doesn't make complete sense at this point. These concepts are a bit more advanced, and we'll cover them fully in Chapter 14.

Next we define the inner loop that will search through the word frequency list to check whether a record for the current word already exists. (Remember that AppleScript normally ignores any differences in capitalization when comparing strings—which is exactly the behavior we want here.) If we find a matching record, we will assign it to a variable named word_info so that it can be used later. If we don't find a matching record... well, we'd better give word_info a default value before we start or else we'll get a "Variable not found" error when we try to use it afterward. Here is the set statement that will assign a default value (missing value is always a good choice for indicating a "nonvalue" value):

```
    -- See if the word frequency list already has an entry for this word
    set word_info to missing value
```

And here is the inner "search" loop in its entirety:

```
repeat with record_ref in word_frequency_list
    if the_word of record_ref = the_current_word then
        -- Assign the record to word_info, then end the search
        set word_info to contents of record_ref
        exit repeat
    end if
end repeat
```

Notice that once we find a matching record, we don't need to bother searching the rest of the loop, so I've added an exit repeat statement that will exit the loop early in that case. This should help to speed things up a little bit.

Next we check the value of the word_info variable to see whether or not we found a matching record:

```
-- Check to see if we found an existing entry for the current word
if word_info = missing value then
    -- No matching record was found, so create a new one
    set word_info to {the_word:the_current_word, the_count:1}
    set end of word_frequency_list to word_info
else
```

If the value has not changed from missing value, then we know that no match was found. In this case, the code within the if statement will execute, creating a new record for this word and adding it to the word frequency list. Otherwise, we increase the count of the existing record by 1:

```
    -- Increment the word count
    set the_count of word_info to (the_count of word_info) + 1
    end if
end repeat
```

At this point, the core logic of the script is complete, so it's a good idea to run another test, just to make sure the word frequency list is being built up correctly. Add the following temporary line and run the script:

```
return word_frequency_list
```

The result should be a list of records that looks like this:

```
--> {{the_word:"It", word_count:10}, {the_word:"was", word_count:11},
    {the_word:"the", word_count:14}, {the_word:"best", word_count:1},
    {the_word:"of", word_count:12}, {the_word:"times", word_count:2}, ...}
```

At this point, you could use the generated word frequency list in any way you like. For this exercise, we will turn it into return-delimited text that looks like this:

```
"It" appears 10 times.
"was" appears 11 times.
"the" appears 14 times.
"best" appears 1 times.
...
```

To do this, we will use another list and another loop, as follows:

```
-- Build the report
set the_report_list to {}
repeat with word_info in word_frequency_list
    set end of the_report_list to quote & the_word of word_info & ¬
        quote & " appears " & the_count of word_info & " times."
end repeat
```

Here, we go through each record in the word frequency list, extract the values of its properties, and assemble them into a string. We then add this string to a new list stored in a variable named the_word_list. We could just as easily have built up the report string directly; however, this approach becomes increasingly inefficient as the string grows large, whereas adding items to the end of an existing list remains fairly fast.

To create the return-delimited string at the end, we set AppleScript's text item delimiters to the return character and then coerce the list to text:

```
-- Coerce the list into a single return-delimited string
set AppleScript's text item delimiters to return
set the_report to the_report_list as text
```

Now that we have our final string (you did remember to run another test at this point, didn't you, just to be sure?), we can send a make command to TextEdit, telling it to create a new document containing the finished report text:

```
-- Create a new TextEdit document containing the finished report
tell application "TextEdit"
    make new document with properties {name:"Word Frequencies", text:the_report}
end tell
```

Figure 10–4 shows a typical result.

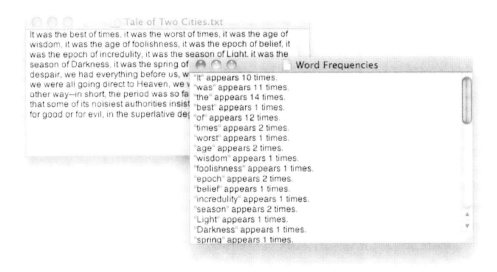

Figure 10–4. *Viewing the word frequency report for a TextEdit document*

Conclusion

Congratulations on the completion of your word frequency script. Before you try it out on larger texts, I suppose I should warn you that the design we've used here isn't as efficient as it could be, nor is AppleScript the fastest language for this sort of heavy data crunching, so running it on the whole of *A Tale of Two Cities* might take a bit longer than you're willing to wait.

All the same, for small texts, the script should perform reasonably, and it demonstrates some very interesting concepts that we will return to again later in the book—in particular, the idea of constructing your own custom data structure (an "associative list") using simpler AppleScript classes (lists and records) in order to store and retrieve values (in this case, word counts) using arbitrary keys (word strings).

Summary

This chapter introduced you to AppleScript lists and records, which allow you to store other objects as either an ordered sequence (list) or a collection of properties (records). You found out how to access the elements of a list by numerical index, and how to access the properties of a record by referring to the property name. You were briefly introduced to repeat loops as a means of processing the items of a list one at a time, and you developed a simple bubble sorting routine for putting lists of numbers, strings, or dates into ascending order.

Now that we've covered the most important classes of objects in AppleScript, it's time to move on to other aspects of working with data in AppleScript, beginning with storing your objects in variables.

Chapter 11

Storing Objects in Variables

Often, a script will create objects that it needs to use again later. Obviously, what the script needs is some way to store those objects and then retrieve them when they're needed. AppleScript's *variables* provide just such a storage system.

Variables consist of two parts: the identifier and the value. The *identifier* is a name that describes the value, and the *value* is the object you actually want to use. Here's an example:

```
set first_name to "Sponge"
```

This example assigns the value "Sponge" to the variable `first_name`. If you want to retrieve the value of that variable somewhere else in the script, you use the identifier `first_name`. When the script is run, AppleScript evaluates the variable's identifier and retrieves and returns the associated value.

Chapters 2 and 6 provided a very brief introduction to variables, and many of the scripts we've written since then have used them, but there are still many details that we haven't covered yet. The following sections will explore in detail the three kinds of variables you can define in your scripts—locals, properties, and globals—and why, where, and how you use them. We'll also look at some predefined variables that are built into AppleScript itself, providing easy access to a number of useful values.

Creating Variables

You can define three kinds of variables in AppleScript: local variables, properties, and global variables. I'll discuss the similarities and differences between these throughout this chapter, but I'll start here with how they're created.

Declaring Your Variables

The type of variable you'll use most is a local variable. A local variable is normally defined automatically the first time you assign a value to it using a set or copy command. For example, the following script implicitly declares i and j as local variables and assigns to them the values 0 and 1, respectively:

```
set i to 0
copy 1 to j
```

Since variables i and j have not been previously defined, AppleScript automatically makes them local variables by default. Alternatively, you can use the local statement to explicitly declare them as local variables first, and then assign values to them later:

```
local i, j

set i to 0
copy 1 to j
```

> **NOTE:** You may be wondering why AppleScript provides two different commands, set and copy, for assigning values to variables. Briefly, the set command simply assigns the given object as is, whereas the copy command makes a copy of the original object and assigns the copy instead. We'll discuss these commands in more detail in Chapter 12.

Another way to create a variable is by declaring a property or a global variable. The most obvious difference between the two is that when you declare a property, you also assign an initial value to it.

You define a property like this:

```
property main_folder_path : "Macintosh HD:Users:hanaan:Work:"
```

You define a global variable like this:

```
global main_folder_path
```

It is important to understand that although you can implicitly declare a local variable anywhere in the script by simply assigning a value to it, you have to explicitly declare global variables and script properties. Also, these declarations *must* appear before the code that uses them, otherwise your script will not work correctly. I recommend always putting them at the top of the script before all your other code, which also makes them easy to see. Script 11–1 shows the start of a well-structured script.

Script 11–1.

```
property identifier1:"starting value"
property identifier2:"starting value"
global identifier3, identifier4

on run
    local identifier5, identifier6 -- optional declarations
    -- other statements
end run
```

```
-- other handlers
```

You'll explore some other differences between locals, properties, and globals throughout this chapter.

Choosing Your Variable Names

Variable identifiers—which you use to refer to variables in your scripts—are words you make up, and there are a few rules you need to follow in order for your identifiers to work. Fortunately, you usually don't have to wait until you run your script to discover that you can't use a variable name. For the most part, the script simply will not compile because the AppleScript compiler will detect and reject invalid identifiers.

The basic rules for naming variables are as follows:

- The variable name must start with an alphabetic character (a–z, A–Z) or an underscore (_).

- It can contain any number of additional alphabetic characters, digits (0–9), and underscores.

- It cannot be a reserved keyword.

Here are some valid identifiers:

```
my_total_score
x
RatioBetweenTaxibleIncomeAndCharitableContribution
```

And here are some invalid ones:

```
2TimesDose
is_address_missing?
count
```

When Keywords and Identifiers Conflict

AppleScript has quite a few words it reserves for its own use, including if, then, data, log, month, file, and so on. (If you are really curious, you can find links to lists of all AppleScript- and Apple-defined keywords in the AppleScript Language Guide on the Apple web site, though be warned: these lists are rather long.) In addition to the words reserved by the AppleScript language, every scriptable application or scripting addition can reserve its own words. For example, FileMaker Pro reserves the words database, record, field, cell, and more.

Trying to use a reserved word as a variable will often cause an error when the script tries to compile. For example, if you try to compile the following line in AppleScript Editor,

```
set repeat to true
```

AppleScript will report a syntax error: "Expected expression but found 'repeat'." repeat is a keyword reserved by AppleScript, so it cannot be used as a variable name.

In some cases—for example, if the reserved word is a property name—then the script will compile but will probably throw an error or behave unexpectedly when it is run. For example,

```
set count to 5
```

will compile, even though count is a reserved command name, but it causes a nonsensical "Can't set count of 5 to." error when run.

Tips for Avoiding Problems with Variable Names

As you become more familiar with the AppleScript language and the scriptable applications and scripting additions you work with, you will tend to remember commonly used keywords and know not to use them as variable names. It's unlikely you'll remember them all, however (and even if you do, the list will change whenever you introduce new applications or scripting additions), so here are some general tips for avoiding problems.

The first tip is to make your variable names stand out. AppleScript, scriptable applications, and scripting additions often use single words as keywords—for example, name, file, document, or log—so you are best to avoid those altogether. Multiword keywords are almost always written with spaces between each word, however, so multiword identifiers are much less likely to conflict. I always use at least two words in my variable identifiers—for example, user_name or documentFile.

The second tip is to get the AppleScript compiler to help you. As I mentioned earlier, many reserved keywords will refuse to compile if you try to use them as identifiers. However, even if they do compile, you can rely on AppleScript's built-in syntax coloring to identify them for you. AppleScript applies different styles to different words, depending on whether they are keywords or identifiers. In Mac OS X 10.6 and later, AppleScript also distinguishes between different types of keywords—command names, property names, class names, and so forth—and indicates whether they were defined by AppleScript itself, a scriptable application, or a scripting addition. By default, keywords are colored in various shades of blue and purple depending on their exact meaning, while user-defined identifiers are colored green. You can view and modify these formatting settings in the Formatting panel of AppleScript Editor's Preferences window, as shown in Figure 11–1.

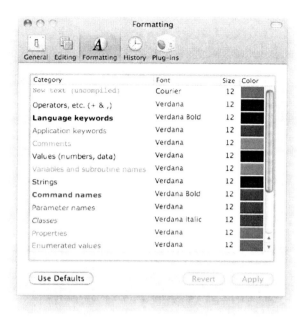

Figure 11–1. *AppleScript Editor allows you to set AppleScript's syntax coloring.*

You will notice right after compiling your script whether the variables you typed have the color and formatting you assigned to the "Variables and subroutine names" style. If they appear in a keyword style, you will know to change them.

One last bit of advice when choosing variable names: never use a user-defined handler name as a variable name as well. If you do, assigning a value to the variable will replace the original handler, causing subsequent calls to the handler to fail! It's a pity that AppleScript doesn't automatically raise a "Can't set *handler name*" error if you try to set a handler (which makes no sense) as this can lead to some rather mystifying error messages. But as it doesn't, you just need to take extra care: a good technique is to begin all of your handler names with a verb (for example, **count**_sheep) and all of your variable names with a noun (such as **sheep**_count).

Follow Good Naming Practices

Picking your variable names wisely can help to make the difference between a script that works, and a script that works *and* is easy to understand and change as well. The following are some simple guidelines you ought to consider when deciding what to call your variables:

▩ Each variable's name should describe its value's purpose, rather than its type. For example, if the variable holds a piece of text representing a user's name, you could call it the_text. However, user_name would be a much better choice as it tells anyone reading the code what the value is actually *for*.

▩ Variable names should be concise, but not so short that their meaning is cryptic. For example, the meaning of source_file_path is immediately obvious, whereas src_pth might require some guessing and p could mean just about anything! Avoid excessively long names, though, as they will make your code bloated and tedious to read. For example, the_folder_to_save_processed_files_into is twice as long as destination_folder but doesn't really tell you anything extra, so why not use the shorter name?

▩ Choosing good names is not so important when creating quick-and-dirty "throwaway" scripts, as they will not be around long enough for you to forget their meaning. On the other hand, when writing large scripts that you will develop and maintain over a long period of time, well-chosen names will make it much easier to remember what the code does when you come back to it later on. (Well-written comments and extra design notes are also a big help here.)

▩ Using more generic names for minor, temporary variables (for example, temp_list) and more descriptive names for major, longer-lasting variables (such as movie_files_to_process) can help the reader to identify which parts of the code are the most important. Similarly, variable names that appear in reusable, general-purpose code can often be more generic; for example, a standard find_and_replace handler would probably name its parameters the_text, search_text, and replacement_text. By comparison, in one-off, specialized code, you should pick variable names that describe each value's exact meaning; for example, customer_name, images_folder_path, US_zip_codes_list.

▩ Single-character names are not always a bad choice. Certain characters are commonly assumed to have specific meanings when used as variable names. For example, i and j may be used to represent unimportant integer values, most commonly loop variables in repeat with ... from ... to ... loops; c and s are often used for temporary variables containing single-character and multicharacter strings; and x, y, w, h may be used to indicate x and y coordinates and width and height values, respectively.

▩ In large scripts, always adding a standard prefix such as p_ or g_ to property and global names can help the reader to distinguish them from local variables; for example, p_log_file_path would obviously be a property containing the path to a log file, rather than a local variable.

> You may or may not find that it helps to add a suffix that indicates the exact class of value stored in some variables; for example, `message_text`, `isbn_list`, `output_folder_alias`, etc. This can be a useful reminder of the type of value to expect, although you shouldn't be lazy and use this approach as a substitute for picking good descriptive names in the first place. Also, if you do use this approach, make sure you don't then store a different class of value than the name suggests, otherwise this will cause some confusion.

Of course, following any or all of the preceding guidelines is not compulsory—ultimately it is up to you to decide which practices are appropriate for your particular needs. Just remember that some day, long after you've forgotten what it does, you may have to read your own code. So if you discover at that point that you can't make heads nor tails of it, you'll have nobody to blame but yourself!

Break All the Rules!

Okay, so now that you've recited all the rules and know them perfectly, I'll show you how to bypass them! Use spaces, start with a number, and use reserved words—anything you want. All you have to do is wrap your identifier in a pair of pipes, like this:

```
|my variable|
```

This shields the variable from any naming rules. Doing this allows you to use spaces, use special characters, start the name with a number (inside the pipes), and so on. Here are some legal names:

```
|#$%@ That!|
|2b or not 2b|
|ユーザ名|
```

When AppleScript decompiles a previously compiled script to source code, it automatically applies pipes to any identifiers that would otherwise conflict with application- or scripting addition–defined keywords. There may also be times when you need to wrap certain identifiers in pipes yourself. For example, because `count` is an AppleScript-defined command name, it will always compile as a keyword, so if you are working with Snow Leopard's new AppleScript-Cocoa bridge (which always uses identifiers), then you must write the equivalent Cocoa command as `|count|`.

Working with Local Variables

So far, you know that assigning a value to a variable allows you to retrieve that value later. That is true to some extent, but as your scripts become more sophisticated, you will need to understand for how long each of the variables you create lives and which parts of your script can and can't see the variable during that time.

As stated earlier in the chapter, when you simply assign a value to a new variable, you are actually getting AppleScript to perform two actions: declaring a local variable and assigning a value to it.

Local variables are simple to understand until you start creating your own handlers. Once handlers enter the scene, you must also consider the *scope* of the variables—that is, which parts of the script can see them.

Understanding Local Variable Scope

The scoping rules for properties and global variables are quite simple: they can be accessed from anywhere in your script. The scoping rules for local variables are a little more complicated: when you declare a local variable in a handler, only the code *within* that handler can see it.

To help you understand this, let's work through some examples. Script 11–2 shows a very simple script.

Script 11–2.

```
1. set user_name to "Ben"
2. display dialog ("Hello " & user_name & "!")
```

When you run the script, line 1 assigns the value "Ben" to a local variable, user_name. Line 2 retrieves the value of user_name and displays it in a dialog box, as shown in Figure 11–2.

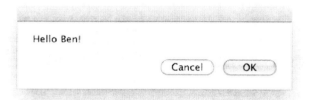

Figure 11–2. *Hello Ben! dialog box*

The script doesn't contain any handlers, so all the code is in a single scope. So far, so good.

What you'll do now is put the display dialog statement from line 2 in the preceding script into a handler. Script 11–3 shows what it looks like.

Script 11–3.

```
1. set user_name to "Ben"
2. say_hello()

3. on say_hello()
4.    display dialog ("Hello " & user_name & "!")
5. end say_hello
```

The handler, which is named say_hello, is declared between lines 3 and 5. It is called to action on line 2.

If you try to run the preceding script, you will get the error shown in Figure 11–3.

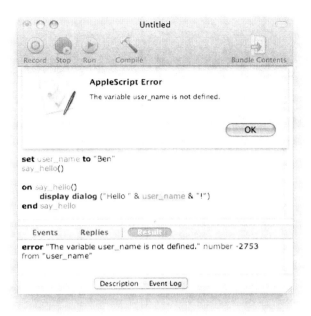

Figure 11–3. *Apparently, the variable user_name has not been declared.*

So, what went wrong? You specifically assigned a value to the user_name variable in line 1, so why did line 4 raise the error it did? Because the user_name variable defined on line 1 was visible in the body of the script (lines 1–2) but *not* to the code inside the say_hello handler (line 4).

The scope of a local variable—and since you didn't specify otherwise, user_name is a local variable—is the current handler only. What handler is that exactly? In Script 11–3, lines 1 and 2 are actually part of the script's run handler. The two lines that declare the beginning and end of the run handler—on run and end run—can be left out, but even without the declaration, any top-level code that is not a property or a handler is part of the implied run handler.

Let's make the run handler by explicitly declaring it, as shown in Script 11–4.

Script 11–4.

```
1. on run
2.     set user_name to "Ben"
3.     say_hello()
4. end run

5. on say_hello()
6.     display dialog ("Hello " & user_name & "!")
7. end say_hello
```

Now things come into focus a bit. The user_name variable was declared in the run handler, which defines one scope, and therefore is not recognized in the say_hello handler, which defines a different scope.

Fortunately, you can remedy this problem in a couple of ways.

The first approach is to make the variable visible to all handlers in the script by declaring it as a property or global variable. In Script 11–5, user_name is declared as a global variable on line 1. When subsequent lines refer to user_name, they are using the same global variable.

Script 11–5.

```
1. global user_name

2. on run
3.     set user_name to "Ben"
4.     say_hello()
5. end run

6. on say_hello()
7.     display dialog ("Hello " & user_name & "!")
8. end say_hello
```

The second approach is to pass the value into the say_hello handler by using it as a parameter to the say_hello command.

Before I explain how to do this, though, let's consider why you would want to do this. Up front, using a global variable sounds simpler: why pass a value as a parameter to multiple handlers when you can just make it directly visible to all handlers?

One good reason is portability. This may not seem like a big deal at the start, but later, when you try to take those brilliant handlers you created and use them in a different script, figuring out which global variables or properties are used by the handler may just drive you out of your mind. You may also start with code that is part of the run handler, then choose to move it to a handler, and finally, when the script gets too long, choose to port some of the handlers to a separate library.

Another reason is that global variables make handlers harder to test and debug individually. If a handler uses only local variables, it should be easy to call it directly, passing it test data as parameters and checking that the value it returns is correct. If a handler uses global variables too, you'll also need to assign test data to those before calling the handler and then check that their values are still correct once the handler is finished.

Perhaps the best reason to avoid gratuitous globals, however, is that they make your scripts harder to read and understand. One of the big advantages of handlers is that they allow you to split up a large, complex script into lots of small, simple units that can be understood and worked on independently while ignoring the rest. Because a global variable is visible to every part of the script, any part of the script is able to use or change it at any time. This means to work safely on a piece of code that uses global variables, you must also pay close attention to all the other parts of the script that share this variable. That's a lot of extra factors to juggle in your head when you want to concentrate on just one!

Although these issues aren't so important in small scripts where the code is simple and easy to understand all at once, in a large script with many handlers and lots of global variables, keeping track of all these extra connections and making sure they all interact correctly can be a lot of extra work.

Despite a handler needing many variables in some cases, it is almost always better to pass them as parameters rather than declare them as global variables, especially if the reason for it is blatant laziness. I'll discuss the justifiable exceptions to this rule later in the chapter, in the "When to Use Properties and Global Variables" section.

Passing Values to and from User-Defined Handlers

Although I don't want to spend too much of this chapter talking about user-defined handlers (which are a fairly advanced topic), now that I've told you that you can pass values in and out of a handler, it's only fair that I briefly show you how to do it.

User-defined handlers actually allow you to specify their parameters in a couple of ways: by position or by label. As this section is only a brief introduction to the subject, we'll use the by-position approach, which is the simpler way.

To pass a value to a handler, you include it in the parentheses following the command name. To call the say_hello handler, you would write the handler name, say_hello, followed by a pair of parentheses containing an expression that returns the value to be passed; for example:

```
say_hello("Ben")
```

or:

```
on run
    set user_name to "Ben"
    say_hello(user_name)
end run
```

When you define the say_hello handler, the parentheses following the handler name should contain the name of the variable to which the passed value will be assigned:

```
on say_hello(user_name)
    display dialog ("Hello " & user_name & "!")
end say_hello
```

What's important to understand is that you are not passing the variable itself, but the value that is stored in it. In the preceding example, the user_name variable in the run handler is completely separate from the one in the say_hello handler—that is, they're two different variables in two different scopes that just happen to use the same name.

You could just as easily use two completely different names, as shown in Script 11–6.

Script 11–6.

```
1. on run
2.    set user_name to "Ben"
```

```
3.    say_hello(user_name)
4. end run

5. on say_hello(somebody)
6.    display dialog ("Hello " & somebody & "!")
7. end say_hello
```

In the preceding script, the say_hello command on line 1 uses the value, "Ben", of the variable user_name as its parameter. When the say_hello handler handles the command, line 5 assigns the "Ben" value to the somebody variable, which is automatically a local variable. Line 6 then retrieves the "Ben" value again by referring to the somebody variable.

However, even if you use the same variable names in both handlers, as long as they are local variables they will be completely independent, as proven by Script 11–7.

Script 11–7.

```
1. on run
2.    set user_name to "Ben"
3.    say_hello(user_name)
4.    display dialog ("Goodbye " & user_name & "!")
5. end run

6. on say_hello(user_name)
7.    set user_name to "Jane"
8.    display dialog ("Hello " & user_name & "!")
9. end say_hello
```

Here, the say_hello handler assigns a new value, "Jane", to its user_name variable on line 7, causing line 8 to display the message "Hello Jane!" Once the say_hello handler finishes and returns control to the run handler, you can see that this change has not affected the run handler's user_name variable, which still contains the value "Ben", as line 4 displays "Goodbye Ben!"

To pass multiple values to a handler, you must separate the values you pass in the command with commas and do the same with the parameter variables in the handler definition. The command must provide a value for each parameter variable in the handler definition. Here is an example:

```
on run
    say_hello("Ben", "Brown")
end run

on say_hello(first_name, last_name)
    display dialog ("Hello " & first_name & space & last_name & "!")
end say_hello
```

Finally, user-defined handlers can also return values using the return statement followed by an expression of some sort that provides the value you want to return. For example, the square_root handler shown in Script 11–8 calculates the square root of the given number and returns the result.

Script 11–8.

```
on square_root(the_number)
    return (the_number ^ 0.5)
end square_root
```

```
square_root(49)
--> 7
```

The `square_root` command calls the `square_root` handler, passing it the value 49. The handler performs some work and returns the result, 7, which becomes the result of the command.

We'll discuss user-defined handlers in a lot more detail in Chapter 18. As you can already see, though, handlers provide you with lots of control over which parts of your scripts can or can't use and modify your local variables, while still allowing you to pass values freely from one handler to another.

Working with Properties and Global Variables

As I mentioned earlier, properties and global variables are variables that are visible to all handlers in a script.

Here is a typical property declaration:

```
property my_name : "Jane Smith" -- Declare a property and assign it an initial value
```

Notice how the two steps of declaring the property's name and assigning an initial value to it are performed by the same statement.

By comparison, when you create a global variable, you must declare it first and then assign a value to it later on using a `set` or `copy` command:

```
global quit_now -- Declare a global variable...
set quit_now to false -- ...and assign it a value
```

Understanding Property and Global Variable Scope

The following script demonstrates how global variables work:

```
1. global g

2. on run
3.    set g to "Hello!"
4.    display dialog "The run handler initially says: " & g
5.    do_something()
6.    display dialog "The run handler finally says: " & g
7. end run

8. on do_something()
9.    display dialog "The do_something handler says: " & g
10.    set g to "Bye!"
11. end do_something
```

The `global` statement at the top of the script tells AppleScript that the g variable should be visible throughout the entire script. When the script is run, the statements in the `run` handler are executed. Line 3 assigns an initial value to the global g variable, and line 4 retrieves the variable's value and displays it. Line 5 then calls the do_something handler. Line 9 retrieves the value from g and uses it; line 10 then assigns a new value to g. Once the do_something handler returns, line 6 of the main run handler executes, displaying the new value that was assigned to g by the do_something handler.

Now replace line 1 with the following:

```
property g : ""
```

This declares g as a property and assigns an initial value to it. When you run the script, the results are exactly the same: lines 3 and 10 assign values to the g property, and lines 4, 9, and 6 retrieve the property's value and use it.

In fact, the scoping rules for properties are slightly different from those for global variables. However, the differences only affect scripts that contain other script objects— an advanced AppleScript feature that you won't need unless your scripts are particularly large and/or complex. (We'll cover this subject in Chapter 19.) The rest of the time, you can use properties and global variables more or less interchangeably, although properties do have the extra advantage that you can give them an initial value at the same time as you define them.

How Properties (and Global Variables) Can Retain Values Between Runs

Both global variables and properties share another important feature: when the script assigns a value to a property, the property will retain that value even after the script is done running. This means the script can remember values you give it from run to run. If local variables are a script's short-term memory—forgotten as soon as the handler they were defined in has finished executing—properties and globals are its long-term memory, remembering values for as long as the script itself remains in existence.

To test this, type the code shown in Script 11–9 into an AppleScript Editor document, compile it, and then run it a few times.

Script 11–9.

```
1. property number_of_runs : 0

2. on run
3.     set number_of_runs to number_of_runs + 1
4.     display dialog "You have now run this script " & number_of_runs & " times."
5. end run
```

When you compile the script, the number_of_runs property is defined and its initial value is set to 0. Each time you run the script, the run handler adds 1 to the value of the number_of_runs property and then displays its new value to the user. So the first time you run it, the dialog box displays the message "You have now run this script 1 times." The second time you run it, however, it tells you that you've run it 2 times; on the next run, 3 times, and so on.

If you save the script as an AppleScript Editor applet, the applet will remember the value for number_of_runs each time you run it. Immediately before the applet quits, it automatically stores the script's current state, including the current values of any properties and global variables. The next time the applet launches, it reloads those values before it proceeds.

> **TIP:** Some, though not all, scriptable applications that load and run AppleScripts also preserve the script's current state between runs. Alternatively, you could read and write any important values from/to a preferences file instead. Later chapters will discuss the various ways you can read and write files in AppleScript.

If you reopen the script after running it, you will not see the new value assigned to the property, because AppleScript Editor displays the original source code, which is not modified. If you recompile the script, the values of the properties will be reset to the original values you gave them.

Although global variables also remember their values between runs, this isn't really useful in practice because your script needs to assign a value to the variable before it can use it the first time. The next time you run the script, the code that assigned the value the first time will probably assign it again, replacing the value that was stored from the previous run. Properties are much easier to work with for storing persistent data, and they also avoid any risk of referring to a variable before it has had a value assigned to it.

> **TIP:** Whether or not you use global variables at all is mostly down to your personal taste. In my own scripts, for example, I tend to avoid them altogether and stick to local variables and properties only.

When to Use Properties and Global Variables

When writing a script, there's always a big question as to whether to use properties (or global variables) instead of local variables.

For simple scripts that don't contain any handlers, it doesn't make such a big difference: using properties will allow your script to retain values between runs, but as all your code appears in the script's run handler, all the variables will be visible to all of the script anyway.

Once you start to use handlers, however, you should think carefully before adding properties or global variables—overusing them, instead of using local variables, can make the script difficult to understand and debug.

In the following sections, you'll look at some typical situations in which utilizing script properties can be useful.

Managing User Preferences

Although requiring users to modify a script themselves in order to use it is often undesirable, some situations just call for it. Take, for example, a droplet script that creates titles in Adobe Illustrator and exports them as TIFF files. You may need to change the font the script uses sometime down the road, so you add the `title_font` property to the top of the script, where it is easy to find and change later on. This approach is often sufficient for scripts that you write for yourself.

With scripts that you distribute to other users, modifying the code by hand is much less desirable: scripts can be difficult to support if the user is messing with the code, and nontechnical users may not be able to cope with making changes themselves. In this situation, it's worth going the extra mile and allowing users to modify these settings via a proper user interface.

If you need to create complex preference panes with radio buttons and so on, you need to go for a full-blown Cocoa application, which is something we'll discuss later in the book. For less complicated preferences, you can present a series of simple dialog boxes intended for collecting different settings from the user. We'll look at that approach here.

The first dialog box appears when the applet is launched, and displays three buttons:

- Quit, in case the user didn't mean to launch the script

- Run, used for normal operation, which should also be the default button

- Settings, which allows the user to change some preferences

If the user clicks the Settings button, they will be presented with a series of dialog boxes whose results will supply values to the script's properties.

Script 11–10 shows the basic outline for an Illustrator script that replaces variables with data in a template and applies the desired font. (Note that the template-rendering code has been omitted for clarity.) The template file path is specified in the `template_path` property and the font name in the `title_font` property.

Script 11–10.

```
1. property template_file : missing value
2. property title_font : missing value

3. on run
4.     if template_file is missing value or title_font is missing value then
5.         set_preferences()
6.     end if
7.     display dialog "Run the script or change settings?" ¬
            buttons {"Quit", "Settings", "Run"} default button "Run"
8.     set button_pressed to button returned of result
9.     if button_pressed is "Quit" then
10.         return
11.     else if button_pressed is "Settings" then
12.         set_preferences()
13.     end if
14.     -- The rest of your code is here...
15. end run

16. on set_preferences()
17.     set template_file to choose file with prompt "Pick an Illustrator template"
18.     tell application "Adobe Illustrator"
```

```
19.        set fonts_list to name of every text font
20.     end tell
21.     set user_selection to choose from list fonts_list ¬
               with prompt "Pick a font for the title"
22.     if user_selection is false then error number -128 -- User canceled
23.     set title_font to item 1 of user_selection
24. end set_preferences
```

In the preceding script, you have a run handler and another handler, set_preferences, that is in charge of collecting settings from the user.

Two scenarios will cause the script to call the set_preferences handler: the first time the script runs, in which case the value of the properties will be missing value, or when the user clicks the Settings button in the startup dialog box. Once invoked, the set_preferences handler allows the user to choose a template path in one dialog box and choose a font in another. Once selected, the chosen font and template are assigned to the properties and are used the next time the script runs.

Enabling Debugging Code

Once in a while some pieces of information belong at the top of the script. For instance, I always include a debug_mode property, which has a Boolean value. I want certain functions to be performed only if I'm debugging, and I don't want to forget to turn them off before I put the script to use or, worse, send it to a client. So, I just wrap any debugging-related function in an if debug_mode then ... end if block, and then all I have to do to turn them all off is to set the debug_mode property to false.

Clarifying the Meaning of Important Hard-Coded Values

Another way you can use properties is to clarify the purpose of literal values whose meaning isn't immediately obvious when reading the code. For example, consider the code shown in Script 11–11.

Script 11–11.

```
display dialog "Please enter item's cost in dollars:" default answer ""
set item_cost to (text returned of result) as real
set total_charge to item_cost * 8.25 + 3.5 + 1.7
display dialog "The total charge is $" & total_charge
```

This script asks the user for the base price of an item, and then adds sales tax, handling fees, and package and posting charges and displays the total cost of purchasing the item. However, although the code does what it's supposed to do, the meaning of all those "magic" numbers on line 3 isn't obvious. We can improve this script by defining each of these numbers as a well-named property and replacing the literal values on line 3 with those property names, as shown in Script 11–12.

Script 11–12.

```
property sales_tax : 8.25
property handling_fee : 3.5
property package_and_postage : 1.7
```

```
display dialog "Please enter item's cost in dollars:" default answer ""
set item_cost to (text returned of result) as real
set total_charge to item_cost * sales_tax + handling_fee + package_and_postage
display dialog "The total charge is $" & total_charge
```

That's much clearer. We can now understand exactly what the calculation is doing, and if any of the tax or fee values change in the future, it will be obvious which literal numbers need modified.

Defining your own "constants" for important values can be especially valuable in larger scripts where the same value is used several times. For example, imagine that you are writing a large financial script and need to apply the sales tax in different parts of the script. You decide to hard-code the literal value, 8.25, at each point in your script. If the tax rate changes in the future, then you will need to very carefully update all instances of 8.25 to reflect the new tax rate. If you miss one instance, or change an identical looking number that means something else, you could end up in big financial trouble! Defining these special numbers as properties just once in your script and then always referring to those properties should prevent such accidents from happening.

Importing Script Libraries

Although I will cover script libraries in detail when I talk about script objects in Chapter 19, it's appropriate to discuss in this section the aspect of using properties to hold *library* scripts that you load into the main script.

A library is just a script containing one or more general-purpose handlers that you regularly use in other scripts. Rather than cutting and pasting these handlers into every script that needs them, you place them in a library script and save it somewhere convenient such as your /Library/Scripts folder. When another script needs to use these handlers, it loads this library into a property. This allows the library's handlers to be called from anywhere in the script, like this:

```
property ListLib : load script (alias "Macintosh HD:Library:Scripts:ListLib.scpt")

on some_handler()
    -- Some statements that create an unsorted list of names...
    set sorted_names_list to ListLib's sort_list(names_list) -- Sort the list
    -- Some statements that use the sorted list of names...
end some_handler
```

Using AppleScript's Built-in Variables

AppleScript has a few predefined variables available for use in your scripts. Some of these variables—namely, it, me, and result—are rather dynamic, with AppleScript automatically updating their values as the script runs, whereas other variables have a predefined value that should not be changed.

The variables return, space, tab, quote, weeks, days, hours, minutes, and pi are constant-like global variables with a preset value. The purpose of these variables is to save you a bit of work and make your script easier to read by supplying a selection of useful values ready for use.

The other variables—it, me, and `result`—are a bit more sophisticated, and you'll get to those variables shortly. The following section describes the built-in variables in detail.

Variables Containing Predefined Values

AppleScript provides a total of nine convenience values: four for working with text, four for working with dates, and one for working with numbers. We've discussed these variables in previous chapters, but it's worth going over them again briefly as a reminder.

> **CAUTION:** Although the following variables all contain preset values, AppleScript does not actually define them as read-only. However, even though it is possible to change them yourself, you should always avoid doing so because this could cause other parts of your code, which are expecting to find the original values, to break.

The *return, linefeed, space, tab,* and *quote* Variables

The `return`, `linefeed`, `space`, `tab`, and `quote` variables each hold a one-character string.

The `return` variable's value is the carriage return character, or ASCII character 13, and it's useful in text concatenations, particularly when dealing with Carbon-based applications, which often use ASCII 13 characters to indicate line breaks.

Here's an example of using the `return` variable:

```
set names_message to "Peter" & return & "Paul" & return & "Mary"
```

The result is as follows:

```
"Peter
Paul
Mary"
```

The `linefeed` variable serves a similar purpose, except that it contains ASCII character 10, which is the line break character normally used by Cocoa applications and Unix shell scripts.

The `space` variable contains a single space character (ASCII 32) and the `tab` variable contains a single tab character (ASCII 9).

The `quote` constant contains a single double quote character (", or ASCII 34). Usually, when you're writing a literal string, such as `"Bob says Hello."`, and want to include a double quote, you have to remember to escape it with a backslash first, or the script won't compile correctly. In other words, you use `"Bob says \"Hello.\""`, not `"Bob says "Hello.""`. However, you can use the `quote` constant instead if you find it more convenient:

```
"Bob says " & quote & "Hello." & quote
```

Using these variables produces the same result as typing the actual character. These variables are useful, though, because you can't always see right away by looking at a string with a few spaces or tabs what characters are used and how many of them are used.

The handler shown in Script 11–13 uses the tab and space variables to trim tabs and spaces from the start or end of a string. It takes one parameter, which is the string you want trimmed.

Script 11–13.

```
1. on trim_tabs_and_spaces(the_text)
2.    considering hyphens, punctuation and white space
3.       repeat while the_text starts with space or the_text starts with tab
4.          if length of the_text is 1 then
5.             set the_text to ""
6.          else
7.             set the_text to text 2 thru -1 of the_text
8.          end if
9.       end repeat
10.       repeat while the_text ends with space or the_text ends with tab
11.          set the_text to text 1 thru -2 of the_text
12.       end repeat
13.       return the_text
14.    end considering
15. end trim_tabs_and_spaces
```

The built-in linefeed variable was introduced in Mac OS X 10.5, so if you need to support Mac OS X 10.4 or earlier, you can define your own linefeed property in a script like this:

```
property linefeed : ASCII character 10
```

The *weeks*, *days*, *hours*, and *minutes* Variables

The weeks, days, hours, and minutes variables each contain an integer representing the number of seconds in a single week, day, hour, or minute:

```
get weeks --> 604800
get days --> 86400
get hours --> 3600
get minutes --> 60
```

These variables are often used when performing date math. For example, if you want to get the date three days earlier, you could use the following:

```
(date "Thursday, August 6, 2009 13:07:26") - (3 * days)
--> date "Monday, August 3, 2009 13:07:26"
```

Or, suppose you want to calculate the whole number of weeks between two dates:

```
((date "Saturday, September 19, 2009 16:47:00") ¬
    - (date "Thursday, August 20, 2009 12:01:20")) div weeks
--> 4
```

The *pi* Variable

The pi variable has the value 3.14159265359 assigned to it. You can use it anytime you need to figure out a circle circumference from its radius, or vice versa. Script 11–14 calculates the length of ribbon you would need to tie around a given number of pies.

Script 11–14.

```
set pie_count to 3
set pie_radius to 14 -- Pie radius in cm

set pie_circumference to pie_radius * pi
set ribbon_length to pie_circumference * pie_count
set ribbon_length to ribbon_length * 1.1 -- Add 10% to allow for bow-tie at end
round ribbon_length rounding up -- Round to a whole number of cm
--> 146
```

Variables Containing Objects of Special Interest

AppleScript provides three special variables—it, me, and result—whose values are automatically updated by AppleScript while the script runs. The following sections look at each of these in turn.

The *it* Variable

The it variable contains a reference to the target of the current tell block. AppleScript sets this value automatically each time it enters or exits a tell block.

When you write a partial reference within a tell block, AppleScript automatically assumes that the reference ends with it; for example,

```
tell application "TextEdit"
   tell document 1
      name
   end tell
end tell
```

is equivalent to writing:

```
tell application "TextEdit"
   tell document 1 of it
      name of it
   end tell
end tell
```

AppleScript allows you to write a reference to the it variable in one of two ways. The first, which you've already seen, looks like this:

```
name of it
```

However, because AppleScript likes to read like regular English where possible, you can also write it like this:

```
its name
```

In most cases, it's neater to leave the "of it" part implicit. Occasionally, however, the use of the it variable is required to clarify the code so that AppleScript understands it correctly. For example, if a property's name is the same as a class or constant name, AppleScript will not realize that you want the property's value unless you qualify your reference to it:

```
tell application "TextEdit"
    tell window 1
        document
    end tell
end tell
--> document

tell application "TextEdit"
    tell window 1
        document of it
    end tell
end tell
--> document "Untitled" of application "TextEdit"
```

Here is another example where an explicit it is required, otherwise the code wouldn't make sense:

```
tell app "TextEdit"
    get every paragraph of document 1 where it is not "\n" -- Find all non-empty lines
end tell
```

The *me* Variable

The variable me refers to the current script object, which is normally the script you're running. (Things get a bit more complicated if you start using script objects in your scripts; because script objects are an advanced topic, we'll ignore them here.)

The me variable is most often used when you want to call a handler in your script from within an application tell block.

Consider the code shown in Script 11–15.

Script 11–15.

```
tell application "Finder"
    say_hello(name of home)
end tell

on say_hello(user_name)
    display dialog ("Hello " & user_name & "!")
end say_hello
```

The aim here is to call the say_hello handler and pass the name of the user's home folder to it. Unfortunately, when you run the script, you get the error shown in Figure 11–4 instead.

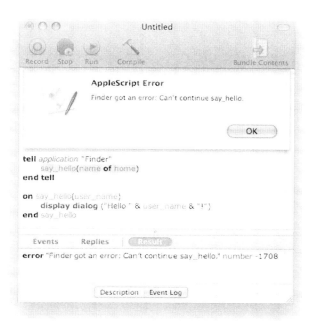

Figure 11–4. *The error you get when running Script 11–15*

The problem here is that when you call a handler from within a `tell` block, AppleScript sends that command to the target object specified by that `tell` block. If the target object contains a handler for that command, it will handle it. If it doesn't, you get an error indicating that the command could not be handled.

I always get a kick from the message "Can't continue." I guess what I want is more details, something like "Can't continue because my feet hurt" or something. Anyway, the message actually means that the Finder didn't know how to handle the `say_hello` command because it is not defined in its dictionary.

What you have to do in this case, or whenever you want to call a local handler from within a `tell application ...` block, is to direct the command toward the script, not the application. Script 11–16 shows how you do that.

Script 11–16.

```
tell application "Finder"
    say_hello(name of home) of me
end tell

on say_hello(user_name)
    display dialog ("Hello " & user_name & "!")
end say_hello
```

Figure 11–5 shows the result of running the script now.

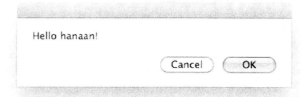

Figure 11–5. *The* say_hello *command is now sent to the script (instead of the Finder), where it is handled successfully.*

As with the it variable, AppleScript allows you to refer to the me variable as either *something* of me or my *something*. When directing user-defined commands at the current script, personally I find that my command_name(...) is much easier to read than command_name(...) of me, although either will work just as well:

```
tell application "Finder"
    my say_hello(name of home) -- This works too
end tell
```

If you want to send several commands to your script, you can even wrap them in a tell block of your own, like this:

```
tell application "Finder"
    set user_name to name of home
    tell me
        say_hello(user_name)
        -- Some other user-defined commands here...
    end tell
end tell
```

Take care, though, not to include any commands in the tell me ... end tell block that need to be sent to the application; otherwise, your script will complain that it doesn't understand how to handle those. Figure 11–6 shows the result of just such an accident.

As a general rule of thumb, I prefer to write my *command* rather than tell me to *command* when sending the script commands from inside a tell application ... block because it is much more specific about what gets sent where.

> **TIP:** The me variable can also be used in the path to command provided by the Standard Additions scripting addition, where it has a slightly different meaning (it causes the path to command to return the path to the script file). See Chapter 20 for details.

Figure 11-6. *Once again, sending a command to the wrong object gives you a (rather cryptic) error.*

The *result* Variable

The result variable is the most often updated variable in AppleScript. After evaluating all the expressions within a statement, AppleScript assigns the final result to the result variable. If the next line needs to use that value, it can obtain it by referring to the result variable.

Examine the simple script in Figure 11-7.

Line 1 of the script in Figure 11-7 contains a simple mathematical expression whose result (6) isn't assigned to any specific variable—it is simply expressed into the air. But, thanks to the result variable, the value it returns is temporarily safe because AppleScript automatically puts it into the result variable. Line 2 retrieves the value of the result variable and shows that it is 6.

Figure 11–7. *The value returned by the expression* 2 + 4 *is automatically assigned to the* result *variable.*

Summary

Although you began using variables in previous chapters, this chapter filled in all the details that you need to know in order to use variables effectively in everyday scripts.

We explored the three different types of variables found in AppleScript—local variables, properties, and global variables—and discussed the roles that they play in your code. You learned that the "scope" of local variables is different from that of properties and global variables: whereas the latter can be seen from anywhere in a script, the former are only visible within a single handler. We also discussed why restricting the scope of most variables is a good thing, although we also considered some situations where it is more appropriate to let them roam free.

We also discussed good practices for naming your variables so that they are clear and easy to understand and (fingers crossed) won't accidentally conflict with keywords defined by AppleScript, scriptable applications, or scripting additions.

Finally, we talked about the various special variables that are built into AppleScript itself, some of which contain useful values that are predefined for your convenience, and others which allow you to access important values that change as the script runs.

Now that you understand variables completely, let's move on to honing your knowledge of perhaps the single most important feature in AppleScript and application scripting: the command.

Chapter 12

More on Commands

As you know by now, commands are an essential tool for manipulating both AppleScript and application objects. In this chapter, you will round out your knowledge of commands as we take a tour of the standard commands provided by many scriptable applications and discuss some of the finer details of commands and their use.

First, though, let's review what you've learned so far.

Understanding How and Where Commands Are Defined

While a command is a command, one of the quirks of AppleScript is that how you type that command depends on how and where it's defined. Commands may be defined in four different places: applications, scripting additions, scripts, and the AppleScript language itself. Let's look at the syntax and usage rules for each in turn, noting where the similarities and differences lie.

Application-Defined Commands

Scriptable application commands have a readable, English-like syntax that uses keywords defined by the application's dictionary.

The name of the command is a keyword. For example, iTunes' dictionary defines command names such as open, play, fast forward, quit, and so on. The following script sends the play command to iTunes, telling it to start playing the current track:

```
tell application "iTunes"
    play
end tell
```

> **NOTE:** If an application is not already running when you send it a command, AppleScript automatically launches it first.

An application command may also take one or more parameters, which are values that it needs to do its job. Some parameters may be required, while others are optional.

Many application commands take a direct parameter, which immediately follows the command's name. For example, TextEdit's open command takes an AppleScript alias value (or list of aliases) as its direct parameter:

```
tell application "TextEdit"
    open alias "Macintosh HD:Users:hanaan:Notes.txt"
end tell
```

Often, the direct parameter is a reference that identifies the application object (or objects) upon which the command should operate. For example:

```
tell application "TextEdit"
    close document 1
end tell

tell application "Finder"
    move every item of desktop to folder "Old desktop stuff"
end tell
```

AppleScript allows some extra flexibility in how you supply the direct parameter for these commands. If the direct parameter is omitted from the command itself, AppleScript will use the default target given by the surrounding tell block:

```
tell application "TextEdit"
    tell document 1
        close -- Closes document 1
    end tell
end tell

tell application "Finder"
    tell every item of desktop
        move to folder "Old desktop stuff" -- Moves all the items on the desktop
    end tell
end tell
```

This can be useful for making code easier to read and is particularly convenient when you want to use the same reference as the target for several commands in a row.

While an application command can have only one direct parameter, it can have any number of labeled parameters, where each value is identified by a different keyword. The application's dictionary explains what each parameter is for and how and when it should be used. The dictionary definition for the Finder's make command is as follows:

```
make v : Make a new element
    make
        new type : the class of the new element
        at location specifier : the location at which to insert the element
        [to specifier] : when creating an alias file, the original item to create an
                alias to or when creating a file viewer window, the target of the window
        [with properties record] : the initial values for the properties of the
                element
--> specifier : to the new object(s)
```

Square brackets indicate optional parameters. (Note that the at parameter in the Finder's make command is actually optional; the Finder's dictionary incorrectly lists it as required.)

For example, the Finder's make command requires you to specify the class of object you want it to create (folder, alias file, window, and so on). To identify this parameter, you must give it the label new:

```
tell application "Finder"
    make new folder
end tell
```

Some application commands allow you to omit some or all of their parameters if you want. You can't omit required parameters; if you do, the application will report an error when it tries to handle the command. However, if you leave out an optional parameter, the command will use a suitable default value instead. For example, you can supply several additional parameters for the Finder's make command if you want; these have the labels at, to, and with properties.

Let's say you want to specify the new folder's name when you create it. You would supply this value via the with properties parameter:

```
tell application "Finder"
    make new folder with properties {name:"Holiday photos"}
end tell
```

HOW APPLESCRIPT FORMATS APPLICATION-DEFINED KEYWORDS

When you compile a script on Mac OS X 10.6 and later, AppleScript highlights each application-defined keyword to indicate its meaning:

- Command names appear as bold, blue text, while parameter labels appear as plain blue.

- Class and element names appear as italic, blue text, while properties and constants (enumerated types) appear as shades of purple.

Scripting addition–defined keywords are formatted in a similar way, but are slightly darker. This formatting can be a big help in making scripts easier to read.

On Mac OS X 10.5 and earlier, AppleScript does not distinguish between different kinds of application- and scripting addition–defined keywords when formatting the script, so all of these keywords appear as plain blue text.

You can change how compiled scripts are formatted in the Formatting panel of AppleScript Editor's Preferences window.

AppleScript has an extra trick up its sleeve when it comes to a labeled parameter whose value is true or false. When a command parameter is written as a literal true or false directly after the parameter label, AppleScript allows it to be written in a more natural way by using the keywords with and without.

For example, the Finder's duplicate command has an optional replacing Boolean parameter that controls whether it replaces an existing item or raises an error if the destination folder contains an item with the same name as the one it's duplicating. Although you can type the command as follows,

```
tell application "Finder"
    duplicate source_item to destination_folder replacing true
end tell
```

when you compile this script, AppleScript will change it to this:

```
tell application "Finder"
    duplicate source_item to destination_folder with replacing
end tell
```

Or, if the replacing parameter is false, AppleScript will change it to this:

```
tell application "Finder"
    duplicate source_item to destination_folder without replacing
end tell
```

You can specify two or more Boolean parameters this way, separating additional parameter labels with commas (the last comma will automatically change to and when you compile):

```
tell application "Finder"
    duplicate source_item to destination_folder ¬
        with replacing, routing suppressed
end tell
```

And you can combine the two forms in the same command when some parameters are true and others are false:

```
tell application "Finder"
    duplicate source_item to destination_folder ¬
        with replacing without routing suppressed
end tell
```

Scripting Addition Commands

The syntax rules for scripting addition commands are the same as for application-defined commands: they have keyword-based names, they may have a single direct parameter and any number of labeled parameters, and parameters may be optional or required.

Unlike scriptable applications, scripting additions can't define their own object models: the only objects they can use are AppleScript values: integers, strings, lists, and so on. This means you won't see scripting additions using object references as their parameters, like applications do.

Unlike application commands, scripting addition commands are always available, and you can use them anywhere in your script. AppleScript will automatically recognize all scripting addition–defined keywords whenever you compile a script, as long as you have that scripting addition installed.

For example, the following,

```
display dialog "Hi there!" giving up after 60
```

will compile whether you put it outside or inside an application tell block.

DEALING WITH TERMINOLOGY CONFLICTS

Because scripting addition terminology is available throughout a script, this can sometimes lead to problems when both a scripting addition and a scriptable application use the same keyword to mean different things. If you try to use a scripting addition command inside the tell block of an application with conflicting terminology, this will often result in errors and other strange behaviors.

For example, the Standard Additions scripting addition defines two commands, read and write, that are used to read and write files in AppleScript. Occasionally you will run into a scriptable application that also defines read and write keywords in its dictionary, using them to mean something else. FileMaker Pro is a good example of this: it defines read and write constant values for use in its access properties.

This means the read and write keywords act as Standard Additions commands when used outside a tell application "FileMaker Pro" ... end tell block and as FileMaker Pro values when used inside the tell block, where FileMaker Pro's dictionary definitions take precedence. If you try to compile the following script,

```
tell application "FileMaker Pro"
    -- Some FileMaker Pro code...
    write the_text to my_file
    -- More FileMaker Pro code...
end tell
```

AppleScript refuses to accept the write the_text to my_file line and gives you an error instead: "Expected end of line but found identifier."

The solution in these situations is to move the scripting addition command outside the application tell block where it will compile correctly:

```
tell application "FileMaker Pro"
    -- Some FileMaker Pro code...
end tell
write the_text to my_file
tell application "FileMaker Pro"
    -- More FileMaker Pro code...
end tell
```

AppleScript Commands

The five commands defined by AppleScript all follow the same English-like style used by application-defined commands, with a few minor differences. The run and count commands follow the same pattern as application- and scripting addition–defined commands and are displayed in the application keyword style (bold blue text) when you compile your scripts. The get, set, and copy commands are styled as language keywords (bold black text). They are written as follows (optional portions appear in brackets):

```
[get] some_expression

set variable_or_reference to some_expression

copy some_expression to variable_or_reference

count some_expression [each some_class]

run [some_expression]
```

More information on these five commands will be presented shortly.

User-Defined Commands

While application- and scripting addition–defined commands take advantage of dictionaries to provide their friendly, English-like syntax, things are a bit more basic for user-defined commands.

Unlike applications and scripting additions, scripters cannot define new keywords for AppleScript to use; they can use only those keywords that already exist. Although it is possible to use command name and parameter label keywords for user-defined command handlers, the normal approach is to use AppleScript identifiers because these can be defined and used by anyone.

A user-defined command can follow one of two syntaxes. In both cases, the command name is a user-defined identifier, which normally appears in a compiled script as green text (the default "Variables and subroutine names" style in the Formatting panel of AppleScript Editor's Preferences window). However, you can specify the command parameters either by position or by label; for example:

```
divide(20, 4)
divide by 4 into 20
```

The by-position form is the simpler of the two and consists of a pair of parentheses that immediately follow the command's name, like this:

```
some_command()
```

If the command has parameters, you place them between the parentheses, each one separated by a comma:

```
some_command("Hello", 3, true)
```

The handler that receives this command will receive these parameter values in the same order as they were given, so it's up to the command to supply them in the order that the handler expects them to be in. In the next example, the variable the_phrase in the handler shout will contain the string "Hello", number_of_times will contain the number 3, and with_feeling will contain the Boolean object true:

```
shout("Hello", 3, true)

to shout(the_phrase, number_of_times, with_feeling)
    -- Some statements here...
end shout
```

The labeled parameter form is more complex, so we won't cover it here. Chapter 18 goes into much greater detail on defining your own commands and using positional and labeled parameters.

One other significant difference from application and scripting addition commands is that user-defined commands cannot have optional parameters. Unfortunately, AppleScript handlers don't provide a way for you to specify a default value to use when a parameter is missing. All parameters are required: if any are missing then an error will occur.

Now that we've reviewed the different command syntaxes found in AppleScript, let's make sure your commands will reach their intended targets.

Picking the Right Target for Your Commands

For your command to work, the target object needs to know how to handle it. Sending a command to an object that doesn't understand it will (usually) result in an error.

For example, if you send a make command to the Finder, the Finder will recognize it and perform the appropriate action:

```
tell application "Finder"
    make new folder
end tell
--> folder "untitled folder" of folder "Desktop" of folder "hanaan"
        of folder "Users" of startup disk of application "Finder"
```

You know that the Finder will recognize this command because make is listed in the Finder's dictionary as one of the commands it understands.

However, if you send the Finder a command such as say_hello, which isn't in its dictionary, you'll get an error instead:

```
tell application "Finder"
    say_hello() -- Finder got an error: Can't continue say_hello.
end tell
```

The error message is a bit cryptic but essentially says that the Finder didn't recognize the say_hello command and couldn't pass it to an object that does (hence the "Can't continue..." bit).

Likewise, if your script sends say_hello to itself but it doesn't have a say_hello command handler defined, you'll get another error:

```
say_hello()
-- Error: «script» doesn't understand the say_hello message.
```

Again, the error description is a bit cryptic, but as with the previous example, it's just telling you that your command wasn't recognized. «script» is the object the command was sent to—in this case, the current script—and message is just another word for command.

If you add a say_hello handler (user-defined command handler) to your script and try again, the say_hello command will now work correctly:

```
say_hello() -- This works now, causing the code in the say_hello handler to run

to say_hello()
    display dialog "Hello!"
end say_hello
```

If your script needs to send a user-defined command to itself from within a `tell application ... end tell` block, make sure you add the `my` keyword in front of the command name, because otherwise AppleScript will send it to the target application instead:

```
tell application "Finder"
    my say_hello()
end tell

to say_hello()
    display dialog "Hello!"
end say_hello
```

NOTE: See Chapter 11 for more information on the me variable and how to use it.

Directing application-defined commands and user-defined commands is fairly straightforward, but what about scripting addition commands? Unlike application commands, where each application is responsible only for handling the commands it defines in its own dictionary (plus a few standard ones such as `run`, `open`, `quit`, `get`, and `set`), *any* application can handle scripting addition commands. How does that work?

First create a new document in AppleScript Editor, and then type the following:

```
display dialog "Hi there!"
```

Compile and run this script, and a dialog box will pop up in AppleScript Editor saying "Hi there!"

Because this command does not appear in a `tell application ... end tell` block, AppleScript starts by trying to handle it itself. First, it checks to see if the script itself contains a script handler named `display dialog`. When it doesn't find one, it forwards the command to the application running the script—in this case, AppleScript Editor—to deal with.

When AppleScript Editor receives a command, it first checks whether it defines the command in its own dictionary. If it does, it handles the command itself. If not, the application automatically loads any available scripting additions to check whether one of them can handle the command. In this case, the `display dialog` command is defined by the Standard Additions scripting addition, so it is handled at last.

If you want to display the dialog box in a different application, wrap the command in an application `tell` block as follows:

```
tell application "Finder"
    display dialog "Hi there!"
end tell
```

Now when you run this script, the "Hi there!" dialog box will appear in the Finder instead. This ability to send scripting addition commands to other applications can be useful at times; for example, if your script needs to bring an application to the front in order to work on it, you'll probably prefer that any confirmation, warning, Open and Save File dialog boxes, and so on, appear in front of that application, instead of bouncing the user back and forth between the application you're scripting and the application running your script each time.

Now that we've discussed how to send commands to the appropriate targets, let's review the five standard commands provided by the AppleScript language itself.

The Five Standard AppleScript Commands

The following sections cover the five basic commands defined by AppleScript: get, set, copy, count, and run. All of these commands operate as both AppleScript and application commands. They also have some interesting and unusual characteristics that set them apart from other commands you use, so it's worth spending a little extra time on them.

The *get* Command

The get command can function both as an AppleScript command and as an application command. When used as an AppleScript command, it returns the value of an expression. The get command in AppleScript is particularly clever because most of the time when you write and run scripts, you're not even aware it's there! It can be written like this,

```
get some_expression
```

where *some_expression* is a regular AppleScript expression or an application reference. For example:

```
get 1 + 2
--> 3

get text 1 thru 3 of "Hi there!"
--> "Hi "
```

In AppleScript code, the get keyword is almost always optional and is normally left out for simplicity.

The *set* Command

The set command works as both an AppleScript command and an application command. In its role as an AppleScript command, set can assign values to variables. It can also assign values to the properties of AppleScript records, dates, and scripts, and can modify the elements in AppleScript lists.

Here is its syntax:

```
set variable_or_reference to some_expression
```

And here are a few examples of its use:

```
set first_name to "Jena"
```

```
set total_area to the_width * the_height
```

```
set end of my_list to new_value
```

The first example assigns a string value, "Jena", to the variable `first_name`. The second assigns the result of the calculation `the_width * the_height` to a variable named `total_area`. The third inserts a value at the end of an AppleScript list.

See Chapter 11 for more information on using the `set` command to assign values to variables.

The *copy* Command

The standard `copy` command is mostly used as an AppleScript command, although it can also operate as various application commands under some conditions. Like the `set` command, AppleScript's `copy` command is commonly used to assign values to variables. Here is its syntax:

```
copy some_expression to variable_or_reference
```

There is one important difference between using `set` and `copy`, however. Although `set` always puts the original value you give it directly into the variable, when used with certain classes of AppleScript values, the `copy` command makes an *identical copy* of the original value and puts this in the variable instead.

This duplicating behavior applies only to values that can have editable properties and elements: lists, records, dates, script objects, and AppleScript references created with the `a reference to` operator. Simpler values such as numbers and strings aren't affected. For example, the following,

```
set variable_1 to "John"
set variable_2 to variable_1
```

and the following,

```
set variable_1 to "John"
copy variable_1 to variable_2
```

do the same thing. The first line assigns a string value, "John", to `variable_1`. The second line assigns the value of `variable_1` to `variable_2`. Both variables contain the same object.

Similarly, if you use the `set` command with a list object, like this,

```
set variable_1 to {"John", "Paul", "George", "Pete"}
set variable_2 to variable_1
```

both variables contain the same object.

You can check this by changing one of the items in the list as follows:

```
set variable_1 to {"John", "Paul", "George", "Pete"}
set variable_2 to variable_1
set last item of variable_2 to "Ringo"
```

If you look at the value of variable_2, it's just what you'd expect it to be:

```
variable_2
--> {"John", "Paul", "George", "Ringo"}
```

If you next check the value of variable_1, you'll find it's the same list object:

```
variable_1
--> {"John", "Paul", "George", "Ringo"}
```

This ability to put the same value into multiple variables can be useful in some situations, although it can also easily catch you out if you're not careful! For example, what if you wanted to keep your original list around so you could use it again later in a different part of the script? Obviously, using set is no good for this.

One solution is to make a perfect copy of the original list by using the copy command instead:

```
set variable_1 to {"John", "Paul", "George", "Pete"}
copy variable_1 to variable_2
```

Now each variable contains a different list object. At first, they still look identical,

```
variable_1
--> {"John", "Paul", "George", "Pete"}
```

```
variable_2
--> {"John", "Paul", "George", "Pete"}
```

but you can now safely alter the contents of the second list without affecting the first one:

```
set last item of variable_2 to "Ringo"
```

```
variable_2
--> {"John", "Paul", "George", "Ringo"} -- Our new list
```

```
variable_1
--> {"John", "Paul", "George", "Pete"} -- Our original list
```

Lastly, like set, you can use copy to assign an application object or list of objects to an AppleScript variable. For example, the following,

```
tell application "Finder"
    copy every folder of home to folder_list
end tell
```

is equivalent to the following:

```
tell application "Finder"
    set folder_list to every folder of home
end tell
```

In each case, you're getting a list of folder references from the Finder and assigning this list to the variable `folder_list`.

The *count* Command

AppleScript's count command returns the number of items in a list, a record, or a string. Its syntax is as follows:

```
count some_expression [each some_class]
```

Here are some simple examples:

```
count "abc"
--> 3
```

```
count {"alef", 2, "gimel", "dalet"}
--> 4
```

```
count {name: "Jerry", occupation: "singer", outlook: "grateful", status: "dead"}
--> 4
```

If you want the count command to count only those items of a particular class, you can use the optional parameter, each:

```
count {"alef", 2, "gimel", "dalet"} each string
--> 3
```

```
count {"alef", 2, "gimel", "dalet"} each number
--> 1
```

Strings, lists, and records also have a length property that allows you to find out the number of items they have:

```
length of {"alef", 2, "gimel", "dalet"}
--> 4
```

Or if you're interested only in a single class of items, you can use a reference like this:

```
length of every number of {"alef", 2, "gimel", "dalet"}
--> 1
```

It's largely a matter of personal preference whether you use AppleScript's count command or an object's length property when dealing with AppleScript strings, lists, and records. Just use whichever one you think looks best.

The *run* Command

The run command also works as both an application command and an AppleScript command. When used as an AppleScript command, the run command tells a script to execute its run handler, which may be implicit or explicit. Here is the syntax for the run command:

```
run [some_expression]
```

An explicit run handler typically looks like this:

```
on run
    -- Some statements...
end run
```

If there's no explicit run handler, AppleScript will treat all top-level statements (except those declaring global variables, properties, handlers, and named script objects) as the script's implicit run handler.

You'll rarely need to send a script a run command. You might occasionally find it useful if you have a script that needs to load another script from disk and run it. For example, save the following script to your home folder as my script.scpt:

```
property i : 1

say i as string
set i to i + 1
```

Now create a new script as follows :

```
set my_script to load script ¬
    alias ((path to home folder as text) & "my script.scpt")
repeat 10 times
    run my_script
end repeat
```

When you run this script, it will load a copy of your saved script and run it repeatedly, causing it to count from 1 to 10.

> **NOTE:** You could also use Standard Additions' run script command to load and run the script in a single step. The only difference with using run script is that it loads a fresh copy of the saved script each time, so it would say "one" each time.

Commands That All Applications Understand

There are several application commands that all GUI applications on Mac OS X should respond to, even ones that are not technically AppleScriptable: run, launch, open, activate, reopen, and quit. The following sections discuss each of these commands in turn.

The *run* Command

You can use the run command with any application. If the application isn't already running, then the run command will cause it to launch. For example:

```
tell application "AppleScript Editor"
    run
end tell
```

You can also write this as follows:

```
run application "AppleScript Editor"
```

If the application is already running, the run command often does nothing, although some applications such as TextEdit may respond by creating a new blank document if they don't already have any documents open.

Most of the time, you don't need to include explicit run commands in your scripts because AppleScript is smart enough to launch applications as needed. For example, if you run the following script,

```
tell application "AppleScript Editor"
    make new document
end tell
```

AppleScript will check whether AppleScript Editor is already running before sending it any commands. If it isn't, AppleScript will automatically start the application before sending it the make command.

> **NOTE:** When AppleScript launches an application, it normally hides it from view. If you want to bring an application to the front, use the `activate` command instead.

The *launch* Command

The launch command works similarly to the run command, with one difference. When you use the run command to start an application, the application will start normally, and a new blank document will be created. If you use the launch command instead, a new document is not created:

```
tell application "TextEdit" to launch
```

The *open* Command

All applications that work with files should respond to the open command. The open command takes a single direct parameter—an alias or list of aliases to the files you want opened:

```
tell application "Safari"
    open alias "Macintosh HD:Users:Hanaan:Sites:index.html"
end tell

tell application "Preview"
    open {alias "Macintosh HD:Users:Hanaan:Pictures:birthday_001.jpg", ¬
        alias "Macintosh HD:Users:Hanaan:Pictures:birthday_002.jpg", ¬
        alias "Macintosh HD:Users:Hanaan:Pictures:birthday_004.jpg"}
end tell
```

Some scriptable applications may define their own enhanced versions of the basic open command; for instance, Adobe Illustrator's open command includes an optional Boolean dialogs parameter that you can use to prevent any warning dialog boxes from appearing when a file is being opened:

```
tell application id "com.adobe.illustrator"
```

```
    open alias "Macintosh HD:Users:hanaan:Work:poster.ai" without dialogs
end tell
```

A number of applications regularly send open commands themselves, including the Finder and the Dock. For instance, when you double-click a document file in the Finder, the Finder sends an open command to the appropriate application, telling it to open the file.

The *activate* Command

The activate command brings a running application to the foreground. This is particularly useful when you need to display dialog boxes, attract the user's attention to a particular application, use graphical user interface (GUI) scripting to manipulate its menu bar, and so on. For example:

```
tell application "iTunes" to activate
```

When writing AppleScript applets that display dialog boxes to users, you may want the applet to send an activate command to itself immediately before it displays a dialog box:

```
activate
display dialog "Enter your name" default answer ""
```

That way, your applet will bring itself to the front, ensuring that the user doesn't miss the dialog box.

The *quit* Command

You can use the quit command to tell a running application to quit itself. For example:

```
tell application "Preview" to quit
```

In many applications, the quit command accepts an optional saving parameter that takes one of three constant values: yes, no, or ask. This allows you to specify how you want documents with unsaved changes to be treated. Use yes to save changes automatically if possible, no to discard any changes, and ask to let the user decide in each case.

The following script will tell TextEdit to quit, saving any changes to existing files automatically:

```
tell application "TextEdit"
    activate
    quit saving yes
end tell
```

If the user has created new documents but not yet saved them, TextEdit will still display a Save As dialog box, requiring the user to save those documents manually. If you want to make sure the user sees these dialog boxes, you can place an activate command before the quit command to bring the application to the foreground first. If the user clicks Cancel in the Save dialog box, the application will halt its shutdown procedure, and the quit command will generate a "User canceled" error instead.

TIP: Another option is to check the modified property of each document object to see if it requires saving, and use the save command to save it if necessary. Once you are sure all documents have been properly saved, you should be able to quit the application without any problems.

Another place where the quit command is used is inside the quit handler of a script applet. More details on this are provided in Chapter 18.

The Standard Suite of Application Commands

While every scriptable application may be different, one of the nice things about AppleScript is that it encourages a degree of consistency across these applications. In addition to the core commands that all applications will respond to—run, open, activate, quit, and the rest—Apple has defined a standard set of commands for manipulating an application's object model.

Whereas more specialized commands for tasks such as sending an e-mail or playing a movie tend to be unique to a particular application, commands for performing basic tasks such as creating new objects and moving, duplicating, and deleting existing objects are very similar, if not identical, across a wide range of applications.

The following sections look at the default commands found in the Standard Suite of most scriptable applications. In pure Cocoa applications, these commands are well standardized thanks to Mac OS X's Cocoa Scripting framework, which provides the core foundation upon which application developers can implement their applications' scripting support. As a result, the syntax and behavior of these commands is the same for most Cocoa applications. You may find a bit more variation in applications that have been around since pre–Mac OS X days, because those developers had to do more of the design and coding work themselves; however, they shouldn't be too different.

The *get* Command

When used as an application command, the get command returns the value of the referenced objects. Here is its syntax:

```
get application_reference
```

And here are some examples of its use:

```
tell application "TextEdit"
    get front document
end tell
--> document 1 of application "TextEdit"

tell application "Finder"
    get name of every folder of home
end tell
--> {"Desktop", "Documents", "Library", "Movies", "Music", "Pictures", ...}
```

What's unusual about the get command is that you hardly ever have to write it yourself because AppleScript is smart enough to send a get command for you whenever you need one. So, you can just as easily write some of the earlier examples as follows,

```
tell application "TextEdit"
    front document
end tell
--> document 1 of application "TextEdit"

tell application "Finder"
    name of every folder of home
end tell
--> {"Desktop", "Documents", "Library", "Movies", "Music", "Pictures", ...}
```

and AppleScript will take care of any "getting" for you—the get commands are *implicit*.

Because get usually works automatically, it's almost always a matter of personal taste whether you write get, although most code looks better if you leave it out. For example, the following,

```
tell application id "com.adobe.indesign"
    set my_doc to document 1
end tell
```

is nicer to read than this:

```
tell application id "com.adobe.indesign"
    set my_doc to get document 1
end tell
```

Occasionally, however, you may do to include an *explicit* get command in your code in order for it to work correctly. We'll discuss how, when, and why you should do this later in the chapter.

The *set* Command

In its role as an application command, set is mostly used to assign values to the properties of application objects, although some applications also allow it to modify certain elements (for example, the text elements of a TextEdit document).

Here is its syntax:

```
set application_reference to some_expression
```

And here are some examples:

```
tell application "Finder"
    set label index of every folder of desktop to 1
end tell

tell application "TextEdit"
    set word 1 of text of document 1 to "Hello"
end tell

tell application "iTunes"
    set name of the_track to new_name
```

```
end tell
```

The first example assigns the value 1 to the `label` `index` property of each `folder` object on the Finder's desktop. The second one will replace the first `word` element in TextEdit's front document with the string `"Hello"`. The third example will assign a new name to an iTunes tiTunes track.

The *make* Command

To create new application objects from scratch, you use the `make` command.

The standard `make` command has the following syntax:

```
make v : Make a new object.
   make
      new type : The class of the new object.
      [at location specifier] : The location at which to insert the object.
      [with data any] : The initial data for the object.
      [with properties record] : The initial values for properties of the object.
   --> specifier
```

As you can see, the `make` command has several labeled parameters. The `new` parameter is required; this the name of the class of object you wish to create—`folder`, `document`, `outgoing message`, and so on:

```
tell application "Finder"
   make new folder
end tell
```

Depending on where you want the new object inserted, you may also have to supply an `at` parameter. In Cocoa applications, this is an insertion location reference, identifying a point either at the start or end of an object's elements, or before or after an existing element. Some older applications such as the Finder and iTunes take a reference to the containing object itself. Application dictionaries are often somewhat vague on the details here, so when you encounter a new application, you may have to experiment a bit to see what works. Here are some examples:

```
tell application "Finder"
   make new folder at folder "Downloads" of home
end tell

tell application "TextEdit"
   make new document at end of documents
end tell
```

When creating new objects within the top-level `application` object, most applications allow you to omit the `at` parameter for convenience:

```
tell application "TextEdit"
   make new document
end tell
```

Some applications may require you to supply an insertion reference, but will work out the class of elements for you based on the `new` parameter; for example, when creating a

new event in iCal, you can shorten the insertion reference from end of events of
calendar 1 to end of calendar 1. Once again, you may have to experiment a bit to see
what works for a particular application.

> **TIP:** As a rough rule, pure Cocoa applications whose scripting support uses the Cocoa Scripting
> framework require an insertion location for the destination location, whereas applications that
> have Carbon roots (the Finder, iTunes, and so on) may expect, or possibly even require, an object
> reference.

When you use the make command to create a new application object, the application will
normally assign default values to all the new object's properties. However, you'll often
want to supply your own values for at least some of these properties, and to do this you
can use the make command's with properties parameter.

The following script creates a new Safari document that displays a very familiar web site:

```
tell application "Safari"
    make new document with properties {URL:"http://www.apple.com"}
end tell
```

> **CAUTION:** Some applications may ignore property values supplied by the with properties
> parameter, due to bugs and other quirks. For instance, in Mac OS X 10.6, the Finder's make
> command can set the name of a new folder but not its label index. In this situation, you will have
> to create the object using make and then use one or more set commands to update the problem
> properties.

The with data parameter is used less often, but can be useful in situations where the
new object will be based upon a value that cannot be supplied via the with properties
parameter. For instance, when you create new text objects in applications such as
TextEdit and Mail, you use the with data parameter to supply the plain text to use:

```
tell application "TextEdit"
    activate
    make new paragraph ¬
        at after first paragraph of text of document 1 ¬
        with data "This is a new line.\n"
end tell
```

If you wish to set the properties of the new text at the same time, just include a with
properties parameter as well:

```
tell application "TextEdit"
    activate
    make new paragraph ¬
        at after paragraph 1 of text of document 1 ¬
        with data "This is a new line.\n" ¬
        with properties {font:"Courier", size:48, color:{65535, 0, 0}}
end tell
```

You should also run some tests to see if the make command returns a reference to the newly created object, as different applications can be somewhat inconsistent here. Many applications return references to newly created objects, but some don't (including a few whose dictionaries claim that they do).

The *exists* Command

The exists command is very simple. Given a reference to an application object, it checks if the object actually exists. Here is the syntax:

```
exists v : Verify if an object exists.
   exists specifier : the object for the command
   --> boolean
```

The following script checks whether an iTunes playlist exists, and creates a new one if not:

```
tell application "iTunes"
   if not (exists user playlist "New Tunes") then
      make new user playlist with properties {name:"New Tunes"}
   end if
end tell
```

For readability, AppleScript also allows you to write the exists command after the reference being checked, so

```
tell application "TextEdit"
   exists document 1
end tell
```

can also be written like this:

```
tell application "TextEdit"
   document 1 exists
end tell
```

The *count* Command

AppleScript isn't the only one to define a count command: many scriptable applications also define count commands for counting their own application objects—documents, windows, tracks, folders, and so on.

The syntax is the same as AppleScript's built-in count command:

```
count v : Return the number of elements of a particular class within an object.
   count specifier : the object for the command
      [each type] : The class of objects to be counted.
   --> integer
```

For example, you can count the number of pages in the front document in InDesign as follows:

```
tell application "Adobe InDesign CS4"
  count document 1 each page
```

```
end tell
```

Personally I find the each parameter a bit awkward to read. Happily, the count command will normally accept a reference directly to the elements being counted as its direct parameter, allowing you to omit the each parameter altogether:

```
tell application "Adobe InDesign CS4"
  count pages of document 1
end tell
```

The *move* Command

The move command is used to move one or more objects to a new location in the object model. The basic move command has the following syntax:

```
move v : Move object(s) to a new location.
    move specifier : the object for the command
        to location specifier : The new location for the object(s).
```

Some applications may provide additional parameters for controlling how the object is moved. For instance, the Finder adds several optional parameters, including a Boolean replacing parameter, which you can set to true if you want to replace an existing item with the same name.

The following script moves all of the files on the Finder desktop into the user's Documents folder:

```
tell application "Finder"
    move every file of desktop to folder "Documents" of home
end tell
```

The Finder's move command returns a reference or list of references to the items at their new location.

As with the make command's at parameter, some applications require an insertion location reference for the to parameter, while others use a reference to the containing object. The next script rotates the tabs in the front Safari window by moving the first tab element to the very end of the window object's tab elements:

```
tell application "Safari"
    tell window 1
        move tab 1 to after last tab
    end tell
end tell
```

This time, you'll notice that the to parameter is an insertion location (beginning of *all_elements*, end of *all_elements*, before *some_element*, after *some_element*).

CAUTION: Remember, the purpose of the move command is to move an object from one position in the object model to another. If you want to, say, move a file from one side of the Finder desktop to the other, you would do this by setting the value of the object's `position` property, not by using the move command.

The *duplicate* Command

The duplicate command copies one or more objects to a new location in the object model. Here is the syntax for the standard duplicate command supported by Cocoa-based applications:

```
duplicate v : Copy object(s) and put the copies at a new location.
   duplicate specifier : the object for the command
      [to location specifier] : The location for the new object(s).
      [with properties record] : Properties to be set in the new duplicated
            object(s).
```

As with the move command, the exact syntax and behavior can vary a bit between applications. Some applications allow you to set the new object's properties as it is being copied—for example, you might want to give it a different name from the original.

Some applications allow you to omit the to parameter entirely, in which case the new objects appear in the same location as the originals. For instance,

```
tell application "Finder"
   duplicate every file of desktop
end tell
```

will create copies of all the files on the desktop, just as if you selected them in the Finder GUI and chose **File ➤ Duplicate**.

Alternatively, if you want to copy the files to a different location, you use the following:

```
tell application "Finder"
   duplicate every file of desktop to folder "Documents" of home
end tell
```

When using the Finder's duplicate command in this way, the to parameter must be a reference to a folder or disk object—in this case, **folder "Documents"** of home. Also, if the destination location already contains any files or folders with the same names as the items being copied, an error will occur: "An item with the same name already exists in this location." If you wish to replace the existing items, the Finder provides an extra Boolean parameter, replacing, that allows you to do this:

```
tell application "Finder"
   duplicate every file of desktop to folder "Documents" of home ¬
         with replacing -- Replaces any existing items; take care!
end tell
```

Just be careful you don't accidentally overwrite anything important, of course!

As with the move command, other applications—particularly pure Cocoa ones—may require an insertion location for the to parameter; for example, **end of every paragraph** of text of document 1.

Here's a script that uses TextEdit to copy all of the text from one RTF document to the end of another:

```
tell application "TextEdit"
    activate
    set source_doc to document "source.rtf"
    set destination_doc to document "destination.rtf"
    make new paragraph ¬
        at end of every paragraph of text of destination_doc ¬
        with data linefeed
    duplicate every paragraph of text of source_doc ¬
        to end of every paragraph of text of destination_doc
end tell
```

The make command simply ensures that the copied text will start on its own line; without this command, the text would be added to the end of the previous last line of the document. The duplicate command then copies all of the paragraphs from the document named source.rtf to the end of the document named destination.rtf.

The nice thing about this approach is that the text never leaves TextEdit itself, so any text styles will be copied over as well. If you tried to perform the same task using separate get and set commands, you would lose any style information when the text is converted into an AppleScript string, because the AppleScript language, unlike the TextEdit application, can't work with styled text.

> **NOTE:** In certain situations, AppleScript's copy ... to ... statement will perform an application duplicate command. More on this in the "Using copy As an Application Command" section later in the chapter.

The *delete* Command

The delete command permanently removes an object or objects from the application's object model. Here is the basic syntax:

```
delete v : Delete an object.
    delete specifier : the object for the command
```

For example, the following script deletes every blank line from the front TextEdit document:

```
tell application "TextEdit"
    delete (every paragraph of text of document 1 where it = "\n")
end tell
```

One application that behaves slightly differently is the Mac OS X Finder. There, the delete command moves files and folders to the user's trash, which must then be emptied with a separate empty command. If you want to delete a file or folder directly, you can use the hidden System Events application instead—more on that in Chapter 20.

> **CAUTION:** Be careful when using the delete command because most scriptable applications do not allow you to undo destructive changes made via AppleScript. (The same warning applies to commands such as move and duplicate if they are allowed to replace existing objects.)

The *print* Command

The print command is used to print documents. Here is the command definition from a typical Cocoa application:

```
print v : Print an object.
   print alias : The file(s) or document(s) to be printed.
      [print dialog boolean] : Should the application show the Print dialog?
      [with properties print settings] : the print settings
```

The direct parameter may be either an AppleScript file object (or list of file objects) or a reference to an application document.

Not all applications will support the print dialog or with properties options. In those that do, you can use the with properties parameter to control how the document is printed. The following example prints the frontmost TextEdit document to a printer named "Office Printer" (the name must match a printer name shown in System Preferences' Print & Fax panel), with four pages to each page:

```
tell application "TextEdit"
   activate
   print document 1 with properties ¬
         {target printer:"Office Printer", pages across:2, pages down:2} ¬
         with print dialog
end tell
```

> **NOTE:** You may see another error occur if the user doesn't click a button within a certain length of time: "TextEdit got an error: AppleEvent timed out." This error is actually generated by the operating system rather than the application itself. Whenever you send a command to another application, AppleScript specifies the length of time that it is willing to wait for a response. If the application doesn't respond within that period—perhaps because it is busy doing something else, or has locked up due to a bug, or simply because the operation you requested takes a long time to process—then a timeout error is generated instead. Later in the chapter, you will look at timeout errors in more detail and discover how to adjust the period of time that AppleScript will wait for a response.

The print dialog parameter is true, so the document will display a dialog box that allows the user to adjust the print settings and click the Print button for himself. If the user clicks Cancel instead of Print, the print command will return an error.

The *save* Command

The save command is normally used to save documents to disk. The standard Cocoa version of this command has the following syntax:

```
save v : Save an object.
   save specifier : the object for the command
      [as text] : The file type in which to save the data.
      [in alias] : The file in which to save the object.
```

Here, the direct parameter is a reference to the object to be saved, which is usually a document object. For instance:

```
tell application "TextEdit"
   save document 1
end tell
```

The optional in parameter indicates where the file should be saved. If you omit this parameter, the document will be saved automatically only if it has been saved to file before and the file is not in an inappropriate location such as the user's trash. Otherwise, the application will display a dialog box asking the user if they wish to save the document, which may not be what you want. If your script needs to check these details before trying to save the document, see if the application's document class defines modified and path properties that tell you if a document has unsaved changes and where the document's file is located, assuming it has one.

In the dictionary definition, the in parameter's class is shown as alias, but this is misleading because it can also be file or POSIX file. This is just as well, as alias objects can only point to existing files, and often when you save a document, you want to save it as a completely new file.

Here is a simple example:

```
set new_file to POSIX file "/Users/hanaan/Documents/notes.txt"
tell application "TextEdit"
   save document 1 in new_file
end tell
```

> **NOTE:** You'll learn more about AppleScript's alias, file, and POSIX file classes in Chapter 17.

Occasionally, you may need to use an older application that doesn't accept a POSIX file object or that requires the file path to be given as a string, so if the usual file-related classes don't work, then experiment until you find something that does.

The optional as parameter is common in Cocoa-based applications. The value is an AppleScript string containing a Uniform Type Identifier (UTI) that indicates the file format to use:

```
tell application "TextEdit"
    save document 1 in file "Macintosh HD:Users:hanaan:Result" as "public.rtf"
end tell
```

In practice, the as parameter generally isn't needed if the file name includes a name extension (.txt, .rtf, .html, and so forth), as most applications can figure out the correct file format from that. Also, working out the correct UTIs to use can require a bit of guesswork as they normally aren't listed in the dictionary.

> **NOTE:** You will learn more about UTIs in Chapter 16.

Some non-Cocoa applications also accept an as parameter in a save command, although there value is more likely to be one of several constants defined especially for this purpose. For example, the save command in Adobe Illustrator defines three constants—Illustrator, eps, and pdf—for use in its as parameter:

```
tell application id "com.adobe.illustrator"
    save document "template.ai" ¬
        in file "Macintosh HD:Users:hanaan:Work:PDFs:A10305.pdf"
        as pdf ¬
        with options {compatibility:Acrobat 4}
end tell
```

The *close* Command

The close command is most often used to close document objects, although some applications may use it for other purposes as well, such as closing windows. Here is the definition of the standard close command:

```
close v : Close an object.
    close specifier : the object for the command
        [saving ask/no/yes] : Specifies whether changes should be saved before
            closing.
        [saving in alias] : The file in which to save the object.
```

For example, to save and close the front TextEdit document in a single command:

```
tell application "TextEdit"
    close document 1 saving yes saving in POSIX file "/Users/hanaan/to finish.txt"
end tell
```

Or, to close all of the tabs in the front Safari window, except for the one that is currently visible:

```
tell application "Safari"
    close (every tab of window 1 whose visible = false)
end tell
```

More on Working with *get*, *set*, and *copy* Commands

While the general concepts behind get, set, and copy are easy enough to learn, some of their behaviors require a bit more effort to understand. The following sections discuss the finer details of working with the get, set, and copy commands.

When Do Implicit *get* Commands Occur?

As you know, if you want an application to do something, you have to send it a command. Even a task as simple as getting the value of an object property involves sending a get command to the application. In practice, though, you hardly ever need to write explicit get commands in your code, as AppleScript very cleverly detects when a get command is needed (or at least when it assumes one is needed) and sends it automatically on your behalf.

Consider the code in Script 12–1.

Script 12–1.

```
tell application "Finder"
    set the_name to name of folder 1 of startup disk
end tell
--> "Applications"
```

This code actually involves two commands:

- An implicit application command, get, to get the value identified by the literal reference name of folder 1 of startup disk [of application "Finder"]

- An explicit AppleScript command, set, to assign the value to variable the_name

Here is how the same script would look if you made the get command explicit:

```
tell application "Finder"
    set the_name to (get name of folder 1 of startup disk)
end tell
```

I think you'll agree that the first version is much nicer to read and write.

So, how do implicit get commands work? The key is understanding how AppleScript evaluates literal references—that is, references that you write in your code.

In Script 12–1, there is a literal reference, name of folder 1 of startup disk, on the right side of the set statement. You might think that when AppleScript encounters this reference, it would ask the Finder for the disk object stored in its startup disk property, then ask the disk object for its first folder element, and finally ask the resulting folder object for the value of its name property. However, this is *not* how AppleScript works! Instead, when AppleScript encounters this literal reference, it reads the entire reference in one go and *then* decides what to do with it.

The first thing AppleScript has to work out is whether this is an absolute reference or a relative one—that is, does the reference contain all of the information needed to locate the desired value, or is more work required to complete it? In this case, the reference ends with a property, startup disk, and is located inside a tell block that is targeted at application "Finder", so AppleScript deduces that name of folder 1 of startup disk is a relative reference, and the full reference is this:

```
name of folder 1 of startup disk of application "Finder"
```

Now that AppleScript knows this reference is pointing to another application, its next task is to figure out what to do with the reference. To do this, it must once again look at how the code is constructed. The main question AppleScript asks itself is a simple one: does the literal reference appear as a parameter to an application command?

For example, the following script contains two literal references that are written as parameters to the Finder's move command:

```
tell application "Finder"
    move every file of folder "Downloads" of home to trash
end tell
```

It is clear from this code that the two references—every file of folder "Downloads" of home [of application "Finder"] and trash [of application "Finder"]—are to be processed by the Finder's move command, so AppleScript sends them directly to the Finder as parameters to the move command.

Now compare the following to our earlier example:

```
tell application "Finder"
    set the_name to name of folder 1 of startup disk
end tell
```

The left side of the set command is an AppleScript variable, not an application reference, so all AppleScript is interested in is the expression on the right side. As you can see, the reference name of folder 1 of startup disk is not part of a larger application command, so once AppleScript has read the entire reference, it automatically sends a get command to the application, asking it to process the reference. The value returned by the command—in this case, a string—becomes the result of the expression.

Lastly, the AppleScript set command assigns this string to the variable the_name. Whew!

Let's look at some more examples where implicit get commands would be performed. First, let's get a list of document references from TextEdit:

```
tell application "TextEdit"
    every document
end tell
--> {document "Untitled" of application "TextEdit",
    document "ReadMe.txt" of application "TextEdit"}
```

Or, if we just want their names:

```
tell application "TextEdit"
    name of every document
end tell
--> {"Untitled", "ReadMe.txt"}
```

In both cases, a single get command is sent containing the entire reference.

Now, here's a more complicated example:

```
tell application "iTunes"
    activate
    play
    tell current track
        display dialog "Now playing " & name & " by " & artist
    end tell
end tell
```

As you can see, this time there are three relative references—one to iTunes' current track property, one to the name property, and one to the artist property. We've already discussed that AppleScript does not perform implicit get commands on references that appear as parameters to application commands. Another special case is where references appear as targets to tell blocks—in this case, current track [of application "iTunes"]. Rather than resolve the reference immediately, AppleScript remembers it in case it needs to expand any relative references within the tell block. When it reaches the name property, it knows this is an application object property, so it expands it into a full reference based on the reference supplied by the tell block:

```
name of current track of application "iTunes"
```

Although there is a command, display dialog, on the same line, the reference itself is surrounded by AppleScript operators, so at that point AppleScript knows it cannot resolve the full expression any further until it has performed an implicit get to retrieve the referenced value. The same thing then happens for the artist property. The concatenation operations are then performed, and the assembled string is sent to iTunes as the parameter to the display dialog command.

> **TIP:** Another way to prevent AppleScript from performing an implicit get on a reference is to use the a reference to operator. You'll learn about this in Chapter 13.

When Are Explicit *get* Commands Necessary?

Although AppleScript is good at working out the right time to send an implicit get command, it doesn't always get it 100 percent right when dealing with literal references. As a result, sometimes you need to help AppleScript out a bit by adding the get commands yourself.

Here's a simple script that retrieves the full name of the current user's home folder:

```
tell application "Finder"
    set the_name to name of home
end tell
--> "hanaan"
```

As you can see, AppleScript has performed an implicit get on the name of home [of application "Finder"] reference. So far, so good. As I've said, AppleScript is pretty good at guessing the right thing to do. Now let's look at what happens when it gets it wrong. Let's say that instead of the full folder name, I want only the first three characters of it—"han" instead of "hanaan" in this case. Here's the code I originally wrote to do this:

```
tell application "Finder"
    set abbreviated_name to text 1 thru 3 of name of home
end tell
```

When I try to run this script, however, instead of getting "han", I get an error: "Finder got an error: Can't get text 1 thru 3 of name of home." I know the folder name is at least three characters long, so the problem isn't that I asked for text that was out of range. Something else must have gone wrong, but what?

Well, remember how AppleScript performed its implicit get command in the earlier example? It saw a literal reference that must be intended for the Finder, name of home, so it slurped up the entire reference and sent it off as the direct parameter to a Finder get command. In this example, it's using the same approach, only this time the reference it's sending to the Finder is text 1 thru 3 of name of home.

If you look at the Finder's dictionary, you'll see that the name property defined in the item class (which is where the folder class gets it from) contains a string value (Unicode text, to be precise). Here is the part of the Finder's dictionary you're interested in, the definition for the item class:

```
item n : every item
    ELEMENTS
    ...
    PROPERTIES
name(text) : the name of the item
    ...
```

You already know that AppleScript knows how to get text 1 thru 3 of an AppleScript string...and there's the problem: AppleScript may know how to do it, but right now you're not talking to AppleScript; you're talking to the Finder. And the Finder, like all scriptable applications, knows how to manipulate only the contents of *application* objects.

In other words, the Finder knows how to resolve the name of home part okay, because the home property contains a folder object, and the folder object contains a name property—all things the Finder understands. However, its dictionary clearly states that the content of the name property is a simple string value, not an application object, and the Finder doesn't know how to manipulate the contents of values such as strings, lists, and records: its object model just doesn't stretch that far.

So, what do you do? You know that the Finder understands a reference such as name of home, and you know that AppleScript understands a reference such as text 1 thru 3 of some_string. The answer is clear: you need to split the one big reference into two, giving the Finder one and AppleScript the other.

You can write this in a couple of ways. Here's the first way:

```
tell application "Finder"
    set the_name to name of home
    set abbreviated_name to text 1 thru 3 of the_name
end tell
--> "han"
```

Here you put the two references on separate lines. This makes AppleScript send an implicit get command to resolve the reference name of home on line 2. Line 3 then takes the resulting string value and asks AppleScript to extract the part you want.

Another way you can do it is to insert an explicit get command:

```
tell application "Finder"
    set abbreviated_name to text 1 thru 3 of (get name of home)
end tell
--> "han"
```

Once again, you force AppleScript to send a get command to the application at the exact point you want. You then use AppleScript to deal with the resulting string value. Both approaches are fine, although the second way has the advantage of being a bit more compact.

Another common situation where AppleScript fails to send a get message when you need it to is when using a repeat with ... in ... loop with an application reference. For example:

```
tell application "Finder"
    repeat with folder_ref in every folder of home
        --Do some stuff with folder_ref here...
    end repeat
end tell
```

You might expect the previous code to get a list of folder references from the Finder and loop over that. Unfortunately, somebody must have forgotten to tell AppleScript this, because instead it creates a series of references like item 1 of every folder of home of application "Finder", item 2 of ..., and so on, assigning those to the folder_ref variable instead. As you can imagine, these sorts of references can cause all sorts of problems when you try to use them, because instead of identifying a folder in the home folder, each one points to an item (file, folder, and so on) in each of the folders of the home folder—not what you meant at all!

Once again, you need to help AppleScript, persuading it to send the Finder a get command that returns a list of folder references that you can then loop over yourself. You can do this by moving the every folder of home reference onto its own line, in which case AppleScript will perform an implicit get for you:

```
tell application "Finder"
    set folders_list to every folder of home
    repeat with folder_ref in folders_list
        --Do some stuff with folder_ref here...
    end repeat
end tell
```

Or you can insert an explicit get command to force AppleScript to resolve the reference at the proper time:

```
tell application "Finder"
    repeat with folder_ref in (get every folder of home)
        --Do some stuff with folder_ref here...
    end repeat
end tell
```

You'll explore AppleScript's repeat statements and how to use them in much more detail when you get to Chapter 14.

Telling the Difference Between AppleScript and Application *set* Commands

Because AppleScript uses exactly the same set ... to ... syntax for assigning values to AppleScript variables and to the properties of application objects, it can sometimes be a little tricky working out what a piece of application scripting code is actually doing.

The following example contains two set commands. Can you tell which one is an AppleScript command and which one is an application command?

```
tell application "Finder"
    set the_file to file 1 of folder "Jobs"
    set name of the_file to "1.jpg"
end tell
```

Don't let the surrounding tell block fool you: just because a set command is inside or outside an application tell block doesn't tell you whether it's working as an application or AppleScript command. Remember, to figure out whether a set command is an AppleScript or application command, you have to look carefully at the direct parameter (the part after the set keyword and before the to keyword) and work out what it is. If it's a variable or a literal reference identifying a property/element in an AppleScript value, it's behaving as an AppleScript command. If it's a literal reference to a property/element in an application object, it's working as an application command.

In the previous example, then, the first set command is actually an AppleScript command because the part between set and to is an AppleScript variable, the_file, while the second set command is working as an application command because it's being used on an application reference, name of file 1 of folder "Jobs" of application "Finder". Not only that, but because the file 1 of folder "Jobs" expression is a reference to an application object that doesn't appear within an explicit application command, AppleScript will automatically send it to the application in a get command. So you actually have three commands in all: an AppleScript set, an application set, and an application get too!

Here is another example to try:

```
tell application "Finder"
    set the_list to {}
    set end of the_list to file 1 of folder "Jobs"
end tell
```

Answer: both set commands are working as AppleScript commands.

Here's a third example:

```
tell application "Finder"
    set the_file to file 1 of folder "Jobs"
end tell
set name of the_file to "1.jpg"
```

This one is especially tricky, and you need to think about what it does when it's run. Answer: the first set command is an AppleScript command, and the second one is working as an application command—even though it's outside the application tell block!

Remember that AppleScript can often figure out a command's target by examining its parameters. In this case, although the second set command lies outside the Finder tell block, AppleScript realizes its direct parameter is an application reference when executing it, so it sends the set command to the application indicated by this reference: the Finder.

I don't recommend writing code like this yourself, mind you, given how much more awkward it is to read. It does provide a useful reminder that you shouldn't jump to conclusions about what a command will do based solely on whether it's inside or outside a tell block.

Getting and Setting Multiple Values in a Single Statement

A nice feature of set statements is the ability to assign several values in a single statement, which can be a great space saver in some situations. Let's say you want to assign values to three variables, a, b, and c. While you could write it like this,

```
set a to 1
set b to 2
set c to 3
```

another option is to write it like this:

```
set {a, b, c} to {1, 2, 3}
```

In both cases, the value of a is 1, the value of b is 2, and the value of c is 3. The trick here is to use lists on both the left and right sides of the set statement. The left list contains the variables or references that you want values assigned to, while the right list contains the values themselves. The first value is assigned to the first variable, the second value to the second variable, and so on.

Ideally the two lists should be the same length, so that the values and variables match up exactly. If the right list is longer than the left list, any extra values are ignored. In the next example, the first three values are assigned to the variables, while the last two values are discarded:

```
set {a, b, c} to {1, 2, 3, 4, 5}
```

However, if the right list is shorter, an AppleScript error will occur:

```
set {a, b, c} to {1, 2}
-- Error: Can't get item 3 of {1, 2}.
```

You can use a similar technique with get commands:

```
tell application "iTunes"
    get {name, artist, album} of current track
end tell
--> {"Teardrop", "Massive Attack", "Mezzanine"}
```

This statement actually sends three get commands to iTunes: get name of current track, get artist of current track, and get album of current track.

The next example sends three get commands to iTunes and assigns the results to three AppleScript variables:

```
tell application "iTunes"
    set {the_name, the_artist, the_album} to {name, artist, album} of current track
end tell
```

Although lists are the usual choice when performing multiple assignments, it is possible to use records as well. For example, the following statement assigns the value 1 to x and 2 to y:

```
set {x:a, y:b} to {x:1, y:2, z:3}
```

With this approach, the property names that appear in the left record must also appear on the right, although the order in which they appear is not important. The next script extracts the values returned by the display dialog command and assigns them to two variables, button_name and the_input:

```
set {button returned:button_name, text returned:the_input} to ¬
    (display dialog "Please enter a value:" default answer "")
display dialog "You clicked: " & button_name
display dialog "You entered: " & the_input
```

Using *copy* As an Application Command

So far you've seen how the standard copy command works when used with AppleScript values and variables. What happens when you start using it as an application command? Here is the syntax:

```
copy some_expression to application_reference
```

Once again, the target is a reference to a property or element of an application object (or objects). However, the way this statement actually behaves varies according to how it's used. Most of the time, it behaves the same as an application's set command. For example, when you run the following script,

```
tell application "Finder"
    copy "new name" to name of folder "old name" of desktop
end tell
```

AppleScript looks at the parameters to the copy command and then internally translates it to a standard set command before sending it to the Finder. It's equivalent to writing this:

```
tell application "Finder"
    set name of folder "old name" of desktop to "new name"
end tell
```

How does AppleScript know to do this? Well, AppleScript already knows that applications always use set to assign values to their properties. Because the copy command's direct parameter is a string and its to parameter is a property of an application object, it helpfully converts your original instruction to one that the application will understand.

Similarly, the following,

```
tell application "Finder"
    tell desktop
        copy label index of first folder to label index of every folder
    end tell
end tell
```

is equivalent to this:

```
tell application "Finder"
    tell desktop
        set label index of every folder to label index of first folder
    end tell
end tell
```

The one exception is when both parameters are references to the elements of application objects (the to parameter must be a literal reference, though the direct parameter can be either a literal reference or an application reference stored in a variable). In this case, AppleScript will internally translate the copy command into a standard application duplicate command and send that to the application.

Consider the following example:

```
tell application "Finder"
    copy every file of desktop to folder "Archive" of home
end tell
```

The direct parameter is a literal reference to all the desktop object's file elements, and the to parameter is a literal reference to the home folder's Archive folder element. Once again, AppleScript helpfully converts your original instruction into one that the application will understand. Because you're working with an application object's elements here, it figures that what you really want it to do is duplicate those objects to another location. In other words, it's equivalent to writing this:

```
tell application "Finder"
    duplicate every file of desktop to folder "Archive" of home
end tell
```

In both cases, all the files on the Finder's desktop will be copied to a folder named Archive in the user's home folder. Be careful, though: copy acts only as a duplicate command in particular conditions. For example, the following,

```
tell application "Finder"
    set destination_folder to folder "Archive" of home
    duplicate every file of desktop to destination_folder
end tell
```

will duplicate every file of the desktop to the Archive folder the same as before. However, if you now try to substitute copy for duplicate, you will change its behavior:

```
tell application "Finder"
    set destination_folder to folder "Archive" of home
    copy every file of desktop to destination_folder
```

```
end tell
```

Now AppleScript will ask the Finder for a list of references to the desktop's files and assign this list to the variable destination_folder instead!

When duplicating application objects, it's probably best if you always use the application's duplicate command and use copy only when you need to make a perfect copy of an AppleScript list, record, or date. That way, there's no misunderstanding about what you really meant your script to do.

> **NOTE:** Some applications also define their own copy commands that are completely unrelated to the standard copy command you've looked at here. These application-specific copy commands are used to copy the current selection in that application to the Mac OS's clipboard, similar to choosing **Copy** from the application's **Edit** menu. You can tell the difference between these clipboard-copying commands and AppleScript's copy command because they don't have a to parameter and are formatted as application commands, not AppleScript keywords, when you compile the script. See Chapter 23 for more information on clipboard-related commands.

Now that you are familiar with the most commonly used application commands, let's move on to discuss how you can fine-tune the ways in which commands are handled.

Changing How Commands Are Handled

Whenever AppleScript sends a command to another application, it usually waits a certain length of time to get some communication from the application. This communication may be information your script wanted from the application or an indication that a command has executed properly.

Two issues are related to the exchange between AppleScript and the scriptable application: should AppleScript wait for a response in the first place, and if it does, then just how long should it wait? By default, AppleScript will wait up to two minutes for an application to respond to a command. However, you can use its considering, ignoring, and with timeout control statements to modify this behavior in various ways.

Considering and Ignoring Application Responses

Using the considering and ignoring control statements with the application responses attribute determines whether AppleScript will wait to see what response the application gives after AppleScript sends it a command.

By default, when AppleScript sends a command to an application, AppleScript will wait for the application to finish handling the command before it proceeds any further. Although this is usually okay, sometimes you may want to send a command to an application and move on with the script.

To tell AppleScript not to wait for a response to specific application commands, wrap those commands in an `ignoring application responses` block. Here is its syntax:

```
ignoring application responses
    -- One or more application commands go here...
end ignoring
```

This will cause AppleScript to ignore any result values or error messages the application may generate in response to the commands within the `ignoring` block. Using this feature means you trust the application to complete the appointed task or you have other ways to verify that the task has been completed.

The following script tells Photoshop to play an action but does not hang around to see how things worked out:

```
tell application id "com.adobe.photoshop"
    ignoring application responses
        do script "Convert folder to JPG" from "Conversion action set"
    end ignoring
end tell
```

The following script asks Adobe Acrobat Distiller to distill an Adobe PostScript file. Although it tells AppleScript to ignore any responses from Acrobat, it does check whether the file has been generated before it reports that the job completed. In between, the script is free to get on with any other work you may want it to do.

```
set input_path to "/Users/hanaan/Desktop/temp_document.ps"
set output_path to "/Users/hanaan/Desktop/final.pdf"

-- Start the distilling process without waiting for it to complete:
tell application id "com.adobe.distiller"
    ignoring application responses
        Distill sourcePath input_path destinationPath output_path
    end ignoring
end tell

(*
    While waiting for Acrobat to finish distilling the file, the script
    can perform any other unrelated tasks here.
*)

-- Wait here until we know that Acrobat has created the finished PDF file:
tell application "Finder"
    repeat until POSIX file output_path exists
        delay 0.1
    end repeat
end tell

(*
    Perform any remaining operations involving the PDF file here.
*)

-- Let the user know when the script is finished:
display dialog "PDF Done!"
```

One limitation of the previous script is that if Acrobat encounters a serious problem while distilling the file, the script will end up looping forever as it waits for a file that will never appear! (Remember, ignoring application responses ignores application errors too.) You could solve this problem by improving the repeat loop so that, in addition to checking for the finished PDF file, it also looks to see whether Distiller has created an error log file; if it has, then the script can raise an error itself.

When using considering and ignoring blocks, be aware that they affect *all* the statements that are executed while inside the block. If you call a script handler from inside a considering/ignoring block, all the statements within that handler will be affected too.

In the following script, you call a delete_file handler that uses the Finder to delete a file, but on this occasion you ask it to delete a nonexistent file. The delete command in the handler will usually generate an error if the file isn't found, but in this case the ignoring application responses block surrounding the handler call means AppleScript will ignore this response:

```
ignoring application responses
    delete_file("path:to:non-existent:file")
end ignoring

on delete_file(file_path)
    tell application "Finder"
        delete file file_path
    end tell
end delete_file
```

You may find this ability to change the considering/ignoring behavior of the handler code from outside the handler useful in some situations. Be careful, though: it could also cause unexpected problems if the code in your handler depends on specific considering/ignoring settings to do their job correctly. (Incidentally, this is true when using any considering/ignoring attribute, not just application responses.)

If you want to override the current ignoring application responses behavior while executing the delete_file handler, you can wrap the delete_file call in a considering application responses block as follows:

```
ignoring application responses
    considering application responses
        delete_file("lala:bimbim")
    end considering
end ignoring
```

If you want to guarantee that the code in your handler always considers application responses, even if called from inside an ignoring application responses block, you may prefer to put the considering block inside it instead:

```
on delete_file(file_path)
    considering application responses
        tell application "Finder"
            delete file file_path -- This command's response will always be considered
        end tell
    end considering
end delete_file
```

Considering and Ignoring Other Attributes

When working with commands, `considering`/`ignoring` blocks are usually used with the `application responses` clause; however, other clauses—case, `diacriticals`, white space, and the rest—may also be used, although whether they have any effect will depend on the command's destination.

In principle, any scriptable application or scripting addition may consider or ignore these attributes when processing text, though in practice the majority sticks with the default behavior, which is to ignore case and consider everything else. Occasionally, you may encounter a command that is affected by these attributes; one example is the `offset` command provided by Standard Additions:

```
ignoring case
   offset of "h" in "Happy holidays!"
end ignoring
--> 1

considering case
   offset of "h" in "Happy holidays!"
end considering
--> 7
```

On the other hand, if you wrap a user-defined command in a `considering` or `ignoring` statement, the handler for that command will always be affected. For example, when using the `find_and_replace` handler from Chapter 7, you can perform case-sensitive searches by wrapping your `find_and_replace` commands in a `considering case ... end considering bconsidering case ... end considering` block:

```
find_and_replace("Hi-ho!", "H", "M")
--> "Mi-Mo!"

considering case
   find_and_replace("Hi-ho!", "H", "M")
end considering
--> "Mi-ho!"
```

Controlling the Timeout Delay for Long-Running Commands

By default, when AppleScript sends a command to an application, it waits 120 seconds for a response. If the application returns no response by then, AppleScript throws a timeout error. You can use the `with timeout` control statement to tell AppleScript to wait for a longer or shorter length of time when executing certain commands. This is especially useful when you have to send an application a time-consuming command that is likely to take more than two minutes to complete.

For example, the following script is intended to back up the entire startup disk:

```
tell application "Finder"
   duplicate disk "Macintosh HD" to folder "BU" of disk "Backup Disk" replacing yes
end tell
```

With so much data to copy, however, the Finder is bound to take longer than 120 seconds to perform this duplicate command. When the timeout delay expires, the result is an error like this:

```
error "Finder got an error: AppleEvent timed out." number -1712
```

It is important to understand that even though AppleScript gives up on the application and throws a timeout error, the application will continue to perform the task assigned to it. In the case of the preceding script where you duplicate the entire hard drive to the backup folder, the duplication will still continue despite that the script that initiated the command has already errored out and stopped.

You can increase (or decrease) the maximum amount of time AppleScript allows an application to perform a command with the with timeout control statement. Here is its syntax:

```
with timeout of some_integer seconds
  -- One or more application commands here...
end timeout
```

For example, to allow up to five minutes for a command to complete, you would use this:

```
with timeout of 300 seconds
  -- Your application commands here...
end timeout
```

Any application command sent from within this with timeout block will be given five minutes to reply—if it takes any longer, a timeout error will occur.

You can include any statements in a with timeout block, but only application commands will be affected by it. As with considering and ignoring blocks, if you call a handler from inside a with timeout block, the code in that handler will also be affected.

The following script allows up to 20 minutes for a script to resize an image in Photoshop:

```
with timeout of (20 * minutes) seconds
    tell application id "com.adobe.photoshop"
        tell document 1
            resize image resolution 120 resample method none
        end tell
    end tell
end timeout
```

If you want, you can tell AppleScript to wait virtually forever for a command response just by specifying a really large number of seconds in the with timeout block. Most times, however, you'll want to set a more reasonable upper limit so your script isn't left waiting forever if some sort of holdup problem occurs.

Even though you can use with timeout to allow extra time for a command to complete, sometimes the command takes longer than you're willing to wait for it. In this case, you may want to provide extra protection by placing the with timeout block inside a try statement that catches and handles any timeout errors that occur.

The following script lets the user choose a file. It will allow the dialog box to remain open for one hour before automatically exiting the script. The problem is that even after the choose file command times out and causes the script to stop, the Choose File dialog box still displays. To deal with this issue, the script uses a try block to trap the timeout error (error –1712) and uses GUI scripting to gracefully dismiss the dialog box.

```
try
    with timeout of (1 * hours) seconds
        tell application "Finder"
            set the_alias to choose file with prompt "Select a file to process:"
        end tell
    end timeout
on error number -1712 -- The command timed out, so cancel the script
    tell application "System Events"
        tell application process "Finder"
            click button "Cancel" of window "Choose a File"
        end tell
    end tell
    error number -128 -- Throw a "User canceled" error
end try
-- Rest of the script...
```

> **NOTE:** You'll learn more about AppleScript's try statement in Chapter 15.

Sending Commands to Remote Applications

Did you know you can use AppleScript to control applications across the network or across the world? One of AppleScript's features is the ability to run a script on one Mac that controls applications on another Mac. You do this with remote Apple events over Internet Protocol (IP). Except for some slightly modified tell application ... blocks, the scripts themselves are the same as if they were made to run locally.

Enabling Remote Apple Events

Before you can even start scripting remote Macs, the Mac you want to script has to be able to accept remote Apple events. By default, Macs are set to not allow access by remote Apple events. This issue is crucial to security: imagine the risk if anyone who knew your IP address could control your Mac from afar. Well, they would also need your username and password, but in a multi-Mac environment, those may not be the most difficult things to get.

To activate remote Apple events on any Mac OS X machine, check the Remote Apple Events check box in the Sharing panel of System Preferences, as shown in Figure 12–1.

Figure 12–1. *The System Preferences Sharing panel, where you turn on remote Apple events*

When you first activate remote Apple events, the "Allow access for: All users" radio button is selected by default. This allows any user who has a user account on the Mac to control it remotely. If you want to limit access to specific users for security reasons, select the "Only these users" option, and then click the + and – buttons to add and remove individual users or groups of users to and from the list below it.

NOTE: Attention network administrators: Mac OS X uses port 3031 for remote Apple events.

You may also need to modify the system's security settings to allow remote Apple events to pass through the Mac OS X firewall. The firewall can be configured from the Firewall tab in the Security panel of System Preferences. Click the Advanced button to adjust individual firewall settings, as shown in Figure 12–2 (older versions of Mac OS X may have different arrangements).

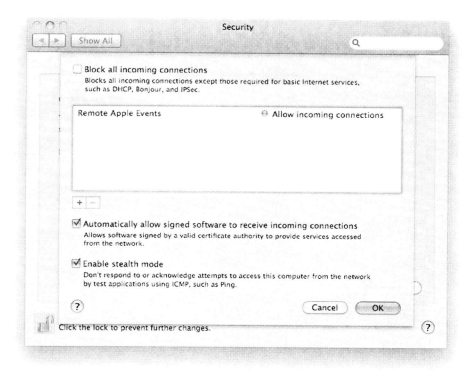

Figure 12–2. *The System Preferences Security panel, where you configure the Mac OS X firewall*

If the "Block all incoming connections" option is checked in the firewall settings, the system will automatically reject all remote Apple events sent to it. If this is the case, you need to uncheck that option. Please consult the Mac OS X documentation for further instructions on configuring the firewall.

> **CAUTION:** *Always* consult your system administrator and/or documentation before changing any sharing or security settings. A weak or incorrect configuration could easily leave the system vulnerable to network-based attacks!

Talking to Remote Machines

When scripting other Macs over IP, you need to specify the Mac (or machine as it is referred to in the script) to which you want to send events. You can specify the remote machine either by using its IP address or, if it is on your local network, by using its Bonjour name. You can obtain both values from the remote Mac's System Preferences. The IP address can be found in the Network panel; for example, 192.168.2.7. The Bonjour name consists of the computer's name, which appears at the top of the Sharing panel, with .local added to the end; for example, hanaans-mac.local.

Once you know the IP address or Bonjour name of the target machine, the next step is to construct a URL string. The beginning of the URL is always `eppc://` followed by either the IP address or the Bonjour name; for example, `eppc://192.168.2.7` or `eppc://hanaans-mac.local`.

Finally, you need to identify the application you want to control. When targeting a local application, you normally specify it like this:

```
application "AppName"
```

To identify a remote application, you must also specify the machine the application is running on:

```
application "AppName" of machine "eppc://..."
```

For example, you would use the following to create a folder on a Mac whose IP address is 192.168.2.7,

```
tell application "Finder" of machine "eppc://192.168.2.7"
    make new folder
end tell
```

or use the following on a Mac whose Bonjour name is hanaan-rosenthals-computer.local:

```
tell application "Finder" of machine "eppc://hanaan-rosenthals-computer.local"
    make new folder
end tell
```

> **CAUTION:** Remote application names are case sensitive. If the application name in your script does not exactly match the remote application's name, an error will occur when you try to compile or run it.

Authenticating Access to Remote Machines

And you thought for a second that Mac OS X security would let you by without identifying yourself? Not a chance! In fact, even if the target Mac allows incoming remote Apple events over IP, you still need to have a username and password of a user on that Mac with sufficient privileges.

You can embed the username and password for that Mac in your machine name string, like this:

```
machine "eppc://username:password@hanaan-rosenthals-computer.local"
```

Storing usernames and passwords in a script creates a serious security risk, however, as anyone with access to that file can easily extract your login details from it—even if you save it as read-only!

Fortunately, Mac OS X provides a safe way to input your username and password when a script is compiled or run. Just write the `eppc://` URL as normal without including any login information, and when you compile or run the script for the first time, your Mac will ask you to enter the login information in a dialog box similar to the one shown in Figure 12–3.

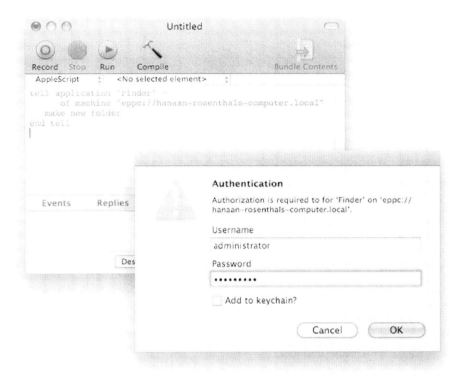

Figure 12–3. *The authentication dialog box for remote Apple events*

Normally you will be asked for these details each time you run the script. If you want your Mac to remember your login details for future use, just check the "Add to keychain" option in the dialog box before you click OK.

NOTE: If you select the "Add to keychain" option, your remote login details will be stored securely in your personal keychain. You can view and modify your keychains using the Keychain Access application (/Applications/Utilities/Keychain Access).

Compiling Scripts Offline

Although you can connect and talk to applications on remote Macs, you may not have a live connection to them while you're writing and compiling the script. To work around this limitation, you can enclose any code that is aimed at a remote application with the using terms from block. This tells AppleScript to compile the code intended to be executed by a remote application, using terms from the same application locally. This makes the `tell` block look like Script 12–2.

Script 12–2.

```
tell application "Finder" of machine (get "eppc://192.168.2.7")
    using terms from application "Finder"
        get name of every Finder window
    end using terms from
end tell
```

The reason why the machine URL is in parentheses is to allow the script to compile even if the remote machine isn't available on the network for some reason. Using the code (`get "eppc://..."`) prevents AppleScript from identifying the machine during compilation. The script will compile using the terms taken from the application identified by the `using terms from` block, and the real machine will be evaluated and found only when the script runs.

Using the *choose remote application* Command

Another thing you can do is allow the user to specify which application they're controlling, by using Standard Additions' `choose remote application` command. This can be useful if the user needs to pick the machine to control, for example. Script 12–3 prompts the user to select a running iTunes application, tells it to play, and then gets a reference to the currently playing track. Notice that a `using terms from` block is needed to compile the iTunes-specific keywords inside the `tell btell` block.

Script 12–3.

```
set remote_app to choose remote application ¬
    with prompt "Please select the remote iTunes application:"

tell remote_app
    using terms from application "iTunes"
        play
        get current track
    end using terms from
end tell

--> file track id 41764 of user playlist id 41668 of source id 41 of
        application "iTunes" of machine "eppc://192.168.2.3/?uid=501&pid=4997"
```

Targeting Remote Applications by User and Process IDs

If you need precise control in targeting a remote application, you can include a user ID (uid) and/or a process ID (pid) in the `eppc://` URL.

A user ID allows you to specify which logged-in user account is running the desired application. This is useful when more than one user is logged into the Mac at a time.

You can determine the ID number for a particular user in a couple of ways. One option is to run the Unix `id` command on the remote machine's terminal. To get the user ID for the current user, just type `id -u`. For example:

```
$ id -u
501
```

To get the user ID for any other user on the machine, add the user's Unix name to the end of the command:

```
$ id -u olivia
503
```

If you need to find out the names of all the currently logged-in users, just run the `users` command first:

```
$ users
hanaan olivia
```

Another option is to use the `choose remote application` command to see what applications are running on the remote machine. Choose an application name, and the uid will be given in the resulting URL; for example:

```
choose remote application
--> application "Finder" of machine "eppc://192.168.2.7/?uid=502&pid=339"
```

From here, you can figure out the username associated with that uid by asking the Finder of that Mac for the name of that user's home folder:

```
tell application "Finder" of machine "eppc://192.168.2.7/?uid=502"
    get name of home
end tell
--> "olivia"
```

Here is a simple script to do both:

```
set remote_app to choose remote application ¬
        with prompt "Please select a remote Finder application:"

tell remote_app
    using terms from application "Finder"
        set user_name to name of home
    end using terms from
end tell

{remote_app, user_name}
--> {"olivia",
        application "Finder" of machine "eppc://192.168.2.4/?uid=502&pid=339"}
```

A process ID allows you to specify the exact application process you want. Each time Mac OS X launches an application, it assigns a unique process ID number to the application process to distinguish it from all the other processes running on the same machine. The process ID for an application will be different each time the application is launched. If the target application is quit and relaunched while a long-running script is using it, the previous process ID will no longer be valid and your script will get an error the next time it tries to use the application, which might be just what you want it to do in this situation.

You can look up the process ID for a particular application by looking at the first column in the remote Mac's Activity Monitor application, or by running the Unix top command in its terminal. The result of the choose remote application command also includes the pid of the selected remote application.

Here's an example of targeting a remote Finder application by its pid:

```
tell application "Finder" ¬
        of machine "eppc://hanaan-rosenthals-computer.local/?pid=131"
    get home
end tell
--> folder "hanaan" of folder "Users" of startup disk of application "Finder"
        of machine "eppc://hanaan-rosenthals-computer.local/?pid=131"
```

Launching Remote Applications

Another caveat of scripting remote applications is that if the application isn't already running when you send it a command, you will get a "Cannot find process on host" error. Although AppleScript can automatically launch local applications if they are not already running, it cannot do the same for remote applications, even if you use a run or launch command.

What you have to do is first use the Finder on the remote machine to launch the application file and only then target it with commands. (The Finder is usually the best choice for this job because it is almost certain to be running.) For example:

```
tell application "Finder" of machine "eppc://Jane-Smiths-Computer.local"
    open file "Macintosh HD:Applications:TextEdit.app"
end tell
tell application "TextEdit" of machine "eppc://Jane-Smiths-Computer.local"
    -- TextEdit code goes here...
end tell
```

Summary

In Chapter 5, you learned the basics of application commands, while Chapters 6 to 11 showed you how to use various commands defined by AppleScript, by scripting additions, and by script handlers that you wrote yourself. In this chapter, we started by reviewing what you've learned so far, then moved on to fill in most of the remaining gaps. (We'll cover user-defined commands and handlers fully in Chapter 18.)

First, you learned about the various commands that all applications support, whether they're scriptable or not: run, launch, open, activate, and quit. Next, we discussed the standard suite of commands that most scriptable applications provide for manipulating objects in their object models: get, set, make, exists, and the rest. While the exact syntax and behavior of these commands may vary a bit from application to application, having a general idea of what they do and how to use them will serve you well as you explore new applications for yourself.

We then discussed in some detail the various responsibilities and quirks of the get, set, and copy commands, which are used both by AppleScript and by scriptable applications. In particular, you learned how to recognize AppleScript's clever "implicit get" behavior, where it sends get commands automatically in certain situations to resolve application object references for you. You also learned about the limitations of this behavior, and when and how to send explicit get commands for yourself.

You discovered how to use considering and ignoring blocks to control the way that commands are handled, most commonly to ignore any application responses so that your script does not wait for the application to return a result or an error before proceeding to the next task.

Finally, you learned about Mac OS X's remote Apple events feature, which allows you to send commands to applications running on other Macs.

In the next chapter, we will tie up two other topics that we have previously touched on when discussing how to manipulate AppleScript objects: operators and coercions.

Chapter 13

More on Operators and Coercions

As you have seen, working with data in AppleScript is not a small topic. Over the last seven chapters, we have looked at seven of the main object classes provided by AppleScript—boolean, integer, real, text, date, list, and record—along with the features used to work with them: commands, operators, and variables. We still haven't covered everything—for example, file system–related classes (alias, file, and POSIX file) will be covered later, in Chapter 17—but we've covered enough to do useful work for now.

The purpose of this chapter is to tie up some loose ends from the previous chapters. We'll start by exploring a couple of less important but still useful features: the a reference to operator and unit type conversions. This will be followed by overviews of all the standard coercions and operators provided by AppleScript. All of these features have been discussed previously, but as most of them apply to more than one class of objects, a side-by-side comparison is also useful. We'll finish with a full review of operator precedence rules—briefly introduced in Chapter 8—which determine the order in which operations within complicated expressions are evaluated.

Understanding the *a reference to* Operator

The a reference to operator allows you to turn a reference literal into a reference object that can be assigned to variables and passed to and from handlers just like any other AppleScript object.

What do I mean by this? Well, as we discussed in Chapter 12, when AppleScript evaluates a literal reference that isn't the target of a tell block or a parameter to a particular command, it normally sends an implicit get command to retrieve the value from the specified location:

```
tell application "Finder"
    set the_disks to every disk
end tell
```

```
--> {startup disk of application "Finder", disk "Backup" of application "Finder"}
```

Most of the time this is what you want, but occasionally it's useful to put off retrieving the referenced value until later on in the script.

A common situation where this happens automatically is AppleScript's repeat with ... in ... loop, where the loop variable is assigned a reference to each list item in turn. This allows the code within the loop to not only obtain each item in the list but also replace that item with a new value if it wants.

For example, the following script uses a repeat with ... in ... loop to iterate over the items in a list object:

```
1. set the_list to {1, 2, 4, 5}
2. repeat with number_ref in the_list
3.    set contents of number_ref to contents of number_ref * 2
4. end repeat
5. the_list
--> {2, 4, 8, 10}
```

The repeat statement on lines 2 to 4 creates a reference to each item of the list in turn (item 1 of *the_list*, item 2 of *the_list*, ...). Line 3 then uses the reference to retrieve the actual object from the list (contents of number_ref), multiplies it by 2, and puts the result back into the *original* list, replacing the old number (set contents of number_ref to ...).

You can also create your own reference objects by placing the a reference to operator in front of a literal reference:

```
tell application "Finder"
   set the_disks_ref to a reference to every disk
end tell
--> every disk of application "Finder"
```

To obtain the current value of the referenced location, just ask the reference object for the value of its contents property:

```
set the_disks to contents of the_disks_ref
--> {startup disk of application "Finder", disk "Backup" of application "Finder"}
```

Similarly, to replace the value at the referenced location with a new value, assign a new value to the reference's contents property:

```
set person_rec to {name: "John", age: 18}
set age_ref to a reference to age of person_rec
set contents of age_ref to 19
get person_rec
--> {name: "John", age: 19}
```

Should the original value change at some point, then the new value will be returned the next time you get the reference's contents:

```
tell application "Finder" to eject (every disk whose ejectable is true)
get contents of the_disks_ref
--> {startup disk of application "Finder"}
```

The a `reference` to operator can be useful when you want to store a reference to an application object in a variable for later use. With some applications, it's fine just to use the reference returned by the application:

```
tell application "Finder"
    set source_folder to folder "Movies" of home
end tell
--> folder "Movies" of folder "Hanaan" of folder "Users"
        of startup disk of application "Finder"
```

A reference that identifies elements by name or ID should be quite reliable over time. Some applications, however, return references that identify elements by position. For example, in Script 13–1, say you'd like to set variable `images_layer` to a specific layer in an Adobe Illustrator document.

Script 13–1.

```
tell application "Adobe Illustrator CS4"
    set images_layer to layer "images" of document "brochure.ai"
end tell
--> layer 1 of document 1 of application "Adobe Illustrator CS4"
```

As you can see, AppleScript takes the original "by name" reference on line 2 and immediately sends it to Illustrator, which trades it for a less precise "by index" reference. If you'll be moving documents or layers, then this sort of reference isn't desirable because it could easily end up identifying a completely different object than the one you want.

This script would be much more reliable if you could keep the original, more precise "by name" reference and always use that. Thanks to the a `reference` to operator, you can. Script 13–2 shows how.

Script 13–2.

```
tell application "Adobe Illustrator CS4"
    set images_layer to a reference to layer "images" of document "brochure.ai"
end tell
--> layer "images" of document "brochure.ai" of
application "Adobe Illustrator CS4"
```

Now, instead of immediately asking Illustrator to get `layer "images"` of document `"brochure.ai"`, line 2 assigns the original reference directly to the `images_layer` variable. The script can use this reference later just like it would any other reference. The only difference is that it'll be more reliable than the one Illustrator would have given you otherwise.

At this point, you might think AppleScript's reference objects are extremely simple, and in many ways they are. However, they do have one really big surprise up their sleeves. Consider the following example:

```
1. set person_rec to {name:"John", age:18}
2. set name_ref to a reference to name of person_rec
3. set the_name to contents of name_ref
4. get length of the_name
--> 4
```

This code is straightforward enough. Line 1 defines a record and line 2 creates a reference to the record's name property. Line 3 then asks for the reference object's contents property, which returns the string value from the record's name property. Finally, line 4 asks the string for the value of its length property.

What makes reference objects special is that you do not have to retrieve the object at the referenced location before referring to that object's properties and elements. Compare the previous script to the next example:

```
1. set person_rec to {name:"John", age:18}
2. set name_ref to a reference to name of person_rec
3. get length of name_ref
--> 4
```

The first two lines are the same as before, but lines 3 and 4 have been replaced by a new line 3. Now, instead of getting the referenced value on line 3 and working with it on line 4, the new line 3 asks the reference object for the value of its length property. The reference object doesn't have a length property, of course, but instead of throwing a "Can't get length of ..." error as you might expect, the reference automatically passes on the request to the object at the referenced location, and returns the result of that.

In effect, the reference object itself is virtually invisible to the code that is using it. This clever behavior makes reference objects extremely convenient to work with, since you can treat the reference object almost as if it was the object at the other end. However, there are a couple of exceptions to this rule which can very easily catch you out if you don't realize that you are talking to a reference object.

The first catch is if the object you want to deal with has a contents property of its own. If you want to get the value of the original object's contents property, then you first have to ask the reference for its contents property, which gives you the original object, and then ask that object for its contents property to get the value you actually want.

The second catch is that if you compare two values for equality, and one of them is a reference, then the result will *always* be false. For example:

```
set person_rec to {name:"John", age:18}
set name_ref to a reference to name of person_rec
name_ref = "John"
--> false -- Why isn't this true?!
```

This caveat applies to both the = and ≠ operators; other operators such as <, >, and as still behave as if they were dealing with the original object. The solution, once again, is to retrieve the original value by asking the reference for its contents property, and then using that in the comparison:

```
set person_rec to {name:"John", age:18}
set name_ref to a reference to name of person_rec
contents of name_ref = "John"
--> true
```

As you will learn in Chapter 14, this is a common gotcha when working with repeat with ... in ... loops, which use references to identify the items of the list being looped over. So even though you may rarely, if ever, need to use the a reference to operator yourself, you still need to understand how AppleScript's reference objects work—and how they can easily trip you up if you aren't careful.

One last thing... AppleScript's reference objects do not have a class property of their own, so asking a reference for the value of its class property will actually give you the class of the object at the referenced location, not reference as you might have hoped. If you really need to find out whether or not an object in AppleScript is a reference, try the following trick instead:

```
set is_object_a_reference to (count references of {the_object}) = 1
```

Although you cannot directly ask a reference object for its class property and get an honest answer, if you wrap up the object in a list and then ask the list for its reference elements, the result will be either an empty list (if the object isn't a reference) or a new list containing a single item (if it is). From there, it's simply a case of turning this information into a straightforward true or false answer that can be understood by the rest of your code.

Introducing Unit Type Conversions

Unit types are an obscure but useful feature that allow you to perform conversions between different units of measurement. AppleScript defines a number of unit type classes so that you can coerce numbers to units and back again. These classes fall into six different categories: length, area, cubic volume, liquid volume, weight, and temperature. Table 13–1 lists the classes available in each category.

Table 13–1. *The Built-in Unit Type Classes*

Type of Measurement	Class Name	Synonyms
Length	centimeters meters kilometers feet inches yards miles	centimeters metres kilometres
Area	square meters square kilometers square feet square yards square miles	square metres square kilometres
Cubic volume	cubic centimeters cubic meters cubic inches cubic feet cubic yards	cubic centimeters cubic metres

Type of Measurement	Class Name	Synonyms
Liquid volume	liters quarts gallons	litres
Weight	grams kilograms ounces pounds	--
Temperature	degrees Celsius degrees Fahrenheit degrees Kelvin	--

You convert a number from one type of unit to another as follows: first, coerce it to the unit class you want to convert from, then coerce it to the class of units you want, and finally coerce it back to a number again. Both unit classes must belong to the same category; you cannot coerce an area measurement to a length, or a weight to a temperature, for obvious reasons.

Here are some examples:

```
3.5 as meters
--> meters 3.5

3.5 as meters as yards
--> yards 3.827646544182

3.5 as meters as yards as number
--> 3.827646544182

20 as degrees Celsius as degrees Fahrenheit as number
--> 68.0

15 as grams as kilograms as number
--> 0.015
```

You cannot use unit type objects for anything else in AppleScript—all you can do is coerce them to and from numbers.

A Summary of AppleScript Coercions

Chapters 6 to 10 described the coercions supported by seven of the main AppleScript classes. This section provides an overview of the coercions that are available by default, and fills in a few other details.

> **TIP:** Third-party scripting additions can also add their own coercions to AppleScript, although they may not indicate this in their dictionaries so you'll need to check their other documentation for details.

Figure 13–1 shows the standard coercions that can be performed in AppleScript. White arrows indicate coercions that will only work for some values of a class.

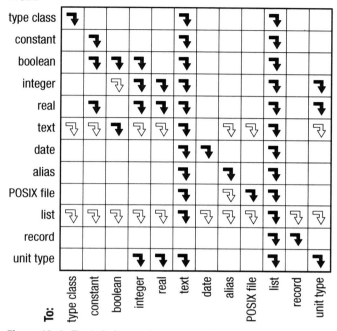

Figure 13–1. *The built-in coercions provided by AppleScript*

As you can see, any object can be coerced to its current class, in which case the result is the original object. Other types of coercions may be supported for all values, supported for only certain values, or not supported at all. When a coercion is not supported, or the object that is being coerced cannot be represented by an object of the new class, a coercion error, number –1700, will occur. The following sections discuss the limitations that apply.

Coercing Class and Constant Names

You can coerce class and constant names to text:

```
document as text
--> "document"

yes as text
--> "yes"
```

This can be particularly useful if you want to display an object's class in a dialog box while debugging a script. Try running the following script:

```
tell application "Finder"
    set the_object to item 1 of home
```

```
end tell
display alert (class of the_object)
```

The result will be a four-character string containing the raw Apple event code for the corresponding class name; for example, folder will appear as "cfol", document file as "docf", and so on. This is because the object is passed to the display dialog command as a class or constant, not as a string. When display dialog coerces the object to a string, it does not have access to any AppleScript- or application-defined terminology, so it uses the raw Apple event code because that is the only information available.

Now try the following:

```
tell application "Finder"
    set the_object to item 1 of home
end tell
display alert (class of the_object as text)
```

This time, the dialog box displays the human-readable name, "folder", "document file", etc.

There is one slight catch: if you run the script outside of AppleScript Editor—for example, as a stand-alone applet—the compiled script will not have access to the application terminology, which AppleScript only loads when compiling a script. The result will be a dialog box showing the raw, chevron-style representation of the object («class cfol», «class docf», or similar).

Fortunately, you can trick AppleScript into loading the Finder's dictionary when the script runs by using Standard Additions' run script command to compile a trivial Finder script on-the-fly:

```
run script "tell application \"Finder\" to launch"
```

Coercing Numbers and Text

When coercing numbers, you can coerce an integer to a Boolean only if the integer is 0 or 1; any other value will cause a coercion error (−1700). You can coerce strings to numbers, but only if the content of the string is some sort of number to begin with:

```
"1705" as real
--> 1705.0

"3.6" as integer
--> 4

"-0.49" as number
--> -0.49

"49e17" as real
--> 4.9E+18

"nineteen" as number
-- Error: Can't make "nineteen" into type number.
```

Notice that when coercing a real to an integer, AppleScript automatically rounds the number for you if the fractional part is not already zero. Also, if the number is too large to be represented as an integer, a coercion error will occur instead:

```
1.0E+300 as integer
-- Error: Can't make 1.0E+300 into type integer.
```

If you coerce a string to a unit type, it will be coerced to a number first, so the same rules apply to that conversion.

If you want to coerce a string to a number, but aren't sure if you want an integer or a real, coerce it to class number instead. The result will be an object of either class integer or class real—AppleScript will decide which class is most appropriate depending on the size of the number and whether or not it has a decimal point in it.

You can coerce text to other types as well, though one noticeable gap is that you can't coerce a date string into a date object; you need to use a date specifier instead.

Coercing File Objects

We haven't really covered alias and POSIX file objects yet, so all I'll say for now is that you can create a file object from a string either by coercing it or by constructing it using the appropriate specifier. Both approaches require a legal path string: a colon-delimited HFS-style path for aliases and a slash-delimited POSIX-style path for POSIX file objects. In addition, when creating an alias object, make sure that the path string points to a disk, folder, or file that already exists. If not, an error will occur because alias objects cannot identify nonexistent items.

The following examples show how to create alias and POSIX file objects using coercions:

```
"Macintosh HD:Applications:" as alias
--> alias "Macintosh HD:Applications:"

"/Applications" as POSIX file
--> file "d1:Applications"
```

In the second example, notice that AppleScript displays the POSIX file object as a file "..." style specifier. However, if you ask it for its class, the result will be «class furl», which tells you that it is really a POSIX file object (for some reason, AppleScript uses a raw code rather than a human-readable keyword here):

```
"/Applications" as POSIX file
class of result
--> «class furl»
```

When coercing file objects to text, the result will *always* be an HFS-style path string. If you want a POSIX-style path string, ask the object for the value of its POSIX path property instead:

```
(POSIX file "/Applications") as text
--> "Macintosh HD:Applications"

POSIX path of (POSIX file "/Applications")
--> "/Applications"
```

Coercing Lists

Any class of object can be coerced to a list, and in almost all cases the result is a single-item list containing the original object. The most obvious exception is if the original value is a list, in which case the result is the same list unchanged.

Record-to-list coercions are another special case. Here, the result is a list containing only the value of each record property; the properly labels are lost:

```
{a:1, b:2} as list
--> {1, 2}
```

If this is an issue for you—for example, when ensuring that a parameter passed to a handler is always a list of some sort—then a safer option than coercing is to check the class of a given value and, if it isn't already list, just wrap it in a list yourself:

```
on do_something(the_list)
    -- Make sure the_list really is a list, even if the user passed something else
    if class of the_list ≠ list then set the_list to {the_list}
    -- Rest of the code...
end do_something
```

When coercing from a single-item list to another class, as long as the list item itself can be coerced to that class, then the coercion will succeed. The result will be the same as if you asked for item 1 of *the_list*.

When coercing a multi-item list, you are rather more limited: in this case, you can only coerce it to a list (no change, in other words) or to text. Thus, coercing a list to text will only work if *all* the items in the list (and any sublists) can be coerced to text themselves.

Oh, and don't forget that when AppleScript joins the items together, it will insert AppleScript's current text item delimiter between each item, so make sure you set the text item delimiters property to the separator string you want *immediately before* performing any list-to-text coercion; otherwise, you could get a very different result from the one you intended! This rule applies regardless of whether the coercion is performed explicitly using the as operator or implicitly, such as when concatenating a list onto the end of a string. For example, the following code sets the text item delimiters before performing an explicit list-to-text coercion,

```
set AppleScript's text item delimiters to {", "}
set the_string to file_name_list as text
```

whereas this code sets them before performing an implicit list-to-text coercion:

```
set AppleScript's text item delimiters to {", "}
display dialog "Processed file names: " & file_name_list
```

Now that we've tied up AppleScript's coercions, let's move on and wrap up operators as well.

A Summary of AppleScript Operators

The following sections provide a brief overview of the operators available in AppleScript. AppleScript's operators can be separated into seven different groups according to purpose: Boolean logic, concatenation, math, comparison tests, containment tests, coercion, and reference creation.

> **NOTE:** Most AppleScript operators are binary operators; that is, they take two operands: one on the left of the operator and one on the right. The only exceptions are the not, negation, and a `reference to` operators. These are unary operators that take a single, right operand only.

Boolean Logic Operators

The and, or, and not operators are used in Boolean logic operations. See the "Working with Boolean Objects" section of Chapter 6 for details.

Table 13–2 provides a brief summary of each operator's syntax, plus the classes of its operand(s) and result, and is followed by some notes.

Table 13–2. *Boolean Logic Operators*

Name	Operator	Class of Operands	Class of Result
AND	and	boolean	boolean
OR	or	boolean	boolean
NOT	not	boolean	boolean

- not is a unary operator that takes a single, right operand, which must be a Boolean object.

- and and or are both binary operators. The left operand must be a Boolean object (true or false). The right operand should also be a Boolean, although any object that can coerce to a Boolean will do.

The Concatenation Operator

The concatenation operator is used to join two objects together. See Chapter 7 and Chapter 10 for details.

Table 13–3 provides a brief summary of the operator's syntax, plus the classes of its operands and result, and is followed by some notes.

Table 13-3. *The Concatenation Operator*

Name	Operator	Class of Operands	Class of Result
Concatenation	&	text, list, record	text, list, record

▨ If the left operand is text and the right operand is text or can be coerced to text, the result is also text.

▨ If the left operand is a record, the right operand must also be a record. The result will be a record.

▨ Otherwise, both operands will be coerced to lists if they aren't already lists, and the result will be a list.

Math Operators

Math operators are mostly used to perform calculations on numbers, although the addition and subtraction operators can also be used on dates. See Chapter 8 and Chapter 9 for details.

Table 13-4 provides a brief summary of each operator's syntax and any synonyms, plus the classes of its operands and result, and is followed by some notes.

Table 13-4. *Math Operators*

Name	Operator	Class of Operands	Class of Result
Addition	+	integer, real, date	integer, real, date
Negation (with one operand)	-	integer, real	integer, real
Subtraction (with two operands)	-	integer, real, date	integer, real, date
Multiplication	*	integer, real	integer, real
Division	/ ÷	integer, real	real
Integral division	div	integer, real	integer
Remainder (modulo)	mod	integer, real	real
Exponent	^	integer, real	real

▨ When both operands are numbers, the result will be a number too. Integers and reals can be used interchangeably with one another.

▨ If text is used for either operand, AppleScript will try to coerce it to a number first.

- If a date is used as the left operand to the addition operator, the right operand must be an integer representing the number of seconds to add. The result will be a new date.

- If a date is used as the left operand to the subtraction operator, the right operand may be either an integer (the number of seconds to subtract) or a date. If the right operand is an integer, the result will be a date. If the right operand is a date, the result will be an integer representing the number of seconds between the two dates.

Comparison Operators

Comparison operators are used to compare two values for equality or relative order. See Chapters 6 to 10 for details.

Table 13–5 provides a brief summary of each operator's syntax and synonyms, plus the classes of its operands and result. Words indicated by square brackets can be omitted when typing the code and AppleScript will add them automatically when the script is compiled.

Table 13–5. *Operator Names and Synonyms*

Name	Operator	Class of Operands	Class of Result

Is equal to	`=`
	`is`
	`equals`
	`[is] equal [to]`
		Any	boolean

Is not equal to	`≠`
	`is not`
	`isn't`
	`isn't equal [to]`
	`is not equal [to]`
	`doesn't equal`
	`does not equal`
		Any	boolean

Is less than	`<`
	`[is] less than`
	`comes before`
	`isn't greater than or equal [to]`
	`is not greater than or equal [to]`
		integer, real, text, date	boolean

Is less than or equal to	`≤`
	`<=`
	`[is] less than or equal [to]`
	`isn't greater than`
	`is not greater than`
	`does not come after`
	`doesn't come after`
		integer, real, text, date	boolean

Name	Operator	Class of Operands	Class of Result

Is greater than	`>`
	`[is] greater than`
	`comes after`
	`isn't less than or equal [to]`
	`is not less than or equal [to]`
		integer, real, text, date	boolean

Is greater than or equal to	`≥`
	`>=`
	`[is] greater than or equal [to]`
	`isn't less than`
	`is not less than`
	`does not come before`
	`doesn't come before`
		integer, real, text, date	boolean

Containment Operators

Containment operators test whether one value can be found inside another. They can be used with lists and strings, and in some cases records too. See Chapter 7 and Chapter 10 for details.

Table 13–6 provides a brief summary of each operator's syntax and synonyms, plus the classes of its operands and result, and is followed by some notes.

Table 13–6. *Containment Operators*

Name	Operator	Class of Operands	Class of Result

Starts with	`starts with`
	`start with`
	`begin with`
	`begins with`
		text, list	boolean

Ends with	`ends with` `end with`	text, list	boolean
Contains	`contains` `contain`	text, list, record	boolean
Does not contain	`does not contain` `doesn't contain`	text, list, record	boolean
Is in	`is in` `is contained by`	text, list, record	boolean

Is not in	`is not in`
	`isn't in`
	`isn't contained by`
	`is not contained by`
		text, list, record	boolean

- The contains and is in operators are mirror images of each other. This means that A is in B is functionally identical to B contains A, and vice versa, so just use whichever one reads best in your code. Not surprisingly, the does not contain and is not in operators are also mirror images of each other, so the same advice applies to them.

- Both operands must be of the same class when the containment check is performed. Fortunately, all of these operators can automatically coerce the operand being looked for into the same class as the operand being searched if their classes are different. For example, when checking for a string in a list, AppleScript will coerce the string into a single-item list first.

- Remember, the containment operators are really checking to see if one operand is a *subset* of the other. This means that when checking for a list within a list of lists, you must write it as {sub_list} is in list_of_lists, not as sub_list is in list_of_lists, otherwise it will never match the sublist you want.

The Coercion Operator

The coercion operator is used to convert an object of one class into an equivalent object of another class. See Chapters 6 to 10 plus the "Summary of AppleScript Coercions" section in this chapter for details.

Table 13–7 provides a brief summary of the operator's syntax and operand and result classes.

Table 13–7. *The Coercion Operator*

Name	Operator	Class of Operands	Class of Result
As	as	Left operand can be anything; right operand must be a class name (type class)	The class specified by the right operand

The *a reference to* Operator

The a reference to operator is used to create an AppleScript reference object that identifies a property or element(s) of another object. See the "Understanding the a reference to Operator" section in this chapter for details.

Table 13–8 provides a brief summary of the operator's syntax and operand and result classes.

Table 13–8. *The a reference to Operator*

Name	Operator	Class of Operand	Class of Result
A reference to (with one operand)	a reference to	Single operand can be anything	The result is a reference, though asking for its class will return the class of the object being referenced, not reference

Now that we've completed our review of AppleScript operators, let's finish off with a full look at how operator precedence works.

Operator Precedence in Detail

Chapter 8 introduced you to the concept of operator precedence when looking at how complex mathematical expressions are evaluated. This section will expand that earlier discussion to cover the full set of AppleScript operators.

First, take a look at Table 13–9, which lists in order of precedence the always useful parentheses followed by all the AppleScript operators.

Table 13–9. *AppleScript's Operators in Order of Precedence*

Order	Operators	Form of Association	Type of Operator
1	()	Innermost to outermost	Grouping
2	-	Unary	Negation (also unary +)
3	^	Right to left	Exponentiation
4	*, /, div, mod	Left to right	Multiplication and division
5	+, -	Left to right	Addition and subtraction
6	&	Left to right	Concatenation
7	as	Left to right	Coercion
8	<, ≤, >, ≥	None	Comparison
9	starts with, ends with, contains, is in, etc.	None	Containment
10	=, ≠	None	Equality and inequality

Order	Operators	Form of Association	Type of Operator
11	not	Unary	Boolean NOT
12	and	Left to right	Boolean AND
13	or	Left to right	Boolean OR
14	a reference to	Unary	Reference

Understanding Precedence

As you can see from Table 13–9, AppleScript defines a clear set of rules for deciding the order in which operations should be performed when evaluating an expression containing two or more operators. If you need to, you can control the order of evaluation by inserting parentheses into your expression, but for now we'll just consider the default behavior.

For example, the following calculation follows the same precedence rules that you would have learned in high school math classes:

```
4 / 2 + 3 * 5 - 1
```

The division and multiplication operators have higher precedence than the addition and subtraction operators, so these calculations are performed first:

```
2 + 15 - 1
```

After this, the operations with the next highest precedence are performed, and so on until the final result is obtained:

```
16
```

You can combine additional operators to perform more complex tasks. For example, if you want to add two numbers and check that the result matches a third:

```
3 + 7 = 10
--> true
```

The equality operator has lower precedence than all of the math operators, so the math operation will be performed before the comparison is done. For example, you can write the preceding as follows and it will be evaluated in precisely the same way, even though the operations are written in a different order:

```
10 = 3 + 7
--> true
```

If you need to perform multiple comparisons and then make a decision based on their combined answers, you can tie them together using the Boolean operators. For example:

```
3 + 7 = 10 and 10 = 3 + 7
--> true
```

Since comparison tests have a higher precedence than Boolean logic tests, the operations on the left and right sides of the and operator are both performed first. Their results are then used as the operands to the and operator, which calculates the final result.

> **TIP:** As an aside, don't forget that the Boolean and and or operators use lazy evaluation and thus may skip evaluating the entire right expression if the result of the left expression provides them with a definitive answer. For example, if the left operand to the and operator is `false`, there is no way the result can ever be `true`, regardless of what the right expression would return.

If two adjoining operators have the same level of precedence, then AppleScript decides which one comes first based on the operators' association rules.

Understanding Forms of Association

Although the order of precedence resolves some of the confusion, quite a few operators have the same order of precedence, such as addition and subtraction. The Form of Association column in Table 13–9 explains how AppleScript deals with statements that contain multiple operators with the same precedence level.

Operators marked "left to right" are evaluated in that order when two or more operators with the same precedence appear next to each other. For instance, 12 - 5 + 30 will be resolved as follows:

```
    12 - 5 + 30
--> 7 + 30
--> 37
```

The left operation is evaluated first. Its result is then used as the left operand to the operator on the right, and so on.

With right-to-left association, the order of evaluation is reversed. There is only one operator that uses this form, the exponent operator. Let's try an example:

```
2 ^ 3 ^ 4
```

When you compile this code, AppleScript will actually help you out by adding parentheses to indicate which subexpression will be evaluated first:

```
2 ^ (3 ^ 4)
```

There, that's much more obvious. When you run the script, the right operation will raise 3 to the power of 4, giving 81.0 as the result. The left operation is then performed, raising 2 to the power of 81.0 to give...well, it's a pretty huge number, whatever it is!

A unary operator is one that takes a single operand to its right; for instance:

```
-7
```

The negation operator in this case turns the positive number to its right into a negative number and a negative number into a positive one.

If you type multiple unary operators of equal precedence all in a row, they start evaluating from the one closest to the operator, going further and further away. Look at the following statement:

```
not not not true
```

Here's how AppleScript looks at the preceding statement:

```
not (not (not true))
```

In fact, if you do use the statement without the parentheses, when you compile the script, AppleScript will add parentheses for you!

Understanding when You Should Use Parentheses

Although AppleScript's precedence rules are helpful, they may not always perform calculations in the order you want. Fortunately, you can use parentheses to change the order in which AppleScript evaluates subexpressions within a larger expression.

For instance, without parentheses, the following expression will have one result:

```
2 + 5 * 7
--> 37
```

The multiplication operator has higher precedence than the addition operator, so the 5 and the 7 will be multiplied first. Alternatively, if you want the 2 and the 5 to be added together and the result of that calculation multiplied by 7, you just need to enclose the 2 + 5 operation in parentheses, like so:

```
(2 + 5) * 7
--> 49
```

You can add as many parentheses as you like to an expression, and AppleScript will automatically start evaluating the subexpressions within the innermost parentheses, then work its way out.

Incidentally, enclosing individual expressions in parentheses can also help to make complex expressions easier to read, even if AppleScript itself does not require them. Adding parentheses can also be handy when you haven't yet memorized the exact order in which AppleScript will evaluate the various expressions; that way, you don't have to worry about it. For example, you might find that

```
(bankruptcies = 0 and credit_ratings > 500 and debt > 10000)
```

is easier to follow if you insert extra parentheses around each of the comparison operations, like this:

```
((bankruptcies = 0) and (credit_ratings > 500) and (debt > 10000))
```

The order of evaluation of this particular expression hasn't been changed in any way, but the start and end of each subexpression are now easier to spot.

Summary

Operators and coercions are not new to you—Chapters 6 to 10 already introduced them and explained how to use them to manipulate various classes of AppleScript objects— but this chapter provides a convenient all-in-one overview of these features and fills in a number of details such as operator precedence rules, the a reference to operator, and unit type coercions.

We have now covered nearly all of our first two key concepts in AppleScript: how information is represented as objects, and how these objects can be manipulated using commands and operators, and stored in variables for later use. There are three AppleScript classes (alias, POSIX file, and script) that have yet to be covered, but we are going to leave these for later chapters and move on to the third of our key concepts: how AppleScript makes decisions on what to do and when to do it.

Chapter 14

Making Decisions Using Conditionals and Loops

Previous chapters have explored in detail the first two key concepts behind AppleScript: how information is represented as objects, and the features used to manipulate those objects (commands, operators, and variables). However, there is one more key concept that you need to grasp before you can really use AppleScript effectively: how your script can make decisions on what to do and when to do it.

In AppleScript, the ability to make decisions is what gives your script "artificial intelligence." The AppleScript language provides three important features for making these decisions:

- *Conditional statements* decide whether or not a section of code should be executed.

- *Repeat statements* decide how many times a section of code is executed.

- *Try statements* decide what to do when something goes wrong in a section of code.

This chapter explores conditionals and repeat loops, while Chapter 15 will deal with error handling. Let's get started.

Choosing Your Course with Conditional Blocks

The AppleScript language, like other programming languages, revolves around two things: a few simple concepts and a lot of syntax. One of these concepts is the conditional, or `if`, statement. A conditional statement decides whether or not to execute a specific section of code depending on whether or not a certain condition is met.

Conditions are everywhere! They do not need a conditional statement to exist. The state of every property of every object of every application, the text or buttons that are returned from a dialog box, the value and properties of any variable you use in your script—these are all conditions you can test and use to your advantage. The only thing limiting you is your imagination.

The idea of a condition is that as complex as a conditional expression may be, its result is primal: it can be either true or false. Even the most complex conditions boil down to true or false; for example:

```
my_age < 35

user_name is in {"Mary", "Sue", "Rob", "Phil"}

class of the_finder_item is folder ¬
    and label index of the_finder_item is 2 ¬
    and name of the_finder_item does not start with "~"
```

Understanding the Basic Conditional Statement

The basic conditional statement is written as follows:

```
if boolean_expression then
    -- One or more statements to execute only if boolean_expression is true...
end if
```

The first line of the statement block starts with the word if, followed by a conditional test (written here as boolean_expression), and ends with the word then. The last line of the block is always end if. Between these two lines you put the statements that you want executed when the conditional test in the first line is met.

The conditional test itself can be any expression that returns true or false. These are often referred to as *Boolean expressions* because they are expressions that always return a Boolean result. Consider the following script:

```
1. set customer_age to 17

2. if customer_age < 21 then
3.     display alert "Sorry, cannot serve under-21s."
4. end if
```

Line 2 contains the conditional test, which tests whether the value of the variable customer_age is less than 21. The execution of the second line depends on the condition being true. This means the code in line 3 will execute only if the test in line 2 returns true. If the test returns a false value, then AppleScript will skip the rest of the code in the conditional statement block and proceed directly to the next statement that follows it.

> **TIP:** When writing a conditional block in AppleScript Editor, you can save yourself some typing by omitting the then keyword from the end of the first line and the if keyword from the end of the last line. When the script is compiled, AppleScript will conveniently add the missing words for you.

The Different Flavors of Conditional Statements

AppleScript's conditional block is a very flexible structure, and the basic if ... then ... form can be easily extended to make additional decisions. This section provides dictionary-style definitions of all the different flavors of if statement. Later sections will explore these flavors in more detail.

Here is the basic if ... then ... block again:

```
if boolean_expression then
    -- Statement/s to execute only if boolean_expression is true
end if
```

If the basic if ... then ... block contains only a single statement, it can be shortened to the following form for neatness:

```
if boolean_expression then single_statement
```

The following is an if ... then ... else ... conditional statement:

```
if boolean_expression then
    -- Statement/s to execute only if boolean_expression is true
else
    -- Statement/s to execute only if boolean_expression is false
end if
```

The following is an if ... then ... else if ... statement block, where there are two or more different conditional tests to perform:

```
if boolean_expression_1 then
    -- Statement/s to execute only if boolean_expression_1 is true
else if boolean_expression_2 then
    -- Statement/s to execute only if boolean_expression_2 is true
...more else if clauses...
end if
```

The following is an if ... then ... else if ... statement block with a provision in case none of the conditional tests used is true:

```
if boolean_expression_1 then
    -- Statement/s to execute only if boolean_expression_1 is true
else if boolean_expression_2 then
    -- Statement/s to execute only if boolean_expression_2 is true
...more else if clauses...
else
    -- Statement/s to execute only if none of the previous expressions is true
end if
```

Offering an Alternative Ending with the *else* Clause

The following script contains a single conditional statement. If the condition is false, then line 4 of the script will be skipped, and the statement will end without anything happening.

```
1. set new_text to "Hello!"
2. tell application "TextEdit"
3.    if exists document 1 then
```

```
4.        set text of document 1 to new_text
5.    end if
6. end tell
```

The preceding script will execute the statement on line 4 only when the condition in line 3, in this case whether document 1 exists, is true. But what will happen if the statement is false? What if you want the script to make a new document if none exists? In that case, you use the else clause. The else clause divides the conditional statement into two parts: what happens when the condition is true and what happens when it is false. It's that simple! Script 14–1 shows how the improved script will look.

Script 14–1.

```
1. set new_text to "Hello!"
2. tell application "TextEdit"
3.    if exists document 1 then
4.        set text of document 1 to new_text
5.    else
6.        make new document with properties {text:new_text}
7.    end if
8. end tell
```

Offering Multiple Choices with *else if* Clauses

Often, a conditional statement will test for multiple conditions. In this case, AppleScript will look for the first test clause whose condition is true and execute its statements, and then the conditional statement will end.

Here's how it might work logically—you're at a party, and you want something to drink. If there's soda, you drink that. If there isn't, you look for beer. If there's no beer, you check for vodka instead. If there's no vodka left, the party has run dry, and you'll probably want to think about heading home.

Script 14–2 shows how the conditional statement for this search for liquid might look in AppleScript.

Script 14–2.

```
property sodas_left : 4
property beers_left : 1
property vodkas_left : 5

if sodas_left > 0 then
    set my_drink to "soda"
    set sodas_left to sodas_left - 1
else if beers_left > 0 then
    set my_drink to "beer"
    set beers_left to beers_left - 1
else if vodkas_left > 0 then
    set my_drink to "vodka"
    set vodkas_left to vodkas_left - 1
else
    set my_drink to "nothing"
end if

display dialog "I'm drinking " & my_drink
```

```
display dialog "Drinks remaining:" & return & ¬
    sodas_left & " soda, " & beers_left & " beer, " & vodkas_left & " vodka"
```

The first condition checks for soda. If there is soda, it makes no difference whether there's also beer or vodka—you will fill your glass with soda and skip the beer and vodka parts. If there's no soda, the beer gets a chance. If there's no beer, it'll try for vodka. If there's no vodka, it means nothing is left, and it's time to head home.

You can see this process in action by re-running the script until no drinks are left—the numbers of available drinks are stored in properties, so the script will remember them between runs. Though once you do run out, you can instantly restock the bar just by recompiling the script in AppleScript Editor. (If only that worked for real parties too!)

Tips for Writing Conditional Statements

Before we move on to discussing repeat loops, let's finish this section with a few tips for making your conditional blocks clean and easy to read.

Using a Condition in a Single Line

Conditional statements that execute a single statement can start and end on a single line, like in the following script:

```
if time_left = 0 then blow_whistle()
```

This form of conditional statement is useful when the statement is simple because it makes the statement more concise and easier to read.

Avoiding Unneeded Conditional Statements

Sometimes you want to check whether a condition is true or false simply to set the value of a variable to that true or false value. You may be tempted to write the script like this:

```
if stoplight_color is "green" then
    set walk_now to true
else
    set walk_now to false
end if
```

This works, but it is unnecessarily complex. Instead, you should just use the following:

```
set walk_now to stop_light_color is "green"
```

The expression stop_light_color is "green" evaluates to either true or false. That value can be directly assigned to the walk_now variable without a conditional statement.

Is It True?

To check whether a Boolean value assigned to a variable is true or false, it isn't necessary to perform a full-blown equality test like this:

```
if boolean_variable = true then do_something()
```

Simply use the variable, like this:

```
if boolean_variable then do_something()
```

If you want to perform the action when the variable's value is false instead of true, simply add the not operator before the variable, like this:

```
if not tired_yet then write_another_chapter()
```

Now, if the value of variable tired_yet is false, the write_another_chapter handler will be called.

Testing a Value Against Multiple Options

One point made earlier is worth discussing in more detail here. Let's explore a situation in which you want to check whether the value of a variable is one of several possibilities. For instance, say you want the script to do something if the month of a given date, for example, is between September and November. In this case, you can create a compound test expression, like this:

```
set the_month to month of some_date
if the_month is September or the_month is October or the_month is November then
    -- Do something
end if
```

Although this works, you will be better off with the following simpler if statement that uses the is in containment operator along with a list of months to achieve the same result:

```
if {the_month} is in {September, October, November} then
    -- Do something
end if
```

Running an Assembly Line with Repeat Loops

A repeat loop allows you to perform a single set of actions multiple times. Here is an example of a simple repeat statement:

```
repeat 3 times
    beep
    delay 1
end repeat
```

Okay, so this didn't do much; it just beeped. Also, the operation was performed identically each time, without any variation. But that's the idea being demonstrated here—an assembly line that performs the same operation every time. If you have an assembly line in a soda can factory, for instance, you may want a tool to apply a label to each can. There may be millions of cans to label, but the labeling operation will be performed in exactly the same way every time, so a single labeling tool can process them all—saving you a lot of time!

This is the most basic form of repeat loop:

```
repeat
    -- Do something...
end repeat
```

Notice that the statement starts with the word repeat and ends with an end repeat line. This is a requirement for all repeat statements. Between these two lines, you put all the statements that will be executed every time the loop repeats. What's sorely missing in the preceding repeat statement is a consideration that the sorcerer's apprentice didn't take into account: what will make the repeat loop stop?

AppleScript has two basic ways to specify when a repeat statement should stop looping and move on to the next statement:

  ▨   The loop will repeat a predetermined number of times.

  ▨   The loop will continue repeating until a condition is met.

For instance, if you loop through a list of folders and do something to each folder, the number of repetitions will normally depend on the number of folders, which is unknown at the time you write the script but will be determined by the script when it runs. Alternatively, if you are looping through the list looking for one folder in particular, you would use a conditional test to exit the loop as soon as the desired folder is found.

What follows are the variations of the repeat control statement, followed by a detailed explanation of each one.

The Different Flavors of Repeat Loops

This section lists the different flavors of repeat loops. These flavors are explained in detail later in the chapter.

The following statement repeats forever:

```
repeat
    -- Statement/s to execute on each loop
end repeat
```

The following statement repeats a specific number of times:

```
repeat n times -- (n is an integer)
    -- Statement/s to execute on each loop
end repeat
```

This statement repeats by counting from one number up to another:

```
repeat with i from start_integer to end_integer
    -- (i increments by 1 on each loop)
    -- Statement/s to execute on each loop
end repeat
```

The current count is assigned to a loop variable (in this case i) which can be used by the statements in the block.

You can also extend this type of loop to jump by intervals other than 1:

```
repeat with i from start_integer to end_integer by step_interval
```

```
    -- (i changes by the step_interval on each loop)
    -- Statement/s to execute on each loop
end repeat
```

This repeats over the items in a list, assigning a reference to each item to a loop variable (in this case item_ref):

```
repeat with item_ref in some_list
    -- (item_ref contains a reference to each item of the list in turn)
    -- Statement/s to execute on each loop
end repeat
```

This repeats until a certain Boolean condition becomes true:

```
repeat until boolean_expression
  -- Statement/s to execute on each loop
end repeat
```

This repeats while a certain Boolean condition is true:

```
repeat while boolean_expression
  -- Statement/s to execute on each loop
end repeat
```

Repeating Forever

Well, you never would really repeat forever, although I'm sure Mac OS X is capable of running continuously for that long! By "forever," I mean that the repeat statement itself doesn't contain any provisions for ending the loop.

Although you can loop forever, you can, and should, include a way for the loop to terminate inside the repeat loop block. One of the ways to terminate the simple repeat statement without specifying an end to it is by using the exit repeat statement. This statement is normally contained in a conditional statement—when the condition is met, the exit repeat statement immediately exits the loop.

Here is an example of a repeat loop with an exit repeat statement inside a conditional statement:

```
repeat
    -- Do stuff...
    if boolean_expression then
        exit repeat
    end if
    -- Do more stuff...
end repeat
```

The advantage of using the basic repeat statement with exit repeat rather than one of the other types of loop is that the exit condition can be placed anywhere in the repeat block. This can be convenient if the code that decides when to exit the loop has to appear in the loop itself. The downside is that it makes the code harder to understand, since you have to read through the entire block to figure out where and when the loop will be terminated. With other types of loops, you only have to look at the first line to see this.

You may be asking yourself what happens if the condition is never met. Well, then AppleScript will run the script forever. It is your job as a scripter to make sure your loops run their course and come to an end when appropriate.

> **TIP:** A script that is in the middle of an endless loop, or a loop that doesn't appear to end, can be interrupted only by pressing Cmd+period. This can be particularly useful during testing. If Cmd+period doesn't work, you may have to force-quit the application using Cmd+Option+Escape.

Repeating *n* Times

This simple repeat variation is intended to be simple and concise. It is useful when you want to perform the same set of actions a certain number of times with no variation from one loop to the next. Here is an example of a repeat loop that repeats five times:

```
repeat 5 times
    -- Do stuff
end repeat
```

You can also use a variable to specify the number of repetitions, as shown in Script 14–3.

Script 14–3.

```
display dialog "How many times should I beep?" default answer "5"
set beep_count to (text returned of result) as integer
repeat beep_count times
    beep
    delay 1
end repeat
```

Script 14–3 first asks the user to enter a number. The user's response, which comes as a string, is coerced into an integer so that it can be used in the repeat loop. The loop then executes a beep command the number of times dictated by the user.

> **TIP:** If you use a real number instead of an integer in the repeat loop, AppleScript will automatically round it to the nearest whole number.

Repeating with Numbers in a Range

When you repeat with numbers in a range, you include a variable that automatically changes in value based on the current loop count. This allows you to specify a numerical range, and while the loop is repeating, the value of that variable increases (or decreases) in value with each repetition.

In the following example, the value of variable n starts at 1 and then increases by 1 (the default increment) all the way to 10:

```
repeat with n from 1 to 10
    display dialog "This is repetition number " & n
end repeat
```

Loop variables are variables whose values change with every loop repetition. Like kids playing jump rope and counting each jump aloud, AppleScript automatically updates the value of that special variable with every loop.

Let's say you have a list of US phone numbers and want to add area codes to the ones that have only seven digits. Looking at the loop requirements, you see that each repetition will treat each item of the phone number list in turn. Script 14–4 shows how you might write this code. The loop variable i changes its value starting with 1 and incrementing up by 1 with every repetition.

Script 14–4.

```
set default_area_code to "201"
set phone_list to {"475-5556145", "5559132", "5557040", "317-5551437", "5556421"}

repeat with i from 1 to count phone_list
    if length of (item i of phone_list) is 7 then
        set item i of phone_list to default_area_code & "-" & (item i of phone_list)
    end if
end repeat

phone_list
--> {"475-5556145", "201-5559132", "201-5557040", "317-5551437", "201-5556421"}
```

As you might imagine, you can use any expressions to specify the start and end of the range, as long as they return integers. This is useful when you don't know in advance the range of numbers you want to count over.

For example, the phone list in Script 14–4 currently contains five items. You could hard-code the loop to count from 1 to 5, but if the number of items in the list later changes, the script won't work correctly unless you remember to modify the repeat statement too. It is simpler and more reliable to use the count command to get the number of applicable objects at the time, which in turn becomes your repeat loop's number of repetitions.

Let's look at another example. Script 14–5 uses two nested repeat loops to calculate the entire multiplication table, and presents the result in HTML.

Script 14–5.

```
1. set html to "<html>" & return & "<head>" & return
2. set html to html & "<title>Multiplication Table</title>" & return
3. set html to html & "</head>" & return & "<body>" & return
4. set html to html & "<table border=1 cellpadding=2>" & return

5. repeat with i from 1 to 10
6.    set html to html & "<tr>" & return
7.    repeat with j from 1 to 10
8.        set html to html & "<td>" & (i * j) & "</td>"
```

```
9.     end repeat
10.    set html to html & "</tr>" & return
11. end repeat
12. set html to html & "</table>" & return & "</body>" & return & "</html>"
```

The outer repeat loop simply counts from 1 to 10, assigning the loop value to the variable i. Each time the outer loop repeats, the inner repeat loop counts from 1 to 10, assigning the value to the variable j. The two numbers are then multiplied and formatted as HTML.

Figure 14–1 shows the resulting web page.

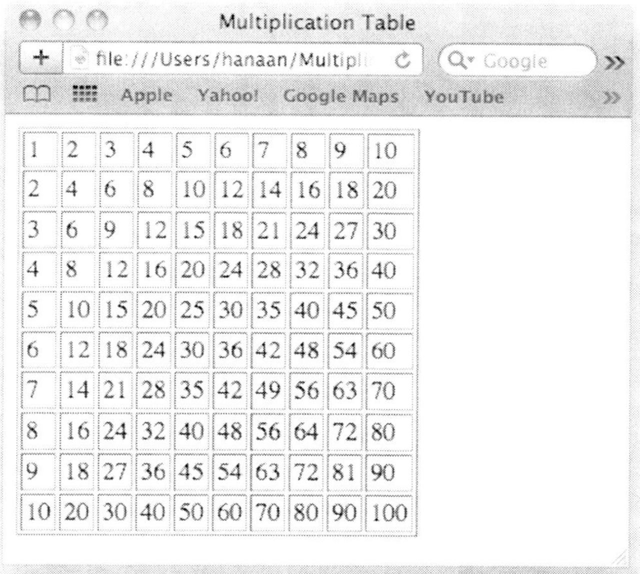

Figure 14–1. *The web page resulting from the multiplication table script*

This type of loop also allows you to play with the way the loop variable increases or decreases. In the previous examples, the loop variable increased by 1 each time, but what happens if you want to increase it by another number? All you have to do is add the keyword by followed by the increment you want to use.

For example, the following script builds a list of numbers in multiples of 5, starting at 0 and counting up to 50 in steps of 5:

```
set the_list to {}
repeat with i from 0 to 50 by 5
    set end of the_list to i
end repeat
the_list
--> {0, 5, 10, 15, 20, 25, 30, 35, 40, 45, 50}
```

The following example will change every third word in the front TextEdit document into the word "carrot":

```
tell application "TextEdit"
    tell document 1
        repeat with i from 3 to (count every word) by 3
            set word i to "carrot"
        end repeat
    end tell
end tell
```

Don't worry if the number of words in the document is not exactly divisible by 3. The repeat loop will keep counting only as long as the value of the loop variable is less than or equal to the end number. For example, if the document contains 14 words, the loop will count 3, 6, 9, 12, and then stop.

A repeat loop can also count backward, starting with a high number and ending at a lower one. To do this, you must use a negative integer for the step value:

```
repeat with i from 100000 to 1 by -1
    display dialog "Shuttle launch in " & i & " seconds" giving up after 1
end repeat
```

Although the preceding script won't land you a job at NASA, it shows how a repeat loop starts high and counts down. Note that it is not enough to specify from high to low numbers; you must include the by *negative_number* clause at the end.

> **TIP:** If you use real numbers instead of integers in the repeat loop, AppleScript automatically rounds them to the nearest whole numbers.

Repeating with Items in a List

In many cases, you will have a list and want to perform one or more actions using each item in the list in turn. For instance, if you have the following list of names,

```
{"Ben", "Jen", "Stan"}
```

you can assign the value of a different list item in every loop, like this:

```
set name_list to {"Ben", "Jen", "Sten"}
repeat with the_name_ref in name_list
    display dialog (contents of the_name_ref)
end repeat
```

This script will repeat over the list, displaying each of its items one at a time.

There are a couple of things you might notice about this script. The first is that the loop variable is called the_name_ref rather than the_name. The second is that when getting the value to display, contents of the_name_ref is used rather than just the_name_ref.

You could also write the loop as shown in Script 14–6, and in this case it would work just as well:

Script 14–6.

```
set name_list to {"Ben", "Jen", "Sten"}
repeat with the_name in name_list
    display dialog the_name
end repeat
```

However, it's important to understand exactly what is going on in the loop, as this type of loop frequently catches out novice users—and even more-experienced users if they aren't careful.

The key to mastering repeat with ... in ... loops is to realize that the value of the loop variable on each repetition is not a value from the list, but a *reference to* an item of the list. So the values of the loop variable in Script 14–6 are not string objects as you might expect,

```
"Ben"
"Jen"
"Sten"
```

but the following reference objects:

```
item 1 of {"Ben", "Jen", "Sten"}
item 2 of {"Ben", "Jen", "Sten"}
item 3 of {"Ben", "Jen", "Sten"}
```

This difference isn't obvious when you run the loop, because in most situations AppleScript references appear completely transparent. For example, in Script 14–6, AppleScript automatically fetches the value being referenced before passing it to the display dialog command.

The problem is that although AppleScript automatically expands these references in most situations, in a few cases it does not. For example, take a look at Script 14–7.

Script 14–7.

```
set name_list to {"Ben", "Jen", "Sten"}
repeat with the_name in name_list
    display dialog the_name
    if the_name is equal to "Jen" then
        display dialog "Hiya, Jenny!"
    end if
end repeat
```

The goal here is to loop through the name list, and when it gets to "Jen" display a friendly "Hiya, Jenny!" greeting. Sounds simple, right?

Now try running it. Uh-oh—the script ran to completion but the greeting dialog box never appeared! What went wrong?

Well, the answer itself is simple enough once you know what you're looking for. However, it certainly isn't obvious at first glance, so let's work through exactly what's going on here.

Each time the `repeat` statement loops, it assigns a reference to a list item to the loop variable the_name. For example, the second time it repeats, the value of the_name is item 2 of {"Ben", "Jen", "Sten"}. Next, the conditional expression on line 4 compares this value against the string "Jen" to see if they are equal, as in:

```
(a reference to item 2 of {"Ben", "Jen", "Sten"}) is equal to "Jen"
```

If you run this line by itself in AppleScript Editor, you will see that the result of the comparison is false. Whereas most operators and commands are fairly flexible in that they will automatically retrieve the object that the reference points to before trying to use it, the is equal to and is not equal to operators are much more strict and compare their two operands exactly as they are. Because one operand is a reference and the other is a string, AppleScript determines that they are not equal. This means that the conditional expression in line 4 returns false, so the code within the conditional block is not executed.

Happily, once you understand what is going on, there is a simple solution: just retrieve the referenced object before trying to use it. To do this, you refer to the reference object's contents property, which contains the value being referenced. For example:

```
set the_reference to a reference to item 2 of {"Ben", "Jen", "Sten"}
set the_value to contents of the_reference
--> "Jen"
```

Let's put this into practice by fixing Script 14–7 so that the greeting dialog box appears as intended. Script 14–8 shows the corrected version.

Script 14–8.

```
set name_list to {"Ben", "Jen", "Sten"}
repeat with the_name_ref in name_list
    display dialog the_name
    if (contents of the_name_ref) is equal to "Jen" then
        display dialog "Hiya, Jenny!"
    end if
end repeat
```

Run the script now, and the extra greeting dialog box will appear as intended.

Notice that line 3 now gets the contents of the reference object stored in the loop variable before comparing it to the string "Jen".

I've also added _ref to the end of the loop variable's name to remind me that it contains a reference to a value rather than the value itself. Good variable naming practices can be a valuable tool for reminding yourself exactly what sort of value to expect to find in a variable. For example, by adding _ref to the end of a variable name to remind myself that the variable contains a reference object, I am much less likely to forget to expand the reference object later on when using it in an is equal to test.

Now, by this stage you might be wondering why AppleScript should go to all the trouble of assigning list item references to the loop variable rather than the items themselves. Well, reference objects have one notable advantage: not only can you get the value being referenced; you can set it too.

For example, in the previous section, Script 14–4 used a `repeat with ... from ... to ... loop` to count from 1 up to the number of items in the phone list. Each time you needed to get or set a list item, you had to refer to it like this: `item i of phone_list`. Using a `repeat with ... in ... loop`, you can do this a bit more elegantly. Script 14–9 shows the revised script—notice how it replaces the list items by setting the contents of the reference object in the `phone_ref` loop variable.

Script 14–9.

```
set default_area_code to "201"
set phone_list to {"204-5556145", "5559132", "5557040", "307-5551437", "5556421"}

repeat with phone_ref in phone_list
    if length of phone_ref is 7 then
        set contents of phone_ref to default_area_code & "-" & phone_ref
    end if
end repeat

phone_list
--> {"204-5556145", "201-5559132", "201-5557040", "307-5551437", "201-5556421"}
```

> **TIP:** Remember that AppleScript reference objects are almost entirely transparent to your code, so asking for `length of phone_ref` in Script 14–9 is effectively the same as asking for `length of contents of phone_ref`. See Chapter 13 for more information on how reference objects work.

Let's finish off this discussion with a practical example. In this exercise, you will take your list of names and generate a personalized letter for each person in the list. The script will open the template you're about to create, replace the name placeholder text, and save the letter with the person's name in the file name.

To start, you'll create the template. Start a new TextEdit document, and type the following text:

```
"Dear NAME_PLACEHOLDER,
You're invited to join us in the office on Monday for pizza"
```

Save the document on the desktop to a file named `letter template.rtf`. (For simplicity, this exercise assumes you created a rich text document, which should be saved with an `.rtf` file name suffix. If it is a plain text document, make sure you use the `.txt` suffix instead.)

Script 14–10 shows the letter generation script. For each name in the list, the script reopens the template file, replaces the placeholder phrase with the person's name, and then saves the finished letter to the desktop under a new file name based on the person's name.

Script 14–10.

```
set names_list to {"Ben", "Jen", "Stan"}
set desktop_path to (path to desktop) as text

repeat with name_ref in names_list
```

```
    tell application "TextEdit"
        open alias (desktop_path & "letter template.rtf")
        tell document 1
            set (every word where it is "NAME_PLACEHOLDER") to contents of name_ref
            save in file (desktop_path & name_ref & " letter.rtf")
            close saving no
        end tell
    end tell
end repeat
```

Notice that the repeat block uses the name_ref loop variable twice: once when inserting the person's name into the report template and again when assembling the file path where the finished letter will be saved.

Repeating While/Until a Condition Is Met

In some situations, the termination of a loop will be determined by a condition being met rather than by a predetermined count.

Using repeat while and repeat until, you can attach a condition to the repeat loop that will stop the loop repeating when the result of the condition changes. For instance, if you have a cookie jar you're trying to empty (one cookie at a time), the condition is whether the jar is empty. Here's how you can script it:

```
repeat until (jar is empty)
    eat cookie
end repeat
```

In the preceding script, which won't run on any of my Macs, the condition jar is empty comes back false as long as there are still cookies in the jar. As soon as there aren't, the loop stops repeating.

Now in the preceding example, theoretically, you could've counted the cookies and repeated a number of times that is equal to the number of cookies; however, in some cases, there's no way to know in advance just how many times a loop is going to repeat. We'll look at a couple of examples later.

Two forms of repeat loop can break on a condition: repeat while and repeat until. Both forms use a condition: when using repeat while, the loop goes on *while* the condition is true, and when using repeat until, the loop repeats *until* the condition is true:

```
repeat while condition_is_true
-- Do something
end repeat

repeat until condition_is_true
-- Do something
end repeat
```

Note that you can use the repeat while and repeat until methods interchangeably by adding the not operator before the condition. For example,

```
repeat while not boolean_expression
    -- Do something
end repeat
```

will behave exactly the same as:

```
repeat until boolean_expression
    -- Do something
end repeat
```

You choose one over the other simply by how it sounds and how well it fits what you do. Scripts 14–11 and 14–12 show simple examples of repeat until and repeat while.

In Script 14–11 you have a virtual pile of playing cards. You want to see how many cards you flip until the card total exceeds 21. So, you have a variable that adds the card values and a variable that counts the cards. The script will loop while the cards total is 21 or less. When the total exceeds 21, the loop exits and returns a record containing the card count and the total card value; for example {card_count:4, total_value:28}.

Script 14–11.

```
set cards_counter to 0
set total_value to 0
repeat while total_value ≤ 21
    set card_value to random number 13
    set total_value to total_value + card_value
    set cards_counter to cards_counter + 1
end repeat
{card_count:cards_counter, total_value:total_value}
```

In Script 14–12, the loop simply repeats until the specified file (~/Desktop/temp.pdf) exists. When distilling an Adobe PostScript file into a PDF file using Acrobat Distiller 5, for instance, Acrobat Distiller won't tell you when the PDF is complete. This loop can come in handy for delaying the script until the PDF file has been created.

Script 14–12.

```
tell application "Finder"
    repeat until file "temp.pdf" of desktop exists
        delay 1
    end repeat
end tell
```

Script 14–13 shows a more advanced example. The script arranges files in folders for archiving and has to make sure each folder has files whose accumulated file size is almost, but not quite, 600MB (or any other specified size) so that they can fit on a disk.

Script 14–13.

```
1. set max_archive_size to 600 * 1024 * 1024 -- 600MB
2. set source_folder to path to pictures folder
3. tell application "Finder"
4.     set files_to_process to document files of source_folder ¬
            whose size < max_archive_size
5.     set archive_number to 0
6.     repeat until files_to_process is {}
7.         set archive_number to archive_number + 1
8.         set archive_folder to make new folder at desktop ¬
                with properties {name:"folder " & archive_number}
9.         set total_size to 0
10.         repeat until files_to_process is {}
11.             set file_size to size of item 1 of files_to_process
```

```
12.            if total_size + file_size > max_archive_size then exit repeat
13.            move item 1 of files_to_process to archive_folder
14.            set files_to_process to rest of files_to_process
15.            set total_size to total_size + file_size
16.        end repeat
17.    end repeat
18. end tell
```

Notice that the script contains two loops.

The first loop starts at line 6. Its job is to create new archive folders as they are needed. It will repeat until the folder you're archiving is empty. Notice that there's no mention of how many files there are or should be, only a simple condition: keep looping until there are zero files to process. (This test also ensures that the loop will never execute unless the Finder command on line 4 returns one or more files to process.)

The second repeat loop, starting on line 10, is responsible for moving files into the current archive folder until it is full. Before starting the inner loop, the outer loop creates a variable named total_size whose value is initially 0. Each time the inner loop archives a file (line 13), it adds the size of the file to the total_size variable (line 15). Before archiving a file, the conditional statement on line 12 checks whether adding the file to the current archive folder would make the archive larger than the maximum allowed size specified by the max_archive_size variable. If so, it immediately exits the inner loop, allowing the outer loop to create a fresh archive folder. Otherwise, the file is processed, and line 14 removes the reference to it from the list of files to process.

Eventually, of course, the script will run out of files to process. At this point, the files_to_process is {} test on line 10 returns true, causing the repeat until ... end repeat block to stop looping. The outer loop then performs the same test on line 6, causing it to exit as well, and the script ends.

Tips for Writing Repeat Statements

Now that you've seen all the different types of repeat statements that AppleScript offers, let's finish this chapter with some useful tips for writing effective repeat loops.

Using Loops to Avoid Repetition

Often in AppleScript you need to perform several very similar tasks one after the other. For example, let's say you want to escape a piece of text on the clipboard as HTML. At minimum you need to replace the & and < characters. If you're being thorough, you might replace the > and " symbols as well.

As you saw in Chapter 7, you can easily replace one piece of text with another using just four lines of code:

```
set AppleScript's text item delimiters to search_text
set temp_list to every text item of the_text
set AppleScript's text item delimiters to replacement_text
set the_text to temp_list as text
```

If you are only replacing a few phrases, it is easy to copy and paste this code a few times, replacing the old_phrase and new_phrase portions with the literal strings to use. As you add more phrases to find and replace, however, your code starts to become very long and unwieldy. The next script uses 16 lines of code to replace just four characters, for example:

```
set the_text to the clipboard
set AppleScript's text item delimiters to "&"
set temp_list to every text item of the_text
set AppleScript's text item delimiters to "&amp;"
set the_text to temp_list as text
set AppleScript's text item delimiters to "<"
set temp_list to every text item of the_text
set AppleScript's text item delimiters to "&lt;"
set the_text to temp_list as text
set AppleScript's text item delimiters to ">"
set temp_list to every text item of the_text
set AppleScript's text item delimiters to "&gt;"
set the_text to temp_list as text
set AppleScript's text item delimiters to "\""
set temp_list to every text item of the_text
set AppleScript's text item delimiters to "&quot;"
set the_text to temp_list as text
set the clipboard to the_text
```

By the time you've copied and pasted the same piece of code three or four times, you should probably start to think about how you can shorten your script to make it simpler and easier to manage.

One solution for avoiding this sort of duplication is to insert the find-and-replace logic just once, and then use a repeat loop to supply the strings to use each time, as shown in Script 14–14.

Script 14–14.

```
set the_text to the clipboard
repeat with replacement_ref in ¬
    {{"&", "&amp;"}, {"<", "&lt;"}, {">", "&gt;"}, {"\"", "&quot;"}}
    set {search_text, replacement_text} to replacement_ref
    set AppleScript's text item delimiters to search_text
    set temp_list to every text item of the_text
    set AppleScript's text item delimiters to replacement_text
    set the_text to temp_list as text
end repeat
set the clipboard to the_text
```

As you can see, using a loop instead of copy-and-paste has made this script quite a bit shorter. It also makes it easier to read—for example, you can easily see which characters will be replaced and by what, as all those values can now be found on a single line (line 2) instead of spread throughout the code.

Lastly, this approach makes it easy to expand the script later on. To find and replace additional phrases, you only have to insert an extra pair of strings into the list instead of copying and pasting another four lines each time.

> **TIP:** AppleScript's user-defined handlers provide another powerful way to avoid unnecessary repetition of code. We'll discuss this feature in Chapter 18.

Naming Loop Variables

As discussed in Chapter 11, picking your variable names wisely can make the difference between a script that works, and a script that works *and* is easy to understand and modify as well.

As you now know, AppleScript provides two types of repeat loops that assign values to their own loop variables as they repeat. Depending on which type of loop you use and what you use it for, you will want to name the loop variable appropriately.

A `repeat with ... from ... to ...` loop is normally used for counting, and the value it assigns to its loop variable is an integer, so you will want to pick a variable name that reflects this.

Short counting loops whose loop variable does not have a particularly important meaning typically use short variable names like i and j. This avoids clogging up the code with wordy identifiers and gives them a suitably mathematical look.

On the other hand, as loops become longer they become harder to follow, so in that situation you should use a longer variable name that describes what the value represents; for example, user_number or vertical_offset.

When using `repeat with ... in ...` loops, it always helps to add _ref to the end of the variable name to remind yourself that you are dealing with a reference to a list item, not the item itself.

It also helps to pick a name that indicates the item's relationship to the list it came from. For example, if you're repeating over a list of names, then it's only fitting that the loop variable will be called something like name_ref, particularly if the original list came from a variable called names_list.

Choosing the Right Loop for the Job

With so many different kinds of `repeat` statements to choose from, it is not always immediately obvious which one is best for a particular job. Here is a modified version of Script 14–11, which repeats while the card total is less than or equal to 21:

```
set cards_counter to 0
set total_value to 0
set cards to {}
repeat while total_value ≤ 21
    set card_value to random number 13
    set total_value to total_value + card_value
    set cards_counter to cards_counter + 1
    set end of cards to card_value
end repeat
```

```
{cards:cards, total_value:total_value}
```

This time, however, you'd like to get as many cards as you can *without* going over 21.

The problem? You asked the script to loop while the card value is less than or equal to 21, but the value of the cards at the end is greater than 21; for example, {cards:{6, 6, 9, 5}, total_value:26}. This happens because when the repeat loop condition executes, the card value has already exceeded 21! At that point, all the repeat loop can do is stop, but the damage has already been done, and the card total has climbed beyond 21.

So how do you fix this problem? You use a simple repeat loop with a conditional statement that exits the loop before the card total would exceed 21, as shown in Script 14–15.

Script 14–15.

```
1. set cards_counter to 0
2. set total_value to 0
3. set cards to {}
4. repeat
5.    set card_value to random number from 1 to 13
6.    if (total_value + card_value) > 21 then exit repeat
7.    set total_value to total_value + card_value
8.    set end of cards to card_value
9. end repeat
10. {cards:cards, total_value:total_value}
```

In the preceding script, the condition to stop the loop isn't part of the repeat statement but rather a separate conditional statement on line 6 that checks whether the new total would exceed 21. If it would, it immediately exits the loop without adding the new card to the hand, giving you the result you're after; for example, {cards:{3, 12, 4}, total_value:19}.

Avoid Looping when Possible

Although the repeat statement is a staple you can't do without when working with the elements of an AppleScript list, when dealing with scriptable applications, you can often operate on several or all elements of an application object at once.

For example, let's say you want to close all the windows that are currently open in the Finder. You could get a list of window references and then tell the Finder to close them one at a time, like this:

```
tell application "Finder"
    repeat with window_ref in (get every window)
        close window_ref
    end repeat
end tell
```

However, it is simpler and quicker just to tell the Finder to close them all at once:

```
tell application "Finder"
   close every window
end tell
```

For some tasks, you may need to manipulate only some elements of an application object, depending on whether or not they match certain conditions. If your tests are particularly complex, you may have to resort to using a loop and testing each object yourself one at a time. However, in many cases, you can refer to the needed objects using the standard whose clause. Because the whose clause is implemented inside the application, it generally runs much faster than having a repeat loop check each element individually.

Imagine standing in front of 100 people who're all wearing different colored hats and having to ask all the red-hat wearers to take off their hats. Using a repeat statement, it would go like this: first person, if your hat is red, take it off; second person, if your hat is red, take it off; third person, if your hat is red, take it off; and so on. With a whose clause, it would go like this: every person whose hat is red, take your hat off.

In the following example, we will delete from the desktop all files that have the word "temp" in the name. First, here is the loop-based version:

```
tell application "Finder"
   repeat with file_ref in (get files of desktop)
      if name of file_ref contains "temp" then
         delete file_ref
      end if
   end repeat
end tell
```

And here is the smart version that uses the whose clause instead of a loop:

```
tell application "Finder"
   delete every file of desktop whose name contains "temp"
end tell
```

It's not only that the code is shorter and more to the point, but the execution time will be shorter—much shorter in situations where there are many objects to loop through. When using the whose clause, you're not sending individual commands to filter and manipulate each object one at a time; instead, a single command that applies to all objects will be sent and the application will do all the filtering work for you.

Summary

In this chapter, we looked at the two main AppleScript features used to control program flow during normal operation: conditionals and loops.

In the first part of the chapter, you saw how the basic conditional, or if, statement can be used to execute one or more statements only if a particular condition is met. You saw how a simple if ... end if block could be expanded with else if ... clauses to perform multiple tests and execute a block of code for the first condition that is met.

You also saw how to add a final `else` clause that would be executed if none of the previous conditions was met.

In the second part, you learned about the various types of `repeat` statements that you can use to execute a block of code zero or more times. You saw how the simplest `repeat` statement can be used to loop indefinitely, although in practice you will normally want to use an `exit repeat` statement to break out of it at some point. You met the two "counting" loop types, `repeat ... times` and `repeat with ... from ... to ...`, both of which repeat a certain number of times. You also met `repeat with ... in ...`, which provides an elegant way to repeat over the items in a list...just as long as you remember how to use its loop variable correctly! Finally, you met the `repeat while ...` and `repeat until ...` forms, which continue looping as long as or until a Boolean condition is met.

In the next chapter, we will continue with the theme of decision making in AppleScript by examining what happens when something goes wrong in your script—and, more importantly, how you can respond to this.

Chapter 15

Making Decisions When Dealing with Errors

Errors in AppleScript fall into one of the following categories: bugs that prevent scripts from compiling, bugs that cause scripts to work incorrectly when run—either failing completely or doing something other than what you wanted—and errors caused by external factors beyond your script's control. Some of these errors may occur when the script is being compiled, others when it is run.

Compilation errors are those that occur when the script tries to compile. Typical compilation errors include misspelled keywords; not including a `tell` block when using application-specific terms; forgetting an end keyword at the end of a compound statement; and so on. Obviously, if you encounter a compile-time error, you will have to fix it before you can run the script.

Runtime errors are those that happen only while the script runs. Typical runtime errors include trying to manipulate an application object that doesn't exist; evaluating a variable whose value has not yet been defined; dividing a number by zero; and so on. By default, runtime errors cause the script to stop, and usually AppleScript will display a dialog box containing the grim details to the user.

Fortunately, it is possible to have your script intercept, or "trap," runtime errors and deal with them itself by using AppleScript's third big decision-making feature: the `try` statement. This is especially useful with errors caused by factors outside of your control, such as a missing folder or file that your script needs to use.

Since compile errors are easy to discover and usually easy enough to fix, this chapter will concentrate mainly on runtime errors. However, it's still worth taking a brief look at some of the common mistakes you can make when typing a script. After all, the cleverest script in the world won't be of much use if you can't get it to run in the first place!

Understanding Compilation Errors

Compilation errors occur when AppleScript is unable to understand your script's source code. The bad news is that they happen a lot when you start to script simply because the syntax is still foreign to you. Later, you often get them when your syntax is correct but some literal expression you used didn't work. The good news is that a compilation error is a bit like losing your car keys down the drain. It's irritating, but at least it can't be made worse by someone driving away in your car....

Most compilation errors are fairly straightforward to identify and solve, although a few may take a bit more thought—for example, a date specifier such as date "9/30/09" would compile for some users but not others, depending on the Date and Time format settings in the International preferences of the Mac on which it is being compiled.

Let's look at a few common mistakes that keep your code from compiling.

Simple Typos

The following script will not compile because of two simple typing errors. First, there's no space between the to and the 10 in line 1; AppleScript expects the word to but instead it gets what it would consider to be a variable name (to10). Second, on line 2 the command display dialog is misspelled.

```
repeat with i from 1 to10
    disply dialog i
end
```

Unbalanced Statements

One mistake that's easy to make is not balancing your block statements, as in the following example:

```
repeat with i from 1 to 20
    if i > 10 then
        display dialog "Second half"
end repeat
```

Although the missing end if is not difficult to spot in this case, block statements such as if, try, tell, and repeat can sometimes span dozens of lines in your script. Detecting where the missing end should be can be a challenge.

When typing block statements, you may find it easier to enter the opening and closing lines of the block first, and then fill in the statements in the middle. Clicking the Compile button in AppleScript Editor after typing each block will also help you spot any errors sooner rather than later.

Unbalanced Parentheses and Unescaped Quotes

When forming complex expressions containing multiple sets of parentheses, it is all too easy to omit or include extra parentheses on either side of the expression. A common related mistake is using quotes in a string but not escaping them properly. Look at the following script:

```
if ((x < 0) or (x > 10) then display dialog "The "x" variable is out of range."
```

In this example, the expression ((x < 0) or (x > 10) is missing a closing parenthesis, and the string literal provided for the display dialog command contains unescaped quotes. Here's the fixed script:

```
if ((x < 0) or (x > 10)) then display dialog "The \"x\" variable is out of range."
```

Unrecognized Keywords

Another easy mistake is using keywords from applications not included in the application tell block. The following line will not compile since the element names track and playlist aren't defined by AppleScript. They are defined by iTunes, however, which is presumably what they're meant for.

```
get every track of playlist 1
```

To fix this problem, wrap the line in a tell application ... end tell block, like this:

```
tell application "iTunes"
    get every track of playlist 1
end tell
```

Here's a less obvious example:

```
folder "Applications"
```

If you compile the word folder by itself, you'll see it gets formatted as an application keyword. When you try to compile folder "Applications", though, you get an error. Why?

By itself, folder compiles as an application keyword because Standard Additions adds its own keyword definition for folder to AppleScript. However, Standard Additions defines folder as a property name (see the file information record defined by the File Commands suite), not a class name, and an object specifier like folder "Applications" needs to start with a class name. But stick the phrase inside a tell application ... end tell block for the Finder or System Events and it'll compile correctly, since both those applications define their own folder classes:

```
tell application "Finder"
    folder "Applications"
end tell

tell application "System Events"
    folder "Applications"
end tell
```

Reserved Word Mishaps

Using reserved words in ways that aren't allowed will cause the script to not compile. One common mistake is trying to use a class name as a variable name:

```
set list to {1, 2, 3, 4, 5}
```

Installed scripting additions often reserve words in addition to the ones reserved by AppleScript. Scriptable applications can also reserve words, though only within `tell application` blocks.

You can greatly reduce the risk of collisions with reserved words by using camel case or underscore-separated multi-word variable names such as `theList` or `the_list`, as applications and scripting additions normally don't spell keywords this way.

Invalid Date Literals

Since the way date literals are compiled depends on the date format set on the Mac you're using, some dates may compile incorrectly or not compile at all. For instance, `date "3/14/10"` will compile as March 14th, 2010 using the default settings of a U.S. Mac system, but it won't compile on a European system.

> **NOTE:** Date specifiers can be a common source of runtime errors too. For example, `date "3/12/10"` could generate three different dates, depending on the current system settings, only one of which is correct.

Understanding Runtime Errors

Runtime errors in AppleScript aren't all-out unanticipated mistakes that can't be recovered from. Rather, runtime errors are designed to let you know that the data provided for a certain statement doesn't fit and that AppleScript's next resort is to throw an error and terminate the script. Errors are the way out when the result of a statement isn't within the range of acceptable possibilities.

How Runtime Errors Work in AppleScript

There are two categories of runtime errors to consider: those that are caused by bugs in your code, which you should obviously fix, and those that are caused by external factors, which your script needs to cope with when they occur. To understand the difference, I'll present a simple script that looks at a set of files in a folder and extracts the first six characters of each file's name. Here's the first attempt:

```
1. tell application "Finder"
2.    set file_list to name of every file in (path to documents folder)
3.    repeat with file_ref in file_list
4.        set the_short_name to text 1 thru 6 of name of file_ref
5.        -- Do something with the short name...
6.    end repeat
7. end tell
```

Figure 15–1 shows what happens when you run the script.

Figure 15–1. *AppleScript Editor reports a runtime error when the script is executed.*

Notice how AppleScript Editor displays a message describing the problem and highlights the code where the error occurred.

The problem is that although the script's syntax is correct, it has a bug that doesn't allow it to run past line 4. The bug is that the variable file_ref in the repeat loop *already* has the filename in it, not a reference to the file. This is a typical programmer's bug that's easy to fix in this case but can sometimes be quite difficult to locate.

Once you fix the first problem, as shown here, the script seems to run well:

```
1. tell application "Finder"
2.    set file_name_list to name of every file in (path to documents folder)
3.    repeat with file_name_ref in file_name_list
4.       set the_short_name to text 1 thru 6 of file_name_ref
5.       -- Do something with the short name...
6.    end repeat
7. end tell
```

The script won't produce an error until you encounter a file whose name is shorter than six characters. Figure 15–2 shows an example.

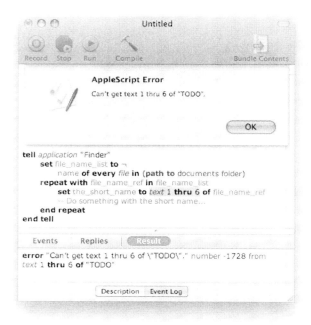

Figure 15–2. *An error occurs when a file name is too short.*

This condition is a different kind of error. Instead of being buggy code, the script makes an incorrect assumption, namely, that all file names will be six characters or longer. You can handle this problem rather easily with a simple conditional statement, as shown in lines 4 to 8 here:

```
1. tell application "Finder"
2.    set file_name_list to name of every file in (path to documents folder)
3.    repeat with file_name_ref in file_name_list
4.       if length of file_name_ref ≥ 6 then
5.          set the_short_name to text 1 thru 6 of file_name_ref
6.       else
7.          set the_short_name to contents of file_name_ref
8.       end if
9.       -- Do something with the short name...
10.   end repeat
11. end tell
```

So, are errors good or bad? Errors are actually good, much like pain is a good thing for our health for one reason—we do our best to avoid it.

Can you avoid errors altogether? Not really. But although you can't avoid them, you can anticipate them, trap them, analyze them, and sentence them to community service.

Understanding the Psychology of an Error

I've come up with four basic rules you should keep in mind with regard to errors when building scripts:

- As the scripter, you subconsciously avoid using your script in ways that will generate errors, so you should have someone else test your script for you.

- As the scripter, you think you know best how your script will behave. Wrong! Give it to a novice user, and that user will likely provoke unexpected behavior and errors within the first three seconds.

- People don't read instructions. If you think to yourself, "I wrote an instruction in the dialog box telling the user to enter a date, so it's not my fault if they don't," you're wrong; it is your fault. The blame does not lie with what the user entered but that you didn't anticipate all the different data that could be entered.

- Remember, Murphy's Law applies to your scripts: any statement in your script that can generate an error because of user incompetence will generate an error. Furthermore, the error yet again reflects on you, the AppleScript genius, not on the just-started-yesterday user.

By considering the psychology of both users and the developer—you—and by sticking to these four rules, you should be much better equipped to prepare for and fix errors.

Understanding the Anatomy of an Error

Every error that is thrown includes various bits of information that help you identify its cause. The two main values are the error message, a string that provides a human-readable description of what went wrong, and the error number, which indicates exactly what type of error it is and which can be used by the script to decide what action it should take next.

The other pieces of information that may be available are the offending object, the partial result, and the expected type. The offending object is the object that caused the error. The partial result value applies only to commands that return results for multiple objects. In this case, the value is a list that can contain the objects that were handled correctly until one object caused an error. The expected type is the type of data the script would have liked to have gotten instead of the offending object.

To understand a bit better, start a script and type the following:

```
1 + "abc"
```

When you run this script, you'll get the error message "Can't make 'abc' into type number." The error number is –1700, which indicates it's a coercion error. There's no partial result, but you do have an offender. The offending object is the string "abc", and the expected type is number. AppleScript tried to coerce "abc" into a number but couldn't.

The error number and the error message are particularly important, both when you want to trap potential errors and when you conspire to take the offender's role and throw an error yourself! You'll learn more about this in the Generating Errors section.

> **NOTE:** In Mac OS X 10.5 and earlier, when AppleScript Editor reports an AppleScript error, the only information it displays is the error message. To obtain the other values, you will need to trap the error and extract the values yourself using a `try` statement. See the next section for details.

Trapping Runtime Errors

How much effort you put into trapping errors is up to you. You may be writing a script for your own use or for a limited purpose, and don't want to turn it into a big production. In such cases, you may want to test the script and explain to the user how to write down any error and let you know about it.

On the other hand, if you have to distribute the script among many users—or worse, to unknown users all over the place—you want to take every precaution that no potential error remains untrapped.

In the following sections, I will show how to trap errors.

Using the *try* Block

The one and only way to trap errors in AppleScript is by using `try` statement blocks, which start with a line containing a single word, `try`, and end with a line containing two words, `end try`. Most `try` blocks also have an additional line in the middle that starts with `on error`, but you'll learn more about that in the Knowing What to Do in Case of an Error section.

The script that follows shows the basic `try` block:

```
try
    -- One or more statements that may throw an error
end try
```

If no errors occur in any of the statements within the `try` block, then the `try` block has no effect. However, if one of the statements does throw an error, then subsequent statements from there until the `end try` statement will be skipped. In fact, every time an error is thrown, AppleScript immediately stops executing the statement where the error occurred and looks to see whether this statement is enclosed by a `try` statement. If it doesn't find a `try` statement, then AppleScript has no choice but to air your dirty laundry and let the user know an error has occurred.

If AppleScript does find a `try` statement, it looks to see whether the `try` statement has an `on error` line. This example doesn't have an `on error` line, just an `end try`. This means AppleScript continues to execute the script from the line following the `end try` line, and you may never know that an error has occurred. (Just take care that the statements that follow the try block are not dependent on statements within the block that may have been skipped if an error occurred.)

Using the Full *try* Statement

The following is the official definition of the try statement. Optional parameters appear in square brackets.

```
try
    -- One or more statements that may throw an error
on error [error_message] [number error_number] ¬
        [from offending_object] [to expected_type] [partial result result_list]
    -- One or more statements that will execute in case of an error
end try
```

As you can see in this example, the full try statement is fairly complex, although you'll usually need to deal with only the error message and the error number parameters.

The error message is a string that provides a convenient, human-readable description of the problem. The error number indicates the type of error that has occurred—very useful if your script needs to perform different actions in response to different kinds of errors.

> **TIP:** The Understanding Common Error Numbers section at the end of the chapter provides a convenient summary of standard error numbers used by AppleScript and many scriptable applications and scripting additions.

The other three parameters are used less often, but occasionally provide additional information that can help in identifying the cause of the error. If a particular object or reference caused the problem, it is often supplied via the from parameter. When a coercion error occurs, the to parameter provides the name of the class that the object could not be coerced to. The partial result parameter is hardly ever used in practice, though in theory it can be used by commands that normally return a list of values to provide the values that were successfully obtained before the error occurred.

Knowing What to Do in Case of an Error

So far you have dealt with the try statement as a simple block with a start and an end. Now, however, you'll learn how to add the on error line at the heart of the try statement. From now on, your try statement block will have two compartments:

```
try
    -- Compartment 1
on error
    -- Compartment 2
end try
```

In compartment 1 you'll put all the statements you want to execute under normal operation. In compartment 2 you'll put all the statements you want to execute if anything goes wrong in compartment 1. Here's another way you can put it:

```
try
    light candles on cake
on error
    call fire department
end try
```

Do you usually invite firefighters to birthday parties? I know my wife wouldn't mind—she has a thing for firemen—but they always seem so busy. However, it is a good idea to have a plan to call the firefighters in case something goes wrong with the candles.

One of the most common uses of the on error clause is to trap error number –128, the "User canceled" error. The "User canceled" error can occur in various ways; for example, it is normally thrown by the display dialog command when the user clicks the Cancel button. Error –128, however, will not generate an ugly error message to the user. All that'll happen if the Cancel button is clicked is that the script will immediately stop whatever it is doing and silently exit.

> **NOTE:** For more information about how the display dialog command works, see Chapter 16.

Script 15–1 shows a simple example of trapping the Cancel button error.

Script 15–1.

```
try
    display dialog "What's next?" buttons {"Cancel", "Go", "Run"}
on error
    display dialog "I'm out of here..." giving up after 5
end try
```

Now this is OK, but what you want to do in many cases is take action *only* if the error is a specific error. In this case, you want the "I'm out of here..." dialog box displayed only for the "User canceled" error.

For that, you need to know the error number. Just for adventure's sake, let's pretend you don't know exactly what error is thrown or what the error number is. To figure it out, you need to create a little script, make sure that AppleScript throws an error at you, trap it, and analyze it. You do that with the error message and error number values that are provided by the error.

To get the error message, you can add a variable identifier immediately after on error. The error message will be assigned to this variable. Examine Script 15–2.

Script 15–2.

```
try
    display dialog "Do it?"
on error the_error_message
    display dialog "An error occurred. The message was:" & return & the_error_message
end try
```

Figure 15–3 shows the message of the second dialog box. It shows that the value of the variable the_error_message you placed after the on error line was "User canceled."

Figure 15–3. *The error message trapped in the variable `the_error_message` is "User canceled."*

To trap the error number, you add the keyword number followed by the variable you want to hold the error number. For now, add the phrase number `the_error_number` as shown in Script 15–3, run the script, and click the Cancel button.

Script 15–3.

```
try
    display dialog "Do it?"
on error number the_error_number
    display dialog "An error occurred. The number is:" & return & the_error_number
end try
```

Figure 15–4 shows the dialog box displayed as a result of clicking Cancel on the "Do it?" dialog. Check out the error number the dialog box revealed.

Figure 15–4. *The dialog box reveals the "User canceled" error number.*

Ah, the satisfaction of attaining hard-earned knowledge! Now, let's mix the error message with the error number—see Script 15–4.

Script 15–4.

```
try
    display dialog "Do it?"
on error the_error_message number the_error_number
    display dialog "An error occurred:" & return & the_error_message & ¬
        return & the_error_number
end try
```

If you return to the original `1 + "abc"` example for a moment, you can use the same approach to capture the error message and number, plus all the other available error information:

```
try
    1 + "abc"
on error error_text number error_number ¬
        from offending_object partial result result_list to expected_type
    return {error_text, error_number, offending_object, result_list, expected_type}
end try
--> {"Can't make \"abc\" into type number.", -1700, "abc", {}, number}
```

Putting Error Numbers to Use

Now that you know how to figure out the error numbers, you can begin using them. To start, modify the preceding script to display the second dialog box only if the error number is –128. To do that, you just have to replace the variable following the word number with the actual error number. Script 15–5 shows how the script will look.

Script 15–5.

```
try
    display dialog "Do it?"
on error number -128
    display dialog "You canceled the script. Bye!"
end try
```

The preceding script is OK, but it lets you act upon only one error. What if you anticipate two or more errors? For that you have two possible options: you can either put the error number into a variable and use an `if-else if` block to test for the different possible errors or you can nest multiple `try` statement blocks inside each other.

Testing For Multiple Error Numbers

In many cases, the same statement may throw more than one type of error. To treat each error independently, you will need to use a simple conditional statement. You'll also need to identify the number of the errors you want to treat and to leave one last open `else` clause to deal with any unspecified error that may occur. This script will take two variables, one with a path pointing to a folder and one with a path pointing to a file. The script will attempt to duplicate the file in the folder.

Two things that can go wrong are that one path points to a nonexistent item, in which case the Finder will throw error number –10006, and that the file you're copying already exists in the destination folder, which is error number –15267.

Watch how the script acts differently based on the error, as shown in Script 15–6.

Script 15–6.

```
try
    tell application "Finder"
        duplicate file source_file_path to folder dest_folder_path
    end tell
on error error_message number error_number
```

```
    if error_number is -10006 then
        display dialog "The file or folder you specify doesn't exist."
    else if error_number is -15267 then
        display dialog "The folder already has a file with the same name."
    else -- Report any other errors
        display dialog "An error has occurred:" & return & error_message
    end if
end try
```

Nesting *try* Handlers

Another way to achieve a similar result is to use several nested `try` statements, as shown in Script 15–7.

Script 15–7.

```
try
    try
        try
            tell application "Finder"
                duplicate file source_file_path to folder dest_folder_path
            end tell
        on error number -10006
            display dialog "The file or folder you specify doesn't exist."
        end try
    on error number -15267
        display dialog "The folder already has a file with the same name."
    end try
on error error_message -- Report any other errors
    display dialog "An error has occurred:" & return & error_message
end try
```

In this example, the code whose error you want to trap is actually inside three nested `try` statements. Each of the first two will trap only a specific error. If the error that occurred is not that error, the error will trickle down to the next `try` statement. At the end, the error will get to the outermost `try` block that you've designed to trap any error.

Generating Runtime Errors

Having spent the last portion of the chapter trying to contain and control errors, why in the world would you want to go around creating them yourself? Well, in some situations during a script's execution, you will realize that the best way to proceed is to throw an error. In many cases, this error will be handled by the same error trapping mechanism you set up to trap other possible errors.

To throw an error yourself, you use AppleScript's `error` statement. The most basic form of this statement is simply this:

```
error
```

Running this statement causes AppleScript to raise an unknown error with the generic message "An error has occurred" and with an error number of –2700. However, in most situations you'll want to supply a more meaningful error message and error number. Here's the full definition of the `error` statement:

```
error [error_message] [number error_number] ¬
    [from offending_object] [to expected_type] [partial result result_list]
```

As you can see, the error statement has the same parameters as the `try` statement's on error line. The error message and error number are the two parameters you'll usually use for throwing errors. For example:

```
error "E.T. could not phone home: wrong number." number 411
```

Figure 15–5 shows the error dialog box that this error, unhandled, will display.

Figure 15–5. *The error message shown in an AppleScript application error dialog box.*

Throwing your own errors is a good idea when part of your script hits a problem it can't deal with itself. Not only does this let other parts of the script know there's a problem, but it also gives them a chance to deal with it if they want by trapping and handling that error in a `try` block.

As an example, let's say you're writing a script where one part involves looking up a phone number based on a person's name. The names and phone numbers are stored in a list of records like this:

```
set contact_table to { ¬
    {the_key:"Joe", the_value:"555-3712"}, ¬
    {the_key:"Pam", the_value:"555-0232"}, ¬
    {the_key:"Sam", the_value:"555-6795"}}
```

This list works as a simple lookup table: to get a phone number, you loop through each item in the main list, checking to see whether the name matches the one you want. When the loop finds a matching name, it returns the corresponding phone number. For example, if the name is "Sam", the value returned will be "555-6795".

You'll encounter one other possibility, though: what if none of the entries in the table matches the desired name? Well, let's take a page out of AppleScript's book here. Just as saying get item 10 of {1, 2, 3, 4, 5} will cause AppleScript to raise a "Can't get item ..." error, I'll have my table-searching handler generate a similar error when it can't find the entry that was requested. Here's the error statement I'll use:

```
error "The item was not found." number -1728
```

Since the type of error being reported is similar to an existing AppleScript error, I've used the same error code as AppleScript, –1728. But I could make up my own error code for it if I preferred, such as error number 6000, "Can't find an entry with the given key in a lookup table."

Here's the full table lookup handler:

```
on get_value_for_key(key_value_list, key_to_find)
    repeat with item_ref in key_value_list
        if the_key of item_ref = key_to_find then return the_value of item_ref
    end repeat
    error "The item wasn't found." number -1728
end get_value_for_key
```

And here are some examples of its use:

```
get_value_for_key(contact_table, "Pam")
--> "555-0232"
get_value_for_key(contact_table, "Frank")
-- Error: The item wasn't found.
```

Now when the get_value_for_key handler raises the error number –1728, the part of the script that called it can handle that error in any way it wants. For example, it might catch that particular error number and record the problem in a log file before continuing to the next task:

```
try
    set the_phone_number to get_value_for_key(contact_table, the_person)
on error number -1728
    add_to_log("Couldn't call " & the_person)
    set the_phone_number to missing value
end try
if the_phone_number is not missing value then
    -- Call the person at that number...
end if
```

Or, it might choose to ignore the error completely, letting the script stop straightaway, and display the standard AppleScript error dialog box. As the designer of the script, the choice is up to you.

Tips for Handling Runtime Errors

The following sections provide useful tips for designing your own error-trapping code.

Being Careful Not to Trap Too Much

Error trapping is not a solution to errors! Well, it kind of is the solution, but only for errors you anticipate or for freak, once-in-a-lifetime errors. During your testing and debugging stage, you should stay away from trapping errors. You want to see the errors as they come and treat them. Once you've managed to account for almost all situations, add some `try` statements just to be sure.

You may also consider deactivating any error-trapping `try` statements. Simply comment out the individual `try`, `on error...`, and `end try` lines, and any code between the `on error...` and `end try` lines. When all is done, uncomment the `try` statements to make them active again. You do this because during the testing stages you actually want to see the errors so you can possibly find better solutions for them.

Providing More Detailed Error Messages

Sometimes you'll want AppleScript's own errors to be displayed but want to add some explanatory text of your own. One way to do this is by using a `try...on error...end try` block to trap an error, expand the original the error text with some detailed script-specific information, and then use the error statement to throw a new error containing the new error message along with any other error information that the original `try` block caught.

In the following example, the script is looking for a file that's needed for normal operation:

```
property work_folder : "Macintosh HD:Users:Hanaan:Work:"
property manifest_file_name : "manifest.txt"

try
    set manifest_file to alias (work_folder & manifest_file_name)
    set jobs_list to paragraphs of (read manifest_file)
on error error_message number error_number
    -- Throw a detailed error if the job manifest can't be found...
    error "Can't read the work manifest file (and can't proceed without it): " & ¬
        error_message number error_number
end try
-- Rest of the code goes here...
```

If the file isn't found or can't be read for some reason, the script traps the original error and raises a new error containing a more detailed error message, for example: "Can't read the work manifest file (and can't proceed without it): File Macintosh HD:Users:Hanaan:Work:manifest.txt wasn't found."

Using a Scriptwide *try* Statement

One of the projects I've worked on is a bunch of scripts Sal Soghoian (AppleScript product manager) wrote for Showtime Networks. The scripts automate the creation of the Upcoming Shows menus for about ten of Showtime Networks' affiliate stations. Sal initially created the scripts as a public relations campaign for Showtime, and it really worked well. It also worked well for me to inherit the project, since besides billing for the time, I got to learn a lot from Sal's AppleScript mastery.

One of the neat features in these scripts was that, besides the localized error trapping that was implemented throughout the script, every script had one big `try` statement that covered it from head to toe.

The purpose of this `try` block's `on error` handler wasn't to notify the user that something wrong went down—AppleScript's built-in error dialog box would have done that. The purpose was to cause the script to display the error message in a nice dialog box instead of the typical error message that AppleScript applets display for unhandled errors, with the dreaded Edit button that, no matter what I tell them, users always seem to want to click. Figure 15–6 shows the standard error message dialog box used by applets.

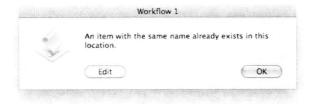

Figure 15–6. *The standard applet error message dialog box with the dreaded Edit button.*

Sal's scriptwide `try` statement worked well, but I needed a way for the user to know exactly where things went bad so I could troubleshoot faster. Unfortunately, AppleScript error messages don't contain a detailed description of where in the script the error occurred, so, I came up with the following solution: I added a global variable called `script_location` and assigned a different number to it throughout the script. Every two or three lines of real code, I added something like this:

```
set script_location to 64
```

At the end, part of the job of that scriptwide `on error` handler was to report to me not only the nature of the error but the value of that script location variable, which allowed me to pinpoint the exact location of the error.

Although adding lines indicating the script location can be useful, what I usually do is remove most of them when the script has been in use for a while. As useful as they can be when an error happens, they do bloat the script quite a bit. Once a script proves that it runs smoothly in a working environment, you no longer need most of these script position indicators.

Logging Errors to a File

An even better error-hunting technique I use is to write the script's activity to a text file. Since doing this every second or third line of the script really hampers performance, you want the user to enable it only when there's a persistent error. You can also choose to log more of the script's activity, in which case the logical place in the script is between tasks the script performs. For instance, you can have comments like the following logged in the proper places throughout your script: "Exporting Excel file <name> to tab-delimited file," "Now reading tab-delimited file into AppleScript," "Now inserting images into page template," and so on.

If your script has a graphical interface, you can add a little check box called Log Activity. Otherwise, if your script has a dialog box that appears at the start, you may want to add a button to it called Settings. Clicking this button would display another dialog box that allows users to turn logging on for the subsequent execution of the script. This will set a scriptwide is_logging_enabled property to true, which will then tell all the handlers in the script to log their activity.

The idea of logging activity is to create a text file on the desktop bearing the date and time and add some text to that file every few lines. The text should describe the location and include some of the actual values used in the script. This can provide clues to the error.

I tell my clients to e-mail me the resulting text file, which is handy for revealing the cause of the error.

Since you will be utilizing the error-logging feature again and again, it is a perfect candidate for a handler with a few parameters, such as the line number, the part of the script it's called from, and maybe the values of a few variables coerced into a string. A handler call is much easier to call multiple times in your script. Script 15–8 shows how you might set this up.

Script 15–8.

```
property is_logging_enabled : true -- Set to false to disable error logging

on log_warning(warning_message)
    if is_logging_enabled then
        -- Write warning message to file...
    end if
end log_warning

on log_error(error_message, error_number)
    if is_logging_enabled then
        -- Write error message to file...
    end if
end log_error

-- Rest of script goes here...
```

Later chapters will look at defining handlers and writing files in more detail.

Understanding Common Error Numbers

The following sections list common AppleScript-related error messages that don't belong specifically to third-party scripting additions or scriptable applications. The errors are divided into operating system errors, Apple event errors, application scripting errors, and AppleScript errors.

Identifying Operating System Errors

An operating system error is an error that occurs when AppleScript or an application requests services from Mac OS X and something goes wrong (see Table 15–1). These errors are rare, and more important, you usually can't do anything about them in a script. A few, such as "File <name> wasn't found" and "Application isn't running," make sense for scripts to handle.

Table 15–1. *Operating System Errors*

Number	Description
–34	Disk <name> is full.
–35	Disk <name> wasn't found.
–37	Bad name for file.
–38	File <name> wasn't open.
–39	End of file error.
–42	Too many files open.
–43	File <name> wasn't found.
–44	Disk <name> is write protected.
–45	File <name> is locked.
–46	Disk <name> is locked.
–47	File <name> is busy.
–48	Duplicate filename.
–49	File <name> is already open.
–50	Parameter error.
–51	File reference number error.
–61	File not open with write permission.
–120	Folder <name> wasn't found.
–124	Disk <name> is disconnected.
–128	User canceled.
–192	A resource wasn't found.
–600	Application isn't running.
–609	Connection is invalid.
–905	Remote access is not allowed.
–906	<name> isn't running or program linking isn't enabled.
–915	Can't find remote machine.
–30720	Invalid date and time <date string>.

Identifying Apple Event Errors

An Apple event error is an error that is generated by a scriptable application or a scripting addition (see Table 15–2). Many of these errors, such as "No user interaction allowed," are of interest to users. Also of interest to users are errors that have to do with reference forms, as well as errors such as "No such object." In addition, AppleScript can generate some of the errors shown.

Table 15–2. *Apple Event Errors*

Number	Description
–1700	Can't make some data into the expected type.
–1701	Some parameter is missing for <commandName>.
–1702	Some data could not be read.
–1703	Some data was the wrong type.
–1704	Some parameter was invalid.
–1705	Operation involving a list item failed.
–1708	<reference> doesn't understand the <commandName> message.
–1712	Apple event timed out.
–1713	No user interaction allowed.
–1715	Some parameter wasn't understood.
–1717	The handler <identifier> is not defined.
–1719	Can't get <reference>. Invalid index.
–1720	Invalid range.
–1721	<expression> doesn't match the parameters <parameterNames> for <commandName>.
–1723	Can't get <expression>. Access not allowed.
–1727	Expected a reference.
–1728	Can't get <reference>.
–1730	Container specified was an empty list.
–1731	Unknown object type.
–1750	Scripting component error.
–1751	Invalid script ID.
–1752	Script doesn't seem to belong to AppleScript.
–1753	Script error.
–1754	Invalid selector given.
–1755	Invalid access.
–1756	Source not available.

Identifying Application Scripting Errors

An application scripting error is an error returned by an application when handling standard AppleScript commands, which are commands that apply to all applications (see Table 15–3). Many of these errors, such as "The specified object is a property, not an element," are of interest to users and should be handled.

Table 15–3. *Application Scripting Errors*

Number	Description
–10000	Apple event handler failed.
–10001	A descriptor type mismatch occurred.
–10002	Invalid key form.
–10003	Can't set <object or data> to <object or data>. Access not allowed.
–10004	A privilege violation occurred.
–10005	The read operation wasn't allowed.
–10006	Can't set <object or data> to <object or data>.
–10007	The index of the event is too large to be valid.
–10008	The specified object is a property, not an element.
–10009	Can't supply the requested descriptor type for the data.
–10010	The Apple event handler can't handle objects of this class.
–10011	Couldn't handle this command because it wasn't part of the current transaction.
–10012	The transaction to which this command belonged isn't a valid transaction.
–10013	There is no user selection.
–10014	Handler only handles single objects.
–10015	Can't undo the previous Apple event or user action.

Identifying AppleScript Language Errors

An AppleScript error is an error that occurs when AppleScript processes script statements (see Table 15–4). Nearly all of these are of interest to users. For errors returned by an application, see the documentation for that application.

Table 15–4. *AppleScript Errors*

Number	Description
–2700	Unknown error.
–2701	Can't divide <number> by zero.
–2702	The result of a numeric operation was too large.
–2703	<reference> can't be launched because it is not an application.
–2704	<reference> isn't scriptable.
–2705	The application has a corrupted dictionary.
–2706	Stack overflow.
–2707	Internal table overflow.
–2708	Attempt to create a value larger than the allowable size.
–2709	Can't get the event dictionary.
–2720	Can't both consider and ignore <attribute>.
–2721	Can't perform operation on text longer than 32K bytes.
–2740	A <language element> can't go after this <language element>.
–2741	Expected <language element> but found <language element>.
–2750	The <name> parameter is specified more than once.
–2751	The <name> property is specified more than once.
–2752	The <name> handler is specified more than once.
–2753	The variable <name> is not defined.
–2754	Can't declare <name> as both a local and global variable.
–2755	Exit statement was not in a repeat loop.
–2760	Tell statements are nested too deeply.
–2761	<name> is illegal as a formal parameter.
–2762	<name> is not a parameter name for the event <event>.
–2763	No result was returned for some argument of this expression.

Summary

In this chapter you learned about the two categories of errors that AppleScript can generate. Compilation errors occur when the grammar of your code is incorrect, for example, if you don't pair your parentheses correctly. Runtime errors occur while the script is running and may be caused by faulty design (bugs!) or outside factors beyond your script's control, such as unexpectedly missing files or folders.

You also learned how to cope with runtime errors by trapping them with a `try` statement. You found out how to use the `on error...` clause to obtain more information about the problem, such as the error message and number, and to execute additional statements that can report it to the user or even try to correct it so that the script can carry on as normal.

Finally, you learned how to use the `error` statement to generate errors of your own—handy if you want to provide a more detailed error message for an existing problem, or even to generate a completely new error from scratch.

Congratulations! You've now covered the first three key concepts of the AppleScript language: how to represent information as values; how to manipulate those values using commands and operators and store them in variables; and how to decide what to do and when using `if`, `repeat`, and `try` statements. At this point, you should know enough about AppleScript to write some very useful scripts of your own.

We still have one more key AppleScript concept to go: how to organize your code using handlers and script objects. However, as these are more advanced features that aren't essential for writing modest scripts, I have left them to the end of Part 2.

In the next chapter, we will move beyond the core AppleScript language by looking at how scripts can interact with the user with the help of Standard Additions' dialog box commands.

Chapter 16

Interacting with the User

You'll often need to get users involved during the execution of your scripts, and AppleScript has a number of basic user interaction commands available. These commands are all part of the Standard Additions scripting addition's User Interaction suite, and they allow your scripts to interact with the user in various ways; for example, you can display informational or warning messages to the user, prompt her to input some text, to select items from a list, or to choose files and folders for your script to process.

Creating Basic Dialog Boxes and Gathering Text Input

In this section, we'll look at three commands for displaying messages and gathering general user input: display dialog, display alert, and choose from list. Let's start with the best-known of these, display dialog.

Introducing the display dialog Command

The display dialog command is one of the most useful and flexible commands you will find in Standard Additions—and one of the first you tried at the start of this book. It's used to display messages and ask the user to click a button or enter text.

The Standard Additions dictionary contains two entries relating to the display dialog command: one describing the command itself and one describing the dialog reply record that the command returns as its result.

From the Dictionary: display dialog

The following is the Standard Additions dictionary definition for display dialog:

```
display dialog v : Display a dialog box, optionally requesting user input
  display dialog text : the text to display in the dialog box
      [default answer text] : the default editable text
      [hidden answer boolean] : Should editable text be displayed as bullets?
```

```
       (default is false)
[buttons list of text] : a list of up to three button names
[default button text or integer] : the name or number of the default button
[cancel button text or integer] : the name or number of the cancel button
[with title text] : the dialog window title
[with icon text or integer] : the resource name or ID of the icon to display…
[with icon stop/note/caution] : …or one of these system icons…
[with icon file] : …or an alias or file reference to a '.icns' file
[giving up after integer] : number of seconds to wait before automatically
       dismissing the dialog
--> dialog reply : a record containing the button clicked and text entered
       (if any)
```

From the Dictionary: dialog reply

The following is the specification for the dialog reply record:

```
dialog reply n : Reply record for the 'display dialog' command
   PROPERTIES
  button returned (text, r/o) : name of button chosen (empty if 'giving up after'
       was supplied and dialog timed out)
  text returned (text, r/o) : text entered (present only if 'default answer' was
       supplied)
  gave up (boolean, r/o) : Did the dialog time out? (present only if 'giving up
       after' was supplied)
```

Using the Basic Form of the Command

In its most basic form, display dialog presents a simple message in a dialog box along with two buttons, OK and Cancel. Figure 16–1 shows the dialog box that is displayed when the following command is run:

```
display dialog "Hello World!"
```

Figure 16–1. *The dialog box resulting from the basic display dialog command*

Clicking on the OK button returns the following result:

```
{button returned:"OK"}
```

As you can see, the result is a record with a single property. The property's label is button returned and its value is a string, "OK", which is the name of the button that was clicked. As we add more parameters to the `display dialog` command, this record will contain more properties.

Dealing with the Erroneous Cancel Button

Run the `display dialog "Hello World!"` command again and this time click the Cancel button. Now, instead of a result value, AppleScript Editor displays the following error information:

```
error "User canceled." number -128
```

What happened here is that the `display dialog` command generates a "User canceled" error when the Cancel button is clicked.

If you do not want the "User canceled" error to bring your script to a halt, you need to trap it using a `try` statement. Script 16–1 will trap any errors from the first `display dialog` command and present that information to the user via a second `display dialog` command.

Script 16–1.

```
try
    display dialog "Hello World!"
on error error_text number error_number
    display dialog "An error occurred." ¬
        & return & "Message: " & error_text ¬
        & return & "Number: " & error_number
end try
```

Figure 16–2 shows the error information displayed when the user cancels the first dialog box.

Figure 16–2. *The error dialog box displayed by Script 16–1*

See Chapter 15 for more information on dealing with errors in AppleScript.

> **NOTE:** Prior to Mac OS X 10.6, Script Editor did not give any indication when "User canceled" errors occur, so if you still have users running Mac OS X 10.5, use the approach shown in Script 16–1 to trap and view the error details.

Creating Custom Buttons

By default, AppleScript's display dialog command gives you the OK and Cancel buttons. However, you can easily define one, two, or three buttons of your own. To define buttons, you use the buttons parameter, which takes a list of button names as strings. Each string will become a button. A list with more than three items will generate an error, and an empty list will prompt AppleScript to use the default OK and Cancel buttons.

The following script displays a dialog box with three custom buttons, as shown in Figure 16–3:

```
display dialog "Do something?" buttons {"Yes", "No", "Maybe"}
```

Figure 16–3. *You can create your own dialog box buttons*

When you click a button in the dialog box, the display dialog command returns a record with a button returned property containing the button's name. For example, clicking the "No" button will give the following result:

```
{button returned:"No"}
```

> **CAUTION:** If you use longer names for your buttons, AppleScript will make the buttons wider to try to accommodate your text. However, if the titles of all buttons force the dialog box to be wider than 600 pixels, the button titles will get truncated from both ends.

Specifying a Default Button

What's missing from the dialog box in Figure 16–3 is a button that will execute when the user presses the Return key. This is called the default button and is automatically highlighted in blue whenever the dialog box is displayed. You can make an existing button into the default button by passing its name as the default button parameter.

For example, the next command produces the dialog box shown in Figure 16–4:

```
display dialog "Do something?" buttons {"Yes", "No", "Maybe"} ¬
    default button "Maybe"
```

Figure 16–4. *The default button is specified*

The default button parameter can also take an integer from 1 to 3, where 1 is the leftmost button in the dialog box and 3 is the rightmost. This means to get the same result as shown in Figure 16–4, you could specify the default button as 3 instead of "Maybe".

> **NOTE:** Deciding which button should be the default can be important. What you have to assume is that, for the most part, people don't read dialog boxes, which means you should make the default button the one with the least harsh consequences. For instance, the default button in a dialog box that reminds users for the last time that the script is about to erase their hard disk should be the Cancel button, not the OK button.

Specifying a Cancel Button

The cancel button parameter allows you to specify which button is executed when the user presses the Esc or Cmd key. This is useful when you want a button that isn't named Cancel to cancel the dialog box. For instance, the following command will display the dialog box shown in Figure 16–5:

```
display dialog "Do something?" buttons {"Yes", "No", "Maybe"} ¬
    default button "Maybe" cancel button "No"
```

Figure 16–5. *The default and cancel buttons are both specified*

Notice that instead of the evenly spaced buttons in the dialog box in Figure 16–4, these buttons have been automatically arranged to send a message. The default (Maybe) and cancel (No) buttons are on the right side of the dialog box. For that to happen, you have to specify both the default and cancel buttons, and you have to order them so that the default button is the rightmost button and the cancel button is the second from the right.

No matter which button you specify as the cancel button, clicking it will generate the benign "User canceled" error number –128.

Adding a Title

Adding a title to a dialog box is a great idea: often you want to use the actual dialog box text to ask a simple question, so a title explaining what the dialog box is about can be useful.

You add a title with the with title parameter. The following example displays the dialog box shown in Figure 16–6:

```
display dialog "Delete older files?" with title "Now performing backup..."
```

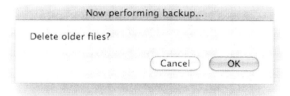

Figure 16–6. *The dialog title tells the user that the script is performing a backup routine*

Showing Icons in Dialog Boxes

Displaying an appropriate icon in a dialog box is a bit like a movie's score: it sets the mood.

Four icon choices are built in:

- stop
- note
- caution
- And, the default, having no icon at all

> **NOTE:** A dialog box that informs the user that the process has completed should probably have the note sign. If something goes seriously wrong in your script, preventing it from continuing, you can alert the user with the stop icon. To warn users that a potentially dangerous action is about to occur—for example, overwriting an existing file—use the caution icon.

You specify an icon by adding the with icon parameter to the display dialog command, followed by the icon you want to display.

For example:

```
try
    -- Your main code here...
on error error_text
    display dialog error_text buttons {"Quit"} with icon stop
end try
```

Notice that stop isn't a string; instead, it's a constant defined by Standard Additions.

You can also specify an icon by number. The number 0 gives you the stop icon, the number 1 displays the note icon, and number 2 shows the yellow caution icon.

Using an Icon File in a Dialog Box

You can go beyond the three built-in icons in a dialog box and display pretty much any icon you want, as long as it is stored in an .icns file.

 You can create your own .icns file with the Icon Composer utility that comes bundled with Apple's free Developer Tools (included on Mac OS X installer disks or available from http://developer.apple.com). Simply drag and drop or copy and paste any graphics into the squares, as shown in Figure 16–7, and save. I prefer to use Adobe Illustrator to compose my icons, then copy the art directly from Illustrator and paste it into Icon Composer.

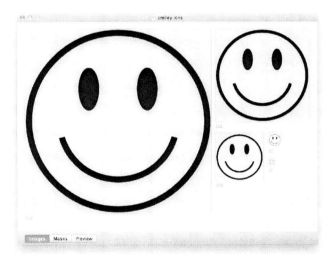

Figure 16–7. *The Icon Composer application window*

In addition, you can use icons from any existing OS X application, but to do that, you have to locate the icon files. They usually reside in the Contents/Resources folder in the application bundle and end with the .icns extension.

Script 16–2 uses the vCard icon from Apple's Address Book application. Figure 16–8 shows the dialog box created when the script is run.

Script 16–2.

```
tell application "Finder"
    set application_alias to application file id "com.apple.addressbook" as alias
end tell
set icon_file to path to resource "vCard.icns" in bundle application_alias
display dialog "Who Are You?" with icon icon_file
```

Figure 16–8. *Specify a path to an* `.icns` *file to use that icon in your dialog box.*

CAUTION: Take care when using your own icons in a `display dialog` command. If the icon file can't be found, an error will occur and the script will stop.

Getting Text Input from the User

Beginning programmers derive special satisfaction from getting information from users, and AppleScript makes that really easy to do. All you need to do is to add a `default answer` parameter to your `display dialog` command, like this:

```
display dialog "Enter your name:" default answer "John Doe"
```

This tells the command to add the input field to the dialog box. The string you supplied as the `default answer` parameter is the text that appears by default in the field when the dialog box is displayed. Figure 16–9 shows the dialog box that is displayed when the above command is run.

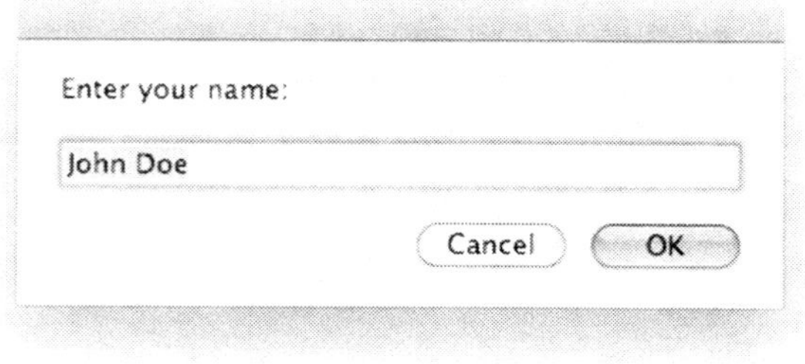

Figure 16–9. *The dialog box with a text entry field containing some default text*

Clicking on the OK button will return a record similar to this one:

```
{text returned:"John Doe", button returned:"OK"}
```

Until now, the result record had a single property labeled `button returned`. Now, it has another property: `text returned`. Only dialog box commands that include the `default answer` parameter will have the `text returned` property in the `dialog reply` record.

> **NOTE:** Later in the "Validating User-Entered Text" section, you will learn different ways to validate the text that users enter.

Creating Password Dialog Boxes

In some instances, you may want the user to enter secret text, such as a password, without having the text actually display. For that, use the Boolean `hidden answer` parameter. The following script asks the user to enter a password, but as you can see in Figure 16–10, the password the user types appears as bullets:

```
display dialog "Enter your database password:" default answer "" with hidden answer
```

Figure 16–10. *The dialog box with the hidden "bullet" text*

Dismissing Dialogs Automatically

A `display dialog` dialog box will normally remain on the screen until manually dismissed by the user. You can, however, control the length of time the dialog box lingers by using the `giving up after` parameter. Consider the following `display dialog` command:

```
display dialog "Click this within ten seconds!" giving up after 10
```

If you click the OK button within ten seconds, the dialog box returns this result:

```
{button returned:"OK", gave up:false}
```

Otherwise, the dialog box automatically closes itself, and the result is as follows:

```
{button returned:"", gave up:true}
```

As you can see, using the `giving up after` parameter is responsible for the `gave up` property in the `dialog reply` record.

The value of the gave up property is Boolean, and it is true if the dialog box gave up since no one clicked any button, or false if the user clicked a button.

Script 16–3 shows how you can use the giving up after parameter for speed quizzing.

Script 16–3.

```
set dialog_reply to display dialog "5472 ÷ 57 =" buttons {"56", "76", "96"} ¬
    giving up after 7
if (gave up of dialog_reply) then
  set the_response to "Not fast enough!"
else if (button returned of dialog_reply is "96") then
  set the_response to "You got it!"
else
  set the_response to "Wrong answer!"
end if
display dialog the_response
```

The preceding script places the dialog reply record in the variable dialog_reply. Next it checks the record's gave up property to see if it is true. If it is, a second dialog tells the user that she is too slow. If not, it checks the record's button returned property to see if the user clicked the right answer, or not, and displays the appropriate congratulatory or commiserative message.

Validating User-Entered Text

When asking users to enter data, you often need to ensure that the resulting value is suitable for your script. For example, if you are asking for a person's name, you might want to check that text was entered before proceeding. If you ask for the age or date of birth, your script could unexpectedly error if the user enters text that can't be converted into a number or date. If you ask for an e-mail address and the user types it incorrectly, it isn't going to be much use for sending e-mail messages.

As we saw earlier, the display dialog command returns the user-entered data in the text returned property of the dialog result record. This value is always a string, so if you're asking for a person's name and want to be sure that something is entered, you can easily check that the string is not empty:

```
set dialog_reply to display dialog "Enter name:" default answer ""
if text returned of dialog_reply is not "" then -- Something was entered
    -- More code here...
end if
```

Similarly, if your script requires an age or a date of birth, you can try coercing the string to an integer or a date, and catch any problems using a try block:

```
set dialog_reply to display dialog "Enter age:" default answer ""
try
    set the_age to (text returned of dialog_reply) as integer
on error number -1700 -- Can't coerce the text to an integer
    -- Handle the error here...
end try
```

Once you've checked whether the value is correct, you can improve the process even further by allowing the user to re-enter the value if it was incorrect the first time. The method I find most effective is to put the dialog box inside an endless repeat loop that won't exit until the user either enters a conforming string or cancels. As an example, suppose you want the user to enter a meeting date and that the date, besides being a valid date, has to be in the future. What you'll need is a variable that will hold the final date. You can start the script by creating the loop and displaying the dialog box:

```
repeat
    set dialog_reply to display dialog "Enter date:" default answer ""
    -- More script here...
end repeat
```

Next, you can try to convert the string the user typed into a date. If that's successful, you check whether the date is after today's date and, if it is, you release the user from eternal bondage and exit the repeat loop. If anything goes wrong, the user is asked to reenter the date, and the loop repeats again.

Script 16–4 shows all this in action.

Script 16–4.

```
1. repeat
2.     display dialog "Enter date:" default answer ""
3.     set user_date to text returned of result
4.     try
5.         set the_date to date user_date
6.         if the_date comes after (current date) then
7.             exit repeat
8.         end if
9.     end try
10.    display dialog "Re-enter date:" buttons {"OK"} ¬
              default button 1 with icon caution
11. end repeat
12. get the_date
```

The try statement that extends from line 4 to line 9 is responsible for capturing the error generated in the event the string the user typed can't be coerced into a date object. No on error portion is needed here: if an error occurs, AppleScript simply proceeds to the next line after the try block. Similarly, if line 6 finds that the entered date isn't later than the current date, the repeat loop simply makes another revolution. Only if both requirements are fulfilled is line 7 executed, exiting the repeat loop and allowing the rest of the script to run.

Introducing the display alert Command

The display alert command is a close cousin of display dialog, but display dialog is a general-purpose command that can be used in several different ways. display alert, in contrast, focuses on just one task: displaying a standard OS X alert box.

From the Dictionary: display alert

The following is the Standard Additions dictionary definition for display alert:

```
display alert v : Display an alert
```

```
display alert text : the alert text (will be displayed in emphasized system font)
      [message text] : the explanatory message (will be displayed in small
system font)
      [as critical/informational/warning] : the type of alert (default is
            informational)
      [buttons list of text] : a list of up to three button names
      [default button text or integer] : the name or number of the default button
      [cancel button text or integer] : the name or number of the cancel button
      [giving up after integer] : number of seconds to wait before automatically
            dismissing the alert
      --> alert reply : a record containing the button clicked
```

As you can see, the buttons, default button, cancel button, and giving after
parameters are identical to those of the display dialog command, so just refer to the
previous section if you need any help with them. The following sections describe
display alert's other parameters.

The display alert command, like display dialog, returns a record as its result. The
alert reply record contains a button returned property and an optional gave up
property identical to those found in display dialog's dialog reply record.

Using the Basic Form of the Command

Like display dialog, display alert requires a direct parameter containing the main text
to be displayed. Figure 16–11 shows the basic alert dialog displayed by the following
command:

```
display alert "Hello World!"
```

Figure 16–11. *The result of a basic* display alert *command*

As you can see, the display alert dialog box is different from display dialog's dialog
box: display alert uses a larger dialog box with smaller controls, only a single OK
button, and it includes the application's icon by default. Further differences will appear
as more parameters are added.

Using the message Parameter

You can use the message parameter to add an explanation or other descriptive text to
the alert box. Figure 16–12 shows the alert generated by the following script:

```
display alert "The script has encountered the wrong file type" message ¬
```

```
"A PDF file should be placed in the 'In' folder. Any other file type" ¬
& " will not process. Please fix the folder and run the script again."
```

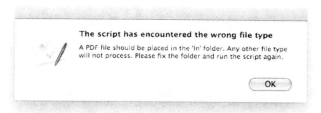

Figure 16–12. *The alert shows its main message in bold, followed by a more detailed explanation of the problem.*

Notice how the text of the alert is now bold and appears a little higher up; also, the text supplied for the message parameter is smaller.

Using the as Parameter

The display alert command's as parameter allows you to manipulate the mood of the alert by specifying one of three constants: informational, warning, or critical.

The difference shows in the icon of the dialog box. The informational constant shows the icon of the current application; warning shows the icon of the current application reduced in the corner of a warning yellow triangle (as shown in Figure 16–13), and critical currently behaves the same as informational.

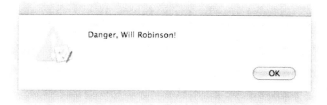

Figure 16–13. *The alert with the* as *parameter set to* warning

Setting the Button Behavior

Unlike in the display dialog command, if you don't specify a default button, the display alert command automatically designates the rightmost button as the default.

Introducing the choose from list Command

The choose from list command displays a list of strings or numbers in a dialog box, then allows users to select just the item or items they want.

From the Dictionary: choose from list

The following is the dictionary specification of the choose from list command:

```
choose from list v : Choose one or more items from a list
  choose from list list of text or number : a list of items to display
      [with title text] : the dialog window title
      [with prompt text] : the prompt to be displayed in the dialog box
      [default items list of text or number] : a list of items to initially select
          (an empty list if no selection)
      [OK button name text] : the name of the OK button
      [cancel button name text] : the name of the Cancel button
      [multiple selections allowed boolean] : Allow multiple items to be selected?
      [empty selection allowed boolean] : Can the user make no selection and then
          choose OK?
      --> list of number or text : the list of selected items
```

Getting the Results of the Command

The choose from list dialog box has two buttons: OK and Cancel. The OK button is always the default and appears to the right of the Cancel button.

Clicking the OK button returns a list containing the selected items. Clicking the Cancel button returns the value false. You can customize the titles of these buttons if you wish; however, you can't change their functions. This means that when using choose from list, you should always check whether it returned false before going any further, as shown in Script 16–5.

Script 16–5.

```
set the_selection to choose from list {1, 2, 3}
if the_selection is false then
    -- The Cancel button was clicked. Do something about it here...
else
    -- The OK button was clicked. Process the user's selection here...
end if
```

If you want choose from list to behave like display dialog and generate a "User canceled" error when the Cancel button is clicked, just add the following one-line conditional statement:

```
set the_selection to choose from list {1, 2, 3}
if the_selection is false then error number -128 -- User canceled
```

Using the Basic Command

In its simplest form, the choose from list command takes a single, direct parameter: the list you want the user to choose items from. Here is a simple example:

```
choose from list {"a", "b", "c"}
```

Figure 16–14 shows the dialog box produced by this command. As you can see, the dialog box conveniently resizes itself to fit the number of items in the list.

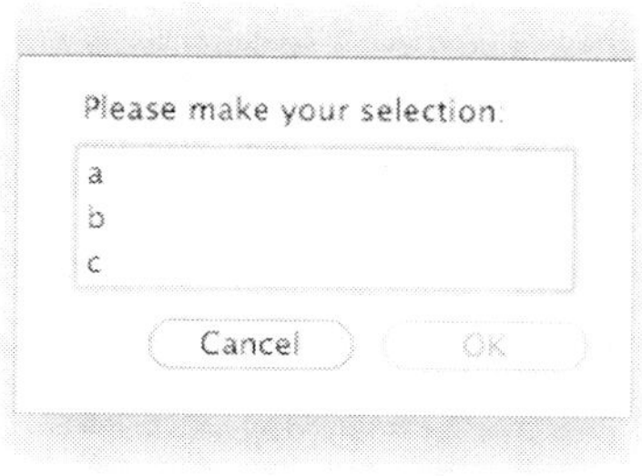

Figure 16–14. *The simplest* `choose from list` *dialog box*

Run this example yourself and you'll notice a couple of interesting things about how the `choose from list` command works.

First, the basic command allows only a single item to be selected, and won't allow the user to click OK until the selection is made. (We'll discuss how to change this behavior later.)

Second, when the user clicks OK, the result is *always* a list, even though only a single item is selected. If your script requires a number or string value, make sure you extract that value from the returned single-item list first.

I often find it convenient to define my own `choose_from_list` handler that first displays the list of items to choose from, then raises a "User canceled" error or returns the item that was selected, depending on which button was clicked. Script 16–6 shows a simple example of this handler, which you can easily customize to suit your own needs (for example, by adding an extra parameter so the user can supply her own prompt).

Script 16–6.

```
on choose_item_from_list(the_items)
    set the_selection to choose from list the_items
    if the_selection is false then
        error number -128 -- User canceled
    else
        return item 1 of the_selection
    end if
end choose_item_from_list
```

Creating a Custom Prompt

The first thing you will want to change about this dialog box is the text that tells the user how to use it. You do that with the `with prompt` parameter, like this:

```
choose from list {"a", "b", "c"} with prompt "Pick a letter"
```

Figure 16–15 shows the dialog box resulting from this script.

Figure 16–15. *A* choose from list *dialog box with a custom prompt message*

Adding a Title

You can also add a title to the choose from list dialog box. The following script displays the dialog box shown in Figure 16–16:

```
choose from list {"Petrol", "Diesel", "Veg Oil"} ¬
    with title "Energy Helper" with prompt "Choose your fuel"
```

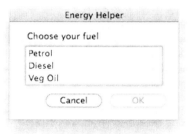

Figure 16–16. *A* choose from list *dialog box with an "Energy Helper" title*

Setting the Default Selection

If you want one or more items to be initially selected when the dialog box displays, you can specify this with the default items parameter.

In the following example, the user runs the script and chooses a city from a list of five cities. A property called favorite_city then remembers the chosen value so that the next time the script is run, the city that was chosen last time is selected by default.

Figure 16–17 shows the dialog box resulting from Script 16–7. The first time it runs, London is selected by default. If the user selects another city and clicks OK, the next time the script runs it will display that city instead (as long as the script isn't recompiled first).

Script 16–7.

```
property favorite_city : "London"

set all_cities to {"London", "Paris", "Moscow", "Sydney", "New York"}

set the_selection to choose from list all_cities with prompt ¬
    "Please pick your favorite city:" default items {favorite_city}
if the_selection is false then error number -128 -- User canceled
set favorite_city to item 1 of the_selection
```

Figure 16–17. *The dialog box resulting from the* choose from list *command with the* default items *parameter*

Restricting the Selection

The choose from list command allows you to restrict the selection the user can make. You can choose to allow or disallow the selection of multiple items and to allow or disallow the user to select nothing.

By default, choose from list allows the user to select one item and one item only. To allow the user to select multiple items, set the multiple selections allowed parameter to true, as shown below:

```
set state_list to {"NY", "RI", "GA", "CA", "WA"}
set chosen_states to choose from list state_list with multiple selections allowed
--> {"RI", "GA", "WA"}
```

In the preceding script, the user selected three items: RI, GA, and WA.

In a similar fashion, you can allow the user to click OK while making no selection at all. Now, the user can always click Cancel, but by default, if the user hasn't picked any item from the list, the OK button will be disabled. You can allow the user to pick no items and still click OK with the empty selection allowed parameter:

```
set chosen_states to choose from list state_list with empty selection allowed
```

If the user clicks OK with nothing selected, the result is an empty list, {}.

Customizing Buttons

The choose from list command has two buttons: OK and Cancel. As discussed earlier, the functions and positions of these buttons are set. The right button will always return a list containing the selected items, and the left button will always return the value false.

You can, however, change the title of these buttons. To do that, you can use the OK button name and Cancel button name parameters. Each of these parameters is a string containing the new title for the button.

The following script displays the choose from list dialog box shown in Figure 16–18.

```
set state_list to {"NY", "RI", "GA", "CA", "WA"}
set chosen_states to choose from list state_list ¬
    OK button name "Make a Pick" cancel button name "Na..."
```

Figure 16–18. *The* choose from list *dialog box with custom button names*

Now that we've discussed how to display messages and obtain basic user input, let's move on to the Standard Additions commands for displaying fil system dialogs.

Choosing Files, Folders, and Disks

Standard Additions provides several commands that allow the user to select files, folders, and disks: choose file, choose file name, and choose folder.

Introducing the choose file Command

The choose file command allows the user to specify an existing file (or files) using the Open dialog box.

From the Dictionary: choose file

The following text is the dictionary definition of the choose file command:

```
choose file v : Choose a file on a disk or server
    choose file
        [with prompt text] : the prompt to be displayed in the dialog box
        [of type list of text] : a list of file types or type identifiers. Only files
            of the specified types will be selectable.
        [default location alias] : the default file location
        [invisibles boolean] : Show invisible files and folders? (default is true)
        [multiple selections allowed boolean] : Allow multiple items to be selected?
            (default is false)
        [showing package contents boolean] : Show the contents of packages? (Packages
            will be treated as folders. Default is false.)
        --> alias : the chosen file
```

Getting the Results of the Command

By default, the choose file command will return a single alias value when the OK button is clicked, or raise a "User canceled" error if the user clicks the Cancel button. However, if the multiple selections allowed parameter is true, clicking OK will always return a list of aliases instead, even if the user chose only one file.

Figuring Out When to Use the Command

You use choose file when you need the user to specify an existing file that the script has to deal with. The choose file command is the AppleScript version of the Open dialog box—not that the command opens anything, but it presents the user with the Open dialog box and allows him to specify a file. From that point on, what happens to the file is up to you and your script.

Suppose you create a script that opens an Adobe InDesign file, exports all the images, and then catalogs them. Sure, if you have a strict filing convention and folder hierarchy, the script may be able to find the files that need processing. However, if the file can be any InDesign file from anywhere on the hard disk or network, you will want to use the choose file command to allow users to specify the file themselves.

One of the most important features of the choose file command is its ability to restrict the user to choosing files of specific types. For example, when you select File ➤ Open in an application, you are restricted to choosing files that the application supports; the same is true for the restrictions you can put on your script's users by specifying which file types they can choose with the choose file command.

Using the Basic Command

The basic `choose file` command requires no parameters. The following command will produce a dialog box similar to the one shown in Figure 16–19:

```
choose file
```

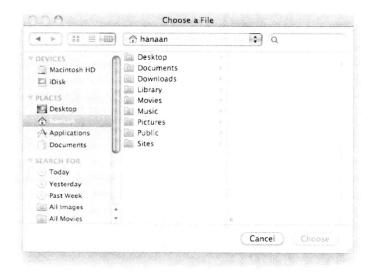

Figure 16–19. *The basic dialog box produced by the* `choose file` *command*

Creating a Custom Prompt

The first parameter you can change is the prompt. The prompt is the text that appears at the top of the dialog box.

The default `choose file` dialog box shown in Figure 16–19 has no prompt. The script that follows adds a custom prompt to the dialog box, as shown in Figure 16–20:

```
choose file with prompt "Pick a file to use as template:"
```

Figure 16–20. *The* `choose file` *dialog box with a custom prompt*

Restricting to Specific File Types

One of the parameters that makes the `choose file` command so useful and powerful is the `of type` parameter. This parameter takes a list of strings, each describing a different type of file. When the dialog box is displayed, the user can choose only those files whose file types appear in the list.

The following example limits the user to choosing a text file:

```
choose file of type {"public.text"}
```

Each string may be a modern uniform type identifier (UTI) or an old-fashioned file type code. For instance, the following script allows the user to choose only Microsoft Word documents (.doc and .docx files):

```
choose file ¬
    of type {"com.microsoft.word.doc", "com.microsoft.word.openxml.document"}
```

while the next script prompts the user to pick an image whose four-character file type code indicates it is a JPEG, TIFF, GIF, or PSD (Photoshop) file:

```
choose file with prompt "Choose an image:" ¬
    of type {"JPEG", "TIFF", "GIFF", "8BPS"}
```

The problem with using Mac OS 9-style file type codes is that Mac OS X prefers to use file name extensions (.txt, .jpg, .mp3, etc.) to identify file types. As a result, many files nowadays do not have file type codes, so if you use file type codes in the `choose file` command's `of type` parameter, users won't be allowed to select these files even though they should be able to do so.)UTIs, on the other hand, are much more flexible: as long as a file has a name extension or a file type code, either will do.

For example, let's say you want to limit the user to choosing only JPEG files. If you use a file type for the `of type` parameter, like so:

```
choose file of type {"JPEG"}
```

only files with the file type code JPEG will be selectable in the resulting `choose file` dialog box. Unfortunately for the user, any JPEG files that don't have a file type—perhaps because they've been downloaded from the Internet or created by a program that doesn't use file type codes—won't be selectable. However, if you use a)UTI, like so:

```
choose file of type {"public.jpeg"}
```

any file that has a JPEG file type *or* a .jpg or .jpeg filename extension will be selectable.

Another advantage of)UTIs is that they allow you to be more general or more specific about the types of files you want to be selectable. For example, if you want to let the user choose *any* kind of image file, just use the following:

```
choose file of type {"public.image"}
```

Mac OS X defines some common)UTIs, and individual applications can add their own. You can find more information about UTIs at this location:

```
http://developer.apple.com/mac/library/documentation/FileManagement/Conceptual/
```

```
understanding_utis/
```

and you can find a list of standard Apple-defined)UTIs here:

```
http://developer.apple.com/mac/library/documentation/Miscellaneous/Reference/UTIRef
```

If you're not sure what the)UTI for a particular kind of file is, don't worry: it's easy to find out using the following script:

```
set the_file to choose file
tell application "System Events" to get type identifier of the_file
```

This script prompts the user to select a file, then returns its UTI. If the chosen file doesn't have an official)UTI, Mac OS X will make one up for it. You can easily spot these made-up UTIs as they always begin with dyn. (short for dynamic).

Setting the Default Location

The optional default location parameter allows you to set a starting point for the choose file dialog box. When the dialog box appears, you may want to direct the user to a specific folder. The following script sets the default location to the Client Jobs folder in my own home folder:

```
set jobs_folder to alias "Macintosh HD:Users:hanaan:Client Jobs:"
choose file with prompt "Pick a job to process:" default location jobs_folder
```

while the next example lets users start the search at the Documents folder of their own home folder:

```
choose file default location (path to documents folder)
```

> **TIP:** The path to command is a very useful Standard Additions command that makes it easy to obtain aliases to important folders in the file system, making it particularly handy here. See Chapter 20 for more details on this command.

If the folder you specify as the default location doesn't exist, the starting location will revert to the default, but no error will be generated.

Picking Invisibles

By default, the choose file command allows users to choose both visible and invisible files. To restrict the user to visible files only, which you should always do unless your script is meant to work with hidden files, set the invisibles parameter to false.

The following script will show the choose file dialog box but will not allow users to pick invisible files:

```
choose file without invisibles
```

Allowing Multiple Selections

You can allow the user to pick multiple files at one time. To do that, set the `multiple selections allowed` parameter to `true`. Users can then Shift- or Cmd-click in the dialog box's file list to select all the files they want.

Setting the `multiple selections allowed` parameter to `true` will change the command's result from a single alias to a list of aliases. If the user ends up choosing one file only, the result will be a single-item list.

The following script allows the user to choose multiple files:

```
choose file with multiple selections allowed
```

Here's a typical result where two files were chosen:

```
--> {alias "Macintosh HD:Users:hanaan:Pictures:image 1.gif",
     alias "Macintosh HD:Users:hanaan:Pictures:image 2.gif"}
```

Showing Package Contents

As other chapters have mentioned, Mac OS X application files and some other kinds of files are really special folders called "bundles." Bundles contain hidden files and folders but normally appear as single files in the Finder and file dialog boxes.

If you set the `showing package contents` parameter to `true`, the `choose file` dialog box will treat these bundles like ordinary folders, allowing you to select files from inside them. For example, the following script uses the `choose file` dialog box in Figure 16–21:

```
choose file default location (path to applications folder) ¬
    with showing package contents
--> alias "Macintosh HD:Applications:Chess.app:Contents:Resources:1.rgb"
```

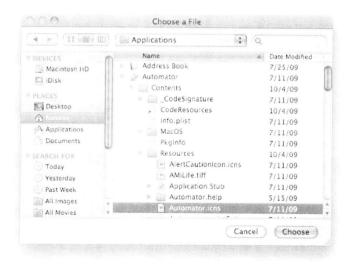

Figure 16–21. The *choose file dialog box with access to bundle contents*

Introducing the choose file name Command

The choose file name command allows you to add a Save As–like dialog box to your scripts. The result is a POSIX file value identifying the location of a file that may or may not already exist.

From the Dictionary: choose file name

The following is the dictionary specification of the choose file name command:

```
choose file name v : Get a new file reference from the user, without creating
the file
  choose file name
      [with prompt text] : the prompt to be displayed in the dialog box
      [default name text] : the default name for the new file
      [default location alias] : the default file location
      --> file : the file the user specified
```

choose file name vs. choose file

The difference between the choose file and choose file name commands is the same as the difference between the Open and Save dialog boxes. When you open, you can choose a file. When you save, you specify a file name and location, but the file may not yet exist. If the file you specified is already there, the usual "Are you sure you want to replace this item?" dialog box will appear.

Figuring Out When to Use the Command

You use the choose file name command whenever you want the user to specify a file that the script has to create in some way—for instance, if the script creates a text log and you want to let the user decide where that log file should be saved and what its file name should be.

Getting the Results of the Command

If the user clicks the OK button, the choose file name command returns a POSIX file value for the chosen file system location. If the user clicks Cancel, then a "User canceled" error will be raised.

> **NOTE:** The reason the choose file name command returns a POSIX file value, and not an alias value like the choose file command provides, is that alias values can identify only those files that actually exist, and the file you specify here may not yet exist. Chapter 17 discusses the differences between alias and file values in more detail.

Using the Basic Command

The basic choose file name command used in the following script will display a dialog box similar to the one shown in Figure 16–22:

```
choose file name
```

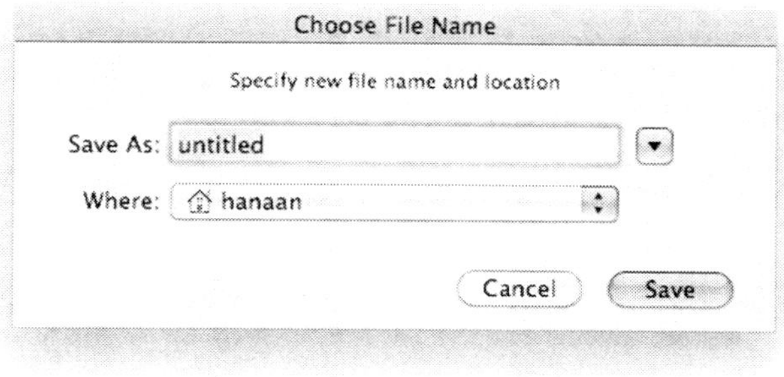

Figure 16–22. *The basic dialog box displayed by the* choose file name *command*

Creating a Custom Prompt

As with other file-related dialog box commands, you can add a custom title to your dialog box. As you can see in Figure 16–22, the default prompt says, "Specify new file name and location." Using the with prompt parameter, as in the following script line, will replace that prompt with a custom message:

```
choose file name with prompt "Save the log file:"
```

Setting a Default Name and Location

The choose file name command allows you to provide a default name for your file via the default name parameter. It can also take an optional default location parameter that allows you to set the initial folder shown in the dialog box.

The next script lets the user choose a file name while directing her to the log files folder and providing a default file name of log.txt. Figure 16–23 shows the resulting choose file name dialog box.

```
set default_log_folder to (path to documents folder as text) & "log files"
choose file name with prompt "Save the log file:" ¬
    default location alias default_log_folder default name "Log.txt"
```

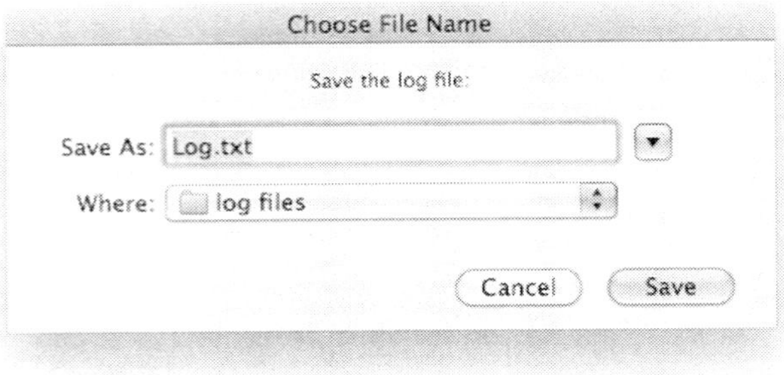

Figure 16–23. *A* `choose file name` *dialog box with a default path and filename*

If the user accepted the defaults and clicked OK, the result would look something like this:

```
file "Macintosh HD:Users:hanaan:Documents:log files:Log.txt"
```

Replacing an Existing File

An interesting feature of the `choose file name` command is that you can choose a file that already exists—if this happens, the dialog will ask if you're sure you want to replace it. However, remember that the command's only purpose is to give you a POSIX file value. It doesn't create or replace any files itself—or even tell you if a file already exists. So merely clicking Replace won't affect an existing file—it's up to your script to move, delete, or simply overwrite that file as appropriate.

Seeing an Example in Action

As a simple example of using the `choose file name` command, I will show how to create a new InDesign document and save it using a name and location the user chooses with the `choose file name` command.

Script 16–8 shows the script, which is followed by the explanation.

Script 16–8.

```
1. set new_file to choose file name ¬
        default location (path to documents folder) ¬
        default name "job name.indd"

2. tell application "Adobe InDesign CS4"
3.    set new_doc to make new document
4.    save new_doc to new_file
5. end tell
```

In line 1, the choose file name command asks the user to specify where she'd like the InDesign file to be saved. The `path to` command is used to obtain an alias value for the user's Documents folder, and the `default name` parameter provides a reasonable default name for the file. The resulting POSIX file value is then stored in the new_file variable to be used later in the script.

Line 3 uses InDesign's make command to create a new document and stores the returned reference to this document in the new_doc variable. Line 4 uses InDesign's save command to store this document, using the POSIX file value created in line 1 as its to parameter.

Introducing the choose folder Command

The choose folder commandlets you ask the user to choose a folder using a standard Choose Folder dialog box.

From the Dictionary: choose folder

The following is the dictionary definition of the choose folder command:

```
choose folder v : Choose a folder on a disk or server
  choose folder
      [with prompt text] : the prompt to be displayed in the dialog box
      [default location alias] : the default folder location
      [invisibles boolean] : Show invisible files and folders? (default is false)
      [multiple selections allowed boolean] : Allow multiple items to be selected?
          (default is false)
      [showing package contents boolean] : Show the contents of packages? (Packages
          will be treated as folders. Default is false.)
  --> alias : the chosen folder
```

Using the Command

The choose folder commandpresents users with the Choose Folder dialog box and allows them to choose a folder. If the user clicks OK, the result is an alias value identifying that folder. If the user clicks Cancel, a User canceled error is raised.

The following script shows the basic form of the command, without any parameters:

```
choose folder
```

Figure 16–24 shows the dialog box that the command generates.

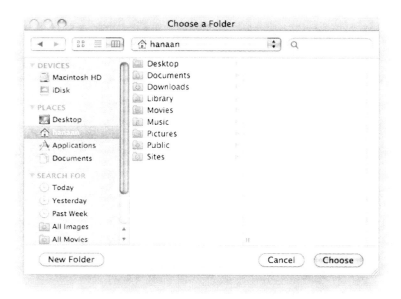

Figure 16-24. *The dialog box shown by the* `choose folder` *command*

Figuring Out When to Use the Command

You should use the `choose folder` command when you need to obtain an alias, path string, Finder reference, etc. to a folder and you want the user to choose the folder for you. For example, you might write a script to batch convert TIFF images to JPEG format. This script would use the `choose folder` command twice, first to ask the user to choose the source folder containing the original TIFF images and then to choose the destination folder for the newly created JPEG files.

Setting the Parameters

The `choose folder` command is pretty similar to the `choose file` command and the following parameters are the same: `with prompt`, `invisibles`, `default location`, `multiple selections allowed`, and `showing package contents`. (The choose file command has one more parameter, `of type`, that is only relevant to files.) Refer back to the section on the `choose file` command if you need help with these parameters.

Choosing a Folder Once

Although allowing users to specify a folder in a Choose Folder dialog box is often more convenient than having them edit the script directly, this can become tiresome if the folder being chosen is the same every time, such as a permanent drop box or log file folder. It'd be much less annoying if the script needed to ask the user to choose a folder only the first time it's run and then remembered that folder for future use. Script 16–9 shows how this might be achieved.

Script 16–9.

```
1. property folder_path : missing value

2. tell application "Finder"
3.    if folder_path is missing value or not (container folder_path exists) then
4.        tell me to set folder_path to (choose folder) as text
5.    end if
6. end tell

7. get folder_path
--> "Macintosh HD:Users:hanaan:Pictures:"
```

The folder_path property in line 1 is used to remember the user's chosen folder from one run to the next. The property starts out having the value missing value assigned to it; later it will hold a path string identifying the chosen folder.

Line 3 checks whether the folder_path property contains a path to an existing folder. If it doesn't, before the script goes any further, line 4 asks the user to choose a different folder and stores it in the folder_path property.

The rest of the script can then retrieve the path from the folder_path property whenever it needs it. The next time the script is run, if the path is still valid, the script will run straight away without asking the user to choose a new folder.

This completes our coverage of the most important GUI commands in Standard Additions. To finish off the chapter, we'll discuss several specialized user interaction commands you may sometimes find useful.

Choosing Other Types of Items

In the following sections, you will read about the user interaction commands that allow users to choose local and remote applications, URLs, and colors.

Introducing the choose application Command

The choose application command lets the user pick an application on the machine running the script. The choose application command can return either an alias value pointing to the application or an application object, as you will see a bit later.

From the Dictionary: choose application

The following is the dictionary definition of the choose application command:

```
choose application v : Choose an application on this machine or the network
    choose application
        [with title text] : the dialog window title
        [with prompt text] : the prompt to be displayed in the dialog box
```

```
[multiple selections allowed boolean] : Allow multiple items to be selected?
    (default is false)
[as type class] : the desired type of result. May be application (the default)
    or alias.
--> application : the chosen application
```

Using the Command

The choose application command, if used by itself with no parameters, displays the dialog box shown in Figure 16–25.

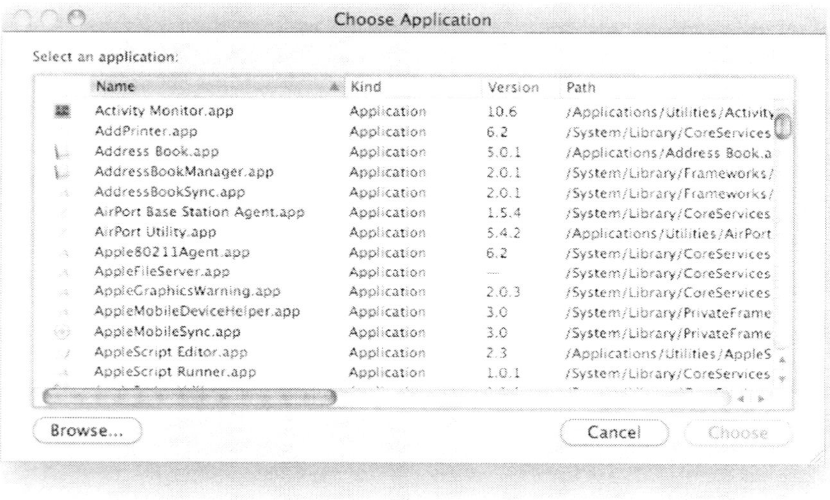

Figure 16–25. *The basic* choose application *dialog box*

The default result is an application object, such as this:

```
application "Finder"
```

Using the as parameter, you can ask for an alias value identifying the application file, as shown here:

```
choose application as alias
--> alias "Macintosh HD:Applications:FileMaker Pro 10:FileMaker Pro.app:"
```

You can also use the with title and with prompt parameters to add a title and a prompt to the dialog box.

Introducing the choose remote application Command

The choose remote application command allows you to choose an application on another Mac on the network.

From the Dictionary: choose remote application

The following is the dictionary definition of the choose remote application command:

```
choose remote application v : Choose a running application on a remote machine or on
     this machine
  choose remote application
     [with title text] : the dialog window title
     [with prompt text] : the prompt to be displayed above the list of applications
     --> application : the chosen application
```

Using the Command

The result of the command is an application object for the remote application, for example:

```
choose remote application
--> application "InDesign" of machine "eppc://franc01.local/?uid=502&pid=1565"
```

Figure 16–26 shows the dialog box resulting from the choose remote application command. The Sending Commands to Remote Applications section in Chapter 12 discusses this command in more detail.

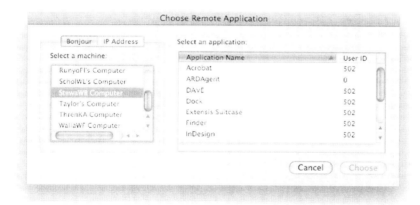

Figure 16–26. *The dialog box resulting from the* choose remote application *command*

Introducing the choose URL Command

The choose URL command allows the user to specify a URL to a server via FTP servers, file servers, remote applications, and so on. The result of the command is a URL string that can be used as a parameter in other commands, such as mount volume (described in Chapter 20).

From the Dictionary: choose URL

The following is the dictionary definition of the choose URL command:

```
choose URL v : Choose a service on the Internet
   choose URL
      [showing list of Web servers/FTP Servers/Telnet hosts/
          File servers/News servers/Directory services/
          Media servers/Remote applications] : which network services to show
      [editable URL boolean] : Allow user to type in a URL?
      --> URL : the chosen URL
```

Using the Command

The `choose URL` command has two parameters. The `showing` parameter allows you to specify a list of protocols that will appear in the protocol pop-up menu at the bottom. By default the list shows eight protocol service types shown above in the dictionary definition. The following script restricts the command to allow only three of these protocols. It also uses the Boolean parameter `editable URL` with a `false` value to prevent the user from typing in his own URL rather than choosing one from the list.

```
choose URL showing {Web servers, FTP Servers, Telnet hosts} ¬
    without editable URL
```

Figure 16–27 shows the dialog box resulting from the preceding script.

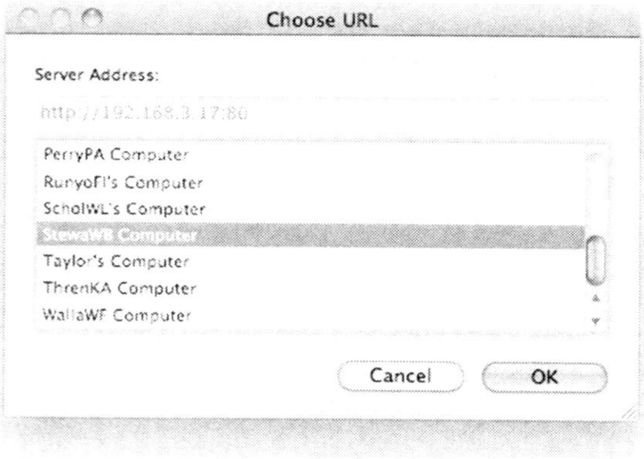

Figure 16–27. *The resulting dialog box from the* choose URL *command*

The following script will ask the user to specify a file server URL, either by choosing it from the displayed list or typing it in by hand, and then mount the specified volume:

```
set server_address to choose URL showing {File servers} with editable URL
mount volume server_address
```

Introducing the choose color Command

The `choose color` commandallows the user to specify a color using the standard color picker dialog box.

From the Dictionary: choose color

```
choose color v : Choose a color
  choose color
      [default color RGB color] : the default color
      --> RGB color : the chosen color
```

Getting the Results of the Command

The result is a list of three integer values, representing the red, green, and blue values of an RGB color. Each number is from 65,535, which corresponds with the bright, full presence of the color, to 0, which means the color is dimmed all the way. For example, this result was returned after specifying a reddish color: {60790, 5233, 6667}. Notice that the first value, indicating the red value, is almost at the full brightness of 65,535, and the green and blue are relatively close to 0. The value of pure red is {65535, 0, 0}.

> **NOTE:** While the color picker dialog allows the user to pick a color using grayscale, RGB, CMYK, HSB sliders, color swatches, and so on, the result will always be an RGB color value.

Figuring Out When to Use the Command

Use this command whenever the user has to specify a color. This feature wasn't intended for precise color use in production or design environments, but rather for picking colors in a more general way: pinkish, light blue, and so on.

Using the Basic Command and Using It with Parameters

The choose color command has one parameter: default color. It allows you to specify the color that is displayed by default when the dialog box appears.

The following script will display the Colors dialog box without a predefined default color:

```
choose color
```

The following script will display the Colors dialog box shown in Figure 16–28:

```
choose color default color {65535, 0, 0} -- default color is red
```

Figure 16-28. *The dialog box resulting from* `choose color`

Summary

In this chapter we looked at the basic GUI commands provided by the User Interaction suite of the Standard Additions scripting addition. These include the `display dialog` and `display alert`, and `choose from list` commands for displaying simple messages and obtaining user input, and a range of `choose...` commands for displaying standard Open and Save file dialogs.

If your solution calls for a more complex interface than the commands covered in this chapter can provide, you'll have to look to other tools. These include third-party scripting additions such as 24U Software's 24U Appearance OSAX (www.24usoftware.com), which allows you to create more complex dialog boxes, and full-blown application development tools such as Satimage's Smile (www.satimage-software.com) and Apple's own AppleScript-Cocoa bridge, AppleScriptObjC. We'll explore some of these advanced options later on in the book.

In the next chapter, we will return to the language itself as we catch up on the different classes of objects that AppleScript uses to identify items in the file system.

Chapter 17

Working with Files

In this chapter, you will learn about the various features AppleScript uses to identify files, folders, and disks, and how to read and write files using Standard Additions.

Identifying Files, Folders, and Disks

When you work with files, you need a way to refer to them. No matter whether your goal is creating a text file, backing up some folders, or deleting the entire contents of a hard disk, the ways you refer to a file are the same.

AppleScript can identify a file, folder, or disk in four general ways, and your job is to choose the method that works best in your situation, with the application you're using:

- An HFS or POSIX path string

- An AppleScript object of class alias, file, or POSIX file (though there is a catch to using file, which we'll get to later)

- A file URL (uniform resource locator) string

- A reference to an application-defined object in Finder or System Events.

Here is a typical example of each approach:

```
--An HFS path string:
"Macintosh HD:Applications:Address Book.app"

--An AppleScript alias object:
alias "Macintosh HD:Applications:Address Book.app"

-- A file URL string:
"file://localhost/Applications/Address%20Book.app"

--A Finder application reference:
application file "Address Book.app" of folder "Applications" of startup disk ¬
      of application "Finder"
```

All four objects identify the same Address Book application file, though in different ways.

The next several sections will concentrate on first three approaches—path strings, file system objects, and file URLs—while Chapter 20 will explain Finder and System Events references in detail.

Using Path Strings

Path strings provide a basic way to describe the location of files, folders, and disks. Since path strings are just ordinary AppleScript strings, they're useful when you want to assemble, modify, or pull apart paths using AppleScript's string-handling facilities: text item delimiters, the concatenation operator, and so on. They are also helpful for creating alias, file, and POSIX file values for use in application and scripting addition commands, and for creating application references in the Finder and the System Events application.

AppleScript understands two types of path strings: HFS paths and POSIX paths. HFS-style paths date back to the original Mac OS and are still used in some parts of Mac OS X, including the AppleScript language. POSIX-style paths are the standard path-name format used on Unix operating systems and are also commonly used on Mac OS X, which is Unix-based.

Here are some examples of HFS path strings:

```
"Macintosh HD:Applications:TextEdit.app"
"Macintosh HD:Users:hanaan:Documents:Manuscript.doc"
"Backup Disk:Work Files:"
```

and here are the equivalent POSIX path strings if we assume that Macintosh HD is the startup volume:

```
"/Applications/TextEdit.app"
"/Users/hanaan/Documents/Manuscript.doc"
"/Volumes/Backup Disk/Work Files/"
```

Let's start with an example of an HFS path: Understanding HFS Paths

```
Macintosh HD:Users:hanaan:reference.pdf
```

This path identifies a file called reference.pdf in a folder called hanaan, which lives in the folder Users on a disk named Macintosh HD. The path starts with the name of the volume the file is on, is followed by the name of each folder in the folder hierarchy that leads to the file, and ends with the name of the file. Each name in the path is separated by a colon character (:), which is reserved for this purpose.

An HFS path that identifies a disk or folder usually has a colon at the end, although this is not essential:

```
Macintosh HD:
Macintosh HD:Users:
Macintosh HD:Users:hanaan:
```

Putting a colon delimiter at the end of disk and file paths is clearer, however, and will matter if you later decide to extend this path string by concatenating it with additional folder and filenames:

```
set the_folder to "Macintosh HD:Users:hanaan:"
the_folder & "reference.pdf"
--> "Macintosh HD:Users:hanaan:reference.pdf" -- Correct

set the_folder to "Macintosh HD:Users:hanaan"
the_folder & "reference.pdf"
--> "Macintosh HD:Users:hanaanreference.pdf" -- Oops!
```

Understanding POSIX Paths

Because of their Unix nature, POSIX paths work a bit differently than HFS paths and require a little more explanation. Here's an example of a POSIX path that identifies the same `reference.pdf` file as the HFS path shown earlier (assuming that `Macintosh HD` is the start-up volume):

```
/Users/hanaan/reference.pdf
```

You'll notice immediately that a POSIX path uses a slash (/), not a colon, to separate each name in the path. In addition, POSIX paths view the file system hierarchy in a slightly different way. HFS paths begin with a disk name, but a POSIX path treats the entire file system as one big tree-shaped structure. The top of this tree structure is called its *root,* which is indicated by the leading slash character, `/`. This represents the disk or volume that Mac OS X started up from. All other volumes then appear further down in this hierarchy, at `/Volumes`.

> **TIP:** The start-up disk also reappears in `/Volumes`, so if you need to refer to a disk by name but aren't sure if it's the start-up disk, just refer to it there. For example, if the start-up disk is named `Macintosh HD`, the path `/Volumes/Macintosh HD/Users/hanaan/reference.pdf` is equivalent to `/Users/hanaan/reference.pdf`.

As with the trailing colon in HFS paths, POSIX paths that identify a folder or disk can be shown with a trailing slash for clarity, although again this is not required:

```
/Users/
/Users/hanaan/
```

You'll look at ways to convert HFS paths to POSIX paths and back again later in the "Converting to and from POSIX Files" section.

> **CAUTION:** In Mac OS X, most files have a file name extension indicating their type: `.mp3`, `.pdf`,
> `.docx`, etc. However, these extensions won't be visible in the Finder unless the Show all
> filename extensions option is enabled in Finder's Advanced preferences. When writing HFS and
> POSIX path strings in AppleScript, make sure you always include any file name extensions,
> otherwise the correct file will not be found. You can double-check a file's name and extension by
> selecting it in the Finder, choosing File ➤ Get Info, and expanding the Name & Extension section
> in the resulting Info panel.

Using File System Objects

AppleScript provides three classes for specifying files, folders, and disks in the OS X file
system: `alias`, `file`, and `POSIX file`. These classes are commonly used by scriptable
applications, particularly in open and `save` commands and in file system-related scripting
addition commands such as `choose file`, `read`, and `write`. AppleScript can easily create
file specifiers from path strings, and vice versa, while the Finder can convert them to and
from Finder-specific references.

Here are some examples of literal file specifiers. Each one identifies the TextEdit
application in the start-up disk's `Applications` folder:

```
alias "Macintosh HD:Applications:TextEdit.app"
file "Macintosh HD:Applications:TextEdit.app"
POSIX file "/Applications/TextEdit.app"
```

As you can see, each file specifier consists of two parts: a keyword—`alias`, `file`, or
`POSIX file`—followed by a path string. The first two take HFS path strings, and the third
takes a POSIX path string.

Let's now look at each class in detail, starting with `alias`.

Understanding Alias Objects

Objects of AppleScript's `alias` class (not to be confused with the Finder's `alias file`
class, by the way) are written as the word `alias` followed by an HFS path string. For
example:

```
alias "Macintosh HD:Users:hanaan:Downloads:About Downloads.pdf"
```

Alias objects refer to files, folders, and disks that already exist. Their most interesting
feature is that, once created, they can keep track of a file or folder even if it is renamed
or moved to another location on the same disk.

Most scriptable applications take an alias (or a list of aliases) as the direct parameter to
their open commands:

```
set the_alias to alias "Macintosh HD:Users:hanaan:Downloads:About Downloads.pdf"
```

```
tell application "Preview" to open the_alias
```

Alias objects are also used by various scripting addition commands; for example, the Standard Additions' choose file command returns an alias identifying a file selected by the user, and its read command can accept an alias (among other things) as its direct parameter.

How Aliases Work

Let's take a closer look at how AppleScript interprets the alias literal that was shown in the previous example:

```
alias "Macintosh HD:Users:hanaan:Downloads:About Downloads.pdf"
```

Whenever AppleScript evaluates this alias specifier, it immediately checks to see whether the item that the path string is pointing to actually exists in the file system. If the item is found, AppleScript creates an alias object and continues on its way, otherwise it raises error number –43, "File not found."

> **NOTE:** In Mac OS X 10.4 and earlier, AppleScript would check all of a script's alias literals when the script was compiled. This would result in a compilation error if any of the alias literals pointed to a file, folder, or disk that didn't exist at the time. Mac OS X 10.5 changed this behavior so that alias literals will always compile correctly and are only checked if a running script uses them.

If you run the preceding example in AppleScript Editor, it will either return an alias object or raise a "file not found" error, depending on whether your Mac has a file named About Downloads.pdf in a folder called Downloads in a folder called hanaan in a folder called Users on a hard disk named Macintosh HD.

Figure 17–1 shows the result of running this script when the path string identifies an existing item in the file system. Figure 17–2 shows what happens if the same item was not found.

Figure 17–1. *AppleScript returns an alias object identifying the file system item.*

Figure 17-2. *AppleScript raises an error when the specified item isn't found.*

Now why would AppleScript go to the trouble of checking the file's existence right away? The answer is that as soon as AppleScript creates an alias object, it finds the specified file or folder and creates an internal reference to it. This internal reference works in a similar way to alias files in the Finder: the file is remembered even if its name or location has changed. Yes! For as long as the alias object exists in the script, AppleScript will keep track of that file. The only way it will lose track of a file is if the file itself is deleted.

All alias objects work this way, whether they're created by an alias literal or returned by an application or scripting addition command. This feature makes aliases especially useful in scripts that rename or move files and folders.

Using Aliases to Keep Track of File System Items

To demonstrate the ability of aliases to keep track of files and folders, even if they're moved or renamed, let's create a script that tracks a file you choose, and reports whether the location or name has changed. For that, you'll need two properties: one for the alias itself, which will keep track of the file even if it's moved or renamed, and one that will hold the previous path name as a string.

Script 17-1 shows such a script. The script starts by checking whether the the_alias property has been set (line 3). If the script is running for the first time and the the_alias property has not been set, the script will ask you to choose a file (line 4). The choose file command returns an alias that will be assigned to the the_alias property.

From there, the script compares the string variable containing the previous location to the alias to check whether the file has moved (line 7). If the file has moved, AppleScript shows you the old path and the new path in a dialog box (line 10).

Script 17–1.

```
1. property the_alias : missing value
2. property last_pathname : ""

3. if the_alias is missing value then
4.    set the_alias to choose file
5. else
6.    set this_pathname to the_alias as text
7.    if this_pathname = last_pathname then
8.       display dialog "The file hasn't moved"
9.    else
10.       display dialog "Old file path:" & return & last_pathname & return & ¬
                "New location: " & return & this_pathname
11.    end if
12. end if
13. set last_pathname to the_alias as text
```

Run the script once to choose the file. Next, change the name of the file you chose, or even move it to a different folder. Run the script again (without recompiling the script!). The script should display a dialog box showing you the old path and the new path of the file.

To force AppleScript to let go of the alias object stored in the the_alias property, recompile the script.

Converting to and from Alias Objects

You can convert an HFS path string to an alias object in two ways. The first way is by using it in an alias specifier:

```
set hfs_path to "Macintosh HD:Applications:TextEdit.app"
alias hfs_path
--> alias "Macintosh HD:Applications:TextEdit.app"
```

The second way is by coercing the string to an alias using AppleScript's as operator:

```
set hfs_path to "Macintosh HD:Applications:TextEdit.app"
hfs_path as alias
--> alias "Macintosh HD:Applications:TextEdit.app"
```

If the item doesn't exist when you do this, you'll get a "File not found" error, of course.

Converting path strings to aliases is useful when you need to assemble the full path while the script is running. For example, to get an alias to a folder named Work on the current user's desktop, you can write this:

```
set desktop_path to path to desktop folder as text
set work_folder to alias (desktop_path & "Work:")
--> alias "Macintosh HD:Users:hanaan:Desktop:Work:"
```

Working out the full path when the script is running makes this code much more portable. If the full path was hard-coded instead, the script would work only for a user named hanaan on a hard disk called Macintosh HD. We'll discuss this technique in more detail when we cover the path to command in Chapter 20.

To convert an alias to an HFS path string, you just use the as operator again:

```
(alias "Macintosh HD:Applications:TextEdit.app") as text
--> "Macintosh HD:Applications:TextEdit.app"
```

You can also obtain a POSIX path string by asking the alias for the value of its POSIX path property:

```
POSIX path of (alias "Macintosh HD:Applications:TextEdit.app")
--> "/Applications/TextEdit.app"
```

Understanding File "Objects"

The most important thing you need to know about file objects in AppleScript is… they don't actually exist!

This statement might sound like complete nonsense at first; after all, you can run a command like this and it works exactly as you'd expect:

```
tell application "Preview"
   open file "Macintosh HD:Users:hanaan:Downloads:About Downloads.pdf" -- Opens file
end tell
```

And yet, if you write it like this:

```
set the_file to file "Macintosh HD:Users:hanaan:Downloads:About Downloads.pdf"
tell application "Preview"
   open the_file
end tell
```

the first line throws an AppleScript error the moment you try to run it:

```
-- Error: Can't get file "Macintosh HD:Users:hanaan:Downloads:About Downloads.pdf".
```

Hey, what gives?

How Files (Really) Work

The truth, as it turns out, is even more bizarre than you think. The first thing you should know is that both of these scripts used to work in Mac OS X 10.4 and earlier. That was because earlier versions of AppleScript actually included a fourth file-related class, called file specification, which was normally abbreviated to file when used in a literal specifier, so that:

```
file specification "Macintosh HD:Users:hanaan:Downloads:About Downloads.pdf"
```

would compile as:

```
file "Macintosh HD:Users:hanaan:Downloads:About Downloads.pdf"
```

File specification objects played a similar role to POSIX file objects, in that they could be used to specify files and folders that didn't yet exist. Unfortunately, they also had a major shortcoming: they dated back to the early days of System 7, when modern file system features such as long file names and Unicode support did not exist. Despite these limitations, Apple somehow managed to continue supporting them in Mac OS X, but their use was strongly discouraged in favor of more capable, modern alternatives.

In Mac OS X 10.5, AppleScript finally dropped its support for file specifications, so you could no longer create objects of class `file specification` within AppleScript. Unfortunately, Apple forgot to provide another object in its place, so now when you ask AppleScript to evaluate a literal specifier like this:

```
file "Macintosh HD:Users:hanaan:Downloads:About Downloads.pdf"
```

the result is a "Can't get file..." error, as AppleScript no longer knows how to resolve this particular object specifier.

All is not lost, however. If you manage to send this specifier to a scriptable application as a regular reference, with a bit of luck the target application will manage to make sense of it for you. This is why the first of our original examples worked.

```
tell application "Preview"
   open file "Macintosh HD:Users:hanaan:Downloads:About Downloads.pdf" -- Opens file
end tell
```

Here, the file specifier is written as a parameter to Preview's open command, and as soon as AppleScript encounters something that looks like a reference in this position, it packs it into the command and sends it directly to the target application to resolve.

However, if you write the file specifier like this:

```
set the_file to file "Macintosh HD:Users:hanaan:Downloads:About Downloads.pdf"
```

AppleScript automatically tries to resolve it. If the statement is inside a `tell application ... end tell` block, AppleScript uses an implicit get command to do this. This is fine for an application like the Finder, which defines its own `file` class and knows how to create objects of that class. However, if the target application doesn't define a `file` class or if AppleScript tries to resolve the specifier itself, an error will occur.

If you really need to write a file specifier in one part of your code and use it in another, the solution is to use the `a reference to` operator, which you met earlier in Chapter 13. Script 17–2 shows how to turn a literal file specifier directly into a reference object that can then be stored in a variable and used later.

Script 17–2.

```
set pdf_file to a reference to ¬
      file "Macintosh HD:Users:hanaan:Downloads:About Downloads.pdf"
tell application "Preview"
   open pdf_file
end tell
```

Despite the practical problems of working with these strange "non-objects," you may still find file specifiers useful for some tasks. Like alias specifiers, file specifiers accept HFS paths, but unlike alias objects, which can only identify an existing file, folder, or disk, a file reference can point to *any* location—even one that doesn't exist yet. The other difference is that file references do not keep track of items that are renamed or moved. Because file references can refer to files that don't yet exist, they are especially useful in application or scripting addition commands such as `save` or `write`, where you often want to create a completely new file.

Converting to and from File References

You can convert an HFS path to a file reference by using it in a `file` specifier, for example:

```
set hfs_path to "Macintosh HD:Users:hanaan:Sites:index.html"
tell application "TextEdit" to open (file hfs_path)
```

Just remember that if your file specifier is not written as a parameter to an application or scripting addition command, you must use the `a reference to` operator to prevent AppleScript trying to resolve the file specifier itself:

```
set hfs_path to "Macintosh HD:Users:hanaan:Sites:index.html"
set file_ref to a reference to (file hfs_path)
tell application "TextEdit" to open (file hfs_path)
```

If the file reference identifies an existing item, you can also coerce it to an alias object or get its `POSIX path` property:

```
(file "Macintosh HD:Users:hanaan:Sites:index.html") as alias
--> alias "Macintosh HD:Users:hanaan:Sites:index.html"

POSIX path of (file "Macintosh HD:Users:hanaan:Sites:index.html")
--> "/Users/hanaan/Sites/index.html"
```

> **TIP:** If file references are too much of a headache, don't worry. You can avoid them completely by using alias and/or POSIX file objects instead.

Understanding POSIX File Objects

AppleScript provides two features that allow scripts to work with the Unix-style POSIX paths used in many parts of Mac OS X:

- a `POSIX file` class
- the `alias`, `file`, and `POSIX file` classes' `POSIX path` properties.

Like file references, POSIX file objects can refer to any location in the file system, even nonexistent files in nonexistent folders on nonexistent disks. For example, the `choose file name` command in Standard Additions will return a POSIX file object identifying a file that may or may not exist yet.

How POSIX Files Work

To create a POSIX file object, you write `POSIX file` followed by a POSIX path string. For example:

```
POSIX file "/Applications/Chess.app"
```

The POSIX path string must provide an absolute path name, that is, one that begins at the file system's root (/) and that describes the full path to the desired file, folder, or disk.

CAUTION: If you're familiar with Unix, you know that the Unix command line understands the concept of *relative* path names. AppleScript doesn't, unfortunately, so make sure you always use absolute paths.

One strange thing you'll notice when you create a POSIX file object is that AppleScript will display the resulting POSIX file object using file specifier syntax, for instance:

```
POSIX file "/Applications/Chess.app"
--> file "Macintosh HD:Applications:Chess.app"
```

Don't worry, it is still a proper POSIX file object. You can find out whether this object is of the POSIX file class by getting the value of its class property:

```
class of posix_file
--> «class furl»
```

I have no idea either why the class name is «class furl» instead of POSIX file as you'd expect, but it works, so it's not a problem.

Converting to and from POSIX File Objects

You can convert a POSIX path string to a POSIX file object by using it in a POSIX file specifier:

```
set path_string to "/Applications/Chess.app"
set posix_file to POSIX file path_string
```

If the POSIX file object identifies an existing file system item, you can coerce it to an alias:

```
posix_file as alias
--> alias "Macintosh HD:Applications:Chess.app:"
```

If the item doesn't exist, AppleScript will raise a coercion error –1700, "Can't make file "…" into type alias."

Application and scripting addition commands that require an alias as a parameter will normally accept a POSIX file object in its place, so you should rarely need to coerce a POSIX file object to an alias—unless you want an alias for its file-tracking abilities, of course.

You can also obtain an HFS path string by coercing the POSIX file object to a string:

```
posix_file as text
--> "Macintosh HD:Applications:Chess.app:"
```

Finally, you can convert a POSIX file object to a POSIX path string by asking it for the value of its POSIX path property:

```
POSIX path of posix_file
--> "/Users/hanaan/ReadMe.txt"
```

File URL Strings

The file URL string is useful for opening local files in a web browser. You can get a file's URL by tapping into the URL property defined in the Finder and System Events dictionaries. Script 17–3 gets the URL property of the file you choose.

Script 17–3.

```
set the_alias to (choose file)
tell application "System Events"
   set the_url to URL of the_alias
end tell
```

For example, if you choose the index.html file in your home folder's Sites folder, the choose file command will return an alias object similar to this:

```
alias "Macintosh HD:Users:hanaan:Sites:index.html"
```

System Events will then convert this alias to the following file URL string:

```
"file://localhost/Users/has/Sites/index.html"
```

Any characters that are not allowed in URLs will be automatically converted to their URL-safe equivalents, for example, space characters will be replaced by %20.

Although you can get the URL of any existing file, folder, or disk, this is really useful only with Internet-related files, such as HTML, JPG, GIF, and so on.

The following script will display the URL in the variable the_url (from Script 17–3) in the front Safari window:

```
tell application "Safari" to set URL of document 1 to the_url
```

You can also use a URL when creating a new Safari document:

```
tell application "Safari" to make new document with properties {URL:the_url}
```

However, if you're opening a local file, it may be easier to use Safari's open command for this, passing it an alias or POSIX file object:

```
tell application "Safari"
   open alias "Macintosh HD:Developer:ADC Reference Library:index.html"
end tell
```

You can also use Standard Additions' open location command to open a URL in the default browser, for example:

```
open location the_url
```

The open location command is defined as follows:

```
open location v : Opens a URL with the appropriate program
   open location [text] : the URL to open
      [error reporting boolean] : Should error conditions be reported in a dialog?
```

Reading and Writing Files

When I started using AppleScript, one of the tasks that fascinated me the most was writing text files. Man, that was almost as much fun as displaying my first dialog box!

Standard Additions' File Read/Write suite provides several commands for reading data from files and writing data into them. For the most part, you use these commands to read and write text, but you can pretty much read and write any data: graphic formats, PDFs, and so on. The reason you will work mostly with text files is that you can easily create text in strings, and see and understand what you created, while other kinds of data are often more complex. You can't really look at a PDF file's data and understand what's going on. When working with complicated binary files, it's usually best to use a scriptable application that already knows how to process them.

But text doesn't have to be dull. Plenty of text-based file formats—including XML, RTF (Rich Text Format, which is used by TextEdit and other applications for styled text documents), and SVG (an XML-based format used to describe line-based graphics)— allow you to create richly formatted files. QuarkXPress and InDesign also define their own tagged text file formats, which you can create.

Commands for Reading and Writing Files

The main Standard Additions commands for reading and writing files are `read` and `write`. Other commands allow you to open and close access to the files you want to use, and get and set their end of file (EOF) positions.

The following sections explain the different file-reading and file-writing commands.

Reading Files

The `read` command allows you to read the text data or binary data of a file.

From the Dictionary

Here's the definition:

```
read v : Read data from a file that has been opened for access
   read any : the file reference number, alias, or file reference of the file
         to read
      [from integer] : starting from this position; if omitted, start at last
            position read from
      [for integer] : the number of bytes to read from current position; if omitted,
            read until the end of the file…
      [to integer] : …or stop at this position…
      [before text] : …or read up to but not including this character…
      [until text] : …or read up to and including this character
      [using delimiter text] : the value that separates items to read…
      [using delimiters list of text] : …or a list of values that separate items
            to read
      [as type class] : the form in which to read and return data
      --> any : the data read from the file
```

Using the read Command

Reading files is fairly straightforward: you furnish the read command with the required file reference, and the result is the contents of the file.

Try the following: Use TextEdit to create a text file. Make sure to convert the file to plain text (not RTF). Type the phrase Hello World!, and then save this document as the file work.txt in your home folder.

Now, start a new script document, and write a line similar to the following, altering the path string to match your own file system:

```
read alias "Macintosh HD:Users:hanaan:work.txt"
```

The result of running the script is the text stored in the file:

```
--> "Hello World!"
```

Opening and Closing Access to Files

Standard Additions defines two closely related commands: open for access and close access. These commands create a longer-lasting connection between AppleScript and the file being worked on, allowing you to perform more complex operations on it.

Although you can read data from files without opening them for access, the read command operates differently depending on whether or not you open the files first. I describe this difference in the "Using the open for access and read Commands Together" section later. When writing to files, you should always open them for access first; otherwise the write command raises an error if the file doesn't already exist.

From the Dictionary

Here are the dictionary definitions for the open for access and close access commands:

```
open for access v : Open a disk file for the read and write commands
    open for access file : the file or alias to open for access. If the file does not
        exist, a new file is created.
    [write permission boolean] : whether to allow writing to the file.
    --> integer : a file reference number; use for 'read', 'write', and
        'close access'

close access v : Close a file that was opened for access
    close access any : the file reference number, alias, or file reference of the
        file to close
```

Opening a File for Reading or Writing

The open for access command has an optional Boolean parameter, write permission. When this parameter is false (the default), you can only read from the file. Setting it to true allows you to write to the file as well. Trying to write to a file that has not been opened with write permission will generate an error.

The open for access command in the following example opens a file for access with write permission:

```
set the_path to "Macintosh HD:Users:hanaan:work12345222.txt"
open for access (file the_path) with write permission
-- Do some stuff to the file...
close access (file the_path)
```

If the specified file does not exist, as long as the rest of the path is valid the open for access command will create a new, empty file for you.

> **CAUTION:** After opening a file for access, make sure you always close it again using the close access command when you are finished with it. Otherwise, the file will remain open until the application that created it (in this case, AppleScript Editor) is quit, which can prevent other applications from using the file in the meantime.

The open for access Result

Notice the result section of the open for access command: it's an integer. When you open access to a file, the result is a unique ID number generated by the open for access command. You can use this ID number to identify the file in Standard Additions' other read/write commands: read, write, get eof, set eof, and close access.

The following script shows how to use the ID number returned by the open for access command:

```
set the_path to "Macintosh HD:Users:hanaan:work.txt"
set file_ID to open for access file the_path
-- (The variable file_ID now contains a unique ID number, e.g. 5680.)
set file_data to read file_ID
close access file_ID
```

This unique ID number refers to the file for only as long as the file remains open, so you don't need to hold onto this number after you close the file. A new ID number will be assigned every time you open a file for access, even if it's the same file.

You can use the original path string, alias, and so on, in all these commands as well—after all, you had to have a normal file reference to the file for the purpose of opening the file for access..

Read Command Parameters

The read command has a number of optional parameters that make it even more powerful.

Reading Different Kinds of Data

By default, the read command reads a file's data into an AppleScript string. The as parameter allows you to read files that contain data in a number of other formats. The most common use for the as parameter is in reading Unicode text files, which we'll look at later in this section.

You can also make the read command read a number of common binary file formats. For example, to read a PICT, TIFF, JPEG, or GIF file, you use picture, TIFF picture, JPEG picture, or GIF picture for the as parameter. The resulting value appears in AppleScript as raw data («data ...») and can—at least in theory—be used in scripting additions and applications that understand it. For example, to read a TIFF file from disk and put it onto the clipboard, you'd use this:

```
set image_file to alias "Macintosh HD:Users:hanaan:Desktop:chocolate.tif"
set tiff_data to read image_file as TIFF picture
set the clipboard to tiff_data
```

Finally, you can use the as parameter to read other AppleScript values, such as lists and records that have been saved as binary files using Standard Additions' write command. You'll look at doing this in the "Writing Files" section.

Using a Delimiter to Read Text into a List

The using delimiter and using delimiters parameters allow you to split up a text file directly into a list. You do that by supplying one or more delimiter strings to the read command, which then automatically splits the string whenever it encounters one of the delimiters. Each delimiter string must consist of a single character. Only non-delimiter characters will appear in the resulting list of strings; the delimiter characters themselves are not included.

For example, if you have multiple lines of text saved in a return-delimited file, you can read that file into a list, where each list item is a paragraph, simply by setting the using delimiter parameter to the return character, like this:

```
set paragraph_list to read text_file using delimiter return
--> {"First paragraph", "second paragraph", "next line"}
```

Be careful, though: older Carbon-based Mac applications often use return characters (ASCII 13) to indicate line breaks, whereas Cocoa-based OS X applications use Unix-style linefeed characters (ASCII 10). Fortunately, the using delimiters parameter can accept a list of characters, allowing you to specify more than one delimiter at a time if you're not sure:

```
set paragraph_list to read text_file using delimiters {string id 10, string id 13}
```

Given that the read command's using delimiters parameter is a bit limited in what it can do, you may often find it easier to read the text as a single string, and then use AppleScript to break it up. For example, to get a list of paragraphs:

```
set paragraph_list to every paragraph of (read text_file)
```

This has the advantage that it will also work with Windows-style line breaks, which consist of two characters, a carriage return followed by a linefeed, instead of one.

If you want to split the text on any other character or phrase, just use AppleScript's text item delimiters feature you learned about in Chapter 7.

> **CAUTION:** The read command's using delimiters parameter will work correctly only if the text file being read represents each character as a single byte of data. If you need to work with Unicode text files, which can use multiple bytes for a single character, you will have to use AppleScript's delimiter features instead.

Reading a Specific Number of Bytes

The for parameter allows you to read a specific number of bytes of data from the current position. This is most useful when your copy of AppleScript and the text file you're reading both use a character set like ASCII or MacRoman where one byte equals one character. (Chapter 7 discussed character sets in detail.) For instance, the following script will read the first ten characters of an ASCII text file:

```
read alias "Macintosh HD:Users:hanaan:logfile.txt" for 10
```

You may also find this parameter useful if you need to extract specific sections of data from binary files whose structure you already know.

It is best to avoid using the for parameter when reading Unicode text files. Because each character may be represented by multiple bytes, it is difficult to know exactly how many bytes you need to read in order to get whole characters only. If you need to extract a section of text from a Unicode file, the safest and easiest method is to read in the whole file first, and then use a reference to get the bit you want. For example:

```
set all_text to read alias "Macintosh HD:Users:hanaan:logfile.txt" as Unicode text
text 1 thru 10 of all_text
```

The from and to Parameters

The from and to parameters allow you to specify the starting and ending points for reading data. Although the for parameter reads a certain number of bytes from the file marker (or from the start), the from and to parameters read data from a specific byte counted from the start of the file.

Let's assume you have an ASCII text file containing the word "applescript". The following script uses the from and to parameters to read the text from character 3 to character 6:

```
read alias "Macintosh HD:Users:hanaan:test 1.txt" from 3 to 6
--> "ples"
```

As with the for parameter, you should avoid using from and to when dealing with Unicode files unless you are know exactly what you are doing.

The *before* and *until* Parameters

The before and until parameters are similar: they both allow you to specify a character at which the read command should stop reading. The before parameter tells the read command to read up to but not including the specified character, and the until parameter includes the indicated character.

Let's assume you have a text file with the contents abcdefabcde. The following scripts illustrate how to use the until and before parameters:

```
read alias "Macintosh HD:Users:hanaan:test 2.txt" before "d"
--> "abc"
```

Notice that the character d is omitted from the end of the returned string, unlike in the next script:

```
read alias "Macintosh HD:Users:hanaan:test 2.txt" until "d"
--> "abcd"
```

You can also combine the before and until parameters with the from parameter. For example, let's start from the fifth byte and read until d:

```
read alias "Macintosh HD:Users:hanaan:test 2.txt" from 5 until "d"
--> "efabcd"
```

This time, the script started from the fifth character and continued until the following instance of d.

As with the using delimiters parameter, you should avoid using before and until when dealing with Unicode files.

Using the open for access and read Commands Together

As mentioned earlier, the open for access and close access commands are used to open and close files for use over a period of time. For simple one-off tasks, the read command does not require that the file is first opened for access:

```
read alias "Macintosh HD:Users:hanaan:some text file.txt"
--> "Contents of the text file"
```

The open for access command is very important for more complex tasks that may require multiple read/write operations to be performed on a single file.

When a file is opened for access, one of the things Standard Additions does is create an internal marker that determines the position in that file where the next read (or write) operation should start, just as you might use a bookmark to keep your place in a book. With a text file that has been opened for access, Standard Additions takes care of moving the bookmark for you. As an example, use TextEdit to create a new document, and type the alphabet: abcde...wxyz. Save it as a "Western (ASCII)" file named work.txt in your Documents folder, and close it.

Now let's see how to write a script that uses the read command with the for parameter. Start a new script as shown in Script 17–4.

Script 17–4.

```
set the_file to alias ((path to documents folder as text) & "work.txt")
open for access the_file
repeat
    set the_text to read the_file for 4
    display dialog the_text
end repeat
```

Now run the script.

The script will loop, each time reading the next four bytes as a four-character string, until it gets to the end of the file. At that point, you will get an "End Of File" error, number –43.

Unless you use the read command's from parameter, you will not be able to read this file again until you use the close access command to close access to it. Try to run your script again and you will get the error right away. To close the file left open by the previous script, create another script file containing the following line, and run it:

```
close access alias ((path to documents folder as text) & "work.txt")
```

This tells Standard Additions to forget the last-read position in this file so the next time you use the read command on it, you will begin reading at the start of the file again.

As you saw above, running Script 17–4 ends up causing the script to try to read bytes that don't exist, resulting in an EOF error. To prevent this error from halting the script, you can add a try block to catch and respond to the error as shown in Script 17–5.

Script 17–5.

```
set the_file to alias ((path to documents folder as text) & "work.txt")
open for access the_file
try
    repeat
        set the_text to read the_file for 4
        display dialog the_text
    end repeat
on error number -39 -- Handle the end-of-file error
    close access the_file -- Close the file now that we're finished with it
end try
display dialog "All done!"
```

Working with the End-of-File (EOF) Commands

Every file is a certain number of bytes in length. That number is known as the "end of file", or EOF, and can be any value from 0 on up. You can retrieve or modify a file's EOF using Standard Additions' get eof and set eof commands.

The value returned by the get eof command is the same as the value of the size property in Finder or System Events, as you can see here:

```
set the_file to alias ((path to documents folder as text) & "work.txt")
tell application "System Events" to set file_size to size of the_file
(get eof the_file) = file_size
--> true
```

From the Dictionary

The following are the dictionary entries of the get eof and set eof commands:

```
get eof v : Return the length, in bytes, of a file
    get eof any : a file reference number, alias, or file reference of a file
        --> integer : the total number of bytes in the file

set eof v : Set the length, in bytes, of a file
    set eof any : a file reference number, alias, or file reference of a file
        to integer : the new length of the file, in bytes. Any data beyond this
                position is lost.
```

Getting a File's EOF

To get the EOF value of a file, you use the get eof command. The get eof command takes a single parameter—a valid file specifier or an ID number returned by open for access—and returns a whole number.

The following script returns the EOF value of the file work.txt from your hard disk:

```
set the_file to alias ((path to documents folder as text) & "work.txt")
set byte_count to get eof the_file
--> 26
```

Setting a File's EOF

When you set a file's EOF, you in fact determine the new end of the file. Setting the EOF to a smaller number than its current value permanently deletes the data after the new EOF. For instance, if the text of an ASCII file is I Love Christina, its EOF is 16 bytes. If you set the EOF to 12, the file now says I Love Chris, which is still perfectly valid but may not be what you intended.

On the other hand, if you set the EOF to a larger number, AppleScript will pad the end of the file with extra bytes, each one equivalent to ASCII 0. These will appear in a text editor as invisible characters, but if you use the arrow keys, you can actually advance through them.

The following script sets the size of the file work.txt to 10 bytes:

```
set the_file to alias ((path to documents folder as text) & "work.txt")
set eof of the_file to 10
```

This script takes the same file and discards the second half of it:

```
set the_file to alias ((path to documents folder as text) & "work.txt")
set byte_count to get eof of the_file
set eof of the_file to (round (byte_count / 2))
```

Writing Files

You can write data to files using Standard Additions' write command. Although you can write any type of data, for the most part you'll stick to what you understand, which is text. You can see it, read it, and understand it.

For writing complex binary files such as JPEGs or PDFs, I recommend you work with scriptable applications that already understand these formats (Adobe Photoshop or Illustrator, Image Events, Satimage's Smile, and so forth). After all, the purpose of AppleScript is to make other programs do all the hard work for you!

From the Dictionary

The following is the dictionary definition of the write command:

```
write v : Write data to a file that was opened for access with write permission
    write any : the data to write to the file
      to any : the file reference number, alias, or file reference of the file
          to write to
      [starting at integer] : start writing at this position in the file
      [for integer] : the number of bytes to write; if not specified, write all
          the data provided
      [as type class] : how to write the data: as text, data, list, etc.
```

Using the write Command

The write command returns no result. It simply writes text or other data to a file. Before writing to a file, you should use the open for access command to get the file ready for use. To grant yourself writing privileges, you must set the open for access command's write permission parameter to true. If you forget this, you'll get a "File not open with write permission" error when you try to write to it.

Using the open for access and close access commands guarantees that there's always a file for the write command to write to. If the file doesn't already exist, open for access creates one automatically. (In fact, it is possible to use the write command without opening a file first, but this works only if the file already exists, otherwise you'll get a "File not found" error.)

Next, unless you plan to insert your new data into the file's existing data (for example, appending a message to the end of a permanent log file), you need to clear any existing file data using the following command:

```
set eof the_file to 0
```

This is another important step when writing to a file; for example, if a text file contains "Hello World" and you write the string "Goodbye" to it without resetting its EOF first, the result will be a file containing "Goodbyeorld"—not "Goodbye" as you intended!

With the preparation complete, you can now write some data to the file. The write command has two required parameters: the data you want to write and a value identifying the file to write to. This value may be a path string, an alias, a file, or a POSIX file object, or a unique ID number returned by the open for access command. Don't forget to use the close access command to close the file when you're done.

The following example creates a new text file if necessary and writes some text into it (you'll need to adjust the file path to suit your own system, of course):

```
set the_path to "Macintosh HD:Users:hanaan:work.txt"
set file_ID to open for access file the_path with write permission
set eof file_ID to 0
write "abc" to file_ID
close access file_ID
```

How Much to Write and Where to Start

Two of the write command's parameters help you specify how much data or text you want to write to the file and at which position in the file you want to start.

The starting at parameter is useful when you want to start writing text or data somewhere in the middle or at the end of an existing file. For example, a script that needs to keep a written record of all its activities would simply add each entry to the end of a permanent log file. To do this, you tell the write command to start writing at the EOF—the end of the file—each time you want to add something. Script 17–6 shows how to write some initial text to a file, first clearing away any existing text. Script 17–7 shows how to append more text to the same file later.

Script 17–6.

```
set file_id to open for access ¬
    file "Macintosh HD:Users:hanaan:work.txt" with write permission
set eof file_id to 0
write "This is the beginning..."to file_id
close access file_id
```

Script 17–7.

```
set file_id to open for access ¬
    file "Macintosh HD:Users:hanaan:work.txt"with write permission
write " and this is the end!" to file_id starting at eof
close access file_id
```

The resulting text file will have the text "This is the beginning... and this is the end!"

Notice that the first write command started writing at the beginning of the file as usual. However, by setting the second write command's starting at parameter to the eof constant, you tell that command to add its data to the end of the file instead.

If you want to limit the amount of data that gets written, you can do that with the for parameter, which takes an integer as an argument and limits the number of bytes written to that number.

In Script 17–8, only the first five bytes of data will be written.

Script 17–8.

```
set file_id to open for access ¬
    file "Macintosh HD:Users:hanaan:work.txt"with write permission
write "abcdefghij" to file_id for 5
```

```
close access file_id
```

Because the `for` parameter works with raw bytes, it is best avoided when writing Unicode text files.

Useful File Writing Handlers

The following are two handlers you can use for basic text-file saving. The first handler saves the given text to a given text file, and the second one adds the given text to the end of the given text file.

```
--Saves a text file
on write_text_to_file(the_file, the_text)
    set file_ref to open for access the_file with write permission
    set eof file_ref to 0
    write the_text to file_ref as «class utf8»
    close access file_ref
end write_text_to_file

--Adds text to a text file
on append_text_to_file(the_file, the_text)
    set file_ref to open for access file theTextFilePath with write permission
    set file_length to get eof file_ref
    write the_text to file_ref as «class utf8» starting at eof
    close access file_ref
end append_text_to_file
```

Notice that both of these handlers write the text in UTF-8 format (as `«class utf8»`), which is one of several ways that the Unicode character set can be encoded when writing it to file. We'll discuss this and other text encoding options shortly.

> **CAUTION:** Make sure you read the Dealing with Text Encodings section before you start reading and writing your own text files. If you don't understand how text encodings work, you could easily end up experiencing surprise errors, nonsense strings, or even corrupted files.

Using the write Command to Create a Script Log

In this exercise you will write a handler, `add_to_log`, similar to the one I use on all my systems. The purpose of this handler is to create a detailed log of script activity. If the script crashes or does something it isn't supposed to do, this log should help you track down the cause of the problem. You can make the log as detailed as you want by calling the handler from many areas in your script.

An important feature of this handler is that each new message is added to the end of the log file as soon as it occurs. This way, if the script gets an error, you can pinpoint the error location in the script by seeing which part of the script wrote the last message in the log file. In contrast, if you saved all your messages in one big string and wrote them to disk only at the end of the script, then any error that caused the script to stop before that point would result in all those messages being lost.

The add_to_log handler in Script 17–9 is pretty simple. It receives a message string and adds it to the log, along with the date and time the message was received. To keep things simple, the handler just saves the log files to the current user's desktop, but you can easily modify it to use a different location.

TIP: If you give your log file the name extension .log, it will automatically open in Mac OS X's Console application when double-clicked.

Script 17–9.

```
1. on add_to_log(the_message)
2.     set {YYYY, MM, DD} to {year, month, day} of (current date)
3.     set MM to MM as integer
4.     if MM < 10 then set MM to "0" & MM
5.     if DD < 10 then set DD to "0" & DD
6.     set log_file_name to (YYYY as text) & "_" & MM & "_" & DD & ".log"
7.     set log_file_path to (path to desktop as text) & log_file_name
8.     set full_message to return & (current date) & return & the_message
9.     set file_ID to open for access file log_file_path with write permission
10.     write full_message to file_ID starting at eof
11.     close access file_ID
12. end add_to_log
```

Lines 2 through 7 create the file path for the log file, consisting of the path to the user's desktop and a filename containing the date when the log file was created. Getting the desktop folder path automatically allows this script to work on any machine without needing to be altered. Using today's date for the filename means that the add_to_log handler will automatically start a fresh log file every day it runs.

NOTE: See Chapter 9 for more information on working with date objects.

Line 8 puts the message together.

Line 9 opens the log file for access, which also creates a new log file if one doesn't already exist. Line 10 appends the message to the end of the file, and line 11 closes the file again.

To add an entry to the log, just call the add_to_log handler, passing it a text message describing your current location in the script along with any other useful information, like this:

```
add_to_log("1044 Adding client name to job ticket")
```

Another technique I use is to include a property called debug at the top of my scripts. This property contains a Boolean value that is used to enable or disable extra debugging code in a script. I then put add_to_log commands inside conditional blocks so they'll call the add_to_log handler only when debug is true. This makes it really easy to turn debugging messages on during testing and off again during normal use. Here's an example:

```
if debug then add_to_log("1044 Adding client name to job ticket")
```

Saving and Loading AppleScript Lists and Records

Another handy feature of the `write` command is its ability to save almost any kind of AppleScript object to a file, not just strings and Unicode text. Besides being able to save binary data for images, PDFs, and so forth, you can write AppleScript lists and records to files and read them right back! This is great for saving script preferences and data that can be shared among scripts or backed up. It's true you can coerce most things into strings and save them as text, but here you can save lists containing real numbers, date objects, and more nested lists; write them all to a file; and later read them back exactly as they were.

All you have to do is specify the object's original class using the `write` command's as parameter. For example, if you want to save a record object to a file, you add as `record` to the end of the `write` command. Script 17–10 demonstrates how to do this, and Script 17–11 shows how to read it back again.

Script 17–10.

```
set the_record to {first_name:"Anthony", age:37, ¬
    date_of_birth:date "Monday, December 4, 1967 12:00:00 AM"}
set full_path to (path to desktop as text) & "record_data"
set file_ID to open for access file full_path with write permission
write the_record to file_ID as record
close access file_ID
```

Script 17–11.

```
set full_path to (path to desktop as text) &"record_data"
set the_record to read file full_path as record
-->{first_name:"Anthony", age:37,
    date_of_birth:date "Monday, December 4, 1967 12:00:00 AM"}
```

Dealing with Text File Encodings

Although reading and writing plain-text files in AppleScript might seem like a simple enough procedure, it's actually a bit more complicated than I've let on so far. Here's the catch: there are many different ways in which characters can be represented, or encoded, as bytes in a text file. When reading and writing text files in AppleScript, it's essential you use the correct text encoding, otherwise the results will appear as gibberish. This applies both to the text files you read and write using AppleScript alone and to the text files that are created by AppleScript for use by other programs, and vice versa.

If you're lucky, you won't run into these issues straightaway. However, you're almost certainly going to run into them sooner or later. When you do, you'll want to know a bit about how text—especially Unicode text—is actually represented in files and how AppleScript reads and writes those files.

About ASCII, MacRoman, and Unicode Character Sets

As we discussed in Chapter 7, AppleScript now uses the modern Unicode character set in all its strings. Unicode is a huge character set—currently it holds around 100,000 characters, but it's large enough to hold over a million if needed! This allows it to contain every character in common use around the world today, plus many that aren't, and still have tons of room for future additions.

Unicode is not the only character set in existence, of course. There are many older, more limited character sets such as ASCII, Latin-1, and MacRoman that are still in use today, but these will become less important in future as more and more applications adopt Unicode as the standard.

Most of the time you work in AppleScript, you don't need to think about the technical details behind Unicode (or any other character set), as AppleScript strings normally "just work." The one big exception is when you read and write text files using Standard Additions' read and write commands.

Remember how, in Chapter 7, we compared the ASCII, MacRoman, and Unicode characters sets. We saw how the ASCII character set is a mere 128 characters in size—enough for an English alphabet, digits 0 to 9, some common punctuation symbols, and a number of special "control" characters—while MacRoman, at 256 characters in length, can hold some non-English characters as well.

While the small size of the ASCII and MacRoman character sets may limit their usefulness compared to Unicode, they do have one slight advantage over it. Because a single byte of computer memory is just a number between 0 and 255, a single ASCII or MacRoman character fits very neatly into one byte. This makes reading and writing ASCII- or MacRoman-encoded plain text files very straightforward, since one byte of data in the file represents one character of text, and vice-versa.

When it comes to reading and writing text that uses the Unicode character set, things become a bit more complex. Obviously there are far too many characters for each to fit into a single byte, so the only solution is to use several bytes to represent, or *encode*, each character. This then raises another question: what combinations of bytes should be used to represent which characters? In the end, Unicode's designers decided to define several standard encoding schemes, each with its own advantages and disadvantages, so that developers and users could pick whichever encoding scheme best suited them for a particular job.

The following sections look at the two most popular Unicode encoding schemes, UTF-8 and UTF-16, since these are the ones that AppleScript supports. We'll also discuss how you can read and write text files using older encodings such as ASCII and MacRoman.

Reading and Writing Text Files in Different Encodings

Text-editing applications such as TextEdit commonly include an option in their Open and Save dialog boxes for specifying which encoding you want them to use when reading and writing a plain-text file. Similarly, Standard Additions' read and write commands give you some control over how you read and write plain-text files in AppleScript by way of the optional as parameter. In both commands, the as parameter takes a class name constant that indicates how the character data is (or should be) encoded in the text file.

You can use three class names for specifying how AppleScript reads and writes text files: `string`, `«class utf8»`, and `Unicode text`.

Reading and Writing UTF-8 Encoded Files

UTF-8 is a cleverly designed encoding scheme that uses a variable number of bytes to represent each character. The first 128 characters in the Unicode character set, which are identical to the 128 characters of the 7-bit ASCII character set, are represented by a single byte each, and all other characters are represented using unique combinations of two to six bytes apiece.

This design means that any ASCII-encoded text file is also a valid UTF-8 file, which provides a degree of backward compatibility with tools that only understand ASCII. For example, most of the text processing tools found on Mac OS X's command line are ASCII-oriented and do not understand the full Unicode character set. However, if you pass them UTF-8-encoded text, they should understand the first 128 characters and leave any other characters as they are. This also makes UTF-8 files that contain mostly English text as compact as possible.

> **TIP:** Many other character sets, including MacRoman, are also supersets of ASCII, giving them a similar degree of backward compatibility with ASCII-based tools.

To read and write UTF-8-encoded text files, use the `«class utf8»` constant as the `read` and `write` commands' as parameter:

```
read the_file as «class utf8»
```

```
write the_text to the_file as «class utf8»
```

Here is a simple handler that lets you write a UTF-8-encoded file with a simple `write_UTF8_file` command:

```
to write_UTF8_file(the_file, the_text)
    set file_ID to open for access the_file with write permission
    -- Clear any existing content if the file already exists:
    set eof file_ID to 0
    -- Add the UTF-8 encoded text:
    write the_text to file_ID as «class utf8»
    close access file_ID
end write_UTF8_file
```

To use this handler in your own code, just call it with two parameters: a file specifier for the file you want to write, and the text to be written, for example:

```
write_UTF8_file(POSIX file "/Users/hanaan/test_utf8.txt", "Copyright © 2009")
```

Reading and Writing UTF-16 Encoded Files

The UTF-16 encoding scheme is a bit more straightforward than UTF-8, although it lacks UTF-8's backward compatibility and compactness when dealing with English text. In

UTF-16, each character is normally encoded as two bytes of data. (Some of the more obscure characters are actually represented using four bytes, but we we'll ignore this detail as they're beyond the scope of this book. You can find links to additional information at the end of this chapter.)

To read and write UTF-16 encoded text files, use the Unicode text constant as the read and write commands' as parameter:

```
read the_file as Unicode text
```

```
write the_text to the_file as Unicode text
```

The UTF-16 format does have one significant twist: although each character is represented as two bytes of data—a "high" byte and a "low" byte—the order in which those two bytes appear can vary. Some processors, such as those in the Power PC family, represent multi-byte numbers with the most significant (highest) byte first; what's known as *big endianness*. Others, including Intel-compatible x86 processors, represent multi-byte numbers with the least significant (lowest) byte first, or *little endianness*. These two UTF-16-based formats are known as UTF-16BE and UTF-16LE—I'm sure you can guess what the BE and LE suffixes mean.

When you use Standard Additions' write command to write a text file as Unicode text, it will always produce a UTF-16 file in big-endian form; that is, UTF-16BE.

When you ask Standard Additions to read a text file as Unicode text, the read command will automatically assume the file is encoded as UTF-16BE, unless it finds a special sequence of bytes at the start that explicitly indicates the byte order used. If it finds one of these special *byte order marks* (BOMs), it will use that to determine whether the file's encoding is UTF-16BE or UTF16-LE and read it accordingly.

Although including a)BOM in a Unicode text file is optional, it's a good idea to add one when writing a UTF-16 file in AppleScript. This lets Unicode-aware applications detect the exact encoding to use when reading the file. Here is a simple handler for writing a UTF-16BE file with the appropriate)BOM at the start:

```
to write_UTF16_file(the_file, the_text)
    set file_ID to open for access the_file with write permission
    -- Clear any existing content if the file already exists:
    set eof file_ID to 0
    -- Add a UTF-16BE byte order mark:
    write «data rdatFEFF» to file_ID
    -- Add the UTF-16BE encoded text:
    write the_text to file_ID as Unicode text
    close access file_ID
end write_UTF16_file
```

As you can see, after setting the file's EOF to 0 to get rid of any previous contents, the handler uses two separate write commands to add the new data. The first one writes the two-byte)BOM to the start of the file, and the second one adds the actual text encoded as UTF-16BE. Notice how I've written the)BOM as a raw data literal:

```
«data rdatFEFF»
```

The opening chevron followed by the data keyword indicates to AppleScript that we are supplying this value as a series of raw bytes. The four-character code after the data keyword, rdat, tell it exactly what kind of data it is (in this case, just generic **raw data**), and this is followed by a series of byte values written in hexadecimal form. In this case, the UTF-16BE byte order mark consists of two byte values, 254 and 255, or FE and FF. While data objects are rarely needed in AppleScript, this is one place where they are actually quite useful as they make it easy to specify the exact bytes we want.

To use this handler in your own code, just call it with two parameters: a file specifier for the file you want to write, and the text to be written, for example:

```
set the_file to POSIX file "/Users/hanaan/test_utf16be.txt"
set the_text to "Wi nøt trei a høliday in Sweden this yër?"
write_UTF16_file(the_file, the_text)
```

Reading and Writing Files in Other Encodings

While Unicode is the default character set used by Mac OS X, and UTF-8 and UTF-16 are the preferred encodings for reading and writing plain text files, Mac OS X can still work with other character sets and encoding schemes for the sake of backward compatibility.

One phrase you will encounter when dealing with encodings is "primary encoding". Because older character sets all interpret the bytes in a text file to mean different characters, it is important that you use the same encoding scheme when reading and writing non-Unicode files. Your Mac's primary encoding is simply the default encoding scheme it uses when interpreting non-Unicode data. Mac OS X decides what your primary encoding should be based on your language settings in System Preferences' International pane. For English-speaking users, this will be MacRoman, for Japanese users it is MacJapanese, and so on.

AppleScript makes it easy to read and write text files in your primary encoding. In Mac OS X 10.5 and later, this is the default encoding used by your read and write commands, so you don't have to do anything special. If you'd rather make your intentions obvious, though, just use the value string for the command's as parameter:

```
read the_file as string
```

```
write the_text to the_file as string
```

WRITING FILES ON OLDER VERSIONS OF MAC OS X

The behavior of Standard Additions' write command has varied quite a bit over the years, which may be an issue for you if your scripts need to support older versions of Mac OS X as well.

Until the release of Mac OS X 10.4, if you didn't specify an as parameter for the write command, it would use string as the default, and the resulting file would contain text data in your primary encoding. This behavior changed a bit in Mac OS X 10.4, however: passing the write command an object of class string as its direct parameter would still write the file using your primary encoding, but an object of class

Unicode text would be written as UTF-16 encoded data instead! In Mac OS X 10.5, the write command's behavior changed again, so that it now writes text using your primary encoding by default.

Fortunately, it's easy to ensure that Standard Additions' write command always uses the encoding you want. Just supply your own as parameter every time you use it, using one of the three text-related objects—string, «class utf8», or Unicode text—so that there can never be any doubt as to which encoding—primary, UTF-8, or UTF-16BE—the resulting file will use.

If you need to read and write ASCII text, the easiest way to do this is by reading and writing the file as UTF-8. (Remember, the UTF-8 encoding scheme is fully backward-compatible with ASCII.) Do remember that this will only work as intended if the string or file really does contain only ASCII characters; otherwise you may get an unexpected result or even an error.

If you want to find out if a plain text file is UTF-16BE encoded, you can use the following handler to read the first two bytes as raw data and check if they match the optional UTF-16BE byte order mark:

```
on is_utf_16_be(the_file)
   try
      return (read the_file to 2 as data) = «data rdatFEFF»
   on error number -39 -- File is less than 2 bytes long
      return false
   end try
end is_utf_16_be
```

If the handler returns true, you can be pretty confident the file is UTF-16BE encoded and can be read using read ... as Unicode text. If it returns false, you know it either uses a different encoding or was saved without a BOM.

Should you need to read or write text files in any encoding other than ASCII, your primary encoding, UTF-8, or UTF-16BE, you will need to look to other tools for help; for example, an advanced scriptable text editor such as TextWrangler or BBEdit (http://www.barebones.com) or the Unix command line, where tools such as textutil can be used to read files in one encoding and convert them to another.

What Happens if the Wrong Encoding is Used?

With so many different text encoding systems in use today, it is quite likely that sooner or later you will read a text file using an encoding different from the one it was written in, or write a file in an encoding different from the one you intended. This can produce bizarre or unintended results, or even cause script errors, so it's a good idea to know the sorts of problems to look out for.

The following script demonstrates the sort of confusion that can easily occur:

```
set test_file to POSIX file (POSIX path of (path to desktop) & "test_utf8.txt")
write_UTF8_file(test_file, "Hello World!")
read test_file as Unicode text
--> "??漠坏枛操"
```

The script uses the previous `write_UTF8_file` handler to write out the ASCII text "Hello World!" to file, then reads this file back in again as if it were UTF-16BE-encoded data. Remember, ASCII uses one byte to represent one character while UTF-16 uses two bytes for each character, and it should be pretty clear what has happened: the write command is interpreting the first two ASCII characters, "He", as a one Unicode character, the next two ASCII characters, "ll", as another Unicode character, and so on. Change the `read` command to read the file as «class utf8», however, and all is well again.

Let's look at another example: what happens if you accidentally read a UTF-8-encoded text file containing the phrase "–15°C" as if it were MacRoman (or whatever your primary encoding is)? Well, we know that the UTF-8 and MacRoman encodings both represent alphanumeric characters as exactly the same bytes, so those should still look correct. But what will happen to the decimal point and degrees symbols, which they represent using different combinations of bytes?

I'll let you try this one yourself. First, create a UTF-8-encoded text file containing the text:

```
–15°C
```

That's an en dash (Option-hyphen on U.S. keyboards), the characters "1" and "5", a degrees symbol (Option-Shift-8) and the character "C".

Next, use the read command to read in the file as if it were written in your primary encoding (`read the_file as string`). The resulting text will look something like this:

```
,Äì15¬∞C
```

As you can see, each of the alphanumeric characters (1, 5, and C) is represented by the same single byte in both the MacRoman and UTF-8 encoding systems, so they will look right either way. However, UTF-8 uses two bytes to represent a degree sign (°) and three bytes to encode an en dash character (–), so they show up as nonsense characters when interpreted as MacRoman instead.

There's one more common mix-up that's worth looking at here, as it's one where the resulting string often looks correct in AppleScript Editor's Results pane, but causes plenty of problems all the same.

If you accidentally read a UTF-16 file as MacRoman, the resulting value may look at first glance like an ordinary string, especially if it contains English text. You'll quickly discover that something is very wrong when you try to use it, however: a common symptom is that each visible character in your "string" seems to have an invisible character in front of it. For example, reading a UTF-16 encoded text file containing the phrase "Hello World!" as a string produces a string like " H e l l o   W o r l d !", where each " " is really an invisible ASCII 0 character.

A Summary of Common Text File Encodings

Figure 17–3 summarizes how the string "−15°C" is represented under each of the four encoding systems described earlier: MacRoman, UTF-8, UTF-16BE, and UTF-16LE.

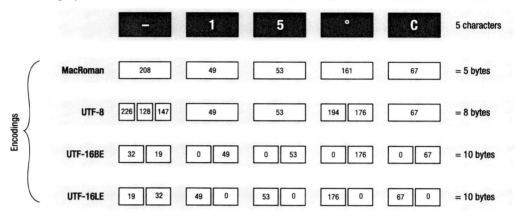

Figure 17–3. *How characters are represented in different text encodings. Each white box indicates a single byte of data in the text file.*

As you can see, in MacRoman each character is represented as a single byte of data. In UTF-8 some characters are represented by a single byte whose value is 0–127, and others are represented by two or more bytes whose values are in the range 128–255. In the two UTF-16 encodings, each character is represented by two bytes, and the order of those bytes depends on whether the encoding is UTF-16BE (big-endian) or UTF-16LE (small endian).

Further Reading on Text Encodings

Character sets and text encodings are much bigger and more complex topics than I can cover in this chapter or would want to bore you with. For further reading, you can start at the following URLs:

```
http://www.joelonsoftware.com/articles/Unicode.html
http://en.wikipedia.org/wiki/Unicode
```

Summary

In this chapter you learned about the various ways you can identify file system objects within AppleScript using HFS and POSIX path strings, alias and POSIX file objects, and the rather quirky but still useful file references, and file URL strings.

You also discovered how to read and write plain text files using Standard Additions' File Commands suite, and you were introduced to the basic principles by which a series of human-readable characters can be encoded as bytes of data in a file on disk.

You even learned how to read and write other kinds of AppleScript objects to binary files, which can be a quick and easy way for your scripts to store important values as simple preferences files.

We will return to the topic of the Mac OS X file system in Chapter 20 when you learn how to manipulate it by scripting the Finder and System Events applications. Meantime, let's move on to the last of our four key AppleScript concepts—organizing your code— by looking at the first of two important features that AppleScript provides for this task: user-defined handlers.

Chapter 18

Organizing Your Code with Handlers

Although user-defined handlers aren't the first thing you create when you learn AppleScript, they are the one facet of writing scripts that will have the most impact on your scripts, especially as they grow bigger and more ambitious. Handlers are your tools for organizing scripts; they make your scripts efficient and give you a perfect way to store and reuse your code.

You do not have to understand handlers in order to write simple AppleScripts, but they are well worth learning about. In addition to enhancing the design of your day-to-day scripts, they are a required feature in more advanced projects such as developing your own GUI applications.

In this chapter, you will learn more about why handlers are useful, how to write your own handlers in AppleScript, and how to pass values in and out of them as parameters and results.

You will then put that knowledge to practical use, developing a new kind of data structure called an associative list, which you can use in your own scripts, along with a set of handlers for manipulating that structure.

> **TIP:** Many of the concepts covered in Chapter 11—choosing identifiers, understanding variable scope, and using AppleScript's special me variable—are especially relevant when creating and using user-defined handlers, so refer to that chapter regularly as you work through this one.

What Are User-Defined Handlers?

A handler is simply a self-contained block of code that does something when the object that contains the handler receives a matching command. For example, the Finder includes a handler named make that creates new files, folders, windows, and so forth when you send a make command to the application.

Handlers exist to make your life easier. A simple command sent from your script might trigger hundreds of lines of complex code in a handler, and you can trigger this code over and over again, wherever and whenever you need to use that functionality.

Scriptable applications and scripting additions conveniently provide your scripts with instant access to many thousands of prewritten handlers, allowing you to perform many common tasks quickly and easily. In addition, you can also write your own handlers using AppleScript code, allowing you to define new commands that fit your own particular needs.

> **NOTE:** User-defined handlers are often referred to as *subroutines*, *functions*, or *procedures*. All these terms, for this book's purposes, have the same meaning.

To better understand handlers, imagine making a list of tasks to complete before throwing a party in your house. These tasks include baking a cake, washing dishes, buying food items, and welcoming the guests. Although this list is a great overview, it doesn't go into the details involved in each step. If the list actually described everything you needed to do to bake a cake or wash each dish in turn, it would no longer be a brief overview that you could glance at to see what needed to be done. Instead, the detailed instructions for each task are written up separately.

So when the day of the party finally arrives, you pick up your list and read the directions. Each item on the list, instead of being the specific instructions for the task, calls your attention to the task, whose specific details you can look up somewhere else.

The same happens with a script that uses handlers. Script 18–1 shows the party plan in AppleScript Editor the way you would organize it as a script with handlers. By looking at the layout of the top-level statements and the various handlers, you can easily differentiate between the master plan and the fine details.

Script 18–1.

```
-- Execute the day of the party
bake_cake("Chocolate cake")
wash_dishes()
buy_food("Chips")
buy_food("Soda")
welcome_guests()

-- Handlers

to bake_cake(cake_type)
    if cake_type is "Chocolate cake" then
        -- Bake chocolate cake
    else
        -- Bake other cake
    end if
end bake_cake

to wash_dishes()
    repeat with the_dish in dish_list
        -- Wash the dish
```

```
    end repeat
end wash_dishes

to buy_food(the_item)
    -- Go to isle containing item
    -- Pick up item
    -- Pay for item
end buy_food

to welcome_guests()
    repeat with the_person in guest_list
        -- Welcome the person to the party
    end repeat
end welcome_guests
```

On their own, none of these user-defined handlers do anything other than occupy bytes in your script file. However, as soon as the script starts sending commands to itself—bake_cake("Chocolate cake"), wash_dishes(), and so on—they leap into action, performing their allotted jobs.

Later, as you gain experience, you can start moving commonly used handlers into separate, reusable script files called *script libraries*. Doing so makes your main scripts smaller and more manageable and allows you to package general-purpose handlers for use by multiple scripts. These libraries may have handlers that all perform related tasks. In the preceding example, you could have a "baker" script library. In this case, you would use this line to bake the cake: tell baker to bake_cake("chocolate cake"). We'll look at script libraries in the next chapter.

Creating a Simple Handler

Before I get into the specifics of user-defined handlers, I'll show how to create one simple handler and call it. In this example, you will create a little handler that displays a dialog box containing the text "Hello!". Script 18–2 shows the basic form of a user-defined handler, along with the corresponding command.

Script 18–2.

```
-- A say_hello command
say_hello()

-- The say_hello handler
to say_hello()
    display dialog "Hello!"
end say_hello
```

The handler statement is made up of a first line and a last line, with any number of statements in between. The first line starts with the keyword to and describes the handler's name and any parameters it takes. As with other multiline statements, the last line starts with the keyword end.

TIP: The on keyword can be used in place of the to keyword to indicate the start of a handler. Both keywords have the same meaning here, so you can use whichever one you prefer.

The handler definition can live almost anywhere in your script, or even in other scripts. The only place it can't appear is directly inside another handler definition. User-defined commands can appear inside expressions or anywhere else, just like any other command in AppleScript. A command can even live inside the handler it triggers, causing the handler to call itself, to call itself, to call itself...and so on, in a process known as *recursion*. Any time your script needs a handler executed, just stick in the appropriate command and off it goes.

CAUTION: When writing a user-defined command inside a tell application ... end tell block, remember that the command will be sent to the target application by default. If you want the command to be handled by your script, put the my keyword before the command name, like this: my some_command(). See the section on AppleScript's special me variable in Chapter 11 for more information.

Using Parameters

Parameters, also referred to as *arguments*, are values passed to the handler by the command. Parameters let you explain to the handler how you want the different commands and statements to be executed.

When you stand at a coffee shop counter, you ask for coffee by giving a command: "Please make me a coffee." The parameters are the details you provide about how you like your coffee: "Make it large and black with one sugar." The "make coffee" handler has three parameters: size, whitener, and sweetener. Anywhere you get coffee in the country, you can supply those parameters to the "make coffee" handler, and people will understand, even though the exact way they'll go about making it may be different.

The following is the "make coffee" handler the way AppleScript would have it:

```
to make_coffee(cup_size, include_whitener, number_of_sweeteners)
    put a cup whose size is cup_size on counter
    fill with coffee
    if include_whitener then add whitener
    repeat number_of_sweeteners times
        add sweetener
    end repeat
    stir
    return cup of coffee
end make_coffee
```

To execute this handler, you'd send the script a `make_coffee` command containing the size, whitener, and sweetener values you want the handler to use in preparing your coffee. For example:

```
make_coffee(large, no, 1)
```

We'll discuss parameters in a lot more detail shortly. Now let's look at how to return results.

What's the Result?

In AppleScript, you may want your handlers to return a value, or you may not. For example, a handler whose job is to close all open documents in InDesign may return no result. It will always just close any open documents, and that's that. You may want to test whether the operation was successful and return a `true` or `false`, or you may return the number of documents you closed. This is entirely up to you.

Using the *return* Statement

By default, a handler will run all the way through and then return the result of the last line executed, if any. However, if you wish, you can make the handler return at any point by using a `return` statement.

The `return` statement starts with the word `return` and is optionally followed by an expression that returns an object, which becomes the command's result. Here is its syntax:

```
return [ some_expression ]
```

If a `return` statement does not include the expression part, no result is returned when it is executed.

Let's look at some examples—the following four handlers will return the sum of the two parameters.

This is the first variation:

```
on add_up(a, b)
    return a + b
end add_up
```

This is the second variation:

```
on add_up(a, b)
    a + b
end add_up
```

This is the third variation:

```
on add_up(a, b)
    set the_sum to a + b
    return the_sum
    -- Any line beyond the return line will be ignored
end add_up
```

This is the fourth variation:

```
on add_up(a, b)
    set the_sum to a + b
end add_up
```

All four handlers will return the same result. Notice that the second and fourth handlers don't explicitly use the return statement, but the last statement contains an expression, so AppleScript just returns the result of that.

One reason to use a return statement in the middle of a handler is if the handler has done everything it needs to do by that point. For example, the conditional statement shown in Script 18–3 uses several intermediate return statements to return a final result as soon as it is available.

Script 18–3.

```
on do_math(a, b, the_operator)
    if the_operator is "+" then
        return a + b
    else if the_operator is "-" then
        return a - b
    else if the_operator is "*" then
        return a * b
    else
        error "Unknown operation."
    end if
end do_math
```

Script 18–4 gives another example of a handler that returns a result part-way through.

Script 18–4.

```
on find_position_in_list(the_list, the_value)
    repeat with i from 1 to count the_list
        if item i of the_list is the_value then return i
    end repeat
    error "Value not found."
end find_position_in_list
```

The find_position_in_list handler searches a list of items and returns the index of the given value within the list. Once you find the item you want, you don't need to keep looking. Executing a return statement on the third line immediately stops the search and returns its result. If a matching item is not found by the time the loop exits, the error statement after it throws an error to indicate that the value is not in the list.

Working with Return Values

Many application and scripting addition commands return a value as their result. AppleScript allows you to put commands inside expressions so that the value returned by the command is used in the expression. The same applies to user-defined commands: you can call a handler from inside an expression, and the result of that call will be used by the expression.

So, you've just seen how generous handlers are in returning results. What you need to do now is collect these results so you can put them to use later in the script. You can do that by assigning the result of the handler call to a variable. Here's an example of a handler that returns a result:

```
on calculate_cubic_feet(ft_tall, ft_wide, ft_long)
    return  ft_tall * ft_wide * ft_long
end calculate_cubic_feet
```

Now you'll call the handler, but you will make sure that the result it returns is assigned to a variable:

```
set this_room_volume to calculate_cubic_feet(8, 12, 10)
this_room_volume -->  960
```

For example, Script 18–5 creates a simple handler that formats a US phone number.

Script 18–5.

```
on format_phone(the_phone_number)
    return "(" & ¬
        (text 1 thru 3 of the_phone_number) & ") " & ¬
        (text 4 thru 6 of the_phone_number) & "-" & ¬
        (text 7 thru 10 of the_phone_number)
end format_phone
```

Now, create a statement that will use that handler, as shown in Script 18–6.

Script 18–6.

```
display dialog "You can reach my office at: " & format_phone("8005551234") & ¬
    " or on my cell at: " & format_phone("2125551234")
```

As you can see in Figure 18–1, the expression in the preceding statement made two calls to the format_phone handler before combining the result into one big string.

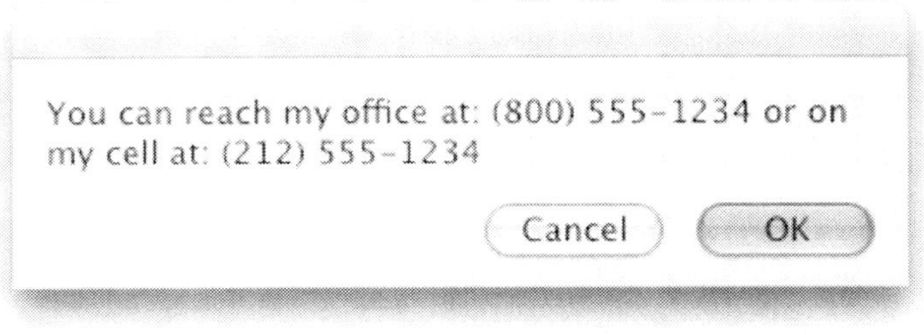

Figure 18–1. *The dialog box produced by the two scripts using the* format_phone *handler*

Can a Handler Return More Than One Result?

By the AppleScript rules, a handler may return only one object as a result. So, what can you do if a handler needs to return more than one value at the same time? The solution is to put all of the objects you want to return into a single list or record and return that.

Script 18–7 will accept a full name as a string and return the first name and last name separately. To return both values to the calling statement, you will use a record.

Script 18–7.

```
on split_name(the_name)
    set first_name to first word of the_name
    set last_name to last word of the_name
    return {forename:first_name, surname:last_name}
end split_name
set name_record to split_name("Paul Revere")
-->{forename:"Paul", surname:"Revere"}
```

In the preceding example, you returned a record as a result. Personally, I like to use lists because they make it easier to map the values to individual variables. Script 18–8 shows how you do that.

Script 18–8.

```
on split_name(the_name)
    set first_name to first word of the_name
    set last_name to last word of the_name
    return {first_name, last_name}
end split_name

set {forename, surname} to split_name("Paul Revere")
-- forename is "Paul", surname is "Revere"
```

As you can see in this example, because the handler returned a list with two items, and the list of variables you assigned the result to also has two items, each item from the returned list was assigned to its corresponding item in the handler's returned variable.

Specifying Handler Parameters

Let's now take a closer look at how you can specify handler parameters. You can pass parameters to a handler in two ways: by position and by label.

Specifying parameters by position is the simpler approach. The handler's name is followed by a pair of parentheses containing one or more parameters, as in

```
do_something(parameter1, parameter2, ...)
```

When using positional parameters, it is essential that both the command's parameters appear in the same order as the handler's; otherwise, the handler won't work correctly. Although commands with many positional parameters can be a bit hard to read, this style of parameter passing is easy to pick up and start using.

Labeled parameters are more complex but allow parameters to be passed to a handler in any order, and they make user-defined commands look more like application and scripting addition commands.

The advantage of using labeled parameters is that labels can clearly describe what each of the parameters stands for. For instance, imagine the following call to an imaginary handler:

```
split_text(file_path, "/", 1, true, true)
```

Just what do all these values stand for? The first two parameters you can probably guess, but what about the rest?

Now try this:

```
split_text of file_path ¬
    with starting_at_end and keeping_delimiters_in_result ¬
    given the_delimiter:"/", max_number_of_splits:1
```

Ah! Now you can look at the handler call and see exactly what the different parameters mean. I can't count how many times I've looked at handler calls I created in the past and had no clue what the different parameters did until I dug back into the handler definition.

Using Positional Parameters

You can start using positional parameter handlers quickly, and they don't get any more complicated than what can be described in two paragraphs.

To understand positional parameter handlers, imagine a cargo train whose cars aren't marked. The person loading the train knows in what order to organize the cars, and the person unloading is aware of the same order. If the first car is supposed to contain lumber but it contains straw instead, then your script will most likely end up trying to build a house of straw.

That's right: what's important in positional parameter handlers is the order, or *position*, of the parameters.

Definition for Positional Parameter Handlers

The following is the dictionary definition of the positional parameter handler (items shown in square brackets are optional):

```
to handler_name ( [ parameter_variable [, parameter_variable ]...] )
    -- Any local and/or global variable declarations
    -- The statement/s to execute
end handler_name
```

If you omit the handler name after the end keyword, AppleScript will automatically add this for you when compiling the script. AppleScript also allows you to start the handler with on instead of to if you want—both mean the same thing.

The corresponding command will look like this:

```
handler_name ( [ parameter_value [, parameter_value ]...] )
```

Defining and Calling Positional Parameter Handlers

You'll start this section by looking at another simple example of a positional parameter handler. The purpose of this handler will be to create a folder somewhere on the hard drive.

You'll start with the naked statements:

```
tell application "Finder"
```

```
    make new folder
end tell
```

Now, wrap it in a handler. For that you will need to give the handler a name, which is normally a user-defined identifier. In this case, call the handler create_folder. The handler name will also be used as the command name when you want to call the handler. Script 18–9 shows the basic handler definition.

Script 18–9.

```
on create_folder()
    tell application "Finder"
        make new folder
    end tell
end create_folder
```

The empty parentheses after the identifier create_folder are required. They are the currently empty home of any parameters the handler may use. To call this handler, you can use this line:

```
create_folder()
```

Note that this command has the same name as the handler, followed by the same set of empty parentheses. Create a new document in AppleScript Editor, enter the handler and the command shown previously, and then run the script. As you can see, the command causes the handler to execute, creating a new folder on the desktop.

Adding Parameters

As it stands, the handler will create a folder named untitled folder on the desktop. This isn't what you want the script to do. What you want is to be able to specify a different location to the script and a different name for it as well.

As mentioned earlier, the important part of adding these parameters to the handler is deciding on their order. Here you will specify the location followed by name. Script 18–10 shows the new handler definition and call with the addition of these two parameters.

Script 18–10.

```
on create_folder(folder_location, folder_name)
    tell application "Finder"
        make new folder at folder_location ¬
            with properties {name:folder_name}
    end tell
end create_folder
```

Then, to call the handler from anywhere in this script, you can use a command such as this:

```
create_folder(path to documents folder, "My Stuff")
```

The result of this command will be a folder named My Stuff placed in the user's Documents folder.

Using Labeled Parameters

If positional parameters are so easy to use, do everything you want, and always work the same, why complicate matters by introducing labeled parameters? Although positional parameters are recognized only based on their position, labeled parameter handlers have a unique way to display parameters. For starters, labeled parameter handlers do away with the parentheses. Instead, they use a combination of special keywords and user-defined labels to define the handler and have a command-like treatment of Boolean values for calling the handler.

To help you understand the structure of labeled parameter handlers, we'll start with the basics and then move on to more complex features later.

Definition for Positional Parameter Handlers

The following is the definition of the labeled parameter handler:

```
to handler_name [ of direct_parameter_variable ] ¬
    [ predefined_label parameter_variable ]... ¬
    [ given user_label:parameter_variable [, user_label:parameter_variable ]...]
    -- Any local and/or global variable declarations
    -- The statement/s to execute
end handler_name
```

If you omit the handler name after the end keyword, AppleScript will automatically add this for you. You can also start the handler with on instead of to, and you can use in rather than of to indicate the direct parameter (both keywords have the same meaning).

And here's the definition for a positional parameter command:

```
handler_name [ of direct_parameter_value ] ¬
    [ predefined_label parameter_value ]... ¬
    [ with user_label [, user_label ]...] ¬
    [ without user_label [, user_label ]...] ¬
    [ given user_label:parameter_value [, user_label:parameter_value ]...]
```

You can substitute the word of in the first line with the word in.

Using Predefined Parameter Labels

We'll start the labeled parameter handler discussion with the predefined handler parameter labels supplied by AppleScript. The handler parameter labels are 23 reserved words that you can use as labels to parameters. Let's look at these labels and at how you can use them.

The 23 labels are about, above, against, apart from, around, aside from, at, below, beneath, beside, between, by, for, from, instead of, into, on, onto, out of, over, since, thru (or through), and under.

You can use these labels in both the handler definition and the corresponding command in a coordinated way, which allows you to determine which objects supplied by the command are assigned to which variables in the handler definition. All 23 labels work in the same way, so choose which ones to use according to how well they fit into the context of the handler.

Say you have a handler that will return the highest number in a list of positive integers. The handler will require one parameter that is the list of integers. Out of the 23 labels, I chose the out of label to be most fitting for the handler parameter label assignment. Script 18–11 shows what my handler looks like.

Script 18–11.

```
to find_highest out of the_list
    set highest_for_now to item 1 of the_list as number
    repeat with the_item_ref in rest of the_list
        if the_item_ref as number > highest_for_now then
            set highest_for_now to the_item_ref as number
        end if
    end repeat
    return highest_for_now
end find_highest
```

To call the handler, I use the following line:

```
find_highest out of {1, 4, 12, 5}
```

As with positional parameter–based commands, the command's name identifies the handler that should be executed, and the parameter label specifies to which variable inside the handler the parameter value will be assigned. In the preceding example, you can clearly see that the value of the variable the_list in the handler will be {1, 4, 12, 5}.

Now let's try that with one more handler parameter. For this example, we'll add a top number. This time, the handler will just return a Boolean value: true if the top number is higher than the highest number in the list and false if the list contains a higher number than the top number we supply.

Script 18–12 shows the second handler definition.

Script 18–12.

```
to check_if_highest out of the_list above the_top
    repeat with the_item_ref in the_list
        if the_item_ref as number > the_top then return false
    end repeat
    return true
end check_if_highest
```

And here's the command:

```
check_if_highest out of {1, 4, 12, 5} above 16
```

Note that since the parameters are recognized by name and not by position, we could also use the following call:

```
check_if_highest above 16 out of {1, 4, 12, 5}
```

Making Up Your Own Labels

You've already seen how to make up custom names for your handlers. Now you'll look at how to define custom names for a handler's parameters as well. All this means is that if you don't find any of the 23 labels reserved by AppleScript suitable for indicating what a parameter's job is, you can choose your own, more descriptive label instead.

There are three differences, however, between using your own labels and using the predefined handler label parameters: you have to precede the use of your own labeled parameters with the word given, your parameters must be separated by a comma, and you have to separate your labels from the variables (or values in the handler call) with a colon. A bit confusing, but together we can do it!

Let's start with a simple single-parameter handler. The handler will take a string and return the reverse of it (for example, "word" will become "drow").

We need to invent three identifiers for this handler: the handler name will be reverse_string, the parameter label will be a_string, and the name of the actual variable used in the handler will be string_to_reverse.

Script 18–13 shows how the handler definition will look.

Script 18–13.

```
to reverse_string given a_string:string_to_reverse
    set text item delimiters to ""
    return (reverse of (characters of string_to_reverse)) as text
end reverse_string
```

This really isn't as bad as it seems. You already know about the handler identifier and the parameter variable. All we did was add our own label to the parameter.

Here is the command for that handler:

```
reverse_string given a_string:"play time"
--> result: "emit yalp"
```

Now let's try it with two parameters. The following handler will calculate the area of a rectangle. The parameter labels will be width and height. Here you go:

```
to calculate_rectangle_area given width:w, height:h
    return w * h
end get_the_area
```

When you use a calculate_rectangle_area command in your code, the parameter labels make it easy to see what the values stand for:

```
calculate_rectangle_area given width:12, height:5
```

Calling Handlers with Boolean Parameters

Another unique feature of the labeled parameter handlers is the ability to specify Boolean values, like you would in any other AppleScript command, using the with and without labels.

As an example, you will create a handler that trims tabs and spaces from strings. As for parameters, you will have four Boolean parameters and one direct parameter.

The direct parameter is the first parameter used in a handler definition. The label of the direct parameter is either in or of, and it always has to be the first parameter. The direct parameter will be the actual string you want to trim white text from. The four Boolean parameters will be from_front, from_back, trimming_spaces, and trimming_tabs. You can assume that for the handler to do anything, either one of the first pair of parameters and either one of the second pair of parameters must be set to true, but that's beside the point.

Now inspect the handler. Mainly pay attention to the first line in the definition and to the corresponding command. Script 18–14 shows the handler definition.

Script 18–14.

```
to trim_characters of the_text ¬
    given from_front:f, from_back:b, trimming_spaces:s, trimming_tabs:t
  -- Assemble a list of characters to trim
  set characters_to_trim to {}
  if s then set end of characters_to_trim to space
  if t then set end of characters_to_trim to tab
  -- Trim from the start of the text
  if f then
    repeat while character 1 of the_text is in characters_to_trim
      if length of the_text is 1 then
        return ""
      else
        set the_text to text 2 thru -1 of the_text
      end if
    end repeat
  end if
  -- Trim from the end of the text
  if b then
    repeat while character -1 of the_text is in characters_to_trim
      if length of the_text is 1 then
        return ""
      else
        set the_text to text 1 thru -2 of the_text
      end if
    end repeat
  end if
  return the_text
end trim_characters
```

Notice that this is a normal labeled parameter definition. You have the labels marking the four labeled parameters, and you're ready to call the handler. In the command, you won't supply values to the parameters in the fashion you learned earlier, which would go something like this:

```
trim_characters of the_text given ¬
    from_front:true, from_back:true, trimming_spaces:true, trimming_tabs:false
```

Instead, you will treat the Boolean parameters like you would treat them in application and scripting addition commands—by using the with and without keywords:

```
trim_characters of the_text ¬
    with from_front, from_back, trimming_spaces and trimming_tabs
```

> **TIP:** If you write the command in the former style, AppleScript will automatically reformat it to use the latter style when you compile it.

In the preceding call, all four Boolean parameters received a true value. In the call that follows, you will assign a false value to the from_front and trimming_tabs parameters:

```
trim_characters of the_text ¬
    with from_back and trimming_spaces without from_front and trimming_tabs
```

Introducing Recursion

Recursion is when a handler calls itself. Technically it means that the handler definition contains the handler call. The following example contains an example of a handler that will call itself an infinite number of times:

```
do_something()

on do_something()
    display dialog "Doing something now..."
    do_something()
end do_something
```

Recursion doesn't necessarily mean that the handler will call itself infinitely. In most cases, the handler calling itself will be subject to a condition.

One thing that recursion is used for is to process files or folders nested in a folder hierarchy. In this case, the script starts by calling the handler and passing the top folder as a parameter. The handler gets the contents of the folder and processes each item; if the item is a folder, the handler then calls itself and passes that folder as the parameter's value.

The recursive handler in Script 18–15 takes an alias to a folder and builds up a string containing the names of all the nested subfolders, each one indented according to its level in the folder hierarchy.

Script 18–15.

```
show_folder_hierarchy(choose folder, "")

on show_folder_hierarchy(the_folder, the_indent)
    -- Process this folder
    tell application "Finder"
        set the_result to the_indent & name of the_folder & return
    end tell
    -- Process each sub-folder in turn
    tell application "Finder"
        repeat with sub_folder_ref in (get every folder of the_folder)
            set the_result to the_result & ¬
                my show_folder_hierarchy(contents of sub_folder_ref, the_indent & tab)
        end repeat
```

```
    end tell
    return the_result
end show_folder_hierarchy
```

You can find more examples of recursive handlers dealing with files and folders in Chapter 20.

Using the *run* Handler in Scripts

The run handler contains all the statements that will be executed when you run the script. A script can have only one run handler at most, but some scripts may have no run handler at all.

I've Never Seen No *run* Handler!

You may be wondering why you already wrote a bunch of scripts, but none of them has anything that looks like a run handler. This is because the run handler doesn't have to be explicitly defined. If a script doesn't contain an explicit run handler, then AppleScript assumes the script has an implicit run handler instead. An implicit run handler consists of all the statements found at the top level of the script, except for any property declarations, named script object definitions, and other handler definitions.

The two script shown in Figures 18–2 and 18–3 are functionally the same; it's just that the one shown in Figure 18–2 has an implicit run handler, whereas in the one shown in Figure 18–3, the run handler is explicitly declared.

Figure 18–2. *The script has a* run *handler, but it is implied. The entire script shown is part of this* run *handler.*

Figure 18–3. *The* run *handler is explicitly written out.*

Now, try this:

```
display dialog "You can run..."
on run
    display dialog "...but you can't compile!"
end run
```

Why won't this script compile? The first display dialog command is inside the implied run handler, and the second display dialog command is in the explicit run handler. Two run handlers don't get along.

When Should You Make the *run* Handler Explicit?

Although in many situations, leaving the run handler implicit (not actually wrapping the top-level statements with on run ... end run) is okay, sometimes you'll want to explicitly identify the run handler.

The one time when you are required to specify the run handler explicitly is when you want to pass parameters to it, like in the following script:

```
on run {value1, value2, etc...}
    ...
end run
```

If you save the preceding script as a plain text or script file, you can load and run it again later using Standard Additions' run script command, like this:

```
run script alias "path:to:script" with parameters {value1, value2, etc...}
```

Another reason you may want to make the run handler explicit is to improve readability, particularly when the script can start running at more than one point. For instance, if the script is a droplet application, it will have another unique handler, called the open handler. This handler will be executed when a file is dropped on the script application. Although for the most part the user will utilize the script by dropping a file on it, you may want to have some code in the run handler that will execute if someone double-clicks the droplet application. Making both handlers explicit helps to emphasize that the script could start with either one.

Script 18–16 defines both the run handler and the open handler in the same script. If you drop a file on the script application, it will show you the file's type, as defined in the open handler, and if you double-click the script application, you will get instructions, as defined in the run handler.

Script 18–16.

```
on open list_of_aliases
    set the_alias to item 1 of list_of_aliases
    tell application "System Events"
        set item_type to type identifier of the_alias
    end tell
    display alert "You dropped a file of type \"" & item_type & "\""
end open

on run
    display alert "Drop something on me and I'll tell you what type it is!"
end run
```

The next section discusses both of these handlers in more detail.

Working with Handlers in Applets

So far you have looked at normal applets and at droplet applets that perform a single run or open event and quit when done. AppleScript Editor also allows you to save applets in stay-open form so they don't quit automatically as soon as they finish handling that first event. Instead, they become idle and wait around until you explicitly quit them, allowing them to handle additional events in the meantime.

Using the Standard Event Handlers

When we talk about commands and handlers, we normally think of commands as compulsory demands that we send to applications or scripts to handle. For some uses, however, it helps to think in slightly different terms. As you've seen in previous chapters, one way you can deploy your scripts is by saving them as "applets," mini-applications created by AppleScript Editor that you double-click in the Finder to run.

In the simplest form, an applet will have a single run handler, which may be implicit or explicit. Some applets may have an open handler, allowing them to receive and process dropped files or folders. To help us think about the different role these handlers play in responding to external, rater than internal, requests, we often refer to them as *event* handlers. The mechanics are exactly the same, mind you; only the intent is different. You'll find the same pattern appears in other situations where scripts respond to external triggers—for example, in Mail rule scripts—but for now, we'll just look at the events sent to applet scripts.

Although a normal script applet or droplet can use only the run/open and quit handlers, the stay-open applet can have two more: reopen and idle. It can also have any number of user-defined handlers that can be called from other scripts.

Let's look at a brief description of all these event handlers before getting into some more details regarding the idle handler and its function. The following handlers aren't ones that your script applet's script would normally call of its own accord. (The only exception might be the quit handler, which will be executed any time another handler sends the applet a quit command.) Instead, they respond automatically to natural events in the life of a script applet. The code inside the event handlers will execute when the specific event occurs.

Any events that you aren't interested in, you can simply ignore—after all, they are intended as polite notifications of events you might want to know about, not compulsory demands for action.

The *run* Event Handler

The run event handler is called once when an applet is launched by double-clicking it in the Finder or by sending it a run command from another script. It won't be called again automatically while the script is running (although other scripts can call it as often as they like).

In a regular applet, the run handler is used to perform all of the applet's duties—once it is done, the applet automatically quits.

In a stay-open applet, most of the work normally is done in other handlers, but the run handler may still be used to initialize values, give instructions, or do anything else the applet has to do once. After the run handler has completed, the idle handler (if one exists) will be called. If your stay-open applet is also a droplet, then any initialization has to happen in a separate handler; otherwise, the same initialization code will repeat in the run handler and in the open handler. Script 18–17 shows the basic code responsible for initialization in a stay-open droplet.

Script 18–17.

```
property is_initialized : false

to initialize()
   if not is_initialized then
      set is_initialized to true
      -- Do initialization here...
   end if
end initialize

on run
   initialize()
```

```
end run

on open dropped_items
    initialize()
    -- Process dropped items here...
end open

on idle
    -- Perform any periodic tasks here...
    return 60 -- Return number of seconds until the next idle call
end idle

on quit
    continue quit
    set is_initialized to false
end quit
```

The *open* Event Handler

If a droplet is launched by dragging files or folders onto it or by sending it an open command from another script, its open handler will be executed instead of its run handler.

A regular droplet will automatically quit as soon as the open handler is done. Saving the droplet as stay-open allows it to accept additional drag-and-drops without quitting each time. After the open handler has finished handling this initial event, the idle handler (if one exists) will be called. Additional files and folders can be dropped onto an already-running droplet; this will cause its open handler to execute again, allowing the new items to be processed.

The *reopen* Event Handler

The reopen event handler will be called when an already-running script applet is relaunched by clicking its Dock icon or by double-clicking it in the Finder again.

The *quit* Event Handler

The quit event handler is called when the user chooses Quit from the **File** menu of the script applet's menu or when the scripter sends a quit command either from the same script or from another script.

If you include a quit event handler in your applet, you are in effect intercepting the normal quit command that tells the applet to stop running. That means the applet will not automatically quit; instead, it will do whatever your script asks it to do. To instruct the applet to stop running, your quit handler needs to execute a continue quit statement. This causes a fresh quit command to be passed to the applet itself.

The following quit event handler asks the user whether they're sure they want to quit, and it quits only if the answer is yes:

```
on quit
    display dialog "Are you sure you want to quit?" buttons {"No", "Yes"}
```

```
    if button returned of result is "Yes" then
        continue quit
        display alert "Daisy, Daisy..." giving up after 5
    end if
end quit
```

In the preceding example, if the user tries to quit the applet but then clicks the No button, the applet will remain open.

If the user clicks Yes, the continue quit statement triggers the applet's built-in quit handler—although this does not stop the application immediately, as you might expect. Instead, the built-in quit handler merely instructs the applet to shut down once the script has finished whatever it is currently doing—in this case, executing the rest of your custom quit handler.

The idle Event Handler

The idle event handler is really where most of the action happens. As you saw earlier, the run handler executes once at the start, the quit event handler executes once at the end, and the reopen handler is really a "just-in-case" handler.

The idle event, however, happens repeatedly. Does that mean the idle handler acts like a huge repeat loop? Well, sort of. The idle event handler works a bit like a repeat loop with a built-in delay.

You can tell the applet to wait for a given period of time before it runs the idle handler again. To do this, use the return statement followed by the number of seconds you want to wait before the next idle event. For instance, the following script, if saved as a stay-open applet, will remind you to take a break every 15 minutes:

```
on idle
    activate
    display dialog "Time to stretch!" giving up after 30
    return (15 * minutes)
end idle
```

In the preceding script, the idle event handler will be executed for the first time as soon as the script has finished executing its run handler. The idle handler will bring the applet to the front and display the "Time to stretch!" dialog box. On returning, it will instruct the script applet to invoke the idle event handler again when 15 minutes have passed.

> **NOTE:** The big advantage of using an idle handler over a repeat statement with a delay command is that when the applet is not executing the idle handler, it is free to respond to menu input and other events such as open and quit. If you use a never-ending repeat loop in your run handler, the applet will never have a chance to respond to other events, and the only way to quit it is by pressing Cmd+period (Cmd+.) or by force quitting.

Using User-Defined Handlers from Other Scripts

Another cool thing about stay-open scripts is that you can call their handlers from an outside script while they are running. In fact, the process of sending a command to a stay-open applet is no different from sending a command to a regular scriptable application, although the applet's handler names will usually be AppleScript identifiers rather than dictionary-defined keywords.

Let's try this now. First, save Script 18–18 as a stay-open applet named My Clock.

Script 18–18.

```
on tell_time()
    display dialog (time string of (current date))
end tell
```

Next, create a new AppleScript Editor document and type in the code shown in Script 18–19.

Script 18–19.

```
tell application "My Clock"
    activate
    tell_time()
end tell
```

When you run this script, it sends an activate command to the My Clock applet, causing it to come to the front. This is followed by a tell_time command, which causes the applet to execute its tell_time handler, displaying the current time to the user.

Tips for Designing and Using Handlers

The following few sections contain tips for creating and using handlers. Handlers can be a boon for efficient script writing, and with the right organization, you will be able to spend more time on the function of the script and less time on messing with syntax.

Organizing Code

One of the brilliant factors handlers add to your scripts is organization. They allow you to tell the story of your script in your language, rather than in a programming language.

You know those people who tell a story about something they did but feel compelled to go into every last detail, until you lose the whole story? Well, without handlers, AppleScript can be like that too. As you read through a script and try to understand it, you don't want to be bothered with the 50 lines of script that made a certain function of the script work. What you want is to quickly get a general idea of the script's organization, what happens in what order, and the basic branching that makes up the script.

For instance, a medium-sized script might contain several dozen conditional blocks and repeat loops, out of which only a few actually play a key role in the overall structure of the script. These statements should be included in the main run handler, making it obvious that they are in overall charge of the script's execution. Less important statements should be tucked away in their own handlers to avoid cluttering up the main body of the script and to make these minor statements easy to find if you do need to check on a specific detail.

So, how do you organize a script with handlers? You think logically as you write the script. You also periodically read the script back and pretend it's a story you're telling someone. If it sounds a bit heavy on the details, you may want to corral the code that has that extra detail you don't want to have in the main body of the script and turn it into a handler. This way, your script becomes more like an easy-to-understand story, and the details are buried in handlers.

Reusing Code

Another big function of handlers, if not the biggest one, is reusing code. The idea is that a handler is a closed nugget of code that, given the expected parameters, will perform reliably and return the expected result. This won't be the same result every time, but it will be a result within the expected range.

Once you have such a handler, even if it has been written for a specific purpose, you may find that you can reuse it elsewhere in the same script and in other scripts too. Another way to instantly know that a piece of a script will make a good handler is if you start copying chunks of script from one part of the script to another. If the same code, or similarly structured code, exists in more than one part of the script, you may want to consider turning it into a handler.

Thinking Ahead

When creating handlers, it is good to consider not only the script you're working on right now but the wider scope of scripts you've created and are likely to create. Think about making your handlers as general-purpose as possible. For instance, if your script needs a handler that takes a list of files as a parameter and returns a new list containing only the names of the Microsoft Word documents from the original list, try to make it more general than that. Rather than hard-code the file type within the handler, pass this information to it as a second parameter. This handler focuses on the process of filtering files by type rather than on a script-specific need such as filtering Word documents.

Thinking Small

Make your handlers as small as you can (while keeping them longer than their own calls). Small, generic handlers are much easier to understand than big, complicated ones that try to do lots of different things at once. They're also much easier to debug because you can often test them in isolation, and they're easier to reuse within the same script or even in other scripts.

What I personally use is a set of about 15 handler library files that has hundreds of handlers dealing with different subjects. Some of the handlers are long, but most have fewer than ten lines of script. As a result, most of my scripts consist of handler calls instead of commands. I name my handlers deliberately and descriptively so that I can easily identify what the script is doing at any given time, such as `Excel handler library.scpt`, `Text manipulation handler library.scpt`, and so on.

Reorganizing Existing Code

One way that handlers are created in your script is that a portion of your script "evolves" into a handler. It happens in the process of writing a script. You suddenly realize that the chunk of script you just created can be its own little thing, responsible for carrying out a single, well-defined task. You may be able to use it somewhere else in the script or in other scripts. Or maybe you just figured that it takes too much space in the body of the script, and you want to move it out of the way where it won't be so distracting.

What you need to do first is identify all the variables on which this part of the script depends. Some variables may be created inside the part you're trying to move, so you don't have to worry about them for the start. The rest will need their values to be passed into the handler, usually as parameters.

After you have some idea of which variables you will need to pass as parameters, you can move the entire part of the script to your handler area and wrap it in an `on ...` end handler wrapper.

This would also be a good time to decide what values the handler call should return. If the portion of the script you're porting into a handler is a single value, you can return that value directly. However, if you need to return more than one value, you will need to wrap them up in a list (or record) before returning them.

In the following example, you will look at extracting part of a larger script into its own handler. The bit you're interested in is used to calculate the age in days of a given file, which is just the sort of nice, well-defined, logical task that can be easily made into a user-defined command.

Script 18–20 shows the script.

Script 18–20.

```
-- Some statements here...
set the_file to choose file
-- Some more statements here...
set file_properties to info for the_file
set file_creation_date to creation date of file_properties
set file_age_in_seconds to (current date) - file_creation_date
set days_old to file_age_in_seconds div days
-- Yet more statements that use the days_old variable here...
```

By looking at the script, you can identify that the part you want to convert into a handler uses a few variables but requires only one variable to start, which is the variable the_file.

The handler will return the value of the days_old variable to the script, which can then assign it to a days_old variable of its own.

It's important to check whether the other variables used in that part of the script (such as file_age_in_seconds, file_creation_date, and so on) are used later in the script. If they are, the handler will need to return their values as well. If that seems a clumsy solution, however, it may be that your handler is trying to do too many different jobs by itself, in which case you should reconsider which parts of the code should stay in this handler and which should go elsewhere.

For example, if file_age_in_seconds is also used later, then it would probably be best to make a handler named get_file_age_in_seconds and leave the code that uses days_old to perform that final division itself. If file_creation_date is used elsewhere, then you should probably think about obtaining the file's creation date as a separate task and then passing it to a handler called calculate_age_in_days that takes a date value as its parameter.

Figuring out the best ways to divide code into separate handlers can be hard at first, but you'll get better and better at it with practice. A good tip is to make a copy of your original script and experiment on that. That way, if you like what you come up with, you can keep it; if not, you can simply throw it away, and no harm has been done in trying.

Script 18–21 shows the new part of the script and the handler definition.

Script 18–21.

```
-- Some statements here...
set the_file to choose file
-- Some more statements here...
set days_old to get_file_age_in_days(the_file)
-- Yet more statements that use the days_old variable here...

on get_file_age_in_days(the_file)
  set file_properties to info for the_file
  set file_creation_date to creation date of file_properties
  set file_age_in_seconds to (current date) - file_creation_date
  set days_old to file_age_in_seconds div days
  return days_old
end get_file_age_in_days
```

Example Project: A Reusable Associative List

While AppleScript has several very useful object classes already built in, there may be times when you wish it would provide more.

For example, imagine you have the names and e-mail addresses for a number of people, and you need a quick way to look up the e-mail address for a particular person according to his name. Obviously, you'll need some way to store these strings in your script—but how? An AppleScript list will let you store multiple items, but you can only look up those items by their numerical index, or position, within the list. An AppleScript record won't help either: while it allows you to associate a name with a value, the name itself must be an AppleScript keyword or identifier defined when the script is compiled, which is no use when your keys are arbitrary strings.

In Chapter 10 we developed a script to measure how often each word appears in a given piece of text. At the heart of this script was a simple data structure that we defined ourselves by using a combination of an AppleScript list and records. This structure, called an *associative list*, allowed us to look up the number of times a word appeared by using the word string itself as the key.

This is such a useful feature that many languages already provide it as a built-in class: for example, the Mac's Objective-C Cocoa frameworks provide an NSDictionary class, while the popular Ruby scripting language includes a Hash class. AppleScript, unfortunately, does not; however, just because associative lists aren't a standard feature doesn't stop us from filling that gap by building our own.

Just as we can use user-defined handlers to provide our own commands, we can also use AppleScript's built-in object classes to assemble new kinds of objects tailored to our specific needs. For this project, we will stick to using lists and records, which you are already familiar with. In the next chapter, we will look at how you can take the design one step further by involving script objects as well.

Designing the Associative List

Our goal is to create a general-purpose associative list that can be used in a wide range of situations. Because we want our associative list code to be portable, reliable, and easy to use, we don't want users fiddling directly with the internal makeup of the data structure. So we will define a set of handlers that will perform all of the operations that users will need: getting values, setting values, and so on.

There are various ways we can implement a key-value based data structure, each with benefits and limitations. For this, we'll use the simplest approach, which is a straight list of records. Each record will have two properties, the_key and the_value, so a typical associative list will have a structure like this:

```
{{the_key:"some key", the_value:"some value"}, ¬
 {the_key:"another key", the_value:"another value"}, ...}
```

Both the key and value properties can hold any object—the only rule is that each key in an associative list must be unique. Because users will only access the associative list using the commands we provide, we can easily enforce that rule in our handlers, preventing the user from accidentally messing up the data.

To look up values, our handlers will loop over the list until they find a record with the key we've asked for. This approach won't be particularly efficient for large numbers of items: if the key the user wants happens to be in the last record of a 10,000-item list, it will take the handlers a while to go through the other 9,999 items looking for it! For smaller collections, it should be adequate, however.

Next, we'll decide what commands to provide.

First off, users will obviously require a pair of commands for getting and setting items, which we'll call get_associative_item and set_associative_item. (Including the word associative in the names makes it obvious that these commands are used to manipulate associative lists in particular, and not other kinds of values.)

Let's also add a command for counting the number of entries, `count_associative_items`. Since our associative list is based on a regular list, we could just use AppleScript's built-in `count` command, but if we ever wanted to redesign the data structure—for example, to store the keys and values in separate lists—then that would cause problems because the standard `count` command would no longer return the correct value.

There are other commands that would also be handy to have, including `delete_associative_item`, `does_associative_item_exist`, `get_keys_of_all_associative_items`, and `get_values_of_all_associative_items`. This chapter will only cover the first of these commands, `delete_associative_item`, but once you understand the basic principles, you can easily implement the others yourself.

Lastly, it might be a good idea to provide a `make_associative_list` command for making a new associative list. In our current design, all this will do is return an empty list, which seems a bit trivial. Once again, though, it does allow us to redesign our data structure in the future without needing users to rework their existing code. As you become more experienced, you will be able to judge for yourself how much functionality is really required and how much is just overkill, but for this exercise let's play it safe and cover all the bases.

Writing the Essential Handlers

Let's start by implementing the simplest command, which is also the one that users will call first: `make_associative_list`. Here is the handler definition for it:

```
on make_associative_list()
    (* Make a new associative list that stores values using any objects as keys.

        Result: an associative list

        Note: Users should not directly manipulate the contents of the returned
        object. Instead, use the handlers provided to work with it safely.
    *)
    return {}
end make_associative_list
```

As you can see, the code itself is trivial, but using a handler will help to protect the user against any future changes. Also, as this code is intended to be used elsewhere, we've added a comment to the start of the handler indicating how it should be used.

Here is how the user will create a new associative list object:

```
set my_assoc_list to make_associative_list()
```

The next step is to write the handlers that will get and set values. The code for looking up items will consist of a repeat loop that compares the value of each record's the_key property in turn until it finds a match or runs out of records. Since the process of looking up records is the same whether we're getting or setting them, let's avoid a bit of unnecessary code duplication by putting this logic into a shared handler that will only be used by our other handlers:

```
on find_record_for_key(the_assoc_list, the_key)
    (* This is a private handler. Users should not use it directly. *)
    repeat with record_ref in the_assoc_list
        if the_key of record_ref = the_key then return record_ref
    end repeat
    return missing value -- The key wasn't found
end find_record_for_key
```

If a matching record is found, the find_record_for_key handler returns the reference to it so that the calling handler can manipulate it. Otherwise it returns missing value so that the calling handler knows that it wasn't found and can decide what to do next.

Next, let's implement the get_associative_item handler:

```
on get_associative_item(the_assoc_list, the_key)
    (*
        Get the value for the given key in an associative list.

        the_assoc_list : associative list
        the_key : anything -- the key to search for
        Result : anything -- the value, if found

        Note: Raises error -1728 if the key isn't found.
    *)
    set record_ref to find_record_for_key(the_assoc_list, the_key)
    if record_ref = missing value then
        error "The key wasn't found." number -1728 from the_key
    end if
    return the_value of record_ref
end get_associative_item
```

This handler first uses our private find_record_for_key handler to look up a record for the given key. It then uses a conditional block to check whether a record was found. If one was found, the handler extracts the value from that record and returns it; otherwise, it throws a clear error to let the user know that the item wasn't found. Since AppleScript already defines a standard error number, -1728, for "Can't get..." errors, we will use it here for consistency, though you can always define your own custom codes if you need to. To help the user figure out exactly why the error occurred, we also supply the key value that caused the problem.

At this point we only need one more handler to complete the core functionality. The set_associative_item handler has a slightly more complicated job. When it is called, it must first check whether a record already exists for that key. If it does, it should change the record's the_value property to the new value given by the user. Otherwise, it should create a new record from scratch and add it to the end of the associative list.

Here is the code:

```
on set_associative_item(the_assoc_list, the_key, the_value)
    (*
        Set the value for the given key in an associative list.

        the_assoc_list : associative list
```

```
        the_key : anything -- the key to use
        the_value : anything -- the new value
    *)
    set record_ref to find_record_for_key(the_assoc_list, the_key)
    if record_ref = missing value then
        set end of the_assoc_list to ¬
            {the_key:the_key, the_value:the_value}
    else
        set the_value of record_ref to the_value
    end if
    return -- No return value; the handler modifies the existing associative list.
end set_associative_item
```

Now that we've created the three essential commands, let's test our associative list. First, we'll create a new associative list object and add some entries to it:

```
set friends_ages to make_associative_list()
set_associative_item(friends_ages, "Bob", 33)
set_associative_item(friends_ages, "Jan", 27)
set_associative_item(friends_ages, "Sam", 29)
set_associative_item(friends_ages, "Bob", 35)
```

Just to be sure it's working so far, let's take a quick peek:

```
friends_ages
--> {{the_key:"Bob", the_value:35},
     {the_key:"Jan", the_value:27},
     {the_key:"Sam", the_value:29}}
```

As you can see, we've added three unique records for three unique keys: "Bob", "Jan", and "Sam". Also, notice that the value of the "Bob" entry is now 35: first we set it to 33, and then we updated it later to 35, changing the contents of the existing "Bob" record in situ.

Next, let's check that we can retrieve values correctly:

```
get_associative_item(friends_ages, "Jan")
--> 27
```

```
get_associative_item(friends_ages, "Bob")
--> 35
```

And, of course, we can't forget to check that the handler behaves correctly when a nonexistent key is used:

```
get_associative_item(friends_ages, "Frank")
--> Error: The key wasn't found.
```

So far, so good, but have we forgotten anything? As the protectors of our associative list's internal structure, it is up to our handlers to guard against any possible uses that might "corrupt" its contents. As it turns out, we have overlooked something: because our lookup code relies on comparing objects for equality, it is susceptible to the influences of considering/ignoring statements when comparing strings.

Try the following experiment to see what I mean:

```
set friends_ages to make_associative_list()
ignoring case -- The default
```

```
        set_associative_item(friends_ages, "Bob", 33)
    end ignoring
considering case
        set_associative_item(friends_ages, "BOB", 35)
    end considering

friends_ages
--> {{the_key:"Bob", the_value:33}, ..., {the_key:"BOB", the_value:35}}
```

Uh-oh. Now our associative list contains two keys that may or may not be equal at any time, depending on the user's current considering/ignoring settings whenever they get or set a value. This could cause all sorts of unexpected problems for unwary users, so let's avoid the possibility by ensuring our associative list keys are always insensitive to case but sensitive to everything else.

Since all of our lookup code is in the find_record_for_key handler, we just need to add a considering/ignoring statement to that:

```
on find_record_for_key(the_assoc_list, the_key)
    (* This is a private handler. Users should not use it directly. *)
    considering diacriticals, hyphens, punctuation and white space but ignoring case
            repeat with record_ref in the_assoc_list
                if the_key of record_ref = the_key then return record_ref
            end repeat
    end considering
    return missing value -- The key wasn't found
end find_record_for_key
```

Run the test script again, and check that there is only a single "Bob" entry in it now.

Writing the Extra Handlers

At this point, you may have all of the functionality you actually need for your current projects, in which case you probably shouldn't worry about creating any more commands for now—after all, time spent writing code you won't use is time you could have spent on other, more pressing tasks. However, as this is a teaching exercise, we'll go ahead and implement our other, nonessential commands as well. Let's start with count_associative_items:

```
on count_associative_items(the_assoc_list)
    (*
        Return the number of items in an associative list.

        the_assoc_list : associative list
        Result : integer
    *)
    return count the_assoc_list
end set_associative_item
```

As you can see, the code for this handler is really trivial, but remember: the point here is to insulate the user's code against any future changes we might make to our associative list code.

Finally, let's create the `delete_associative_item` command. The goal here is to find a matching record and remove it completely from the list. Unfortunately, as you may recall from Chapter 10, AppleScript lists lack a proper "delete" feature, so the only option is to create a new list containing only the items you want from the old one. Since we know our associative list contains only records, we can do this bit easily enough: just replace the unwanted record with `missing value`, and then ask the list for only its `record` elements, as this test code demonstrates:

```
set test_list to {{the_key:"Bob", the_value:33}, {the_key:"Jan", the_value:27}}
set item 1 of test_list to missing value
get every record of test_list
--> {{the_key:"Jan", the_value:27}}
```

At this point it looks like our `delete_associative_item` command now has to return a new associative list object, rather than modify the existing one as the `set_associative_item` command does. This sort of inconsistent behavior could easily trip up users who expect all the commands to work in the same way, so it is hardly ideal. Let's go ahead and implement it that way for now, while we think of other ways to protect the user's code from our own private problems:

```
on delete_associative_item(the_assoc_list, the_key)
   (*
      Delete the value for the given key.

      the_assoc_list : associative list
      the_key : anything -- the key to delete
      Result : associative list

      Caution: Unlike the set_associative_item command, this command returns a new
      associative list object instead of modifying the existing one!
   *)
   set new_assoc_list to every item of the_assoc_list
   set record_ref to find_record_for_key(new_assoc_list, the_key)
   if record_ref is missing value then
      error "The key wasn't found." number -1728 from the_key
   end if
   set contents of record_ref to missing value
   return every record of new_assoc_list
end delete_associative_item
```

Don't forget to test it, of course:

```
set friends_ages to delete_associative_item(friends_ages, "Bob")
--> {{the_key:"Jan", the_value:27}, {the_key:"Sam", the_value:29}}
```

Okay, it's not the perfect design, but it does what it claims to—I've even added a warning to the handler's comment to let users know there's a catch.

Revising the Design

Let's say we've been successfully using the "get" and "set" commands for several months now, and the "delete" command is a new feature we're in the process of adding. At this point, we could just call it a day and move on to something else, but I just know this particular inconsistency is going to catch me out in the future. It would be better to deal with it now—but what to do?

The solution, as it happens, lies with our original design mantra: insulate the user's code from ours. Clearly, we didn't separate them enough: we gave the user's code a bare list object to hold, but now we want to hide that list away from them so that we can manipulate it in private and even replace it completely when we need to. To do this, we will need to hide the original list within another object—so let's wrap it up in a new, formal "associative list" record where it will be safe.

Originally, our `make_associative_list` handler returned a simple list, so let's start by changing that:

```
on make_associative_list()
    (* Make a new associative list that stores values using any objects as keys.

        Result: an associative list

        Note: Users should not directly manipulate the contents of the returned
        object. Instead, use the handlers provided to work with it safely.
    *)
    return {class:"associative list", the_items:{}}
end make_associative_list
```

Next, we'll need to go through all of our other handlers, updating them where needed so that they know how to deal with the modified structure. First, modify the `find_record_for_key` handler so that it gets the actual list from the new record's `the_items` property:

```
on find_record_for_key(the_assoc_list, the_key)
    (* This is a private handler. Users should not use it directly. *)
    considering diacriticals, hyphens, punctuation and white space but ignoring case
        repeat with record_ref in the_items of the_assoc_list
            if the_key of record_ref = the_key then return record_ref
        end repeat
    end considering
    return missing value -- The key wasn't found
end find_record_for_key
```

Next, make sure the `set_associative_item` handler knows where to insert new records now:

```
on set_associative_item(the_assoc_list, the_key, the_value)
    (*
        Set the value for the given key in an associative list.

        the_assoc_list : associative list
        the_key : anything -- the key to use
        the_value : anything -- the new value
    *)
    set record_ref to find_record_for_key(the_assoc_list, the_key)
    if record_ref = missing value then
        set end of the_items of the_assoc_list to ¬
            {the_key:the_key, the_value:the_value}
    else
        set the_value of record_ref to the_value
```

```
    end if
    return -- No return value; the handler modifies the existing associative list.
end set_associative_item
```

A quick check of the get_associative_item handler shows that no alterations are needed there. However, we will need to change the count_associative_items handler:

```
on count_associative_items(the_assoc_list)
    (*
        Return the number of items in an associative list.

        the_assoc_list : associative list
        Result : integer
    *)
    return count the_items of the_assoc_list
end set_associative_item
```

(I'll bet you're glad now that you didn't cut any corners by using the built-in count command before!)

Lastly, let's redesign our delete_value_from_key handler before it goes into production use, where it would cause more disruption to change later on:

```
on delete_associative_item(the_assoc_list, the_key)
    (*
        Delete the value for the given key.

        the_assoc_list : associative list
        the_key : anything -- the key to delete
    *)
    set record_ref to find_record_for_key(the_assoc_list, the_key)
    if record_ref is missing value then
        error "The key wasn't found." number -1728 from the_key
    end if
    set contents of record_ref to missing value
    set the_items of the_assoc_list to every record of the_items of the_assoc_list
    return -- No return value; the handler modifies the existing associative list.
end delete_associative_item
```

Remember to go back and retest all of your handlers when you're done, just to make sure you haven't missed anything.

Conclusion

As you may have noticed, this project is a bit different from the others you have done so far. Whereas previous projects have concerned themselves with solving specific problems, generally by the shortest possible path, this project is concerned with solving a general problem that many AppleScripters will run into more than once in their scripting careers: how to store and retrieve values using other, arbitrary objects as keys. While there are other options that may work as well, or perhaps better, in some situations—for example, using Mac OS X's hidden Database Events application—sometimes the best solution is one written purely in AppleScript (for example, storing lists, records, and application references within AppleScript is easier than storing them in external applications or scripting additions). This project has created a simple but reliable associative list object that you can use in any script that needs to store values using strings or other objects as keys. It won't win any prizes for speed (although, as we'll discuss in later chapters, there are ways to get better performance out of it if needed), but for modest-sized tasks, it should be quite adequate.

Another reason for this project was to show you how handlers can be used to structure a particular solution in a way that makes it easy for other code to use *and* easy for you to modify later on without causing major disruption elsewhere. This is a powerful design technique, known in technical circles as *abstraction*, or "hiding the details from everyone who doesn't need to know them."

As you've seen, not only does hiding the internal workings of our associative list objects behind a set of simple commands—set_associative_item, get_associative_item, and so forth—make them easy for other scripts to use, it also lets us make some pretty big changes to our associative list implementation without needing to make serious changes to all those other scripts that already use it. Following our redesign of the associative list structure, what was originally a list object is now a record—which is about as different from a list as you can get. Yet, except for the change in how the delete_associative_item handler works (which, hopefully, was made before putting it into general use), none of these alterations should affect *any* of the scripts using this code!

The only exception would be if other scripts were messing around with the internal structure of our associative lists. However, because we told users not to do that, they'll have nobody to blame but themselves if their code breaks—if additional associative list features are needed, they should be implemented as new handlers in our existing library of associative list commands.

Depending on the size and complexity of your scripts, you may or may not ever need to think about code in this way. Yet even if most of your scripts are small in size, there may be some areas where you can tuck some details out of the way; for example, hiding the text item delimiter-based code used to find and replace text behind a simple-to-use find_and_replace command.

We will continue discussing this and other handy design techniques in the next chapter, and in Chapter 29.

Summary

In this chapter we looked at how to define our own custom commands by adding handlers to our scripts.

You learned how to pass objects into handlers as parameters, and how to return them as results. We looked at how parameters can be specified either by position, which is the simplest approach, or by label, which allows user-defined commands to use a syntax similar to that used by scriptable application and scripting addition commands, making it easier to see the meaning of each parameter.

We also took another look at how to send user-defined commands to the current script from within `tell application ...` blocks—something that often catches out novice scripters but is easy to remember once you realize that there's no real difference between user-defined commands and application-defined ones apart from their syntax.

We covered the various handlers (`run`, `open`, `idle`, `quit`, etc.) that you can optionally implement in AppleScript Editor applets to respond to incoming events that you are interested in.

Lastly, we rounded off the chapter by developing a general-purpose associative list consisting of a custom data structure built from lists and records and a set of accompanying handlers for working safely and easily with that structure.

In the next chapter, we will conclude our journey through the AppleScript language by exploring its most advanced feature for organizing your code: script objects.

Chapter 19

Organizing Your Code with Script Objects

Script objects are probably the most underutilized complex feature in the AppleScript language. This chapter explains the idea behind script objects and what they can do, and it discusses real-world techniques for putting them to effective use in your projects.

Initially, it is difficult to see what's so great about script objects. After all, many AppleScript users manage to create terrific scripts that do everything they want without ever going near script objects. So, what's all the hoopla about? Well, if your scripts are fairly small and simple, you can just ignore script objects altogether—good tidiness and a smattering of handlers are all you normally need to organize that sort of code effectively. On the other hand, if you plan to develop large, sophisticated AppleScript systems, you will need much more powerful tools to manage that complexity...and that's where script objects really shine.

If you are completely new to scripting, I recommend that you ignore this chapter for the moment and proceed directly to Part 3 of the book, where you will get lots of good, practical experience in automating your Mac. Once you are comfortable performing day-to-day scripting tasks, come back and continue this chapter from where you left off. Otherwise, read on now to learn what script objects can do for you...

Introducing Script Objects

You may not realize it, but script objects are the foundation of every single script you write. As soon as you click the Compile button in AppleScript Editor, AppleScript takes the raw source code and compiles it into a script object. When you click the Run button, AppleScript Editor sends a run command to this object. If you modify the code and click Compile again, AppleScript throws away the previous script object and creates a new one in its place. When you select **File ➤ Save As** and pick the Script format, AppleScript flattens this object into a series of bytes and writes them to disk as a .scpt file. When you open a .scpt file, AppleScript reads the data from the file and uses it to construct a new, identical copy of the original script object.

Now, if this was all that script objects were used for, they really wouldn't be of any interest to us. However, AppleScript goes further by enabling you to create script objects *within* other script objects. There are two ways you can do this:

- Use Standard Additions' load script command to read a compiled .scpt file from disk. The result is an object of class script that you can pass around your script just like any other object.

- Use AppleScript's script statement to define a script object within an existing script. When the script statement is executed, AppleScript creates a new script object, just as it creates a new string object when it evaluates a string literal or a list object when it evaluates a list literal.

Whether a script object is created by compiling some source code in AppleScript Editor, loading a .scpt file from disk, or executing a script statement, it is all the same to AppleScript. Each script object can contain any combination of properties, handlers, and/or top-level statements (the implicit run handler). The difference with the second and third approaches is what they allow *you*, the script developer, to do. As you can tell from the title of this chapter, script objects are a tool for organizing your code. And they are not just any old tool, either—they are the most powerful organizational tool AppleScript has, with not one but *two* advanced uses: script libraries and object-oriented programming.

What Is a Script Library?

Unlike most of the scripts you write, which are designed to be run directly, a script library defines handlers for *other scripts* to use. In organizational terms, think of a script library as the next step up from a handler. Whereas handlers allow you to reuse series of statements from different parts of a script, a script library allows you to reuse a collection of handlers across several different scripts.

To create a library, you simply add some handlers to a script and save it to disk as a compiled script file. To use the library, you load it into another script as a script object and then send to that object commands to handle.

Script libraries can be useful even in fairly small scripts that often need to perform the same general tasks: finding and replacing text, sorting lists, formatting dates, and so on. Since you need to understand how user-defined handlers work before you can proceed to learning about script libraries, they are not for complete beginners. Once you are comfortable defining and using your own handlers and have started building up a collection of general handlers that you regularly use, you should read the "Understanding Script Objects" section followed by the "Working with Script Libraries" section, later in this chapter, to learn about script libraries as well.

What Is Object-Oriented Programming?

A second, more advanced use for AppleScript's script objects is in defining custom objects for use in your scripts—what programmers refer to as *object-oriented programming*, or *OOP*.

Just as handlers allow you to define your own custom commands, script objects allow you to define your own custom objects. For example, although AppleScript lacks a built-in command for sorting lists, you can define a custom `sort_list` handler to provide this feature. Similarly, although AppleScript already defines several basic object classes for you to use in scripts—`integer`, `string`, `list`, `record`, `date`, and so on—you may sometimes find yourself wishing it provided other types as well. For example, in Chapter 18, we developed a simple, reusable associative list that can be used to store and retrieve objects using strings (or any other objects) as keys. The design consisted of two parts: a record containing the key-value data, and a collection of handlers for manipulating that data. This is a perfectly good way to design code—what's known as *procedural programming*—but it is not the only way to do it. Another option is to combine the data *and* the handlers into a single object, so that instead of having a "dumb" data structure, plus a bunch of separate handlers, you have a "smart" object that contains everything it needs to do its job. To make the object do things, you simply send commands to it.

Combining data and functionality into self-contained objects this way is the most powerful organizational tool provided by the AppleScript language. Ironically, it is also the least useful as far as the average AppleScript user is concerned, since most AppleScripts tend to be relatively small and simple, relying on scriptable applications to do most of the work. Small, simple scripts don't need all that much organization to do their jobs successfully, so using object-oriented design techniques on them would be like cracking a walnut with a sledgehammer, and the resulting code would be more complex than if you'd just followed the usual procedural approach.

There are, however, two important groups of AppleScript users who will benefit from learning OOP: professional scripters who write large, complex automation systems for publishing and other industries, and scripters who wish to create full-blown GUI applications using Snow Leopard's new Cocoa Bridge. If you fall into either of these groups, or are just looking for something new to learn after mastering handlers and libraries, you should read all of this chapter.

Understanding Script Objects

Before you begin putting script objects to practical use, you need to understand a few things about how they work. This section doesn't cover every last technical detail—just the ones you need to know to get started. Later sections will fill in any additional details as they are needed.

Defining a Script Object in a Script

As I mentioned earlier, one way to define a script object within another script is by using a `script` statement. The syntax for a `script` statement is as follows:

```
script [ variable_name ]
    -- Properties, handlers, and/or top-level statements go here...
end script
```

The first line of the statement begins with the keyword `script`. If you want the newly created script object to be assigned to a particular variable, just add a variable identifier after `script`. Otherwise, the object can be retrieved from AppleScript's special `result` variable as usual.

The last line of the statement begins with the keyword end, followed by `script`. If you omit the `script` part, AppleScript adds it automatically when the script is compiled.

Between these two lines, you can include any number of properties, handlers, and/or top-level statements. When writing these lines in a script object, the rules are exactly the same as for a top-level script; for example, you can include top-level statements *or* an explicit `run` handler, but not both. You should also take care to declare any properties above the handlers that use them, because otherwise the AppleScript compiler will become confused and the handlers will not be able to see the properties.

How and where you declare the `script` statement determines when the corresponding script object is created. If the statement appears at the top level of your main script and you have given it a name, the corresponding script object will be created as soon as the main script is compiled. If you do not include a variable name or declare it inside an explicit `run` handler or any other handler, a new script object will be created each time the handler executes.

However you create it, once a script object exists, you can send commands to it. Type the following code into AppleScript Editor, click Compile, and then click Run:

```
script HelloWorld
    display dialog "Hello World!"
end script

tell HelloWorld to run
```

When you compile the script, a new script object is created and assigned to the variable named HelloWorld. When you run the script, the last line sends a `run` command to the script object, which executes its top-level statements in response. The result is a dialog box containing the message "Hello World!"

This might not seem all that impressive, but we've only just scratched the surface: in fact, the humble `script` statement is the fundamental building block behind all OOP in AppleScript. But let's not get too deep into that subject right now...

> **NOTE:** This chapter uses a CamelCase naming style for important library and script object names, just so that they stand out from other variable names, which use the usual underscore style. You can use whatever naming convention works best for you.

Loading and Storing Script Objects from Disk

The second way you can create a new script object inside another script is by loading a compiled script file from disk. Since a .scpt file is really just a script object that has been taken out and flattened, it won't surprise you to learn that reading the file into AppleScript and unflattening it again produces a new copy of the original script object.

To read a script file from disk, you use the load script command from Standard Additions' Scripting Commands suite. The load script command takes a single direct parameter, which is an alias or file object identifying the .scpt file to load. The result is, naturally, an object of class script. For example, the following code loads an existing script file from your /Library/Scripts folder and then sends a run command to the resulting script object:

```
set the_script_object to load script ¬
    POSIX file "/Library/Scripts/Mail Scripts/Crazy Message Text.scpt"
tell the_script_object to run
```

The load script command, as you might guess, is the key to working with script libraries. More on that shortly.

Incidentally, the Scripting Commands suite contains a couple of other commands that may be of interest to you. The store script command allows you to save a script object to disk as a .scpt file. The run script command is also pretty neat: you can pass it either a string containing AppleScript code or an alias or file object for a .scpt file, and it will compile the code/load the file and send it a run command. You can even pass parameters into the script and get results back. For example:

```
set the_source_code to ¬
    "on run {first_value, second_value}
        return first_value * second_value
    end run"
run script the_source_code with parameters {7, 6}
--> 42
```

Being able to compile and run AppleScript code on-the-fly allows you to do all sorts of weird and wonderful—not to mention dangerous(!)—things that you can't normally do when your scripts are hard-coded. Mind you, dynamic code generation is almost always the wrong solution to a given problem, but if you do find yourself in a situation where nothing else will do, it is good to know it can be done.

How Variable Scope Works in Script Objects

Up to now, you've been able to use properties and global variables more or less interchangeably in your scripts. Once you introduce script objects to the mix, however, you need to be much more careful because properties and globals behave *very* differently when multiple script objects are involved.

Consider the following script:

```
script A
    property x : "hi"
    display dialog "A says " & x
end script

script B
    display dialog "B says " & x
end script

run A -- Displays the message "A says hi"
run B -- Throws an error: "The variable x is not defined."
```

When you run it, a dialog box containing the message "A says hi" appears. An error then occurs on the second display dialog statement: "The variable x is not defined." That's because the scope of a property is limited to the script object it is defined in, in this case script A. Handlers and script objects defined inside the script object can see that property directly, but statements outside of the script object cannot—if they want to access it, they must refer to the script object first; for example:

```
script A
    property x : "hi"
    display dialog "A says " & x
end script

script B
    display dialog "B says " & x of A
end script

run A -- Displays the message "A says hi"
run B -- Displays the message "B says hi"
```

(Whether it's a good idea for outside code to go poking around a script object's internal properties is another question, but that's not important for now.)

Now try the following script:

```
global x

script A
    set x to "hi"
    display dialog "A says " & x
end script

script B
    display dialog "B says " & x
end script
```

```
run A -- Displays the message "A says hi"
run B -- Displays the message "B says hi"
```

As you can see, now that x is declared as a global variable, there are no limitations to its visibility: any part of the script can see it.

Now, you might be wondering what happens if you move the global declaration into the script object as well. Let's try it:

```
script A
    global x
    set x to "hi"
    display dialog "A says " & x
end script

script B
    display dialog "B says " &  x
end script

run A -- Displays the message "A says hi"
run B -- Throws an error: "The variable x is not defined."
```

Hey, that looks like the same behavior as we originally had when we used properties. But is it really, or is AppleScript just fooling with us? Try this:

```
script A
    global x
    set x to "hi"
    display dialog "A says: " & x
end script

script B
    global x
    display dialog "B says: " & x
end script

run A -- Displays the message "A says hi"
run B -- Displays the message "B says hi"
```

Yep, it was just the AppleScript compiler missing the point before. When it got around to compiling the script B ... end script block, it forgot that x had been declared global earlier on in script object A, so it treated the x variable in B as a local. Put a global declaration in both script objects, though, and as soon as you assign a value to x in either of them, they will both see the change. That sounds like it could be a pretty cool feature when you begin working with script libraries, because it means you can share values across multiple different script objects loaded from multiple different files, but in truth it completely defeats the point of using libraries in the first place. Since the goal of libraries is to parcel up a large program into smaller, self-contained units that are easier to understand and maintain, allowing any library to alter values in any other library means that instead of small *independent* units, you have one big cat's cradle of code where all sorts of less-than-obvious interactions can occur. For example, if the value of a global variable in library C changes, was that assignment made by C itself; or was it intentional fiddling by library A, B, D, E, or F; or perhaps even accidental interference by another, completely unrelated library that also happened to define a global variable with the same name?

Because of the potential that global variables have for creating complexity, confusion, and hard-to-trace bugs, I *strongly* recommend that when you're working with script libraries or OOP, you avoid using global variables altogether and stick to local variables and properties only. Managing and minimizing complexity is key to the successful creation of reliable, large-scale programs, and global variables' total disregard for boundary lines does not help here. On occasions where you really do need to share data between several libraries, you can always pass it as parameters to commands, or even create a single "preferences" library that is loaded once and then assigned to properties in all the libraries that need it. That way, you can see exactly where the shared information is being accessed, because any code that wants to use it will include a reference to the preferences library where it is stored.

Now that we've covered the basic mechanics of script objects, let's look at the first of the two ways they can be used in practice: as script libraries.

Working with Script Libraries

As you know by now, even though the AppleScript language comes with a decent number of built-in features, when it comes to finding useful commands to manipulate your data, you nearly always have to look elsewhere. In Chapter 5 you discovered how to use the many thousands of commands provided by AppleScript-aware applications to carry out a huge variety of tasks. In Chapters 16 and 17, you took advantage of the various commands defined by a scripting addition (Standard Additions) to display dialog boxes and read and write files. Finally, in Chapter 18 you learned how to roll your own commands from scratch, using nothing but AppleScript itself.

Although scriptable applications and scripting additions provide a wealth of ready-to-use commands, there are still plenty of tasks that they do not cover or may not be ideal for. For example, if you want to find and replace some text, there are third-party applications and scripting additions that will do that for you, but if your script needs to be portable, then you may want to avoid any external dependencies. No problem: just copy and paste the `find_and_replace` handler we developed in Chapter 7 into your script, and you're good to go.

The downside is that as your collection of AppleScripts grows and individual scripts become bigger and more complex, this sort of copy-and-paste approach becomes very tedious and painful to manage. The new code you develop becomes bloated as the same old utility handlers appear again and again, and any time you want to fix a bug or make an improvement in one of these handlers, you have to go through each of the scripts that use it and update the code by hand.

After a while, you may be wishing you could organize and access these utilities a bit more efficiently. After all, any time you want to use some scripting addition commands, you only have to install the relevant scripting addition files on your Mac and, like magic, they're instantly available for all your scripts to use. Wouldn't it be great if you could use a similar approach with your own commands? Well, by using script libraries, you can!

What Advantages Do Script Libraries Provide?

Script libraries can help you maintain sanity when working on larger AppleScript projects in two ways: they *reduce the size of your main scripts*, which makes their code more manageable, and they allow you to *reuse handlers across many scripts* without having to copy and paste the handler code each time.

Think of a script library as a kind of do-it-yourself scripting addition. Although there are some technical differences, the ultimate goal is the same: to provide scripts with new commands to use.

Table 19–1 lists the main similarities and differences between scripting additions and script libraries.

Table 19–1. *Scripting Addition and Script Library Features Compared*

Scripting Addition	Script Library
Provides commands for scripts to use	Provides commands for scripts to use
Written in the C language	Written in AppleScript
Can be created by experienced programmers	Can be created by any AppleScript user
Can be used by any AppleScript user	Can be used by any AppleScript user
Can make use of low-level features in the operating system that aren't directly accessible from AppleScript	Can make use of scriptable applications and scripting additions
Can work with simple objects (numbers, strings, lists, etc.) only	Can work with any kind of object, including application references and script objects
Automatically available to all scripts	Must be loaded before use
Commands use the same syntax as scriptable applications	Commands use normal AppleScript syntax
Commands can be sent to the current script	Commands must be sent to the library scripts that define them

As you can see, scripting additions and script libraries both have their own particular benefits and limitations. Think of them as complementing, rather than replacing, each other. For some tasks, a scripting addition is best; for others, a script library provides the ideal solution. Plus, since script libraries are written in AppleScript, they can take advantage of scripting additions, too.

Perhaps the best thing about script libraries, though, is that you can begin using them whenever you like. As long as an existing script is already organized into handlers, you can easily move the simpler, self-contained handlers into their own library files. All you need to do then is make a few tweaks to the remaining code so that it uses those libraries instead. Later on, you may decide those handlers would be useful to other scripts, in which case you just load your existing libraries into those scripts as well.

Creating Your First Script Library

Let's walk through the basic steps of creating and using a script library. Start by creating a new script. In it, type the lines of code in Script 19–1.

Script 19–1.

```
on do_something(action_name)
    display dialog "I'm in ur library, " & action_name & "."
end do_something
```

Next, save your script on your desktop, and name it TestLib.scpt. Then, close the file you just created. Start a new script file, and type the following:

```
set test_lib to load script alias ((path to desktop as text) & "TestLib.scpt")
```

What you should pay particular attention to here is the load script command in the first line. The load script command, which is defined in Standard Additions, loads a compiled script file from disk. The result is a script object, which you can assign to a variable for later use.

In order to make use of the library's handlers, you need to send commands to this script object. Add the following lines to your script:

```
tell test_lib
    do_something("handlin' ur command")
end tell
```

Here we use a tell statement to identify the script object as the default target for all commands within the block. We then send a do_something command to the object. The result is a dialog box containing the message "I'm in ur library, handlin' ur command."

If you don't want to change the default target for all commands, you can direct a single command at the script object by using a reference like this,

```
do_something("handlin' ur command") of test_lib
```

or in this form:

```
test_lib's do_something("handlin' ur command")
```

Where Should You Save Your Library?

Another important aspect of a library is where you save it. Of course, if you're writing scripts for yourself, the location of your library doesn't make too much difference. But sooner or later you will need to make your scripts available to other people on other

Macs. At that point, you must ensure that your script can always find the script library and that the installation procedure isn't too complicated.

The best solution is to find a folder you can later access using the `path to` command. Placing your library in one of these folders allows your scripts to find them no matter which Mac OS X computer they run on. A good choice is somewhere in the current user's `Library` folder, or in the main `/Library` folder if you want them to be accessible to all users. You can use the `Application Support` folder to store libraries that are used by a specific script applet, and use the `Scripts` folders for general-purpose libraries that any script can use.

For now, just move the `TestLib.scpt` file you created earlier into the `~/Library/Scripts/` folder on your hard disk. In the next section, we will explore loading the library from that location.

Alternatively, if you are writing an application that you will distribute to other users, you can put any libraries inside the application bundle's `Scripts` folder so that when you distribute it, its libraries travel with it. When your application runs, it can use Standard Additions' `path to` and `path to resource` commands to locate the library scripts in the `Scripts` folder. Figure 19–1 provides a simple demonstration of this.

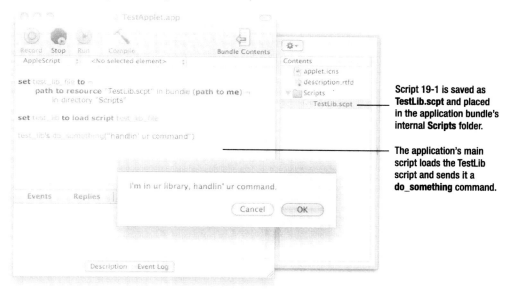

Figure 19–1. *Using a library script embedded in a bundle-based applet*

I started by creating a new document in AppleScript Editor and entering the code shown. I then saved the script as a bundle-based application, allowing me to include additional files within the application's bundle folder. Next, I added a copy of the `TestLib.scpt` file to the bundle's `Scripts` folder. To do this, I clicked the Bundle Contents button in the toolbar to open the drawer on the right, and then I dragged the `TestLib.scpt` file under the `Scripts` folder icon, as shown. Lastly, I tested everything was working correctly by running the script in AppleScript Editor, resulting in the dialog box shown.

What Are the Options for Loading Script Libraries?

So far, you've learned that a script library is just an ordinary compiled script file that is designed to be used by other scripts rather than run directly. You've also been introduced to the load script command and found out how to send commands to the resulting script object. Let's now look at some of the options for managing and loading your libraries in day-to-day use.

Using the *load script* Command

The most basic way to load a script library is to use Standard Additions' load script command directly. This is quite sufficient if your needs are modest and your library files are stored in a fixed location such as ~/Library/Scripts/.

As for when you load the library, you have two choices: you can load it once when the script is compiled, or you can load it each time the script runs. Each approach has its advantages and disadvantages that you should consider when deciding which is most appropriate to your needs.

In both cases, we will use a property to hold the loaded script object. This allows the library's handlers to be used from anywhere in the script, which is normally what you want.

Script 19–2 shows how to load a library (in this case, TestLib) at compile time.

Script 19–2.

```
property TestLib : load script ¬
    alias ((path to scripts folder from user domain as text) & "TestLib.scpt")
```

When the script is compiled, AppleScript evaluates the expression to the right of the colon, and then assigns the resulting script object to the property identifier.

Loading libraries at compile time has two benefits: first, it is simple to write, and second, it makes it easy to distribute already-compiled scripts to other users—since the libraries are already embedded in the main script, you do not need to distribute the library files as well.

Script 19–3 shows how to load a library each time the script runs.

Script 19–3.

```
property TestLib : missing value

on load_libraries()
    set scripts_folder_path to path to scripts folder from user domain as text
    set TestLib to load script alias (scripts_folder_path & "TestLib.scpt")
end load_libraries

on run
    load_libraries()
    -- Rest of the code goes here...
end run
```

Loading libraries at runtime is a bit more complicated to implement correctly than loading them at compile time. For example, if you write an applet containing both a `run` handler and an `open` handler, you will need to add a `load_libraries` command to the start of both handlers to ensure the libraries are loaded at launch. If the user launches the applet by double-clicking it in the Finder, the `run` handler will execute as normal. However, if the user launches the applet by dropping files onto it, the `open` handler will be called instead of the `run` handler.

The big advantage of loading libraries at run time is that if you modify the library code at any time, then the next time you run the main script, these changes will be picked up automatically. If you load libraries at compile time, your main script will continue using the library object it was compiled with, and you will need to recompile it in order to make it use the new version of the library.

If your library code is stable, compile-time loading should not be a problem, but if you regularly modify it, then having to recompile all the scripts that use those libraries can become very tedious, in which case loading libraries at runtime is the better option.

Using AppleMods Loader

The basic `load script` command is often sufficient if your needs are modest, but if you have a large collection of libraries, some of which need to load other libraries, then you could probably use some help.

Many scripting languages include their own built-in systems for locating, loading, and initializing libraries with just a simple "import" statement. Unfortunately, AppleScript is a little short on such home comforts, so you need to either roll your own solution or find an existing third-party one.

One option is the AppleMods Loader system, which you can download from the AppleMods web site at `http://applemods.sourceforge.net/` along with a number of ready-to-use libraries. (Coincidentally, Loader was written by one of the authors of this book, so you'll know who to blame if you have problems using it!)

The Loader system consists of two parts: a scripting addition, `AppleModsTools.osax`, and the Loader library itself. Loader is designed to be flexible, portable, and easy to use; although it is based on Standard Additions' `load script` command, it provides many additional features for locating and loading libraries for you. Loader is free and is released under the very liberal open source MIT license, allowing you to use, distribute, and modify it however you like.

The AppleMods Tools scripting addition defines a single command, `AppleMods Loader`, that you use to load the Loader library into your script. Here is how you use it:

```
property _Loader : AppleMods Loader
```

You only need to install the scripting addition if you are compiling scripts; it is not used to run them. Once the Loader library is stored in the _Loader property, it will remain there until the script is recompiled.

Next, you need to define the properties that will hold the loaded libraries. For this exercise, let's say you want to load the List library that is installed along with Loader itself, so you add the following property to your script:

```
property _List : missing value
```

Now comes the "magic" part. Rather than address Loader directly, you include a handler named __load__ in your script. Each time Loader processes a script, it looks for a handler with this name. If it finds one, it calls it. The __load__ handler should take a single positional parameter, which is the object that does the actual library loading. Loader refers to libraries as "modules," so the command for loading a library is loadModule. To load the List library, you send a loadModule command to the loader object like this:

```
on __load__(moduleLoader)
    tell moduleLoader
        set _List to loadModule("List")
    end tell
end __load__
```

You might wonder why Loader needs you to use a __load__ handler rather than talking to it directly. There are two reasons for this:

- When Loader runs, it does quite a bit of work behind the scenes, so it is simplest if Loader does its own thing first and only calls your code once it's ready.

- It allows the loading process to be recursive: each time Loader loads a script, it checks whether the script has a __load__ handler. If it does, it calls the handler, which can then tell Loader to load additional scripts, and so on. This means that each library can also load any libraries it needs to use: Loader simply keeps going until every required library has been loaded.

To trigger the loading process in your main script, you need to include the following command:

```
_Loader's initScript(me)
```

You only include this command in your main script, not in your library scripts.

If you want to load your libraries at compile time, you can add the following line below the __load__ handler:

```
property _ : _Loader's initScript(me)
```

This line forces AppleScript to call Loader's initScript handler as soon as the script is compiled.

Notice that the initScript command requires a single parameter. This is always the value of the me variable; in other words, your top-level script.

If you want to load your libraries at runtime, you need to send Loader an initScript command at the start of your run handler and/or open handler as described in the previous section.

Script 19–4 shows the full code for loading the List library at runtime, along with some code that uses the library's sortList handler to sort a list of numbers.

Script 19–4.

```
property _Loader : AppleMods Loader

property _List : missing value

on __load__(moduleLoader)
    tell moduleLoader
        set _List to loadModule("List")
    end tell
end __load__

on run
    _Loader's initScript(me)
    set the_list to {3, 7, 1, 9, 2, 0}
    set sorted_list to _List's sortList(the_list)
    return sorted_list
end run
```

> **CAUTION:** If you have the Satimage.osax scripting addition installed, then you will need to write the name of the sortList command as |sortlist|; otherwise it will conflict with the sortlist command defined in the Satimage dictionary.

When you run this script, the result will be as follows:

```
--> {0, 1, 2, 3, 7, 9}
```

As you can see, using the Loader system does add some extra lines to your scripts. On the other hand, this is mostly just the same old boilerplate code each time, so it is easy to get right, and it is still much shorter and easier to manage than if you copied and pasted all the handlers you needed directly into your scripts.

You can also use Loader to manage your own libraries. For example, move your earlier TestLib.scpt library into ~/Library/Scripts/AppleMods/, which is one of the standard folders that Loader searches in. (You may need to create the folder first.)

Now, compile and run the following script:

```
property _Loader : AppleMods Loader

property _TestLib : missing value

on __load__(moduleLoader)
    tell moduleLoader
        set _TestLib to loadModule("TestLib")
    end tell
end __load__

property _ : _Loader's initScript(me)

_TestLib's do_something("making the tea")
_TestLib's do_something("washing the dishes")
_TestLib's do_something("watching tee-vee")
```

In this example, we tell Loader to load the libraries at compile time, so that they are permanently embedded in our main script. Loader will recognize any compiled script file (.scpt or .scptd) that is stored in a known folder and whose name follows certain rules. In this case, the file name is TestLib.scpt, so the name you use to load the library is TestLib. (See the AppleMods documentation for more information about library naming rules.)

Once the library script object is safely stored in our main script (which, after being compiled, is now a script object too, of course), the script can send it do_something commands as often as it likes.

This section has only provided a brief glimpse at what Loader can do, but hopefully it's enough to whet your appetite for more. You can find additional documentation on the AppleMods web site, both on Loader itself and on the various useful libraries that are distributed along with it.

> **TIP:** A couple of other AppleScript library systems are also worth investigating. One alternative is the XModules system from http://homepage.mac.com/tkurita/scriptfactory/, which uses a similar approach to Loader. Another option is to use the built-in library features in Late Night Software's Script Debugger (http://www.latenightsw.com). Unlike the Loader and XModules systems, which load library scripts into properties of your main script, Script Debugger merges your library code directly into your main script when the script is compiled. All of these approaches have their pros and cons, of course, so go with whichever one works best for you.

Beginning Object-Oriented Programming

Learning object-oriented programming can be an interesting challenge, even for fairly experienced scripters. Up to now, you've mostly been concerned with learning individual language features and then putting them together to create working scripts. With OOP, learning the language features is the quick bit, as the number of completely new features is actually very small. The real challenge is wrapping your head around the concepts involved, beginning with: *What is the point of OOP anyway?*

This is a good question. After all, you can already do everything that you need to do using good old-fashioned procedural programming techniques. Not only that, but as you begin studying OOP, you will find that your simple learning scripts tend to grow slightly longer, not shorter, as you add the extra lines needed to define your objects! Surely this is just creating more complexity, rather than less?

Well, yes...and no. It's true that the object-oriented approach does add a bit of complexity due to the extra boilerplate code required to declare and construct objects. However, a good scripter doesn't do extra work without a good reason, and the reason is this: adding a little complexity in one area can often eliminate a much greater amount of complexity elsewhere. In small, simple scripts this doesn't really work—there isn't much complexity in the code to begin with—but in larger, more sophisticated systems, a careful choice of tactics can make a great deal of difference to how quickly and concisely you solve the design challenges involved. If a bit more planning and a few extra lines of code now can eliminate a whole bunch of code further down the line, then that is an overall win. If it can make the structure of your code and the interactions between its various parts easier for you and other developers to follow, then that is a big win as well. As with handlers and libraries, the goal of OOP is to provide your code with a meaningful, well-defined structure and to eliminate unnecessary duplication by enabling and encouraging greater reuse of existing logic.

Of course, until you actually sit down and do some OOP, these benefits are all just theoretical. So rather than talk about how great OOP is, let's just dive in and put it to work.

By the end of this chapter, you'll either see the benefits that OOP can provide, or you won't. If you don't, don't worry about it: even your humble author required a few tries before the concepts involved finally "clicked." It may not be until you're actually in the middle of a problem project, struggling to keep its spiraling complexity under some sort of control, that you will finally think "there *must* be a better way to do this"—at which point, this chapter will still be here for you.

THE DIFFERENT STYLES OF OBJECT-ORIENTED LANGUAGES

There are two styles of object-oriented languages in common use today: class-based and prototype-based.

Class-based languages such as Python, Ruby, and Objective-C use a two-stage approach, where each class is effectively a "template" that describes how usable objects, or *instances* of that class, should be constructed.

Prototype-based languages such as AppleScript and JavaScript prefer a single-step approach where you have only objects. To create a new object, you simply write a literal object in your code and then execute it, or make a copy—or *clone*—of an existing object (the "prototype").

You will learn more about the class-based approach in Chapter 30 when you begin working with Mac OS X's powerful class-based Cocoa frameworks. This chapter concentrates on the particular style of prototype-based OOP used by the AppleScript language itself.

Your First Object: A Better Associative List

For this first exercise, we will take the associative list project from the previous chapter and convert it from a procedural design, where the data and its related handlers are separate, to an object-oriented design, where they are combined into one.

What is the point of doing this? Well, in Chapter 10 the original associative list design was mixed together with the rest of the code, with various parts of the script manipulating it directly. Later, we extracted the associative list functionality and created a set of handlers specifically for manipulating the list structure. This gave us three benefits:

- Because the associative list code was no longer tied to a specific script, it could easily be reused across other scripts.

- It provides the user with a clear set of easy-to-understand commands for manipulating the data.

- The handlers create a safety barrier between the data structure and the rest of the program, protecting the data's integrity and making it easier to improve or change the associative list's internal design later on without breaking existing code that uses it.

An object-oriented design gives us all these advantages, and more.

The first of these new advantages is that you no longer have to keep track of all the different handlers in your script and remember which ones should be used on which objects. By combining the data and the handlers into one, you ensure that only the correct handlers can be used. This reduces the number of separate parts that you have to remember, and makes it impossible to accidentally pass the correct data structure to the wrong handler, or vice versa. We will put this ability to use as we convert the procedural associative list design into an object-oriented one. Subsequent projects will explore other benefits of OOP: extending the behavior of existing objects through inheritance and creating collections of swappable "plug-and-play" objects.

Planning the Conversion

As you will recall, our original associative list library provided four public handlers, whose names and parameters looked like this:

```
set_associative_item(the_assoc_list, the_key, the_value)
get_associative_item(the_assoc_list, the_key)
count_associative_items(the_assoc_list)
delete_associative_item(the_assoc_list, the_key)
```

A fifth handler, make_associative_list, is used to create new associative list objects.

In our object-oriented redesign, we'll keep the "make" handler where it is, but modify it so that instead of returning a record object, it returns a script object.

Like the record, the script object will contain a property named the_items where all of its private data is kept.

We will then move all the other handlers from the body of the main script into the new script object, where we will tweak them to manipulate the object's the_items property directly.

All we're really doing, in other words, is changing the packaging. Though, as you will discover, this new style of packaging makes it very easy to do some really cool things in your code.

NOTE: In OOP jargon, handlers within objects are commonly known as *methods*, and commands sent to those objects are commonly known as *messages*. We'll keep referring to them as handlers and commands here, but you'll often encounter these terms when dealing with other object-oriented systems such as Cocoa.

Converting the *make_associative_list* Handler

Let's begin transforming our old procedural associative list design into an object-oriented one. To remind you, here is the original make_associative_list handler from Chapter 18:

```
on make_associative_list()
    return {class:"associative list", the_items:{}}
end make_associative_list
```

The first step is to replace the original record with a script object containing the same properties, class and the_items:

```
on make_associative_list()
    script AssociativeList
        property class : "associative list"
        property the_items : {}
    end script
end make_associative_list
```

As you can see, the new structure is remarkably similar to the old one: both contain two properties, class and the_items. The make_associative_list handler also serves the same role as it did before: manufacturing new objects. The only difference is that instead of creating new record objects, it now creates new script objects. Each time you call the handler, it executes the script ... end script statement, creating a new script object. Want ten associative list objects to use in your script? No problem: just call make_associative_list ten times.

To use the proper object-oriented jargon, we describe the make_associative_list handler as a *constructor*, because its job is to construct, or create, new objects. Also, we refer to the objects that it returns as *instances*, because each is a separate instance of our original script object definition.

THE DIFFERENT WAYS OF CREATING SCRIPT OBJECTS

There are three ways that you can create a new script object in AppleScript: by loading a compiled script file with the load script command, by executing a script statement, or by copying an existing script object with AppleScript's copy command. The load script command is best used for loading libraries, whereas executing a script statement in a constructor handler is best for object-oriented programming.

You can, in principle, define a prototype script object at the top level of the main script and then use the copy command to clone it, like this:

```
script PrototypeObject
    -- Code goes here...
end script
```

```
copy PrototypeObject to new_object
```

The problem with this approach is that it duplicates not only the script object you defined, but also all of its parent objects. This normally includes your main script. In turn, all the properties and top-level script objects in your main script will be duplicated as well.

This has two unwanted consequences. First, if you have a top-level property that you want all objects to share, this won't work, as each object will end up talking to its own version of the property. Second, it is very inefficient: instead of cloning a single script object, you are copying your entire script each time. At best, this is slower than using a constructor. At worst, the number of AppleScript objects being copied grows so large that the AppleScript interpreter grinds to a halt or crashes altogether.

As a rule, then, when writing object-oriented code in AppleScript, it is best to stick to using constructor handlers to create new script objects rather than using the copy command to clone existing ones.

Repackaging the Remaining Handlers

The second step is to repackage the handlers used to manipulate the associative list data so that they are part of the same AssociativeList script object. Since the handlers are already well designed, this step is surprisingly easy.

Begin by moving the five handlers—the private find_record_for_key handler, and the public set_associative_item, get_associative_item, count_associative_items, and delete_associative_item handlers—into the AssociativeList script object.

Your code should now have the following structure (the contents of each handler have been omitted for space):

```
on make_associative_list()
    script AssociativeList
        property class : "associative list"
        property the_items : {}

        on find_record_for_key(the_assoc_list, the_key)
        end find_record_for_key

        on set_associative_item(the_assoc_list, the_key, the_item)
        end set_associative_item

        on get_associative_item(the_assoc_list, the_key)
        end get_associative_item

        on count_associative_items(the_assoc_list)
        end count_associative_items

        on delete_associative_item(the_assoc_list, the_key)
        end delete_associative_item

    end script
end make_associative_list
```

We aren't done restructuring yet: we still need to modify each handler so that it refers directly to the script object's the_items property. First, remove the the_assoc_list parameter from every handler and command, because it is no longer needed. Then, replace every reference to the_items of the_assoc_list with a reference to my the_items.

Lastly, in Chapter 18 we included the word associative in each handler name to make it clear to users that these handlers were designed to manipulate associative list records only. Now that these handlers are part of the associative list object itself, this naming scheme is no longer needed. To finish the restructuring, rename each handler so that set_associative_item becomes set_item, get_associative_item becomes get_item, and so forth.

> **NOTE:** Now that these handlers operate directly on the script object that contains them, it is impossible to use them to manipulate any other object. This makes them rather more foolproof compared to the handlers in Chapter 18, where it was possible to pass the wrong kind of object as the first parameter—either by accident or by design—with who-knows-what consequences.

Once you have done this, your new associative list object is ready to roll. Script 19–5 shows how the new make_associative_list handler should look.

Script 19–5.

```
on make_associative_list()
    script AssociativeList
        property class : "associative list"
        property the_items : {}

        on find_record_for_key(the_key)
            (* This is a private handler. Users should not use it directly. *)
            considering diacriticals, hyphens, punctuation and white space ¬
                    but ignoring case
                repeat with record_ref in my the_items
                    if the_key of record_ref = the_key then return record_ref
                end repeat
            end considering
            return missing value
        end find_record_for_key

        on set_item(the_key, the_value)
            set record_ref to find_record_for_key(the_key)
            if record_ref = missing value then
                set end of my the_items to {the_key:the_key, the_value:the_value}
            else
                set the_value of record_ref to the_value
            end if
            return
        end set_item

        on get_item(the_key)
            set record_ref to find_record_for_key(the_key)
            if record_ref = missing value then
```

```
                    error "The key wasn't found." number -1728 from the_key
                end if
                return the_value of record_ref
            end get_item

        on count_items()
            return count my the_items
        end count_items

        on delete_item(the_key)
            set record_ref to find_record_for_key(the_key)
            if record_ref is missing value then
                error "The key wasn't found." number -1728 from the_key
            end if
            set contents of record_ref to missing value
            set my the_items to every record of my the_items
            return
        end delete_item
    end script
end make_associative_list
```

> **TIP:** I've omitted most of the handler comments in Script 19–5 for space, but as a conscientious AppleScript developer, you should ensure that your own copy is fully documented. Remember to update the old comments so that they no longer talk about a separate `the_assoc_list` parameter, of course.

Now the reason for using a script object instead of a record object is clear. Whereas records can contain only properties, script objects can contain both properties *and* handlers. Not only that, but these properties and handlers all share the same scope, so the handlers can see and manipulate the properties as they see fit.

> **NOTE:** The technical term for wrapping up some data and the code that manipulates it in a single object is *encapsulation*.

Using the Object-Oriented Associative List

Now let's look at how you can use your object-oriented associative list. The following code shows how you would interact with the original, procedural design:

```
-- Create a new associative list object
set friends_ages to make_associative_list()

-- Store some values
set_associative_item(friends_ages, "Jan", 27)
set_associative_item(friends_ages, "Sam", 29)
set_associative_item(friends_ages, "Bob", 35)

-- Retrieve some values
display dialog "Jan is " & get_item(friends_ages, "Jan") -- "Jan is 27"
```

```
display dialog "Bob is " & get_item(friends_ages, "Bob") -- "Bob is 35"
display dialog "Frank is " & get_item(friends_ages, "Frank") -- Key not found error
```

And here is how you would use the new, object-oriented design:

```
-- Create a new associative list object
set friends_ages to make_associative_list()

-- Store some values
set_item("Jan", 27) of friends_ages
set_item("Sam", 29) of friends_ages
set_item("Bob", 35) of friends_ages

-- Retrieve some values
display dialog "Jan is " & get_item("Jan") of friends_ages -- "Jan is 27"
display dialog "Bob is " & get_item("Bob") of friends_ages -- "Bob is 35"
display dialog "Frank is " & get_item("Frank") of friends_ages -- Key not found error
```

You can also write your references in a more possessive style if you prefer,

```
friends_ages's set_item("Jan", 27)
display dialog "Jan is " & friends_ages's get_item("Jan")
```

or even a tell block (though remember that this will direct *all* commands inside the tell block to your script object by default):

```
tell friends_ages
    set_item("Jan", 27)
    display dialog "Jan is " & get_item("Jan")
end tell
```

Personally, I prefer the possessive style because it's the most compact, but you can use whichever works best for you.

Now that you know how to design a basic object, let's explore the second unique advantage of object-oriented programming: the ability to expand or customize existing objects through the use of *inheritance*.

Extending Objects Through Inheritance

Having already studied application scripting concepts elsewhere in the book, the term "inheritance" should not be new to you. Because the design of the Mac's application scripting system draws many of its influences from object-oriented design, it is not surprising that it borrows a lot of its jargon too. For this section, we'll begin with a quick review of the general concepts behind inheritance; then, we'll look at how inheritance works with script objects in particular; and finally, we'll use inheritance to create separate case-insensitive and case-sensitive variations of our original associative list object.

A Quick Reminder of General Inheritance Concepts

In classic object-oriented terms, "inheritance" means taking all the functionality defined in a "parent" class and adding it to a "child" class, so that this new *subclass* provides all the features of both. For example, in the Finder's dictionary, the classes of the objects you actually interact with—alias file, application file, document file, folder, disk, and so on—are defined in terms of other, more general classes: document, container, and item.

The idea here is that when designing a collection of related classes, you begin by identifying *common* behaviors shared by them all. You then define a general-purpose class, in this case item, that implements those common behaviors; for example, the ability to get and set the object's name and label, the ability to move or duplicate it to another location, and so on.

Next, you identify the behaviors that will be *unique* to each type of object: for example, a disk object should provide a format property and can be used with the eject command; each alias file object should have an original item property that identifies the original item. So, you define a specialized disk class to represent all disk objects, and a specialized alias file class to represent all alias file objects.

You may also find that some behaviors are common to several, but not all, classes of objects—for example, folders can contain other file and folder objects, and so can disks. So, you create some semi-specialized classes that add those behaviors on top of the features provided by the base item class.

Finally, you need a way to indicate which classes get some of their behaviors from which other classes, so you indicate that the document file class inherits from the file class, which inherits from the item class; that the folder class inherits from the container class, which inherits from the item class; and so on. When the user creates a new object of class folder, say, that folder object possesses all of the behaviors that were defined in the folder class, *and* the container class, *and* the item class.

> **NOTE:** In class-based design, a class that is used to construct usable objects is described as a *concrete class*, while a class whose only purpose is to provide functionality for use by other classes is described as an *abstract base class*. In the following sections, we will refer to objects that are used directly by the client code as concrete objects, and the objects that these concrete objects inherit from as base objects.

So what is the point of all this inheriting between classes?

The answer is simple: to avoid unnecessary duplication of code. For example, if the code for getting and setting an item's name is identical regardless of whether the item is an alias file, a document file, a folder, a disk, or whatever, you only want to write that code once and share it between all the objects that need it.

Now, application scripting is a bit of a special case, since it mostly uses concepts like classes and inheritance as a means of presenting an attractive interface to users, and also mixes in ideas from other fields while it is at it. For example, application object references behave a bit like object-oriented references, but they also act a bit like database queries in that some of them can identify multiple objects at once. When you deal with a class-based programming language such as Python, MacRuby, or Objective-C, however, classes are no mere window dressing: they are very real structures that appear in the code and are precisely tied together using inheritance as I've described.

With a language such as AppleScript, inheritance needs to work in a slightly different fashion because there are no actual classes to deal with, only script objects. The overall goal is exactly the same, however—to extend the functionality of one script object by combining in the functionality of another—so let's look at that next.

How Inheritance Works with Script Objects

Inheritance is such a useful feature that it would be a great shame if we couldn't use it simply because the AppleScript language uses prototype-based, not class-based, OOP. Happily, script objects have their own way of doing inheritance. The only difference is that instead of combining the functionality of several classes so that it all becomes available in a single object, you use several separate script objects that are linked together in a chain.

To chain script objects together like this, you use the special parent property. The parent property is read-only, so you can only set it at the time the script object is created. Its value should be an existing script object whose behaviors you want to "inherit."

Script 19–6 shows a simple example of script object inheritance in action.

Script 19–6.

```
script A
    on say_hello()
        display dialog "Script A says hi!"
    end say_hello
end script

script B
    property parent : A
end script

tell B to say_hello()
```

When you run this script, the result is a dialog box containing the message "Script A says hi!"

Let's work through what's going on here. First, you sent a say_hello command to script B. Script B checked whether it had a handler called say_hello. It didn't, so it did the only thing it could, which was to pass on the command to its parent, script A. Script A then checked whether it had a say_hello handler. It found one, so it executed it.

Script objects can also inherit properties in the same way, with one caveat: when addressing a property in another script object, you must precede it with the my keyword; otherwise AppleScript won't search for it correctly. Try running the code in Script 19–7 to see what this means.

> **NOTE:** If you do not define your own `parent` property in a script object, its default parent will be the script object that contains it. In the case of Script 19–6, script B's parent is script A, and script A's parent is the main script. In turn, the parent of the main script is the special `AppleScript` object. The `AppleScript` object is responsible for performing various runtime tasks—for example, defining the `text item delimiters` property and passing any commands that weren't handled by the script on to the host application to see if it can respond to them—so all inheritance chains should ultimately end up there.

Script 19–7.

```
script A
    property x : " says hi!"

    on say_hello()
        display dialog "Script A" & x
    end say_hello
end script

script B
    property parent : A

    on say_hello_again()
        display dialog "Script B" & x
    end say_hello_again
end script

tell B to say_hello() -- This works
tell B to say_hello_again() -- This errors
```

When you run this script, the say_hello handler works okay, but when the say_hello_again handler executes, AppleScript Editor highlights its x variable and displays an error: "The variable x is not defined."

To fix this, add the my keyword before the x variable in the say_hello_again handler, or you can write x of me if you prefer (both mean the same thing):

```
on say_hello_again()
    display dialog "Script B" & x of me
end say_hello_again
```

As you know from Chapter 11, AppleScript's special me variable contains a reference to the current script object, which in this case is script B (the target of the latest tell block). By using a reference to x of me, you are making it clear to AppleScript that you want it to search for property x at the time the script is running. As a result, AppleScript first looks for x in script B, and when it doesn't find it there it tries looking in script B's parent object, which is script A, and so on until it finds x or runs out of places to look.

If you only refer to x, the AppleScript compiler assumes you must be referring to a local variable, property, or global variable somewhere in the current physical scope: that is, in the say_hello_again handler, script B, or the top-level script. When it doesn't find an x property in script B or a global x variable, it decides that x *must* be a local variable and forever marks it as such. Yeah, the AppleScript compiler can be pretty thick at times. Adding a my keyword is your way of telling it to back off and let the code do the right thing when it runs.

Before we move on, there's one more neat trick to script object inheritance that we should look at.

Consider Script 19–6 again. There, we sent a say_hello command to script B, which couldn't handle it itself so it passed it on to script A, which could. The purpose of inheritance, of course, is to provide an easy way to extend existing behaviors with new ones, and this applies as much to individual handlers within objects as the objects as a whole.

Now let's say we want both A *and* B to say hello when B receives the say_hello command. No problem, you may think: let's just add a say_hello handler to script B as well. Script 19–8 shows the modified code; can you guess what happens when it runs? Oh, what the heck—just run it anyway.

Script 19–8.

```
script A
    on say_hello()
        display dialog "Script A says hi!"
    end say_hello
end script

script B
    property parent : A

    on say_hello()
        display dialog "Script B says hi!"
    end say_hello
end script

tell B to say_hello()
```

The problem here is that as soon as the say_hello command hits script B, script B uses its say_hello handler to handle it. Once B's say_hello handler is done, it returns control directly to the caller—script A never even had a chance to respond! We describe the parent script's say_hello handler as being *overridden* by the child script's say_hello handler.

Fortunately, there is a way to give script A a chance to respond as well: the continue keyword.

You met this briefly in Chapter 18 when we looked at the standard handlers you can add to AppleScript Editor applets—specifically, the quit handler. If you define a quit handler in an applet, then any quit events sent to the applet—whether from another application or from within the applet itself when the user selects **File ➤ Quit**—will be intercepted by your custom quit handler instead of the applet's default quit handler. If you want the applet ever to quit, it is essential that your quit handler forwards, or continues, the quit command to the script's parent—in this case, the applet shell—so that the applet's default quit handler can execute as well.

Let's now fix Script 19–8 so that script B's `say_hello` handler does the same thing. Script 19–9 shows the corrected code.

Script 19–9.

```
script A
    on say_hello()
        display dialog "Script A says hi!"
    end say_hello
end script

script B
    property parent : A

    on say_hello()
        continue say_hello()
        display dialog "Script B says hi!"
    end say_hello
end script

tell B to say_hello()
```

In this example, we use a single `continue say_hello()` statement to display script A's greeting before script B's, although you can include as many `continue` lines as you need at any points you want.

If the handler takes parameters and/or returns a result, then you can make use of those too—either passing the previous parameter or a new one, and capturing the returned value for use later on:

```
script A
    on say_hello(the_greeting)
        display dialog "Script A says " & the_greeting
        return "Aloha!"
    end say_hello
end script

script B
    property parent : A

    on say_hello(the_greeting)
        set new_greeting to continue say_hello(the_greeting)
        display dialog "Script B says " & new_greeting
    end say_hello
end script

tell B to say_hello("G'day!")
```

When you run this code, script A wishes you "G'day!" and then script B says "Aloha!"

So, now that you understand the principles behind script object inheritance, it's time to put them to practical use.

NOTE: The process of forwarding a command from one object to another is known as *delegation*. By default, a script object automatically forwards any unhandled commands to its parent object. The continue keyword allows you to explicitly forward a command yourself. This allows object B in the preceding example to do some of the work of handling a say_hello command and then delegate the rest of the work to its parent object, script A.

Implementing Case-Insensitive and Case-Sensitive Associative Lists

Our earlier associative list object was pretty good, but as you may have noticed, it had one particular limitation: when using string-based keys, it always stored them case-insensitively. For most tasks, this is probably what you want, but there may be some occasions when you would prefer case-sensitive behavior. One way you could achieve this is by duplicating the original make_associative_list handler, renaming it make_case_sensitive_associative_list, and then tweaking the considering/ignoring block in the private find_record_for_key handler. But wait; this is a chapter on OOP, and we're supposed to be looking for ways to avoid copy-and-paste coding!

Can OOP help us to avoid this unnecessary duplication? You betcha!

Here's the plan: we will take our original make_associative_list handler and declare it "private"—in other words, it's only for use by our other handlers, and users should not call it themselves. We will then create two new public constructors, make_case_insensitive_associative_list and make_case_sensitive_associative_list, for creating the associative list objects that the user can actually work with. (Yeah, the constructor names are a little long, but sometimes you just have to be descriptive—and besides, users only have to type them when creating new objects, not when using them.)

The cool thing here is that almost all of the actual associative list logic will remain exactly where it is—and because the two new associative list objects will inherit from that parent object, they get to reuse all that existing functionality for free. The only tweak we have to make is to move the ignoring case clause out of the parent object so that the child objects can specify different settings for this attribute themselves.

Let's begin by modifying the original make_associative_list handler. Script 19–10 shows the altered find_record_for_key handler (the other handlers have been omitted for space).

Script 19–10.

```
on _make_associative_list()
    script AssociativeList
        property class : "associative list"
        property the_items : {}

        on find_record_for_key(the_key)
            (* This is a private handler. Users should not use it directly. *)
```

```
        considering diacriticals, hyphens, punctuation and white space
            repeat with record_ref in my the_items
                if the_key of record_ref = the_key then return record_ref
            end repeat
        end considering
        return missing value
    end find_record_for_key

    -- Remaining handlers go here...
  end script
end _make_associative_list
```

As you can see, all we've done to the find_record_for_key handler itself is remove the ignoring case clause. We've also tweaked the name of the make_associative_list handler, adding an underscore to the start of it so that it becomes _make_associative_list. This is a common naming convention for indicating that a handler or property is for private, or internal, use only.

> **TIP:** If you like, you can go through the rest of the code later on and prefix the private the_items property and find_record_for_key handler names with an underscore as well.

The next step is to define the script objects that will specialize the general behavior provided by our parent object to fit their particular needs. Let's begin with the constructors:

```
on make_case_insensitive_associative_list()
    script CaseInsensitiveAssociativeList
        property parent : _make_associative_list()

        -- Other code goes here...
    end script
end make_case_insensitive_associative_list

on make_case_sensitive_associative_list()
    script CaseSensitiveAssociativeList
        property parent : _make_associative_list()

        -- Other code goes here...
    end script
end make_case_sensitive_associative_list
```

Notice how the parent properties for these objects are written. Rather than refer directly to a top-level script object as our earlier inheritance examples did, they use the _make_associative_list constructor to create a new parent object each time. If they referred to a top-level script object, then all of your child objects would share a common parent object—instead of independent objects, they would all share the *same data* as well as the same behavior. This is definitely not what you want!

The next step is to override the parent object's find_record_for_key handler in each of the child objects. Script 19–11 shows the completed code.

Script 19–11.

```
on make_case_insensitive_associative_list()
    script CaseInsensitiveAssociativeList
```

```
        property parent : _make_associative_list()

        on find_record_for_key(the_key)
            ignoring case
                return continue find_record_for_key(the_key)
            end ignoring
        end find_record_for_key
    end script
end make_case_insensitive_associative_list

on make_case_sensitive_associative_list()
    script CaseSensitiveAssociativeList
        property parent : _make_associative_list()

        on find_record_for_key(the_key)
            considering case
                return continue find_record_for_key(the_key)
            end considering
        end find_record_for_key
    end script
end make_case_sensitive_associative_list
```

As you can see, adding the first child object adds a good few lines of code to the script.
However, once you define the second one, the total amount of code, including the
parent constructor, is still less than if you'd created two full copies of the
make_associative_list handler. The more variations you add, the bigger the total
savings becomes. And since all of your key logic only appears once in the script, it is
quicker and easier to understand and modify than if you had half-a-dozen slightly
different versions of the same code to dig through.

Testing the New Associative List Objects

Now that the code is complete, you might want to put it into a self-contained library file,
AssociativeListLib.scrpt, so that other scripts can make use of it. Before you do that,
though, don't forget to run some tests just to make sure that the new functionality is
working correctly.

First, here's some code to check that the case-insensitive version is working correctly:

```
set friends_ages to make_case_insensitive_associative_list()

set_item("Jan", 27) of friends_ages
set_item("Sam", 29) of friends_ages
set_item("Bob", 35) of friends_ages
-- So far, so good...

ignoring case
    if friends_ages's get_item("Sam") ≠ 29 then error "Test 1 failed."
    -- Test 1 passed.
    if friends_ages's get_item("sAM") ≠ 29 then error "Test 2 failed."
    -- Test 2 passed.
end ignoring

considering case
    if friends_ages's get_item("Sam") ≠ 29 then error "Test 3 failed."
```

```
    -- Test 3 passed.
    if friends_ages's get_item("sAM") ≠ 29 then error "Test 4 failed."
    -- Test 4 passed.
end considering
```

We start by creating a new case-insensitive associative list object and adding some values to it. If any errors occur at this point, we know there is a problem. Next we try retrieving a value using different combinations of key case and considering/ignoring blocks. A good test should anticipate all unique combinations of circumstances and check them all; for this example, I haven't bothered confirming that other attributes such as diacriticals and white space work correctly; you can add checks for those yourself. In all cases, neither the case of the key nor the presence of considering/ignoring blocks should have any effect: the get_item command should always return 29. If any errors occur, you know you have a bug, either in the setting code or the getting code, and will need to track it down and fix it.

Next, let's test the case-sensitive version:

```
set friends_ages to make_case_sensitive_associative_list()

set_item("Jan", 27) of friends_ages
set_item("Sam", 29) of friends_ages
set_item("Bob", 35) of friends_ages
-- So far, so good...

ignoring case
    if friends_ages's get_item("Sam") ≠ 29 then error "Test 1 failed."
    -- Test 1 passed.
    try
        friends_ages's get_item("sAM")
        error "Test 2 failed: should have raised error -1728."
    on error number -1728
    end try
    -- Test 2 passed.
end ignoring

considering case
    if friends_ages's get_item("Sam") ≠ 29 then error "Test 3 failed."
    -- Test 3 passed.
    try
        friends_ages's get_item("sAM")
        error "Test 4 failed: should have raised error -1728."
    on error number -1728
    end try
    -- Test 4 passed.
end considering
```

Once again, we want to check all of the combinations that we suspect could break our code if we haven't designed and debugged it correctly. The difference from the previous test code is that, with a case-sensitive associative list, we *want* an error -1728 to occur if the case of the key when getting a value does not exactly match the case of a key already in the associative list.

You could also add more tests of your own—for example, will the case-insensitive object store values with keys "Sam" and "SAM" as the same item, and will the case-sensitive object store them as separate items? It is up to you to anticipate all of the correct and incorrect ways the objects might be used and test them as necessary.

Now that you've added inheritance to your object-oriented toolbox, it's time to look at the final benefit that OOP provides: the ability to create "plug-and-play" code.

Creating Plug-and-Play Objects

So, what is the final benefit that object-oriented programming brings?

Previously, you learned how to structure your code using objects as a more elegant alternative to separate data structures and handlers. You also saw how inheritance can make it easier to reuse existing code. These are important benefits, but they are not, in my opinion, the biggest one.

Imagine you've written a thousand-line script. The techniques you've studied so far might allow you reuse a hundred lines of that, but what if I told you that, in some situations, object-oriented design could let you reuse the other 900 instead?

You might think I'm kidding here, but I'm not: it's just a matter of perspective. Let's say the script you've written sucks some data out of a FileMaker Pro database and pours it into an InDesign document. Now imagine your boss comes to you with an Excel spreadsheet and demands you run a job using the data from that instead. The logical thing to do would be to create a copy of your original Artwork Builder script, delete the FileMaker-specific code, and replace it with some Excel-specific code instead. The rest of the code remains the same, mind; it's just that one hunk of data-reading code that changes. If the FileMaker code was the bulk of your script, that's not so bad, but if it was only a small portion—a hundred lines or so—then you've just duplicated 900 lines of code that hasn't changed a bit.

If the Excel job was a one-off thing, then, hey, who cares? You solved the problem by the quickest practical route. On the other hand, if this is a regular event, then you might want to look for a more efficient long-term strategy for managing your code. Otherwise, any time you need to make a change to your other 900 lines, you will have to make that change twice…and things will only become worse as the boss turns up later on with Numbers spreadsheets, Microsoft SQL Server databases, and every other form of data you can imagine.

Now consider a different approach. Instead of gluing all of your data-reading options directly into your script, wrapping them in large conditional blocks, you keep them more or less independent from each other. The trick, as you might imagine, involves using objects. This time, though, it doesn't involve new language features—it is purely a design technique. All you do is move your FileMaker, or Excel, code into a script object and then hide it behind one or more handlers. What makes this approach work is that the handlers in the `FileMakerReader` and `ExcelReader` objects that return the data accept the *same* number and classes of parameters and return the *same* class of result.

Let's begin with a simple demonstration, as shown in Script 19–12.

Script 19–12.

```
script VisualHello
   on say_hello(the_greeting)
      display alert "Visual object says " & the_greeting
   end say_hello
end script

script AudioHello
   on say_hello(the_greeting)
      say "Audio object says " & the_greeting
   end say_hello
end script

repeat with hello_obj in {VisualHello, AudioHello}
   tell hello_obj to say_hello("Yo-ho-ho!")
end repeat
```

When you run this script, the first thing that happens is that the VisualHello object receives a say_hello command and responds by displaying a dialog box. Then, the AudioHello object receives an identical say_hello command, and responds with an audio announcement. In other words, two very different reactions to the same command are produced. All that your theoretical Artwork Builder script would do is scale things up a bit: instead of a say_hello command, you would send it a fetch_data() command, or something like that. Perhaps you would have a single command that retrieves all the data at once and then returns it as a list or string. Or you might use several commands: an open_for_access() command to prepare the data object for retrieving information, a read_entry() command for fetching each chunk of data one at a time, and a close_access() command for tidying up once you're done.

This is not to say that *all* your commands have to be identical. In particular, the constructor handler for each type of object will very likely be different: the make_excel_data_source constructor might take two parameters—an alias object identifying the Excel file, and a string containing the name of the worksheet in the file that contains the data. The make_sql_server_data_source constructor would take a string containing the information needed to connect to a Microsoft SQL database...and so on. However, the commands that count—the commands that are used by the main part of the system—are identical for all types of object, no matter what might go on behind the scenes. Plug in a different data source object, and the rest of your code is none the wiser: as long as it sends command X and receives data Y, it is happy.

Okay, that's enough theory: let's have some practice. A thousand-line script is a bit ambitious for this book, so let's consider a slightly simpler task: building a flexible system for logging progress information and errors within a larger project. The overall goal is the same, though: allowing you to plug in whatever functionality that suits you best for a particular job.

> **NOTE:** The ability of different classes of objects that present the same interface to be used interchangeably is known as *polymorphism*.

Planning the Logging System

Let's say we're building a large workflow system. Because the system will need to run by itself for long periods without constant supervision, it will need a built-in logging system to record its activity so that we can check and, if necessary, troubleshoot it later on. The main code is already large and complex, so we don't want to clog up its design by strewing lots of custom logging code throughout it. The solution is to design an object, or objects, to manage all of the logging duties. Any part of the system that needs to report something—a normal progress message, a detailed error description, and so forth—will do so by talking to a Log object.

To ensure that all of the Log objects we provide are interchangeable—at least from the point of view of the main script—we will define a standard set of commands that all Log objects will respond to. To keep the project simple, we will define only three logging commands, as follows:

```
log_important(the_text)
log_message(the_text)
log_error(the_text)
```

A full-blown system may well provide a richer interface than this; for example, the log_error command might take an error number and other information that may help the user in debugging a problem; other commands might be provided for indicating the beginning and end of each major stage of the process; and so on. However, it's always good to start small and build up functionality if and only when it is actually needed, so three commands are plenty for now.

Having decided on the standard logging interface we will provide, the only other thing to do is to decide what sort of logging objects we will actually provide. For example, we could provide a FileLog object that writes the messages to a plain text file whose path is specified when the FileLog object is created. We might also define a TextEditLog object for writing messages directly to a TextEdit document, allowing the user to view them as they are reported. Or we could create a MailErrorLog object that reports only errors by e-mailing them to a specified address. The point is, once you have agreed on a standard interface for logging information, Log objects are free to do anything they like with it.

Let's start by designing a basic FileLog object that will write messages to a file. While we're at it, let's also create a LogBase object that provides some common functionality that will be useful to all the different types of Log objects we might create.

Designing the *LogBase* Object

The goal of the LogBase object is simple: to contain any bits of functionality that are relevant to more than one type of Log object. This doesn't mean that all Log objects have to use it—they can still override it if they need to do something different—but it's there if they want it.

In practice, if you were designing this code for yourself, you might well start by creating a complete FileLog object by itself. Later, as you find you need to create other types of Log objects, you would go back and subdivide the existing code into parent and child

objects as and when needed. For this exercise, though, we will assume you have
already decided how you are going to break up the code for maximum reuse, and start
from there.

Let's start by defining the constructor for the `LogBase` object. As both the `FileLog` and
`TextEditLog` objects will format all of their messages in the same way, it makes sense to
put all of the formatting code into the parent object. The only code that will actually vary
between them is the code that writes the formatted messages either to a file or to a
TextEdit document.

Script 19–13 shows the `make_log_base` constructor.

Script 19–13.

```
on make_log_base()
    script LogBase
        property _linefeed : character id 10

        on _write(the_text)
            -- Sub-classes should override this method to write all text
            -- to their preferred output device
            error "Not implemented." number -1708
        end _write

        on log_important(the_text)
            _write("****** " & the_text & " ******")
        end log_important

        on log_message(the_text)
            _write(the_text)
        end log_message

        on log_error(the_text)
            _write("ERROR: " & the_text)
        end log_error
    end script
end make_log_base
```

Notice that we have defined a _write handler here, but the only thing it does when
called is raise an error. That's just to remind us that we need to override this handler in
any child object we define.

Now let's define the `make_file_log` constructor. Remember, if you were developing this
code a step at a time, you might just begin by filling in the _write handler with the file-
writing code and worry about restructuring it later. But as we already know we're going
to create two different types of logging objects, we can jump directly to the defining-the-
child-objects step.

If you have already jumped ahead and read most of Part 3 of the book (as I
recommended at the beginning of this chapter), then you know how to write to the end
of a plain text file using the commands in Standard Additions' File Read/Write suite.
Rather than explain the file-writing process in detail here, I will simply show you the
code. The objective is to open the target file if it already exists, or create a new one if it
doesn't, and then add a text message to the end of it.

Since all of the necessary message formatting code is provided by the LogBase object, the only thing we need to put in the FileLog object is a _write handler that knows how to do this. Script 19–14 shows the code.

Script 19–14.

```
on make_file_log(file_path)
    script FileLog
        property class : "file log"
        property parent : make_log_base()

        on _write(the_text) -- Writes log messages to a UTF8-encoded text file
            set f to open for access file_path with write permission
            try
                write (the_text & my _linefeed) to f starting at eof as «class utf8»
            on error error_message number error_number
                close access f
                error error_message number error_number
            end try
            close access f
        end _write
    end script
end make_file_log
```

Don't forget to include a parent property so that you can inherit the common functionality provided by the LogBase object, of course!

When you want to create a new FileLog object, simply call the make_file_log constructor, passing it an HFS path string (or alias or POSIX file object) specifying the file to write to. For example:

```
property the_log : missing value
set the_log to make_file_log("Macintosh HD:Users:hanann:Work:Logs:log.txt")
```

Now, whenever you send a log_important, log_message, or log_error command to the FileLog object, the message text will be formatted and added to the log.txt file on disk.

Try this for yourself. Create a new document in AppleScript Editor and add the make_log_base and make_file_log constructors to it, along with the following test code:

```
set the_log to make_file_log((path to desktop folder as text) & "test-log.txt")
the_log's log_important("An important message")
the_log's log_message("A message.")
the_log's log_message("Another message.")
the_log's log_error("Oh, no!")
```

When you run it, the result will be a test-log.txt file on your desktop containing the following text:

```
****** An important message ******
A message.
Another message.
ERROR: Oh, no!
```

Run it again, and a fresh set of messages will be added to the end, and so on.

Defining the Concrete Log Objects

At this stage, all we have done is created extra complexity: after all, if all that's needed is a single type of logging object, there's no point in defining a pair of chained objects when one would do. As soon as we start defining more kinds of Log objects, however, the savings become clear.

We'll begin by defining the TextEditLog object. Once again, this exercise assumes you already know how to script TextEdit. Script 19–15 lists the code for the make_textedit_log constructor.

Script 19–15.

```
on make_textedit_log(log_name)
    script TextEditLog
        property class : "textedit log"
        property parent : make_log_base()

        on _write(the_text)
            tell application "TextEdit"
                if not (exists document log_name) then
                    make new document with properties {name:log_name}
                end if
                make new paragraph at end of document log_name ¬
                        with data (the_text & my _linefeed)
            end tell
            return
        end _write
    end script
end make_textedit_log
```

As you can see, the only thing we've had to do here is provide a different _write handler, one that knows how to create a new TextEdit document if one doesn't already exist, and then append the formatted message to it.

Let's test this. Add the make_textedit_log constructor to your previous test script, and then modify the first line of the testing code to create a TextEditLog object instead of a FileLog objects, like this:

```
set the_log to make_textedit_log("test log 1")
```

Now when we run the test script, a new document named "test log 1" is created in TextEdit, and the test messages appear in that, as shown in Figure 19–2.

Figure 19–2. *The logging window that appears in TextEdit when the test script is run*

Notice that we now have two objects that respond to the same commands, but in different ways. None of the code that uses these objects needs to know or care that one writes to files and the other writes to TextEdit; it just trusts that whatever object it is given knows how to do its job.

By now, we're on a roll, so let's invent some other types of logging objects that we know will be useful.

First up, let's say we want to provide a way to disable the logging system completely. One way we could do this is by adding a conditional block around each logging command, like this:

```
if is_logging_enabled
    log_obj's log_message(...)
end if
```

However, if our code already contains a lot of logging commands, this approach would bloat it considerably. Instead, why not define a new type of logging object: one that does absolutely nothing when called! In Script 19–16, the make_null_log constructor returns a NullLog object that responds to all internal _write commands sent by its parent by doing precisely nothing.

Script 19–16.

```
on make_null_log()
    script NullLog
        property class : "null log"
        property parent : make_log_base()

        on _write(the_text)
        end _write -- Did nothing!
    end script
end make_null_log
```

Any time you want to turn off logging, just pass a NullLog object into the system in place of a FileLog or TextEditLog object. You might think that talking to an object that does nothing is rather wasteful, but if you look at the "big picture," the time your script spends waiting for your logging commands to do nothing is pretty insignificant compared to all the other work it is doing. Modern processors are fast and powerful, and you can easily afford to waste a few cycles here and there if it makes your code significantly easier to develop and maintain.

Now that we know how to write messages to no logs, let's turn this around: what if we want to output messages to several types of log at the same time? For example, a GUI-based log is good for keeping an eye on things as the script is running, whereas a file-based log provides a permanent record in case you need to go back and troubleshoot a few days or weeks later. No problem: we'll just define a logging object that can hold one or more other logging objects, and when we send this GroupLog object a command, it will automatically redistribute that command to all of the log objects it contains. The code for this new type of object is shown in Script 19–17.

Script 19–17.

```
on make_group_log(log_objects)
    script GroupLog
        property class : "group log"

        on log_important(the_text)
            repeat with log_ref in log_objects
                log_ref's log_important(the_text)
            end repeat
        end log_important

        on log_message(the_text)
            repeat with log_ref in log_objects
                log_ref's log_message(the_text)
            end repeat
        end log_message

        on log_error(the_text)
            repeat with log_ref in log_objects
                log_ref's log_error(the_text)
            end repeat
        end log_error
    end script
end make_group_log
```

Unlike the previous objects that override the LogBase object's _write handler, this object ignores the LogBase object entirely and defines its own handlers for all logging operations. As long as the different Log objects respond to the same commands, AppleScript doesn't care who inherits from what.

Let's try a few more quick examples. This time, we'll define objects that can be used to extend or modify the behavior of existing Log objects using—you guessed it—inheritance.

The first of these objects, which we'll call ErrorFilter, will override a parent Log object so that only error messages get through. The second, TimestampAdder, will insert the current date and time at the beginning of each log entry. Script 19–18 shows the code.

Script 19–18.

```
on make_error_filter(log_object)
    script ErrorFilter
        property parent : log_object

        on log_important(the_text)
        end log_important

        on log_message(the_text)
        end log_message
    end script
end make_error_filter

on make_timestamp_adder(log_object)
    script TimestampAdder
        property parent : log_object
```

```
   on _write(the_text)
      tell (current date)
         set time_stamp to its short date string & space & its time string
      end tell
      continue _write(time_stamp & tab & the_text)
   end _write
   end script
end make_timestamp_adder
```

Notice how both of these constructors take an existing log object as their parameter and then use it as the parent of the newly created filter object. This is one of the really elegant things about AppleScript's classless OOP system: the ability to build new inheritance relationships on-the-fly. You could not do this in a class-based language where inheritance relationships between classes are fixed at compile time; instead, you would have no choice but to implement your filters as wrapper objects like our earlier GroupLog. In AppleScript you can use whichever approach, inheritance or containment, that best fits your particular needs.

Testing the Finished Logging System

Let's finish off this section by assembling our collection of plug-and-play logging objects into a more complete demonstration. For this exercise, we will create two types of logs: a TextEdit-based log containing only error messages, and a file-based log containing timestamped entries for everything. We will then wrap these two objects in a group log so that the client code only has to deal with a single Log object.

First, gather up all of the log object constructors from Scripts 19–13 to 19–18 and put them in a new document in AppleScript Editor. Now that we've gone to all the trouble of creating this functionality, we should allow as many scripts as possible to take advantage of it, so let's make it a reusable library. Save the document as LogLib.scpt in ~/Library/Scripts/.

Next, begin a fresh script in AppleScript Editor. Before we can do anything else, we need to import the LogLib.scpt library, so let's do that:

```
property LogLib : load script alias ¬
      ((path to scripts folder from user domain as text) & "LogLib.scpt")
```

This will load the library when the main script is compiled and store it in the property named LogLib.

Below this, define a property to hold the main GroupLog object once it is created:

```
property system_log : missing value
```

Now let's define a handler that will prepare the logging system for use:

```
on prepare_system_log()
   set log_file_path to (path to desktop as text) & "full-log.txt"
   set file_log to LogLib's make_file_log(log_file_path)
   set file_log to LogLib's make_timestamp_adder(file_log)
   set textedit_log to LogLib's make_textedit_log("Error Log")
   set textedit_log to LogLib's make_error_filter(textedit_log)
   set system_log to LogLib's make_group_log({file_log, textedit_log})
```

```
end prepare_system_log
```

When the script starts running, the first thing it must do before trying to log any messages is to call this handler. The `prepare_system_log` handler will initialize whatever Log objects are appropriate for this project and then assign a single Log object—in this case, a GroupLog—to the `system_log` property so that the logging system can be accessed from anywhere it the script.

And last but not least, let's test it:

```
on run
    -- Always remember to set up the logging system before use:
    prepare_system_log()

    -- Run some tests:
    system_log's log_important("This is an important test")
    system_log's log_message("This is an ordinary report")
    system_log's log_error("This is a fictional calamity")
end run
```

Figure 19–3 shows how the TextEdit-based log will look when the test script is run.

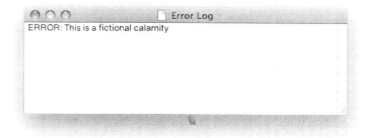

Figure 19–3. *The TextEdit-based error log after the test script is run*

Notice how extending the basic TextEditLog object with an ErrorFilter object causes any log_important and log_message commands to be ignored so that only error messages get through. This can provide the user with a quick heads-up should anything go wrong while the system is running. Once they know there's a problem, they can open up the detailed log file to find further information there:

```
21/08/2009 13:10:34    ****** This is an important test ******
21/08/2009 13:10:34    This is an ordinary report
21/08/2009 13:10:34    ERROR: This is a fictional calamity
```

As you can see, the TimestampAdder object is modifying each entry before it is written to file so that it includes a timestamp at the start. Because the whole system is designed of small, simple, pluggable components, you can extensively customize it to suit whatever needs a project has. And any time you need to provide additional feedback options—for example, you might want error messages to be e-mailed to the developer or displayed to the user in a Growl notification window (http://growl.info)—you can add new kinds of Log objects to your LogLib.scpt library.

Conclusion

As you can see, the time it takes to design and build a flexible, object-based logging system is greater than the time it would take just to hard-code a one-off handler to write messages to a file. On the other hand, if you do a lot of logging in your scripts and need plenty of options in how the logging system is configured, it is worth considering a more modular approach like the one shown here.

Because the entire logging system is implemented using object-oriented techniques, its internal details are safely hidden away from the code that uses it, with all objects providing the same, standard interface for client code to communicate with them. This design will give you flexibility in how the system is configured for each job and allow room to expand it later on by adding new types of logging objects that are interchangeable with the existing ones.

Summary

In this, the final chapter of Part 2, you learned about one of the most advanced features in AppleScript—script objects—and how you can use them to organize your code in two different ways.

In the first half of the chapter, you learned how to create and use libraries of user-defined handlers. These libraries are ordinary compiled script files, but instead of being run directly, they are loaded into other scripts, which then send them commands. This allows you to share commonly used handlers among many scripts without having to copy and paste them every time—with all the code bloat and maintenance headaches that causes.

In the second half of the chapter, you were introduced to a powerful new coding technique known as object-oriented programming (OOP), where simple, "dumb" values and the handlers that operate on them are wrapped up as powerful "smart" objects, which you can pass around your script and manipulate by sending them commands. While object-oriented design is usually overkill for smaller scripts, it can be a terrific tool for organizing some or all of the code in large, sophisticated systems that deal with lots of complicated data structures.

Anyway, congratulations—you've made it to the end of Part 2! At this stage, you should have a good understanding of how the AppleScript language itself works, so now it's time to put that knowledge to work by doing what AppleScript was born to do: automating applications.

In the chapters that follow, you will use all of the important AppleScript features covered in this part of the book: Booleans, numbers, strings, lists, records, and dates; commands, operators, variables, and coercions; conditional, loop, and error handling statements; and handlers.

You will even encounter script objects again in the final chapter of the book. Mac OS X's extensive Cocoa frameworks are highly object-oriented, so if you intend to write your own GUI applications using AppleScriptObjC, then you'll find that this chapter provides an easy introduction to OOP concepts and techniques.

In the next chapter, we will begin Part 3 by returning to the world of the Mac OS X file system. We will look at how the scriptable Finder and System Events applications can be used to manipulate the file system, and also explore some useful file-related commands provided by our old friend, Standard Additions.

Part III

Putting AppleScript to Work

Chapter 20

Scripting the File System

Chapter 17 looked at the various ways you can identify the files, folders, and disks that make up Mac OS X's file system. In this chapter, you'll learn how to manipulate these objects using scriptable applications. We'll also look at some useful file system-related commands provided by the Standard Additions scripting addition.

Mac OS X includes two scriptable applications that can manipulate the file system: Finder and System Events. I'm sure you're already familiar with the Finder, but you may not have heard of System Events before so let's do a quick introduction.

System Events is what's known as a "faceless background application"—a GUI-less program that runs invisibly on your Mac. Such applications are frequently used to provide collections of useful services to other programs. System Events, for example, offers many different suites of commands and classes for AppleScripts to use. Some of these suites allow scripts to control various aspects of Mac OS X, such as Dock preferences and network settings. Others can be used to work with common file formats, including XML and QuickTime movie files. There is even a suite that lets you manipulate applications' GUIs directly from AppleScript—very useful when applications don't have a scripting interface of their own.

Later in this chapter, we'll look at one System Events suite in particular: the Disk-Folder-File Suite. But first, let's review how the Finder's object model represents the Mac OS X file system.

How the Finder Represents the Mac OS X File System

The first items to explore when scripting the file system are the different classes of objects Finder and System Events use to represent files, folders and disks. There are quite a few differences between the Finder's and System Events' object models, so this section will focus on the Finder and the next section will cover System Events.

The top of the food chain in the Finder's inheritance structure is a class called `item`. The `item` class describes the basic features found in every class of file system object you'll meet in Finder scripting: `disk`, `folder`, `application file`, `document file`, and so on.

Figure 20–1 illustrates how Finder's file system–related classes inherit features and behaviors from one another. For example, if you follow the arrows on the diagram, you can see that the `alias file` class inherits many of its properties from the `file` class, which in turn inherits many of its attributes from the `item` class. Similarly, the `disk` and `folder` classes inherit most of their properties and all of their elements from the `container` class.

To give another example: if you look at the Finder's dictionary, you can see that the `item` class defines a name property. From this, you can deduce that every `disk` object, every `folder` object, every `document file` object, and so on, also possesses a name property. This means you can ask any kind of file system object for its name, even when you don't know—or care—exactly what class of object it is. As long as you know it's some sort of `item` object, you know that asking it for its name will always work.

You can also use your knowledge of the Finder's inheritance hierarchy when creating references to file system objects. For instance, if you have an HFS path string and want to use the Finder to delete the corresponding file or folder, you can convert that path to a Finder object reference using an `item` specifier:

```
set the_path to "Macintosh HD:Users:hanaan:some item"

tell application "Finder"
    delete (item the_path)
end tell
```

You don't need to worry whether the path is to a document file, an application file, a folder, or the like, as you know from the Finder's inheritance tree that these are all items. Just use an `item` specifier, and the Finder will automatically work out exactly what type of object it is. For example:

```
tell application "Finder"
    get (item "Macintosh HD:Users:hanaan:ReadMe.txt")
end tell
--> document file "ReadMe.txt" of folder "hanaan"
        of folder "Users" of startup disk of application "Finder"


tell application "Finder"
    get (item "Macintosh HD:Users:hanaan:untitled folder")
end tell
--> folder "untitled folder" of folder "hanaan"
        of folder "Users" of startup disk of application "Finder"
```

Similarly, if you know that the `duplicate` command will work on any kind of item, you can be confident that the item will be duplicated whether it is a document file, an application file, a folder, or a disk.

The `item` class has four subclasses: `container`, `file`, `package`, and `computer-object`.

Understanding Containers

The `container` class defines the properties, elements, and behaviors that are common to all Finder items that can contain other items. It has four subclasses: `disk`, `folder`, `desktop-object`, and `trash-object`.

The Finder represents mounted volumes (hard disk, CD, DVD, etc.) as objects of class `disk`, while `folder` objects represent the folders that live on those disks. Since the purpose of disks and folders is to contain items (files and folders), it's not surprising that they should share many common characteristics, all of which are defined by the `container` class.

However, while the `folder` class does not define any new features beyond those provided by the `container` class, the `disk` class adds several features that are relevant only to hard disks and other kinds of volumes, such as the type of formatting scheme used (Mac OS Extended, NTFS, etc.) and the ability to be ejected when no longer required.

You could almost think of a disk as a top-level folder, and for many scripting purposes they are essentially the same, unless you want to use a command such as `erase` or `eject`. These commands work only with disks.

Figure 20–2 shows how the various classes of file system-related objects can fit together. (Some parts have been truncated for simplicity or because they can, in theory, go on forever—for instance, folders can contain folders that contain folders that contain folders....)

The inheritance hierarchy in Figure 20–1 showed you how similar the various classes of objects are to one another. For instance, application files and document files obtain most of their characteristics from the `file` class, which in turn inherits some features from the `item` class.

The containment hierarchy in Figure 20–2 tells you how you can reach the various classes of objects within the object model. For example, the main `application` object has `disk` elements, each of which has various `file` and `folder` elements. Each folder can contain `file` and `folder` elements of its own, and so on.

For example, on my Mac, the disk `Macintosh HD` contains a folder named `Users`, which contains a folder named `hanaan`, which contains various files and yet more folders. The file system on your Mac will contain different files and folders, of course, so the object model in your Finder will be different, too. However, the overall rules by which Finder objects can fit inside one another are always the same.

You can combine the information in the inheritance and containment diagrams to navigate around the object model more precisely. If you want only the document files of a folder, you would ask for the folder's `document file` elements. If you don't care about the exact type of file, you could ask the folder for its `file` elements. And if you want sub-folders as well as files, just ask for every `item` element.

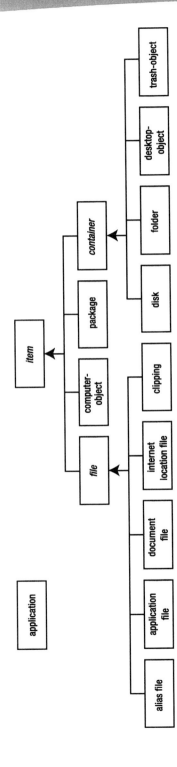

Figure 20–1. *The inheritance hierarchy of the Finder's file system–related classes*

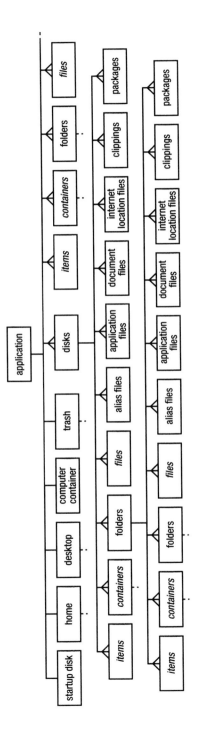

Figure 20–2. *The Finder's containment hierarchy for file system-related objects*

Similarly, referring to `container` elements is great when you want to execute any command on objects or get information about objects that you know are containers but you're not sure exactly what kind—disks or folders. For example, the following script will back up every file of a given container, without caring whether that container object is a disk or a folder:

```
tell application "Finder"
    duplicate (every file of container the_path) to (folder "backup" of home)
end tell
```

You will notice that the Finder's `application` object has several properties that contain other objects (or shortcuts to other objects) in the object model. These properties are named `startup disk`, `home`, `desktop`, `computer container`, and `trash`. These properties make it easy to refer to locations of particular interest.

For example, the `home` property always contains a reference to the current user's home folder

```
tell application "Finder" to get home
--> folder "hanaan" of folder "Users" of startup disk of application "Finder"
```

while the `startup disk` property provides a handy shortcut to the disk from which Mac OS X was booted.

```
tell application "Finder" to get name of startup disk
--> "Macintosh HD"
```

The other three properties contain one-off objects that represent special locations. The `trash` property contains an object of class `trash-object` and the `desktop` property contains an object of class `desktop-object` (we'll cover the `computer container` property in a later section).

The `trash-object` and `desktop-object` classes describe two special container objects that represent the current user's trash and desktop, respectively. These two objects are always found in the `trash` and `desktop` properties of the Finder's application `object`. The following are two examples of using `trash` and `desktop`:

```
tell application "Finder" to set trashed_items to every item of trash
```

```
tell application "Finder" to move every file of desktop to trash -- Be careful!
```

Notice how the two preceding script lines use the words `trash` and `desktop` to refer to the two special Finder containers.

Incidentally, while the `trash` property provides the only way to access items in the user's trash, there are no fewer than three different ways you can reach files and folders on the user's desktop:

- You can refer to the elements of the desktop object found in the `desktop` property.

- You can build your own reference to the `Desktop` folder first, like this:
  `folder "Desktop" of home`.

- You can refer directly to the `file` and `folder` elements of the Finder's main `application` object.

It is an indication of the power and the flexibility of the Finder's object model that it can provide you with a choice of routes to the objects you're interested in. We'll discuss some of the benefits of using the `startup disk` and `home` folder shortcuts later in the chapter, and you'll discover other applications often provide similarly useful shortcuts.

> **NOTE:** Depending on the language settings on your Mac, the Finder may localize the names of some folders and applications when displaying them on screen. However, both Finder and System Events prefer to use the standard English names when communicating with AppleScript. For instance, if you ask the Finder for `name of folder "Bibliothe que" of home` on a French-speaking Mac, the result is `"Library"`. Asking for `folder "Library" of home` still works, too.

Understanding Files

The `file` class has five subclasses: `alias file`, `application file`, `document file`, `internet location file`, and `clipping`. Each subclass may add its own set of properties that no other class has. The `application file` class, for instance, defines a Boolean property called `has scripting terminology`. This property is `true` when the application is scriptable, for example:

```
tell application "Finder"
    tell application file "TextEdit" of folder "Applications" of startup disk
        has scripting terminology
    end tell
end tell
--> true
```

Although for the most part you will just use the class `file` in scripts, distinguishing among the different subclasses may be useful when getting lists of specific items from folders. For instance, you can create a script that goes through a folder and all of its sub-folders and fixes or deletes any nonworking alias files it finds.

Heck, let's create that script right now!

I will show you how to create a script that will loop through folders and delete all the alias files whose original items no longer exist. Later you can modify the script to ask the user to choose a new original item instead, but that is your homework.

Now, writing a script that can process the contents of a single folder is simple enough, but what if you also want it to process all of the folder's sub-folders, each of those folder's sub-folders, and so on? The answer is first to put all the code for processing a single folder into a handler. This handler calls itself in order to process each one of the folder's sub-folders too, and as it processes each of those folders, it calls itself to process their sub-folders too, and so on, and so on, until every single nested folder has been dealt with.

This ability of a handler to call itself (then call itself … then call itself…) is what's known as *recursion*, and it's exactly what is needed to deal with deeply nested structures such as the folders in a file system or the elements in an XML document.

> **NOTE:** Make sure you remember the difference between AppleScript's `alias` class and the Finder's `alias file` class. An alias file is a special "shortcut" file that opens another file or folder when you double-click it in the Finder, whereas an alias is an AppleScript object that points to a file, folder, or disk in the file system. If you write `alias` where you actually mean `alias file`, or vice versa, the script won't work correctly.

Script 20–1 shows the script.

Script 20–1.

```
1. set the_folder to (choose folder)
2. clean_alias_files_in_folder(the_folder)

3. on clean_alias_files_in_folder(the_folder)
4.     tell application "Finder"
5.         -- Check each of the alias files in this disk/folder
6.         set alias_files to every alias file of the_folder
7.         repeat with file_ref in alias_files
8.             if not (exists original item of file_ref) then
9.                 delete file_ref
10.            end if
11.        end repeat
12.        -- Clean the alias files in each sub-folder
13.        set sub_folders to every folder of the_folder
14.        repeat with folder_ref in sub_folders
15.            my clean_alias_files_in_folder(folder_ref)
16.        end repeat
17.    end tell
18. end clean_alias_files_in_folder
```

Line 1 of the script allows the user to choose a folder. This folder will be the top-level folder processed by the script, which will then process all nested files in that folder.

Line 2 calls the main handler, `clean_alias_files_in_folder`. As you'll see in a minute, what makes the script recursive is the fact that the handler calls itself.

The handler, which runs from line 3 through line 18, treats only one folder. First, all the alias files are treated. This happens in lines 6 through 11, and it starts with the creation of a list that contains references to all of the alias files in the folder:

```
set alias_files to every alias file of the_folder
```

Lines 7 to 11 loop through the list, allowing each alias file to be processed in turn. Line 8 builds a reference to an alias file's `original item` property and uses the Finder's `exists` command to check if this new reference points to an existing file, folder or disk. If the original item no longer exists, line 9 deletes the alias file.

Similarly, lines 13 to 17 create a list of references to the current folder's sub-folders and loop through them. What happens with these sub-folder references, however, is different. Line 15 makes the handler call itself, passing it one of these sub-folder references. Now the handler goes off and processes the sub-folder in the same way as before: first deleting any broken alias files, then processing each one of *its* sub-folders, and so on. When no more sub-folders are left to process, AppleScript knows to return to the spot it left off at and continue running through more folders.

Understanding Packages

Packages (also known as *bundles*) are special folders: they appear as single files in a Finder's window, but they're really disguised folders that contain other folders and files. The most common form of package is the OS X application bundle, where the application binary and its various resource files (icons, audio files, help files, and so on) are all wrapped up in a bundle folder with the filename extension .app.

The following script obtains references to all of the items in your Applications folder that are packages:

```
tell application "Finder"
   every package of folder "Applications" of startup disk
end tell
--> {application file "Address Book.app" of folder "Applications" of
      startup disk of application "Finder", application file "Automator.app"
      of folder "Applications" of startup disk of application "Finder", ...}
```

Notice how the Finder neatly identifies each package-based item by its exact class: application file, document file, etc. While it isn't obvious from Finder's dictionary that this will be the result, it seems like a sensible thing to do from the user's point of view. Ask the Finder for a list of references to items that are really packages, and that is exactly what you get.

> **TIP:** You will further explore .app bundles later in this chapter and in Chapters 22 and 30 when learning how to embed various types of resource files in your own AppleScript-based applications.

Understanding the *computer-object* Class

The Mac OS X Finder likes to provide its users with a "worldview" of the entire file system—a special location named "Computer" where all local disks, mounted media, and other network-accessible computers are visible at once. You can easily view this location by choosing Computer from the Finder's Go menu. The Computer location is also represented in the Finder's scripting interface by a single object of class computer-object. You can find this object in the computer container property of the Finder's application object.

The computer-object class itself is a bit odd. The dictionary says that it inherits from the item class, so you can expect it to have all the properties defined by the item class. Most of these properties don't actually contain useful values, though, and can just be ignored. The one useful property you can extract from the computer container object is `displayed name`. The value of this property is the name of your computer, as defined in the Sharing panel in System Preferences.

The `computer container` property is also useful for opening the Computer window from AppleScript:

```
tell application "Finder" to open computer container
```

Now that we've looked at how the Finder's object model describes the Mac OS X file system, let's see what System Events makes of it.

How System Events Represents the Mac OS X File System

System Events' Disk-Folder-File Suite defines a somewhat different object model from the Finder's, although as it describes the same file system objects—files, folders, and disks—it mostly works in similar ways.

One reason you might want to use System Events to manipulate the file system is that some Mac users prefer to disable the Finder and use a third-party file manager such as Cocoatech's Path Finder instead. Clearly, this is a problem for scripts that rely on the Finder for manipulating the file system; fortunately, the System Events application is always available, so you can often use that instead.

Another consideration is that System Events contains a few useful features that don't currently exist in Finder, such as `domain` objects and the ability to work with hidden files and folders (the Finder can only manipulate visible files and folders). In turn, the Finder has several advantages over System Events, such as the ability to access Finder windows and icon positions. One particularly annoying omission in System Events is that it can't yet duplicate files and folders; if you need to do this, the Finder is your best bet.

Figure 20–3 shows the part of the System Events inheritance hierarchy we're interested in, while Figure 20–4 shows the containment hierarchy for objects of these classes.

As you can see, System Events allows you to refer to any file, folder or disk in the file system. It also provides plenty of shortcuts to important locations such as the current user's standard folders—even more than the Finder offers.

For now, let's concentrate on the classes that define individual disk, folder, and file objects. The top class, `disk item`, is also the most general one. Any object in the file system is a disk item of one sort or another: all folders are disk items, all files are disk items, and all disks are disk items.

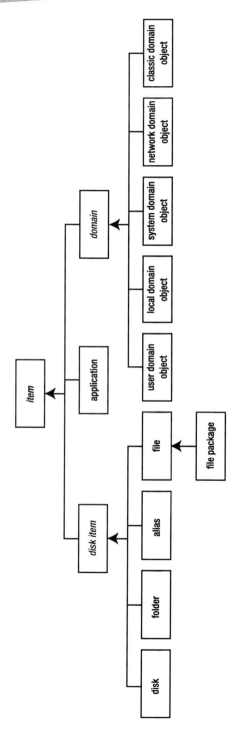

Figure 20–3. *The inheritance hierarchy for System Events' file system–related classes*

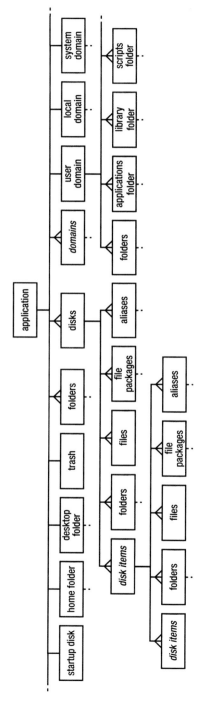

Figure 20–4. *The containment hierarchy for System Events' file system-related objects*

The disk item class has four subclasses: folder, alias, disk, and file. Note how different they are from the Finder's object class hierarchy. For example, System Events doesn't distinguish between different kinds of files to the same degree as the Finder, so if you want to create a reference that identifies only application files, say, you'll find it harder to do in System Events. However different, the System Events' class hierarchy is pretty easy to understand. Let's look at the four subclasses in detail.

Understanding Files

Unlike the Finder, System Events does not distinguish among application files, clippings, document files, and so on. Instead, they are all represented by objects of a single class: file.

Here's a simple script that gets a reference to the first file in the user's home folder, assuming there is one:

```
tell application "System Events"
    file 1 of home folder
end tell
```

As with Finder references, System Events also allows you to identify files by index, name, range, test, and so on. For example:

```
tell application "System Events"
    file 1 of home folder
end tell
```

```
tell application "System Events"
file "Read Me.txt" of home folder
end tell
```

```
tell application "System Events"
    files 2 thru -1 of home folder
end tell
```

```
tell application "System Events"
    every file of home folder whose name extension is "txt"
end tell
```

The following example uses the file class's size property to filter files that are larger than 5MB (or 5 million bytes, to be exact):

```
tell application "System Events"
    set large_files_list to every file of the_folder whose size > 5000000
end tell
```

The following, more complex example gets the names of the HTML files in a selected folder. The script does that by using the file class's type identifier property. You can find more information about type identifiers in Chapter 17.

```
set the_path to (choose folder) as text

tell application "System Events"
    set file_names to name of every file of (disk item the_path) ¬
        whose type identifier is "public.html"
end tell
```

The file class has one subclass, file package. Like the Finder's package class, this can be used to refer to package-based items such as application bundles. For example:

```
tell application "System Events"
   every file package of folder "Applications" of startup disk
end tell
--> {file package "Macintosh HD:Applications:Address Book.app:"
         of application "System Events",
      file package "Macintosh HD:Applications:Automator.app:"
         of application "System Events",
   ...}
```

Understanding Folders

In scripting terms, folders are disk items that can have elements. These elements represent files and other folders that are contained by the folder.

For example, I can build up a reference to my home folder by referring to each disk and folder element in turn:

```
tell application "System Events"
   folder "hanaan" of folder "Users" of disk "Macintosh HD"
end tell
```

Or I can create the same reference using a full path string:

```
tell application "System Events"
   folder "Macintosh HD:Users:hanaan:"
end tell
```

Like the Finder, System Event's application object also provides several useful properties that contain references to important locations. (You can find these and most other properties of the application class defined under the System Events suite.) So, I can also get a reference to my home folder using the following:

```
tell application "System Events"
   home folder
end tell
```

All three methods return a reference that looks like this:

```
folder "Macintosh HD:Users:hanaan:" of application "System Events"
```

Working with a folder object's elements is quite straightforward. For example, to get the name of every folder in the current user's home folder, use this:

```
tell application "System Events"
   name of every folder of home folder
end tell
--> {".Trash", "Desktop", "Documents", "Library", "Movies", "Music", ...}
```

Notice that unlike the Finder's scripting interface, which only shows visible items, System Events lets you see hidden items, too, such as files and folders whose names start with ".". This can be useful for some tasks, but annoying for others; fortunately, you can easily filter out the invisible items if you want using a whose clause and the disk item class's `visible` property. For example, to get a reference to the first visible file or folder in the `Applications` folder, use this:

```
tell application "System Events"
   disk item 1 of folder "Applications" of startup disk whose visible is true
end tell
--> file package "Macintosh HD:Applications:Address Book.app:"
         of application "System Events"
```

Understanding Disks

In the Finder, the `disk` class is a subclass of the `container` class. In System Events, `disk` is a direct subclass of the `disk item` class.

The following script lists the names of all available disks:

```
tell application "System Events"
   name of every disk
end tell
--> {"Macintosh HD", "Number Nine", ...}
```

Understanding System Events' *alias* Class

The `alias` class in System Events' dictionary is a bit of an oddity. It has no relation either to AppleScript's `alias` class or to Finder's `alias file` class; its actual purpose is to make it easier to write references in System Events.

Scriptable applications normally allow you to refer to their objects only by using a full object reference, such as `text of document 1` or `name of every track of playlist "Library"`. When dealing with the file system, however, it's common to refer to files, folders, and disks using AppleScript alias objects.

Of course, you could convert your AppleScript alias object to a path string and use that to construct a new application reference in Finder or System Events. For example:

```
set the_alias to choose file
set the_path to the_alias as text
tell application "System Events" to set file_info to properties of file the_path
```

However, both the Finder and newer versions of System Events allow you to skip these extra conversion steps and just use the original AppleScript alias object directly in the reference:

```
set the_alias to choose file
tell application "Finder" to set file_info to properties of the_alias
tell application "System Events" to set file_info to properties of the_alias
```

So although seeing the nonstandard `alias` class definition in System Events' dictionary may be a bit confusing at first, don't worry about it. It's just System Events' way of making this trick work.

This extra flexibility makes dealing with AppleScript aliases a bit simpler and more convenient. Just remember to be careful if you need to ask for the object's class, since AppleScript alias objects already have a `class` property of their own—a line like this

```
tell application "System Events" to get class of the_alias
```

will return `alias`, not `disk`, `folder`, or `file` (or `alias file`, `document file`, and so on, in the Finder's case), as you probably wanted. So, you still need to use the longer method for that. But the rest of the time, it "just works."

Other Classes of Interest

So far, you have learned about those classes of objects in System Events that deal directly with the file system: `file`, `folder`, and `disk`.

System Events' dictionary defines many other classes besides its disk item classes. Most of these other classes apply to unrelated tasks such as GUI scripting and XML processing, so I won't cover them in this chapter. However, there are three classes of related interest: `user`, `domain`, and `login item`. Let's take a closer look at them.

The *user* Class

No, not only you and your family members are privileged enough to be users on your OS X–equipped Mac. Try this script to see who else has an administrator account or ordinary user account on your Mac:

```
tell application "System Events"
    name of every user
end tell
--> {"johanne", "olivia", "hanaan", "aylam"}
```

Now, let's see what properties each user has. This script checks the properties of user "hanaan":

```
tell application "System Events"
    properties of user "hanaan"
end tell
--> {full name:"Hanaan Rosenthal", name:"hanaan", home directory:"/Users/hanaan",
    picture path:"/Library/User Pictures/Animals/Dragonfly.tif", class:user}
```

The *domain* Class

In Mac OS X, a domain is a region of the startup disk that serves a particular purpose. Files and folders are organized into one of several standard domains according to which user owns them and who else, if anyone, is allowed to use them. For example, operating system files are kept in the system domain; items that need to be accessible to all users go in the local domain; a user's personal files and folders live in the user domain; and so on.

The following script lists the name of each domain:

```
tell application "System Events"
    name of every domain
end tell
--> {"System", "Local", "Network", "User", "Classic"}
```

What tasks are domains good for? Well, each domain can contain a number of "standard" folders: one for applications, another for fonts, another for scripting additions, and so on. The user domain can also have standard folders for items like the user's documents, movies, music, and so on. Each of System Events' domain objects includes a number of properties containing references to that domain's standard folders, making it easy for an AppleScript to locate those folders without needing to know their exact paths.

Later on in this chapter we'll look at the Standard Additions path to command, which you can also use to locate special folders in each domain. However, path to is limited in that it can only obtain one path at a time. What if you want to get the paths to all possible locations a scripting addition can be in, or get the paths for all font folders in the system? To do that the easy way, you need System Events:

```
tell application "System Events"
    get scripting additions folder of every domain
end tell
--> {folder "Macintosh HD:System:Library:ScriptingAdditions:"
          of application "System Events",
      folder "Macintosh HD:Library:ScriptingAdditions:"
          of application "System Events", missing value,
      folder "Macintosh HD:Users:hanaan:Library:ScriptingAdditions:"
          of application "System Events", missing value}
```

As you can see, the resulting list includes references to all of the ScriptingAdditions folders that currently exist on your system. In the above example, the third and last items are missing value because the network and classic domains on my Mac didn't contain ScriptingAdditions folders when I ran the script. You can use a whose clause to filter out the non-existent folders if you want:

```
tell application "System Events"
    get scripting additions folder of ¬
        every domain whose scripting additions folder is not missing value
end tell
```

The following example collects the names of all the scripting additions installed in each domain:

```
tell application "System Events"
    set osax_names to name of (every file whose name extension is "osax") of ¬
        scripting additions folder of ¬
        (every domain whose scripting additions folder is not missing value)
end tell
--> {{"Digital Hub Scripting.osax", "StandardAdditions.osax"},
      {"FITS.osax", "Numerics.osax", "Satimage.osax", "XMLLib.osax"},
      {"Adobe Unit Types.osax", "AppleModsTools.osax"}}
```

The *login item* Class

Before we move on, let's take a quick look at one more System Events class: the `login item` class in its Login Items Suite. Login items are used to identify file system items—usually application files—that should be opened when you log into the system. (Depending on your settings in System Preferences' Accounts pane, Mac OS X may log you in automatically each time it starts up.) While System Preferences' Accounts pane allows you to add and remove login items manually, if you want to automate the process System Events is the way to go.

Script 20–2 prompts the user to pick an application and creates a login item for that application. The next time you log in, Mac OS X will launch the application automatically.

Script 20–2.

```
set the_app to choose application ¬
with prompt "Choose application to startup automatically" as alias
set app_path to POSIX path of the_app
tell application "System Events"
    make new login item at end of login items with properties {path:app_path}
end tell
```

Now, after users have lots of fun with your script, they will have a surplus of unwanted login items. Script 20–3 lets them choose a login item from a list and delete it.

Script 20–3.

```
tell application "System Events"
    set login_item_names to name of every login item
    set the_selection to choose from list login_item_names¬
OK button name "Delete"
    if the_selection is not false then
        set selected_name to item 1 of the_selection
        delete login item selected_name
    end if
end tell
```

Your homework is to allow the user to delete multiple login items at a time and warn the user before deleting ("Are you sure?").

Working with Finder Items

In the following sections, you'll focus not on all the things you can do with the Finder application, but rather on all the things you can do with and to Finder items. Since the System Events commands are so similar to the Finder's commands, the following sections will concentrate on the Finder and just point out any important differences.

Opening and Closing Items

The open command works with any item you can open from the Finder. It acts as if you double-clicked the item. If you use the open command on a disk or folder, the disk/folder will open as a new Finder window. For example, this will open the current user's home folder:

```
tell application "Finder" to open home
```

If you use it to open a file, the Finder will normally tell the file's default application to open it; for example, an HTML file will typically open in your favorite web browser:

```
tell application "Finder"
    open file "index.html" of folder "Sites" of home
end tell
```

You can specify a different application with the open command's optional using parameter:

```
tell application "Finder"
    open file "index.html" of folder "Sites" of home ¬
using application file "TextEdit" of folder "Applications" of startup disk
end tell
```

Incidentally, Finder also lets you specify an application file by its bundle id, which is handy if the application's name or location might change in future:

```
tell application "Finder"
    open file "index.html" of folder "Sites" of home ¬
        using application file id "com.apple.textedit"
end tell
```

The close command can be applied to disks and folders, closing their windows if they're already open:

```
tell application "Finder" to close home
```

In practice, though, it's more commonly used to close windows directly:

```
tell application "Finder" to close window 1
```

Duplicating Files and Folders

The Finder's duplicate command copies files and folders.

In its simplest form, the duplicate command takes a single value as its direct parameter: a reference to one or more items to copy. For example:

```
tell application "Finder" to duplicate file "ReadMe.txt" of desktop
```

This has the same result as selecting Duplicate in the Finder's File menu: creating a copy of the file in the same folder as the original.

The duplicate command, along with other commands such as move and delete, can also accept an alias, or a list of aliases, as its direct parameter. This is handy when you already have a list of alias values obtained from somewhere else, because you don't need to convert them to Finder references before passing them to the command.

The other way you can use the duplicate command is to copy items from one folder to another. To do this, you have to specify a reference to the Finder items you want to duplicate and a reference to the container you want to duplicate them to:

```
tell application "Finder"
    duplicate every file of desktop to disk "Backup Disk"
end tell
```

The most useful feature, however, is being able to decide what to do if an item by that name already exists in the container you duplicate to. By default, the Finder will raise an error: "An item with the same name already exists in the destination." You can make it replace any existing items automatically by making the optional `replacing` parameter true:

```
duplicate file the_file_path to folder the_folder_path replacing true
```

> **NOTE:** While System Events also has a `duplicate` command, it doesn't work with disk items, unfortunately, so this is one area where the Finder definitely has the advantage.

One last bit of advice... AppleScript allows you to write this:

```
tell application "Finder"
    copy the_items to folder "Documents" of home
end tell
```

as another way of saying:

```
tell application "Finder"
    duplicate the_items to folder "Documents" of home
end tell
```

Be careful, though: using `copy items to container` in place of the normal `duplicate items to container` command works *only* if `container` is a literal Finder reference, as shown previously. If it's a variable, AppleScript will get the referenced items and assign the result to the variable instead!

For example, this will duplicate the items to the user's `Documents` folder:

```
tell application "Finder"
    set destination_folder to folder "Documents" of home
    duplicate the_items to destination_folder
end tell
```

but this will assign the items to the variable `destination_folder` instead:

```
tell application "Finder"
    set destination_folder to folder "Documents" of home
    copy the_items to destination_folder
end tell
```

To avoid confusion, I suggest you always use the `duplicate` command for duplicating application objects.

Deleting Files and Folders

The `delete` command in the Finder's dictionary doesn't actually delete anything; it just moves the referenced Finder item to the trash. The following:

```
tell application "Finder" to delete file the_file_path
```

is identical to this:

```
tell application "Finder" to move file the_file_path to the trash
```

As with the `duplicate` command, the `delete` command can accept a reference identifying multiple items. For example, to delete all the labeled files on the desktop with help from the Finder's powerful `whose` clause, you can use this:

```
tell application "Finder"
    delete every file of desktop whose label index is not 0
end tell
```

You can also empty the trash by simply using the `empty` command:

```
tell application "Finder" to empty trash
```

or by using just this:

```
tell application "Finder" to empty
```

> **CAUTION:** System Events can also delete files and folders, but be careful: while the Finder's `delete` command only moves items to the trash, System Events' `delete` command erases them completely!

Moving Files and Folders

Moving files works just like dragging files in the Finder: you have the file or folder you want to move and the folder or disk to which you're moving it. For this task, you use the Finder's `move` command, which takes the item or items to move as its direct parameter and the destination disk or folder as its `to` parameter; for instance:

```
tell application "Finder" to move file the_file_path to container the_folder_path
```

You can also specify whether you want to replace an existing item with the same name using the optional Boolean `replacing` parameter. If it is `true`, the `move` command will automatically replace any existing items without further warning:

```
tell application "Finder"
    move every file of folder source_folder to folder dest_folder with replacing
end tell
```

If you would prefer not to overwrite anything by accident, you can wrap the move command in a try statement that catches the "An item with the same name already exists in this location" error and performs some other action in response. The number code for this particular error is –15267, so if you want to handle only that particular error and not any others, write your try block like this:

```
tell application "Finder"
    try
        move every file of folder source_folder to folder dest_folder
    on error number -15267
        display dialog "Can't replace the files, replace the scripter instead..."
    end try
end tell
```

Checking if Items Exist

The exists command is one of my favorites. It takes one parameter, a reference to the item whose existence is in question, and returns a Boolean: true if the item exists or false if it doesn't:

```
tell application "Finder"
    exists file "I am here!" of desktop
end tell
```

By the way, a neat trick of AppleScript's is that it lets you put the exists keyword *after* the reference if you prefer, making the code read more like English:

```
tell application "Finder"
    file "I am here!" of desktop exists
end tell
```

The exists command is often used to check whether a file, folder, or disk actually exists before trying to use it, which allows your script to take an alternative course of action if it doesn't. For example:

```
tell application "Finder"
    tell document file "HAL9000 Manual.txt" of folder "Documents" of home
        if exists then
            open
        else
            display alert "I'm sorry Dave, I can't do that right now." as warning
        end if
    end tell
end tell
```

Making New Items

The make command allows you to create Finder items such as files, folders, and Finder windows, though most often it is used to create folders.

The Finder's make command has one required parameter, new, which is the class of the object you want to create. Here are the optional parameters:

- at, which is a reference to the folder or disk where a new file or folder should be created

- to, which is used when creating new alias files and Finder windows

- with properties, which allows you to supply initial values for many of the new object's properties, instead of leaving the Finder to use its own default values.

The following script creates a new folder on the desktop. The script uses the with properties parameter to name the folder My Files and assign a comment to it:

```
tell application "Finder"
    activate
    make new folder at desktop with properties ¬
        {name:"My Files", comment:"Place to put stuff"}
end tell
```

You can also use the make command to create blank text files and alias files. For example, to create an empty file on the desktop, you can do this:

```
tell application "Finder"
    make new document file at desktop with properties ¬
        {name:"My File", comment:"Place to put thoughts"}
end tell
```

When making an alias file, you specify the original item that it should point to using the to parameter:

```
tell application "Finder"
    set original_item to folder "Documents" of home
    make new alias file at desktop to original_item
end tell
```

The following script creates a new window in the Finder that displays the contents of the startup disk. You can specify the disk or folder the window should show using the optional to parameter:

```
tell application "Finder"
    activate
    make new Finder window to startup disk
end tell
```

Sorting Lists of Finder References

The Finder's sort command sorts a list of Finder file system references by a particular property, such as name, creation date, or size. The following example sorts a list of folders by name and by creation date:

```
tell application "Finder"
    set folder_list to folders of startup disk
    set folder_list_by_name to sort folder_list by name
    set folder_list_by_date to sort folder_list by creation date
end tell
```

One word of caution: although most Finder commands will accept a reference that identifies several objects at once—for example, every folder of home or every file of desktop whose label is 1—the sort command can work only with a list of one or more single item references. For instance, the sort command in the following script will generate an error:

```
tell application "Finder"
    set folder_list to sort (folders of startup disk) by name
end tell
```

To solve this problem, you need to ask the Finder to resolve the multiple item reference folders of startup disk first—for example, by inserting an explicit get command. The sort command can then process the resulting list of single item references:

```
tell application "Finder"
    set folder_list to sort (get folders of startup disk) by name
end tell
```

Ejecting Disks

The `eject` command takes a disk reference as the parameter and ejects that disk:

```
tell application "Finder" to eject disk "Removable 4000"
```

The following script uses a whose clause to identify only disks that are `ejectable` and ejects them all:

```
tell application "Finder"
    eject (every disk whose ejectable is true)
end tell
```

Selecting Items in a Finder Window

A few commands control how files are displayed in a Finder window but don't really do anything to them. For instance, selecting a file or sorting the contents of a window doesn't change any files or folders, only how they appear in the window.

The `select` and `reveal` commands work similarly in the Finder. They both select a Finder item in the Finder window. If the disk or folder containing the item is closed, both commands will open it as a new window, but will do so using different defaults.

The `select` command will open the container to a window using the last viewing style (icon, outline, or browser). If the `reveal` command has to open a window to reveal the item, it will use the default browser viewing style:

```
tell application "Finder"
    select every folder of home
end tell
```

Revealing files and folders in Finder windows can come in handy. In the interface of any system or script dealing with files, it is a pleasant surprise for the user to have a button that reveals a related file or folder in the Finder. (That is, of course, unless the intention of your script is to keep these users *out* of the file system…).

Converting Finder References to AppleScript Aliases

As you learned in Chapter 5, when you create references to objects in one application, only that particular application can understand these references—you can't pass them to any other application. It can be easy to forget this rule, however, particularly when working with file and folder references in the Finder.

For example, if you run a script like this:

```
tell application "Finder" to set the_file to file "ReadMe.txt" of home
tell application "TextEdit" to open the_file
```

and the `ReadMe.txt` file opens in TextEdit, you might well assume that TextEdit's open command understands the Finder reference created on the first line (file "ReadMe.txt" of folder "hanaan" of ... application "Finder"). But does it really?

What happens if you try it with a different application?

```
tell application "Pages" to open the_file
```

Uh-oh... the file *still* opens in TextEdit! If you check the Event Log in AppleScript Editor, all becomes clear:

```
tell application "Finder"
    get file "ReadMe.txt" of home
        --> document file "ReadMe.txt" of folder "hanaan"
                of folder "Users" of startup disk
    open document file "ReadMe.txt" of folder "hanaan"
          of folder "Users" of startup disk
end tell
```

As you can see, even though the open command was enclosed in a `tell application "Pages" ... end tell` block, AppleScript ignored this `tell` block and sent the command to the Finder instead. This behavior might seem very odd—after all, isn't the point of using `tell application ... end tell` to direct commands to a particular application? The answer is that it usually does... but there are caveats.

When you pass an application object reference as the direct parameter to an application-defined command, it is actually the reference that determines the target application rather than the surrounding `tell` block. In most scripts, you'll put the command inside the same `tell application ... end tell` block where the reference was created, so you simply don't notice this subtle detail in AppleScript's behavior. It's only when you try to use the reference within a `tell` block directed at a different application that you realize things are not quite as simple as you thought. The original script only did what you wanted by accident—because the Finder normally opens .txt files using TextEdit by default. If you associate the text file with a different application in Finder's Get Info window, the next time you open the file using the Finder, it will open in the newly chosen application instead.

If you want to ensure that the open command is sent to the application you want, you have to convert the Finder reference into a something the command can understand—an AppleScript alias object. Fortunately, the Finder provides an easy way to do this: just use the as coercion operator to coerce the reference to class alias, like this:

```
tell application "Finder" to set the_file to file "ReadMe.txt" of home as alias
tell application "Pages" to open the_file
```

If you check the Event Log now, you will see that the open command is being sent to Pages, not Finder, and its direct parameter is an AppleScript alias object.

If you want to coerce a Finder reference that identifies multiple items into a list of aliases, the Finder defines an `alias list` class especially for performing this kind of coercion:

```
tell application "Finder" to get every folder of home as alias list
--> {alias "Macintosh HD:Users:hanaan:Desktop:",
     alias "Macintosh HD:Users:hanaan:Documents:",
     alias "Macintosh HD:Users:hanaan:Downloads:", ...}
```

Finally, if you ever need to convert from an AppleScript alias to a Finder reference, the Finder helpfully allows you to use the alias in an item specifier:

```
set the_alias to alias "Macintosh HD:Users:has:Documents:"
tell application "Finder" to set item_ref to item the_alias
--> folder "Documents" of folder "hanaan" of folder "Users"
        of startup disk of application "Finder"
```

More on Working with Folders

We've discussed the various kinds of objects that Finder and System Events use to represent the Mac OS X file system. Let's now spend a bit more time looking at how to navigate these object models and locate items of interest.

Filtering the Content of Folders

Both Finder and System Events support the powerful filter reference form, or whose clause, allowing you to filter out just the set of items in a folder or disk you want to work with.

The whose clause can be of great assistance in all sorts of different tasks. For example, you might create a script that tidies your Downloads folder by moving all of the image files into your Pictures folder, the video files into Movies, and the audio files into Music. Or you could write a script that searches your Documents folder for large files that haven't been worked on recently and archives them.

Let's look at a few examples of using the Finder to filter files in different folders. Here's a simple script that gets the name of every item in the current user's home folder whose name starts with "m":

```
tell application "Finder"
   get name of every item of home whose name starts with "m"
end tell
--> {"Movies", "Music", "my to-dos.txt"}
```

The next script gets references to all files in a chosen folder that have not been modified in the last ten weeks and that have no label attached to them:

```
set the_folder to choose folder
tell application "Finder"
   get every file of the_folder whose ¬
        (modification date < ((current date) - (10 * weeks)) and label index = 0)
end tell
```

Notice how you can use a single command to look for files (not folders) that are of a certain age and label. If you wanted to move these files to an archive folder or to the user's trash, you could use the same reference in a move or delete command instead:

```
tell application "Finder"
   move every file of the_folder whose ¬
        (modification date < ((current date) - (10 * weeks)) and label index = 0) ¬
        to folder "Archives" of disk "Backup 1"
end tell
```

Script 20–4 looks for files that are larger than 10MB and are not applications. Unlike the previous scripts, this one uses a recursive handler to search through all the sub-folders as well, starting from the folder selected by the user.

Script 20–4.

```
1. set the_folder to choose folder
2. set mb_limit to 10
3. set byte_limit to mb_limit * 1024 * 1024
4. set list_of_large_files to get_large_files(the_folder, byte_limit)

5. on get_large_files(the_folder, minimum_size_in_bytes)
6.    tell application "Finder"
7.       --Find all the matching files in this folder
8.       set found_files_list to every file of the_folder ¬
             whose size ≥ minimum_size_in_bytes and class is not application file
9.       --Process each sub-folder in turn
10.      set sub_folders_list to every folder of the_folder
11.      repeat with sub_folder_ref in sub_folders_list
12.         set found_files_list to found_files_list & ¬
                my get_large_files(sub_folder_ref, minimum_size_in_bytes)
13.      end repeat
14.   end tell
15.   return found_files_list
16. end get_large_files
```

The get_large_files handler appears in lines 5 through 16. The handler starts on line 8 by asking the Finder for a list of references to all the applicable files in the current folder. After that, the script gets all the sub-folders in the current folder so they can be searched through as well. The loop in lines 11 to 13 takes each sub-folder in the list and recursively calls the get_large_files handler to search through that folder—and any sub-folders it has—and return a list of all the files it finds there.

What makes this script so fast and simple is the Finder's ability to filter the right kind of files with the whose clause on line 8. If the Finder didn't have this built-in filtering support, you'd have to loop through each file in the folder to check them yourself, which would make the code more complex and take longer to run.

Getting the Entire Contents of a Folder

Another useful property defined by the container class in the Finder is the entire contents property. You can use the entire contents property to get a reference to every file and folder contained in a disk or folder and all of its nested folders as well.

Here is something *not* to try in practice:

```
tell application "Finder"
   get entire contents of folder "System" of startup disk
end tell
```

This script would—at least in theory—give you a list of every file and folder in /System, which contains way more than 100,000 items. In reality, you'll find that using entire contents to search through hundreds or thousands of folders like this takes far too long to be practical. (In fact, AppleScript will normally give up waiting for the command to complete long before the Finder finished searching the System folder.)

When dealing with a much smaller folder structure, however, the entire contents property can come in handy. For example, you can use it to quickly look for all the files with a particular name extension by combining it with the whose clause:

```
set the_folder to choose folder "Choose the folder to search:"
display dialog "Enter the file name extension to match:" default answer "mp3"
set desired_name_extension to text returned of result
tell application "Finder"
   get every file of entire contents of the_folder ¬
        whose name extension is desired_name_extension
end tell
```

> **TIP:** You can use a with timeout block if you need it to increase the length of time that AppleScript is willing to wait for a long-running application command to finish. See Chapter 12 for details.

Locating Important Files and Folders with Standard Additions

We've already looked at how Finder and System Events can easily locate "standard" folders within the file system. Another way to locate these folders is by using Standard Additions' path to command.

The path to command always takes a direct parameter, which is the item you're looking for. This is usually a constant value identifying a special system folder such as desktop, fonts or home folder, although it could also be a current application constant or the me keyword (we'll look at these later), or even an application specifier. See the Standard Additions dictionary for a full list of options. Here are a few examples:

```
path to desktop
--> alias "Macintosh HD:Users:hanaan:Desktop:"

path to fonts
--> alias "Macintosh HD:System:Library:Fonts:"

path to application "Safari"
--> alias "Macintosh HD:Applications:Safari.app:"
```

> **CAUTION:** When using an application specifier as the path to command's direct parameter, remember that if AppleScript can't find the application itself, it will display a dialog asking the user to locate it manually. If this could be a problem, you can use Finder to locate the application by its bundle id instead, for example: tell application "Finder" to get application file id "com.apple.safari" as alias.

The path to command also accepts several optional keyword parameters. The `from` parameter lets you specify a particular domain to search, otherwise a suitable default is used. For example:

```
path to fonts from system domain
--> alias "Macintosh HD:System:Library:Fonts:"

path to fonts from local domain
--> alias "Macintosh HD:Library:Fonts:"

path to fonts from user domain
--> alias "Macintosh HD:Users:hanaan:Library:Fonts:"
```

The as parameter simply allows you to get the item's location as a path string instead of an alias:

```
path to startup disk as text
--> "Macintosh HD:"
```

The other parameter is `folder creation`. According to the dictionary, `folder creation` means that if the folder you're requesting a path for does not exist, the folder will be created. Also, the dictionary claims that the default is `true`. This works only for a few folders, though, and only in domains where you have sufficient permissions to make such changes.

Avoiding Hardcoded Paths to the Startup Disk and Home Folder

Two of the most useful paths you can get are the paths to the startup disk and the user's home folder. Obtaining these paths automatically instead of hard-coding them in your script can go a long way toward making that script system-independent.

The idea is to make your script as portable and flexible as possible. I know what you're thinking . . . this is just a script that'll run on your Mac, and it has little chance of going anywhere else. That's not necessarily so. As you'll discover, a small bit of code you write to perform a simple task can suddenly grow into a full-blown script and then become part of a larger scheme. At that point, you copy the script to some other Mac to test it, and wham! Nothing works since the other Mac's hard drive has a different name.

So, as much as you just want to get the pesky script working, I urge you to take the time to replace any startup disk or home folder paths with some suitable Finder, System Events, or path to code that will obtain these paths whenever the script runs.

Let's say, for example, that your script refers to a folder called `Client Jobs` in the current user's home folder. You need a variable in your script that'll identify that folder. If you provide the full path as a literal string, your script line may look like this:

```
set client_jobs_folder to "Macintosh HD:Users:hanaan:Client Jobs:"
```

If you move the script to a Mac with a differently named hard drive or home folder, your script will break. Instead, use `path to home folder` to get the first part of the path, and build up the full path from there:

```
set client_jobs_folder to (path to home folder as text) & "Client Jobs:"
--> "Macintosh HD:Users:hanaan:Client Jobs:"
```

Once you've constructed the full path, you can convert it to an alias if you need one; use it to create a Finder or System Events reference, and so on.

Here are some examples using Finder and System Events to identify the same folder using an alias value and POSIX path respectively:

```
tell application "Finder"
    set client_jobs_folder to folder "Client Jobs" of home as alias
end tell
--> alias "Macintosh HD:Users:hanaan:Client Jobs:"

tell application "System Events"
    set client_jobs_folder to POSIX path of folder "Client Jobs" of home folder
end tell
--> "/Users/hanaan/Client Jobs"
```

Getting the Path to the Currently Running Script

One of the most useful pieces of code you can use in your quest for script portability is path to me.

The variable me is usually used to refer to the current script object—for example, when calling a local handler from within a tell application ... end tell block—but it can also be used in the path to command to try to find out the script's location on disk. This doesn't work in every situation but is useful when it does.

A common use for path to me is to allow a script applet to find files and folders relative to its own position on disk. This comes in handy when your applet is part of some sort of folder structure. It's also one of the situations where path to me generally does what you want, which is good news.

The way I like to set things up is to have a folder I call the Main folder. Inside I have all the folders the system needs (even small systems). The folders may be resources, templates, in/out, and so on. I also put the main applet that controls the whole system into Main. Figure 20–5 shows a sample of this folder structure.

The script, however, needs to know where all the related files are. Since the position of these files within the Main folder is already known, all the script needs in order to work out their locations is a reference to the Main folder. To get that, I just need to get the container of the script application's file. Here's the line in the script that assigns a reference to the Main folder to a variable:

```
tell application "Finder"
    set main_folder to container of (path to me)
end tell
--> folder "Main" of folder folder "Work" of folder "hanaan"
        of folder "Users" of startup disk of application "Finder"
```

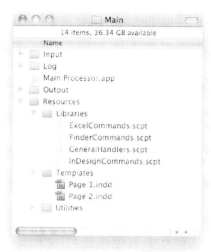

Figure 20–5. *A sample folder structure for an AppleScript workflow system*

I can then use this reference to build up references to the files and folders the script will use as I need them. For instance, the following code creates a reference to the `Main` folder's `Output` folder. Since other scriptable applications don't understand Finder references, it then coerces this reference to an AppleScript alias, which they will accept:

```
tell application "Finder"
    set input_folder to folder "Output" of main_folder as alias
end tell
```

The next snippet obtains a list of AppleScript aliases identifying all of the files in the Templates folder:

```
tell application "Finder"
    tell folder "Resources" of main_folder
        set template_files to every file of folder "Templates" as alias list
    end tell
end tell
```

> **CAUTION:** Prior to Mac OS X 10.4, `path to me` had the same meaning as `path to current application`, returning the path to the application that was running the script, not to the script itself. This wasn't a problem when the script was run as an applet, but running it in most other applications would give you the path to the application instead of to the script file. Most applications that run AppleScripts have since been updated to support the new `path to me` behavior (Script Editor was updated in 10.5) but a few may still use the old behavior, in which case you'll probably have to hard-code the script's path yourself.

Getting Paths to Resources in an Application Bundle

As mentioned earlier in the chapter, a package (or bundle) is a special sort of folder that looks and behaves like a regular file in a Finder window. Almost all Mac OS X applications are packages, and the same format can be used for other sorts of "files," too. For example, TextEdit allows users to create a text document containing embedded images and save it as an .rtfd file, which is really a package containing separate text and image files. However, only TextEdit needs to know about these contents, so it appears in the Finder as a single file to prevent the user from seeing—and possibly interfering with—the private items inside.

You can tell if a file is a package by right-clicking on it in the Finder. If one of the menu items is **Show Package Contents**, as shown in Figure 20–6, you know it's a package-based file you're dealing with, and you can open it and look around.

Figure 20–6. *The Show Package Contents menu item*

Figure 20–7 shows the standard package contents of an AppleScript applet created by AppleScript Editor.

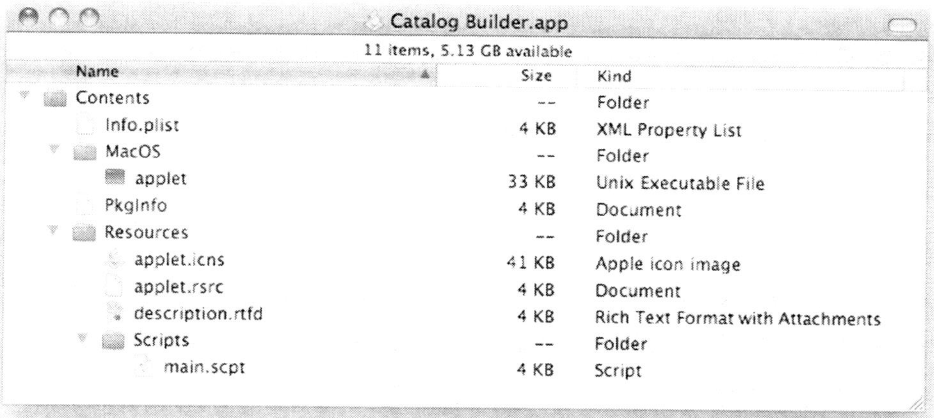

Figure 20–7. *The open package of an AppleScript applet*

Although users may not need to know what's inside a package, there may be times when a developer does need to access a package's contents. Within each package is a single folder, Contents, which contains all of the package's resource files. These files are often organized into sub-folders according to their purpose. For example, an application bundle contains a sub-folder called MacOS that contains the actual program code, and another sub-folder called Resources that contains all of the images, sounds, etc. that the program uses.

Script 20–5 provides a convenient way to open the Contents folder of a bundle-based file directly. Type the code into a new AppleScript Editor document, then save it as an application named Bundle Opener.app. When you drag a bundle-based file onto this application, the bundle's Contents folder will open in a new Finder window.

Script 20–5.

```
on open {the_alias}
    try
        tell application "Finder" to open folder "Contents" of item the_alias
    on error
        display alert "Not a bundle."
    end try
end open
```

An easy way to locate resources within a bundle is by using Standard Additions' path to resource command. This command takes two parameters: the name of the file you want and an alias value identifying the bundle you want to search. The advantage of this approach is that you don't need to know exactly where in the bundle the file is in order to find it. For example, the following script gets an alias to a file named compass.icns in Safari's application bundle:

```
set bundle_file to alias "Macintosh HD:Applications:Safari.app:"
set resource_file to path to resource "compass.icns" in bundle bundle_file
--> alias "Macintosh HD:Applications:Safari.app:Contents:Resources:compass.icns"
```

Bundle-based scripts can use the path to me and path to resource commands to locate custom resource files included within the bundle. The bundle-based AppleScript applet shown in Figure 20–8 uses the path to me command to obtain an alias to itself. It then uses the path to resource command to locate an icon file named help.icns stored within the bundle. The icon file is then used in a display dialog command as shown.

Figure 20–8. *Locating a resource file within a bundle-based AppleScript applet or file*

Notice how the help.icns file is listed in the bundle contents drawer on the right side of the main window, along with other files and folders found in the applet's Resources folder. You will learn how to add your own files here in Chapter 22.

Mounting Volumes

You can mount volumes from servers, remote computers, or iDisks with Standard Additions' mount volume command.

There are two ways to specify the volume to mount. The first way is to supply the volume's name as the direct parameter to the mount volume command, followed by the name of the server as its on server parameter. For example:

```
mount volume "Macintosh HD" on server "OfficeMac.local"
```

The other way is to supply a URL string as the direct parameter and omit the on server parameter:

```
mount volume "afp://OfficeMac.local/Macintosh%20HD"
```

The URL string describes the server address and the protocol used to connect to the server, such as Server Message Block (SMB) or Apple File Protocol (AFP).

> **NOTE:** SMB and AFP are protocols for sharing files and printers across a network. SMB is normally used with Windows and AFP with Macs, although Mac OS X supports both. Your Mac's built-in Help file contains more information if you need it; just select **Help ➤ Mac** Help in the Finder and search for "connecting to servers."

Besides the server name, you can provide several other pieces of information if you want: the name of the volume to mount, a username, and/or a password. We'll look at these shortly.

Here's the mount volume command the way it appears in the dictionary:

```
mount volume v : Mount the specified server volume
  mount volume text : the name or URL path (e.g. 'afp://server/volume/') of the
          volume to mount
    on server text : the server on which the volume resides; omit if URL path
              provided
      [in AppleTalk zone text] : the AppleTalk zone in which the server resides;
              omit if URL path provided
      [as user name text] : the user name with which to log in to the server; omit
          for guest access
      [with password text] : the password for the user name; omit for guest access
```

The basic command looks like this:

```
mount volume "afp://serverNameOrIPAddress"
```

Here are a couple of examples, one using a Bonjour name and the other using an IP address:

```
mount volume "afp://Jean-Grays-Macintosh.local"
mount volume "afp://192.168.200.2"
```

After running this command, the user will be shown a Connect to Server dialog box, allowing him either to connect as a guest user or to enter a username and password and connect as a registered user.

> **NOTE:** That same Connect to Server dialog box allows a user to add the server to the keychain. Adding the server login information to the keychain should not be taken lightly because it makes access to the server much easier from the computer the script ran on. However, if you don't want to have to enter the same login details each time the script is run, then storing this information in the keychain is still *far* more secure than hard-coding it in your script, which isn't secure at all (even if the script is saved as run-only).

If you want, you can supply the name of the specific volume to mount. This might be the name of a mounted disk or a particular user account:

```
mount volume "afp://Jean-Grays-Macintosh.local/Macintosh%20HD"
mount volume "afp://OfficeMac.local/jsmith"
```

If the URL doesn't include a volume name, Mac OS will list all the available volumes for the user to choose from.

You can also supply login information directly to the command in one of two ways. You can either include the username and/or password in the URL itself, or use the command's as user name and with password parameters.

The following two script lines will work the same. The first includes the login information in the URL, and the second one uses parameters:

```
mount volume "afp://username:my_password@serverNameOrIpAddress"
```

```
mount volume "afp://serverNameOrIpAddress" ¬
    as user name "username" with password "my_password"
```

Or you can just supply the username by itself and leave the user to type the password into the Connect to Server dialog box.

> **NOTE:** One of the issues that may cause problems when trying to access volumes with the mount volume command is the keychain. If the volume information is already entered into a keychain but the password has changed, you may get an error. It has been reported that this situation happens when the login information is embedded in the URL. Manually deleting the old login entry from the keychain can solve this problem.

You can also use other protocols instead of AFP, such as SMB. The protocol you use depends on the server setup.

For example, you can use the following handler as a general handler for mounting server volumes:

```
on mount_volume(userName, pswd, serverIP, volumeName)
    set serverString to ¬
        "afp://" & userName & ":" & pswd & "@" & ¬
        serverIP & "/" & volumeName
    mount volume serverString
end mount_volume
```

When using this mount_volume handler, it's useful to note that Standard Additions' mount volume command is pretty relaxed about URL encoding issues. For example, a volume name such as Macintosh HD should really be encoded as Macintosh%20HD, but in practice the unencoded version seems to work OK, too. However, if any of your mount_volume parameters contain special URL characters such as forward slashes, you will need to encode these first, or they won't work as intended.

CAUTION: The other three file system-related commands in Standard Additions' File Commands suite are info for, list disks, and list folder. Although you can still use these commands for now, Standard Additions' dictionary indicates these commands are deprecated in Mac OS X 10.5 and later. This means Apple strongly discourages their use and may eventually remove them altogether in a future release, so you should use the Finder or System Events instead.

Summary

In this chapter, you learned how to manipulate the Mac OS X file system using the scriptable Finder and System Events applications. You looked at the various classes and commands that these applications define for the job, and the similarities and differences between them.

You saw how to make, move, duplicate, and delete files and folders in the file system by manipulating objects in the Finder's object model. While every scriptable application's object model may be different, many of the underlying concepts are the same from application to application. As a result, the standard commands used to manipulate other applications' object models usually work in similar ways, so the knowledge and experience you gain in learning one application may help when learning another.

Lastly, you explored three utility commands provided by the Standard Additions scripting addition—path to, path to resource, and mount volume—which you can use to locate important files and folders and mount local and remote volumes.

In the next chapter, you will continue to develop your knowledge and experience with desktop automation by exploring several more popular and important Apple applications, including iTunes, iCal and Mail.

Chapter 21

Scripting Apple Applications

Many of the standard Apple applications that ship with Mac OS X provide some level of AppleScript support. As you can imagine, covering every aspect of scripting every Apple application would easily fill its own book (or three), so my intention in this chapter is just to give you a solid start in scripting the five most important ones: iTunes, Mail, iCal, Address Book, and Automator.

> **CAUTION:** Remember to back up your data before running potentially destructive scripts (or performing automation of any sort, for that matter). Accidents will happen, even to the most careful of scripters.

Scripting iTunes

iTunes has long provided a solid object model for working with its tracks and playlists. Scripts for iTunes generally fall into two categories: easing maintenance and improving usability. Maintenance scripts are great for features such as cleaning up your library and managing your tracks and playlists. With the ability to manage many thousands of tracks, AppleScript can be a saving grace when you want to organize the iTunes part of your life. Usability scripts can help you enjoy music more easily and efficiently on a day-to-day basis. You can easily create little AppleScript utilities that perform tasks that would require several steps in the iTunes GUI.

The following sections will introduce the three main types of objects in the iTunes object model—sources, playlists, and tracks—and show you how to manipulate them using various iTunes commands.

> **TIP:** Doug's AppleScripts for iTunes (http://dougscripts.com/itunes) provides hundreds of free iTunes scripts you can use and learn from.

Understanding the iTunes Object Model

Whenever you start scripting a new application, the first thing to do is to open its dictionary in AppleScript Editor and study the classes that describe the contents and structure of the application's object model. iTunes has a well-designed object model, a quality that can make scripting easier.

To complement how you think about music organization in general, iTunes has three main types of object: sources, playlists, and tracks. Most other object classes are variations of the `playlist` and `track` classes. In fact, the iTunes object model has five types of playlists and five types of tracks, as shown in Figure 21–1. Notice, for example, how the different classes of tracks all inherit from a common `track` class. This means that a `file track` object will support all of the features defined by the `track` class along with any additional features of its own (for example, a `location` property identifying the file in question).

Now that you know about the different classes of objects defined by iTunes objects, the next step is to look at how these objects are assembled into an object model.

As you would expect, the iTunes object model starts out with an object of class `application`, representing the iTunes application itself. Before accessing iTunes playlist and track objects, however, you will have to go through an object of class `source`. The source object you will work with most is the main library source. On English-speaking systems this source object is named "Library," although the name may differ for other languages. In the library source, you will find your playlists and, in there, your tracks.

Other sources may be useful as well. If an iPod is connected to your Mac, for example, the iPod becomes its own source with playlists and tracks. Audio CDs, MP3 CDs, and shared libraries are also represented by source objects.

In turn, each source object can contain various playlist elements. For example, the library source contains a special playlist object of class `library playlist`. This library playlist is also called "Library" (or its equivalent in other languages) and contains every file-based track, URL-based track, and shared track that iTunes is aware of. The library source can also contain any number of user-defined playlists, each one containing whatever file, URL, and shared tracks you put in it. So, in order to work with a particular track (or tracks), you have to refer to a specific playlist in a specific source.

Figure 21–2 illustrates this part of the iTunes containment hierarchy, showing how different kinds of tracks are contained by different kinds of playlists, which in turn are contained by the source elements of the application.

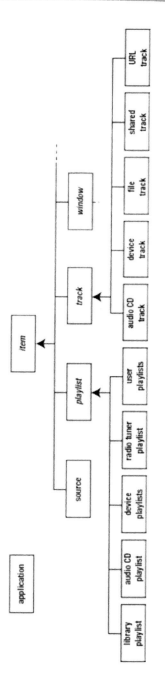

Figure 21–1. The inheritance hierarchy for the main classes of objects that make up iTunes' object model (minor classes are omitted for simplicity)

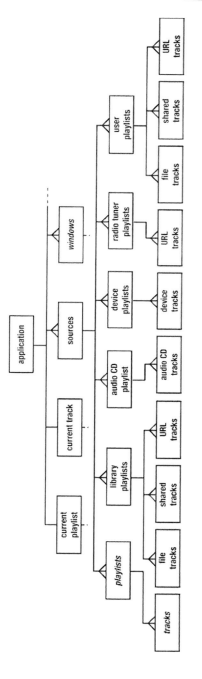

Figure 21–2. Part of the containment hierarchy for iTunes' object model, showing how source, playlist, and track elements are contained by one another

Working with Sources

As you can see from iTunes' dictionary, source objects are quite simple. Like most iTunes classes, the source class inherits five basic properties from iTunes' item class: container, id, index, name, and persistent ID. On top of this it defines three properties of its own—capacity, free space, and kind—along with a bunch of elements representing the various kinds of playlist objects that a source object can contain.

Source elements can be referred to in various ways, including all at once:

```
tell application "iTunes"
   get every source
end tell
--> {source id 43 of application "iTunes",
     source id 56324 of application "iTunes",
     source id 56495 of application "iTunes"}
```

By index:

```
tell application "iTunes"
   get source 1
end tell
-->source id 43 of application "iTunes"
```

By name:

```
tell application "iTunes"
   get source "Library"
end tell
--> source id 43 of application "iTunes"
```

By unique ID:

```
tell application "iTunes"
   get source id 43
end tell
--> source id 43 of application "iTunes"
```

Or by test (whose clause):

```
tell application "iTunes"
   get every source whose kind is audio CD
end tell
--> {source id 56495 of application "iTunes"}
```

Although AppleScript Editor's dictionary viewer doesn't indicate exactly which reference forms can be used with source elements, it's pretty easy to work out. By-index references should always work, and a well-designed object model will normally support by-range and by-test references as well. Lastly, since the iTunes dictionary shows that all source objects have name and id properties, we can assume that sources can be identified by name and ID as well.

When referring to the main library source by name, bear in mind that this name may vary according to the user's language settings and/or personal preferences. So a reference to source "Library" may work on some computers but fail on others, unless you modify the code each time. If your script needs to be portable, you might find it safer to refer to the source by index instead.

By-ID references are unique to a single iTunes application, of course. So while the by-ID references returned by iTunes commands provide a highly reliable way to identify objects while the script is running, you should avoid hard-coding these IDs in your code.

What else can we do with source objects, apart from referring to them in order to reach the real goodies, playlists and tracks? Well, we can find out some useful information about them by querying their properties:

```
tell application "iTunes"
    get name of source 1
end tell
--> "Library"
```

```
tell application "iTunes"
    get name of every source
end tell
--> {"Library", "Radio", "Post"}
```

```
tell application "iTunes"
    get kind of every source
end tell
--> {library, radio tuner, audio CD}
```

Searching the iTunes dictionary also turns up a couple of source-related commands that will be of particular interest to iPod users: update and eject. The update command updates the track contents of a connected iPod, while the eject command will eject an iPod. As discussed previously, when an iPod is connected to your computer, iTunes regards it as another source. For example, you can specify the iPod to eject by referring to the source object pointing to the iPod. If you know the iPod's name, you can refer to it that way,

```
tell application "iTunes" to eject source "Hanaan's iPod"
```

or you can just eject all connected iPods if you prefer:

```
tell application "iTunes" to eject every source whose kind is iPod
```

> **TIP:** While iTunes' eject command only works with iPods and not other kinds of sources, you can easily eject audio CDs and MP3 CDs by scripting the Finder instead.

Working with Tracks and Playlists

Let's now look at the best part of scripting iTunes: manipulating tracks and playlists.

In order to refer to track and playlist objects, we need to know exactly where they lie in iTunes' containment hierarchy. If you look back at Figure 21–2, you will see that tracks are elements of playlists, and playlists are elements of sources. This means that to identify a track object, we must first identify the playlist that contains the track, and the source that contains that playlist:

```
tell application "iTunes"
    tell source 1
```

```
    tell playlist 1
        track 1
    end tell
  end tell
end tell
--> file track id 414 of library playlist id 381
        of source id 43 of application"iTunes"
```

Or, if you prefer to construct the reference in a single line, you can write it like this:

```
tell application "iTunes"
  track 1 of playlist 1 of source 1
end tell
--> file track id 414 of library playlist id 381
        of source id 43 of application"iTunes"
```

> **TIP:** iTunes is quite flexible in how it interprets references in that you can omit the parent containers. For instance, track 1 and track 1 of playlist 1 are equivalent to track 1 of playlist 1 of source 1.

Like sources, track and playlist elements can be identified by index, by name, by ID, or by test, as shown in Script 21–1.

Script 21–1.

```
tell application "iTunes"
  tell source 1
    tell library playlist 1
      every track whose artist is "Björk"
    end tell
  end tell
end tell
--> {file track id 425 of library playlist id 381 of source id 43
        of application "iTunes",
    file track id 426 of library playlist id 381 of source id 43
        of application "iTunes", ...}
```

When referring to the main library playlist, remember that the playlist's name may vary according to the user's language settings and/or personal preferences. A more portable approach is to refer to library playlist 1, as shown in the previous script.

We can also get and set the properties of the playlists:

```
tell application "iTunes"
  get name of every playlist of source "Library"
end tell
--> {"Library", "Music", "Movies", "Podcasts", ...}

tell application "iTunes"
  get time of playlist "My Top Rated" of source "Library"
end tell
--> "1:03:49"

tell application "iTunes"
  set shuffle of playlist "My Top Rated" of source "Library" to true
end tell
```

```
tell application "iTunes"
    get {name, artist, album} of track 1 of playlist "Library" of source "Library"
end tell
--> {"Stardust", "Nat King Cole", "Let's Fall in Love"}

tell application "iTunes"
    get name of every track of playlist 1 of source "Post"
end tell
--> {"Army Of Me", "Hyper-Ballad", "The Modern Things", ...}

tell application "iTunes"
    tell source "Library"
        tell library playlist 1
            tell (every track whose album is "Post")
                set rating to 100 -- The rating value is given as a percentage
                set comment to "I love this album!"
            end tell
        end tell
    end tell
end tell
```

iTunes also provides a range of commands for manipulating track and playlist objects directly. The Standard Suite defines all of the basic commands for working with elements: count, exists, make, duplicate, delete, and so forth. For example, to check if a playlist exists:

```
tell application "iTunes"
    exists user playlist "My First Playlist" of source "Library"
end tell
--> false
```

Or to count the number of tracks in the main library playlist:

```
tell application "iTunes"
    count every track of playlist "Library" of source "Library"
end tell
--> 7192
```

The iTunes Suite lists various commands for controlling how tracks are played—play, pause, previous track, next track, and so on. The following example plays a random song from the main library:

```
tell application "iTunes"
    play some track of playlist "Library" of source "Library"
end tell
```

Script 21–2 plays the first five seconds of each track.

Script 21–2.

```
tell application "iTunes"
    play
    repeat
        delay 5
        next track
    end repeat
end tell
```

Creating new playlists in iTunes is simple: just use the make command, optionally passing it the new playlist's name via the with properties parameter:

```
tell application "iTunes"
    make new user playlist with properties {name:"My First Playlist"}
end tell
```

You don't need to specify a location because iTunes will automatically add the new playlist object to your library source.

To delete an unwanted user playlist, just use the delete command:

```
tell application "iTunes"
    delete user playlist "My First Playlist" of source "Library"
end tell
```

Creating new track objects is a little different. To import new audio files into iTunes, use the add command. iTunes will automatically create the corresponding track objects for you in the main library playlist. Script 21–3 prompts the user to select some audio or movie files, and then adds them to iTunes' library playlist.

Script 21–3.

```
set file_aliases to choose file ¬
    with prompt "Please select one or more files to import into iTunes:" ¬
    with multiple selections allowed without invisibles
tell application "iTunes" to add file_aliases
```

If you want, you can use the optional to parameter to add the newly imported tracks to a user-defined playlist at the same time:

```
tell application "iTunes"
    if not user playlist "Latest Imports" exists then ¬
        make new user playlist with properties {name:"Latest Imports"}
    add file_aliases to user playlist "Latest Imports"
end tell
```

To add existing track objects to a user playlist, use the duplicate command to copy the desired track objects from one playlist (usually the main library playlist) to the other. Script 21–4 creates a new playlist named "Everything Yellow" and duplicates to that new playlist every track object whose name contains the word "yellow".

Script 21–4.

```
tell application "iTunes"
    set everything_yellow_playlist to make new user playlist ¬
        with properties {name:"Everything Yellow"}
    duplicate (every track of library playlist 1 whose name contains "yellow") ¬
        to everything_yellow_playlist
end tell
```

To remove one or more tracks from a playlist, use the delete command. Deleting tracks from the main library playlist will remove them from the iTunes library completely.

> **TIP:** The "Common AppleScript Optimizations" section in Chapter 29 includes some useful information on maximizing the performance of your application commands when working with large numbers of application objects—a common requirement when working with large iTunes libraries.

Example Project: My Themed Playlist

One of the nice features of iTunes is that you can set up a "smart" playlist that automatically contains all of the tracks that match one or more conditions. iTunes comes with several default smart playlists already set up, including Recently Played and My Top Rated, and you can create your own as well; for instance, you could create smart playlists to list all of the episodes of your favorite TV show or the five jazz tracks you play most often.

Sometimes, however, smart playlists may not be flexible or powerful enough to choose tracks according to the rules you want, in which case it's time to roll your own playlists from scratch—with a little help from AppleScript, of course.

For this exercise, we will develop a simple utility script that fills a playlist named "My Themed Playlist" with tracks according to a particular theme requested by the user. The script will consist of three main parts:

- The first stage will prompt the user to enter a word or phrase to search for and specify how many tracks the playlist should contain.

- The second stage will check whether the themed playlist already exists. If it doesn't exist, the script will create it. If it does, the script will clean out any old tracks.

- The third stage will add the newly found tracks to the playlist and start it playing.

Gathering the User Input

The first step is to gather all the information that our script needs to do its job. The script will always use the same playlist to avoid creating lots of clutter, so we can hard-code the playlist's name at the top of the script for simplicity:

```
set playlist_name to "My Themed Playlist"
```

We will use `display dialog` commands (previously covered in Chapter 16) to obtain the user input. As this is an iTunes script, we will send the `display dialog` commands to iTunes so that the dialog boxes appear within iTunes itself.

First, we start a `tell` block to target iTunes and send it an `activate` command to bring it to the front so that the user can see our dialog boxes:

```
tell application "iTunes"
    activate
```

Next, we need to ask for the phrase to search for and find all of the tracks that match it. There is a potential problem here that our script will need to cope with somehow: what if the user enters a phrase that does not show up anywhere in their iTunes library? One option would be to stop the script there and then, but a nicer solution is to enclose this part in a loop that keeps prompting the user for a new search phrase until it is successful:

```
-- Ask the user for a theme and find all of the matching tracks
repeat
    set search_phrase to text returned of ¬
        (display dialog "Please enter a phrase to search for:" ¬
        default answer "")
```

To actually look up the tracks, we will use iTunes' search command. We could also have used a whose clause here, but the search command provides an easy way to search in several fields—name, artist, album, and so on—without much code. Here is the search command's definition from the iTunes dictionary:

```
search v : search a playlist for tracks matching the search string. Identical
    to entering search text in the Search field in iTunes.
    search playlist : the playlist to search
        for text : the search text
        [only albums/all/artists/composers/displayed/songs] : area to search
            (default is all)
        --> track : reference to found track(s)
```

> **NOTE:** One slight disadvantage of using the search command rather than a whose clause is that search returns a list of references, one reference for each track, so we will have to use a repeat statement to process these references one at a time. If a large number of tracks are returned, it may take some time for the script to process them all individually. whose-based references can really shine in these situations: for instance, if you pass a multitrack reference as the direct parameter to iTunes' duplicate command, it will copy all of the tracks at once.

Our search will be performed on all of the available areas of the main library playlist, so our search command appears as follows:

```
set found_tracks to search library playlist 1 for search_phrase
```

If the result is an empty list, then we inform the user that the search phrase was not found and ask them to try again:

```
if length of found_tracks = 0 then
    display dialog "Sorry, no matching tracks were found." ¬
        buttons {"Cancel", "Try Again"} default button 2
```

Because we are using the basic infinite repeat statement, it will simply keep on looping until we deliberately exit it:

```
    else
        exit repeat
    end if
end repeat
```

Once some tracks have been found and the first loop has exited, we should ask the user if they want to include all of the found tracks in the themed playlist, or only some of them. Once again, we will use an infinite loop to keep trying until the user provides some valid input:

```
-- Ask the user for the number of tracks to include
repeat
    try
        set number_of_tracks_to_include to text returned of ¬
            (display dialog "Please enter the number of tracks to include" & ¬
            " (1-" & length of found_tracks & "):" ¬
            default answer length of found_tracks) as integer
        if number_of_tracks_to_include ≥ 1 and ¬
                number_of_tracks_to_include ≤ length of found_tracks then
            exit repeat
        end if
    on error number -1700 -- The user didn't enter a number
    end try
    display dialog "Sorry, that is not a valid number." ¬
        buttons {"Cancel", "Try Again"} default button 2
end repeat
```

Notice how a try block is used here to catch any coercion errors (–1700) that might occur when coercing the user's input to an integer. And even if the user does enter a number of some sort, we still need to check that it is in the right range: negative numbers are obviously no good, and any number that is larger than the number of found tracks doesn't make much sense either. Only when both requirements are satisfied does the exit statement execute, breaking us out of the loop.

Now that our script has all of the information it needs to do its job, it's time to prepare the playlist.

Preparing the Playlist

For the second stage, we need to ensure that our themed playlist exists and is empty.

First, we use iTunes' exists command to check if a playlist named "My Themed Playlist" can be found:

```
-- Create the themed playlist if it doesn't already exist, or clean it if it does
if (exists user playlist playlist_name) then
```

The exists command returns a Boolean result, which we use to control the behavior of the if ... then ... else ... block. If the result is true (that is, the playlist object exists), then the first part of the conditional block executes:

```
set my_playlist to user playlist playlist_name
delete every track of my_playlist
```

The first line assigns a reference to the playlist to a variable, making it easier to work with. The second line uses a delete command to get rid of any old tracks. Notice how we use a reference to every track ... here. We don't need to retrieve a list of track references and delete them one by one—it's simpler and safer to let the delete command do all the hard work for us.

CAUTION: If the `every track ...` reference does not identify any objects (because the playlist is already empty), then iTunes' `delete` command simply does nothing. This is not the case with all commands, however. For instance, the `duplicate` command requires that the reference identifies one or more objects, otherwise a "Can't get *reference*" error (−1728) will occur.

If the `exists` command returns `false`, we need to use the `make` command to create a new user playlist, like this:

```
else
    set my_playlist to make new user playlist with properties {name:playlist_name}
end if
```

iTunes' `make` command conveniently returns a reference to the newly created playlist, so we capture that in the same variable as before so that it can be used again later.

Adding the Tracks to the Playlist

The third and final phase of our script involves adding the desired tracks to the themed playlist.

First, let's make the playlist visible to the user:

```
-- Add the tracks to the playlist
reveal my_playlist
```

Next, we check if the user requested all or only some of the found tracks to be added to the playlist. If all the tracks are to be added, we simply loop over the `found_tracks` list, copying each track reference to the target playlist using iTunes' `duplicate` command:

```
if number_of_tracks_to_include = length of found_tracks then
    repeat with track_ref in found_tracks
        duplicate track_ref to my_playlist
    end repeat
else
```

If only some tracks are to be added, we make things a bit more interesting by choosing the tracks at random:

```
    repeat number_of_tracks_to_include times
        set i to random number from 1 to length of found_tracks
        duplicate item i of found_tracks to my_playlist
        set item i of found_tracks to missing value
        set found_tracks to every reference of found_tracks
    end repeat
end if
```

While we could use AppleScript's `some item of` *the_list* reference form, that may pick the same item more than once. To ensure each track in the themed playlist is unique, we use Standard Additions' `random number` command to pick an index number at random. We then get the chosen track reference from the list (`item i of found_tracks`) and use iTunes' `duplicate` command to copy it to the themed playlist.

The last two lines in the repeat loop are responsible for "removing" the chosen track from the found_tracks list. As you learned in Chapter 10, although AppleScript allows scripts to add items to an existing list, it doesn't provide a way to remove them. The solution is to construct a new list containing all of the previous list's items except for the item we don't want. One option would be to use the remove_item_from_list handler from Chapter 10. However, as we know this list will only ever contain references, a simpler solution is to replace the item we don't want with a non-reference value such as missing value, and then ask the list for all of its reference elements. We then assign this new list to the found_tracks variable, replacing the previous list, and continue looping until we have processed the desired number of tracks.

Finally, we send iTunes a play command, passing it a reference to the playlist we want it to play:

```
    play my_playlist
end tell
```

> **TIP:** If you have previously enabled the system-wide Scripts menu, why not save this script as ~/Library/Scripts/Applications/iTunes/Update My Themed Playlist.scpt (creating any intermediate folders as necessary)? In addition to providing a quick and easy way to update the themed playlist, the script will only appear in the Scripts menu when iTunes is frontmost and won't clutter up the Scripts menu when you are working with other applications. See Chapter 4 for more details.

Now that you have had some practice in scripting iTunes, let's move on to discuss the next Apple application on our list, Mail.

Scripting Mail

Mac OS X's Mail application provides fairly extensive support for manipulating accounts, mailboxes, and incoming and outgoing e-mail messages from AppleScript. The structure of Mail's object model is simple. Each account has mailboxes, and mailboxes can contain both messages and other mailboxes. Shortcuts to important mailboxes and mailboxes that do not belong to a particular account appear as properties and elements of the main application object. Figure 21–3 shows how it all fits together.

The following sections explain how to work with mailboxes and the e-mail messages that they contain. You will also learn how to create and send e-mails to other people, and how to automate the processing of incoming e-mails using the Mail rules feature.

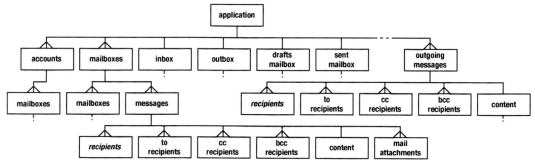

Figure 21–3. *Part of the containment hierarchy for Mail's object model, showing how account, mailbox, and message objects can be contained by one another*

Working with Mailboxes

This script lists the mailboxes of the first account:

```
tell application "Mail"
    return name of every mailbox of account 1
end tell
--> {"INBOX", "Drafts", "Sent Messages", "Deleted Messages", "Junk"}
```

Mailboxes can also be elements of the main application object without having to belong to a specific account. Mailbox objects can contain other mailboxes too. Six standard top-level mailboxes are also accessible via properties of Mail's application object: drafts mailbox, inbox, junk mailbox, outbox, sent mailbox, and trash mailbox.

Mailbox objects are fairly simple, with only a few properties, all of which are read-only except for the name property. Each mailbox object also has two types of elements, messages and mailboxes, that you can manipulate from AppleScript to work with the messages and/or sub-mailboxes that are inside that mailbox.

The account class is much more extensive, with three subclasses, pop account, imap account, and MobileMe account (which is actually a subclass of imap account), that represent the different types of e-mail accounts that Mail supports. Each account object contains plenty of properties for manipulating the account's settings. (These are the same settings you see in the Accounts panel of Mail's Preferences window.) In addition, each account object has mailbox elements representing all the mailboxes that belong to that particular account.

The following sections look at how to work with existing e-mail messages, how to create and send e-mails, and how to set up new mailboxes and Mail rules.

Working with Messages

To get information from a message, you first have to provide a reference to it. You can locate messages in Mail's object model in several ways: you can obtain a list of references to the currently selected messages from the application object's selection property, you can refer to one or more messages in a top-level mailbox, and you can refer to one or more messages in a mailbox that belongs to a specific account. Which method you use depends on what you want to do, of course.

Let's say I'm about to cancel one of my e-mail accounts with my service provider. I will want to notify every person who previously sent mail to that address. Assuming all those messages are still in the original Inbox for that account, Script 21–5 shows how I can get a list of the senders' addresses. I start by referring to my soon-to-be-canceled Flybynight.net account and then to the mailbox named "INBOX" within that account. Finally, I ask Mail to get the sender of every message in that mailbox.

Script 21–5.

```
tell application "Mail"
    tell account "Flybynight.net"
        tell mailbox "INBOX"
            set address_list to sender of every message
        end tell
    end tell
end tell
--> {"Jo Brown <jo@example.org>", "Alan Green <alan.green@example.com>", ...}
```

EXTRACTING INFORMATION FROM E-MAIL STRINGS

For your convenience, Mail's dictionary includes two string-related commands that can be helpful when you need to extract information about a message's sender: extract name from and extract address from. These commands will accept a string containing the sender's name and e-mail address in angle brackets (<>). Here's an example of how they work:

```
tell application "Mail"
    set the_sender to sender of message 1 of inbox
    -- the_sender contains the string "Donald F. Duck <donald@disney.com>"
    set sender_name to extract name from the_sender
    set sender_address to extract address from the_sender
end tell
return {sender_name, sender_address}
--> {"Donald F. Duck", "donald@disney.com"}
```

If the message is in a local mailbox you created, you can start by referring to a mailbox element of the top-level application object. Let's say I've created a top-level mailbox called "Clients" that contains sub-mailboxes for each of the organizations I do business with. If I want to count all the messages in the sub-mailbox named "Brown & Black Inc.", I refer to it as shown in Script 21–6.

Script 21–6.

```
tell application "Mail"
    tell mailbox "Clients"
        tell mailbox "Brown & Black Inc."
            count messages
        end tell
    end tell
end tell
--> 74
```

One other way to refer to messages is via the six standard mailbox properties in Mail's application object: inbox, outbox, drafts mailbox, and so on. These are equivalent to the standard large mailbox icons that appear on the left side of a viewer window in Mail and are used in much the same way. For example, the mailbox object in the inbox property acts as a convenient shortcut that allows you to refer to all the messages in all your accounts' "INBOX" mailboxes at once. So, a command like this,

```
tell application "Mail"
    get every message of inbox
end tell
```

would return a long list like this:

```
--> {message id 21 of mailbox "INBOX" of account "Work" of application "Mail",
     message id 52 of mailbox "INBOX" of account "Work" of application "Mail",
     ...
     message id 38 of mailbox "INBOX" of account "Personal" of application "Mail",
     ...
     message id 97 of mailbox "INBOX" of account "Temp" of application "Mail"}
```

Yet another option is to get the contents of the main application object's selection property, which holds an AppleScript list containing references to any messages that are currently selected in the GUI. This can be particularly useful in Mail scripts that require some user interaction. It also provides a quick and easy way to get a reference to specific e-mail messages for testing and debugging purposes.

Once you have a reference to the message or messages you want to work with, you can obtain various pieces of information. Header information can be found in properties such as sender, subject, and reply to—which contain AppleScript strings—and date sent and date received, which contain AppleScript date objects. Script 21–7 asks Mail for a list of currently selected messages and extracts some useful details from the first message in the list.

Script 21–7.

```
tell application "Mail"
    set the_message to item 1 of (get selection)
    {sender, subject, date sent, date received} of the_message
end tell
--> {"applescript-users-request@lists.apple.com",
     "AppleScript-Users Digest, Vol 7, Issue 110",
     date "Friday, February 26, 2010 10:23:17 PM",
     date "Friday, February 26, 2010 10:23:18 PM"}
```

> **CAUTION:** If you don't have any messages selected, the second line in Script 21–7 will throw an error when it tries to get item 1 of the empty list. In a practical script, you would typically trap and handle this error in a try block, or check that the selection list is not empty before trying to extract its first item.

Also of interest is the message class's content property (not to be confused with AppleScript's contents property). This contains a rich text object representing the body of the e-mail message. You will find the class for this object in Mail's Text Suite, which is a standard suite of classes found in most Cocoa-based applications (it is also used by the text property of TextEdit documents, for example).

If you ask Mail for the value of the content property, it assumes that you want to process the body text in AppleScript, so it returns it as an AppleScript string:

```
tell application "Mail"
    set the_message to item 1 of (get selection)
    content of the_message
end tell
--> "Send AppleScript-Users mailing list submissions to
    applescript-users@lists.apple.com
However, if you want to examine the message body in more detail, you can.
    To subscribe or unsubscribe via the World Wide Web, visit
        http://lists.apple.com/mailman/listinfo/applescript-users
    or, via email, send a message with subject or body 'help' to
        applescript-users-request@lists.apple.com
    ..."
```

However, because the text object is an application-defined object, it is still part of the Mail object model. This means you can also ask Mail to manipulate the properties and elements within the object:

```
tell application "Mail"
    set the_message to item 1 of (get selection)
    {font, size, color} of character 1 of content of the_message
end tell
--> {"Helvetica", 15.0, {8525, 14769, 26519}}
```

This is not something you can do with properties such as subject that contain ordinary AppleScript strings, as only AppleScript understands how to manipulate those:

```
tell application "Mail"
    set the_message to item 1 of (get selection)
    word 1 of subject of the_message
end tell
-- Mail got an error: Can't make word 1 of subject of message id 88424
        of mailbox \"AppleScript\" into type reference."
```

As with the selection property, you must first get the entire value from the subject property, and then manipulate it within AppleScript:

```
tell application "Mail"
    set the_message to item 1 of (get selection)
    word 1 of (get subject of the_message)
end tell
--> "AppleScript"
```

A word of warning here: because both AppleScript and Cocoa Scripting identify their text-related objects using the same class name, text, the AppleScript Editor dictionary viewer cannot properly distinguish between properties that contain AppleScript strings and properties that contain application-defined text objects.

As a rough rule of thumb, if the property contains text that appears in a large, scrollable or styled text view in the GUI, it will contain an application-defined text object. If the text only appears in the GUI as a single-line text field or not at all, the corresponding property almost certainly contains an AppleScript string.

You can confirm that a property contains a rich text object by asking it directly for one of its properties or elements—for instance, get every paragraph of the_property—and seeing if the command succeeds or fails.

> **TIP:** If you want to get the entire e-mail in raw form, get the message object's `source` property instead.

The `message` class also defines several classes of elements. The `recipients` class has several subclasses—`to recipients`, `cc recipients`, and `bcc recipients`—that describe the different types of recipients for this mail.

To get a list of all the message recipients, regardless of their exact type, just ask for all the message's recipient elements:

```
tell application "Mail"
    set the_message to item 1 of (get selection)
    every recipient of the_message
end tell
--> {to recipient 1 of message id 75008 of mailbox "INBOX"
        of account "john.smith@example.org" of application "Mail",
    cc recipient 1 of message id 75008 of mailbox "INBOX"
        of account "john.smith@example.org" of application "Mail"}
```

Each recipient object has a couple of properties containing the recipient's name (if known) and e-mail address:

```
tell application "Mail"
    set the_message to item 1 of (get selection)
    properties of to recipient 1 of the_message
end tell
--> {address:"applescript-users@lists.apple.com",
        class:recipient, name:missing value}}
```

Another useful class of elements is `mail attachment`, which represent any attachments the message has. Script 21–8 loops over each attachment in each of the selected messages and saves it to the user's Downloads folder.

Script 21–8.

```
tell application "Mail"
    repeat with message_ref in (get selection)
        repeat with attachment_ref in every mail attachment of message_ref
            tell attachment_ref
                set download_path to POSIX path of (path to downloads folder) & name
                save in (POSIX file download_path)
            end tell
        end repeat
    end repeat
end tell
```

Notice that the `save` command will fail if a file of the same name already exists in the Downloads folder. I will leave you to decide how you might want to deal with this possibility: perhaps by using the Finder to create a new, empty folder and saving all the files into that, or perhaps by inserting a numbered suffix before the file name extension (file.txt, file-1.txt, file-2.txt, ...). See Chapter 20 for help with scripting the file system, and Chapter 7 for more information on AppleScript string manipulation.

To finish our discussion of messages, one thing that you will notice when looking at the message class in Mail's dictionary is that most properties are read-only. Only the mailbox property and a few status properties can be changed. This makes sense, because there isn't a good reason for modifying the headers and contents of messages you've already sent or received.

As you cannot edit objects of class message, you might be wondering how you create new messages to send. Don't worry, though: Mail defines another class for this task, outgoing message, which we shall look at next.

Creating Outgoing Messages

Creating a new message to send is pretty straightforward: just use Mail's make command to create a new object of class outgoing message, and assign suitable values to its properties and elements. See Mail's dictionary to figure out the different properties and elements this object can have. Script 21–9 shows an example of a script that creates a new e-mail message.

Script 21–9.

```
set the_subject to "Hello there"
set the_body to "Please read the attached file:"
set the_file to choose file with prompt "Choose the file to attach:"

tell application "Mail"
    set new_message to make new outgoing message ¬
        with properties {subject:the_subject, content:the_body, visible:true}
    tell new_message
        -- Add the recipients:
        make new to recipient ¬
            at end of to recipients ¬
            with properties {name:"Simon", address:"simon@example.net"}
        make new cc recipient ¬
            at end of cc recipients ¬
            with properties {name:"Georgia", address:"georgia@example.net"}
        -- Add the attachment:
        make new paragraph ¬
            at end of last paragraph of content ¬
            with data (linefeed & linefeed & linefeed)
        make new attachment ¬
            at end of last paragraph of content ¬
            with properties {file name:the_file}
    end tell
end tell
```

The preceding message has two recipients. Mail's dictionary defines three kinds of recipients you can use when adding new recipients to a message: to recipient, cc recipient, and bcc recipient. All three are subclasses of the recipient class, which defines the name and address properties used to store the person's details.

CAUTION: When creating new recipients, make sure you specify either to recipient, cc recipient, or bcc recipient in the make command. If you use recipient by accident, you'll get an error because Mail can't make objects of that class.

Notice that when you create the attachment, you insert it into the message's content. In normal messages, attachments are defined as mail attachment elements of the message itself. In outgoing messages, however, attachment objects appear as attachment elements of Mail's text class.

This approach seems a bit odd at first, but it does make sense if you think about how Mail works: When you view an e-mail message on the screen, attachments appear within the message's body. By adding attachments to the text itself, you can control where the attachment icons appear in the text. This means that whenever you want to attach a file to a message, you must tell the make command to insert the new attachment object somewhere within the text object that lives in the outgoing message's content property. In Script 21–9, I added some blank paragraphs to the end of the message for neatness and added the attachment there; you could insert the attachment somewhere in the middle of the content text if you prefer.

You can top it off by sending your message with the send command, like this:

```
tell app "Mail" to send new_message
```

Working with Mail Rules

In addition to extensive AppleScript support, Apple Mail provides a second powerful automation feature: Mail rules.

The idea behind rules is simple: whenever a new e-mail message arrives or is about to be sent, it is checked to see if any of its attributes—sender, subject, content, junk mail status, and so on—match certain conditions defined by the user. You can also run rules manually by right-clicking one or more messages and choosing the **Apply Rules** option in the context menu.

For instance, a rule might check whether the sender's e-mail address ends in apple.com, or whether Mail thinks the message is junk. When a message matches the conditions set by the rule, Mail applies the actions specified by the rule to the message. These actions might include playing an alert sound, moving the message to another mailbox, or even running an AppleScript (my personal favorite).

NOTE: The ability to hook an AppleScript into a scriptable application so that the script is notified when something interesting happens in the application is known as *attachability*. Other attachable applications include System Events (folder actions), iCal (event alarms), Address Book (rollover actions), Adobe InDesign (the Scripts panel), and Satimage Smile (which has so many hooks that a good portion of the application is actually written in AppleScript).

To create or edit a Mail rule, go to the Rules panel of Mail's Preferences window and click the Add Rule or Edit button. You can also enable and disable existing rules or delete them altogether. To attach an AppleScript to Mail as a rule action, create a new rule with the conditions you want, and then choose the Run AppleScript action and select the .scpt file you want.

Let's say you have a workflow script running on a server that sends a report to you via e-mail whenever a job is run. Figure 21–4 shows a rule that looks for incoming e-mails sent from the server's e-mail address whose subject lines start with an easy-to-spot phrase. When one or more matching messages are detected, the rule runs an AppleScript, Save Log to File.scpt, that saves the content of the e-mail to disk for later reference. Additional actions could be added to move the message to another mailbox or delete it altogether.

Figure 21–4. *Running an attached AppleScript from a Mail rule*

The Mail suite of the Mail dictionary includes a single command definition, perform mail action with messages, especially for attached scripts to use. Unlike other commands in the Mail dictionary, you do not send this command yourself. Instead, Mail will send this command to your scripts when the Run AppleScript action is triggered. Your script can then decide what, if anything, it wants to do with the message or messages that triggered the rule.

> **TIP:** Notification commands such as perform mail action with messages that are sent from an application to a script are often referred to as *events* in order to distinguish them from regular commands that are sent from a script to an application to perform a specific action.

To handle the perform mail action with messages event, your script will need to define a handler named perform mail action with messages. Here is the dictionary definition for your handler:

```
perform mail action with messages v : Script handler invoked by rules and menus
       that execute AppleScripts. The direct parameter of this handler is a list
       of messages being acted upon.
   perform mail action with messages list of message : the message being acted upon
       [in mailboxes mailbox] : If the script is being executed by the user selecting
               an item in the scripts menu, this argument will specify the mailboxes
               that are currently selected. Otherwise it will not be specified.
       [for rule rule] : If the script is being executed by a rule action, this
               argument will be the rule being invoked. Otherwise it will not be
               specified.
```

As you can see, the handler accepts three parameters: a required direct parameter, which is a list of references to the messages that triggered the rule, and two optional named parameters, in mailboxes and for rule, which you can include if you need to know how the rule was triggered (either automatically or via the context menu).

Script 21–10 shows the code for Save Log to File.scpt. (It includes the pad_with_zero handler from Chapter 8 and the write_UTF16_file handler from Chapter 17.)

Script 21–10.

```
1. using terms from application "Mail"
2.     on perform mail action with messages message_list
3.         repeat with message_ref in message_list
4.             set {the_date, the_text} to {date received, content} of message_ref
5.             set the_file to POSIX file (POSIX path of (path to documents folder) ¬
                   & "Automation Logs/" & format_date_stamp(the_date) & ".txt")
6.             write_UTF16_file(the_file, the_text)
7.         end repeat
8.     end perform mail action with messages
9. end using terms from

10. on format_date_stamp(the_date)
11.     set date_stamp to year of the_date as text
12.     repeat with number_ref in {month, day, hours, minutes, seconds} of the_date
13.         set date_stamp to date_stamp & "-" & pad_with_zero(number_ref as integer)
14.     end repeat
15.     return date_stamp
16. end format_date_stamp
```

The main part of this script is the perform mail action with messages handler on lines 2 to 8. We are only interested in the incoming messages, so the in mailboxes and for rule parameters can be omitted from line 3.

Lines 3 to 7 loop over the supplied list of message references, processing each message in turn. Line 4 gets the date that the message was received on, which we'll use to construct the file name, and its content, which we will write to file.

Line 5 is responsible for creating an AppleScript POSIX file object identifying the location of the file we want to create. (See Chapter 17 for more information on the POSIX file class.) This particular script saves the log files in an existing folder named Automation Logs in the user's Documents folder, so we use concatenation to assemble the full folder path and the parts of the file name. To create the main part of the file name, we use the format_date_stamp handler (lines 10 to 16) to convert the date object into a YYYY-MM-DD-HH-MM-SS style date string.

Finally, line 6 uses the write_UTF16_file handler to save the file to disk.

Notice how the entire perform mail action with messages handler is wrapped in a using terms from block. Normally, when you deal with a scriptable application, you write application-specific keywords within a tell ... end tell block. The AppleScript compiler then looks at the target of that tell block, for example, application "Mail", to figure out where those keywords are defined.

With the Mail rule script, it is not possible to enclose the perform mail action with messages handler within a tell block because script handlers can only appear within a script (or script object). We still need some way to tell AppleScript where to find the definition of the perform mail action with messages keyword, however, because otherwise the script will not compile.

The solution is to wrap the handler (or even the entire script) within a using terms from block. Unlike a tell block, which is also used to target commands, the only purpose of a using terms from block is to instruct the AppleScript compiler to look in the specified application's dictionary when compiling keywords within the block. In Script 21–10, the using terms from block identifies the Mail application, ensuring that the handler name on line 2 compiles correctly.

Before installing the folder action, it's a good idea to test it first. You can call the perform mail action with messages handler yourself by temporarily adding the following code and running it:

```
tell application "Mail"
    set test_list to selection
    tell me to perform mail action with messages (test_list)
end tell
```

This gets a list of the currently selected messages in the Mail GUI and passes those references to the Mail rule handler to process. Once you're happy that everything is working correctly, comment out or delete the test code, attach the script to the rule, and check that the rule is triggered correctly when the desired e-mails are received or sent.

Example Project: Building a Monthly Message Archive

As a longtime subscriber to the various AppleScript-related mailing lists at
http://lists.apple.com, I have built up quite a collection of AppleScript-related e-mail
digests. Early on, I created a Mail rule that files these messages away in their own
"AppleScript Lists" mailbox as soon as they arrive, but over time this mailbox has grown
rather large.

Recently I decided to tidy the mailbox by moving the messages into dated folders
according to the months in which they were received. To save myself the trouble of
rearranging many hundreds of e-mails by hand, I put together a quick-and-dirty script to
do it for me. The script works by calculating the date of the start of each month, starting
with the current month, and working backward from there. If the "AppleScript Lists"
mailbox contains any messages that were received on or after that date, it creates a new
sub-mailbox for that month and moves the messages into them. Once that's done, the
script jumps to the month before, and repeats the process until no messages are left.

Preparing to Write the Script

As I don't script Mail on a daily basis, I needed to do a bit of research and
experimentation first. A key part of this script involves creating new sub-mailboxes from
AppleScript, so let's start there.

> **CAUTION:** Before starting to experiment on important data such as Mail messages, it is a very
> good idea to make a backup of that data just in case anything goes wrong. Before developing
> this script, I made a copy of the ~/Library/Mail folder so that if I messed up the existing
> Mail folder I could easily replace it with the previous version.

First, I created a new mailbox named "AppleScript Archive":

```
tell application "Mail"
    make new mailbox ¬
        at end of mailboxes ¬
        with properties {name:"AppleScript Archive"}
end tell
```

As this is a one-off task, I could have created the mailbox by hand, but doing it with an
application command is good practice. One thing I noticed in doing so is that Mail's
make command does not return a reference to the newly created mailbox. So whenever a
mailbox object is created, any references to it must be constructed separately.

The next step is to figure out how to create sub-mailboxes, named "2010-03", "2010-
02", "2010-01", and so on.

Earlier in Script 21–6, you saw how to refer to sub-mailboxes by referring to the mailbox
elements of a mailbox object. In a well-designed AppleScriptable application, you would
expect to use a similar approach, like this:

```
tell application "Mail"
    make new mailbox ¬
            at end of mailboxes of mailbox "AppleScript Archive" ¬
            with properties {name:"2010-03"}
end tell
```

Unfortunately, running this script produced the following, completely unhelpful error message:

```
error "Mail got an error: AppleEvent handler failed." number -10000
```

At first I was perplexed: the code looked like it should work, but it didn't. I experimented with different styles of at reference—omitting the of mailboxes and end of mailboxes portions to see if that would make any difference.

> **NOTE:** Some applications require the at parameter to be a reference to the containing object—the Finder is one good example—while other applications (particularly Cocoa ones) require an insertion location before or after the object's elements. Often, the only way to find out which form is correct is to try both and see which one works.

Alas, none of these tests were successful, so next I created a sub-mailbox by hand and asked Mail for a reference to it, just to make sure that this bit was working:

```
tell application "Mail" to mailbox "2010-03" of mailbox "AppleScript Archive"
--> mailbox "AppleScript Archive/2010-03" of application "Mail"
```

Straightaway, I noticed that the returned reference pointed to a mailbox element of the main application object, with the mailbox object's name being made up of the main mailbox name, followed by a slash, followed by the sub-mailbox name. So I deleted the previous sub-mailbox, and tried re-creating it with a new make command, this time leaving out the at parameter altogether (which you can often do when adding elements to the main application object) and using the same slash-delimited name:

```
tell application "Mail"
    make new mailbox with properties {name:"AppleScript Archive/2010-03"}
end tell
```

This time, the command worked. (If it doesn't work for you, check that your new mailbox name isn't the same as the name of an existing mailbox, as Mail requires that each one has a unique name.)

The next step was to make sure that I could calculate a date for 12:00 AM on the first day of a given month. Fortunately, I already had a set of useful date-manipulation handlers created for an earlier job, so I didn't need to develop this code from scratch:

```
on calculate_start_of_month(the_date)
    copy the_date to new_date
    set day of new_date to 1
    set time of new_date to 0
    return new_date
end calculate_start_of_month
```

```
on calculate_start_of_previous_month(the_date)
    copy the_date to new_date
    set day of new_date to 1
    set time of new_date to 0
    set new_date to new_date - 1 * days
    set day of new_date to 1
    return new_date
end calculate_start_of_previous_month
```

The `calculate_start_of_month` handler works by setting the day property of a date object to 1 and the `time` property to 0 (12:00 AM). For safety, the handler makes a copy of the given date and modifies the copy, not the original. If the handler modified the original date, other parts of the script still using that date would get a nasty surprise when the date unexpectedly changed on them!

The `calculate_start_of_previous_month` handler uses a similar approach, except that once it finds the start of the month, it subtracts a day (in seconds) to calculate the last day of the previous month. Once it has obtained that date, it simply sets its day to the first of the month.

Here are some examples of use:

```
calculate_start_of_month(date "Monday, March 15, 2010 6:30:00 PM")
--> date "Monday, March 1, 2010 12:00:00 AM"

calculate_start_of_previous_month(date "Monday, March 15, 2010 6:30 PM")
--> date "Monday, February 1, 2010 12:00:00 AM"
```

Creating the Sub-Mailboxes

Having figured out how to create sub-mailboxes in principle, the next step was to develop some working code to create the dated sub-mailboxes. As this is a fairly self-contained task, I wrote it as a handler for neatness:

```
on make_sub_mailbox_for_month(main_mailbox_name, the_date)
    set the_year to year of the_date as text
    set the_month to pad_with_zero(month of the_date as integer)
    set sub_mailbox_name to main_mailbox_name & "/" & the_year & "-" & the_month
    tell application "Mail"
        if not (exists mailbox sub_mailbox_name) then
            make new mailbox with properties {name:sub_mailbox_name}
        end if
        return mailbox sub_mailbox_name
    end tell
end make_sub_mailbox_for_month
```

This handler has two main parts. The first part gets the year and month values from a date object and formats them as a four-digit year, followed by a hyphen, followed by a two-digit month, padding the month number with a leading zero if necessary. (You will need to include the `pad_with_zero` handler from Chapter 8 for this.) The second part checks whether the desired mailbox already exists and, if it doesn't, creates it. It then returns a reference to the mailbox for the calling code to use. While it might have made more sense to split this code into two separate handlers, it's good enough for the job at hand.

To check that this handler worked correctly, I simply sent some test commands using a good mix of dates—including dates for the first and last days of a month, and more than one date in the same month—to check that I hadn't missed anything:

```
make_sub_mailbox_for_month("AppleScript Archive", current date)
repeat with date_string in {"February 1, 2010", "March 15, 2010", ¬
      "February 28, 2010", "September 30, 2009", "June 4, 2009 6:30 PM"}
   make_sub_mailbox_for_month("AppleScript Archive", date date_string)
end repeat
```

After confirming that the correct mailboxes appeared in Mail, I pasted the two date-manipulation handlers into the script and moved on to the final stage: processing the messages in the "AppleScript Lists" mailbox a month at a time.

Putting It All Together

With my supporting handlers tested and working, all that remained was to write the code to calculate the start of each month and move any messages received on or after that date to a new sub-mailbox. Script 21–11 shows the completed script. (It includes the calculate_start_of_month, calculate_start_of_previous_month, and make_sub_mailbox_for_month handlers from the previous two sections and the pad_with_zero handler from Chapter 8.)

Script 21–11.

```
1. set current_mailbox_name to "AppleScript Lists"
2. set archive_mailbox_name to "AppleScript Archive"

3. set start_date to calculate_start_of_month(current date)
4. tell application "Mail"
5.    tell mailbox current_mailbox_name
6.       repeat while (count every message) > 0
7.          tell (every message whose date received ≥ start_date)
8.             if (count) > 0 then
9.                set archive_mailbox to my make_sub_mailbox_for_month(¬
                     archive_mailbox_name, start_date)
10.                  set its mailbox to archive_mailbox
11.            end if
12.          end tell
13.          delay 2
14.          set start_date to my calculate_start_of_previous_month(start_date)
15.       end repeat
16.    end tell
17. end tell
```

First, lines 1 and 2 define a pair of variables at the top of the script to hold the mailbox names that will be used later on. If I use this script in the future to create other archives, I can easily see which lines need to be modified.

Next, line 3 calculates the date for the first day of the current month to use as my starting point. While I could have started from the oldest month and worked forward to the current date, I would have had to figure out first when the oldest message was received. By starting with the most recent month (which is easy to determine using current date) and working backward, all I needed to do was keep going until no messages were left—an easy test using Mail's count command (line 6).

Line 7 uses a whose clause to identify only those messages that were received on or after the starting date. For neatness, the script only creates a sub-mailbox if one or more messages are found for that month (line 8).

To get a reference to the appropriate sub-mailbox, line 9 sends a make_sub_mailbox_for_month command to obtain a reference to the mailbox for the month. As this command is inside a tell application ... end tell block, I've added the my keyword in front of the command so that AppleScript knows to send it to the script, not the Mail application.

Once I had a reference to the destination mailbox, I simply needed to move the messages identified by the enclosing tell block into it. In most applications, this type of action would be performed using the move command, but I found Mail's move command to be a bit buggy and unreliable—some messages would end up duplicated into the wrong mailboxes; other times, the command would throw an error for no obvious reason.

Another way to move messages in Mail is to set their mailbox properties to a new mailbox reference, as shown on line 10. Although this made a bit of difference, it still wasn't perfect. After a few test runs of the assembled script, I suspected there might be some sort of timing issue with moving large numbers of messages at once—almost as if Mail was starting on the next move before the previous one was finished. To see if this was the case, I added a simple "kludge": a two-second pause on line 13 that executes before the next loop starts.

Once I did this, the script ran without any more problems—if a bit more slowly. (Time to send another bug report to Apple...)

Finally, line 14 calculates the start of the preceding month and updates the start_date variable before proceeding with the next loop.

Success! My AppleScript mailboxes were tidy at last, and while automating the task took me a bit longer than I'd expected (thanks to the bugs and other quirks in Mail's scripting support), I gained some valuable knowledge on Mail scripting along the way. Plus, the next time my mailboxes get messy, tidying them up again is only a Cmd+R away.

Scripting iCal

iCal has a modest but reasonably well-crafted scripting dictionary. In iCal you normally have one or more calendars, each of which can contain any number of to-do and event items. These are represented in iCal's object model by objects of class calendar, todo, and event.

A to-do object represents a task that you need to do sometime, such as write an article or arrange a vacation. A to-do object is fairly simple, with a summary and description of the task to do, an optional due date for the task to be done, and a few other useful properties such as the date the task was finally completed (if it has been). To-do objects can also have `alarm` elements, used to trigger various reminders for tasks that haven't been completed yet.

An event object represents a particular occurrence at a specific time (or times) and place, such as a 90-minute meeting with several colleagues that you need to attend every Monday morning at 9:30 AM for three weeks, or the much-anticipated summer vacation you'll be taking from July 15 to July 30. Not surprisingly, event objects are a bit more complex than to-do objects, with properties for the start date, end date, and location of the event and whether the event repeats at regular intervals, and with elements for specifying who'll be attending the event and triggering various alarms.

> **NOTE:** Although iCal can have multiple calendars, they all appear in the same calendar window. You can identify which events belong to which calendars by their color.

iCal's inheritance hierarchy is almost completely flat: every class directly inherits from Cocoa Scripting's standard `item` class. Figure 21–5 shows the containment hierarchy for iCal's object model. As you can see, it's also fairly simple and quite straightforward.

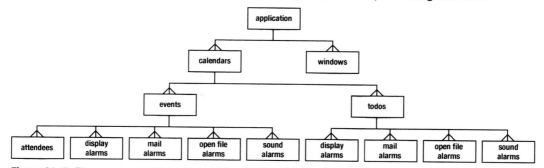

Figure 21–5. *The containment hierarchy for iCal's object model*

> **TIP:** One class that is listed in the iCal dictionary's Standard Suite but isn't shown in Figure 21–5 is the document class. The document class is one of the three default classes defined by the Cocoa Scripting framework, but it's only really relevant to document-based applications such as TextEdit and Safari. Ideally, application developers should remove any unused class and command definitions from their dictionaries to avoid confusion, but sometimes they forget, so just ignore this and any other irrelevant Standard Suite entries when you encounter them.

The following sections look at how to work with calendar and event objects. To-do objects are also scriptable, but as the `todo` class is really just a simplified version of the event class, we won't cover it here.

Working with Calendars

The `calendar` class is the core element of any iCal application. Any event you want to manipulate or create has to belong to a calendar.

To create a calendar named "Sports", run the following script:

```
tell application "iCal"
    make new calendar with properties {name:"Sports"}
end tell
--> calendar 9 of application "iCal"
```

Calendar objects can be identified all the usual ways—by index, by name, by ID, by test, and so on:

```
tell application "iCal"
    get calendar "Sports"
end tell
--> calendar id "72E8F46F-9DA7-4710-BE15-F5978A0EA49C" of application "iCal"
```

Oddly, the make command returns a by-index reference, whereas the get command returns a more robust by-ID reference. If you want to create a by-ID reference to your newly created calendar, you can ask iCal for the ID of the newly created calendar, like this:

```
set the_id to uid of (make new calendar with properties {name:"Sports"})
```

You can then construct a new by-ID reference for yourself:

```
set the_calendar to calendar id the_id
```

> **TIP:** For historical reasons, the object ID property in iCal is named `uid` instead of the more familiar `id`. Don't worry, though, because iCal accepts `id` as a synonym, and `uid` behaves as a regular `id` property would.

As you would expect, you can get and set the properties of calendar objects, either individually or via the properties property:

```
tell application "iCal" to get properties of calendar "Work"
--> {class:calendar, description:"", id:"D24745F6-75C3-4901-9C29-0B5D7CCAF4ED",
    title:"Work", writable:true, color:{11308, 41377, 2827}}
```

To view a particular date in a calendar, use the `view calendar` command:

```
tell application "iCal"
    view calendar "Work" at date "Monday, June 21, 2010 12:00:00 AM"
end tell
```

Each calendar object can also have zero or more event and/or todo elements. Let's look at working with calendar events next.

Working with Events

As you can imagine, one of the most useful classes in iCal is the event class. Events are what make the calendar useful in the first place: dinner party Tuesday at 6 PM, sales meeting Friday from 3 to 4:30 PM, and so on.

The event class has a few obvious properties, such as start date and end date, both of which hold AppleScript date values. You can also get and set the summary, location, description, and other values displayed in the iCal window, as shown in Script 21–12.

Script 21–12.

```
tell application "iCal"
    get properties of last event of calendar "Home"
end tell
--> {stamp date:date "Monday, March 1, 2010 8:21:11 AM",
    allday event:false,
    end date:date "Wednesday, April 14, 2010 1:00:00 PM",
    class:event,
    start date:date "Wednesday, April 14, 2010 12:00:00 PM",
    description:missing value,
    summary:"Lunch with Phil",
    location:"Cafe Bar",
    ...
    id:"D684D6EB-F3AA-4439-8C06-1A0A34505E63"}
```

Script 21–13 shows a simple script that creates a new event and assigns it a few basic properties.

Script 21–13.

```
tell application "iCal"
    set feed_ferret_event to make new event ¬
        at end of events of calendar "Home" ¬
        with properties { ¬
            summary:"Feed ferret", location:"Providence", ¬
            start date:date "Saturday, May 1, 2010 4:00:00 PM", ¬
            end date:date "Saturday, May 1, 2010 4:30:00 PM", ¬
            allday event:false, status:confirmed, ¬
            recurrence:"FREQ=DAILY;INTERVAL=2;UNTIL=20100601"}
end tell
```

Let's look at the seven properties of the new event object set in this example. The first two properties are start date and end date. These are probably the most important properties that define the date and time boundaries of the event.

The summary and location properties are two strings that provide information about the event.

The event's status property can be none, confirmed, tentative, or cancelled, and the allday event property's value is a Boolean that determines whether the event appears as a variable-sized block that runs between the start and end times given by your date values or as an all-day block that automatically runs from midnight to midnight.

The recurrence property is one area where Apple engineers could have definitely spent more time. Right now, the recurrence property is an ugly string that includes information about the recurrence frequency, intervals, and duration of the event. Here is an example of the string again:

```
FREQ=DAILY;INTERVAL=2;UNTIL=20100601
```

The string contains three labels: FREQ, INTERVAL, and UNTIL or COUNT. Each label is followed by a value as follows:

- FREQ is the frequency at which the event recurs. The FREQ label is followed by one of the following values: DAILY, WEEKLY, MONTHLY, or YEARLY.

- If the frequency is set to DAILY, for instance, INTERVAL specifies how many days between event occurrences. In the preceding example, the interval is 2, which means the feed ferret event will recur every two days.

- The duration either can be the label UNTIL followed by a YYYYMMDD style date string or can be the label COUNT followed by the number of occurrences that will happen before the event repetition expires. In the earlier example, I used the following UNTIL value: 20100601. This means the event will stop recurring at midnight on May 31, 2010. An UNTIL duration of -1 indicates that the event never expires.

NOTE: The recurrence string format is part of the iCalendar specification, which is a standard format for transferring calendar and schedule information between many different programs. If you are feeling brave, you can find the full 147-page technical specification at http://www.ietf.org/rfc/rfc2445.txt; recurrence rules are covered in section 4.3.10.

When working with iCal, you will often want to identify events that fall on certain dates. Because AppleScript dates contain both date and time information, to get a list of the events that start on a particular day, you need to check for all of the events whose start dates fall on or after midnight of the day you want and before midnight of the following day:

```
set the_date to current date
tell application "iCal"
    summary of every event of every calendar ¬
        whose start date ≥ (date "12:00 AM" of the_date) ¬
        and start date < (the_date + 1 * days)
end tell
--> {{"Dentist", "Lunch with Phil"}, {"New Client Meeting"}}
```

Unfortunately, iCal will only return events that are defined on that day—recurring events that are defined on an earlier date and which happen to recur on the day you are interested in are not included. (Hmm…perhaps a recurring feature request to Apple is in order…) Detecting multiday events that start on an earlier date and finish on or after the day you want will also require a separate test:

```
set the_date to current date
tell application "iCal"
```

```
    summary of every event of every calendar ¬
        whose start date < (date "12:00 AM" of the_date) ¬
        and start date ≥ (date "12:00 AM" of the_date)
end tell
```

Event objects can also have attendee elements and four types of alarm elements: open file alarm, sound alarm, display alarm, and mail alarm. For instance, to send an e-mail alarm to yourself an hour before the ferret needs to be fed, simply insert the following make command at the end of the tell block in Script 21–13:

```
make new mail alarm ¬
    at end of mail alarms of feed_ferret_event ¬
    with properties {trigger interval:-60}
```

Another neat feature of iCal is that you can schedule AppleScript files to run at specific times. You'll discover how to do this in Chapter 23.

> **TIP:** See the "Transferring Meeting Arrangements from Mail to iCal" project in Chapter 7 for a good demonstration of iCal and Mail scripting combined with some AppleScript string manipulation.

Scripting Address Book

One of the hidden jewels scripters get with Mac OS X is the ability to script Address Book. The reason why it is so nice is that you get access to the operating system's contact database. Other Apple applications such as Mail use this database, which is open to any developer who wants to use it.

What makes Address Book scripting so nice is the well-structured object model, which reflects the database structure itself. The object model in Address Book is designed for flexibility. It does not limit you to a specific number of addresses or phone numbers per person. Instead of numbers and addresses being properties of the person, they are elements. As you are aware, an object can have only one of each property, but you can add as many elements as the application allows.

The two main classes of objects you work with are person and group. Each person object contains all of the details describing a single person or company entered into your address book. If you wish, you can also organize people into groups—for instance, you might put your friends in a group named "Friends" and work colleagues in a group named "Work" to make them easier to find.

Figure 21–6 shows the inheritance hierarchy for the classes defined in the Address Book dictionary.

Notice that the topmost item class is not visible in the Address Book dictionary. Cocoa-based applications sometimes leave this definition out of their dictionaries because it's a standard feature provided by Cocoa itself, and so is always present. The item class defines only two standard properties, class and properties, which you can use to obtain basic information about an object. All other properties and elements are defined in the application's own subclasses.

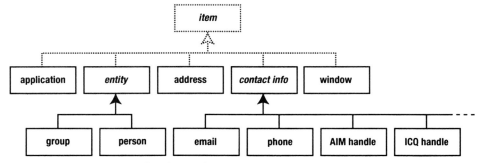

Figure 21–6. *Address Book's inheritance hierarchy*

Figure 21–7 shows the main part of the containment hierarchy for Address Book's object model.

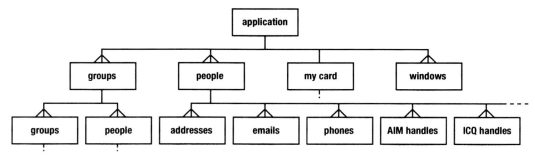

Figure 21–7. *Address Book's containment hierarchy*

As you can see, you can refer to person elements as elements of the top-level application object; every person in the Address Book is accessible this way. You can also refer to person elements within specific groups; for example: every person of group "Friends".

Working with People

The single most important class in Address Book is person. You can identify individual person elements by index, name, ID, or before or after another person; or you can refer to a number of people by range, whose test, or all at once. Most of these reference forms should always work in Cocoa applications because they are a standard Cocoa feature. However, you will need to check a particular class's definition to see if by-name and/or by-ID references work: if the class (or one of its parent classes) lists name and/or id properties, then you know those reference forms will work as well. In the case of Address Book, the person class defines a name property and its parent entry class defines an id property, so you know that you can also refer to people objects by name and ID:

```
tell application "Address Book"
    name of every person
end tell
--> {"Mita Singh", "Apple Inc.", "Dr David Andrew Smith", ...}
```

When you get a person reference back from Address Book, it will identify the person object by ID, which means that when you use the reference again later, you are guaranteed to get the same person object every time (assuming that the object hasn't been deleted, of course). For example, the following script returns a list of references to the currently selected people:

```
tell application "Address Book" to get selection
--> {person id "6F99ADB1-F15F-4317-B7AA-B6562A2C476D:ABPerson"
        of application "Address Book"}
```

When working with person objects, you will often need to find out more information about that person. Each person object has various properties containing their title, first name, middle name, last name, birth date, and so on:

```
tell application "Address Book"
    {title, first name, middle name, last name, suffix} of person 3
end tell
--> {"Dr", "David", "Andrew", "Smith", missing value}
```

Properties that don't hold any useful information will contain AppleScript's missing value constant.

You can set as well as get most person properties, although a few are read-only. An obvious case is the name property, whose value is automatically assembled from the other name-related properties:

```
tell application "Address Book"
    name of person 3
end tell
--> "Dr David Andrew Smith"
```

Properties are only good for holding one-of-a-kind values, of course, so other information such as addresses, phone numbers, and e-mail addresses are represented as elements of the person object. Address objects have a number of properties, as you can see:

```
tell application "Address Book"
    properties of address 1 of person "Apple Inc."
end tell
--> {street:"1 Infinite Loop", city:"Cupertino", country:"United States",
     formatted address:"1 Infinite Loop\nCupertino  CA  95014\nUnited States",
     class:address, zip:"95014", label:"work", country code:"us", state:"CA",
     id:"A29C86A2-9534-4C72-A7C3-DF466BD97D95"}
```

Other types of contact information are much simpler, consisting of label-value pairs. The labels do not have to be unique. For instance, a person's work phone number would typically appear in Address Book's main window as follows:

work 401-555-1212

This would be represented by an object of class phone, which is a specific subclass of the general contact info class that defines the label and value properties. Its label would be "work" and its value "401-555-1212." To get every work-related phone number of the currently selected person in Address Book, you would use the following:

```
tell application "Address Book"
    set the_person to item 1 of (get selection)
    get value of every phone of the_person whose label is "work"
end tell
--> {"401-555-1212", "401-555-5237"}
```

Script 21–14 shows how to create people and contact information using the standard make command.

Script 21–14.

```
tell application "Address Book"
    set new_person to make new person at end of people with properties ¬
        {first name:"Janet", last name:"Brown", organization:"Brown & Black Inc."}
    make new phone at end of phones of new_person with properties ¬
            {label:"Mobile", value:"901-555-2124"}
    save -- Remember to save your changes!
end tell
```

Notice the save command at the end—this is essential! Until you save your changes, they will not become visible in the Address Book GUI and, more importantly, they will be lost without any warning when you quit Address Book.

Incidentally, you may notice that the Address Book dictionary contains two different descriptions for save. The one in the Standard Suite is redundant, so just ignore it. The definition under the Address Book Script Suite is the one you want:

```
save v : Save all Address Book changes. Also see the unsaved property for
    the application class.  syn save addressbook
  save
    --> any
```

In older versions of Address Book, the command for saving changes was called save addressbook, but in Mac OS 10.6 it was renamed to save. The save addressbook keyword is still supported for the sake of backward compatibility, however. As you can see from the command definition, it is now treated as a synonym ("syn") of the save keyword, so any save addressbook keywords will automatically be reformatted as save when you compile the script.

Similarly, you can delete objects using the standard delete command:

```
tell application "Address Book"
    delete person "Andrew Scott"
    save
end tell
```

Working with Groups

Groups are a great way to organize large address books effectively. The Address Book GUI allows you to create two types of groups: normal groups, whose contents you manage manually or using AppleScript, and groups, which automatically list all people that match a particular set of conditions.

You can work with the person elements of a particular group just as you would refer to the person elements of the main `application` object. For instance, Script 21–15 builds a tab-delimited table listing all of the people in the group named "Work" along with their phone numbers.

Script 21–15.

```
1. tell application "Address Book"
2.    tell every person of group "Work"
3.       set the_names to name
4.       set phones_by_name to value of every phone
5.    end tell
6. end tell

7. set table_rows to {}
8. repeat with i from 1 to length of the_names
9.    set end of table_rows to item i of the_names & tab & item i of phones_by_name
10. end repeat
11. set AppleScript's text item delimiters to linefeed
12. set table_text to table_rows as text
```

Lines 1 to 6 retrieve the information we want from Address Book. The `tell` block on lines 2 to 5 specifies the default target, `every person of group "Work"`, for lines 3 and 4.

Line 3 gets the name of every person in the group. A typical result might look like this:

```
{"Janice Smith", "Carlos Hernández", "Samantha Brown", ...}
```

Line 4 retrieves all of the phone numbers for each of these people:

```
{{"901-555-4980"}, {}, {"401-555-5629" "310-555-7422"}, ...}
```

Notice how we asked for a property of every subelement of every element of an object. This is quite a complex request, but Address Book resolved it without any problem, helpfully grouping the phone numbers for each person into a sublist.

Lines 7 to 12 then turn these raw lists into the finished text:

```
"Janice Smith       901-555-4980
Carlos Hernández
Samantha Brown     401-555-5629/310-555-7422
..."
```

You can use the `make` command to create regular groups from scratch (smart groups can only be created via the GUI, unfortunately). To add and remove people to and from a particular group, use the `add` and `remove` commands. Script 21–16 asks the user to enter a new group name, creates a new group by that name, and then moves the currently selected people into that group.

Script 21–16.

```
tell application "Address Book"
    activate
    set group_name to text returned of ¬
            (display dialog "Enter name of new group:" default answer "")
    set new_group to make new group with properties {name:group_name}
    repeat with person_ref in (get selection)
        add person_ref to new_group
    end repeat
    save
    set selected of new_group to true
end tell
```

As you can see, making new groups is very straightforward. As with creating new person objects, the make command returns a by-ID reference to the newly created group, so we store that reference in a variable for later use.

If you check the Address Book dictionary, you will see that the selection property contains an ordinary AppleScript list object rather than an application object. While the add command can operate on more than one object at a time if you use a multi-item reference (for instance, add every person whose title = "Dr" to *some_group*), it won't understand a list of references. This means we have to retrieve the list of references from the selection property, and then loop over that list, adding each person to the group one at a time.

A common mistake here is to forget to get the list object from Address Book before trying to loop over it. If we wrote

```
repeat with person_ref in selection
    ...
end repeat
```

AppleScript would send a series of get commands to Address Book, asking it to do all the work: get item 1 of selection, get item 2 of selection, and so on. This might seem an odd way of doing things, but that is just how repeat with ... in ... loops work, so it is something we have to live with. Unfortunately, these commands cause Address Book to throw an error because it only knows how to get elements of application objects, not AppleScript objects. In Script 21–16, the explicit get command ensures that the list object is retrieved from the selection property before it is used by the repeat loop. Alternatively, you could write the code like this:

```
set selection_list to selection
repeat with person_ref in selection_list
    ...
end repeat
```

Now that the selection expression is on its own line, AppleScript will automatically send an implicit get to retrieve the value. Personally, I prefer the approach used in Script 21–16 as it is shorter and makes my intentions clear, but you can use whichever style you feel most comfortable with.

TIP: See Chapter 12 for more information on implicit versus explicit get commands.

Lastly, the script saves the changes that have been made (don't forget to do this!), and sets the group object's selected property to true so that the content of the new group is displayed in the GUI.

Working with Rollovers

There is one more neat, if obscure, feature in Address Book where AppleScript can be used: rollover plug-ins. When the user clicks the label for a piece of contact information, Mail displays a pop-up menu listing any special actions that can be performed on that particular type of item.

For instance, Figure 21–8 shows the result of clicking the label of a phone number entry. The standard Show in Large Type action displays the phone number across the entire screen, while the Add to Phone List action is a custom action written in AppleScript. Each time you choose it, it adds the person's name and number to a TextEdit document named "Phone List"—ideal for creating a list of people to call later.

Figure 21–8. *Clicking a contact entry's label displays a list of rollover actions.*

Script 21–17 shows the script behind the Add to Phone List action.

Script 21–17.

```
using terms from application "Address Book"
    on action property
        return "phone"
    end action property

    on action title for thePerson with theEntry
        return "Add to Phone List"
    end action title

    on should enable action with the_element for the_person
```

```
        return true
    end should enable action

    on perform action with the_element for the_person
        set person_name to name of the_person
        set phone_number to value of the_element
        tell application "TextEdit"
            if not (exists document "Phone List") then
                make new document with properties {name:"Phone List"}
            end if
            make new paragraph ¬
                    at (end of paragraphs of document "Phone List") ¬
                    with data (person_name & tab & phone_number & linefeed)
        end tell
    end perform action
end using terms from
```

As you can see, the script consists of four handlers: action property, should enable action, action title, and perform action. The names for these handlers are defined in the Address Book Rollover suite of the Address Book dictionary. As they are application-defined keywords, a using terms from block is used to ensure that the handler names compile correctly.

The first three handlers are quite simple.

The action property handler must return a string that indicates the type of contact information that the action can be used on—address, e-mail, phone, and so on. When the user clicks an entry, Address Book calls this handler to decide whether or not to include this action in the pop-up menu. If the answer is yes, then it calls the action title handler, which should return the name of the action as it should appear in the menu.

The should enable action handler gives the script an opportunity to disable the action if it would be inappropriate to run it on the selected value. The handler is passed two parameters that it can use to make a decision: the with parameter contains a reference to the address or contact info object for this entry; the for parameter contains a reference to the person object that contains it. The handler should return true if it is safe for the user to run this action, or false if it is not.

If the user chooses to run this action, then Address Book calls the perform action handler, which is where the real work is done. The perform action handler starts by getting the name of the person along with the selected phone number. As the script is being run within Address Book, these commands do not need to be enclosed in a tell application "Address Book" ... end tell block.

Next, the perform action handler checks whether TextEdit already contains a document named "Phone List" and, if not, creates one. Finally, it creates a new paragraph at the end of the document containing the person's name and phone number, separated with a tab. Notice how the text for the paragraph is being passed via the make command's with data paragraph—we are creating the paragraph element directly from this data, rather than setting a property within it. You can use the with properties parameter if you want to set attributes of the new paragraph such as the font name or size.

To install the action, save the script as Add to Phone List.scpt in ~/Library/Address Book Plug-Ins, or in /Library/Address Book Plug-Ins if you want to make them visible to all users on your Mac, creating the plug-ins folder if necessary. If Address Book is already running, you will need to restart it for the new action to appear.

Now, you can build up your reminder list simply by flicking through the people you need to phone, clicking their phone numbers, and choosing the Add to Phone List action as you go.

Example Project: Looking Up Contact Information by Name

Let's finish our exploration of Address Book scripting with another look at people and contact info objects, and performing lookups using the powerful whose clause.

Script 21–18 shows a little utility for quickly looking up contact information by a person's first or last name. The script taps the contact database structure and shows only the available phone numbers and e-mail addresses.

The script starts by letting the user pick a character from the alphabet. Then it gets the full name of all people in the Address Book database whose first or last name starts with the chosen character. Once the user picks a name, the script will show the e-mail addresses and phone numbers of the chosen contact and will create an e-mail message for that person if the user wants.

Script 21–18.

```
1.  -- Ask user to select a letter from A to Z
2.  set character_list to characters of "ABCDEFGHIJKLMNOPQRSTUVWXYZ"
3.  set the_selection to choose from list character_list
4.  if the_selection is false then return -- User canceled
5.  set chosen_character to item 1 of the_selection

6.  -- Get the names of people whose first/last names start with that letter
7.  tell application "Address Book"
8.     set name_list to name of every person ¬
           whose first name starts with chosen_character ¬
           or last name starts with chosen_character
9.  end tell
10. if name_list is {} then
11.    display alert "No matching people were found." as warning
12.    return
13. end if

14. -- Ask user to select a person's name
15. set the_selection to choose from list name_list
16. if the_selection is false then return -- User canceled
17. set chosen_name to item 1 of the_selection

18. -- Get all the email and phone contact info for the chosen person
19. tell application "Address Book"
20.    set chosen_person to first person whose name is chosen_name
21.    tell chosen_person
22.       set {email_labels, email_values} to {label, value} of every email
23.       set {phone_labels, phone_values} to {label, value} of every phone
```

```
24.    end tell
25. end tell
26. if email_labels is {} and phone_labels is {} then
27.    display alert ¬
              "The person you selected has no email or phone details." as warning
28.    return
29. end if

30. -- Assemble a string containing the contact information
31. set the_message to "Contact information for " & chosen_name & ":" & return
32. repeat with i from 1 to (count email_labels)
33.    set the_label to item i of email_labels
34.    set the_value to item i of email_values
35.    set the_message to the_message & the_label & " email: " & the_value & return
36. end repeat
37. repeat with i from 1 to (count phone_labels)
38.    set the_label to item i of phone_labels
39.    set the_value to item i of phone_values
40.    set the_message to the_message & the_label & " number: " & the_value & return
41. end repeat

42. -- Display the contact information, with the option of creating a new email
43. if email_labels is {} then
44.    display alert the_message
45. else
46.    set dialog_reply to display alert the_message buttons {"Make E-mail", "OK"}
47.    if button returned of dialog_reply is "Make E-mail" then
48.       tell application "Mail"
49.          activate
50.          set new_message to make new outgoing message ¬
                   with properties {visible:true}
51.          tell new_message to make new to recipient with properties ¬
                   {name:chosen_name, address:item 1 of email_values}
54.       end tell
55.    end if
56. end if
```

After the user picks a letter from the alphabet, the script needs to create a list of full names whose first or last name starts with that letter. This takes place in lines 7 through 9.

In the Address Book dictionary, the person class defines several name-related properties: name, first name, middle name, last name, title, suffix, nickname, maiden name, and then phonetic first name, phonetic middle name, and phonetic last name. That makes 11 name options—better safe than sorry, I guess. Actually, you can control only 10 name-related properties. The property name is a read-only property that is composed of the person's title; first, middle, and last names; and suffix details.

Once you collect the list of names, the user gets to pick the one they want. That happens in line 15.

In line 20 you get the reference to the person based on the full name the user picks from the list. Note that if there are two identical names, the script will arbitrarily pick the first one. Just make sure you fix that little issue before you package this script and sell it as shareware.

Once you assign the person to a variable, you can collect the phone numbers and e-mail addresses assigned to that person. As you saw earlier, phone numbers and e-mail addresses are represented as elements of a `person` object.

Since you need both the label and the value of the e-mail addresses and phone numbers, you collect both. This takes place in lines 22 and 23. First you create a pair of lists containing all the person's e-mail details: one list contains all the labels (home, work, and so on), and the other list contains all the values (that is, the e-mail addresses). Then you create another pair of lists containing the person's phone number details.

Each label string in the first list corresponds to the value string at the same position in the second address. For example:

```
phone_labels --> {"home", "work", "work"}
phone_values --> {"401-555-7999", "401-555-1212", "401-555-5237"}
```

Why do it this way? You could have built up a single list of label-value pairs using the following method:

```
tell application "Address Book"
    set phone_infos to {}
    repeat with phone_ref in (get every phone of chosen_person)
        set end of phone_infos to {label, value} of phone_ref
    end repeat
end tell
phone_infos
--> {{"home", "401-555-7999"}, {"work", "401-555-1212"}, {"work", "401-555-5237"}}
```

However, it's often simpler just to write this:

```
tell application "Address Book"
    tell chosen_person
        set {phone_labels, phone_values} to {label, value} of every phone
    end tell
end tell
```

This gives you two separate lists, but as long as you remember how the labels in one list relate to the values in the other list, this isn't a problem when using that data.

> **NOTE:** The second approach also has performance advantages when retrieving data from large numbers of objects. See Chapter 29 for more information.

Between lines 31 and 41 you construct a string using the values from these lists. This string is stored in the variable the_message and will be used to display the collected information to the user at the end.

Finally, the contact information appears to the user in a dialog box. If the script has detected one or more e-mail addresses, it will display a dialog box containing an extra "Make E-mail" button. If the user clicks that button, the script will create a new e-mail message in Mail with the selected person's e-mail address.

Scripting Automator

AppleScript is not the only automation technology you can use in Mac OS X. Automator, which was introduced in Tiger, provides a friendly, drag-and-drop graphical interface for performing simple automation tasks such as renaming files or sending e-mails to people in your Address Book.

There are two important concepts in Automator: *actions* and *workflows*. Actions serve a similar role to Mac OS X's Unix command-line tools, but with checkboxes and text fields instead of textual flags. Each action performs a specific task, and several actions can be linked together to form a more complex workflow. These workflows can then be run directly from Automator, or saved as applet-style applications and run separately. Some applications—for example, Microsoft Word—even allow Automator actions to be run directly from built-in script menus.

Automator comes with over 200 built-in actions, and Automator-aware applications can add more actions of their own. You can also download additional actions and workflows from web sites such as these:

http://www.apple.com/downloads/macosx/automator

http://www.automatoractions.com

Automator can interface with AppleScript in a couple of ways:

- The Run AppleScript action can be used to run AppleScript code within an Automator workflow. This action can take an input value from the previous action, manipulate it, and return a result to be used as input in the next action.

- Automator is a scriptable application, so it can be controlled by external AppleScripts.

The following sections will look at each of these options.

> **NOTE:** Prior to Mac OS X 10.6, it was also possible to create your own Automator actions using AppleScript Studio. AppleScript Studio is deprecated in Mac OS X 10.6, however, and Xcode currently does not provide an AppleScript Automator Action template for the new AppleScriptObjC bridge. Hopefully this omission will be addressed in a future Mac OS X release.

Using the Run AppleScript Action

To add the Run AppleScript action to your workflow, you have to first create a new workflow window if none exists. Choose **File ➤ New in Automator** and pick a template as your starting point. For this exercise, choose the Workflow template (or Custom template if you are on Mac OS X 10.5).

The Run AppleScript action is found in the Utilities category, so click the Utilities icon in the Library column on the left of the window to display all of the actions in that category.

Now, drag the Run AppleScript action to your workflow on the right of the window. Your workflow window should look similar to the window in Figure 21–9.

Figure 21–9. *An Automator workflow containing a newly added Run AppleScript action*

As you can see, the Run AppleScript action already has some code in it:

```
on run {input, parameters}
   (* Your script goes here *)
   return input
end run
```

In short, any code you place inside the run handler will execute when the action is executed. In this case, this will happen as soon as the workflow is run, since this is the first action in the workflow. The real power of Automator comes from connecting several actions together, so let's look at how that works next.

Understanding the Action's Input and Output

By examining the short script in the Run AppleScript action's body, you probably see two things that may need explanation: the two parameters passed to the run handler, input and parameters, and the return input statement at the end.

As you can imagine, the script in its current form doesn't do much. It does, however, do something. First, Automator takes the output value from the previous action and passes it to your Run AppleScript action via the run handler's input parameter. The last line of the run handler, return input, faithfully returns that value as the Run AppleScript action's output value, allowing Automator to use that value as the input to the next action in the workflow. This means that although the action doesn't do anything spectacular, it also doesn't ruin the flow.

What is the input, however? Which data class is it, and what sort of values can you expect? That completely depends on the previous action, whichever it may be, and the type of data it produces. For the most part, however, that data is arranged in a list. For instance, a Finder action may return a list of file references or aliases, and a Mail action may return a list of references to Mail messages.

To see the input, you will use the Run AppleScript action's Result area. This area is right below the script in the Run AppleScript action's pane but is initially hidden, so click the Results button to make it visible.

To see a typical action's result, drag the Get Selected Finder Items action from the Finder category and drop it above the Run AppleScript action.

> **TIP:** It is easy to locate an action if you enter the action's name or part of it in the Search Actions search field at the top-left corner of the Automator window.

Once the workflow contains the two actions, go to the Finder, and select a few files on your desktop (if you're like me, at least 20 random files are lurking there in disarray).

After you've selected the files, return to Automator, and run the workflow. Click the Results button at the bottom of the Run AppleScript action to view the value returned by the run handler, as shown in Figure 21–10.

What you get is a list of AppleScript aliases supplied by the Get Selected Finder Items action. You can control how these values are displayed by clicking the three view buttons directly beneath the Results button. Different types of values will be displayed in different ways.

In this case, we are looking at a list of files and folders, so click the left button to view the items as icons and file names, the middle button to see their POSIX paths, and the right button to see the list in AppleScript format:

```
{alias "Macintosh HD:Users:hanaan:Desktop:cover.tiff",
 alias "Macintosh HD:Users:hanaan:Desktop:DropBox:",
 alias "Macintosh HD:Users:hanaan:Desktop:log.txt"}
```

We'll shortly add some code to the Run AppleScript action to process this list of files.

Figure 21–10. *The workflow containing the two actions and the Run AppleScript's action result*

Understanding the Action's Parameters

Okay, so the input can be almost anything, such as a list of files or anything else the previous action spits out. What are the parameters, though? To find out, change the `return` line in the script from `return input` to `return parameters`. Now run the workflow. The value in the Result area should look something like this:

```
{|ignoresInput|:false,
 |temporary items path|:"/var/folders/.../com.apple.Automator.RunScript",
 |action|:item id 14,
 |source|:"on run {input, parameters}

    (* Your script goes here *)

    return parameters
end run"}
```

As you can see, the action's parameters are supplied as a record containing a number of properties describing the action and its environment. For instance, the `|ignoresInput|` property tells you whether the user chose to have the action ignore any input to this action that was supplied by the preceding action.

Filtering Files with Run AppleScript

Let's put the Run AppleScript action to practical use by creating a workflow that filters files larger than a certain size, specified by the user. Although the Run AppleScript action doesn't allow you to create complex GUIs, it can still use Standard Additions' user interaction commands, so we'll use the `display dialog` command to allow the user to input the minimum desired file size when the action is run.

The backbone of the script is a repeat loop that will loop through the files in the `input` variable (remember, the `input` variable is going to have a list of files returned from the previous action), checking the size of each one. If the file size is greater than the size specified by the user, then the file reference will be added to a new list. This new list will be returned at the end of the script.

Script 21–19 shows the rather simple script you will enter for the Run AppleScript action.

Script 21–19.

```
1. on run {input, parameters}
2.    set file_list to input as list
3.    set dialog_reply to ¬
            display dialog "Enter minimum file size in KB:" default answer "20"
4.    set min_size_in_kb to text returned of dialog_reply as number
5.    set filtered_files to {}
6.    tell application "Finder"
7.       repeat with file_ref in file_list
8.          if (size of file_ref) > (min_size_in_kb * 1024) then
9.             set end of filtered_files to contents of file_ref
10.            end if
11.         end repeat
12.      end tell
13.      return filtered_files
14. end run
```

Because we'll want to loop over a list of file references later on, line 2 just makes sure that the input really is a list of values. It also picks a more descriptive name for the input value to make the rest of the code easier to read. Lines 3 and 4 get the minimum file size to check for from the user, while line 5 creates an empty list into which we'll add the files that pass the minimum-size test.

Lines 7 through 11 loop over the input list, processing each item in turn. First, line 8 checks the file's size is greater than the user's desired minimum size. (Notice that because the Finder measures file size in bytes, we need to multiply the value of the `min_size_in_kb` variable by 1,024 to convert it to a size in bytes as well.) Then, if the file passes the test, line 9 adds it to the list of found files.

The final line of the script's run handler may be the most important: `return filtered_files`. This line ensures that the following action in the workflow gets the new file list as its input.

To keep this example simple, I haven't included any error handling code, so if the previous action provides something other than a list of alias values or file/folder references, then an error will probably occur on line 8 when the script tries to get the item's `size` property. Similarly, if the user enters something other than a number into the dialog box, a coercion error will occur on line 4. When writing actions for other people to use, I would normally add `try` blocks to catch these sorts of errors and provide helpful error messages so that they know exactly what went wrong.

Now that our Run AppleScript action is complete, let's finish the rest of the workflow. What this workflow will do is apply a red label to the files that are larger than the value specified by the user. To do that, add the Label Finder Items action to the end of the workflow, and check the red label in the action's interface.

Now run the workflow. It will apply a red label to the selected files that are larger than the size you specified. Figure 21–11 shows the completed workflow.

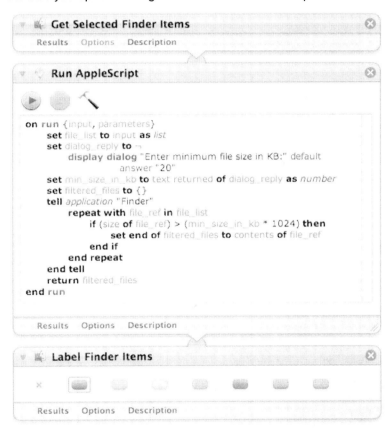

Figure 21–11. *The finished workflow containing the three actions*

Scripting the Automator Application

The Automator application is scriptable, as would be expected, and several classes and commands are useful for automating the automation program. The classes of objects you will be using are `workflow` and `Automator action`. As you would imagine, Automator action objects are elements of workflow objects. There are a few other classes, but they are less important than these two.

> **NOTE:** You can find the relevant classes and commands under the Standard Suite and Automator Suite sections of the Automator dictionary. (The remaining suites define legacy terminology used by AppleScript Studio–based Automator actions.)

Three commands are defined in the Automator Suite of Automator's dictionary: add and remove add and remove Automator action elements to and from a workflow object. The execute command can execute a workflow.

Let's look at a simple script using Automator. Script 21–20 will ask the user to pick an iTunes Automator action, add that action to the workflow, save the workflow, and execute it.

Script 21–20.

```
tell application "Automator"
    activate
    set itunes_action_names to name of Automator actions ¬
        whose target application contains "iTunes"
    set the_selection to choose from list itunes_action_names
    if the_selection is false then return -- User canceled
    set action_name to item 1 of the_selection
    set my_workflow to make workflow with properties {name:action_name & "Workflow"}
    add Automator action action_name to my_workflow
    save my_workflow in file ((path to desktop as string) & action_name)
end tell
```

Note that the script creates the workflow object, assigning the string containing the action's name and the word Workflow to its name property, and assigns the resulting reference, workflow "My Random Workflow" of application "Automator", to the variable my_workflow. If the name of the workflow changes later, the reference stored in that variable would no longer refer to that workflow, since it uses the workflow's name, not its unique ID, to identify it.

> **NOTE:** When using the make command to create a new workflow, it's a good idea to specify a name for your workflow in the with properties parameter. If you don't, the new workflow window will automatically display a "Choose a template for your workflow" sheet, which probably isn't what you want.

One area where the execute command can be useful is if you need to automate non-AppleScriptable applications from AppleScript. Although the GUI Scripting feature of Mac OS X's System Events application allows you to manipulate the buttons, text fields, and other controls that make up an application's GUI, it can be fairly complicated to use. If your needs are modest, a simpler option may be to use Automator's Watch Me Do feature (**Workflow ➤ Record**) to record your mouse clicks and keystrokes as an Automator action. You can then save this action as a workflow and use the execute command to trigger it from your AppleScripts whenever you need this action replayed.

Summary

In this chapter, you continued your exploration of popular scriptable applications included in Mac OS X. You've covered a lot of ground in this chapter, so let's spend a bit of time reviewing what you've learned.

Starting with iTunes, you familiarized yourself with the main classes of objects that make up the application object model—sources, tracks, and playlists—and the various commands you can use to manipulate those objects, including the standard get, set, make, duplicate, and delete commands found in most applications, as well as the add and search commands that are specific to iTunes scripting. You saw how iTunes commands like to return by-ID references to tracks and playlists, providing your scripts with a reliable way to identify the same objects later on, even if their indexes or names change. You also discovered some of the features and quirks particular to iTunes scripting, including the ability to omit parts of the references to track objects in the main library playlist, and the use of duplicate and delete to add and remove items to and from user playlists (other applications usually use add and remove commands for these tasks).

Next, you got to grips with Apple's Mail application, where you learned how to refer to mailboxes and the e-mail messages within them, and examine their properties and elements, including senders, subject lines, recipients, and message bodies. You also found out how to create and send new e-mail messages to other people, using the standard make command to create objects of class outgoing message and the Mail-specific send command to dispatch them. You then explored Mail rules and the Run AppleScript rule action, discovering that some applications have the ability to trigger AppleScripts to inform them that something of interest has happened, allowing those scripts to respond in any way you like—a concept known as attachability.

Following Mail, you spent a bit of time exploring iCal's modest but still useful object model, creating and manipulating calendars and events.

Moving on to Address Book, you learned how to work with person and group objects, examining some of the main properties and elements defined by the person class that tell you who a person is and how and where you can contact them. In addition to accessing multiple people's information with some fairly fancy references, you saw how to create and delete person objects and how to add new contact information. You also learned the importance of always sending a save command after making changes, if you want those changes to stick. You also explored Address Book's attachability support, which allows you to develop custom rollover actions that allow users to manipulate selected contact info entries from within the Address Book GUI.

Finally, you took a quick tour of one of AppleScript's close cousins in Mac OS X: Automator. You learned how to create simple AppleScript-based actions that can sit within a larger Automator workflow, filtering input data and/or generating output data, while interacting with scriptable applications in between. You also found out how to control the Automator application from AppleScript—handy if you wish to make use of Automator features such as Watch Me Do within a larger AppleScript-based system.

Along the way, you have gained some valuable perspective on the similarities and differences that exist between scriptable applications. For instance, Address Book has some strong similarities to iTunes—people are a bit like tracks, and groups are used to catalog people just as user playlists can catalog tracks—and their object models represent this information in similar ways. Then there are the differences; for example, iTunes uses `duplicate` and `delete` to add and remove tracks to and from user playlists, whereas Address Book uses `add` and `remove`. Consistency across different scriptable applications is a good thing as it allows you to reuse existing knowledge when learning to script new applications; however, you cannot always rely on this to be the case. So always read the dictionary and any supplementary examples, study existing scripts, check on the AppleScript mailing lists and bulletin boards, and don't be afraid to explore and experiment—though remember always to back up your data first, just in case of accidents.

In the next chapter, we will take a detour from discussing general application scripting to look at how the functionality of the AppleScript language can be enhanced using two types of extensions: scripting additions and scriptable faceless background applications.

Chapter 22

Extending AppleScript with Scripting Additions

Although AppleScript is extremely powerful in its ability to control any scriptable application, the language itself comes with only a limited number of features built into it. Fortunately, there are several ways to add extra functionality that your scripts can take advantage of: scripting additions, scriptable faceless background applications, and script libraries. Script libraries have already been explained in Chapter 19, so we won't cover them again here. Instead, this chapter concentrates on the two most popular options, scripting additions and scriptable faceless background applications.

> **NOTE:** Although using scripting additions and scriptable faceless background applications is easy, writing new ones requires a bit more programming experience because they normally have to be written in a lower-level language such as C. Because programming in other languages is beyond the scope of this book, this chapter will concentrate on using existing scripting additions from Apple and third-party developers.

Introducing Scripting Additions and Scriptable Faceless Background Applications

Scripting additions, also referred to as OSAXen, are special files that add extra AppleScript commands to applications. Mac OS X ships with a couple of scripting additions included as standard, while many more are available as free or commercial downloads. You can find many third-party scripting additions at http://www.osaxen.com.

> **NOTE:** The acronym OSAX stands for Open Scripting Architecture eXtension. Modern scripting additions have the file name extension .osax.

Another method of adding functionality to AppleScript is by using scriptable faceless background applications, or FBAs. These invisible applications play a similar role to scripting additions, providing additional commands for AppleScripts to use. The main difference is that whereas scripting additions are chunks of code that are loaded into existing programs, FBAs are complete applications that run by themselves. The only technical differences between FBAs and regular Mac applications are that FBAs do not have a graphical user interface (GUI) and do not show up in the Dock when they are running.

There are several benefits to using scripting additions and scriptable FBAs:

- They may allow you to perform tasks that vanilla AppleScript simply can't do. A lot of the functionality provided by the Mac operating system—file system access, GUIs, audio features, and so on—is accessible only through lower-level languages such as C.

- They may make your scripts run faster. Scripting additions and FBAs are normally written in lower-level languages such as C that run faster than AppleScript.

- They may make your development cycle shorter. Using commands in ready-made extensions saves you the time it would take to write the same functionality yourself in AppleScript.

- While scripting addition commands are usually used within the application that is running the script, they can be sent to other applications as well. This can be useful when you need to display a dialog box in a particular application; for example:

```
tell application "Finder"
    activate
    display alert "The Finder says Hello!"
end tell
```

There are also some limitations to be aware of:

- Scripting additions can define new commands but cannot provide an elegant object model to go with them. Only applications can do that. This is one reason why more complex extensions are usually written as scriptable FBAs instead.

- Scripting additions must be loaded into a running application in order to use them. This means that both the scripting addition and the application must support the same processor architectures—for example, an Intel-only application cannot load a PowerPC-only scripting addition. This will be explained in more detail in a later section, "Understanding Scripting Addition Compatibility Issues."

- If you distribute scripts to other users, you need to make sure that any third-party scripting additions and scriptable FBAs used by those scripts are also present on those users' systems. In some cases it is possible to include these "dependencies" within your script; otherwise, you need to instruct your users on how to obtain and install the required items for themselves. More on this later.

- Only applications run by ordinary users and administrators can load scripting additions. A security restriction introduced in Security Update 2008-005 (http://support.apple.com/kb/HT2647) prevents application processes owned by the system from loading scripting additions themselves.

Scripting Additions in Detail

Scripting additions are plug-ins that add extra commands for scripts to use. Scripting additions actually install handlers into a running application rather than into the AppleScript language itself, but because these handlers are provided for AppleScript's benefit, we generally refer to them as AppleScript extensions.

The following sections look at how scripting additions work, and how they interact with the AppleScript language and the applications that host them.

Scripting Additions and the AppleScript Language

The biggest difference between application-defined commands and scripting addition–defined commands is that whereas application commands normally require a tell block to direct them to a specific application, scripting addition commands do not. For example, the following script sends a make command to the TextEdit application,

```
tell application "TextEdit"
    make new document with properties {text:"Hello World!"}
end tell
```

whereas this script sends a display dialog command to the current application (that is, the application running the script):

```
display dialog "Hello World!"
```

You can script for a long time and not realize that commands such as display dialog are not actually part of AppleScript, but are instead defined by the Standard Additions scripting addition that is included in Mac OS X by default.

You can send scripting addition commands to other applications if you want, although you usually don't need to do this. For example, the following script uses the standard activate command to bring the TextEdit application to the front where the user can see it, and then displays the "Hello World!" dialog box there:

```
tell application "TextEdit"
    activate
    display dialog "Hello World!"
end tell
```

Another difference from scriptable applications is that scripting addition terminology is not limited to a `tell application ... end tell` block. Instead, all scripting addition terminology is available throughout your scripts, allowing scripting addition commands to be compiled regardless of where they appear.

> **CAUTION:** The fact that scripting additions lack a `tell` block forces developers to use the same keyword universe with other scripting addition developers and with AppleScript itself. This means any variable you use anywhere in your script can potentially be a word reserved by a scripting addition. Although scripting addition developers are generally careful to use unique word combinations for their classes and commands, you may also want to stick to camel case or underscore word separation when naming variables, which should keep name collision to a minimum.

Installing Scripting Additions

Unlike scriptable applications, which you can install and use anywhere, scripting additions need to be installed into a special `ScriptingAdditions` folder before AppleScript can use them. Mac OS X defines `ScriptingAdditions` folders in three standard locations:

- The system domain, which is for Apple's scripting additions only: `/System/Library/ScriptingAdditions/`

- The local domain, which makes scripting additions available to all users: `/Library/ScriptingAdditions/`

- The user domain, which is where you can place scripting additions that will be available to you only: `~/Library/ScriptingAdditions/`

> **NOTE:** You may have to create the `ScriptingAdditions` folders in the local and/or user domains if they don't already exist. The name of the folder has no space between the two words.

The standard icon for scripting additions is an unmistakable LEGO®-style cube, shown in Figure 22–1.

Figure 22–1. *The standard scripting addition icon*

The following script will create a neatly formatted string describing the contents of all of your ScriptingAdditions folders:

```
set osax_info to {}
tell application "System Events"
    set osax_folders to scripting additions folder of every domain
    repeat with folder_ref in reverse of osax_folders
        if (contents of folder_ref is not missing value) then
            set AppleScript's text item delimiters to return & tab
            set end of osax_info to POSIX path of folder_ref & return & tab & ¬
                (name of every file of folder_ref whose visible is true)
        end if
    end repeat
end tell
set AppleScript's text item delimiters to return & return
osax_info as text
```

Here is a typical result:

```
"/Users/hanaan/Library/ScriptingAdditions
    XMail.osax

/Library/ScriptingAdditions
    Adobe Unit Types.osax
    FITS.osax
    Numerics.osax
    Satimage.osax
    XMLLib.osax

/System/Library/ScriptingAdditions
    Digital Hub Scripting.osax
    FontSyncScripting.app
    Keychain Scripting.app
    StandardAdditions.osax
    URL Access Scripting.app"
```

> **CAUTION:** If you install different versions of the same scripting addition in both the user and local domains, the one in the user domain will be used.

Missing Additions and Garbled Scripts

Anytime you're counting on a third-party addition, you should also count on the day you (or someone else) will open the script on a Mac that doesn't have those scripting additions installed.

If the script is supplied in compiled form (that is, as a .scpt file), then when you open it in AppleScript Editor, the scripting addition commands will appear in their raw forms. If the script is in source code form, then the scripting addition commands won't compile unless written in raw form («event...»). Either way, you'll get an error when the script tries to execute that command.

For example, if you open a compiled script that uses the change command from the Satimage scripting addition but don't have that addition installed on your Mac, then a line like this

```
change old_text into new_text in the_text
```

will appear instead as this

```
«event SATIRPLl» old_text given «class by  »:new_text, «class $in »:the_text
```

and the script will raise an error saying that the value of the old_text variable doesn't understand the «event SATIRPLl» message.

Fortunately, the problem isn't permanent: as soon as the required scripting addition is installed, the script will run normally, and AppleScript Editor will compile and decompile it normally using the familiar English-like terminology from the addition's dictionary.

If it's important to you not to get an error in these cases, you can make your script check whether the scripting addition is installed before it tries to use it. The simplest way to do this is by sending a command that you know will work if the scripting addition is installed, and catching the error that occurs if it isn't. For example, Script 22–1 checks whether the Satimage scripting addition is installed by sending a simple change command.

Script 22–1.

```
is_satimage_addition_installed()
--> true

on is_satimage_addition_installed()
    try
        change "a" in "abc" into "d" -- Send a Satimage-specific command
        return true
    on error number -1708 -- Command not found
        return false
    end try
end is_satimage_addition_installed
```

Distributing Scripting Additions with Your Scripts

Just as we like to travel light, so do our scripts. They just don't like to have too many strings attached. If you use scripting additions in your script, installing your script correctly on other Macs isn't quite as simple as copying the script itself across. You also need to make sure all the required scripting additions are installed on those Macs; otherwise users could get an unexpected error when they try to use the script. So if you want to make a script foolproof, you need to supply all the scripting additions it uses along with it *and* make sure your script can find those additions when it needs them.

There are a couple of ways you can do this. You can create an installer package for your script and scripting additions, or you can save your script as a bundle-based application with the required scripting additions embedded in it.

> **CAUTION:** Always check the license agreements for third-party extensions before redistributing them with your own scripts. While some developers may be happy for you to redistribute their products without any restrictions at all, others (particularly commercial products) do not allow this or may impose certain requirements on you (for example, including their copyright information as part of your distribution).

Embedding Scripting Additions Within a Script Application

The most elegant way to package scripting additions with your scripts is to save your script as a bundle-based application (either an AppleScript Editor applet or a full AppleScriptObjC-based Cocoa application), and embed the required scripting additions within the application bundle.

Let's say you want to create an AppleScript applet that uses the Satimage scripting addition to escape any special HTML characters (<>&"') in a piece of copied text.

> **NOTE:** If you don't already have the Satimage scripting addition installed, you'll need to download a copy from the Satimage web site first: `http://www.satimage.fr/software/en/downloads/downloads_companion_osaxen.html`

Start a new script in AppleScript Editor, and type the code shown in Script 22-2.

Script 22-2.

```
set the_string to the clipboard as Unicode text
set the_html to encode entities the_string
set the clipboard to the_html
```

When this script is run, it will retrieve the text from the user's clipboard, use the Satimage scripting addition's `encode entities` command to encode any special HTML characters in the text, and then place the modified text back onto the clipboard.

Now, save the script as an application named `EscapeAsHTML`. (If you are using Mac OS X 10.5 or earlier, make sure you use the Application Bundle file format when saving the script.) Once the script is saved, click the Bundle Contents button in the script window's toolbar. This will open a drawer that lists the contents of the bundle's `Resources` folder, as shown in Figure 22-2.

Figure 22–2. *The contents of the application bundle's* Resources *folder are shown in the Bundle Contents drawer.*

By default, the bundle does not contain a scripting additions folder, so you will need to create one yourself. To do this, click the button with the gear icon at the top of the drawer (see Figure 22–2), and select the New Folder option. Name this folder Scripting Additions, taking care to include a space in the name this time.

Lastly, drag the Satimage.osax file onto the Scripting Additions entry to add the scripting addition to your bundle. Figure 22–3 shows how the Bundle Contents drawer should look once this is done.

Figure 22–3. *The Bundle Contents drawer showing the embedded Satimage scripting addition*

You can now distribute the EscapeAsHTML applet to other users and it will automatically use the embedded Satimage scripting addition.

> **CAUTION:** Before you distribute this application, make sure you have met all of the licensing requirements for the embedded Satimage scripting addition. (The same rule applies to any other embedded third-party extensions, of course.) You can find Satimage's licensing terms here: http://www.satimage.fr/software/en/pricing/licensefree.html

Using the Mac OS X Installer to Install Your Script and Scripting Additions

The first option is to create an installer package for your script and the scripting additions it needs. You can create an installer package using the PackageMaker utility included in Apple's Developer Tools. This packages everything into a .pkg file, which users can install simply by double-clicking it and walking through the standard installation process in Mac OS X's Installer application.

Working with the PackageMaker application is beyond the scope of this book, but you can find out more from the PackageMaker user guide at:

```
http://developer.apple.com/DOCUMENTATION/DeveloperTools/Conceptual/
    PackageMakerUserGuide/Introduction/Introduction.html
```

> **TIP:** If you want to automate the creation of installer packages and don't mind a bit of Unix scripting, a command-line version of PackageMaker is also provided as part of the Developer Tools. Type man packagemaker in the Terminal application for more information.

Understanding Scripting Addition Compatibility Issues

Although the AppleScript language may not have evolved much over the years, the Macintosh itself has gone through some massive changes: moving from 68K to PowerPC processors, replacing Mac OS 9 with Mac OS X, and then switching from PowerPC to Intel chips while introducing 64-bit support along the way.

With each transition, Apple engineers have quietly worked to update the AppleScript language to support these changes. As a result, AppleScript itself runs just as smoothly on the newest 64-bit Mac OS X Intel systems as it did on the original 68K System 7 machines (though a lot faster!).

These software and hardware changes have also had a big impact on applications and scripting additions. Like the Apple engineers, many third-party developers have upgraded their products over the years to keep them compatible with the latest and greatest hardware and software combinations. Some third-party products have not kept pace, however—either because other changes in the Mac world have meant that they are no longer needed, or because the cost of updating them was too high.

Throughout these changes, Apple has been pretty good at maintaining backward support for older software that hasn't yet been upgraded. For example, PowerPC applications continue to run on Intel hardware thanks to Mac OS X's built-in PowerPC emulator, Rosetta. Systems like Rosetta only work for entire applications, however, which means you have to pay a bit more attention when dealing with application plug-ins such as scripting additions.

Caution: Mac OS 9 Scripting Additions Don't Work on Mac OS X

The first limitation you need to watch out for is that Mac OS X cannot use scripting additions that were written for Mac OS 9. You can still find old OS 9–era scripting additions as well as newer OS X ones when searching for third-party scripting additions on sites such as http://www.osaxen.com. However, if you try to use OS 9 scripting additions in an OS X script, you will just get an error because AppleScript cannot compile or run commands defined by non-OS X additions.

Using PowerPC-Only Scripting Additions on Intel-Based Macs

The second limitation you may encounter is that some older Mac OS X scripting additions are PowerPC-only, which can cause problems on Intel-based Macs if you aren't careful.

Since the new Intel-based Macs were introduced, Apple has encouraged third-party developers to create "Universal" versions of their software that will run on both PowerPC and Intel Macs. Some scripting addition developers have already done this, but others have not.

You can find out if a scripting addition is Universal or PowerPC-only by selecting it in the Finder and choosing File ➤ Get Info. The file's kind will be listed as "Scripting addition (PowerPC)" or "Scripting addition (Universal)" under General information.

If you try to use a PowerPC-only scripting addition in an application that is running natively on an Intel Mac, you will find that the script compiles okay, but will give an "object doesn't understand message" error when it tries to execute the command. You can confirm the problem by looking in OS X's Console application (/Applications/Utilities/Console.app) for a message similar to this:

```
Error loading/Library/ScriptingAdditions/NAME.osax/Contents/MacOS/NAME:
    dlopen(/Library/ScriptingAdditions/NAME.osax/Contents/MacOS/NAME, 262):
    no suitable image found. Did find:
        /Library/ScriptingAdditions/NAME.osax/Contents/MacOS/NAME: mach-o,
    but wrong architecture
```

The giveaway here is the phrase "wrong architecture." In other words, the operating system can see the scripting addition file, but cannot load its handlers into an application that is running in native Intel mode because the scripting addition does not include Intel support.

Fortunately, it is still possible to use PowerPC-only scripting additions on an Intel-based Mac—as long as you only use them within an application that is running under Rosetta. If the application is PowerPC-only as well, then you don't have to do anything special because it will always run in PowerPC mode anyway. If the application is Universal, you can force it to run in PowerPC mode by selecting the application file in the Finder, choosing File ➤ Get Info, and checking the "Open using Rosetta" option, as shown in Figure 22–4.

Figure 22–4. *Setting a Universal application to run in Rosetta*

The next time you launch the application, it will run in PowerPC mode, allowing it to load handlers from both PowerPC and Universal applications.

> **CAUTION:** In Mac OS X 10.6 and later, Apple's own applications—including AppleScript Editor—are Intel-only applications. This means you have to use a third-party Universal editor such as Satimage's Smile to write and compile your PowerPC-dependent scripts. Also, make sure that the applications you use to run these scripts are set to run in Rosetta too (this applies to applets too, of course). Lastly, don't forget to contact the scripting addition developers, politely requesting that they release Universal or Intel-only versions before PowerPC-only additions become impossible to use.

Using 32-Bit-Only Scripting Additions on 64-Bit Macs

The third and final limitation that scripting addition users need to watch out for is that some Universal scripting additions may only be compiled with 32-bit support. Most of Apple's own applications and many third-party applications now provide 64-bit support, and Mac OS X 10.6 will normally launch these applications in 64-bit mode when running on 64-bit-capable hardware.

To force an application to launch in 32-bit mode, you need to bring up the application's Info window in the Finder and then tick the "Open in 32-bit mode" check box. Figure 22–5 shows how to do this for an applet created by AppleScript Editor.

Figure 22–5. *Setting an application to run in 32-bit mode*

TIP: Whereas AppleScript Editor itself only provides 32- and 64-bit Intel support, the applets it saves include 32-bit PowerPC support as well; so as long as the applet code doesn't depend on any 10.6-only features, you should be able to run the applet on older PowerPC machines as well.

Working Around Scripting Addition Limitations

If you do run into problems using a third-party scripting addition, here are some possible solutions for you to consider:

▓ If you need to use a PowerPC-only scripting addition from an Intel-only application, one solution is to write an applet that wraps the scripting addition commands you need in ordinary AppleScript handlers, like this:

```
on some_osax_command(value_1, value_2, ...)
    return some osax command value_1 some_label value_2 ...
end some_command
```

▓ You can then send commands from your original script to this applet in order to have them processed. Remember to set the applet to run in Rosetta, of course. The same trick will work if you need to use a 32-bit scripting addition from a 64-bit process.

▓ Look around for another scripting addition or scriptable application that provides the same functionality, and use that instead. Scriptable FBAs are a particularly good choice when it comes to portability—because they are stand-alone applications, not plug-ins, they can run almost anywhere.

▓ Use a Unix command-line tool via the do shell script command in Standard Additions. Much of the functionality that scripters used to rely on additions for is now available freely with different shell commands, which can be invoked right from AppleScript. Shell commands are fast, relatively easy to master, and prolific in the variety of commands they offer. Chapter 27 will look at this technique in much more detail.

▓ Write your script as an AppleScriptObjC-based application, allowing it to access many features of Mac OS X's powerful Cocoa libraries directly. The Cocoa frameworks can be a bit intimidating to newcomers, but they provide a huge number of useful features, and there are plenty of experienced Cocoa developers who can help you out if you get stuck, both inside and outside the AppleScript community.

▓ Define your own equivalent command using a script handler. Many scripting addition commands provide access to system features that cannot be reached from AppleScript itself, so this is not always a practical solution. Some tasks, however, can be performed just as well (or even better) using AppleScript code alone; for example, trimming white space from a string, or sorting a list of values.

Understanding Scriptable Faceless Background Applications

Like scripting additions, scriptable FBAs provide extra commands for scripts to use. Although scriptable FBAs do not provide a GUI, in other ways they work a lot like regular scriptable applications: you can launch them, send commands to them, and quit them when you're done.

Scriptable FBAs have a couple of advantages over scripting additions. Firstly, scriptable FBAs can implement full object models, making it easier for users to work with complex data. Secondly, because scriptable FBAs run as independent applications, they do not care if the applications that call them are PowerPC- or Intel-based, or 32-bit or 64-bit.

Scriptable FBAs also have one disadvantage: they tend to be a bit slower than scripting additions because you are sending commands between two different applications, whereas scripting addition commands can be handled within the application that is running the script. However, you are unlikely to notice the difference unless your script needs to send many hundreds or thousands of commands.

Installing Scriptable FBAs

Because scriptable FBAs are applications, you do not have to install them in a specific location in order to use them. However, as they will be used by AppleScript, it is often convenient to keep them in one of the two standard ScriptingAdditions folders (/Library/ScriptingAdditions/ or ~/Library/ScriptingAdditions/), along with the rest of your AppleScript extensions.

Distributing Scriptable FBAs with Your Scripts

Like scripting additions, scriptable FBAs can be embedded within a bundle-based applet for distribution. Apple recommends that embedded helper applications go in a different location from scripting additions, however, so adding them requires a slightly different approach.

The first step, of course, is to save your script as an application bundle. Next, go to the Finder, Ctrl-click the application file, and select the Show Package Contents option. Within the main bundle folder, you will see a single folder named Contents. Open this folder, and create a new subfolder named Support. Copy your scriptable FBA and any other helper applications into the Support folder, and then close the window once you're done.

Examples of AppleScript Extensions

Mac OS X comes with a variety of scripting additions already built in, and you can install more yourself. The following sections should give you an idea of the types of extensions that are available for you to use.

Built-in Extensions

Mac OS X comes with two scripting additions and several scriptable FBAs already included:

- Database Events is a simple scriptable object database. (Chapter 25 will explore Database Events in more detail.)

- The Digital Hub Scripting scripting addition provides terminology for several media-related event handlers. The CDs & DVDs panel in System Preferences can be used to trigger scripts containing these handlers when CDs and DVDs are inserted.

- FontSyncScripting can be used to compare fonts installed on different Macs.

- Image Events is used to perform simple image processing tasks.

- Keychain Scripting allows AppleScript to access usernames and passwords that are securely stored in a user's keychain.

- The Standard Additions scripting addition defines several dozen commonly used commands covered throughout this book.

- System Events defines over a dozen different suites of classes and commands for performing a wide range of tasks, including working with the file system, controlling nonscriptable applications via their GUIs, working with XML, and accessing various system preferences.

- URL Access Scripting provides basic commands for uploading and downloading Internet files.

Third-Party Extensions

The one-stop place to shop (or more likely, browse) for scripting additions is http://www.osaxen.com, which is part of MacScripter (http://www.macscripter.net). The folks at MacScripter are mostly volunteers who put a good bit of effort into a well-organized and fresh AppleScript web site. Among other features, they boast the most complete and up-to-date searchable collection of scripting additions.

The following are some of the scripting additions worth investigating:

- 24U Appearance is a commercial scripting addition that can be used to display more sophisticated dialog boxes than Standard Additions provides.

- List & Record Tools provides useful commands for working with AppleScript's list and record values.

- Property List Tools can be used to read and write property list (.plist) files.

- The Satimage scripting addition provides several suites of commands for advanced text processing, working with the file system, and performing mathematical calculations.

- The free XMail scripting addition allows you to send e-mail messages directly from AppleScript without having to go through a scriptable e-mail application such as Mail or Entourage.

- XMLLib provides a suite of commands for reading and writing XML data.

Using the Standard Additions Scripting Addition

The Standard Additions scripting addition comes preinstalled with AppleScript and contains a variety of useful, basic commands. You can see the definitions of the commands and records used in Standard Additions by selecting File ➤ Open Dictionary in AppleScript Editor and choosing StandardAdditions.osax from the list, as shown in Figure 22–6.

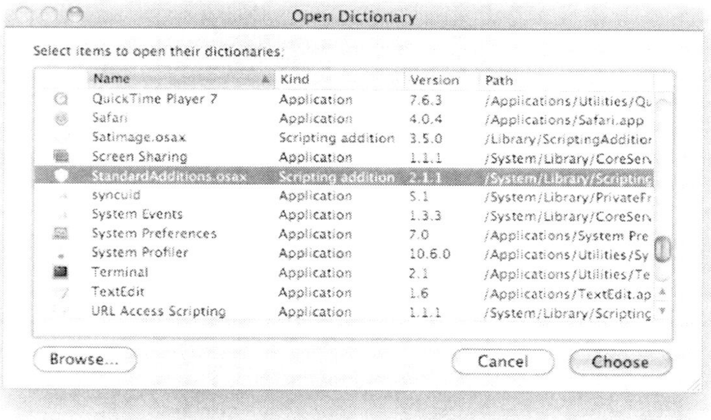

Figure 22–6. *Choosing Standard Additions from the list in the Open Dictionary dialog box*

Standard Additions commands are divided into nine suites based on functionality: User Interaction, File Commands, String Commands, Clipboard Commands, File Read/Write, Scripting Commands, Miscellaneous Commands, Folder Actions, and Internet Suite.

Most Standard Additions commands are already covered elsewhere in this book; Table 22–1 provides a list of chapter references.

Table 22–1. *Chapters That Cover Standard Additions Commands*

Suite Name	Where Its Commands Are Covered
User Interaction	Chapter 16 covers the dialog box commands; beep, say, and delay are covered later in this chapter
File Commands	Chapter 17
String Commands	Chapter 7 covers offset, ASCII number, and ASCII character
Clipboard Commands	Chapter 23
File Read/Write	Chapter 17
Scripting Commands	Chapter 19 covers load script, store script, and run script
Miscellaneous Commands	Chapter 8 covers random number and round; Chapter 9 covers current date and time to GMT; Chapter 27 covers do shell script; other commands are covered in this chapter
Folder Actions	Chapter 23
Internet Suite	This chapter

Other useful commands are described in the following sections.

Providing Audio Feedback

In addition to GUI-related commands, Standard Additions' User Interaction suite also defines two simple commands, beep and say, for providing simple audio feedback to users.

The *beep* Command

This command sounds a beep or a number of beeps using the system alert sound. For example:

```
beep -- Beep once
beep 3 -- Beep three times
```

The *say* Command

This command speaks any text you provide using one of Apple's built-in speech voices. Note that the voice names are case sensitive. Here's an example:

```
say "Hello" using "Victoria"
```

You can also use the optional saving to parameter to output the sound to an AIFF audio file:

```
say "The Lord is my Shepherd, I shall not want." saving to (choose file name)
```

Pausing Your Scripts

The User Interaction suite also provides a handy delay command that you can use to temporarily pause your script.

The *delay* Command

This command delays the script by the specified number of seconds:

```
delay 3 -- Pause for three seconds
delay 1.5 -- Pause for one-and-a-half seconds
```

Getting and Setting the System Volume

The Miscellaneous Commands suite defines a pair of commands, get volume settings and set volume, for getting and setting your Mac's volume settings.

The *get volume settings* Command

The get volume settings command simply returns a record describing your current volume settings:

```
get volume settings
--> {output volume:56, input volume:46, alert volume:100, output muted:false}
```

The output volume, input volume, and alert volume properties contain percentage values from 0 to 100. The output muted property is a Boolean that indicates whether or not your output volume is temporarily muted.

The *set volume* Command

You can use the set volume command to adjust your output, input, and alert volumes, or to mute or unmute the output volume. The parameter names and values for this command are the same as the properties in the volume settings record returned by the get volume settings command.

For example, to set the alert volume to 50 percent:

```
set volume alert volume 50
```

Or to set all volume settings to 100 percent:

```
set volume output volume 100 input volume 100 alert volume 100
```

You can also mute the sound output altogether with the output muted parameter, like this:

```
set volume with output muted
```

Or, to turn sound back on, use this:

```
set volume without output muted
```

Getting System Information

The Miscellaneous Commands suite contains two commands for obtaining information about the host Mac: system attribute and the newer system info command.

The *system attribute* Command

Experienced programmers use the system attribute command to look up low-level hardware and software information. Although the system info command introduced in Mac OS X 10.4 provides a much easier way to look up common system information, system attribute is still useful if your script needs to run on older systems.

You can get two types of information using the system attribute command: Gestalt values and shell environment variables.

Gestalt values are a low-level legacy technology inherited from Mac OS 9 and earlier, so you'll find them to be rather cryptic to use. Although most Gestalt values aren't of any interest to AppleScripters (and many are obsolete in OS X anyway), you may find that a few of them are useful, such as those for getting the system number, the processor speed, or the amount of RAM installed. You can find a full list of available Gestalts in the Gestalt Manager documentation on Apple's web site:

```
http://developer.apple.com/documentation/Carbon/Reference/Gestalt_Manager
```

To obtain a Gestalt value, you pass a string containing its four-letter code as the command's direct parameter. If the code is recognized, the result will be a 32-bit number containing the requested system information. Depending on how that information is represented, you may have to do some additional processing to make sense of it.

For example, to get the version of Mac OS X that is running on your computer, use this command:

```
system attribute "sysv"
```

The resulting value will be a decimal number such as 4194. That number translates into the hexadecimal value 1062, which indicates the current system version is 10.6.2. Here's a handy subroutine to calculate this for you:

```
get_system_version()
--> {10, 6, 2}

on get_system_version()
    set n to system attribute "sysv"
```

```
set major_version_number to (n div 4096 * 10) + (n div 256 mod 16)
set minor_version_number to n div 16 mod 16
set patch_number to n mod 16
return {major_version_number, minor_version_number, patch_number}
end get_system_version
```

Whereas OS X inherits Gestalt values from its classic Mac OS side, shell environment variables come from its Unix side. To obtain a list of available shell environment variable names, just run the system attribute command without any parameters:

```
system attribute
--> {"PATH", "SECURITYSESSIONID", "HOME", "SHELL", "USER", ...}
```

You can then use any of these strings as the direct parameter to the command to look up the corresponding value:

```
system attribute "USER"
--> "hanaan"

system attribute "SHELL"
--> "/bin/bash"
```

The *system info* Command

Available in Mac OS X 10.4 and later, this useful command simply returns a record containing system information. When I run it on my Mac, I get this result:

```
system info
--> {AppleScript version:"2.1.1",
     AppleScript Studio version:"1.5.1",
     system version:"10.6.2",
     short user name:"hanaan",
     long user name:"Hanaan Rosenthal",
     user ID:501,
     user locale:"en_US",
     home directory:alias "Macintosh HD:Users:hanaan:",
     boot volume:"Macintosh HD",
     computer name:"Hanaan Rosenthal's Computer",
     host name:"hanaan-rosenthals-computer.local",
     IPv4 address:"127.0.0.1",
     primary Ethernet address:"00:0b:85:dc:16:20",
     CPU type:"Intel 80486",
     CPU speed:2400,
     physical memory:4096}
```

Working with URLs

The Internet Suite provides a couple of useful features for working with URLs: the open location command and the URL coercion.

The *open location* Command

This command opens a URL with the default application for that type of URL.

For example, a URL using the http (Hypertext Transfer Protocol) scheme will open in your default web browser:

```
open location "http://www.apple.com"
```

A URL using the mailto scheme will create a new e-mail message in your default e-mail client:

```
open location "mailto:news@example.com" & ¬
    "?subject=subscribe&body=Please%20subscribe%20me%20your%20newsletter%2E"
```

> **TIP:** You can also send open location commands directly to applications such as Safari, Firefox, and Mail. This is useful if you want a specific application to open the URL; for example, tell application "Safari" to open location "http://www.apple.com".

Coercing URLs

Standard Additions installs a special coercion into AppleScript that allows you to break down URL strings and extract various information from them. The URL and Internet address entries define the structure of the records returned by this coercion. For example:

```
"http://www.apple.com" as URL
--> {class:URL, scheme:http URL, path:"http://www.apple.com",
    host:{class:Internet address, DNS form:"www.apple.com",
        port:80, dotted decimal form:"17.149.160.10"}}
```

> **TIP:** The other two entries in the Internet suite, handle CGI request and Web page, define some basic terminology for use by third-party applications that need to interface AppleScript with a web server. I'm not aware of any applications that currently use these terms, however, so just ignore them.

Using the Image Events Faceless Background Application

Image Events is another scriptable utility that has only a handful of commands and classes but can be invaluable when you don't want to use a full-blown application such as Adobe Photoshop or Lemke Software's GraphicConverter (http://www.lemkesoft.com) to perform basic operations such as rotating, flipping, and resizing.

One task that Image Events is ideal for is getting information about image files. You can open an image file and then use the properties defined by the image class to get that image's bit depth, resolution, size, color space, file type, and more. This can prove invaluable in publishing workflows.

Script 22–3 changes the comment of a chosen file into a description of the image containing the resolution, file type, bit depth, and so on.

Script 22–3.

```
1. set image_file to choose file with prompt "Please select an image file:" ¬
        of type "public.image"

2. try
3.     tell application "Image Events"
4.         set the_image to open image_file
5.         tell the_image
6.             set {the_width, the_height} to dimensions
7.             set file_type to file type
8.             set color_space to color space
9.             set bit_depth to bit depth
10.            set res to resolution
11.            close
12.         end tell
13.     end tell
14. on error error_text
15.     display dialog "The file you picked couldn't be analyzed for some reason." ¬
            buttons {"OK"} default button 1 with icon stop
16.     return
17. end try

18. tell application "Finder"
19.     set comment of image_file to ¬
            "Image information:
            File type: " & file_type & "
            Width: " & the_width & ", height: " & the_height & "
            Resolution: " & res & "
            Color space: " & color_space & "
            Bit depth: " & bit_depth
20. end tell
```

The main parts to notice in the preceding script are that the open command on line 4 returns a reference to an object of class image representing the newly opened file, and lines 6 to 10 then get information about that image file by referring to the image object's properties. If an error occurs—for example, because the chosen file wasn't of a type Image Events understands—the surrounding try block informs the user there's a problem and stops the script. Lines 18 to 20 set the file's comment to a description of the image.

Image Events can also be used to perform basic image conversions: changing size, rotation, format, and so forth. For example, the following script will resize image files to the desired image size:

```
on open files_list
    set max_size to (text returned of (display dialog ¬
        "Enter the maximum width/height in pixels:" default answer "600")) ¬
```

```
            as integer
    set output_folder to choose folder with prompt "Save the resized files to:"
    repeat with file_ref in files_list
        try
            tell application "Image Events"
                set the_image to open file_ref
                scale the_image to size max_size
                save the_image in file ((output_folder as text) & name of the_image)
                close the_image
            end tell
        on error error_string
            display dialog "Skipping file " & (file_ref as text) & ¬
                " due to error:" & error_string buttons {"OK"} default button 1
        end try
    end repeat
end open
```

Save the script as an application in AppleScript Editor, and then drag and drop one or more bitmap files onto it. Enter the number of pixels you want on the longer edge, followed by the folder to save the resized files to, and the script will convert each file in turn. If an error occurs while converting an image, the try block will report the problem before proceeding to the next file.

Processing Text with the Satimage Scripting Addition

AppleScript's support for text handling has always been a little limited. This gap has been filled by Scripting Additions like the Satimage text processing library.

Satimage produces a development environment called Smile, which is based on AppleScript. The kind folks at Satimage have made many of the underlying libraries available free of charge, and we are going to take a look at one of them here.

After you download and install the Satimage scripting addition, described next, the following sections will cover these topics:

- Performing simple find and replace tasks

- Counting occurrences of a substring in a string

- Finding and replacing substrings in a file

- Searching and replacing across many files

- Finding and replacing text with regular expressions

- Batch-changing file names

Downloading and Installing the Satimage Scripting Addition

You can find the Satimage scripting addition at the following web site:

`http://www.satimage.fr/software/en/downloads/downloads_companion_osaxen.html`

Satimage provides a collection of scripting additions, and I recommend that you take a look at all them, as they provide a highly polished and easy-to-use set of additional tools for the AppleScripter. For now, though, choose the Satimage osax file: at the time of writing this is at version 3.5.0, and all the examples in this section are based on this version.

Just download the Satimage osax .pkg file and double-click it to install the Satimage scripting addition into /Library/ScriptingAdditions (note that you will need an administrator password for this).

Once in place, the Satimage commands are ready for use. You might want to check out the Satimage dictionary:
`http://www.satimage.fr/software/en/dictionaries/dict_satimage.html`. I found it useful to print out the basic pages, but the web pages are also very useful for their examples. In any case, you can always get to the dictionary locally by choosing File ➤ Open Dictionary in AppleScript Editor.

> **NOTE:** For the examples in the following sections, I have used an e-book from Project Gutenberg: Lewis Carroll's *Through the Looking Glass*; please download a copy of this e-book from `http://www.gutenberg.org/files/12/12.txt` before proceeding. (Obviously, you can use any piece of text in your own work, but using this e-book is convenient for following the examples.)

Performing Simple Find and Replace Tasks

We're going to start with some simple demonstrations of find and replace in text. For the first example, use TextEdit or another text editor to open and find the following piece of text in *Through the Looking Glass* (the first verse of the poem "Jabberwocky"):

> "'Twas brillig, and the slithy toves
> Did gyre and gimble in the wabe;
> All mimsy were the borogoves,
> And the mome raths outgrabe."

This is famous as a nonsense poem, but as you will know from reading it, this verse is explained thoroughly in the book (finding this explanation is an exercise for the reader). So we're going to "improve on" Carroll's original by changing the text to read more clearly. Create a new script in AppleScript Editor and type the code shown in Script 22–4.

Script 22–4.

```
set the_string to "'Twas brillig, and the slithy toves
     Did gyre and gimble in the wabe;
     All mimsy were the borogoves,
     And the mome raths outgrabe."
set the_string to change "brillig" into "four o'clock" in the_string
set the_string to change "slithy toves" into "lithe lizards" in the_string
set the_string to change "gyre and gimble" into "span and made holes" in the_string
set the_string to change "wabe" into "grass around the sun-dial" in the_string
set the_string to change "mimsy" into "flimsy and miserable" in the_string
set the_string to change "borogoves" into "thin shabby birds" in the_string
set the_string to change "mome raths" into "homeless green pigs" in the_string
set the_string to change "outgrabe" ¬
     into "bellowed and whistled, with a kind of sneeze in the middle" ¬
     in the_string
```

This is what you should see in AppleScript Editor after you have run the script:

```
--> "'Twas four o'clock, and the lithe lizards
     Did span and made holes in the grass around the sun-dial;
     All flimsy and miserable were the thin shabby birds,
     And the homeless green pigs bellowed and whistled, with a kind of sneeze
          in the middle."
```

There: that makes *much* more sense than the Reverend Dodgson's original verse, doesn't it? Okay, this is a trivial example, but it illustrates the basic operation of one command: change. Here we have taken a piece of text and then used the change command to identify and modify specified strings within that text. The basic syntax for this command is

```
change substring_to_change into replacement_substring in input_string
```

The change command has a number of useful parameters to help you to tune its behavior. Check out the Satimage dictionary to see how these work.

There is an important point here about the way in which commands like change work. The change command does not, as its name suggests, actually change the original string, which is stored in the variable the_string. Instead, it returns a new string. Unless we assign the new string to a variable (by using the set command as in Script 22–4), the change is lost. So in each line in the script, we are assigning the changed text back to the original the_string variable.

The change command also has several optional parameters that give you extra control over how the find and replace operation is performed.

Counting Occurrences of a Substring in a String

Now, let's look at something slightly different. Suppose we want to know how many times the word "Alice" appears in *Through the Looking Glass*? We would use another Satimage command: find text. First take a look at the code, and then we will step through it:

```
-- Get the source file
set source_file to choose file with prompt "Select the file:"
-- Read in the contents of the file
set source_text to read source_file
set the_list to find text "Alice" in source_text ¬
    with all occurrences and string result
set number_of_occurrences to length of the_list
```

We started by using the choose file command to pop up a dialog box where the user picks the file to process. This passes a file reference back. The read command then puts the entire content of the text file into the variable source_text. The next line is more complex. We are using the find text command to find every occurrence of the word "Alice" obviously, but there are some Satimage subtleties here that are worth unpacking. The basic command looks and works like this:

```
set the_list to find text "Alice" in source_text
--> {matchPos:1588, matchLen:5, matchResult:"Alice"}
```

The find text command returns the position, length, and text of the first match. Adding the all occurrences parameter returns, well, all occurrences, but still as a structure like the original command:

```
set theList to find text "Alice" in theSourceText with all occurrences
--> {{matchPos:1588, matchLen:5, matchResult:"Alice"},
    {matchPos:1767, matchLen:5, matchResult:"Alice"},
    {matchPos:2037, matchLen:5, matchResult:"Alice"},
    {matchPos:2826, matchLen:5, matchResult:"Alice"},
    {matchPos:3172, matchLen:5, matchResult:"Alice"}, ...}
```

You can probably see where we need to go with this: to get the number we are looking for, we can trim this result down to a simple list using the string result parameter:

```
set the_list to find text "Alice" in source_text with all occurrences and string result
--> {"Alice", "Alice", "Alice", "Alice", "Alice", "Alice", "Alice", "Alice", ...}
```

Finally, we can simply get the length of this list:

```
set number_of_occurrences to length of the_list
--> 454
```

Finding and Replacing Substrings in a File

What if we wanted to change Alice's name throughout the whole of the book? We would use the change command again—by default it changes every occurrence of a substring within a string. Here's how we would do it:

1. Open the file.

2. Find every occurrence of "Alice".

3. Change every occurrence to "Zelda".

4. Save the file (with a new name—let's not change the original).

Here is the AppleScript to do this:

```
-- Read in the contents of the source file
set source_file to choose file with prompt "Select the file:"
set source_text to read source_file
-- Do the text replacement
set modified_text to change "Alice" into "Zelda" in source_text
-- Write the new text to the destination file
set output_file to (path to desktop as text) & "ttlg_modified.txt"
set output_file_id to open for access output_file with write permission
write modified_text to output_file_id
close access output_file_id
```

Most of this example is straightforward non-Satimage AppleScript: as in the earlier example, the script allows us to choose the text file, which is then read using Standard Additions' read command. Then comes the Satimage change command, which replaces every occurrence of the word "Alice" with "Zelda" and saves the result in the variable modified_text. The script then sets up a separate output file (ttlg_modified.txt), which enables us to save the changes while leaving the source file untouched. The new text is saved to the output file, which is finally closed.

Searching and Replacing Across Many Files

You can use the Satimage commands to directly change the content of a group of files in a folder—that is, without specifically opening and saving the individual files. Personally, I would advise caution in this approach because it is destructive—I would always advise saving the changed file with a new name. Nevertheless, here is how to do it: this will change "Alice" to "Zelda" in all files with a .txt extension in the current folder. Note, by the way, that I am also using the Satimage list files command to get the list of files.

```
set the_folder to choose folder
set the_files to list files the_folder of extension "txt"
repeat with file_ref in the_files
    change "Alice" into "Zelda" in file_ref
end repeat
```

Finding and Replacing Text with Regular Expressions

The Satimage commands include excellent support for regular expressions. If you have never used regular expressions, or have been daunted by the learning curve, don't worry: I'm going to provide some simple but extensible examples here.

A Brief Background on Regular Expressions

In a nutshell, a regular expression is a way of finding a small piece of text in a larger piece of text by the use of a pattern. The pattern indicates the shape and content of the text you are looking for. So you define the pattern, then point that pattern at the document you want to search, and the regular expression engine goes off and matches that pattern to all of the text in the document. For example, to find all occurrences of "Alice" in our sample file, we could simply use the pattern "Alice".

Let's take a look at this pattern in a bit more detail. In effect, each of the characters in the string "Alice" are used to match themselves. This is a very precise match. Obviously a pattern like that is so simple that there is no benefit to using a regular expression over just doing a simple search. Where regular expressions really start to come into their own is when you need to identify more complex patterns. Such patterns will include not just the literal characters that we want to match (such as "Alice") but also *metacharacters* that are used to represent concepts of quantity and position. Some of the most common metacharacters that you are likely to encounter are "." (meaning "match any character"), "+" (meaning "one or more occurrences"), and "*" (meaning "zero or more occurrences").

Let's try out some of these on our "Jabberwocky" text:

> *"'Twas brillig, and the slithy toves*
> *Did gyre and gimble in the wabe;*
> *All mimsy were the borogoves,*
> *And the mome raths outgrabe."*

Here are some simple regular expressions applied to this text. First, let's get the text into a variable:

```
set source_text to "'Twas brillig, and the slithy toves
Did gyre and gimble in the wabe;
All mimsy were the borogoves,
And the mome raths outgrabe."
```

As a start, let's find the word "borogoves":

```
find text "borogoves" in source_text with regexp, all occurrences and string result
-->{"borogoves"}
```

The regular expression has matched the pattern "borogoves", character by character, with anything that looked like that pattern in the source text and returned the resulting match. Suppose we wanted to find every word that begins with "g". We could start by constructing a regular expression like this:

```
find text "g.+" in source_text with regexp, all occurrences and string result
```

This regular expression can be translated as "match the letter 'g' followed by one or more of any other characters" (we could have used "*" to match zero or more characters). This is what comes back:

```
--> {"g, and the slithy toves", "gyre and gimble in the wabe;", "goves,", "grabe."}
```

Hmm. This is not at all what we want. The string that we found does start with a "g" but that's about all that is right with it. Clearly this regular expression has a way to go until it does what we want. We could look for the space at the end of the word by adding a space to the regular expression:

```
find text "g.+ " in source_text with regexp, all occurrences and string result
--> {"g, and the slithy ", "gyre and gimble in the "}
```

This may look a bit better, but actually it hides a potential problem. To test this case, change the word "borogoves" to "boro goves" (with an apology to Lewis Carroll) in the source text and then run the find command again:

```
set source_text to "'Twas brillig, and the slithy toves
Did gyre and gimble in the wabe;
All mimsy were the boro goves,
And the mome raths outgrabe."
```

```
find text "g.+ " in source_text with regexp, all occurrences and string result
--> {"g, and the slithy ", "gyre and gimble in the "}
```

So why didn't the regular expression find the word "goves"? This is a word beginning with a "g", so what has gone wrong? The problem is the space character: we can't rely on it being there when a word is at the end of a line, as it is in the case of "goves". Instead, we need to use the construct "\b" in our regular expression, to match a word boundary (note that when using the Satimage scripting addition for regular expressions, we need to escape characters like "\" by adding another "\" in front):

```
find text "g.+\\b" in source_text with regexp, all occurrences and string result
--> {"g, and the slithy toves", "gyre and gimble in the wabe", "goves", "grabe."}
```

Well, this time we have all of the words beginning with "g", but we still have a lot of excess text in the result. Why?

It's important to know that regular expressions are *greedy*. That means that unless you tell it otherwise, a regular expression will try to grab the largest result it can. In this case, the longest string that matched the pattern we asked for is what came back. So we need to add the "?" to the quantifier:

```
find text "g.+?\\b" in source_text with regexp, all occurrences and string result
--> {"g, ", "gyre", "gimble", "goves", "grabe"}
```

It's looking a lot better, but there is still a problem. The regular expression is finding text beginning with a "g" wherever it occurs, not just at the beginning of a word. Word boundaries to the rescue again: add "\b" to the beginning of the regular expression and try again:

```
find text "\\bg.+?\\b" in source_text with regexp, all occurrences and string result
--> {"gyre", "gimble", "goves"}
```

Great. The regular expression has found the two original words plus the bogus word "goves". This illustrates the workflow you often need to adopt in building regular expressions: start simple and build in complexity as you need it. By the way, having done all of the preceding work, it's worth mentioning that there is almost always a simpler way of expressing ourselves: we could have used another modifier, "\w", that finds word characters (that is, characters other than spaces, punctuation, and so on):

```
find text "\\bg\\w*\\b" in source_text with regexp, all occurrences and string result
->{"gyre", "gimble", "goves"}
```

Still, if we had gone straight to this solution, we would have missed out on an interesting detour.

A good and common example of a use for regular expressions is where you need to find e-mail addresses in a body of text. E-mail addresses come in all shapes and sizes, but they do conform to a pattern: a string of characters (which may include letters, numbers, and some additional characters), followed by an "@" sign, followed by more characters, then a ".", and finally some more characters. Searching for every e-mail address in a document by conventional searching would be very difficult. However, with a regular expression, things become much easier: here is a typical regular expression to find e-mail addresses:

`\b[a-zA-Z0-9._%-]+@[a-zA-Z0-9.-]+\.[a-zA-Z]{2,4}\b`

At first this appears quite daunting, but it breaks down quite logically, as shown in Table 22–2.

Table 22–2. *How the E-Mail Address Pattern Is Constructed*

Subpattern	What It Matches
`\b`	This string at the beginning and end of the expression means "word boundary" and in this case defines that we are searching for something that has no spaces.
`[a-zA-Z0-9._%-]+`	Describes the first part of the e-mail address: a collection of characters comprising the upper- and lowercase letters A–Z, the numbers 0–9, dot, underscore, percent, and minus. The plus sign means multiple occurrences. For example, **the.author**@thisbook.apress.com.
`@`	Finds an @ symbol. For example, the.author**@**thisbook.apress.com.
`[a-zA-Z0-9.-]+`	Finds the second part of the address: letters, numbers, dot, and minus. For example, the.author@**thisbook.apress**.com.
`\.`	Finds a dot (note that this dot is escaped so that it is interpreted as a literal). For example, the.author@thisbook.apress**.**com.
`[a-zA-Z]{2,4}`	Matches the last portion of the address, provided that it is between two and four characters in length. For example, the.author@thisbook.apress.**com**.

Assembled together, this expression will find any e-mail address that conforms to this pattern (I will show an example of this in the next section).

> **NOTE:** This is not meant to be a treatise on regular expressions, but in passing it is worth noting that the preceding pattern is not comprehensive. If you would like to see a really systematic regular expression for a fully RFC 822–compliant e-mail address, look here (but get yourself a stiff drink before you do): `http://www.ex-parrot.com/~pdw/Mail-RFC822-Address.html`.

Using Satimage Regular Expression Commands

It's time for a real example. Returning to our *Through the Looking Glass* text for this example, first we are going to seed the text with a few e-mail addresses, using the find and replace commands that we used earlier:

```
-- Read in the contents of the source file
set source_file to choose file with prompt "Select the file:"
set source_text to read source_file
-- Do the text replacement
set modified_text to change "Tweedledee" ¬
    into "Tweedledee (dee@tweedle.com)" in source_text
set modified_text to change "Tweedledum" ¬
    into "Tweedledum (dum@tweedle.com)" in modified_text
set modified_text to change "White Knight" ¬
    into "White Knight (white.knight@lookingglass.com)" in modified_text
-- Write the new text to the destination file
set output_file to (path to desktop as text) & "ttlg_emails.txt"
set output_file_id to open for access output_file with write permission
write modified_text to output_file_id
close access output_file_id
```

Note: You may have noticed that the preceding script does not find and change all of the strings that you might expect it to. Why not, and what would you do to solve it? Answer: There are examples of all three strings in uppercase. This script misses them because, unlike the normal text handling behavior of AppleScript, the default for the Satimage find text and change commands is to do *case-sensitive* searching. To include upper- and lowercase strings, simply set the optional case sensitive parameter to false, like so:

```
set modified_text to change "tweedledee" ¬
    into "Tweedledee (dee@tweedle.com)" in source_text without case sensitive
```

So now we have a file containing some e-mail addresses. In a new AppleScript Editor window, add this code:

```
set source_file to choose file with prompt "Select the file:"
set source_text to read source_file
find text "\\b[a-zA-Z0-9._%+-]+@[a-zA-Z0-9.-]+\\.[a-zA-Z]{2,4}\\b" ¬
    in source_text with regexp, all occurrences and string result
```

Figure 22–7 shows the result of running this script.

Figure 22–7. *AppleScript Editor showing e-mail addresses found in Through the Looking Glass*

Note that, as mentioned earlier, we had to escape the "\" symbols by putting another "\" in front of them.

As an exercise, try modifying this script to sort the e-mail addresses and remove duplicates (hint: look at the Array and List Utilities suite in the Satimage dictionary). The solution is shown in Figure 22–8.

Figure 22–8. *AppleScript Editor showing de-duplicated and sorted e-mail addresses*

Batch-Changing File Names

The final example in this section will be to use the Satimage commands to modify file names. If you use software that creates files containing letters and numbers in the file name, there may be occasions where you want to change them all in a consistent way. You may already be familiar with the Rename Finder Items action in Automator, which is great for simply changing one part of a file name into another. This example will allow you to do some more-sophisticated file name mangling.

I frequently use the built-in screen capture tools on my Mac: Cmd+Shift+3 to take a quick shot of the entire screen, Cmd+Shift+4 to grab just a region, or Cmd+Shift+4 followed by the spacebar to grab a specific window. In Mac OS X 10.6, these actions create files with file names like Screenshot on 2010-03-04 at 20.38.57.png.

Suppose I have collected a set of screenshots for my latest project and want to be able to identify them uniquely for this project. Just to complicate things, these files are currently categorized into subfolders under my parent Screenshots folder, as shown in Figure 22–9.

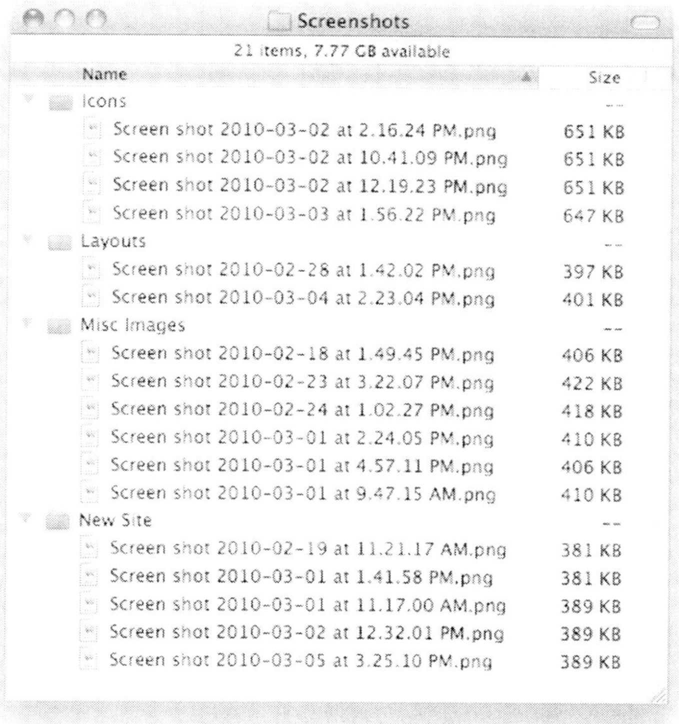

Figure 22–9. *Source files for batch file renaming*

What I would really like is for all of my screenshot files to conform to a common naming pattern:

```
category_screenshot_yyyymmdd_xxx.png
```

Each file name will therefore have the project category name, the type of resource (screenshot), a datestamp derived from the file name, an incrementing number, and the .png extension.

For example, the file at this path,

```
New Site/Screenshot on 2010-03-24 at 14.09.01.png
```

would become:

```
newsite_screenshot_20100324_013.png
```

Script 22–5 shows the finished code, and is followed by a more detailed walkthrough.

Script 22–5.

```
1. set source_folder to choose folder ¬
        with prompt "Where are the current files?"
2. set destination_folder to choose folder ¬
        with prompt "Where do you want to save the new files?"
3. set all_source_files to list files source_folder ¬
        of extension {"png"} with recursively
4. set file_number to 1

5. repeat with file_ref in all_source_files
6.     -- Get the names of the file and the folder that contains it
7.     set file_path to file_ref as text
8.     set path_items to splittext file_path using ":"
9.     set {folder_name, file_name} to items -2 thru -1 of path_items
10.    -- Extract the YYYY-MM-DD style date and reformat it as YYYYMMDD
11.    try
12.        set date_string to find text ¬
                "^Screen shot ([0-9]{4})-([0-9]{2})-([0-9]{2})" in file_name ¬
                using "\\1\\2\\3" with regexp and string result
13.        set is_screenshot to true
14.    on error -- Not a standard file name for a Mac OS X 10.6 screenshot
15.        set is_screenshot to false
16.    end try
17.    if is_screenshot then
18.        -- Assemble the new file name
19.        set folder_name to lowercase (change " " into "" in folder_name)
20.        set file_number to format file_number into "#####000"
21.        set file_name_extension to last item of (splittext file_name using ".")
22.        set new_file_name to folder_name & "_screenshot_" & ¬
                date_string & "_" & file_number & "." & file_name_extension
23.        set file_number to file_number + 1
24.        -- Duplicate and rename the file
25.        tell application "Finder"
26.            set new_file to duplicate file_ref to destination_folder
27.            set name of new_file to new_file_name
28.        end tell
29.    end if
30. end repeat
```

Lines 1 and 2 begin by putting up dialog boxes to allow the user to choose the source (the root of the image files) and destination folders (all of the modified files will go into this one folder). Line 3 then uses the Satimage list files command to recursively bring all of the files into a list. Because Mac OS X 10.6 saves screenshot files in the PNG file format, I can save myself some work by asking the list files command to list only files with a .png file name extension.

Next, the repeat loop on lines 5 to 30 processes each of the items in the list. For each item, lines 7 to 9 extract the file name and the name of its parent folder (these provide components of the final file name) into two variables, folder_name and file_name.

The next step is to obtain the components of the new file name.

First, line 12 uses a simple regular expression to check that the file name begins with the word Screenshot, followed by a YYYY-MM-DD style datestamp. ([0-9]{4} means match any four digits in a row; [0-9]{2} means match any two digits in a row.) If the file name doesn't match this pattern, the find text command will throw an error, so I wrap it in a try statement that traps the error and prevents the script from trying to process this particular file any further.

If the file is a screenshot, then the rest of the processing is quite straightforward. Line 19 tidies up the parent folder name by lowercasing it and removing any spaces. Line 20 ensures that the incrementing file number is at least three digits long by adding leading zeros to it as necessary. Line 21 extracts the file name extension—while I could just hard-code it as "png", this approach ensures that the code will still work if the screenshot file format ever changes.

Once all the information is collected, line 22 reassembles the file name as I want it.

Now that I have the new file name, the final steps are to increment the file name number counter on line 23, and to use the Finder's duplicate and set commands to copy the existing file to the new location and then rename it (lines 26 and 27).

That's it. To test this, create a set of folders similar to the ones shown in Figure 22–9 somewhere on your system, and populate them with screenshots. Then run the script, choosing the New site folder as the source and a suitable destination. If all goes well you will see a result similar to the one shown in Figure 22–10.

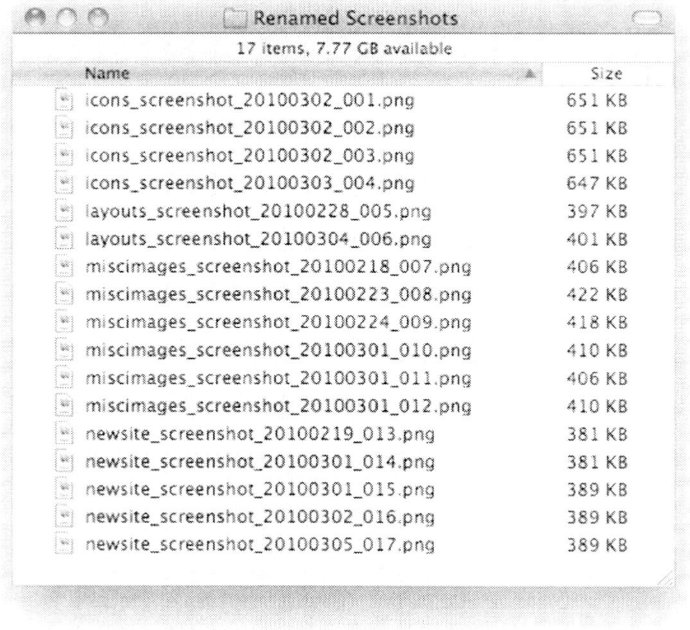

Figure 22-10. *Output from batch file-renaming AppleScript*

Summary

In this chapter we explored the practical aspects of installing, using, and redistributing scripting additions and scriptable faceless background applications (FBAs). We looked at two of the extensions that come with Mac OS X as standard, Standard Additions—which is used throughout this book—and Image Events. We then wrapped up the chapter by using the popular third-party Satimage scripting addition to significantly enhance AppleScript's text processing capabilities.

In the next chapter we will look at how to enhance the AppleScript language itself, through the use of extensions.

Chapter 23

AppleScript Amenities

In this chapter we will look at some useful supporting features available to AppleScript users. We will begin by looking at how AppleScript can integrate with the Mac OS X Services menu. Next, we will look at ways to trigger scripts automatically, first by scheduling them to run at specific times, and then by configuring them to run in response to user actions in the Finder. After that, we will take a look at the GUI Scripting features of System Events that allow AppleScript to control desktop applications that do not provide a scripting interface of their own. Lastly, we'll look at the various ways you can work with the Mac OS X clipboard.

Using the Services Menu

The Services menu is a submenu of the Application menu of almost all Mac OS X applications. It allows software vendors to make some of the useful features found in their applications available from within any other application that supports services. Some great services are New Email With Selection (provided by Mail), Search With Google (supplied by Safari), and the three AppleScript-related services provided by AppleScript Editor, which we'll get to shortly.

Figure 23–1 shows a typical Services submenu.

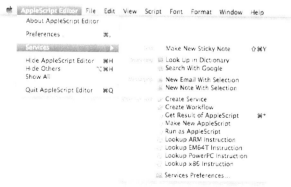

Figure 23–1. *The services that can be used on a text selection in AppleScript Editor*

The Services menu in Mac OS X 10.6 is context-sensitive. If you, say, select a piece of text in Safari or a file in the Finder, the Services menu will automatically include all of the services that it thinks are relevant for the selection.

A particularly neat feature of the Services menu is that you can set up your own keyboard shortcuts for services you use often—just click the Services Preferences option at the bottom of the Services menu, which takes you directly to the Keyboard Shortcuts tab of the Keyboard panel of System Preferences. Click to the right of the service's name and press the keys you want to use (avoid key combinations that are already in common use, of course).

You can also use the Keyboard Shortcuts tab to enable or disable individual services or groups of services. For example, if you never use the "Lookup … Instruction" services in the Development section, you can hide them by unchecking the check boxes next to their names.

AppleScript Editor Services

AppleScript Editor installs three services for you to use: Get Result of AppleScript, Make New AppleScript, and Run as AppleScript. This means that you can highlight a piece of text in any application that supports services, and then choose one of these services in the application's Services menu to perform the corresponding action in AppleScript Editor.

To try it, open TextEdit, type 12 * 7, highlight it, and choose TextEdit ➤ Services ➤ Get Result of AppleScript (or TextEdit ➤ Services ➤ Script Editor ➤ Get Result of AppleScript if you are on Mac OS X 10.5). This compiles and runs the selected text as AppleScript code, and then replaces the selection with the result.

If you choose Make New Script, AppleScript Editor creates a new document containing the text you highlighted.

The Run as AppleScript option also runs the selected text as AppleScript code, but does not replace the selection when it is done.

Creating Your Own Services

You can also create your own services. Mac OS X 10.6 makes this easy to do by using Apple's own Automator application (/Applications/Automator.app).

For example, when posting a comment online, I often want to include a signature at the end of the post:

```
--
Learn AppleScript: The Comprehensive Guide to Scripting and Automation on Mac OS X
http://apress.com/book/view/9781430223610
```

To create a simple AppleScript-based service that does this task for you, first launch Automator and create a new workflow using the Service template, shown in Figure 23–2.

Figure 23-2. *The different types of workflow templates provided by Automator*

When you create a workflow based on the Service template, Automator adds some extra options to the workflow window:

■ The "Service receives" menu allows you to specify the type of input that the service should accept, if any. For example, if your service is designed to work on text files, you would select the text files option from the menu.

■ The "in" menu allows you to restrict the service so that it only appears in a particular application, or you can make it visible to any suitable application if you prefer (the default).

■ The "Replaces selected text" check box determines whether or not the service will produce any output. For example, if the service is designed to replace a piece of selected text (or insert text at the cursor's current position), you should enable this option.

For this exercise, your service doesn't require any input but does produce output, so set the "Service receives" menu to the "no input" option and tick the "Replaces selected text" check box.

Now you need some way to generate the text to insert. Because this book is all about scripting, you'll use some AppleScript.

First, click the Utilities entry under the Library section on the left side of the workflow window. This will display the names of all the general-purpose actions provided by Automator, including the one you want: Run AppleScript.

Next, drag the Run AppleScript entry to the right side of the window to add the action to the workflow, as shown in Figure 23–3.

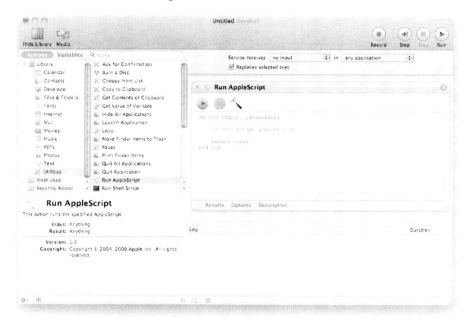

Figure 23–3. *An Automator window with a Run AppleScript action added to the workflow*

As you can see, the Run AppleScript action provides a text box for entering your AppleScript code, along with various buttons for compiling and test-running it.

The script initially contains a single run handler that takes a list of two values: the input data plus a parameters record containing some useful information about the workflow. The handler also returns a value—by default, the object it received as its input, but you can change this if you wish.

Your action doesn't require any input but it does need to return your signature text as output, so change the handler to look like this (you can use your own choice of signature text, of course):

```
on run {input, parameters}
    return "--
Learn AppleScript: The Comprehensive Guide to Scripting and Automation on Mac OS X
http://apress.com/book/view/9781430223610"
end run
```

Finally, choose File ➤ Save As and type in the name of the service, in this case Add My Signature.

As this is a text-based service, you can easily test it. Just create a temporary document in TextEdit and select TextEdit ➤ Services ➤ Add My Signature. If everything is working correctly, the signature text should appear at the cursor's current position.

Once you're satisfied that everything is working correctly, don't forget that you also can set up a keyboard shortcut for the Add My Signature service (by clicking the Services Preferences option on the Services menu to access the Keyboard Shortcuts tab).

> **TIP:** If you need to support older versions of Mac OS X, you can also create services using waffle software's free ThisService utility (`http://wafflesoftware.net/thisservice/`).

Scheduling Scripts with iCal

Most AppleScripts are run by users at the time the users need them. But what if you want a script to run automatically at any time of the day or night? What you need is some sort of tool to trigger your scripts at certain intervals or on specific dates.

The good news is, you have quite a few options to choose from here—some already built into Mac OS X; others available from third-party developers. In this section, we will look at scheduling script execution using Apple iCal, which is very easy to do.

First, create a new event in iCal, and set the start date and time to the date and time on which you want the script to execute. Give your event a good, clear name so that you remember later what it does. You might even want to set up a special calendar named, say, "Scheduled Scripts" to keep all of your script scheduling events in the same place.

After you have named the event and set the start date and time, choose Run Script as the alarm option and select the script file you want to run. Set the alarm to execute 0 minutes before the event.

To have your script run at regular intervals, choose one of the available options from the Repeat menu: Every day, Every week, Every month, Every year, or Custom if you need more precise control.

Once you've finished setting up the event, click the Done button and it's good to go.

Figure 23–4 shows an iCal event that will run a script called `Backup user folders.scpt` every night at 12:20 AM.

If iCal isn't your cup of tea, other options for scheduling AppleScripts include:

- Apps and More Software Design, Inc.'s commercial Script Timer application (`http://www.appsandmore.com/`), which can trigger scripts written in AppleScript and other languages

- The traditional Unix `cron` tool, which can run AppleScripts via Mac OS X's command-line `osascript` tool, which you'll learn about in Chapter 27

▓ Apple's powerful launchd utility—a sort of supercharged cron that manages a huge range of scheduling tasks on Mac OS X, from coordinating operating system startups, to relaunching crashed processes automatically, to starting third-party housekeeping scripts. You can find out more about launchd at http://developer.apple.com/macosx/launchd.html.

Figure 23–4. *The event shown will run the* Backup user folders.scpt *script every night at 12:20 AM.*

CAUTION: Because scriptable applications need to access the Mac OS X GUI in order to run, running AppleScripts via launchd or cron will only work if a normal user is logged in.

Triggering Scripts with Folder Actions

Folder actions allow you to create hot folders on your Mac that trigger a script whenever the folder is modified. You create a folder action by attaching a script to a folder. This script can contain one or more special event handlers that activate when the folder window opens, closes, or moves, or when items are either added to or removed from the folder.

Folder actions are great for any hot-folder setup you need to create. Imagine any workflow in which files need to be processed automatically but a person has to trigger the automation by telling the script which file or files to process. Although you could have created the same workflow using a script application saved as a droplet (that is, containing an open handler), folder actions give you a wider variety of action-triggering events and allow users to trigger scripts by dropping files into a folder, which may be more workflow-like than dragging and dropping files on an application droplet.

Defining Event Handlers for Folder Actions

While the most common use for folder actions is to perform some action when items are added to the folder, your scripts can respond to up to five different types of folder action events. The terminology for these handlers is defined in the Folder Actions suite of the Standard Additions scripting addition and is as follows:

```
opening folder v : Called after a folder has been opened into a window
    opening folder alias : the folder that was opened

closing folder window for v : Called after a folder window has been closed
    closing folder window for alias : the folder that was closed

moving folder window for v : Called after a folder window has been moved or resized
    moving folder window for alias : the folder whose window was moved or resized
        from bounding rectangle : the previous coordinates of folder window
            (you can get the new coordinates from the Finder)

adding folder items to v : Called after new items have been added to a folder
    adding folder items to alias : Folder receiving the new items
        after receiving list of alias : a list of the items the folder received

removing folder items from v : Called after items have been removed from a folder
    removing folder items from alias : the folder losing the items
        after losing list of alias : a list of the items the folder lost. For
            permanently deleted items, only the names (in strings) are provided.
```

Where Are Folder Action Scripts Stored?

Folder action scripts reside in the Folder Action Scripts folder in the Scripts folder of either the current user's Library folder or the Library folder in the startup disk. Out of the box, the /Library/Scripts/Folder Action Scripts folder already exists, and it contains several samples of folder action scripts you can open and play with or attach to folders.

Managing Your Folder Actions

For folder actions to work, you have to meet a couple of conditions. First, you must have folder actions activated on the Mac that the actions should run on. Second, you must attach to a folder a script containing at least one folder action event handler.

You can enable folder actions and manage your folder action scripts in a couple of ways: using the Folder Actions Setup utility or using AppleScript itself.

Using the Folder Actions Setup Utility

The Folder Actions Setup utility allows you to enable and disable folder actions. If the system-wide Script menu is enabled in the menu bar, you can launch Folder Actions Setup by choosing Script ➤ Folder Actions ➤ Configure Folder Actions. Another option is to right-click a folder in the Finder and select the Folder Actions Setup option in the context menu.

> **NOTE:** On Mac OS X 10.5, you can launch the Folder Actions Utility from the system-wide Script menu, from the More submenu of Finder's context menu, or by going to /Applications/AppleScript/ and double-clicking Folder Actions Setup.app.

Figure 23–5 shows the Folder Actions Setup utility before any actions have been set up.

Figure 23–5. *The Folder Actions Setup utility*

Folders that have folder action scripts attached to them are shown in the left pane. Selecting a folder in the left pane displays the scripts currently attached to it in the right pane.

Using Scripts

You may be in a situation where you need to be able to set up multiple Macs with some folder action functionality—for example, if you are administering a Mac network in a school or business. You can easily automate this process by scripting System Events, an invisible Mac OS X application that provides a wide range of valuable features for AppleScript to use. The commands and classes used to manage folder actions are defined in the Folder Actions suite of System Events.

To get started, check out the scripts that come with the Mac in the
/Library/Scripts/Folder Actions folder. In this folder you will find ready-made scripts
for enabling and disabling the folder actions system, and for attaching and removing
folder actions to and from folders:

- Enable Folder Actions.scpt
- Disable Folder Actions.scpt
- Attach Script to Folder.scpt
- Remove Folder Actions.scpt

You can run these scripts either from AppleScript Editor or from the system-wide Script
menu. All of the scripts are editable, and you're encouraged to copy parts of them into
your own scripts. For example, this one enables folder actions:

```
tell application "System Events" to set folder actions enabled to true
```

Creating Your First Folder Action

After you enable folder actions, you can get started by creating a folder action script,
attaching it to a folder, and testing it. You'll create a simple script that will randomly
change the labels of the items you drop in the folder. You will use the Folder Actions
Setup utility to administer the operation.

Create Your Folder Action Script

Create a new script document in AppleScript Editor and type in the code shown in
Script 23–1.

Script 23–1.

```
on adding folder items to this_folder after receiving dropped_items
    repeat with alias_ref in dropped_items
        set label_index to random number from 1 to 6
        tell application "Finder"
            set label index of alias_ref to label_index
        end tell
    end repeat
end adding folder items to
```

Script 23–1 contains a single folder action event handler, adding folder items to. This
handler will be called automatically when any files or folders are added to the folder that
this script is attached to.

When the handler is called, it receives two parameters: a direct parameter that is an alias
value identifying the folder itself, and a parameter labeled after receiving that is a list
of aliases identifying the items that were dropped into it. Depending on your needs, you
can use or ignore either or both of these parameters. In this script, you only need the
after receiving parameter.

Within the handler, you loop across the list of alias values, processing each one in turn.
First you decide which color of label to apply by picking a random number between one

and six. You then use the Finder to set the item's label index property to this number. (A real folder action script would normally do something a bit more practical—convert image files to a different format, upload each file to an FTP site, etc.—but the point of this example is to show how you can easily process each alias value in the list of dropped items using a repeat loop.)

> **TIP:** You can include up to five different folder action event handlers in a single script.

Save Your Script

For your script to become folder action material, you need to save (or move) it to a Folder Action Scripts folder. There is an existing Folder Action Scripts folder at /Library/Scripts, or you can create one at ~/Library/Scripts if you want a folder action script to be available to the current user only. Save the script in one of these locations as Hot Folder Test.scpt.

Create Your Hot Folder

Create a folder on the desktop, and call it My Hot Folder. This will be the folder that triggers the adding folder items to event handler in your folder action script.

Activate the Folder Actions Setup Utility

Launch the Folder Actions Setup utility. If folder actions are not already enabled, select the Enable Folder Actions check box (shown earlier in Figure 23–5).

Attach the Folder Action Script to the Folder

To attach the folder action script you created, you start by adding the folder to the folder list, and then you attach the script to it.

In the Folder Action Setup utility, click the "+" button under the folder list on the left. This opens the Choose Folder dialog box. Choose the hot folder you created on the desktop, and click OK. This adds the folder to the folder list and brings up a list of all the folder action scripts that you currently have installed in your Folder Actions Scripts folders, as shown in Figure 23–6.

Figure 23–6. *Choosing one or more folder action scripts to attach to a folder*

TIP: If you right-click a folder in the Finder and choose the Folder Actions Setup option from the context menu, Folder Actions Setup will automatically add the selected folder to the folder list for you.

Choose your Hot Folder Test script, and click OK. Figure 23–7 shows how the Folder Action Setup utility window should look when you have done this.

Figure 23–7. *The Folder Actions Setup utility after an action has been added to a folder*

Each folder can have more than one folder action script attached to it. If you need to add more folder action scripts to an existing folder entry, clicking the "+"button beneath the right pane will bring up the list of available actions. To remove an action or a folder, click the "–" button beneath the appropriate pane.

You also can enable and disable individual scripts by clicking the check boxes in the right pane, or you can check and uncheck folders in the left pane to enable or disable all of their attached actions at once.

Test Your Folder Action

To finish off, test your new folder action in the Finder by dragging some test files or folders onto the hot folder. If all goes well, when you open the hot folder, you should find a collection of randomly labeled items waiting for you.

Controlling Applications with GUI Scripting

When applications have good AppleScript support, a working object model, and a solid dictionary, scripting the graphical user interface (GUI) is simply not needed. GUI Scripting is used to plug holes in the scriptability of your system, including applications, utilities, and any other thing you'd want to automate.

Although GUI Scripting is not a replacement for a real application scripting interface, it generally works well within its limitations and allows you to automate almost any feature that can be invoked from the application's GUI.

The main disadvantage is that scripts that rely on GUI Scripting tend to be less portable than scripts that use a proper application scripting interface. If the application GUI changes from one version to the next, a script written for one version of the application can easily break if used on other versions.

> **NOTE:** The GUI Scripting examples in this chapter are written for Mac OS X 10.6. If you are running a different version of Mac OS X, you may need to modify them to suit.

Another disadvantage of GUI Scripting is that the code is often harder to read and to write, as you are poking around the actual objects that make up the application's GUI, rather than working with a scripting interface that is specifically designed for AppleScript to use.

A third problem you might encounter is that the script sometimes works faster than the user interface can respond and therefore trips over itself. You can often work around this situation, however, by inserting a small delay in the script.

Despite these issues, GUI Scripting is a welcome feature, and in many cases it is the only option you have to bridge the scriptability gaps in the applications you use in your workflows.

Enabling GUI Scripting

Before you can run any scripts that use GUI Scripting commands, you will need to enable GUI Scripting support on your Mac. To do this, launch System Preferences, and in the Universal Access panel, select the "Enable access for assistive devices" check box at the bottom of the window. (GUI Scripting uses the same technology as Mac OS X's Accessibility features.) Alternatively, you can run the following script:

```
tell application "AppleScript Utility"
    set GUI Scripting enabled to true
end tell
```

> **NOTE:** You may need to enter an administrator password before you can enable or disable access for assistive devices. You can leave it turned on all the time without any noticeable effects.

The GUI Scripting Dictionary

The GUI Scripting commands and objects are defined in the System Events dictionary under the Processes suite. The Processes suite defines five commands and many classes. The five commands are click, perform, key code, keystroke, and select. The list of classes in the Processes suite is a bit longer. It contains 45 classes, almost all of them being subclasses of the class named UI element. On top of that, each UI element has many elements and properties of its own. You can set the values of many of the properties using AppleScript's set command, and you can evaluate them using the get command.

Although some logic applies to the hierarchy of the elements—such as a window element can contain a button element, a button cannot contain a window, and a menu bar contains menus that contain menu items—the dictionary doesn't hint at any of that. Once you've identified the application process you want to control—for example, tell process "Preview" ... end tell—it's up to you to locate the UI elements you want.

So, figuring out which element in the GUI of a given application contains which other elements is difficult—unless, of course, you have the right tool. The best tool for this job is PreFab Software's UI Browser, created by Bill Cheeseman and available at http://prefabsoftware.com/uibrowser/. A less powerful but free utility called Accessibility Inspector is also available as part of Apple's Developer Tools. You can install the Developer Tools from your Mac's installation discs, or download the latest version from http://developer.apple.com.

GUI Scripting Object Structure

Even though the dictionary isn't much help when it comes to the GUI object model, I can try to shed some light on the situation. In GUI Scripting, two main types of objects contain all others: windows and the menu bar. Windows, then, can contain all elements that belong in a window such as text fields, buttons, and pop-up buttons. Menu bars can contain menus, and menus contain menu items, and so on. Figure 23–8 shows the inheritance hierarchy for some commonly used GUI Scripting–related classes, which helps you to understand which classes of objects share similar features and behaviors. Figure 23–9 shows the corresponding containment hierarchy, which describes how objects of these classes can fit together in the System Events object model.

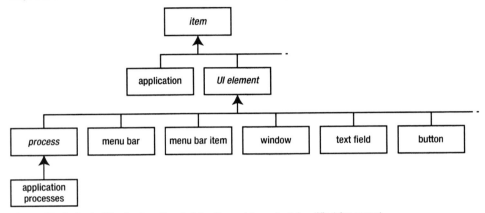

Figure 23–8. *Part of the System Events inheritance hierarchy (simplified for space)*

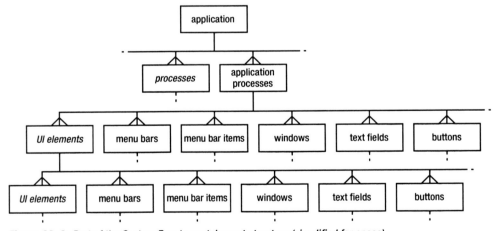

Figure 23–9. *Part of the System Events containment structure (simplified for space)*

If you study the System Events dictionary, you will notice that the many different classes of objects that represent GUI controls inherit all of their properties and elements from the UI element class, so that is the main class you should look at when figuring out what System Events' GUI Scripting objects can do. The process class also inherits from UI element, but adds various properties and elements of its own for describing running applications. In turn, the process class's attributes are inherited by application process.

In Mac OS X 10.6, System Events represents every running application as an object of class `application process`:

```
tell application "System Events" to get every process
--> {application process "loginwindow" of application "System Events",
    application process "Dock" of application "System Events",
    application process "SystemUIServer" of application "System Events",
    application process "Finder" of application "System Events",
    ...}
```

When determining the containment hierarchy for the various classes of GUI-related objects, notice how System Events allows any class of GUI control element to contain (in theory) any other class of GUI control element. It is up to you to figure out how an application's GUI objects are actually nested within the object model—for example, by using PreFab Software's UI Browser to explore a specific application's GUI objects directly—and construct your System Events references appropriately.

It is also important to note that any object (such as a table) that appears to have a scrollbar really doesn't. In reality, the scrollbar is part of a scroll view in which the object resides. This means that, in some cases, to get to the UI element you want to change, you have to dig through the scroll element. See the "Introducing PreFab UI Browser" section later in this chapter.

GUI Scripting also lets you get and set attributes of a UI element that are not defined in the System Events dictionary, and it lets you perform actions that aren't defined in that dictionary by using technical terms defined by Apple and by third-party applications to support Apple's Accessibility technology—such as `get value of attribute "AXPosition" of window 1` or `perform action "AXRaise" of window 1`. For example, the Finder responds to several new technical terms of this nature, and GUI Scripting can use this technique to get at them. You can use tools such as Apple's Accessibility Inspector and PreFab's UI Browser to learn what these technical terms are.

Basic GUI Scripting Examples

Let's look at a few examples of putting GUI Scripting to use. The first example will help you to discover the basic structure of an application's GUI. Launch Mac OS X's Preview application and open a bitmap image file in it (for example, take a screenshot and open it). Now, run the following script:

```
tell application "Preview" to activate

tell application "System Events"
    return every UI element of process "Preview"
end tell
```

The result will be a list similar to this:

```
--> {window "Screenshot on 2010-03-04 at 16.38.10.png"
            of application process "Preview" of application "System Events",
    menu bar 1 of application process "Preview" of application "System Events"}
```

Notice that the only command you sent to the Preview application was the `activate` command. When scripting an application's GUI, you usually activate the desired application first and then send the rest of the commands to System Events, using a `process` element to identify the running application you want. In this case, the element is `process "Preview"`. Also notice that the result of the script has two elements: a window and a menu bar. The menu bar is the main element you use to identify and select menu items. The rest of the UI elements usually are part of some window.

In the next example, you will flip the front image that is open in Preview. To do that you will use the `click` command to click a specific menu item:

```
tell application "Preview" to activate

tell application "System Events"
    tell process "Preview"
        click menu item "Flip Vertical" of menu "Tools" of menu bar 1
    end tell
end tell
```

Using GUI Scripting Commands

Having only five commands makes it seem like your options are limited; however, what you can do in this case has more to do with which object you perform the command on than with the command itself. On top of that, every UI element has many properties that can be manipulated with the standard `get` and `set` commands. This by itself will account for a lot of what you can do with GUI Scripting. You can also use System Events' `exists` command to check if a UI element exists before you try to manipulate it.

The following sections describe the three most useful commands provided specifically for GUI Scripting: `click`, `keystroke`, and `key code`.

The *click* Command

The `click` command makes the UI element behave as if you clicked it with the mouse. This applies to buttons, text fields, menu items, and so on. If you were going to the desert and could take just a single GUI Scripting command with you, `click` would be it. Most GUI Scripting tasks you will perform will boil down to clicking some UI element. It is finding that element that will pose the challenge.

In the following script, the `click` command selects a UI element of the dock process:

```
tell application "System Events"
    tell process "Dock" to click UI element "iTunes" of list 1
end tell
```

The *keystroke* Command

The keystroke command allows you to simulate the action of a user pressing keys on the keyboard. All you have to do is follow the `keystroke` command with a string you want System Events to enter via your keyboard.

This command is handy in two situations: one is when you want to type text, and the other is when you want to execute a keyboard shortcut with the Cmd key (or other key).

For example, to type some text into an existing TextEdit window:

```
tell application "TextEdit" to activate
tell application "System Events"
   keystroke "Hello World!"
end tell
```

You can use the keystroke command's optional using parameter to specify one or more modifier keys just for the next keystroke, like this:

```
keystroke "n" using command down
```

To use multiple modifiers, put them in a list, like this:

```
keystroke "n" using {command down, shift down}
```

> **CAUTION:** When testing scripts that use the keystroke command in AppleScript Editor, always click the Run button or choose the Script ➤ Run menu item. Don't type Cmd+R to run your scripts; otherwise, the Command modifier could affect the characters being "typed" by script.

The *key code* Command

The key code command is a bit like keystroke, but instead of typing based on a character, it uses the hardware-based integer key code of a particular key. This method has the advantage of giving you access to keys that aren't characters, such as the Delete key, the arrow keys, and the function keys on the top row of your keyboard.

Like the keystroke command, the key code command provides an optional using parameter for specifying one or more modifier keys to "hold down" at the same time.

Useful key codes include 123 through 126, which are the left, right, down, and up arrow keys, and code 51, which is the Delete key. Utilities such as PreFab's UI Browser can show you the key code of any key you press.

Script 23–2 will start a new document in TextEdit and type the word *Apple*. Then it will go back one character and select the middle three characters by using the left arrow with the Shift key.

Script 23–2.

```
tell application "TextEdit" to activate
tell application "System Events"
   keystroke "n" using command down
   keystroke "Apple"
   key code 123
   key code {123, 123, 123} using shift down
end tell
```

In a few pages you will look at using the get and set commands to get and set the values of UI elements.

> **NOTE:** While the other Processes suite commands can be targeted at a specific application using a `process` element, the `keystroke` and `key code` commands *always* affect the frontmost application, so make sure you active the right application first.

Example Project: Searching in Preview

In this exercise, you will create a search script for Preview. First, you will develop a simple script that enters a search string into the search field of a Preview window. Then, you will enhance it to extract the search results directly out of the window.

> **NOTE:** The script in this project is developed with the help of UI Browser, so if you don't yet own a copy, go to `http://prefabsoftware.com` and download the demo.

Introducing PreFab UI Browser

Working with AppleScript's GUI Scripting means working with UI elements, and the only sane way to do that, especially when dealing with complex windows containing lots of nested elements, is by using the UI Browser tool from PreFab Software.

The reason why UI Browser is so useful is that the Mac GUI wasn't designed with you scripting it in mind. The internal structure of application GUIs can be surprisingly complicated, and finding your way around them often takes a lot of time. For instance, if you want to know what's in the first row of the sidebar in Apple's Mail, you have to use the following syntax:

```
tell application "System Events"
    tell process "Mail"
        value of static text 1 of row 1 of outline 1 ¬
            of scroll area 1 of splitter group 1 of splitter group 1 of window 1
    end tell
end tell
--> "MAILBOXES"
```

Using UI Browser is simple. You start by picking the application whose interface you want to script from the Target pop-up menu. This pop-up menu shows all open applications and also allows you to choose an application. Figure 23–10 shows UI Browser with the Target menu exposed. Once you choose an application, the main browser view shows you the main set of UI elements. These usually are the menu bar and the main open windows.

Figure 23–10. *UI Browser with the Target menu exposed*

Beginning the Script

Start by opening a text-based PDF file with Preview. For this example, I'll use the `AppleScriptLanguageGuide.pdf` file, which you can download from:

```
http://developer.apple.com/mac/library/documentation/AppleScript/
     Conceptual/AppleScriptLangGuide/AppleScriptLanguageGuide.pdf
```

You can use a different PDF file if you want.

Next, choose Preview from UI Browser's Target menu. (If you already have, you may want to refresh your screen.)

> **NOTE:** To keep things simple, this example assumes the window's toolbar is currently visible, so make sure the toolbar isn't hidden or, if it is, reveal it manually. You can always add your own code to reveal a hidden toolbar automatically later on.

Next, click the `standard window` element representing your PDF document in the second browser column, and continue clicking the objects listed in the subsequent browser columns until you've located the search field in the toolbar, as shown in Figure 23–11. If you check the Highlight check box, UI Browser will highlight the interface element with a yellow rectangle. You can also expand the Path to Element disclosure triangle to show the path to the currently selected element.

Figure 23–11. *UI Browser's main browser with the Search button element selected*

You will use the set command to enter a search phrase into this field, but you first need to create an AppleScript tell block that identifies the text field.

In GUI Scripting you don't tell applications what to do. Instead, everything you do happens under the System Events application. You tell different process objects of System Events what to do. Script 23–3 shows a typical tell block to start off a GUI Scripting script.

Script 23–3.

```
activate application "Preview"
tell application "System Events"
    tell process "Preview"
        -- insert GUI Scripting statements here
    end tell
end tell
```

In UI Browser, choose Tell Block Wrapper (Short) from the AppleScript menu to generate this code. Then, copy and paste the result into a new script window in AppleScript Editor.

Performing the Search

After you have clicked the last text field element, choose Set Value of Selected Element from the AppleScript menu. This will give you a line of code similar to the following:

```
set value of text field 1 of group 3 of tool bar 1
    of window "AppleScriptLanguageGuide.pdf (page 1 of 262)" to "<string>"
```

Copy this line into your script, but first, because you will work more with this text field, separate it and give it its own `tell` block, like this:

```
tell window 1
  set value of text field 1 of group 3 of tool bar 1 to "beep"
end tell
```

Notice that I changed the code to point to the frontmost window instead of a window with a specific name, allowing this code to work with other PDF files as well. For demonstration purposes, I also switched the search string to a word that I know exists in the file, in this case "beep". In practical use, you might prompt the user to enter this string via a `display dialog` command.

Here is the script so far:

```
activate application "Preview"
tell application "System Events"
   tell process "Preview"
      tell window 1
         -- Perform the search
         set value of text field 1 of group 3 of tool bar 1 to "beep"
      end tell
   end tell
end tell
```

Run this script, and it should enter the word "beep" into the search field of the front Preview document. If you are lucky and everything works as intended, Preview will automatically list all of the found occurrences in the window's sidebar, as shown in Figure 23–12.

Unfortunately, when testing this script myself, I found that the search would work on some occasions but not on others. The script was setting the search field's content okay, but Preview didn't seem to realize that text had been entered.

These sorts of hiccups are common in GUI Scripting—after all, you are dealing with objects that are designed to recognize human, not AppleScript, interactions. So if your GUI Scripting code doesn't immediately work as intended, you might need to think for a moment about what a human user does that your script isn't doing.

In this case, after performing a mixture of manual and automated experiments on the window, I realized that the automated approach would only work if the search field was already highlighted, either by clicking in it or by choosing the Edit ➤ Find ➤ Find menu option; otherwise, Preview wouldn't notice when the field's content was changed by the script.

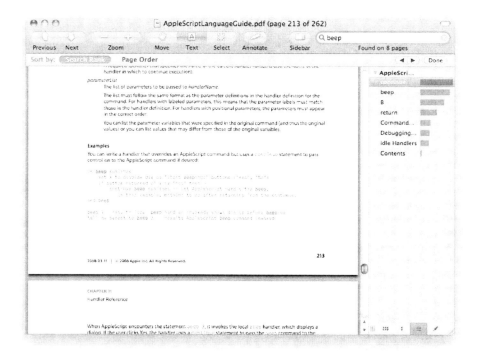

Figure 23–12. *The search results in the Preview window*

Once the problem was identified, it was easy to figure out the answer: just use Preview's Find menu item to activate the search box before setting its content. Because the Find option already has a keyboard shortcut, Cmd+F, a quick solution is to send the menu item's keyboard shortcut, like this:

```
activate application "Preview"
tell application "System Events"
    keystroke "f" using command down
    tell process "Preview"
        -- Rest of the code...
    end tell
end tell
```

Using `activate application "Preview"` to ensure Preview is frontmost is especially important here, as System Events always sends keystrokes to whichever application is frontmost at the time.

A more polished approach is to use System Events' `click` command to trigger the menu item itself. Browse to Preview's Edit ➤ Find ➤ Find menu item in UI Browser, and then choose AppleScript ➤ Click Selected Element to obtain a complete command for clicking it:

```
click menu item "Find…"  of menu 1 of menu item "Find"
    of menu 1 of menu bar item "Edit"  of menu bar 1
```

Script 23–4 shows how the script looks once this line is added to it.

Script 23–4.

```
activate application "Preview"
tell application "System Events"
   tell process "Preview"
      click menu item "Find…" of menu 1 of menu item "Find" ¬
            of menu 1 of menu bar item "Edit" of menu bar 1
      tell window 1
         -- Perform the search
         set value of text field 1 of group 3 of tool bar 1 to "beep"
      end tell
   end tell
end tell
```

Run the script now, and the script should activate the search field before it enters the text, ensuring the search works every time.

Getting Data from the Search Table

In addition to highlighting the search phrase within the PDF document, Preview can also list all the pages that contain the search phrase. You can view this list in the window's sidebar following a search, and use GUI Scripting to extract additional information on the search results.

The first thing to do is to locate the outline view that contains the search results. Rerun Script 23–4 if necessary and make sure the sidebar containing the search results is visible.

Next, use UI Browser to locate the outline view, and then choose AppleScript ➤ Reference to Selected Element to obtain a reference to it. The reference should look something like this:

```
outline 1 of scroll area 2 of splitter group 1 ¬
    of window "AppleScriptLanguageGuide.pdf (page 1 of 262)"
```

Conveniently, clicking the Find menu option automatically opens the sidebar where the search results will appear, so you won't have to open it yourself.

The last step is to extract the information from the outline view, so locate it again in UI Browser. As you will see, the outline view has a number of row elements: the first is the heading for the search results; the rest are the results themselves. Dig down further, and you will find that each of these result rows has two UI elements of their own: a text field, which contains the page number as text, and a relevance indicator. Figure 23–13 shows an example of this.

Figure 23–13. *UI Browser's main browser with the second row of the search results outline view selected*

To retrieve the values of the text field and relevance field elements, just get their value properties. Script 23–5 shows the finished script, which retrieves all of the search result information.

Script 23–5.

```
activate application "Preview"
tell application "System Events"
    tell process "Preview"
        click menu item "Find…"  of menu 1 of menu item "Find" ¬
            of menu 1 of menu bar item "Edit"  of menu bar 1
        tell window 1
            -- Perform the search
            set value of text field 1 of group 3 of tool bar 1 to "beep"
            delay 1
            -- Get the search results from the sidebar
            tell rows 2 thru -1 of outline 1 of scroll area 2 of splitter group 1
                set page_numbers to value of text field 1
                set page_relevances to value of relevance indicator 1
            end tell
        end tell
    end tell
end tell
{page_numbers, page_relevances}
--> {{"continue", "beep", "B", "return", "Commands Reference", ...},
    {2056.9306640625, 1879.22546386719, 1519.01831054688, 1044.01293945312, ...}}
```

You'll notice I've added a short delay between performing the search and getting the results. Once again, when testing the script, I found it would sometimes throw an error or return the results of the previous search.

This is not an uncommon problem in GUI Scripting. While the commands you send to System Events return almost immediately, the application you are controlling may take a moment or two to respond to the action—by which time your script may already have sent several more commands. Inserting a Standard Additions `delay` command at these problem points can give the target application a chance to catch up before the next GUI Scripting command is sent.

For this exercise, I have simply guessed a reasonable amount of time (one second) for the script to wait. Of course, if a particular search takes longer than this, then the script will run into problems again unless the delay is increased some more.

A less crude approach would be to wrap the `delay` command in a repeat loop that uses GUI Scripting to detect when the information you're waiting on—in this case, a list of search results—has appeared. That way, if the search takes a bit longer, the `delay` command will execute again, ensuring that the script only proceeds once the target application is ready for the next step.

Once you have retrieved the raw values, you can reorganize and present them however you like. You could also enhance this script in other ways—for example, by using the standard open command (which even nonscriptable applications like Preview support) to open the PDF to be searched, and GUI Scripting to select the File ➤ Close menu item to close it again when done.

Understanding the Limitations of GUI Scripting

As you have seen in this section, application GUIs can have a surprisingly complex internal structure that is difficult to navigate without help, and this structure can easily change while the application is running—for example, toolbars, sidebars, and so on may be hidden or revealed at any time.

You should also not be surprised if GUI Scripting code written for one version of an application breaks on other versions. Unlike scripting interfaces, where backward compatibility with existing scripts is an important requirement, graphical interfaces can significantly change in layout and appearance from one version to another.

Whereas human users can easily cope with such changes, the changes will almost certainly break existing GUI Scripting code, which heavily relies on the internal structure of GUI menus and windows. If you are writing a GUI Scripting–based script for general use, you will need to plan carefully for these possibilities. For example, your script might automatically detect and reveal hidden elements as it needs them, run different variations of your GUI Scripting code for specific application versions, or display informative error messages telling the user how to correct a problem manually and run the script again.

Despite these limitations, however, GUI Scripting can be a real savior when you absolutely must automate an otherwise nonscriptable application. Oh, and don't forget to contact the application's developers and politely ask them to add a proper AppleScript interface in future releases!

Working with the Clipboard

To finish off the chapter, we will look at scripting clipboard operations such as copying and pasting between applications and manipulating data residing in the clipboard. As you will see, you can get values in and out of the clipboard in a few ways, and the clipboard can move information that can't be handled as an AppleScript object.

Getting Clipboard Data into AppleScript

The Standard Additions command the `clipboard` will return the contents of the clipboard. The class of the result of the the `clipboard` command depends on what sort of data was copied, however.

For example, if you copy some text from a TextEdit document, the `clipboard` will return a string of some sort:

```
the clipboard
--> "Some text from TextEdit."
```

If you get the class of this returned value, you'll see that it's text:

```
the clipboard
class of result
--> text
```

The the `clipboard` command also has an optional parameter, as. To understand how to use this parameter, you first need to look at how the Mac clipboard actually works.

Understanding How the Mac Clipboard Works

The Mac clipboard is a clever piece of software; it's simple to use but surprisingly sophisticated beneath the surface.

When a user copies some data from an application, the clipboard has no idea what kind of application the user is going to paste that data into next. To provide as much flexibility as possible when copying and pasting between applications, the clipboard doesn't just get the data in the native format used by that application; it gets it in as many different formats as the application can provide. This gives the clipboard a sort of "backup plan" when pasting the data into other applications. Less sophisticated formats may not contain as much of the original data as the native format, but they are likely to be understood by a greater number of applications—and something is better than nothing.

For example, when you copy text from a rich text document in TextEdit, the Mac clipboard obtains this text in as many formats as it can, from the basic (string) to the richest (Rich Text Format, or RTF). It does this so that when you paste this text into another application, the receiving application can pick whichever format is best for it. For instance, Microsoft Word understands RTF data, so it will ask the clipboard for this because RTF contains not only character data but also lots of valuable style information that Word can put to good use. An application such as Terminal would take the UTF-8 encoded character data, because that's the richest format it can understand and use. An elderly, Carbon-based application that doesn't support Unicode text would make do with MacRoman-encoded text, with any characters outside of that encoding being lost altogether.

Finding Out What's on the Clipboard

The `clipboard info` command returns some information about the contents of the clipboard, as shown in the following example:

```
set the clipboard to 50000
clipboard info
--> {{integer, 4}}
```

The result shows that the clipboard contains 4 bytes of integer data. Next, here's an example of the clipboard information after copying some text from a rich text document in TextEdit:

```
clipboard info
--> {{Unicode text, 1142}, {scrap styles, 62}, {string, 571},
    {uniform styles, 564}, {«class ut16», 1144}, {«class utf8», 575},
    {«class RTF », 914}}
```

The result is a list describing all the data formats TextEdit used to place a single piece of data on the clipboard. It shows that the basic character information is available as MacRoman-encoded text (`string`) or as Unicode text in three different encodings (`Unicode text`, `«class ut16»`, and `«class utf8»`). Also, some separate style information is available (`scrap styles` and `uniform styles`) for applications that know how to combine this with one of the previous character-only formats. Finally, the data is available in RTF (`«class RTF »`), which combines both character and style information in a single format.

Getting Specific Types of Data from the Clipboard

Although the the `clipboard` command tries to return clipboard data in a format AppleScript can use, sometimes you want to retrieve data in one of the other available formats. You can specify which of the available formats you want by using the optional as parameter. For example, if RTF data is available, you might want to retrieve it so you can write it to a file:

```
set rtf_data to the clipboard as «class RTF »
set the_file to choose file name default name "untitled.rtf"
set file_ID to open for access the_file with write permission
write rtf_data to file_ID
close access file_ID
```

Setting the Clipboard Data

Your scripts can set the contents of the clipboard in several different ways: by using cut and copy commands in applications that provide them, by using Standard Additions' set the `clipboard to` command, and by using GUI Scripting to manipulate the application's Edit menu directly. The following sections look at each of these techniques in turn.

Using the *cut, copy,* and *paste* Commands in Applications

Some applications define cut, copy, and paste commands that perform the same operations as the standard Cut, Copy, and Paste menu options in their Edit menus. For example, Adobe Photoshop's copy command (not to be confused with AppleScript's own copy ... to ... statement) will copy the user's current selection to the clipboard. The following example copies the selection in the front Photoshop document to the clipboard,

```
tell application id "com.adobe.photoshop"
    activate
    copy
end tell
```

while this example does the reverse:

```
tell application id "com.adobe.photoshop"
    activate
    paste
end tell
```

Notice that the first command is activate. Clipboard-related operations require that the application you copy from or paste to is the frontmost application.

Other applications define their own version of the copy and paste commands. The following example copies the current selection in the front document in Word 2008 to the clipboard. The command in Word is copy object, and the direct parameter is selection:

```
tell application "Microsoft Word"
    copy object selection
end tell
```

Script 23–6 shows how to convert an RGB Adobe Illustrator document to a CMYK document. It does this by copying all the artwork from the current document (presumably an RGB one) and pasting it into a newly created CMYK document.

Script 23–6.

```
1. tell application id "com.adobe.illustrator"
2.     set selected of every page item of document 1 to true
3.     activate
4.     copy
5.     make new document with properties {color space:CMYK}
6.     paste
7. end tell
```

Note that in the preceding example, the script is responsible for two critical tasks. The first task, performed on line 2, is to select the items that need to be copied. (To keep things simple, we'll assume that all page items are already visible and unlocked.) The second task, performed on line 3, is to activate the Illustrator application so that the subsequent copy and paste commands work correctly.

Using the *set the clipboard to* Command

Use the set the clipboard to command to set the contents of the clipboard to a string or other value:

```
set the clipboard to "Paste me!"
```

The following script sets the clipboard to the short version of the date:

```
set the_date_string to short date string of (current date)
set the clipboard to the_date_string
```

Using GUI Scripting

You can usually copy selections from any application by using GUI Scripting to manipulate the application's Edit menu directly. The example project in the next section shows how you can do this.

Example Project: Creating PDF Cuttings from Selections in Preview

Finally, you are going to put into practice some of the knowledge you gained, by creating a neat little utility script to enhance Apple's Preview application.

You may already be familiar with Mac OS X's "clippings" feature, which lets you drag a text selection from an application on to your desktop to create a .textClipping file. While Preview allows you to create text clippings from PDF documents this way, it only works for selections made with the text selection tool (Tools ➤ Text Tool). Wouldn't it be useful if you could turn marquee selections into file "cuttings" just as easily? With AppleScript's help, you can.

Script 23–7 shows the code used to create "cuttings" from PDF documents in Preview. When run, it copies a selection you've made with Preview's marquee selection tool (Tools ➤ Select Tool) and saves it to a file you specify.

> **NOTE:** To run this script, you must have GUI Scripting support enabled on your Mac. See the "Controlling Applications with GUI Scripting" section earlier in the chapter for more information.

Script 23–7.

```
1. -- Use GUI Scripting to click on Edit -> Copy in Preview's menu bar
2. tell application "Preview" to activate
3. tell application "System Events"
4.    tell application process "Preview"
5.       click menu item "Copy" of menu "Edit" of menu bar item "Edit" of menu bar 1
6.    end tell
7. end tell

8. -- Get the PDF data from the clipboard
9. delay 1
10. activate
```

```
11. try
12.    set pdf_data to the clipboard as «class PDF »
13. on error number -1700 -- The clipboard doesn't contain any PDF data
14.    display alert "Please make a marquee selection " & ¬
              "in a PDF document in Preview, then try again." as warning
15.    return
16. end try

17. -- Write the PDF data to file
18. set destination_file to choose file name default name "cutting.pdf"
19. set file_ID to open for access destination_file with write permission
10. set eof file_ID to 0
21. write pdf_data to file_ID as «class PDF »
22. close access file_ID
23. tell application "Finder"
24.    set file type of file destination_file to "PDF "
25. end tell

26. -- Preview the new file
27. tell application "Preview" to open destination_file
```

> **TIP:** If you're a fan of Mac OS X's built-in Script menu, save this script as `Make PDF`
> `Cutting.scpt` in the `~/Library/Scripts/Applications/Preview/` folder. Now the
> script will conveniently appear in the Script menu whenever Preview is active. See Chapter 4 for
> more information on the Mac OS X Script menu.

Let's now look at how this script works.

Because Preview isn't yet scriptable, you have to use GUI Scripting to trigger its Edit ➤
Copy menu item directly. Line 2 brings the Preview application to the front so that its
graphical interface is active. Lines 3 to 7 use System Events' GUI Scripting features to
"click" Preview's Copy menu item. To keep this example simple, the script will assume
that the user has remembered to open a file and make a marquee selection in it before
running it. Preview's lack of proper scripting support would make this difficult to check
automatically anyway.

Line 9 makes the script wait for a second before continuing. Without a brief pause here,
I found that the the `clipboard` command would sometimes raise an error, as if it didn't
have time to catch up with the recent change to the clipboard. It's not an elegant or
foolproof way to make the script behave (it's what experienced scripters would call a
kludge), but it seems to do the trick here.

The `activate` command on line 10 brings the current application—that is, the one
running the script—back to the front before using the the `clipboard` command.

Line 12 uses the the `clipboard` command to get the raw PDF data (`«class PDF »`) from
the clipboard. If the clipboard doesn't contain any PDF data—perhaps the user selected
part of a JPEG file, not a PDF file like they're supposed to do—the the `clipboard`
command will raise a coercion error, number –1700, instead. If that happens, the
surrounding `try` block will catch this error, tell the user there's a problem, and stop the
script from going any further.

Lines 18 to 25 create a new PDF file on disk. Line 18 asks the user to choose the name and location for the new PDF file, and lines 19 to 22 write the raw PDF data to this file using the commands in Standard Additions' File Read/Write suite. (These command are discussed in detail in Chapter 17, if you need to refresh your memory.) Lines 23 to 25 use the Finder to set the new file's file type code to "PDF ". This bit isn't absolutely essential—as long as the file's name includes a .pdf extension, then Mac OS X will know it's a PDF file. However, if the user forgets to add a .pdf extension when choosing a new file name, the OS can still work out that it's a PDF file by looking at its file type.

Finally, line 26 tells Preview to open the new file so the user can look at it. Even though Preview isn't scriptable, it can understand the basic run, activate, open, and quit commands that all Mac applications should understand.

TESTING TIP

When testing this script, you can insert the following temporary line after line 9 to check what types of data have just been put on the clipboard:

```
return clipboard info
```

The value in AppleScript Editor's Result area will probably look something like this:

```
{{picture, 33546}, {TIFF picture, 29542}, {«class PDF », 59627}}
```

Notice how the clipboard contains PICT and TIFF versions of the copied data, as well as the obvious PDF version, so that other applications will have a range of formats from which to choose. For example, a bitmap graphics editor probably won't understand PDF data, but it can use TIFF or PICT data just fine. For this project, what we're interested in is the PDF data, which is indicated by the «class PDF » entry. If you don't see «class PDF » in the list, it's probably because the front document in Preview isn't a PDF, so you'll need to open one that is. Once you're finished testing this part of the script, remember to delete or comment out this temporary line so that the rest of the script can execute.

TIP: If you find this script useful, why not expand it to create plain text, RTF, and TIFF cuttings as well as PDF cuttings? Use the clipboard info command to find out which types of data are available on the clipboard—Unicode text, «class RTF », TIFF picture, and/or «class PDF »—and create a separate .txt, .rtf, .tif, and/or .pdf file for each one that's found.

Summary

This chapter has provided you with a tour around some of the useful AppleScript-related amenities available to you in Mac OS X: integrating with the Services menu, running scripts automatically at specific times or in response to file system changes, controlling nonscriptable applications by directly manipulating their graphical interfaces, and working with the Mac OS X clipboard.

In the next chapter we will put AppleScript to serious use, automating the popular Apple iWork and Microsoft Office application suites.

Chapter 24

Scripting iWork and Office

While AppleScript is always great for fun jobs such as organizing your iTunes playlists or iPhoto albums, for many scripters it is a key tool for automating more serious tasks too. In this chapter, we will be looking at how AppleScript can be used to manipulate two important office application suites on Mac OS X: Apple's iWork, a relative newcomer to the Mac scene, and the venerable Microsoft Office, which dates back to the days of System 7 and is still going strong today.

As these application suites are rather large and complicated, we won't cover every single application in comprehensive detail. Instead, we will mostly focus on iWork's Pages and Keynote applications, and Entourage and Excel from Microsoft Office, with a brief look at Numbers and Word along the way.

Scripting iWork

Apple's office productivity suite is called iWork and it is targeted to home users, small businesses, and professionals working in education. The suite features a word processor (Pages), a spreadsheet (Numbers), and a tool for professional presentations (Keynote). All three titles ship with a variety of stationery and templates that can be extended. The whole iWork suite supports import and export of Microsoft Office documents and ties heavily into Apple's iLife product.

We will not cover every aspect of iWork scripting here, as that would fill a long chapter on its own. However, the following sections will give a decent overview of iWork's two most-used applications, Pages and Keynote; enough for home, business, and university users of those two applications to get started automating their tasks. A quick introduction to Numbers' scripting features will be given as well.

> **NOTE:** The current version at the time of writing is iWork '09.

Since iWork does not feature macros like Microsoft Office, the only way to extend a workflow is by using AppleScript. The following pages give you information on what is and what is not possible with each application.

Scripting Pages

Pages is a word processor that integrates a page layout application. The application comes with more than 180 templates designed by Apple, making it easy to create documents that range from simple letters to brochures and newsletters.

Pages' latest major upgrade—version 4—includes a variety of interesting additions, including full-screen editing, dynamic outlines, and native support for MathType and EndNote (third-party applications used to write technical papers).

This section will give you some quick snippet examples on how to create new Pages documents, work with the documents' text, and make use of the new features that have been recently introduced to Pages.

Creating a New Document

When you create a new document in Pages using the File menu, the Template Chooser appears. Similarly, when creating a document via AppleScript, you need to specify a template to create a new document successfully. The following script shows you how to create a new document based on a template and put some text inside the document's body:

```
tell application "Pages"
    make new document with properties {template name:"Blank"}
    set body text of document 1 to "This is my first example with Pages"
end tell
```

The template name property is implemented as a write-only property. This means that it is not possible to find out what the current document's template is via scripting. Also, you can only set this property during a make new document ... command. The explanation for this behavior lies in the way Pages uses templates. A template can only be set once, when the document is created. We will later see that Keynote is built around a different concept, which uses themes. A document's theme can be changed any time; however, a template can only be set at the document's creation.

A Pages document is divided into different sections. Figure 24–1 provides an overview of the main scriptable parts of a Pages document.

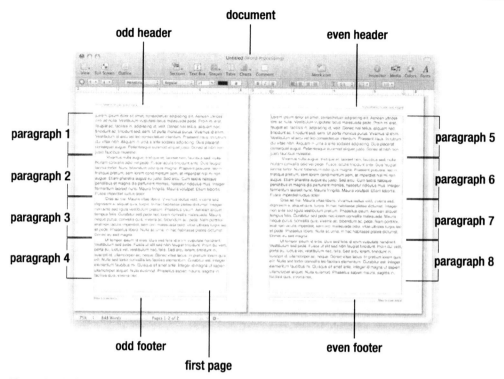

Figure 24–1. *Overview of a Pages document*

Working with a Document's Paragraphs

This section shows you how to create different paragraphs within the document's body text.

In an application like TextEdit, you can add a new line by using a command like the following:

```
tell application "TextEdit"
    make new paragraph ¬
        at end of paragraphs of document 1 ¬
        with data ("This is my text" & return)
end tell
```

This command also works in Pages to add new text inside the document. However, the make command does not set the cursor to the end of the inserted text, which is a requirement for a command like insert page break. Therefore, it is recommended that you use the set command if needed. Be aware that the set command replaces text if there is already content at the specified paragraph:

```
tell application "Pages"
    tell document 1
        set last paragraph to "The new text." & return
```

```
      end tell
end tell
```

Script 24–1 sets the content of different paragraphs within the document. After adding each paragraph, it starts a new page by telling Pages to insert a page break after the placed text.

Script 24–1.

```
tell application "Pages"
    tell (make new document with properties {template name:"Blank"})
        set paragraph 1 to "Pages Version 4 Features"
        tell body text to insert page break
        set paragraph 2 to "Full-screen view. When your desktop is cluttered, " & ¬
            "it can be hard to focus on what you're writing."
        tell body text to insert page break
        set paragraph 3 to "Dynamic outlines. It's easier to write when " & ¬
            "your ideas are structured."
        tell body text to insert page break
        set paragraph 4 to "Mail merge with Numbers. Now it's even easier " & ¬
            "to address invitations, create invoices, personalize letters, " & ¬
            "and build mailing lists."
        tell body text to insert page break
        set paragraph 5 to "Enhanced Template Chooser. Find inspiration for " & ¬
            "your writing or design project even faster."
        tell body text to insert page break
        set paragraph 6 to "More ways to share. Share your Pages documents " & ¬
            "with anyone on a Mac or PC."
    end tell
end tell
```

When you run this script, the result will be a six-page document containing one paragraph of text on each page.

Before we move on, we are quickly going to format the first page's content. Script 24–2 sets the font type and size for the first paragraph. Furthermore, it sets the paragraph's shadow and bold properties to true, and changes its alignment property to center the whole paragraph. After the formatting is done, the document will be saved as Examples.pages in the system's Shared folder.

Script 24–2.

```
tell application "Pages"
    tell paragraph 1 of document 1
        set font size to 45
        set font name to "Times New Roman"
        set bold to true
        set shadow to true
        set alignment to center
    end tell
    save document 1 in POSIX file "/Users/Shared/Examples.pages"
end tell
```

> **NOTE:** When using the `save` command, the file name extension in the path string can be `.pages` (Pages), `.txt` (plain-text), `.doc` (Word), or any other document type that Pages can export to.

Figure 24–2 shows how the first two pages should look after you run Script 24–1 and Script 24–2.

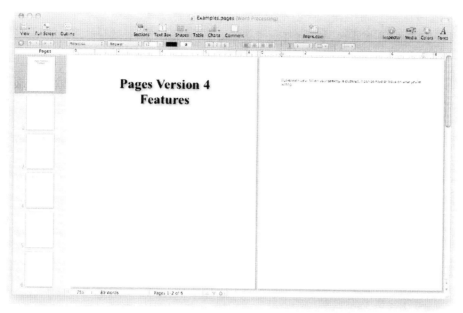

Figure 24–2. *The first two pages of the* `Examples.pages` *document*

Adding Headers and Footers to a Document

The text used in Script 24–1 to create an example document is taken from Apple's iWork web site. To give Apple credit for its work, headers and footers with the appropriate information need to be added. As shown in Figure 24–1, Pages can distinguish between odd and even footers. To use different headers and footers on opposite pages, the Boolean property `different left and right pages` needs to be set beforehand. If you want to place the same header or footer on all of your pages, all headers or footers are treated and addressable as an odd header or odd footer.

Script 24–3 shows how to add headers and footers and align them. Because the document created in the previous example has a nice cover page, Script 24–3 sets the first page to be different insofar as the script does not place any type of header or footer on that page.

Script 24–3.

```
tell application "Pages"
    tell every section of document 1
        set different first page to true
        set different left and right pages to true
        set odd header to "iWork '09"
        set even header to "Pages Features"
        set odd footer to "http://www.apple.com/iwork/pages/"
        set even footer to "(c) Apple Inc., 2010"
        set alignment of odd footer to left
        set alignment of even footer to right
    end tell
end tell
```

Drawing Shapes in Pages

In Pages '09 you are able to script 12 different shapes to be drawn. Script 24–4 shows how to draw shapes within a document.

Script 24–4.

```
tell application "Pages"
    tell body text of document 1
        make new shape at after word 1 of paragraph 2 ¬
            with properties {shape type:diamond, name:"Shape of a diamond"}
        set object text of shape "Shape of a diamond" to "I am a diamond"
        set shadow of shape "Shape of a diamond" to true
        set shadow color of shape "Shape of a diamond" to {25000, 0, 25000}
    end tell
end tell
```

Using the command make new shape ... and providing two properties, shape type and name, a new graphic is drawn in the document. In the script I placed a diamond shape after the first word of the second paragraph. Pages' dictionary has a list of all supported shape types. After that, the script adds a shadow to the diamond shape, changing the color of the shadow from its default black to purple.

The drawn diamond shape should look like the one shown in Figure 24–3.

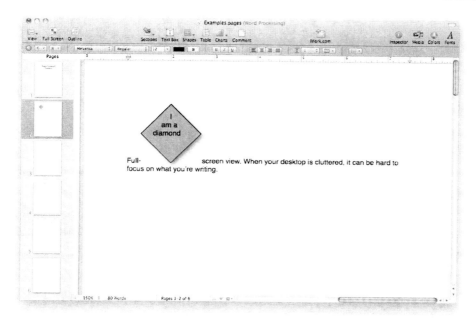

Figure 24–3. *Examples.pages with a diamond shape*

Adding Tables and Charts

The following example shows how to add a table to a document:

```
tell application "Pages"
    activate
    tell document 1
        add table data {{"Year", "Visual Basic", "AppleScript"}, ¬
            {2008, 100, 140}, {2009, 80, 220}} with header column and header row
    end tell
end tell
```

To create a new table, the command add table is used. The data for the table is provided as a list of lists, with each sublist holding the values for one row. If the header column and header row parameters are true, Pages will format the first column and first row as headings.

Figure 24–4 shows how the finished table will look.

Year	Visual Basic	AppleScript
2008	100	140
2009	80	220

Figure 24–4. *The created table in Pages*

Let's now use the same data to create a chart.

A chart can be created with the add chart command. Row names and column names need to be specified, followed by the data the chart needs to process. The type parameter can draw a chart in more than 15 ways. The last parameter that needs to be set is the group by option. You can group the result either by row or by column. The following example uses the same data for creating the chart that we used in the preceding "add table" script:

```
tell application "Pages"
    activate
    tell document 1
        add chart row names {"2008", "2009"} ¬
            column names {"Visual Basic", "AppleScript"} ¬
            data {{100, 140}, {80, 220}} ¬
            type "vertical_bar_3d" group by "row"
    end tell
end tell
```

After applying the preceding script to a new document, the chart should look like the one shown in Figure 24–5.

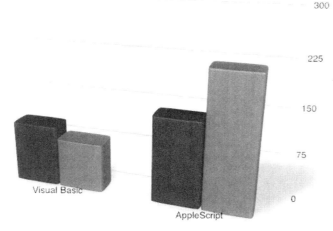

Figure 24–5. *The created chart in Pages*

Tips for Scripting Pages

As previously mentioned, a recently introduced feature to Pages is full-screen editing. Unfortunately, a couple of Pages' features, like uploading to iWork.com, can only be automated by scripting clicks in Pages' Share menu. To make sure Pages' Full Screen feature does not block your GUI scripting, you can simply deactivate it with the following command:

```
tell application "Pages"
    tell window of document 1
        set full screen to false
    end tell
end tell
```

> **NOTE:** Alongside the latest upgrade, iWork will be extended in the future with a web-based, up-in-the-cloud document repository for sharing and reviewing iWork '09 documents, simply called `iWork.com` (this service is still in beta at the time of writing).

The other tip is quite useful if your workflow includes printing. If you have to change the document's margins for an appropriate printout, you can easily achieve this in a single line:

```
tell application "Pages"
    tell document 1
        set {top margin, bottom margin, left margin, right margin} to {1, 1, 1, 1}
    end tell
end tell
```

Scripting Keynote

Keynote lets you create presentations and ships with over 40 built-in themes. All slides can be extended with tables, 3D charts, and shapes. In addition, you can embed QuickTime videos. Mac OS X's Core Graphics enhancements provide the technology base for the application's cinematic animations that are used for slide and text transitions.

> **CAUTION:** You will find out that typical AppleScript commands won't work in Keynote, which I am going to highlight where needed.

Creating a Slideshow

To get started, let's create a new presentation (`make new slideshow`) using Keynote's default theme, and start and stop the slideshow. The reference returned by the `make` command can be used with the `start` and `stop slideshow` commands as illustrated in the following short example script:

```
tell application "Keynote"
    tell (make new slideshow)
        start
        delay 2
        stop slideshow
    end tell
end tell
```

The Keynote presentation software is currently in its fifth revision. Similar to other presentation software titles on the market, Keynote already includes a number of themes for slides, and others are commercially available or free of charge. To get an overview of themes that are currently installed on your system and that can be used for scripting, the next section will show you how to create your own Theme Chooser.

TIP: The iWorkCommunity web site, at `http://www.iworkcommunity.com`, is a great place to get add-ons and templates for Keynote and other applications of the iWork suite.

Choosing a Theme

By default, Keynote allows you to create presentations with the default sizes of 800 × 600 or 1024 × 768 pixels and up to 1920 × 1080 pixels with the newer HD themes. It is still possible to change the resolution by setting a custom size from the Inspector palette's Document tab, after you have created the new document. In cases where you want to use the machine's screen for the presentation instead of a projector, you'll want to create the presentation to use the machine's full screen resolution.

Script 24–5 shows how to obtain the current machine's main screen resolution and create a new full-screen slideshow using the chosen theme.

NOTE: In order for the following examples to work, make sure that Keynote doesn't have the Theme Chooser window open on the screen.

Script 24–5.

```
set display_info to do shell script "system_profiler SPDisplaysDataType | " & ¬
    "grep 'Main Display:' -B 4 | grep 'Resolution:'"
set theme_width to (word 2 of display_info) as number
set theme_height to (word 4 of display_info) as number

tell application "Keynote"
    activate
    set the_selection  to choose from list (get name of every appTheme)
    if the_selection  is false then error number -128 -- User canceled
    set chosen_theme to item 1 of the_selection
    set this_slideshow to make new slideshow ¬
        with data {theme:chosen_theme, slideSize:{theme_width, theme_height}}
end tell
```

The screen resolution is retrieved with the help of the command-line version of the System Profiler application, `system_profiler`. By using the `grep` tool to extract only the Resolution entry of System Profiler's Main Display part, we get a string similar to this one: "Resolution: 1280 x 800".

NOTE: Please refer to Chapter 27 for additional information on how to use command-line utilities from within AppleScript with do `shell script`.

Now we can simply take the second and fourth word of that string. Since the `slideSize` data of a slideshow object can only understand integer numbers, we need to convert them to numbers.

Note that making a new slideshow requires a `with data` parameter rather than the more common `with properties` parameter that is used in other applications.

Figure 24–6 shows how the created Theme Chooser dialog box will look.

Figure 24–6. *Theme Chooser created with AppleScript*

Filling Slides with Content

Once we have successfully created a presentation, the next step is to fill the presentation with content. However, there are a couple of things you need to be aware of before you begin. First of all, when a new slideshow is created, the first slide will be created automatically, so you can start adding content to it straightaway.

Secondly, you can add more slides with the following command:

```
tell application "Keynote"
    tell slideshow 1
        make new slide at end of slides
    end tell
end tell
```

However, because of a bug in Keynote '09, the `make new slide ...` command does not return a valid slide reference that you can use in other commands. For example, the following code will not run:

```
tell application "Keynote"
    tell slideshow 1
        tell (make new slide at the end of slides)
            set title to "My title"
            set body to "This is my example text"
        end tell
    end tell
end tell
```

To work around this problem, I recommended you first create a new slide and afterward refer to it by position when setting its content:

```
tell application "Keynote"
    tell slideshow 1
        make new slide at the end of slides
        set my_slide to last slide
        set my_slide's title to "My title"
        set my_slide's body to "This is my example text"
    end tell
end tell
```

In Script 24–6 we are going to create a white-themed, 800 × 600 pixel slideshow with four slides. I will show you how to set the title and body on each individual slide. After that I will save the file as a Keynote document in the system's Shared folder.

Script 24–6.

```
tell application "Keynote"
    tell (make new slideshow with data {theme:"White", slideSize:{800, 600}})
        tell slide 1
            set title to "Keynote features"
            set body to "(c) Apple, Inc."
        end tell
        make new slide at the end of slides
        tell slide 2
            set title to "Magic Move"
            set body to "The new Magic Move feature lets you add " & ¬
                "a sophisticated animation using a quick and simple process."
        end tell
        make new slide at the end of slides
        tell slide 3
            set title to "Enhanced Theme Chooser"
            set body to "Now choosing the right theme " & ¬
                "for your presentation is easier than ever."
        end tell
        make new slide at the end of slides
        tell slide 4
            set title to "Text- and object-based transitions"
            set body to "Let your words and graphics really play onscreen."
        end tell
    end tell
    save slideshow 1 in POSIX file "/Users/Shared/Examples.key"
end tell
```

Figure 24–7 shows how the generated slideshow document will look when the script is run.

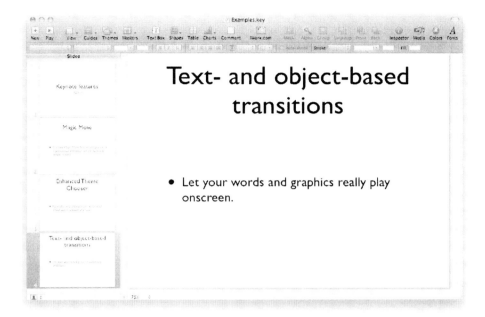

Figure 24–7. *The newly created Keynote slideshow*

> **NOTE:** In comparison to Pages, the save command in Keynote only allows presentations to be saved in the default .key format and cannot be used to export them into different formats. At the time of writing, the only way to automate exporting presentations to PDFs or another format is by using GUI Scripting to control Keynote's File menu.

Working with Transitions

Another challenge when scripting Keynote is working with transitions. All transition effects are listed in the Transition table of the Inspector palette, as shown in Figure 24–8.

Figure 24–8. *Keynote transitions*

Unfortunately, when scripting Keynote, the names of the slideTransition elements are different from the names that appear in the Inspector palette. Instead of identifying a slide transition by its human-readable name, you have to use its unique identifier. For example the Text transition named "Swing" is addressable in AppleScript as "apple:ca-swing".

Since this is quite confusing, Script 24–7 shows how to create a Transition Chooser similar to the Theme Chooser that lists all available transitions with their scriptable name.

Script 24–7.

```
1. tell application "Keynote"
2.    activate
3.    set the_selection to choose from list (get name of every appTransition)
4.    if the_selection is false then error number -128 -- User canceled
5.    set chosen_transition to item 1 of the_selection
6.    tell slideshow 1
7.       set appTransition of slideTransition of every slide to chosen_transition
8.    end tell
9. end tell
```

First, line 3 generates a list of all available transition names and displays them in a dialog box for the user to choose from, shown in Figure 24–9. After a transition is chosen, line 7 applies it to every slide of the document.

Figure 24–9. *The Transition Chooser dialog box*

Scripting an Advanced Screen Reader

One of the new features introduced with Mac OS X 10.6 is an enhanced version of the text-to-speech command-line say utility. Among other improvements, the enhanced say can create files in several different audio formats by just giving the desired file name extension.

Script 24–8 shows you how to export the text of a Keynote slideshow to an audio file. The script uses Apple's default AAC (Advanced Audio Coding) format by providing the .m4a extension. This creates a file encoded with 32 kbps in mono quality.

Script 24–8.

```
1. tell application "Keynote"
2.    set slideshow_content to "Presentation name: " & (name of slideshow 1) & space
3.    tell slideshow 1
4.       repeat with i from 1 to count slides
5.          set slideshow_content to slideshow_content & (title of slide i) & space
6.          set slideshow_content to slideshow_content & (body of slide i) & space
7.          set slideshow_content to slideshow_content & (notes of slide i) & space
8.       end repeat
9.    end tell
10. end tell
```

```
11. set file_path to POSIX path of (choose file name with prompt ¬
        "Save the presentation's content as:" default name "My Presentation.m4a")
12. if file_path does not end with ".m4a" then set file_path to file_path & ".m4a"
13. do shell script "say -o" & space & quoted form of file_path & space & ¬
        quoted form of slideshow_content
```

First, line 2 gets the slideshow's name. After that, lines 4 to 8 work through all slides and get the slide's title, body text, and speaker notes. The results are assembled into a string stored in the slideshow_content variable, ready to be passed to the command-line say tool.

Line 11 displays a Save dialog box that prompts the user to specify the output file. (The choose file name command is covered in Chapter 16.)

Once the path to the .m4a output file is obtained (lines 11 and 12), line 13 executes the Unix say command through Standard Additions' do shell script command to create the compressed audio file from the slideshow's content.

Tips for Scripting Keynote

The look and feel of a slide is defined in its master slide. A newly created slide automatically inherits its appearance from the master slide when it is created. By default, the first slide in a slideshow inherits from the "Title & Subtitles" master slide, while all following slides inherit from the "Title & Bullets" master slide.

If you want to change the look of an individual slide, you can simply set the value of the slide's master property to a new master slide reference. Script 24–9 shows you how to change the format of the first slide from the default "Title & Subtitles" to "Title & Bullets."

Script 24–9.

```
tell application "Keynote"
    activate
    tell slideshow 1
        set master of slide 1 to master slide "Title & Bullets"
    end tell
end tell
```

Scripting Numbers

Numbers is an application that comes with over 30 templates to create visually appealing spreadsheets. It enables you to embed pictures and videos inside tables. The built-in help gives an overview and explanations for more than 250 functions to apply to the content of cells. An additional new feature in Numbers '09 is the support of AppleScript.

The following sections will give you a basic demonstration of how to interact with specific cells of a document and how to change a cell's value once a document has been created.

NOTE: At the time of writing, it is not possible to create new documents in Numbers 2.0 via scripting, unless you use GUI Scripting. This also applies to generating charts or graphs from data contained in a sheet. Hopefully these shortcomings will be fixed in a future release.

Creating Sheets and Tables

One of Numbers' concepts is to have multiple sheets inside a table and multiple tables inside a sheet. New sheets and tables can be created with the make command, optionally specifying properties such as the sheet's name or the number of rows and columns in the table:

```
tell application "Numbers"
    activate
    tell document 1
        tell (make new sheet with properties {name:"my new sheet"})
            make new table with properties {name:"my new table", row count:4, column ¬
 count:4}
        end tell
    end tell
end tell
```

Running this script on a new empty document results in the following output:

```
--> table "my new table" of sheet "my new sheet" of document "Untitled"
        of application "Numbers"
```

Working with Cells

The following example sets the value of specific elements inside our newly created table:

```
tell application "Numbers"
    activate
    tell document 1
        tell sheet "my new sheet"
            tell table "my new table"
                -- setting value for column "B"
                set value of cell 2 of row 1 to "units sold"
                set value of cell 2 of row 2 to 200
                set value of cell 2 of row 3 to 600
                set value of cell 2 of row 4 to 700
                -- setting value for column "C"
                set value of cell 3 of row 1 to "year"
                set value of cell 3 of row 2 to 2007
                set value of cell 3 of row 3 to 2008
                set value of cell 3 of row 4 to 2009
            end tell
        end tell
    end tell
    save document 1 in POSIX file "/Users/Shared/Examples.numbers"
end tell
```

As you can see, a `table` element contains `row` elements, which in turn contain `cell` elements. To modify the contents of each cell, I set its `value` property.

The `save` command at the end of the script saves the document in the `Shared` folder. As with Pages, it is possible to save the document in formats other than `.numbers` by using different file name extensions. For example, to save it as an Excel sheet, just use the `.xls` extension.

Figure 24–10 shows how the modified spreadsheet document will look.

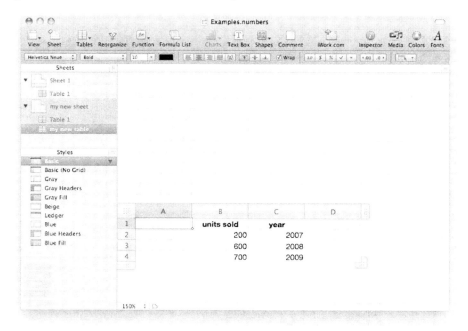

Figure 24–10. *The edited Numbers document*

Unfortunately, the Numbers application still suffers from a lack of important spreadsheet features like pivot tables, which holds it back from being heavily used in a professional environment. More advanced spreadsheet functionality can be achieved using Microsoft's Excel, as explained in the next section.

Scripting Microsoft Office

It has been claimed that, outside of Apple itself, Microsoft has the largest Mac developer team in the world. Certainly, the Office for Mac application suite is a huge undertaking and, despite its obvious and natural links to its bigger brother, is definitely a suite of Macintosh applications. The Office for Mac applications stick as closely as they can to the Apple Human Interface Guidelines and leverage core OS X technologies throughout, including AppleScript. Far gone are the days when the AppleScript dictionary in Microsoft Excel was limited to little more than a `do visual basic ...` command.

Microsoft Entourage was written from the ground up as a Mac application and has made very effective use of AppleScript from the start. Microsoft Word, Excel, and PowerPoint, having a much older history, had some catching up to do, but with the introduction of Office 2004 for Mac, they made a huge leap forward. Office 2008 for Mac enhanced and improved the scriptability of all the applications—a necessary move in a release that saw the removal of the Visual Basic for Applications (VBA) support that had previously been the mainstay of most Office scripting.

Whatever the past, AppleScript is here to stay in Office for Mac. The developers of Office for Mac, the Macintosh Business Unit at Microsoft, make massive use of AppleScript routines for automated testing of the Office applications during development, so it is a key tool for them too.

Is it perfect? Certainly not—there are bugs, oddities, and curiously missing features in the implementation in all the applications. However, it remains the most scriptable suite of applications available for the Mac so far. What I present here barely scratches the surface of what is possible. Writing a full tutorial on any of the applications could fill a complete book, let alone part of one chapter. However, I hope to give you a taste of what can be done and a small step on the way to help you start your own voyage of discovery. If the next few pages inspire you to try writing your own script for the Office applications, I will have achieved my objective. Enjoy yourself, and don't be afraid to step out on your own and just "try it."

I haven't attempted to cover all aspects of any of the applications in the Office for Mac suite. I give fairly thorough introductions to Entourage and Excel, barely touch on Word, and do not mention PowerPoint at all. I made this selection based simply on what I judge to be the most-used applications and the areas in which scripting may benefit the most people. I'm very sorry if my selections don't match your usage or expectation, but in the very limited space available in this chapter, some fairly major sacrifices had to be made.

I have used Microsoft Office 2008 for Mac as my base point for the scripts presented. Most, if not all of them, will work perfectly well in Office 2004 for Mac. I point out in the text where significant differences exist in the implementation. Any versions older than Office 2004 will have considerable difficulties running almost all the scripts included here, and you are probably better off skipping to the next chapter if you use an earlier version. That is an unfortunate side effect of the continued development of AppleScript in Office for Mac—a side effect of an otherwise thrilling and encouraging trend.

Working with Microsoft Entourage

E-mail applications seem to be the most scripted applications around. Maybe this is because they are primarily a "productivity" application and so feature centrally in people's workflows, or maybe it is because e-mail application writers have a particular liking for AppleScript! Whatever the reason, there are hundreds of example scripts available on the Internet for a wide variety of e-mail applications. Obviously, in this section I am going to concentrate on Microsoft Entourage.

Entourage has great AppleScript support. You can script most activities the application can undertake, but scripting the interface is fairly limited. Unlike other Microsoft Office for Mac applications, Entourage has a fairly traditional AppleScript dictionary. The development of Entourage can be traced back through several releases to its roots in Outlook Express for Macintosh, and even before that to Claris Emailer because many of the development team members that wrote Claris Emailer joined Microsoft to work on Outlook Express for Mac.

As with other applications, start learning what is possible by exploring the AppleScript dictionary. Looking in there will reveal, apart from the standard and common suites, three Entourage-specific suites: the Entourage Contact suite, the Entourage Mail and News suite, and the Entourage Search suite. Unfortunately, the Entourage Search suite, while powerful and very useful for more complex scripts, is beyond the scope of what can be covered in a chapter of this size, so I will concentrate on the Contact and Mail and News suites.

Disable the Security Warning

Microsoft Entourage has a security feature built into it that will throw open a dialog box if any external application tries to automate the sending of a message. This is intended to forestall any malicious scripts, viruses, or other malware from using Entourage for their own nefarious purposes. An "external application," however, also includes a script being run deliberately by the current user, so to make use of Entourage's script ability, you need to disable this warning.

Open the Entourage preferences and select the Security pane. Make sure the first option box, "Warn before allowing an external application to send mail," is unchecked, as shown in Figure 24–11.

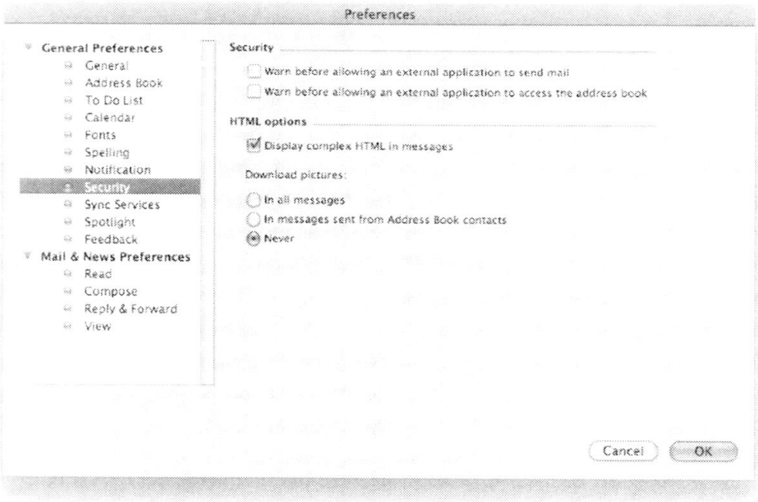

Figure 24–11. *Disabling the security warning*

You can now use scripts to create and send mail through Entourage. The additional risk involved in unchecking this option is almost insignificant. At this time there have been no examples of malware in the wild that can exploit Entourage.

Creating Messages

Look in the dictionary—there are two different types of message: incoming messages and outgoing messages. Both inherit the majority of their properties from the message class.

Like other objects, messages can be created with a simple make command; for example:

```
tell application "Microsoft Entourage" to make new outgoing message
```

This will create a completely empty "sent" message in the local drafts folder (the one under the "On My Computer" folder hierarchy). Obviously, other information can be added to the outgoing message so created, either at the same time the message is created or in separate script steps. Also, the location in which the message will be created can be specified in the make command. This command can be useful when scripting the importing of messages, for example, because the messages can be created in a particular folder rather than in the inbox. Indeed, a complete hierarchical folder structure could be created!

The command returns a unique by-ID reference that identifies the message so created. Storing the returned reference in a variable will allow the same message to be easily modified in future script steps. For example:

```
tell application "Microsoft Entourage"
    -- 'Import' is a top level folder under 'On My Computer'
    set new_message to make new outgoing message at folder "Import"
    set subject of new_message to "This is a new message"
end tell
```

> **TIP:** When passing locations to create a new message, you can refer to "special" folders (folders "Inbox", "Outbox", "Sent Items", "Drafts", "Deleted Items", "Junk E-mail") by their ID numbers (1 to 6 respectively). This will ensure that the same folder is always referenced whatever language option of Entourage the user is running.

The other option, more commonly used where a message is being created for actual sending and the user is expected to add information to the message before sending it, is to create a draft window instead of a message. This is an exact parallel to selecting **File** ➤ **New** ➤ **Mail Message** in the Entourage menus. A new draft window for writing a message is created and (by default) the addressing pane is activated.

This method has the disadvantage that no by-ID message reference is returned—the draft window is not a message until the window contents have been saved. Instead, the command returns a result containing a reference to the window by name (`window "untitled" of application "Microsoft Entourage"`—unless you passed a subject to the window when it was created). This returned result is not a lot of help, especially because it is possible for many windows to share the same name. A better approach is to remember that the window is always created as the frontmost window and can be addressed as window 1 in future script commands. As always, there is a tiny risk that the user could click another window to the front while the script is still operating, but there is little that can be done to prevent that.

So, without further ado, let's make a useful message. I'll assume that you want to create a message, attach a file, and send it to two "to" recipients and one "cc" recipient. By reading the AppleScript dictionary, you could probably come up with a script like Script 24–10.

Script 24–10.

```
1. set the_file_name to "test data.txt"
2. set the_file to alias ((path to desktop as text) & the_file_name)
3. tell application "Microsoft Entourage"
4.     set new_message to make new outgoing message at folder id 2
5.     set subject of new_message to "Here is the file you requested"
6.     set content of new_message to "Please find attached the file " & the_file_name
7.     make new attachment at end of new_message with properties {file:the_file}
8.     make new recipient at end of new_message with properties ¬
              {recipient type:to recipient, address:{display name:"Fred Flintstone", ¬
              address:"ff@hardrock.com.invalid"}}
9.     make new recipient at end of new_message with properties ¬
              {recipient type:to recipient, address:{display name:"Mickey", ¬
              address:"mmouse@disney.com.invalid"}}
10.    make new recipient at end of new_message with properties ¬
              {recipient type:cc recipient, address:{display name:"Shrek", ¬
              address:"shrek@dreamworks.com.invalid"}}
11. end tell
```

> **NOTE:** I have used a .invalid top-level domain (TLD) on the e-mail addresses used in these examples. .invalid is a reserved TLD defined by RFC 2606, and using it will avoid real domains getting "spammed" by your test messages as you develop these scripts.

The AppleScript dictionary tells you that attachments and recipients are elements of a message and implies that you have to make each one separately. It's long-winded, untidy, and inefficient (it uses a separate application call event for each line). What is worse, it won't work! Before I tell you what will work, and work much more efficiently, let's look at some of the detail in this script.

First, line 4 creates a new message in the outbox and will work whatever the outbox is called in your localized version of Entourage. The settings of the subject and content (lines 5 and 6) are fairly self-explanatory—you can put whatever text you want in these properties (subject to a length limit in the subject line).

The dictionary says that an attachment is an element of a message and is available for creation with a make new attachment ... command. This works very well (line 7). It needs the location of the file to be attached, which is accomplished by using the alias object obtained in line 2 as the new attachment's file property.

The dictionary also says that a recipient is an element of a message as well and you should be able to create one in the same way, but it doesn't work on lines 8 to 10! Entourage throws an error when you try to run this script: "Microsoft Entourage got an error: Can't make class recipient." It should work, it used to work, but there seems to be a new bug in Entourage 2008 that prevents it from working. The same syntax will still work if you apply it to a draft window, but it is broken for outgoing messages. It's just as well that we don't need it, but before we move on, let me point out another quirk of the Entourage AppleScript dictionary.

See the properties of the recipient we are trying to attach (lines 8 to 10)? It has two: recipient type and address. The value of the recipient type property can be to recipient, cc recipient, or bcc recipient—fairly straightforward so far. The value of the address property is a record with a class of address. This type of duplication of property and class names is common enough in AppleScript, and it causes little confusion because the one is the name of a property and the other is the class of that property. However, look at the properties of the address record class itself: a display name property and another address property! Therefore, two different properties called "address" exist, and it is only the fact that they are used in different contexts that prevents AppleScript from becoming totally confused. This does not always stop the user from being confused, though. You need to be careful how you use "address."

Some Shortcuts

Having shown you the way *not* to script message creation in Script 24–10, Script 24–11 shows what you can do.

Script 24–11.

```
1. set the_file_name to "test data.txt"
2. set the_file to alias ((path to desktop as text) & the_file_name)
3. tell application "Microsoft Entourage"
4.    set new_message to make new outgoing message at folder id 2 with properties ¬
            {subject:"Here is the file you requested", ¬
            content:"Please find attached the file " & the_file_name, ¬
            attachment:{the_file}, ¬
            recipient:{"Fred Flintstone <ff@hardrock.com.invalid>", ¬
                {display name:"Mickey", address:"mmouse@disney.com.invalid"}, ¬
                {recipient type:cc recipient, address:{display name:"Shrek", ¬
                address:"shrek@dreamworks.com.invalid"}}}}
5. end tell
```

This script is a lot more efficient. It sends only one command to Entourage instead of the seven that would have been made by Script 24–10. Better still, it actually works! Let's look at what we did a little more closely.

Line 4 starts off exactly the same as before, but we have now included a with properties parameter to set all the message properties and elements as the message is created instead of in separate code lines.

The subject and content properties are set in a similar manner to the first example, but now as properties of the record block passed to Entourage.

The attachment and recipient properties of the record are a little strange. According to the Entourage AppleScript dictionary, these are elements of a message, not properties, yet this code works! What has happened is that the developers have put in place a silent shortcut that can be used *only* at the time a message (or draft window or draft news window) is created. There is no hint of it in the dictionary and no way that you would know that this would work. It is something you will only discover by reading supplementary documentation, studying existing Entourage scripts, or asking other AppleScripters for advice.

The attachment property can take a single alias as its value, or can take a list of aliases. I prefer to stick with a list, even though it is a list of one in this case.

The recipient property is also unusual. It can take its data in any of three ways—Script 24–11 uses all three examples. The first method is to pass a text string containing the display name and e-mail address. The display name is optional, but if it is used, then the e-mail address has to be enclosed in "<...>" braces. You can pass as many of these text entries as you like in a simple string, delimited with commas. The second method is to use an address class record ({display name: "Mickey Mouse", address: "mickey@disney.com"}), which is convenient if you are assembling the addressee list from external data where the names and addresses are already separate. The third example uses the full recipient class record:

```
{recipient type:cc recipient, address:{display name:"Shrek",
    address:"shrek@dreamworks.com.invalid"}}
```

You need to use a record like this to define cc or bcc recipients—the recipient type created by the first two shortcuts is always a "to" recipient.

Many other properties could be set using this example—the account to be used, character sets, signatures, attachment encoding, and so forth. Entourage's outgoing message class defines over 40 different properties, but you can explore those on your own. This example will get you started with scripting messages.

> **TIP:** You can also send the message immediately after creating it by adding a simple final send new_message command before the end tell line. This will send the message using the standard method set up in Entourage already.

Working with Contacts

Just as messages can be contained in folders, contacts can be held in different address books. How many address books are available to the user depends on what types of accounts are set up. For POP, IMAP, and Hotmail accounts, there is only one address book—the one that appears in the "On My Computer" hierarchy.

However, if the user has Exchange accounts set up, there could be many address books available. There will certainly be at least two—the default "local" address book and the default Exchange address book. Depending on how Exchange is configured, there could be many more address books—they can even be nested address books within address books. Exchange address books have a special class of exchange address book that inherits all the properties of address book and adds just four more: account (a reference to which Exchange account "owns" the address book), category (more on categories later), kind (there are six different types of Exchange address book—see the AppleScript dictionary for a description of the "kind" constants), and URL (the path to the location of the address book on the server).

When scripting contacts, you can either specify which address book you want to use or, if you don't specify, use the default address book. This will be the primary address book of the default mail account. So, if your default mail account is of type POP, IMAP, or Hotmail, then the default address book is the one under "On My Computer." If your default mail account is an Exchange account, then the default address book is the first address book of that account (remember, Exchange accounts can have multiple address books!).

So, if we ask for every contact, we will get a list of contacts in the default address book. Alternatively, we can say every contact of address book 2, in which case that specific address book is targeted. If you specifically want to target the local address book, it is always address book ID 14.

Creating Contacts

Okay, let's create a new contact. Script 24–12 shows how.

Script 24–12.

```
tell application "Microsoft Entourage"
    make new contact with properties ¬
            {first name:"Billy", last name:"Baxter", nickname:"Bobo", ¬
            home address:{street address:"1 Apple Court", ¬
                        city:"Hemmingford Abbots", state:"Cambridgeshire", ¬
                        zip:"CB4 9HG", country:"UK"}, ¬
            category:{category "Family", category "Christmas Card", ¬
                        category "Private"}}
end tell
```

Making a new contact is pretty straightforward (although this example will run on your machine only if you have the three categories listed in the category property's value already defined!). This example uses only a few of the 73 different properties that can be got or set for a contact! Take a look through them all in the AppleScript dictionary. Many of them you will never use—those properties with furigana in the name will only ever be used for a contact that has been marked as Japanese Format in the Contact menu in Entourage. Others you will use very rarely (the "custom" fields, for example), but there is lots of stuff in there that can be used all the time.

When you looked through the AppleScript dictionary for a contact earlier, you may have noticed that there are two address properties for a contact—home address and work address. There is also a flag to determine which of these addresses is the default postal address (called, naturally enough, default postal address). All of these properties have their equivalent display in the GUI. The default postal address property can have one of three values, home, work, or other, which seems a little strange at first—with just two addresses available, how can the default postal address be anything else apart from home or work? The reason is that the same values (which are AppleScript constants) are used in other places; for applying to labels in e-mail addresses and IM addresses—these can be home, work, or other. The developers have simply reused these constants in this contact property.

Selecting and Changing Multiple Contacts

We have spent quite a bit of time creating new items in Entourage—let's look now at modifying some contacts in bulk.

Imagine, for example, that you have lots of contacts where the default postal address property wasn't set properly when the contacts were created—maybe you imported them from another personal information manager and this information wasn't available. It would be a tedious exercise to manually go through all your contacts looking for those misfiled contacts, so let's use the power of AppleScript to do it for us in Script 24–13.

Script 24–13.

```
1. tell application "Microsoft Entourage"
2.    set empty_address to ¬
         {city:"", country:"", state:"", street address:"", zip:""}
3.    set misfiled_contacts to ¬
         every contact whose home address is not empty_address ¬
         and business address is empty_address and default postal address is work
4.    repeat with this_contact in misfiled_contacts
5.       set default postal address of this_contact to home
6.    end repeat
7. end tell
```

This script starts by setting a variable to an empty postal address class record on line 2: set empty_address to {city:"", country:"", state:"", street address:"", zip:""}. We will use it in two places, so it is less typing and makes for more readable code to define it as a variable.

On line 3 we use that empty record and also see the power of the whose clause in Entourage. Instead of going through each contact individually and checking the home address, the business address, and the default postal address flag, we can do it all in one query. This command will return a list of contacts where the home address has some data in it, the business address doesn't, but the default address is set to work—obviously something is wrong in these contacts.

The repeat block in lines 4 to 6 simply loops through all the misfiled contacts that were found and sets the default postal address property to home. Remember to always use home and work as values for this property without quotes (line 5)—the default postal address is a constant, not a string. You can't say set default postal address ... to "home"—it will cause an error.

> **NOTE:** The Entourage developers haven't been entirely helpful with their naming conventions. The work address property is named `business address`, but the default postal address property has a value of `work`. This will likely cause you to make a few mistakes at first, until you get used to the names.

Setting Categories

This is a good place to mention categories, since we just used them without a proper introduction in Script 24–12. Categories are a great feature in Entourage. Any item in the Entourage database can have one or more categories assigned. They are really useful when used in conjunction with Saved Searches or used as a filter for selecting items in AppleScript.

Let's expand the script we wrote in Script 24–12 for creating a contact to do some error checking for categories that haven't been created yet. Script 24–14 shows the new and improved version.

Script 24–14.

```
1. tell application "Microsoft Entourage"
2.     set category_names to name of categories
3.     repeat with this_name in {"Family", "Christmas Card", "Private"}
4.         if this_name is not in category_names then
5.             make new category with properties {name:this_name}
6.         end if
7.     end repeat
8.     make new contact with properties { ¬
            first name:"Billy", last name:"Baxter", nickname:"Bobo", ¬
            home address:{street address:"1 Apple Court", ¬
                    city:"Hemmingford Abbots", state:"Cambridgeshire", ¬
                    zip:"CB4 9HG", country:"UK"}, ¬
            category:{category "Family", category "Christmas Card", ¬
                    category "Private"}}
9. end tell
```

There is so much that can be done with categories in Entourage it is worth spending some time exploring them on your own. From an AppleScript perspective, they are relatively simple—they have only three properties, and one of them (id) is read-only. The others are name (used in Script 24–14) and color, which is a simple record of three integers giving the red, green, and blue values for the color to display the category in.

Script 24–14 has simply added lines 2 to 7 to the original script in Script 24–12. These lines ask Entourage for the name of every category (line 2), loop through each of the category names we are using (lines 3 to 7), and then create a new category (line 5) if that new name doesn't already appear in the list of category names in the application (categories are defined for the whole application—they can be used anywhere in Entourage and so are application properties). Because we are not declaring a color in line 5, a default color will be added, just as if we had created a new category in the GUI.

> **CAUTION:** When scripting categories, it is possible via AppleScript to apply a list of categories to an item in Entourage where a category is duplicated. You can end up with an item that has categories {"Private", "Family", "Private"} for example. This can't be done in the user interface and can cause some confusion, so be sure to take care that you don't add an already present category to the end of the list of categories for an item.

Creating Calendar Events

Like the address book, there can be multiple calendars, of different types, *if* you have an Exchange account. If no Exchange account is defined, you are limited to just the local calendar. Also like the address book, the default calendar is the calendar associated with the default mail account, and omitting a specific reference to any other calendar will target it. The local calendar is always calendar ID 13.

Creating calendar events is done in the same manner as creating other items in Entourage, as shown in Script 24–15.

Script 24–15.

```
tell application "Microsoft Entourage"
    set new_event to make new event at calendar id 13 with properties { ¬
        subject:"Test Event", ¬
        content:"This is an event created to test AppleScript", ¬
        all day event:true, ¬
        start time:date (date string of ((current date) + 1 * days))}
end tell
```

As before, this represents only a small number of the properties that can be set when creating an event. The subject property contains the data that shows up in the calendar view—the title of the event, if you like. The content property is what shows up in the notes field of the event. In the GUI, an event can be set as either a timed event or an all-day event. The same can be done through AppleScript by setting the all day event property to true or false. If an event is an all-day event that covers only a single day, you don't need to explicitly set an end time.

Another important property of an event is its recurrence. If the recurring property is set to true, then the event repeats according to the string of rules set in the event's recurrence property. These arcane rules are not defined in the AppleScript dictionary but are derived from the iCal recurrence rules defined in RFC 2445 (which you can find at http://tools.ietf.org/html/rfc2445, although you'll have to dig through quite a lot of irrelevant text to find the syntax for the recurrence string).

Let's do something useful with recurrence. While we're at it, I'll link it into scripting contacts and introduce a new concept—how to check for a selected item. Script 24–16 will set up an annually recurring event for the birthday of each contact selected in Entourage. The title of each event will be taken from the name of the contact.

Script 24–16.

```
1. tell application "Microsoft Entourage"
2.     set selected_contacts to my get_selection_as_class(contact)
3.     if selected_contacts is missing value then
4.         beep 2
5.         return
6.     end if
7.     repeat with this_contact in (selected_contacts)
8.         set birthday_text to birthday of this_contact
9.         set the_birthday to AppleScript's date birthday_text
10.         set month_day to day of the_birthday
11.         set month_number to month of the_birthday as integer
12.         set recurrence_string to "FREQ=YEARLY;INTERVAL=1;BYMONTHDAY=" ¬
                & month_day & ";BYMONTH=" & month_number & ";WKST=SU"
13.         set the_name to ¬
                first name of this_contact & " " & last name of this_contact
14.         set event_label to "Birthday - " & the_name
15.         make new event with properties {subject:event_label, ¬
                start time:the_birthday, all day event:true, ¬
                recurring:true, recurrence:recurrence_string}
16.     end repeat
17. end tell

18. on get_selection_as_class(required_type)
19.     tell application "Microsoft Entourage"
20.         try
21.             set the_selection to selection
22.             set the_class to class of the_selection
23.             if the_class is list then
24.                 set the_class to class of item 1 of the_selection
25.             end if
26.             if the_class is not required_type then error
27.         on error
28.             return missing value
29.         end try
30.         return the_selection
31.     end tell
32. end get_selection_as_class
```

First, line 2 gets the user's selection only if it is of the correct class (in this case a contact object). Because this is such a useful technique, I have defined it as a separate handler, get_selection_as_class (lines 18 to 32). Many useful AppleScripts act on a single selected item or on all selected items. It is best, for that type of script, to check that the right thing is selected first or the AppleScript may error while running or, even worse, do nasty things to the wrong item.

Unfortunately, Entourage can be put into a state where just asking for get selection can cause an error. This typically happens when either no window is open or one of the "service" windows is frontmost (the progress window, for example). To avoid this, we wrap the command in a try ... end try code block (lines 20 to 29). The next problem is that some selections are a single item (a mail folder, for example) and some are lists (one or more messages in that folder). Line 24 takes care of this problem by resetting variable the_class to the class of the first item in that list (all items in a selection list will always be of the same type).

The get_selection_as_class handler is called at the start of the script's main run handler (line 2) and passed the type of item that you want to test for. In this case it is contact. In other cases it could be event, note, incoming message, and so on. Note that because these are all Entourage class types, they must appear inside a tell application "Microsoft Entourage" ... end tell code block to compile correctly as an Entourage keyword.

If the selected item matches the required type, the handler returns the selection to the calling code on line 30. If it doesn't match, it returns the value missing value (line 28).

The result of the get_selection_as_class command on line 2 is checked in line 3. If the result is missing value, then the script terminates on line 5 with a couple of beeps (line 4). You could put up a dialog box with some explanatory text here—I leave that as an exercise for you.

Now we enter a repeat loop (lines 7 to 16) to check through each contact selected. On line 8 we get the birthday information from the first contact. Look in the AppleScript dictionary and you will see the class of object returned is text—not much good to set up a calendar event. So, we need to convert it to an object of class date.

> **CAUTION:** Here we hit a bit of a snag—a terminology conflict. It *should* be pretty straightforward just to say set the_birthday to date birthday_text. Try it in this script and you will get an error. This happens because the conversion is being done inside a tell application "Microsoft Entourage" ... end tell block. Entourage has its own definition of date and it appears to conflict with the AppleScript language definition. The simple way around this is to spell out which definition of date you want to use. I do this in line 9 with set the_birthday to AppleScript's date birthday_text. (Using ... my date birthday_text will also work.) I could also have closed the tell block before using the date specifier, but that is messy, since I want to use the Entourage AppleScript terms almost immediately afterward.

Having now converted the date text to a date object, we can extract the day and month of the date (lines 10 and 11).

Now we have all the information we need to set up the recurrence string that we discussed earlier. When the recurrence string is complete (line 12), we can build the display name of the contact in line 13 (putting error checks in here for missing first or last names is another improvement I leave to you), and create a title for the event (line 14). Now it only remains to create the event itself, starting on the original birthday date and recurring every year on the same date (line 15).

Finally, the repeat loop comes to an end (line 23) and the whole process is repeated with the next contact—until they are all finished.

If you want to work on the script even more, try setting a "birthday" category to each event as it is created (hint: category: {category "birthday"}). Remember, before you enter the loop, you will need to check whether the "birthday" category already exists and create it if it doesn't.

Extracting Information from a Whole Lot of Messages in a Folder

Before we leave Entourage, let's look at extracting some information from it, instead of just creating new things. Because AppleScript is at its most useful when interacting with different applications, we will use the data extracted in the next section—in Microsoft Excel.

Let's say that you filter messages of a particular topic into a single folder. Also, you would like to find out who is sending the most messages of that type. Script 24–17 will extract a list of all the senders and count how many messages they have sent.

> **NOTE:** Because the script is quite a long one, I have included comments in it to document the code. Thus, when you return to the code at a later date, you will have reminders of what is happening.

Script 24–17.

```
1. tell application "Microsoft Entourage"
2.     -- Check selection
3.     try
4.         set the_selection to selection
5.     on error
6.         -- No sensible selection at all!
7.         display dialog "Please select a folder and run the script again" ¬
                buttons {"Abort"}
8.         return
9.     end try

10.     set the_folder to missing value
11.     if class of the_selection is in {folder, news group} then
12.         -- Folder selected - use this folder
13.         set the_folder to the_selection
14.     else
15.         -- Something else selected - find out what
16.         try
17.             set the_messages to current messages
18.             if (count the_messages) = 1 then
19.                 -- Just one message - could be in list or open in its own window
20.                 -- Use the folder that contains this message
21.                 set the_folder to storage of item 1 of the_messages
22.             end if
23.         on error
24.             -- Nothing useable selected - abort run
25.             display dialog "Please select a folder and run the script again" ¬
                    buttons {"Abort"} default button 1 with icon stop
26.             return
27.         end try
28.     end if

29.     -- Start processing
```

```
30.    if the_folder ≠ missing value then
31.        -- A folder was selected - get the data directly
32.        set folder_name to name of the_folder
33.        -- List of email addresses
34.        set sender_list to (address of sender of every message of the_folder)
35.        -- List of display names
36.        set name_list to (display name of sender of every message of the_folder)
37.    else
38.        -- Multiple messages were selected - loop though to get the data
39.        set folder_name to "Selected Messages"
40.        set sender_list to {} -- List of email addresses
41.        set name_list to {} -- List of display names
42.        repeat with this_message in the_messages
43.            set end of sender_list to address of sender of this_message
44.            set end of name_list to display name of sender of this_message
45.        end repeat
46.    end if
47. end tell

48. -- Write the data out to a file
49. -- (Temporary items folder will be emptied on next restart)
50. set the_file to ((get path to temporary items folder) as text) & "SenderScript"
51. set data_file to open for access the_file with write permission
52. set eof data_file to 0
53. set AppleScript's text item delimiters to {linefeed}
54. set sender_text to sender_list as text
55. write sender_text to data_file as «class utf8»
56. close access data_file

57. -- Use shell script to sort and count unique email addresses...
58. set the_script to "sort -f " & quoted form of (POSIX path of the_file) ¬
            & " | tr '[:upper:]' '[:lower:]' | uniq -c"
59. set frequency_info to paragraphs of (do shell script the_script)

60. -- ...and parse the result
61. set result_list to ¬
            {"Display Name" & tab & "Email Address" & tab & "Message Count"}
62. repeat with this_item in frequency_info
63.    set message_count to word 1 of this_item
64.    set email_address to (text 6 thru -1 of this_item)
65.    -- Loop through list of email addresses to find this one...
66.    repeat with i from 1 to (count sender_list)
67.        if item i of sender_list is email_address then
68.            -- ...and get the display name from the list of display names
69.            set display_name to item i of name_list
70.            exit repeat
71.        end if
72.    end repeat
73.    if display_name = "" then set display_name to contents of email_address
74.    set end of result_list to ¬
            display_name & tab & email_address & tab & message_count
75. end repeat

76. set AppleScript's text item delimiters to {return}
77. set the clipboard to result_list as text
```

The first thing to do is to find out which messages the user wants to count. I could have used the get_selection_as_class handler introduced in Script 24–16, like this,

```
set the_folder to my get_selection_as_class(folder)
```

but I want to give the user several different methods of dictating which messages should be counted. This also has the advantage of introducing a few new concepts to you as well!

First, in lines 2 through 9 we get the selection, but wrap it up in a try ... on error ... end try block just in case there is no suitable selection to get—we don't want our script to crash!

Now we check what class the selection is (line 11), but unlike previously, when we were only testing for a single class, I now want to check whether the selection is a folder or a newsgroup—this script will work equally well on both. This is also the first reason I did not use my get_selection_as_class handler. If the user has highlighted either a folder or a newsgroup in the left pane of a standard Entourage mail window, then the test passes and line 13 sets a variable to a reference to the folder selected.

If the selection wasn't a folder or newsgroup, then the else clause at line 14 kicks in and the block of code up to line 27 is run. Again, we wrap it up in a try statement, just in case something strange is selected. This time, instead of looking directly at the selection, I have used current messages to find the messages selected (see the "Using the Current Messages Property" sidebar), and line 17 sets a variable, the_messages, to a list of references to the selected messages.

The script from line 30 onward will operate on this list of messages, but before we get there, there is one last test to carry out. Line 18 checks whether the list of selected messages contains just a single message. It would be a bit silly to use a script to count the sender of just one message, so we assume the user intended to select this whole folder rather than this single message. Line 21 uses the storage property of a message to determine what folder contains it, and sets the the_folder variable to contain a reference to that folder.

Finally, for this section, lines 23 through 27 are put in place just in case the user did anything unexpected before running the script, to catch any errors and exit gracefully from the script.

Now, either the_folder contains a reference to the folder or newsgroup we want to operate on, or the_messages contains a list of references to the messages that were selected and we can get on with the business of extracting the data we want.

USING THE CURRENT MESSAGES PROPERTY

This is a great and very useful property of the Entourage application that returns different things in different circumstances. If one or more messages are selected in the folder listing or if a message is open in its own window for reading or editing, then current messages contains a reference to those messages (as a list of one item, if necessary); for example:

```
tell application "Microsoft Entourage" to get current messages
```

```
--> {incoming message id 30356 of application "Microsoft Entourage"}
```

If, however, the script is being run as the result of a mail rule action, then `current messages` contains a single-item list of the message being filtered by the mail rule at that time. The `current messages` property is also very useful if the user has selected several messages in a "saved search" (what used to be called a custom view in older versions of Entourage) or in a window displaying the found results of a Spotlight search. In these situations, getting `current messages` will return a list of by-ID references to those selected messages, even if those messages are scattered across many different mail folders. It is a very flexible, powerful, and useful property!

Line 33 checks whether the_folder contains anything useful. It was set to an empty string in line 10, and will only contain suitable data if the user selected a folder (line 13) or selected just one message (line 21). If the_folder is not an empty string, then lines 34 and 36 get lists of e-mail addresses and display names directly. However, if multiple messages were selected, the test at line 30 fails and the else clause at line 37 operates. Unfortunately, no quick method exists for extracting the data from a list of messages, so we have to loop through each one of them in lines 42 through 45 to obtain our lists of e-mail addresses and display names.

We have now extracted all the data we need from Entourage and so can close the tell block at line 47. All the remaining processing is purely AppleScript based and doesn't involve Entourage any more.

The data we have now is in the form of two AppleScript lists, one containing all the e-mail addresses of the senders of messages we worked on, the other containing all the display names. These lists will not be in any particular order—the names will be jumbled up in the order of the messages as they are stored in Entourage. We want to count how many messages each individual sender has sent. I could write AppleScript handlers to sort the lists and count the number of times that each sender appears, and a quick web search would soon find AppleScript sorting routines that would do that part of the job. Once sorted, looping through the lists several times would achieve the counting operation. However, I'm going to use a couple of the Unix commands built into the operating system that will achieve these tasks a lot more quickly and easily. Don't worry too much if you don't understand how these commands work; the result is the main thing here. Shell scripting will be covered in more detail in Chapter 27.

We want to sort and count the e-mail addresses, so first (lines 48 to 55) we write the list of e-mail addresses out to a temporary file that can be accessed by the shell script. I write this to the Temporary Items folder—a special system folder that is emptied whenever the system is shut down. This means I don't need to worry about having to "tidy up" the file after the script is finished. Line 55 sets AppleScript's text item delimiters to a Unix line feed character and line 56 coerces the sender list to text so that the e-mail addresses are delimited by line feed characters—just what the Unix commands like to work with. Line 57 writes the resulting text to file.

The sorting and counting is achieved with three Unix commands: sort, tr, and uniq. If you want to delve into these commands, plenty of information is available on the Web, but here's a brief summary. The sort command is run on the temporary file we just saved, and sorts the lines into order. The result of this is "piped" into the next command, `tr`, which converts all uppercase characters into lowercase (just in case someone has different variants of their e-mail address listed), and the result of this is piped into the `uniq` command. This is used to count the number of times each unique value occurs. This combination of three commands returns a result to AppleScript in the form of a line feed–delimited chunk of text. Each line in the result contains a unique e-mail address preceded by the number of times that this e-mail address appeared in the data passed to the shell scripts. In line 59 we call the shell script and store the result in a variable, `frequency_info`. The `paragraphs of` ... reference used in this line splits the lines of the returned result into an AppleScript list again.

So, entering into the final section at line 60, we have three lists: `sender_list` still contains all the e-mail addresses in the order of the messages in Entourage; `name_list` contains the display names of the messages in the same order as `sender_list`; and `frequency_info` contains a much shorter list of unique e-mail addresses, with the count of how often they occur. Line 62 sets up a repeat loop, looping through each item in `frequency_info`. The first five characters of each line is the count of the number of occurrences—this is pulled into a temporary variable at line 63. The remainder of this line is the e-mail address and is likewise stored in another temporary variable at line 64. There now remains the problem of finding the display name that goes with this e-mail address. Lines 62 to 72 loop through the original list of e-mail addresses and find a match for the unique e-mail address being worked on. The display name is looked up in the corresponding item in the list of display names (line 69). Line 73 just adds a sanity check for missing display names (not all e-mail senders have their e-mail clients set up properly) and substitutes the e-mail address if the display name is missing. Line 74 writes these temporary variables out as tab-delimited text to an AppleScript list.

Finally, lines 76 and 77 put the tab-delimited text on the clipboard, with lines separated by return characters. The script then ends. This data can now be pasted into a spreadsheet or word processor or any other suitable application. We will make use of this script and its data in the next section.

Working with Excel

Microsoft Excel has a very large and complex AppleScript dictionary that may appear daunting and somewhat off-putting to the new scripter. It is also an unusual dictionary in comparison to many other applications' scripting dictionaries in the terminology and the layout of the commands and classes. The reason for this is that the scripting methodology in Excel has been inherited from the VBA Object Model that was originally in Excel, before Office 2008 removed all VBA support from Office for Mac. However, don't despair! There is an excellent (and essential) document produced by Microsoft to assist the scripter for Excel. It is called the *Excel 2004 AppleScript Reference* and is available from `http://www.microsoft.com/mac/developers/default.mspx`. Do not be put off by the "2004" in the title—most of the functionality in Office 2008 is identical to that found in 2004, and this guide will certainly put you on the right track with regard to some of the basic principles for working with Excel. It really is essential reading, and you should download your copy right away!

Creating Workbooks and Worksheets

Most of the stuff you are going to do in Excel requires a worksheet to put it in. Let's start with the easy stuff, making a new workbook and saving it to a file:

```
tell application "Microsoft Excel"
    set new_book to make new workbook
    save workbook as new_book filename "aPress2010.xls"
end tell
```

Well, it works, but where has the file been saved? Excel by default saves the file in the "current" folder—whichever folder was last used for saving by Excel. This is the folder that will be shown when you choose the **File ➤ Save As** menu item in the Excel GUI. You can't always tell what it will be. A look in the dictionary for the parameters of the save workbook as command (make sure you look at the correct command—there are nine different commands associated with saving) shows that the filename parameter takes a text object. If you put in the full file path here, you can define exactly where the file is to be saved:

```
1. set file_name to (path to desktop as text) & "aPress2010.xls"
2. tell application "Microsoft Excel"
3.     set new_book to make new workbook
4.     save workbook as new_book filename file_name
5. end tell
```

By default, the save workbook as command will save the file as a .xlsx file. Take a look in the AppleScript dictionary for Excel—this command can be used to save a file in any one of more than 30 different file formats! If you substitute line 4 with

```
save workbook as new_book filename file_name file format Excel98to2004 file format
```

you will have the file saved as the older .xls format.

If you have an existing workbook file that you want to open, you can use the open workbook command. You specify the full path to the file using the workbook file name parameter, like this:

```
1. set file_name to (path to desktop as text) & "aPress2010.xls"
2. tell application "Microsoft Excel"
3.     set new_book to open workbook workbook  file name file_name
4. end tell
```

The somewhat curious and repetitive syntax in line 3 is quite typical of AppleScript in Excel. It does take some getting used to, and you really need to study both the dictionary and the Microsoft guide referred to in the introduction to this section until you are familiar and comfortable with the way it all works together. Note especially that whereas the save workbook as command uses a filename parameter without spaces, the open workbook command uses a workbook file name parameter with a space in "file name." Great, isn't it?

As in the GUI, starting a new workbook by AppleScript also creates a single worksheet in the new workbook. But what if you want to start a second worksheet? Here's how you do that:

```
tell application "Microsoft Excel"
```

```
    set new_book to make new workbook
    make new worksheet at active workbook
end tell
```

In the GUI, many of the commands you choose from a menu are applied to whatever part of the current document is active—it may be a cell, a chart, a whole row, or some other item. In the previous script, in order for Excel to know where to make the new worksheet, you can specify that it is in the active workbook, which you identify by referring to the `active workbook` property. This obviously raises the question of how to make some item active (the new_book worksheet is automatically active, having just been created). This is accomplished with the `select` command; for example: `select sheet "sheet1"`.

Working with Ranges

Well, it's good that we have now been able to open, create, and save a file, but unless we can put some data into it, it's not a lot of use, is it?

Absolutely key to manipulating data in Excel is the concept of ranges. Look in the AppleScript dictionary for Excel and you will see the `range` class defined as a cell, row, column, or a selection of cells containing one or more contiguous blocks.

RANGES CAN BE TRICKY!

A range is a very flexible thing. The trouble is, the way it is used in Excel can be quite rigidly constrained. So, for example, even though a range can be almost any shape (or mixture of shapes in the same range), some commands will error unless the range is defined in exactly the right way. Take the `autofit` command, for example. The AppleScript dictionary just says that it takes a reference to a range as its direct parameter. But, unless the range is defined as just one or more columns, the command will error:

```
tell application "Microsoft Excel"
    autofit range "A:A" of worksheet 1 of active workbook
end tell
-- Microsoft Excel got an error: range "A:A" of worksheet 1
        of active workbook doesn't understand the autofit message.
```

Even though the range reference identifies only a single column, `autofit` will error unless you refer specifically to a `column` element (or elements), rather than a range that identifies a column. This leads to all sorts of awkward contortions, like this:

```
tell application "Microsoft Excel"
    autofit every column of range "A:A" of worksheet 1 of active workbook
end tell
```

The dictionary should really declare `autofit` as requiring an object of class `column` or `row` as its parameter rather than a range, but unfortunately it doesn't.

In general, when a command asks for a range as a parameter, take some time to understand exactly what kind of range it is expecting. Be prepared for lots of trial and error as you first start out scripting Excel—it is very complex and will take some time to master. However, once you have learned some of its vagaries, it does begin to make more sense.

To add data to a worksheet, you set the value property of a range element to an AppleScript list. If you want to add data to rows and columns, you use a list of lists. The easiest way to explain is by example, as shown in Script 24–18.

Script 24–18.

```
set my_data to {{1, 2, 3}, {4, 5, 6}, {7, 8, 9}, {10, 11, 12}}
tell application "Microsoft Excel"
    set my_range to range "A1:C4" of worksheet 1 of active workbook
    set value of my_range to my_data
end tell
```

The data to be added can be objects of any basic AppleScript class—integer (as we have in these examples), real, text, or date:

```
set my_data to {{1, 2, 3}, {4.5, 5.6, 6.7135462}, {"this", "is", "text"}, ¬
        {current date, (current date) + 1 * days, date "01/01/2009"}}
tell application "Microsoft Excel"
    set my_range to range "A1:C4" of worksheet 1 of active workbook
    set value of my_range to my_data
    autofit columns of my_range
end tell
```

So, adding data is pretty easy to accomplish. One thing to be aware of is that the target range should be the same size and shape of the data you are adding. If the target range is larger than the data being passed, the undefined cells will receive a value of N/A. If you modify Script 24–18 as follows and run it, you get the result shown in Figure 24–12:

```
set my_data to {{1, 2, 3}, {4, 5, 6}, {7, 8, 9}, {10, 11, 12}}
tell application "Microsoft Excel"
  set my_range to range "A1:F9" of worksheet 1 of active workbook
    set value of my_range to my_data
end tell
```

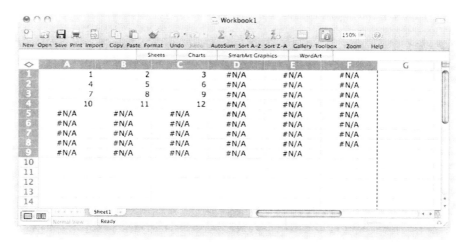

Figure 24–12. *Target range is greater than data size*

Make the target range too small and the data simply gets truncated to the size of the range you have targeted. Any data outside this range is discarded.

Let's expand on the data we add, by including some formulae and formatting. A cell (or range) object includes a formula property that the user can get or set, in just the same way as the value property has been used in Script 24–18. Script 24–19 expands on Script 24–18 to add formula, number, and text formatting.

Script 24–19.

```
tell application "Microsoft Excel"
    set my_data to {{1, 2, 3}, {4, 5, 6}, {7, 8, 9}, {10, 11, 12}}
    set my_range to range "A1:C4" of worksheet 1 of active workbook
    set value of my_range to my_data
    set sum_range to range "a5:c5"
    set formula of sum_range to {{"=sum(a1:a4)"}, {"=sum(b1:b4)"}, {"=sum(c1:c4)"}}
    set bold of font object of sum_range to true
    set italic of font object of sum_range to true
    set new_range to union range1 my_range range2 sum_range
    set number format of new_range to ¬
        "_-£* #,##0.00_-;-£* #,##0.00_-;_-£* \"-\"??_-;_-@_-"
end tell
```

The font object property, which contains an object of class font, is crucial to text formatting of cells in Excel. Explore the possibilities with a simple line of code: properties of font object of cell "a1". This will return a list of properties that can be got or set to format the text within the cell. Script 24–19 uses only two of these properties—bold and italic. Both of these are Boolean properties of the font object, so they are set to either true or false. There are 14 properties of the font object. Most are self-explanatory, and asking the font object for its properties property will list them all for you to explore. However, color requires a little explanation. Consider Script 24–20.

Script 24–20.

```
tell application "Microsoft Excel"
    set color of font object of cell "a1" to {255, 0, 0}
    set font_color to color of font object of cell "a1"
end tell
--> {221, 8, 6}
```

Excel has only a limited number of colors available to it—these are the colors in the current color palette. If you set a color to a font object (or any other object that carries a color property) by using a list of RGB values as in Script 24–20, then the actual color set is converted to the nearest match in the current color palette. An alternate way to set the color property is to use the palette index directly. The following command will set the font color to the same red as was returned previously:

```
set font color index of font object of cell "a1" to 3
```

Determining to which color a specific font color index relates is not straightforward. The following script will create a worksheet with 56 cells containing text of each color index available:

```
tell application "Microsoft Excel"
    make new workbook
    repeat with x from 0 to 3
```

```
        set the_column to item (x + 1) of {"a", "b", "c", "d"}
        repeat with y from 1 to 14
            set the_cell to the_column & y
            set color_index to x * 14 + y
            set value of cell the_cell of worksheet 1 to "Color Index " & color_index
            set font color index of font object of cell the_cell to color_index
        end repeat
    end repeat
    autofit column "a:d"
end tell
```

This will give you a chart like the one shown in Figure 24–13 (but yours will be in color).

Figure 24–13. *The generated color index chart*

(Note that "Color Index 2" is white. The cell appears empty, but it isn't.)

Now that we can get data and formulae into a spreadsheet and apply simple formatting, let's have a look at working with some real data. To do this, I'll use a variation of the script used in the Entourage section to count the senders of e-mails (Script 24–17). Script 24–21 shows the end of Script 24–17 again (lines 1 to 59 are exactly the same as in Script 24–17 and thus are not repeated), with a few subtle changes (shown in bold) to present the data in a form suitable for transferring to Excel.

Script 24–21. (Includes the next two sections of code, lines 60 to 89)

```
60. -- ...and parse the result
61. set result_list to {{"Display Name", "Email Address", "Message Count"}}
62. repeat with this_item in frequency_info
63.     set message_count to word 1 of this_item
64.     set email_address to (text 6 thru -1 of this_item)
```

```
65.    -- Loop through list of email addresses to find this one...
66.    repeat with i from 1 to (count sender_list)
67.        if item i of sender_list is email_address then
68.            -- ...and get the display name from the list of display names
69.            set display_name to item i of name_list
70.            exit repeat
71.        end if
72.    end repeat
73.    if display_name = "" then set display_name to contents of email_address
74.    set end of result_list to {display_name, email_address, message_count}
75. end repeat
```

Lines 61 and 74 change the output of the script to a two-dimensional list—a list of three-item lists. These are ideal for entering straight into Excel. The last two lines of Script 24–17 (lines 76 and 77) have been deleted because we are not using the clipboard any more.

Now, extend the script by adding these lines:

```
76. tell application "Microsoft Excel"
77.    activate
78.    make new workbook
79.    set the view of window 1 to normal view
80.    set the display page breaks of the active sheet to false
81.    set name of active sheet to "Count Senders"
82.    set the_rows to count result_list
83.    set the_columns to count (item 1 of result_list)
84.    set the_range to get resize (range "a1" of active sheet of active workbook) ¬
            row size the_rows ¬
            column size the_columns
85.    set value of the_range to result_list
86.    set bold of font object of row 1 to true
87.    sort the_range ¬
            key1 (column 3 of the_range) ¬
            order1 sort descending ¬
            header header yes
88.    autofit (columns of the_range)
89. end tell
```

Line 77 just brings Excel to the front so you can see what is going on—you can omit this line if you want to. Line 78 we have seen before, in the "Creating Workbooks and Worksheets" section. Lines 79 to 81 are new commands, but probably don't need any explanation. Lines 82 and 83 count how much data is in the data set ready for line 84, which creates a range of the right size.

> **TIP:** Now, we know that for this script we can only have three columns of data, because we hard-coded those columns on lines 61 and 74, so there isn't really any need to count the columns in line 83. However, suppose that in the future we were to add another column to the data collected. Counting columns before using them means that we won't have to look through the script to see what has been hard-coded and what hasn't.

Line 84 contains a new Excel command, get resize, so it is worth looking up in the dictionary:

```
get resize v : Resizes the specified range. Returns a Range object that represents
      the resized range.
   get resize range
      [row size integer] : The number of rows in the new range. If this argument
            is omitted, the number of rows in the range remains the same.
      [column size integer] : The number of columns in the new range. If this
            argument is omitted, the number of columns in the range remains the
            same.
      --> range : A range object that represents the resized range.
```

get resize (note that the "get" is compulsory here—it is part of the command name, not the optional get keyword encountered elsewhere in AppleScript) extends the range declared in the first parameter (range "a1", in this example) by the number of rows and columns declared in the second and third parameters. The command here is used to create a range the same size as the data extracted from Entourage. Remember what happens when the range is smaller or larger than the data you try to put in it? See the sidebar for a fuller description of how get resize is used.

USING GET RESIZE

Data inserted into a worksheet needs to exactly match the size and shape of the range you are trying to put it into. Determining the size of the data is easy enough—just count the length of the lists of data you are handling. Determining the size of the range to put it in is not so easy. Since a range is declared with cell references, as in set my_range to range "A1:C4", it would be possible to construct the cell references as a text string. That would be awkward to code, though, turning a count of the number of columns into the letter references needed. How do you convert column 127 into "DW" to build range "A1:DW32,687"?

Using get resize solves this problem. It takes three parameters: a starting range, which can be a single cell or a multicell range—only the top-left cell is used to set the starting point for your new range; a row size value to set the number of rows in your new range; and a column size value to set the number of columns. Here's an example:

```
tell application "Microsoft Excel"
   set active workbook to workbook of window 1
   set the_range to get resize (range "a1:c3") ¬
         row size 10 ¬
         column size 3
end tell
--> range "[Workbook1]Sheet1!$A$1:$C$10" of application "Microsoft Excel"
```

This makes defining a range of the right size so much easier, as you are dealing only with integers to set the number of rows and columns, and these integers can easily be obtained from counting the rows and columns in the data you are inserting in your script.

Note that in the short script above, I have declared the starting point as a 3 × 3 range—this is completely arbitrary. The get resize command uses only the top-left cell to define the start point for the new range—you could use range "A1" or Range "A1:XFD1048576" (the maximum size of a worksheet) and get exactly the same result.

Line 85 puts the data into our new range, and line 86 formats the first row. Again, we have used these commands before. Line 87 is another new command, and sorts the data on the third column. The optional parameters to the `sort` command reflect what is available through the GUI. You can specify up to three worksheet columns to sort on using the key1, key2, and key3 parameters. The order1, order2, and order3 parameters specify the sort order applied to each of those columns. The sort order can be `sort ascending`, `sort descending`, or `sort manual` (although `sort manual` makes no sense for the sort order in this command, the same constants are used elsewhere, where it does make more sense). The final parameter used here is header, which declares whether or not a header row is present. The options are header `yes` (used here), header `no`, or header `guess` (which takes a guess depending on the type of data in the first row compared to the rest of the column).

Finally, line 88 adjusts the column width to suit the data we have entered. Remember what I wrote about `autofit` earlier in this chapter? The AppleScript dictionary states that `autofit` requires a parameter of class `range`. However, it errors unless the range is declared as either columns or rows, so we use the syntax here of `columns of the_range`.

Figure 24–14 shows a typical result from running this script on one of my mail folders (although names and e-mail addresses have been changed to protect identities). Note the formatting applied to the top row by line 86, the data sorted by the "Message Count" column (line 87), and the columns opened out to show the full width of the data (line 88).

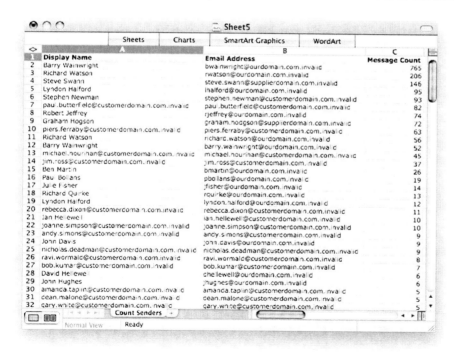

Figure 24–14. *The results of the Count Senders script*

Creating Charts

Now that we have some "real world" data to work with, let's make our spreadsheet even more useful by adding a chart to present the data in a more visual manner.

Continuing with the script from the previous section, replace the last line (line 89) with the following lines:

```
89.    select sheet "Count Senders"
90.    select (intersect range1 the_range range2 range "$a:$a,$c:$c")
91.    make new chart sheet at active workbook
92.    set properties of active chart to ¬
             {chart type:column clustered, ¬
              has legend:false, ¬
              has data table:false, ¬
              name:"All Senders Chart"}
93.    set name of series 1 of active chart to ¬
             " All Senders of \"" & folder_name & "\""
94. end tell
```

Line 89 just makes the current sheet active. It shouldn't be necessary in an example like this, where you have just created a workbook with just the one sheet, but making the current object active is a good habit to get into with Excel, if you want to avoid unpleasant things from happening in the more complicated scripts you will be writing in the future.

Line 90 contains an example of one of the range manipulation commands in Excel. intersect will return a range defined by the common areas of the range1, range2, ..., range30 parameters. Note that the range that follows each of these parameter labels can be a range defined in any way that Excel understands. Here, I have used two methods. The value for the range1 parameter is provided by the variable the_range, since that is already defined. the_range carries the data that has just been entered into the worksheet, and consists of three columns. range2 passes a region as range "$a:$a,cc", which consists of columns A and C in their entirety—see how the range is declared as two distinct regions separated by a comma. The purpose of this line is to select just the display name and count columns in the data set to be plotted as a chart.

Line 91 creates a new chart sheet, which will initially contain a chart in the user's default format. Line 92 applies the particular format we require. Line 93 names the data series and, since only one series is plotted, adds the name as a chart title.

Now, if you selected a lot of messages before running this script (or a folder containing a lot of messages), two things happen. First, the script takes quite a while to run. This can be improved slightly by tweaking the code, but that's an exercise beyond the scope of this chapter. Secondly, the chart produced is not very useful, since so much data is squeezed into a small place that it becomes unreadable. Let's improve things by just charting the first 25 data points. This is a reasonable cut, since the chart resulting will be unreadable and in such a large data set most of the "tail end" senders will probably have a very low sent message count.

Script 24–22 demonstrates how to do this. Replace the lines we just added (lines 89 to 94) as shown. (Lines 1 to 89 are exactly the same as in Script 24–21.)

Script 24–22.

```
89.    if (count result_list) > 25 then
90.        select sheet "Count Senders"
91.        select (get intersect range1 the_range range2 range "$c:$c")
92.        make new chart sheet at active workbook
93.        set properties of active chart to ¬
                {chart type:column clustered, ¬
                has legend:false, ¬
                has data table:false, ¬
                name:"All Senders Chart"}
94.        set name of series 1 of active chart to ¬
                " All Senders of \"" & folder_name & "\""
95.        select sheet "Count Senders"
96.        select (get intersect range1 the_range ¬
                range2 range "$A$1:$a$25,$c$1:$c$25")
97.        make new chart sheet at active workbook
98.        set properties of active chart to ¬
                {chart type:column clustered, ¬
                has legend:false, ¬
                has data table:false, ¬
                name:"Top 25 Chart"}
99.        set name of series 1 of active chart to ¬
                " Top 25 Senders of \"" & folder_name & "\""
100.   else
101.      select sheet "Count Senders"
102.      select (get intersect range1 the_range range2 range "$a:$a,$c:$c")
103.      make new chart sheet at active workbook
104.      set properties of active chart to ¬
                {chart type:column clustered, ¬
                has legend:false, ¬
                has data table:false, ¬
                name:"All Senders Chart"}
105.      set name of series 1 of active chart to ¬
                " All Senders of \"" & folder_name & "\""
106.   end if
107. end tell
```

The charting section now starts with a test of the data to see if it exceeds 25 entries. If it doesn't, the script continues with the else clause at line 100. The remainder of the script from here is exactly the same as that just considered in the previous example.

However, if the count of data contains more than 25 entries, two charts are drawn. The first (lines 90 to 94) uses all the data in a similar manner to the previous example, but this time (in line 91) we select only column "c" which contains the count data—the display names are not charted because they will be unreadable at this scale. The second chart is drawn by lines 95 to 99 and just uses the first 25 rows of data. You should end up with a chart sheet looking similar to the one shown in Figure 24–15.

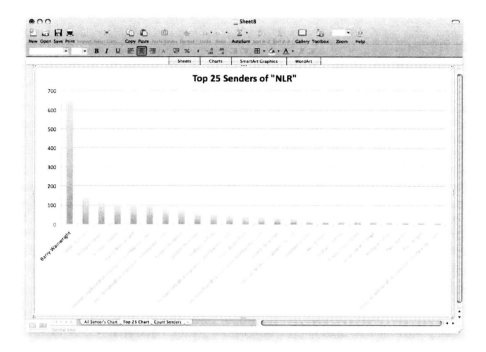

Figure 24–15. *The finished "Top 25 Senders" chart*

Working with Word

Like Excel, Word has a tremendously large and complex AppleScript dictionary. The Microsoft web site provides a *Word 2004 AppleScript Reference* to complement the Excel guide mentioned earlier in this chapter.

One of the key concepts to get to grips with when scripting Word is the *text range* concept. An object of class text range refers to a contiguous area in a document. Each text range object is defined by a starting and ending character position.

Unfortunately, this chapter is too short to spend much time on Word scripting. I will cover a few simple tasks to get you started and leave you to explore and learn more on your own. Spend time studying these concepts—they are essential to progressing in scripting Word.

Creating a Word Document

Just like with Excel, starting a Word document is easy:

```
tell application "Microsoft Word"
    set new_document to make new document
    set content of text object of new_document to "Here is some text."
end tell
```

Note that a document doesn't have content; it is the text object property of the document that does.

Saving the file is not much more difficult, using the save as command:

```
set the_path to (path to desktop as text) & "My New Document.docx"
tell application "Microsoft Word"
    set new_document to make new document
    set content of text object of new_document to "Here is some text."
    save as new_document file name the_path
end tell
```

Just be warned that if the file already exists, it is overwritten without warning!

Opening an existing document is also straightforward. For example:

```
set the_path to (path to desktop as text) & "My New Document.docx"
tell application "Microsoft Word"
    open the_path
end tell
```

Working with Selected Text

Much of what you script in Word will be taking actions on selected text. Word's selection object is used here—it is a special object type in Word that allows you to manipulate the text and properties of the selection. To demonstrate its use, I will present one final script in this section that operates on the selection object.

Script 24–23 is a script that I used while writing this section of the book in Word. It is used for pasting in a script from AppleScript Editor, applying the particular formats required by the publisher, and changing all tabs to spaces (another requirement of the publisher).

Script 24–23.

```
1. tell application "AppleScript Editor"
2.     compile document 1
3.     set script_text to text of document 1
4. end tell

5. set line_number to 1
6. set formatted_lines to {}
7. set is_continuing_line to false
8. repeat with line_ref in paragraphs of script_text
9.     ignoring white space
10.        if contents of line_ref = "" then -- Empty lines are blank
11.            set end of formatted_lines to ""
12.        else if is_continuing_line then -- Don't number continuing lines
13.            set end of formatted_lines to "    " & line_ref
14.        else -- Add a line number
15.            set end of formatted_lines to (line_number as text) & ". " & line_ref
16.            set line_number to line_number + 1
17.        end if
18.        set is_continuing_line to line_ref ends with "¬"
19.    end ignoring
20. end repeat
21. set text item delimiters to {return}
```

```
22. set formatted_text to formatted_lines as text

23. tell application "Microsoft Word"
24.     set content of selection to formatted_text
25.     clear formatting selection
26.     set style of paragraphs of selection to ¬
            Word style "code" of active document
27.     set style of first paragraph of selection to ¬
            Word style "code first" of active document
28.     set style of last paragraph of selection to ¬
            Word style "code last" of active document
29.     tell find object of selection
30.        clear formatting
31.        set content to tab
32.        clear formatting of its replacement
33.        set content of its replacement to "    "
34.        execute find wrap find find continue ¬
               replace replace all with match forward
35.     end tell
36. end tell
```

The first part of the script (lines 1 to 4) gets the code to insert from the front document in AppleScript Editor. The second part (lines 5 to 22) adds line numbers to the text.

> **NOTE:** If you are still on Mac OS X 10.5 or earlier, replace application "AppleScript Editor" on line 1 with application "Script Editor" before compiling the script, or use application id "com.apple.ScriptEditor2" if you need to support both 10.5 and 10.6.

Line 24 simply inserts the text we have into the selection, replacing any text existing there. Note that, unlike Entourage and many other scriptable applications, we don't simply set the selection property to the text, but have to refer to content of selection instead. This is because a selection object holds much, much more information than just the plain text. Take a look in the dictionary—there are dozens of properties (many of them records with many properties of their own) and 19 different elements defined. However, setting the value of the content property of the selection object will achieve what we are after.

> **TIP:** If no text is selected in Word, the selection object refers to the insertion point, so setting the content of an empty selection will insert text into the document at the current cursor position—very useful.

Line 25 clears any existing format applied to the selection (such as the compiled script formatting applied by AppleScript Editor) and lines 26 to 28 apply specific styles to the selection. The Apress style guidelines require code text to have different styles from the rest of the document and require the first and last lines of a code block to have their own unique styles as well. When setting a style to a text object, you have to define the origin of the style as well. In this case (and most cases you will come across) you will set a defined style from the document you are working with—the active document.

However, you could set a style that was defined in some other document or template. Obviously, your scripts will have to be written with style names that exist on your system.

Now, we have to replace any tabs in the script block with spaces—this is a requirement for the book formatting. So, I've made use of Word's find-and-replace feature to automate this task.

Find-and-replace works in a bit of a strange way in Word. There is a simple `execute find` command, with parameters, but the details of what is to be searched and what has to be replaced need to be set up first. This requires an object of the `find` class to be defined first. A find object is a complicated thing, but fortunately it appears as a property of a text object in Word and also, luckily for us, as a selection object. So, in line 29 we target the find object we are going to work on, which is simply the find object already existing in the selection. That's not all, though; a find object has many properties, and we need to set a few to our own particular use here. The main ones are the `content` property (line 31), which contains the text we want to look for (a tab character), and the `replacement` property (lines 32 and 33), which contains an object of class `replacement` where we can set the content to the text we want to replace each tab with (three spaces, in this case). Lines 17 and 19 simply ensure that the format of the selected text and replacement text is ignored. Look in the dictionary for other possible properties that can be set.

> **CAUTION:** Because Word uses the `replacement` keyword as a property name, a class name, *and* a constant, you must write `its replacement` (or `replacement of it`), not `replacement`, inside the `tell find object ... end tell` block on lines 29 to 35. The `its` keyword makes it clear to AppleScript that you are talking about the `replacement` property of the `tell` block's target object, not the class name or constant. See Chapter 11 for more information on AppleScript's special `it` variable.

The hard work is then done by the `execute find` command on line 34. This command has several parameters that mimic the options available in the Find and Replace dialog box in the GUI. Because the command is inside a `tell find object ... end tell` block (lines 29 to 35), the `execute find` operates on that find object.

Where Next?

As I warned in the introduction to this section, these scripts barely scratch the surface of AppleScripting Office for Mac. However, if they have whetted your appetite and you want to take things further, there are lots of sources on the Web.

The Mactopia web site (http://www.microsoft.com/mac) has a very good Help And How-To section that is certainly worth browsing. In particular, the AppleScript Reference guides (http://www.microsoft.com/mac/developers) provide searchable documentation and example code to supplement the information provided by the Office applications' built-in dictionaries.

Also, take a look at ScriptBuilders (http://www.scriptbuilders.net); they have lots of scripts available there for Office applications, most of which are freeware and are editable, so you can explore their inner workings.

Apart from that, simply start playing and trying new things. In the end, that's the only way to learn, especially with the rather curious dictionary structure in Word, Excel, and PowerPoint.

Summary

As you have seen, both iWork and Office have fairly extensive support for AppleScript-based automation, so large and often complex dictionaries are the order of the day. The applications in each suite also have their own particular approaches to supporting AppleScript (complete with plenty of quirks and bugs, just to keep things interesting), which you will need to learn your way around in order to use them effectively.

Scripting support in iWork applications is still rather new, and the design of some features can seem a bit rushed or not very well thought out. Office's scripting support is far more mature, although the Word and Excel dictionaries are based on the original VBA interfaces, so they may take a bit more getting used to than other application dictionaries.

Despite a few challenges, though, if you use these applications on a regular basis, learning to script them can bring significant rewards, from minor productivity enhancements all the way up to fully automated multi-application workflows.

In the next chapter, we will continue our investigation of AppleScriptable workflow tools, by looking at how to manage and manipulate important data in databases.

Chapter 25

Scripting Data and Databases

A frequent theme in this book is the importance of AppleScript in managing and manipulating user data. While applications such as iTunes and Mail provide their own custom storage systems for managing specific types of data such as music and e-mail collections, there are many other data management tasks which require a more flexible, user-customizable solution. To meet these needs, users can turn to general-purpose database applications, and—naturally—AppleScript can play an key role in working with these applications too.

Three factors make a database what it is: the data structure, which basically consists of the fields and field definitions; the data itself; and the functionality, such as sorting, searching, and exporting. Two common types of databases are

- *Relational databases*: Information is stored as records within tables. Records in one table can be easily cross-referenced against related records in another (the relational part).

- *Object databases*: Objects are stored in a tree-shaped structure, much like the object models you deal with in scriptable applications.

Although the AppleScript language itself has no built-in database features, you can get a bit done with lists and records. For instance, you can collect data in a list of records, as shown here:

```
set people_table to { ¬
    {first_name:"Jo", last_name:"Brown", age:31}, ¬
    {first_name:"Sam", last_name:"Green", age:24}, ¬
    {first_name:"Adam", last_name:"Smith", age:29}, ¬
    }
```

Later, you can loop through the records in this list, getting and setting the values of their properties as needed. However, although this approach works for basic operations on small amounts of data, more advanced tasks such as sorting or searching the data will be slow and complicated to do using AppleScript alone.

In this chapter, you will look at three ways AppleScript can interact with external databases. You will start with scripting FileMaker Pro 10, and then move on to connecting to SQL databases using MacSQL 3.1, and finally investigate the Database Events application that is included in Mac OS X.

> **NOTE:** The FileMaker Pro and MacSQL sections assume prior experience with the respective application and with basic database concepts and terminology.

Automating FileMaker Pro with AppleScript

FileMaker Pro is one of the oldest and most loved applications used on the Mac. It started out through Claris, an Apple subsidiary, and is now created and sold by FileMaker, Inc. (http://www.filemaker.com). FileMaker Pro is known for its ease of use, robust scripting, and layout tools, which give developers the ability to develop database-driven applications quickly.

One thing you should know about FileMaker Pro's AppleScript support is that it's designed for manipulating the data in existing databases, not constructing new ones. You still have to do tasks such as creating new databases and editing their layouts using FileMaker Pro's graphical interface. As a result, you'll find that many properties and elements are noneditable. For example, you can't use AppleScript to create and delete database or layout elements, and you can change only one important property, cellValue, using the set command.

Although this might sound like a significant limitation, it really isn't. The beauty of scripting FileMaker Pro isn't in how you can construct the database but rather in how you can use an already established database to help you with script execution. Given an existing database, you can use AppleScript to get and set the values of records' cells, create and delete records, and perform advanced operations such as finding and sorting records. As a scripter, I like that I can use FileMaker Pro to put together a back-end database for my script with minimal effort. I can give the users a nice user interface, set up reports, control security in a jiffy, and best of all, have full access to the underlying data.

The following sections describe the important aspects of FileMaker Pro scripting. While these sections cover FileMaker Pro 10, versions 7 to 9 will work as well.

> **NOTE:** The downloadable source code for this book includes sample files for use with the scripts in this chapter. You can find it at http://www.apress.com.

The FileMaker Object Model and the Commands You Can Use

The FileMaker Pro object model is reasonably simple. Figure 25–1 shows a slightly simplified diagram of the containment structure of the main FileMaker objects.

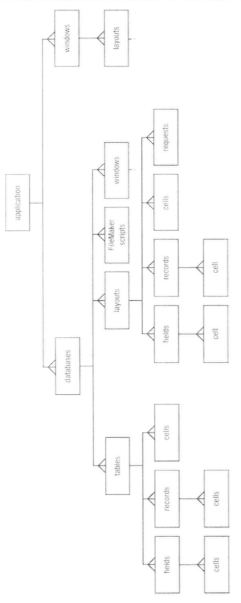

Figure 25–1. *The containment structure for the main objects in FileMaker Pro's object model*

A few less important element classes have been omitted for simplicity, as have a number of properties that provide convenient shortcuts to objects of interest (for example, window objects have properties containing references to the current layout, record, table, and cell objects.) However, the diagram should give you a pretty good idea of how the object model fits together overall, and you can always look up the FileMaker Pro dictionary in AppleScript Editor to fill in the remaining details.

Here's a quick overview of the main object classes, to help you get started:

- Database objects represent open FileMaker Pro files. Databases consist of tables and layouts.

- Tables, which consist of rows and columns (records and fields) of cells, store your data.

- Layouts control exactly how and where that data is presented, and can be used to perform searches and sorts.

- Windows allow you to organize and view your data using layouts.

The following sections will discuss all of these objects in much more detail.

The *database* Class

The main elements of the top-level application object are database and window. There's also menu, but I will not cover it here.

The application object's database elements represent open FileMaker Pro database files. (In fact, FileMaker Pro's dictionary defines another class, document, but you'll find that database and document are interchangeable in practice.)

You can refer to database elements either by index (which depends on the current window order) or by name (which is the same as its file name, except that the name extension bit is optional). For example:

```
tell application "FileMaker Pro"
   open alias "Macintosh HD:Users:hanaan:Desktop:Inventory.fp7"
end tell

tell application "FileMaker Pro"
   database 1
end tell
--> database "Inventory.fp7" of application "FileMaker Pro"

tell application "FileMaker Pro"
   database "Inventory"
end tell
--> database "Inventory.fp7" of application "FileMaker Pro"
```

A modern FileMaker Pro database file contains one or more tables, which hold your data, and defines one or more layouts for viewing that data in various ways. Not surprisingly, FileMaker Pro's dictionary defines table and layout classes to represent database tables and layouts too. Using table objects is good when you want direct access to all the data in that table, and using layouts is useful when you want to work with a found set of records. You'll look at using tables and layouts in later sections.

The *window* Class

Windows display some or all of a database's data. Although you can generally ignore window objects in other applications when scripting them, in FileMaker Pro scripting, you need to refer to window objects and their layout elements whenever you want to work with found sets.

Window objects appear both as elements of the top-level `application` object and as elements of each database object. The latter is particularly useful when you already have a reference to a particular database and want a reference to the window (or windows) that belongs to it. For example:

```
tell application "FileMaker Pro"
    tell database "Inventory"
        window 1
    end tell
end tell
--> window "Inventory" of database "Inventory.fp7" of application "FileMaker Pro"
```

Each database can have one or more windows open at the same time, and each window can show its own found set of records. For example, one window might show all the records in your database, although another shows only the records that match a recent `find` request. You can refer to windows either by index (which depends on their onscreen order) or by name. If a database has multiple windows open, make sure you refer to the window that contains the found set you want.

Each window uses a layout from the database to display the records in its found set, and you can switch between layouts whenever you like, to display that data in different ways. To get and set values in a found set, you need to use a layout that includes fields that show those values. In the later section on the `layout` class, I'll discuss how to go to different layouts in a window, how to use them to manipulate the found set, and how to get and set values.

The *table* Class

Tables are where your actual data is stored. Simple databases will have just a single table, but more sophisticated relational designs can contain multiple tables whose records are related to one another in various ways.

For example, a sales database might have one table containing its product details, a second table containing its customer details, and a third table for keeping track of which customers buy which products. FileMaker Pro will use the predefined relationships between the database's tables and unique IDs stored in the key fields of each table to determine which records are related to one another (hence the phrase *relational database*).

FileMaker Pro allows AppleScripts to have direct access to a database's table objects. This is useful when you want full access to all the fields in that table and to the data in every cell of every record.

Script 25–1 shows a typical script for getting values from a table.

Script 25–1.

```
tell application "FileMaker Pro"
    tell database "Inventory"
        tell table "equipment"
            tell record 1
                set the_date to cell "date purchased"
                set the_cost to cell "cost"
            end tell
        end tell
    end tell
end tell
{the_date, the_cost}
--> {"12/2/2008", "740"}
```

Note that this script asks for the first record in the table. In a table, records always appear in the order they were added, so the first record is the oldest and the last record is the newest. You cannot change the order of records in a table; you can only add and delete them. New records are automatically added at the end, of course.

The *layout* Class

Layouts present particular views of a database's data to its users, both human and AppleScript. You can use layouts to find only those records that match certain criteria (the found set) and to sort records in a particular order. A layout may show some or all of the fields from a single table or from several related tables if portal views are used.

For example, the sales database mentioned earlier might provide one layout for viewing the company's product details (name, model number, description, and price) and another layout for viewing its customer details (contact name, mailing address, and account number). In addition, since this is a relational database, the customer layout could include a portal view showing which of the company's products a customer has purchased.

Working with layouts in AppleScript is a lot like working with them by hand. To use a layout, you first have to refer to a window in which it's displayed. FileMaker Pro's database objects helpfully include window elements, which makes it easy to locate the window (or windows) currently displaying the data for a particular database.

Script 25–2 shows a typical script for getting values from a layout.

Script 25–2.

```
tell application "FileMaker Pro"
    tell database "Inventory"
        tell window 1
            go to layout "equipment"
            tell current record
                set the_date to cell "date purchased"
```

```
            set the_cost to cell "cost"
          end tell
        end tell
      end tell
end tell
{the_date, the_cost}
--> {"12/2/2008", "740"}
```

As you can see, this script has some similarities to the previous one but also some differences. Notice that instead of referring to `table "equipment"` of database `"Inventory"`, you now start by referring to `window 1` of database `"Inventory"`. Next you use the `go to` command to tell the window which layout you want it to display. In this case, you go to a layout named "equipment", which is set up to display various data from the equipment table. Once the desired layout is visible, you can identify the record you're interested in and get the values from its cells.

Since windows and layouts are used for controlling how data is displayed, they have some extra abilities that tables don't; for example, you can ask FileMaker Pro for the currently selected record by referring to the window's `current record` property. If you wanted the first record currently shown in that layout, you could get that by referring to `record 1 of layout "equipment" of window 1`. Of course, which record that is will depend on which records are in the window's found set and the order in which they are sorted.

One other difference when working with layouts rather than tables is that you can refer only to fields that are actually present on the layout itself. For example, if a table includes a "product code" field but the layout you're using doesn't display this field, you won't be able to get the product code from that particular layout—you'll need to use a different layout or access the table directly instead. On the other hand, a single layout can have portal views that allow you to access data held in multiple tables, whereas a table object allows you to access the data only in that particular table.

Incidentally, if you're designing a FileMaker Pro database yourself, you might sometimes find it useful to set up some layouts especially for your AppleScripts to use, in addition to the layouts you provide for human users. That way, your scripts can get access to additional fields that human users don't need to see, and you can still enjoy the extra benefits that working with layouts rather than tables provides (found sets, sorting, and so on).

The *record*, *field*, and *cell* Classes

In FileMaker Pro you can get and set the data of an individual cell or of an entire record or field at once.

Although the `cell` class has a `cellValue` property, just referring to the cell object returns its value, as shown in Script 25–3.

Script 25–3. *(Includes the next two scripts)*

```
tell application "FileMaker Pro"
    tell database "Inventory"
        tell record 3 of table "equipment"
            get cellValue of cell "cost"
```

```
      end tell
   end tell
end tell
--> "495"
```

As you can see, getting the value of the cell's cellValue property returns a string, but FileMaker Pro also allows you to retrieve the same value just by using this:

```
tell application "FileMaker Pro"
   tell database "Inventory"
      tell record 3 of table "equipment"
         get cell "cost"
      end tell
   end tell
end tell
--> "495"
```

Getting either the cell element or its cellValue property always returns a string, no matter from where the field type the data comes.

Script 25–4 sets the value of a cell in certain records of a table.

Script 25–4.

```
tell application "FileMaker Pro"
   tell database "Inventory"
      tell table "equipment"
         tell (every record whose cell "model" is "DP-121")
            set cell "status" to "obsolete"
         end tell
      end tell
   end tell
end tell
```

The preceding script represents more than merely a way to set data. As you can see, you can also use a whose clause to specify *which* records you want a command to act on. Think of the whose clause as AppleScript's own answer to FileMaker Pro's Find Mode, although you can use AppleScript to control that too if you want; you'll look at doing this later in this chapter.

You can also set or get data of an entire field or record at once. For example, the following script gets all the values from the "test scores" field of the database's "score" table:

```
tell application "FileMaker Pro"
   tell database "Test Scores"
      get field "score" of table "test scores"
   end tell
end tell
--> {"80", "65", "76", "83", "95", "47", ...}
```

Here's another example that gets all the cell values from a record:

```
tell application "FileMaker Pro"
   get record 5 of table "test scores" of database "Test Scores"
end tell
--> {"Janet", "Smith", "95"}
```

You can even retrieve all the data in the table at once either by writing this,

```
tell application "FileMaker Pro"
    get table "test scores" of database "Test Scores"
end tell
```

or by writing this,

```
tell application "FileMaker Pro"
    get every field of table "test scores" of database "Test Scores"
end tell
```

depending on whether you want the cell values grouped by record or by field. Both commands will return a list of lists.

When you work with table and layout objects, you have to be aware of the order FileMaker Pro uses when it sets and returns data.

As explained earlier, the field order in a table is the field creation order, and the record order is the record creation order. You can't change that order, even by sorting the records. However, when you get data from the layout instead of the table, the records will be returned from the found set in the current sort order.

This means that although the table object is more flexible and has greater access to the data, it may be beneficial sometimes to use the layout object to get or set the same data, because you can specify the sort order and found set you want before you change or get the data, which gives you more control over what you do.

Script 25–5 first uses FileMaker Pro's show command with a whose reference to tell FileMaker Pro to show the records you want in the current window. It then sorts the displayed records based on the contents of the "cost" field before retrieving the data from this field.

Script 25–5.

```
tell application "FileMaker Pro"
    tell database "Inventory"
        tell table "equipment"
            show (every record whose cell "category" is "miscellaneous")
        end tell
        tell layout "equipment" of window 1
            sort by field "cost"
            set cost_list to field "cost"
        end tell
    end tell
end tell
cost_list --> {"50", "185", "200", "200", "450"}
```

In the preceding script, you use FileMaker Pro's show command as a simpler alternative to its find command. The actual find command in FileMaker Pro's AppleScript dictionary will perform a find using the most recent find settings. Although you can use AppleScript to create and execute new find requests from scratch, for most tasks it's easier just to use the show command with a whose reference.

Notice that for the show command, you turn to the table object, not the layout object. Remember, the layout object knows only about the currently found set, so it will show the records that fit the criteria you set, if they are already in the found set. Even if you use the following line, FileMaker Pro may not show all the records in the table:

```
show every record of layout "equipment"
```

To show all the records in the table, you will need to use the following:

```
show every record of table "equipment"
```

To sort records, on the other hand, you have to use a layout object because the table object doesn't handle the sort command.

Just as you get data from the database a whole field at a time, you can also insert data a whole field at a time.

Script 25–6 sets the "asset tag" cell of every record in the found set to values from a list. The values will be applied to the records in the order in which they happened to be sorted at the time.

Script 25–6.

```
set asset_tags to {"AB-222", "AB-223", "AB-224", "AB-225", "AB-226"}
tell application "FileMaker Pro"
    tell database "Inventory"
        tell layout "equipment" of window 1
            set field "asset tags" to asset_tags
        end tell
    end tell
end tell
```

If the inner tell block had been directed at the table object instead of the layout object, then the data in the field would apply to the records in the table, starting from the first one in the creation order, going up until the last record or the last item in the list (whichever comes first), completely ignoring the found set and the sort order.

> **NOTE:** When performing layout-based searches and sorts, make sure your layout reference points to a layout element of a window object, not a database object, otherwise it won't work.

Finding Data Quickly with the *whose* Clause

You probably have used the **Find Mode** menu option in FileMaker Pro many times. When writing scripts for FileMaker Pro, however, you may want to avoid using either the dictionary's find command or any reference to a FileMaker Pro script that performs a find command—not necessarily because they don't work, but rather because there's a better way to refer to the set of records you want to use. That way is AppleScript's powerful filtering whose clause.

For most operations, such as getting and setting data with the get and set commands, you don't even need to actually find the data and display the found set, but rather isolate the records you want to work with inside your script. The whose clause is great for that.

As you've seen, you can use a single *whose* clause to retrieve complex sets of data. Script 25–7 shows an example.

Script 25–7.

```
tell application "FileMaker Pro"
    tell database "Campaign"
        tell table "donors"
            tell (every record whose ¬
                cell "state" = "RI" and ¬
                cell "income" > 100000)
                set address_list to cell "address"
                set phone_list to cell "tel01"
                set name_list to cell "full name"
            end tell
        end tell
    end tell
end tell
```

The preceding script allows you to get data quickly from a specific set of records without changing any interfaces, running any scripts, or invoking any FileMaker Pro find commands.

Using the *whose* Clause to Retrieve Relational Data

Using the *whose* clause search techniques you saw previously, you can perform complex relational searches with minimal effort and without having to set up or refer to any FileMaker Pro relationships.

The idea is to first find the key field and then use the value in that key field to find related records. For example, let's say you have a contacts database. In that contacts database you have two tables: "People" and "Numbers". The "Numbers" table contains all the fax and phone numbers for all the contacts, and every number is linked to the contacts with the "person id" field. Each number record has four cells then: "number id", "person id", "number label", and "number value".

Now let's imagine you have a person named John L. Smith from Boulder, Colorado, and you need to get all the numbers related to his record. All you have to do is find the value of the "person id" field in the "People" table and then find all the records in the "Numbers" table that have that same number in that table's "person id" field. Script 25–8 shows how the script goes.

Script 25–8.

```
tell application "FileMaker Pro"
    tell database "Customers"
        tell table "People"
            tell (first record whose ¬
                cell "first name" = "John" and ¬
                cell "middle name" starts with "L" and ¬
                cell "last name" = "Smith" and ¬
                cell "city" = "Boulder" and ¬
                cell "state" = "CO")
                -- Note: the next line will error if the person isn't found
                set person_id to cell "person id"
```

```
        end tell
      end tell
      tell table "Number"
        tell (every record whose cell "person id" = person_id)
          set person_number_list to cell "number value"
        end tell
      end tell
    end tell
end tell
```

Using the *find* Command

Using the whose clause for filtering records is great in many cases, but FileMaker Pro
still may have search criteria that perform filtering functions not available in
AppleScript, such as searches for duplicates and searches that need to perform
complex tests on cells' values. In these situations you'll want to use FileMaker Pro's
find command instead.

For example, Script 25–9 will find all the Wednesday morning meetings that will be
attended by employee John Smith. A whose clause is no good here because there's no
way to make it match only records whose dates fall on a Wednesday, so you have to
use find.

Script 25–9.

```
tell application "FileMaker Pro"
  tell database "Company Calendar"
    show every record of table "Meetings"
    tell window 1
      tell layout "Meeting Details"
        go to it
        if requests exists then delete requests
        set my_request to create request
        tell my_request
          set cell "Date" to "=Wednesday"
          set cell "Start Time" to "8 AM...12 PM"
          set cell "Attendees::First Name" to "==John"
          set cell "Attendees::Last Name" to "==Smith"
        end tell
      end tell
      find
    end tell
  end tell
end tell
```

Figure 25–2 shows a typical result after this script is run.

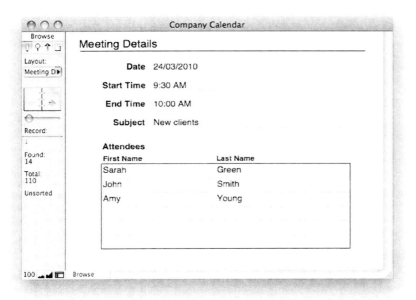

Figure 25–2. *The result of running the* find *script; FileMaker Pro has found 14 out of 110 records matching the request.*

You start by identifying the window you want to work with, window 1 of database "Company Calendar". Next you tell this window to go to the "Meeting Details" layout, which lets you view the information you want. You then tell this layout to delete any previous find requests; otherwise, these would interfere with your new search.

Now you can construct the new search request. First you use the create (make) command to add a new request element to the layout. You then add the search values to this request. To match a particular day in the date field named "Date", you use a string containing an equals (=) sign followed by the name of the day. To match a range of times in the "Start Time" field, you write the starting time followed by three dots and then the finishing time. The "Meeting Details" layout uses a portal view of the database's "Attendees" table to show the first and last names of the employees who will be attending each meeting, so you refer to those cells as "Attendees::First Name" and "Attendees::Last Name". To exactly match the text in those fields, you add two equals signs to the start of your strings. You can find full instructions on how to use FileMaker Pro's special find symbols in its built-in Help.

Once you've finished setting up the request, you tell the window (not the layout) to perform the find command. Any records that don't match all the criteria in the search request will be eliminated from the found set, leaving just the ones you want.

Running AppleScripts from Inside FileMaker Pro

FileMaker Pro allows you to run AppleScripts that are embedded in FileMaker Pro scripts. To do that, you use the Perform AppleScript script step in a FileMaker Pro script.

Figure 25–3 shows the dialog box in FileMaker Pro that allows you to specify the AppleScript you want to run.

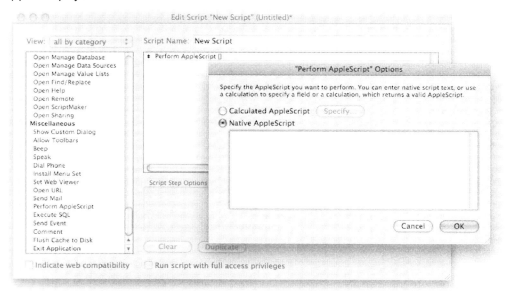

Figure 25–3. *The Perform AppleScript script step in a FileMaker Pro script*

This script step is used to execute AppleScript code in the middle of a FileMaker Pro script. As you can see in Figure 25–3, you have two ways to perform AppleScripts from FileMaker Pro scripts. You can either specify a calculation, whose text result is a valid AppleScript, or dictate the actual script text.

If you choose to enter the native AppleScript code, FileMaker Pro will attempt to compile your script and check your syntax when you click the OK button. You will be able to exit the dialog box only if the script you entered compiles or if you click Cancel. Note that unlike other AppleScript editors, FileMaker Pro does not reformat your source code or colorize its keywords after it has been compiled. For instance, if you typed `tell app "Finder" ... end` instead of `tell application "Finder" ... end tell`, that is the way your source code will remain. Don't worry, though; as long as you can click the OK button, you'll know it has been compiled correctly.

> **TIP:** When running AppleScripts from a FileMaker Pro script step, FileMaker Pro is considered to be the default application. This means if you choose, you don't have to use the `tell application "FileMaker Pro"` line. I recommend you do, though, in order to make your scripts also usable outside the context of a FileMaker Pro script. This also lets you develop your script in your usual script editor and paste it into FileMaker Pro once you're happy with it. Writing AppleScripts in AppleScript Editor or Script Debugger is a lot nicer than doing it in FileMaker Pro!

In the case of calculated fields, FileMaker Pro compiles the script right before execution, because the script can change any time leading up to that point.

You can use the Native AppleScript option when you want the database to execute the same script every time. The Calculated AppleScript option is great when you need the database to choose from a selection of prewritten scripts or generate the script's code on-the-fly; for example, you might want it to run a different script depending on what day of the week it is.

I prefer to put all my scripts into calculation fields—even the ones that could be typed into. The actual code for these scripts is stored in an extra table I call "AppleScript". Each record contains the text for a different AppleScript used by the entire database. That way, whenever I need to make manual changes to a script, I need to edit only a field in the database, rather than having to dig up the original FileMaker Pro script step each time.

> **CAUTION:** Because FileMaker Pro acts as the default application when you run AppleScripts from inside FileMaker Pro, some scripting addition commands normally won't compile because of conflicts with existing keywords in FileMaker Pro's dictionary. For example, FileMaker Pro's dictionary defines `read` and `write` constants for describing the access privileges for tables, records, and so on. This means Standard Additions' `read` and `write` commands don't compile unless you place them in another application's `tell` block, such as the Finder.

Scripting Runtime Labs' MacSQL

In many cases your AppleScripts have to connect to different enterprise SQL databases. These databases span Microsoft SQL Server, MySQL, Oracle, FrontBase, OpenBase, Sybase, and others. When your AppleScript solution calls for integration with a SQL database, one product stands out: Runtime Labs' MacSQL (http://www.rtlabs.com).

MacSQL is a simple program that gives you GUI access to many flavors of SQL databases, including the few I mentioned previously. In addition to helping you create queries and view the schema of the SQL database, MacSQL is "AppleScriptable" to a point that you can perform any SQL command with AppleScript code. You will, of course, need the proper SQL statements that will get the job done, but these are usually easy to get. The best thing to do, if you are not familiar with SQL syntax, is to find a good reference book that details the syntax of the specific SQL flavor you're using and ask someone from IT to help you get a handle on the SQL statements you need.

Getting Connected

The biggest challenge you will face when scripting a SQL database with MacSQL is the initial stage of getting access to your database. Once you're over that part, it's usually smooth sailing.

To get connected, you will need database access settings such as the host, database name, and user login information. Start by choosing **File ➤ New**. In the New Connection dialog box, shown in Figure 25–4, choose the database type you will be using. Once you do that, MacSQL will display the fields you need to fill in order to establish a connection with your database. Write down the settings you will require, and ask someone from IT for the values to enter.

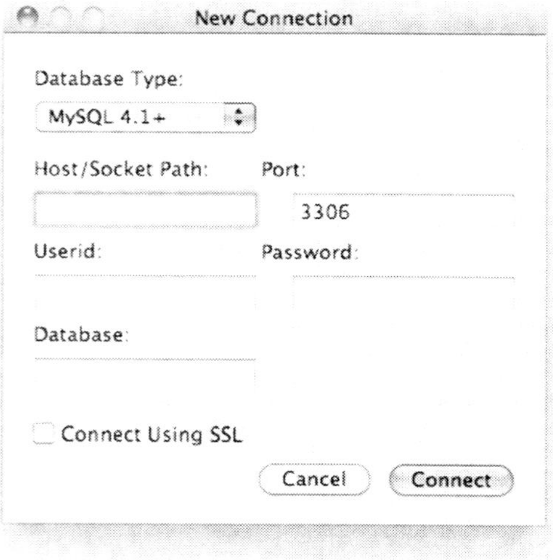

Figure 25–4. *MacSQL's New Connection dialog box*

After some consultation with IT, you should be able to establish a connection with the database. This connection will represent itself in the form of a MacSQL document. Save this document to the hard drive, and keep a note somewhere safe with the settings the administrator gave you (for example, use Keychain Access to make a secure note in your keychain).

The document you saved is your new best friend. Every time your script needs to connect to that database, all you have to do is open that document. Then, you will direct any SQL statement to MacSQL's front document object, which has all the settings.

Using a Simple *select* Command

Interacting with SQL databases using MacSQL is a bit more complicated than just using the do query command. Script 25–10 gets data from two fields from the entire "contact_table" table. Let's look at the script and then analyze it line by line.

Script 25–10.

```
1. set query_text to "SELECT first_name, last_name FROM contact_table"
2. tell application "MacSQL3"
3.    tell front document
4.       set the_result_set to ¬
              do query query_text results as none with prefetching results
5.    end tell
6.    set the_data to values of every row of the_result_set
7.    delete the_result_set
8. end tell
9. return the_data
--> {{"Liz", "Brown"}, {"Jason", "Green"}, ...}
```

Line 1 of the script is simply the string that makes up the SQL command. Usually, you will be concatenating strings in AppleScript to get to the final SQL statement you want.

Next, line 3 declares that you want to talk to the front document. Remember, this is the document you saved in the "Getting Connected" section. This script assumes that this document is already open and frontmost in MacSQL.

In line 4, you do the query. You supply the do query command with a direct string parameter that contains the raw SQL command. The SQL statement you use has been put in the variable query_text in the first line of the script.

When the do query command's results as parameter is none and the command is successful, the result is a reference to a result set. A result set is a MacSQL object that can contain rows and columns (more on that later). In this script you assign the reference returned by the do query command to the variable the_result_set. Line 6 then extracts the values from every row of the result set and assigns the result to the variable the_data.

Now, the value of the variable the_data contains a list of lists, and it contains all the data you fetched from the SQL table.

Line 7 deletes the result set. This is essential housecleaning. If you don't delete the result set once you've finished with it, MacSQL will jam after a number of queries.

More on Result Sets

Because of the way MacSQL communicates with database applications, result set objects behave a bit differently from other application objects. Depending on the type of database (such as Microsoft SQL Server) and how you use the do query command, the rows of the result set may be "indeterminate"—that is, MacSQL doesn't know how many rows there are or what they contain until you actually ask for each one. This means a command such as get every row of the_result_set won't work as intended when a result set has indeterminate rows. Instead, you have to loop an unlimited number of times, getting the next row of the result set until an error occurs. You can then trap that error, using it to break out of the repeat loop.

Another option is to use the do query command's prefetching results parameter, as shown in Script 25–10. If prefetching results is true (the default is false), MacSQL will obtain the data for all the rows from the database in advance. However, the MacSQL documentation warns that this could cause problems if there is a large amount of data, so sometimes you may want to use the looping approach instead.

Script 25–11 is adapted from one of the sample scripts that come with MacSQL, which forces you to loop through the rows and then through the items in each row for the purpose of generating a tab-delimited string.

Script 25–11.

```
tell application "MacSQL3"
    tell front document
        set result_set to do query "select * from some_table" results as none
    end tell
    set result_text to ""
    set row_num to 1
    try
        repeat
            set the_values to tab delimited values of row row_num of result_set
            set result_text to result_text & the_values & linefeed
            set rowNum to rowNum + 1
        end repeat
    on error err
    end try
    delete result_set
end tell
return result_text
```

Although this is a good example of the row and result set objects, know that each row object has not only the values property, whose value is a list, but also the tab delimited values property, which contains the string version of the data in the row.

> **NOTE:** When working with Microsoft SQL Server, it is important to always retrieve all the rows for a result set; otherwise, it won't behave correctly. If you use prefetching results, this will be done for you; otherwise, you *must* loop through every single row in the result set yourself until no more are found.

Some Useful Handlers

The next two scripts provide useful handlers for working with a Microsoft SQL Server database. Script 25–12 returns data that the SQL statement gets from the database. Script 25–13 sets data, so it doesn't need to return anything.

Script 25-12.

```
set query_text to "SELECT first_name, last_name FROM contact_table"
set the_result to sql_query_select(query_text)

on sql_query_select(query_text)
    try
        tell application "MacSQL3"
            tell front document
                set rs to do query query_text results as none with prefetching results
            end tell
            set the_data to values of every row of rs
            delete rs
        end tell
        return the_data
    on error err_msg number err_num
        -- Uncomment the next line during testing and debugging
        -- display dialog err_msg & return & query_text
        try
            delete rs
        end try
        error err_msg number err_num
    end try
end sql_query_select
```

Script 25-13.

```
set query_text to ¬
    "INSERT INTO contact_table (first_name, last_name) VALUES ('Dan', 'Smith')"
set the_result to sql_query_insert(query_text)

on sql_query_insert(query_text)
    try
        tell application "MacSQL3"
            tell front document
                set rs to do query query_text results as none
                delete rs
            end tell
        end tell
    on error err_msg number err_num
        try
            delete rs
        end try
        -- Uncomment the next line during testing and debugging
        -- display dialog err_msg & return & query_text
        error err_msg number err_num
    end try
end sql_query_insert
```

As discussed previously, deleting each result set once you're finished with it is essential. Each result set object uses a separate connection to the database, and database applications put a maximum limit on the number of connections you can have open at the same time (the exact number depends on the database setup). So, if you don't clean up after yourself, you will eventually get the error "Connection pool limit reached."

Notice how each handler attempts to delete the result set if there has been any error in the script. This ensures that if the error occurred after the result set was created but before it was deleted, you won't eventually get a "Connection pool limit reached" error.

Database Events

Database Events is a small scriptable faceless background application (FBA) included in Mac OS X. You can use Database Events to create simple, free-form object databases for storing strings, numbers, and other AppleScript values in any structure you like.

Each Database Events database you create is stored as a file on your hard disk. The database name and folder path you specify while creating them determine the file path where the data is stored. Each record in the database is created individually and can contain any number of field elements, each of which has its own name and value properties.

Database Events Classes and Commands

You can find the Database Events application in /System/Library/CoreServices/. Here are the database-related classes from its dictionary:

```
database n [inh. item] : A collection of records, residing at a location in
      the file system
  ELEMENTS
  contains records; contained by application.
  PROPERTIES
  location (alias, r/o) : the folder that contains the database
  name (text, r/o) : the name of the database

record n [inh. item] : A collection of fields, residing in a database
  ELEMENTS
  contains fields; contained by databases.
  PROPERTIES
  id (integer, r/o) : the unique id of the record
  name (text, r/o) : the name of the record, equivalent to the value of the
          field named "name"

field n [inh. item] : A named piece of data, residing in a record
  ELEMENTS
  contained by records.
  PROPERTIES
  id (integer, r/o) : the unique id of the field
  name (text, r/o) : the name of the field
  value (any) : the value of the field
```

As you can see from the dictionary, there are three main classes, besides the application class, of course. These classes are database, record, and field. Unlike FileMaker Pro, there is no table class or cell class. Also, Database Events doesn't require that neighboring records all have the same structure. Each record can have completely different fields, with different names and data types.

While Database Events does not provide any special commands for working with objects in the database, you have the full range of Standard Suite application commands to work with—make, move, duplicate, delete, and so on—and you can use whose clauses to filter records according to the field values you want.

Database Events Examples

To see how Database Events scripting works, let's create two scripts: one will create the database and populate it with records, fields, and data; the second script will read the data.

Script 25–14 will create a database named "cars" that has two records; each record will hold information about one car in three fields, say, "make", "model", and "year". When the script is run, a file named cars.dbev will be created automatically on your desktop if it doesn't already exist; otherwise, the existing file will be used.

Script 25–14.

```
set the_folder to path to desktop
tell application "Database Events"
  set the_db to make new database with properties {name:"cars", location:the_folder}
  tell the_db
    set the_record to make new record with properties {name:"Toyota"}
    make new record with properties {name:"Mercedes"}
  end tell
  tell the_record
    make new field with properties {name:"Make", value:"Toyota"}
    make new field with properties {name:"Model", value:"Camry"}
    make new field with properties {name:"Year", value:1993}
  end tell
  tell record "Mercedes" of the_db
    make new field with properties {name:"Make", value:"Mercedes-Benz"}
    make new field with properties {name:"Model", value:"300TD"}
    make new field with properties {name:"Year", value:1997}
  end tell
  save the_db
end tell
```

Let's take a look at a few points in this script. First, note the use of variables for referencing database elements and the database object itself. The script starts by creating a new database and assigning it to the the_db variable. Later in the script, you refer to the database using this variable.

Also, references to the records you create in the database are assigned to variables as they are created. The first record the script adds fields to is assigned to the variable the_record. Later on, the script retrieves the record reference from the variable and uses it as the target for further commands. Just for comparison, the second record isn't assigned a variable. Instead, it's referenced using its name in the script line tell record "Mercedes" of the_db.

The last command in the script is the save command: save the_db. This line saves the changes to the cars.dbev database file on your desktop.

The following script will get data from a single field from the database:

```
tell application "Database Events"
  tell database "~/Desktop/cars.dbev"
    set car_model to value of field "Model" of record "Mercedes"
  end tell
end tell
car_model
--> "300TD"
```

Notice how you identify the database using a POSIX path to the existing database file. The ~ character is shorthand for the path to the current user's home folder, which Database Events understands.

After you established a link with the database, you can go down the object hierarchy: database ➤ record ➤ field.

Database Events supports the usual range of AppleScript reference forms, allowing you to perform basic database-style operations. For example, to get the make of every car, use this:

```
tell application "Database Events"
    tell database "~/Desktop/cars.dbev"
        set car_makes to value of field "Make" of every record
    end tell
end tell
car_make
--> {"Toyota", "Mercedes-Benz"}
```

Remember, though, that Database Events doesn't require every record in a database to contain the same fields, so this script will work only if all records contain a field named "Make".

Similarly, to delete all the records for cars made before 1995, use this:

```
tell application "Database Events"
    tell database "~/Desktop/cars.dbev"
        delete every record whose value of field "Year" < 1995
    end tell
end tell
```

To extract all the values from the database as a list of lists (assuming that every record contains identically named fields in the same order), use this:

```
tell application "Database Events"
    tell database "~/Desktop/cars.dbev"
        set field_names to name of every field of first record
        set record_values to value of every field of every record
    end tell
end tell
{field_names:field_names, record_values:record_values}
--> {
    field_names:{"name", "Make", "Model", "Year"},
    record_values:{{"Toyota", "Toyota", "Camry", 1993},
                   {"Mercedes", "Mercedes-Benz", "300TD", 1997}}
}
```

Summary

In this chapter, you learned about three different options for managing and manipulating large amounts of data using AppleScript.

First, we explored the venerable FileMaker Pro application, which provides an extensive, if slightly quirky, AppleScript interface. You learned how to interact directly with database tables, retrieving and modifying their contents in various ways, and performing simple searches using the standard whose clause. You also learned how to manipulate layouts, which control the display of records onscreen and can also be used by AppleScript to perform complex searching and sorting operations.

Next, we discussed Runtime Labs' MacSQL application, which allows you to send SQL queries to popular relational database systems such as MySQL and process the results.

Finally, we looked at Mac OS X's Database Events application, a simple object database which AppleScript can use to store simple values such as numbers, strings, and lists and retrieve them again later.

In the next chapter, we will complete our tour of scriptable productivity applications by getting to grips with one of the biggest names in AppleScript automation: Adobe InDesign.

Chapter 26

Scripting Adobe InDesign

One of the hard facts of scripting life is that before you work out how to do something, you often need to find out if you can do it at all. Applications that make nearly all their abilities available to scripters are still too rare. But one application that stands out in this area is Adobe InDesign (see Figure 26–1).

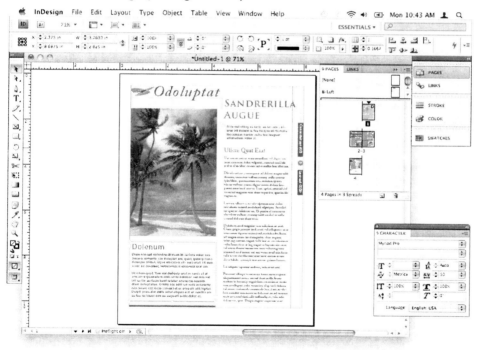

Figure 26–1. *The Adobe InDesign application*

InDesign is a poster child for scriptability. It's a very complex application, and just about everything it does can be scripted. It has a Scripts panel you can run scripts from. You can attach scripts so that they are run when menu items are chosen, and you can add your own scripts to any menu. You can set scripts to be run when the application is launched, or when events such as a document opening occur. It supports versioning, which enables you to instruct a version to behave like an older version, to keep your older scripts running until you update them. It ships with several sample utility scripts preinstalled, and its detailed documentation can be freely downloaded. There is an Adobe User to User forum devoted to scripting InDesign. It even "talks" three languages, depending on the platform: AppleScript, Visual Basic, and Adobe's version of JavaScript.

> **NOTE:** You can download sample scripts, tutorials, and documentation for versions CS3 and CS4 from `http://www.adobe.com/products/indesign/scripting/`. And you can navigate to Adobe's InDesign Scripting User to User Forum from `http://forums.adobe.com`.

InDesign does some things differently from how other applications do them, and the approach it takes to harness some of its capabilities into a manageable form may be confusing at first. But the scripting implementation follows closely the structure of how the application works in the user interface. This means that, for a scripter, understanding how InDesign works is just as important as understanding AppleScript.

This chapter covers the latest version of InDesign, CS4, also known as version 6.0. But most of the scripts will also work in CS3 and earlier versions—most changes with new versions involve accommodating new features or expanding old ones. Perhaps the most significant change for scripts was between CS2 and CS3, where the introduction of find-change capabilities for objects, glyphs, and grep patterns meant the way of scripting find-change had to be overhauled.

> **NOTE:** Grep is InDesign's version of regular expressions, previously covered in Chapter 23. Although InDesign uses a different pattern-matching syntax from that used by the Satimage scripting addition, the overall idea is the same.

In a well-designed scriptable application, the "power" is locked up in the objects and their properties. This is true of InDesign, but it also has many custom commands, often mirroring commands in the user interface. This approach has both pros and cons, but in a complex application, it sometimes makes hunting down the correct command easier for the newcomer.

Learning by Example

One of the best ways to learn how to script an application is to look at existing scripts, especially ones that do something similar to what you want to do. With InDesign, there are plenty of scripts available. There are about 20 sample utility scripts preloaded in the Scripts panel, which is shown in Figure 26–2 (you may need to download them for versions before CS4).

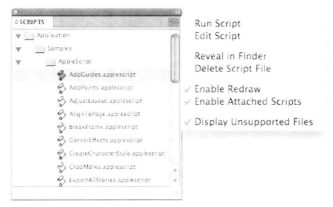

Figure 26–2. *The Scripts panel, showing some of the sample scripts included in CS4*

When you download the scripting tutorial from the Adobe web site, it is accompanied by more than 200 snippet files covering a broad range of areas. The *Adobe InDesign CS4 Scripting Guide: AppleScript* document alone is almost 200 pages.

So, rather than throw out a whole lot more code here, we will start off by looking at how the main objects in a typical InDesign document relate to each other, and explore some of the less obvious, unconventional, and sometimes undocumented aspects of InDesign scripting. You may want to have a look at some of the sample code first, or refer to the relevant sections of it as you make your way through this chapter.

Just be aware that the sample code is just that: it shows the use of particular commands, classes, and properties. The sample code sometimes is not the most efficient—stylistically, some reads as if it were ported from JavaScript rather than taking advantage of AppleScript features and approaches—and in some cases it makes assumptions that are not always warranted. And because it has to be written well before the application ships, it sometimes contains bugs. But it's free, it's comprehensive, and much of it is perfectly useable code you can just copy and paste.

For reasons that are probably historical, the sample scripts, including those in the Scripts panel, all ship as .applescript text files. Although they work fine like that, it is better to save scripts meant to be run from the panel as compiled scripts (.scpt files) or even script bundles (.scptd). That saves them having to be recompiled, lets you take advantage of script properties' persistence, and can make changing versions of InDesign less a chore.

> **TIP:** Where the Scripts panel's scripts are stored has changed with recent versions, and there are both machine-level and user-level homes for them. The best way to find them is to select one in the panel and choose **Reveal in Finder** from the flyout menu (shown in Figure 26–2).

Understanding the InDesign Object Model

One of the most common scripting mistakes is to refer to objects incorrectly, sometimes inadvertently but more often because of confusion over their position in the application's object hierarchy. So, one of the first steps you should take when approaching a new application is to draw a clear diagram of its object model. The diagram doesn't need to cover every class—in the case of a complex application like InDesign, that's likely to be so detailed as to be useless, if not impossible to draw—but it should cover the main things you are likely to deal with regularly. Figure 26–3 shows a simplified version of the containment hierarchy for InDesign's object model.

As space is limited, Figure 26–3 shows only the main classes of elements and a couple of properties. In addition, the page item and text classes have several subclasses; these details appear as inserts. Page item–related elements appear as medium-gray boxes; text-related elements appear as light-gray boxes.

> **TIP:** A larger version of this diagram is included in the source code download for this book, available from http://www.apress.com.

Figure 26–3 will help you to understand how the various classes of objects discussed in the following sections fit together in the InDesign object model, so refer back to it regularly.

How InDesign Organizes Its Many Properties

Once you have an idea of the object model, the next step is to start looking at the properties of the various object classes. If you open InDesign CS4's dictionary in a script editor, you will see that the application class contains more than 110 properties. If you look at the document class, the situation is similar. (The exact numbers depend on what plug-ins are installed.) That's a lot of properties! Yet some of the basic attributes of a document you will want to work with, such as page height and width, are not among a document's properties. What's going on?

It turns out that the application and document have many more attributes, but most of them can only be accessed indirectly. If every attribute were a property, the number of properties would be much, much larger, to the point of being very hard to manage. To help manage all the attributes, InDesign creates a whole lot of objects that have no equivalent in the user interface—things that exist just for the purpose of holding a collection of related properties. This is done throughout InDesign's object model, so it is important that you understand how it works.

Many of these classes are recognizable by their names—they are often named *something* preference, and many can be found in the Preferences suite. They are similar to the preferences class in the Finder, which can only be accessed via a read-only property of the application, but they are used more widely and for many attributes that are not preferences. If you search the dictionary for "width" or "height," you will come across a class called document preference that contains properties called page height

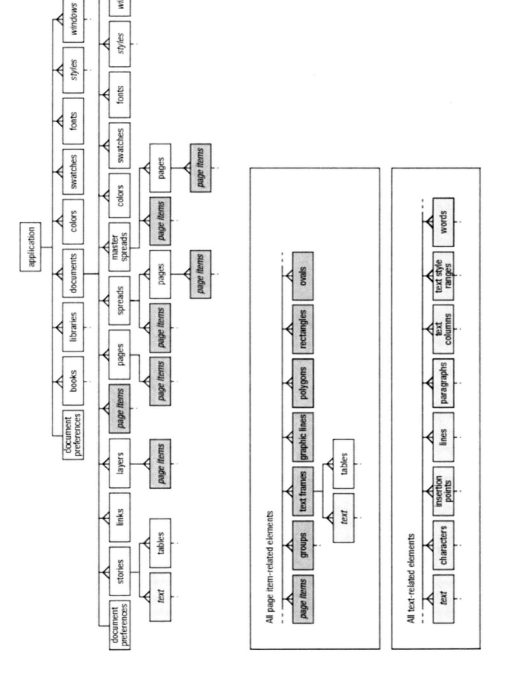

Figure 26–3. A simplified view of InDesign's containment hierarchy, showing how the main classes fit into it

and page width. These look like what you need, but there's a problem: how do they fit into the object hierarchy? The dictionary gives no immediate clue about how you might get to them.

The answer is that you access these objects indirectly: you must find an object that contains the preference object you want to manipulate, and address it there. The preference object is stored in a property whose name is usually the same as the preference class's name, except that the class name is singular and the property name is plural, which makes it easy to search for. So if you look at the document (or application) class, you will see a property called document preferences that contains an object of class document preference. Don't be put off by the read-only designation—the property returns a reference to the object, and so is read-only, but you can read and write to the properties of the object.

Script 26–1 shows how to make a new document and set the page size.

Script 26–1.

```
tell application "Adobe InDesign CS4"
    make new document
    tell document 1
        tell document preferences
            set page height to "8i"
            set page width to "6i"
        end tell
    end tell
end tell
```

Notice that the script uses strings for the sizes. InDesign will accept via scripting whatever it will accept in the GUI, so if you provide just a number, it will be interpreted in whatever measurement units are set for the rulers. When you read a measurement-related property, you will get back just a number. By default, this number will reflect the current ruler units. Some properties will allow you to specify your own choice of units when getting values—get page width as points, for example—although this doesn't work for properties that return lists, such as geometric bounds.

The application also has a document preferences property. Why? Think of the user interface: in most cases if you change a preference without a document open, you're setting a preference for future documents, but if a document is open, you're changing it for just the open document. Similarly, in scripting, if you address a preference object via the application, you're setting the default for future documents. The difference is that you can do this via scripting while documents are open. You will find many cases where more than one class has the same preference property—for example, you will find the text frame preferences property in the application, document, object style, and text frame classes.

TIP: A common mistake by newcomers is to accidentally target commands at the application rather than at a document. So you might be trying to create new styles, and nothing appears to be happening—until you close all documents, and see that the application contains the missing styles.

How InDesign Manages Units of Measurement

When manipulating the size of frames and graphics, you need to know what units you are measuring in. Many scripts do all calculations in points or some other unit; they store the preexisting units, change to points, do all their calculations and manipulation, and reset to the original units at the end. That means the script will run fine, whatever units the document's user has chosen in the user interface.

How to change the units? A search for "measurement" in the dictionary will find properties called horizontal measurement units and vertical measurement units, which belong to another preference class, view preference, accessed by the view preferences property of a document object (or the main application object).

So you might set up a new document as shown in Script 26–2.

Script 26–2.

```
tell application "Adobe InDesign CS4"
   make new document
   tell document 1
      tell view preferences
         set horizontal measurement units to inches
         set vertical measurement units to inches
      end tell
      tell document preferences
         set page height to 11
         set page width to 8
         set facing pages to false
         set pages per document to 1
      end tell
   end tell
end tell
```

TIP: Script 26–2 addresses document 1, but it could use the active document property of the application and say tell active document ... end tell instead. You will probably see examples of both methods, and most of the time there is no difference, but there a couple of occasions where it matters, so using tell document 1 ... end tell is a good habit to get into.

When you create an object, it can be more efficient to set properties at the same time, using the make command's with properties parameter. So you could write Script 26–2 as follows:

```
tell application "Adobe InDesign CS4"
   make new document with properties { ¬
       view preferences:{ ¬
           horizontal measurement units:inches, ¬
           vertical measurement units:inches}, ¬
       document preferences:{ ¬
           page height:11, page width:8, ¬
           facing pages:false, pages per document:1}}
end tell
```

But if you run this, you might get an unexpected result. That's because you have no control over the order in which the properties are processed, and in this case the page height and width are set before the measurement units. So if your default units were not vertically and horizontally inches, you might get a bit of a surprise.

How to Set Properties Safely when Making New Objects

In most cases, the order in which properties are processed doesn't matter; the preceding example is a very rare case where the order can make a difference. But there is another good reason to consider using the step-by-step approach, at least until you are familiar with InDesign scripting. Run the following script:

```
tell application "Adobe InDesign CS4"
   make new document with properties { ¬
       view preferences:{ ¬
           horizontal measurement units:inches, ¬
           vertical measurement units:inches, ¬
           allow page shuffle:false}, ¬
       document preferences:{ ¬
           page height:11, page width:8, ¬
           facing pages:false, pages per document:1}}
end tell
```

Now if you go to the flyout menu on the Pages panel, **Allow Document Pages to Shuffle** may still be checked; it will be set to whatever your default was, and unchanged by the script. Why? It's because the script addressed the allow page shuffle property as if it belonged to the view preference object, whereas it belongs to the document preference object.

In such cases, InDesign behaves differently from most other applications, and this is as much a potential trap for experienced scripters as it is for newcomers. Most applications would simply generate an error. In InDesign, when you make an object using with properties, you get an error only if you try to set a valid, direct, read-write property to an invalid value. If you try to set the value of a read-only property, the attempt will just be silently ignored. If you try to set a nonexistent property, as in the previous example, it too will be ignored.

So at least while you are developing your scripts, the longer approach makes more sense:

```
tell application "Adobe InDesign CS4"
   make new document
   tell document 1
       tell view preferences
           set horizontal measurement units to inches
```

```
            set vertical measurement units to inches
            set allow page shuffle to false
        end tell
        tell document preferences
            set page height to 11
            set page width to 8
            set facing pages to false
            set pages per document to 1
        end tell
    end tell
end tell
```

In this case you will get an error when the script tries to set the allow page shuffle property.

You might also be tempted to try a bit each way—create the document, then set the properties, perhaps like this:

```
tell application "Adobe InDesign CS4"
    make new document
    tell document 1
        set properties of view preferences to { ¬
                horizontal measurement units:inches, ¬
                vertical measurement units:inches, ¬
                allow page shuffle:false}
        set properties of document preferences to { ¬
                page height:11, page width:8, ¬
                facing pages:false, pages per document:1}
    end tell
end tell
```

In this case—where you are setting properties of something that already exists, as opposed to setting them at creation time—InDesign is even less likely to complain. As long as there is one valid read-write property being set to a valid value, InDesign will silently ignore any errors.

Don't be put off using this form—it's efficient and useful. Just be aware that it can mask problems, so sometimes breaking it down to one property at a time is a useful way to track down problems. And as you will see later, InDesign's tolerance can also be used to your advantage.

Working with Documents

The relationship between application and document is obvious, but the relationship between the document and the things that belong to it is a bit more complicated. Documents are made up of spreads and pages, and on these we put what are collectively known as page items: text frames, rectangles, polygons, ovals, graphic lines, groups, and form fields. Some of these page items in turn contain other elements, such as various types of graphics and text, as well as other page items.

The structure is hierarchical, and you can get some idea of where an item sits in the hierarchy by looking at its parent property, which naturally enough returns a reference to its parent. The problem is that items can only have one parent, yet they can belong to more than one container.

Consider a single-page document containing one text frame. The parent of the page is the spread it's on, not the document, yet the page is an element of both spread and document. The text frame is an element of page 1 of the document, of spread 1 of the document, and of the document itself. The parent of the text frame is the page. Figure 26–4 shows the containment hierarchy for these elements—notice how the document's text frame objects can be reached by several different routes.

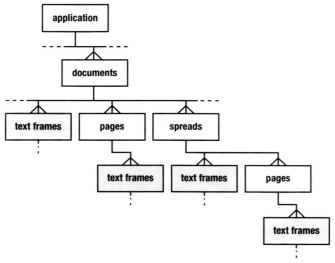

Figure 26–4. *The containment model used by InDesign document, spread, page, and text frame objects*

So you can refer to that text frame using any of the following references:

```
text frame 1 of document 1
text frame 1 of page 1 of document 1
text frame 1 of spread 1 of document 1
text frame 1 of page 1 of spread 1 of document 1
```

One more thing...if you look at the InDesign dictionary, you will see that the text frame class inherits from the page item class:

```
text frame n [inh. page item] : A text frame.
   ...
```

So you can also refer to the text frame as page item 1 of ..., because a text frame is also a page item.

> **NOTE:** The numbering, or index, of elements is generally front-to-back order, based on each element's position within its parent.

Now suppose you add a second text frame to the page, and group the two. Script 26–3 shows how to do that via AppleScript.

Script 26–3.

```
tell application "Adobe InDesign CS4"
    make new document
    tell document 1
        tell view preferences
            set horizontal measurement units to inches
            set vertical measurement units to inches
        end tell
        tell document preferences
            set page height to 11
            set page width to 8
            set facing pages to false
            set pages per document to 1
        end tell

        set text_frame_a to make new text frame at page 1 ¬
            with properties {geometric bounds:{1, 1, 6, 3}}
        set text_frame_b to make new text frame at page 1 ¬
            with properties {geometric bounds:{1, 5, 6, 7}}
        make new group at page 1 with properties ¬
            {group items:{text_frame_a, text_frame_b}}
        get every page item of page 1
    end tell
end tell
--> {group id 246 of page id 190 of spread id 185 of document "Untitled-1"
        of application "Adobe InDesign CS4"}
```

> **TIP:** The group items property used in Script 26–3 is not listed in the InDesign scripting dictionary. Also, ungrouping is done with the ungroup command.

The group belongs to the page, spread, and document, but the text frames no longer do—they belong to the group, which is now their parent. Rectangles, polygons, ovals, graphic lines—all page items behave the same.

This presents a problem if you want to write a script that involves every page item, or particular type of page item, in a document. Some might be in groups, or in groups within groups, and they might also be anchored in text. The solution is a property called all page items that returns a list of references to all the page items the target contains, regardless of where they are in its hierarchy. So if you ask for

```
all page items of document 1
```

the document with the two grouped text frames will return a list of three items: the two text frames, plus the group.

Figure 26–5 shows how the all page items property fits into the containment hierarchy.

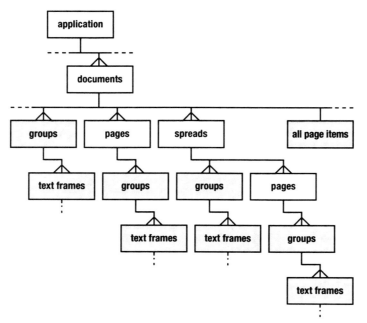

Figure 26–5. *The* all page items *property allows you to refer directly to all the page items in a document, even if they're nested inside other page items.*

The all page items property is often used in a filtered reference, or whose clause. So if you want a list of all the text frames in a document, you can use

```
set the_text_frames to every item of all page items whose class is text frame
```

> **TIP:** A mistake many newcomers make is to type every page item of all page items ..., instead of every item of all page items ...—remember that in this case you are extracting items from a list.

This distinction between all page items and every page item is important to understand, and a similar construction is used for several classes. For example, a document can contain paragraph styles, and it can contain paragraph style groups that contain other paragraph styles. The document has the property all paragraph styles to refer to all the styles, regardless of their parent. The same goes for other types of styles.

There is even a property all graphics, which returns a reference to all the graphics used in a document. Graphics do not actually sit on pages or documents—they are owned by the rectangles, ovals, or polygons they have been placed in—so this property can be especially useful.

Working with Document Layers

At this point, you might be wondering how layers fit into this scheme. Surely page items can also belong to layers. Well, no they can't, at least in the scripting sense of "belong."

When you create a page item, it appears on the active layer—the one active in the GUI. You can control this using the appropriately named active layer property of a document. Let's make a document with two layers and try it:

```
tell application "Adobe InDesign CS4"
    make new document
    tell document 1
        make new layer with properties {name:"Text"}
        set active layer to layer 1
        set active layer to layer "Text"
        set active layer to "Text"
    end tell
end tell
```

This does the same thing three ways. Referring to objects by their index can become a bit tricky because if you add or delete an item, you risk changing the index of the remaining items, so this method is best avoided if possible. Both the other methods work fine. But rework the script slightly and try again:

```
tell application "Adobe InDesign CS4"
    make new document
    make new layer at document 1 with properties {name:"Text"}
    set active layer of document 1 to "Text"
    set active layer of document 1 to layer "Text"
end tell
```

This time the second-to-last line generates an error: "Invalid value for set property 'active layer'. Expected layer or string, but received nothing." That's because this time the script is looking for a layer of the application—the layer "Text" specifier is no longer inside a tell document block. To avoid this problem—which can happen with all the classes you refer to by name, such as styles, presets, and colors—you should use either the name alone or a full reference to the item. You make and use a reference either like this,

```
tell application "Adobe InDesign CS4"
    tell document 1
        set text_layer to layer "Text" -- Store a reference
        set active layer to text_layer
    end tell
end tell
```

or, if it fits your script better, like this:

```
tell application "Adobe InDesign CS4"
    set text_layer to layer "Text" of document 1 -- Store a reference
    set active layer of document 1 to text_layer
end tell
```

It would be nice to be able to say you should always use references, or always use names, but in practice that's not the case. Either will work in most cases, but there are some situations where you have to use references, and others where you have to use just names. Earlier version of InDesign required references in most cases, and using them is a good habit to get into. One area where you should use names only is when searching, which we will come to later.

> **CAUTION:** Referring to items by index can be especially confusing with layers. Make a document and make a second layer, keeping the default names. The one named "Layer 1" will be layer 2, and the one named "Layer 2" will be layer 1. Ouch.

The preceding method might be fine for making new page items, but you will also need a way to find out what layer existing items are on, and to move them from layer to layer. The answer lies in a property of page items called item layer. So if you want to move the frontmost rectangle to a layer called "Text", you would use this:

```
tell application "Adobe InDesign CS4"
    tell document 1
        set text_layer to layer "Text" -- Store a reference
        set item layer of rectangle 1 to text_layer
    end tell
end tell
```

To find out the name of the layer an item is on, you could use

```
tell application "Adobe InDesign CS4"
    tell document 1
        set text_layer_name to name of item layer of rectangle 1
    end tell
end tell
```

You can also set the item layer property when you create an item, rather than relying on the active layer. So if you want to make a black circle of one-inch diameter at the top left of page 1, on a layer called "Text", you could use the code shown in Script 26–4.

Script 26–4.

```
tell application "Adobe InDesign CS4"
    tell document 1
        tell view preferences
            set horizontal measurement units to inches
            set vertical measurement units to inches
        end tell
        set text_layer to layer "Text"
        set black_color to color "Black"
        make new oval at beginning of page 1 with properties { ¬
            geometric bounds:{0, 0, 1, 1}, ¬
            item layer:text_layer, ¬
            fill color:black_color}
    end tell
end tell
```

I haven't mentioned geometric bounds before. It is the values for the smallest unrotated rectangle that could contain the item, excluding stroke thickness. Importantly, the values are in the order top, left, bottom, and right. If you want to include stroke widths as well, use the visual bounds property instead.

Understanding InDesign References

We talk above of commands returning references, but what are these references? If you look in the dictionary, every class has a property called object reference, and in the case of all but the text-related classes, that's what gets returned when you refer to an object. When InDesign returns a reference to a non-text object, you will typically see something like this:

```
--> rectangle id 2532 of page id 539 of spread id 526
        of document "Sample table.indd" of application "Adobe InDesign CS4"
```

This lists the position of the item in the object hierarchy, and it refers to it by ID. These IDs are what is returned for the id property—each is unique to a document, although they can change if you close and reopen a document.

You may find this a bit daunting at first—what is page id 539?—but by being based on a unique ID, these references are very robust. They hold if you rename an item or move it around. In fact, they are nearly indestructible: you can move a page item to another page, or group it, and the reference will still hold (it matches on the item's ID, and will ignore the fact that other IDs or containers may have changed).

These references are so robust that you can do this:

```
tell application "Adobe InDesign CS4"
    make new document
    set text_frame to make new text frame ¬
        at end of page 1 of document 1 ¬
        with properties {geometric bounds:{0, 0, "2i", "4i"}})
    set (content type of text_frame) to graphic type
    select text_frame
    get class of text_frame
end tell
--> rectangle
```

By changing the content type property, the script is turning the text frame into a rectangle—but still the reference works. (Incidentally, notice how the parentheses are used here to separate the words set and content; otherwise InDesign interprets them as the set content command instead.)

Working with Text

The most important element in InDesign for most people is probably text, and there are several text classes. Some of the classes will be familiar to you, like word, character, and paragraph, and some might be new to you.

If you take a text frame, it contains just one item of the text class. So if you have a document containing a text frame, you can get its contents like this:

```
text 1 of text frame 1 of document 1
```

You can also refer to pieces of text. For example, you can ask for character 1, or word 1, or paragraph 1, or line 1, and work back up the hierarchy by asking for things like paragraph 1 of character 256, or line 1 of word 28. Less obvious but very important are two other classes: insertion point and text style range.

The insertion point class often confuses people because they assume it relates to where the cursor is in text. It can be—if you click between two characters, you have selected an insertion point—but it doesn't have to be. Every character is preceded by, and followed by, an insertion point. Even an "empty" text frame contains a single insertion point. And insertion points have the same properties as characters, so if you want to add some large text to a text frame, you can do it like this:

```
tell application "Adobe InDesign CS4"
    tell document 1
        tell text frame 1
            set point size of insertion point -1 to 36
            set contents of insertion point -1 to "Some more text"
        end tell
    end tell
end tell
```

> **TIP:** Try setting the contents of the last insertion point of a paragraph to something. The result might surprise you—the last insertion point of a paragraph is also the first insertion point of the following paragraph (except for the last paragraph in a story, obviously).

The other class that is very useful is text style range. This refers to a range of identically styled text. So if you have a text frame containing "This is some text" and you make the word "some" bold, you have three text style runs: one before the bold, one where the text is bold, and one after the bold. Where text style ranges are particularly useful is in checking for attributes—rather than checking every character for a particular attribute, it is much quicker to loop through the text style ranges.

Working with Text Stories

Text gets a bit more complicated because it can flow from one frame to another as stories. If you look in the dictionary, you will see that "stories" are elements of documents, not text frames. But when you want to do something to the text in a frame, often you want to act on the whole story, no matter how many frames it passes through—or even if it is overset, and some of it appears in no frame.

To deal with this, text frames have a property called parent story. This read-only property returns a reference to the story that passes through that text frame. In a sense, we can treat it a bit like an object, and use it like this:

```
tell application "Adobe InDesign CS4"
    tell document 1
        tell parent story of text frame 1
            set font style to "Bold"
        end tell
    end tell
end tell
```

This will style the whole story bold (assuming a bold variant of the typeface used is available; otherwise an error will occur).

You can still address stories via the document. For example:

```
tell application "Adobe InDesign CS4"
    tell document 1
        tell every story
            set point size to 18
        end tell
    end tell
end tell
```

And this being AppleScript, you can use stories at the document level with whose clauses, like this:

```
tell application "Adobe InDesign CS4"
    tell document 1
        try
            set strike thru of every story whose contents begins with ¬
                "It was a dark and stormy night" to true
        on error
            -- None were found, so do nothing
        end try
    end tell
end tell
```

> **TIP:** If you ask for a property other than contents of a paragraph, word, line or story— say the point size, the index, or the applied font—the result will be the value for the first character of that paragraph, word, line, or story.

Working with References to Text

When you "get" some text—for example, set some_text to word 2 of parent story of text frame 1 of document 1—what is returned is the contents of the text. It is really the same as saying, set some_text to contents of word 2 of parent story of text frame 1 of document 1. This is consistent with AppleScript in general:

```
set some_text to "A good time was had by all"
word 2 of some_text --> "good"
```

But sometimes what you need—or what you are provided with—is not the contents, but a reference to some text. For example, suppose a text frame contains a story, and you want to find every occurrence of the word "script" in it, and you want to do something only to those instances that obey some rule you can't express in a whose clause. You may wish to use a simple whose clause to get the instances of the word, and then loop through testing them in turn.

If you try this,

```
tell application "Adobe InDesign CS4"
    tell document 1
```

```
      tell parent story of text frame 1
         set the_words to every word whose contents = "script"
      end tell
   end tell
end tell
```

the variable the_words will end up containing something like {"script", "script", "script", "script"}. That's accurate, but it's hardly useful. The solution is to use the object reference property:

```
tell application "Adobe InDesign CS4"
   tell document 1
      tell parent story of text frame 1
         set the_words to object reference of every word whose contents = "script"
      end tell
   end tell
end tell
```

Now the_words will contain a list of text references, with each reference looking something like this:

```
 text from character 11 to character 16 of story id 228 of document "Sample.indd"
```

Unlike references to page items and objects like styles, these references are not based on ID. The text classes have no id property—giving every character, insertion point, word, and so on its own ID would probably bring the application to its knees. Instead, they are based on the index, or offset from the beginning of the containing story.

Text object references are used extensively. For example, if you perform a search using find text or find grep, the result will be a list of object references, and if you ask for the selection when text is selected, the result will include an object reference.

Because these references are index-based, they are far more fragile than other references. You may have a reference to text from character 11 to character 16, but if something is done to add or delete text at the beginning of the story, when you get the contents of the reference, you might not get what you expected.

Because of this, whenever you loop through a series of text references, it is best to do it from last to first. That way, even if what you do alters the length of the story, it won't affect references to earlier in the story.

> **TIP:** You may be tempted to try reversing a list of references using AppleScript's reverse property, like set the_words to reverse of the_words. Unfortunately, InDesign also uses the term reverse, and this terminology conflict means reverse of ... won't work within a tell application "Adobe InDesign CS4" ... block.

Working with Graphics

The other common classes we haven't looked at are the various classes of graphics. The graphic class is a hold-all superclass for the various types of graphics InDesign can import: EPS, image (bitmap file), imported page, PDF, PICT, and WMF. As mentioned earlier, they are not page items—they are contained by page items. You usually put them there using the place command, just as in the user interface, and if you place them on something other than a frame—like a document or insertion point—a containing page item will be created automatically.

So if you have a rectangle on a page, and it contains, say, a PDF, you can refer to the PDF like this:

```
tell application "Adobe InDesign CS4"
    tell document 1
        set the_PDF to PDF 1 of rectangle 1 of page 1
    end tell
end tell
or this:
tell application "Adobe InDesign CS4"
    tell document 1
        set the_PDF to graphic 1 of rectangle 1 of page 1
    end tell
end tell
```

Just as you have links in the user interface, so too you have links in scripting. The link object contains information about graphics such as their path, whether they are missing or out of date, their type, and so on.

It's important to understand the relationship between links and graphics. As stated earlier, graphics don't belong to pages or documents—they belong to page items. Links, on the other hand, belong to the document.

If you are dealing with a link and want to deal with the graphic it refers to, you ask for the parent of the link. Even though links belong to documents, their parent property refers to their related graphic. Let's say you are checking the status of links, and you want to find the graphic a missing link relates to. Script 26–5 finds the graphics frame that contains the first missing link in the document.

Script 26–5.

```
tell application "Adobe InDesign CS4"
    tell document 1
        if exists (link 1 whose status is link missing) then
            set the_graphic to parent of link 1 whose status is link missing
            set the_graphics_frame to parent of the_graphic
            select the_graphics_frame
            -- The next line is a simple trick to scroll to the page if necessary,
            -- and center the selection on screen
            set zoom percentage of layout window 1 to ¬
                (get zoom percentage of layout window 1)
        end if
    end tell
end tell
```

If you are dealing with a graphic and want to deal with its link—perhaps the user has selected a graphic, and you want to put a caption underneath it containing its path—you can get a reference to the related link by using the graphic's item link property, as shown in Script 26-6.

Script 26-6.

```
tell application "Adobe InDesign CS4"
    -- The next line ensures that InDesign can show our dialogs
    set user interaction level of script preferences to interact with all
    tell document 1
        set the_selection to selection -- Returns a list
        set the_graphic to item 1 of the_selection
        if class of the_graphic is in {EPS, image, imported page, PDF, PICT, WMF} then
            set the_graphics_link to item link of the_graphic
            set path_to_graphic to file path of the_graphics_link
            display dialog "The path to the selected graphic is: " & path_to_graphic ¬
                    buttons {"OK"}
        else
            display dialog "You don't have a graphic selected." buttons {"Cancel"}
        end if
    end tell
end tell
```

Drawing Lines

When you want to draw a rule on a page, you make an object of the graphic line class. Graphic lines have a lot of properties in common with other page items, so you could do something like this:

```
tell application "Adobe InDesign CS4"
    tell document 1
        make new graphic line at page 1 with properties { ¬
                stroke weight:1, geometric bounds:{"1i", "1i", "1i", "7i"}}
        make new graphic line at page 1 with properties { ¬
                stroke weight:1, geometric bounds:{"1i", "1i", "10i", "1i"}}
    end tell
end tell
```

You now have a vertical line and a horizontal line. But what if you want a diagonal line? The problem is that whether the line starts top left and goes to bottom right, or starts top right and goes to bottom left, its bounds will be the same. So for angled lines, you need another step: you need to address the entire path property of the path element that makes up the rule. Because rules only have one path, you address path 1 of the rule, and the entire path property takes a list of coordinate pairs. So:

```
tell application "Adobe InDesign CS4"
    tell document 1
        set line1 to make new graphic line at page 1 with properties {stroke weight:1}
        set entire path of path 1 of line1 to {{"1i", "1i"}, {"7i", "10i"}}
        set line2 to make new graphic line at page 1 with properties {stroke weight:1}
        set entire path of path 1 of line2 to {{"1i", "10i"}, {"7i", "1i"}}
    end tell
end tell
```

> **TIP:** The shape of other page items can be modified like this—the result can be that what was a rectangle becomes a polygon, or even what was a graphic line becomes an oval.

Example Project: An InDesign Scripts Launcher

Now that you have an idea of InDesign's main objects and how they fit together, it's time get down to writing some scripts.

You may have found that some of the supplied scripts in InDesign's Scripts panel (shown earlier in Figure 26–2) are useful—you might sometimes need to put crop marks around an item, or apply some path or corner effects. If you use the scripts regularly, you might find it convenient to give them keyboard shortcuts. The problem with keyboard shortcuts is remembering them, and if you use a lot of scripts, it's easy to lose track.

> **TIP:** Many of the sample scripts are useful! It's a shame that so few users know about them. Take the time to familiarize yourself with them.

One solution is to write a new script, assign it a keyboard shortcut, and have that script bring up a dialog box that you can navigate, via the keyboard, and use it to choose the script to run. That's much more convenient than dealing with the Scripts panel, which you can then hide. The basic version of this script will work in versions CS2, CS3, and CS4—we will take advantage of a new CS4 feature a little later.

The first thing the script needs to do is get a list of the other scripts. To make this easy, you will save the new script in the same folder as the sample scripts. Then, when the script is run, it will use a property of InDesign called `active script` to get the path to itself; from there, the path to the containing folder can be extracted.

> **CAUTION:** You can also get the script's path using Standard Additions' `path to` command (previously covered in Chapter 20), but in InDesign's case this only works within compiled (`.scpt` or `.scptd`) script files. If you use `path to me` in uncompiled (`.applescript`) scripts run from the Scripts panel, it will return the path to InDesign itself. Also, `active script` does not work in stand-alone script applications (`.app`).

So the script begins by getting the path. Because the script is going to bring up a dialog box, it also needs to make sure that InDesign hasn't been told to skip dialog boxes when running scripts. We'll discuss this later in the chapter, but for now you can just enter the line as it appears here:

```
tell application "Adobe InDesign CS4"
    set path_to_me to (active script) as text
    set user interaction level of script preferences to interact with all
end tell
```

If you try to run this script in a script editor, you'll get an error: "No script is active." The active script property only works in a script while it is being run from the Scripts panel (technically, while it's being run by InDesign itself). Let's push on and extract the folder path, using text item delimiters:

```
set old_delims to AppleScript's text item delimiters
set AppleScript's text item delimiters to {":"}
set path_to_folder to (text 1 thru text item -2 of path_to_me) & ":"
set AppleScript's text item delimiters to old_delims
```

Now the script needs to get all the script files in the folder. There are a few ways you can do this. You could ask the Finder or System Events, although they can be a bit on the slow side. In this case we're going to call a couple of shell commands, using AppleScript's do shell script command:

```
set script_file_names to paragraphs of (do shell script "ls " & ¬
    quoted form of POSIX path of path_to_folder & " | grep '\\.applescript$'")
```

If you are unfamiliar with shell scripting, ls is a command for listing the names of items in a folder, and the | character is a "pipe" that passes the result to the next command, grep, which weeds out all those entries that don't end with .applescript. (Chapter 27 will cover shell scripting in more detail.) The result of the shell script is a string containing one or more file names separated by linefeed (ASCII 10) characters. This string can be converted to a list of file names by asking for the paragraphs of it.

You could use that list as is, but let's face it, the sample script names are unwieldy enough because of the lack of spaces in them. Stripping off the .applescript extension from the entries in our dialog box will help a bit:

```
set script_names to {} -- Store names here
repeat with i from 1 to count script_file_names
    set end of script_names to text 1 thru -13 of item i of script_file_names
end repeat
```

Now you can show the dialog box, and end the script if the user clicks the Cancel button:

```
set the_selection to choose from list script_names ¬
    with prompt "Choose a script to run:"
if the_selection is false then error number -128
set chosen_name to item 1 of the_selection
```

Finally, the script tells InDesign to run the chosen script, using its do script command:

```
tell application "Adobe InDesign CS4"
  do script alias (path_to_folder & chosen_name & ".applescript")
end tell
```

Save the script in the same folder as the provided .applescript Scripts panel files folder, and assign it a shortcut if you wish. (Use the panel's flyout menu to reveal the folder in the Finder.)

Make sure you save the script as a compiled script (.scpt file); otherwise you could end up having it call itself (or change the code to filter out its own name). Now run it: a dialog box similar to the one shown in Figure 26–6 will open, listing all the scripts. You can navigate it using the cursor keys or by typing part of a script's name. That's much more convenient.

Figure 26–6. *The dialog box produced by the script; no need to use the mouse or remember dozens of keyboard shortcuts*

The script could be expanded further to cover other folders. One of the great things about scripting is that you can customize your tools to fit your own requirements exactly.

> **NOTE:** There's one small visual glitch when you run scripts that call standard AppleScript dialog boxes from InDesign's Scripts panel: the cursor changes into the spinning pizza. It behaves like a normal cursor, but it can be a bit disconcerting at first. You could use InDesign's built-in GUI feature to build the dialog box instead, but then you would have to use a pop-up menu that is not navigable via the keyboard.

Okay, the script works: you select a rectangle, press the assigned keyboard shortcut, and the dialog box comes up; you type "cro" and CropMarks is selected, you click OK or press Return, and you choose the type of crop marks you want. But what if you selected the wrong rectangle? You can try the Undo menu, but when you do, you will see that each step the script took requires a separate undo. So you'll be undoing more than 40 times for the default crop marks settings. So much for automation.

Fortunately, this problem has been addressed in CS4, where the do script command has been enhanced so that you can undo the whole sequence in one go, and even set what appears in the Undo menu. So our new do script line becomes

```
do script alias (path_to_folder & chosen_name & ".applescript") ¬
    undo mode entire script undo name (chosen_name & " Script")
```

Now after you run the script and call CropMarks, you can go to the Undo menu and choose **Undo CropMarks Script**. Remember, this option is in CS4 only.

The do script command is very powerful. Not only can you run another AppleScript file from it like this, but you can also pass it AppleScript code as text, or even JavaScript code or a JavaScript file. And if you use it in a script saved as an application, which usually results in scripts running slower than when run from the Scripts panel, the code called will run significantly faster.

> **TIP:** CS4 has another option for the do script command's undo mode parameter, called fast entire script. It makes scripts run faster, but there are implications when errors occur that are beyond the scope of this chapter. In most cases, just using entire script is fast enough.

When working on scripts, being able to go into InDesign and use the Undo command to step backward, one command at a time, can be very useful in diagnosing problems.

Working with Tables

Working with tables is one of the more complicated and fiddly areas of InDesign. Table styles and cell styles can help, but they're far from perfect—and lots of people still don't use them. Working with tables is an area where scripting can shine.

In this section we're going to work through two samples: in the first we'll update the contents of a table from a spreadsheet without losing the formatting, and in the second we'll copy some formatting from one cell to one or more others.

> **NOTE**: The downloadable source code for this book includes sample files for use with the scripts in this chapter. You can find it at http://www.apress.com.

Importing Table Text from a Spreadsheet

As a simple example, suppose you have a table formatted and ready to print (see Figure 26–7), when someone sends you a spreadsheet containing new figures (see Figure 26–8).

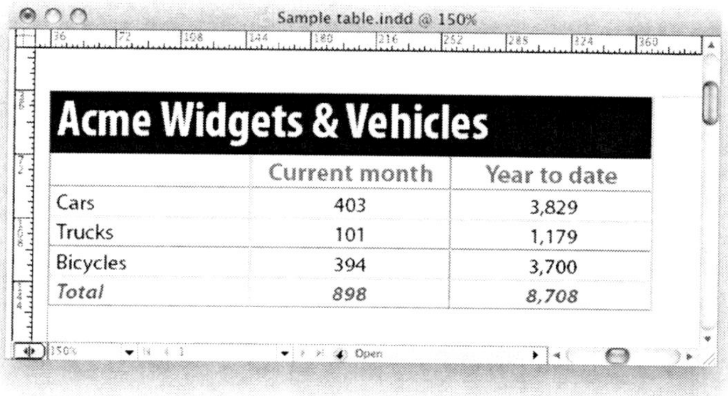

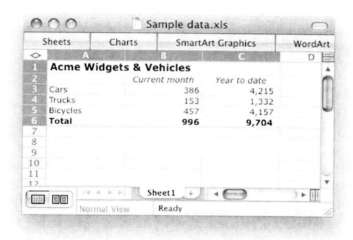

Figure 26–7. *The original table in InDesign*

Figure 26–8. *The new spreadsheet figures to import*

Open the spreadsheet in Excel, select some cells, and run the following:

```
tell application "Microsoft Excel"
    set value_list_of_lists to string value of selection
end tell
```

(If you are using Excel 2004, you need to ask for the formula of selection, and if the cells include dates, they may be formatted differently in the resulting lists.)

The result is a list of lists, one for each row selected. For example, if you select all the used cells of the sample file, you will get the following:

```
--> {{"Acme Widgets & Vehicles", "", ""},
    {"", "Current month", "Year to date"},
    {"Cars", "386", " 4,215 "},
    {"Trucks", "153", " 1,332 "},
    {"Bicycles", "457", " 4,157 "},
    {"Total", "996", " 9,704 "}}
```

Before you can use this data in InDesign, you need to manipulate it a bit because InDesign tables—unlike Excel spreadsheets—do not use nested lists. You can check this for yourself by selecting an existing InDesign table and getting the contents:

```
tell application "Adobe InDesign CS4"
    contents of selection
end tell
```

In this case the result is a single, flattened list; for example, using the sample InDesign table:

```
--> {"Acme Widgets & Vehicles", "", "Current month", "Year to date",
    "Cars", "403", " 3,829 ", "Trucks", "101", " 1,179 ",
    "Bicycles", "394", " 3,700 ", "Total", "898", " 8,708 "}
```

So to move the copy from your spreadsheet to InDesign, you need to flatten the original list of lists into a single list, like this:

```
set value_list to item 1 of value_list_of_lists
repeat with i from 2 to count value_list_of_lists
    set value_list to value_list & item i of value_list_of_lists
end repeat
```

Now it's a simple matter of setting the contents property of the selected table in InDesign. The complete script looks like this:

```
tell application "Microsoft Excel"
    set value_list_of_lists to string value of selection
end tell
set value_list to item 1 of value_list_of_lists
repeat with i from 2 to count value_list_of_lists
    set value_list to value_list & item i of value_list_of_lists
end repeat
tell application "Adobe InDesign CS4"
    set contents of selection to value_list
end tell
```

Try it for yourself, using the sample files or files of your own. Make sure that the range of cells you select in the spreadsheet matches the range selected in the InDesign table, because otherwise results can be unpredictable.

NOTE: This ability to deal with more than one application from a single script is one of the great strengths of AppleScript. It means you can build workflows based on a range of tools.

Copying Formatting Between Cells

Sometimes it's not the content of a table you want to change, but the formatting. Styles can sometimes help, but not always.

Suppose you have a table in which one or more cells are formatted how you want, but some others aren't. Figure 26–9 shows a typical table.

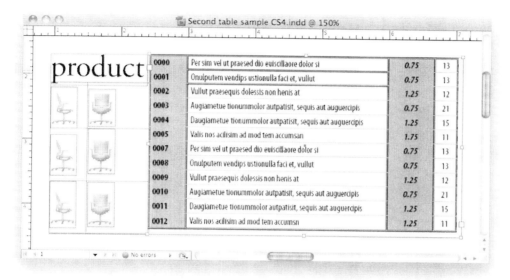

Figure 26–9. *The sample table*

For a start, try to make cell 2 of row 2 look like cell 1 of row 2. You might think that the solution is to get the value of each property from one cell and set the same properties in the other cell. But cells have nearly 100 properties, and even though you can skip quite a few, that's going to take some hefty typing to run.

You could speed things up by getting all the properties, extracting just the ones you want, and setting the required ones all at once—but dealing with all those properties is still going to be a mammoth typing exercise.

This time assume you have selected the frame containing the table, so you could consider something like this:

```
tell application "Adobe InDesign CS4"
   set the_table to table 1 of selection
   tell the_table
      set the_props to properties of cell 1 of row 2
      set properties of cell 2 of row 2 to the_props
   end tell
end tell
```

But if you are an experienced scripter, you might see an immediate problem: you're trying to set some properties that are read-only, and some to values that would be invalid, things that normally trigger an error. As you discovered earlier, though, InDesign is more tolerant; it will just ignore what doesn't make sense.

There's also another problem: if you run the preceding script on a sample, you will also change some things you may not want to, like the contents and width properties of the cell (see Figure 26–10).

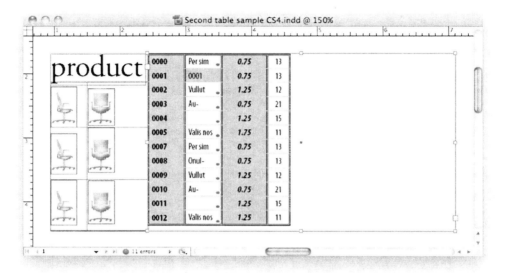

Figure 26–10. *If all the properties of cell 1 of row 2 are applied to cell 2 of row 2, the width and content also get changed.*

So, you need some way to remove a couple of the properties from the record of all the properties. That's actually something hard to do in AppleScript, but there is a workaround. When you concatenate two records in AppleScript, and the same label appears in both, the resulting record uses the first value. So you can set up a dummy record with nonsense values; for instance, InDesign's nothing value works nicely here:

```
set dummy_props to {contents:nothing, width:nothing}
```

> **TIP:** InDesign's nothing is a bit similar to AppleScript's missing value. It can be used as here, and it is also used to set properties to indeterminate values (something done in character styles, for example). In the preceding case, you could use any other value that doesn't make sense in the content, such as a Boolean.

You can then concatenate the dummy record with the record containing the properties from cell 1, before applying the new record to cell 2:

```
tell application "Adobe InDesign CS4"
set dummy_props to {contents:nothing, width:nothing}
    set theTable to table 1 of selection
```

```
tell theTable
    set actual_props to properties of cell 1 of row 2
    set the_props to dummy_props & actual_props
    set properties of cell 2 of row 2 to the_props
end tell
end tell
```

Now the cell will ignore the attempts to change the `contents` and `width` properties, but still make the other changes. Figure 26–11 shows the InDesign document once the correct changes have been made.

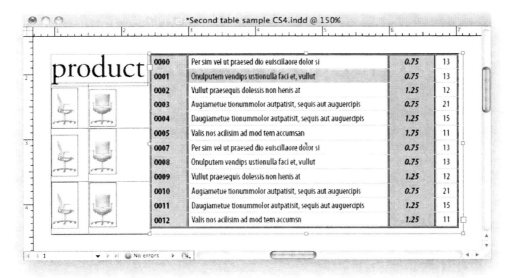

Figure 26–11. *Success—this is the result when invalid values are supplied for the width and contents.*

> **NOTE:** Tables can be addressed as elements of text frames, as in the previous discussion, but they are also elements of stories and the various text classes. If you want to know where in a story a table falls, you can use the `story offset` property of a table. This property has changed: in CS3 and earlier it returned the offset of the insertion point containing the table, but as of CS4 it returns a reference to the insertion point containing the table.

Working with Selections

Most scripts are in one of two categories: general-purpose utility scripts that assist InDesign users in their day-to-day work, and large, specialized workflow scripts that run without user interaction. The sample scripts in the Scripts panel are good examples of utility scripts, and the thing many of them have in common is that they act on the selection.

Like many other applications, InDesign has a selection property. It is a read-write property of the application itself, of documents, and of windows, and returns a list of object references of the selected items. If nothing is selected, it returns an empty list.

In some applications—for instance, Mail—to work with the selected items, you must first retrieve a list of single-item references from the selection property, and then process each of those references one at a time. That's not necessary in InDesign, where you can manipulate the selected item or items via the selection property, so if you have a rectangle selected and you ask for class of selection, the result will be rectangle, even though get selection returns a list.

Example Project: Captioning a Selected Graphic

Suppose you want to write a script to put a caption under a graphic, containing the graphic's path. You might want to put the caption on a separate layer, and use its own paragraph style. You know that you need to be using known units when calculating dimensions, so your solution might look like Script 26–7.

Script 26–7.

```
tell application "Adobe InDesign CS4"
   -- Get the path
   set graphics_link to item link of graphic 1 of selection
   set graphics_path to (file path of graphics_link) as text
   tell document 1

      -- Make a new layer if it doesn't exist
      try
         set caption_layer to layer "Captions"
      on error
         -- It doesn't exist, so...
         set caption_layer to make new layer at beginning ¬
              with properties {name:"Captions", printable:false}
      end try

      -- Make a new paragraph style if it doesn't exist
      try
         set caption_style to paragraph style "Path captions"
      on error
         -- It doesn't exist, so...
         set caption_style to make new paragraph style ¬
              with properties {applied font:"Myriad" & tab & "Roman",
              point size:8, justification:center align, hyphenation:true}
      end try

      -- Store old ruler units and change to points
      tell view preferences
         set old_units to properties
         set properties to {horizontal measurement units:points, ¬
              vertical measurement units:points}
      end tell

      -- Get the dimensions
      set {y1, x1, y2, x2} to geometric bounds of selection
```

```
      -- Make the new frame
      set caption_frame to make new text frame at in front of selection
      set properties of caption_frame to { ¬
            geometric bounds:{y2 + 3, x1, y2 + 27, x2}, ¬
            item layer:caption_layer, contents:graphics_path}
      set properties of parent story of caption_frame to ¬
            {applied paragraph style:caption_style}

      -- Reset the rulers
      set properties of view preferences to old_units
   end tell
end tell
```

To caption a graphic, just click a frame containing an image and run your script.

> **NOTE:** Notice in Script 26–7 how you refer to the name of a font: you provide the family name, followed by a tab, followed by the font style; in this case, `"Myriad" & tab & "Roman"`.

It's a good start, but what if you give the script to someone else, and they try to run it, this time with the graphic selected with the Direct Selection tool, or with nothing selected ("Hey, this is a computer, it should know what I want.")? They will get an error. So you need to check that there actually is a selection, and that it contains an image. And it makes sense to do the checking at the beginning, before bothering to make the layer and paragraph style, or change the ruler units. So your script would begin something like this:

```
tell application "Adobe InDesign CS4"
   -- Ensure InDesign can display dialogs
   set user interaction level of script preferences to interact with all

   -- Check that only one item is selected
   set selections_list to selection
   if length of selections_list ≠ 1 then
      display dialog ¬
            "Please select a single frame containing a graphic and try again." ¬
            buttons {"Cancel"}
      error number -128
   end if
   set the_selection to item 1 of selections_list

   -- If the user selected a graphic within a frame then get the frame itself,
   -- otherwise check that the selection is a frame with a graphic in it
   set item_class to class of the_selection
   if item_class is in {EPS, image, imported page, PDF, PICT, WMF} then
      set the_selection to parent of the_selection
   else if not ((item_class is in {rectangle, oval, polygon}) ¬
         and (exists graphic 1 of the_selection)) then
      display dialog ¬
            "Please select a single frame containing a graphic and try again." ¬
            buttons {"Cancel"}
      error number -128
   end if
```

```
-- If we get this far then all is well, so proceed with the rest of the script...

-- Get the path
set graphics_link to item link of graphic 1 of the_selection
...
```

That's a fair bit of extra code, but the thing to do is to file it away to use again, so you don't have to reinvent the wheel.

> **NOTE:** The last conditional expression in the preceding script performs two important tests. First, the item_class is in {rectangle, oval, polygon} operation finds out if the selection is some type of frame. If that test returns true, then the exists graphic 1 of the_selection command finds out if the frame contains a graphic. However, if the first test returns false, then the second test is *not* performed (AppleScript's and operator only evaluates the right operand if the left operand is true). This is important as exists graphic 1 of ... will error if used on an object that is not capable of containing a graphic.

Example Project: Cleaning Up Selected Text

In the case of scripts meant to operate on text, the number of possible selection types can make it more complex. When you have some text selected, the class of the selection can be any of insertion point, character, word, line, paragraph, text column, text style range, or text itself. In this project, you'll write a simple utility script to perform some cleaning up of selected text.

The guts of the script will use InDesign's find-change facility. First, you have to do the equivalent of returning the Find/Change dialog box to default settings. In fact, you *are* returning it to its default settings—you can see the results in the Find/Change dialog box. If you don't, you will start off with the settings the user last set in the user interface. All the various things you can set in the Find/Change dialog box—what to look for, what font it's in, what style, and so forth—can be returned to default by setting two properties to the value referred to earlier, nothing:

```
set find text preferences to nothing
set change text preferences to nothing
```

There are a few other options in the Find/Change dialog box when doing a text search, and you can also set them:

```
set properties of find change object options to {case sensitive:true, ¬
    include footnotes:false, include hidden layers:false, ¬
    include master pages:true, whole word:false}
```

Now for the search. The idea is to have a list of strings to find, and a list of their replacements. For the sake of this exercise, assume you are fixing some spacing issues, so:

```
set the_finds to {space & space, return & space, return & return}
set the_changes to {space, return, return}
```

These are just examples (and one of the sample scripts includes a much more detailed and powerful find-change capability if you need such a thing). Finally, you need to loop through, setting the find what and change to properties, and issue the change text command—and that's where you need to specify the target:

```
repeat with i from 1 to count the_finds
    set find what of find text preferences to (item i of the_finds)
    set change to of change text preferences to (item i of the_changes)
    change text selection
end repeat
```

To make the script flexible, you might design it like this: if a text frame, an insertion point, or a single character is selected, assume the user wants to act on the related story; otherwise, act just on the selected text. Script 26–8 shows the finished code.

Script 26–8.

```
set the_finds to {space & space, return & space, return & return}
set the_changes to {space, return, return}

tell application "Adobe InDesign CS4"
    -- Make sure InDesign can display dialogs
    set user interaction level of script preferences to interact with all

    -- Check that only one item is selected
    set selections_list to selection
    if length of selections_list ≠ 1 then
        display dialog "Please select some text or a text frame." buttons {"Cancel"}
        error number -128
    end if
    set the_selection to item 1 of selections_list

    -- If an insertion point or character is selected then get its containing story;
    -- if it's a text frame then get its parent story; otherwise check that it's
    -- some other type of text
    set item_class to class of the_selection
    if item_class is in {insertion point, character} then
        set the_selection to parent of the_selection
    else if item_class is text frame then
        set the_selection to parent story of the_selection
    else if item_class is not in ¬
        {word, line, paragraph, text column, text style range, text} then
        display dialog "Please select some text or a text frame." buttons {"Cancel"}
        error number -128
    end if

    -- If we get this far then all is well, so do the actual work...

    -- Set the find-change options
    set find text preferences to nothing
    set change text preferences to nothing
    set properties of find change object options to {case sensitive:true, ¬
            include footnotes:false, include hidden layers:false, ¬
            include master pages:true, whole word:false}

    -- Perform the changes
    repeat with i from 1 to count the_finds
```

```
      set find what of find text preferences to (item i of the_finds)
      set change to of change text preferences to (item i of the_changes)
      change text the_selection
    end repeat
end tell
```

Depending on what your utility script does, you may need to use variations on these—for example, scripts to format tables have to deal with issues of tables, cells, and their content. But the principle is the same: get the class, and use a process of elimination.

Labeling Objects for Use in Workflow Scripts

Workflow scripts are scripts that carry out a series of steps, often using templates, sometimes involving more than one application, and often producing completed documents from a bunch of text and graphic files. You can't rely on the selection to guide the script where to act, so you need some other mechanism.

The various page item subclasses have a label property (as do other classes, including documents and even the application itself, but their greatest usefulness is with page items). You can set a label to more or less any text—it can run to thousands of words, if you really want it to—and you can even set a label in the user interface, using the Script Label panel shown in Figure 26–12. Labels are an ideal way to identify the various elements of a document in order to place text and graphics.

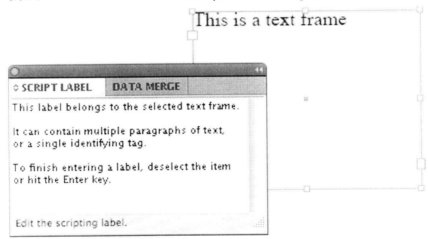

Figure 26–12. *The Script Label panel can be used to edit the* label *property of a selected page item.*

You are probably used to referring to items like styles by their name. Page items don't have names, but you can use their labels as if they were names. So you might have a template with a series of text frames labeled "Head", "Byline", "Intro", and "Body". Your stories might come as documents containing the information in that order. Rather than running the script from the Scripts panel, you might save the script as an application, so you can drag and drop the source files over it. Typically, such a script would be similar to Script 26–9.

Script 26–9.

```
-- This property should contain the path to our template
property template_path : "Macintosh HD:Users:sstanley:Documents:Template.indd"

on open file_list
    set desktop_path to path to desktop as text
    tell application "Adobe InDesign CS4"
        -- Turn off interaction for the duration; we don't want 'missing font'
        -- dialogs and the like
        set user interaction level of script preferences to never interact

        repeat with i from 1 to count file_list
            set the_document to open file template_path
            tell the_document
                -- Place the text from the file into the "Body" text frame
                place item i of file_list on text frame "Body"

                -- Move the first three lines into the "Head", "Byline", and "Intro"
                -- text frames, deleting the trailing returns
                move paragraph 1 of parent story of text frame "Body" ¬
                    to after parent story of text frame "Head"
                delete character -1 of parent story of text frame "Head"
                move paragraph 1 of parent story of text frame "Body" ¬
                    to after parent story of text frame "Byline"
                delete character -1 of parent story of text frame "Byline"
                move paragraph 1 of parent story of text frame "Body" ¬
                    to after parent story of text frame "Intro"
                delete character -1 of parent story of text frame "Intro"

                -- Apply the various styles and do whatever else is required here...

                -- Save the document to the Desktop and close it when done
                save to file (desktop_path & "Finished file " & i & ".indd")
                close saving no
            end tell
        end repeat

        -- Turn interaction back on again
        set user interaction level of script preferences to interact with all

        -- With longer scripts it's a good idea to let the user know when you are done
        activate
        beep
        with timeout of 10000 seconds -- In case the user has gone to make a coffee
            display dialog "Done, " & (count file_list) & " files processed." ¬
                buttons {"OK"} default button 1
        end timeout
    end tell
end open
```

Labels do not have to be unique; you can have more than one page item with the same name. This can be put to good use—you might have a text frame labeled "Copy" on every page of a document, and you could address them in turn as text frame "Copy" of page n. Addressing page items by label also has the same limitation as other references, in that text frame "Copy" means a text frame with a label of "Copy" that lives directly on a page or the pasteboard. If you need to refer to a page item that is part of a group or otherwise not directly on a page or spread, you need to use a filtered reference, like this:

```
set theFrame to item 1 of all page items ¬
    whose class is text frame and label is "Copy"
```

> **TIP:** The Script Labels panel accepts returns in labels, so to finish an entry, you need either to click somewhere else or to use the Enter key.

InDesign objects also have other, hidden labels. You set them by using the insert label command, and read them by using extract label. You can have as many of these labels as you like on any object, and they can handle masses of text. Each of them has a key you identify them with, and a value you store and retrieve. You can use InDesign as your own hidden database! Here is a simple example of adding a couple of custom labels, in this case to a document:

```
set system_info to system info
set my_name to long user name of system_info
set this_date to (current date) as text
tell application "Adobe InDesign CS4"
   make new document
   insert label document 1 key "User name" value my_name
   insert label document 1 key "Creation date" value this_date
end tell
```

Later on, you can read these labels as follows:

```
tell application "Adobe InDesign CS4"
   if exists document 1 then
      set creator_name to (extract label document 1 key "User name")
      set creation_date to (extract label document 1 key "Creation date")
   end if
end tell
if creator_name is not "" and creation_date is not "" then
   display dialog "This document was created by " & creator_name ¬
        & " on " & creation_date & "." buttons {"OK"}
else
   display dialog "This document was created somewhere else." buttons {"OK"}
end if
```

Taking Advantage of AppleScript-Specific Preferences

There's one property of the application that is for scripters only, script preferences. If you look in the dictionary entry for the script preference class, you will see several useful and important properties. Perhaps the most important of these properties is user interaction level, and we've used it quite a bit in this chapter already. This property has three options, or enumerations: interact with alerts, interact with all, and never interact. The default setting is interact with all, but by setting the user interaction level to never interact, you tell InDesign to disallow dialog boxes—you avoid messages about missing fonts and out-of-date links, and a range of other dialog boxes it can otherwise pop up at inopportune times. It will even stop your own `display dialog` commands if you send them to InDesign. (The other setting, `interact with alerts`, is rarely used, except perhaps in testing.)

Often a script will turn off user interaction while it runs (after any required dialog boxes), and then turn it back on at the end. So a script might be written like this:

```
tell application "Adobe InDesign CS4"
    set user interaction level of script preferences to never interact
    -- Do stuff here...
    set user interaction level of script preferences to interact with all
end tell
```

> **NOTE:** The `user interaction level` setting has no effect outside of scripts.

You need to be careful with setting the user interaction level because it affects all scripts. Suppose you run a script and it has a bug in it so it never gets to the command that would turn user interaction back on; subsequent scripts that use dialog boxes may seem not to work. So it is a good habit to turn on user interaction before you attempt to display a dialog box in InDesign, just in case, as we have done in several of our examples. (The user interaction level is also reset each time InDesign is launched.)

The `script preference` class has a few other useful properties: `scripts folder` gives you the path to the folder containing the scripts that appear in the Scripts panel, and `version` tells you what version of scripting is active (6.0 for CS4, 5.0 for CS3, and so on). This `version` property can also be written to. So if you have a script that has been written for InDesign CS2 (version 4.0), you can try to make it run as is under CS4 by starting with

```
tell application "Adobe InDesign CS4"
    set version of script preferences to 4.0
```

All subsequent commands will then be interpreted as if the running InDesign application were version CS2. Like the user interaction level, this setting applies to all subsequent scripts until the application is relaunched, so use it with care and make sure you reset it at the end of each script you use it in.

This is not perfect in all cases; you still might need to make some changes to make your old scripts run. It can also be problematic where the terminology has changed, requiring the use of AppleScript's `using terms from ...` statement to ensure that your script compiles correctly. This, in turn, means you need to publish the alternative terminology using InDesign's `publish terminology` command, which makes a mock copy of the previous version that contains only the required terminology. It's a one-off procedure, and it is best to follow the step-by-step instructions in Adobe's documentation.

Example Project: Replacing Tags with Images

For our final example, let's get a bit more adventurous. The next script will involve several features: grep searching, placing images, and a special guest appearance from cousin Photoshop.

So this is the situation: you have a document containing a story or stories that have references to various items, and you want to insert anchored thumbnail pictures next to the references. The text has already been prepared, and where a graphic should appear is a tag containing the name of the relevant file in angled brackets. Figure 26–13 shows the InDesign document with the tagged text already inserted and awaiting the addition of the inline graphics.

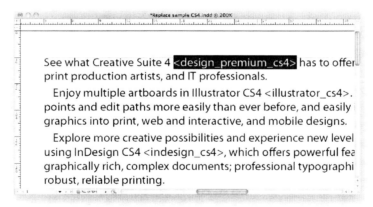

Figure 26–13. *The page containing the story with tags where the graphics are meant to go*

The images are all in a folder, as shown in Figure 26–14. Notice that the file names do not exactly match the tag names—your script will need to allow for this when matching files to tags.

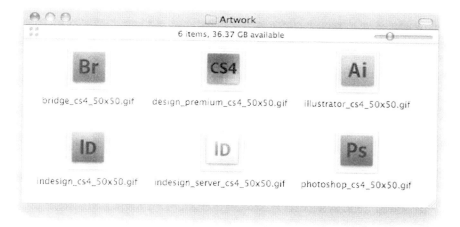

Figure 26–14. *The sample graphic files*

Before you place the graphics, you want to process them in Photoshop—scale them to size, convert them to monochrome, and do some gratuitous fiddling. (InDesign still won't convert color graphics to monochrome when exporting to PDF, so keep sending feature requests to Adobe if you want that feature added.)

Preparing InDesign

The script will start by asking the user to choose the folder containing the graphics, and setting a variable where you can record any problems:

```
tell application "Adobe InDesign CS4"
    set user interaction level of script preferences to interact with all
    set graphics_folder_path to (choose folder ¬
        with prompt "Choose the folder containing the graphics:") as text
    set error_string to "" -- This will contain any error info
```

Once the user input is gathered, dialog boxes are turned off, in case importing the graphics provokes any:

```
set user interaction level of script preferences to never interact
```

Then it will change the measurement units. Depending on how you do the scaling, this step may not be necessary, but if you put it in, it's not going to do any harm:

```
    -- Store old ruler units and change to points
    tell view preferences
        set old_units to properties
        set properties to {horizontal measurement units:points, ¬
            vertical measurement units:points}
    end tell
```

Next, the grep find is set up. This is similar to the text find earlier in the chapter. The grep pattern it will look for is an opening angle bracket, followed by a series of characters that are not a closing angle bracket, then a closing angle bracket:

```
-- Set up to do the search
set find grep preferences to nothing
tell find change grep options
    set include footnotes to false
    set include hidden layers to false
    set include locked layers for find to false
    set include master pages to false
end tell
set find what of find grep preferences to "<[^>]+?>"
```

Next you need to make a folder in the same folder as the document, call it Links, and use it to store the processed graphics. The path to the file's folder is actually a property called file path, and because making the folder is none of InDesign's business, that section will be put in a handler called make_links_folder:

```
tell document 1
    -- Make a folder in the same folder as the document, calling it Links
    set doc_folder_path to file path as text
    my make_links_folder(doc_folder_path)
```

The handler is simple enough—see if the folder exists, and if not, create it:

```
on make_links_folder(doc_folder_path)
    tell application "Finder"
        if not (exists folder "Links" of folder doc_folder_path) then
            make new folder at folder doc_folder_path with properties {name:"Links"}
        end if
    end tell
end make_links_folder
```

Processing the Tags

Now it's time to do the search:

```
-- Do the grep search and store the results
set the_instances to find grep
```

As you may remember from earlier in the chapter, you should loop through text references from back to front, so:

```
-- Loop through from the back
repeat with i from (count the_instances) to 1 by -1
```

The name will be the contents of the string each reference refers to, minus the first and last characters, and you want the height to match the ascent of the text:

```
-- The name will be the contents minus the first and last characters
set the_graphic_name to text from character 2 to character -2 ¬
    of contents of item i of the_instances
-- Get the ascent of the characters for the height of the images
set required_height to ascent of character 1 of item i of the_instances
```

Now you need a reference to the original file, and again you can put this in a handler:

```
-- Get a reference to original file
set the_original_file to ¬
      my find_graphic_file(graphics_folder_path, the_graphic_name)
```

This time the handler will trap for missing graphics, and return missing value in such cases. For this example, you are not requiring an exact match, but rather matching beginnings:

```
on find_graphic_file(graphics_folder_path, the_graphic_name)
   try
      tell application "Finder"
         return to (file 1 of folder graphics_folder_path ¬
               whose name begins with the_graphic_name) as alias
      end tell
   on error
      return missing value
   end try
end find_graphic_file
```

Preparing the Image Files

The variable the_original_file contains the result of this handler. If the result is missing value, an error message is generated; otherwise the script continues on to process the image, this time in a handler that calls on Photoshop:

```
      if the_original_file = missing value then
         set error_string to error_string & ¬
               "Missing file for " & the_graphic_name & return
      else
            -- Process the image in Photoshop, and return the path to the new image
            set graphics_path to my prepare_graphic(the_original_file,  ¬
               the_graphic_name, doc_folder_path, required_height)
```

The Photoshop handler turns off dialog boxes, opens the file, resizes it, changes it to grayscale, does some level adjustments and unsharp masking, and then saves the file as a .tiff file in the Links folder. If there are any errors, it returns missing value; otherwise it returns the path to the new file:

```
on prepare_graphic(the_original_file, ¬
      the_graphic_name, doc_folder_path, required_height)
   -- Process the file
   tell application "Adobe Photoshop CS4"
      set display dialogs to never
      try
         open the_original_file
         tell current document
            -- Resize it and make it grayscale
            resize image resolution 200 resample method none
            resize image height required_height as points resample method bicubic
            change mode to grayscale
            -- Fiddle with it a bit
            adjust art layers using levels adjustment with options { ¬
                  input range start:0, input range end:255, ¬
                  output range start:0, output range end:255, input range gamma:2.0}
            filter art layers using unsharp mask with options {amount:200, radius:0.5,
threshold:0}
```

```
                    -- Save it as a tiff and close it
                    save in file (doc_folder_path & "Links:" & the_graphic_name & ".tif") ¬
                        as TIFF appending no extension with options { ¬
                            class:TIFF save options, byte order:Mac OS, ¬
                            image compression:none, save layers:false, ¬
                            transparency:false}
                close saving no
            end tell
        on error
            -- The error might have left the pic open, so try to close it
            try
                set display dialogs to always
                close current document saving no
            end try
            return missing value
        end try
        set display dialogs to always
    end tell
    return (doc_folder_path & "Links:" & the_graphic_name & ".tif")
end prepare_graphic
```

> **CAUTION:** The prepare_graphic handler uses Adobe's Adobe Unit Types.osax scripting
> addition to perform a unit type coercion (required_height as points). Unfortunately, older
> versions of this scripting addition are 32-bit only, so if you are running Photoshop CS4 or earlier
> on Mac OS X 10.6 or later, you need to download and install a newer version from the Adobe
> web site (http://kb2.adobe.com/cps/516/cpsid_51615.html). Otherwise, you may get
> unexpected coercion errors when running this and other Photoshop-related scripts.

Placing the Graphics

The variable graphics_path holds the result of the handler. If the result is missing value, an error message is generated; otherwise the script continues on to delete the placeholder tag and place the graphic on the first insertion point. The place command returns a reference to the placed graphic, in a list, so the script stores this:

```
            if graphics_path = missing value then
                set error_string to error_string & ¬
                    "Problem processing " & the_graphic_name & return
            else
                -- Delete the marker text
                delete item i of the_instances
                -- Put in the graphic
                set {the_new_graphic} to place alias graphics_path ¬
                    on insertion point 1 of item i of the_instances
```

In the user interface, you can set various parameters for anchored items, but when you create one using the place command in a script like this, the preferences are ignored and you will always get an inline graphic placed on the baseline. That's exactly what is required here, but if it weren't, the script would make changes by addressing the anchored object settings property of the anchored frame.

Photoshop should have scaled the graphic to the right size, but let's not make any assumptions. There are many ways to scale a page item or graphic, from the powerful but inordinately complex transform and resize commands, to setting the scale properties of the item, to redefining the bounds of the item. In this case the script will use the scale properties.

One potential disadvantage of using the scale properties is that there is no reference to the point you are scaling about—the graphic is scaled about the point set in the Transform Point proxy in the user interface. You can set this via script and the transform reference point property of a layout window (not document), but in this case there is no need because the fit command will fix things up when you ask for the frame to fit the image:

```
-- Get geometry, scale graphic, make frame fit it
tell the_new_graphic
    set {y1, x1, y2, x2} to geometric bounds
    set actual_height to y2 - y1
    set needed_scale to required_height / actual_height * 100
    set properties to ¬
        {vertical scale:needed_scale, horizontal scale:needed_scale}
    fit given frame to content
end tell
```

You might wonder about the earlier place command, which referred to insertion point 1 of an item that had been deleted, but it works because references are based on character offsets. In fact, you can use the reference again, this time to keep the graphic and any punctuation following it on the same line:

```
-- Stop it from splitting from any following punctuation
set no break of text from character 1 of item i of the_instances ¬
    to character 2 of item i of the_instances to true
```

Then it's time to end the if, repeat, and tell blocks, reset the rulers, and put up a final dialog box:

```
            end if
        end if
    end repeat
end tell
-- Reset the rulers
set properties of view preferences to old_units

-- Report the result
set user interaction level of script preferences to interact with all
if error_string = "" then
    set final_message to "Finished."
else
    set final_message to "The following errors occurred:" & ¬
        return & return & error_string
end if
beep
with timeout of 10000 seconds
    display dialog final_message buttons {"OK"} default button 1
end timeout
end tell
```

Testing the Script

Now it's time to test the script, using the supplied files. To see that the InDesign scaling part is working correctly, you can comment out the two resizing lines in the Photoshop section (although having prescaled graphics makes the script run much faster, because it avoids lots of text reflow).

Figure 26–15 shows the finished page with the icons inserted.

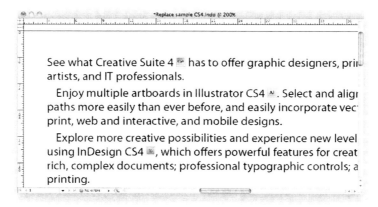

Figure 26–15. *The page after the script has been run and the graphics imported*

Using InDesign on a Server

By now you should be aware of some of the power of InDesign scripting—you can produce all sorts of complex documents completely automatically. You might start thinking about taking it further, perhaps using it as a back end to a web site, or having a server in your office produce documents from input to a watched folder.

The bad news is that such uses are beyond the scope of the normal InDesign license, which doesn't permit server-based use. The good news is that you can buy a special version of InDesign, called InDesign Server. Not only is it licensed for use on a server (and priced accordingly), but it is also designed to be run only via scripting—there is no interface to slow it down. The best part is that it will run your existing scripts with only a few changes.

Because it has no user interface, your scripts cannot deal with selections, or copy and paste; you can't refer to windows; you can't undo; and you can't use the `active document` property. The `user interface level` property is effectively fixed at `never interact`, so you can't show dialog boxes. There are a few other, more obscure gotchas, but a lot of code will run unchanged.

InDesign Server is sold directly by Adobe, and also by specialist value-added resellers.

Summary

InDesign is a wonderful application to script. This chapter touched on only some of the many features, for obvious reasons of space, but you can read about them in Adobe's documentation and see them used in the accompanying sample scripts. This chapter has given you an idea of how to approach scripting InDesign, and pointers to some of the common pitfalls, causes of confusion, and undocumented behaviors.

In the next chapter, we will take a brief break from the familiar GUI desktop to explore the Unix-based command line that lies beneath the surface of Mac OS X. You will learn how AppleScript can interact with this very different but also very powerful environment.

Chapter 27

Interacting with the Unix Command Line

Although the main purpose of AppleScript is to manipulate GUI-based applications, it can also interact with other types of applications. Beneath Mac OS X's graphical desktop lies a very different user interface—the Unix command line—and AppleScript can work with this too.

The world of Unix offers scripters an endless source of free scriptable applications. Many free Unix applications are available, each performing little commands and actions. You can utilize these applications by running Unix command-line scripts, or *shell scripts*. In turn, you can run shell scripts from your AppleScripts by means of the Standard Additions do shell script command.

Not only can you use the Unix command line from AppleScript, you also can run AppleScripts from the command line using the osascript command.

This chapter will explore both approaches: controlling the Unix command line from AppleScript, and triggering AppleScripts from the command line. It will also discuss useful techniques and warn of various gotchas to help you combine these two very different environments into elegant, reliable solutions.

Before we begin all that, however, let's start with a brief introduction to Unix scripting for the benefit of readers who are completely new to it.

Why and When Are Shell Scripts Used in AppleScript?

Although working with the Unix command line is different from working in AppleScript, in many situations the two can complement one another nicely. Many tasks where AppleScript is known to be weak, such as advanced text processing, raw performance, and access to lower-level operating system features, are long-time strengths of the Unix world. Decades of Unix development have produced a wide range of powerful, fast, and reliable command-line applications, many of which are freely available over the Internet or already installed on Mac OS X ready for you to use. At the same time, AppleScript provides terrific support for controlling scriptable GUI applications on Mac OS X— something that's crucial to many Mac users and an area where its Unix side is still playing catch-up.

By combining the two, you get the best of both worlds. Your AppleScripts can call into Unix scripts to help out with heavy-duty data-crunching tasks, and the Unix scripts can call into AppleScript when they want to work with Apple iTunes or Apple iCal. Although the integration isn't completely seamless and you still need to watch out for a few issues, it is still a highly valuable addition to an AppleScripter's toolbox, alongside traditional AppleScript solutions such as scriptable applications, scripting additions, and script libraries.

Even in areas where AppleScript is already strong, such as manipulating the file system, sometimes you may prefer to use Unix commands instead, perhaps because they perform a task in a slightly different way or provide extra options that aren't available elsewhere. For example, when working with the file system, Unix commands won't produce a Finder progress dialog box when deleting or copying files. Also, a shell script can process a large number of files much more rapidly than an AppleScript script can. If you need to extract a few files from a folder that contains several thousand items or search for a file in a directory tree, Unix commands can do that much faster than Finder commands.

Sometimes it's not that the Finder lacks a command; it's just that the shell script equivalent is a bit more convenient. For instance, if you need to duplicate a file to a different folder and rename it, with the Finder you first need to use the duplicate command to copy it and then use the set command to change the name of the new file. However, this can cause problems if the target location already contains a file with either the old name or the new name. If you use the Unix cp (copy) command instead, you can copy and rename the file in one shot.

Understanding Unix Scripting Concepts

In the following sections, you will learn about some basic concepts of Unix scripting that will be useful when you start to work with the command line on your Mac.

The Unix Command Line and Mac Desktop Compared

The Unix command line is like a giant toolbox, packed full of really useful tools for performing a huge range of tasks. Each tool in this toolbox is designed to do a single job and do it well. This is a bit different from the way that graphical user interface (GUI) applications such as the Finder, TextEdit, and Mail work, because each of these is designed to perform a range of related tasks. For example, you can use the Finder to eject a disk, copy a file or folder, list the contents of a folder, mount an iDisk, and so on. In the Unix world, you would perform each of these actions using a *separate* application: the Unix application for copying items is called cp, the one for listing the contents of folders is ls, and so on.

Another difference is that many Unix applications are designed to launch, perform a single task, and quit as soon as that task is done. By comparison, a GUI application such as Mail takes much longer to start up and then stays open so you can perform any number of e-mail–related tasks until you quit it. Some Unix applications do provide similar interactive options: for example, you can use the top application to get a one-off list of running processes, or you can have it display a constantly updating list of process information. (Incidentally, AppleScript can interact only with those Unix applications running in noninteractive mode.)

A third difference between the Unix world and the Mac desktop is that Unix applications are designed to connect to one another easily so that the output from one can be fed, or "piped," directly into the next. Some Mac applications are designed to interact with one another to a limited degree; for example, Safari allows you to Ctrl-click an image in a web page and add it directly to your Apple iPhoto library. For anything more serious, however, you have to resort to AppleScript—and hope the applications you're using provide the commands you need. By comparison, Unix applications are designed from the ground up so that users can seamlessly plug them together with little or no effort.

Even if you've never used Unix before, you may still find that all of this sounds a bit familiar if you've used Apple's Automator application at all. An Automator *action* is equivalent to a Unix application and performs a single, specific task; the Automator application fills a similar role to the Unix command line in that it allows you to link multiple actions together and run them as a single unit. Of course, some differences exist: for example, Automator has a friendly, easy-to-use GUI, whereas the Unix command line has many advanced (and cryptic!) power-user features. Overall, though, you can probably guess where Apple got the original idea for Automator from!

You should be able to see the similarities between what AppleScript lets you do (connect GUI applications to create powerful workflows) and what the Unix command line lets you do (connect Unix applications to create powerful workflows), even if the ways they go about it are a bit different.

How the Unix Command Line Works

You need to understand a number of key concepts before you start to work with the Unix command line. The following sections summarize these concepts to give you a feel for the subject if you're new to Unix scripting; for a much more detailed discussion, you should refer to the many books and tutorials that are dedicated to the topic. (For example, our technical reviewer, David Coyle, recommends Dave Taylor's *Wicked Cool Shell Scripts* book, which includes a chapter on Mac OS X–specific shell scripting. See http://www.intuitive.com/wicked for more details.)

The Shell

When you open a new Terminal window or call do shell script, you'll first meet a Unix command line, or *shell*. A Unix shell application is basically a scripting language, a command-line interface (for working interactively), and a script interpreter all rolled into one.

When a shell application is running interactively, you can enter commands and other code at the command line. As soon as you press Return, the line of code you've just entered will be read and executed. For example, if you open a new Terminal window, type in ls, and then press Return, the shell will read that line of text, figure out that ls is the name of a command, look for a Unix application with the same name, and run it for you. In Figure 27–1, you can see the ls command being executed in Terminal.

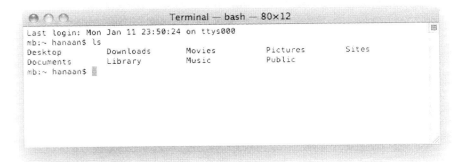

Figure 27–1. *The ls command executed in the Terminal application with the result below it*

NOTE: Another approach is to write a shell script in a text editor, save it as a text file, and then tell a shell application to read and execute that file. Because this chapter is about using the Unix command line from AppleScript, I won't discuss this approach here. However, I will show you how to create a Unix shell script as an AppleScript string and then use Standard Additions' do shell script command to execute that script.

Mac OS X includes a number of Unix shell applications as standard. These have names such as sh, tcsh, zsh, and bash, and each one offers to users a slightly different set of features for working on the Unix command line. You don't need to worry too much about the differences between these shell applications as long as your shell scripts are simple, because they all deal with basic tasks such as issuing commands in the same way. More advanced shell scripting features such as setting variables and using repeat loops do vary from shell to shell, however, so you'll need to read the manual for the particular shell you're working in if you want to use the advanced features.

NOTE: Terminal uses your default shell, which is bash (unless you've changed it), but the do shell script command always uses sh.

Commands

I discussed earlier how Unix uses lots of small, single-purpose applications to perform tasks. To run Unix applications from the Unix shell, you use *commands*. A command is just the name (or the path) of the application to run, followed by any options and arguments you want passed to the application.

You'll find that Unix commands are not unlike AppleScript commands, which consist of the name of a command handler you want to execute followed by the parameters you want to pass to the handler. Here is a typical Unix command:

```
ls -l /Applications/
```

The command's name is ls, which is the name of the Unix application for listing a folder's contents. The -l bit is an *option*, and the /Applications/ part is an *argument*. Notice that each option and argument in a command is separated by a space. In general, arguments are values for the application to process, and options control exactly how that processing is performed. In the previous example, /Applications/ is the path to the folder whose content you want to list, and the -l option is a simple on/off flag that tells ls to provide a detailed description of each item rather than just its name (the default).

Many Unix applications provide an additional way to pass in data, known as *standard input* (often abbreviated to stdin). Although arguments are useful for passing in small pieces of data such as file and folder paths, you can pass any amount of data via standard input. This data is usually (though not always) plain text, and many Unix programs process this input on a line-by-line basis, where each line is separated by a linefeed (ASCII 10) character.

Most Unix applications also return a result, which is often also plain text. Not surprisingly, this is known as *standard output* (or stdout). For example, the ls application returns a list of file and folder names/descriptions as text, with each item separated by a newline.

NOTE: When running the ls command by itself in Terminal, it may format its output into several columns for readability. Don't worry, though: when you use ls in a longer shell script or via AppleScript's do shell script command, it will return each file name on a separate line as expected.

Finally, when a Unix application encounters a problem that it's unable to cope with, it will generate an error. These error codes are given as numbers. Code 0 normally indicates success, while any non-zero number indicates a particular error occurred. In addition, a description of the problem is often given; this appears as *standard error* (stderr). Standard error works a bit like standard output, except that it's used for error messages, not normal results. Standard error is also used for warning messages describing nonfatal problems that the application was able to deal with by itself but still wants the user to see.

Pipes

By default, a Unix application takes its input from the Unix shell that started it, and its output is displayed by that same shell. You can see this for yourself by typing ls -l /Applications/ in a Terminal window and pressing Return.

One of Unix's key features is that it enables you to link multiple applications together to create powerful data-processing workflows, or *pipelines*. It does this by allowing you to redirect the standard output of one Unix application to the standard input of another. These connections are called *pipes*, and on the command line they are written as a single vertical bar, |.

For example, let's say you want to list the name of every item in your home folder whose name contains the letter *D*. To get the name of each item, you'll use the ls command, which outputs the item names as linefeed-delimited text. To extract only the lines containing the letter *D*, you'll use a second command, grep, which is used to match lines that contain a particular pattern of text. grep takes the text to search as its standard input and the pattern to look for as its argument. To join the two commands, you put a pipe character between them:

```
ls | grep D
```

When you run this script, the result is—you guessed it—a list of names containing the letter *D* as newline-delimited text.

> **NOTE:** You may notice that when you run the previous example, only names containing an uppercase *D* are matched. If you want to make grep ignore case, add the -i option between the grep command's name and its argument, as shown here: ls | grep -i D.

Other Redirections

Usually the first command in a pipeline takes its standard input from the shell that started it, and the last command's standard output and standard error are displayed by the same shell. Sometimes it's useful to use a different source for standard input or different destinations for standard output and/or standard error.

For example, let's say you want to use grep to match lines in a plain text file. To do this, you need to tell the shell to read the standard input data for the grep command from your text file. (grep can also read files directly, but don't worry about that here.)

To redirect standard input, you use the < symbol followed by the path of the file to read from:

```
grep some-pattern < /path/to/input/file
```

Similarly, to specify a different destination for standard output, use the > symbol followed by the file to write to:

```
ls -l /Applications/ > /path/to/output/file
```

You can use other redirection symbols for redirecting standard error, appending standard output to an existing file, and so on, but I won't cover them here.

Getting Help

For users who are used to the comforts of the Mac desktop, learning to use the Unix command line and the many powerful tools it offers can be a bit intimidating at first. Fortunately, plenty of assistance is available.

Built-in Help

Unix comes with extensive built-in documentation that you can easily access from the command line. Almost every Unix application comes with a detailed manual that describes what it does and how to use it. To view a manual, you use the man tool. For example, to view the manual for ls, type the following:

```
man ls
```

You can use the cursor keys to scroll through longer manuals. When you're done, just type q to exit the manual viewer.

Some Unix applications also provide built-in help. For example, the popular curl tool (used to upload and download files via File Transfer Protocol [FTP] and Hypertext Transfer Protocol [HTTP]) will provide a short description of each option you can use, which is handy when you don't want to search through its full manual just to look up something. To view curl's built-in help, just type curl followed by the -h option:

```
curl -h
```

Another handy tool is apropos. This searches through a list of brief descriptions for every installed Unix application and displays those that contain a given search word or phrase. For example, try typing this:

```
apropos text
```

This will return dozens of matching manuals, not only for Unix tools but also for things such as low-level operating system calls that are of interest only to C programmers, Perl and Tcl libraries, and so on. Fortunately, apropos puts a number in parentheses after the manual name that tells you what section it came from. The most useful section is section 1, which contains general commands, while section 8, which contains system administrator tools, might also be of occasional interest. (Other sections are usually only of interest to Unix programmers.)

For example, to do a quick and dirty filter for section 1 manuals, you could use this:

```
apropos text | grep '(1)'
```

The man tool also provides some powerful manual search tools if apropos doesn't find what you're after; see its manual (man man) for details.

Other Sources of Help

Unix is a popular operating system that has been around for many years now, so plenty of good books and tutorials about Unix scripting are available; you'll also be able to find online newsgroups and other sources of information and assistance. A quick online search for the phrase *Unix tutorial* will produce thousands of links for you to rummage through and find one you like!

Things to Watch Out For

Although the Unix command line is sophisticated in some respects, it can be quite primitive in others. I'll quickly cover some common issues that you may encounter, particularly when using the Unix command line from AppleScript.

Data in Unix Is "Dumb"

Although AppleScript provides a variety of well-defined object classes for representing different kinds of data (integers, reals, strings, dates, lists, records, and so on), to the Unix command line all data is just a dumb series of bytes, and it's up to individual applications to interpret that data in a particular way.

Many Unix applications treat data as plain ASCII text, and when they want to represent a "list" of "strings," they use a single block of ASCII text where each "list item" is a single line followed by a linefeed (ASCII 10) character. For example, if you're passing data to a command that expects linefeed-delimited text as its standard input, make sure that's what you're giving it.

An easy mistake is to use return characters (ASCII 13) to separate your lines because AppleScripts and many older Mac applications often use return characters for this purpose. As of Mac OS X 10.5, AppleScript provides a built-in linefeed constant, so make sure you use that and not the return (ASCII 13) constant. (If you need to support Mac OS X 10.4 or earlier, then use the command ASCII character 10 instead.)

Script 27–1 shows a join_lines handler that will join a list of strings into a linefeed-delimited string as required by the Unix command line.

Script 27–1.

```
on join_lines(the_list)
    set old_tids to AppleScript's text item delimiters
    set AppleScript's text item delimiters to linefeed
    set the_text to the_list as text
    set AppleScript's text item delimiters to old_tids
    return the_text
```

```
end join_lines
```

For example,

```
set the_list to {"some item", "some other item", "yet another item"}
join_lines(the_list)
```

will return a three-line string with each line separated by an ASCII 10 character.

Unix Doesn't Know About Different Character Sets

Another difference is that few Unix applications that work with text understand character sets such as MacRoman and Unicode: the only character set they know about is ASCII. Perhaps some day these applications will finally catch up, but for now it's just something command-line users have to accept.

To compensate for Unix's ignorance of modern (and not-so-modern) text encodings, a common technique is to represent non-ASCII text as UTF-8 encoded Unicode. This provides a reasonable degree of compatibility because the first 128 characters in UTF-8 also happen to be the same 128 characters that make up the ASCII character set. Most Unix tools that deal with ASCII text will understand these 128 characters as usual and pay no special interest to any others. For example, the ls command actually returns file and folder names in UTF-8 format, so if a filename or folder name contains non-ASCII characters, these characters will be preserved.

Fortunately, you don't have to worry too much about text encodings when using the do shell script command, since it will convert AppleScript strings to UTF-8 data and back again for you. However, you do need to watch out when using Standard Additions' read and write commands to read and write text files that are used by shell scripts. See Chapter 17 for more information about how to read and write UTF-8 encoded text files in AppleScript.

Unix Understands POSIX File Paths Only

Although AppleScript prefers to use colon-delimited HFS paths to identify files and folders—for example, Macintosh HD:Applications:TextEdit.app—the Unix shell always uses slash-delimited POSIX paths—for example, /Applications/TextEdit.app.

Watch Where You Use Spaces and Other Special Characters!

Because Unix shells already use spaces to separate command options and arguments from one another, you have to be careful not to add any extra spaces where you shouldn't when constructing shell scripts. You also need to watch out for other special characters used by Unix shells (this includes most punctuation characters).

For example, the following command will list the items in the Applications folder:

```
ls /Applications/
```

However, the following command, which is supposed to list the contents of the folder named `FileMaker Pro 8`, won't work as expected:

```
ls /Applications/FileMaker Pro 8/
```

Instead of treating `/Applications/FileMaker Pro 8/` as a single argument, the Unix shell actually sees three arguments: `/Applications/FileMaker`, `Pro`, and `8/`. At best, this sort of mistake results in the shell script immediately halting with an error message. At worst, the script may perform a different action than the one you intended. This could be bad news if your script is performing a potentially dangerous task such as writing or erasing files: you could easily end up deleting a completely different part of your file system instead!

Fortunately, Unix shells allow you to escape or quote spaces and other special characters, and you should take great care always to do so whenever appropriate. I'll discuss this further in the "Quoting Arguments" section later in the chapter.

Unix Assumes You Know What You're Doing

Unlike the Mac OS desktop, Unix was designed by programmers for programmers. It places few restrictions on what you can do and rarely provides "Are you sure?" warnings before performing potentially dangerous operations such as replacing or deleting files. A simple mistake such as forgetting to escape spaces in a file path when using the `rm` command to delete files and folders could easily lead to disaster. See the "Quoting Arguments" section for some examples of how dangerous mistypes can be in Unix.

Some Useful Unix Commands

Table 27–1 lists some particularly useful Unix applications that are included with Mac OS X. Because this book is about AppleScript, not Unix, I won't be covering most of them here, but you might like to check them out sometime. I've included a brief description of what each one does to help you get started.

Table 27–1. *Useful Unix Commands*

Command	Description
cd	Changes the working directory (that is, the default folder used by other commands).
ls	Lists the items in a folder.
mkdir	Makes new folders.
mv, cp, rm	Move, copy, and delete files and folders.
find	Searches for files and folders.
chown, chmod	Change the owner and access permissions for files and folders.

Command	Description
date	Gets the current date as a custom-formatted string.
curl	Uploads and downloads files using HTTP, FTP, and so on.
grep, awk, sed	Extract lines or parts of lines that match specific patterns.
iconv	Converts plain text files from one encoding to another (for example, from UTF16-BE to UTF16-LE).
textutil	Converts text files from one format to another (.txt, .rtf, .html, .doc, .webarchive, etc.).
afplay	Plays audio files.
mdfind	Performs Spotlight searches.
sips	Examines and manipulates image files and their ColorSync profiles.
zip, unzip	Pack and unpack ZIP archive files.
perl, python, ruby, tcl	Access powerful general-purpose scripting languages.

Running Shell Scripts from AppleScript

You can run shell scripts from AppleScript in two ways: scripting the Terminal application and using Standard Additions' do shell script command.

Scripting the Terminal Application

Apple's Terminal application provides a basic scripting interface. Its dictionary defines just four classes, application, settings set, tab, and window. It also defines several commands, including the main do script command, which tells Terminal to run a Unix shell script.

Understanding Terminal's Object Model

Terminal's window objects include the usual properties for manipulating the window's bounds, whether or not it is miniaturized, and so on. Each window can have one or more tabs, so window objects also contain tab elements. You can get the current tab by referring to the window's selected tab property.

Tab objects are where the main action happens. Each tab represents a running Unix shell application and provides various properties for getting information on both the tab itself and the programs being run.

Objects of the `settings set` class define the presentation and behavior of tabs—for example, the size of font and the number of rows and columns shown. Each settings set is an element of the main application object—several ready-made sets are already provided, and you can define more yourself using Terminal's Preferences dialog box or `make` command.

To find out the names of all available settings sets:

```
tell application "Terminal"
    get name of every settings set
end tell
--> {"Basic", "Homebrew", "Ocean", "Red Sands", "Grass", "Pro", "Novel"}
```

You can apply a settings set to a tab by setting the tab object's `current settings` property. For example, the following script applies a random settings set to each tab in every window:

```
tell application "Terminal"
    repeat with window_ref in every window
        repeat with tab_ref in every tab of window_ref
            set current settings of tab_ref to some settings set
        end repeat
    end repeat
end tell
```

Using the *do script* Command

Here's the definition of the `do script` command:

```
do script v : Runs a UNIX shell script or command.
    do script [text] : The command to execute.
        [in tab, window, or any] : The tab in which to execute the command
        --> tab : The tab the command was executed in.
```

This takes a shell script string as a direct parameter and executes it either in a new window or in an existing one depending on whether you supply an `in` parameter.

Note that `do script` doesn't wait for the shell script to complete; it just starts it and returns immediately. It doesn't return a result, and it doesn't raise an error if the shell script fails.

A Simple *do script* Example

The following example will open a new Terminal window and use the `ls` Unix command to list the contents of a folder (or *directory* in Unix jargon):

```
tell application "Terminal"
    do script "ls /Applications/"
end tell
```

Alternatively, if you want to run the script in an existing window or tab, use the `in` parameter to supply a reference to the window or tab you want to use:

```
tell application "Terminal"
```

```
    do script "ls /Applications/" in window 1
end tell
```

Like many other shell script commands, the ls command may take no arguments, in which case it uses the current working directory. In this example, a single argument passed to the ls command is a POSIX path pointing to the Applications folder (/Applications/). The slash at the start of the pathname indicates that the path is an absolute path and not a relative path. (You'll learn more about working directories and relative vs. absolute paths in the "Absolute Paths, Relative Paths, and the Working Directory" section later in the chapter.) The result is a string listing the names of the files and folders in the folder.

Limitations of the *do script* Command

The following are the limitations of scripting the Terminal application:

- You can't pass data directly via stdin and stdout (you need to read to/write from separate files for that).

- The do script command won't wait for the script to complete before returning.

- The do script command won't raise an error if the shell script fails (you need to write any error information to a separate file and then check that; this requires extra work and is often clumsy to do).

Using the *do shell script* Command

The do shell script command is simple: it takes a string containing a Unix command or script and executes it as if you had typed it in the Terminal application and pressed Return. (There are a few differences, though, which I'll discuss along the way.)

> **NOTE:** Apple provides a very good FAQ on using do shell script at
> http://developer.apple.com/mac/library/technotes/tn2002/tn2065.html.

From the Dictionary

The do shell script command is defined in the Miscellaneous Commands suite of Standard Additions:

```
do shell script v : Execute a shell script or command using the 'sh' shell
    do shell script text : the command or shell script to execute. Examples are 'ls'
        or '/bin/ps -auxwww'
        [as type class] : the desired type of result; default is text (UTF-8)
        [administrator privileges boolean] : execute the command as the administrator
        [user name text] : use this administrator account to avoid a password dialog
            (If this parameter is specified, the "password" parameter must also be
            specified.)
```

```
[password text] : use this administrator password to avoid a password dialog
[altering line endings boolean] : change all line endings to Mac-style and
        trim a trailing one (default true)
--> text : the command output
```

Understanding the *do shell script* Command's Parameters

The following sections discuss the do shell script command's parameters.

The Direct Parameter

The direct parameter is a string containing the Unix shell script to execute.

The *as* Parameter

The as parameter allows you to control how the shell script's result is converted back into an AppleScript object. More on this in the upcoming "How *do shell script* Deals with Unicode" section.

The *administrator privileges* Parameter

The administrator privileges parameter allows you to enter the Mac administrator's username and password in the operating system's Authenticate dialog box. This authentication will hold for as long as the script is open. Every time it's opened, it will require authentication the first time it runs. If it's a script applet, it will require authentication every time it runs. This may be annoying, but it ensures that someone can't use AppleScript and do shell script to bypass the Mac's security system without the user's knowledge.

The *user name* and *password* Parameters

You can use user name and password together as an alternative to the administrator privileges parameter, although you can supply any username and password, not necessarily an administrative one. Here's an example:

```
do shell script "cd /secure/server/directory/" user name "admin" password "URaQT"
```

> **CAUTION:** Hard-coding sensitive login information right into your script can create a serious security risk! Always use the Keychain or automatic authentication if you want to keep your login details safe.

The *altering line endings* Parameter

This Boolean parameter allows you to alter the line endings of the do shell script command's result from the original Unix line endings (ASCII 10) to classic Mac-style line endings (ASCII 13). By default, the line endings will be altered and become Mac line endings. However, you will want to prevent this if you plan on feeding the result of one do `shell script` command to another, as Unix applications do not recognize ASCII 13 characters as line endings.

For example,

`do shell script "ls"`

will return a list of file names as an ASCII 13–delimited string, while

`do shell script "ls" without altering line endings`

will return the names as an ASCII 10–delimited string with a trailing ASCII 10 character at the end.

How *do shell script* Deals with Unicode

As I mentioned earlier in the chapter, most Unix command-line tools only understand ASCII-encoded text. To work around this limitation, applications that need to pass Unicode text to the Unix shell normally encode that text as UTF-8 data. The first 128 characters in the UTF-8 format are the same as in ASCII, which makes those characters compatible with an ASCII-oriented shell. Other Unicode characters are represented as a sequence of 2–6 bytes, which the shell just leaves as is.

When you call do `shell script`, the direct parameter you hand it (which is the shell script you want to execute) is automatically converted from a Unicode-based AppleScript string to UTF-8 encoded text data.

By default, do `shell script` assumes that the shell script returns text data encoded as ASCII or UTF-8, and converts it back into an AppleScript string for you. Most Unix commands do return ASCII-encoded text or UTF-8 encoded text, so this is usually what you want. However, you might occasionally need to override this behavior—for example, if your script returns UTF-16 encoded text or raw binary data. To do this, just use the name of the AppleScript class you want as the command's as parameter.

For example, the default is «class utf8», which reads the shell script's result as UTF-8 encoded text data. If the script's result uses your primary encoding (e.g., MacRoman), use `string`, or if it uses the UTF-16 encoding, use `Unicode text`. If the script returns pure binary data, your safest bet is to use `data`; for example:

```
do shell script ("curl " & quoted form of the_url) as data
--> «data rdat4170706C...»
```

Although you can't manipulate the contents of raw data objects in AppleScript, you can pass these objects to other commands such as Standard Additions' `write` command that know how to handle them.

> **TIP:** When reading and writing ASCII or UTF-8 encoded text files in AppleScript, remember to use «class utf8» as the as parameter to Standard Additions' `read` and `write` commands. See Chapter 17 for more information.

A Simple *do shell script* Example

Figure 27–2 shows an example of using the do shell script command to return the names of all the items in the Applications folder.

Figure 27–2. *Running the* ls *Unix command from AppleScript using the* do shell script *command*

The result is a Unicode text string containing the names of the items in the folder. Each name appears on a separate line in the string, separated by a return (ASCII 13) character. (Remember to use the altering line endings parameter if you want the original ASCII 10 characters instead.) Many Unix commands will represent a list of values in this way. You can easily split this multiline string into a list of strings by asking for all of its paragraph elements:

```
every paragraph of (do shell script "ls /Applications/")
--> { "Address Book.app", "Automator.app", "Calculator.app", "Chess.app", ...}
```

Limitations of the *do shell script* Command

The following are some known limitations to using the do shell script command.

No User Interaction

In some cases, you may need to run shell scripts that require user interaction. Because the do shell script command doesn't allow this, you will have to run these shell scripts in the Terminal application instead. See the previous "Scripting the Terminal Application" section for more details.

Performance Overheads

Although shell scripts often execute quickly, do `shell script` has to start a new shell each time it's called, which can add overhead time. This can start to add up if you're calling do `shell script` frequently.

Can't Directly Supply Data to Standard Input

Unfortunately, the do `shell script` command doesn't provide any way to supply data directly to standard input. I'll cover a couple of ways to work around this limitation in the "Passing Data to Standard Input" section a bit later.

Assembling Shell Script Strings

The following sections discuss ways to assemble AppleScript strings that can be used as shell scripts.

Unix File Paths

Whereas AppleScript uses colon-delimited HFS paths to describe the locations of files and folders on a hard disk, Unix requires slash-delimited POSIX paths. This means any time you want to pass a path from AppleScript to a shell script or back, you have to convert from one format to the other.

Chapter 17 discusses how to convert between HFS- and POSIX-style paths, but here's a quick refresher. When going from AppleScript to a shell script, use an alias or file object's POSIX path property to get the equivalent POSIX path string (this can also work on HFS path strings):

```
set posix_path_string to POSIX path of alias "Macintosh HD:Applications:"
--> "/Applications/"
```

When going from a shell script to AppleScript, use a POSIX file specifier to convert a POSIX path string back into a file object:

```
set the_file_object to POSIX file posix_path_string
--> file "Macintosh HD:Applications:"
```

Because of some long-time bugs, all these conversions will work correctly only when the named hard drive is mounted; otherwise, you'll get a malformed path as a result. For example, the following,

```
POSIX path of "Non-existent Disk:Folder:"
```

returns the following,

```
"/Non-existent Disk/Folder/"
```

but it should be the following:

```
"/Volumes/Non-existent Disk/Folder/"
```

In addition, the following,

```
POSIX file "/Volumes/Non-existent Disk/Folder/"
```

returns the following,

```
file "Macintosh HD:Volumes:Non-existent Disk:Folder:"
```

but it should be the following:

```
file "Non-existent Disk:Folder:"
```

Quoting Arguments

Forgetting to quote arguments is a common mistake and is also potentially serious because, unlike the Mac's GUI, the Unix command line is extremely unforgiving of user mistakes (it assumes you already know what you're doing). For example, it's all too easy to accidentally ask the command line to delete your entire home folder, and before you know it, you'll be restoring your entire account from backups (you do always keep up-to-date backups, don't you?). There are few "Are you sure?" confirmations and no Undo.

Although the most common result of a missing or misplaced quote is that the script halts with an error or produces an incorrect result, you really can do serious damage if you're not careful.

For example, the Unix file deletion command, rm, will just delete what you ask it to and not think twice about it. Imagine if I wanted to use the POSIX path /Users/hanaan/Documents Backup in an rm command and forgot to quote it:

```
set the_path to "/Users/hanaan/Documents Backup"
do shell script "rm -rf " & the_path -- DO NOT RUN THIS CODE!
```

Running this script would erase my Documents folder and the item named Backup in the current working directory, not my Documents Backup folder as I'd intended!

Assuming you're not quite that careless, you'll remember to quote the path first, but here's where unsuspecting folk run into another pitfall. If you try to add the quotes yourself, such as in the following,

```
do shell script "rm -rf '" & the_path & "'"
```

then you avoid the previous, more obvious bug, but you still leave yourself open to another bug. Specifically, what happens if the string you're quoting *also contains a single quote*? The shell will see that character, assume it's the closing quote, and treat what follows as regular code. Here's a relatively benign example that causes an error when run:

```
set the_text to "Use a pipe '|' symbol"
do shell script "echo '" & the_text & "'"
-- Error: sh: line 1:  symbol: command not found
```

What the shell sees is the line like this (with extra spaces added to make it more obvious):

```
echo 'Use a pipe' | symbol
```

It executes the echo command and then tries to pipe its output to a command named symbol. In this case, the script errors because a symbol command isn't available, but imagine what damage it could do if some destructive command *was* triggered, either accidentally or possibly even deliberately. (For example, malicious Internet hackers often use carefully crafted strings to trick carelessly written programs that have these flaws into executing code that hijacks the whole machine.)

Therefore, before using an AppleScript string as a literal string in a shell script, *always* make sure it's correctly quoted and escaped first. Asking a string for the value of its quoted form property will do this for you easily and effectively. Quoting POSIX path strings is an obvious example, but you should do it for *any* string whose contents should be treated as data, not code. For example:

```
set shell_script to "rm -rf " & quoted form of the_posix_path
```

And:

```
set shell_script to "echo " & quoted form of input_text & ¬
    " | grep " & quoted form of match_pattern
```

Absolute Paths, Relative Paths, and the Working Directory

When executing file-related shell script commands either in AppleScript or in Terminal, you need to pass the path of the target file or directory as arguments to the Unix command. You can specify file paths in Unix commands in two ways: either as an absolute path or as a relative path.

Passing an absolute path means you disregard your current location and assume that the starting point (which is also the top directory, in this case) is either the startup disk or the current user's home directory. Relative paths start from the current working directory.

When specifying an absolute path starting from the startup disk level, you start the path with a slash. To indicate the startup disk only, you pass a slash by itself. The following shell script will list the content of the startup disk:

```
do shell script "ls /"
```

In a way, when executing the do shell script command from AppleScript, it is easier to use absolute paths starting from the startup disk because this is the path that is returned by the POSIX path property of alias and file objects. The following script gets an alias to the user's Documents folder using AppleScript's path to command, and then retrieves the POSIX path string from the alias's POSIX path property and uses it with the ls command in a shell script (remembering to quote it first, of course):

```
set the_alias to path to documents folder from user domain
--> alias "Macintosh HD:Users:hanaan:Documents:"
set posix_path to POSIX path of the_alias
```

```
--> "/Users/hanaan/Documents/"
do shell script ("ls " & quoted form of posix_path)
```

If you want to start from the current user's home directory, you have to precede the slash with a tilde: ~/. The following script will have the same result as the previous one, listing the contents of the Documents folder in the home directory:

```
set posix_path_relative_to_home to "Documents"
do shell script ("ls ~/" & quoted form of posix_path_relative_to_home)
```

You can also refer to disks other than the startup disk. To do that, you need to precede the name of the disk with /Volumes/. The script that follows lists the contents of the hard disk External 2000:

```
do shell script ("ls '/Volumes/External 2000'")
```

When writing shell scripts in the Terminal application, where they belong, the most common way to pass path arguments is as relative paths. Relative paths use an implied working directory for all your file-related commands. You can add on to that working directory or change the working directory and work from there.

Imagine giving someone directions to the kitchen in your house. You may tell that person to go to the front door or a room and start from there (absolute paths), or you may ask that person where they are standing at the moment and give directions from that point (relative path). After all, they might be one doorway away, so why send them all the way to the front door to start?

You can change the working directory with the cd command, after which you can see the path to the working directory in Terminal as the prefix to the commands. Figure 27–3 shows the Terminal window after the working directory was changed with the cd command.

The first line (after the welcome line) shows the cd command change the working directory to the Applications folder on the startup disk. The next line shows that path as part of the command prompt.

Figure 27–3. *The Terminal window shown after the* cd *command. Watch how the command prompt changes.*

When using relative paths, you can use `../` to indicate the parent directory of the one you're in. The following script lists the directory that encloses the current working directory:

```
do shell script to "ls ../"
```

The problem with using the working directory in AppleScript's do shell script is that, unlike Terminal, AppleScript forgets the working directory between executions of the do shell script command. You can still make good use of cd within a single do shell script command, though. To execute multiple commands in the same shell script, just separate them with a semicolon. For example, the following script will change the working directory with the cd command and list the working directory with the ls command:

```
do shell script "cd ~/Documents; ls"
```

The fact that AppleScript doesn't retain the working directory between do shell script calls does make working directories less helpful, though, and for most tasks absolute paths are the method of choice.

Passing Data to Standard Input

Although the do shell script command doesn't provide any way to feed data directly to standard input, you can supply standard input yourself in a couple of ways, each with its own advantages and disadvantages.

Using *echo*

The simplest way to get data into a Unix application's standard input is to include it in the shell script. To do this, you use the Unix echo command, which takes your input data as an argument (correctly quoted, of course!) and passes it directly to standard out. You can then use a pipe to redirect this output to the standard input of a second command.

To demonstrate, here's how you could use grep to find all lines in a linefeed-delimited string containing the specified pattern (also correctly quoted):

```
do shell script ¬
     "echo " & quoted form of input_text & ¬
     " | grep " & quoted form of pattern_to_match
```

For example, to find all the strings in a list that contain at least one digit (0–9):

```
set the_list to {"hello", "bob42", "three", "0.197"}
set pattern_to_match to "[[:digit:]]"

set input_text to join_lines(the_list)
do shell script ¬
     "echo " & quoted form of input_text & ¬
     " | grep " & quoted form of pattern_to_match
every paragraph of result
--> {"bob42", "0.197"}
```

(Notice that this script uses the `join_lines` handler shown earlier in Script 27–1, so you will need to paste that handler into your script as well.)

This echo-based approach has a couple of disadvantages, however. The first is that the Unix shell sets a maximum length for scripts (usually something like 256KB, though it may be less on older versions of Mac OS X), so if you try to pass a string that is too big, you'll get an error. The second disadvantage is that if your string contains any ASCII 0 characters, you'll get an error because Unix often interprets ASCII 0 to mean "end of string" and will stop reading your shell script before it gets to the actual end.

For some tasks these limitations won't be an issue, but when they are, you'll need to use the next approach.

Using Temporary Files

Another way to get data from AppleScript to a Unix application's standard input is to write it to a temporary file and then redirect the shell script's standard input to read from that file. Although this approach takes a bit more work, it doesn't have the limitations of the echo-based approach you just saw.

This approach has three steps:

1. Create a temporary file.

2. Write the data to the temporary file using Standard Additions commands.

3. Tell your shell script to read its standard input from this file.

If you want, you can add some code that uses the `rm` command to erase the temporary file once it's no longer needed. This step isn't strictly necessary if you write the file to one of Mac OS X's temporary folders, however, because Mac OS X will eventually clean up any leftovers in those locations for you. To keep the following example simple, I've left out this cleanup stage, but you can add it if you want.

Creating the Temporary File

The simplest way to create a temporary file is by using the Unix `mktemp` command. This creates an empty temporary file with a unique name, and then returns the path to that file. You can create the file at a specific location, or use the `-t` option to create it in a temporary folder.

Script 27–2 shows the finished handler. I've told `mktemp` to create the file in a temporary folder and prefix the file name with "dss" (short for "do shell script").

Script 27–2.

```
on make_temp_file()
    return do shell script "mktemp -t dss"
end make_temp_file
```

This handler returns a POSIX-style file path; for example:

```
"/var/folders/p+/p+pBAQxKE-S81g-RmJ1K8U+++TI/-Tmp-//dss.dvrJvv1J"
```

You'll need to convert this path to a POSIX file object before passing it to the file-writing handler, but you can use it in other shell scripts as is.

Writing the Temporary File

This step is easy. You'll write the file's content as UTF-8 encoded Unicode text («class utf8»), because that gives you a good level of compatibility with the ASCII-oriented Unix shell while also preserving any non-ASCII characters. You can use the write_UTF8_file handler from Chapter 17 for this:

```
to write_UTF8_file(the_file, the_text)
    set file_ID to open for access the_file with write permission
    set eof file_ID to 0
    write the_text to file_ID as «class utf8»
    close access file_ID
end write_UTF8_file
```

Redirecting the Shell Script

To make the shell script read its standard input from a temporary file, you use the < symbol followed by the path to the temporary file:

```
grep 'pattern to match' < '/path/to/input text'
```

The do shell script equivalent of this is as follows:

```
do shell script ¬
    "grep " & quoted form of pattern_to_match & ¬
    " < " & quoted form of temp_path
```

Script 27–3 uses grep to find all the strings in a list that contain at least one digit (you will need to include the make_temp_file and write_UTF8_file handlers from the previous sections and the join_lines handler shown in Script 27–1).

Script 27–3.

```
set the_list to {"hello", "bob42", "three", "0.197"}
set pattern_to_match to "[[:digit:]]"

set temp_path to make_temp_file()
set input_text to join_lines(the_list)
write_UTF8_file(POSIX file temp_path, input_text)

do shell script ¬
    "grep " & quoted form of pattern_to_match & ¬
    " < " & quoted form of temp_path
every paragraph of result
--> {"bob42", "0.197"}
```

Running AppleScript from Shell Scripts

Reversing the tables on the do shell script command is the osascript shell command. This command allows you to run AppleScript scripts from the command line.

Using the *osascript* Command

The osascript command can run scripts in three different ways:

- It can compile and run AppleScript source code you supply as a string.

- It can run a compiled or uncompiled AppleScript file.

- It can appear in a special line (#!/usr/bin/osascript) at the start of an uncompiled AppleScript file, allowing you to run that file directly from the command line.

To execute a line of AppleScript code directly, use the -e option followed by the code itself. Make sure to wrap the code in single quotes so that the Unix shell recognizes it as a single string. For example, the following shell script will tell iTunes to start playing:

```
osascript -e 'tell app "iTunes" to play'
```

You can supply multiple lines of script by including more -e options, each one followed by a line of code. The following shell script will run a four-line AppleScript that activates the Finder and tells it to display a dialog box containing the name of the startup disk:

```
osascript -e 'tell app "Finder"' -e 'activate' \
    -e 'display dialog (get name of startup disk)' -e 'end tell'
```

> **TIP:** osascript cannot run GUI-related commands such as display dialog directly because it is not a GUI application itself, but you can work around this limitation by sending the command to a GUI application such as the Finder or System Events instead. Remember to activate the application first so that the dialog box doesn't get hidden by other applications' windows.

To run a script stored in a file, you specify the file path right after the command name. For example, create a plain text file containing the text date string of (current date) and save it in your home folder with the name today.applescript. Next, create a new shell window in Terminal, type the following command, and then press Return:

```
osascript today.applescript
```

The osascript command will compile and run the today.applescript file and return its result; for example:

```
Wednesday, July 1, 2009
```

To run an uncompiled AppleScript in the same way that you run other Unix commands, first create a new document containing the line #!/usr/bin/osascript followed by the AppleScript code you want to run; for example:

```
#!/usr/bin/osascript
```

```
date string of (current date + 1 * days)
```

Save this script in your home folder as a plain text file called `tomorrow.applescript`.

> **TIP:** I've kept the `.applescript` file name extension here for clarity, but you can omit the extension and just call the file `tomorrow` if you prefer to keep things short. This is a common naming practice for shell scripts that will be run as commands.

Next, go to your Terminal window and type the following command:

```
chmod +x tomorrow.applescript
```

The `chmod` command is used to set the read, write, and execute permissions for a given file. It's a bit cryptic to follow, but in this case you're setting the permissions for the `tomorrow.applescript` file to allow anyone to execute it directly.

Lastly, to run the script, type the following command:

```
./tomorrow.applescript
```

If all goes well, your new "Unix command" should run and return tomorrow's date; for example:

```
Thursday, July 2, 2009
```

> **TIP:** By default, when you run a Unix command, the Unix shell will look for that command only in certain predefined directories. Adding `./` in front of your script's name tells the Unix shell to look in the current directory for the `tomorrow.applescript` command. If you move your script to a different location from the current working directory (your home folder is the default), you will need to type the full path to your script or else ensure that the folder you moved it to is included in your Unix shell's PATH environment variable. (The PATH variable contains a list of all the folders that the shell can look in when searching for a command—a good Unix scripting book or online tutorial can provide more information on this.)

Passing Parameters to the Script

`osascript` can also pass parameters to the AppleScript's `run` handler. What you have to do is include a parameter variable at the end of the `on run` line. The value of this variable will be a list containing the arguments passed from the command line.

The simplest way to pass parameters is to create a new document in AppleScript Editor and type the following:

```
on run folder_names
    tell application "Finder"
        repeat with name_ref in  folder_names
```

```
            make new folder at desktop with properties {name:name_ref}
        end repeat
    end tell
end run
```

Save this script as a text file in your home folder, and name it `make folder.applescript`.

Now, enter the following text into the Terminal window:

```
osascript 'make folder.applescript' 'My Cool Folder' 'An Even Cooler Folder'
```

`osascript` will compile script in the text file and call its `run` handler, passing it the list `{"My Cool Folder", "An Even Cooler Folder"}` as its parameter. The script in turn will loop through each item in this list, creating a new folder on the desktop and using the string as the name of the folder.

> **NOTE:** To pass multiple parameters to your AppleScript script, separate each argument in the `osascript` command with a space. Remember to enclose each argument in single quotes if it contains spaces or other special shell characters.

Other Related Commands

Other AppleScript-related commands, which I won't be covering here, are `osalang`, which lists all the Open Scripting Architecture (OSA) languages you have installed, and `osacompile`, which compiles text and saves it as a compiled script. Use `man` to find out more about these commands.

Example Projects

Let's finish this chapter with some projects that combine the strengths of AppleScript with the strengths of Unix scripting.

In the first project, you'll implement a couple of utility handlers, `encode_URL` and `uppercase_text`, that use the popular Python scripting language (included in Mac OS X) to perform basic text processing tasks. In the second project, you'll create a simple drag-and-drop applet that uses the Unix `chmod` command to modify file and folder permissions. In the final project, you'll use a third-party Unix tool, `pdffonts`, to extract font information from PDF files.

Simple Text Processing Handlers

Mac OS X ships with several popular general-purpose scripting languages installed as standard: Perl, Python, Ruby, and Tcl. Because this is a book about AppleScript, I don't want to spend lots of time teaching you how to use those languages as well, but scripters who already know a little about using these languages (or are willing to learn) can easily call them from AppleScript via the `do shell script` command.

You'll now look at a couple of quick examples using Python (http://www.python.org), a popular general-purpose scripting language with a clean syntax and plenty of useful libraries included as standard.

Encoding URLs

The following script uses Python's `urllib` module to convert an AppleScript string for use in URLs:

```
on encode_URL(txt)
    set python_script to ¬
        "import sys, urllib; print urllib.quote(sys.argv[1])"
    set python_script to "/usr/bin/python -c " & ¬
        quoted form of python_script & " " & ¬
        quoted form of txt
    return do shell script python_script
end encode_URL

encode_URL("photos ƒ")
--> "photos%20%C6%92"
```

In a URL, only numbers, characters *a* to *z* and *A* to *Z*, and a few symbols (such as - and _) are left untouched. Everything else should be converted to the UTF-8 equivalent and then formatted as hex numbers with a % symbol in front of each one. As you'll recall, do shell script already converts text to UTF-8 when passing it to the Unix shell, and UTF-8 is just what the quote function in Python's `urllib` module wants, so you can pass it to that without any extra conversions. Similarly, the quote function returns ASCII text, so you don't need any extra conversion there either.

In the Python script, the `import` statement imports the libraries you need. The `sys.argv[1]` bit gets the text to convert; this is supplied as an extra argument to the python shell command, which passes it to the script. The quote function converts this to the desired format, and the result is printed to standard out.

In the previous example, the command executed by the Unix shell will look like this:

```
/usr/bin/python -c 'import sys, urllib; print urllib.quote(sys.argv[1])' 'photos ƒ'
```

The -c option is followed by the script you want Python to execute. This is followed by the argument you want it to pass directly to the script for processing.

Changing Case

The following script is quite similar to the previous one, except this time you're using Python to convert a string to uppercase. Here's the handler, followed by an example of its use:

```
on uppercase_text(txt)
    set python_script to ¬
        "import sys; print sys.argv[1].decode('utf8').upper().encode('utf8')"
    return do shell script "/usr/bin/python -c " & ¬
        quoted form of python_script & " " & ¬
        quoted form of txt
```

```
end uppercase_text
```

```
uppercase_text("Il fera beau cet été!")
--> "IL FERA BEAU CET ÉTÉ!"
```

Since you'll want any non-ASCII characters to be converted correctly, you'll use Python's Unicode support. You do this by asking Python to convert the UTF-8 data it receives into a unicode object (equivalent to an AppleScript text object, only more powerful), change the case of that, and then convert the result into UTF-8 data. As you can see from the example result, non-ASCII characters, in this case the two é characters, are correctly converted.

You can easily adapt this code to take advantage of other basic text manipulation features built into every unicode object in Python. For example, to change the text to lowercase, sentence case, or title case instead, replace the upper() call with lower(), capitalize(), or title(), respectively. If the input text is large, you'll want to pass it via stdin instead of argv, in which case you'd need to use the temporary file technique described earlier in the chapter, and then change the Python script to this:

```
"import sys; print sys.stdin.read().decode('utf8').upper().encode('utf8')"
```

Changing File System Permissions

One of the biggest headaches Unix integration brought to the Mac platform is permissions. I know, it's all for the best, but it is still a pain. Although you can use the Finder's Get Info dialog box or third-party GUI applications such as BatChmod (http://macchampion.com/arbysoft/) to do this, sometimes you may want to use the powerful chmod Unix command to do this.

Since this is not a Unix book and many Unix books are available, I will not go into it too deeply; however, I do want to cover the basics of using chmod and how to integrate it with AppleScript. chmod, which is short for change mode, changes the permission modes of a file or folder. Besides the file you want to change, it takes a mode argument, which is a single code that describes the new permissions settings for the file.

> **NOTE:** Mac OS X 10.4 and later also support access control lists (ACLs), a newer and more flexible way to specify file permissions for different users. chmod supports full ACLs, but for our purposes, we'll keep it simple and stick to the traditional Unix permissions (user/group/everyone).

chmod also takes several options, allowing you to customize the way it works. An important option is -R, which determines whether folders are processed recursively so that any permissions you apply to a folder are also applied to all the files and folders in it.

The mode argument is a bit more complicated because it allows the same information to be specified in different ways. For this exercise, you'll specify the mode in its absolute form, which is easy to calculate in AppleScript. Imagine a three-digit number in which the first digit represents the owner, the second digit represents the group, and the third represents anyone else. Now, say the number 4 stands for "allow to read," number 2 stands for "allow to write," and 1 is for "allow to execute." As an example, the mode 444 means allow the owner to read, the group to read, and anyone else to read. What if, however, you want to let the owner read and write? Well, read is 4 and write is 2, so read and write is 6. The mode number in that case would be 644. Table 27–2 offers a quick reference.

Table 27–2. *Mode Numbers for Different User Permissions Settings*

Permission Level	Mode Number
Read	4
Write	2
Execute	1
Read/write	6
Read/execute	5
Write/execute	3
Read/write/execute	7

Looking at Table 27–2, you can tell why a popular choice is 644, which allows a file's owner to read and write the file and provides everyone else with read-only access. Also, 755 is commonly used for Unix command-line applications and executable shell scripts, because it allows everyone to run a command but prevents anyone other than the owner from modifying it.

To learn more about chmod, type man chmod in the Terminal application to read its manual. (I won't be discussing ACLs here, so you can ignore the "ACL Manipulation Options" section for now.)

Script 27–4 is an AppleScript Editor droplet that loops through nine dialog boxes that represent the nine options: owner read, owner write, owner execute, and the same for group and others. After collecting the information from the user, the script assembles a string that will be run as a shell script. The script is followed by a brief explanation.

Script 27–4.

```
1. on open the_item_list
2.     set shell_script to "chmod"

3.     -- Ask the user what mode to use
4.     set this_mode to 0
5.     repeat with the_entity_ref in ¬
              {{"owner", 100}, {"group members", 10}, {"others", 1}}
6.         set {entity_name, entity_val} to the_entity_ref
7.         repeat with the_action_ref in ¬
                {{"read", 4}, {"write to", 2}, {"execute", 1}}
```

```
8.          set {action_name, action_val} to the_action_ref
9.          display dialog ¬
                "Allow " & entity_name & " to " & action_name & "?" ¬
                buttons {"No", "Yes"} default button "Yes"
10.           if button returned of result is "Yes" then
11.              set this_mode to this_mode + (entity_val * action_val)
12.           end if
13.        end repeat
14.     end repeat

15.     -- Ask if folders should be processed recursively
16.     display dialog ¬
                "When processing folders, change all enclosed items as well?" ¬
                buttons {"No", "Yes"} default button "Yes"
17.     if button returned of result is "Yes" then
18.        set shell_script to shell_script & space & "-R"
19.     end if

20.     -- Add the mode argument to the command string
21.     set shell_script to shell_script & space & this_mode

22.     -- Add the file path arguments to the command string
23.     repeat with item_ref in the_item_list
24.         set shell_script to shell_script & space & ¬
                 quoted form of POSIX path of item_ref
25.     end repeat

26.     -- Run the shell script
27.     display dialog "Make these changes as an administrator?" ¬
                buttons {"No", "Yes"}
28.     set run_as_admin to button returned of result is "Yes"
29.     try
30.        do shell script shell_script administrator privileges run_as_admin
31.     on error err_msg
32.        display dialog "The following error(s) occurred:" & return & err_msg ¬
                buttons {"OK"}
33.     end try
34. end open
```

The preceding script consists of a few parts.

Lines 4 to 14 find out what permissions the user wants to use. The outer loop cycles through each entity (owner, group, and everyone else), and the inner loop goes through the permission options for that entity (read, write, execute). Each time, a dialog box asks the user to choose whether to allow or disallow a particular permission. It starts with the owner's read permission, then the owner's write permission, and so on. If the user clicks Yes, the script adds the appropriate number to the value in the this_mode variable.

Lines 16 to 19 ask the user whether items inside folders should be changed as well. If the user clicks Yes, the -R option is added to the chmod command.

Once the command's options have been added, the next step is to add its arguments. Line 21 adds the mode argument that was constructed earlier. Lines 23 to 25 loop through the list of dropped items, getting the POSIX path of each, quoting it (don't forget this bit!), and adding it to the command.

Lines 27 and 28 let the user decide whether they want to make the changes as an administrator or as a regular user. Line 30 executes the shell script. If the user decides to perform it as an administrator, the do shell script command will ask for an administrator name and password to be entered before running the shell script. Users who don't have administrator access can still change the permissions on files they already own. Any errors that occur will be trapped by the surrounding try block and reported to the user.

> **TIP:** You can find out the current permissions for a file or folder in the Finder by choosing File ➤ Get Info and looking at the Ownership & Permissions tab or by using AppleScript (open the Finder's dictionary in AppleScript Editor, and look for the three privileges properties defined in the item class). The ls Unix command also provides an l option for displaying detailed information about a file or a folder's contents, as in ls -l /Applications/. If the file has an ACL (indicated by a "+" after the permissions), use ls -le ... to view those too.

Analyzing PDF Files

In addition to the Unix applications that come as standard on Mac OS X, many free Unix applications are available, and you can figure out how to script many of them with the do shell script command.

As a small example, I will show how to script a Unix application called pdffonts, which is part of the open source Xpdf package by Glyph & Cog (http://www.glyphandcog.com). You can download Xpdf from its website at http://www.foolabs.com/xpdf/. (There should be a link to a Mac OS X binary installer on the downloads page.)

pdffonts takes the path of a PDF file and returns detailed information about the fonts in that PDF file—whether the font is embedded, the font type, and so on. The following is sample output from pdffonts:

```
Name                                 Type         Emb Sub Uni Object ID
------------------------------------ ------------ --- --- --- ---------
TZJIIJ+Palatino-Roman                CID Type 0C  yes yes yes    17  0
RJPWGN+Palatino-Bold                 CID Type 0C  yes yes yes    23  0
QBFQSP+Palatino-Italic               CID Type 0C  yes yes yes     9  0
```

The meaning of the different columns is as follows:

> *Name*: The font name. The text before the + is a subset prefix. (This is added to the font name when a subset of that font is embedded in the PDF.) The part after the + is the font's proper name, which is the bit you normally want.

> *Type*: The font type. (Type 1, Type 3, TrueType, CID Type 0, and so on.)

> *Emb*: Whether the font is embedded in the PDF.

Sub: Whether the font is a subset.

Uni: Whether the PDF contains an explicit "to Unicode" map. For details, see http://www.glyphandcog.com.

Object ID: The font dictionary object ID, which includes the number and generation.

It is up to you to extract the information you want from this.

Script 27–5 creates a droplet that accepts a PDF file and tells you how many fonts it uses and how many of them are embedded.

Script 27–5.

```
1. on open {pdf_file}
2.    set shell_script to "/usr/local/bin/pdffonts " & ¬
            quoted form of POSIX path of pdf_file
3.    try
4.       set shell_result to do shell script shell_script
5.    on error error_message
6.       display dialog "Error:" & return & error_message
7.       return
8.    end try
9.    -- The first 2 lines are table headings, so we ignore those
10.    if (count paragraphs of shell_result) > 2 then
11.       set font_info_list to paragraphs 3 thru -1 of shell_result
12.       set embedded_font_count to 0
13.       repeat with font_info_ref in font_info_list
14.          -- The embedded column is fifth from the right
15.          set is_embedded to word -5 of font_info_ref
16.          if is_embedded is "yes" then
17.             set embedded_font_count to embedded_font_count + 1
18.          end if
19.       end repeat
20.       display dialog "This PDF contains " & ¬
                (count font_info_list) & " fonts, out of which " & ¬
                embedded_font_count & " are embedded."
21.    else
22.       display dialog "No fonts were found."
23.    end if
24. end open
```

In line 2 of the script you get the POSIX path to the dropped PDF, quote it, and construct the shell command.

Lines 3 to 8 are responsible for running the shell command and reporting any errors that might occur (for example, whether the file dropped is not a PDF).

Line 10 checks whether any fonts were found in the PDF. The first two lines of the result string are table headings, so you ignore those. If it contains more than two lines, you can start extracting the data from the remaining lines; otherwise, you just let the user know that no fonts were found.

In line 11 you create a list that includes all the paragraphs of the result, starting from the third paragraph (paragraphs 1 and 2 are the title and underscore).

Once you have the list, you loop through each font information line and pick out the information you need. Although the finished solution looks simple enough, coming up with one that will work reliably isn't always as easy, so let's look at how this one was arrived at and some of the potential traps discovered along the way.

As is common for command-line tools, table-style data isn't presented as simple tab-delimited text but arranged as vertical columns designed for viewing in a monospace font on a command-line display. This sort of format is rather trickier to parse reliably because the number of spaces between each item in a table row will vary as the application tries to arrange everything into vertical columns.

If you're lucky, the columns will all be fixed widths that never change, in which case you can extract the bits you want using references like this:

```
text start_position thru end_position of the_line
```

Unfortunately, this is not always the case. For example, if a left column contains a long value, then all the remaining columns may be pushed to the right to fit it in. These sorts of issues often aren't obvious at first glance, so be careful; otherwise, you could introduce all sorts of subtle, hidden bugs into your code. Faulty code that happens to produce correct results most of the time but occasionally slips in an incorrect answer can easily go unnoticed for a long time if it doesn't cause an actual error.

In this case, testing pdffonts with a PDF file whose font names are known to be longer than 37 characters (the width of the first column) quickly shows that this approach won't be an option here.

Another common way to break down these sorts of tables is to use another Unix application, awk. awk is a basic pattern-matching language for identifying and extracting sections of data from a single line. It's ideal for dealing with command-line table data where spaces appear between items but never appear inside them, because it treats any number of adjoining spaces as a single divider. For example, to extract the third column from such a table, you would pipe the table data from the previous command into an awk command like this:

```
some_command | awk '{print $3}'
```

Alas, this won't help you either, because the values in the second column of the table may often contain spaces (for example, Type 1), so a value that appears as item 3 on one line could be item 4 or 5 on the next.

Still, it feels like you're getting closer to a solution, doesn't it? Looking at the columns on the right, notice that they're all a lot more regular; therefore, I reckon you'll be okay if you count columns from the right instead of from the left. Using awk would be trickier here because it normally counts from left to right. However, the values in the right columns are all either numbers or words, so you should be able to get the one you want using a word -5 of ... reference in AppleScript. Problem (you hope) solved!

Once you've extracted the desired yes/no value from the line's Embedded column, you can see whether it's a yes and increment the value of embedded_font_count if it is. This happens on lines 16 to 18.

Finally, on line 20, the finished message is assembled and displayed.

Summary

In this chapter, you discovered how to take advantage of the Unix command line from AppleScript, and vice versa. You saw how Standard Additions' do shell script command and Terminal's do script command can be used to run individual Unix commands or larger shell scripts, and you were introduced to the osascript command that allows text-based or compiled AppleScripts to be run from the command line. You also learned the importance of using the quoted form property of strings to safely escape them for use in shell scripts, and other limitations and gotchas.

Obviously, this chapter only scratches the surface of Unix shell scripting itself, so if you do work in this area, you should consult a good book or online tutorial on the subject before going much further. This chapter should, however, give you a decent idea of where to start, and how you can combine these two great technologies, Unix scripting and AppleScript, to enjoy the best of both.

In the next chapter we will return to the world of AppleScript as we explore one of its more powerful and interesting multipurpose tools: Satimage Software's Smile application.

Chapter 28

Using Smile: The AppleScript Integrated Production Environment

Smile is an integrated development environment (IDE) for writing and executing scripts— and much more. Satimage, located in Paris, is the creator of Smile. You can download Smile from the Satimage web site at http://www.satimage.fr/software.

Introducing Smile

In the following sections, I'll introduce you to Smile and its main features.

Introducing Smile's Integrated Engine Architecture

Although the interface of Smile looks simple—the menus are not especially long, and the dialog boxes do not have loads of buttons and pop-up lists—Smile can perform many tasks for you. How does that work? Well, most of Smile's features, including some of the more powerful ones, do not have an interface but are available in the software, waiting for you to call them in a script.

Smile's interface was designed to help you edit and test your scripts efficiently. For instance, if you are writing a script to process text files, Smile lets you test it in an interactive command-line window first. And when you make a PDF or an image, you view the document in a window as you are building it.

Smile's architecture enables it to offer a particularly wide range of well-implemented technologies. Indeed, when you work with Smile, you work simultaneously with the following:

- An AppleScript command-line interpreter

- An editor (and runner) of scripted Aqua interfaces, including palettes that you can associate with any application

- A Unicode-based text editor, including an extended (XML) validator

- A text search-and-replace tool

- A regular expression engine

- An XML engine

- A graphic generation engine capable of producing high-quality vector PDFs, JPEGs, and movies

- A scientific environment with fast computational libraries for numbers and for arrays of numbers

- A data visualization environment with the finest features: ready-to-publish vector PDF production; 1D, 2D, and 3D plots; 3D objects library; 3D triangular mesh generation; easy animations; easy customization of figures using the graphic generation engine; Unicode support; and more

- An industrial interface able to handle RS232 serial communication and some digital input/output (I/O) universal serial bus (USB) devices.

Since you control everything by script, you can use any of these technologies in any automated process.

About Smile's Terminal

To operate the various features available in Smile, you communicate with your machine through the AppleScript language. To that effect, Smile includes a unique command-line interpreter for AppleScript, called *AppleScript terminal*, which is basically the AppleScript version of Mac OS X's Terminal application.

Smile does include a traditional AppleScript editor too, but the AppleScript terminal is more than that—it's a fully interactive command-line environment. In fact, even if you don't use any of Smile's special features, you will still find it helpful to use the AppleScript terminal as the environment in which to control your machine: the Finder, the shell commands, the scripting additions, and your preferred applications.

Why Should You Use Smile?

Smile is the perfect complement to AppleScript because it makes the most of some of AppleScript's features:

- AppleScript supports persistent contexts. Smile embeds you in a context that augments as you work. You can see the benefits right away and also in the long term. In other words, once you program a routine, it is straightforward to include it in the context as a library. Smile's context is itself a script, and you can dynamically load new handlers into that context easily.

- In AppleScript, you can compile and execute in one operation a single line or a block of lines. In the standard AppleScript Editor, you must run all lines every time, but Smile is way more versatile—in an AppleScript terminal, you can run any part of a script independently, and that execution will happen in a persistent context.

- In AppleScript, scripts are scriptable. Any script, running or not, is an object (it owns handlers and properties) that can be scripted. A script can send commands to another script and change its properties. Furthermore, whether it's running or not, a script retains its current state. All of Smile's objects (including the application itself) are scriptable objects; each one has its own script, which can provide it with specific properties and behaviors.

- An AppleScript program supports handling quantities belonging to any class, including classes that did not even exist at the time the program was written. For instance, it will seem natural to the AppleScript user that the same commands that used to work with ASCII now work transparently with Unicode text.

Downloading Smile

At the time of writing, the latest version of Smile is 3.5.1. It is free to download and use, although some advanced features such as data visualization and web services require paid licenses (SmileLab and SmileServer). However, if you do not pay to register, the SmileLab features will run in demo mode, which is enough for testing all the examples in this chapter.

To install Smile, visit Smile's home page at `http://www.satimage.fr/software`, where you can download an installer file. Once the download is complete, double-click the Smile `.pkg` file you downloaded and just follow the instructions in the installer.

Using Smile

The following sections will get you a bit more familiar with Smile and some of its components.

Using the AppleScript Command-Line Environment

Launch Smile by double-clicking the saucer icon in /Applications/Smile/. If this is the first time you are launching a copy of Smile, a splash screen offers several options that introduce Smile's features. You can practice a moment using the splash screen and then proceed.

Smile's primary tool is its unique AppleScript terminal. This text window is an interpreter for AppleScript; pressing Cmd+R executes the current line or the selected lines. To run a single line, you do not need to select the line. When no text is selected, pressing Cmd+R runs the line where the insertion point is located, and then the insertion point moves to the beginning of the next line, making it natural to run a script line by line (see Figure 28–1).

Try it—create a new AppleScript terminal window in Smile (File ➤ New ➤ New AppleScript terminal) and type the following line:

```
tell application "Finder" to set s to name of startup disk
```

When the cursor is blinking somewhere in the line, press Cmd+R to compile and run it. Now delete that line and type the following:

```
display dialog "The startup disk's name is " & s
```

Press Cmd+R again. As you can see, Smile remembers the value of s, which you would not expect if you were working in AppleScript Editor.

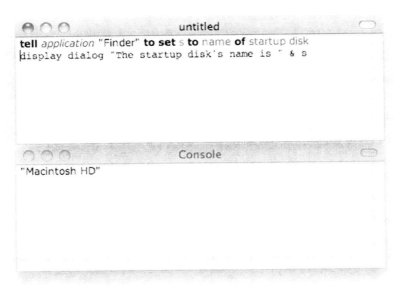

Figure 28–1. *A line is compiled and executed by pressing Cmd+R, and the result is then displayed in the console.*

> **NOTE:** The preceding example was possible because Smile maintains a persistent AppleScript context. When you run one line or a block of lines in an AppleScript terminal, the variables and handlers remain defined until you quit. They are available at a global level—that is, to any script running from any terminal window. You'll get familiar with this as you work more with Smile.

Now type in these two lines:

```
set pdf_url to "http://www.satimage-software.com/downloads/mc0306.pdf"
set pdf_path to (POSIX path of (path to desktop)) & "mc0306.pdf"
```

Click anywhere in the first line to put the insertion point in that line, and then press Cmd+R. Do the same for the second line. Now pdf_url and pdf_path are defined. Unless you assign them different values later, their contents will be preserved.

If your computer is connected to the Internet, you can now execute the following line. To confirm that all AppleScript terminal windows share the same context, type it into a new terminal window and then press Cmd+R to run it.

```
do shell script "curl " & quoted form of pdf_url & " -Lo " & quoted form of pdf_path
```

This will download a PDF file that you will use in the "Adding Text to a PDF Document" project later in this chapter. As long as the command executes, the script is suspended; the insertion point will blink again once the download is complete. As you see, the latest line uses the variables that were defined in a previous run. In the PDF application you'll build in this chapter, you will use the pdf_path variable again.

Such variables compiled on-the-fly in terminal windows live in Smile's persistent context.

Using Smile's Custom Dialog Boxes

Smile consists of an editor—and creator of graphical interfaces—known as Smile's *custom dialog boxes*. Later in the chapter, I'll show you how to create a graphical interface, but I suggest you experiment now with custom dialog boxes. In the following two sections, I'll show you how to create a simple application interface to display a date. It should take you less than one minute.

Creating the Interface

To create the user interface, do the following:

1. Select File ➤ New ➤ New Dialog. This opens a new dialog box and also the Controls palette (which is a Smile dialog box).

2. Click the "new button" button in the Controls palette, and drag it to the empty dialog box.

3. Close the Controls palette.

4. Double-click your newly placed button, and enter "Date & Time" for its name.

Programming the Functionality

Now that the interface of the first dialog box is done; let's program it:

1. Select Action ➤ Edit Dialog Script, or click in an empty part of the dialog box with the Cmd and Opt keys pressed. This opens a new colored window, which is where we'll add the dialog box's script.

2. By default, the dialog box's script contains two empty handlers: `prepare` and `click in`. Remove the `prepare` handler. In the `click in` handler, insert the following line:

```
dd(current date)
```

3. Verify that your handler now looks like this:

```
on click in theDialog item number i
   dd(current date)
end click in
```

4. Select File ➤ Save to save the script, and then select File ➤ Close to close the script's window.

5. Select Edit ➤ Edit Mode to toggle your dialog box from edit mode to normal mode. You should also now save the dialog box to disk, so select File ➤ Save. Then provide a name.

6. You can now test your first dialog box by clicking the button. Doing this will send the `click in` event to the dialog box, which will execute your script line. Figure 28–2 shows the dialog box and script.

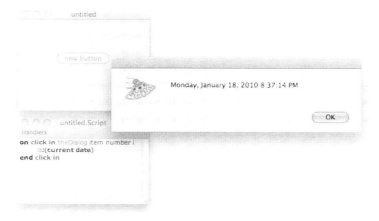

Figure 28–2. *The simplest working dialog box ever: one button, one line of script*

Note that your script uses `click in`, a term not included in native AppleScript. Smile's built-in libraries include a number of handy terms documented in Smile's built-in dictionaries. To get information about a specific term such as `click in`, select the term, and then select Edit ➤ Find Definition. (You can also press Cmd+Shift+F or right-click the selection and choose Find Definition.)

Using Regular Expressions

Smile offers an AppleScript implementation of regular expressions. Regular expressions are the basic tools for most text-matching tasks, such as extracting a given substring or finding all the e-mail addresses contained in a file; therefore, regular expressions are useful in a wide range of situations.

The Find dialog box understands regular expressions and is the best place to test a regular expression on text windows before using it in a script. The same Find dialog box works both in AppleScript terminal and Unicode text windows.

For example, to find the next sequence of one or more (+) digits ([0-9]) in the front window:

1. Select Edit ➤ Find. This opens the Find dialog box.

2. Enter [0-9]+ as the Find string.

3. Enable the Regexp check box.

4. Click the Find button.

You can also perform searches and substitutions using the `find text` and `change` commands. These commands are normally provided by the Satimage scripting addition, but when you use them within Smile, the `in` parameter can be a reference to a Smile window (for example, `window 2`) as well as a string or file.

Figure 28–3 shows how the previous search can be performed using the `find text` command. When you run it, make sure that the terminal window is frontmost and the window being searched (`window 2`) is immediately behind it.

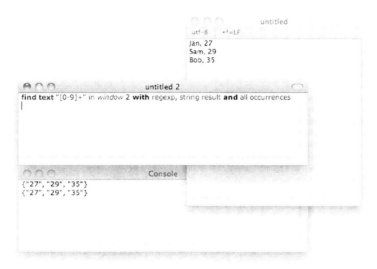

Figure 28–3. *Searching a Smile text window using the* `find text` *command*

If you are curious to experiment further with regular expressions, you will want to have the list of the regular expressions' metacharacters handy. You will find one in the pop-up list in the Find dialog box, on the right of the Regular Expression check box.

Satimage's web site provides exhaustive documentation on regular expressions. You can find it at `http://www.satimage.fr/software/en/smile/text/`.

> **Tip:** Chapter 22 also provides an introduction to using the Satimage `find text` and `change` commands to process strings and files outside of Smile.

Using the Graphic Engine

Smile includes an AppleScript PDF graphic library. This is the facet of Smile that you will explore most in the "Adding Text to a PDF Document" project later on. Here, you'll get a small taste of it first.

Create a new script window (File ➤ New ➤ New Script), type in the code shown in Script 28–1, and press Cmd+R to compile and run it.

Script 28–1.

```
set c to {250, 250}
set r to 100
set i to first character of (system attribute "USER")
BeginFigure(0)
SetPenColor({1 / 8, 1 / 4, 1 / 2})
SetFillColor({1 / 4, 1 / 2, 1, 1 / 2})
CirclePath(c, r)
DrawPath("fill-stroke") -- or: 3
```

```
TextMoveTo(c)
SetTextSize(1.5 * r)
SetTextFont("Courier")
SetFillGray(1)
DrawString("[h]" & i)
DrawPath("fill") -- or: 0
EndFigure()
```

Running this script will create an image similar to the one shown in Figure 28–4. Alternatively, you can produce JPEGs, BMPs, PNGs (often an optimal solution for synthetic graphics), and so on, as well as Apple QuickTime movies.

Figure 28–4. *The PDF document created by Script 28–1*

Here you are using Smile's graphic library: BeginFigure(0) prepares a default graphic window for drawing. SetPenColor and SetFillColor let you specify a color, either as RGB or as RGB-alpha (alpha being the opacity).

In a PDF document, you define shapes (*paths*), and then you draw them—usually in "stroke" mode or in "fill" mode. However, you have other options. Here CirclePath defines a circular path, with the center and radius as specified in points (1 point equals 1/72 inch), and then DrawPath draws it, using the current graphical settings such as the pen color and fill color.

Finally, EndFigure is what terminates the PDF record and displays the final graphic in the default graphic window.

Again, if you are curious about a particular term, select the term, and then press Cmd+Shift+F (or select Edit ➤ Find Definition). To open the documentation for the graphic engine, select File ➤ Open Dictionary ➤ Graphic Library.

Using SmileLab

Smile includes graphical objects for numerical data visualization and additional libraries that go together to form SmileLab. The graphical objects can make curves, plots, color maps, 3D surfaces, and so on, to represent numerical data and to change them into PDF vector graphics.

Smile also has a set of mathematical functions that allows you to program, in AppleScript, extremely fast computations on numbers and on arrays.

Next, you will learn how to generate some data and then plot it.

Enter Script 28–2 as shown.

Script 28–2.

```
-- Create data
set n to 1000
set x to createarray n
set y to runningsum (randomarray n range {-1, 1})
set y to multlist y with sqrt (3)

-- Display data as a curve
set c to QuickCurve(x, y, 0)
set v to c's container -- The curve belongs to a plot ...
set w to v's container -- ... which belongs to a window

-- Display equations as curves
set c1 to QuickCurve(x, "sqrt(x)", v)
set c2 to QuickCurve(x, "-sqrt(x)", v)

-- Customize appearance
set name of v to "A random walk of " & n & " steps"
set legend kind of v to 3
set legend abscissa of v to n / 2
set legend text size of v to 14
set legend fill color of v to {1, 1, 1, 1}
set label text size of v to 14
set xlabel of v to "n"
set name of c to "\\Sigma_{i=1.." & n & "}\\ Rnd_i"
set name of c1 to "n^{1/2}"
set name of c2 to "-n^{1/2}"
draw w
```

Run the whole script (or run it block by block if you'd like—you can run a block by pressing Cmd+R once the lines are selected). Figure 28–5 shows the results.

Block 1 creates the data. Smile introduces a datatype equivalent to an AppleScript list of numbers such as {1.0, pi, 300}, the array of real. Computations on arrays of real are fast, and arrays of real have virtually no size limit (AppleScript native lists are not adapted for extensive calculations).

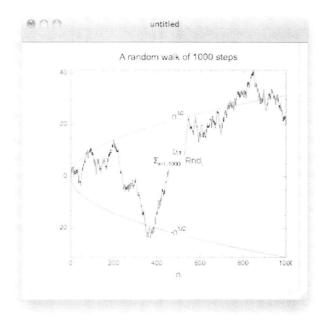

Figure 28–5. *A typical graph generated by Script 28–2*

createarray is one way of making a new array of reals. By default, createarray n creates an array of the n-first integers. The dictionary shows that createarray accepts optional parameters. To view the entry for createarray in the dictionary where it belongs (namely, the dictionary of the Satimage OSAX), select createarray, and then select Edit ➤ Find Definition.

As its name suggests, randomarray returns an array of random numbers in the given range, [-1 .. 1].

y contains * as its item of rank k, the sum of the previous k random numbers. This is called a *random walk* (on the line); after k steps, the random walker's position may be any value between -k and k.

Block 2 will display the random walk as a curve: position vs. time. QuickCurve belongs to QuickPlotLib, a library included with SmileLab: pressing Cmd+Shift+F on QuickCurve will open the documentation for the command.

As you see, the curve you made lives in a plot view, which in turn requires a graphic window to exist.

Which class of objects may contain which other class of objects is part of the information that the dictionary supplies: select Smile ➤ Smile dictionary, and then use the Index menu in the dictionary's toolbar to view the entry for curve. Be aware that the entry for a given class shows which classes of objects it can contain (its elements), not which class of object can contain itself (its container).

Scientists know that a random walk (with n steps chosen randomly in [-1 .. 1]) will essentially scale like $\sqrt{n}$. Let's confirm the fact and plot the two curves $-\sqrt{n}$ and $+\sqrt{n}$: this is what the two lines in block 3 do. You can run the script several times to observe different draws. Also, you can increase n.

Finally, the fourth block controls the visual appearance of the graph; you can adjust each visual feature of an object by setting the corresponding property to the desired value. The Graphic Settings dialog box has a script button to generate such scripts automatically. The list of the properties of an object in a given class is provided in the dictionary, in the entry for that class. To view the entry for a given class, you do the same as when viewing the entry for a given command: select the class's name, such as plot view, and then press Cmd+Shift+F.

For convenience, all Smile objects include a properties property, intended for setting several (and getting all) properties in one instruction. Here's an example:

```
set properties of v to { ¬
    name:"A random walk of " & n & " steps", ¬
    legend kind:3, legend abscissa:n / 2, legend text size:14, ¬
    legend fill color:{1, 1, 1, 1}, label text size:14, xlabel:"n"}
```

You can use this as a shortcut for the following:

```
set name of v to "A random walk of " & n & " steps"
set legend kind of v to 3
set legend abscissa of v to n / 2
set legend text size of v to 14
set legend fill color of v to {1, 1, 1, 1}
set label text size of v to 14
set xlabel of v to "n"
```

Example Project: Adding Text to a PDF Document

You'll now learn how to make a program in Smile to add some text to an existing PDF document. Usually, you'd do this with Adobe Acrobat. However, Acrobat is not free, so it's great to be able to write a program to update PDFs for free! So that you can test your program on a real PDF document as you develop it, you have been given clearance by the state of California to use one of its forms from the Department of Health Services. However, you can use any PDF document for this tutorial.

Preparing the PDF

If you ran the sample scripts earlier in the chapter, the PDF file should already be downloaded to your desktop, and its path will be stored in the pdf_path variable.

Otherwise (or if you have quit Smile since), execute the following lines to download the PDF file to your desktop (remember that you need to be connected to the Internet):

```
set pdf_url to "http://www.satimage-software.com/downloads/mc0306.pdf"
set pdf_path to (POSIX path of (path to desktop)) & "mc0306.pdf"
do shell script "curl " & quoted form of pdf_url & " -Lo " & quoted form of pdf_path
```

If you want to use another file, store its path (as a string) in the pdf_path variable. It's useful to know that dropping a file on a text window inserts its path in the window.

Now open the PDF file in Smile. If you double-click the file's icon, Finder will choose to open it in Acrobat Reader or in Preview; explicitly tell Smile to open it by executing the following line:

```
set w to open POSIX file pdf_path
```

As you can see in Figure 28–6, the result returned (the value of w) is a graphic window.

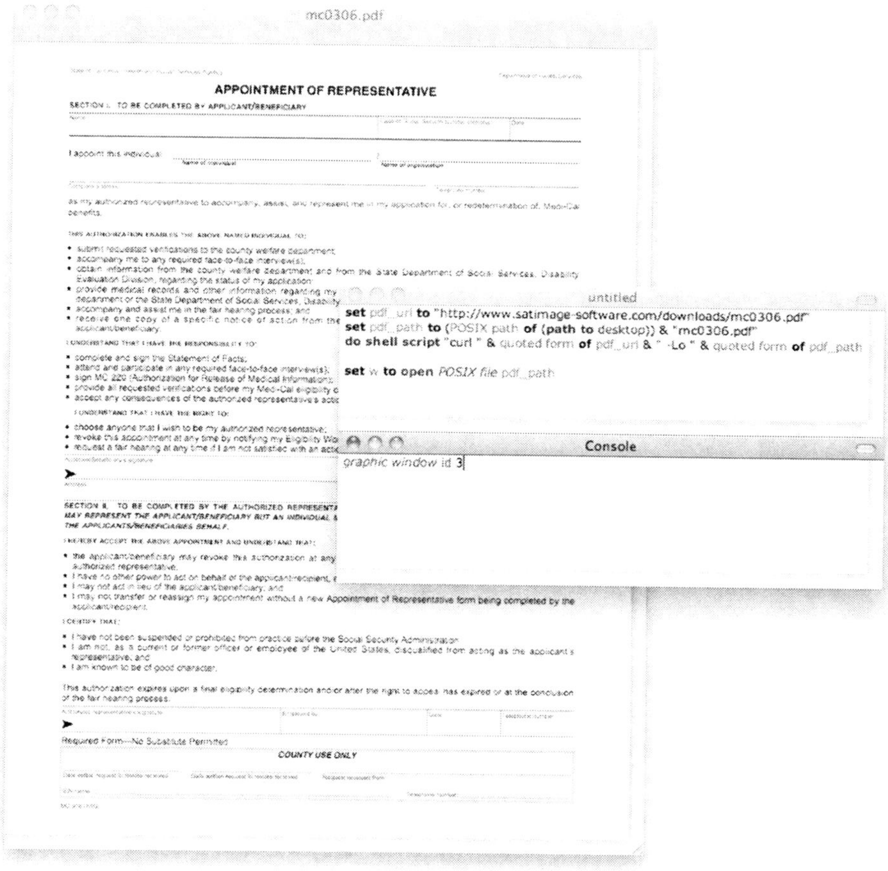

Figure 28–6. *Smile opens PDF files in graphic windows, where you can make custom graphics.*

Select the graphic window keyword and choose Edit ➤ Find Definition to display the entry for the graphic window class. For this project, you'll focus only on two properties: back pdf and front pdf; those are where the graphic window stores PDF data. Here is an excerpt of Smile's dictionary describing the class graphic window:

```
graphic window n [inh. window > basic object] : a window where you can draw
    pictures of various kinds by script, and that you can save as a PDF file
```

or as a jpg, png or tiff file.
ELEMENTS
    contains graphic views, widgets.
PROPERTIES
    ...
    back pdf (string) : the PDF data for the background of the window. Can be set
        to a file, to some Graphic Kernel output or to raw PDF data as string.
    front pdf (string) : the PDF data drawn after the background and the graphic
        views of the window. Can be set to a file, to some Graphic Kernel output
        or to raw PDF data as string.
    ...

Making a PDF drawing consists of filling the back pdf and/or the front pdf fields of a
new graphic window with PDF data (a string, actually). Here is an excerpt of the PDF
data in the file you just opened:

```
%PDF-1.3
%fÂÚÂÎßÛ −f?
2 0 obj
<< /Length 1 0 R /Filter /FlateDecode >>
stream
xú+T_T(_c}?\C_ó|dæ_ú_
endstream
[...]
xú•?k"-?m&·??:ÛIûrñöwrÊì,ÀâO?_KI*)WMŸgíÂ_..._ÎH_Â?_>Ï^k_Ïáç~ÀÂ*K[__lÇ
[...]
```

As you can see, PDF is not as intuitive as AppleScript. Thus, you will not make PDF data
directly; rather, Smile's graphic library will. You will use natural commands such as
MoveTo, LineTo, and DrawString, and Smile's graphic library will turn them into regular
PDF data.

When you program the graphic library, you will find the documentation useful, which is
available in several forms:

- File ➤ Open Dictionary ➤ Graphic Library will display a dictionary of all
  graphic library commands, including examples of use.

- The hypertext documentation for all commands is available via the
  Help menu.

- A chapter in the online documentation is available from Smile's home
  page (and includes guide and reference).

> **NOTE:** To enjoy this tutorial, you do not have to use the documentation. I merely mention it for
> further reading.

To have Smile generate the PDF and provide it to the back pdf property of a given
graphic window, w, your script proceeds in three steps. First, you initiate the PDF with
BeginFigure(w). Second, you include the graphic commands specific to your graphic.
Finally, you close the PDF with EndFigure(). This is the instruction that will notify Smile

to compile the graphic commands into PDF data and to load the PDF data into the back pdf field of w so the window will display your graphic.

When you open the PDF file mc0306.pdf, Smile loads the PDF into back pdf. You do not want to replace the original graphic; rather, you want to superimpose a new graphic. Here you have to use the foreground layer—the front pdf field of the window. The instructions are the same as for drawing in the background layer, except you must call BeginFrontFigure() and EndFrontFigure() instead of BeginFigure() and EndFigure(). Try it by drawing a line from one corner to the other, over the opened PDF. Here you'll use basic graphic commands: MoveTo and LineTo. Both want a point as their parameter, the list {x, y} of two numbers (MoveTo moves the pen without drawing; LineTo defines a line starting from the current pen location). The scale is 1 point (1 point = 1/72 inch ≈ 0.35 mm). x/y coordinates increase rightward/upward.

```
BeginFrontFigure(w)
MoveTo({0, 0})
LineTo({600, 840})
EndFrontFigure()
draw w
```

As usual, select the text, and press Cmd+R. Ouch! Nothing happens. This is because the program does not draw! All it does is define a shape (a *path*)—here, the diagonal line. After having defined a path, you then have to draw it in a separate operation, which is why you use DrawPath. The parameter of DrawPath will specify whether to draw the stroke of the path, will specify whether to fill the path (which makes little sense for this line, of course), and will propose more options such as using the path, not to draw but as a mask. The most often used values are DrawPath("fill-stroke"), which draws the stroke and fills the path; DrawPath("fill"); and DrawPath("stroke").

Usually, before firing a DrawPath command, you specify the pen and fill settings you want it to use. Here you'll use the default settings; by default the pen and the fill colors are black, and the pen size is 1 point:

```
BeginFrontFigure(w)
MoveTo({0, 0})
LineTo({600, 840})
DrawPath("stroke") -- or: 2
EndFrontFigure()
draw w
```

Select the text, and then press Cmd+R—you'll notice that a slash has been drawn on the page, as shown in Figure 28–7.

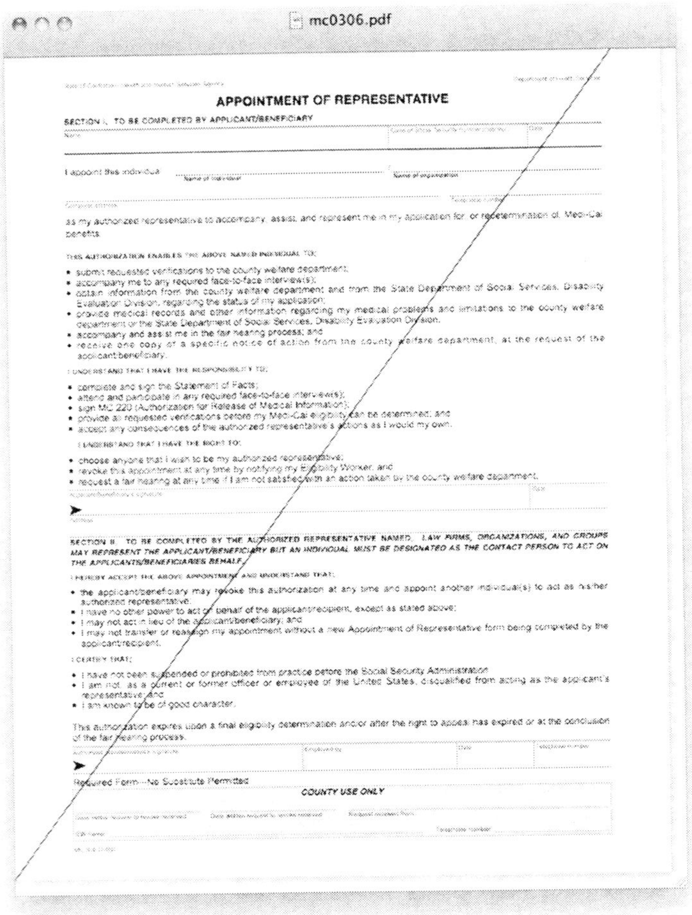
mc0306.pdf

APPOINTMENT OF REPRESENTATIVE

SECTION I. TO BE COMPLETED BY APPLICANT/BENEFICIARY

I appoint this individual

as my authorized representative to accompany, assist, and represent me in my application for, or redetermination of, Medi-Cal benefits.

THIS AUTHORIZATION ENABLES THE ABOVE NAMED INDIVIDUAL TO:

- submit requested verifications to the county welfare department;
- accompany me to any required face-to-face interview(s);
- obtain information from the county welfare department and from the State Department of Social Services, Disability Evaluation Division, regarding the status of my application;
- provide medical records and other information regarding my medical problems and limitations to the county welfare department or the State Department of Social Services, Disability Evaluation Division;
- accompany and assist me in the fair hearing process; and
- receive one copy of a specific notice of action from the county welfare department, at the request of the applicant/beneficiary.

I UNDERSTAND THAT I HAVE THE RESPONSIBILITY TO:

- complete and sign the Statement of Facts;
- attend and participate in any required face-to-face interview(s);
- sign MC 220 (Authorization for Release of Medical Information);
- provide all requested verifications before my Medi-Cal eligibility can be determined; and
- accept any consequences of the authorized representative's actions as I would my own.

I UNDERSTAND THAT I HAVE THE RIGHT TO:

- choose anyone that I wish to be my authorized representative;
- revoke this appointment at any time by notifying my Eligibility Worker; and
- request a fair hearing at any time if I am not satisfied with an action taken by the county welfare department.

SECTION II. TO BE COMPLETED BY THE AUTHORIZED REPRESENTATIVE NAMED. *LAW FIRMS, ORGANIZATIONS, AND GROUPS MAY REPRESENT THE APPLICANT/BENEFICIARY BUT AN INDIVIDUAL MUST BE DESIGNATED AS THE CONTACT PERSON TO ACT ON THE APPLICANTS/BENEFICIARIES BEHALF.*

I HEREBY ACCEPT THE ABOVE APPOINTMENT AND UNDERSTAND THAT:

- the applicant/beneficiary may revoke this authorization at any time and appoint another individual(s) to act as his/her authorized representative;
- I have no other power to act on behalf of the applicant/recipient, except as stated above;
- I may not act in lieu of the applicant/beneficiary; and
- I may not transfer or reassign my appointment without a new Appointment of Representative form being completed by the applicant/recipient.

I CERTIFY THAT:

- I have not been suspended or prohibited from practice before the Social Security Administration
- I am not, as a current or former officer or employee of the United States, disqualified from acting as the applicant's representative; and
- I am known to be of good character.

This authorization expires upon a final eligibility determination and/or after the right to appeal has expired or at the conclusion of the fair hearing process.

Required Form—No Substitute Permitted

COUNTY USE ONLY

Figure 28–7. *With five script lines, you have programmed your first graphic.*

By default, Smile did not refresh the window. It is designed that way so you can avoid unnecessary or incomplete updates. To request that the window refresh explicitly, use the following:

```
draw w
```

Now you'll go further with the text-drawing experiments.

First you have to position the text. So, click in the form under the Name prompt; the toolbar of the window displays the values for x and y—values close to 55 and 702, respectively (see Figure 28–8).

Figure 28–8. *The graphic window's toolbar displays the location of the mouse pointer.*

A command analogous to MoveTo sets the position of the pen for writing. This is TextMoveTo. The following script uses the simplest command for writing text, DrawText (see Figure 28–9):

```
BeginFrontFigure(w)
TextMoveTo({55, 702})
DrawText("John Smith")
EndFrontFigure()
draw w
```

Figure 28–9. *Writing the text in the PDF document*

You'll now change the look by writing the text using 12pt Courier instead of the default 10pt Monaco (see Figure 28–10). The commands for setting the text font and size are SetTextFont (which wants a string as its parameter, the name of a font) and SetTextSize (which accepts any positive real number). The script is now the following; run it:

```
BeginFrontFigure(w)
SetTextFont("Courier")
SetTextSize(12)
TextMoveTo({55, 702})
DrawText("John Smith")
EndFrontFigure()
draw w
```

Figure 28–10. *Now the string is in the right place with the right font and size.*

You still have one task to perform. You want to be able to address several strings, so you have to put each string in independent objects in picture view, each containing one string.

First, you can empty the front layer to reinitialize the PDF:

```
BeginFrontFigure(w)
EndFrontFigure()
draw w
```

Then, you make a new picture view and fill it with the string. A *picture view* is a rectangular object living in a graphic window, which has the front pdf and back pdf properties, like a graphic window. Its frame property specifies its position inside its container window and its size.

```
set {the_width, the_height, dy} to {100, 50,-3}
set v to make new picture view at w ¬
     with properties {frame:{55, 702 + dy, the_width, the_height}}
BeginFrontFigure(v)
SetTextFont("Courier")
SetTextSize(12)
TextMoveTo({0, 0-dy})
DrawText("John Smithson")
DrawPath("stroke")
EndFrontFigure()
draw w
```

You have finished the program! You now have a (small) script capable of writing any text in any location of a PDF, using any font. You can even enhance it. For example, you could adjust the frame of the picture view by using the measuretext command to compute what the rectangle's sizes must be exactly to display a given string using a given font.

Here is the entire script listing:

```
-- Replace with actual document's path
set pdf_path to (POSIX path of (path to desktop)) & "mc0306.pdf"
set w to open POSIX file pdf_path
-- Run the following block as many times as needed, adapting the parameters to suit
set text_font to "Arial"
set text_size to 12
set s to "John Smithson"
set {dx, dy, the_width, the_height} to ¬
```

```
    measuretext s font {text font: text_font, text size: text_size}
set v to make new picture view at w ¬
    with properties {frame:{55, 702 + dy, the_width, the_height}}
BeginFrontFigure(v)
SetTextFont(text_font)
SetTextSize(text_size)
TextMoveTo({0, 0-dy})
DrawText(s)
DrawPath("stroke")
EndFrontFigure()
draw w
```

Keeping productivity gains as large as possible sometimes means making the minimal effort required to have the work done. Here you are not implementing any error checking, any user notifications, or any of the other bells and whistles you would expect for an application that you would distribute. You have just externalized the variables and added a few comments to make the program reusable later.

Rolling Up the Scripts into a Graphical Interface

In this section, you will add a user interface to the script you created earlier. Once you have made a task doable in Smile, you may want to make it available for nonscripters to use. This interface will allow users to select the PDF they want to edit and specify the text they want to add to it.

Smile makes creating a graphical interface easy using *custom dialog boxes*. When you save a custom dialog box, you get a document that will open in Smile when double-clicked: each graphical interface can be seen as a separate application able to run in Smile's environment.

For your first experience of a custom dialog box, you'll keep it simple: you'll have the user enter each quantity as a string, in text fields. So far, you have identified the following inputs: the string, the font, the text size, and the location, which consists of two numbers; so, you need five text entry fields (*editable text boxes*) and five *static text boxes* to let the user know what to type there.

In your tests, you obtained a reference to the graphic window (w) because you opened the PDF file yourself. In a real situation, the user opens a PDF file, and then they may use the custom dialog box to edit the PDF. So that the user is able to target any open PDF file (any graphic window), you'll add a sixth text field in which the user will type the name of the window to target. Obviously, you could design a user-friendly way of targeting the desired window, but for the purposes of this example, I'll restrict the tutorial to a simple tool.

The user will trigger the actions with buttons. You won't update the window's display each time the user changes any quantity in the text fields, but rather you'll have the user decide when to show the result: a first button will display the new string with the current settings. You also want to validate the current drawing before editing a new string; you need a second button for that.

To have the dialog box open with one click, you will install it in the User Scripts menu (the S-shaped icon between the Window and Help menus). To install a new item in the User Scripts menu, you copy it into a specific location in the user's domain, namely, `~/Library/Application Support/Smile/User Scripts/`.

This makes you ready to create your Smile tool. In the first step, you'll build the interface—the dialog box the user will see. Then you'll provide the scripts that will bring the dialog box to life.

Building the Interface

The first action is to make a new dialog box. Select File ➤ New ➤ New Dialog. This opens a new dialog box and also the Controls palette from which you will copy the desired controls (see Figure 28–11). Note that the Controls palette is merely a dialog box. It is part of Smile's philosophy to define a limited number of window classes so that you can script Smile more easily. The Controls palette is where you find one copy of each of the controls you can install in your dialog box.

Figure 28–11. *The Controls palette is in edit mode; you copy a control into your dialog box by dragging and dropping.*

As you can check by selecting the Edit menu, both windows are in edit mode, which is the mode where you can make structural changes to the dialog box. This is because you used File ➤ New ➤ New Dialog. When you open an existing dialog box by the usual means, it opens in running mode, the normal use mode. Selecting Edit ➤ Edit mode lets you toggle the dialog box into edit mode and immediately make any change.

You can also check that, since the dialog boxes are in edit mode, the menu bar displays a Dialog menu with several commands to help with editing a dialog box.

Now you'll populate the empty, new dialog box. Enlarge the new dialog box. Click the "new static text" control in the Controls palette, hold down the mouse button, and drag the control to the new dialog box, close to the upper-left corner. You have installed your first control.

Sooner or later you'll have to save the dialog box to disk, so do that now. Select File ➤ Save, and save the dialog box as Add text to PDF file in ~/Library/Application Support/Smile/User Scripts/. This changes the dialog box's name into the file's name. Check that the User Scripts menu now offers one new item, with the name you supplied.

Proceeding as you did for the static text, install a "new editable text" control in the dialog box. Place it to the right of the "new static text" control. It is better that the two controls do not overlap. Drag the new editable text control sufficiently to the right, and/or resize the static text control to a shorter size: select it with the mouse, and then move its frame's bottom-right corner.

Instead of dropping more items, you'll duplicate the two existing items. Select them both, in the creation order ("new static text", then "new editable text"), using the Shift key. Or, deselect any item by clicking in an empty spot in the dialog box, and then select Edit ➤ Select All. Now press Cmd+D, or select User Scripts ➤ More Smile Commands ➤ Edit ➤ Duplicate. (Duplicate is better than copying and pasting, because Duplicate leaves the clipboard untouched.) The duplicated items are created with an offset of 20 pixels to the right and to the bottom, as seen in Figure 28–12. You can move them with the arrows on the keyboard; press the Shift key to have the items move by 20 pixels, and use the left and the bottom arrows to align the new controls with the first ones.

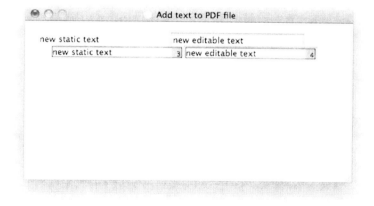

Figure 28–12. *New items are created with increasing indexes. The Duplicate menu command creates new copies at an offset of (20, 20) with respect to the original.*

Repeat this step four times (to end up with six copies of each).

Still using drag and drop from the Controls palette, create two new buttons (for instance, both at the same height, under the array of text fields). Now you can resize the dialog box so as to enclose the controls only.

When you write the script for the dialog box, you'll refer to the controls by their indexes. A control's *index* is the number that its frame displays in the bottom-right corner when selected. Check that the indexes are in the natural order; that is, from left to right and then from top to bottom. The rightmost button in the bottom should assume the index 14. If you have more items, use Edit ➤ Clear to suppress the extra controls. If the order is not what it should be, proceed as follows. Unselect any item by clicking an empty spot. Then press the Shift key, and click each item once in the desired order so as to finally select them all. Finally, select Edit ➤ Cut and then Edit ➤ Paste; the controls will be pasted in the same order as you selected them.

The script will handle the contents of the editable text boxes, but you have to name the other eight controls. For the editable text boxes, I suggest "Text to display:", "Text font:", "Text size:", "x (points):", "y (points):", and "Current target:"; for the buttons, I suggest "Refresh" and "Validate" (see Figure 28–13). For each of the eight controls to be renamed successively, double-click each to open its Control dialog box, set its name to the desired string, and then close the Control dialog box.

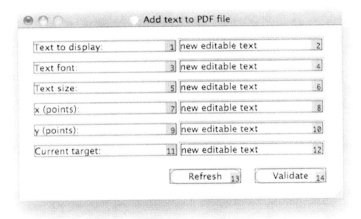

Figure 28–13. *The dialog box with all the controls laid out. Notice how selecting a control in editing mode displays its index number.*

You will not need another new control for the moment, so close the Controls palette.

The interface of the dialog box is now operational—if not fully finalized from a cosmetic point of view. I won't demonstrate cosmetic-oriented features here. It may be enough to say that in addition to moving and resizing, you can, using the Dialog ➤ Align Items menu item, copy the sizes from a control to another and align and/or distribute the controls vertically or horizontally. More sophisticated, user-contributed editing tools are available for free at Satimage's web site.

Programming the Dialog Box

Last but not least, you have to program the dialog box by providing it with scripts. All the lines you wrote for the first tests are still available, so your task will have much to do with copying and pasting.

In Smile, when the user acts on a control (for instance, typing a character in an editable text box or clicking a button), Smile notifies the script of the control's container—the dialog box; the control itself is not notified. More precisely, the script of the dialog box will receive the following event:

```
click in d item number n
```

where d is a reference to the dialog box (the owner of the script) and n is the index of the control that the user's action addresses. Thus, you won't write as many `click in` handlers as you have active controls—you need only one.

The other handler you need to write is `prepare`. When a custom dialog box opens, Smile sends the following event to its script just before making it visible:

```
prepare d
```

where d is a reference to the dialog box. Any initialization should be performed in the `prepare` handler. Most often, the job of the `prepare` handler is to prepare the appearance of the dialog box and to assign initial values to the global variables that the script of the dialog box may use. However, at this step you won't use global variables (`properties`); the `prepare` handler will mainly reset the entry text fields.

Now write the `prepare` handler. With the dialog box still in edit mode, select Action ➤ Edit Dialog Script; this will open the script of the dialog box. The name of the new (colored) window is the same as the dialog box's name, with `.Script` appended. It may be helpful to note here that the script of the dialog box is different from, say, the script of an applet, in that it will never "run"; the script will receive events that it will handle in the handlers you'll write, but under normal conditions it will never receive a `run` event.

Type or copy the following `prepare` handler into the script window:

```
on prepare theDialog
    repeat with i from 2 to 12 by 2
        set contained data of dialog item i of theDialog to ""
    end repeat
end prepare
```

(By default, the script of the dialog box already includes the first and last lines of the handler, so you have only three lines to type. A script may not contain two handlers with the same name.)

Now save the script into the dialog box. Select File ➤ Save. If you introduced a typo, Smile throws an alert to notify you of a compilation error, and the script does not get saved; fix the typo, and try again.

In Smile, you test as you develop, so test the handler now. Bring the dialog box to the front, and then create a new AppleScript terminal window. The dialog box is now the second window. Execute the following line in the terminal window:

```
set d to window 2
```

This returns to d an absolute reference to the dialog box, which will remain valid even when the dialog box is no longer the second window and until it gets deleted. Now to test the handler, execute the following:

```
tell d to prepare it
```

This should clear the editable text fields.

If it does not, the first thing to do—if you are sure the script was saved—is to install an error output. Indeed, in the spirit of a behavior ready for automatic applications, Smile keeps silent the errors triggered in a prepare handler, unless the scripter explicitly handles them. You'll now see how you would install an error handler. Specifically, you'll introduce a typo into the script that follows and see how the error code you will insert handles the error.

To experiment with the error handler, bring the dialog box's script window to the front, and replace its content with the following lines:

```
on prepare theDialog
    try
        repeat with i from 2 to 12 by 2
            set contained data of dialog item i of dlog to ""
        end repeat
    on error s
        FatalAlert(s)
    end try
end prepare
```

Do not forget to save the script with File ➤ Save to make the change effective. Now, as you have done already, put the cursor in the following line, and press Cmd+R:

```
tell d to prepare it
```

AppleScript attempts to run the prepare handler. But in the set contained data... line, it will choke on a variable that was not defined before: dlog (the variable passed as the parameter to prepare is theDialog, not dlog). This is a typical runtime error. AppleScript thus jumps to the first line after the on error clause. There you see FatalAlert; FatalAlert is nothing but a shortcut that Smile defines for convenience, which is really one option of display alert, and is adapted for displaying error messages.

Now correct the typo (replace dlog with theDialog), and save the script.

You are finished with the prepare handler; now you are going to program the click in handler. It is good practice not to directly handle the event in the click in handler but instead to write routines that click in will call.

Reviewing the sequence of test scripts, you see that you can reuse the picture view to enable text modifications. You just have to store its reference to address it later or to reinitialize it when validating. It will be a good idea, as a visual confirmation, to blank the string to display once the current front graphic is merged in the background graphic.

Bring the script of the dialog box back in view if needed, and type (or copy) the three new handlers shown in Script 28–3. Remove the built-in sample click in handler, but keep the prepare handler you entered previously.

Script 28–3.

```
property v : 0

on prepare theDialog
     set v to 0
     repeat with i from 2 to 12 by 2
         set contained data of dialog item i of theDialog to ""
     end repeat
end prepare

on RefreshDisplay(d)
   tell d
       set s to contained data of dialog item 2
       set text_font to contained data of dialog item 4
       set text_size to contained data of dialog item 6
       set x to contained data of dialog item 8
       set y to contained data of dialog item 10
       set w_name to contained data of dialog item 12
   end tell
   set w to graphic window w_name
   set {dx, dy, the_width, the_height} to ¬
       measuretext s font {text font:text_font, text size:text_size }
   try
       set frame of v to {x, y + dy, the_width, the_height}
   on error
       set v to make new picture view at w ¬
           with properties {frame:{x, y + dy, the_width, the_height}}
   end
   BeginFrontFigure(v)
   SetTextFont(text_font)
   SetTextSize(text_size)
   TextMoveTo({0, -dy})
   DrawText(s)
   DrawPath("stroke")
   EndFrontFigure()
   draw w
end RefreshDisplay

on MergeCurrent(d)
   set v to 0
   set contained data of dialog item 2 of d to ""
end MergeCurrent

on click in d item number n
   if n = 13 then
       RefreshDisplay(d)
   else if n = 14 then
       MergeCurrent(d)
   end if
end click in
```

Save the script, and select File ➤ Close to close its window. Bring the dialog box to the front, and save it as well. This will save to disk the changes you made to the dialog box, including the script you just wrote.

You are now ready to test and use the new Smile tool. If it is still open, close the PDF file, discarding the changes. If it is still open, close the dialog box, too.

Now, open the PDF file in Smile like a user would do normally. In other words, drop its icon on the Smile icon, use File ➤ Open in Smile, or use a script as shown here:

```
open POSIX file pdf_path
```

Open the dialog box. If you followed the instructions verbatim, your new dialog box should be available as an item in the User Scripts menu. Otherwise, just double-click the icon of the dialog box in the Finder.

Now you can use your new tool. To start, try adding a first string to the document; for this example, suppose you want to set the name information to Bart Simpson. To fill in the x/y (points) information, click the graphic window at the location where "Bart Simpson" should print. The toolbar displays the values for x and y—something like 55 and 702. Now you can fill the text fields in the dialog box, such as "Bart Simpson", "Lucida Grande", "13", "55", "702", and "mc0306.pdf". At this point, you'll need to fill all the fields; you have not installed any error handling or any system of default values.

To view the result, click Refresh. If nothing happens, probably a field is not filled in or is incorrectly filled in—for instance, a letter in a numeric field.

If some setting does not suit you, change it, and click Refresh again until you are satisfied with the result. Then, to validate that first string, click Validate. This resets the string to display to the empty string, suggesting you can now work on a second string. Proceed for the second string like you just did for the first string. If the second string is on the same horizontal as the first one, keep the same value for y (points).

Handling User Clicks

Obviously, reading the window's toolbar and copying its content manually into the dialog box is not productive. You should have the graphic window send the location of the click to the dialog box.

When the user clicks in an active graphic window, Smile sends `pick in` to the graphic window's script, so you will need to add a handler for `pick in` to the graphic window's script. Open the script of the graphic window. As for the dialog box, you must first change the graphic window to edit mode. With the graphic window being the active window, select Edit ➤ Edit Mode (or press Cmd+Y), and then select Action ➤ Edit Dialog Script. This will open its script; by default, the script is empty.

Type the following lines. (This assumes you named the dialog box "Add text to PDF file". Otherwise, change the string in the script accordingly.)

```
on pick in w at {point:{x, y}, step:i}
    set d to dialog "Add text to PDF file"
    set contained data of item 8 of d to x
```

```
    set contained data of item 10 of d to y
end pick in
```

Note that `pick in` passes a `step` parameter. The value of `step` is 1 when the user presses the button ("mouse down"), 2 when the user is moving the mouse while the button is down ("drag"), and 3 when the user releases the button ("mouse up"). For more sophisticated handling—for instance, if you wanted to implement the ability to constrain the drag with the Shift key—you would use the value of `step`.

Also, if you look carefully at the script, you'll observe that you set the `contained data` property of an editable text field not to a string but to a number. This is something special to Smile. Text fields can be filled with numbers, and you can customize the way they will display numbers by setting their `number formatting` property. You can do this by right-clicking the text field while in edit mode and choosing the Format option.

On the other hand, reading the `contained data` property of an editable text field always returns a string unless you coerce the string to a number by specifying `as real`.

Select File ➤ Save and then File ➤ Close to close the script's window, and then select Edit ➤ Edit Mode (or press Cmd+Y) to change the PDF's graphic window to running mode.

Now click and drag the mouse; the dialog box should display the mouse's location in the x/y (points) field.

Note that the graphic window's toolbar does not display the coordinates any longer when you drag the mouse. This is because your custom `pick in` handler overrides the window's standard behavior. If you want the toolbar to update as well, add the following `continue` statement to your handler:

```
    continue pick in w at {point:{x, y}, step:i}
```

If you want nonprogrammers to use your tool, you should have the script installed "automagically." You'll make a third button that will implement the `pick in` handler in the target graphic window. For this, change the dialog box to edit mode (Edit ➤ Edit Mode), click the Refresh button to select it, duplicate it (User Scripts ➤ More Smile Commands ➤ Edit ➤ Duplicate), and align the new button to its left (arrow keys with or without the Shift key pressed). Double-click the new button, and name it "Auto click".

Now program the new button. Cmd+Opt-click the dialog box to open its script (or select Action ➤ Edit Dialog Script). Add the handler in Script 28–4 to the script (in addition to `RefreshDisplay`, `MergeCurrent`, and `click in`) at any location in the script (not inside another handler, though).

Script 28–4.

```
on InstallScript(d)
    set w_name to contained data of item 12 of d
    set w to graphic window w_name
    set script of w to "
        on pick in w at {point:{x, y}, step:i}
            set d to dialog \"" & name of d & "\"
            set contained data of item 8 of d to x
            set contained data of item 10 of d to y
```

```
              continue pick in w at {point:{x, y}, step:i}
         end pick in"
   postit ("Loaded")
   smilepause 5
   postit ("")
end InstallScript
```

In this handler you use a sophisticated feature, scripted scripting. In Smile you can dynamically provide a script to an object; you can set the `script` property of an object to a string—provided the string is an AppleScript source that can be compiled. Smile lets you manipulate—by script—scripts as well as the individual handlers and properties of a script.

You have chosen to display feedback when the action is done: the floating Message window will display "Loaded" for 5 seconds (`postit ("")` closes the Message window).

The handler uses a unique command of Smile's: `smilepause`. Inserting `smilepause` in a script pauses the script (for the time specified, which can be 0) while letting the application be fully responsive. You can use `smilepause` for a wide variety of occasions. Here you use it to have the message go away after five seconds yet let the user work normally as soon as the action is done.

Of course, you must have the new handler called when the user clicks the Auto Click button. This is the job of the `click in` handler, where you should insert (before end `if`) the two following lines:

```
else if n = 15 then
   InstallScript(d)
```

You can check your script against the code download. The order of the routines is arbitrary. If there is no error, save and close the script. Once the dialog box is the front window, save it as well.

Now you can click the new Auto click button and finish filling in the form as shown in Figure 28–14, and then you can save it too.

Finally, you can view the file by double-clicking its icon in the Finder. Depending on your settings, this will open the file in Preview or in Adobe Reader (or Acrobat Reader), and you can see the strings you have added. You can use a high magnification to check that you have vector graphics.

Figure 28–14. *Filling in the PDF form with the completed dialog box*

Further Exercises

Obviously, you have made a working tool, but its functionality is minimal. What you should do now depends mostly on who will be using the tool and how often they will use it.

Here are some standard improvements you may want to implement later. For the sake of brevity, I leave them as exercises for you to do on your own.

- Have the dialog box systematically work on the first graphic window (even if the window is not the second window) while also displaying its name as a visual feedback. Or, install a `load window 2` button.

- Install a menu for the text font. For the text size, install the small arrows control.

- Modify the `pick in` handler to support the Shift key to pin one coordinate.

- Enable the user to type a numeric expression such as 55+200 as x or y.

- Install a live check box for live update.

- Allow the user to switch between picture views so that all the text remains editable until the user saves it as PDF.

- Graphic windows support widgets that you can use like scriptable handles to an object. Rewrite Adobe Illustrator using the widgets.

Summary

In this chapter you explored some of the powerful and flexible features provided by Satimage's Smile environment, including its interactive AppleScript terminal, dialog box development tools, and PDF-based graphics engine.

In the next chapter, we will discuss some general tips and techniques for designing, debugging, and optimizing your AppleScript code.

Chapter 29

Tips and Techniques for Improving Your Scripts

Up until now, the main goal of this book has been to teach you AppleScript and application scripting, providing you with the essential knowledge and skills for automating your Mac. You know how to use AppleScript objects, commands and operators, flow control statements, and perhaps even handlers and script objects. You understand how scriptable applications present information as objects in an object model, and how to manipulate those objects by sending commands to the application. And you have put this knowledge to practical use in a wide range of exercises throughout the preceding chapters. At this point, you have a powerful set of tools under your belt—more than enough to solve many common automation tasks.

The only question now is: where next? The answer to this question will depend very much on your reasons for learning AppleScript and the kinds of projects you intend to develop with it. While we have talked a lot about what the various features in AppleScript do and how to use them yourself, less has been said about how to use those features to maximum effect.

Think of the difference between a competent do-it-yourself (DIY) enthusiast and a master craftsman who has many years of experience. As a DIY enthusiast, you may know how to paper walls, paint doors and windows, replace taps, and so on. With a bit of practice, you may even do a respectable job of it. If you enjoy this kind of work, have the time to spend on it, and find that the results satisfy your needs, then more power to you for doing it yourself.

Just for a minute, though, consider how the master craftsman approaches the same tasks. In the time it takes you to paper a wall, a professional decorator will finish a room. While your plumbing joins may sometimes leak a little and need to be redone, a skilled plumber will solder a perfect connection the first time, every time.

I do a little DIY myself, and it never ceases to amaze me how a skilled professional makes the same tasks look so quick and easy. Of course, what those guys and gals do is hardly effortless—it's all due to a deep knowledge of their field and years of practice. Unlike me, they don't need to stop every five minutes to check a manual or undo a simple mistake, nor do they waste effort on trivial details that make no real difference to the end result.

With programming, as with DIY, as with painting, or writing, or any of myriad other pursuits, some tasks can be either easy to do or hard to do depending on your knowledge and experience. In this chapter, we are going to look at how you, as an AppleScripter, can get the most out of your AppleScript knowledge to ensure that you are scripting efficiently and not wasting time doing things the hard way.

We will start with a discussion of some of the ways you can improve the design of your scripts. We will then look at various tools and techniques for testing and debugging your scripts effectively. Finally, we will explore some of the ways you can maximize the performance of your scripts.

Design, in a Nutshell

The first thing I'll say about design is this: it's hard. Testing, debugging, and optimizing performance are hard, too—but at least the end benefits are easy to recognize: fast, reliable scripts. With design, it's easy to think: "My script works; that's good enough for me." And you know what? In many cases, that is good enough! A script that fulfills a need is a successful script, even if it isn't the most beautiful of code to look at.

As an AppleScripter, many of the scripts you develop will be fairly quick and simple, performing straightforward tasks such as renaming files, tidying iTunes libraries, perhaps even scrubbing InDesign documents for dodgy text and links. For these sorts of tasks, a good practical knowledge of AppleScript and InDesign features is essential, allowing you to dive in, write some lines of code, and run the script to achieve the desired result. Time spent learning fancy design theory or honing the structure and presentation of such scripts is time you could have spent doing much more interesting and productive things elsewhere. So if these are the kinds of scripts you use, then "dive in, write it, run it" is an ideal strategy for you.

The problem with this quick-and-dirty approach is this: it works great for short, straightforward utility scripts, but as soon as you attempt large, sophisticated workflow systems, you have an excellent chance of digging yourself into an enormous hole. The "just do it" approach that served you so well in solving small, simple problems simply does not scale to large, complex problems.

If you wish to take on large-scale development, and do so both efficiently and effectively, then perhaps it is time to become not only a skillful AppleScripter but also, dare I say, a little bit of a "real programmer."

Taking Your Scripting Skills to the Next Level

If you do decide to develop your design skills, realize that it is not something you can achieve overnight. To reap the long-term benefits, you will have to invest quite a bit of time and work in the beginning. Furthermore, as a self-taught scripter, you will often have to make your own way through the subject—as much as I'd like to cover every aspect of program design here, doing so would be impossible without doubling the size of this book.

Fortunately, a number of excellent guides on general programming techniques already exist. Although they are not aimed specifically at AppleScripters, once you are comfortable with the nuts and bolts of AppleScript itself, you can adapt the general knowledge presented in these books to your specific AppleScripting needs.

My own personal favorite is *Code Complete*, by Steve McConnell (http://www.cc2e.com), which I've found to be of enormous assistance over the years (it's now in its second edition). In addition to being written in a very friendly, accessible style, it is not the sort of book you need to read from cover to cover before it makes sense. Although you can do that if you wish, it is also easy to dive into an individual chapter if and when you need to improve your understanding of one particular area. Another highly regarded book is *The Pragmatic Programmer: From Journeyman to Master*, by Andrew Hunt and David Thomas (http://www.pragprog.com/the-pragmatic-programmer).

The great thing about these books is that they not only teach you new things, but also help you to realize just how much you *don't* know…yet. Once you are aware of the gaps in your knowledge, you can start to fill them in as necessary.

Although we are not going to go into significant detail here, it is worth spending a little time discussing some of the challenges you will face as you tackle larger and more sophisticated projects, which will give you an idea of how a good set of general design skills can play a key role in overcoming those challenges.

How Much Design Do Your Scripts Need?

The world of programming is full of smart folks with lots of interesting and valuable insights into the art and craft of creating code, so let's start with a couple of them:

> *"Any fool can write code that a computer can understand. Good programmers write code that humans can understand."*

> —Martin Fowler

> *"Controlling complexity is the essence of computer programming."*

> —Brian Kernighan

As an AppleScript user, I'm sure you already appreciate the value of human-readable code, as readability is the biggest benefit of AppleScript's English-like syntax. Even if you've never used AppleScript before, chances are that you can look at a typical utility script and get a reasonable idea of what it does.

Of course, as your scripts grow larger, you will need more help than AppleScript alone can provide in order to maintain order and clarity in your code. Features such as user-defined script handlers become a valuable tool here, allowing you to tuck all of the fine details of a complex operation behind a single, descriptively named command. However, don't forget about the basics: carefully named variables; flow control blocks that are not too long or deeply nested; comments that explain *why* you've done a certain thing rather than comments that just restate what the code does; and so forth. As a rough rule of thumb, a single section of code that fits onscreen is easier to understand than one that requires you to scroll up and down.

This then leads us to the second of the preceding insights: programming is all about *controlling complexity*. If your own code is too complicated for you to understand yourself, what are the chances that it will even work, much less be easy to develop and maintain in future?

To put it another way: a 10-line script is pretty simple however you look at it; a 100-line script is much more complicated; a 1,000-line script is more complicated still. How much more complicated? Well, you could almost certainly memorize the entire workings of the 10-line script, but it's unlikely you could remember every detail of the 100-line one, and, unless you have a perfect photographic memory, it's almost impossible that you could remember the entire 1,000-line script, much less understand how each of the lines in that script interact with all the others.

So does this mean that a 1,000-line script is 100 times harder to understand than a 10-line one? The answer is: it depends. Specifically, it depends on whether you designed it in such a way that it is easy to identify the main sections of code and see how they interact with one another, without having to follow all of the fine details involved. If you can break your 1,000-line script down into, say, twenty 50-line sections, each of which has a clearly defined purpose and connects only to those other sections that it needs to interact with, you can tackle each of those sections independently. I don't know about you, but given the choice of figuring out 50 lines or a 1,000 lines at a time, I know which option I'd pick.

We touched on this topic in Chapter 18, when I introduced the term *abstraction*, which is just a fancy way of saying you should hide the minor details so that the important bits stand out. We have already covered the essential AppleScript features required to do this; the only question is when you should start to use them. As a rule of thumb, I would suggest the following milestones:

- If you are writing small, simple scripts that mainly just manipulate scriptable applications, you don't need any design skills to do so.

- If your scripts go over a few dozen lines of code, or have crazy, deep nesting, or use lots of copied-and-pasted code, it's time to learn handlers.

- If your scripts run to hundreds of lines and are getting hard to navigate or contain lots of copied-and-pasted handlers, it's time to learn libraries.

- If your scripts run to thousands of lines, contain complex, fiddly-to-manage record-based data structures, or deal with AppleScriptObjC, you should learn OOP.

Starting Out Is Hard (But Gets Easier with Practice)

Naturally, when you begin working with handlers (or libraries, or OOP), you won't be very good at it. Sometimes, you won't divide up the code as much as you could, resulting in bloated, hard-to-understand, "Swiss Army knife" handlers that try to do too many things at once. Other times, you will break the code into too many parts, resulting in handlers that are too fragmented to follow easily. Sometimes you will divide up the code in the wrong places, requiring complicated, confusing connections between the handlers.

The more you practice, however, the more you will develop a feel for what works and what doesn't. If something seems harder than it ought to be, that may be a sign that you're approaching it in the wrong way, in which case you should back up and try a different path.

For instance, I often find it useful to block out the rough structure of my code by defining the main handlers without filling in the actual code. Once the names make sense and the parameters are easy to follow, I know I have a good starting point from which to work on the details.

This is a completely different approach from the one I use when writing cheap and cheerful utility scripts. In those cases, I just start with the first line and keep on writing until I get to the end. Then, if I feel like it, I might tidy the script a little by moving any obvious bits of copied-and-pasted code into shared handlers—a `find_and_replace` here, a `sort_list` there. Overall, though, these sorts of scripts work in exactly the same way that I wrote them: perform one step, then the next step, then the step after that, and so on. In the early days of my scripting career, I would use exactly the same approach even with fairly large projects, so a script to generate a product catalog from an InDesign template might have the following structure:

```
on run
    tell application "FileMaker Pro"
        -- Retrieve the raw text and image data from a particular record
    end tell
    -- Tidy up the raw text using text item delimiters, Satimage.osax commands, etc.
    tell application "Finder"
        -- Locate each of the required image files
        repeat with image_file_ref in the_files
            tell application "Adobe Photoshop CS4"
                -- Open, resize, adjust, and save the image in the required format
            end tell
        end tell
    end
    tell application "Adobe InDesign CS4"
        -- Open the InDesign template file
        repeat with text_frame_ref in all_frames
            -- If the frame has a template tag attached, extract the tag's name
            -- Search the cleaned up FileMaker data for the tag name
            -- Insert the found value into the text frame
```

```
      end repeat
      -- Repeat the basic process for each image frame
      -- Save the finished document
   end tell
end
```

As you can see, I've omitted the actual details for the sake of space and inserted brief comments that summarize what each part does. In fact, the preceding "pseudocode" would not be a bad way to begin planning a medium-sized script. After all, it describes the main tasks that will be performed by the script; all we really need to do is reorganize it a bit:

```
on run
   get_data_from_FileMaker(record_number)
   repeat with image_file in image_files
      reformat_image(image_file, the_size, save_as_format)
   end repeat
   -- Open the InDesign template file
   -- Replace text and images
   insert_tagged_text(the_template, the_copy)
   insert_tagged_images(the_template, image_files)
   -- Save the finished document
end run

on get_data_from_FileMaker(record_number)
end get_data_from_FileMaker

on reformat_image(image_file, the_size, save_as_format)
end reformat_image

-- etc...
```

As you can see, this is far from being working code; it is merely a sketch to help us think about how we might structure this script. We can quickly change and refine this outline to see how different ideas might look, to add things we've missed or remove bits that aren't needed, or to completely revise the structure if a better arrangement comes to mind.

For instance, we should probably have the get_data_from_FileMaker handler take the database file as a parameter so that this key piece of information appears at the top of the script and can easily be changed without having to recode the handler itself.

Looking at the InDesign-related section, we could move all those steps into their own render_InDesign_template handler, which would then call additional subhandlers to perform the smaller steps as needed, further simplifying our script at the top level.

We can also consider whether the text-cleaning code should be called inside or outside the get_data_from_FileMaker handler. If the data must always be cleaned before it is used, then the text-cleaning code is probably best called by the handler itself. However, if the cleaning is optional, or requires the text to be treated in different ways depending on where it is used, then it is probably best to make it a completely separate step.

You don't even need to go near AppleScript Editor to do any of this; you could just as easily jot down your notes in a TextEdit document, in an OmniGraffle chart, or even on a piece of paper. The important bit is that, instead of tackling the entire problem all at once, working in a linear order, you start at the top of the problem and break it down into smaller, simpler problems. Once you are at a point where you can easily understand these small problems, you are ready to begin writing the code to address each of these problems one at a time, gradually solving the entire problem from the bottom-up.

How the Design-Driven Approach Changes the Way You Think About Code

In our previous, hypothetical example, we tackled the big questions before writing a single line of real code. Playing around with ideas is quick and easy; writing polished, tested code takes time. Even if you don't figure out all the answers before you begin coding—or even identify all the questions that need to be asked—you are giving yourself a head start.

Once we begin working on the code itself, we may discover that our initial answers weren't right after all, in which case we just have to stop for a bit and rethink them. But at least we have some idea of where we want to go and aren't just jumping in blind. The result, hopefully, is that we run into fewer major problems along the way—problems that might otherwise require us to throw away large amounts of recently written code or, worse, try to make do with code that is confusing and difficult to work with, assuming it even works properly in the first place.

In our hypothetical example, we also stopped considering the script as a long series of statements to be executed one after another; instead, we began thinking about it in terms of a collection of components, where each component is tasked with certain roles and responsibilities, and interacts with related units to achieve a larger goal.

It's a little like the difference between a one-person business and a large company with many different employees. Instead of treating the code as a long list of instructions to be performed by a lowly, unquestioning clerk, we are creating a kind of "management structure." The "big boss" of the script—in this case, the run handler—does not do any of the grunt work itself, but instead delegates various responsibilities to the appropriate "middle managers," additional handlers specifically created to oversee the main activities in the code. Those handlers might then delegate smaller tasks to the junior employees—handlers written to perform one specific task each.

This doesn't mean that the big boss can't spend her time sticking stamps on envelopes, just as the owner of a one-person business would; it means only that this probably is not the most productive use of her energies. Instead, she should hire a mailroom clerk to perform this task for her, with the added benefit that everyone else in the company who needs to send mail can make use of this service, too.

The ability to think about a program in terms of the "big picture" as well as the individual details is key to effective design. From there, it is a matter of using the AppleScript language's organizational features—handlers and script objects—to "explain" the structure of your program in the same way. If your design is successful, you should then spread the overall complexity of your program evenly across several levels, and then break it down further within each level.

Now that you have gained a little insight into the value that well-honed design skills can provide (assuming it is worth your time to develop these skills in the first place, of course), let's move on to the next topic in this chapter: the tools and techniques you can use to test and debug your scripts effectively.

Testing and Debugging Your Code

"Everyone knows that debugging is twice as hard as writing a program in the first place. So if you are as clever as you can be when you write it, how will you ever debug it?"

—Brian Kernighan

Let's face it, if reliability isn't any concern to you, you might as well save yourself a huge amount of time and work by writing all your scripts as follows:

```
on run
end run
```

Okay, so it doesn't do anything *useful*, but it's incredibly quick to write and run—a real timesaver!

Seriously, though, testing and debugging your code is not something you do as an afterthought. A good scripter will test and debug his code at every step of development. While this might sound like a chore and a good way to slow down progress, frequently testing small sections of code as you write them actually turns out to be less time consuming and a lot more pleasant than piling up all of your testing work to do right at the end.

Although there are many tricks to debugging, there's no better overall way than to do it with Script Debugger from Late Night Software (http://www.latenightsw.com). I know, it does cost US$199, but if you spend a good chunk of your time writing scripts, it will pay for itself. It is currently the only AppleScript editor written for Mac OS X that gives you step-by-step debugging.

Script Debugger, as the name suggests, has useful tools for debugging scripts. The main debugging feature, and the one Script Debugger is most known for, is the ability to run through the script step by step and set breakpoints where the script pauses. I'll return to some Script Debugger debugging techniques later in the chapter. In the meantime, you'll learn about some other ways you can get the bugs out of your scripts with any script editor.

General Testing Tips and Techniques

In Chapter 15, we discussed the various types of runtime errors that may occur in your code. Although some of these errors may be due to circumstances outside your control—for example, if the user enters an invalid date or deletes an essential data file used by your script—plenty of other runtime errors inevitably are caused by programmer error. If you want your scripts to run correctly when released, sooner or later you are going to have to beat those bugs out of your code. The following sections discuss some of the general techniques that will help you in this process.

Design Your Scripts for Easy Testing

One of the benefits of a well-designed script is that it is much easier to test and debug than a similar sized script that was simply thrown together. If complex code is broken down into small, simple, self-contained handlers, it becomes much easier to test because you can test each handler in isolation. Just call the handler with suitable test values and check that the result is what you expected it to be.

Let's say you're writing a templating script that pulls a bunch of data from a FileMaker Pro database, converts a folder full of images into CMYK `.tiff` files using Adobe Photoshop, and finally inserts the text and images into an Adobe Illustrator document. If you mix the code for all three tasks together, then the only way to test it is by running the entire process from start to finish.

Now, let's say you are doing some maintenance work on the page layout code. Ideally, you would run a quick test after each modification just to check that you haven't broken anything, but if the entire script takes several minutes to run, then you will naturally be reluctant to do this. Instead, you make all your changes, run the code when you're done…and spend even more time hunting down the errors, as it's no longer obvious which change caused which error.

On the other hand, if you design the templating system as three separate components that plug together to form the complete system, you could replace the real database code with a fake "database" made up of AppleScript lists and records filled with a range of dummy data that gives your templating code a thorough workout. Because there is little real code in your fake data source, there is very little to go wrong in it—so any time an error occurs, you can be pretty much certain that the bug is in your templating component, and not anywhere else.

Test Your Code with Bad Data As Well As Good

While testing that your script produces the correct results when given the correct input is important, you should also think about what could happen if your script is passed invalid values instead. Will it fail gracefully with a helpful explanation of what the user did wrong? Will it throw a raw AppleScript error and quit unceremoniously? Might it even damage or destroy valuable data in the process?

As you know, Murphy's law states that anything that can go wrong, will go wrong. One of the aims of your tests should be to make as many things go wrong as possible. After all, if a script breaks on you, you just find the problem and fix it. If you deliver a script to a user and something goes horribly wrong with it some time later, not only will you still have to find and fix the problem, you will have to deal with a very irate user as well. Obviously, if a script is going to break, the safest person to break it is you.

For example, if a handler expects numbers as parameters, what happens when you pass, say, a non-numerical string? Will it do the sensible thing and report a descriptive error? Or might it do something completely unexpected? If this handler is at all important, you should test it and find out. What about testing a handler that does string manipulation using AppleScript's text item delimiters (TIDs)? Have you tried setting TIDs to a nonempty string such as "BADTIDS" before calling the handler? If "BADTIDS" shows up in the handler's results, you know your handler has forgotten to set TIDs before performing a list-to-text coercion. What other dirty tricks could you try in order to make your handlers fail?

Once you get into the habit of looking for weaknesses in your code, you will find and squash a lot more bugs than if you only bother to check it with values you already know will work.

Test Your Code As You Go

A key habit to develop is that of frequently testing small sections of code as you write them. It is tempting to write the entire script in one go and debug it once it's complete, but this rarely goes smoothly in practice. Not only is a large, untested script likely to contain more bugs, but these bugs are more likely to interact with each other in all sorts of weird and hard-to-understand ways—making them even harder to track down and diagnose accurately.

It is easier to write a little bit of code, test it, write a bit more, test that, put them together, and test the result. This reduces the number of bugs that are introduced at any one time and gives them fewer places to hide.

If your script is large, it may be worth taking some time to create proper test scripts that call individual handlers with a variety of test values. The test script can then check that the handler's result matches the expected value—or, in tests where the input values are intentionally invalid, the test script can catch the resulting error in a `try` block and confirm that the error code and message are as expected. Don't forget that if the handler fails to throw an error when it should, your test script should report the absence of the expected error as a failure.

If you need to test individual application commands before adding them to your main script, a nice little feature introduced in Mac OS X 10.6 is the new "tell application" menu. This allows you to target another application by default, avoiding the need to type out a full `tell application ... end tell` block. To enable the menu, go to the Editing panel of AppleScript Editor's Preferences window and tick the Show "tell" application pop-up menu option. The "tell" menu will now appear in the middle of the navigation bar, immediately under the toolbar, as shown in Figure 29–1.

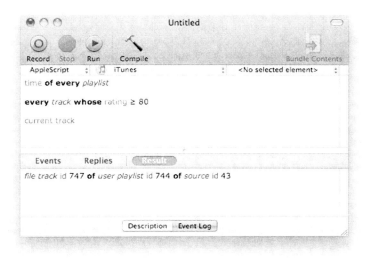

Figure 29–1. *Using AppleScript Editor's "tell application" menu to target a default application (in this case, iTunes)*

Why Testing Matters

It is easy for me to say you should test and retest your code constantly throughout development. Now let me give a practical example of how I learned this lesson for myself—the hard way.

Many years ago, when working under deadline to complete one of my first "large scale" projects (around 2,500 lines of code), I found myself plunged into the longest and toughest bug hunt of my entire scripting career. It took me a whole week just to identify the major bugs and knock them out of that script. Admittedly, the code wasn't terribly well structured to begin with, and its tangled nature often made it difficult or impossible to test smaller sections of code in isolation. However, I had a deadline to meet, and getting the code completed as soon as possible was the important thing, right?

Alas, when the entire script was finally assembled and run for the first time, it immediately broke. And as soon as I figured out and fixed that problem, the script broke again. With dozens, if not hundreds, of suspect lines to comb through each time a new error came to light, tracking down each problem one at a time was a slow process. Plus, as I fixed the bugs that occurred early in the script's progress, bugs that occurred later on would come to light. So each time I ran the script, it would take longer to arrive at the next problem, causing the whole testing process to slow down even as it progressed.

The biggest single problem I found was that the script used a lot of nested lists and records to store data and move it around the script. Unfortunately, one part of the code would modify the content of these data structures while processing them—these changes would then be visible to all the other parts of the script that also used these structures.

Unfortunately, because these problems only occurred after the script had been running for a couple of minutes, running the tests to track it down was a slow and frustrating process. Furthermore, because all the parts of the script had been assembled at the same time, I had no clues as to which one of these parts might actually be causing the problem, and which parts were merely experiencing the consequences secondhand. I had to search the entire script, from one end of the program to the other.

Eventually I got the script more or less working, and for a while I felt that my heroic debugging session was a great achievement. Later on, though, I realized what I had really achieved: I had created a lot of difficult and unpleasant work for myself, much of which would have been entirely unnecessary had I not treated testing and debugging as a complete afterthought. Oh well, it was a lesson learned.

A year or so later, I developed a replacement system. This time, I planned my design more carefully. Instead of writing all of the code and then trying to organize it, I worked out what the main sections would be, and then wrote and tested each section in turn. Once each section was working, I put a couple of them together, tested them in combination, and fixed any new bugs that shook out of that. When all of the pieces were finally put together, the whole script pretty much worked straightaway.

Although the total number of bugs probably wasn't all that different from the system being replaced, because I tested and debugged as I went, they never got the chance to pile up on me. At every stage of development, the code was working—or as close to working as was practical—so that if something did break along the way, I quickly spotted it and tracked it to its source, which in the majority of cases was the most recent change.

> **TIP:** With hindsight, I could have avoided the accidental data sharing problems in various ways. One option would have been to use AppleScript's copy command to make copies of the original data structures that could be modified locally without affecting the originals. Better yet, I could have developed a set of handlers or a custom script object to control all access to the data, ensuring inappropriate changes could not be made to it. See Chapters 12, 18, and 19 for more advice.

Debugging in AppleScript Editor

Although AppleScript Editor does not provide many debugging-related features, it does include a number of useful tools and techniques that you can use during testing.

Viewing Intermediate Results with *return* and *error* Statements

The first value-exposing debugging method you'll use is the return statement. Inserting a return statement allows you to return any value currently set in the script:

```
return some_value
```

The advantage of using `return` is that it will return the value in a pure AppleScript format for you to examine in AppleScript Editor's Result pane, on the Event Log tab. The downside of this approach is that it will also stop the script right then and there, so you can't inspect values from different points in the script at the same time. However, when working with simple scripts or fragments of larger scripts that you are testing in isolation, it can be a useful technique.

Using `return` within handlers is less convenient, since it will simply return the value from the handler to the part of the script that called it. In that case, you'll need to add further `return` statements to return the value all the way.

Another option is to use an `error` statement, passing the value you want to inspect as the error's `from` parameter:

```
error from some_value
```

AppleScript Editor will display the full error description in the Result pane, allowing you to view the value in its original form. The limitation here is that any `try` statements in your code may intercept your deliberate error before it reaches AppleScript Editor.

Obviously, both of these techniques are only useful when you want the script to run up to a certain point and then stop. If you want to monitor the script's progress while it runs, you will have to use one of the following approaches.

Monitoring a Script's Progress Using Dialog Boxes

One of the basic forms of debugging is to use the `display dialog` command. All you do is display a dialog box showing the value in question.

The `display dialog` command is best for debugging string values or values that can be coerced into strings, such as numbers, Booleans, and dates. If you are dealing with application references, you might be able to get a name or ID, or some other piece of identifying information, from the object being referenced.

> **TIP:** If you can convert values to text for displaying in dialog boxes, don't forget that you can write them out to log files as well for a more permanent record of your script's activity. See Chapters 15, 17, and 19 for more advice and suggestions on logging messages to file.

Using the Event Log

As you know from Chapter 4, you can use a script window's Event Log tab to view all the commands sent to scriptable applications and scripting additions, along with any values or errors that are sent back. Just click the tab's Events and Replies buttons to show and hide this information.

The Event Log can be especially useful when debugging code that deals with scriptable applications and scripting additions, because you can see exactly what information is being sent and received by your script.

So far, so good—but did you know that you can also use the Event Log to record your own debugging messages as well? To do this, you use the `log` command. The `log` command will take almost any value as its direct parameter and display it in the Event Log as a comment, like this: (* *some value* *). The value is wrapped in a comment because anything that appears in the Event Log is actually legally compiled AppleScript code.

The `log` command displays objects in human-readable rather than literal form, so some syntactic details such as quote marks and braces are not shown. This is fine for general text messages, although it's not ideal if you want to inspect the value in its original form. Once again, it's a limitation you'll have to live with if you develop and test scripts in AppleScript Editor.

Figure 29–2 shows the Event Log in action.

Figure 29–2. *AppleScript Editor's Event Log displays messages logged by the script as well as commands sent to applications and scripting additions.*

> **TIP:** Normally the log messages are mixed in with all the other events, but if you click the Events button so that it displays all events and then click it again, everything except the log messages will be hidden, making them far easier to read.

You can also use AppleScript Editor's Event Log History window (**Window ➤ Event Log History**) to keep a record of all the Apple events and `log` commands that your script sends across several runs.

Debugging in Script Debugger

As mentioned, Script Debugger is the best debugging tool for AppleScript. If you own Script Debugger, then check the following sections out for a few debugging how-tos; if you don't own it, read on and consider getting it.

To debug with Script Debugger, you switch to a special debugging mode called AppleScript Debugger X. This mode is similar to AppleScript in any respect having to do with running the scripts, but you have to switch back to normal AppleScript mode before deploying your script in any way.

To switch to debugging mode in Script Debugger, choose **Script ➤ Enable Debugging**.

Using the *start log* and *stop log* Commands

If you're using Script Debugger, you have two more commands at your disposal: `start log` and `stop log`. These two commands will start and stop logging to the Apple Event Log panel. For these commands to work, the Apple Event Log panel must be open (**Window ➤ Apple Event Log**).

When you want to log only specific statements or parts of your script, you can add a `start log` line before the part you want to log and a `stop log` line after that part. Since the log starts automatically when the Event Log panel is open, you may want to start your script with the `stop log` command. To use these commands inside an application `tell` block, make sure you direct them to the current script, not the target application, like this:

```
stop log
tell application "AppName"
    -- Some commands...
    tell me to start log
    -- The commands to monitor...
    tell me to stop log
    -- More commands...
end tell
```

Using the Script Window

The most notable part of the Script Debugger script window is the Result drawer, shown at the right of the window in Figure 29–3. This drawer shows all the script's properties, global variables, top-level variables, declared local variables, and their values. To open and close the drawer, click the Show/Hide Result button in the window toolbar.

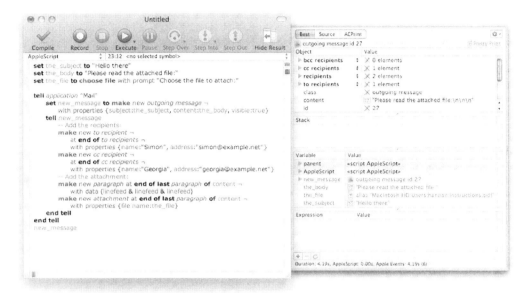

Figure 29–3. *Script Debugger's script window with the Result drawer open*

The little icon to the left of each value indicates its class. Unicode text has a square containing the letters "UTF XVI" (UTF-16) next to it, application references show the application's icon, alias and file objects are indicated by the file's icon, and so on.

This properties and variables list is great when you want a glimpse of the script's current state. The result of the last line to execute is displayed in the Result area at the top of the Result drawer; in this example, `outgoing message id 27` of Mail. You'll also notice that the drawer lets you inspect the current properties and elements of application objects—a highly helpful feature!

Using the Debugging Mode

Next, you will convert the example script to AppleScript debugger language. You do that by choosing **Script ▶ Enable Debugging**. When the script is in debugging mode, the Result drawer displays debugging-related information.

The most notable addition to the main scripting window is a row of diamonds to the left of the script. Each diamond represents a potential breakpoint next to a line of code. Clicking that diamond turns it red, which indicates that the script should stop at this line the next time it runs. The script's "playback head," shown as a blue arrow, stops at the line with the breakpoint before this line is executed.

Figure 29–4 shows Script Debugger's script window in debugging mode.

Figure 29–4. *Script Debugger's script window in debugging mode*

The Stack section of the Result drawer now shows a list of handler calls. When the playback head is stopped inside a handler, that handler is selected in the list and all of its variables appear in the property area to the right.

By default, undeclared local variables do not appear in the list. If you want to examine the values of local variables, you have to declare them as local variables at the top of the handler definition. After doing so, these declared local variables and their values will appear in the yellow-shaded area in the Variable section of the Result drawer.

Stepping Through Scripts

When in debugging mode, Script Debugger allows you to perform five additional script navigation actions besides the usual Execute and Stop. The actions are Pause, Step Over, Step Into, Step Out, and Resume, and are available as menu items in the Script menu and as buttons on the window toolbar.

The Pause option (z+ +period) is good when you want to pause a long-running script just to see where you are, although you can't use this command to pause at an exact point.

Stepping is really where things heat up. The Step Into (z+I) and Step Over (z+Y) actions allow you to execute one line of script at a time. The difference is that Step Into will go into handler calls and step through every line there, whereas Step Over will skip the handler call and move right to the next line.

The Step Out action is handy if you stepped into a handler but want to get out of it.

Once you have finished inspecting the script's state at a particular breakpoint, click the Resume button (z+R) to proceed to the next one.

As the script runs, the blue arrow at the left of the script will always show you where you are, and the Result area at the top of the Result drawer will always show you the result returned from the previous line the script executed.

Keeping Track of Changes

It is said that there are two certainties in life: death and taxes. To this list, I would add a third: any time you write some code, sooner or later you will want to change it.

In Chapter 4 we took a quick look at AppleScript Editor's Event Log History window, which not only allows you to view all of the Apple events sent by a script, but also allows you to view earlier versions of the script itself, just by selecting its name in the left pane and clicking the Show Script button in the window's toolbar.

Although the Event Log History window can be very useful for tracking the changes you make to a script during a single editing session, you may also need to review and compare changes over a much longer period. Let's take a quick look at a couple of more advanced options that are open to you.

Comparing Scripts with FileMerge

One of my favorite coding tools is FileMerge, a text file comparison tool included in Apple's Xcode Developer Tools suite. The FileMerge application provides a very nice GUI for identifying and resolving all of the differences between two scripts—ideal if you need to recombine two slightly different versions of the same script, or compare an older version against a newer one to see what's changed. Figure 29–5 shows FileMerge in action.

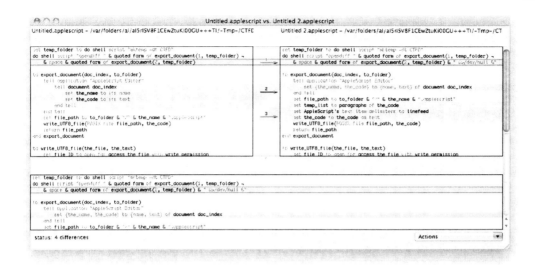

Figure 29–5. *Using FileMerge to compare two different versions of a script*

> **NOTE:** If you don't already have Apple's Developer Tools on your Mac, you can download the latest Xcode installer from Apple's web site (http://developer.apple.com/mac/) or use the copy that's included on your Mac OS X installation disk. You'll also use Apple's Developer Tools in Chapter 30 when you learn how to develop GUI applications using Xcode and the powerful new AppleScriptObjC bridge.

FileMerge is not AppleScriptable, but it does come with opendiff, a command-line tool for opening plain text files in FileMerge. Of course, most AppleScripters prefer to save their scripts in binary .scpt format, making comparisons of AppleScript files a bit more of a challenge, but nothing we can't solve for ourselves.

Script 29–1 uses a combination of AppleScript and Unix scripting features to compare the contents of the front two AppleScript Editor documents in FileMerge.

Script 29–1.

```
1. set temp_folder to do shell script "mktemp -dt CTFD"
2. do shell script "opendiff " & quoted form of export_document(1, temp_folder) ¬
        & space & quoted form of export_document(2, temp_folder) & " &>/dev/null &"

3. to export_document(doc_index, to_folder)
4.     tell application "AppleScript Editor"
5.         set {the_name, the_code} to {name, text} of document doc_index
6.     end tell
7.     set file_path to to_folder & "/" & the_name & ".applescript"
8.     set temp_list to paragraphs of the_code
9.     set AppleScript's text item delimiters to linefeed
10.    set the_code to the_code as text
11.    write_UTF8_file(POSIX file file_path, the_code)
```

```
12.    return file_path
13. end export_document

14. to write_UTF8_file(the_file, the_text)
15.    set file_ID to open for access the_file with write permission
16.    set eof file_ID to 0
17.    write «data rdatEFBBBF» to file_ID
18.    write the_text to file_ID as «class utf8»
19.    close access file_ID
20. end write_UTF8_file
```

The code is mostly straightforward but it does include several interesting details, so let's look at how it works.

As you can see, Script 29–1 contains two handlers, export_document and write_UTF8_file, followed by a do shell script command that calls the opendiff command. Some of the code comes from Chapter 27, though it has been modified a bit to meet our requirements here.

The first thing to notice is that the opendiff command on line 2 takes two arguments: the paths to the files to compare. As the AppleScript Editor documents may be unsaved, or saved in compiled form, we will have to create our own temporary text files for the task. Since there is more than one AppleScript Editor document to export, we define our own command, export_document, to do the job.

To avoid making a mess, we will write both of these files to a temporary folder, which we create on line 1 using the mktemp shell command, previously covered in Chapter 27. (Incidentally, this script doesn't delete the temporary folder once it's done, so you might want to add your own code for that later.)

Lines 3 to 13 define the handler for our custom export_document command. The handler takes two parameters: the index of the desired document element, and a POSIX path string to the output folder.

Line 5 sends two get commands to AppleScript Editor, one to get the document's name, which we'll use as part of the temporary file name, and one to get the document's code. By performing two assignments using the same set statement on line 3, I've kept the code nice and compact, but you can split it into two separate lines if you find it easier to read.

Line 7 assembles the full POSIX path to the temporary .applescript file.

During testing, I found that FileMerge doesn't recognize return (ASCII 13) characters as line breaks, so lines 8 to 10 use AppleScript string manipulation to convert any return characters to Unix-style linefeeds instead. If you want to tidy this code a bit, you could move these lines into their own reusable use_Unix_line_breaks handler later on.

Line 11 then writes the file to disk using a modified version of the write_UTF8_file handler from Chapter 27. The one difference in this handler is that line 17 adds a UTF-8 Byte Order Mark (hexadecimal code EFBBBF). The first time I tried to compare two scripts containing non-ASCII characters, FileMerge read them using my primary encoding, causing those characters to appear as nonsense. Adding the UTF-8 BOM ensures that FileMerge knows the file contains UTF-8 encoded data.

Lastly, notice the final part of the shell script on line 2: " &>/dev/null &". This was another late addition, and is basically the shell script equivalent of an `ignoring application responses ... end ignoring` block.

Originally, I saved the script as `Compare Front Two Documents.scpt` in `/Library/Scripts/Script Editor Scripts`, allowing them to be run from either the system-wide Script menu or from AppleScript Editor's context menu. However, when running it from the context menu, I found AppleScript Editor would act strangely, often becoming unresponsive. With a little testing. I found that the `do shell script` command on line 2 didn't return straightaway, so I modified my shell script to allow it to return without waiting for the `opendiff` command to complete.

First, the `&>` operation redirects the `opendiff` command's `stdout` and `stderr` so that the `do shell script` does not wait for them. If necessary, I could direct them to additional temporary files for later examination, but this script doesn't need them, so I've just redirected them to `/dev/null`, which is a special Unix file that ignores anything written to it. Second, the lone ampersand at the end of the line "detaches" the shell script process so that it runs completely independently of the process that launched it (in this case, AppleScript Editor). This allows the `do shell script` command to return while the `opendiff` command is still running, allowing the AppleScript to finish without any more delay.

> **NOTE:** The FileMerge application will warn you when opening files that contain any non-ASCII characters, just in case you have accidentally asked it to compare image, audio, or other nontext files. However, it will understand UTF-8 encoded files as long as they start with the correct BOM (line 17), so just click the Proceed Anyway button to continue as normal.

Managing Your Code with Source Control

One of the great innovations in the world of software development has been the introduction of powerful, free source control systems, allowing developers to track and organize the changes they make to their project files over time. Although using a source control system to store quick-and-dirty utility scripts would be overkill, if you develop large commercial workflows, then investigating them further may be worth your time.

For example, I use the Mercurial source control system (http://mercurial.selenic.com) to look after my larger Xcode-based projects. Xcode also provides built-in support for several server-based source control systems, but I prefer Mercurial for one-man projects because it is quick and easy to set up for stand-alone use on a single machine. With the aid of a good GUI-based client such as Murky (http://bitbucket.org/snej/murky), checking in changes is quick and easy, and if I later need to retrieve an older version of a file, I can easily do so. It also encourages me to add comments describing what changes I've made each time.

A longer discussion of source control systems is beyond the scope of this book, but you can find plenty of articles and documentation online and in print, plus lots of existing users who can provide advice and assistance.

Improving the Performance of Your Code

John Thorsen, of AppleScript training company TECSoft (http://www.tecsoft.com), claims that the value AppleScript automation adds to any workflow is so drastic that the actual speed in which the script runs doesn't really matter. After all, does it really matter whether the process that used to take 3 hours now takes 20 seconds or 30 seconds?

Although this is true, some scripts do need to perform as fast as possible, because after a while, people start comparing how fast they are in relation to other scripts, not how fast the manual process was. People forget quickly...

The following sections explore some of the principles and practices you should consider when trying to speed up your scripts.

The Dos and Don'ts of Optimization

When it comes to performance-tuning your code, nothing expresses the challenges and pitfalls that await you better than the following quote:

> *"We should forget about small efficiencies, say about 97 percent of the time: premature optimization is the root of all evil."*

> —Donald Knuth

To put it another way, if you dive into your code without a clear plan of action, the likely outcome is that you'll spend a lot of time fiddling with minor details that make little difference to your overall running time, while messing up the original design and introducing new bugs.

If you want to optimize your code *effectively*, you should follow these three rules:

- Don't try to optimize a script unless you know for certain that it actually needs optimized.

- If optimization is required, don't start modifying the code until you have identified exactly where the main bottlenecks lie.

- Once you have identified the biggest bottlenecks, don't change any more than is necessary to achieve the level of performance that is required.

However, before you even think of optimizing *at all*, make sure that your code is reasonably well structured and thoroughly debugged and tested. There is little point in trying to fine-tune code that is a mess, and even less point if it doesn't actually work! So keep your priorities in order: *make it work*, *make it right*, and then, only if you need to, *make it fast*.

When Should You Optimize?

Determining if a script needs to be optimized is relatively simple. Just ask yourself: "Is it fast enough?" If the answer is "yes," then your job is already done. Only if the script is too slow in its current form should you consider trying to make it faster.

The reason you should resist the temptation to optimize a script that doesn't need optimizing is also fairly simple: you've already written and tested the code, and it does the job it was designed to do. Even if a workflow script takes an hour to complete a job, that may not be a problem if you don't need the results urgently, in which case you can just run it during a lunch break or overnight.

As soon as you start trying to make your code faster, you're going to use up time that could have been spent doing something else instead, and you run the risk of introducing fresh bugs into code that was previously working perfectly.

There are other challenges too. If the code works but is a bit messy, you will probably need to spend time cleaning it up first, because poorly organized code is harder to optimize effectively than well-structured code, for much the same reasons that it is harder to test and debug, too. And depending on how aggressively you have to optimize, your code may not be as simple or cleanly structured by the time you're done, making it harder to maintain and update the script in the future.

Where Should You Optimize?

Okay, so now you're aware of the potential pitfalls of optimizing your code and have determined that, yes, your script really does need to run faster. What next? Well, before you start making any changes, it is essential that you identify where the major bottlenecks actually lie.

While you may have a hunch as to what is causing the slowdown, don't dive in until you have checked that you are right. It is all too easy to end up tinkering with a piece of code that is obviously inefficient in design—but if that code is only called once or twice in your script, then it may well be that it only contributes a very small part of the total running time.

In business and other fields, there is a rule of thumb known as the Pareto Principle which states that roughly 20 percent of an activity is responsible for 80 percent of the outcome. The programmer's version of this observation, which is also known as the 80/20 rule, states that perhaps 20 percent of the code in a computer program is responsible for 80 percent of the execution time. For instance, a setup handler that prepares the script at the beginning of a large batch processing job might take 5 seconds to run, but because it only runs once, it probably isn't part of the 20 percent of performance-critical code. On the other hand, a handler that is called from within a deeply nested series of job processing loops might take only half a second to execute, but if it is called a 1,000 times, then it consume 500 seconds!

Of course, even after you do identify the 20 percent of your code in which 80 percent of your running time is spent, there is no guarantee that you will be able to reduce the time that code takes to run. But it should always be the point at which you start looking for improvements. Don't be tempted to mess with the 5-second startup routine unless you have managed to eliminate that 500-second bottleneck first. Even if you cut the startup time by half, you will only have made your script 1 percent faster—an insignificant difference in running time, and probably only a fraction of the time it took you to design, test, debug, and test again. Not a very effective way to save time!

There are two tools you can use to identify potential bottlenecks: performance profiling and big O notation. Big O notation is an advanced topic that involves a fair bit of theory, so we'll cover it later in the chapter. For now, let's discuss how to identify bottlenecks using practical measurement techniques.

Profiling Your Code with Timing Commands

The practical way to identify performance bottlenecks is simply to time how long various sections of your code take to execute. There are a couple of scripting addition commands that you can use to do this: Standard Additions' current date command and the AMTime command found in the AppleMods Tools scripting addition on the AppleMods web site (http://applemods.sourceforge.net).

Timing code is easy. At the point in your script where the "stopwatch" should start, add a line like this:

```
set start_time to current date
```

Then, at the end of the timed task, use this line:

```
set time_taken to (current date) - start_time
```

One advantage of using the current date command is that you can leave that code in the script even if you distribute it to other users—handy if you need to get feedback on how well it is performing for them. The big downside is that the current date command only measures time to the nearest second. If you are profiling a handler that, say, takes half a second to run, you will need to compensate for the limited accuracy of your timing command. A good solution is to call your handler perhaps 10 or 100 times in a row, like this:

```
set start_time to current date
repeat 10 times
    do_something()
end repeat
set time_taken to ((current date) - start_time) / 10
```

Another advantage of timing your code over a series of runs is that it averages out any random variations. For example, if you run the handler once and it takes over a second, that might just be because another running application chose that moment to hog the hard disk or something. Averaging out a whole series of runs will give you a more accurate measurement.

If you find current date to be too imprecise, the AMTime command provides the current time in milliseconds rather than seconds. This doesn't mean that you can reliably measure an operation that only takes one or two milliseconds—once again, the amount of "background noise" due to other activities on your Mac will be significantly greater—but measuring to the nearest tenth of a second should be pretty trustworthy.

One more thing: when profiling routines that deal with varying amounts of data—for example, a handler that loops over a folder full of files or a list sorting routine—make sure you take measurements using different quantities and types of data.

For example, consider the bubble sort routine from Chapter 10. You might assume that sorting a 1,000-item list would take ten times as long as sorting a 100-item list...but does it? The only way to find out for sure is to run timing tests for both and compare the results. In addition, you might use a list of numbers in mostly ascending order as a convenient test value, as it is quick and easy to generate. You would also be surprised at just how speedy your handler sorts it—but is that a true reflection of its performance? Try it with a truly random list, and you may be surprised by the difference.

We will touch on the topic of efficiency a bit more in the remainder of this chapter, but let's now move away from the theory to look at some practical optimizations you can use in your code.

Common AppleScript Optimizations

While some of the bottlenecks you discover may be unique to a particular script, others seem to pop up quite often. The following sections look at simple design improvements that can help speed up your code in these common cases:

- Building up large lists one item at a time
- Building up large strings one piece at a time
- Manipulating multiple application objects with a single command
- Filtering multiple application objects with whose clause references

> **TIP:** In the "Advanced Optimization Techniques" section later in the chapter, we will also look at a clever, if ugly, code trick for improving performance when manipulating AppleScript lists, along with more efficient routines for searching and sorting large lists. You can use these routines in your own scripts even if you aren't interested in learning how they work.

Building Up Large Lists

When you have a list to which you want to add an item at the end, you can do so in two ways.

One option is to concatenate the existing list and the new item, like this:

```
set the_list to the_list & {the_item}
```

The other option is to insert the new item at the end of the existing list:

```
set end of the_list to the_item
```

Since adding items to a list often happens many times inside a repeat loop, you should consider how this might affect your script's performance.

Script 29–2 uses the AMTime command to measure how long it takes to assemble a 10,000-item list using each technique.

Script 29–2.

```
-- List concatenation test
set t to AMTime
set the_list to {}
repeat with i from 1 to 10000
    set the_list to the_list & {i}
end repeat
set t1 to (AMTime) - t
-- List appending test
set t to AMTime
set the_list to {}
repeat with i from 1 to 10000
    set end of the_list to i
end repeat
set t2 to (AMTime) - t
-- Compare the results
"concatenating=" & t1 & ", appending=" & t2
--> "concatenating=6.234330892563, appending=0.049731016159"
```

Try running the same script for 100- and 1,000-item lists. (I don't recommend attempting 100,000-item lists, though, because you may be waiting for a *very* long time!) Run each test several times, just to make sure that the results you get each time are roughly average.

As you can see, appending to an existing list takes very little time compared to concatenating a value to form a new list each time. Using the concatenation approach, 100 items takes perhaps 1ms, 1,000 items takes 60ms, and 10,000 items takes a very noticeable 6,000ms—definitely not linear behavior. When the values are appended, the timings look more like this: 0.7ms, 3ms, and 50ms, respectively. Okay, so it's still not exactly a linear increase (AppleScript has to do a bit of internal magic in order to grow the list structure), but it's a lot closer.

Clearly, if you are going to be building small lists of 100 items or fewer, there is no significant difference and either approach will do. However, as the lists become larger, the performance gap rapidly widens and using the more efficient appending technique really pays off. Therefore, you should generally use the list appending technique.

Building Up Large Strings

You can see a similar effect when building up large strings. Generally, when you assemble a string from smaller strings, you use the & operator to concatenate two strings at a time to form a longer string. In a repeat loop, it looks something like this:

```
set the_string to ""
repeat until is_done
```

```
    -- Do some stuff...
    set the_string to the_string & new_text
end repeat
```

Each time the loop repeats, AppleScript creates a new string by copying the contents of two strings to a new location in memory. This code is simple and works well enough for small numbers of items. However, if the final string you're generating is very large, all that internal copying will start to have a noticeable impact on your script's performance. If this is the case, you may want to modify the script so that it adds all the strings to a long list and then coerces the final list into one big string, like this:

```
set temp_list to {}
repeat until is_done
    -- Do some stuff...
    set end of temp_list to new_text
end repeat
set AppleScript's text item delimiters to ""
set the_string to temp_list as text
```

Now AppleScript only has to copy each of the original strings once when it assembles the finished string in the last line. Try running your own timing experiments to see how the two approaches compare. Script 29–3 provides some rough code. Try using different sizes of strings for s—say, 1, 10, 100, and 1,000 characters—and different values of n—10, 100, 1,000, and 10,000. (As you gather the results for smaller combinations, you might want to think twice before trying to copy 1,000 characters 10,000 times, or you may have quite a wait!)

Script 29–3.

```
set s to "1234567890"
set n to 10000

set t to AMTime
set the_string to ""
repeat n times
    set the_string to the_string & s
end repeat
set t1 to (AMTime) - t

set t to AMTime
set temp_list to {}
repeat n times
    set end of temp_list to s
end repeat
set AppleScript's text item delimiters to ""
set the_string to temp_list as text
set t2 to (AMTime) - t

"concatenating=" & t1 & ", appending=" & t2
```

In my own tests, for example, I saw that the appending approach was noticeably quicker throughout, but the difference didn't become really significant until I tried to copy a 100-character string 10,000 times: all of a sudden, the concatenation approach jumped to a whopping 30 seconds, while the list appending technique still came in at under a tenth of a second.

The downside of this new code is that it is more complicated than the first version, which is why it is better to avoid making this sort of optimization unless you know that it will make a significant difference to the performance of your script.

Manipulating Multiple Application Objects with a Single Command

Interacting with applications slows AppleScript down. Although you can't eliminate this interaction altogether, you can try to limit it. As a rough rule of thumb, if you have a large number of objects to process, you want the application to do as much work as possible using the fewest commands. Fortunately, one of the most impressive capabilities found in many scriptable applications is that they allow you to apply a single command to multiple objects.

To take advantage of this feature, you create a single multiobject reference that identifies all the objects you want the command to operate on. This is much more efficient than getting a list of references to the individual objects, looping over the list, and applying the same command to each object in turn.

You can use three sorts of multiobject reference: those that identify all the elements of an object, those that identify a range of elements, and those that identify all the elements that match certain conditions (otherwise known as the whose clause). Some application commands are better than others at dealing with these sorts of complex references, but it's always worth a go, especially when you know you have a lot of objects to process. It helps to make your code shorter and simpler too.

For example, to get the name, artist, album, and playing time of every track in iTunes' main library playlist, you could write the following:

```
set track_info_list to {}
tell application "iTunes"
   set track_list to every track of library playlist 1
   repeat with track_ref in track_list
      set end of track_info_list to {name, artist, album, time} of track_ref
   end repeat
end tell
track_info_list
--> {{"Army Of Me", "Björk", "Post", "3:54"},
     {"Hyper-Ballad", "Björk", "Post", "5:21"},
     {"The Modern Things", "Björk", "Post", "4:10"}, ...}
```

The problem here is that to fetch all of this information, the script is sending four get commands per track, plus an initial get command to retrieve a large list of track references. If your iTunes library contains thousands of tracks, the time it takes for AppleScript and iTunes to process all of these get commands will really add up— meaning a "simple" script like this could easily take several minutes to run.

To improve performance, it is necessary to reduce the number of get commands being sent by your script. The following script will perform the same task far more quickly since it uses four get commands in total, regardless of how many tracks there are:

```
tell application "iTunes"
   tell every track of library playlist 1
```

```
      set name_list to name
      set artist_list to artist
      set album_list to album
      set time_list to time
   end tell
end tell
{name_list, artist_list, album_list, time_list}
--> {{"Army Of Me", "Hyper-Ballad", "The Modern Things", ...},
     {"Björk", "Björk", "Björk", ...},
     {"Post", "Post", "Post", ...},
     {"3:54", "5:21", "4:10", "3:38", ...}}
```

The only difference is that instead of being arranged by track, the track information is grouped according to property.

All you need to do now is process the contents of these lists—although, as we'll discuss later in the "Improving the Efficiency of AppleScript Lists" section, looping over large AppleScript lists has a few performance problems of its own.

Filtering Multiple Application Objects with whose Clause References

Earlier chapters have also demonstrated the value of using the whose clause when filtering objects in applications, but it is such a valuable feature that it bears repeating. Using the whose clause instead of looping through objects and testing each one yourself in AppleScript can add a real time boost to the script execution, especially when dealing with application commands that can accept these multiobject references directly.

The following script retrieves a list of track references from iTunes and then loops over it, duplicating each track whose artist is "Björk" to a newly created playlist:

```
tell application "iTunes"
   set new_playlist to make new playlist with properties {name:"Björk"}
   set track_list to every track of library playlist 1
   repeat with track_ref in track_list
      if artist of track_ref is "Björk" then
         duplicate track_ref to new_playlist
      end if
   end repeat
end tell
```

This works, but if the list of tracks is large, it may take some time to process since the script sends one get command for each track in the playlist. It also sends a duplicate command for each track that matches the test condition, though this will only make a noticeable difference if a large number of matches are found.

To achieve the same result in less time—and less code—use the following code instead:

```
tell application "iTunes"
   set new_playlist to make new playlist with properties {name:"Björk"}
   duplicate (every track of library playlist 1 whose artist is "Björk") ¬
         to new_playlist
end tell
```

Not only have you saved yourself from testing each artist name in AppleScript, you've also reduced the entire operation to one make command and one duplicate command in total.

Of course, there are limits to what you can do with whose clauses, and even where a whose clause appears valid, some applications are better than others at resolving complex references. For instance, consider the following script:

```
tell application "iTunes"
    set new_playlist to make new playlist with properties {name:"Björk 2"}
    duplicate (every track of library playlist 1 ¬
        whose album is in {"Post", "Vespertine", "Volta"}) to new_playlist
end tell
```

This code looks fine; unfortunately, when you try to run it, iTunes doesn't like it very much:

```
error "iTunes got an error: Handler only handles single objects." number -10014
```

Alas, it looks like we just exceeded the capabilities of iTunes' scripting interface. All is not lost, however; we can still minimize the number of application commands being sent if we retrieve all of the values being tested in advance and loop over them in AppleScript:

```
tell application "iTunes"
    set new_playlist to make new playlist with properties {name:"Björk 2"}
    set album_list to album of every track of library playlist 1
    set track_list to every track of library playlist 1
    repeat with i from 1 to length of album_list
        if item i of album_list is in {"Post", "Vespertine", "Volta"} then
            duplicate item i of track_list to new_playlist
        end if
    end repeat
end tell
```

This time, we send two get commands—one to retrieve all the album names, the other to get a list of the corresponding track references. The repeat loop counts over the album name list, and each time a match is found, it sends a duplicate command containing the corresponding track reference to iTunes. Although this takes a bit more time and code to perform, it gives us the result we want while keeping the number of commands being sent to a minimum.

Advanced Optimization Techniques

To finish our discussion of efficient optimization techniques, we will now look at big O notation, which is one of the more sophisticated theoretical tools that professional software developers often use to assess the overall efficiency of their code and identify likely performance black spots.

Of course, the key word here is "efficient," so if your scripts are already fast enough, you can optimize the use of your own time by skipping over the theory and just stealing the practical pieces of code from the following sections! The two most useful items are the script object trick for improving performance when looping over large lists, and the quicksort handler, which provides much better performance when sorting lists compared to the bubblesort handler we looked at in Chapter 10.

Later on, if you need to improve your understanding of efficiency and big O notation in order to optimize your own code effectively, you can always come back here and work through the text in more detail.

Assessing Your Code's Efficiency with Big O Notation

When optimizing code, there are two things to consider: speed and efficiency. You might think these are the same thing, but they are not.

Speed is simply how fast your code runs when performing a certain task. For example, a Finder script that processes 100 files might take 10 seconds. Efficiency, on the other hand, tells you how fast the script will run in comparison when it is fed 1, 10, 1,000, or 10,000 files instead. For example, you might assume the same script would take 1 second to process 10 files and 100 seconds to process 1,000 files. It's a logical guess, but is it actually correct?

The answer is: it depends. Some scripts may indeed behave this way, while others may perform very differently. For instance, some scripts might always take roughly 10 seconds, regardless of how many files they process. Others could take a lot less than 1 second to process 10 files, and spend absolutely ages working their way through 1,000 files. To help them understand what is going on here, professional software developers often use a "pen and paper" programming tool known as big O notation.

Strictly speaking, understanding big O is a bit outside the scope of this book, but I know you like your scripts to run fast, and so do I—so let's have a quick look at how it works.

The goal of big O is simple: to work out how well your script will perform under increasing amounts of load. To do this, you identify any structures that are directly affected when the *number* of items being processed changes, ignoring everything else. For our purposes, this mostly means identifying any repeat statements or recursive handler calls in your code that loop over lists of arbitrary length. It is these loops that primarily determine the efficiency of your script. To help you understand this, let's look at some examples.

First, consider a script without any repeat statements in it. For instance, Script 29–4 uses a single get command to retrieve the names of all the files in a Finder folder. This command will take roughly the same amount of time whether there is 1 file or 100.

Script 29–4.

```
tell application "Finder"
   get name of every file of folder "Macintosh HD:Users:hanaan:src:"
end tell
```

The Finder, of course, may take longer to process the command for 100 files, since it has its own performance characteristics, but we'll ignore that here because what the Finder does internally is beyond our control; all we're interested in here is how well our own code performs.

Now consider Script 29–5.

Script 29–5.

```
set file_names to {}
tell application "Finder"
   set the_files to every file of folder "Macintosh HD:Users:hanaan:src:"
   repeat with file_ref in the_files
      set end of file_names to name of file_ref
   end repeat
end tell
return file_names
```

This time we have a repeat statement in the middle of the script that loops over a list. Not every repeat block is significant—if the list is of a fixed length, then the time it takes to execute will not vary, so we ignore it. In this case, though, the list could be any length, so this loop will definitely take longer to run as the list grows larger.

Script 29–4 is said to run in *constant* time, since it takes (roughly) the same amount of time in all situations. By comparison, Script 29–5 is described as having *linear* efficiency: if it takes N milliseconds to loop over 1 file, it will take 10N milliseconds to loop over 10 files, 100N milliseconds to loop over 100 files, and so on.

> **CAUTION:** I have simplified this example on paper to make it easy to understand. In fact, AppleScript lists throw a fly in the ointment that means looping over a list has worse than linear efficiency. We will discuss this problem in the next section, and how to work around it.

Let's now describe the performance characteristics of these two scripts in big O notation. Basically, big O is written as $O(...)$, where the bit in the middle expresses its efficiency. Constant efficiency is expressed simply as $O(1)$. Linear efficiency is written as $O(n)$, where n stands for the number of items being processed by the main loop.

Let's consider a few more examples. First, suppose there are two loops, one inside the other:

```
repeat with x in list_1
   repeat with y in list_2
   end repeat
end repeat
```

If both lists are fixed size, we ignore them both—that is, constant, or $O(1)$, efficiency. If one list varies in size, we have linear, or $O(n)$, efficiency.

Another common case is *quadratic* efficiency. For instance, the bubble sort routine in Chapter 10 (Script 10-4) uses two nested repeat blocks to process a single list of variable size. The inner block counts over each item in the list, swapping it with its neighbor if necessary. The outer block keeps looping until no more items need swapped. In big O notation, this is expressed as $O(n*n)$, or $O(n^2)$. If the number of items in the list doubles, then the processing time typically becomes four times as long (2^2). Of course, there may be exceptions: if you pass an already sorted list to a bubble sort routine, it will only loop over it once, detect that all items are already in ascending order, and return immediately after (linear performance). However, when assessing the efficiency of a routine, we are really only interested in typical behavior, so we ignore this sort of corner case on the basis that in everyday use most lists being sorted will be in pretty random order.

Figure 29–6 shows how constant, linear, and quadratic performance profiles compare. As you can see, some approaches scale better than others!

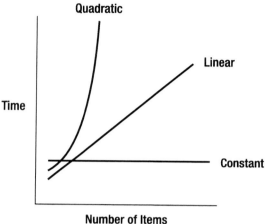

Figure 29–6. *Comparing constant, linear, and quadratic efficiency*

At this point, there is still a lot to learn about big O notation and measuring efficiency. While a comprehensive guide is beyond the scope of this book, hopefully this section has given you some appreciation of the design factors that affect the efficiency of your code and how to assess those factors in broad terms. Combined with a good timing tool such as the AMTime command, you will be much better equipped to identify and rework grossly inefficient logic in areas where it is a problem. For instance, if timing tests point toward a central handler with $O(n^2)$ efficiency as the main culprit, perhaps you can look for ways to turn it into an $O(n)$ routine, or something in between.

Improving the Efficiency of AppleScript Lists

If you have worked with AppleScript lists for a while, you may have noticed that their performance when getting and setting list items is not exactly impressive. In particular, the time it takes to get or set a list item seems to increase as the list itself gets longer. This time, though, don't feel bad: it's nothing to do with your code. The problem lies within the AppleScript interpreter itself.

Unfortunately, as many experienced AppleScript users have discovered, the way in which the AppleScript interpreter implements list object behaviors is somewhat flawed. In theory, looking up a list item should take a constant amount of time, regardless of the list's length: just take the item index and jump directly to that position in the list. (If you are really curious, the technical term for this type of list is *vector*.) Unfortunately, a quick test shows this is not what happens in practice. Take a look at the performance profiling code in Script 29–6, and the typical result that it produces when run.

Script 29–6.

```
on run
    set my_list to {1, 2, 3, 4, 5, 6, 7, 8, 9, 0}
    set lookup_times to {}
    repeat 16 times
        set t to AMTime
        repeat 100 times
            get middle item of my_list
        end repeat
        set end of lookup_times to round (((AMTime) - t) * 1000)
        set my_list to my_list & my_list -- Double the size of the list
    end repeat
    lookup_times
end run
--> {1, 0, 1, 1, 1, 2, 4, 8, 15, 30, 60, 120, 240, 480, 959, 1917}
```

Script 29–6 starts by setting up a ten-item list that will double in length each time the loop repeats. In the middle of the loop, we look up the middle item of the list (when testing this yourself, also try getting the first and last items, just to see if that makes a difference). The item lookup is surrounded by timing code that measures the time it takes to do 100 of these lookups. Since a single lookup should be very quick, we repeat it a fixed number of times to give us a larger time to measure, making our timing results more reliable and less prone to influence by any random factors.

In theory, no matter how long the list is, the lookup time should be the same every time, but when we look at the results, we see that the time it takes to get the list item grows twice as large each time we double the size of the list—a linear increase, in other words, or $O(n)$ efficiency. So if, for example, we were writing a script to loop over a variable number of items in a list, we would see the time it takes increase quadratically compared to the number of items in the list, or $O(n*n)$. Ouch! That could really start to bite if you have, say, several thousand items to get through, perhaps even becoming the major performance bottleneck in your code.

Fortunately, there is a "solution" of sorts that tricks AppleScript lists into performing constant-time lookups. If you wrap up your list in a script object property and refer to it there (see Script 29–7), something in the way that AppleScript references work causes whatever piece of the interpreter that is causing the slowdown to be bypassed.

Script 29–7.

```
on run
    script FastList
        property my_list : {1, 2, 3, 4, 5, 6, 7, 8, 9, 0}
    end script
    set lookup_times to {}
    repeat 16 times
        set t to AMTime
        repeat 100 times
            get middle item of FastList's my_list
        end repeat
        set end of lookup_times to round (((AMTime) - t) * 1000)
        set FastList's my_list to FastList's my_list & FastList's my_list
    end repeat
    lookup_times
```

```
end run
--> {1, 0, 0, 0, 0, 0, 0, 1, 0, 0, 0, 0, 0, 0, 0, 0}
```

Okay, so the code is really rather ugly now—more complex and easier for bugs to hide in, making it harder to read and maintain—but we've just fixed our performance problem. As to exactly how and why this hack works, I have no idea; only an Apple engineer could tell you that. But on this occasion, I'm just glad it does. For example, if you have a large list you need to loop over, you can modify your code from this,

```
repeat with i from 1 to length of some_list
    -- Do some stuff...
    set an_item to item i of some_list
    -- And more stuff...
    set item i of some_list to new_value
    -- And yet more stuff...
end repeat
```

to this:

```
script FastList
    property fast_list : some_list
end script
repeat with i from 1 to length of FastList's fast_list
    -- Do some stuff...
    set an_item to item i of FastList's fast_list
    -- And more stuff...
    set item i of FastList's fast_list to new_value
    -- And yet more stuff...
end repeat
```

> **CAUTION:** Because the modified code uses a named script object, make sure you put it inside a handler. If you put it at the top level of your script, the AppleScript compiler will see the `script` statement and assume you want the script object created and assigned to the identifier `FastList` when the script is compiled...and promptly throw a compiler error because it cannot find the value of the `some_list` variable to assign to the object's `fast_list` property. Putting the `script` statement inside a handler ensures it is only evaluated at the point at which it is needed.

Obviously, you do not want to use this workaround if you don't have to, but at least the option is there for when you do. (And don't forget to bug Apple to someday fix the problem at source.)

Now that we've discussed an ugly if valuable guerilla optimization, let's balance things out with some civilized examples of list processing algorithms, and see how different designs can provide better (or worse) efficiency.

Linear Search vs. Binary Search

Suppose you have a list of strings and want to find out the position of a given string within that list. The most obvious approach would be to loop over that list, counting the indexes until you find the item you want, and return the index value—that is, a linear search. Script 29–8 shows how you might implement this linear search algorithm in a user-defined handler, offset_of_list_item.

Script 29–8.

```
index_of_item_in_list("Jim", {"Mary", "Al", "Jim", "Sal"})
--> 3

on index_of_item_in_list(the_item, the_list)
    script FastList
        property fast_list : the_list
    end script
    repeat with i from 1 to length of FastList's fast_list
        if item i of FastList's fast_list = the_item then return i
    end repeat
    error "Item not found." number -1728 from the_item
end index_of_item_in_list
```

I've used the script object trick to ensure that the list search code really does have 0(n) efficiency, and provided a simple example of use. Try running some timing tests of your own to see how it performs when, say, searching for the first and last items of 10-, 100-, and 1,000-item lists. You will find that looking up the first item takes almost no time in every case; however, that is the best-case scenario, and when judging the code's efficiency, you need to look at its worst-case behavior. In this case, that means the time it takes to locate an item when it has to go through the entire list. As you will see in your timing tests, the time taken increases at the same rate as the list length grows. Alternatively, if you think about the code in terms of big O notation, you can see that it has a single repeat statement that counts over an arbitrary number of items, which means it has 0(n) efficiency.

Can we improve on this? The answer is: it depends. If the list is completely random, then no, not really. A linear search is the best we can do. On the other hand, if the list happens to be presorted, then yes, we can improve on this.

Consider how you would quickly search a very large book index. You flip it open part way through, see if the words you're at come before or after the word you're looking for, then flip to an earlier or later page accordingly, and so on. We can use the same "divide and conquer" strategy in our code too, minus the guesswork. First, we look at the middle item of the list: if it comes after the string we want, we know our string is in the first half, so then we compare the item at the one-quarter point, and then the item that is either one-eighth or three-eighths of the way through…and so on until we happen to hit on the item we're after. This *binary search* algorithm is much more efficient than the linear one: if the number of items in the list doubles, then at most we only have to perform one additional search step. This is known as *logarithmic* efficiency, or 0(log n), since a graph of size versus time follows a logarithmic curve, as shown in Figure 29–7.

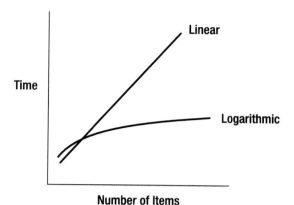

Figure 29–7. *Comparing the performance characteristics of linear and binary searches*

Script 29–9 shows the binary search code itself.

Script 29–9.

```
on index_of_item_in_sorted_list(the_list, the_item)
    -- Caution: this only works on fully sorted lists
    script FastList
        property fast_list : the_list
    end script
    set lo to 0
    set hi to length of FastList's fast_list
    repeat while lo < hi
        set mid to (lo + hi) div 2
        if the_item < FastList's fast_list's item (mid + 1) then
            set hi to mid
        else
            set lo to mid + 1
        end if
    end repeat
    if item lo of FastList's fast_list ≠ the_item then
        error "Item not found." number -1728 from the_item
    end if
    return lo
end index_of_item_in_sorted_list
```

As you can see, the binary search code is significantly more complex than the linear search code. It is not uncommon for the faster algorithm to be more complex than the slower one, simply because it needs to be smarter in how it operates. Still, let's take a quick look at how it works.

The main thing you will notice about this routine is that it defines three new variables: lo, hi, and mid. Remember, the binary search operates by comparing your value against a list item that is halfway between two points. Initially, those two points are the start and the end of the list, but each time the loop repeats, one of those points moves to the previous midpoint, narrowing the gap until the desired item is found. The conditional block in the middle determines if the object you're after comes before or after the current midpoint item, and updates either the lo or hi variable accordingly. Figure 29–8 shows how a typical search might go.

Start	(12, 17, 25, 31, 37, 42, 49, 56, 60, 67, 72, 76, 89, 91, 93, 97)
After 1st loop	(12, 17, 25, 31, 37, 42, 49, 56, 60, 67, 72, 76, 89, 91, 93, 97)
After 2nd loop	(12, 17, 25, 31, 37, 42, 49, 56, 60, 67, 72, 76, 89, 91, 93, 97)
After 3rd loop	(12, 17, 25, 31, 37, 42, 49, 56, 60, 67, 72, 76, 89, 91, 93, 97)
After 4th loop	(12, 17, 25, 31, 37, 42, 49, 56, 60, 67, 72, 76, 89, 91, 93, 97)

Figure 29–8. *Using the divide-and-conquer approach to search a sorted list*

If this still sounds too complicated, don't worry. The nice thing about these kinds of practical algorithms is that many other programmers have already done all the hard work for you. A quick online search for "list search algorithms" should help you to find an existing routine that you can, with a bit of time and work, convert into AppleScript code. Often, the only thing you need to watch out for is that the examples are usually written in languages that use zero-indexed lists, so you need to remember to increase the index number by 1 when using it to identify an item in an AppleScript list (the item (mid + 1) bit in this case).

> **TIP:** If you're lucky, you may find that another AppleScripter has already created an AppleScript version of the algorithm you're looking for, so don't forget to ask around on the AppleScript mailing lists, too.

Bubble Sort vs. Quicksort

Chapter 10 showed you how to sort lists using a simple bubble sort routine, so called because out-of-position items gradually "bubble" along the list until they reach the appropriate positions. Earlier in this chapter we discussed how bubble sort is not very efficient. With two nested loops operating on the same list, we calculate it as having only quadratic, or $O(n^2)$, efficiency. In fact, when we take into account the performance problems of AppleScript lists, we get cubic, or $O(n^3)$, efficiency. This tells us that performance will drop off *very* quickly as the number of list items increases. Using the script object trick in the bubble sort code will give us the expected $O(n^2)$ behavior, but that's still nothing to shout about.

Can we do better? Yes, we can. In fact, list sorting is such a common task that computer scientists have spent decades coming up with all sorts of ingenious algorithms for making the process more efficient. The disadvantage of these improved algorithms is that they also tend to be more complex, which is why bubble sort is often used as a teaching example.

One of the classic list sorting routines is the quicksort algorithm invented by Tony Hoare. Quicksort provides much better performance than bubble sort, yet is still relatively easy to understand. Like the binary search algorithm we looked at earlier, quicksort uses a "divide and conquer" strategy where it splits the original list into smaller and smaller chunks, gradually rearranging it along the way. Script 29–10 shows the basic quicksort routine written in AppleScript.

Script 29–10.

```
1. on quicksort(the_list)
2.     script FastList
3.         property fast_list : the_list
4.     end script
5.     if (count FastList's fast_list) ≤ 1 then
6.         return FastList's fast_list
7.     else
8.         set pivot_index to (count FastList's fast_list) div 2
9.         set pivot_value to item pivot_index of FastList's fast_list
10.        set lesser_list to {}
11.        set greater_list to {}
12.        repeat with range_ref in {¬
               {start_index:1, end_index:pivot_index - 1}, ¬
               {start_index:pivot_index + 1, end_index:count FastList's fast_list}}
13.            repeat with i from start_index of range_ref to end_index of range_ref
14.                set the_item to item i of FastList's fast_list
15.                if the_item ≤ pivot_value then
16.                    set end of lesser_list to the_item
17.                else
18.                    set end of greater_list to the_item
19.                end if
20.            end repeat
21.        end repeat
22.        return quicksort(lesser_list) & {pivot_value} & quicksort(greater_list)
23.    end if
24. end quicksort
```

Using this handler couldn't be simpler. Just pass it a list of numbers, dates, or strings, like this:

```
set the_list to {6, 18, 13, 5, 12, 20, 9, 36, 8, 20, 31, 1, 23}
set sorted_list to quicksort(the_list)
--> {1, 5, 6, 8, 9, 12, 13, 18, 20, 20, 23, 31, 36}
```

As you can see, I have used the script object trick to optimize away the unnecessary extra costs of looping over an AppleScript list. This makes the code slightly harder to read, but is worth doing here as you may want to sort thousands of items at a time. The quicksort algorithm itself runs from lines 5 to 23.

The purpose of lines 5 and 6 should be pretty obvious: eventually the divide-and-conquer strategy will produce a list that contains one or fewer items, so return it straightaway as it requires no further sorting.

If the list contains more than one item, lines 8 to 21 run instead. First, lines 8 and 9 pick a value from the list—the middle item is a decent choice. The goal is to divide the current list into two smaller lists. One list will contain all the items from the original list that are less than or equal to this "pivot" value; the other will contain all the items that are greater than it. On average, each of these lists should contain about half of the original list's items. This is similar to the strategy we used in our binary search: halve the original list, then quarter it, and so on.

Once the two smaller lists have been created, line 22 sorts each list recursively. So, for instance, if you start with a 16-item list, this will be split into two smaller lists of roughly 8 items each. Each of those lists then divides into two 4-item lists, and so on. If you need to sort a 32-item list, then that adds one more level of recursion.

Let's look at this handler in terms of efficiency. As you can see, it contains two repeat statements, one inside the other. The repeat statement starting on line 12 loops over a fixed-length list, so we just ignore that. The loop on lines 13 to 20 counts over a variable-length list, so that is $O(n)$. On top of that, we have recursive calls happening on line 22. Doubling the number of list items adds roughly one more level of recursion, which is logarithmic, or $O(\log n)$, behavior. Since the looping happens inside the recursion, multiplying the two gives us the efficiency of quicksort as a whole: $O(n \log n)$—not as good as $O(n)$ but much better than $O(n^2)$.

In practice, the efficiency of quicksort tends to be a bit less than this, since you only get $O(\log n)$ efficiency on the recursion stage if the two sublists are equally split. If one list is larger than the other, it will take longer to get through. Some quicksort implementations add extra code to try to improve this balancing act, but even a "pure" quicksort design like this one will, on average, provide pretty impressive performance.

Studying algorithms can be an educational experience, providing you with greater insight into the design and performance of your own code. In the end, though, perhaps what matters most is that you can put this quicksort handler to good use in your own scripts, taking advantage of all the hard work that other people have done in creating and sharing really useful code—all the way from the humble quicksort routine to mighty productivity suites such as Microsoft Office and Adobe Creative Suite. And that, surely, is one of the best optimizations of all.

Summary

Getting to be an experienced scripter is a funny thing: the more I work with AppleScript, the slower and more deliberate I become at writing the scripts, but because of that, the systems I create are more solid and well thought out. I used to rush into things by writing scripts, but now I jot down diagrams and flow charts before I even get to the script editor.

Furthermore, I can appreciate the time I spend on writing better scripts when I have to refer to some of my older work. It spreads out on a sort of an evolutionary timeline, with older scripts looking a bit childish and "bad habits" slowly disappearing from them the more current they are.

The takeaway from this chapter is that although there is rarely One True Way of developing code, and you can go a long way in AppleScript even without learning "proper" programming skills, you may find some problems are far more easily solved if you have a good range of tools in your scripting toolbox to choose from.

While a single chapter cannot hope to teach you every piece of knowledge you might need to achieve this goal, with any luck it has given you some interesting ideas to think about, a handy set of practical tricks and techniques to put to work in your code today, and perhaps a little inspiration and confidence should you decide to pursue this aspect of your scripting career further.

In the final chapter of this book, we will step into the bigger world of Mac OS X programming with an introduction to Cocoa-based GUI application development using Snow Leopard's new AppleScriptObjC bridge.

Chapter 30

Creating Cocoa Applications with AppleScriptObjC

With the release of Snow Leopard, Apple has introduced an exciting new framework called AppleScriptObjC. This framework allows full access to the Cocoa frameworks through AppleScript, allowing you to write Cocoa-based applications using AppleScript instead of Mac OS X's lower-level Objective-C language. Whether you are a seasoned Objective-C developer or an AppleScript user just starting out in GUI programming, the power and flexibility of AppleScriptObjC has something for you.

Because of its flexibility, AppleScriptObjC offers many ways to accomplish a given task. You can use AppleScript by itself, use AppleScript and AppleScriptObjC together, or use a combination of AppleScript, AppleScriptObjC, and Objective-C. Objective-C–based applications can even import AppleScriptObjC to gain full access to the AppleScript language. The choice is yours.

You will hear the terms Objective-C and Cocoa used frequently, so you should be aware of what each means. Objective-C is a programming language that extends the procedural C language with object-oriented features. Cocoa is a collection of *frameworks*, or large libraries, for building GUI applications. Objective-C is the main language used to access the Cocoa frameworks but any language that knows how to talk to Cocoa can be used. With the advent of AppleScriptObjC, AppleScript is now one of the languages that knows how to talk to Cocoa.

> **NOTE:** Cocoa application development is an advanced topic. Before tackling this chapter, make sure you have read Chapters 11, 18, and 19, as AppleScript properties, handlers, and script objects are all essential to AppleScriptObjC.

This chapter will introduce you to various aspects of Cocoa development as you develop the following four applications:

- HelloAppleScriptObjC is a twist on the standard "Hello World!" application. Instead of displaying "Hello World!", this application will have a text field where the user will enter text, and when they click a button, it will display whatever they just typed into the text field. This exercise will teach you how to create a new Xcode project, add a text field and a button to the application window, and build, run, and test the application. We come back to this project a few sections later to add to it the ability to set values in the text field as well.

- PlaySound will introduce you to Cocoa's NSSound class and teach you how to play sounds from your application. Later on, we will enhance this project by adding our own sound files to the application bundle and use Cocoa's NSBundle class to locate these resource files.

- SnapShot will hide itself when a button is clicked, take a screenshot, and save the screenshot to a specified location. We'll come back to this application and rework it to use Cocoa bindings. The comparison of this application with its first version will help you to understand how to use bindings and will show off their benefits by reducing the amount of code you need to write.

- KitchenTimer demonstrates how to use Cocoa's NSTimer class, which is the Objective-C equivalent of the AppleScript idle handlers. You'll continue to learn how to build an AppleScriptObjC application and, in this example, begin using multiple files to hold our code.

Cocoa applications are developed using Apple's powerful Developer Tools package, which includes the Xcode project editor and the Interface Builder GUI designer. Xcode does not come pre-installed on your system, so unless you've previously installed it yourself, you need to download a copy from Apple's website (http://developer.apple.com/mac/) or install it from your Mac OS X installation disk.

Application development, Xcode, Interface Builder, and Objective-C are, in their own right, large subjects themselves. This chapter merely touches the surface of these subjects while introducing you to AppleScriptObjC. The end of the chapter provides references to training, books, web sites, and videos that you can access to further your knowledge and understanding of these topics.

You're probably chomping-at-the-bit to get started, so let's create our first application.

Example Project: HelloAppleScriptObjC

In this example, we are going to create a simple project that allows the user to type text in a text field, click a button, and have that text displayed in a normal AppleScript display dialog box.

There are four main steps to developing this application:

1. Create a new project in Xcode.

2. Add AppleScript code to the project.

3. Add the GUI objects to the application's window in Interface Builder.

4. Build, run, and test the application.

Creating the Project in Xcode

After you have installed Xcode, launch it. You will find it in `/Developer/Applications/`. When Xcode first launches, it displays the window shown in Figure 30–1. Select the "Show this window when Xcode launches" check box at the bottom of this window if you would like this window to appear each time you launch Xcode.

Figure 30–1. *Xcode's introductory screen when launching the application*

Choose "Create a new Xcode project." When you do this, Xcode displays the New Project window, shown in Figure 30–2.

Choose Application from the Mac OS X section of the left column and then Cocoa-AppleScript Application from the right side of the window. Lastly, click the Choose button and save your project to disk with the name `HelloAppleScriptObjC`.

When the application window first opens, the folders in the Groups & Files pane might not be expanded. If they are not, toggle open the `Classes` and `Resources` folders. Inside the `Classes` folder there is one file that has been created for you, `HelloAppleScript ObjCAppDelegate.applescript`. Select it, and in the right side of the window, the file's code will appear, as shown in Figure 30–3. The right side of the window is the editor and is where you will spend the majority of your time. We will cover what this code means shortly.

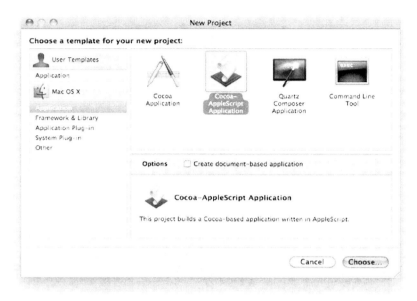

Figure 30–2. *Xcode's New Project window*

Figure 30–3. *Xcode's editor view displaying the code contained within the* HelloAppleScriptObjAppDelegate.applescript *file*

Adding the AppleScript Code in Xcode

Before we go any further, click the Build and Run button in the toolbar or choose **Build ➤ Build and Run**. As you can see, this is a fully functioning application but it doesn't do much. We should add some code to remedy that.

Quit the application and go back to Xcode. Add the following code right under the property parent : class "NSObject" declaration:

```
property textField : missing value

on buttonClick_(sender)
    set theText to textField's stringValue()
    display dialog "Here is the text you entered: " & return & theText
end buttonClick_
```

> **CAUTION:** Previous chapters used the underscore style for variable and command names (for example, underscore_naming). However, the Cocoa frameworks, and consequently AppleScriptObjC, use the camel case naming convention (camelCaseNaming). You will see in later examples why following this naming convention is so important.

Save your work and double-click the MainMenu.xib file in the Resources folder of the Groups & Files pane. This is the file that describes the layout of HelloAppleScriptObjC's GUI. Interface Builder will launch if it is not already running and open the MainMenu.xib file so that you can edit it.

Constructing the Interface in Interface Builder

Interface Builder is where you lay out your application's GUI objects—buttons, text fields, table views, and so forth. It is also where you connect them to the code you have written in Xcode. Figure 30–4 shows the various windows and palettes you will work with in Interface Builder.

Understanding Interface Builder's Interface

There are several windows and palettes shown in Figure 30–4. Let's look at each one in turn.

MainMenu window   Library palette

MainMenu.xib – English window

Figure 30–4. *Interface Builder windows and palettes*

The MainMenu Window

The MainMenu window shows all the menus that will appear in your application's menu bar. This menu bar is completely configurable by you. You can remove items from it and add items to it. You can connect menu items to your code the same as you would connect a button. (You will learn how to connect buttons later in this project.)

> **TIP:** It is a good idea to remove items from this default menu when your application does not use them. An example of this would be to remove the Save options if your application lacks this ability.

The Application Window

The application window is the window that is displayed when your application launches. This is where you will add GUI objects such as buttons, table views, text fields, and sliders. The window itself also has many configurable options.

The MainMenu.xib – English Window

The MainMenu.xib – English window contains all the objects within the MainMenu.xib file.

It lists the following top-level GUI objects:

- *MainMenu*: Represents your application's menu bar. You can double-click this entry to open the MainMenu window.

- *Window*: Represents your main application window. Double-clicking this item opens the window for editing, as previously described. If your application needs more than one kind of window, you can drag additional window objects from the Library palette into the MainMenu.xib – English window.

It also lists several important non-GUI objects in your application:

- *Font Manager*: Provides support for the default Font menu in your application's menu bar (Format ➤ Font)—useful if your GUI has text fields that contain styled text.

- *Application*: Identifies the main NSApplication object that is in overall charge of your application. We'll discuss the NSApplication class a little more later on, although you shouldn't often deal with it directly.

- *File's Owner*: The object that is in overall charge of the GUI objects defined in this .xib file. In a simple, single-window application like HelloAppleScriptObjC, this is the main NSApplication object. In a more complex, document-based application, you might have several .xib files, each owned by a different class of object.

- *First Responder*: Identifies whichever GUI object has the user's focus. For instance, if the user clicks in a text field, the text field object will become the first responder—that is, the first object to receive the user's keyboard and menu bar input. You can usually ignore this item.

You will learn shortly how to add additional objects to the MainMenu.xib – English window and create connections between the GUI and non-GUI objects so they can talk to each other.

The Library Palette

The Library palette contains three tabs: Objects, Classes, and Media.

The Objects tab lists all the GUI objects you can use in your application—windows, table views, buttons, controllers, menus, and so on. It is divided into three panes:

- The top Groups pane has a hierarchal outline view making it easy to find GUI objects by category. Selecting any one of these groups will cause the middle pane to display only the objects in that category.

- The middle Items pane lists all the GUI objects in the currently selected category. It has four view options: View Icons, View Icons and Labels, View Icons and Descriptions, and View Small Icons and labels. You can change the view options by clicking the pop-up menu with the sprocket icon in the lower-left corner of the Library palette window.

- The bottom Details pane contains a short description of the item selected in the Items pane. It also displays an icon representation of the item and its Objective-C class.

The Classes tab provides details about all the object classes you can use in Interface Builder, including any custom classes you have defined in Xcode. This feature is only used in more advanced projects; you will not need it for this chapter.

The Media tab contains various media files you can use in your application. Apple provides a few, but the most useful are the ones you will add yourself. Graphics, images, and sound files that you add to your Xcode project will show up here. To add an icon to your application window, just drag it from the Media tab to the position you want.

> **NOTE:** Before you start constructing your GUI, set the Items pane's view options to View Icons and Labels. This will make it easier for you to find the GUI objects used in this chapter.

Adding the GUI Objects

Add a text field and a button to the application window. Open the Library palette by choosing **File ► Tools ► Library**. Under the Objects tab, toggle open the **Library ► Cocoa ► Views & Cells** group, and then choose **Inputs & Values**. Select the Text Field object and drag it onto the HelloAppleScriptObjC application window, as shown in Figure 30–5.

Once the text field is on the window, resize the text field by dragging the circular handle on the field's right edge to the right until you see the blue-dotted guide appear near the window's edge. The blue-dotted guides provide an alignment reference that helps you make your application look better.

Next, select the Buttons group under Views & Cells and drag a Push Button object onto the window (see Figure 30–6).

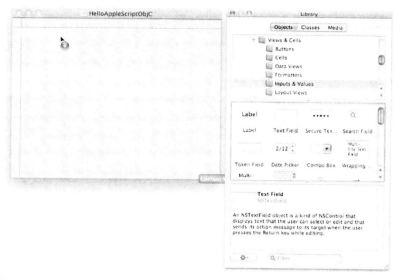

Figure 30–5. *Adding a text field to the application window in Interface Builder*

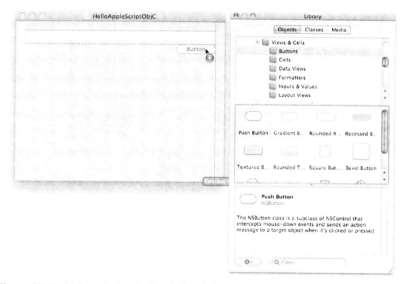

Figure 30–6. *Adding a button to the window in Interface Builder*

Rename the button to Display Dialog, and then resize the window by selecting the bottom-right corner of the window with your mouse and dragging upward. As the window is reduced in size and you get closer to the button, the blue-dotted guides will appear below the button to let you know when to stop.

Making Connections

In the MainMenu.xib – English window, Ctrl-click the blue cube labeled Hello Apple S...
and the connections panel will appear. Drag from the circle next to `textField` to the text
field on the window, as shown in Figure 30–7, and release. This connects the text field
on the window with the `textField` property we defined in Xcode.

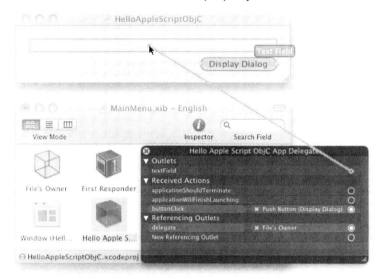

Figure 30–7. *Connecting the `textField` property to the* NSTextField *object in Interface Builder. This is also how the finished window looks after resizing using the blue-dotted guides.*

Connect the button in the same way by dragging from the circle next to the
`buttonClick:` action to the button on the window (see Figure 30–8). This connection
creates the link from the button to the `buttonClick_` handler we created in Xcode. When
the button is clicked, the code in this handler will be executed.

> **NOTE:** Notice how Interface Builder displays the handler's name as `buttonClick:`, not
> `buttonClick_`. Because Interface Builder was originally designed for Objective-C developers, it
> displays your `buttonClick_` handler's name in Objective-C, not AppleScript, format. Don't
> worry, though: the process of translating Objective-C and AppleScript syntax is quite
> straightforward. By the end of this chapter, you will have had plenty of experience with this
> translation.

Figure 30–8. *Connecting the* `buttonClick_` *handler to the NSButton in Interface Builder*

Building and Testing the Application

Save your work, go back to Xcode, and click Build and Run. When the application finishes launching, type some text into the text field and click the Display Dialog button. If all goes well, you will see a dialog box appear with the text you typed into the text field as its message. Figure 30–9 shows a typical example of this.

Figure 30–9. *Using the finished HelloAppleScriptObjC application*

Understanding How Cocoa Works

Wow! If you think about it, that was incredibly easy to create our first application. If you have previously used AppleScript Studio, you should be even more excited about the simplicity of connecting GUI objects to their respective code. Speaking of code, let's review how the code works.

Understanding Outlets

The first thing we added to our HelloAppleScriptObjC project was a property declaration for a text field:

```
property textField : missing value
```

> **TIP:** At this point in the book, being the last chapter and all, you should be very familiar with script properties. If not, refer to Chapters 11 and 19 for more information.

A script property has a special meaning to Interface Builder when its value is missing value. Interface Builder sees these properties as *outlets* and displays them in the connections panel as such. An outlet provides a connection from your script object to another Cocoa object—usually an interface object such as a text field, button, table view, progress indicator, and so forth.

When AppleScriptObjC creates a new script object, it uses the connection information you set up in Interface Builder to assign the appropriate Cocoa objects to the script object's outlet properties. Whenever the handlers in your script object need to manipulate those interface objects, they simply refer to those properties.

In our example, we created a script property named textField inside of our script object, which is the script HelloAppleScriptObjCAppDelegate inside the HelloAppleScriptObjCAppDelegate.applescript file. We then connected the textField script property to the Objective-C NSTextField object in Interface Builder. When our application launches, the textField script property is our direct link to the NSTextField object in our application's window. When we send messages to the textField script property, we are talking directly to this NSTextField object.

Understanding Targets and Actions

Cocoa applications use an event-driven model. This means that once the application is running, it waits patiently for someone to click something, move something, or enter text into something. It is waiting for an event to act upon. When an interface object receives an input event, it sends a *message* to your script object ("message" is just Objective-C jargon for "command"). Because the message is being sent by a GUI object, it is known as an *action* and the script object it is sent to is the action's *target*. In order for your script object to respond to the action, it must define a handler (what Objective-C calls a *method*) with the corresponding name and parameters.

In the HelloAppleScriptObjC application, we set up the Display Dialog button to send a buttonClick: message to the buttonClick_ handler we had previously added to the application's HelloAppleScriptObjCAppDelegate script object.

TRANSLATING OBJECTIVE-C METHOD NAMES TO APPLESCRIPT SYNTAX

Notice how the AppleScript handler name is not exactly identical to the action name. Objective-C method names can contain colons as well as the usual alphanumeric characters. In Objective-C code, each colon indicates where a parameter appears; for example:

```
doSomethingWithParameter1: someValue parameter2: anotherValue
```

Don't be fooled by the superficial resemblance to the labeled parameter syntax used by scriptable applications and scripting additions. What you are looking at is the method's name:

```
doSomethingWithParameter1:parameter2:
```

It just so happens that in Objective-C syntax, the method's parameters appear mixed in with the name itself. The parameters are all positional, however.

As AppleScript does not support Objective-C's unusual method syntax, each colon must be replaced with an underscore and all of the parameters must be enclosed in parentheses after the name:

```
doSomethingWithParameter1_parameter2_(someValue, anotherValue)
```

With a little practice, converting method names between Objective-C and AppleScript syntax will soon become second nature to you.

In Interface Builder, we connected the buttonClick_ handler directly to the button on the application's window. When the button is clicked, the handler's code is executed. The button has a direct link to the code. You can connect the code this way to multiple GUI objects on the window and each will have its own link to the code. What I mean by this is that you could have several GUI objects on a window all connected to the same action handler. Each GUI object could have a different title, and the handler could perform separate actions depending on the button's name.

Just as the properties have a specific required format, so does an action. Interface Builder will see a handler as an action if it has two things: an underscore at the end of its name and a single parameter named sender. Actually, the parameter does not have to be named sender, but it is the preferred syntax and makes it easy for you, and any other developer that might see your code, to see that this method is an action method:

```
on buttonClick_(sender)
    set theText to textField's stringValue()
    display dialog "Here is the text you entered: " & return & theText
end buttonClick_
```

How AppleScript Interacts with Cocoa Objects

AppleScriptObjC uses Objective-C methods to interact with the application's Cocoa objects. For instance, to access the text contained in an interface object of class NSTextField, we use the object's stringValue method:

```
set theText to textField's stringValue()
```

The result is a Cocoa object of class NSString.

> **TIP:** You will not find stringValue in the Xcode documentation for the NSTextField class. Instead, you will find it in its parent class, NSControl. Inheritance is a beautiful thing but may take some time to get used to. If you know that a method exists for a class but cannot find it in its documentation, begin looking up the inheritance chain.

In AppleScript, we are accustomed to using strings, lists, and records. In AppleScriptObjC applications, we use these as well, but now we also have access to their Objective-C class counterparts: NSString, NSArray, and NSDictionary. AppleScriptObjC also translates Booleans and numbers to and from the equivalent C types. Table 30–1 lists the main AppleScript classes and their Objective-C equivalents.

Table 30–1. *How AppleScriptObjC Converts Values Between AppleScript and Objective-C*

AppleScript Class	Objective-C Type/Class
boolean	BOOL
integer	int/unsigned int/long/unsigned long/NSInteger/NSUInteger
real	float/double
string	NSString
list	NSArray
record	NSDictionary

AppleScriptObjC will normally convert AppleScript objects to their Cocoa equivalents, though you may need to convert Cocoa objects to AppleScript objects in order to use them in situations where an AppleScript object is required, or vice versa.

For instance, if you want to use an NSString method on an AppleScript string, you will first need to change the AppleScript string into an NSString object, like this:

```
set theObjCString to current application's ¬
    class "NSString"'s stringWithString_("AppleScript string")
set theObjCString to theObjCString's uppercaseString()
```

The same goes when getting the string back after calling NSString methods on it. For example, if you want to use the string in an application command, you will need to change it back to an AppleScript string by coercing it to the text class:

```
set theAppleScriptString to theObjCString as text
tell application "TextEdit"
   make new document with properties {text:theAppleScriptString}
end tell
```

Modifying HelloAppleScriptObjC to Set the Text Field

Our next example will build on the previous HelloAppleScriptObjC project. We will add to the display dialog command the default answer parameter. Then we will set the window's text field to the text returned from the dialog box.

Updating the Code and Testing the Changes

Go back to Xcode and change the buttonClick_ handler to the following:

```
on buttonClick_(sender)
   set theText to textField's stringValue()
   set dialogText to text returned of ¬
      (display dialog "Here is the text you entered: " & return & theText ¬
         default answer "")
   textField's setStringValue_(dialogText)
end buttonClick_
```

Click Build and Run. When the application finishes launching, enter some text into the text field and click the Display Dialog button. When the dialog box appears, enter text into its field and click OK. The dialog box goes away and the text you entered into it is now displayed in the text field on the window. How much easier can it get!

What Is All That Code in the Default AppleScript File?

When the project is first created, there is one default AppleScript file created with it, *ProjectName*AppDelegate.applescript. Inside this file is a single script statement similar to the one shown in Script 30-1.

Script 30-1.

```
script ProjectNameAppDelegate
   property parent : class "NSObject"

   on applicationWillFinishLaunching_(aNotification)
      -- Insert code here to initialize your application before any files are opened
   end applicationWillFinishLaunching_

   on applicationShouldTerminate_(sender)
      -- Insert code here to do any housekeeping before your application quits
      return current application's NSTerminateNow
   end applicationShouldTerminate_

end script
```

Notice the parent property declaration at the top of this script statement:

```
property parent : class "NSObject"
```

This states that this script's parent is the class NSObject, which is the top-level class from which all other Cocoa classes inherit their basic behaviors. This means that Cocoa will treat our *ProjectName*AppDelegate script object just like any other Cocoa object.

When the application is first launched, each object created in Interface Builder is brought to life. Once it has been fully instantiated with all its outlets and actions, each object is sent an awakeFromNib message. The awakeFromNib handler is a good place to set up user default information. You can use this method in any and all files as needed. We will be using this method in our next example.

```
on awakeFromNib()
    -- Code here
end awakeFromNib
```

In all of the simple examples in this chapter and for applications containing only one .xib file, the application delegate is the only object that has an applicationWillFinishLaunching_ handler. This handler is called after the awakeFromNib message has been sent to all other objects in the main .xib. If you need to perform any tasks after all other objects have been fully instantiated, then this is the place to put that code.

WHAT IS AN APPLICATION DELEGATE ANYWAY?

When a Cocoa-based application launches, the Cocoa framework automatically creates an object of class NSApplication that takes care of the low-level housekeeping tasks that every Cocoa application must perform when launching, running, and quitting. Naturally, many applications need to perform their own housekeeping tasks on top of this, but because NSApplication is so critical to the correct running of all parts of the application, Apple generally advises against messing with it directly. The solution is to put your housekeeping code into a separate object, which the NSApplication object will send messages to in response to certain events.

In Cocoa jargon, this process is known as "delegation" because one object—in this case, the NSApplication object—is delegating the responsibility for performing certain tasks to another object—in this case, one of yours. To connect the two objects together, the NSApplication object provides an outlet named, naturally, delegate, to which you assign your AppDelegate object. This connection is normally set up in Interface Builder, and to make things even easier, the standard AppleScriptObjC project template comes with a basic AppDelegate object predefined in an AppleScript file and already connected to the NSApplication object in the MainMenu.xib file for you. So all you need to do is add your own code to the default AppDelegate object, and you're good to go.

The applicationShouldTerminate_ handler is called before the application quits. Place code here that your application needs to take care of before it quits; saving data to disk, updating user preferences, and so forth.

Notice the last line of the applicationShouldTerminate_ handler:

```
return current application's NSTerminateNow
```

Like AppleScript, Objective-C often uses named constants as parameters and results. NSTerminateNow is one of three constants defined by Cocoa that your applicationShouldTerminate_ handler can return. These constants are shown in the Cocoa documentation like this:

```
enum {
    NSTerminateCancel = 0,
    NSTerminateNow    = 1,
    NSTerminateLater  = 2
}
```

enum is short for "enumeration," which is what C calls a set of related constants. Each constant that is defined in a particular enumeration has a corresponding integer value; however, your code will be much more readable if you refer to constants by name. For convenience, AppleScriptObjC allows you to refer to Cocoa constants as properties of the current application object, so to use these constants in AppleScript you must refer to them like this: current application's *SomeConstant*.

When your applicationShouldTerminate_ handler has finished doing its thing, it must return one of these three constants. Normally you would use NSTerminateNow to confirm that the application should quit as normal. However, if you want to cancel the shutdown, then return NSTerminateCancel instead. (NSTerminateLater is an advanced option that we won't discuss here.)

Example Project: PlaySound

In this example, we will build an application that plays system sounds using Cocoa's NSSound class. Having access to Cocoa classes makes this an easy task.

Creating the Project and Adding the Code

Open Xcode, create a new AppleScript-Cocoa Application project, and name it PlaySound. You might be surprised at how little code this will take. In the PlaySoundAppDelegate.applescript file, add the following code. We will go over how the code works shortly.

```
property soundNameTextField : missing value

on playSound_(sender)
    set soundName to soundNameTextField's stringValue()
    set soundFilePath to "/System/Library/Sounds/" & soundName & ".aiff"
    tell class "NSSound" of current application
        set soundInstance to its alloc()'s ¬
            initWithContentsOfFile_byReference_(soundFilePath, true)
    end tell
    soundInstance's setVolume_(1.0)
    soundInstance's |play|()
end playSound_
```

Constructing the Interface

Save your work and double-click the `MainMenu.xib` file. Just as you did before, add a text field and a button to your window. Ctrl-click the Play Sound A... blue cube in the MainMenu.xib – English window to bring up the connections panel. Drag from the circle, next to `playSound:` in the connections panel, to the button and release. Drag from the circle, next to `soundName` in the connections panel, to the text field. Adjust the text field, button, and window to look like the image shown in Figure 30–10.

Figure 30–10. *The finished PlaySound application*

Let's have our button execute when the Return key is pressed. This way we can use the mouse or the keyboard to see our results. For this, we will need the Inspector palette. You can find it under **Tools ➤ Inspector** or with the keyboard shortcut Cmd+Shift+I.

Select the button and then choose the first tab in the Inspector palette, named Button Attributes. Click inside the Key Equiv area and press Return. A small curved arrow will appear in the box, as shown in Figure 30–11.

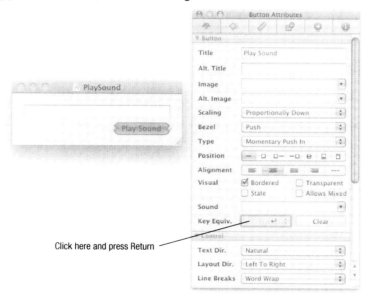

Figure 30–11. *Setting the key equivalent for the button to the Return key*

While we are here, go ahead and set the Title for the text field, as shown in Figure 30–12. The Title will represent the initial value the text field contains when the application launches. First, select the text field and then type in the Title field the word Glass. This will also set the text field's default value when the application launches.

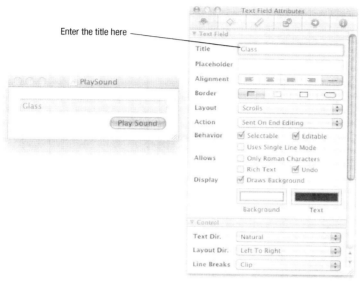

Figure 30–12. *Setting the text field's Title property*

Building and Testing the Application

Save your work, go back to Xcode, and click Build and Run. When the application finishes launching, click the Play Sound button. You should hear a ding.

If you open up a Finder window and navigate to /System/Library/Sounds/, you will find 14 different sounds to play with (see Figure 30–13). Type any name from the list, leaving off the .aiff of course, into the text field and click the Play Sound button to hear it.

Figure 30–13. *A listing of system sounds found in* `/System/Library/Sounds/`

Understanding How It Works

As in the HelloAppleScriptObjC project, we created a property in our code to link to a text field in Interface Builder. We named this one `soundNameTextField` and gave it a default value of `missing value`, as follows. Remember, `missing value` is a requirement for Interface Builder to see this property as an outlet.

```
property soundNameTextField : missing value
```

The `playSound_` handler contains the entire code needed to play a system sound, as shown next. There is a lot going on here, but I find this incredibly exciting to have so much power at our fingertips, right from inside AppleScriptObjC!

```
1. on playSound_(sender)
2.     set soundName to soundNameTextField's stringValue()
3.     set soundFilePath to "/System/Library/Sounds/" & soundName & ".aiff"
4.     tell class "NSSound" of current application
5.         set soundInstance to its alloc()'s ¬
                   initWithContentsOfFile_byReference_(soundFilePath, true)
6.     end tell
7.     soundInstance's setVolume_(1.0)
8.     soundInstance's |play|()
9. end playSound_
```

Line 2 is almost identical to the one in our HelloAppleScriptObjC project. We are sending a message to the text field and asking it for its string. We then capture that value into a local variable named soundName.

Line 3 constructs the path to the desired sound file.

Lines 4 to 6 are the exciting part. Here we are talking directly to a Cocoa class named NSSound. The first thing that is required to use Objective-C classes is to tell our application the name of the class we are targeting:

```
class "NSSound" of current application
```

AppleScriptObjC presents Cocoa classes as class elements of the current application object. When you refer to a Cocoa class from inside a handler, you must use a full reference as shown here. If you only write class "NSSound", AppleScript will try to get the class element from the script object's parent (in this case, NSObject) instead, which causes an error because Cocoa classes don't have AppleScript-style elements.

If you refer to a particular Cocoa class often and want to save yourself some typing, you can store it in an AppleScript property like this:

```
property NSSound : class "NSSound"
```

You can then refer directly to the NSSound property instead of writing the full class "NSSound" of current application reference each time.

In line 5, we are telling the class NSSound to make an instance of itself and to use the file we specify in the first parameter as its sound. At the same time, we capture the new sound object into the variable soundInstance. The second parameter (the byReference part) controls how this object should be archived. (It has nothing to do with AppleScript-style references.) Archiving is beyond the scope of this chapter, and it is not important here, so we just pass true.

HOW TO CREATE COCOA OBJECTS

Creating a new Cocoa object is a two-step process, compared to the single-step process used by scriptable applications. To create a new folder object in the Finder, for instance, you send a single make command to the Finder's main application object, passing any initial property values for the new object in the with properties parameter.

When creating a new NSSound instance, however, you must first send an alloc message to the NSSound class to create a new instance of that class, and then call one of the instance object's init... methods to set up its initial values and ensure that it is ready to use.

Incidentally, a common mistake when learning to use Cocoa is to forget the alloc call and to try to send the init... message directly to the class object—more about this in the next section.

On line 7, we send the message setVolume: to our sound object, passing the value 1.0 as the parameter. Possible values for the sound are 0.0 to 1.0. This specifies the level at which the sound will play as a fraction of the current system sound volume.

Lastly, on line 8 we send the play message to our object. Notice how the |play| identifier is surrounded with pipe symbols. This is necessary because the word play is a reserved word in AppleScript. Any Objective-C method name that conflicts with an AppleScript keyword needs pipes around it to ensure that it compiles as an identifier, not as a keyword.

Viewing the Cocoa Documentation in Xcode

Now that you know the basic concepts behind Objective-C, the next step is to learn about the Cocoa frameworks themselves. Now, if you thought Adobe InDesign was large and complicated, you ain't seen nothing yet! Mac OS X's Cocoa library is huge, containing hundreds of classes and thousands upon thousands of methods. Even the two main Cocoa frameworks you will use in AppleScriptObjC, Foundation and AppKit, contain far more features than you are ever likely to learn or use. This may seem scary at first but you'll discover that it is a good thing. These frameworks contain an incredible amount of functionality already built and tested for you.

Fortunately, Xcode comes with excellent tools for exploring the Cocoa documentation and finding the information you need. Let's start our investigation by looking up the documentation for one of the features we just used: the NSSound class's initWithContentsOfFile:byReference: method. Open Xcode's documentation by selecting **Help ➤ Developer Documentation**, as shown in Figure 30–14.

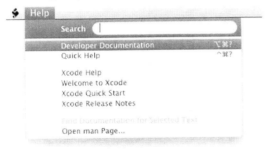

Figure 30–14. *Opening Xcode's documentation to explore the NSSound class*

When it opens, type NSSound into the search field and press Return. Figure 30–15 shows a typical documentation viewer window. One thing I must say about the developer documentation is that "I love it!" Apple has done an outstanding job with this version.

Figure 30–15 shows the Xcode documentation window displaying the class reference for NSSound. If you look at the leftmost pane, you will see all the search results for NSSound. The reason there are so many results is that I have *Contains* selected in the options located just above this pane. You can narrow the search by choosing one of the other options.

The middle pane contains links to organized categories for the methods of a class. Clicking the Overview link will take you to the Overview section. It is a good idea to read the Overview section, as this will give you some valuable information about the class.

1. Type "NSSound" into the search field

2. Click the "NSSound Class Reference" entry

3. Click to toggle open the table of contents

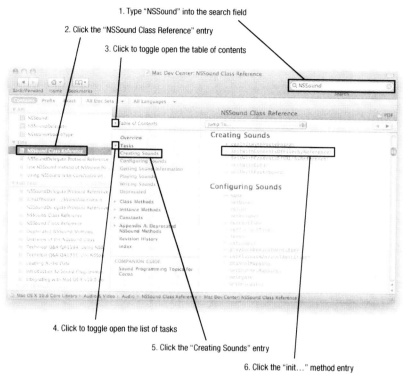

4. Click to toggle open the list of tasks

5. Click the "Creating Sounds" entry

6. Click the "init…" method entry

Figure 30–15. *Navigating the NSSound documentation in Xcode*

You can either click or toggle open the Tasks link. Clicking it will take you to the top of the Tasks section. When toggling the Tasks link open, as shown in Figure 30–15, you are presented with more links that will take you directly to the methods, which fall under each link's type of task. These methods are direct links to the full method documentation.

The right pane is where you read about the class and explore its methods.

How Cocoa Classes Are Documented

Once you have located a class in the documentation, you will need to make sense of it. At the top of the class description is the class's name, followed by a table of basic information, as shown in Figure 30–16.

NSSound Class Reference

Inherits from	NSObject
Conforms to	NSCoding
	NSCopying
	NSPasteboardWriting
	NSPasteboardReading
	NSObject (NSObject)
Framework	/System/Library/Frameworks/AppKit.framework
Availability	Available in Mac OS X v10.0 and later.
Companion guide	Sound Programming Topics for Cocoa
Declared in	NSSound.h
Related sample code	AttachAScript
	BundleLoader
	CustomSave
	GeekGameBoard
	TrackIt

Figure 30–16. *The NSSound class reference begins with a table of useful information.*

The most important part of the table is the "Inherits from" section, as this tells you which class this class inherits at least some of its functionality from. The NSSound class is quite straightforward in that it inherits directly from NSObject, so it will contain all the methods defined by NSObject as well as the methods it lists for itself. Other useful items are the "Availability" section, which will become important to you as new features are introduced in future Mac OS X releases, and the "Companion guide" and "Related sample code" sections, which lead you to additional documentation and examples of use.

The rest of the class reference is divided into a number of sections, including Overview, Tasks, Class Methods, Instance Methods, and Constants.

TIP: Use the left sidebar to navigate quickly to different sections in the class reference.

The Overview section provides a general description of the class and hints on how to use it, so it's a good idea to read this first.

The Tasks section lists all the methods by functionality. In addition to giving you a good idea of what this class can do, you can click a name to jump directly to a method description. It is a great place to start when you are not sure what methods handle your specific need.

Under Creating Sounds you will see a method with a "+" symbol to its left, but all the others have a "−" symbol next to them. You may be wondering what the difference is between the two symbols. All methods with the "+" next to them are called class methods. This means you do not have to have an instance of the class to use it. As a matter of fact, you can't use a class method on an instance. The opposite is true for methods that have a "−" next to them. They must have an instance of the class to be used.

UNDERSTANDING "UNRECOGNIZED SELECTOR" ERRORS

When a Cocoa object receives a message that it does not understand, you will see an error in Xcode's console similar to this:

```
+[NSSound initWithContentsOfFile:byReference:]: unrecognized selector sent to object
```

This error message is the Cocoa equivalent of error −1708 ("*some_object* doesn't understand the *command_name* message") in AppleScript.

The bracket notation is commonly used in Objective-C documentation and logs to tell a reader the name of a particular method and the class it's in. The square brackets contain the name of the class followed by the name of the method you tried to call. The "+" symbol to the very left of the error informs you that you sent this message to a class object. A "−" symbol would indicate that you sent this message to an instance of that class.

From the error message, we can see that the script tried to send an `init...` message to the NSSound class object. However, this won't work because `init...` methods are defined as instance methods, not class methods. The correct approach is to create a new instance of NSSound first by sending an `alloc` message to the NSSound class object, and then call `init...` on that.

So whenever you see this type of error message, make sure you check not only that you wrote the method name correctly, but that you sent it to the right kind of object—class or instance—as well.

Class methods are described in detail under the Class Methods section of the class reference, while instance methods are covered in the Instance Methods section.

There are several more sections, whose functionality should be self-explanatory by their title.

Now let's look at how individual methods are documented.

How Cocoa Methods Are Documented

The documentation for our `initWithContentsOfFile:byReference:` method has a lot of valuable information to help us use it effectively and correctly. Figure 30–17 shows the definition as it appears in Xcode's documentation viewer.

initWithContentsOfFile:byReference:

Initializes the receiver with the the audio data located at a given filepath.

```
- (id)initWithContentsOfFile:(NSString *)filepath
byReference:(BOOL)byRef
```

Parameters

filepath
  Path to the sound file with which the receiver is to be initialized.

byRef
  When YES only the name of the sound is stored with the NSSound instance when archived using encodeWithCoder:; otherwise the audio data is archived along with the instance.

Return Value
Initialized NSSound instance.

Availability
Available in Mac OS X v10.0 and later.

Related Sample Code
AttachAScript

Declared In
NSSound.h

Figure 30–17. *Xcode's documentation detail for the* NSSound *method* `initWithContentsOfFile:byReference:`

The Method Name

The method name, `initWithContentsOfFile:byReference:`, is the full method name. The fact that the parameters are separated is one of the things that make Objective-C unique and easy to read. Code written well can often times read like a story.

Make note that these are not "named parameters." In many languages, you can have named parameters and they can be in any order you choose. Objective-C does not have named parameters. This *is* the method name. Even though all the parameters are named, they must be in the order specified.

Beneath the method name is a short description of what the method does. This is followed by the full method name with specific information about the types of parameters it expects to receive and the type of value it will return to its caller. Figure 30–18 shows how the method name breaks down.

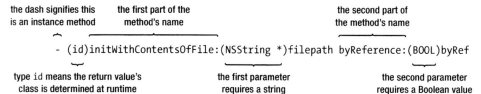

Figure 30–18. `initWithContentsOfFile:byReference:` *broken down*

Notice that the method name has a "–" symbol next to it, which tells us that it is an instance method, not a class method. That means we have to create an instance of NSSound to use it. To create an instance, an `alloc` message is sent to the class object, followed by an init... message. It is most common to combine these into one statement and wrap it in a tell class ... end tell block:

```
tell class "NSSound" of current application
    set soundInstance to its alloc()'s ¬
        initWithContentsOfFile_byReference_(soundFilePath, true)
end tell
```

Parameters

This section tells us exactly what the parameters are expecting, whether it can be nil, and in some cases its meaning.

UNDERSTANDING OBJECTIVE-C'S SPECIAL NIL VALUE

You may be wondering what the special nil value you see mentioned in Objective-C documentation means. Objective-C's nil value has a couple of important uses that you should be aware of when working with Cocoa in AppleScriptObjC:

- Objective-C methods, like AppleScript handlers, do not support optional parameters. However, some methods let you pass nil—or missing value if you are using AppleScriptObjC—as a way of saying "use a default value" for a parameter.

- Unlike AppleScript, Objective-C hardly ever throws errors ("exceptions") to indicate that something has gone wrong. Instead, some Objective-C methods that normally return a Cocoa object will return nil (or missing value in AppleScriptObjC) to indicate that an error has occurred. Make sure your code knows how to deal with this.

Notice that AppleScriptObjC automatically converts Objective-C's nil values to AppleScript's missing value constant, and vice versa. Make sure you always write missing value, not nil, in your AppleScript code; otherwise an error will occur.

Return Value

The return value is the type of object the calling code will get when this method is invoked.

Discussion, Availability, See Also, Related Sample Code, and Declared In

A method description may contain one or more additional sections providing further help and advice. The Discussion section can provide extra information on how to use the method and any nuances it may have. Availability specifies what OS versions can utilize this method. See Also provides links to similar or opposing methods. Related Sample Code, when available, provides a way for you to see how this method is used in context by experienced developers. This code is presumably written in Objective-C, but using

AppleScriptObjC requires learning at least how to read and convert Objective-C code to AppleScriptObjC.

Hopefully, this short tour through the documentation has given you confidence to use it more often and more effectively.

Example Project: SnapShot

I don't know about you, but I am ready to write some more code! In this example, we will create a program to take full-screen screenshots of our computer screen. Until now, the examples have been very simple and demonstrated only a few techniques. It's time to up the ante! I will introduce several more techniques and the code will be larger and slightly more complex. Nothing you can't handle, though.

There will be two iterations of this project. In the first iteration, we are going to write out the code required to get and set GUI object data. In the second iteration, we will reduce the amount of code by using Cocoa bindings. I strongly believe that you should understand how things work, by doing them manually, before using the bindings mechanism.

Creating the Project and Starting the Code

Open Xcode, create a new application, and name it SnapShot. In the SnapShotAppDelegate.applescript file, add the following property declarations to the SnapShotAppDelegate object. These properties are all outlets we will connect to in Interface Builder.

```
property folderPath : missing value
property pictureName : missing value
property resize : missing value
property delayTime : missing value
property stepperValue : missing value
property mainWindow : missing value
property maxWidthHeight : missing value
```

Declare an action called snapShot_ as well:

```
on snapShot_(sender)
end snapShot_
```

Due to the way we are building this application, you may get varying results if you click Build and Run before the Building and Testing section, so just be patient.

Constructing the Interface

Save your work and double-click the MainMenu.xib file to launch Interface Builder. Drag the GUI objects onto the window and arrange them as indicated in Figure 30–19, then Ctrl-click the SnapShot Ap… app delegate in the MainMenu.xib – English window to open the connections panel.

Figure 30–19. *How to connect the PlaySound application's interface in Interface Builder*

Connect the interface to the application delegate by dragging a line from each of the numbered points on the Snap Shot App Delegate panel to the corresponding GUI object. Once you have made all the connections, save your work and go back to Xcode.

Completing the Code

Here is what the SnapShot application is going to do:

1. When the Snap button is clicked, the application will hide its window.

2. Wait the specified number of seconds delay time.

3. Take a screenshot of the screen and save it to the specified location.

4. Play the system sound Glass, alerting that it is finished with its task.

5. Show its window.

With a slight modification, we will add the playSound handler from our previous example. Instead of hard-coding the path and using the alloc and init... methods, we will use one of NSSound's factory methods to return an instance for us. The factory method we will use is soundNamed: and it is a class method:

```
on playSound()
   tell class "NSSound" of current application
      set soundInstance to its soundNamed_("Glass")
   end tell
   soundInstance's setVolume_(1.0)
   soundInstance's |play|()
end playSound
```

Not only does the soundNamed: method return an instance of NSSound, it automatically searches several directories to locate the sound file by the name we provide. It is common practice to leave off the extension when supplying the sound's name. The first place this method looks for the sound file is in our application's bundle. If it is not found there, then the following directories are searched in order:

1. ~/Library/Sounds

2. /Library/Sounds

3. /Network/Library/Sounds

4. /System/Library/Sounds

Next, we add code to the snapShot_ handler that is connected to the Snap button:

```
on snapShot_(sender)
   mainWindow's orderOut_(me)
   delay (delayTime's integerValue())

   set folderPathString to folderPath's stringValue() as string
   set pictureNameString to pictureName's stringValue() as string
   set targetFile to folderPathString & "/" & pictureNameString & ".jpg"
   set quotedTargetFile to quoted form of targetFile

   do shell script "screencapture -t jpg -x " & quotedTargetFile

   if (resize's state as integer) = 1 then
      set maxWidthHeight to maxWidthHeight's integerValue()
      do shell script "sips --resampleHeightWidthMax " & maxWidthHeight ¬
            & space & quotedTargetFile & " --out " & quotedTargetFile
   end if

   my playSound()
   mainWindow's makeKeyAndOrderFront_(me)
end snapShot_
```

> **CAUTION:** The examples in this chapter are designed to give you a feel for how the AppleScriptObjC bridge works, and are not always production ready. The preceding code does not check that the folderPathString variable points to a valid folder or that the pictureNameString variable contains a valid file name before constructing the file path. As an exercise, add the necessary validation code yourself.

Understanding How It Works

One of the outlet properties we set up was `mainWindow`. The connection we created in Interface Builder will set this property to an instance of `NSWindow` when the application launches. The two `NSWindow` methods we will use are `orderOut_` and `makeKeyAndOrderFront_`. The first one will hide the window and the second will bring it back. Both methods take a single parameter, which is the object that called them—in this case, the `SnapShotAppDelegate` object, which we get from AppleScript's special `me` variable:

```
-- First line in handler where we hide the window
mainWindow's orderOut_(me)

-- Last line in handler where we bring it back
mainWindow's makeKeyAndOrderFront_(me)
```

> **NOTE:** AppleScript's special `me` variable always contains a reference to the current script object. See Chapter 11 for details.

In each of the previous examples, we retrieved text from a text field using the method `stringValue`. `NSTextField` has several methods for retrieving values as a specified type: `integerValue`, `intValue`, `floatValue`, and so forth. Standard Additions' `delay` command requires a number, so we call the text field's `integerValue` method first:

```
delay (delayTime's integerValue())
```

The next few lines retrieve the string values from the `folderPath` and `picturePath` text fields. The text field's `stringValue` method returns an `NSString` instance, of course, so we have to coerce this value to an AppleScript string before we can manipulate it with AppleScript commands and operators—in this case, `&`. The last line creates a quoted path to be used in the `do shell script` command.

```
set folderPathString to folderPath's stringValue() as string
set pictureNameString to pictureName's stringValue() as string
set targetFile to folderPathString & "/" & pictureNameString & ".jpg"

set quotedTargetFile to quoted form of targetFile
```

The next line uses Standard Additions' `do shell script` command to run the command-line `screencapture` tool:

```
do shell script "screencapture -t jpg -x " & targetFile
```

If you want to learn more about how the `screencapture` utility works, type `man screencapture` into a Terminal window to display all of its capabilities. The two options we are using here are `-t` and `-x`. Here is what the man page says about these two options:

```
-t     <format> Image format to create, default is png
       (other options include pdf, jpg, tiff and other formats).

-x     Do not play sounds.
```

> **TIP:** See Chapter 27 for more information on interacting with the Unix command line.

We added a check box to our window to determine if we need to resize the image after it has been created. A simple `if` statement will do, but we need to coerce the button's state to an integer to test it. If the check box has been checked, its value is 1; otherwise it is 0. If the conditional test passes, then the screenshot file is resized using the command-line `sips` utility:

```
if (resize's state as integer) = 1 then
    set maxWidthHeight to maxWidthHeight's integerValue()
    do shell script "sips --resampleHeightWidthMax " & maxWidthHeight ¬
        & space & quotedTargetFile & " --out " & quotedTargetFile
end if
```

`sips` is an incredible command-line tool that is capable of manipulating images in many ways. To see the full list of options, type `man sips` in a Terminal window.

> **TIP:** Viewing man pages in the Terminal can be no fun at all. If you would like to view the man page in Preview instead, use this Terminal command: `man -t sips | open -f -a /Applications/Preview.app`. (You can substitute the word `sips` with any other Unix command name to view its man page in Preview as well.)

First, we retrieve the integer value from the `maxWidthHeight` text field. This value and the path to the newly created screenshot are then given as parameters to the `sips` command. The `--resampleHeightWidthMax` option is very nice for our purpose because it will resize the image to a maximum height or width while maintaining the image's proportion. Notice that the resizing is destructive, because we are overwriting the file with the new size. If you want to keep both files, you will need to provide another path for the `--out` option. This is the file path `sips` will use to save the converted image to disk.

Once the file is generated, we play a sound to notify the user:

```
my playSound()
```

Preparing the Text Fields Using an *awakeFromNib* Handler

As previously promised, I will now demonstrate using the `awakeFromNib` handler. If you were to click Build and Run in Xcode, all the text fields would be empty. This is not very user-friendly behavior. We remedy this by setting up default values in an `awakeFromNib` handler. Insert this just above the `applicationWillFinishLaunching_` handler:

```
on awakeFromNib()
    folderPath's setStringValue_(POSIX path of (path to pictures folder))
    delayTime's setIntegerValue_(2)
    stepperValue's setIntegerValue_(2)
    pictureName's setStringValue_("TestPic")
    maxWidthHeight's setIntegerValue_(680)
    resize's setState_(1)
```

```
end awakeFromNib
```

You have already used the setStringValue: method in the HelloAppleScriptObjC project. The two new methods are setIntegerValue: and setState:. The purpose of the setIntegerValue: method should be clear. The other method, setState:, is a method of NSButton, which our check box is. The state is either 1, meaning ON, or 0, meaning OFF.

Building and Testing the Application

Save your work and then click Build and Run. You now have an application to take screenshots with a delay and automatically resize them. Next up, we will change this application to use bindings!

Modifying SnapShot to Use Cocoa Bindings

Now that you have learned how to get and set GUI object values programmatically, it's time to experience some magic. Bindings are very cool and can save you from writing a lot of code. So far, we have been getting and setting values for the properties using Objective-C methods. Using bindings will eliminate this "controller" code and directly update the properties as the values change in the GUI, and vice versa.

A full discussion of Cocoa bindings is beyond the scope of this book. However, for simple tasks, they are fairly straightforward to use. What this means is that you can update the value of your properties from AppleScript by referring to the property using AppleScript's special my keyword. When the values are updated in your code this way, the GUI objects they are bound to will update automatically. The reverse is also true. When a value is changed in the GUI, the property it is bound to will be updated. It is a very cool mechanism!

To get or set the value of a bound property in your code, use the my keyword like this:

```
my someProperty
set my someProperty to newValue
```

> **CAUTION:** If you do not use the my keyword when getting or setting a property's value, your bindings will not work as expected.

Adjusting the Code for Bindings

The majority of the work in setting up bindings is performed in Interface Builder, but first we need to make some adjustments to our code.

Remove everything except the set folderPath to ... line from inside the awakeFromNib handler and make the following changes to the code. Notice, we no longer need a stepperValue property.

```
property folderPath : missing value
property pictureName : "TestPic"
property resize : 1
property delayTime : 2
property mainWindow : missing value
property maxWidthHeight : 680

on awakeFromNib()
    set my folderPath to (POSIX path of (path to pictures folder))
end awakeFromNib

on snapShot_(sender)
    mainWindow's orderOut_(me)
    delay my delayTime

    set folderPathString to my folderPath as string
    set pictureNameString to my pictureName as string
    set targetFile to folderPathString & "/" & pictureNameString & ".jpg"
    set quotedTargetFile to quoted form of targetFile

    do shell script "screencapture -t jpg -x " & quotedTargetFile

    if (my resize as integer) = 1 then
        set maxWidthHeight to my maxWidthHeight as integer
        do shell script "sips --resampleHeightWidthMax " & maxWidthHeight ¬
            & space & quotedTargetFile & " --out " & quotedTargetFile
    end if

    my playSound()
    mainWindow's makeKeyAndOrderFront_(me)
end snapShot_
```

Setting Up Bindings in Interface Builder

As I stated earlier, the majority of the work will be done in Interface Builder. Double-click the MainMenu.xib file to open it. Before doing the additional work of setting up bindings, we need to remove all of the current references by clicking the "×" symbols in the connections panel, as shown in Figure 30–20.

CAUTION: If you do not remove missing references, the application will crash upon launch.

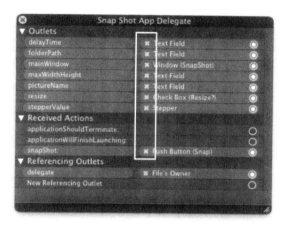

Figure 30–20. *Removing connections in Interface Builder*

Next, open the Bindings tab in the Inspector palette (the shortcut is Cmd+4) and select the first text field. Choose Snap Shot App Delegate from the pop-up menu and set the Model Key Path to `folderPath`. Continue setting up the bindings as shown in Figures 30–21 to 30–26.

> **CAUTION:** It is *very* important that you spell the property names correctly. If you do not, the application will crash, stating that it is not key value coding-compliant for the key *whateverKeyWasMisspelled*.

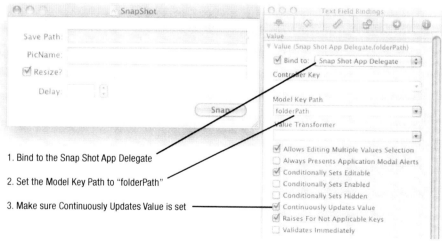

Figure 30–21. *Setting up the bindings for the Save Path text field*

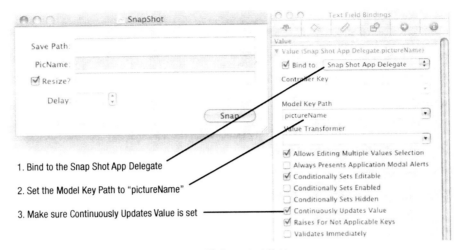

Figure 30–22. *Setting up the bindings for the PicName text field*

The Resize text field is special, in that we are going to bind its Enabled property to the Resize check box. When the check box is checked, the text field will be editable; when it is unchecked, the text field will turn gray and not be editable.

We can do this in code, but one of the beauties of bindings is that it takes care of that for you.

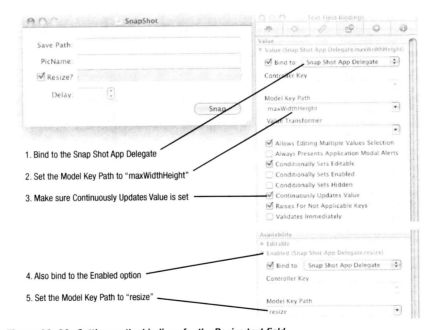

Figure 30–23. *Setting up the bindings for the Resize text field*

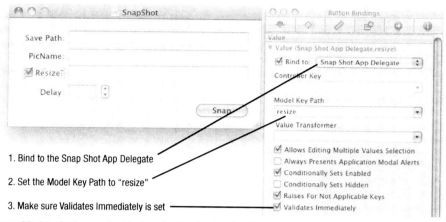

Figure 30–24. *Setting up the bindings for the Resize check box*

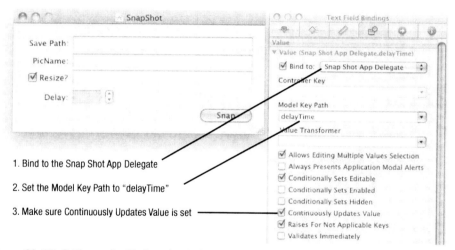

Figure 30–25. *Setting up the bindings for the Delay text field*

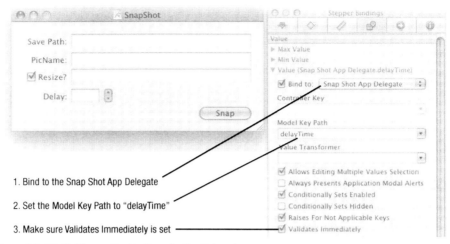

Figure 30–26. *Setting up the bindings for the Delay stepper*

Both the Delay text field and stepper are bound to the same property. In the previous example, we had to manually set this up and use two properties. With bindings, we need only one.

Building and Testing the Application

Save your work, go back to Xcode, and click Build and Run. The application is working with less code and more functionality (remember, we added a binding for the Enabled property of the maximumWidthHeight text field).

Bindings are an exciting feature, and this example is just the tip of the iceberg of what you can accomplish using them.

Modifying PlaySound to Use Bundled Sound Files

One thing you will do often is to include items in your bundle that will ship with your application. The most common items are sound files, command-line utilities, and images.

In this example we will modify the PlaySound application and add to it the ability to play sound files located in its own bundle.

Adding the Sound File Resources to the Project

Open the PlaySound Xcode project, right-click the Resources folder, and select **Add ➤ New Group**. Name it Sounds. This will not create a physical folder within the application but it will help you to manage the sound files that you're about to add to the project.

Now right-click the Sounds group and select **Add ➤ Existing Files**. Navigate to /System/Library/Sounds and select all the files. It's a good idea to check the "Copy items into destination group's folder (if needed)" option at the top of the confirmation window so that the resource files are included in your project folder. That way, your project will contain its own copies of these files, so even if the original files are moved or deleted in the future, your project will still build correctly.

Adding the Code

In order to use the sound files, we will use an `awakeFromNib` handler, one property, and one button click handler. It will be used to play the sounds. Add the following code to the `PlaySoundTwoAppDelegate.applescript` file:

```
property popupButton : missing value

on playSound_(sender)
    set soundName to popupButton's titleOfSelectedItem

    tell class "NSBundle" of current application
        tell its mainBundle
            set soundFilePath to its pathForResource_ofType_(soundName, "aiff")
        end tell
    end tell

    tell class "NSSound" of current application
        set soundInstance to its alloc()'s ¬
                initWithContentsOfFile_byReference_(soundFilePath, true)
    end tell
    soundInstance's setVolume_(1.0)
    soundInstance's |play|()

end playSound_

on awakeFromNib()
    popupButton's addItemsWithTitles_({"Basso", "Blow", "Bottle", "Frog", ¬
            "Funk", "Glass", "Hero", "Morse", "Ping", "Pop", "Purr", "Sosumi", ¬
            "Submarine", "Tink"})
end awakeFromNib
```

Adding the Pop-Up Button

Double-click the `MainMenu.xib` file to open Interface Builder. Remove the existing text field and then drag an NSPopUpButton and an NSButton onto the application's window. Name the button Play Sound. Ctrl-drag from the class instance to the pop-up button and select `popupButton`. Ctrl-drag from the button to the class instance and choose `playSound:`.

Building and Testing the Application

Arrange the window items appropriately and then save and close. Go back to Xcode and click Build and Run. Select a sound from the pop-up list and click the Play Sound button to hear it.

Understanding How It Works

First we will go over the awakeFromNib handler. When we set the property popupButton and connected it in Interface Builder, we gave ourselves a connection to an instance of NSPopUpButton. One instance method that NSPopUpButton has is addItemsWithTitles:. When provided an array of strings, it will populate the pop-up with all the sound names we added to the project.

```
on awakeFromNib()
    popupButton's addItemsWithTitles_({"Basso", "Blow", "Bottle", "Frog", ¬
        "Funk", "Glass", "Hero", "Morse", "Ping", "Pop", "Purr", "Sosumi", ¬
        "Submarine", "Tink"})
end awakeFromNib
```

In the playSound_ handler, we first get the title of the current pop-up selection by calling the NSPopUpButton object's titleOfSelectedItem method:

```
set soundName to popupButton's titleOfSelectedItem
```

Next, we use NSBundle to obtain the full path to the sound file. Here is the definition for NSBundle from the documentation:

> *"An NSBundle object represents a location in the file system that groups code and resources that can be used in a program."*

When you create an application using Xcode, the application file that is created is a bundle. A bundle is a special folder that acts as an executable when double-clicked. It contains your compiled code, application icon, Info.plist file, and other resources needed by your application. NSBundle is the class we use to access these resources.

```
tell class "NSBundle" of current application
    tell its mainBundle()
        set soundFilePath to its pathForResource_ofType_(soundName, "aiff")
    end tell
end tell
```

USING NSBUNDLE TO FIND RESOURCE FILES

Using the pathForResource:ofType: method provided by NSBundle is a great way to get paths to resources in the Resources folder. Here are a few more examples:

```
-- Get the path to a Ruby file named search_path.rb
set soundFilePath to its pathForResource_ofType_("search_path", "rb")

-- Get the path to a PNG file named moonlight.png
set soundFilePath to its pathForResource_ofType_("moonlight", "png")
```

If you want to obtain the paths to all files of a particular type, then use the pathsForResourcesOfType:inDirectory: method. It requires a specific directory inside the Resources folder to hold the files. To create this folder, open your project folder in the Finder. Create a new folder and name it appropriately, and copy the image, graphic, music, and other files into this folder.

Back in Xcode, right-click the `Resources` folder and select **Add ➤ Existing Files**. Navigate to your project's folder and select the folder of files you just created. When the window drops down, do not check the option to have the items copied, because they are already in the project folder, but do check Create Folder References for any added folders.

This example returns an array of file paths:

```
set mp3Paths to pathsForResourcesOfType_inDirectory_("mp3", "Sounds")
```

Finally, we play the sound as we have done previously using the NSSound class:

```
tell class "NSSound" of current application
    set soundInstance to its alloc()'s ¬
        initWithContentsOfFile_byReference_(soundFilePath, true)
end tell
soundInstance's setVolume_(1.0)
soundInstance's |play|()
```

Example Project: KitchenTimer

KitchenTimer is a simple application that will allow text entry of a number, and then count down to zero from that number. We will demonstrate how to use a separate file for the application's controller and let the application delegate *be* a delegate for NSApplication only. We will also be demonstrating how to use NSTimer, which is Cocoa's answer to the `idle` handlers used in AppleScript Editor applets.

Creating the Project and Starting the Code

Create a new project in Xcode and name it `KitchenTimer`. Right-click the `Classes` folder and choose **Add ➤ New File**. Select AppleScript class and click Next. Name the file `Controller.applescript` and save.

The Controller file is where we will be adding most of the code. Until now, we have put all of the code inside the AppDelegate file: however, the AppDelegate's intended job is handling messages sent to it by NSApplication: `awakeFromNib`, `applicationWillFinishLaunching:`, `applicationShouldTerminate:`, and so on. To keep the code well organized and easy to maintain, we should really put other code in their own objects.

Open the `Controller.applescript` file. As you can see, Xcode has already added a new script object named `Controller`, representing your new `Controller` "class." Add the following just above the `script Controller ... end script` block. This will give us easy access to the NSTimer class throughout our Controller script without having to use a lengthy `tell class "NSTimer" of current application ... end tell` declaration each time.

```
property NSTimer : class "NSTimer" of current application
```

Add the following code just below the `parent` property declaration:

```
-- IBOutlets
property displayTime : missing value
```

```
property startStopButton : missing value
property timeInMinutesTextField : missing value
```

These property declarations will be used as outlets from Interface Builder. The displayTime property contains the text field used to show the current time during the countdown. The startStopButton property allows us to set the title of the button. The timeInMinutesTextField property contains the text field where the user enters the value of time to count down from.

Next, we set some script properties. The myTimer property will hold the NSTimer instance we will create and it allows us to keep track of whether it is running or not. The totalSecondsRemaining property will be used to decrement the timer.

```
-- Script properties
property myTimer : missing value
property totalSecondsRemaining : 0
```

Create a startTimer_ handler to begin the timer's execution. We will fill in the details right after we lay out the application's interface and make the connections in Interface Builder.

```
on startTimer_(sender)
end startTimer_
```

> **TIP:** In simple applications, having only one .xib file is common. In more complex applications, multiple .xib files are a good way of organizing your application GUIs by functionality. For example, a more complex application might have the menu bar defined in one .xib, the main document window in another .xib, and the preferences window in a third .xib file.

Constructing the Interface

Double-click the MainMenu.xib file to launch Interface Builder. Drag an NSObject from the Objects & Controllers folder in the Library pallet (see Figure 30–27).

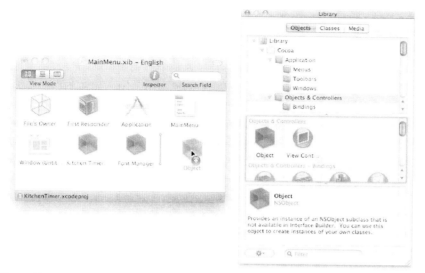

Figure 30–27. *Dragging an NSObject to the MainMenu.xib window*

Set the class identity of the object to `Controller`, as shown in Figure 30–28.

Figure 30–28. *Setting the class's actual identity*

This gives us a way to visually connect objects in Interface Builder to the `Controller` object's handlers and properties. When the `.xib` file is loaded, the application will create a new `Controller` object automatically.

Of course, we still need to add the window controls and set up their connections to the `Controller` object, so let's do that next.

Open the window object for editing and use the Size tab of the Inspector palette to resize it to 305 wide by 129 high.

Now drag a Multi-line Text Field onto the window and resize it to fill the entire window. With the text field selected, go to the Attributes tab of the Inspector palette and set the border to no border and align the text to center alignment. Set the Title to 00:00:00 and uncheck the Selectable, Editable, Undo, and Draws Background check boxes as demonstrated in Figure 30–29.

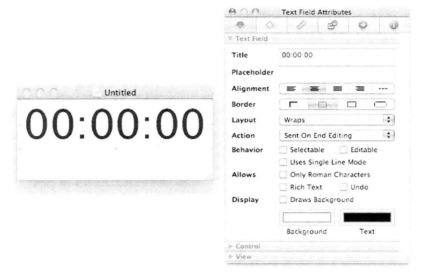

Figure 30–29. NSTextField *attribute settings*

Set the font to Lucida Grande with a point size of 64. You do this by bringing up the Font window using Cmd+T on the keyboard or **File ➤ Font ➤ Show Fonts**. To make the connection, Ctrl-drag from the text field to the `Controller` instance and choose `displayTime`.

Now drag another `NSTextField` object onto the window along with a button. Arrange as shown in Figure 30–30. Ctrl-drag from the text field to the instance of the Controller and choose `timeInMinutesTextField`.

Figure 30–30. *KitchenTimer layout*

Add a push button and name it Start Timer, and then Ctrl-drag from the button to the `Controller` instance and choose `startTimer:`.

We are all done in Interface Builder so save your work and go back to Xcode.

Completing the Code

Now let's fill in the code for the `startTimer_` handler in our `Controller` file. This handler is responsible for starting the timer when the Start Timer button is clicked (or stopping it if it is already running):

```
on startTimer_(sender)
    set buttonTitle to sender's |title|()

    if (buttonTitle as text) is equal to "Start Timer" then
        if timeInMinutesTextField's integerValue() ≠ 0 then
            sender's setTitle_("Stop Timer")
            set numberOfMinutes to timeInMinutesTextField's integerValue()
            set totalSecondsRemaining to (numberOfMinutes * 60)

            set myTimer to NSTimer's ¬
                scheduledTimerWithTimeInterval_target_selector_userInfo_repeats_ ( ¬
                1, me, "updateTime:", missing value, true)
        end if
    else
        sender's setTitle_("Start Timer")
        cancelTimer()
        displayTime's setStringValue_("Stopped!")
        playSound()
    end if
end startTimer_
```

The handler starts by getting the button name, which it uses to decide whether it should start or stop the timer. (A more sophisticated design would store this information in a Boolean script property and update the button label whenever the property's value changes, but we're keeping it simple here.)

If the timer is not running, then the first half of the conditional block executes. This checks whether the user has entered a time value into the text field. If a time is found, several things happen. First, the button label is changed to "Stop Timer". Next, the number of seconds that the timer should run for is calculated and the result is assigned to the `totalSecondsRemaining` property. Finally, a new `NSTimer` instance is created and assigned to the `myTimer` property. This timer will trigger the `Controller` script's `updateTime_` handler once every second.

If the timer is already running when the button is clicked, then the second part of the conditional block executes instead. This cancels the timer object and updates the GUI objects accordingly.

As you can see, the `startTimer_` handler uses several other handlers to perform various tasks, so let's add these next.

The `cancelTimer` handler is called when the time remaining reaches zero or the user manually cancels the countdown:

```
on cancelTimer()
    if myTimer ≠ missing value then
        myTimer's invalidate()
        set myTimer to missing value
    end if
```

```
end cancelTimer
```

First we check whether the value of myTimer is missing value. If it is, then nothing happens. If it is not, we invalidate the timer object, causing it to stop, and then set the myTimer property's value back to missing value.

The updateTime_ handler is responsible for updating the GUI and time remaining, or playing the alarm when the time reaches zero:

```
on updateTime_(myTimer)
    if totalSecondsRemaining = 0 then
        cancelTimer()
        displayTime's setStringValue_("Complete")
        startStopButton's setTitle_("Start Timer")
        playSound()
    else
        set newTime to formatTime()
        displayTime's setStringValue_(newTime)
        set totalSecondsRemaining to totalSecondsRemaining - 1
    end if
end updateTime_
```

We start by checking if the value of the totalSecondsRemaining property is zero. If it is, we cancel the timer, change the displayTime text field's value to "Complete", set the startStopButton's title to "Start Timer", and play the system sound Glass.aiff to notify the user.

If it is not zero, meaning the timer is still running, we create a new time string using the formatTime handler, update the displayTime text field with the new string, and reduce the value of the totalSecondsRemaining property by one.

The formatTime handler is used to format the time in a consistent way for viewing. It gets the current number of seconds from the totalSecondsRemaining property, determines hours, minutes, and seconds, and returns the formatted string to the calling code:

```
on formatTime()
    set hoursLeft to totalSecondsRemaining div 3600
    set minutesLeft to (totalSecondsRemaining div 60) mod 60
    set secondsLeft to totalSecondsRemaining mod 60
    return padWithZero_(hoursLeft) & ":" & padWithZero_(minutesLeft) ¬
        & ":" & padWithZero_(secondsLeft)
end formatTime
```

The padWithZero_ handler is a convenience handler to add a zero to any single digit for display purposes:

```
on padWithZero_(the_number)
    if the_number < 10 then
        return "0" & the_number
    else
        return the_number as text
    end if
end padWithZero_
```

The playSound handler, which we are so familiar with, is used to alert the user that the timer has finished:

```
on playSound()
    tell class "NSSound" of current application
        set soundInstance to its soundNamed_("Glass")
    end tell
    soundInstance's setVolume_(1.0)
    soundInstance's |play|()
end playSound
```

You now have a very simple timer and you have learned how to use an NSTimer instance to perform the same type of functionality that the idle handler performs in an AppleScript Editor applet.

Extra Exercises

Now that you've completed the projects in this chapter, why not try enhancing them for yourself? Here are some ideas to get you started.

Enhance the KitchenTimer application as follows:

- Currently the time counts the seconds down one by one, but as the updateTimer_ handler takes a number of milliseconds to run itself, your timer may end up going a few seconds longer than it should. To avoid this cumulative timing error, modify the startTimer_ handler to calculate the time when the alarm should go off, and store that in a property instead of the number of seconds remaining. The updateTimer_ handler should then check whether the current date is equal to or greater than the alarm date.

- Embed your own choice of audio file and have it play that as the alarm sounds. Or you could have it play a track in iTunes if you prefer. After all, what's the point of writing an application in AppleScript if you can't do a bit of application scripting on the side?

Enhance the SnapShot application as follows:

- Add code to check that the folderPath and pictureName properties contain valid values before constructing the target file path.

- Add a Choose button next to the Save Path field that, when clicked, displays a standard Choose Folder dialog box (hint: you'll need to define a new action handler for this button). When the user picks a folder and clicks OK, set the folderPath property to the POSIX path of the chosen folder. Make sure that your AppleScript code refers to the folderPath property as my folderPath; otherwise the text field won't automatically update with the new path.

- Add a pop-up menu that lists the different image file types supported by the command-line screencapture tool, allowing the user to pick the type of file to create (TIFF, PNG, etc.).

▓ Put the screenshot code into its own `makeScreenshot` handler and replace the Standard Additions delay command with `NSTimer` code that will call the `makeScreenshot` handler after the delay time. This will prevent the GUI becoming unresponsive between clicking the Snap button and the screenshot being taken.

Where Next?

Obviously, you have only scratched the surface of AppleScriptObjC development in this chapter. AppleScriptObjC is a new technology, so the amount of documentation dedicated to the subject is currently limited. No doubt more material will become available in time; for now, though, here are some links to get you started:

▓ AppleScriptObjC Release Notes

`http://developer.apple.com/mac/library/releasenotes/ScriptingAu tomation/RN-AppleScriptObjC/index.html`

▓ Apple's AppleScriptObjC mailing list

`http://lists.apple.com/mailman/listinfo/applescriptobjc-dev`

▓ Five AppleScriptObjC in Xcode tutorials at MacScripter.net

`http://macscripter.net/viewforum.php?id=31`

▓ The AppleScriptObjC and Xcode forum at MacScripter.net

`http://macscripter.net/viewforum.php?id=63`

▓ Scripting Events LLC

`http://www.scriptingmatters.com/ASObjC`

▓ John C. Welch's blog (www.bynkii.com)

`http://www.bynkii.com/archives/2009/09/a_look_at_applescriptobj c.html`

▓ AppleScriptObjC training videos by Craig Williams

`http://allancraig.net`

If you don't mind learning a bit of Objective-C along the way, then there are plenty of good books, online resources, and other resources available that cover general Cocoa development:

▓ *Introduction to the Objective-C Programming Language*

`http://developer.apple.com/Mac/library/documentation/Cocoa/Conc eptual/ObjectiveC`

▓ Cocoa Programming for Mac OS X, by Aaron Hillegass

`http://www.bignerdranch.com/books`

- Beginning Mac Programming: Develop with Objective-C and Cocoa, by Tim Isted

  http://www.pragprog.com/titles/tibmac/beginning-mac-programming

- Cocoa Programming: A Quick-Start Guide for Developers, by Daniel H. Steinberg

  http://www.pragprog.com/titles/dscpq/cocoa-programming

- Objective-C and Xcode Essential Training, by Craig Williams

  http://www.vtc.com/modules/products/titleDetails.php?sku=34088&affiliate=allancraig

- Becoming Productive in Xcode, by Mike Clark

  http://pragprog.com/screencasts/v-mcxcode/becoming-productive-in-xcode

- Coding in Objective-C 2.0, by Bill Dudney

  http://pragprog.com/screencasts/v-bdobjc/coding-in-objective-c-2-0

Summary

In this final chapter, you were introduced to the powerful new AppleScriptObjC framework introduced in Mac OS X 10.6.

You discovered how to create new AppleScript-Cocoa projects in Xcode and how to construct your application GUI in Interface Builder.

You learned how AppleScriptObjC enables script objects that inherit from Cocoa classes to operate as if they were Objective-C class and instance objects. Within these script objects, you can define handlers that act as Objective-C–style class and instance methods, just as long as you follow the proper naming convention. In particular, you can use handlers as action methods that are called when the user clicks a button or performs some other GUI input. You can also define properties to act as Objective-C outlets, providing your code with easy access to text fields, check boxes, and other GUI objects.

After adding your GUI controls and defining outlet properties and action methods in your code, you used the connections palette in Interface Builder to define the connections between them. This allows Cocoa to connect your GUI to your code automatically when your application runs.

After exploring the essential mechanics of Cocoa and AppleScriptObjC in the HelloAppleScriptObjC project, we looked at how to create and use Cocoa objects within AppleScript. In the PlaySound project, we created an instance of Cocoa's NSSound class to play an audio file. Later on, the KitchenTimer project used an instance of the NSTimer class to trigger a handler every second—the Cocoa equivalent of using an AppleScript idle handler. We also touched on the powerful Cocoa bindings feature, which reduces the amount of code you must write to connect your GUI to your script objects.

Obviously, this chapter has only scratched the surface of Cocoa application development, but hopefully it has given you a taste of what is possible with AppleScriptObjC should you choose to explore this area further.

Conclusion

Well, this concludes our journey into the sometimes wild and whacky, yet also undeniably wonderful world of AppleScript and application scripting.

The AppleScript language may not be perfect and some scriptable applications may not be as capable or well designed as you might hope; nevertheless, the potential for simplifying and streamlining repetitive desktop tasks is considerable, and arguably unparalleled on any other platform. With a bit of knowledge and a spot of practice, it is possible for even casual scripters to achieve some extremely impressive results.

So whether you are only an occasional dabbler in desktop automation or a professional AppleScript developer creating the next big thing in automated publishing systems, we hope that you find this book to be an essential traveling companion both now and in the future.

Happy scripting!

Index

Characters and Numerics

B

P

X

Y

Z

CPSIA information can be obtained at www.ICGtesting.com
Printed in the USA
LVOW110159041212

309984LV00014B/126/P